GREECE

THE RO[UGH]

KU-350-549

THE ROUGH GUIDES

OTHER AVAILABLE ROUGH GUIDES

AMSTERDAM • AUSTRALIA • BARCELONA • BERLIN • BRAZIL
BRITTANY & NORMANDY • BULGARIA • CALIFORNIA & WEST COAST USA
CANADA • CRETE • CZECH & SLOVAK REPUBLICS • CYPRUS • EGYPT
EUROPE • FLORIDA • FRANCE • GERMANY • GUATEMALA & BELIZE
HOLLAND, BELGIUM & LUXEMBOURG • HONG KONG • HUNGARY • IRELAND
ISRAEL • ITALY • KENYA • MEDITERRANEAN WILDLIFE • MEXICO • MOROCCO
NEPAL • NEW YORK • NOTHING VENTURED • PARIS • PERU • POLAND
PORTUGAL • PRAGUE • PROVENCE • PYRENEES • ST PETERSBURG
SAN FRANCISCO • SCANDINAVIA • SICILY • SPAIN • THAILAND • TUNISIA
TURKEY • TUSCANY & UMBRIA • USA • VENICE • WEST AFRICA
WOMEN TRAVEL • ZIMBABWE & BOTSWANA

FORTHCOMING
CORSICA • ENGLAND • SCOTLAND • WALES

Rough Guide Credits

Text Editors: Mark Ellingham, Marc Dubin, Martin Dunford and John Fisher
Series Editor: Mark Ellingham
Editorial: Jack Holland, Jonathan Buckley, Richard Trillo, Kate Berens
Production: Susanne Hillen, Gail Jammy, Andy Hilliard, Vivien Antwi
Finance: Celia Crowley

Acknowledgements

For **fresh research** we're greatly indebted to Carol Phile for overhauling most of the the Cyclades and Corfu, John Hartle for adding no less than eight new islands (and finally covering Áyios Efstrátios!), John Watkins for looking over the Thrace section, and, once again, Richard Hartle for encouragement, Peloponnesian updates and a brand new Kefalloniá. For their contributions to the **Contexts** chapter, thanks to Pete Raine for the *Wildlife* section, Michael House and Diane Fortenberry for *250 Years of Archaeology*, and Nick Edwards for updating the politics. For the advice for disabled travellers, thanks to Alison Walsh. From previous editions, continuing thanks to Tim Salmon and Stephen Lees for sharing their knowledge of Greece. Thanks to Kate Berens for proofreading.

We'd also like to thank all those **readers of the previous editions** of the guide who took time to annotate our errors, omissions and lapses of taste. On this edition, we were helped enormously by letters from Geoff Garvey, Mike Gerrard, Gordon McLachlan, Ted Sumner, Liz Raymont, Matthew Hancock and Amanda Tomlin, Stuart and Diane Gray, Alex Woodfield, Steve Pottinger, James Dale, Ronald Ti, Victoria Thompson, Barney McCullagh, Michael O'Hare, Carola Scupham, Steve Smith, Harry Hinde, RJ Blakeway-Phillips, Mary Castelberg-Kouma, Graham Nevill and Hazel Walmsley. Lastly, for **help on the ground in Greece**, thanks to Greg Koutsomitopoulos, Manolis and Sofia Hadzinikolau, Apostolos and Jo Sikelianos, Eleanor Guralnick and Kevin Consodine, Marianne and Sotiris Nikolis, Yasmin Gy, Heidi Abbühl, Katerina Tsakiris, Liz Tamalunas, Panayiotis Boudouris, Barbara Fields, Sandra Klein, the Valaoritis family, Nikos Stavroulakis, Julie Hardenberg, Toula Chryssanthopoulou, Michael Hathaway, Eva Hedin, Thales and Maria Aryiropoulos, and Piers and Iris Townshend.

The publishers and authors have done their best to ensure the accuracy and currency of all information in *The Rough Guide to Greece*; however, they can accept no responsibility for any loss, injury, or inconvenience sustained by any traveller as a result of information or advice contained in the guide.

This **fifth edition** published in July 1992 by Rough Guides Ltd, 1 Mercer Street, London WC2H 9QJ. Reprinted twice in 1993.

Distributed by the Penguin Group:

Penguin Books Ltd, 27 Wrights Lane, London W8 5TZ
Penguin Books USA Inc., 375 Hudson Street, New York 10014, USA
Penguin Books Australia Ltd, 487 Maroondah Highway, PO Box 257, Ringwood, Victoria 3134, Australia
Penguin Books Canada Ltd, 10 Alcorn Avenue, Toronto, Ontario, Canada M4V 1E4
Penguin Books (NZ) Ltd, 182–190 Wairau Road, Auckland 10, New Zealand

Originally published in the UK by Routledge & Kegan Paul and by Harrap Columbus.
Previously published in the United States and Canada as *The Real Guide Greece*.

Typeset in Linotron Univers and Century Old Style to an original design by Andrew Oliver.
Printed in the United Kingdom by Cox and Wyman Ltd (Reading).
Illustration on p.1 by Helen Manning; Illustration on p.643 by Jane Strother.
Illustrations in Part One and Part Three by Edward Briant.

720p. Includes index.
A catalogue record for this book is available from the British Library.

SBN 1-85828-020-6

GREECE

THE ROUGH GUIDE

Written and researched by

Mark Ellingham, Marc Dubin, Natania Jansz and John Fisher

With additional contributions by

Tim Salmon, Carol Phile, Richard Hartle and John Hartle

THE ROUGH GUIDES

PLACE NAMES: A WARNING!

The art of rendering Greek words in Roman letters is in a state of chaos: a major source of confusion with **place names**, for which seemingly each local authority, and each map-maker, uses a different system. The word for "saint", for instance, one of the most common prefixes, can be spelt Áyios, Ágios, or Ághios. And, to make matters worse, there are often two forms of a name in Greek – the popularly used *dhimotikí*, and the old "classicising" *katharévoussa*. Thus you will see the island of Spétses written also as Spétsai, or Halkídha, capital of Évvia, as Halkís (or even Chalcís, on more traditional maps). Throw in the complexities of Greek grammar – with different case-endings for names – and the fact that there exist long-established English versions of classical place names, which bear little relation to the Greek sounds (Mycenae for Mikínes, for example), and you have a real mare's nest.

In this book, we've used a modern and largely phonetic **system**, with *Y* rather than *G* for the Greek gamma, and *DH* rather than *D* for delta, in the spelling of all modern Greek place names. We have, however, retained the accepted "English" spellings for the **ancient sites**, and for familiar places like Athens (Athiná, in modern Greek). We have also accented (with an acute) the stressed letter of each word; getting this right in pronunciation is vital in order to be understood.

CONTENTS

Introduction viii

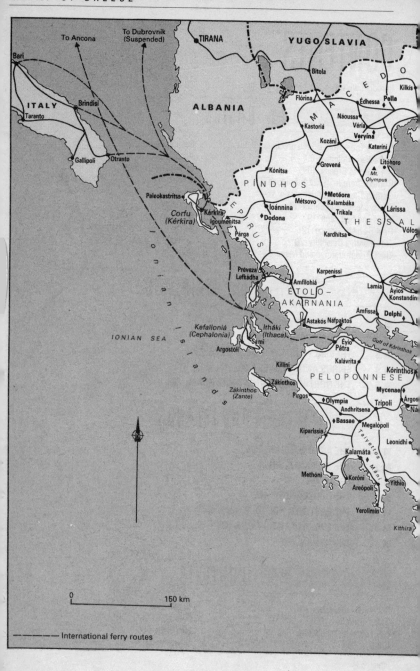

To Ancona

To Dubrovnik
(Suspended)

TIRANA

YUGOSLAVIA

Bari

Bitola

ITALY

Brindisi

Taranto

ALBANIA

Flórina

MACEDO

Edhessa

Pella

Kilkis

Náoussa

Véria

Veryína

Gallipoli

Otranto

Kastoriá

Kozáni

Katerini

Litóhoro

Kónitsa

Grevená

Mt.
Olympus

Paleokastrítsa

PÍNDHOS

Métsovo

Metéora

Kalambáka

Lárissa

Corfu
(Kérkira)

Kérkira

Ioánnina

Trikala

THESSAL

Igoumenítsa

E

P

I

R

U

S

Dodona

Kardhítsa

Vólos

Párga

Prévaza

Karpeníssi

Lamía

Lefkádha

Amfilohía

Áyios
Konstandin

ÉTOLO –

AKARNANIA

Amfissa

Delphi

Ionian

Islands

Astakós

Náfpaktos

Kefalloniá
(Cephalonia)

Itháki
(Ithaca)

Éyio

Pátra

Gulf of Kórinthos

IONIAN SEA

Sámi

Argostóli

Kalávrita

Kórinthos

Killini

PELOPONNESE

Zákinthos

Mycenae

Árgos

Pirgos

Olympia

Tripoli

Ná

Zákinthos
(Zante)

Andhritsena

Kiparíssia

Bassae

Megalópoli

Leonídhi

Taiyetos

Kalamáta

Máni

Methóni

Koróni

Yíthio

Areópoli

0   150 km

Yerolímin

Kíthira

International ferry routes

INTRODUCTION

With over one hundred and sixty inhabited islands and a territory that stretches from the Mediterranean to the Balkans, Greece has interests enough to fill months of travel. The **historic sites** span four millennia of civilisation, encompassing the legendary and renowned, such as Mycenae, Olympia, Delphi or the Parthenon, and the obscure, where a visit can still seem like a personal discovery. The **beaches** are parcelled out along a convoluted coastline equal in length to that of (far larger) France, and they range from those of islands where the boat calls once a week to resorts as cosmopolitan as any in the Mediterranean. Perhaps less expected by visitors, the country's mountainous interior offers some of the best and least exploited **hiking** in Europe.

Modern Greece is the sum of an extraordinary diversity of **influences**. Romans, Arabs, French, Venetians, Slavs, Albanians, Turks, Italians, to say nothing of the great Byzantine empire, have all been here and gone since the time of Alexander the Great. All have left their mark: the Byzantines in countless churches and monasteries, and in ghost towns like Mystra; the Venetians in impregnable fortifications at Náfplio, Monemvassía and Methóni in the Peloponnese; the Franks in crag-top castles. Most obvious of all is the heritage of four hundred years of Ottoman Turkish rule which, while universally derided, exercised an inestimable influence on music, cuisine, language and way of life. The contributions, and continued existence, of substantial minorities – Vlachs, Muslims, Jews, Gypsies – round out the list of those who have helped to make up the Hellenic identity.

All of these groups have left an indelible stamp on the character of the people, which combines with that powerful and hard to define strain of **Greekness** that has kept alive the people's sense of themselves throughout their turbulent history. With no ruling class to impose a superior model of taste or patronise the arts, the last few centuries of Greeks – peasants, fishermen, shepherds – created a vigorous and truly popular culture. Its works can be seen in the songs and dances, costumes, embroidery, woven bags and rugs, furniture, the white cubist houses of popular image – in a thousand instinctively tasteful manifestations. Its vigour may be failing under the impact of western consumer values, but much survives, especially in remoter regions.

Of course there are formal cultural activites as well: **museums** that shouldn't be missed, in Athens, Thessaloníki and Iráklion; equally compelling buildings, like the **monasteries** of the Metéora and Mount Áthos; **castles** such as those in the Dodecanese, Lésvos, central Greece and the Peloponnese; as well, of course, as the great Mycenaean, Minoan, Classical, Macedonian and Roman sites. The country hosts some excellent summer **festivals**, too, bringing international theatre groups and orchestras to perform in ancient theatres at Epidaurus, Dodona and Athens – magical settings in themselves.

But the call to cultural duty should never be too overwhelming on a Greek holiday. The **hedonistic pleasures** of languor and warmth – always going lightly dressed, swimming in the sea without a hint of a shiver, talking and drinking under the stars – are just as appealing. Be aware, though, that Greece is a land for simple sybarites. If you're into the five-star stuff – super-soft beds, faultless plumbing, exquisite cuisine, attentive service – forget it. Hotel accommodation is mostly plain. Rooms can be box-like and stuffy. Campsites offer the minimum of facilities. Food at its best is fresh, colourful and uncomplicated.

The Greek people

To begin to get an understanding of the Greek people, it is important to realise just how recent and profound were the events that created the **modern state** and national character. Up until the early decades of this century many parts of Greece – Crete, Macedonia, the islands of the Ionian and Dodecanese – were in Turkish (or in the latter case, British and Italian) hands. Meanwhile, as many ethnic Greeks lived in Asia Minor, Egypt and in the north Balkans as in the recently forged kingdom. The Balkan Wars of 1912–13 and the exchange of "Greek" and "Turkish" populations in 1922–23 changed everything in a sudden, brutal manner. Worse still was to come during World War II, and its aftermath of civil war between the Communists, who formed the core of wartime resistance against the German occupation, and the western-backed rightist, "government" forces. The viciousness of this period found a more recent echo in nearly seven years of military dictatorship under the colonels' junta between 1967 and 1973.

Such memories of brutal misrule, diaspora and catastrophe remain uncomfortably close for all Greeks, despite the last decade or so of democratic stability and economic growth as a member of the European Community. The resultant identity is complex, an uneasy coexistence of opposing impulses, which cannot be accounted for merely by Greece's position as a natural bridge between Europe and the Middle East. Within a generally extroverted outlook is a strong streak of pessimism, while the poverty of, and enduring paucity of opportunity in, their homeland spurs the resourcefulness of Greek entrepreneurs, many of whom choose to emigrate. Those who remain may be lulled by an (until recently) humane full-employment policy which has resulted in the lowest jobless rate in Western Europe. The downside of this is an occasionally staggering lack of initiative, but official attempts to impose a more austere economic line have been met by waves of popular strikes.

On the other hand, the meticulousness of Greek craftworkers is legendary, even if their values and skills took a back seat to the demands of crisis and profiteering when the evacuation of Asia Minor and the rapid depopulation of rural villages prompted the graceless urbanisation of Athens and the other cities. Amid the contemporary sophistication that resulted, it's easy to forget the nearness of the agricultural past and the fact that Greece is still as much a part of the Third World as of the the First. You may find that buses operate with Germanic efficiency, but ferries sail with an unpredictability little changed since the time of Odysseus.

Attitudes, too, are in a state of flux as Greece has adapted to mass tourism and the twentieth century, neither of which had made much impact up until the last twenty to thirty years. The encounter has been painful and at times destructive, as a largely rural, traditional and conservative society has been lost. Though the Greeks are adaptable and the cash registers ring happily, at least in tourist areas, visitors still need to be sensitive in behaviour towards the older generations. The mind boggles to imagine the reaction of the black-clad grandparents to nudism, or even scanty clothing, in a country where until recently the Orthodox church was all but an established faith and the guardian of national identity.

Where and when to go

There is no such thing as a typical Greek island; each has its distinctive character, appearance, history, flora, even a unique tourist clientele. And the same is true of the mainland provinces. **Landscapes** vary from the mountainous northwest and rainy, shaggy forests of the Pílion to the stony deserts of the Máni, from the soft theatricality of the Peloponnesian coastal hills to the poplar-studded plains of Macedonia, from the resin-scented ridges of Skíathos and Sámos to the wind-tormented rocks of the central Aegean. The inky plume of cypress, the silver green of olive groves, the blue outline of distant hills, an expanse of shimmering sea: these are the enduring and unfailingly pleasing motifs of the Greek landscape.

Most places and people are far more agreeable, and recognisably Greek, outside the **peak period** of late June to the end of August, when the soaring temperatures and crowds can be overpowering. You won't miss out on warm weather if you come in **early June or September**, excellent times everywhere but particularly amid the Sporades and north or east Aegean islands. In **October** you might hit a stormy spell, especially in western Greece or in the mountains, but most of the time the "summer of Áyios Dhimítrios", the Greek equivalent of Indian summer, prevails. Autumn in general is beautiful; the light is softer, the sea often balmier than the air, the colours subtler.

December to March are the coldest and least reliable months, though there are many fine days of perfect crystal visibility, and the glorious lowland flowers begin to bloom very early in spring. The more northerly latitudes and high altitudes of course endure far colder and wetter conditions with the mountains themselves snowed under from November to April. The most **dependable winter weather** is to be found in the Dodecanese, immediately around Rhodes, or in the southeastern parts of Crete. As spring slowly warms up, **March and early April** are still uncertain, though fine for visiting the Ionians or Dodecanese; by **May** the weather is more generally dependable, and Crete, the Peloponnese, and the Cyclades are perhaps at their best, even if the sea's still a little cool for swimming.

Other factors that can affect the timing of your Greek travels are mainly concerned with the level of tourism. Standards of service invariably slip under the high-season pressures, and room rates are already at their highest in July and August. If you can only visit in high season, then you'll do well to plan your itinerary a little away from the beaten track. Explore the less obvious parts of the Peloponnese, or the northern mainland, for example; or island-hop with an eye for the more obscure – the places where ferries don't call more than once a day, and there's not yet an airport.

Out of season, especially between November and March, you may have to wrestle with uncertain ferry schedules to the islands, and often fairly skeletal facilities when you arrive. However, you will find reasonable service on all the main routes and at least one hotel open in the port or main town. On the mainland, out-of-season travel poses no special difficulties.

	AVERAGE TEMPERATURES AND RAINFALL											
	Jan		March		May		July		Sept		Nov	
	°F Max Min	Rain days	°F Max Min	Rain days	°F Max Min	Rain days	°F Max Min	Rain days	°F Max Min	Rain days	°F Max Min	Rain days
Athens	54 44	13	60 46	10	76 60	9	90 72	2	84 66	4	65 52	12
Crete (Haniá)	60 46	17	64 48	11	76 56	5	86 68	0	82 64	3	70 54	10
Cyclades (Míkonos)	58 50	14	62 52	8	72 62	5	82 72	0.5	78 68	1	66 58	9
North Greece (Halkithikí)	50 36	7	59 44	9	77 58	10	90 70	4	83 64	5	60 47	9
Ionian (Corfu)	56 44	13	62 46	10	74 58	6	88 70	2	82 64	5	66 52	12
Dodecanese (Rhodes)	58 50	15	62 48	7	74 58	2	86 70	0	82 72	1	68 60	7
Sporades (Skíathos)	55 45	12	58 47	10	71 58	3	82 71	0	75 64	8	62 53	12
East Aegean (Lésvos)	54 42	11	60 46	7	76 60	6	88 70	2	82 66	2	64 50	9

PART ONE

THE
BASICS

GETTING THERE FROM BRITAIN AND IRELAND

It's close on 2000 miles from London to Athens, so for most visitors flying is the only viable option. There are direct flights to a variety of Greek destinations from all the major British airports, and to Athens from Dublin and Belfast. Flying time is around three and a half hours and the cost of economy or charter flights is reasonable – from around £120 return out of season, £200 or so in midsummer or over Easter. Costs can often be highly competitive, too, if you buy a flight as part of an all-in package: see p.6–7 details of holiday operators.

Road or rail alternatives take a minimum of three days but are obviously worth considering if you plan to visit Greece as part of an extended trip through Europe. The most popular route is down through Italy, then across to Greece by ferry. Depending on conditions, alternative overland routes are through what was Yugoslavia – a standard trip until the civil war – or via Hungary, Romania and Bulgaria.

FLIGHTS FROM BRITAIN

Most of the cheaper flights from Britain to Greece are **charters**, which are sold either with a package holiday or, through "consolidators", as a flight-only option. The flights have fixed and unchangeable outward and return dates, a maximum stay of one month, and must meet the somewhat peculiar conditions of Greek law – more on which in the section following.

For longer stays or more flexibility, or if you're travelling out of season (when few charters are available), you'll need a **scheduled** flight. As with charters, these are offered under a wide variety of fares, and are again often sold off at discount by consolidators.

Although **Athens** remains the prime destination for cheap fares, there are also **direct flights** from Britain to **Thessaloníki** and **Préveza** on the Greek mainland, and to the islands of **Crete**, **Rhodes**, **Corfu**, **Lésvos**, **Páros**, **Zákinthos**, **Skíathos**, **Sámos** and **Kós**. And with any flight to Athens, you can buy an additional **domestic connecting flight** (on the national carrier, *Olympic*) to one of a dozen or so additional Greek mainland and island airports.

CHARTER FLIGHTS

Travel agents throughout Britain sell **charter flights** to Greece. Even the high street chains frequently promote "flight-only" deals, or discount all-inclusive holidays, when their parent companies need to offload their seat allocations. Obviously, the more flexible you can be on dates the better your chances of a bargain fare; if you're prepared to take a "leaving tomorrow at 2am from Luton Airport" flight, you might pick up a flight at a fraction of the normal cost. In any case, phone around agents for a range of offers.

The greatest variety of **flight destinations** tends to be from the London airports. In summer, if you book in advance, you should have a choice of most of the dozen Greek regional airports listed above. Flying from elsewhere in Britain, or looking for last-minute discounts, you'll find options more limited, most commonly to Athens, Corfu, Rhodes and Crete.

Some words of **warning** about Greek aviation law. This specifies that a charter ticket must be a return, of no fewer than three days and no more than four weeks, and must be accompanied by an **accommodation voucher** for at least the first few nights of your stay – check that your ticket satisfies these conditions or you could be refused entry. In practice, the "accommodation voucher" has become a formality; it has to name an existing hotel but you're not expected to use it (and probably won't be able to if you try). As for the time limit, a cheap return flight can often prove advantageous even just using the outbound half.

FLIGHT AGENTS IN BRITAIN

In addition to the **recommended agents** listed below, useful **sources for finding a flight** are classified advertisements in the travel sections of newspapers like *The Independent* and *The Guardian* (Saturday editions), *The Sunday Times*, or – in London – *Time Out* and the *Evening Standard*.

High street travel agents are also worth a look for reductions on package holidays and charter flights, and you might also contact some of the holiday companies (see box on p.6–7) direct. Some of these sell flight-only deals as well as full packages.

STA AND CAMPUS/ *USIT*

The *STA* and *Campus* chains are worth a call for most travel requirements. Both are reliable agents, whose scale of operations ensures a range of good deals; both maintain offices throughout Britain, cater for all travellers and have special deals for students.

STA Travel

74 Old Brompton Rd, London W7
(☎071/937 9962).

UK branch offices include:
25 Queen's Rd, Bristol.
38 Sidney St, Cambridge.
75 Deansgate, Manchester.
36 George St, Oxford.

Campus Travel

52 Grosvenor Gardens, London SW1W 0AG
(☎071/730 8111).

UK branch offices include:
39 Queen's Rd, Bristol (☎0272/292 494).
5 Emmanuel St, Cambridge (☎0223/324 283).
5 Nicholson Sq, Edinburgh (☎031/668 3303)
13 High St, Oxford (☎0865/242 067).

Campus usually have their own student/youth charter flights to Athens during the summer months.

GREEK SPECIALISTS/DISCOUNT AGENTS

Alecos Tours, 3a Camden Rd, London NW1 (☎071/267 2092). Regular *Olympic Airways* consolidator.

Euro Express, 1 Charlwood Court, County Oak Way, Crawley, West Sussex RH11 7XA (☎0293/511125). Features budget flights valid for up to two months and with unusually civilised arrival/departure hours.

Goldair, 321–322 Linen Hall, 162–168 Regent St, London W1 (☎071/287 1003). Good for all Greek flight enquiries, especially if you want flights to Athens and then on to Turkey, Israel or Egypt.

Springways Travel, 15 Gillingham St, London SW1V 1HN (☎071/976 5833). Reliable discount flight agent.

OTHER STUDENT-ORIENTED AGENTS

South Coast Student Travel, 61 Ditchling Rd, Brighton BN1 4SD (☎0273/570226). A good agent with plenty to offer non-students as well.

Travel Cuts, 295 Regent St, London W1 (☎071/255 1944). Often has discount flights.

Council Travel, 28a Poland St, London W1 (☎071/287 3337).

CTS, 44 Goodge St, London W1P 2AD (☎071/637 5601). UK branch of Italian student agency.

AIRLINES

Air UK, Stansted House, Stansted Airport, Stansted (☎0345/666777).

Balkan Airlines, 322 Regent St, London W1R 5AB (☎071/637 7637).

Britannia, 25 Tavistock Place, London WC1H 9SE (☎071/388 2881).

British Airways, 156 Regent Street, London W1R 5TA (☎081/897 4000).

ČSA Czechoslovak Airlines, 72 Margaret St, London W1N 7HA (☎071/255 1898).

Dan Air, 45 Victoria Rd, Horley, Surrey RH6 7QG (☎0293/820222).

LOT Polish Airlines, 313 Regent St, London W1R 7PE (☎071/580 5037).

Malev Hungarian Airlines, 10 Vigo St, London W1X 1AJ (☎071/439 0577).

Olympic Airways, 164 Piccadilly, London W1V 9DE (☎071/493 3965).

The other important condition regards **travel to Turkey**. If you travel to Greece on a charter flight, you may visit Turkey (or any other neighbouring country) only as a day trip; if you stay overnight, you will invalidate your ticket. This rule is justified by the Greek authorities because they subsidise charter airline landing fees, and are therefore reluctant to see tourists spending their money outside Greece. Whether you buy that excuse or not, there is no way around it, since the Turkish authorities clearly stamp all passports, and the Greeks check them. The package industry on the east Aegean and Dodecanese islands bordering Turkey, however, do sometimes prevail upon customs officials to back-date re-entry stamps when bad weather strands their tour groups overnight in Anatolia.

Student/youth charters are exempt from the voucher restriction and are allowed to be sold as one-way flights only. By combining two one-way charters you can, therefore, stay for over a month. Student/youth charter tickets are available to anyone under 26, and to all card-carrying full-time students under 32.

SCHEDULED FLIGHTS

The advantages of scheduled flights are that they can be pre-booked well in advance, remain valid for three months (sometimes longer) and involve none of the above restrictions on charters.

As with charters, discount fares on scheduled flights are available from most high street travel **agents**, as well as from a number of specialist flight and student/youth agencies (for details, see box opposite). Again, you will usually do well to phone around a number of outlets.

The biggest choice of scheduled flights is with the Greek national carrier **Olympic Airways**, who offer the choice of Athens, Thessaloníki and, depending on season, some of the major island airports. *Olympic* shares the UK–Athens routes with **British Airways**. Both airlines have a range of special scheduled fares available, though at £250–325 they generally work out a fair bit more more than a charter.

East European airways like *ČSA*, *Balkan*, *Malev* and *LOT* are often substantially cheaper – £115 single, £210 return for much of the year – but nearly always involve delays, with connections in (respectively) Prague, Sofia, Budapest and Warsaw. It is not always possible to book discount fares direct from these airlines, and you'll often pay no more by going through an agent (see box).

Certain of the **smaller airlines**, such as *Air UK*, *Britannia* and *Dan Air*, offer both charter and scheduled services, and are worth asking after at a travel agency or contacting directly.

FLIGHTS FROM IRELAND

Comments above on charters and scheduled flights apply equally to Ireland as a starting point. Costs, however, are generally higher – count on nearly £250 for a charter in season – and if you want to fly **direct from Dublin** (*Aer Lingus* services only) or **Belfast** (*British Airways* and *Balkan Tours*), you'll be limited to the major Greek destinations such as Crete, Corfu and Athens.

The cheaper flights, including most youth/student offers, are invariably **via London**, with a tag-on fare from Ireland for the connection. As ever, it's worth shopping around agents.

FLIGHT AGENTS IN IRELAND

USIT. Student and youth specialist. Branches at: 19/21 Aston Quay, Dublin 2 (☎01/778 117); 10–11 Market Parade, Cork (☎021/270 900); 31a Queen St, Belfast (☎0232/242 562).

Balkan Tours, 37 Ann St, Belfast BT1 4EB (☎0232/246795). Direct charter flights.

Joe Walsh Tours, 8–11 Baggot St, Dublin (☎01/789 555). General budget fares agent.

Thomas Cook, 118 Grafton St, Dublin (☎01/771 721). Mainstream package holiday and flight agent, with occasional discount offers.

AIRLINES

Aer Lingus, 59 Dawson St, Dublin (☎01/795 030); 46 Castle St, Belfast (☎0232/245151).

British Airways, 60 Dawson St, Dublin (☎01/610 666); 9 Fountain Centre, College St, Belfast (☎0232/245151).

BY RAIL THROUGH EUROPE

Travelling from Britain to Greece by train takes around three and a half days, with minimum stops en route. Fares work out more expensive than a charter flight, though if you plan to take in Greece as part of a rail trip around Europe, InterRail passes – now available in "youth" and "26-plus" versions – represent good value.

ROUTES

Up until the outbreak of civil war in Yugoslavia in 1991, most rail travellers to Greece did a circuit: down **through France and Italy and across on the ferry** from Bari, Brindisi or Otranto, then **back through Yugoslavia** – or vice versa.

At the time of writing (mid-1992), services are suspended on what was the fastest and for years the most popular Yugoslav route: Venice–Zagreb–Belgrade–Thessaloníki. However, *British Rail* are still selling tickets, on a day to day basis, for travel on the **Budapest–Belgrade–Skopje–Thessaloníki** route – which bypasses Croatia and Bosnia-Hercegovina.

If political conditions forbid this route, or if your curiosity takes you further east, a somewhat rambling alternative is to travel from **Budapest to Thessaloníki via Bucharest and Sofia**.

Note that **Thessaloníki** is suggested as a first Greek stop on all these overland rail routes. Athens is nearly nine hours further on the train.

Note also that the disruption caused by the suspension of Yugoslav routes has put an extra burden on the **trains to the Italian ports** – and on the ferries themselves. Book seats on both well in advance, especially in summer.

PACKAGE HOLIDAYS: BRITISH-BASED SPECIALISTS

Virtually every British **tour operator** includes Greece in its programme, though with many of the larger groups you'll find choices limited to the established resorts – notably the islands of Rhodes, Kos, Crete, Skíathos, Zákinthos and Corfu, plus Toló and the Halikidhikí on the mainland. If you buy one of these at a last-minute discount, you may find it costs little more than a flight – and you can use the accommodation offered as much or as little as you want. For a rather more low-key and genuinely "Greek" resort, however, it's better to book your holiday through one of the smaller **specialist agencies** listed below.

VILLA OR VILLAGE ACCOMMODATION

These companies are all fairly small-scale operations, offering competitively priced packages with flights plus accommodation. They make an effort to find local, village accommodation and to offer islands without over-developed tourist resorts.

CV Travel, 43 Cadogan St, London SW3 2PR (☎071/581 0851). High quality villas on Corfu and Paxí.

Corfu à la Carte, 8 Deanwood House, Stockcross, Newbury, Berkshire RG16 8JP (☎0635/30621). Selected beach and rural cottages on Corfu, Paxí and Skíathos.

Greek Islands Club, 66 High St, Walton-on-Thames, KT12 1BU (☎0932/220477). Holidays on the Ionian islands, including Kíthira. Also offer sailing holidays through their "Sailing Club" wing.

Greek Sun Holidays, 1 Bank St, Sevenoaks, Kent TN13 1UW (☎0732/740317). Offer a variety of packages, including fly-drive, on a wide range of islands and on the Pílion peninsula.

Ilios Island Holidays, 18 Market Square, Horsham, West Sussex RH12 1EU (☎0403/59788). Features mainly Ionian and Sporades islands, plus Naxos and the west coast of Pílion.

The Best of Greece, 100 Week St, Maidstone, Kent, ME14 1RG (☎0622/692278). Limited number of exclusive villa and hotel arrangements from a long-established operator.

Kosmar Villa Holidays, 358 Bowes Rd, Arnos Grove, London N11 1AN (☎081/368 6833). Villas at Toló and on the Argo-Saronic isles and Crete.

Laskarina Holidays, St Marys Gate, Wirksworth, Derbyshire DE4 4DQ (☎0629/822203). Emphasis on a dozen of the less visited islands of the Dodecanese and Sporades.

Manos Holidays, 168–172 Old St, London EC1V 9BP (☎071/608 1161). Operates in most of the major resorts.

Simply Crete, 8 Chiswick Terrace, London W4 5LY (☎081/994 4462). High-quality apartments and small hotels around Crete.

Skiathos Travel, 4 Holmesdale Rd, Kew Gardens, Richmond, Surrey GU13 8AA (☎081/940 5157). Flights and accommodation to the other Sporades as well as Skíathos.

Sunvil Holidays, Sunvil House, 7–8 Upper Square, Old Isleworth, Middlesex TW7 7BJ (☎081/568 4499). Good choice of smaller resorts, including Límnos and mainland showcase villages.

REGULAR AND BIJ TICKETS

Regular train tickets from Britain to Greece are not good value. London to Athens costs anywhere from £300 to £350 return, depending on whether you transit via Belgrade, opt for the quieter Italy passage, or for the circuitous route via Budapest, Bucharest and Sofia. If you are **under 26**, you can get a **BIJ ticket**, discounting these fares by around 30 percent; these are available through *Eurotrain* and *Wasteels* (see box overleaf).

None of these prices compares well with InterRail passes (see below), though they do have advantages if you want to stay for a longer period in Greece. Both regular and BIJ tickets have two months' return validity, or can be purchased as one-ways, and the Italy routes include the ferry crossing. The tickets also allow for stopovers, so long as you stick to the route prescribed.

INTERRAIL PASSES

Anyone resident in Europe for six months is eligible for an **InterRail pass**. Available from *British Rail* (or any travel agent), this offers the flexibility of go-where-you-please, stop-where-you-please, travel on most European rail networks, for a 15-day or month-long period. There are two types:

● **InterRail Youth Pass** (£180 for a month). Covers travel on 24 rail networks. The only extras you pay are supplements on certain express trains, plus half-price fares in Britain (or the country of issue) and on the Channel ferries. The pass includes the ferry from Brindisi in southern Italy to Pátra (Patras) in Greece.

● **InterRail 26-plus Pass** (£260 for a month, £180 for 15 days). As above, though the pass gives no reductions on travel in Britain, or on the Channel ferries and doesn't cover Spain.

Timsway Holidays, Astley House, 33 Notting Hill Gate, London W11 3JQ (☎071/221 2656). Good for some of the remoter islands, such as the small Dodecanese, and the Peloponnese; also special-interest holidays such as *kaíki* cruising.

Voyages Ilena, Old Garden House, The Lanterns, Bridge Lane, London SW11 3AD (☎071/924 4440). Peloponnese specialist, with a careful selection of accommodation in the Máni and Argolid.

HIKING TOURS

All the operators below run trekking groups, which generally consist of 10 to 15 people, plus an experienced guide. The walks tend to be day-hikes from one or more bases, or point-to-point treks staying in village accommodation en route; camping is not usually involved.

Exodus Expeditions, 9 Weir Rd, London SW12 0LT (☎081/675 5550). Treks in the Píndhos, or a less strenuous itinerary in Crete.

Explore Worldwide, 1 Frederick St, Aldershot, Hants GU11 1LQ (☎0252/344161). Organised rambles in western Crete and island sailing.

Ramblers Holidays, Box 43, Welwyn Garden City, Hertfordshire AL8 6PQ (☎0707/331133). Easy walking tours on Kefalloniá, Itháki and Crete.

Sherpa Expeditions, 131a Heston Rd, Hounslow, Middlesex TW5 0RD (☎081/577 2717). Good range of programmes.

Waymark Holidays, 44 Windsor Road, Slough SL1 2EJ (☎0753/516477). Spring and autumn walking holidays on Sámos and Mílos.

NATURE AND WILDLIFE

Peregrine Holidays, 40/41 South Parade, Summertown, Oxford OX2 7JP (☎0865/511642). Natural history tours around the Peloponnese, the Macedonian lakes, Crete, and select other islands; the emphasis on each tour is on wildlife – though combined with visits to archaeological sites.

SAILING

Dinghy sailing and windsurfing holidays based on small flotillas of four- to six-berth yachts. Prices start at around £320 per week; all levels of experience. If you're a confident sailor and can muster a group of people, it's possible simply to hire a yacht from a broker; the Greek National Tourist Organisation has lists of companies.

Falcon, Groundstar House, 390 London Rd, Crawley RH10 (☎ 0293/599944).

Greek Islands Sailing Club, 66 High St, Walton-on-Thames KT12 1BU (☎0932/220416).

Sunsail The Port House, Port Solent, Portsmouth PO6 4TH (☎0705/210345).

World Expeditions, 8 College Rise, Maidenhead, Berkshire SL6 6BP (☎0628/74174).

MIND AND BODY

Skyros Centre, 92 Prince of Wales Rd, London NW5 3NE (☎071/267 4424). Holistic health, fitness and "personal growth" holidays on the island of Skíros, as well as writers' workshops and "mythological journeys".

RAIL AND BUS TICKET OFFICES

RAIL

British Rail European Travel Centre, Victoria Station, London SW1 (☎071/834 2345).

Eurotrain, 52 Grosvenor Gardens, London SW1 (☎071/730 3402).

Wasteels, 121 Wilton Rd, London SW1 (☎071/834 7066).

BUSES

Citysprint, Maybrook House, Queens Gardens, Dover, Kent CT17 9BR (☎0304/240202).

Eurolines, 52 Grosvenor Gardens, London SW1 (☎071/730 0202).

SENIOR CITIZENS

Anyone over 60 and holding a British Rail Senior Citizen Railcard, can buy a **Rail Europe Senior Card** (£7.50 for one year). This gives up to fifty percent reductions on rail fares throughout Europe and thirty percent off sea crossings.

EURAIL PASSES

Most North Americans and Australasians fail to meet the residency requirement for InterRail – though some travel agents have been known to bend the rules. The official alternative is a **Eurail pass**, which must be bought before arrival in Europe. This gives unlimited travel in seventeen countries – Austria, Belgium, Denmark, Finland, France, Germany, Greece, Hungary, Ireland, Italy, Luxembourg, Norway, The Netherlands, Portugal, Spain, Sweden and Switzerland. It covers fewer countries than Interrail, and gets discounts only on *Hellenic Mediterranean services* on the Italy–Greece ferries. However, on the plus side, it is valid for more express trains, thus saving money on supplements.

If you're under 26, you can buy the **Eurail Youth Pass** (US$470/Aus$590 for one month; US$640 for two months), or the **Eurail Youth Flexipass**, which is valid for any 15 days within two months (US$420). These all cover second-class travel.

Regular Eurail passes – available to all ages – cover first-class travel for a choice of five **periods**: 15 days (US$430), 21 days (US$550), one month (US$680), two months (US$920) and three months (US$1150). Additionally, there are: the **Eurail Saverpass** (US$340 for 15 days); the **Eurail Flexipass** (5 days' travel within 15 consecutive days for US$280; 9 days within 21 days for US$450; 14 days within one month for US$610); and the **Eurail Drive Pass** (any 3 days' rail travel and any 3 days' car rental for US$269 per person; extra days US$40 per person).

LUGGAGE TRANSIT

Note that, for a nominal fee, you can have the bulk of your **luggage registered through to Athens** (or any other stage of the journey), saving the hassle of carting it around at every change. Furthermore, if the railway authorities lose, damage or delay your baggage, you are entitled to compensation. When registering the luggage, insist on obtaining the supporting documentation.

BY BUS/COACH FROM BRITAIN

Unless you're lucky enough to get a rock-bottom flight, coaches are the cheapest form of transport between London and Athens, perhaps 25 percent less than the equivalent train ride. Prices advertised through the summer – both in London and Athens – can start very low indeed, at under £70 one way for the three to four day journey.

As with flights, the best source for **adverts** in London are the classified sections of *Time Out*, the *Evening Standard* and the free Australasian magazines. However, **be very wary** about going for the cheapest company unless you've heard something about them. There have been a string of accidents in recent years with operators flouting the terms of their licence, and horror stories abound of drivers getting lost or their coaches being refused entry. Some of the more disreputable operators actually start their journeys in modern, air-conditioned coaches to comply with British regulations then, once across the Channel, transfer passengers to old beaten-up buses. Be equally aware of these cowboys in Athens.

All things considered, it's probably best to opt for **Eurolines**. These coaches are operated by *National Express*, along with a consortium of other European state bus companies. They're comparatively expensive (£80 one way) but are safe, reliable and bookable through any *National Express* office.

The **route** is usually via Belgium, Germany, Austria and (conditions permitting) what-was-Yugoslavia. Stops of about twenty minutes are made every five or six hours, with the odd longer break for roadside café meals. If you've booked with one of the more reliable operators you'll have three drivers working in shifts; most companies make do with two, and driving can become correspondingly hairy.

DRIVING FROM BRITAIN

If you have the time, driving to Greece can be a pleasant proposition. The most obvious route is down through France and Italy to catch one of the Adriatic ferries. Overland routes through ex-Yugoslavia are, at the time of writing, unsafe and uncertain. However, if an overland loop through eastern Europe appeals, you can drive by way of Hungary, Romania and Bulgaria.

VIA ITALY

Heading for Western Greece, or the Ionian islands, it has always made most sense to drive via Italy – and whatever your final destination, taking a ferry on the final leg makes for a more relaxed journey. From Italy there's a choice of six **ports** (though the closest, Venice and Trieste, are expensive options); in Greece you can dock at either Igoumenítsa in Epirus, Pátra in the Peloponnese, or (coming from Venice or Bari) at Pireás, the port of Athens. See below for details of routes and operators.

Routes down **to Italy through France and Switzerland** are very much a question of personal taste. The fastest is probably Calais–Paris–Dijon–Geneva–Chamonix, which will get you to Milan with just one night en route if you follow the autoroutes (and pay their tolls).

Whichever route you choose, you're likely to emerge in Italy around the Milan ring road. From here **Ancona** is under a day's drive on the autostrada; for the southern ports of **Bari**, **Brindisi** or **Otranto** you will need to count on at least one Italian overnight stay.

VIA HUNGARY, ROMANIA AND BULGARIA

Avoiding ex-Yugoslavia involves a pretty substantial diversion through Hungary, Romania and Bulgaria. This is not a drive to contemplate unless you actively want to see some of the countries en route – it's too exhausting and too problematic. However, it's all easier than it was, with visas now more or less routinely available at the borders, if you haven't fixed them in advance.

From **Budapest**, the quickest route **through Romania** is via Timisoara (4–5hr) then through Drobeta-Turnu-Severin to Calafat (6–8hr), where a car ferry runs across the Danube to the Bulgarian town of Vidin. This is very much B-road driving – and not easily rushed.

Heading from Vidin **through Bulgaria**, the roads improve, with an approximation of a highway down to Sofia and on across the Rila mountains to the border at Kulata. All in all, this would be about ten to twelve hours' driving. Once at the **Greek border**, it's a three to four-hour drive to Thessaloníki or Kavála.

VIA EX-YUGOSLAVIA

The two main highways through what-was-Yugoslavia cut across most of the republics. It is thus very hard to make any predictions about their status, even if the fighting comes to an end.

The **inland highway** heads through Ljubjana (Slovenia) and Zagreb (Croatia), then into a swathe of Bosnia-Hercegovina on its way to Belgrade (Serbia), and finally through Skopje (Macedonia) to reach Flórina or Thessaloníki in Greek Macedonia. Even before the conflicts, this was one of Europe's poorest road arteries, with thundering trucks on what was often little more than a two-lane highway.

The alternative approach is the **coast road**, which includes sections of Slovenia, Croatia, Bosnia-Hercegovina and Montenegro. In Montenegro, you need to head inland, joining the inland highway in Kosovo or Macedonia.

HITCHING FROM BRITAIN

The best plan for hitchers is to talk yourself into a lift on the ferry across to France or Belgium: the Channel ports are miserable places to hitch out of, and a sympathetic TIR truck-driver might offer a single lift most of the way to Italy or Hungary. You will thus bypass the legendary French indifference to hitchers.

The choice of routes are outlined under "Driving", above. Travelling via **Italy** will involve more outlay on ferries, but saves travelling time – and therefore money. If you take the **Romania/Bulgaria** route, you have the option of getting a very cheap Romanian/Greek-operated bus from Bucharest to Thessaloníki or Athens. Numerous (cowboy) companies operate these.

FERRIES TO GREECE: ROUTES AND AGENTS

Regular car and passenger ferries link the Italian ports of **Ancona**, **Bari**, **Brindisi** and **Otranto** with **Igoumenítsa** (the port of Epirus in western Greece) and/or **Pátra** (at the northwest tip of the Peloponnese). Most sail via the island of **Corfu**, and a few link other Ionian islands en route to Pátra; you can stop over at no extra charge if you get these stops specified on your ticket. Most are year-round services.

Ferries also sail – less frequently – from **Venice** to Pireás, the port of Athens, from **Trieste** to Pátra, and from **Ortona** to Corfu. At the time of writing, ferries down the **Croatian coast**, from Rijeka, Split and Dubrovnik to Corfu, have been suspended due to the war in ex-Yugoslavia.

Booking

The hostilities in ex-Yugoslavia – which have also suspended overland rail and road services through Zagreb and Belgrade – have led to severe strains on the Italy–Greece ferries. In summer, it is essential to **book tickets** a few days ahead, especially in the peak July–August season. During the winter you can usually just turn up at the main ports (Ancona, Bari, Brindisi, Igoumenítsa/Corfu), but it's still wise to book in advance, certainly if you are taking a car or want a cabin.

A few phone calls and brochure-collection jaunts before leaving are, in any case, advisable, as the range of fares and operators (from Brindisi especially) is considerable; if you do just turn up at the port, spend an hour or so shopping around the agencies.

THE ITALY–GREECE ROUTES

*Note that crossing to **Igoumenítsa** is substantially cheaper than to **Pátra**; the cheapest of all the crossings are from **Brindisi** or **Otranto** to Igoumenítsa. However, drivers will discover that the extra cost in Italian petrol – double the British price – offsets the routes' savings over those from Bari or Ancona; the shipping companies are well aware of this and set their prices accordingly.*

From Ancona *Marlines*, *Strintzis*, *ANEK* and *Minoan* to Igoumenítsa (24hr) and Pátra (34hr); *Karageorgis* direct to Pátra (33hr); daily or nearly so year-round. *Minoan* sails via Corfu, with a separate line for Kefalloniá, Pireás, Páros, Sámos and Kusadasi (Turkey) half the year; *Strintzis* and *ANEK* via Corfu; *Marlines* has a summer extension from Pátra to Iráklio (Crete), Rhodes and Limmasol (Cyprus). Most sailings between 8 and 10pm, but there are a number of afternoon departures.

From Bari *Ventouris* to Pátra direct (20hr), nearly daily; to Corfu, Igoumenítsa (12hr) and Pátra (20hr); daily departures year-round between 8 and 9pm. To Pátra via Corfu and/or Igoumenítsa on *Poseidon Lines*, *Arkadia Lines*. *Adriatica* stops here en route to/from Venice.

From Brindisi *Fragline* and *Adriatica* to Corfu, Igoumenítsa (11hr) and Pátra (20hr). *Hellenic Mediterranean Lines* to Corfu and Pátra, three to seven a week depending on season; Kefalloniá and Pátra, or Paxí and Igoumenítsa, served on separate daily sailings during summer. *European Seaways* to Corfu, Igoumenítsa and Pátra. *Marlines* to Igoumenítsa and Brindisi. *Mediterranean Line* to Igoumenítsa/Pátra; allows drivers to sleep in their camper-vans, thus saving on cabin. Several ferries leave every day in season, most between 8 and 10.30pm; at least one daily in winter.

From Ortona *Hellenic Mediterranean* to Corfu/ Igoumenítsa (20/21hr), summer only.

From Otranto *R-Lines* to Corfu and Igoumenítsa (9hr.); five weekly, May–Oct only.

From Venice *Adriatica* to Pireás (42hr.) and Iráklio, (Crete), three monthly, continuing to Alexandria (Egypt); *TML* to Pireás en route Ito zmir (Turkey), one weekly in low season.

From Trieste *ANEK* to Pátra (43hr). One weekly in summer, tagged on to Ancona service.

DALMATIAN ROUTES

Jadrolinja Lines used to operate ferries down the Dalmatian coast to Corfu and Igoumenítsa, starting at **Rijeka** and calling at (Rab), Zadar, Split, (Hvar), Korçula and Dubrovnik; ports in brackets are stops in peak season only.

This service is suspended at time of publication – mid-1992 – but if hostilities cease, should be renewed in 1993. In previous years, there were one to two departures weekly from April to October. Note that *Jadrolinija* itself may reform under another name, since so many of the Adriatic ports now lie in independent Croatia.

UK AGENTS

For details on local agents in Greece, see the respective listings for Pátra and Igoumenítsa. The following are UK agents for advance bookings:

Mak Travel, 36 King St, London W1 (☎071/836 8216). *Karageorgis.*

Mediterranean Passenger Services, 9 Hanover St, W1 (☎071/499 0076). *Hellenic Mediterranean Lines.*

P&O European Ferries, Channel House, Channel View Rd, Dover, Kent CT17 9TJ (☎0304/22300). *Minoan Lines.*

Sealink, Charter House, Park St, Ashford, Kent TN24 8EX (☎0233/647047). *Adriatica.*

Sunquest Holidays, 9 Grand Parade, Green Lanes, London N4 (☎081/800 8030). Agent for *TML* ferries between Turkey, Italy and Greece.

Viamare Travel Ltd, 33 Mapesbury Rd, London NW6 (☎081/452 8231). *ANEK, Arkadia, Fragline, Marlines, R-Lines, Strintzis, Ventouris.*

Yugotours, Chesham House, 150 Regent St, London W1 (☎01/734 7321). *Jadrolinija Lines.*

SAMPLE FARES

*Prices range below are indicated as for low/high season; **port taxes** (£3–5 per person in each direction) are not included.*

Igoumenítsa from Bari, Brindisi or Otranto: deck class £15–£20/£20–£30; car from £20/£45.

Pátra from Bari, Brindisi or Otranto: deck class £20–£30/£30–50; car from £20/45.

Igoumenítsa from Ancona: deck class £30/40; car from £50/£70.

DISCOUNTS

Note that substantial reductions apply on most lines for both **InterRail** or **Eurail** pass-holders, and those **under 26**. Slight discounts are usually available on **return fares**.

FERRIES TO CYPRUS, TURKEY, ISRAEL AND EGYPT

Greece also has regular **passenger ferry links** with **Turkey**, **Cyprus**, **Israel** and **Egypt**. Details of these are to be found throughout the guide under entries for the various ports of exit/arrival – Pireás, Pátra and Igoumenítsa on the mainland, and the islands of Rhodes, Crete, Lésvos, Híos, Sámos and Kós.

TURKEY

Ferry links between Greece and Turkey have relaxed over the past few years, as relations have softened between the two countries. Note, however, that if you travelled to Greece on a **charter flight**, staying overnight in Turkey will invalidate the return half of the ticket (see p.5).

Crossings are:

Ancona–Corfu–Kefalloniá–Pireás–Páros–Sámos–Kuşadasi Weekly in season on the C/F *Ariadne. Minoan Lines.*

Pireás–Izmir Out of season only on the C/F *Ankara. Turkish Maritime Lines.*

Lésvos–Ayvalik Local service.

Híos–Çesme Local service.

Sámos–Kuşadasi Local service.

Kós–Bodrum Local service.

Rhodes–Marmaris Local service.

CYPRUS

Ferries from Greece to Cyprus offer slight savings over flights from Athens and Rhodes; the island is, however, a stopover on routes to Haifa (Israel),

Port Said/Alexandria (Egypt) and Lattakia (Syria), which may appeal to Med-hoppers.

Crossings to the Greek part of the island are:

Pireás/Rhodes/Crete to **Limassol**.

Pireás to **Larnica**.

ISRAEL

Ferries run from **Pireás to Haifa**, calling en route at **Cyprus** and often at **Crete** or **Rhodes**. It's usually possible to buy stopover tickets taking in two of these islands at no extra cost.

EGYPT

Ferries from Pireás to Egypt also include stops en route at Cyprus or Crete.

Routes are:

Pireás–Limassol (Cyprus)–Port Said. *Louis Cruise Lines.*

Pireás–Iraklion (Crete)–Alexandria. *Adriatica Lines.*

Pireás–Larnica (Cyprus)–Lattakia (Syria)–Alexandria. *Black Sea Shipping.*

GETTING THERE FROM NORTH AMERICA

Only a few carriers fly directly to Greece from North America, so most North Americans travel to a gateway European city, and pick up a connecting flight on from there with an associated airline. If you have time, you may well decide that it's cheaper and easier to arrange the Europe–Greece leg of the journey yourself, in which case your only criterion will be finding a suitable and good value North America–Europe flight. Seat consolidators, who buy blocks of seats on major airlines and advertise in the travel sections of the Sunday newspapers, are the best way to find a cheap fare; useful companies to start your search with are listed in the box opposite.

In general there just isn't enough traffic on the Athens route to make for many very cheap fares, partly because the American FAA limits the Greek national airline, *Olympic Airways* (☎1-800/223-1226), to flying only out of New York (JFK). The main advantage to buying a ticket from *Olympic*, who also fly out of Montreal and Toronto, is that they can offer add-on flights within the country, especially to the Greek Islands, for only US$50–75, leaving from the same Athens terminal that you will fly into.

FROM THE USA

With **direct flights**, there's usually a big difference in cost depending upon where you start your journey. Fares from New York to Athens cost around US$300 less than they do from other US cities, so it may be worth making your way to the Big Apple. On **indirect flights**, via London, Paris or Frankfurt, for example, the price differentials aren't so great, while the budget-minded will probably do best of all booking a flight to London and then contacting agents there for the leg to Greece (see previous sections for details).

Note that tickets bought through **seat consolidators** are usually difficult and expensive to **change** once you've bought them, though if you're willing to plan ahead they can open up lots of options, such as flying "open jaw", for example landing in Athens and leaving out of Rome, London or another European city.

FROM THE EAST COAST

Non-stop flights to Athens out of **New York** on *Olympic* start at around US$700 round-trip in winter, rising to around US$1100 in summer for a maximum thirty day stay with seven-day advance purchase. *Delta*, which has recently assumed the transatlantic routes of defunct *Pan Am*, currently has a daily service to Athens via Frankfurt but intends to begin direct flights by summer 1992.

Fares on other carriers such as *TWA* cost around US$300 more, though seat consolidators offer flights on major airlines for around half the cost the airlines themselves quote: round-trips run from around US$600 in winter, US$900 in summer. One-way fares usually cost a little more, say US$20, than half the round-trip price.

Seat consolidators are generally the best-value outlets for travellers starting off in other eastern cities: flights from Atlanta, for example, cost around US$700 round-trip in winter, US$900 in summer.

FROM THE WEST COAST

Since all scheduled flights to Athens from the West Coast go via New York or another eastern city, you basically end up paying for a transcontinental flight on top of the transatlantic fare: round-trip APEX tickets from Seattle, San Francisco or Los Angeles on *TWA* or *Delta* start at US$1275 in winter, rising to over US$1600 in summer. Student/youth fares through the likes of *STA* or *Council Travel* can sometimes save you money, though again the best deals are usually those offered by seat consolidators advertising in Sunday newspaper travel sections.

FLIGHT AGENTS IN NORTH AMERICA

The **agents, travel clubs and consolidators** listed below are included either because they feature Greece on their itineraries or because they offer good value access to Europe (usually London). Most should be able to sell you an add-on flight to Greece from the European point of entry they favour. Alternatively, you could travel on overland (see previous section).

USA

Council Travel, 205 E 42nd St, New York, NY 10017 (☎212/661-1450). Head office of the nationwide US student travel organisation. Branches in San Francisco, Berkeley, Los Angeles, Washington, New Orleans, Chicago, Seattle, Portland, Minneapolis, Boston, Atlanta and Dallas, to name only the larger ones.

STA Travel, 48 E 11th St, Suite 805, New York, NY 10003 (☎212/986-9470); 166 Geary St, Suite 702, San Francisco, CA 94108 (☎415/391-8407). Main US branches of the worldwide specialist in independent and student travel. Other offices in LA, Berkeley, Boston and Honolulu.

CANADA

Travel Cuts, 187 College St, Toronto, ON M5T 1P7 (☎416/979-2406). Main office of the Canadian student travel organisation. Many other offices nationwide.

CANADA/USA

Nouvelles Frontières, 800 bd de Maisonneuve Est, Montréal, PQ H2L 4L8 (☎514/288-9942); 12 E 33rd St, New York, NY 10016 (☎212/779-0600). Main Canadian/American branches of the French discount travel outfit. Other branches in Quebec City, LA and San Francisco.

EAST COAST/CENTRAL USA

Access International, 101 West 31st St, Suite 104, New York, NY 10001 (☎1-800/TAKE-OFF). Good East Coast/central US consolidator.

EAST COAST

Airhitch, 2790 Broadway, Suite 100, New York, NY 10025 (☎212/864-2000). Operates a scheme whereby, for a flat, heavily discounted fee, you are flown to any one of a selection of points in Europe within a five-day time range which you specify.

Discount Club of America, 61–33 Woodhaven Blvd, Rego Park, NY 11374 (☎718/335-9612). Discount travel club.

Discount Travel International, Ives Bldg, 114 Forrest Ave, Suite 205, Narbeth, PA 19072 (☎215/668-2182 or 1-800/221-8139).

Encore Short Notice, 4501 Forbes Blvd, Lanham, MD 20706 (☎301/459-8020 or 1-800/638-0830). East Coast travel club.

Last-Minute Travel Club, 132 Brookline Ave, Boston, MA 02215 (☎617/267-9800 or 1-800/LAST-MIN).

Moment's Notice, 425 Madison Ave, New York, NY 10017 (☎212/486-0503). Travel club that's good for last-minute deals.

TFI Tours, 34 W. 32nd St, New York, NY (☎212/736-1140 or 1-800/825-3834)

Travel Brokers, 50 Broad St, New York, NY 10004 (☎1-800/999-8748). New York travel club.

WEST COAST

Airkit, 1125 W 6th St, Los Angeles, CA 90017 (☎213/957-9304). West Coast consolidator with seats from San Francisco and LA.

Global Access, San Francisco (☎800/229-5355 or 415/227-4641).

Scan the World, Palo Alto (☎415/325-0876).

Travel Time, San Francisco (☎800/235-3253 or 415/677-0799).

Travel Warehouse, Los Angeles (☎213/551-3181). West Coast consolidator/agent.

SOUTHEASTERN/SOUTHERN USA

Interworld, 3400 Coral Way, Miami, FL 33145 (☎305/443-4929). Southeastern US consolidator.

Travelers Advantage, 49 Music Square, Nashville, TN 37203 (☎1-800/548-1116). Reliable travel club.

Worldwide Discount Travel Club, 1674 Meridian Ave, Miami Beach, FL 33139 (☎305/534-2082).

MIDWEST USA

Stand Buys, 311 W Superior St, Chicago, IL 60610 (☎1-800/331-0257). Good travel club.

Travel Avenue, 130 S Jefferson, Chicago, IL 60606 (☎312/876-1116 or 1-800/333-3335). Discount travel agent.

Travac, 1177 N Warson Rd, St Louis, MO 63132 (☎1-800/872-8800). Useful consolidator.

Unitravel, 1177 N Warson Rd, St Louis, MO 63132 (☎1-800/325-2222). Reliable consolidator.

FROM CANADA

As with the US, air fares from Canada to Athens vary tremendously depending upon where you start your journey. The best-value scheduled fare is on *Olympic*, who fly non-stop out of Montréal every weekend in winter for CDN$1100 round-trip, twice a week in summer for CDN$1500.

Air Canada, who fly to Vienna with connections to Athens on *Olympic*, are your best bet from elsewhere in Canada, with flights from Vancouver costing CDN$1600 in winter, CDN$1800 in summer. If you're eligible, student/youth fares offer good value for travelling from outside Montréal: fares from Vancouver cost CDN$900–1400 depending on season.

AIRLINES IN NORTH AMERICA

DIRECT FLIGHTS TO GREECE

Olympic Airways, 647 Fifth Ave, New York, NY 10022 (☎212/838-3600 or 1-800/223-1226); 168 N Michigan Ave, Chicago, IL 60601 (☎312/329-0400 or 1-800/223-1226); 500 South Grand St, Suite 1500, Los Angeles, CA 90014 (☎212/624-6441); 80 Bloor St West, Suite 502, Toronto, ON M5S 2V1 (☎416/920-2452).

Delta Airlines, Hartsfield Atlanta International Airport, Atlanta, GA 30320 (☎404/765-5000 or 1-800/241-4141).

INDIRECT FLIGHTS

Air France, 888 Seventh Ave, New York, NY 10106 (☎212/830-4000 or 1-800/237-2747); 875 N Michigan Ave, Chicago, IL 60611 (☎312/440-7922); 2000 rue Mansfield, Montréal, PQ H3A 3A3 (☎514/284-2825); 151 Bloor St W, Suite 600, Toronto, ON M5S 1S4 (☎416/922-5024).

Alitalia, 666 Fifth Ave, New York, NY 10103 (☎212/582-8900 or 1-800/223-5730); 2055 Peel St, Montréal, PQ H3A 1V8 (☎514/842-5201); 120 Adelaide St West, Toronto, ON M5H 2E1 (☎416/363-2001).

American Airlines, PO Box 619616, Dallas/Fort Worth International Airport, Dallas, TX 75261 (☎817/267-1151 or 1-800/433-7300).

British Airways, 530 Fifth Ave, New York, NY 10017 (☎1-800/2479297); 1001 bd de Maisonneuve Ouest, Montréal, PQ H3A 3C8 (☎1-800/668-1059); 112 Kent St, Ottawa, ON K1P 5P2 (☎613/236-0881); 1 Dundas St West, Toronto, ON M5G 2B2 (☎416/250-0880).

Continental Airlines, 2929 Allen Parkway, Houston, TX 77019 (☎713/821-2100 or 1-800/231-0856).

ČSA Czechoslovak Airlines, 545 Fifth Ave, New York, NY 10017 (☎212/682-5833 or 1-800/223-2365); 2020 University St, Montréal, PQ H3A 2A5 (☎514/844-4200); 401 Bay St, Toronto, ON M5H 2Y4 (☎416/363-3174).

Icelandair, 360 W 31st St, New York, NY 10001 (☎212/967-8888 or 1-800/223-5500).

KLM, 565 Taxter Rd, Elmsford, NY 10523 (☎212/759-3600 or 1-800/777-5553); 225 N Michigan Ave, Chicago, IL 60601 (☎212/861-9292); 1255 Green Ave, West Mount, MontréalPQ H3Z 2A4 (☎514/933-1314 or 1-800/361-5073).

LOT Polish Airlines, 500 Fifth Ave, New York, NY 10110 (☎212/869-1074); 333 N Michigan Ave, Chicago, IL 60601 (☎312/236-3388); 2000 Peter Elizabeth London, Montréal, PQ H3A 2W5 (☎514/844-2674).

Lufthansa, 1640 Hempstead Turnpike, East Meadow, NY 11554 (☎718/895-1277 or 1-800/645-3880); 875 N Michigan Ave, Chicago, IL 60611 (☎312/751-0111); 55 Yonge St, Toronto, ON M5E 1J4 (☎416/368-4777); 2020 University St, Montréal, PQ H3A 2A5 (☎514/288-2227).

Malev Hungarian Airlines, 630 Fifth Ave, New York, NY 10111 (☎212/757-6446 or 1-800/223-6884 for east coast, 1-800/262-5380 for west coast); 175 Bloor St East, Toronto, ON M4W 3R8 (☎1-800/334-1284).

Northwest Airlines, Minneapolis/St Paul International Airport, St Paul, MN 55111 (☎612/726-1234 or 1-800/225-2525).

Sabena, 720 Fifth Ave, New York, NY 100022 (☎1-800/955-2000); 5959 W Century Blvd, Los Angeles, CA 90045 (☎213/642-7735); 1001 bd de Maisonneuve Ouest, Montréal, H3A 3C8 (☎514/845-0215).

Trans World Airlines, 100 South Bedford Rd, Mount Kisco, NY 10549 (☎212/290-2141 or 1-800/892-4141).

United Airlines, PO Box 66100, Chicago, IL 60666 (☎708/952-4000 or 1-800/241-6522 or 538-2929).

US Air, Crystal Park Four, 2345 Crystal Drive, Arlington, VA 22227 (☎703/418-7000 or 1-800/622-1015).

Virgin Atlantic Airways, 96 Horton St, New York, NY 10014 (☎212/206-6612 or 1-800/862-8621).

TRAVELLING VIA WESTERN EUROPE

Unless you're setting off from New York or Montréal, you can save a lot of money, not to mention see a lot more of Europe, by travelling to **London**, **Frankfurt**, **Paris** or **Amsterdam**, and continuing on to Greece from there. Flights to these cities often cost as little as half the price of a flight direct (or even with add-on fare) to Athens, and travel within Europe, whether by plane or train or a combination of both, is relatively cheap. For details of routes, operators and agents, see the previous section on "Getting There from Britain".

Because of international regulations, it's illegal to sell or even advertise **air fares** for trips wholly within Europe in the US or Canada, so you'll have to make arrangements once you're in Europe. **Train journeys** are another, generally enjoyable, option: a round-trip train ticket, including all ferry crossings, between London and Athens costs around US$550, and is valid for two months with unlimited stopovers en route. If you're under 26, the same ticket costs around US$425. Train fares from Amsterdam, Paris or Frankfurt are marginally lower still. Unless you plan extended rail travel in Europe, these individual tickets are considerably better value than a **Eurail Pass** – the European train pass marketed in North America (see p.8). Except in the peak summer months, trains through Europe are rarely fully booked, so you can usually travel comfortably by reserving seats a day or two ahead.

As detailed in the "From Britain" overland sections, the continuing instability and upheaval in ex-**Yugoslavia** – long the main overland link between Greece and western Europe – make it best to plan your route through **Italy**, taking the ferries from Bari or Brindisi via Corfu to Pátra or Igoumenítsa in Greece. Alternative train routes run via **Hungary**, **Romania** and **Bulgaria** to Thessaloníki in northeastern Greece.

GETTING THERE FROM AUSTRALASIA

Australians and New Zealanders have the possibility of direct and reasonably competitive flights from Sydney or Melbourne to Athens. However, it's almost always cheaper to transit via London, picking up flights or rail tickets on from there. For a summary of these possibilities, see the "Travelling via Western Europe" section above; for details of routes and operators, see previous section on "Getting There from Britain and Ireland".

FLIGHTS AND ROUTES

There are frequent **flights** from **Melbourne** and **Sydney** to **Athens** on *Qantas*, *Olympic Airways*, *Singapore Airlines* and *Thai International*. All involve a stop in either Singapore or Bangkok, and there's usually not a great deal of difference in fares; a single to Athens should set you back around Aus$780, with a return ticket costing minimally less than twice that. With the large Greek populations of Sydney and Melbourne, however, there may sometimes be bargain deals to Athens on *Olympic*.

Flights from **Perth** to **Athens**, when available, often work out at about Aus$100 less than from the other Australian centres, while a flight from **Auckland** to **Athens** will cost approximately NZ$300 extra for a single, NZ$420 for a return.

For these and other low-price tickets, the most reliable operator is *STA* (*STS* in New Zealand). They can issue **rail tickets** and passes if you prefer to get a flight to London and make your way on from there.

AGENTS AND AIRLINES

AUSTRALIA

STA: 1a Lee St, Railway Square, Sydney 2000 (☎02/519 9866); 224 Faraday St, Carlton, Victoria, 3053 (☎03/347 4711).

Olympic Airways, 84 William St, 3000 Victoria, Melbourne (☎03/602 5400).

NEW ZEALAND

STS Head office: 10 High St, Auckland (☎09/309 9723).

Olympic Airways, 44 Pitt St, NSW 2000, Sydney (☎02/251 1047).

VISAS AND RED TAPE

UK and all other EC nationals need only a **valid passport** for entry to Greece; you are no longer stamped in on arrival or out upon departure, and in theory at least enjoy uniform civil rights with Greek citizens. US, Australian, Canadian, and most non-EC Europeans, receive entry and exit stamps in their passports and can stay, as tourists, for ninety days; New Zealanders get sixty days.

If you are planning to **travel overland**, you should check current visa requirements (if any) for Hungary, Romania and Bulgaria, or for newly independent Slovenia and Croatia at their closest consulates; transit visas for most of these territories are at present issued at the borders, though at a higher price than if obtained in advance at a local consulate.

VISA EXTENSIONS

If you wish to stay in Greece for longer than three months, you should officially apply for an **extension**. This can be done in the larger cities like Athens, Thessaloníki, Pátra and Iráklio through the *Ipiresía Allodhapón* (Aliens' Bureau); prepare yourself for concerted bureaucracy. In remoter locations you can visit the local police station, where staff are apt to be more cooperative.

The first extension is free, while subsequent ones currently cost 1200 drachmas. It is vital to begin the procedure a couple of weeks before your time runs out, and also to present pink, personalised bank exchange slips (see "Costs, Money and Banks", below) as proof that you can support yourself without working.

Some individuals get around the law by leaving Greece every three months and re-entering a few days later for a new tourist stamp. However, with the recent flood of Albanian refugees into the country, and a smaller influx of east Europeans, either looking for work or causing trouble according to their disposition, security and immigration personnel don't always look very kindly on this practice.

If you overstay your time and then leave under your own power – ie are not deported – you'll be fined a small amount upon exit. The amount is usually equivalent to the 200-drachma-per-month revenue stamps that would have accompanied a formal application. Overstaying for a short period, you may, therefore, prefer just to profess ignorance and pay up.

GREEK EMBASSIES ABROAD

Australia 9 Turrana St, Yarralumla, Canberra, ACT 2600 (☎062/273-3011).

Britain 1a Holland Park, London W11 (☎071/727 8040).

Canada 80 Maclaren St, Ottawa, ON K2P 0K6 (☎613/238-6271).

Ireland 1 Upper Pembroke St, Dublin 2 (☎01/767254).

New Zealand Cumberland House, 237 Willis St, PO Box 27157, Wellington (☎04/847-556).

USA 2221 Massachusetts Ave NW, Washington, DC 20008 (☎202/667-3168).

COSTS, MONEY AND BANKS

CURRENCY

Greek currency is the **drachma** (*dhrahmí*), currently rated at around 325dr to the pound sterling, 185dr to the US dollar.

The most common **notes** in circulation are those of 100, 500, 1000 and 5000 drachmas (*dhrahmés*), while **coins** come in denominations of 1, 2, 5, 10, 20, 50 and 100dr.

The drachma is theoretically subdivided into 100 *leptá*, though the unit is more or less defunct.

The costs of living in Greece have spiralled over the past decade of EC membership: the days of renting a house for a few thousand drachmas a week are long gone, and food prices at corner shops now differ little from those of other member countries. However, outside of the established resorts, travel in the country remains quite a bargain, with the prices of restaurant meals, accommodation and public transport as cheap as anywhere in northern or western Europe.

COSTS

Needs are simple in Greece. Once you've negotiated a room or campsite, it is only really meals, your choice of transport, and admission tickets to ancient sites that make inroads on your budget. You don't seem to spend money without noticing it – as in France or Italy, for example.

Travelling as one of a pair or a group, sharing rooms and food, you could get by on £11–14/US$20–25 a day if you eat only one meal out a day and stick to public transport and the humbler grades of accommodation. On £16–20/US$28–36 per day you could be living quite well, ordering a top-quality bottle of wine at one of two daily taverna meals and treating yourself and a friend to motorbike or car rental, plus the occasional internal plane flight.

SOME SAMPLE COSTS

Domestic Aegean **ferries**, a main unavoidable expense, are quite reasonably priced, helped by government subsidies to preserve island commu-

nities. A deck-class ticket from Pireás, the port of Athens, to Crete or Sámos, both 12-to-14hr trips, costs about £10/US$18. For half the cost, there are dozens of closer islands in reach.

Long-distance **buses** now cost nearly the same as their equivalents elsewhere in Europe, but city services are still very cheap, as are **trains** – for example Athens–Thessaloníki, the longest single journey you're likely to make, is just £9/US$16 second -class.

The simplest double **room** can generally be had for £8–12/US$14.50–21 a night, depending on the location and the plumbing arrangements. Organised **campsites** cost little more than £1.50/US$2.50 per person, with similar charges per tent and perhaps 25 percent more for a camper van. With discretion you can camp for free in the more remote, rural areas.

Meals are also good value. A basic taverna **meal** can be had for around £6/US$10 a head. Add a better bottle of wine, seafood, or more careful cooking, and it could be up to £10/US$16 a head – but you'll rarely pay more than that.

OTHER COST FACTORS

All costs are of course subject to **where and when** you go. You'll pay much more for the same calibre room in Athens or at major island resorts than in the provinces or on the lesser-known islands. Similarly, high season rates are generally 25 to 50 percent above the rest of the year.

Solo travellers will experience some frustration. Even in city hotels, single rooms are relatively rare, and in summer on the islands you'll invariably pay the full double rate. Food likewise is cheaper if shared, but even in the resorts with their inflated "international" menus you'll usually find a reasonable taverna where the locals (and penniless soldiers) eat.

For **students**, an ISIC or FIYTO card gives a fifty percent discount off admission fees at most archaeological sites, plus many reductions on transport – including international air tickets, plus local trains and ferries.

CARRYING MONEY

There is no need to change foreign currency into dhrachmas before arrival unless you're coming in at some ungodly hour at one of the remoter land or sea frontier posts. Airport arrival lounges will always have an exchange booth operating for passengers on incoming international flights.

Most people bring their funds in the form of travellers' cheques, though if you've a European bank account you might prefer to carry Eurocheques, or if you've a Girobank current account, Postcheques. A certain amount of small- and medium-sized sterling, US dollar or Deutschmark notes are also very useful for unexpected last-minute expenses.

CHEQUES AND EXCHANGE

Travellers' cheques can be cashed at all banks and most post offices and, when they're closed, at quite a number of hotels, agencies and tourist shops – though nearly always on poorer terms. **Eurocheques**, which most British banks issue along with a Eurocheque card, are widely accepted at banks or post offices and are written out in drachmas.

Commission on travellers' cheques is paid when you buy them and also to the exchanging bank or post office. With most Eurocheques you pay a charge of around 1.6 percent to the exchanging bank plus a handling fee of around 30p per transaction against your British account when they're presented for payment, usually around three weeks later.

Postcheques, available to European Girobank customers, work in a similar way to Eurocheques (again in conjunction with a cheque card) but are exchanged only at post offices. They are issued, with a small commission, in amounts of the equivalent of £100 in local currency.

Exchanging money at the **post office** has some considerable advantages in Greece. You miss out on the queues at banks and have access to exchange almost anywhere you go. There are a number of small islands that have no bank but they almost all have a post office. Commissions levied for both cheques and cash tend, at about 300dr, to be lower than at banks.

Note that Eurocheques and Postcheques can be cashed at post offices during the frequent strikes and computer crashes which plague Greek banks, since their negotiation does not depend on knowing the exact exchange rate for that day.

In addition, **travel agents**, **shipping agents** and larger **hotels** will generally exchange travellers' cheques or foreign currency.

PLASTIC: CREDIT AND CASHPOINT

Major **credit cards** are accepted only by the more expensive shops, hotels and restaurants. They're useful – indeed almost essential – for renting cars, for example, but not much use in the cheaper tavernas or hotels.

If you run short of money, you can get a **cash advance on a credit card**, but be warned that the minimum amount is 15,000dr. The *Emborikí Trápeza* (Commercial Bank) handles *Visa*; the *Ethnikí Trápeza* (National Bank) services *Access/ Mastercard* customers.

It is much easier to use the small but growing network of Greek **cashpoint (autoteller) machines**. The most useful and well-distributed are those of the *Trápeza Písteos* (Credit Bank), which will accept not only Visa and American Express but also Barclaycards. In the largest cities and airports the Commercial and National banks have a number of machines catering for a range of card-holders.

EMERGENCY CASH

In an emergency, you can arrange to have **money sent** from home to a bank in Greece. Though this is theoretically very quick, you should in practice count on delays of three to six days for receipt of telexed funds. You can pick up the sum in foreign currency, or even travellers' cheques, on payment of an additional premium.

RECEIPTS AND CURRENCY REGULATIONS

Travellers' cheques are freely importable into Greece, but more than £600 in **cash** should be declared upon entry by EC citizens to minimise hassles if you want to take it out again. A lower limit of approximately £300 applies to non-EC nationals.

If you have any reason to believe that you'll be acquiring large quantities of drachmas — from work or sale of goods — declare everything on arrival, then request (and save) pink, personalised **receipts** for each exchange transaction. Otherwise you may find that you can only re-exchange a limited sum of drachmas on departure. These pink receipts are also essential for obtaining a residence permit.

Try, though, not to have substantial amounts of leftover drachmas to sell back. You may have to visit four or five banks to find the currency of your choice, and the red tape, as European unity looms, seems paradoxically greater. The best bets are usually the airport exchange booths.

BANKS AND COMMISSIONS

Greek **banks** are normally open Mon–Thurs 8am–2pm, Fri 8am–1.30pm. Certain branches in the major cities and tourist centres are open extra hours in the evenings and on Saturday mornings for exchanging money. Always take your passport with you as proof of identity and be prepared for at least one long queue — usually you have to line up once to have the transaction approved and again to pick up the cash.

Commissions vary within the range of 400 to 700 drachmas, depending on the bank and the size of the transaction — ask first. Both commission and rate will be worse if you change money at a **hotel** or **travel agent**.

HEALTH AND INSURANCE

There are no required inoculations for Greece, though it's wise to have a typhoid-cholera booster, and to ensure that you are up to date on tetanus and polio.

The water is safe (and tastes wonderful) pretty much everywhere, though you will come across shortages or brackish supplies on some of the drier and more remote islands. Bottled water is widely available if you're feeling cautious.

SPECIFIC HAZARDS

The main health problems experienced by visitors have to do with overexposure to the sun, and the odd nasty from the sea. To combat the former, wear a hat and drink plenty of fluids in the hot months to avoid any danger of **sunstroke**, and

don't underestimate the power of even a hazy sun to **burn**. For sea-wear, a pair of goggles for swimming and footwear for walking over wet rocks are useful.

HAZARDS OF THE DEEP

In the sea, you may just have the bad luck to meet an armada of **jellyfish**, especially in late summer; they come in various colours and sizes including invisible and minute. Various over-the-counter remedies are sold in resort pharmacies; baking soda or ammonia (your own urine is the simplest solution) also help to lessen the sting.

Less vicious but more common are **sea urchins**, which infest rocky shorelines year-round; if you step on or graze one, a needle (you can crudely sterilise it by heat from a cigarette lighter) and olive oil are effective for removing spines from your anatomy; they should be extracted, or they will fester.

The worst maritime danger — fortunately very rare — seems to be the **weever fish**, which buries itself in tidal zone sand with just its poisonous dorsal and gill spines protruding. If you tread on one the sudden pain is unmistakably excruciating, and the venom is exceptionally potent. Consequences can range up to permanent paralysis of the affected area, so the imperative first aid is to immerse your foot in water as hot as you can stand. This serves to degrade the toxin and relieve the swelling of joints and attendant pain.

SANDFLIES, MOSQUITOES AND SNAKES

If you are sleeping on or near a **beach**, a wise precaution is to use insect repellent, either lotion or wrist/ankle bands, and/or a tent with a screen to guard against **sandflies**. You are unlikely to be infected by these, but they are potentially dangerous, carrying visceral leishmaniasis, a rare parasitic infection characterised by chronic fever, listlessness and weight loss.

Mosquitoes (*kounóupia*) are less worrying – in Greece they don't carry anything worse than a vicious bite – but they can be infuriating. The best solution is to burn pyrethrum incense coils (*spíres* or *fidhákia* in Greek); these are widely and cheaply available, though smelly. Better if you can get them are the small electrical devices which vaporise an odourless insecticide tablet.

The **adder** and **scorpion** are found in Greece, though both are shy; just take care when climbing over dry-stone walls where snakes like to sun themselves, and don't put hands/feet in places, ie shoes, where you haven't looked first.

PHARMACIES AND DOCTORS

For **minor complaints** it's enough to go to the local **farmakío**. Greek pharmacists are highly trained and dispense a number of medicines which elsewhere could only be prescribed by a doctor. In the larger towns there'll usually be one who speaks good English.

Homeopathic and herbal remedies are quite widely available, with homeopathic pharmacies in many of the larger towns. There is a large homeo-

TRAVEL WITH A DISABILITY

It is all too easy to wax lyrical over the attractions of Greece: the stepped, narrow alleys, the ease of travel by bus and ferry, the thrill of clambering around the great archaeological sites. It is almost impossible, on the other hand, for the able-bodied travel writer to see these attractions as potential hazards for anyone who has some difficulty in walking or is wheelchair-bound or suffers from some other disability. The cheering line "facilities for the disabled are not well developed in Greece" is often the only reference to disabled people in the available travel literature.

In all honesty this guide is barely more practical in this respect than any other. However, don't be discouraged. It is possible to enjoy an inexpensive and trauma-free holiday in Greece if some time is devoted to gathering information before arrival. The following guidelines come from a rheumatoid arthritis sufferer, but the general principles should be applicable to all physically challenged travellers.

ATTITUDES

There are **organised tours and holidays** specifically for disabled people, but if you want to be more independent that is perfectly possible, provided that you do not leave home with the vague hope that things will turn out all right, and that "people will help out" when you need assistance. The best form of assistance, unexpected and unasked for, is likely to be cheerfully given in Greece, but it cannot be relied on. Local attitudes – and comments – may be astonishingly outdated. You must either be completely confident that you can manage alone, or travel with an able-bodied friend (or two). When you have special personal needs, the confidence to travel alone or with one other person, to plan and organise your trip, comes only with preparation.

Become an authority on where you must be self-reliant and where you may expect help, especially regarding transport and accommodation. For example, to get between the terminals at Athens airport, you will have to fight for a taxi; it is not the duty of the airline staff to find you one, and there is no trace of an organised queue.

Be wary, too, since much existing or readily available information is **out of date** – you should always try to double-check. A number of addresses of contact organisations are published below. The EOT (Greek Tourist Office) is a good first step as long as you have specific questions to put to them; they publish a useful questionnaire which you could send to hotels or owners of apartment/villa accommodation.

It is also vital to **be honest** – with travel agencies, insurance companies, the organisations you write to for information, companions, the people you meet, and, above all, with yourself. Know your limitations and make sure others know them. If you do not use a wheelchair all the time but your walking capabilities are limited, remember that you are likely to need to cover greater distances while travelling (often over tougher terrain and in hotter weather than you are used to). So if you use one, take a wheelchair with you, have it serviced before you go, and carry a repair kit; rough roads play havoc with nuts, bolts and tyres.

pathic centre in Athens at Nikosthénous 8, Platía Plastíra, Pangráti (☎709-8199) and a nearby homeopathic pharmacy at Ivíkou 8, corner Eratosthénous (☎722-2774). Others are delineated by the characteristic green cross sign.

If you regularly use any form of **prescription drug** you should bring along a copy of the prescription together with the generic name of the drug – this will help should you need to replace it and also avoid possible problems with customs officials. In this context, it's worth being aware that codeine is banned in Greece. If you import any, even the common American Empirin-Codeine compound, you just might find yourself in serious trouble, so check labels carefully.

Contraceptive pills are more readily available every year, but don't count on local availabil-

ity – unfortunately abortion is still the principal form of birth control. **Condoms**, however, are inexpensive and ubiquitous – just ask for *profilaktiká* at any pharmacy or corner *períptero* (kiosk).

Lastly, **hay fever** sufferers should be prepared for the early Greek pollen season, at its height from April to June. If you are taken by surprise, pharmacists stock tablets and creams.

DOCTORS AND HOSPITALS

For serious **medical attention** you'll find English-speaking doctors in any of the bigger towns or resorts; the tourist police (☎171 in Athens) or your consulate should be able to come up with some names if you have any difficulty.

In **emergencies**, treatment is given free in **state hospitals** – for cuts, broken bones, etc –

INSURANCE AND PREPARATIONS

If you're getting travel **insurance**, read the small print carefully to make sure that people with a pre-existing medical condition are not excluded. And use your travel agent to make your journey simpler: **airlines** or coach companies can cope better if they are expecting you, with a wheelchair provided at airports and staff primed to help. A medical certficate of your fitness to travel, provided by your doctor, is also extremely useful; some airlines or insurance companies may insist on it.

The best place to start is with a **list** of all the facilities that will make your life easier while you are away. You may want a ground-floor room, or access to a large elevator; you may have special dietary requirements, or need level ground to enable you to reach shops, beaches, bars, and places of interest. Again, be realistic, and accept that you may not be able to expect the level of comfort and convenience you have at home. You should also keep track of all your other special needs, making sure, for example, that you have extra supplies of drugs – carried with you if you fly – and a prescription including the generic name in case of emergency. Any kind of drug, clothing or equipment that might be hard to find in Greece you should carry spares of; if there's an association representing people with your disability, contact them for information on what to take and what to leave behind.

And if all of this sounds like hard work, the rewards should be worth it.

USEFUL CONTACTS

Evyenia Stravropoulou, Lavinia Tours: Egnatía 101, 541 10 Thessaloníki.
Will advise disabled visitors and has tested many parts of Greece in her wheelchair. She also organises tours within Greece.

Holiday Care Service, 2 Old Bank Chambers, Station Rd, Horley, Surrey GU9 8RW (☎0293/774535).
Publishes a fact sheet, and also runs a useful "Holiday Helpers" service for disabled travellers.

Mobility International, 228 Borough High St, London SE1 1JX (☎071/403 5688) and PO Box 3551, Eugene, OR 94703 (☎503/343-1284).
Issues a quarterly newsletter on developments in disabled travel.

National Foundation of Disabled (KAPAS): Leofóros Dhiamantídhou, Paléa Psihikó, Athens.
Contact in case of emergency.

National Institution of Rehabilitation for the Handicapped: Odhós Hassías, Néa Lióssia, KA 1322, Athens.
Will advise disabled visitors.

National Tourist Organisation of Greece (EOT): Addresses on p.23.
Their specific information for travellers with disabilities is skimpy and out of date, but they try, and can at least usually advise on terrain and climate.

RADAR: 25 Mortimer St, London W1N 8AB (☎071/637 5400).
Publishes fact sheets and an annual guide to accommodation and facilities abroad, and issues a list of insurance companies who arrange policies

though you will only get the most basic level of nursing care. Greek families routinely take in food and bedding for relatives, so as a tourist you'll be at a severe disadvantage. Somewhat better are the ordinary state-run **outpatient clinics** (*yatría*) attached to most public hospitals and also found in rural locales; these operate on a first-come, first-served basis; usual hours are 8am to noon.

TRAVEL INSURANCE

British and other EC nationals are officially entitled to free medical care in Greece upon presentation of an E111 form, obtained by filling in form CM1 at a DSS office, post office or travel agent at least a month before departure. "Free", however, means admittance only to the lowest grade of state hospital (known as a *yenikó noso-komío*), and does not include nursing care or the cost of medications. In practice, hospital staff tend to greet E111s with uncomprehending looks, and you may have to request reimbursal to the NHS upon return home. If you need prolonged medical care, you'll prefer to make use of private treatment, which is, as everywhere, expensive.

Some form of **travel insurance**, therefore, is advisable – and almost essential for **North Americans and Australasians**, whose countries have no formal health care agreements with Greece. For medical claims, keep receipts, including those from pharmacies. You will have to pay for all private medical care on the spot (insurance claims can be processed if you have hospital treatment) but it can all be (eventually) claimed back.

EUROPEAN COVER

Among **British/Irish** insurers, *Endsleigh* are about the cheapest, offering a month's cover for around £20. Their policies are available from most youth/student travel specialists or direct from their offices at 97–107 Southampton Row, London WC1 (☎071/436 4451).

Most **banks** and **credit card** issuers also offer some sort of vacation protection, often automatic if you pay for the holiday with a card.

NORTH AMERICAN COVER

Before purchasing special **travel insurance**, whether for medical or property mishaps, check to see that you won't duplicate the coverage of any **existing plans** you may have.

For example, **Canadians** are usually covered for medical expenses by their provincial health plans (but may only be reimbursed after the fact).

Holders of **ISIC** cards are entitled to US$3000 worth of accident coverage and sixty days of hospital in-patient benefits for the period during which the card is valid. University **students** will often find that their student health coverage extends for one term beyond the date of last enrolment. Bank and charge **accounts** (particularly *American Express*) often have certain levels of medical or other insurance included. **Homeowners' or renters'** insurance may also cover theft or loss of documents, money and valuables while overseas.

If after checking policies and cards, you still feel you need specialist travel insurance, good companies to approach include: *Travel Guard*, 110 Centrepoint Drive, Steven Point, WI 54480 (☎715/345-0505 or 800/826-1300), *Travel Assistance International*, 1133 Fifteenth St NW, Suite 400, Washington, DC 20005 (☎1-800/821-2828) or *Access America International*, 600 Third Ave, New York, NY 10163 (☎212/949-5960 or 800/284-8300).

Travel insurance offerings are quite comprehensive, anticipating everything from charter companies going bankrupt to delayed (as well as lost) baggage, by way of sundry illnesses and accidents. If you think that you might rent a car or motorbike, make sure that such activities are included – a good proportion of tourist accidents in Greece involve falling off two-wheelers.

A most important thing to keep in mind – and a source of major disappointment to would-be claimants – is that *none* of the currently available **North American policies** insure against **theft** of *anything* while overseas. The policy cover applies only to items lost from, or damaged in, the custody of an identifiable, responsible third party, ie a hotel porter, airline, luggage consignment, etc. If you are travelling for some period of time in Europe, or are stopping en route in Britain, you should consider a **British** travel insurance policy, which normally include theft cover (see above).

INSURANCE REPORTS

In all cases of loss or theft of goods, you will have to contact the local police to have a **report** made out so that your insurer can process the claim. This can occasionally be a tricky business in Greece, since many officials simply won't accept that anything could be stolen on their turf, or at least don't want to take responsibility for it. Be persistent and if necessary enlist the support of the local tourist police or tourist office.

THE EOT, INFORMATION AND MAPS

The **National Tourist Organisation of Greece** (*Ellinikós Organismós Tourismoú*, or *EOT*) publishes an impressive array of free, glossy, regional pamphlets, which are good for getting an idea of where you want to go, even if the actual text should be taken with an occasional grain of salt. Also available from the EOT are a reasonable fold-out **map** of Greece, a large number of sheets on special interests, from annual festivals to lead-free petrol stations, and a (highly approximate) ferry timetable.

The EOT maintains **offices abroad** in most European capitals, plus major cities in Australia and North America (see box below).

In Greece, you will find EOT offices in most of the larger towns and resorts. The principal

Athens offices are on Síntagma Square, one inside the National Bank of Greece, and an annexe handling the overflow nearby at the General Bank. Here, in addition to the usual leaflets, you can pick up weekly **schedules for the inter-island ferries** – not 100 percent reliable but useful as a guideline. The EOT staff are themselves very helpful for advice on **ferry, bus, and train departures**.

Where there is no EOT office, you can get information (and often a range of leaflets) from municipally run **tourist offices** or from the **Tourist Police**. The latter are basically a branch (often just a single delegate) of the local police. They can sometimes provide you with lists of rooms to let, which they regulate, and they are in general helpful and efficient.

MAPS

Maps are an endless source of confusion in Greece. Each cartographic company seems to have its own peculiar system of transcribing Greek letters into English – and these, as often as not, do not match the transliterations on the road signs.

The most reliable **road maps** of Greece are *Michelin #980* (1:700,000) and *Freytag-Berndt* (1:650,000). These are widely available in Britain and North America, though less easily in Greece. *Freytag-Berndt* also publishes a series of more detailed maps on various regions of Greece, such as the Peloponnese and the Cyclades; these are best bought overseas, from specialist outlets.

Maps of **individual islands** are more easily available on the spot. They span the range of usefulness: some are wildly inaccurate or obsolete, with strange hieroglyphic symbology, others are reliable and up-to-date. The most comprehensive, though not always the most accurate series, covering most islands of any size and available overseas, is published by *Toubi*.

The most useful map of **Athens**, easy to use and with a decent index, is the *Falkplan* – available from most specialist outlets. If you can read Greek, and plan to stay in the city some time, the *Athina-Pireas Proastia Alpha-Omega* street atlas, published by Kapranidhis and Fotis, is invaluable. It has a complete index, down to the tiniest alley – of which there are many.

HIKING/TOPOGRAPHICAL MAPS

Hiking/topographical maps, subject to uneven quality and availability, are gradually improving.

The Greek mountaineering magazine *Korfes* began in 1982 to publish 1:50,000 maps of select alpine areas, with Latin-alphabet lettering appearing in the last few years. More than fifty are in print and a new one is issued every other month as a centrefold in the magazine. To get back issues you may need to visit the magazine's office at Kentrikí Platía 16, Aharnés, Athens (☎24 1 528), although the more central bookstore *Polia tou Vivliou* (see "Specialist Shops" in the Athens chapter) also has a backstock.

The *Korfes* maps are, unfortunately, unreliable in the matter of trails and new roads, but extremely accurate for natural features and village position, based as they are on the older maps of the **Army Geographical Service**

(*Yeografikí Ipiresía Stratoú*). If you want to obtain these for islands, and mainland areas not covered by *Korfes*, visit the *YIS* at Evelpídhon 4, north of Áreos Park in Athens, on Monday, Wednesday or Friday from 8am to noon only. All foreigners must leave their passport with the gate guard; EC citizens may proceed directly to the sales hall, where efficient, computerised transactions take just a few minutes. Other nationals will probably have to go upstairs for an interview; if you don't speak reasonably good Greek, it's best to have a Greek friend get them for you.

As of writing, maps covering Crete, the Dodecanese, the east Aegean, Skiros, parts of Corfu and much of Epirus, Macedonia and Thrace are still off-limits to all foreigners, but *YIS* staff anticipates that EC nationals at least will have unrestricted access to 1:50,000 sheets covering the entire country by 1993.

Recently, a German company, **Harms**, has released a series of five maps at 1:80,000 scale which cover Crete from west to east and show many hiking routes – invaluable until and unless the *YIS* declassifies this area.

In **Britain**, general touring maps, the *Harms* sheets and a limited number of the *Korfes* products are available through *Stanfords*, 12 Long Acre, London WC2 (☎071/836 1321). In **North America**, there's a similar selection available from *Map Link*, 25 E Mason St, Santa Barbara, CA 93101 (☎805/965-4402 – they do mail-order business). Possibly more convenient for walk-in trade are branches of the *Rand McNally* chain; they have outlets in New York at 150 E 52nd St, NY 10022 (☎212/758-7488); in Chicago at 444 N Michigan Ave, IL 60611 (☎312/321-1751); and in San Francisco at 595 Market St, CA 94105 (☎415/777-3131).

GETTING AROUND

The standard means of land transport in Greece is the bus. Train networks are usually slow and limited, though service on the northern mainland lines is improving. Buses, however, cover just about every route on the mainland – albeit infrequently on minor roads – and provide basic connections on the islands. The best way to supplement buses is to rent a moped, motorbike or car, especially on the islands, where at any substantial town or resort you can find a rental outlet.

Inter-island travel of course means taking ferries. These again are extensive, and given time will get you to any of the 166 inhabited isles. Planes are expensive, at double the cost of ferries, but useful for saving time at the start or finish of a visit.

BUSES

Bus services on the **major routes** – both on the mainland and islands – are highly efficient: On **secondary roads** they're less regular, with long halts, but even the most remote villages will be connected – at least on weekdays – by a school or market bus to the provincial capital. As these often leave for the major centre shortly after dawn, an alarm clock can be a useful travel aid. On the **islands**, there are usually buses to connect the port and main town for ferry arrivals or departures.

Most of the network consists of green-and-cream-coloured buses, privately run by a syndicate of companies known as the **KTEL**. However, even in medium-sized towns there can be several scattered terminals for services in different directions, so make sure you have the right station for your departure. As a rough estimate to cost, figure on about 11–13 drachmas per kilometre travelled.

Buses are amazingly **prompt** as a rule, so be there in plenty of time for scheduled departures. For the major, inter-city lines such as Athens–Pátra, ticketing is now computerised, with assigned seating and sold-out vehicles common. On smaller rural/island routes, it's generally first-come, first-served with some standing allowed, and tickets dispensed on the spot by a peripatetic *ispráktoros* or conductor. Most operations fall somewhere in between.

A few long-distance and international routes are also served by express buses operated by **OSE**, the State Railway Organisation. These always leave from the train station and can be useful supplements to regular services.

TRAINS

The Greek railway network, run by **OSE**, is limited to the mainland, and with few exceptions trains are invariably slower than the equivalent buses. However, they're also much cheaper – about fifty percent less on non-express services, even more if you buy a return ticket – and some of the lines are

enjoyable in themselves. The best, a real treat of a ride, is the rack-and-pinion line between **Diakoftó and Kalávrita** in the Peloponnese.

Timetables are sporadically available during May or June, printed in Greek only; the best place to obtain one is the *OSE* offices in Athens or Thessaloníki. Always check the station placards, since with the once-yearly printing, changes often crop up in the interim. Trains tend to leave promptly at the outset, though on the more circuitous lines they're invariably forty minutes late by the end of the journey.

If you're starting a journey at the initial station of a run you can (at no extra cost) **reserve** a seat; a carriage and seat number will be written on the back of your ticket. At most intermediate points, it's first-come, first-served.

There are two basic **classes**: first and second. First class may be worth the extra money, insomuch as the cars may be emptier and seats more comfortable. Of late a luxury, **sleeper** category, the so-called *tréna/ksenodhohía*, has been inaugurated on certain routes between Alexandhroúpoli, Thessaloníki, Athens and Vólos – these are very sleek overnighters, and much faster than the bus if the timetable is to be trusted.

InterRail pass holders must secure reservations like everyone else, and must pay express supplements on a few lines. InterRail passes and Eurotrain tickets are available in Greece through *ISYTS*, Níkis 11, Second Floor, Athens.

OSE also sells its own **pass**, offering unlimited travel for 10, 20 or 30 days,. This is unlikely to be worthwhile unless you're touring extensively in the northern mainland.

See overpage for train route map.

FERRIES

Ferries are of use primarily for travel to, and between, islands, though you may also want to make use of the routes between Athens and Monemvassía in the Peloponnese. There are three different varieties of boats: medium-sized to large **ordinary ferries** (which operate the main services), **hydrofoils** (run by the *Ceres* "*Flying Dolphins*", *Ilios*, and *Dodecanese Hydrofoils*, among other companies), and local **kaíkia** (small boats which in season cover short island hops and excursions). Costs are very reasonable on the longer journeys, though proportionately more expensive for shorter, inter-island connections.

GREECE: TRAINS

0   100 km

We've indicated most of the **ferry connections**, both on the maps (see p.366–67 for a general picture) and in the "Travel Details" at the end of each chapter. Don't take our listings as exhaustive or wholly reliable, however, as schedules are notoriously erratic, and be aware that we have given details essentially for summer departures. **Out-of-season** departure frequencies are severely reduced, with many islands connected only once or twice a week. However in spring or autumn those ferries that do operate are often compelled by the transport ministry to call at extra islands, making possible some interesting connections.

The most reliable, up-to-date information is available from the local **port police** (*limenarhío*), which maintains offices at Pireás (☎108 or 143) and on virtually all fair-sized islands. They rarely speak much English, but keep complete schedules posted – and, meteorological report in hand, are the final arbiters of whether a ship will sail or not in stormy weather conditions. Another good resource is *The Thomas Cook Guide to Greek Island Hopping*, which features a comprehensive overview of past ferry patterns and what they're likely to be in the future.

REGULAR FERRIES

On most ferry routes, your only consideration will be getting a boat that leaves on the day, and for the island, that you want. However, when sailing from **Pireás (Piraeus)**, the port of Athens, to the

Cyclades or Dodecanese islands, you should have quite a range of choice and may want to bear in mind a few of the factors below.

Most importantly, bear in mind that **routes** taken and the speed of the boats vary enormously. A journey from Pireás to Thíra (Santoríni), for instance, can take anything from nine to fourteen hours. Before buying a ticket it's wise to establish how many stops there'll be before your island, and the estimated time of arrival. Many agents act only for one specific boat (they'll happily tell you that theirs is the only available service), so you may have to ask around to uncover alternatives. Especially in high season, early arrival is critical in getting what may be a very limited stock of accommodation.

The **boats** themselves have improved somewhat recently, with a fair number of garbage scows consigned to the scrap heap or dumped overseas – just about the only ferries you might want to avoid if you have the choice are the odiferous *Ayios Rafael*, on the Kavála–Rhodes run, and the elderly *Golden Vergina* on the Páros–Sámos route. You will more often than not be surprised to encounter a former English Channel or Scandavian fjord ferry, rechristened and enjoying a new lease on life in the Aegean.

The pattern of **sailings from Pireás** has changed in recent years. There are now relatively few early-morning sailings for the Cyclades and Sámos/Ikaría, with the bulk of departures for the major Dodecanese at about 1pm, and a broad mix among the Cyclades and Dodecanese between 2 and 6pm. There is a final spate of departures between 6 and 9pm for Crete, Híos and Lésvos, as well as Sámos, Ikaría and a large number of the Cyclades.

Regular ferry **tickets** are, in general, best bought on the day of departure, unless you need to reserve a cabin berth or space for a car. Buying tickets in advance will tie you down to a particular ferry at a particular time – and innumerable factors can make you regret that. Most obviously there's **bad weather**, which, particularly off-season, can play havoc with the schedules, causing some small boats to remain at anchor and others to alter their routes drastically. There are only three periods of the year – March 23–25, the week before and after Easter, and mid-August – when ferries need to be booked at least a couple of days in advance. Otherwise, you can always buy a ticket once on board with no penalty, despite what travel agents may tell you. Ticket prices for each route are currently set by the transport ministry and should not differ among ships or agencies.

The cheapest class of ticket, which you'll probably automatically be sold, is **deck class**, variously called *tríti* or *gámma*. This gives you the run of most boats except for the upper-class restaurant and bar. On the shorter, summer journeys the best place to be, in any case, is on deck – space best staked out as soon as you get on board. However, boats acquired recently seem, with their glaring overhead lights and moulded-plastic bucket seats, expressly designed to frustrate those attempting to sleep on deck. In such cases it's well worth the few thousand extra drachmas for a cabin bunk, especially if you can share with friends. Class consciousness has increased of late, so deck-class passengers will find themselves firmly locked out of second-class facilities at night to prevent them from crashing on the plush sofas. First-class cabin facilities usually cost scarcely less than a plane flight and are not terrific value – the only difference between first and second being the presence of a bathroom in the cabin. Most cabins, incidentally, are apt to be overheated, stuffy and windowless.

Motorbikes and **cars** get issued extra tickets, in the latter case up to four times the passenger fare. This obviously limits the number of islands you'll want to drag a car to – it's really only worth it for the larger ones like Crete, Rhodes, Híos, Lésvos, Sámos or Kefalloniá. Even with these, unless you're planning a stay of more than four days, you may find it cheaper to leave your car in Pireás and rent another on arrival.

Most ferries sell a limited range of **food** aboard, though it tends to be overpriced and mediocre in quality. Honourable exceptions are the decent, reasonable meals served by *ANEK* lines, which operates the ferries from Pireás to Haniá and Iráklio on Crete; most of the boats plying to Híos and Lésvos; and as a general rule any overnight sailing where the galley is used to serving supper to a captive audience. On other lines, particularly the short hops in the Argo-Saronic, Cyclades and Sporades, it is well worth stocking up with your own provisions.

HYDROFOILS

"Flying Dolphin" and other **hydrofoils** are roughly twice as fast (and at least twice as expensive) as ordinary ferries. They are a useful alternative to regular ferries if you are pushed for time; their network seems to be growing each year, so it's worth asking after services, even if they are not mentioned in this guide. Their drawback is that, owing to their design, they are extremely sensitive to bad weather and most of the services don't operate – or are heavily reduced – out of season.

At present, hydrofoils operate among the **Argo-Saronic islands** close to Athens, down the **east coast of the Peloponnese** to Monemvassía and Kíthira, among the **northern Sporades** (Skíathos, Skópelos and Alónissos), among certain of the **Cyclades** (Ándros, Tínos, Míkonos, Páros, Náxos, Amorgós, the minor islets, Íos, Thíra – and Crete), and in the **Dodecanese** among Rhodes, Kós and Pátmos, with occasional forays up to Sámos or over to Tílos and Níssiros. The principal **mainland ports** are Zea and Flisvos marinas in Pireás and Paleó Fáliro respectively, Rafína, Vólos, Áyios Konstandínos and Thessaloníki.

Schedules and tickets for the *Ceres* company, which operates most of the *"Flying Dolphin"* lines, are available in Athens from *Wagons-Lits*, Stadhíou 5, off Síntagma square (☎01/324 2281), and in Pireás from *Ceres Hydrofoils*, Aktí Miaoúli 69 (☎01/452 7107); in Vólos from *Tsoulos*, Antonopoúlou 9–11 (☎0421/39 786); and in Thessaloníki from *Egnatia Tours*, Kamvouníon 9 (☎031/22 3811). *Ilios* has offices at Goúnari 2, Pireás (☎01/41 73 453), while the head office of *Dodecanese Hydrofoils* is at Platía Líprou 6, Ródhos (☎0241/24 000).

KAÏKIA AND OTHER SMALL FERRIES

In season *kaïkia* (caiques) and small ferries of a couple hundred tonnes displacement sail between adjacent islands and to a few of the more obscure ones. These can be extremely useful and often very pleasant, but are no cheaper than mainline services; indeed if they are technically tourist agency charters, and not passenger lines controlled by the transport ministry, they tend to be quite expensive, with some pressure to buy return fares.

We have tried to detail the more regular links in the text, though many, inevitably, depend on the whims of local boat-owners or fishermen. The only firm information is to be had on the quayside.

Kaïkia and small ferries, despite appearances, have a good safety record; indeed it's the larger, overloaded car-ferries that have in the past run into trouble.

MOTORBIKES, MOPEDS AND BIKES

Motorcycles, **scooters**, **mopeds** and **bicycles** are available for rent on many of the islands and in a few of the popular mainland resorts. Motorcycles and scooters cost around £10/US$18 a day up; mopeds from £5–6/US$9–11; push-bikes as little as £2/US$3.50. All rates can be reduced with bargaining outside of peak season, or if you negotiate for a longer period of rental. To rent motorcycles (usually 125cc) you will need to show a driver's licence; otherwise all you need is a passport to leave as security.

MOPEDS – AND SAFETY

Mopeds are perfect for all but the hilliest islands, and you can obtain them literally everywhere. Make sure you check them thoroughly before riding off since many are only cosmetically maintained and repaired. If you break down it's your responsibility to return the machine, so it's worth taking down the phone number of whomever rents it to you in case it gives out in the middle of nowhere.

A warning should also be given about **mopeds and safety**. There are a stream of accidents each year involving tourists coming to grief on rutted dirt tracks or astride a mechanically dodgy machine. In many cases accidents are due to attempts to cut corners, in all senses, by riding two to an underpowered scooter simply not designed to support such a load. You won't regret getting two separate mopeds, or one powerful 125cc bike to share. Keep in mind, too, that you're likely to be charged an exorbitant price for any repairs if you have an accident.

If you intend to stay for some time in the warmer months, it's well worth considering the **purchase** of a moped or motorbike once in Greece. They are relatively inexpensive to run, do not cause passport problems, can be taken on the ferries very cheaply, and can be resold easily upon departure.

CYCLING

Few people seem to **cycle** in Greece but it's not always such hard going as you might imagine. If you have a bicycle – especially a mountain bike, which is ideal for Greek terrain – you might consider taking it along by train or plane (it's free if within your twenty-kilo allowance).

Within Greece you should be able to take a bike for free on most of the **ferries**, in the guard's van on most **trains** (for a small fee – it goes on a later goods train otherwise), and with a little persuasion on the roof of **buses**. Any spare parts you might need, however, are best brought along, since there are specialist bike shops only in Athens.

Alternatively, you can **rent** an old bone-shaker, with three speeds at the very most, on many of the larger islands.

CAR RENTAL

Cars have obvious advantages for getting to the more inaccessible parts of mainland Greece. If you're thinking of **renting** one, though, bear in mind that this is one of the more expensive countries in Europe to do so – £140–200/US$240–360 a week (depending on season) for a compact model on an unlimited kilometrage basis, once you have added on the mandatory extras like insurance and VAT. Outside of peak season you can sometimes get terms of about £20/US$36 per day, all inclusive.

If you want to rent a car from the outset, you may get a better price from one of the **British companies** that deal with local firms than if you negotiate for rental in Greece itself. One of the most competitive of these outlets, which can arrange for (reliable and fully insured) cars to be picked up at most airports is *Holiday Autos* (12 Bruton St, London W1X 7AJ; ☎071/491 1111). Most travel agents can also offer car rental in Greece, though their rates are generally higher than the specialist rental agents.

From a costs standpoint, you might prefer to spend most time on public transport, with just the occasional strategic week (say in the Máni or Pílion peninsulas, where buses are sparse) in your own vehicle. **In Greece**, *EuropCar, Kenning, Budget, Ansa* and *Just* are reliable medium-sized companies with branches in many towns; all are considerably cheaper than (and just as reputable) as the biggest international operators *Hertz* and *Avis*. Specific local recommendations are given in the guide.

All agencies will want either a credit card or a large cash deposit up front; minimum age requirements vary from 21 to 25. In theory an International Driver's Licence is also needed but in practice European, Australasian and American ones are honoured. If you're forced to get an international permit in Greece, *ELPA* (the Greek automobile association) offices sell them for the hefty fee of £10/US$18 – you'll need a handful of small photos, too.

Note that initial rental prices quoted almost never include tax, collision damage waiver fees and personal insurance; the coverage included by law in the basic rental fee is generally inadequate, so check the fine print on your contract.

TAXIS

Greek **taxis**, especially Athenian ones, are among the cheapest in western Europe and well worth making use of (though see the caveats on fares in the *Athens* chapter).

Within **city or town limits**, use of the meter is mandatory if one is present, and the flag falls at 200dr throughout the country. Double tariff applies between 1 and 6am, and outside city or town limits at any time of the day. There are also surcharges for entering a ferry harbour (currently 100dr), an airport (200dr), and per large bag (50dr), as well as the hefty Christmas and Easter bonuses. All of these may legitimately hike the fare up by as much as a third more than shown on the display.

In **rural areas**, taxis occasionally have no meters – you bargain. A reasonable per-vehicle (*not* per-person) charge for a ten-kilometre trip will be the equivalent of about £5/US$8.50. Occasionally a taxi returning empty from a drop-off will offer you a ride for not much more than the bus fare, just to pay for the petrol.

A special warning needs to be sounded about **unlicenced (ie pirate) taxi-drivers** which congregate outside major trains stations, particularly Athens and Lárissa. These shady characters may offer to shuttle you several hundred kilometres for the same price as the train/*KTEL* bus, or less; upon arrival you will discover that the fare quoted is per person, not per vehicle, and that along the way stops are made to cram several more passengers in – who again do not share your fare. Moreover, the condition of the vehicles usually leaves a lot to be desired. Beware.

HITCHING

Hitching is fine in Greece as long as you're not too concerned about time; lifts are fairly frequent but tend to be short. Most important, it's also one of the safer countries for women travellers, though as always confidence is boosted by numbers – the best being two, one man and one woman.

Although Greek traffic is sparse, much of it is **trucks and vans**, which are good for thumbing. Rides are easiest to come by in remote areas

DRIVING IN GREECE

If you drive your own vehicle to and through Greece, you'll need international third party insurance, the so-called **Green Card**, which British insurers issue for a minimum period and fee of about one month for £40. Upon arrival your passport will get a **carnet stamp**; this normally allows you to keep a vehicle in Greece for up to six months, exempt from road tax.

It is difficult, though not impossible, to leave the country without the vehicle; the nearest customs post will seal it for you – while you fly back home for a family emergency, for example – but you must find a Greek national to act as your guarantor. This peron will assume ownership of the car should you ultimately abandon it.

ACCIDENTS, ROADS AND ASSISTANCE

Keep in mind that Greece has the highest **accident rate** in Europe after Portugal, and many of the roads, particularly if you're unfamiliar with them, are quite perilous. Asphalt can turn into a dirt track without warning on the smaller routes, and railway crossings are rarely guarded. If you are involved in any kind of accident it's illegal to drive away, and you can be held at a police station for up to 24 hours. Often the talk will be way out of proportion to the incident, but if it is serious ring your consulate immediately, in order to get a lawyer (you have this right). Don't make a statement to anyone who doesn't speak, and write, very good English.

There are a limited number of **express highways** between Pátra, Athens, Vólos and Thessaloníki, on which modest tolls are levied – currently about 400dr at each sporadically placed gate. They're nearly twice as quick as the old roads, and well worth using, especially if you're a novice driver here.

Tourists with proof of AA/RAC or similar membership are given free **road assistance** from **ELPA**, the Greek equivalent, which runs breakdown services based in Athens, Pátra, Lárissa, Vólos, Ioánnina, Corfu, Trípoli, Crete and Thessaloníki. The information number is ☎174. In an **emergency** ring their road assistance service on ☎104, anywhere in the country.

Some car rental companies have an agreement with *ELPA*'s competitors, *Hellas Service* and *Express Service*, but they're prohibitively expensive to summon on your own – over 20,000 drachmas to enrol you as an "instant member" in their scheme.

MAINTENANCE

In terms of **maintenance**, the easiest models to have serviced and buy parts for in Greece are VWs, Mercedes, Ladas, Skodas, Dacias, Zastavas and virtually all French, Italian and Japanese makes. British models are a bit more difficult but you should be okay as long as you haven't brought anything too esoteric.

In general, both mechanics' **workshops and parts** retailers are clustered at the approach and exit roads of all major towns, usually prominently signposted. For the commonest makes, emergency spares like fan belts and cables are often found at surprisingly remote petrol stations, so don't hesitate to ask at an unlikely looking spot. Rural mechanics are okay for quick patch-up jobs like snapped clutch cables, but for major power-train problems it's best to limp into the nearest sizeable town for a mechanic factory-trained for your make.

PETROL/GASOLINE

Petrol/gasoline currently costs slightly less per litre than in the UK – 130 drachmas, or 38p/ US$0.70. However, deregulation of the government-set price is constantly threatened, and prices may well be in for a dramatic rise.

It is easy to run out of petrol after dark or on weekends in both rural and urban Greece. Most stations close at 7pm sharp, and nearly as many are shut all weekend. There will always be at least one pump per district open at the weekend, but no rota list is posted, and you'll often just be lucky to stumble on the single station open for miles around. This is not so much of a problem on the major highways, but it's a factor everywhere else, even in the largest cities, where pumps take turns being open 24 hours one day in every ten – too bad if it's the wrong day. So always fill, or insist on full rental vehicles at the outset, and if you've brought your own car, keep a jerrycan full at all times.

where most people know that buses are scarce. Hitching on commercial vehicles is nominally illegal, so if you're offered a ride in a large van or lorry, especially in the load space, don't be offended if you're set down just before an upcoming town and its police checkpoints.

Thumbing may even prove the quickest form of travel if you want to take an unusual route that would otherwise involve a string of bus connections. At its best, it's a wonderful method of getting to know the country – there's no finer way to take in the Peloponnese than from the back of a truck that looks like it has been converted from a lawnmower – and a useful means of picking up some Greek. While you'll often get lifts from Greeks eager to display or practice their English, there will be as many where to communicate you're forced to try the language. As it can be all too easy to stay in Greece without picking up more than restaurant talk, this is one way of breaking out.

DOMESTIC FLIGHTS

Olympic Airways and its subsidiary *Olympic Aviation* operate all **domestic flights** within Greece. They cover a fairly wide network of islands and larger towns, though most routes are to and from Athens, or the northern capital of Thessaloníki. They are both in the throes of being privatised, however, so expect fares to continue rising and routes to keep changing, as they've been doing for the past few years. **Schedules** can be picked up at *Olympic* offices abroad (see "Gettinh There" sections) or through their branch offices or representatives in Greece, which are maintained in almost every town or island of any size.

Fares usually work out around three to four times the cost of an equivalent bus or ferry journey, but on certain inter-island hauls poorly served by boat (Rhodes–Kastellórizo or Kefalloniá-Zákinthos, for example), you might consider this time well bought. For obscure reasons, flights between Athens and Mílos, Kíthira or Kalamáta are slightly better value per kilometre, so take advantage.

Island flights are often full in midseason; if they're part of your plans, **reserve** at least a week in advance. Domestic air tickets are **non-refundable** but you can change your flight details, space permitting, as late as a day before your original intended departure without penalty.

Like ferries, **flights can be cancelled** in bad weather, since most services are on small, 20- to 50-seat turbo-prop planes that won't fly in strong winds.

Size restrictions also mean that the 15-kilo baggage **weight limit** is fairly strictly enforced; if, however, you've just arrived from overseas, you are allowed the 20-kilo standard international limit. Overweight charges, if you're caught, are fairly reasonable.

Incidentally, there is no longer an *Olympic*-run **shuttle bus** from each airport into town – most were axed in 1991 as part of a cost-cutting exercise. In the cases where a municipal service has picked up the slack, it is detailed in the guide; otherwise you're at the mercy of the taxi drivers who congregate outside the arrivals gate.

ACCOMMODATION

There are huge numbers of beds for tourists in Greece, and most of the year you can rely on turning up pretty much anywhere and finding a room – if not in a hotel, then in a private house or block of rooms (the standard island accommodation). Only in late July and throughout August, the country's high season, are you likely to experience problems. At these times, it is worth striking a little off the standard tourist routes, turning up at each new place early in the day, and taking whatever is available in the hope that you will be able to exchange it for something better later on.

HOTELS, ROOMS AND VILLAS

Hotels are categorised by the tourist police from "Luxury" down to "E-class", and all except the top category have to keep within set price limits. D- and E-class hotels are usually very reasonable, costing around £7–11/US$12–17.50 for a double room, £5–8/US$9–13.50 for a single. The

ROOM PRICE SCALES

All establishments listed in this book have been price-graded according to the scale outlined below. The **rates quoted** represent the **cheapest available room in high season**; all are prices for a double room, except for category ①, which are per person rates. Out of season rates can drop by up to fifty percent.

You should expect rooms in all ① and most ② range accommodation to be without private bath, though there may a basic washbasin in the room. In the ③ category and above there are usually private facilities. Scales designated to establishments should not be regarded as absolutely rigid: some of the cheap places will also have more expensive rooms including en suite facilities – and vice versa, especially in the case of singles tucked in less desirable corners of the building.

① 1000–1500dr (£3–4.50/US$5.50–8)
Official/unofficial hostel rooms.

② 2000–3000dr (£6–9.50/US$11–16.50)
Simple private rooms.

③ 3000–5500dr (£9.50–17/US$16.50–30)
Comfortable private rooms and basic hotels.

④ 5500–7500dr (£17–23/US$30–41.50)
C-class hotels, cheaper EOT lodges

⑤ 7500–9000dr (£23–28/US$41.50–50)
Less expensive B-class hotels.

⑥ 9000dr and upwards (£28/US$50 upwards)
Fancy EOT lodges and worthwhile luxury hotels.

Prices for rooms and hotels should by law be **displayed** on the back of the door of your room. If you feel you're being overcharged at a place which is officially registered, threatening to report it to the tourist office or police – who will generally adopt your side in such cases – should be enough to elicit compliance. Small amounts over the posted price may be legitimately explained by tax or out-of-date forms. And occasionally you may find that you have bargained so well, or arrived so far out of season, that you are actually paying less than you're supposed to.

better-value places tend to be in the less touristed areas, as ratings depend partly on location; in Athens, inevitably, you get least for your money.

If you want a roof over your head while travelling about the mainland towns, you're generally going to have to depend on these small hotels – specific recommendations for which appear throughout the guide. In resorts, however, and throughout the islands, you can supplement them with privately let **rooms** (*dhomátia*). These are again officially controlled and are divided into three classes (A down to C). They are usually slightly cheaper than hotels, and are in general spotlessly clean. These days the bulk of them are in new, purpose-built low-rise blocks, but some are in people's homes, where you'll occasionally be treated to disarming hospitality.

At its simplest, *dhomátia* implies a bare, concrete room, with a hook on the back of the door and toilet facilies (cold water only) outside in the courtyard; at its fanciest it could be a modern, fully furnished place with an attached, marble-dressed bathroom. Between these two extremes you may find that there's a well-equipped kitchen on the property, and a choice of rooms at various prices (they'll usually show you the most expensive first). Price and quality are

not necessarily directly linked: always ask to see the room before agreeing to take it and settling on the price.

Areas to look for rooms, and some suggestions for the best, are again included in the guide. But as often as not, the rooms find you: owners descend on ferry or bus arrivals to fill any space they have, sometimes waving photos of the premises. In smaller places you'll often see rooms advertised (sometimes in German – *zimmer*), or you can just ask at the local taverna or *kafenío* (café). Even if there are no official places around, there is very often someone prepared to earn extra money by putting you up.

In **winter**, designated to begin in November and end in early April, private rooms are closed pretty much across the board to keep the hotels in business. There's no point in traipsing about hoping to find exceptions – most rooms owners obey the system very strictly. If they don't, the owners will find you themselves and, watching out for hotel rivals, guide you back to their place.

It has become standard practice for rooms proprietors to ask to **keep your passport** – ostensibly "for the tourist police", but in reality to prevent you skipping out with an unpaid bill. Some owners may be satisfied with just taking down the details, as in hotels, and they'll almost always return the documents once you get to know them, or if you need them for another purpose (to change money, for example).

LONG-TERM RENTALS

Houses or flats – and, out of season, **villas** – are often rented by the week or month. If you have two or three people to share costs, and want to drop roots on an island or a mainland coastal resort for a while, it's an option well worth considering. To arrange a rental, find a place you want to stay, get yourself known around the village, and ask around, particularly at the central *kafenía*; you can occasionally pick up reasonable deals in less visited spots.

If you want to rent a villa in season, see p.6–7 for details of British-based **package holiday operators** who arrange them.

HOSTELS, ROOFSPACE, MONASTERIES AND REMOTE VILLAGES

In addition to hotels and rooms, Greece has quite a few budget or oddball accommodation alternatives.

YOUTH HOSTELS

Greece is not exactly packed with **youth hostels** (*ksenón neótitos*) but those that there are tend to be fairly easy-going affairs: slightly run-down and a far cry from the harsh institutions you find in northern Europe. Very few of them ever ask for an IYHF card, and if they do you can usually buy one on the spot, or maybe just pay a little extra for your bed. Charges are around £3/US$5.50 a night.

The only annoying factor about hostels is the imposition of a **curfew**, most often around 11.30pm or midnight, but occasionally as early as 10pm. However, this is usually offset by the company of fellow travellers, with the hostel simply turning into a kind of members-only club. With their noticeboards, hostels can also be a good source of up-to-date information, and are sometimes handy for finding work, such as when farmers march down to the rural ones at harvest time to pick up casual labour.

Hostels on the **mainland** are at Athens (3), Náfplio, Mycenae, Olympia, Pátra, Delphi, Litohóro (Mount Olympus) and Thessaloníki. On the **islands** you'll find them only on Corfu (2), Thíra, and Crete (where there are seven – at Iráklio, Mália, Ierápetra, Réthimno, Haniá, Sitía and Mírthios).

STUDENT HOUSES AND ROOFSPACE

In Athens there are a number of cheap dormitory-style "**Student Houses**", non-YHA hostels which despite their name are in no way limited to students. Conditions are in general fairly insalubrious, but if you're on your own, the prices are likely to be the best deal in town.

Student hostels – and sometimes rural/island tavernas – also sometimes let "**roofspace**" providing a mattress for you to lay a sleeping bag down on, or even full bedding. If a place is full it's worth asking about this, as it can be a cheap cool and pleasantly uncramped alternative.

MONASTERIES

Greek **monasteries and convents** have a tradition of putting up travellers (of the same sex). On the mainland, this is still customary practice; on the islands, much less so. Wherever you should always ask locally before heading out to one for the night. Also, dress modestly – shorts on either sex, and short skirts on women, are total anathema – and try to arrive early evening, not later than 8pm or sunset (whichever is earlier).

For **men**, the most exciting monastic experience is a visit to the "Monks' Republic" of **Mount Áthos**, on the Halkidhikí peninsula, near Thessaloníki. This is a far from casual travel option, involving a fair bit of advance planning and bureaucratic procedure to obtain a permit. If you are interested, see p.339 for details.

IN THE MOUNTAINS

If you are stranded, or arrive very late, in a **remote mountain village** with no tourist facilities whatsoever, you may very well find that you are invited to spend the night in someone's home. This should not be counted on, but things work out more often than not. The most polite course is to have a meal or drink at the taverna, *kafenío* (there will always be at least one of the latter) and then, especially if it is summer enquire as to the possibility of sleeping either in the vacant schoolhouse or in a spare room at the *kinotikó grafío* (community records office).

CAMPING

Official campsites range from ramshackle compounds on the islands to highly organised (and rather soulless) *EOT* (Greek Tourist Organisation) – run complexes. Cheap, casual places rarely cost much above £1.50/US$2.50 a night per person; at the larger sites, though, it's not impossible for two of you and one tent (all separately charged) to almost add up to the price of a basic room.

Generally, you don't have to worry about leaving tents or **baggage** unattended; the Greeks are one of the most honest races in Europe. The main risk, sadly, comes from other campers, and every year a few items disappear in that direction.

"FREELANCE" CAMPING

Freelance camping – outside authorised campsites – is such an established element of Greek travel that few people realise that it's officially forbidden. Since 1977, however, it has indeed been forbidden by law, and increasingly the regulations are enforced.

If you do camp freelance, therefore, it is vital to exercise **sensitivity and discretion**. Obviously the police crack down on people camping rough (and littering) on or near popular tourist **beaches**, and they get especially concerned when a large community of campers is developing. Off the beaten track, however, and particularly in **rural inland areas**, nobody is very bothered. Wherever you are, it is always best to ask permission locally – in the village taverna or café – before pitching a tent.

EATING AND DRINKING

Greeks spend a lot of time socialising outside their homes, and sharing a meal is one of the chief ways of doing it. They're not great drinkers, but what drinking they do is mainly done at the café. The atmosphere is always relaxed and informal, and pretensions (or expense-account prices) are rare outside of the more chi-chi parts of Athens or major resorts.

RESTAURANTS

Greek cuisine and **restaurants** are simple and straightforward. There's no snobbery about eating out; everyone does it some of the time, and for foreigners with strong currencies it's fairly inexpensive – around £6–8 for a substantial meal with a good quantity of house wine.

In choosing a restaurant, the best strategy is to go where the Greeks go. And they go late: 2 to 3pm for **lunch**, 9 to 11pm for **dinner**. You can eat earlier, but you're likely to get indifferent service if you frequent the purely touristic establishments. Chic appearance is not a good guide to quality; you'll mainly be paying for the linen napkins and stemmed wine glasses. Often the most basic are the best, so don't be put off by a restaurant that brings your order in a sheet of paper and plonks it directly on the table-top, as *psistariés* (see below) often do.

It's wise to keep a wary eye on the **waiters**. They are inclined to push you into ordering more than you want and then bring things you haven't ordered. They often don't actually write anything down and may work your **bill** out by examining your empty plates. Itemised tabs, when present, may be in totally illegible Greek scribble, so the opportunities for slipping in a few extra drachmas here and there are pretty good, especially in establishments which disdain menus and published prices altogether. The **service charge** is always included, although a small tip (75–100 dr) is standard practice for the "boy" who lays the table, brings the bread and water, and so on.

If you have **children**, have no fears for them. Wherever you go they'll be welcome, and no one gives a damn if they chase the cats or play tag between the tables.

ESTIATÓRIA

There are two basic types of restaurant: the **estiatório** and the *taverna*. Distinctions between the two are slight, though the former is more commonly found in towns and it tends to have slightly more complicated dishes.

An *estiatório* will generally feature a variety of **oven-baked casserole dishes**: *moussakás*, *pastítsio*, stews like *kokinistó* and *stifádho*, *yemistá* (stuffed tomatoes or peppers), the oily vegetable casseroles called *ladherá*, and oven-baked meat and fish. Choosing these dishes is commonly done by going to the kitchen and pointing at the desired trays.

The cooking is done in the morning and then left to stand, which is why the food is often **lukewarm** or even cold. Greeks don't mind this (most actually believe that hot food is bad for you), and in fact in summertime it hardly seems to matter. Besides, dishes like *yemistá* are actually enhanced by being allowed to cool off and stand in their own juice. Similarly, you have to specify if you want your food with little or no **oil** (*horís ládhi*), but once again you will be considered a little strange since Greeks regard olive oil as essential to digestion (and indeed it is one of the least pernicious oils to ingest in large quantities).

Desserts of the pudding-and-pie variety don't exist, although fruit is always available in season and you may occasionally be able to get a yoghurt served at the end of a meal. Autumn treats worth asking after include *kidhóni* or *ahládhi sto foúrno*, baked quince or pear with some sort of syrup or nut topping.

TAVERNAS

Tavernas range from the glitzy and fashionable to rough-and-ready cabins with a bamboo awning set up by the beach. The primitive ones have a very limited menu, but the more established will offer some of the main *estiatório* dishes mentioned above as well as the standard **taverna fare**. This essentially means *mezédhes* (hors d'oeuvres) and *tis óras* (meat and fish fried or grilled to order).

Since the idea of courses is foreign to Greek cuisine, starters, main dishes and salads often arrive together. The best thing is to order a selection of *mezédhes* and salads to share among yourselves; that, after all, is what Greeks do. Waiters encourage you to take the *horiátiki* **salad** – the so-called Greek salad – because it is the most expensive one. If you only want tomato or tomato and cucumber, ask for *domatosaláta* or *angourodomáta*. *Láhano* (cabbage) and *maroúli*

(lettuce) are the typical winter and spring salads.

The most interesting **starters** are *tzatzíki* (yoghurt, garlic and cucumber dip), *melitzanosaláta* (aubergine dip), corgette or aubergine fried in batter (*kolokithákia tiganitá*, *melitzánes tiganités*), *yígandes* (white haricot beans in vinaigrette or hot tomato sauce), small cheese and spinach pies (*tiropitákia*, *spanakópittes*), *saganáki* (fried cheese), octopus (*okhtapódhi*), and *mavromatiká* (black-eyed peas).

Of **meats**, *souvláki* (shish kebab) and *brizóles* (chops) are reliable choices. In both cases, pork (*hirinó*) is usually better and cheaper than veal (*moskharísio*). The best *souvláki* is lamb (*arnísio*), but it is not often available. The small lamb cutlets called *païdhákia* are very tasty, as is roast lamb (*arní psitó*) and roast kid (*katsíki*) when obtainable. *Keftédhes* (meatballs), *biftékia* (a sort of hamburger) and the spicy sausages called *loukánika* are cheap and good.

Seaside tavernas of course also offer **fish**, though the choicer varieties, such as *barboúnia* (red mullet), *tsípoura* (gilt-head bream), *fangrí* (sea bream), are expensive. The price is quoted by the kilo, and the standard procedure is to go to the glass cooler and pick your own. The cheapest widely available fish are *gópes* (bogue) and *marídhes* (tiny whitebait, eaten head and all).

Kalamarákia (fried baby squid) and *okhtapódhi* (octopus) are a summer staple of most seaside tavernas, and occasionally, exotic **shellfish** such as *mídhia* (mussels), *kidhónia* (cherrystone clams) and *garídhes* (small prawns) will be on offer for reasonable amounts. Keep an eye out, however, to freshness and season – mussels in particular are a common cause of stomach upsets or even mild poisoning.

As in **estiatória**, **desserts** are more or less nonexistent. Watermelons, melons and grapes are the standard summer fruit.

SPECIALIST TAVERNAS

Some tavernas specialise. **Psarotavérnes**, for example, feature fish, and **psistariés** serve spit-roasted lamb and goat or *kokorétsi* (grilled offal).

A very few other tavernas concentrate on game (*kinígi*): wild boar, hare, quail or turtle dove in the autumn, when the migrating flocks fly over Greece on their way south. In the mountains of the north where there are rivers, trout, pike and freshwater crayfish are to be found in the local eating places.

A FOOD AND DRINK GLOSSARY

Basics and terms

Neró	Water	Fitofágos/Hortofágos	Vegetarian
Psomí	Bread	Avgá	Eggs
Oktáspora psomí	Wholemeal bread	Tirí	Cheese
Sikalénio psomí	Rye bread	(Horís) ládhi	(Without) oil
Aláti	Salt	Katálogo/lísta	Menu
Yiaoúrti	Yoghurt	O logariasmós	The bill
Méli	Honey	Sto foúrno	Baked
Kréas	Meat	Psitó	Roasted
Psári(a)	Fish	Stí soúvla	Spit roasted
Lahaniká	Vegetables	Tis óras	Grilled/fried to order

Soups and starters

Soúpa	Soup	Tzatzíki	Yoghurt and cucumber dip
Avgolémono	Egg and lemon soup	Melitzanosaláta	Aubergine dip
Dolmádhes	Stuffed vine leaves	Kopanistí, Ktipití	Semi-fermented cheese purée with hot chilli
Fasoládha	Bean soup		
Taramosaláta	Fish roe paté	Florínes	Canned red Macedonian peppers

Vegetables

Patátes	Potatoes	Briám	Ratatouille
Hórta	Greens (usually wild)	Kolokithákia	Courgette
Radhíkia	Wild chicory	Spanáki	Spinach
Piperiés	Peppers	Fakés	Lentils
Domátes	Tomatoes	Rízi/Piláfi	Rice (usually with sáltsa – sauce)
Fasolákia	String beans	Saláta	Salad
Angoúri	Cucumber	Horiátiki (saláta)	Greek salad (with olives, feta etc)
Angináres	Artichokes	Yemistá	Stuffed vegetables
Yígandes	White haricot beans	Papoutsákia	Stuffed aubergine
Koukiá	Broad beans	Bouréki	Courgette, potato and cheese pie
Melitzána	Aubergine	Bámies	Okra, lady fingers

Meat and meat-based dishes

Kotópoulo	Chicken	Kelftiko	Meat, potatoes and veg cooked together in a pot or foil; a Cretan speciality traditionally carried to bandits in hiding
Arní	Lamb		
Hirinó	Pork		
Moskhári	Veal		
Sikóti	Liver	Pastítsio	Macaroni baked with meat
Patsás	Tripe and trotter soup	Païdhákia	Lamb chops
Biftéki	Hamburger	Brizóla	Pork or beef chop
Moussaká	Aubergine, potato and mince pie	Keftédhes	Meatballs
Stifádho	Meat stew with tomato and onion	Loukánika	Spicy sausages
Yuvétsi	Baked clay casserole of meat and Kritharáki (pasta)	Kokorétsi	Liver/offal kebab
		Tsalingária	Garden snails

Fish and seafood

Garídhes	Prawns	Glóssa	Sole	Soupiá	Cuttlefish
Okhtapódhi	Octopus	Barbóuni	Red mullet	Marídhes	Whitebait
Astakós	Lobster	Xifías	Swordfish	Gávros	Mild anchovy
Kalamária	Squid	Sinagrídha	Dentex	Galéos	Dogfish, squale
Kalamarákia	Baby squid	Gópes	Bogue	Mídhia	Mussels
Kidhónia	Cherrystone clams				

Sweets and Fruit

Karidhópita	Walnut cake	*Graviéra*	Gruyère-type	*Pepóni*	Melon
Baklavás	Honey and nut pastry		hard cheese	*Karpoúzi*	Watermelon
Rizógalo	Rice pudding	*Fráoules*	Strawberries	*Míla*	Apples
Galaktobóureko	Custard pie	*Kerásia*	Cherries	*Síka*	(Dried) figs
Pagotó	Ice cream	*Stafília*	Grapes	*Fistíkia*	Pistachio nuts
Pastéli	Sesame and honey bar	*Portokália*	Oranges	*Kidhóni*	Quince
Kasséri	Medium cheese				

Drinks

Metalikó neró	Mineral water	*Tsái*	Tea	*Gazóza*	Generic fizzy
Bíra	Beer	*Kafés*	Coffee		drink
Krasí	Wine	*Galakakáo*	Chocolate milk	*Boukáli*	Bottle
Mávro	Red	*Portokaládha*	Orangeade	*Potíri*	Glass
Áspro	White	*Limonádha*	Lemonade	*Stinyássas!*	Cheers!
Rosé/Kokkinéli	Rosé				

WINES

Both *estiatória* and tavernas will usually offer you a choice of **bottled wines**, and some may have their own house variety, kept in barrels and served out in metal jugs.

Among the **bottled wines**, *Cambas, Boutari Lac des Roches,* the Rhodian *CAIR* products, and the Cretan *Logado* are good inexpensive whites, while *Boutari Naoussa* is perhaps the best mid-range red. If you want something better, *Tsantali Agioritiko* is an excellent white or red; *Boutari* do a fine *Special Reserve* red; and, in addition, there are three small, premium wineries whose products are currently fashionable: *Hatzimihali, Athanasiadh* and *Lazaridhi.*

Otherwise, go for the **local wines**. Retsina – pine-resinated wine, a slightly acquired taste – is invariably better straight from the barrel. Not as many tavernas keep it as once did, but always ask whether they have wine *varelísio* or *híma* – both mean, in effect, "from the barrel". Non-resinated bulk wine is almost always more than decent.

CAFÉS AND BARS

The Greek eating and drinking experience encompasses a variety of other places beyond restaurants. Most importantly, there is the institution of the **kafenío**, found in every town, village and hamlet in the country. In addition, you'll come across **ouzeris**, **zaharoplastía** and **bars**. Distinctions among these follow.

THE KAFENÍO

The **kafenío** is the traditional Greek coffee shop or café. Although its main business is Greek coffee – prepared *skéto* (unsweetened), *métrio* (medium) or *glikó* (cloying) – it also serves spirits such as *oúzo* (aniseed-based spirit), brandy (*Metaxa* brand, in three grades), beer, tea (either herbal mountain tea or British-style *Liptons*) and soft drinks. Another summer drink sold in the more modern cafés is *kafés frappé,* a sort of iced instant coffee – uniquely Greek despite its French-sounding name.

Usually the only edibles sold in cafés are *glikó koutalíou* (sticky, syrupy preserves of quince, grape, fig, citrus fruit or cherry), and the old-fashioned *ipovríhio*, which is a piece of mastic submerged in a glass of water like a submarine, which is what the word means in Greek.

Like tavernas, *kafenía* range from the plastic and sophisticated to the old-fashioned, spit-on-the-floor variety, with marble or brightly painted metal tables and straw-bottomed chairs. An important institution anywhere in Greece, they are the central pivot of life in the country villages. In fact, you get the impression that many men spend most of their waking hours there. Greek **women** are rarely to be seen in the more traditional places – and foreign women may sometimes feel uneasy or unwelcome in these establishments. Even in holiday resorts, you will find there is at least one café that the local men have kept intact for themselves.

Some *kafenía* close at siesta time, but many remain open from early in the morning until late at night. The chief socialising time is 6pm, immediately after the siesta. This is the time to take your pre-dinner **oúzo**, as the sun begins to sink and the heat cools (see below).

OÚZO, MEZÉDHES AND OUZERÍ

If you order **oúzo**, you will be served two glasses, one with the *oúzo*, and one full of water, to be tipped into your *oúzo* until it turns a milky white. You can drink it straight, but its strong, burning taste is hardly refreshing if you do. There are more than a dozen brands of **oúzo** in Greece; the best are reckoned to come from Lésvos, Tírnavos and Sámos, the least distinguished being the mass-produced *12* label.

Until not long ago, every *oúzo* you ordered was automatically accompanied by a small plate of **mezédhes**, on the house: bits of cheese, cucumber, tomato, a few olives, sometimes octopus or even a couple of small fish. Unfortunately these days you have to ask and pay, for them.

Though they are confined to the better resorts and select neighbourhoods of the bigger cities, there is a kind of drinking establishment which specializes in *oúzo* and *mezédhes*. These are called an **ouzerí** (same in the plural) or *ouzádhiko*, and are well worth trying for the marvellous variety of *mezédhes* they serve. Several plates of these plus drinks will effectively substitute for a more involved meal out at a taverna.

ZAHAROPLASTÍO

A somewhat similar institution to the *kafenío* is the **zaharoplastío**. A cross between café and patisserie, it serves coffee, alcohol, yoghurt and honey, sticky cakes, etc, both to consume on the premises and to take away.

The good establishments offer an amazing variety of pastries, cream and chocolate confections, honey-soaked Greco-Turkish sweets like *baklavás, kataífi* (honey-drenched "shredded wheat"), *loukoumádhes* (puffs of batter fried in olive oil, dusted with cinnamon and dipped in syrup; if you have a sweet tooth they'll transport you), *galaktoboúreko* (a soft-centred, milky-eggy pie), and so on.

If you want a stronger slant toward the dairy products and away from the pure sugar, seek out a **galaktopolío**, where you'll often find *rizógalo* (rice pudding), *kréma* (custard), and home- or at least locally made *yiaoúrti* (yoghurt), best if it's *próvio* (from sheep's milk). A sign at either establishment with the legend *pagotó politikó* or *kaïmáki* means that the shop concerned makes its own Turkish-style ice cream, and the proprietors are probably from Istanbul (Konstantinoúpoli to them, of course) – as good as or better than the usual Italian-style fare.

Both *zaharoplastía* and *galaktopolía* are more family-oriented places than the *kafenío*, and many also serve a basic continental-type **breakfast** of *méli me voútiro* (honey poured over a pat of butter) or jam (all kinds are called *marmeládha* in Greek; ask for *portokáli* – orange – if you want proper marmalade) with fresh bread or *friganiés* (melba-toast-type slivers). You are also more likely to find proper (*evropaïkó*) tea and different kinds of coffee. *Nescafé* has become the generic term for all instant coffee, regardless of brand.

BARS – AND BEER

Bars – *barákia* in the plural – are a recent transplant, confined to big cities and holiday resorts. They range from clones of Parisian cafés to seaside cocktail bars by way of mindless, imitation English "pabs" (sic), with equally mindless videos running all day. Drinks are invariably more expensive than at a café.

They are, however, most likely to stock a range of **beers**, which in Greece are all foreign labels made under licence, since the old Fix brewery closed in the 1980s. *Kronenberg* and *Kaiser* are the two most expensive brews, with the former much preferable and also offering the only dark beer in the country. *Amstel* and *Henninger* are the two ubiquitous cheapies, rather bland but inoffensive. A possible compromise is the sharper-tasting *Heineken*, universally referred to as a "*prássini*" by bar and taverna staff after its green bottle.

Incidentally, try not to be stuck with the one-third litre cans, vastly more expensive (and more of a rubbish problem) than the returnable half-litre bottles.

BREAKFAST, PICNIC FARE AND SNACKS

Greeks don't generally eat **breakfast**. So the only egg-and-bacon kind of places are in resorts where foreigners congregate; they're expensive compared to a taverna meal. The alternatives are the sort of bread/jam/yoghurt compromises obtainable in some *zaharoplastía* or *galaktopolía*, or having a picnic breakfast with your own ingredients.

PICNIC FARE

Picnic fare is good, cheap, and easily available. When buying **olives**, go for the fat Kalamáta or Ámfissa ones; they're more expensive, but tastier

Τοιχογραφία από τις Μυκήνες. 13ος αι. π.Χ.
Fresco from Mycenae. 13th cent. B.C.

ΓΕ

ENTRANCE
TICKET
ΔΡΧ. 200
DRS.

3069236

and more nourishing. *Fétta* **cheese** is ubiquitous – often, ironically, imported from Holland or Denmark. It can be very dry and salty, so it's wise to ask for a piece to taste before buying. If you have access to a fridge, dunking it overnight in a plastic container with water will solve both problems. That sampling advice also goes for other cheeses, the most palatable of which are the expensive gruyère-type *graviera*.

Yoghurts are superlative (and good stomach settlers); honey is also wonderful, though it costs an arm and a leg. The **fruit** is generally good, though not especially cheap; **salad vegetables** are usually more reasonable.

SNACKS

Snacks can be one of the distinctive pleasures of Greek eating, though they are being increasingly edged out by an obsession with *tóst* (toasted sandwiches) and pizzas. However, small kebabs (*souvlákia*) are on sale at bus stations, ferry crossings, and all over the place in towns.

The same goes for *tirópites* (cheese pies), which can usually be found at the baker's, as can *kouloúria* (crispy baked pretzel rings sprinkled with sesame seeds) and *boutímata* (bagged biscuits heavy on the molasses, cinnamon and butter). Another city staple is *yíros* (doner kebab), in *píta* bread with garnish and often *tzatzíki.*

COMMUNICATIONS: MAIL, PHONES AND THE MEDIA

POSTAL SERVICES

Post offices are open from about 7.30am to 2pm, Monday to Friday; in the largest towns and important tourist centres, there are usually supplementary weekday evening hours and short shifts on weekend mornings. At such times you can have money exchanged, in addition to handling mail.

MAIL

Air mail letters from the mainland take three to six days to reach the rest of Europe, five to eight days to get to North America, and a bit more for Australia and New Zealand. Allow an extra four or five days when sending from any island – with the new generation of smaller planes, mail now goes on a space-available basis. Services to Greece take similar times.

Aerograms are faster and surer. **Postcards** can be inexplicably slow: up to two weeks for Europe, a month to North America or the Pacific. A modest (about 300dr) fee for **express** (*katapígonda*) service cuts letter delivery time by a few days to any destination. **Registered** (*sistiméno*) delivery is also available, but it is quite slow unless coupled with express service.

For a simple letter or card, **stamps** (*grammatósima*) can also be purchased at a *períptero* (corner kiosk). However, the proprietors are entitled to a ten percent commission and never seem to know the current international rates. **Post boxes** are bright yellow; if you are confronted by two slots, *esoterikó* is for domestic mail, *exoterikó* for overseas.

If you are sending large purchases home, note that **parcels** should and often can only be handled in sizeable towns, preferably a provincial capital. This way your bundle will be in Athens, and on the plane, within a few days.

RECEIVING MAIL

Receiving mail, the *poste restante* system is reasonably efficient, especially at the post offices of larger towns. Mail should be clearly addressed and marked *poste restante*, with your surname underlined, to the main post office of whichever town you choose. It will be held for a month and you'll need your passport to collect it.

Alternatively, you can use the ***American Express*** one-month mail-holding service, free of charge if you carry their cheques or hold their card, but because of new security regulations they will no longer accept delivery of even small packages. *Amex* offices are open Monday to Friday, plus Saturday mornings, and are conveniently spaced:

ATHENS: *American Express International*, Síntagma/Ermoú 2, PO Box 325.

THESSALONÍKI: c/o *Doukas Tours*, Venizélou 8.

IRÁKLION (CRETE): c/o *Adamis Tours*, 25 Avgoústou 23.

RHODES TOWN: c/o *Rodhos Tours Ltd.*, Ammohóstou 23, PO Box 252.

KÉRKIRA (CORFU): c/o *Greek Skies Travel*, 20A Kapdhistríou, PO Box 24.

PHONES

Local calls are relatively straightforward. In many hotel lobbies or cafés you'll find fat, **red pay-phones** which presently take a ten-drachma coin and are for local calls only. On street corners you may still find conventional phone **booths**, though these are slowly being phased out. Those with a blue band on top are for local (*topikó*) calls and require ten-drachma coins; those with an orange strip are intended for long-distance (*iperastikó*), and are fed ten-, twenty-, and fifty-drachma pieces. A tone in mid-conversation warns you when you need to insert more.

It's probably easier, though a bit noisier, to phone from a *períptero*, or **street kiosk**. Here the phone is connected to a meter, and you pay after you have made the call, thus eliminating the need to juggle small change. Local calls are very cheap, but **long-distance** ones, at 8.5 drachmas per unit, add up quickly to some of the most expensive rates in the EC – and definitely the worst **connections**. You will generally have to try four or five times to get through, waiting for a critical series of six electrical crunches on the line after dialling the country and area codes, and then tolerate sudden cut-offs, ghastly echoes, one party being inaudible, etc.

For **international** (*exoterikó*) calls, it's better to visit the nearest **OTE** (*Organismós Tiliepikinoníon tis Elládhos*) office, where there's often a slightly better-wired booth reserved for overseas calls only. You'll also have to do this if you want to reverse charges or do anything else exotic. Operator-assisted calls can take well over an hour to connect, but even if you are going to dial direct on their metered phones you should be prepared for a long wait.

In the very largest towns there is at least one branch open 24 **hours**, or more commonly 7am to 10 or 11pm. In smaller towns *OTE* can close as early as 3pm, though in a few resorts there are a few *OTE* Portakabin booths keeping weird, useful hours such as 2–10pm.

When *OTE* is **closed** you'll have no choice but to use a kiosk, or to find a *kafenío* with a metered phone: look for a sign saying *Tiléfono meh metrití*. Try never to make a long-distance call from a hotel, as they slap a fifty percent surcharge onto the already outrageous rates.

If you have access to a private phone you can dial the **international operator** (☎161) to get a reversed-charges/collect call put through, or dial direct: ☎00, followed by the country code (44 for the UK, 1 for the US and Canada) and the local number without its initial zero. Greece participates in the *AT&T* USA Direct scheme, so with an *AT&T* Calling Card you can save considerably on the Greek rates when phoning North America.

Otherwise, calls will **cost**, very approximately, £2.25 for three minutes to all EC countries and most of the rest of Europe, or US$10 for the same time to North America or Australasia. **Cheap rates**, such as they are, apply from 3 to 5pm and 9pm to 8am daily, plus all weekend, for calls within Greece. There is a very slight discount for international calls after 10pm, dialled from the mainland only.

MEDIA: PUBLICATIONS AND AIRWAVES

If you want to stay in touch with home events in Greece, you can buy international papers and pick up BBC/VOA broadcasts. Details of these follow, along with a brief rundown on local media.

NEWSPAPERS AND MAGAZINES

British newspapers are fairly widely available in Greece for 200–300dr, 400–500dr for Sunday editions. You'll find day-old copies of the better papers, including *The Independent* and *The Guardian*'s European edition, in all the resorts as well as in major towns, and a few of the tabloids can be found too. **American and international** alternatives are represented by *USA Today* and the *International Herald Tribune*.

Local English-language alternatives include the daily *Athens News*, heavily dependent on wire-service dispatches but with an interesting (and in its police-blotter section, bizarre) round-up of selections from the Greek press. It's on sale widely in Athens and at some of the larger cities and resorts. The *Greek Weekly News* is more literate, with a good summary of Athens cinema and concert offerings. The expatriate community in Rhodes also puts out a creditable weekly sheet.

Among **magazines**, the best – despite having gone through a bad patch recently and almost folding – is *The Athenian*, an English-language monthly sold in Athens and all major resorts. It's usually worth a read for its cultural/festival listings, updates on Greek life and politics, and often excellent features.

RADIO

If you have a **radio** you may pick up something interesting. Greek music progammes are always accessible despite the language barrier, and with various recent challenges to the government's former monopoly of wavelengths, regional stations have mushroomed; the airwaves are now positively cluttered, as every town of more than a few thousand sets up its own studio and transmitter. There are regular news bulletins and bouts of tourist information in English on local Greek stations (try 412 MW at 7.30am daily).

The **BBC World Service** can be picked up on short wave frequencies throughout Greece. For programme times and frequencies (15.07 and 12.09 Mhz are the most common), pick up a copy of "London Calling" from the library of the British Council in Athens.

The **Voice of America** and **American Armed Forces Radio** can also be picked up on medium wave.

GREEK TV

Greece's two centralised, government-controlled **TV stations**, ET1 and ET2, nowadays lag far behind a trio of private channels – Mega-Channel, New Channel and Antenna – in the ratings. On ET1, news summaries in English are read daily at 6pm, and generally followed by a plethora of American serials and old movies, most of which are subtitled and with the original soundtrack.

With the appropriate aerial, satellite dish or cable hookup, you can routinely pick up the French Channel Five, Italian Rai Due, Sky Channel, CNN and Super Channel in most of the country.

OPENING HOURS AND PUBLIC HOLIDAYS

It is virtually impossible to generalise about Greek opening hours, except to say that they change constantly. The traditional timetable starts at a relatively civilised hour, with shops opening between 8.30 and 9.30am, and runs through until lunchtime, when there is a long break for the hottest part of the day. Things may then reopen in the mid-to late afternoon.

Tourist areas tend to adopt a slightly more northern timetable, with shops and offices probably staying open right through the day. Certainly the most important archaeological sites and museums do so.

BUSINESS AND SHOPPING HOURS

Most **government agencies** are open to the public from 8am to 2pm. In general, however, you'd be optimistic to show up after 1pm expecting to be served the same day. Medium to large white-collar, **private businesses**, or anyone providing a service – eg film processor, osteopath, electronics repair – is likely to operate on a

unitary, 9am–6pm schedule. If someone is actually selling something, than they are more likely to follow a split shift.

Shopping hours during the hottest months are theoretically Monday, Wednesday and Saturday from approximately 9am until 2pm, and Tuesday, Thursday and Friday from 9am to 1.30pm and 5.30 to 8.30pm; during the cooler months with shorter daylight hours the morning schedule shifts slightly forward, the evening trade a half or even a full hour back. There are so many **exceptions** to these rules, though, by virtue of holidays and professional idiosyncrasy that you can't count on getting anything done except from Monday to Friday from 9.30am to 1pm or so.

Pharmacies are usually closed evenings and Saturday morning but are supposed to have a sign on their door referring you to the nearest one open.

ANCIENT SITES AND MONASTERIES

All the major **ancient sites** are now fenced off and, like most **museums**, charge admission. This ranges from a token 100dr to a whopping 1500dr, with an average fee of around 500dr. Anomalies are common, with some tiny one-pot museums charging the same as major atttractions. At most, there are reductions of 50 to 100 percent (the latter applying to EC nationals) for student card holders. In addition, entrance to all state-run sites and museums is **free** to everyone on Sundays and public holidays.

Opening hours vary from site to site. As far as possible, individual times are quoted in the text, but bear in mind that these change with exasperating frequency and at smaller sites may be subject to the whim of a local keeper. The times quoted are generally summer hours, which operate from around April to the end of September. Reckon on similar days but later opening and earlier closing in winter.

Smaller sites generally close for a long lunch and **siesta** (even where they're not supposed to), as do **monasteries**. Most monasteries are fairly strict on visitors' dress, too, especially for women; they don't like shorts on either sex and often expect women to cover their arms and wear skirts, with the necessary wraps sometimes provided on the spot. They are generally open from about 9am to 1pm and 5 to 8pm (3.30–6.30pm in winter) for limited visits.

PUBLIC HOLIDAYS

All of the above will be regularly thrown out of sync by any of a vast range of **public holidays and festivals**. The most important, when almost everything will be closed, are:

January 1
January 6
March 25
First Monday of Lent (February or March)
Easter weekend (according to the Orthodox festival calendar, see below)
May 1
Whit Monday (usually in June)
August 15
October 28
December 25 & 26
There are also a large number of local holidays.

VARIABLE RELIGIOUS FEASTS 1992–996		
Lent Monday	**Easter Sunday**	**Whit Monday**
March 9	April 26	June 15
March 1	April 18	June 7
March 14	May 1	June 20
March 6	April 23	June 12
February 27	April 17	June 3

FESTIVALS

Many of the big Greek popular festivals have a religious base so they're observed in accordance with the Orthodox calendar.

This is similar to the regular Catholic liturgical year, except for Easter, which can fall as much as three weeks to either side of the western festival.

EASTER

Easter is by far the most important festival of the Greek year – infinitely more so than Christmas – and taken much more seriously than it is anywhere in western Europe. From Wednesday of Holy Week the state radio and TV networks are given over solely to religious progammes until the following Monday.

The festival is an excellent time to be in Greece, both for the beautiful and moving religious ceremonies and for the days of feasting and celebration that follow. The mountainous island of **Ídhra** with its alleged 360 churches and monasteries is the prime Easter resort, but unless you plan well in advance you have no hope of finding accommodation there at that time. Probably the best idea is to make for a medium-sized village where, in most cases, you'll be accepted into the community's celebration.

The first great public ceremony takes place on **Good Friday** evening as the Descent from the Cross is lamented in church. At dusk the *Epitafión*, Christ's funeral bier, lavishly decorated by the women of the parish, leaves the sanctuary and is paraded solemnly through the streets. In many places, Crete especially, this is accompanied by the burning of effigies of Judas Iscariot.

Late **Saturday** evening sees the climax in a majestic *Anástasi* mass to celebrate Christ's triumphant return. At the stroke of midnight all lights in each crowded church are extinguished and the congregation plunged into the darkness which envelopes Christ as He passes through the underworld. Then there's a faint glimmer of light behind the altar screen before the priest appears, holding aloft a lighted taper and chanting "*Avtó to Fós . . .* " (This is the Light of the World). Stepping down to the level of the parishioners, he touches his flame to the unlit candle of the nearest worshipper intoning "*Dévthe, lévethe Fós*" (Come, Take the Light). Those at the front of the congregation and on the aisles do the same for their neighbours until the entire church is ablaze with burning candles and the miracle affirmed.

Even solidly rational atheists are likely to find this moving. The traditional greeting, as fireworks explode all around you in the streets, is "*Hristós Anésti*" (Christ is risen), to which the response is "*Alithós Anésti*" (Truly He is Risen). In the week leading up to Easter Sunday you should wish people a Happy Easter: "*Kaló Páskha*".

The burning **candles** are then taken home through the streets by the worshippers, and it brings good fortune on the house if the candle arrives without having been blown out in the wind. On reaching the front door it is common practice to make the sign of the cross on the lintel with the flame, leaving a black smudge visible for the rest of the year. The Lenten fast is traditionally broken early on Sunday morning with a meal of *mayarítsa*, a soup made from lamb tripe, rice and lemon. The rest of the lamb will be roasted for Sunday lunch, and festivities often take place through the rest of the day.

The Greek equivalent of **Easter eggs** are hard-boiled eggs (painted red on Holy Thursday), which are baked into twisted, sweet bread-loaves (*tsouréki*) or distributed on Easter Sunday; people rap their eggs against their friends' eggs, and the owner of the last uncracked egg is considered lucky.

THE FESTIVAL CALENDAR

Most of the other Greek festivals are celebrations of one or another of a multitude of **saints**. The most important are detailed below: wherever you are, it is worth looking out for a village, or church, bearing the saint's name, a sure sign of celebrations – sometimes across the town or island, sometimes quiet and local. Saints' days are also celebrated as **name-days**; if you learn that it's an acquaintance's name-day, you wish them "*Hrónia Pollá*" (Many Happy Returns).

Detailed below, too, are a scattering of more **secular** holidays, most enjoyable of which are the pre-Lenten carnivals.

It is important to remember the concept of the ***paramoní****, or eve of the festival. Most of the events listed below are celebrated on the night before, so if you show up on the morning of the date given you will very probably have missed any music, dancing or drinking.*

January 1
New Year's Day in Greece is the feast day of **Áyios Vassílios**, their version of Santa Claus, and is celebrated with church services and the baking of a special loaf, *vassilópitta*, in which a coin is baked which brings its finder good luck throughout the year. The traditional New Year greeting is "*Kalí Hroniá*".

January 6
The **Epiphany**, when the *kalikántzari* (hobgoblins) who run riot on earth during the twelve days of Christmas are rebanished to the nether world by various rites of the Church. The most important of these is the blessing of baptismal fonts and all outdoor bodies of water. At lakeside and seaside locations, the priest traditionally casts a crucifix into the deep, with local youths competing for the privilege of recovering it.

Pre-Lenten Carnivals
These span three weeks, climaxing during the seventh weekend before Easter. **Pátra Carnival**, with a chariot parade and costume parties, is one of the largest in the Mediterranean, with events

from January 17 until "Clean Monday", the last day of Lent; on the last Sunday before Lent there's a grand parade. Interesting, too, are the *boúles* or masked revels which take place around **Macedonia** (particularly at Náoussa), and the outrageous "Goat Dance" on **Skíros** in the Sporades. The **Ionian islands**, especially Kefalloniá, are also good for Carnival, while **Athenians** celebrate by going around hitting each other on the head with plastic hammers.

March 25
Independence Day and the **Feast of the Annunciation** is both a religious and national holiday, with, on the one hand, parades and dancing to celebrate the beginning of the revolt against Turkish rule in 1821, and, on the other, church services to honour the news being given to Mary that she was to become the Mother of Christ. There are major festivities on **Tínos**, **Ídhra (Hydra)**, and many other places, particularly any monastery or church named Evangelístria or Evangelismós.

April 23
The **Feast of St George (Áyios Yióryios)**, the patron of shepherds, is a big rural celebration. Good places for dancing and feasting include **Aráhova**, near Delphi. Saint George is also the patron saint of **Skíros**, so this day is celebrated in some style there too. If the date falls before Easter, ie during Lent, the festivities are postponed until the Monday after Easter.

May 1
May Day, the great urban holiday when townspeople traditionally make for the countryside to return with bunches of wild flowers. Wreaths are hung on their doorways or balconies until they are burnt on Midsummer's eve. The demise of communism in eastern Europe notwithstanding, there are still likely to be large demonstrations by the left, claiming the *Ergatikí Protomayiá* (Working-Class First of May) as their own.

May 21
The Feast of **Áyios Konstantínos** and his mother, **Ayía Eléni**, the first Orthodox Byzantine rulers. There are firewalking ceremonies in certain **Macedonian villages**, and elsewhere the day is celebrated rather more conventionally as being the name-day for two of the more popular Christian names in Greece.

June 29
The **Feast of Saints Peter and Paul (Áyios Pétros and Áyios Pávlos)**. More name-day celebrations to watch out for.

June 30
The **Feast of the Holy Apostles (Ayíi Apostolí)**. Widely celebrated.

July 17
The **Feast of Ayía Marína**; a big deal in rural areas, as she's an important protectress of crops.

July 18–19
The **Feast of Profítis Ilías (the Prophet Elijah)** is widely celebrated at the countless hill- or mountain-top shrines of Profítis Ilías. The most famous is on **Mount Taíyettos**, near Spárti.

July 26
Feast of Áyia Paraskeví, with big village festivals, especially in **Epirus**.

August 6
The **Feast of the Metamórfosi (Transfiguration)** provides another excuse for celebrations. In fact, between mid-July and mid-September there are religious festivals every few days, especially in the rural areas, and between these and the summer heat ordinary business comes to a virtual standstill.

August 15
The **Apokímisis tis Panayías (Assumption of the Blessed Virgin Mary)**. This is the day when people traditionally return to their home village, and in many places there will be no accommodation available on any terms. Even some Greeks will resort to sleeping in the streets. There is a great pilgrimage to **Tínos**, and major festivities at **Páros**, at Ayiássos on **Lésvos**, and at Olímbos on **Kárpathos**.

September 8
The **Yénesis tis Panayías (Birth of the Virgin Mary)** sees special services in churches dedicated to the event, and a double cause for rejoicing on **Spétses** where they also celebrate the anniversary of the **Battle of the Straits** of Spétses, which took place on September 8, 1822. A re-enactment of the battle takes place in the harbour, followed by fireworks and feasting well into the night.

September 14

A last major summer festival, the **Exaltation of the Cross**.

October 26

The **Feast of Áyios Dhimítrios**, another popular name-day, particularly celebrated in **Thessaloníki**, of which he is the patron saint. New wine is traditionally tapped on this day, a good excuse for general inebriation.

October 28

Óhi Day, the year's major patriotic shindig – a national holiday with parades, folk-dancing and feasting to commemorate Metaxas' apocryphal one-word reply to Mussolini's 1940 ultimatum: "*Ohi!*"(No!).

November 8

Another popular name-day, the **Feast of the Archangels Michael and Gabriel (Mihaíl and Gavriél)**, with rites at the numerous rural monasteries and chapels named for them.

December 6

The **Feast of Áyios Nikólaos**, the patron of seafarers, with many chapels dedicated to him.

December 25

A much less festive occasion than Greek Easter, **Christmas** is still an important religious feast celebrating the birth of Christ, and in recent years it has started to take on more of the trappings of the western Christmas, with decorations, Christmas trees and gifts. December 26 is not Boxing Day but the *Sínaksis tis Panayías*, or Meeting of the Virgin's Entourage.

December 31

New Year's Eve, when, as on the other twelve days of Christmas, children go door-to-door singing the traditional *kalénda* (carols). Adults tend to sit around playing cards, often for money. The *vassilópitta* may be cut at midnight, to mark the start of another year of what sometimes seems like a non-stop round of celebrations.

In addition to the specific dates mentioned, there are literally scores of **local festivals**, or *paniyiriá*, celebrating the patron saint of the village church. With some 330-odd possible name–saints' days you're unlikely to travel around Greece for long without stumbling on something.

ENTERTAINMENT AND SPORTS

Outlined below are the country's main cultural festivals – highlights of which include ancient drama in ancient theatres; other cultural events and activities; and sport – both participatory and spectator.

CULTURAL FESTIVALS

The major summer cultural events in Greece take place under the aegis of the **Athens Festival** (mid-June to mid-September). This encompasses a wide range of performances, including modern and ancient theatre, ballet, opera, jazz and classical music.

For most people the highlights are the open-air **performances of Classical drama** in the ancient theatres of **Epidaurus** (in the Peloponnese) and the Herodes Atticus in **Athens**. Those at Epidaurus take place at weekends (when there are special buses from Athens); at Herodes Atticus (which also hosts ballet and symphony concerts) they are usually spread through the week.

The **Athens International Jazz and Blues Festival**, with consistently big name acts, occurs the latter half of June at another (modern) open-air theatre on Likavitós hill.

Details and tickets for both festivals can be obtained from the Athens Festival offices (see p.111). It's worth calling in very soon after you arrive in Greece, since the more prestigious events often sell out.

REGIONAL EVENTS

You might also pick up – from the Athens Festival Office or tourist offices abroad – an annual leaflet published by the EOT called "Greek Festivals". This includes details of smaller, **local festivals** of music, drama and dance, which take place on a more sporadic basis. Among these are performances of Classical plays in the ancient theatres of **Thássos**, **Dodona** and **Philippi**.

Other important **regional events** include the **Pátra Festival** (mid-June to August); the **Thíra/Santorini music festival** (late August to

September); a festival of song on **Itháki** (July); the **Rhodes festival** (August to October); on Crete, the **Iráklio festival** and **Réthimno Renaissance fair** (early August); the **Kavála festival** (through August); a general arts jamboree on **Lefkádha** (through most of August), including poetry, theatre, and great dancing by foreign and Greek troupes; the **Makrinítsa/ Vólos festival** during the first half of August; the "*Politistikó Kalokéri*" (Cultural Summer) events from mid-July to mid-August in **Ioánnina**; and two biggies in **Thessaloníki**, the "*Dhimitría*" general festival in October, plus a film festival in November (recently moved from September and thrown open to international entrants).

CINEMA AND THEATRE

Greek **cinemas** show a large number of American and British movies, always undubbed with Greek subtitles. They are highly affordable, currently 600 to 900dr depending on location, and in summer a number set up outside on vacant lots. An **outdoor movie** is worth catching at least once – indoor shows never quite seem the same once you've seen an open-air screening of Kirk Douglas in *The Odyssey* on Ithaca.

Theatre gets suspended during the summer months but from around September to May there's a lot of activity; Athens alone has some 45 theatres, with playbills ranging from the classics to satirical revues (both in Greek).

SPORTS

The Greek seashore offers endless scope for water sports, with **windsurfer-boards** for rent in most resorts, and, less regularly, **waterskiing** facilities. On land, the greatest attraction lies in **hiking**, through what is one of Europe's more impressive mountain terrains. Winter also sees possibilities for **skiing** at one of a dozen or so underrated centres.

Spectating, the twin Greek obsessions are **football** (soccer) and **basketball**. Both are constantly to be seen on TV, as well as by attending matches. **Volleyball** runs a close third in popularity, with the European championship recently held in Athens.

WATER SPORTS

The last few years have seen a massive growth in the popularity of **windsurfing** in Greece. The country's bays and coves are ideal for beginners, and boards can be hired in literally hundreds of resorts. Particularly good areas include the islands of Lefkádha, Zákinthos, Náxos, Sámos, Lésvos, Corfu and Crete, and Methóni in the Peloponnese. You can almost always pay for an initial period of instruction, if you've not tried the sport previously. Rates are very reasonable – about £5/US$9 an hour.

Waterskiing is available at a number of the larger resorts, and a fair few of the smaller ones, too. By the crippling rental standards of the ritzier parts of the Mediterranean it is a bargain, with twenty minutes' instruction often available for around £8–10/US$14–18. At many resorts, for example Párga in Epirus, **parasailing** (*parapént* in Greek) is also possible.

Sailboats and dinghies are rented out by the day or week at many of the country's naval clubs. For details, contact the Greek Sailing Federation, Xenofóndos 15a, Athens (☎01/32 35 560).

Because of the potential for pilfering submerged antiquities, **scuba diving** is restricted to a very few recognised centres, on the islands of Míkonos, Rhodes, Corfu, Paxí and Lefkádha, and on the mainland's Halkidhikí peninsula. A leaflet, "Sea Areas for Underwater Activities", is published by the EOT.

Greece also has lots of white water, especially in the Peloponnese and Epirus, so if you're into **river rafting** there is much potential. There are periodic articles and advice (in Greek) in the outdoors magazine *Korfés*.

SKIING

Skiing is a comparative newcomer to Greece, in part because snow conditions are unpredictable, and runs generally short. However, there are now a dozen **ski centres** scattered about the mountains, and what they lack in professionalism is often made up for by a very easy-going and unpretentious *après-ski* scene. Costs are an attraction, too – much lower than in northern Europe, at around £6/US$11 a day for rental of skis and boots, plus £4/US$5.50 a day for a lift pass. The **season** generally lasts from the beginning of January to the end of April, with a few extra weeks possible at either end depending on snow conditions.

The most developed of the resorts is on **Parnassós**, the legendary mountain near Delphi. It's easily accessible from Athens; throughout the season Athenian operators run buses up to the resort, returning the same day. Avoid weekends (which can be chaos) and you may have the resort more or less to yourself. The leading operator is *Klaoudatos*, a big department store on Dhimarhíou street, near Omónia square. In winter they devote a floor to skiing, including ski rental (though this is simpler at Parnassós itself). The resort has slopes for beginners and enough to keep most experienced skiers happy, at least for a couple of days. Its main problem is that the lifts are often closed due to high winds.

Other major **ski centres** include **Veloúhi**, near Karpeníssi in central Greece; **Helmós**, near Kalávrita on the Peloponnese; **Vérmion**, near Náoussa in Macedonia; nearby **Pisodhéri** near Flórina, also in Macedonia; and **Métsovo** in Epirus, which has ample other attractions besides the skiing. **The Pílion** is another enjoyable region to ski in as part of a general holiday. Buses run to its ski centre at Haniá from Vólos. All of these centres rent out ski equipment for casual visitors. The last two are at a lower altitude than the others, so seasons are shorter.

Further details are available from the EOT, which publishes a leaflet entitled "Ski Centres and Mountaineering Shelters", or from the Greek Mountaineering and Skiing Federation, Karayióryi Servías 7, Síntagma, or Milióni 5, Kolonáki, Athens (☎01/32 34 555).

WALKING

Greeks are just becoming used to the notion that anyone should want to walk for pleasure, yet if you have the time and stamina it is probably the single best way to see the country. This guide includes descriptions of a number of the more accessible mountain hikes, as well as suggestions for more casual walking.

In addition, you may want to acquire one or both of the specific Greek **hiking guidebooks**; both of these are written by contributors to this guide – see "Books" in *Contexts*. See also p.24 for details of **hiking maps** available, and p.7 for details of companies offering walking holidays in the mountains.

FOOTBALL AND OTHER SPECTACLES

Football (soccer) is far and away the most popular sport in Greece – both in terms of participating and watching. The most important (and most heavily sponsored) teams are *Panathanaïkós* and *AEK* of Athens, *Olympiakós* of Pireás, and *PAOK* of Thessaloníki. Other major teams in the provinces include *Lárissa* and the Cretan *Ofí*. If you're interested, matches are easy enough to catch during the winter/spring season. In mid-autumn you might even see one of the Greek teams playing European competition, though the clubs, and the national squad, have fallen on somewhat hard times of late.

Not so the nation's **basketball** team, which recently won the European Championship – cheered all the way with enormous enthusiasm. At club level, many of the football teams maintain basketball squads.

POLICE, TROUBLE AND HARASSMENT

It's now nearly two decades since the colonels' junta was dislodged and Greece ceased to be a police state. As everywhere, there are a few mean characters around, but in general your average Greek policeman is not likely to have too much of a power complex, and you need to do something pretty insensitive to risk arrest. The most common causes of a brush with authority – all of them technically illegal – are nude bathing or sunbathing, camping outside an authorised site, and (a major crime in the Greek book) taking or possessing cannabis products or any other drug.

From the other side of things, you'd be unlucky to have possessions stolen –

though increased caution, alas, is in order. For women, harassment is a (relatively low-key) fact of life, given the classically Mediterranean machismo of the culture.

OFFENCES

Nude bathing is, currently, legal on only a very few beaches (on Míkonos, for example), and is deeply offensive to many more traditional Greeks – exercise considerable sensitivity to local feeling and the kind of place you're in. Generally, if a beach has become fairly established for nudity, or is well secluded, it's highly unlikely that the police are going to come charging in. Where they do get bothered is if they feel a place is turning into a "hippie beach" or nudity is getting too overt on mainstream tourist stretches. But there are no hard and fast rules; it all depends on the local cops. Most of the time, the only action will be a warning but you can officially be arrested straight off – facing up to three days in jail and a stiff fine.

Topless (sun)bathing for women is technically legal nationwide, but specific locales often opt out of the "liberation" by posting signs to that effect. It is best to follow their dictates.

Very similar guidelines apply to **freelance camping** – though for this you're still less likely to incur anything more than a warning to move on. The only real risk of arrest is if you are told to move on and fail to do so. In either of the above cases, even if the police do take any action against you, it's more likely to be a brief spell in their cells than any official prosecution.

Drug offences are a far more serious matter, as with a growing local use and addiction problem the Greeks are very nearly hysterical on the topic. The maximum penalty for "causing the use of drugs by someone under 18", for example, is life imprisonment and a 10-million-drachma fine. Theory is by no means practice, but foreigners caught in possession of small amounts of grass do get jail sentences of up to a year – more if there's evidence that they've been supplying others.

If you get arrested for any offence, you have a right to contact your **consulate** who will arrange a lawyer for your defence. Beyond this, there is little they can, or in most cases will, do. Details of consulates in Athens and Thessaloníki appear in their respective "Listings" sections.

THEFTS

Greece is traditionally one of the safest and most crime-free parts of Europe – and in most respects

it remains so. Leave a bag or wallet at a café and you'll find it scrupulously looked after, pending your return. Similarly, the Greeks are very relaxed about leaving possessions unlocked or unattended on the beach, in rooms, or on campsites.

Sadly, since the influx of desperately poor, underemployed **Albanian refugees** in 1991, there has been an astronomical increase in the number of car and house break-ins, and crimes against persons in the larger cities especially. The police have reacted harshly, deporting large numbers of Albanians who have entered the country illegally since Greece and Albania agreed to place a ban on refugee emigration. Overtones of racism seem unavoidable but it still seems wisest to keep cars and rooms religiously locked and a sharp eye on bags, treating Greece like any other European destination.

SEXUAL HARASSMENT

Many women travel independently about Greece without being harassed or feeling intimidated. Greek machismo, however, is strong, if less upfront than in, for example, Spain or Italy. Most of the hassle you are likely to get is from a small minority of Greeks who migrate to the **main resorts and towns** in summer in pursuit of "liberated, fun-loving" tourists.

Indigenous Greeks, who are increasingly hospitable as you become more of a fixture in any one place, treat these outsiders, known as **kamákia** ("harpoons"), with contempt. Their obvious stake-outs are beach bars and discos. Words worth remembering for an unambiguous response include "*Stamáta*" (stop it), "*afísteme*" (leave me alone) and "*fíyete*" (go away).

Camping is generally easy and unthreatening, although away from recognised sites it is often wise to attach yourself to a local family by making arrangements to use nearby private land. In the more **remote mountains and inland areas** you may feel more uncomfortable travelling alone. The intensely traditional Greeks may have trouble understanding why you are unaccompanied, and might not welcome your presence in their exclusively male *kafenía* – often the only place where you can get a drink. Travelling with a man, you're more likely to be treated as a *kséni*, a word meaning both (female) stranger and guest.

Very few Greek women **hitch**, although a fair number of tourists do. Much the same rules of caution apply as elsewhere in Europe: accept rides from couples and you'll feel secure enough.

FINDING WORK

The EC notwithstanding, short-term work in Greece is always on an unofficial basis and for this reason it will generally be where you can't be seen by the police or you're badly paid – or, more often, both. The recent influx of nearly 100,000 Albanians, Poles, Yugoslavs, Russian Greeks and assorted orther refugees from the upper Balkans has resulted in a surplus of unskilled labour and severely depressed wages. There's a little more dignity to permanent employment, though as elsewhere in Europe this is largely limited to teaching English.

SHORT-TERM WORK

A few ideas to get you started – from **bars** to **harvests**. Note that **youth hostels** are a good source of information on temporary work – indeed a few may even offer you a job themselves, if you turn up at the right time.

TOURISM-RELATED WORK

Most tourists working casually in Greece find jobs in **bars or restaurants** around the main resorts. Women will generally find these jobs easier to obtain than men – who should generally count themselves lucky to get work washing up. "Trained" chefs, however, sometimes fare better.

If you're waiting or serving, most of your wages will probably have to come from tips but you may well be able to get a deal that includes free food and lodging; evening-only hours can be a good shift, leaving you a lot of free time. The main drawback may be the machismo and/or chauvinist attitudes of your employer. (Ads in the local press for "girl bar staff" are certainly best ignored.)

Corfu, with its big British slant, is usually the most rewarding place to look for bar work, though its resorts are perhaps less of an attraction for living. Rhodes and Crete are promising, too. Start looking, if you can, around April or May; you'll get better rates at this time if you're taken on for a season.

On a similar, unofficial level you might be able to get a sales job in **tourist shops** on Corfu, Rhodes or Crete, or (if you've the expertise) helping out at one of the **windsurfing** "schools" that have sprung up all around the coast.

Perhaps the best type of tourism-related work, though, is that of **courier/greeter/group co-ordinator** for a package holiday company. All you need is EC nationality and language proficiency compatible with the clientele, though knowledge of Greek is a big plus. English-only speakers are pretty well restricted to places with a big British package trade, namely Crete, Rhodes, Skíathos and the Ionian islands.

Many such staff are recruited through ads in back-home papers, but it's by no means unheard of to be hired on the spot in April or May. A big plus, however you're taken on, is that you're usually guaranteed about six months of steady work, and that if things work out you may be re-employed the following season with contract and foreign-currency wages from the home company, not from the local affiliate.

Outside the tourist season there can be **building/painting/signpainting** work preparing for the influx; ask around at Easter time. **Yacht marinas** can also prove good hunting-grounds though less for the romantic business of crewing (still a possibility if you've got the charm and arrogance) than scrubbing down and repainting. Again, the best possibilities are likely to be on Rhodes, Corfu, or Crete; the Zéa port at Pireás is actually the biggest marina, but non-Greek owners don't tend to rest up there for long.

SELLING AND BUSKING

You will almost certainly do better by working for yourself. Travellers report rich pickings during the tourist season from **making and selling jewellery** (or importing it from Turkey to sell) on island beaches, or on boats. Once you've managed to get the stuff past the customs officials (who will be sceptical, for instance, that all those trinkets are presents for friends), there rarely seem to be problems with the local police, though it probably pays to be discreet.

Busking can also be quite lucrative. Playing on the Athens metro, it's possible to make around 2000dr in a two-hour session. In resorts, you might just strike luckier if you've talent, and even back in Athens the western-style pubs occasionally hire foreign musicians for gigs.

AGRICULTURE

Harvesting and other **agricultural jobs** are invariably low-paid, more so now with the glutted labour pool, but they provide a winter fallback for some long-term travellers. It's predominantly male work, however, with the fields often quite a rough scene, while in addition some Greeks, see fit to pay women a lower daily rate.

If you're still intent on doing it, the most promising course is to ask around among fellow travellers at youth hostels – at some of which you'll find employers recruiting casual labour.

The best **areas, month by month** are:

November–February: Oranges, in the region bounded by Mycenae, Árgos, Náfplio and Tólo – though be aware that the police here are among the most unpleasant in Greece. Lemons at Mistrás, near Spárti, and Kiáto on the coast by Kórinthos, after the oranges are gone. On Crete the season may continue into **April or May**, especially at Paleohóra and Falásarna in the west.

March: Artichokes at Iría, near Tólo.

June: Peaches around Véria in Macedonia.

October–November: Olive harvest, most notably around Ámfissa, near Kalamáta, and on Crete.

TEACHING ENGLISH

Language schools (*frondistíria*) have expanded massively through Greece over the past decade, and English remains by far the most popularly required tongue. To get a job in a school you need to have a TEFL (Teaching of English as a Foreign Language) **certificate**, or a university degree (preferably in English), though with just

the latter you'll be paid less. Speaking Greek helps but isn't essential.

The simplest way to get a teaching job is to apply before leaving – preferably in **Britain**. There are ads published weekly, particularly from August to October, in *The Guardian* newspaper (Tuesday Education) and in the weekly *Times Educational Supplement*. Once accepted, you should get one-way air fare from London paid, (usually) accommodation found for you, and a contract of employment. The other big advantage of arranging work from abroad is that the red tape of **work permits** and teaching licences will be cleared up for you before you set off. You'll always be asked for a translated copy of your degree or TEFL certificate, more cheaply done at a Greek consulate abroad than in Greece itself. You may also be obliged to present a medical certificate of good health.

If you're already in Greece and want teaching work, obtaining a work permit is harder but not impossible. **EC nationals** are at a distinct advantage in this respect, though non-EC citizens of Greek descent will find it just as easy and in fact qualify to operate their own schools. In practice, however, schools are rarely bothered, and if they like you and your qualifications, and you're around at the right time, you're likely to find a place. Try in late August/early September, or again in January – some teachers don't last the isolation of Greek winters.

The best technique is to approach *frondistíria* directly – dozens are listed in the phonebook for all larger towns, and many are jointly owned and will send you to an affiliate if they don't have a vacancy. Teaching is essentially a winter/spring exercise; most, though not all, schools close down from the end of May until September, operating only a few special courses in June and July.

The current minimum gross **salary** is about 120,000dr per month (equivalent to about £380/US$680), or 1000–1300dr per hour. Wage increases are indexed to approximately the rate of inflation. Often you will be paid a net salary, with a portion of the Greek income tax and IKA (social security payments) deducted by your employers.

It's general practice to supplement your income by giving **private lessons**, and for this the going rate is around £10––/US$18–23 an hour. Many teachers finance themselves exclusively on private lessons and, although you still officially need a teaching permit for this, few people experience any problems with it (though some schools don't like their employees to indulge, and/or may demand a cut).

The *British Council* in Athens can put you in touch with people wanting lessons or you can advertise in the *Athens News* or *Greek Weekly News*.

RECRUITING ORGANISATIONS
Pan-Hellenic Association of Language School Owners (PALSO), Kallíróis 37, 117 43 Athens.

English Teachers for Greece (ETFG), Nikifórou Plastíra 3, Réthimno, Crete (☎0831/20 750), and 160 Littlehampton Road, Worthing, West Sussex BN13 1QT (☎0903/690729).

Teachers in Greece (TIG), Taxílou 79, Zográphou, 157 71 Athens (☎01/77 92 587), or 53 Talbot Rd, London W2 (☎071/243 9260).

The popularity and scale of private English teaching also means that English-speaking women are heavily in demand as **au pairs**. As ever, such positions tend to be exploitive and low-paid, but if you can use them to your own ends – living reasonably well and learning Greek – there can be mutual benefits.

It's unwise to arrange anything until you're in Greece, so you can at least meet and talk terms with your prospective family, and in Athens you should find little difficulty fixing something up. Posts are advertised in the daily *Athens News* and there are quite a number of specialist agencies. These include:

International Staff (Th. N. Camenos), Botási 12, Athens.

Miterna, Ermoú 28, Athens.

Working Holidays, Níkis 11, Athens.

XEN (Greek YWCA), Amerikís 11, Athens.

DIRECTORY

AIRPORT TAX There is no tax on exit or arrival.

ANIMAL WELFARE is not a Greek strongpoint: cats, dogs, donkeys, horses, etc, are rarely considered worthy of veterinary treatment. The *Greek Animal Welfare Fund* has a network of (English-speaking) contacts around the country, willing to help animals in distress. For the local representative, phone their Athens office (☎01/64 35 391 or ☎01/64 44 473).

BARGAINING isn't a regular feature of life, though you'll find it possible with private rooms and some off-season hotels. Similarly, services such as shoe or camera repair don't have iron-clad rates, though as a foreigner you're more likely to be undercharged than the opposite.

CONSULATES/EMBASSIES See listings for Athens and Thessaloníki.

CONTRACEPTIVES Condoms (*profilaktiká*, or more slangy, *kapótes*) are available from city kiosks or *farmakía*; the pill, too, can be obtained from a *farmakío*.

ELECTRICITY is 220 volt AC, just possibly 110 DC in a dwindling number of remote spots. Wall outlets take double round-pin plugs as in the rest of continental Europe. North American appliances will require both a step-down transformer and a plug adapter.

FERRY DEPARTURE TAX A departure tax is levied on all international ferries – currently 1500dr per person *and* per car or motorbike.

FILMS *Fuji* films are reasonably priced and easy to have processed; *Kodakchrome* and *Ektachrome* slide films are expensive, and the former cannot be processed in Greece.

GAY LIFE is centred on Míkonos, still the most popular European gay resort after Ibiza in Spain. Lesser action occurs on Rhodes and Íos; for women, to a modest extent, at Erissós on Lésvos (appropriately). Homosexuality is legal over the age of 17, and (male) *bi*sexuality quite widely accepted. See also "Gay discos and clubs" and "Listings" in the *Athens* chapter.

GREEK LANGUAGE COURSES abound in Athens – again see the city's "Listings" section for addresses.

KIDS/BABIES are worshipped and indulged in Greece, perhaps to excess, and present few problems when travelling. Baby foods and nappies are ubiquitous and reasonably priced, plus concessions are offered on most forms of transport. Private rooms establishments are more likely to offer some kind of babysitting service than the more impersonal hotels.

LAUNDRIES (*plintíria*) are beginning to crop up in most of the main resort towns; sometimes an attended service wash is available for little or no extra charge over the basic cost of 800–1000dr per wash and dry. Otherwise, ask rooms owners for a *skáfi* (laundry trough), a bucket (*kouvás*), or the special laundry area often available; they freak out if you use bathroom sinks, Greek plumbing (and wall-mounting) being what they are.

MEDICAL EMERGENCIES ☎166 summons an ambulance throughout the country.

PERÍPTERA are street-corner kiosks. They sell everything from pens to disposable razors, stationery to soap, sweets to condoms, cigarettes to plastic crucifixes . . . and are often open when nothing else is.

TIME Greek **summertime** begins at 4am on the last Sunday in March, when the clocks go forward one hour, and ends at 4am the last Sunday in September when they go back. Be alert to this, as scores of visitors miss planes, ferries, etc every year; the change is not well publicised. Greek time is two hours ahead of Britain, three hours when the countries' respective changes to summertime fail to coincide. For North America, the difference is seven hours for Eastern Standard Time, ten hours for Pacific Standard Time, with again an extra hour for those weeks in April and October. A **recorded time message** (in Greek) is available by dialling ☎141.

TOILETS Public ones are usually in parks or squares, often subterranean; otherwise try a bus station. Throughout Greece you toss paper in adjacent wastebaskets, *not* in the bowl. Except in areas frequented by tourists, public toilets tend to be pretty filthy – best to use the much cleaner ones in restaurants and bars.

USEFUL THINGS TO BRING should include an alarm clock (for early buses and ferries) and a torch (if you camp out). You can buy just about anything you've forgotten in Athens, arguably the largest de facto bazaar in the Mediterranean.

PART TWO

THE
MAINLAND

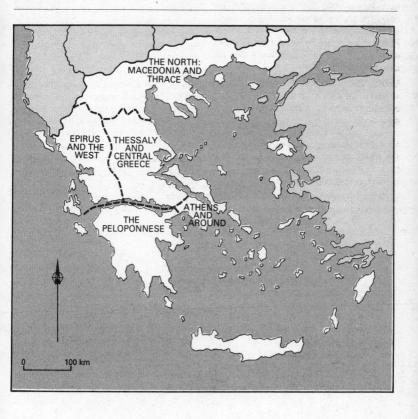

THE NORTH:
MACEDONIA AND
THRACE

EPIRUS
AND THE
WEST

THESSALY
AND
CENTRAL
GREECE

ATHENS
AND
AROUND

THE
PELOPONNESE

0   100 km

CHAPTER ONE

ATHENS AND AROUND

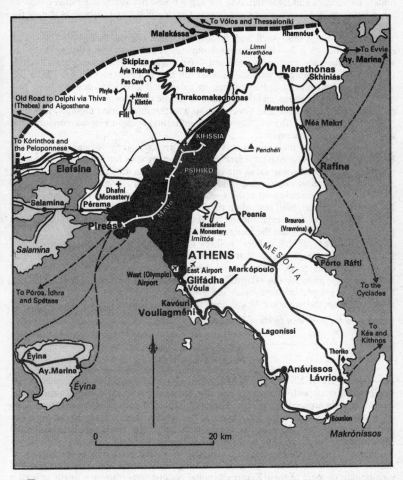

A **thens** is not a graceful city. It looks terrible from just about every approach; its air pollution is dire; and its traffic and postwar architecture are a disaster. For many of the three million-plus visitors who pass through each year, it can seem a dutiful stop. Time is spent at the Acropolis; more at the vast National Archaeological Museum; and an evening or two amid the tavernas of Pláka, the one surviving old quarter. Most tourists then get out fast, disillusioned at such sparse evidence of the past and so little apparent charm.

Such are the basic facts – yet somehow the city has the character to transcend them. An exhausting but always stimulating mix of metropolis and backwater, First and Third World, West and East, Athens has seen its population soar from 700,000 to four million – over a third of the nation's people – since World War II. The speed of this process is reflected in the city's chaotic mix of urban and rural: goats graze in yards, horsecarts are pulled along streets thick with traffic, Turkish-style bazaars vie for space with outlets for Armani and Benetton. And the city's hectic modernity is tempered with an air of intimacy and hominess; as any honest Greek will tell you, Athens is merely the largest village in the country.

Once you accept this, you'll find the **ancient sites** and the **Acropolis** – supreme monument though it is – only the most obvious of **Athens' attractions**. There are some beautiful cafés, garden tavernas and street markets; startling views from the hills of **Likavitós** and **Filopáppou**; and, around the foot of the Acropolis, the **Pláka** has scattered monuments of the Byzantine, medieval and nineteenth-century town that seemed so exotic to Byron and the Romantics. As you might expect, the city also offers the best **eating** to be found in Greece, as well as the most varied nightlife, including traditional **music and films** in the winter months, and open-air cinema, **concerts** and **Classical drama** in summer.

Outside Athens, the travel focus shifts more exclusively to ancient sites; the beaches along the Attic coast are functional enough escapes for Athenians, but hardly priorities if you are moving on to the islands. Of the sites, the Temple of Poseidon at **Sounion** is the most popular trip, and rightly so, with its dramatic cliff-top position above the cape. Lesser-known and less-visited are the sanctuaries at **Rhamnous** and **Brauron** (Vravróna), both rewarding ruins with beaches nearby; while the committed might also take in the burial mound at **Marathon** – though this is more Classical pilgrimage than sight – and the Sanctuary of Demeter at **Eleusis** (Elefsína).

For relief from all this culture, walkers may want to head for the **mountains** – **Párnitha**, most compellingly – that ring the city, where springtime hikes reveal some of the astonishing range of Greek wild flowers. Hedonists, however, will already be making escape plans for **the islands**, which are served by ferries and hydrofoils from the Athenian port-suburb (and heavy industrial centre) of **Pireás** (Piraeus), and more selectively from the two other Attican ferry terminals at **Ráfina** and **Lávrio**.

Coverage of the ports and sights of Attica starts on p.118.

ATHENS

For visitors, **ATHENS** (ATHINÁ in modern Greek) has obvious highlights in the vestiges of the ancient, Classical Greek city, stunningly present in the **Acropolis** and its surrounding archaeological sites. These form the first section of this chapter – "The Acropolis Area" – and, if it's your first trip to the city, they're likely to occupy a fair portion of your time. An essential accompaniment is the **National Archaeological Museum**: the finest collection of Greek antiquities anywhere in the world.

Even on a brief visit, however, it is a shame to see Athens purely as the location of ancient sites and museums. Although the **neighbourhoods** may lack the style and monuments of most of their European-capital counterparts, they are worth at least a casual exploration. The old nineteenth-century quarter of **Pláka**, in particular, is a delight, with its mix of Turkish and Greek island architecture, and array of odd little museums, devoted to traditional arts, ceramics and music. Just to its north, the **bazaar** area, around Athinás and Eólou, retains an almost Middle Eastern atmosphere in its life and trade, while the **National Gardens**, elegant **Kolonáki** and the hill of **Likavitós** offer escape from the maelstrom. Further afield, but still well within the limits of Greater Athens, are the monasteries of **Kessarianí** and **Dhafní**, the latter with Byzantine mosaics the equal of any in Greece.

A brief history of modern Athens

Athens has been inhabited continuously for over 7000 years. Its *acropolis*, supplied with springwater, protected by a ring of mountains, and commanding views of all approaches from the sea, was a natural choice for prehistoric settlement and for the Mycenaeans, who established a palace-fortress on the rock. Its development into a city-state and artistic centre continued apace under the Dorians, Phoenicians and various dynastic rulers, reaching its apotheosis in the fifth century BC. This was the **Classical period**, when the Athenians, having launched themselves into an experiment in radical democracy, celebrated their success with a flourish of art, architecture, literature and philosophy that has pervaded Western culture ever since. (An account of the Classical Period is given with the main sites of Ancient Athens on p.70–72; later, Roman, history is outlined on p.85).

For all the claims of this ancient past, and despite the city's natural advantages, Athens was not the first-choice capital of modern Greece. That honour went to Náfplio in the Peloponnese, where the War of Independence was masterminded by Capodistrias, and where the first Greek National Assembly met in 1828. Athens at the time was still a provincial backwater, whose population – 250,000 in Classical times – had declined to around 1500 Greek and 400 Turkish families under Ottoman rule.

Had Capodistrias not been assassinated, in 1831, the capital would most likely have remained in the Peloponnese; if not at Náfplio, then at Trípoli, Kórinthos (Corinth) or Pátra, all much more established and sizeable towns. But following Capodistrias' death, the "Great Powers" of Western Europe intervened, inflicting on the Greeks a king of their own choosing – **Otho**, son of Ludwig I of Bavaria – and in 1834 transferring the capital and court to Athens.

The reasoning was almost purely symbolic and sentimental. Athens was not only insignificant in terms of population and physical extent but was at the edge of the territories of the new Greek state, which was yet to include Northern Thessaly, Epirus and Macedonia, or any of the islands beyond the Cyclades.

Medieval and Turkish Athens

The break from ancient to medieval in Athens was due, essentially, to the emergence of **Christianity**. Having survived with little change through years of Roman rule, the city lost its pivotal role in the Roman-Greek world after the division of the Roman empire into eastern and western halves, and the establishment of Byzantium (Constantinople) as capital of the eastern – **Byzantine** – empire. There, a new Christian focus soon outshone the prevailing ethic of Athens, whose schools of philosophy continued to teach a pagan Neoplatonism. In 529 the schools were finally closed by Justinian I and the city's temples, including the Parthenon, were reconsecrated as churches. Athens was designated an archbishopric but it features little in the chronicles of the age.

The city underwent a brief revival under the foreign powers of the Middle Ages. In the aftermath of the piratical Fourth Crusade, Athens – together with the Peloponnese and much of Central Greece – passed into the hands of the **Franks**. At the Acropolis they established a ducal court (of some magnificence, according to contemporary accounts) and for a century Athens was back in the mainstream of Europe. Frankish control, however, was based on little more than a provincial aristocracy. In 1311 their forces battled **Catalan** mercenaries, who had a stronghold in Thebes, and were driven to oblivion in a swamp. The Catalans, having set up their own duchy, in turn gave way to **Florentines** and, briefly, **Venetians**, before the arrival in 1456 of **Sultan Mehmet II**, the Turkish conqueror of Constantinople.

Turkish Athens was never much more than a garrison town. The links with the West, which had maintained some sense of continuity with the Classical and Roman city, were severed. The Acropolis became the home of the Turkish governor, and the Parthenon a mosque; visitors were reduced to a handful of French or Italian ambassadors to the Sublime Porte and the occasional traveller or painter. The town does not seem to have been oppressed by Ottoman rule; the Greeks enjoyed some autonomy, and both Jesuit and Capuchin monasteries were permitted. However, life in the village-like quarters around the Acropolis drifted back to a rural, market existence, while the great port of **Pireás** – still partially enclosed within its ancient walls – was left to serve just a few dozen fishing boats.

Records of the Ottomans' four centuries of occupation largely concern the city's **monuments**. In 1687 the Venetians, under the Doge Francisco Morosini, laid siege to the Acropolis. A "fortunate shot", fired by a Swedish mercenary general from the hill of Filopáppou, ignited the Turkish powder-store in the Parthenon and blew the temple in two. At the end of the eighteenth century came the Western looters: **Elgin** levering away sculptures from the Parthenon, the French ambassador **Fauvel** gathering his share for the Louvre. **Byron**, a sympathetic luminary amidst all this activity, visited in 1810–11, in time to see the last of Elgin's ships loaded with the marbles.

Independence was just two decades away. In 1821, in common with a score of other towns across the country, the Greeks of Athens rose in rebellion. They occupied the Turkish quarters of the lower town – the current Pláka – and laid siege to the Acropolis. The Turks withdrew, but five years later were back to reoccupy the Acropolis fortifications, while the Greeks evacuated to the countryside. When the Ottoman garrison finally left in 1834, and the Bavarian architects of the new German-born monarchy moved in, Athens was arguably at its nadir.

Modern Athens

The **nineteenth-century development** of Athens was a gradual and fairly controlled process. While the archaeologists stripped away all the Turkish and Frankish embellishments from the Acropolis, a modest city took shape along the lines of the Bavarians' neoclassical grid. **Pireás**, meanwhile, grew into a port again, though until this century its activities continued to be dwarfed by the main Greek shipping centres on the islands of Síros and Ídhra (Hydra).

The first mass expansion of both municipalities came suddenly, in 1923, as the result of the tragic Greek-Turkish war in **Asia Minor**. The peace treaty concluding this involved the exchange of Greek and Turkish ethnic populations, the determination of identity being made solely on the basis of religion. A million and a half Greeks, mostly from the age-old settlements along the Asia Minor coast, but also many Turkish-speaking communities from inland Anatolia, arrived in Greece as refugees. Over half of them settled in Athens, Pireás, and the neighbouring villages, changing at a stroke the whole make-up of the capital. Their integration, and survival, is one of the great events of Athens' history – ancient and modern. It is still evident today. The web of suburbs that straddle the metro line from Athens to Pireás, and sprawl out into the hills, bear nostalgic names of their refugees' origins: *Néa Smírni* (New Smyrna), *Néa Iónia*, *Néa Filadhélfia*, and so on. At the beginning they were exactly that: refugee villages with populations primarily from one or another Anatolian town, built in ramshackle fashion, often with a single water source for two dozen families.

The merging of these shanty-suburbs and their populations with the established communities of Athens and Pireás dominated the years before **World War II**. With the war, however, new concerns emerged. Athens was hit hard by German occupation; during the winter of 1942 there were an estimated 2000 deaths from starvation each day. In late 1944, when the Germans had finally left (Allied policy was to tie them down in the Balkans), the capital saw the first skirmishes of **civil war**, with British forces being ordered to fight against their previous Greek partners in the Communist-dominated resistance army, ELAS. Physical evidence of the ensuing month-long Battle of Athens, the *Dhekemvrianá*, can still be seen in a handful of bullet-pocked walls. From 1946 to 1949 Athens was a virtual island in the civil war, with road approaches to the Peloponnese and the north only tenuously kept open.

During the 1950s, however, after the cival war, the city started to expand rapidly. A massive **industrial investment** programme – financed largely by the Americans, who had won Greece for their sphere of influence – took place, and, concurrently, the capital saw huge **immigration** from the war-torn, impoverished countryside. The open spaces between the old refugee suburbs began to fill and, by the late 1960s, Greater Athens covered a continuous area from the slopes of mounts Pendéli and Párnitha down to Pireás and Elefsína.

This enormous and rapid population increase and attendant industrial development have had disastrous **environmental effects**. On a visual level, much of the modern city is unremittingly ugly; old buildings were demolished wholesale in the name of quick-buck development, particularly during the colonels' junta of 1967–73. Only now – too late – are planning and preservation measures being enforced. More seriously, with a third of the Greek population, half the country's industry and over two-thirds of its cars crammed into Greater Athens, the capital has found itself with one of the world's worst **pollution** problems. A noxious cloud, the *néfos*, makes regular appearances, trapped by the circle of mountains and aerial inversion layers, hovering above the city. Despite what your burning eyes and throat may tell you, some improvement in the situation has been registered in the past decades, though not in the critical pollutant nitrogen dioxide, and not enough to prevent any current opposition party from scoring points against the party in power. It still, moreover, aggravates acute respiratory diseases and arguably contributed to the high death toll during the freak heat waves or *kávsones* during the summers of 1987–88.

Symbolically, some might say, the *néfos* is eating away at the Parthenon marbles: sulphur dioxide settles on the columns and statuary, becomes a friable coating of calcium sulphate, and washes off in the winter rains, taking a thin layer of stone with it. For the last ten years, however, the only antipollution measures have been restrictions on the use of **private cars**. Recent governments have played about with limitations on weekday use of vehicles, stipulating alternate days for odd- and even-numbered plates. But still most shops, offices and businesses persist in closing for a three-hour summer siesta, making for four rush hours a day and doubling the pollution and traffic problems that most cities have to face. Additionally, short-sighted governmental taxation and duty policies mean that Athenians keep their beloved autos until they die of metal fatigue, rarely maintaining or tuning them to optimum, low-exhaust running conditions.

Not all is gloom. Dimitris Beïs, the former PASOK mayor, endowed the city with thousands of trees, shrubs, and patches of garden, and an ever-growing number of pedestrian-only streets – though Athens still lags far behind Paris or London in terms of open space. There is also increasing awareness of the nineteenth-century architectural heritage – what's left of it – with many old houses being restored and repainted.

It's the **long-term solutions** that are more problematic: decanting industry and services into the provinces, where there is little infrastructure and where no self-respecting Athenian wishes to live, and creating a mass transport network capable of meeting the needs of a modern capital city. The current Néa Dhimokratía mayor, Andonis Tritsis – a renegade from PASOK, American-trained and an ex-Minister of the Environment – is nominally committed to finally beginning the metro, and the extra Spáta airport, in earnest. However, with air inversion layers still prompting pollution alerts in both summer and winter, there is still a very long way to go.

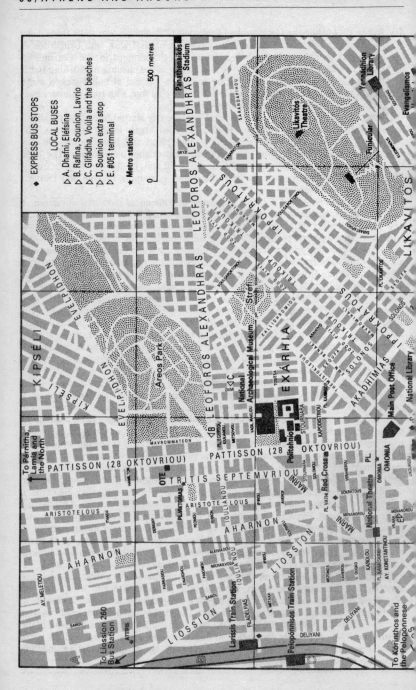

EXPRESS BUS STOPS

LOCAL BUSES
△ A. Dhafní, Eléfsina
△ B. Rafína, Soúnion, Lávrio
△ C. Glifádha, Voúla and the beaches
△ D. Soúnion extra stop
△ E. #051 terminal

★ Metro stations

0   500 metres

KIPSÉLI

Areos Park

EVELPÍDHON

LEOFOROS ALEXANDHRAS

LIKAVITOS

Panathenaïkós Stadium

Likavitos Theatre

Funicular

Vensadhion Library

Evangelismós

Gennadhion Library

IPPOKRÁTOUS

Stréfi

EXÁRHIA

National Archaeological Museum

Politehnio

AKADHIMIAS

National Library

Main Post Office

To Párnitha, Lamia and the North

PATTISSON (28 OKTOVRIOU)

OTE

TRITIS SEPTEMVRIOU

ARISTOTELOUS

ARISTOTE LOUS

AHARNON

Red Cross

National Theatre

OMONIA

PL.

OMONIA

MARNI

LIOSSION

AHARNON

LIOSSION

To Liossion 260 Bus Station

Larissis Train Station

Peloponnisos Train Station

To Kórinthos and the Peloponnese

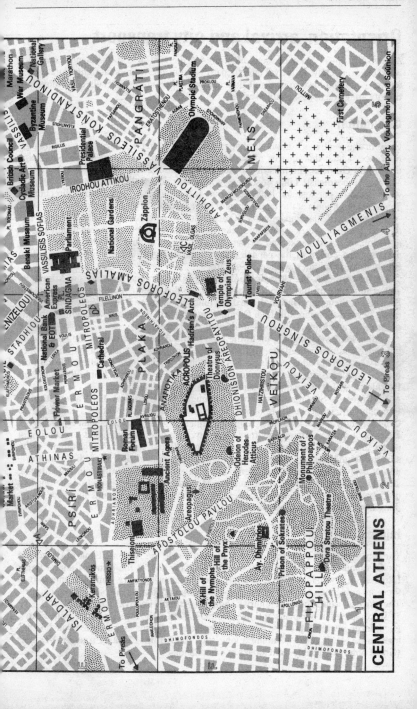

CENTRAL ATHENS

To Piréas

ISALDARI

Keramikós

ERMOU

THISSIO ★

PL. ELEFTHERIAS

DIMIOU

AMFIKTYONOS

POULOPINRATOU

AKTAIOU

DHIMOFONDOS

Hill of the Nymphs
Hill of the Pnyx

APOSTOLOU PAVLOU

FILOPAPPOU HILL

Ay. Dimitrios

Prison of Sokrates

Monument of Philopappos

Dora Stratou Theatre

DHIMOFONDOS

APOLLONOS

Thisseíon

Ancient Agora

Roman Forum

PSIRÍ

ATHINAS

EOLOU

ERMOU

MITROPOLEOS

Market

Flower Market

Cathedral

National Bank & EOT

STADHIOU

VENIZELOU

ERMOU

MITROPOLEOS

VOULIS

NIKIS

PLAKA

ANAFIOTIKA

ACROPOLIS

Hadrian's Arch

Odeion of Herodes Atticus

Theatre of Dionysos

DHIONISION AREOPAYITOU

Areopagus

VEIKOU

VEIKOU

LEOFOROS SINGROU

To Piréas

Temple of Olympian Zeus

Tourist Police

VOURVAHI

LEOFOROS AMALIAS

SINDAGMA

American Express

Parliament

VASSILISIS SOFIAS

Benaki Museum

Cycladic Art Museum

British Council

Byzantine Museum

War Museum

National Gallery

Marathon

VASSILEOS KONSTANDINOU

PANGRÁTI

Olympic Stadium

National Gardens

Záppion

IRODHOU ATTIKOU

Presidential Palace

RIGILLIS

VASSILIS

METS

First Cemetery

ARDHITTOU

VOULIAGMENIS

LEOFOROS VOULIAGMENIS

To the Airport, Vouliagméni and Soúnion

Orientation, arrival and city transport

As a visitor, you're likely to spend most time in the central grid of Athens, a compact, walkable area. Only on arrival at or departure from the various far-flung stations and terminals do you have to confront the confused urban sprawl. Details on coming into the city are given opposite and overleaf.

Orientation

Once in the centre, it's a simple matter to **orient** yourself. There are four strategic reference points: the squares of **Síndagma** ("Syntagma" on many English-language maps) and **Omónia**, the hills of the **Acropolis** (unmistakable with its temple crown) and (to the northeast) **Likavitós**. Once you've established these as a mental compass you shouldn't get lost for long – anyone will point you back in the direction of Síndagma or Omónia at the (approximate) pronunciation of their names.

Síndagma (Platía Sindágmatos, "Constitution Square", to give it its full title) lies midway between the Acropolis and Likavitós. With the Greek Parliament building on its uphill side, and banks and airline offices grouped around, it is to all intents and purposes the centre of the capital. Almost everything of daytime interest is within twenty to thirty minutes' walk of the square.

To the northeast, the ritzy **Kolonáki** quarter curls around the slopes of **Likavitós**, with a funicular up the hillside to save you the final climb. To the east, behind the Parliament, the jungly **National Gardens** function as the city's chief lung and meeting place; beyond them are the 1896 Olympic stadium and the attractive neighbourhoods of **Pangráti** and **Méts**, both good for drinking and eating.

To the southwest, lapping up to the base of the **Acropolis**, spread the ramshackle but much-commercialised lanes of **Pláka**, the lone surviving area of the nineteenth-century, pre-independence village. Beyond the Acropolis itself huddles **Filopáppou hill**, a parkland ringed by the neighbourhoods of **Veïkoú**, **Koukáki** and **Áno Petrálona**, which offers more possibilities of a good bed or a meal.

Northwest of Síndagma, two broad thoroughfares, **Stadhíou** and **Panepistimíou** (officially but ineffectually renamed Venizélou), run in just under a kilometre to **Omónia** (fully, Platía Omonías, "Concord Square"). This is an Athenian equivalent of Piccadilly Circus or Times Square: a bit seedy, with fast-food cafés and a scattering of porno shows in the backstreets around. To the northeast, beyond Panepistimíou, is the student neighbourhood of **Exárhia**, a slightly "alternative" district, with a concentration of lively tavernas and bars there and in its extension **Neápoli**. South of Omónia, stretching down to **Ermoú** street and the **Monastiráki** bazaar district on the borders of Pláka, lies the main commercial centre, crammed with offices and shops for everything from insurance to machine tools.

Information

The city's main **EOT tourist office** is located inside the National Bank of Greece on the Stadhíou corner of Síndagma, with an overflow post at the nearby General Bank. Either is an invaluable source of information, dispensing ferry timetable sheets (use these as guidelines only), along with maps and pamphlets for all parts of the country. The office is useful, too, for enquiries about the **Athens Festival** (see p.111).

To complement our plans and the free EOT map, is the street-indexed **Falk-Plan** a good, **large-scale map** of the city (hard to obtain in Athens, but see the bookshop listings on p.114). If you're planning a long stay, the **Athína-Pireás Proastia A-Ω** atlas (Greek only) is available from kiosks and bookshops.

Points of arrival

The section below details points of arrival and transport into the city centre. For more details on the Athens transport system, see overleaf.

The airport terminals

Athens airport – **Ellinikón** – is 9km out of the city, southeast along the coast towards Glifádha. It has two distinct sections – **West** (Thíssi) and **East** (Anatolí) – whose separate entrances are five minutes' drive apart on either side of the perimeter fence. When you leave, it's important to specify which one you want: **Olympic Airways** flights, domestic and foreign, operate from the western terminal; all **other airlines** from the eastern. Both terminals have **money exchange** facilities, open 24 hours at the eastern terminal, though only from 7am to 11pm at the western one; insist on some small denomination notes for paying for your bus ticket or taxi ride.

To get into the city, the quickest and simplest way is to get a **taxi**, which, at around 1000dr to central Athens or Pireás, is a modest cost split two or more ways. Make sure before setting out that either the meter is switched on, and visible, or that a price has been established; overcharging of tourists can be brutal. You may find (see comments on taxis overleaf) that you'll have fellow passengers in the cab; each drop-off will pay the full fare.

If you're willing to wait a bit, and carry your bags around, a blue-and-yellow, double-decker **express bus** (see box overleaf) calls at both terminals on a variable schedule around the clock, dropping you at selected points in the city centre. The fare is currently 160dr (240dr between midnight and 5.30am); tickets can usually be bought on the bus if you're forearmed with small change.

The train stations

There are two train stations, almost adjacent, a couple of hundred metres northwest of Omónia, off Dheliyáni street. The **Stathmós Laríssis** handles the main lines coming from the north (Lárissa, Thessaloníki, the Balkans, Western Europe and Turkey). The **Stathmós Peloponníssou**, three blocks south, is the terminal for the narrow-gauge line circling the Peloponnese, including the stretch to Pátra (the main port for the ferries from Italy and Corfu).

From either station, you are within five or ten minutes' walk of the concentration of hotels around Platía Viktorías and Exárhia, both handy for the National Archaeological Museum and excellent eateries. For hotels elsewhere, yellow trolley **bus #1** passes right by the Laríssis station (to get to it from the Peloponníssou terminal, use the giant metal overpass) and makes a strategic loop down through Omónia, along Stadhíou to Síndagma, then down Fillelínon to Hadrian's Arch (for Méts), and finally along Veïkoú to Koukáki (on the southeast side of Filopáppou hill).

Be wary of **taxis** (both official and unlicensed) at the train stations – some thrive on newly arrived tourists, shuttling them a couple of blocks for highly inflated fares.

The bus stations

Again, there are two principal terminals. Coming into Athens **from Northern Greece or the Peloponnese**, you'll find yourself at **Kifissoú 100**, a ten-minute bus ride from the centre. The least expensive way into town is to take city bus #051 to the corner of Vilára/Menándhrou, just off Omónia and only a block or two from a yellow trolley-bus stop.

Routes from central Greece (see p.65 for specific destinations) arrive at a terminal at **Liossíon 260**, north of the train stations; to get into the centre, take the blue city bus #024 to Síndagma.

In addition, there are international **OSE buses**, run by the railway company, which arrive at the two train stations. Private **international bus companies** arrive at, and leave from, a variety of locations. Most will take you to the train station or to Kifissoú 100; a few drop passengers right in the city centre.

Pireás: the ferries

If you arrive by boat at **Pireás**, the simplest access to Athens is by **metro** to the stations at Monastiráki, Omónia or Viktorías. Trains run from 6am to midnight, with fares varying from 75 to 100dr according to a zone system. For the airport, take express **#19** (see box).

Taxis between Pireás and central Athens should cost around 1000dr, including baggage, fifty percent more at night rates – but again see the comments below. There's a **map of Pireás**, showing the metro station and harbours, on p.120.

City transport: buses, the metro and taxis

Athens public transport networks operate from around **5am to midnight**, with a skeleton service on some of the buses in the small hours. Certain of the yellow trolleys, including the useful #1 route, run all night on Saturdays.

City buses

The **bus network** is extensive and cheap, with a 75dr flat fare. Tickets must be bought in advance from kiosks, certain shops and newsagents, or from the limited number of booths run by bus personnel near major stops – look for the brown, red and white logo proclaiming "*Isitiria edho*" (tickets here). They're sold individually or in bundles of ten, and must be cancelled in a special machine when boarding. Fare-dodgers risk an on-the-spot fine equivalent to twenty times the current fare. Cancelled tickets apply only to a particular journey and vehicle; there are no transfers. If you're staying long enough, there's a monthly pass for 1600dr – a two-thirds savings if you ride twice daily.

Buses are very crowded at peak times, unbearably hot in summer traffic jams, and chronically plagued by strikes and slow-downs; where you can walk instead, you probably will. Individual **routes**, where relevant, are detailed in the text. The most straightforward are the **yellow trolley buses** #1–19. The **#1** connects the Laríssis train station with Omónia, Síndagma and Veïkoú/Koukáki; **#2**, **#3**, **#4**, **#5** and **#12** all link Síndagma with Omónia and the National Archaeological Museum on Patissíon.

In addition, there are scores of **blue city buses**, all with three-digit numbers and serving an infinity of lines out into the straggling suburbs and beyond.

The Metro

The single-line **metro** (75dr single-zone fare, 25dr supplement for passing Omónia in either direction) runs from Pireás in the south to Kifissiá in the north; in the centre, there are stops at Thissío, Monastiráki, Omónia and Platía Viktorías. Long-awaited work on lateral extensions to the system has allegedly begun, but don't expect much before the new millennium. Metro and bus tickets are not interchangeable.

Taxis

Athenian **taxis** are the cheapest of any EC capital – fares around the city centre will rarely run above 700dr, with the airport and Pireás only 1000dr. All officially licensed cars are painted yellow and have a special red-on-white number plate. You can wave them down on the street; pick them up at ranks at the train station, airport or the National Gardens corner of Síndagma; or get your hotel to phone for one for you. They are most elusive during the rush hours of 1.30–2.30pm and 7.30–8.30pm.

EXPRESS BUS LINES

Five blue-and-yellow double-decker **express bus lines** connect the airport terminals, the centre of the city and the port of Pireás.

The **Athens routes** are:

Line A Airport (east terminal)–Stilés–Síndagma–Omónia.

Omónia–Síndagma–Stíles–Airport (east terminal).

Line Á As above, but running to and from the west (Olympic) air terminal, and stopping at the Olympic headquarters at Singroú 96 instead of at Stilés.

Line B Airport (east terminal)–Stilés–Síndagma–Omónia.

Omónia–Síndagma–Stilés–Airport (east terminal).

Line B́ As above, but running to and from the west (Olympic) air terminal, and stopping at Singroú 96 instead of at Stilés.

The most obvious stops for the centre of town are Omónia and Síndagma; the Stilés and Singroú 96 stops are useful if you plan to stay in the Veikoú/Koukáki area. Heading out to the airport, it's safest to flag the buses down at the ticket booth near the corner of Othónos and Amalías, where they all make a short halt.

The **Pireás route** is:

#19 Airport (east terminal)–Airport (west terminal)–Fáliro–Mégaro–Telonío–Platía Karaïskáki/Aktí Tselépi.

Platía Karaïskáki/Aktí Tselépi–Telonío–Fáliro–Airport (west terminal)–Airport (east terminal).

For hydrofoils from the Zéa port, the best stop is Telonío; Mégaro is by the international ferry dock; Aktí Tselépi and the landscaped Platía Karaïskáki front the main harbour, where most island ferries leave and ticket agents are concentrated.

Lines A, Á, B, and B́ run **every twenty minutes** from 6am to midnight and roughly every hour at night. The Pireás #19 bus runs **every thirty minutes** from 6am to midnight and every ninety minutes at night. Each service has a 160dr **flat fare** (240dr from midnight to 6am). Useful free **plans** indicating the lines and the metro are widely available in hotels, travel agents, tourist offices, etc, in Athens.

Make sure the **meter** is switched on when you get in, with its display visible and properly zeroed; it is theoretically illegal to quote a flat fare for a ride within city limits – the meter must be used. If it's "not working", find another taxi or fix the fare in advance. Attempts at **overcharging** tourists are particularly common with small-hours arrivals at the airport; a threat to have a policeman adjudicate the disagreement usually elicits cooperation, as they'll very likely take your side and threaten the driver with revocation of his operating permit.

Legitimate surcharges can bump the final bill up considerably from the total showing on the meter. Currently there's an automatic 100dr supplement for entering the confines of the airport of Pireás harbour; luggage is about 50dr extra per piece; double tariff applies between 1 and 6am; and there are Easter and Christmas bonuses which seem to extend for a week or two to either side of the actual date. Every taxi must have a plastic dash-mounted placard listing extra charges in English and Greek.

To try and make ends meet on government-regulated fare limits, taxi drivers will often pick up a whole **string of passengers** along the way. This is technically illegal but universally practised. There is no fare-sharing: each passenger (or group of passengers) pays the full fare for their journey. So if you're picked up by an already-occupied taxi, memorise the meter reading at once; you'll pay from that point on, plus the 200dr minimum. When hailing an occupied taxi, yell out your destination. The kerb-crawling driver then decides whether you suit him or not.

Finding a place to stay

Hotels and **hostels** can be packed to the gills in midsummer – August especially – but for most of the year there are enough beds in the city to go around, and to suit most wallets and tastes. The **recommendations** below are geared towards the lower end of the range – hostels, D- and E-class hotels, C- and B-class pensions – and are listed in roughly ascending order of price. At the end of each area section, however, we've included a few more upmarket and comfortable C- and B- class hotels.

Looking for a room, it makes sense to phone before turning up. If you just set out and do the rounds, you'll find somewhere, but in summer, unless you're early in the day, it's likely to be at the third or fourth attempt. If you have the money for a hotel categorised C-class (③ or above – see opposite), you can book through the **hotel reservations desk** inside the National Bank of Greece on Síndagma.

For cheaper places, you're on your own. Find a street kiosk (there are hundreds in Athens) and ask to use their phone; you pay after you've finished making all the calls – there's no need to find coins. Virtually every hotel and hostel in the city will have an English-speaking receptionist. Once you locate a vacancy, ask to see the room before booking in. Standards vary greatly even within the same building, and you can avoid occasional overcharging by checking the government-regulated room prices displayed by law on the back of the door in each room.

Hotels: an area-by-area guide

The following listings are organised according to **area** – an important consideration for more than just ease of access. Many of the hotels around Pláka and the bazaar, for instance, are victim to round-the-clock noise; if you want uninterrupted sleep, better to head for the neighbourhoods south of the Acropolis (Méts, Veïkoú, Koukáki) or to the north between the National Archaeological Museum and the railway stations.

Grid references (in italics) refer to the map on p.60–61.

In and around Pláka/Síndagma

Pláka is a good area to consider if you're after a middle-budget hotel. The whole quarter, despite its commercialisation, is highly atmospheric, and above all very central, within easy walking distance of all the sites, Síndagma, and the Monastiráki metro station (a useful gateway for the port of Pireás).

Thisseus Inn, Thisséos 10, *E3* (☎32 45 960). You don't get much more central than this – three blocks west of Síndagma – nor much cheaper. No frills, but clean enough. ①

George's Guest House, Níkis 46, *E3* (☎32 36 474). One of the cheapest and most enduring of the hostel-type places, located just a block west of Síndagma. Various-sized dorms (mattresses on floor) and some doubles, but cramped bathrooms are consistently grubby. ①

Student Inn, Kidhathinéon 18, *E3* (☎32 44 808). Another central hostel that's gone downhill over the years, and is prone to night-time noise outside; 1.30am curfew. ②

XEN (YWCA), Amerikís 11, *D3* (☎36 26 970). **Women-only** hostel just north of Síndagma – *not* in Pláka – that provides clean, relatively quiet rooms, a self-service restaurant, a small library, and Greek classes. Well worth considering. The YMCA (**men-only**) equivalent nearby, the **XAN** (Omírou 28, *D3*; ☎36 24 291), is less inspiring.

Solonion, Spírou Tsángari 11, *F3* (☎32 20 008). Eccentric and (usually) friendly staff in a slightly run-down 1950s building. ②

Pension Kouros, Kódhrou 11, *E3* (☎32 27 431). Okay facilities and on a pedestrianised street (the continuation of Voulís – two blocks southwest of Síndagma). ②

Phaedra, Herefóndos 16 at the Adhrianoú junction, *F3* (☎32 27 795). Plain, clean, and dead quiet at night, at the junction of two pedestrian malls. Prices fluctuate wildly with season. ③

Cleo's Guest House, Patróoü 3, *E3* (☎32 29 053). Cell-like but comfortable; doubles only. ③

John's Place Patróoï 5, *E3* (☎32 29 719). Somewhat cheaper and more basic (no en suite baths) than its neighbour. ③

Pension Dioskouri, Pittákou 6, *F3* (☎32 48 165). Gloomy rooms, though well-furnished, with a garden and a good locale (one block in from Leofóros Amalías). ③

Phoebus, Pétta 12 – off Níkis, *F3* (☎32 20 142). Probably the best C-class in Pláka, and charges accordingly. Three minutes walk from Síndagma down Filellínon. ④

Myrto, Níkis 40, *E3* (☎32 27 237). Good value for its class, with baths in all rooms and a small bar. Just off Síndagma. ④

Acropolis House, Kódhrou 6, *E3* (☎32 22 344). A very clean, well-sited pension (see *Kouros* above for directions) and surprisingly good value. ④

Adonis, Kodroú 3, *E3* (☎32 49 737). A modern but unobjectionable low-rise pension across the street from *Acropolis House*, with some suites. ④

Nefeli, Iperídhou 16, *E3* (☎32 28 044). Another mid-range hotel, usually not block-booked by tour groups. ④

Byron, Víronos 19, *F3* (☎32 53 554). Smallish, pleasant pensión that should certainly be booked in advance. ④

The Bazaar area

If the Pláka is bohemian/chic Athens, this district is the city at its (occasionally gritty) most authentic. Noise there is in abundance, plus the odd bordello or cockroach, but also every other material thing you could possibly want – and it's a very short walk to the major sites.

Ideal, Eólou 39, corner Voréou, *E2* (☎32 13 195). Nineteenth-century Neoclassical building with the odd balcony facing the Acropolis; reasonable if somewhat decayed rooms, and friendly management. ②

Tembi, Eólou 29, *E2* (☎32 13 175). Just around the corner from the *Ideal*, marginally more comfortable. ③.

Hermion, Ermoú 66c, *E2* (☎32 12 753). Not the most salubrious part of the bazaar, but the hotel itself is okay, with an excellent coffee shop, *Hermes*, down the road at no. 56. ③

Carolina, Kolokotróni 55, *E3* (☎32 28 148). A quieter and and more savoury location; favoured by North American visitors, and charges accordingly. ④

Note that most of the hotels on Sofokléous street, and on adjacent Athinás, up towards Omónia, are worked by prostitutes. The area is tame enough, even at night, but you wouldn't want to actually stay in these places unless you're a compulsive slummer.

South and east of the Acropolis: Veïkoú and Koukáki, Méts and Pangráti

Veïkoú and **Koukáki** are adjacent districts just south of the Acropolis, edging up to the hill of Filopáppou; **Méts** and **Pangráti** spread behind the Olympic Stadium, over to the east. Both are attractive parts of the city, and though slightly out of the way – twenty minutes' walk from Síndagma or the heart of Pláka – compensate with excellent neighbourhood tavernas and cafés. Veïkoú/Koukáki are easiest reached from Pireás via the #9 trolley bus, whose terminus is just outside the Petrálona metro station.

Youth Hostel #5, Damaréos 75, Pangráti, off map beyond *G5* (☎75 19 530). A bit out of the way but friendly, no curfew and in a decent, quiet neighbourhood; trolleys #2, #11 or #12 from downtown will get you most of the way there. ①

Joseph's House, Márkou Moussoúrou 13, Méts, *F4* (☎92 31 204). This elegant old building is one of the city's most attractively sited budget pensions – though a bit seedy. It has a few non-dorm rooms, summer roofspace, plus a self-service kitchen. ②

Villa Olympia, Karatzá 16, Koukáki, *G2* (☎92 37 650). A helpful, British-managed pension which offers full English breakfast. Call ahead as there are only sixteen beds. ②

Leto, Missaraliótou 15, corner of Kariatídhon/Zítrou, Veïkoú, *C3* (☎92 31 768). Comanaged with *Phaedra* in Pláka, but rather cheaper. ③

Marble House, in a quiet cul-de-sac off A. Zínni 35, Koukáki, *G3* (☎92 34 058). Probably the best value in Koukáki, with a very helpful French/Greek management. It's often full, however, so call ahead. Rooms by the month in winter. ③

Tony's, Zaharítsa 26, Koukáki, *G2* (☎92 36 370). A quiet and clean pension. ③

Art Gallery, Erekhthíou 5, Veïkoú (☎92 38 376). Original paintings on the walls lend this upmarket pension its name. ③

Hera, Falírou 9, Veïkoú, *G3* (☎92 36 682). Big cement pile popular with tour groups; nice location across the road from a branch of *Floca* patisserie. ④

Austria, Moussón 7, Veïkoú, *G2* (☎92 35 151). One of a row of hotels on this street beneath the Acropolis; again popular with groups. ④

Around the National Archaeological Museum: Exárhia and Platía Viktorías

These areas north of Omónia – **Exárhia** to the east of the National Archaeological Museum, **Platía Viktorías** to the west – are again out of the tourist mainstream. The local restaurants are good value, the train stations (and metros Omónia or Viktorías) a short walk away, and there are the cinemas north of Platía Viktorías plus the clubs and bars around Exárhia. Due to all of these factors, these areas now have the main concentration of budget lodging in the city; most places are very well run, offering a choice of private rooms or dorm beds, friendly advice and useful services. Exárhia and the hillside above it also have a cluster of very good-value, mid-range hotels.

Youth Hostel #1, Kipséli 57, Kipséli, just north of *A3* (☎82 25 860). A second choice to the hostels listed below – due to its remote location out in Kipséli, a 15-min ride from the centre on yellow trolley #2, #4 or #9. Phone first as it's often full in season. ①

Athens Connection, Iouliánou 20, just east of Patission, Platía Viktorías, *B2* (☎82 24 592). One of the better student hostels, with single and double rooms as well as four-bed dorms, knowledgeable reception, money change and ticket-booking facilities, and a basement bar. ①

Iokastis' House, Aristotélous 65, corner of Ioulianoú, Platía Viktorías, *B2* (☎82 26 647). Basically a dive, but cheap and friendly, with a bar, travel agency, luggage storage, etc. ①

Orion, Anexartisías 5, corner Benáki, Exárhia, *C3* (☎36 27 362). Very quiet, well-run hotel across from the Lófos Stréfi park – a steep uphill walk. Self-service kitchen and common area on the roof with amazing view of central Athens. ②

Alex, Mézonos 4, Platía Váthis, *C2* (☎52 40 657). A hostel recently upgraded to bona-fide hotel status, but still with low rates, a nice bar and friendly, helpful staff. ③

Orpheus, Halkokondhíli 58, Platía Váthis, *C2* (☎52 24 996). Again recently upgraded from hostel to proper hotel. ③

Museum, Bouboulínas 16, corner Tossítsa, Exárhia, *C3* Nicely placed, good-value hotel right behind the National Archaeological Museum and parkland. ③.

Dryades, Dhriadón 4, off Anexartisías, Exárhia, *C3* (☎36 20 191). A small, quiet hotel, co-managed with the *Orion*, behind the National Archaeological Museum. ③

Exarhion, Themistokléous 55, Platía Exárhia, *C3* (☎36 01 256). Big 1960s high-rise hotel that's surprisingly inexpensive and well-placed, if a bit noisy. Doubles only. ③

Athenian Inn, Háritos 22, Kolonáki, *D5* (☎72 38 097). Not actually in Exárhia but listed here as it's virtually the only semi-affordable place in this posh neighbourhood. Small, elegant and dead convenient for most of the museums around the National Gardens. ⑤

Campsites

The city's **campsites** are out in the suburbs, not especially cheap, and only worth using if you have a camper-van to park. If you do, phone ahead to book space in season.

Dhafni Camping, on the main road towards Kórinthos, near the Dhafní monastery (☎59 81 150). Accessible by any Dhafní bus (prefixed #8) from Platía Eleftherías, halfway between Omónia and Keramikós. Driving, head down towards Keramikós and take Ierá Odhós, which later becomes the main highway to Dhafní and Elefsína. Poor and often crowded facilities.

Camping Acropolis (☎80 75 253) and **Camping Nea Kifissia** (☎80 71 494), a kilometre or so apart in the cool, leafy suburb of Kifissiá. Both have swimming pools. To reach either, take bus #528 from just north of Omónia to the final stop, from where the sites are just a short walk. Alternatively, you can take the metro all the way to its end in Kifissiá, flagging down the #528 from behind the station for the final stretch.

Camping out rough in Athens is not a good idea. Police patrol many of the parks, especially those by the train stations, and muggings are commonplace. Even the train stations are no real refuge, closing up when services stop and cleared of any stragglers. If you can't afford a night in a hostel, spend it in a bar.

Long-term Residence

Finding a flat in Central Athens, if you decide to stay and work, is quite tricky at present. Your best bet is probably a scan of the adverts in the Greek-language daily *Ta Nea*. Otherwise, everyone just paces the streets, looking for rectangular stickers, usually red on white, announcing *ENOIKAZETAI* (To Let). They are all over the city, stuck on doors, walls, windows, or lamp posts, but give little information other than the number of rooms, the presence or absence of furniture, and a phone number.

Average **rents** have risen lately to the European standard of two-fifths to one-half of the average income; you would be doing well to find a tiny studio apartment for under 45,000dr a month. On top of the rent, you will nearly always have to pay *kinóhrista*, an all-encompassing term for services, lighting, heating and sometimes cleaning, too. Kolonáki/Pefkáki, Ilisía/Ambelókipi, and Méts are the fashionable central **neighbourhoods**; one notch below are Pangráti (beyond Méts), Pláka/Anafiótika, or Koukáki (east of the Filopáppou hill), with Exárhia/Neápoli still further down the scale.

If you are planning to live in Athens, the expatriate-produced *Network Directory*, listing every conceivable service from immigration problems to pet-sitting, is invaluable. *Athens: A Survival Handbook* (Efstathiadhis) may also be useful but is way out of date.

The Acropolis and Ancient Athens

This section covers the **Acropolis** and the assorted Classical and Roman sites on its slopes; the hills of the **Pnyx** and **Philoppapus (Filopáppou)** over to the southwest; and the neighbouring **Ancient Agora** (marketplace) and **Keramikos** (cemetery) to the northwest. This is essentially, this is the core of the ancient, Classical Greek city, though a few further pockets and Roman extensions are covered in the Pláka section, beginning on p.82.

Classical Athens: some history

Perhaps the most startling aspect of ancient, Classical Athens is how suddenly it emerged to the power and glory for which we remember it – and how short its heyday proved to be. In the middle of the **fifth century BC**, Athens was little more than a country town in its street layout and buildings. These comprised a scattered jumble of single-storey houses or wattled huts, intersected by narrow lanes. Sanitary conditions were notoriously lax: human waste and rubbish were dumped outside the town with an almost suicidal disregard for plague and disease. And on the rock of the Acropolis, a site reserved for the city's most sacred monuments, stood blackened ruins – temples and sanctuaries burnt to the ground during the Persian invasion of 480 BC.

There was little to suggest that the city had entered a unique phase of its history in terms of power, prestige and creativity. But following the victories over the Persians at Marathon (470 BC) and Salamis (460 BC), Athens stood unchallenged for a generation. It grew rich on the export of olive oil and of silver from the mines of Attica, but

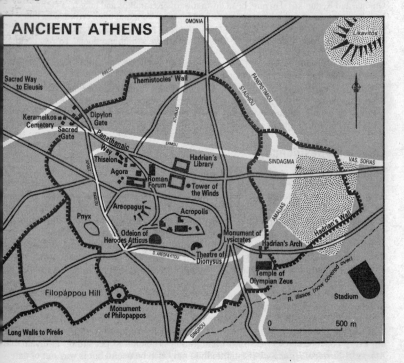

above all from the control of the Delian League, an alliance of Greek city-states formed as insurance against Persian resurgence. The Athenians removed the League's treasury from the island of Delos to their own acropolis, ostensibly on the grounds of safety, and with its revenues their leader Pericles was able to create the so-called **Golden Age** of the city. Great endowments were made for monumental construction; arts in all spheres were promoted; and – most significantly – a form of **democracy** emerged.

This democracy had its beginnings in the sixth-century BC reforms of Solon, in which the political rights of the old land-owning class had been claimed by farmer- and craftsmen-soldiers. With the emergence of **Pericles** the political process was radically overhauled, aided in large part by the Delian League's wealth – which enabled office-holders to be paid, so making it possible for the poor to play a part in government. Pericles's constitution ensured that all policies of the state were to be decided by a general assembly of Athenian male citizens – six thousand constituted a quorum. The assembly, which met outside at either the **Agora** or the **Pnyx**, elected a council of five hundred members to carry out the everyday administration of the city and a board of ten *strategoi* or generals to guide it. Pericles, one of the best known and most influential of the *strategoi*, was as vulnerable as any other to the electoral process. If sufficient numbers had cast their lot (*ostra*) against him, his citizenship would be forfeited (he would be literally ostracised); as it was, he managed to stave off such a fate and died with his popularity intact.

In line with this system of democratic participation, a new and exalted notion of the Athenian citizen emerged. This was a man who could shoulder political responsibility, take public office, and play a part in the **cultural and religious events** of the time. The latter assumed ever-increasing importance. The city's Panathenaic festival, honouring its protectress deity Athena, was upgraded along the lines of the Olympic Games to include drama, music, and athletic contests.

Athenians rose easily to the challenge. The next five decades were to witness the great dramatic works of **Aeschylus**, **Sophocles** and **Euripides**, and the comedies of **Aristophanes**. Foreigners such as **Herodotus**, considered the inventor of history, and **Anaxagoras**, the philosopher, were drawn to live in the city. And they, in turn, were surpassed by native Athenians. **Thucydides** wrote *The Peloponnesian War*, a pioneering work of documentation and analysis; **Socrates** posed the problems of philosophy that were to exercise his follower **Plato** and to shape the discipline to the present day.

But it was the great civic **building programme** that became the most visible and powerful symbol of the age. Under the patronage of Pericles and with vast public funds made available from the Delian treasury, the architects **Iktinos**, **Mnesikles** and **Callicrates**, and the sculptor **Pheidias**, transformed the city. Their buildings, justified in part as a comprehensive job-creation scheme, included the Parthenon and Erechtheion on the Acropolis; the Thiseion (or Hephaisteion) and several *stoas* (arcades) in the Agora; a new Odeion (theatre) on the south slope of the Acropolis hill; and, outside the city, the temples at Sounion and Rhamnous.

Athenian culture flourished under democracy, but the system was not without its contradictions and failures. Only one in seven inhabitants of the city were actual citizens; the political status and civil rights that they enjoyed were denied to the many thousands of women, *metics* (foreigners) and slaves. While the lives of men became increasingly public and sociable, with meetings at the Agora or Pnyx and visits to the gymnasiums and theatres, **women** remained secluded in small and insanitary homes. Their subordination was in fact reinforced by a decree (451 BC) restricting their property rights, which placed them under the control of fathers, husbands or guardians. Only forty women were appointed priestesses – one of the few positions of female power – at any one time. Aeschylus summed up the prevailing attitude when he declared that the mother does no more than foster the father's seed.

The city's democracy was also sullied by its **imperialist** designs and actions, which could be as brutal and exploitative as any force before or since. Atrocities included the wholesale massacre of the male population of Melos – although acts of mercy against rebellious allies were also documented – and the building programme of Pericles itself relied on easy pickings from weaker neighbours and allies. In the *polis* of Athens the achievements of democracy could be overshadowed, too, with attacks on the very talents it had nurtured and celebrated. Aristophanes was impeached; Pheidias and Thucydides were exiled; Socrates was tried and executed.

But, historically, the fatal mistake of the Athenian democracy was allowing itself to be drawn into the **Peloponnesian war** against Sparta, its persistent rival, in 431 BC. Pericles, having roused the assembly to a pitch of patriotic fervour, died of the plague two years after war began, leaving Athens to a series of far less capable leaders. In 415 BC a disastrous campaign in Sicily saw a third of the navy lost; in 405 BC defeat was finally accepted after the rest of the fleet was destroyed by Sparta in the Dardanelles. In a demoralised state, Athens succumbed to a brief period of oligarchy.

Through succeeding decades Athens was overshadowed by Thebes, though it recovered sufficiently to enter a new phase of democracy, the **age of Plato**. However, in 338 BC, nearly one and a half centuries after the original defeat of the Persians, Athens was again called to defend the Greek city-states, this time against the incursions of **Philip of Macedon**. Demosthenes, said to be as powerful an orator as Pericles, spurred the Athenians to fight, in alliance with the Thebans, at Chaironeia. There they were routed, in large part by the cavalry commanded by Philip's son, Alexander, and Athens fell under the control of the Macedonian empire.

The city continued to be favoured, particularly by **Alexander the Great**, a former pupil of Aristotle, who respected both Athenian culture and its democratic institutions. Following his death, however, came a more uncertain era, with periods of independence and Macedonian rule, until 146 BC when the **Romans** swept through southern Greece, subjugating it as an imperial province (see p.85).

The Acropolis

Open Mon–Fri 8am–7/5.45pm, Sat & Sun 8.30am–3pm (Acropolis Museum Mon 10am–3pm, Tues–Sun 8.30am–3pm); site and museum entrance 1500dr, students 750dr.

The **rock of the Acropolis**, with the ruins of the Parthenon rising above it, is one of the archetypal images of western culture – and a first glimpse of it above the traffic feels both a revelation and utterly familiar. Pericles had intended the temple to be a spectacular landmark, a "School for Hellas" and a symbol of the city's imperial confidence – and, as such, it was famous throughout the ancient world. Even Pericles, however, could not have anticipated that the ruin of his temple would come to symbolise no less than the emergence of Western civilisation – nor that, two millennia on, it would draw some three million tourists a year.

As Donald Horne points out in *The Great Museum*, it would be hard to imagine the ruins having such a wide appeal if they had retained more of their former glory: if the Parthenon "still had a roof, and no longer appealed to the modern stereotype for outline emerging from rough stone", or if "we repainted it in its original red, blue and gold and if we reinstalled the huge, gaudy cult-figure of Athena festooned in bracelets, rings and necklaces". Yet it's hard not to feel a sense of wonderment as you catch glimpses of the ancient ruins from the city below. The best of these street-level **views** are along Eólou, where the Parthenon forms the focal point of the horizon. Up above, calmer and quieter vantage points include the nearby hills of **Likavitós**, **Ardhittós** and **Filopáppou**, where you can look on undisturbed from among the pine groves; a walk to one of these is highly recommended.

APPROACHES

The main **approach** to the ruins is the path that extends above Odhós Dhioskoúron, where it joins Theorías at the northwest corner of Pláka. Two alternatives – though both perhaps better as ways down from the rock – are to make your way through the ancient Agora (entrance on Adhriánou, *E2*; see p.80) or, from the south side of the slope, around the footpath beside the Odeion of Herodes Atticus (*F2*).

The Propylaia and Athena Nike temple

Today, as throughout its history, the Acropolis offers but one entrance – from a terrace above the Agora. Here in Classical times the Panathenaic Way extended along a steep ramp to a massive monumental double-gatehouse, the **Propylaia**; the modern path makes a more gradual, zigzagging ascent through an arched Roman entrance, the **Beule Gate**, added in the third century AD.

THE PROPYLAIA

The **Propylaia** were constructed by Mnesikles upon completion of the Parthenon, in 437 BC, and their axis and proportions aligned to balance the temple. They were built from the same Pentelic marble (from Mount Pendéli, northeast of the city), and in grandeur and architectural achievement are no mean rival to the Parthenon temple. In order to offset the difficulties of a sloping site, Mnesikles combined for the first time standard Doric columns with the taller and more delicate Ionic order. The ancient Athenians, awed by the fact that such wealth and craftsmanship should be used for a purely secular building, ranked this as their most prestigious monument.

The halls had a variety of uses, even in Classical times. To the left of the central hall (which before Venetian bombardment supported a great coffered roof, painted blue and gilded with stars), the Pinakotheke exhibited paintings of Homeric subjects by Polygnotus. Executed in the mid-fifth century BC, these were described 600 years later by Pausanias in his Roman-era *Guide to Greece*. There was to have been a similar wing-room to the right, but Mnesikles's design trespassed on ground sacred to the Goddess of Victory and the premises had to be adapted as a waiting room for her shrine – the Temple of Athena Nike.

TEMPLE OF ATHENA NIKE

Simple and elegant, the **Temple of Athena Nike** was begun late in the rebuilding scheme (probably due to conflict over the extent of the Propylaia's south wing) and stands on a precipitous platform overlooking the port of Pireás and the Saronic Gulf. Pausanias recounts that it was from this bastion that King Aegeus, watching for the return from Crete of his son Theseus, threw himself to his death; Theseus, having slain the Minotaur, had forgotten his promise to change his black sails for white. The temple's frieze, with more attention to realism than triumph, depicts the Athenians' victory over the Persians at Plataea.

Amazingly, the whole temple was reconstructed, from its original blocks, in the nineteenth century; the Turks had demolished the building two hundred years previously, using it as material for a gun emplacement. Recovered in this same feat of jigsaw-puzzle archaeology were the reliefs from its parapet – among them *Victory Adjusting Her Sandal*, the most beautiful exhibit in the Acropolis Museum.

THE ACROPOLIS: PERICLES TO ELGIN – AND BEYOND

The Acropolis's natural setting, a craggy mass of limestone plateau, watered by springs and rising an abrupt 100 metres out of the plain of Attica, has made it a focus and nucleus during every historical (and prehistorical) phase of the city's development.

The site was one of the earliest settlements in Greece, drawing a **Neolithic** community to its slopes around 5000 BC. In **Mycenaean** times it was fortified with Cyclopean walls (parts of which can still be seen), enclosing a royal palace and temples where the cult of Athena was introduced. City and goddess were integrated by the **Dorians** and, with the union of Attic towns and villages in the ninth century BC, the Acropolis became the heart of the first Greek city-state, sheltering its principal public buildings. So it was to remain, save for an interval under the **Peisistratid tyrants** of the seventh and sixth centuries BC, who re-established a fortified residence on the rock. But when the last tyrant was overthrown in 510 BC, the Delphic Oracle ordered that the Acropolis should remain forever the **province of the gods**, unoccupied by humans.

It was in this context that the monuments visible today were built. More or less all of the substantial remains date from the **fifth century** BC or later. There are outlines of earlier temples and sanctuaries but these are hardly impressive, for they were burnt to the ground when the Persians sacked Athens in 480 BC. For some decades, until Pericles promoted his grand plan, the temples were left in their ruined state as a reminder of the Persian action. But with that threat removed, in the wake of Athenian military supremacy and a peace treaty with the Persians in 449 BC, the walls were rebuilt and architects set to draw up plans for a reconstruction worthy of the city's cultural and political position.

Pericles's rebuilding plan was both magnificent and enormously expensive but it won the backing of the democracy, for many of whose citizens it must have created both wealth and work– paid for from the unfortunate Delian League's coffers. The work was under the general direction of the architect and sculptor **Pheidias** and it was completed in an incredibly short time. The Parthenon took only ten years to finish: "every architect", wrote Plutarch, "striving to surpass the magnificence of the design with the elegance of the execution".

Their monuments survived unaltered – save for modest Roman embellishments – for close to a thousand years, until in the reign of the Emperor Justinian the temples were converted to **Christian** worship. In subsequent years the uses became secular, too, and embellishments increased, gradually obscuring the Classical designs. Fifteenth-century Italian princes held court in the Propylaia, the entrance hall to the complex, and the same quarters were later used by the **Turks** as their commander's headquarters and as a powder magazine. The Parthenon underwent similar changes from Greek to Roman temple, from Byzantine church to Frankish cathedral, before several centuries of use as a Turkish mosque. The Erechtheion, with its graceful female figures, saw service as a harem. A Venetian diplomat, Hugo Favoli, described the Acropolis in 1563 as "looming beneath a swarm of glittering golden crescents", with a minaret rising from the Parthenon. For all their changes in use, however, the buildings would have resembled – very much more than today's bare ruins – the bustling and ornate ancient Acropolis, covered in sculpture and painted in bright colours.

Sadly, such images remain only in the prints and sketches of that period. Having survived all its various occupations and uses, the Acropolis buildings finally fell victim to

In front of this small temple stood a **Sanctuary of Brauronian Artemis**. Its precinct was home to a colossal bronze representation of the Wooden Horse of Troy, but the sanctuary's function remains obscure, and only scant remains of its foundations can be seen. More noticeable is a nearby stretch of **Mycenaean wall** (running parallel to the Propylaia) that was incorporated into the Classical design.

the demands of war, blown up during the successive attempts by the Venetians to oust the Turks. In 1684 the Turks demolished the temple of Athena Nike to gain a brief tactical advantage. Three years later the Venetians, laying siege to the garrison, ignited a Turkish gunpowder magazine in the Parthenon, and in the process blasted off its roof and set a **fire** that raged within its precincts for two days and nights. The apricot-coloured glow of the Parthenon marbles so admired by the neoclassicists of the eighteenth century was one of the more aesthetic results.

Arguably surpassing this destruction, at least in the minds of modern Greeks, was **Lord Elgin**'s "removal" of the Parthenon's frieze in 1801. As British Ambassador to the Porte he obtained permission from the Turks to erect scaffolding, excavate, and remove stones with inscriptions. He interpreted this concession as a licence to make off with almost all of the bas-reliefs of the Parthenon's frieze, most of its pedimental structures and a caryatid from the Erechtheion – which he later sold to the British Museum. There were perhaps justifications for Elgin's action at the time – the Turks' tendency to use Parthenon stones in their lime kilns, and possible further ravages of war – though it was controversial even then and opposed notably by Byron. Today, however, the British Museum's continued retention of the "Elgin Marbles" (a phrase that Greek guides on the Acropolis, who portray Elgin unequivocally as a vandal, do not use) rests on legal rather than moral claims. Hopefully the British Museum will soon find a graceful pretext to back down; the completion of the new Acropolis Museum, slated to occupy land around the Makriyánni barracks just south of the bluffs, would be a perfect opportunity.

As for the Acropolis **buildings**, their fate since the Greeks regained the Acropolis after the war of independence has not been entirely happy. Almost immediately, Greek archaeologists began clearing the Turkish village that had developed around the Parthenon-mosque; a Greek regent lamented in vain that they "would destroy all the picturesque additions of the Middle Ages in their zeal to lay bare the ancient monuments". Much of this early work was indeed destructive. The iron clamps and supports that were used to reinforce the marble structures early this century were, contrary to ancient example, not sheathed in lead, so they have since rusted and warped, causing the stones to crack. Meanwhile, earthquakes have dislodged the foundations; generations of feet have slowly worn down surfaces; and, more recently, sulphur dioxide deposits, caused by vehicle and industrial pollution, has been turning the marble to dust.

Since a 1975 report predicted the collapse of the Parthenon, visitors have been barred from its actual precinct, and a major, long-term restoration scheme embarked upon. Inevitably this has its frustrations, with many of the buildings scaffolded and the whole Acropolis at times taking on the appearance of a building site. However, attempts have been made to keep this as discreet as possible: a giant crane was designed that could be folded and concealed nightly behind the temple columns. In late 1990 the first phase of the project was finished, and some scaffolding removed, but further progress on the pronaos to the east has been halted by a bitter dispute between purists in the archaeological service who want no new, bright marble introduced to the structure, and those who essentially propose a reconstruction to give the five million yearly, non-specialist tourists a clearer idea of the building in its heyday. The purists have demanded the installation of plaster casts of the proposed new work to evaluate its visual effect, much to the irritation of such pragmatists as Manolis Korres, architect in charge. The Minister of Culture is currently reviewing this strategy.

The Parthenon

Seen from the Propylaia, the Acropolis is today dominated by the Parthenon, set on the rock's highest ground. In Classical times, however, only the temple's pediment could be viewed through the intervening mass of statues and buildings. The ancient focus was a ten-metre-high bronze statue of *Athena Promachos* (Athena the Champion), moved to Constantinople in Byzantine times and there destroyed by a mob who believed that its beckoning hand had directed the Crusaders to the city in 1204. The statue was created by Pheidias as a symbol of the Athenians' defiance of Persia; its spear and helmet were visible to sailors approaching from Sounion.

To the right of the statue passed the Panathenaic Way, the route of the quadrennial festival in honour of the city's patroness, the goddess Athena. Following this route up today, you can make out grooves cut for footholds in the rock and, to either side, niches for innumerable statues and offerings.

The **Parthenon** was the first great building in Pericles's scheme. Designed by Iktinos, it utilises all the refinements available to the Doric order of architecture to achieve an extraordinary and unequalled harmony. Its proportions maintain a universal 9:4 ratio, not only in the calculations of length:width, or width:height, but in such relationships as the distances between the columns and their diameter. Additionally, any possible appearance of malproportion is corrected by meticulous mathematics and craftsmanship. All straight-appearing lines are in fact slightly curved, an optical illusion known as *entasis* ("intensification"). The columns (themselves swelled slightly to avoid seeming concave) are slanted inwards by 6cm, while each of the steps along the sides of the temple was made to incline just 12cm over a length of 70 metres.

Built on the site of earlier archaic temples, the Parthenon was intended as a new sanctuary for Athena and a house for her cult image, a colossal wooden statue of *Athena Polias* (Athena of the City) decked in ivory and gold plate, with precious gems as eyes and sporting an ivory gorgon death's-head on her breast. Designed by Pheidias and considered one of the Seven Wonders of the Ancient World, the statue was installed in the semi-darkness of the *cella* (cult chamber), where it remained an object of prestige and wealth, if not veneration, until at least the fifth century AD. The sculpture has been lost since ancient times but its characteristics are known through numerous later copies (including a fine Roman one in the National Archaeological Museum).

The name "Parthenon" means "virgins' chamber" and initially referred only to a room at the west end of the temple occupied by the priestesses of Athena. However, the temple never rivalled the Erechtheion in sanctity and its role tended to remain that of treasury and artistic showcase, devoted rather more to the new god of the *polis* than to Athena herself. Originally its columns were painted and it was decorated with the finest frieze and pedimental sculpture of the Classsical age, depicting the Panathenaic procession, the birth of Athena, and the struggles of Greeks to overcome giants, Amazons and centaurs. Of these, the best surviving examples are in the British Museum, but the greater part of the pediments, alongside the central columns and the *cella*, were destroyed by the Venetian bombardment in 1687.

The Erechtheion

To the north of the Parthenon, beyond the foundations of the Old Temple of Athena, stands the **Erechtheion**, the last of the great works of Pericles to be completed. It was built over ancient sanctuaries which in turn were predated by a Mycenaean palace. Here, in symbolic reconciliation, were worshipped both Athena and the city's old patron of Poseidon-Erechtheus; the site, according to myth, was that on which they had contested possession of the Acropolis. The myth (which probably recalls the integration of the Mycenaeans with earlier pre-Hellenic settlers) tells how an olive tree sprung from the ground at the touch of Athena's spear, while Poseidon summoned forth a seawater spring. The Olympian gods voted Athena the victor.

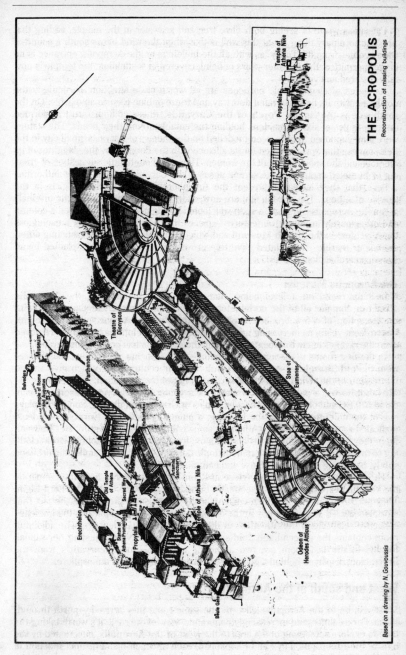

THE ACROPOLIS
Reconstruction of missing buildings

Temple of Athena Nike

Propylaia

Parthenon

Erechtheion

Belvedere

Museum

Parthenon

Temple of Rome and Augustus

Asklepieion

Stoa of Eumenes

Halikotheke

Artemis Sanctuary

Statue of Athena Promachos

Temple of Athena

Erechtheion

Sacred Way

Propylaia

Temple of Athena Nike

Beulé Gate

Odeon of Herodes Atticus

Theatre of Dionysos

Based on a drawing by N. Gouvoussis

Pausanias wrote of seeing both olive tree and seawater in the temple, adding that "the extraordinary thing about this well is that when the wind blows south a sound of waves comes from it". Today, as with all the buildings on the Acropolis, entrance is no longer permitted, though after years of being covered in scaffolding, the temple is now fully restored and visible.

Its series of elegant Ionic porticoes are all worth close attention, particularly the north one with its fine decorated doorway and frieze of blue Eleusinian marble. On the south side is the famous **Porch of the Caryatids**, whose columns are transformed into the tunics of six tall maidens holding the entablature on their heads. The statues were long supposed to have been modelled on the widows of Karyai, a small city in the Peloponnese that was punished for its alliance with the Persians by the slaughter of its menfolk and the enslavement of the women. There is, though, little suggestion of grieving or humbled captives in the serene poses of the Caryatid women. Some authorities believe that they instead represent the Arrephoroi, young, high-born girls in the service of Athena. The ones in situ are now, sadly, replacements. Five of the originals are in the Acropolis Museum, a sixth was looted by Elgin, who also removed a column and other purely architectural features – pieces that become completely meaningless out of context in the British Museum and which are replaced here by casts in a different colour marble. The stunted olive tree growing in the precinct was planted by an American archaeologist in 1917.

The Acropolis Museum

Placed discreetly on a level below that of the main monuments, the **Acropolis Museum** contains all of the portable objects removed from the site since 1834 (with the exception of a few bronzes displayed in the National Archaeological Museum). Over recent years, as increasing amounts of stone and sculptures have been removed from the ravages of environmental pollution, the collection has grown considerably.

In the first rooms to the left of the vestibule are fragments of pedimental sculptures from the **old Temple of Athena** (seventh- to sixth- century BC), which give a good impression of the vivid colours that were used in temple decoration. Further on is the **Moschophoros**, a painted marble statue of a young man carrying a sacrificial calf, dated 570 BC and one of the earliest examples of Greek art in marble. Room 4 displays one of the chief treasures of the building, a unique collection of **Korai**, or maidens, dedicated as votive offerings to Athena at some point in the sixth century BC. Between them they represent a shift in art and fashion, from the simply contoured Doric clothing to the more elegant and voluminous Ionic designs. The figures' smiles also change subtly, becoming increasingly loose and natural.

The pieces of the **Parthenon frieze** in Room 7 were sundered from the temple by the Venetian explosion, and subsequently buried, escaping the clutches of Lord Elgin. They portray scenes of Athenian citizens in the Panathenaic procession; the fact that mortals featured so prominently in the decoration of the temple indicates the immense collective self-pride of the Athenians at the height of their Golden Age. The adjoining room contains the graceful and fluid sculpture of **Athena Nike** adjusting her sandal. Finally, in the last room are two authentic and semi-eroded **caryatids** from the Erectheion, displayed behind a glass screen in a carefully rarified atmosphere.

West and south of the Acropolis

Most visitors to the Acropolis leave by the same route they arrived – north through Pláka. For a calmer, and increasingly panoramic, view of the rock, it's worth taking the time to explore something of the area to the **west of the Acropolis**, punctuated by the hills of the Areopagus, Pnyx and Filopáppou, each of which had a distinct function in the life of the ancient city.

The **south slope** is rewarding, too, with its Greek and Roman theatres and the remains of *stoas* and sanctuaries. It can be approached from the Acropolis, with an entrance just above the Herodes Atticus theatre, though its main entrance is some way to the south along Leofóros Dhionissíou Areopayítou.

No less important, these sites all give access to the neighbourhoods of Veïkoú, Koukáki and Áno Petrálona, three of the least spoilt quarters in Athens, and with some of the city's best tavernas (see p.100).

The Areopagus, Pnyx and Filopáppou Hill

Rock-hewn stairs ascend the low hill of the **Areopagus** immediately below the entrance to the Acropolis. The "Hill of Mars" was the site of the Council of Nobles and the Judicial Court under the aristocratic rule of ancient Athens. During the Classical period the court lost its powers of government to the Assembly (held on the Pnyx) but it remained the court of criminal justice, dealing primarily with cases of homicide. Aeschylus used this setting in *The Eumenides* for the trial of Orestes, who, pursued by the Furies' demand of "a life for a life", stood accused of murdering his mother Clytemnestra.

The hill was used as a campsite by the Persians during their siege of the Acropolis in 480 BC, and in the Roman era by Saint Paul, who preached the *Sermon on an Unknown God* here, winning amongst his converts Dionysius "the Areopagite", who became the city's patron saint. Today, there are various foundation cuttings on the site, and the ruins of a church of Áyios Dhioníssios (possibly built over the court), though nothing is actually left standing. The Areopagus's historic associations apart, it is notable mainly for the views, not only of the Acropolis, but down over the Agora and towards Kerameikos – the ancient cemetery (see p.81).

Following the road or path over the flank of the Acropolis, you come out on to Leofóros Dhionissíou Areopayítou, by the Herodes Atticus theatre. Turning right, 100m or so down (and across) the avenue, a network of paths leads up **Filopáppou Hill**, also known as the "Hill of the Muses" (*Lófos Moussón*). This strategic height has played an important, if generally sorry, role in the city's history. It was from here that the shell that destroyed the roof of the Parthenon was lobbed; more recently, the colonels placed tanks on the slopes during their coup of 1967. (Avoid the area at night, when it has a reputation for rapes and muggings.)

The hill's summit is capped by a somewhat grandiose monument to a Roman senator and consul, Filopappus, who is depicted driving his chariot on its frieze. Again, it is a place above all for views. To the west is the Dora Stratou Theatre (or Filopáppou Theatre) where Greek music and dance performances (see p.111) are held. Northwest, along the main path, and following a line of truncated ancient walls, is the church of **Áyios Dhimítrios**, an unsung gingerbread gem, preserving its original Byzantine frescoes. In the cliff face across from this to the south you can make out a kind of cave dwelling, known (more from imagination than evidence) as the **prison of Socrates**.

Further to the north, above the church, rises the **Hill of the Pnyx**, an area used in Classical Athens as the meeting place for the democratic assembly. All except the most serious political issues, such as ostracism, were aired here, the hill on the north side providing a convenient semicircular terrace from which to address the crowds of at least 6000 citizens (a quorum) that met more than forty times a year. All could vote and, at least in theory, all could voice their opinions, though the assembly was harsh on inarticulate or foolish speakers. There are remains of the original walls, used to form the theatre-like court, and of *stoas* for the assembly's refreshment. The arena is today used for the *son-et-lumière* (not greatly recommended) of the Acropolis, which takes place on most summer evenings.

Beyond the Pnyx, still another hill, **Lófos Nimfón** (Hill of the Nymphs), is dominated by a nineteenth-century observatory and gardens, occasionally open to visitors.

The south slope of the Acropolis

Entrances above the Herodes Atticus theatre and on Leof. Dhionissíou Areopayítou. Open daily 8.30am–2.30pm; entrance 400dr .

The second-century Roman **Odeion of Herodes Atticus**, restored for performances of music and Classical drama during the summer festival (see p.111), dominates the south slope of the Acropolis hill. It is open, however, only for shows, and the main interest on the slope lies in the earlier Greek sites to the east.

Pre-eminent among these is the **Theatre of Dionysos**, beside the main site entrance. One of the most evocative locations in the city, it was here that the masterpieces of Aeschylus, Sophlocles, Euripides and Aristophanes were first performed. It was also the venue for the annual festival of tragic drama, where each Greek citizen would take his turn as member of the chorus. The ruins are impressive; rebuilt in the fourth century BC, the theatre could hold some 17,000 spectators – considerably more than the Herodes Atticus's 5000–6000 seats. Twenty-five of the theatre's sixty-four tiers of seats survive. Most notable are the great marble thrones in the front row, each inscribed with the name of an official of the festival or of an important priest; in the middle sat the Priest of Dionysos and on his right the representative of the Delphic Oracle. At the rear of the stage along the Roman *bema* (rostrum) are reliefs of Dionysos flanked by squatting Sileni.

To the west of the theatre extend the ruins of the **Asclepion**, a sanctuary devoted to the healing god Asclepius (see p.152) and built around a sacred spring. The curative centre was probably incorporated into the Byzantine church of the doctor-saints Kosmas and Damian, of which there are prominent remains. Nearer to the road are the foundations of the Roman **Stoa of Eumenes**, a colonnade of stalls that stretched to the Herodes Atticus Odeion.

The Ancient Agora

South entrance by the Areopagus; north entrance on Adhriánou, (*E2*); open Tues–Sun 8.30am–3pm; entrance 800dr.

The **Agora** (market) was the nexus of ancient Athenian city life. Competing for space were the various claims of administration, commerce, market and public assembly. The result was ordered chaos. Eubolus, a fourth-century poet, observed that "you will find everything sold together in the same place at Athens: figs, witnesses to summonses, bunches of grapes, turnips, pears, apples, givers of evidence, roses, medlars . . . water clocks, laws, indictments." Before shifting location to the Pnyx, the assembly also met here, and continued to do so for cases of ostracism for most of the fifth and fourth centuries BC.

Originally the Agora was a rectangle, divided diagonally by the Panathenaic Way and enclosed by temples, administrative buildings, and long porticoed *stoas* (arcades of shops) where idlers and philosophers gathered to exchange views and listen to the orators. Women were not in evidence; secluded by custom, they would delegate any business in the Agora to slaves. In the centre of the rectangle was an open space, defined by boundary stones at the beginning of the fifth century BC, that was considered sacred and essential to the life of the community. Those accused of homicide or other serious crimes were excluded from it by law.

Perhaps appropriately, the site is today a confused, if extensive, jumble of ruins, dating from various stages of building between the sixth century BC and the fifth century AD. The best overview, as stated, is from the Areopagus, by the north entrance. For some idea of what you are surveying, however, the place to head for is the **Museum**, housed in the totally reconstructed **Stoa of Attalos**. Here you can get some measure of the original buildings and also find your bearings from plans of the site displayed within. The stoa itself was a US$1.5 million project of the American School of Archaeology in Athens. It is, in every respect bar one, an entirely faithful reconstruction of the original. What is missing is colour. In Classical times the exterior would have been painted in bright red and blue (like the Minoan palaces of Crete).

Around the site, the most prominent ruins are those of various other stoas– including the recently excavated "Painted Stoa", where Zeno expounded his Stoic philosophy– and of the city's gymnasiums and council hall (*bouleuterion*). Somewhat above the general elevation, to the west, is the **Thiseion**, or Temple of Hephaistos. The best preserved, though perhaps least admired, of all Doric temples, it lacks the curvature and "lightness" of the Parthenon's design. It was the first building begun in Pericles's programme, though not the first completed, and was dedicated to the patron of blacksmiths and metalworkers. Its remaining metopes depict the labours of Hercules and the exploits of Theseus, hence the popular name. The barrel-vaulted roof dates from the Byzantine conversion of the temple into a church of Saint George.

Kerameikos (Keramikós)

Entrance at Ermoú 148, (*E1*); open Tues–Sun 8.30am–3pm; entrance 400dr.

The Kerameikos site, encompassing the principal cemetery of ancient Athens, provides a fascinating and quiet retreat from the Acropolis. It is little visited and in addition has something of an oasis feel about it, with the lush Iridhanós channel, speckled with water lilies, flowing across it from east to west.

From the entrance can be seen the double line of the **Long Walls**, which ran to the port at Pireás; the inner wall was hastily cobbled together by the men, women and children of Athens while Themistocles was pretending to negotiate a mutual disarmament treaty with Sparta in 479 BC. The barriers are interrupted by the great **Dipylon Gate**, where travellers from Pireás, Eleusis and Boeotia entered the ancient city, and the **Sacred Gate**, used for the Eleusinian and Panathenaic processions. These followed the Sacred Way, once lined by colonnades and bronze statues, into the Agora. Between the two gates are the foundations of the **Pompeion**, where preparations for the processions were made and where the main vehicles were stored.

Branching off from the Sacred Way is the **Street of the Tombs**, begun in 394 BC and now excavated along a hundred or so metres. Both sides were reserved for the plots of wealthy Athenians. Some twenty, each containing numerous commemorative monuments, have been excavated, and their original stones, or replicas, replaced on the site. The flat vertical *stelai* were the main funerary monuments of the Classical world; the sarcophagus belonged to Hellenistic and Roman times. The sculpted crescent with the massive conglomerate base to the left of the path is the *Memorial of Dexileos*, the twenty-year-old son of Lysanias of Thorikos, who was killed in action at Corinth in 394 BC. The adjacent plot contains the *Monument of Dionysios of Kollytos*, in the shape of a pillar *stele* supporting a bull carved from Pentelic marble. As with any cemetery, however, it is the more humble monuments, such as the statue of a girl with a dog on the north side of the street, that connect past and present in the shared experience of loss. From the terrace overlooking the tombs, Pericles delivered his famous funeral oration dedicated to those who died in the first years of the Peloponnesian War. His propaganda coup inspired thousands more to enlist in a campaign in which one-third of the Athenian force was to be wiped out.

The **Oberlaender Museum**, named after the German-American manufacturer who financed it, contains an extensive collection of *stelai*, terracotta figures, vases and sculptures from the site. Among them, Room 1's *Ampharete Holding Her Infant Grandchild*, and *The Boxer*, with a cauliflower ear and thongs of a glove tied around his wrist, are remarkable in their detailed execution. The terracotta figures and vases of Room 2 include some of the earliest art objects yet found in Greece.

Pláka and Monastiráki

Pláka, with its alleys and stairs built on the Turkish plan, is the most rewarding Athenian area for daytime wanderings. In addition to a scattering of Roman sites and various offbeat and enjoyable museums, it offers glimpses of an exotic past, refreshingly at odds with the concrete blocks of the metropolis. An attraction, too, is its pedestrianisation, with cars banished from all but a few main streets. And if you can coincide, there is plenty to look at, if few bargains to be found, in the Sunday morning **flea market** (smaller on other days) around Monastiráki square.

The district was basically the extent of nineteenth-century, pre-independence Athens, and provided the core of the city for the next few decades. Its area is roughly delineated by Síndagma, Odhós Ermoú and the Acropolis. Once away from Síndagma, the narrow winding streets and stairs are lined with nineteenth-century neoclassical houses, some grand, some humble and home-made. The tiled roofs are edged with terracotta medusa-heads, goddesses and foliage designs, ornaments known collectively as *akrokerámata*. The grander facades are decorated with pilasters and capitals and wrought-iron balconies. Gateways open onto courtyards filled with greenery and overlooked by wooden verandas. Poor and working-class for most of this century, the district has lately been extensively gentrified and physically renovated.

From Síndagma to Adhriánou

An attractive approach to Pláka is to follow **Odhós Kidhathinéon**, a pedestrian walkway that starts near the **English and Russian churches** on Odhós Filellínon, south of Síndagma. It leads gently downhill, past the Popular Arts Museum, on a leafy square with one of the few remaining old-time cafés on the corner, on through café-crowded Platía Pláka to Hadrian's street, **Odhós Adhriánou**, which runs nearly the whole length of Pláka from Hadrian's Arch to the Thiseíon.

The **Museum of Greek Folk Art** (Tues–Sun 10am–2pm; 200dr), at Kidhathinéon 17, is one of the most enjoyable displays in the city. A tiny museum in the heart of Pláka, its first floor is devoted to collections of weaving, pottery and embroidery, which reveal both the sophistication and the strong Middle Eastern influence of Greek popular arts. On the upper levels are traditional and ceremonial costumes from almost every region of the country. Most compelling of all – if it is back on display after recent removal – is the reconstructed village house with a series of murals by the "primitive artist" Theophilos (1873–1934). Theophilos was one of the characters of nineteenth-century Athens, dressing in War of Independence outfits and painting tavernas and cafés for a meal or a small fee. Several examples of his work – usually scenes from peasant life or of battles from the War of Independence – survive in situ in the Peloponnese and on Mount Pílion, though they have only in the last few decades been recognised as worth preserving.

Two other musums, close by, provide interesting supplements. A couple of blocks to the northwest, at Angelikís Hatzimiháli 6, the **Centre for Popular Arts and Traditions** (Tues & Thurs 9am–9pm, Wed, Fri & Sat 9am–1pm & 5–9pm, Sun 9am–1pm if staff available; free) features costumes, cloth, musical instruments, and so forth, in another grand Pláka mansion.

A similar distance to the southeast of the Popular Arts Museum, above the French Chamber of Commerce at Amaliás 36, is the **Jewish Museum of Greece** (9am–1pm; closed Sat; free but donations welcome). Here are displayed art and religious artifacts from the very ancient Jewish communities scattered throughout Greece. The centrepiece is the reconstructed synagogue of Pátra, dating from the 1920s, whose furnishings have been moved here en bloc and rededicated.

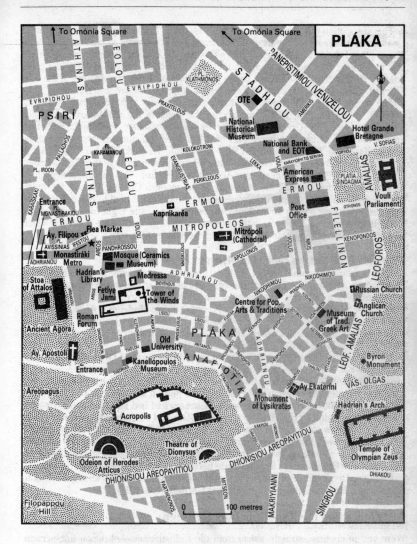

The Monument of Lysikrates and Temple of Olympian Zeus

At the eastern end of Pláka, Odhós Lissikrátous gives on to a small, fenced-off archaeological park at one end of Odhós Tripódhon, the **Street of the Tripods**, where winners of the ancient dramatic contests dedicated their tripod-trophies to Dionysos. The park can't be entered, but you can walk around the outside to admire the **Monument of Lysikrates**, a tall and graceful stone and marble structure from 335 BC, which stands as a surprisingly complete example of these ancient exhibits. A four-metre-high stone base supports six Corinthian columns rising up to a marble dome on which, in a flourish of acanthus leaf carvings, a winning tripod was placed.

The inscription on its architrave tells us that "Lysikrates of Kikyna, son of Lysitheides was *choregos*; the tribe of Akamantis won the victory with a chorus of boys; Theon played the flute; Lysiades of Athens trained the chorus; Evainetos was archon". The monument was incorporated into a French Capuchin convent in 1667, and tradition asserts that Byron used it as a study, writing part of *Childe Harold* here; at the time Athens had no inn and the convent was a regular lodging for European travellers.

The street beyond, **Víronos**, is named after the poet ("O Lórdhos Víronos" to Greeks). At its far end, facing you across the road, is the old Makriyánni police barracks, revered by Greek rightists for its stout resistance to Communist attack during the 1944 Battle of Athens. Part of it has been transformed into the so-called **Acropolis Study Centre** (Mon–Fri 9am–2pm, Mon, Weds & Fri also 6–9pm, Sat & Sun 10am–2pm; free), so far containing little beyond plaster casts of the Elgin Marbles and models of the Italian-planned, new **Acropolis Museum**. This was originally scheduled for completion in 1996, the centenary of the modern Olympic Games, for which Greece made an unsuccessful bid. Nonetheless, the Greeks intend to proceed with the museum, reserving a wing for its hoped-for centrepiece – the Elgin Marbles. A major obstacle to overcome, however, is the purchase of a large tract of the quarter – which property owners and businesses are resisting every step of the way.

Hadrian's Arch and the Temple of Olympian Zeus

Had you taken the other street at the Lysikrates monument crossroads, Ódhos Lissikratoús, you would emerge at the edge of Pláka near one of the most hazardous road junctions in Athens, the meeting of Dhionissíou Areopayítou, Amalías and Singroú. Across the way, facing Leofóros Amalias, stands **Hadrian's Arch**, erected by that emperor to mark the edge of the Classical city and the beginning of his own. On the near side its frieze is inscribed "This is Athens, the ancient city of Theseus", and on the other "This is the City of Hadrian and not of Theseus".

Directly behind the arch, the colossal pillars of the **Temple of Olympian Zeus** (site open Mon–Sat 9am–3pm, Sun 10am–2pm; entrance on Leofóros Amalías) make some justification for this show of arrogance. The largest temple in Greece, and according to Livy, "the only temple on earth to do justice to the god", it was dedicated by Hadrian in 131 AD, some 700 years after the tyrant Peisistratos had laid its foundations. Hadrian marked the occasion by contributing a statue of Zeus and a suitably monumental one of himself (both now lost). Of the temple, just fifteen of the original 104 Pentelic marble pillars remain erect, though the column drums of another (which fell in 1852) litter the ground, giving a startling idea of the project's size. Almost equally impressive is the fact that in the Byzantine era a stylite made his hermitage on the temple architrave.

From the Olympian Zeus temple, you could, if you wanted, take a shady route up to Síndagma or Kolonáki through the **National Gardens** (see p.94).

Anafiótika and the Kanellópoulos Museum

Were you to continue straight ahead from the Kidhathinéon–Adhriánou intersection, up **Odhós Thespídhos**, you would reach the edge of the Acropolis precinct. Up to the right, the whitewashed cubist houses of **Anafiótika** cheerfully proclaim an architect-free zone amidst the highest crags of the Acropolis rock.

The buildings here were erected by workers from the island of Anáfi in the southern Aegean, who were employed in the mid-nineteenth century construction of Athens. Unable to afford land, they took advantage of a law stating that if a roof and four walls could be thrown up overnight, the premises were yours at sunrise. In appearance, the houses, and the two churches that serve them, are the image of those the Cycladic islanders had left behind. Today, sadly, many stand empty on their mule-width lanes and steps.

ROMAN ATHENS

When the **Romans** ousted the Macedonian rulers of Athens, incorporating the city into the vast new province of Achaia in 146 BC, Athens continued to enjoy rare political privileges. The city's status as a respected seat of learning and great artistic centre had already been firmly established throughout the ancient world. Cicero and Horace were educated here and Athenian sculptors and architects were supported by Roman commissions. Unlike Corinth, though, which became the administrative capital of the province, the city was endowed with relatively few imperial Roman **monuments**, Hadrian's Arch being perhaps the most obvious. Athenian magistrates, exercising a fair amount of local autonomy, tended to employ architects who would reflect the public taste for the simpler *propylaion*, gymnasium and old-fashioned theatre, albeit with a few Roman amendments.

The city's Roman **history** was shaped pre-eminently by its alliances, which often proved unfortunate. The first major onslaught on what became a prestigious backwater of the empire occurred in 86 BC, when Sulla punished Athens for its allegiance to his rival Mithridates by burning its fortifications and looting its treasures. His successors were more lenient. Julius Caesar proferred a free pardon after Athens had sided with Pompey; and Octavian, who extended the old *agora* by building a forum, showed similar clemency when Athens harboured Brutus following the Ides of March. The most frequent visitor was the **Emperor Hadrian**, who used the occasions to bestow grandiose monuments, including his eponymous arch, a magnificent and immense library and (though it had been begun centuries before) the Temple of Olympian Zeus. A generation later **Herodes Atticus**, a Roman senator born in Marathon, became the city's last major benefactor of ancient times. His great wealth came purely and simply from a lucky find; his father had stumbled upon a vast treasure buried in an old house and, with permission from the Emperor, kept it all.

Follow Rangáva or Stratoús anticlockwise around the Acropolis rock and you will eventually emerge on Theoriás, outside the eclectic **Kanellópoulos Museum** (Tues–Sun 8.30am–3pm; 400dr). Though there is nothing here that you won't see examples of in the bigger museums, this collection of treasures, exhibited in the topmost house under the Acropolis, has a calm appeal of its own. The bulk of the exhibits are icons but there is also Byzantine jewellery, Coptic textiles, plus odds and ends of Cycladic, Minoan and Classical art. (Among the pots, on the top floor, hides a miniature "Kama Sutra" vase, which the guard points out to male visitors.)

A block east of the museum, straddling Klespídhras and Alimbérti, is a building thought to be the oldest of post-Independence Athens – the **Panepistímio**; the site of the first university in in modern Greece, it was established in the 1830s.

The Roman Forum and Tower of the Winds

The western reaches of Adhriánou, past the newly restored neoclassical Demotic School, is largely commercial – souvenir shops and sandals – as far as the **Roman Forum** (entrance corner Pelopídha/Eólou; Tues–Sun 8.30am–3pm; 400dr), a large irregularly shaped excavation site bounded by railings.

The forum was built by Julius Caesar and Augustus (Octavian) as an extension of the older ancient Greek agora to its west. It has been under substantial excavation in recent years, and usually much of it is closed to visitors. Its main entrance was through the relatively intact Gate of Athena Archegetis, which consisted of a Doric portico and four columns supporting an entablature and pediment. On the pilaster facing the Acropolis is engraved an edict of Hadrian announcing the rules and taxes on the sale of oil.

The Tower of the Winds and Medresse

The best preserved and easily the most intriguing of the forum ruins is the graceful, octagonal structure known as the **Tower of the Winds** (*Aéridhes* in Greek). It was designed in the first century BC by Andronikos of Kyrrhos, a Syrian astronomer, and served as a compass, sundial, weather vane and water clock – the latter powered by a stream from one of the Acropolis springs.

Each face of the tower is adorned with a relief of a figure floating through the air, personifying the eight winds. On the **north** side (facing Eólou) is Boreas blowing into a conch shell; **northwest**, Skiron holding a vessel of charcoal; **west**, Zephyros tossing flowers from his lap; **southwest**, Lips speeding the voyage of a ship; **south**, Notos upturning an urn to make a shower; **southeast**, Euros with his arm hidden in his mantle summoning a hurricane; **east**, Apiliotis carrying fruits and wheat; and **northeast**, Kaikias emptying a shield full of hailstones. Beneath each of these it is still possible to make out the markings of eight sundials.

The semicircular tower attached to the south face was the reservoir from which water was channelled in a steady flow into a cylinder in the main tower; the time was read by the water level viewed through the open northwest door. On the top of the building a bronze Triton used to revolve with the winds. In Ottoman times dervishes used the tower as a *tekke* or ceremonial hall, terrifying their superstitious Orthodox neighbours with their chanting, music and exercises.

Other forum ruins – and Hadrian's library

The other forum ruins open to view are somewhat obscure. Among the more prominent Roman bits and pieces are a large public latrine, a number of shops and a stepped *propylaion* or entrance gate (at the southeast corner). In another corner of the forum, an old Ottoman mosque, the **Fetiye Jami** (Mosque of the Conquest), serves as an archaeological warehouse.

Bordering the north end of the forum site, stretching between Áreos and Eólou, stand the surviving walls of **Hadrian's Library**, an enormous building which once enclosed a cloistered court of a hundred columns. **Odhós Aréos**, alongside, signals the beginning of the Monastiráki flea market area (see below). At its end, round behind the forum, are some of the quietest, prettiest and least spoiled streets in the whole of Pláka – many of them ending in steps up to the Anafiótika quarter (see p.84).

Another Turkish relic stands across the street from the Tower of the Winds – a gateway and single dome from a **Medresse**, an Islamic college or "seminary". Here in 1821 the Ottoman judge Hatzi Halil successfully dissuaded a Turkish mob from indiscriminate massacre of the entire male population of Attica; the Greek rebels were not so scrupulous, and indeed Hatzi Halil's clemency was repaid by the destruction of the *medresse* during or shortly after the War of Independence.

The Museum of Musical Instruments

Almost opposite the *medresse* mentioned above, at Dioyénous 1–3, is a **Museum of Musical Instruments** (Tues & Thurs–Sun 10am–2pm, Wed noon–6pm; free). This is a wonderful display, superbly designed (in 1991) in the rooms of another neoclassical building. It traces the history and distribution of virtually everything that has ever been played in Greece, including (in the basement) some not-so-obvious festival and liturgical instruments such as triangles, strikers, livestock bells and coin garlands worn by Carnival masquers. Reproductions of frescoes show the Byzantine antecedents of many instruments, and headphone sets are provided for sampling the music made by the various displays.

It's difficult, after all this plenty, to resist the stock of the museum shop, which includes virtually the entire backlist of the Society for the Dissemination of Greek Music's excellent "Songs of . . . " series (see "Music" in *Contexts*).

Monastiráki: the Flea Market area

The northwest districts of Pláka, along Ermoú and Mitropóleos, are noisier, busier and more geared to the Greek life of the city. Neither street lays any claim to beauty, though the bottom (west) half of **Ermoú**, with its metalworkers and other craftsmen, has an attractive workaday character; the top half has unhappily transformed the pretty Byzantine church of the **Kapnikaréa** into a traffic island.

Churches, too, are the chief feature of **Odhós Mitropóleos** (Cathedral Street). A dusty, tiny chapel of **Ayía Dhinamí** crouches surreally below the concrete piers of the Ministry of Education and Religion; the **Mitrópolis** itself, an undistinguished nineteenth-century cannibal of dozens of older buildings, carves out a square midway along; and the **old cathedral** stands alongside it, a beautiful little twelfth-century church cobbled together from plain and carved blocks as ancient as Christendom itself.

Pandhróssou, Platía Monastiráki and the Mosque of Tzistarákis

From the bottom corner of the cathedral square, recently reclaimed for pedestrians, **Odhós Pandhróssou** introduces the **Monastiráki Flea Market** – not that its name is really justified by the rich and conventional jewellery and fur shops that pack the first section. In fact, not many genuine market shops remain at all this side of Platía Monastirakíou. With the exception of a couple of specialist icon dealers, everything is geared to the tourist. The most quirky among them is the shop of *Stavros Melissinos*, the "poet-sandalmaker of Athens", at Pandhróssou 89. Melissinos enjoyed a sort of fame in the 1960s, hammering out sandals for The Beatles, Jackie Onassis and the like; it is said that Lennon sought him out specifically for his poetic musings on wine and the sea, which Melissinos continues to sell alongside the footwear.

Platía Monastirakíou, full of nut sellers, lottery sellers, fruit stalls, kiosks and cars, gets it name from the little monastery church (*monastiráki*) at its centre, tenth-century in origin and currently undergoing restoration. The area around has been a marketplace since Turkish times, and maintains a number of Ottoman features.

On the south side of the square, rising from the walls of Hadrian's Library and the shacks of Pandhróssou, is the eighteenth-century **Mosque of Tzistarákis**, nowadays secularised, minus minaret, and home to the **Kyriazopoulos Ceramic Collection of the Museum of Greek Folk Art** (9am–2.30pm; closed Tues; 400dr). This collection, donated by a Thessaloníki professor, recently reopened after lengthy building repairs of damage from the 1981 earthquake. The ground floor is devoted to folk sculpture and pottery, mostly by refugee artists from Asia Minor. The mezzanine features decorated household items from various points in the Hellenic world.

The mosque itself, especially its striped *mihrab* (the niche indicating the direction of Mecca) is equally interesting. Outside, by the entrance gate, are calligraphic inscriptions stating the mosque's founder and date, and a series of niches used as extra *mihrabs* for occasions when worshippers could not fit into the main hall.

West of Monastiráki square: the flea market proper

West of Monastiráki square, the **flea market** caters more and more for local needs, with clothes, iron- and copperware, tools, records and second-hand books in **Odhós Iféstou**; old furniture, bric-a-brac and camping gear in **Platía Avissinías**; chairs, office equipment, wood-burning stoves, mirrors, canaries and sundry other goods in **Astíngos**, **Ermoú**, and around.

Beside the church of **Ayíou Filípou**, there's a market in hopeless jumble-sale rejects, touted by a cast of eccentrics (especially on Sundays); of late this extends around the corner, along Adhriánou, as far as Platía Thisíou. At Ayíou Filípou there's a tiny *kafenío*, too, and the *Estiatorio Ipiros*, not much to look at, but serving good, inexpensive Greek fare.

The north entrance to the **Agora** (see p.80) is just south of Platía Avissinías on Adhriánou, across the cutting where the metro line for Pireás re-emerges into open air after tunnelling under the city centre. Odhós Adhriánou is here at its most appealing, with a couple of interesting antique shops, a shady *kafenío* beloved of cats, and the best views of the Acropolis. Following the Agora fence around to the southwest, you'll come to another good café vantage-point on busy **Apostólou Pávlou**, which shares the same view. On the hill above is the old **Observatory**, surrounded by a last enclave of streets untroubled by tourism or redevelopment: no special features, just a pleasant wander through the very north end of Áno Petrálona.

North from Pláka: the Bazaar, Omónia square and the National Archaeological Museum

When the German neoclassicists descended on Athens in the 1830s, the land between Pláka and present-day **Omónia square** was envisioned as a spacious and European expansion of the Classical and medieval town. Time and the realities of Athens's status as a commercial capital have made a mockery of that grandiose vision: the main **bazaar area** is no less crowded and oriental than Monastiráki, while Omónia itself stubbornly retains a mix of gritty Balkan and Greek-American bad taste. For visitors, the focus of interest is the **National Archaeological Museum**, which, with its neighbour, the **Politehnío**, fronts the student/alternative quarter of **Exárhia**, currently the city's liveliest option for nights out.

The Bazaar: Athinás to Omónia

A broad triangle of streets, delineated by Piréos (officially Tsaldhári) in the west and Stadhíou in the east, reaches north to its apex at Omónia square. Through the middle run **Athinás** and **Eólou streets** – the modern **bazaar**, whose shops, though stocked mainly with imported manufactured goods, still reflect their origins in their unaffected decor, unsophisticated packaging, and – most strikingly – by their specialisation.

Each street has a concentration of particular shops and wares, almost untouched by any modern notions of marketing. Hence the Monastiráki end of Athinás is dedicated to tools; food shops are gathered around the central market in the middle, especially along Evripídhou; there's glass to the west; paint and brasswork to the east; and clothes in Eólou and Ayíou Márkou. Praxitélous is full of lettering merchants; Platía Klafthmónos of electrical goods. Department stores are close to Omónia. Always raucous and teeming with shoppers, *kouloúri* (bread-ring) sellers, gypsies and other vendors, the whole area is great free entertainment.

The best single bit is the **central meat and seafood market**, on the corner of Athinás and Evripídhou. The building itself is a grand nineteenth-century relic, with fretted iron awnings sheltering forests of carcasses and mounds of hearts, livers and ears – no place for the squeamish. In the middle section of the hall is the fish market, all manner of luscious fruits of the sea squirming and glistening on the marble slabs, while across the street brilliant displays of fruit and vegetables are flanked by miserably caged pullets, rabbits and canaries (the latter not for eating). A little to the west is the temporary **fruit and vegetable bazaar**, open-air stalls arrayed around a giant, suspended archaeological dig. On the surrounding streets are rows of grocers, their stalls piled high with sacks of pulses, salt cod, barrels of olives and wheels of cheese.

To the north is the **flower market**, gathered around the church of Ayía Iríni on Eólou. This has stalls through the week but really comes alive with the crowds on a Sunday morning. An additional feature of **Eólou** is its views. Walk it north to south, coming from Omónia, and your approach takes you towards the rock of the Acropolis, with the Erechtheion's slender columns and pediment peeking over the crag edge.

Around Omónia square

Omónia itself has little to offer. A continuous turmoil of people and cars, it is Athens at its sleaziest and most urban. There are sporadically functioning escalators (the only public ones in Greece) down to the **metro**, and, at the top, every kind of junk food imaginable – the pride of returned Greek-Americans. The central fountain, playing on a hideous glass-shard sculpture, works only occasionally and the baby palms are remorseful replacements for their predecessors, cut down in the 1950s lest foreigners think Greece "too Asiatic". The square has recently developed a reputation for hustle, due largely to the Albanian refugees, while after dark the area is frequented by prostitutes and their customers (the main red-light district is on nearby Sofokléous).

To the north, just beside the National Archaeological Museum on Patissíon, a more interesting landmark is the **Politehnío**, a neoclassical building housing the university's school of engineering and science. It was here in late 1973 that the students launched their protests against the repressions of the colonels' junta, occupying the building and courtyards, and broadcasting calls for widespread resistance from a pirate radio transmitter. Large numbers of Greeks defied the military cordons to demonstrate support and to smuggle in food and medicines. The colonels' answer came on the night of November 16. Snipers were positioned in neighbouring houses and ordered to fire indiscriminately into the courtyards while tanks broke down the gates – with students still clinging on. Nobody knows how many of the unarmed students were killed – official and unofficial figures range from twenty to three hundred – since their bodies were secretly buried in mass graves. Although the junta's leader, Papodopoulos, was able publicly to congratulate the officers involved before being sacked in favour of secret police chief Ioannidhes, a new, more urgent sense of outrage was spreading; within a year of the massacre the dictatorship was toppled.

Evidence of the incident can still be seen today, in the bullet-marked pillars and staircases, and the anniversary of the massacre is invariably commemorated by a march on the US Embassy, outpost of the colonels' greatest ally; it's a bit apathetic nowadays, but still a day out for the left. The date is also commemorated in the name of the shadowy terrorist group *Dhekaeftá Noemvríou* (17 November), who have operated, with not a single member caught or arrested, since the early 1980s.

The National Archaeological Museum

Patissíon 28 (*C2/3*); Mon 12.30–7pm, Tues–Fri 8am–7pm, Sat & Sun 8.30am–3pm; pottery section open Mon 12.30–5.30pm, Tues–Sun 8.30am–3pm; entrance1500dr, students 750dr.

The National Archaeological Museum is an unrivalled treasure house of Cycladic, Minoan, Mycenaean, and Classical Greek art – and an essential Athens visit. In superb Greek fashion, it forces its way into the world's list of top ten museums, despite haphazard labelling and generally unimaginative displays. To avoid all-too-possible disappointment, make sure you check the latest opening times and give yourself a clear morning or afternoon for a visit. Better still, take in the collection – which is overwhelming if you want to delve beyond the obvious highlights – in two or more separate trips.

The museum's main divisions are **Prehistoric**, with Mycenae predominating; **Sculpture** from the Archaic (eighth century BC) to Hellenistic (third to second century BC) periods; and **Pottery** from Geometric (ninth century BC) to the end of the fourth century AD. Smaller self-contained collections include **bronzes** in Rooms 36 to 40; immensely covetable **jewellery** in Room 32; and the brilliant Minoan-style **frescoes from Thira (Santorini)** upstairs in Room 48.

Mycenaean and Cycladic art

The biggest crowd-puller is the **Mycenaean hall** (Room 4), facing the main entrance, with all of Schliemann's gold finds from the grave circle at Mycenae. To the left, as hard to get a look at on a summer's day as the Louvre's Mona Lisa, is the so-called funerary *Mask of Agamemnon* [a] in Case 3. Modern dating techniques prove this must have belonged to some more ancient Achaian king, yet it fits the Homeric myth so well that such facts scarcely seem to matter.

The Mycenaeans' consummate art was small-scale decoration – rings, cups, seals, inlaid daggers – and requires eye-tiring scrutiny of the packed showcases to appreciate. Don't be entirely mesmerised by the death masks, or the superb golden-horned *Bull's Head* [b] in Case 27. In Case 5 there's a lovely duck-shaped vase of rock crystal; in Case 3, with the "Agamemnon" mask, a magnificent inlaid dagger. Case 8 has jewellery, daggers and a miniature golden owl and frog from Nestor's palace at Pylos; alongside, in Case 9, are baked tablets of Linear B, the earliest Greek writing.

On the wall in this section are Cretan-style frescoes from Tiryns of chariot-borne women watching spotted hounds in pursuit of boar, and bull-vaulting reminiscent of Knossos. More finds from Tiryns in Case 15 include a huge ring depicting four demons presenting gifts to a goddess.

Another superb exhibit – in Case 32 [c] – are the *Vafio cups*, with their scenes of wild bulls and long-tressed, narrow-waisted men, while in Case 33 an equally eye-catching cup is decorated with twining octopuses and dolphins. Further references to Homer abound. In Case 18 there's a magnificent *Boar's Tusk Helmet* and an ivory lyre with sphinxes adorning the soundboard; on the frescoes in the corner of the room you can pick out Achilles-style figure-of-eight shields.

To the right of the Mycenaean hall, Room 6 houses a large collection of **Cycladic art** – pre-Mycenaean pieces from the Aegean islands. Many of these suggest the abstract forms of modern Cubist art – a link at its most striking in the much-reproduced *Man playing a Lyre* [d]. Another unusual piece, at the opposite end of the room, is a sixteenth-century BC cylindrical vase depicting a ring of fishermen carrying fish by their tails. The most common and characteristic of the sculptures are folded-arm figurines, among them a near full-size nude.

To the left of the Mycenaean hall, Room 5 contains **Neolithic** finds, primarily from excavations in Thessaly.

Sculpture

Most of the rest of the ground floor is occupied by **Sculpture**. Beginning in Room 7, on the left of the museum's main entrance, the exhibition evolves chronologically (and this is the best way to see it) from the Archaic through the Classical and Hellenistic periods (Rooms 7–31) to the Roman- and Egyptian-influenced (Rooms 41–43). The gradual development from the stiff, stylised representations of the seventh century BC towards ever freer and looser naturalism is excitingly evident as you go through these cold and rather shabby rooms.

Early highlights include the Aristion *Stele of a Young Warrior* [e], with delicately carved beard, hair, and tunic folds in Room 11, and the Croesus *kouros* (statue of an idealised youth) in Room 13 [f]; both are from the late sixth century BC. You need sharp eyes not to miss some of the less obvious delights. Behind the Croesus *kouros*, for instance, and quite untrumpeted, a statueless plinth is carved with reliefs showing, on one side, young men exercising in the gymnasium, on the other a group of amused friends setting a dog and cat to fight each other – a common enough sight in contemporary Greece.

Room 15, which heralds the **Classical art** collection, leaves you in rather less doubt as to its central focus. Right in the middle stands a mid-fifth-century BC *Statue of Poseidon* [g], dredged from the sea off Évvia in the 1920s. The god stands poised to

NATIONAL ARCHAEOLOGICAL MUSEUM

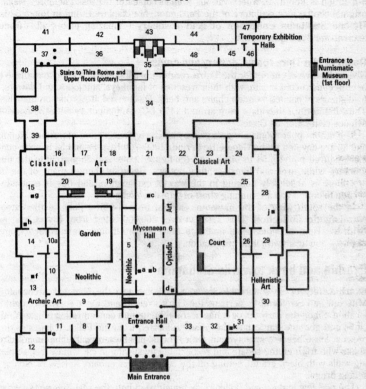

throw his trident, weight on the front foot, athlete's body perfectly balanced, the model of idealised male beauty. A less dramatic, though no less important, piece in the same room is the *Eleusinian Relief* **[h]**, highly deliberate in its composition, showing the goddess of fertility, accompanied by her daughter Persephone, giving to mankind an ear of corn – symbol of the knowledge of agriculture.

Other major classical sculptures include the virtuoso *Little Jockey* (Room 21; **[i]**) urging on his galloping horse, found in the same shipwreck as the *Poseidon*; the fourth-century BC bronze *Ephebe of Antikithira* **[j]** in Room 28; and the three portrait heads in Room 30: a *Boxer*, burly and battered; the furrowed brow and intellectual's unkempt hairdo of the third-century BC *Philosopher*; and the expressive, sorrowful first-century face of the *Man from Delos*. The most reproduced of all the sculptures is in Room 31: a first-century AD statue of a naked and indulgent *Aphrodite* **[k]** about to rap Pan's knuckles for getting too fresh – a far cry (a long fall, some would say) from the reverent, idealising portrayals of the gods in Classical times.

Too numerous to list, but offering fascinating glimpses of everyday life and changing styles of craftsmanship and perception of the human form, are the many **stelai** or carved gravestones. They are to be found in several of the Classical rooms. Also worth a mention is Room 20, where various Roman copies of the lost Pheidias *Athena*, the original centrepiece sculpture of the Parthenon, are displayed. And in Room 32 is the **Hélène Stathatos Collection of gold jewellery** – amazing pieces all – from the ancient and Byzantine worlds.

Upstairs: the Thira rooms, pottery and coins

Keep a reserve of energy for the **Thíra rooms** upstairs. A visual knockout, these have been reconstructed in situ, with their frescoes of monkeys, antelopes and flowers, and furnishings of painted wooden chairs and beds. Discovered at Akrotiri on the island of Thíra (Santoríni), they date from around 1450 BC, contemporary with the flourishing Minoan civilisation on Crete.

The other upper rooms are occupied by a dizzying succession of **pottery**. Rooms 49 and 50 are devoted to the Geometric Period (1000–700 BC); 52 and 53 to sixth-century black-figured pottery; 54 to black- and red-figured pots; and 55 and 56 to the mainly funerary white urns and fourth-century pottery. Beautiful though many of the items are, there is absolutely nothing in the way of explanation, and this is probably the section to omit if you are running short of time or stamina.

In the south wing of the museum, entered from the first floor, is the extensive **Numismatic Collection**. This takes in over 400,000 coins, from Mycenaean times (with the Homeric double-axe motif) to Macedonian, though only a fraction are on display – and again with little imagination.

Exárhia and back towards Síndagma

Exárhia, fifty or so square blocks squeezed between the National Archaeological Museum and Stréfi hill, is perhaps the city's liveliest and most enjoyable night-time location. Since the early 1980s it has become home to a concentration of *ouzerí*, night-clubs and genuine music tavernas, many relocated from the Pláka. It has also, in the press at least, become synonymous with Athens' disaffected youth, the so-called anarchists who frighten the sedate and respectable by staving in car windscreens, splattering walls with black graffiti, setting off the occasional incendiary device, or buying and selling drugs.

The odd few junkies and police raids notwithstanding, the reality is not so extreme as Athenians – who like their city pretty savoury – would lead you to believe. Most disturbances that do take place tend to be the settling of private scores, and disorderly drunkenness is positively tame by north European standards; student budgets confronting bistro prices results in the nursing of a single drink all evening.

Back towards Síndagma

Between the counter-culturality of Exárhia and the occasional frowsiness of the bazaar, the broad busy avenues of Stadhíou, Panepistimíou and Akadhimías are lined with mainstream retailers, usually tucked into cavernous, occasionally opulent arcades that would have gained the approval of the original Bavarian planners.

Except for the blue city buses peeling off behind on Akadhimías, the grounds of the neoclassical **National Library** and **University** buildings, bang in the middle of all this, are an oasis of calm. The scattered buildings, designed by the Dane Christian Hansen, deserve a look, since their garish decoration gives an alarming idea of what the Classical monuments must have looked like when their paintwork was intact. Also worth a stop if you've time are two minor but quite enjoyable museums, devoted to the city's and nation's history.

The first of these, housed in the original Parliament building, in use from the 1860s until 1935, on Platía Kolokotróni, is the **National Historical Museum** (Tues–Fri 9am–1.30pm, Sat & Sun 9am–12.30pm; 200dr; *D3*). Its exhibits are predominantly Byzantine and medieval, though there is also a strong section on the War of Independence that includes Byron's sword and helmet.

The other, the **City of Athens Museum** (Mon, Wed, Fri & Sat 9am–1.30pm; 100dr; *D3*) occupies the original Royal Palace at Paparigopoúlou 7, on Platía Klafthmónos. This was the residence of the German-born King Otho in the 1830s before the new palace – now the Parliament, on Síndagma – was completed in 1842. Exhibits (prints mainly, and still somewhat sparse) feature an interesting – if also, in the modern light, depressing – model of the city as it was in 1842, with just 300 houses.

Síndagma, the National Gardens and south

All roads lead to Platía Sindágmatos – **Síndagma** (Syntagma) square – so you'll find yourself there sooner or later. Geared to tourism, with the main EOT information posts (in the National and General banks), post office (extended hours), American Express, airline and travel offices grouped around, it has convenience but not much else to recommend it. The cafés, well patrolled through the summer by Greek males on the lookout for foreign affairs, are overpriced and dangerously exposed to exhaust fumes, but make an easy rendezvous spot.

The square

Most of the square's buildings are modern and characterless, though earlier times prevail on the uphill (east) side where the **Voulí**, the Greek National Parliament, looks over proceedings. This was built as the royal palace for Greece's first monarch, the Bavarian King Otho, in the 1830s. In front of it, goose-stepping **Evzónes** in tasselled caps, kilt and woolly leggings – a prettified version of traditional mountain costume – change their guard at intervals in front of the **Tomb of the Unknown Soldier**, to the rhythm of camera shutters. Hemingway, among others, impugned their masculinity but they are in fact a highly trained elite corps who must be two metres or over in height, with weight proportionate; formerly they were recruited almost exclusively from mountain villages.

Other flanking buildings to have survived postwar development include the vast **Hotel Grande Bretagne** – Athens' grandest. In the course of one of the more nefarious episodes of British meddling in Greek affairs, it nearly became the tomb of Winston Churchill. He had arrived on Christmas Day 1944 to sort out the *Dhekemvrianá*, the "events of December": a month of serious street-fighting between British forces and the Communist-led ELAS resistance movement, whom the British were trying to disarm. ELAS saboteurs had placed an enormous explosive charge in the drains, intending to blow up various Greek and Allied VIPs; according to whom you believe, it was either discovered in time by a kitchen employee, or removed by ELAS themselves when they realised they might get Churchill as well.

"Síndagma" means "constitution" and the name derives from the fact that Greece's first one was proclaimed by a reluctant King Otho from a palace balcony in 1843. The square is still the principal venue for mass **demonstrations**, whether trade-union protests against government austerity programmes or "drive-in" sabotages by taxi drivers outraged at proposals to limit their movements in the interest of cleaner air. At election times the major political parties always stage their final campaign rallies here – a pretty intimidating sight, with around 100,000 singing, flag-waving Greeks packed into the square. At such times overground city transport comes to a halt, with the metro the only way around the bottleneck.

The National Gardens

At the back of the Voulí, the **National Gardens** (open sunrise to sunset; free) form the most refreshing acres in the whole city – not so much a flower garden as a luxuriant tangle of trees, shrubs and creepers, whose shade, duck ponds, and murmuring irrigation channels provide palpable relief from the heat and smog of summer. They were originally the private palace gardens – a pet project of Queen Amalia in the 1840s; purportedly the main duty of the minuscule Greek navy in its early days was the fetching of rare plants, often the gifts of other royal houses, from remote corners of the globe.

Of late, however, the gardens have fallen on hard times: pond-cleaning and pruning are neglected, a botanical museum is closed more often than not, and a sorry excuse for a mini-zoo has become the target of criticism by environmental and animal-welfare groups. To add insult to injury, the newly created metro construction commission is demanding ten percent of the gardens' area for the construction of tunnel vents – a requisition so far denied by the parks commission. Adding to the air of dereliction are the packs of half-wild cats, abandoned in such numbers here that the city has recently seen fit to post a sign forbidding the practice. Despite all this, there are few better places in the city than the gardens to read or wait for an evening ferry or plane.

The southern extension of the gardens, open twenty-four hours, is comprised by the graceful crescent-shaped grounds of the **Záppion**. This grand neoclassical exhibition hall, another creation of the Danish architect Hansen (he of the University), was for a period the Greek State Radio headquarters but is now used mainly for press conferences and commercial exhibitions.

The café-ouzeri *Aigli*, adjacent to the Záppion, was formerly one of the most elegant in town, though it appears to have closed for the present. There's a more basic but shaded **café**, the *Oasis*, up at the east (uphill) exit of the park on to Iródhou Attikoú.

Iródhou Attikoú also fronts the **Presidential Palace**, the royal residence until Constantine's exit from the scene in 1967, where more *evzónes* stand sentry duty. The surrounding streets, with a full complement of foreign embassies and hardly a store or taverna, are very posh and heavily policed. The centre-right party, *Néa Dhimokratía*, has its headquarters in Odhós Rigílis nearby, as does the army's Officers' Club, scene of much anti-democratic intriguing in the past.

The Olympic Stadium

A walk to the base of Iródhou Attikoú and across busy Leofóros Ardhittoú will bring you to the **Olympic Stadium** (free entrance), a nineteenth-century reconstruction on Roman foundations, slotting tightly between the pine-covered spurs of Ardhittós hill.

This site was originally marked out in the fourth century BC for the Panathenaic athletic contests, but in Roman times, as a grand gesture to mark the reign of the Emperor Hadrian, it was adapted for an orgy of blood sports, with thousands of wild beasts baited and slaughtered in the arena. Herodes Atticus (see p.80) later undertook to refurbish the 60,000 seats of the entire stadium; his white marble gift was to provide the city with a convenient quarry throughout the ensuing seventeen centuries.

The stadium's reconstruction dates from the modern revival of the Olympic Games in 1896 and to the efforts of another wealthy benefactor, the Alexandrian Greek, Yiorgos Averoff. Its appearance – pristine whiteness and meticulous symmetry – must be very much as it was when first restored and reopened under the Roman senator, and indeed it's still used by local athletes despite the tight curves. Above the stadium to the south, on the secluded **Hill of Ardhittós**, are a few scant remnants of a Temple of Fortune, again constructed by Herodes Atticus. Unfortunately, it is currently inaccessible, since the entire hill is fenced off to protect its pine groves from the risk of fires –which would be catastrophic for the city.

Méts and Pangráti

South and east of Ardhittós are the only two central neighbourhoods outside Pláka to have retained something of their traditional flavour – **Méts** and **Pangráti**. Particularly in Méts, a steep hillside quarter on the southwest side of the stadium, there are still nearly intact streets of pre-World War II houses, with tiled roofs, shuttered windows, and courtyards with spiral metal stairs and potted plants. They're a sad reminder of how beautiful this out-of-control city once was, even quite recently.

Méts and the Próto Nekrotafío

More specific attractions in **Méts** are the concentration of tavernas and bars around Márkou Moussoúrou and Arhimídhous (see p.104), and the Próto Nekrotafío (First Cemetery), at the top end of Anapáfseos (Eternal Rest) street, itself lined with shops specific to the funerary trade.

The **Próto Nekrotafío** shelters just about everybody who was anybody in twentieth-century Greek public life; the humbler tombs of singers, artists and writers are interspersed with ornate mausolea of soldiers, statesmen and "good" families, whose descendants come to picnic, stroll and tend the graves. One of "the unregarded wonders of Athenian life", Peter Levi called it; "the neoclassical marbles run riot, they reflower as rococo, they burst into sunblasts of baroque". The graveside statuary occasionally attains the status of high art, most notably in the works of Ianoulis Halepas, a Belle Époque sculptor from Tínos generally acknowledged to be the greatest of a school of fellow-islanders. Halepas battled with mental illness for most of his life and died in extreme poverty during the 1930s; his masterpiece is the idealised **Kimiméni** (Sleeping Girl), on the right about 300 metres in.

Pangráti

Pangráti is the unremarkable but pleasant quarter to the north and east of the Stadium. Platía Plastíra, Platía Varnáva and Platía Pangratíou are the focal points, the first with a vast old-fashioned *kafenío* where you can sit for hours on a leafy terrace for the price of a coffee. Pangratíou, fringed by the local *álsos* or grove-park, is the rallying place for the neighbourhood's youthful posers; between (and on) Varnáva and nearby Odhós Arhimídhous are several good tavernas, and the latter has an impressive *laikí agorá* – **street market** – every Friday.

Another Pangráti eating area lies down towards Leofóros Konstandínou, among the rather claustrophobic alleys opposite the **statue of Harry Truman**, recently restored to his pedestal after being blown off it by leftists in reprisal for his notorious doctrine promulgated in 1947 to justify US intervention in the Greek civil war. The Nobel-laureate poet **Goerge Seferis** lived not far away in Odhós Ágras, an attractive stair-street flanking the northeast wall of the Olympic Stadium.

North of Síndagma: Kolonáki, Likavitós and the Benáki and Cycladic Art museums

Athens is at its trendiest north of Síndagma, and if you have money to spend, **Kolonáki** is the place to do it, catering to every western taste from jazz bars to high fashion. The quarter is not especially interesting for visitors to the city – though it's a fond haunt of expatriates – but it does give access to **Likavitós hill**, where a funicular hauls you up for some of the best views of the city. Also close by are two fine museums, one devoted to **Cycladic Art**, the other, the **Benáki**, an assembly of just about all matters Greek, from Mycenaean artefacts to twentieth-century historical memorabilia.

Kolonáki

Kolonáki is the city's most chic central address and shopping area. Although no great shakes architecturally, it enjoys a superb site on the southwest-facing slopes of Likavitós (Lycabettus), looking out over the Acropolis and National Gardens. From its summit, on one of those increasingly rare clear days, you can just about make out the mountains of the Peloponnese. The lower limits of Kolonáki are defined by Akadhimías and Vassilísis Sofías streets, where in grand neoclassical palaces Egypt, France and Italy have their embassies. The middle stretches of the quarter are for shopping, and the highest purely residential.

The heart of the district is **Kolonáki square**, officially called Platía Filikís Eterías; the ancient "little column" of which name hides in the trees on the southwest side. The square's location should be committed to memory, for beneath the central garden, where kids, pensioners, nannies and pigeons compete for limited bench space, glistens the city's almost unique and certainly cleanest public toilet. Other possible lures include the kiosks with their stocks of foreign papers and magazines, the **British Council library** on the downhill side, where you can read the paper for free and browse upcoming programme flybills, and numerous cafés on Patriárhou Ioakím to the east – the principal display ground for Kolonáki's well-heeled natives. The assorted cafés, pubs and sandwich bars on pedestrianised Tsakálof are a better bet for sustenance.

Kolonáki's streets also contain an amazing density of small, classy **shops**, with the accent firmly on **fashion and design**. In a half-hour walk around the neighbourhood you can view the whole gamut of consumer style. Patriárhou Ioakím and Skoufá with its cross-streets to the northwest, comprise the most promising area, along with the pedestrianised Voukourestíou-Valaorítou-Kriezótou block, just below Akadhimías.

For more random strolling, the highest tiers of Kolonáki are pleasant, with vertical streets ending in long flights of steps, planted with oleander, jasmine and other flowering shrubs. The one **café** spot up here is at **Platía Dhexamenís**, a small and attractive square close to the Likavitós loop road, where in summertime tables are set under the trees around the **Dhexamení**, a covered reservoir begun by the Emperor Hadrian.

Likavitós

Not far away from Kolonáki square, at the top of Ploutárhou, a **funicular** (8am–10pm, every 20min in summer, less frequent at other times; 200dr) begins its ascent to the summit of **Likavitós Hill**. For the more energetic, the principal path up the hill begins here, too, rambling through woods that are a favourite with amorous couples. On the summit, the chapel of **Áyios Yióryios** provides the main focus – a spectacular place to celebrate that name-day if you're around on April 23. There's a **café** on the adjacent terrace, and another, less plastic, halfway down. Both have morning and sunset views – you're eyeball-to-eyeball to the Acropolis – spectacular enough to excuse the inflated prices and unenthusiastic service.

Various other paths lead up and around the hill, and a **road** runs by the southwest tip, overlooking another quarter of narrow lanes and steep stairs near the junction of Ítis and Sína streets, where the French Institute puts forth the Gallic message.

Most paths and driveways up the hill from here converge at the open-air **Likavitós Theatre**, used primarily as a music venue during the Athens Summer Festival (see p.111). If you come down by the southeast slopes, you emerge in the very lovely but privileged little enclave that the British and American archaeological schools have managed to retain for themselves on Odhós Souidhías. Here too is the **Yennádhion Library**, with large collections of books on Greece and an unpublicised drawer full of Edward Lear's watercolour sketches; good-quality and reasonably priced reproductions are on sale.

The Benáki Museum

Koumbári 1/corner Vassilísis Sofías, *D4*; 8.30am–2pm; closed Tues; admission 200dr.

Not to be missed – as it is by ninety percent of tourists – is this private collection, given to the state by an Egyptian-Greek collector, **Emmanuel Benáki**, who had grown wealthy on the Nile cotton trade. Constantly surprising and fascinating, the exhibits range through Ottoman ceramics, Mycenaean jewellery, Coptic textiles, Greek costumes and folk artefacts, Byronia, and other memorabilia of the Greek War of Independence – even a reconstructed Egyptian palace reception hall. These and displays of jewellery and other items from the Hélène Stathatos collection are worth an hour or two of anyone's time. Unfortunately the upper floor, with period paintings and engravings of Athens, is closed for renovation at time of writing.

Among the more unusual exhibits, not easily accessible elsewhere, are collections of early Greek gospels, liturgical vestments and church ornaments rescued by Greek refugees from Asia Minor in 1922 (Rooms 4 and 10); some dazzling embroideries and body ornaments from various parts of the islands and mainland (in the basement); and some unique historical material – on the Cretan statesman Eleftherios Venizelos, Asia Minor, and the Cretan Revolution (Room 9), and material on the 1821 rising against the Turks upstairs. Don't miss the museum's two very early **El Greco** panels, either. These include the artist's earliest known work, dating from the time when he painted in the Byzantine style on his native Crete.

An additional attraction, if you've been dodging traffic in the streets all day, is the **rooftop café**, with good snacks and views over the nearby National Gardens. A **shop**, by the entrance, stocks a fine selection of books on Greek folk art, records of regional music and some of the best posters and postcards in the city.

Museum of Cycladic and Ancient Greek Art

Neofítou Dhouká 4 – second left off Vassilísis Sofías after the Benáki museum, *D4*; Mon & Wed–Fri 10am–3.30pm, Sat 10am–2.30pm; admission 200dr.

For display, labelling, explanation and comfort, this small, private museum is way ahead of anything else in Athens. Though the collections are restricted – to the Cycladic civilisation (third millennium BC), pre-Minoan Bronze Age (second millennium BC), and the period from the fall of Mycenae to the beginning of historic times around 700 BC, plus a selection of Classical pottery – you can learn far more about these periods than from the corresponding sections of the National Archaeological Museum.

If Cycladic art seems an esoteric field, don't be put off. This display establishes the characteristic marble bowls and folded-arm figurines with their sloping wedge heads as objects of supreme purity and simplicity. Their interest for twentieth-century artists like Moore, Picasso and Brancusi becomes immediately obvious. And you can see in the figurines the remote ancestry of the Archaic style that evolved into the great sculptures of the Classical period. The exact purpose of the mostly female effigies has been disputed, but given their frequent discovery in grave-barrows, it has been variously surmised that they were spirit-world guides for the deceased, substitutes for the sacrifice of servants and attendants, or representations of the Earth Goddess in her role of reclaiming yet another of her children.

Much of the top floor is devoted to a collection of painted Classical bowls, often ingeniously showing two unrelated scenes on opposite sides. The curators consider the one with a depiction of revellers on one face and three men in cloaks conversing on the other, to be the star exhibit, but there is not one dud. Most of the more exquisite items date from the fifth century BC – not for nothing was it referred to as a "Golden Age".

To round off the experience, there's a **shop**, **snack bar** and shaded courtyard.

Other nearby museums

A number of other museums – of somewhat more specialist interest – are grouped conveniently close together near the angled intersection of Vassilísis Sofías and Vassiléos Konstandínou, close by the Benaki and Cycladic Art museums.

Byzantine Museum

Vassilísis Sofías 22, 400m from the Benakí, *D5*; Tues–Sun 8.30am–3pm; 1000dr.

The Byzantine Museum's setting is perhaps its best feature: a peaceful, courtyarded villa that once belonged to the Duchesse de Plaisance, a French philhellene and widow of a Napoleonic general who helped to fund the War of Independence. To enjoy the exhibits — almost exclusively icons, housed in two restored side galleries – requires some prior interest, best developed by a trip to the churches at Mystra, Dhafní or Óssios Loukás. Labelling is generally Greek-only and you are told little of the development of styles, which towards the sixteenth century show an increasing post-Renaissance Italian influence, due to the presence of the Venetians in Greece. The rear hall contains marble artefacts, plus a reconstructed basilica.

War Museum

Vassilísis Sofías 24, just beyond the Byzantine museum, *D5*; Tues–Sat 9am–2pm, Sun 9.30am–2pm; free.

The only "cultural" endowment of the 1967–74 junta, this museum becomes predictably militaristic and right-wing as it approaches modern events: the Asia Minor campaign, the civil war, Greek forces in Korea, etc. Earlier times, however, are covered with a more scholarly concern and this gives an interesting insight into changes in warfare from Mycenae through to the Byzantines and Turks. Among an array of models are a fascinating series on the acropolises and castles of Greece, both Classical and medieval.

National Gallery of Art

Vassiléos Konstandínou 50, past the War Museum by the Hilton, *E5*; Tues–Sat 9am–3pm, Sun 10am–2pm; admission 150dr.

The National Gallery has a rather disappointing core collection of Greek art from the sixteenth century to the present. One of the few modern painters to stand out is Nikos Hatzikyriakos-Ghikas (Ghika), who is well represented on the ground floor. On the mezzanine is a small group of canvases by the "Primitive" painter Theophilos (more of whose work can be seen in the Pláka – see p.82). Temporary exhibitions can be worth catching; keep an eye out for posters or check the listings in *The Athenian* magazine.

The outskirts: Dhafní, Kessarianí and Kifissiá

Athens pushes its suburbs higher and wider with each year and the **monasteries of Dhafní and Kessarianí**, once well outside the city limits, are now approached through more or less continuous cityscape. However, each retains a definite country-side setting and makes for a good respite from the central sights.

The monasteries are easily reached by taxi or by local **city transport**. For Dhafní (9km west of the centre), take more or less any bus prefixed #8 (#818, #853, #862, #880 are most frequent) from Platía Eleftherías (*D1*); the monastery is signposted on the right of the road, about twenty minutes' ride. For Kessarianí, take blue bus #224 from Akadhimías (*D3/4*) to the last stop, from where the church is a thirty- to forty-minute climb up the lower slopes of Mount Imittós.

The northern suburb of **Kifissiá** is included in this section as an insight into wealthy Athenian life – it has long been where the rich have their villas – and for natural history enthusiasts, who may want to check out the Goulandhrís Museum. The suburb is the most northerly stop on the metro.

Classical enthusiasts may want to continue from Dhafní to the site of **Eleusis** (see p.128), a further twenty-minute ride on many of the same bus routes.

Dhafní

Dhafní Monastery (daily 8.30am–3pm; 500dr) is one of the great buildings of Byzantine architecture. Its design – the classic Greek-cross-octagon – is a refinement of a plan first used at Óssios Loukás, on the road to Delphi (see p.233), and its mosaics are considered among the great masterpieces of the Middle Ages.

The monastic church replaced a fortified fifth-century basilica, which in turn had been adapted from the ruins of a sanctuary of Apollo – the name is derived from the *daphnai* (laurels) sacred to the god. Both the church and the fortifications which enclose it incorporate blocks from the ancient sanctuary; a porch, present until two centuries ago, featured complete Classical columns, but was among the targets of Lord Elgin's looting. The fortifications (and remains of a Gothic cloister) also show evidence of later building under the Cistercians, who replaced Dhafní's Orthodox monks after the Frankish conquest of Athens in 1204.

The Byzantines, ironically, had occupied their building for little over a century. When the monastery was established, in 1070, the Greek church was undergoing an intellectual revival but the state was in terminal collapse. The following year the Normans took Bari, the last Byzantine possession in southern Italy, and the Seljuk Turks defeated the Byzantine army in Armenia – a prelude to the loss of Asia Minor and, before long, Greece itself.

Inside the church, the **mosaic cycle** is remarkable for its completeness, giving a full display of Byzantine iconography as well as artistic power. There are scenes from the life of Christ and the Virgin, saints (a predominance of Eastern figures from Syria and elsewhere in the Levant), archangels and prophets. But the great triumph is the *Christ Pandokrátor* (Christ in Majesty) on the dome. Lit by the sixteen windows of the drum, and set against a background of gold, this stern image directs a tremendous and piercing gaze, his finger poised on the Book of Judgement. It is a perfect encapsulation of the strict orthodoxy of Byzantine belief, rendered poignant by the troubled circumstances in which it was created.

The monastery today is unoccupied; the Cistercians were banished by the Turks, and Orthodox monks, allowed to return in the sixteenth century, were expelled in turn for harbouring rebels during the War of Independence.

Kessarianí

What it loses in an architectural comparison with Dhafní, **Kessarianí monastery** makes up for in its location. Although just five kilometres from the centre of the city, it is high enough up the slopes of Mount Imittós to escape the *néfos* and the noise. The sources of the River Ilissos provide for extensive gardens hereabouts, as they have since ancient times (Ovid mentions them), and today's Athenians still come to collect water from the local fountains.

The monastery buildings date, like Dhafní, from the eleventh century, though the frescoes in the chapel are much later – executed during the sixteenth and seventeenth centuries. In contrast to Dhafní's clerics, Kessarianí's abbot agreed to submit to Roman authority when the Franks took Athens, so the monastery remained in continuous

Greek (if not quite Orthodox) occupation through the Middle Ages. It today maintains a small group of monks, who allow **visits** to the monastery proper Tuesday to Sunday from 8.30am to 3pm (500dr admission). Outside these hours you can while the time away in the well-maintained grounds, full of picknickers until sunset in summertime.

On the **way up to the monastery**, which is fairly obvious from the bus terminal, don't overlook the neighbourhood of Kessarianí. It has an attractively casual, ramshackle aspect about its streets, which were used as a 1920s location for the Greek movie *Rembetiko*. There are a handful of good tavernas around the square off to the left, four stops before the end of the bus line.

Kifissiá

Kifissiá, Athens' most desirable suburb, edges up the leafy slopes of Mount Pendéli, about eight kilometres north of the city centre. A surprising 300m above sea level and a good 5°F cooler than central Athens, it appealed to the nineteenth-century bourgeoisie as a suitable site for summer residence. Their villas – neoclassical, Swiss, Alsatian and fantasy-melange – still hold their own amid the newer concrete models. Indeed, despite the encroachments of speculators' apartment blocks and trendy boutiques, the suburb's village character prevails.

The centre of the old "village" is the crossroads called Plátanos, though the mighty plane tree that gave it its name has long since fallen to the demands of the traffic planners. It's just at the uphill end of the gardens opposite the Kifissiá metro station. The hub is the two or three streets around Plátanos, with *Varsos*, the old-fashioned patisserie specialising in home-made yoghurts, jams and sticky cakes, a magnet for the whole neighbourhood. The young (and rich) hangout is the *Edelweiss* café, ten minutes' walk away in Kefalaríou. A good lunchtime stop that will serve most people's purposes is the *Estiatorio O Platanos* by the above-mentioned crossroads.

If you need a more purposeful focus than merely wandering among trees and gardens, you could find it in the collections of the **Goulandhrís Natural History Museum** (9am–2.30pm; closed Fri; entrance 200dr) at Levídhou 13, ten minutes' walk from the metro. The modest but well-displayed collection has especially good coverage on Greek birds and butterflies and endangered species like the monk seal (*Monachus monachus*) and sea turtle (*Caretta caretta*). Housed in a grand marble mansion, with a 250,000-specimen herbarium attached, the museum also boasts a café and a shop selling superb illustrated books, postcards, posters and prints.

Eating and drinking

As you'd expect in a city that houses almost half the Greek population, Athens has the best and the most varied **restaurants and tavernas** in the country – and most places are sources of not just good food but a good night out. The listings below are devoted mainly to **restaurant meals**, grouped according to district and divided into cheap (under 2000dr per person) and less so (2000–3500dr).

Folllowing these are rundowns on **breakfast** (most Athenians don't take it), **snacks** (on which you could contentedly live), **ouzerí** (ditto – but better), **bars** and **tea houses** (which are among the few fallbacks for vegetarians).

Restaurants

If it is character you are after, **Pláka**'s hills and lanes still provide a pleasant evening's setting for a meal, despite the aggressive touts and general tourist hype. But for good-value and good-quality fare, only one in ten of the quarter's restaurants and tavernas is these days worth a second glance. For quality Greek cooking, if you're staying any length of time in the city, it's better to strike out into the ring of neighbourhoods around: to **Méts**, **Pangráti**, **Exárhia/Neápoli**, **Veïkoú/Koukáki**, **Áno Petrálona**, or the more upmarket **Kolonáki**. None of these is more than a half hour's walk, or a quicker trolley bus or taxi ride, from the centre – effort that is well repaid in increased menu choice and a more authentic and often livelier atmosphere.

Note that several of our recommendations are closed in summer (usually June to August); this is usually due to hot, un-air-conditioned locales, or the exodus of their regular business trade. All grid listings refer to the map on p.60–61.

Pláka

Selections here represent just about all of note that **Pláka** has to offer, and most, sadly, are on the periphery of the quarter, rather than on the more picturesque squares and stairways. At these, don't be bamboozled by the touts, positioned at crucial locations to lure you over to their tavernas' tables – invariably a bad sign.

UNDER 2000DR

O Platanos, Dhioyénous 4, *E3*. One of the oldest tavernas in the district, with outdoor summer seating under the namesake tree. Closed Sun.

Damingos, Kidhathinéon 41, *F3*. Dour service, but good value; barrelled wine, excellent *bakaliáro skordhaliá* (cod with garlic sauce). Evenings only; closed midsummer.

MORE UPMARKET

To Ipoyio, Kidathinéon 30 (in the basement), *E3*. Wide range of grills, vegetable *mezédhes*, bulk wine. Evenings only; closed May 15–Sept 30.

O Zafiris, Thespídhos 4a, *F3*. Renowned game taverna, at its best in autumn and winter.

Eden, Fléssa 3, *E3*. The city's best vegetarian restaurant provides dishes that you'll pine for on travels around the country; the setting is pleasant, too – an old mansion plus terrace. In summer, from time to time, the cooks and staff are overstretched and standards plummet.

To Yerani (Kouklis), Tripódhon 14, corner Epihármou, *F3*. Attractive split-level taverna serving a good selection of *mezédhes*; it has a perennially popular summer terrace.

Monastiráki and the Bazaar

The shift from Pláka to Monastiráki is refreshing. In the streets of the commercial quarter people eat for a serious fill. There is a definite character about the quarter, too, at its best around the flea market.

UNDER 2000DR

Ipiros, Platía Ayíou Filíppou, *E2*. An old restaurant in a great location, right at the heart of flea market. If the food – casserole dishes – is occasionally a bit listless, the prices and quantity are fair enough.

Kea, Panós 6, *E2*. Average food but a fine outdoor setting, beside an old mosque and with a terrace trailed with vines. Open April –Nov, evenings only.

Bairaktaris, Platía Monastirakioú 2, *E2*. Huge old restaurant whose walls are lined with retsina barrels. Straightforward menu. Closes 11pm.

Psistaria I Platia, Platía Iróön (a couple of minutes' walk from Monastiráki along Miaoúli), *E2*. Specialises in vegetable *mezédhes* and grilled northern Greek dishes. Always packed with locals at lunchtime.

In the meat market (entrances at Eolóu 80 and off Athinás), *D2*. The meat-market building is not everyone's prime eating site but the restaurants within know how to cook the goods – and feature *patsás* (tripe soup) for the more hardened. Most of them are open from around 6am until 3am; the best is probably **To Monastiri**.

Exárhia/Platía Viktorías

Exárhia is still surprisingly untrodden by tourists, considering its proximity to the centre. Its eating and drinking establishments are conveniently close to the National Archaeological Museum and several recommended hotels, and exploring them gives some insight into how the student/youth/alternative crowd carries on.

UNDER 2000DR

Vangelis, Sahíni, off Liossíon (100m up from Platía Váthis), *C2*. Simply one of the friendliest and most traditional tavernas in the city.

O Lefteris, Iouliánou 84. Walled-in garden taverna with casserole food.

Ouzeri, Elpídhos 14, Platía Viktorías. Seafood and *pikilíes* with your drinks.

To Monastiri, Kallidhromíou 30, corner Zoödhóhou Piyís, Exárhia, *C3*. Oven food at lunchtime, *tis óras* grills in the evening.

Barba Yannis, Emmanuíl Benáki 94, Exárhia, *C3*. Limited menu but good cooking and a very relaxed atmosphere.

Maïnas, Kallidhromíou 27, Exárhia, *C3*. Fine pizza and other entrées to eat in or take away.

MORE UPMARKET

Kostoyiannis, Zaími 37 (behind the National Archaeological Museum, off Ioulianoú), *C3*. One of the city's best restaurants – much frequented by crowds from the theatres and cinemas around. Quality *mezédhes* and delicacies like rabbit stew. Evenings only; closed Sun.

FOREIGN CUISINE RESTAURANTS

Healthy as it may be, it's not difficult to get tired of Greek food, especially during an extended visit, and you may find your imagination turning to other cuisines. Unlike the rest of the country, Athens offers a fair selection – from highly chi-chi French places, through Armenian and Arabic, Spanish and Balkan, to Japanese and Korean. Listed below are some of the more central places – others are to be found at the beach suburbs to the south – which don't require a large outlay in taxi fares to reach. Economy ends there, however, since except for the Asian restaurants they are all comparatively expensive – budget for 3000–5000dr per person depending on what you order.

Unless otherwise indicated, the places listed below are closed in summer and on Sunday, but stay open until 1.30am. Reservations are advisable.

ARMENIAN-TURKISH

Tria Asteria, Mélitos 7/corner Plastíra, Néa Smírni (☎93 58 134; off map, at end of #10 trolley line). Specialities include *tandir kebab* and *kionefe*, a special stuffed-filo dessert.

CHINESE

Golden Flower, Níkis 30, Síndagma (☎32 30 113; *E3*). Open daily and in summer.

Golden Dragon, Olimbíou 27–29/Singroú 122, Koukáki (☎392 32 315; off map, below *G2/3*). A cut above average: ginger chicken, stuffed chicken wings, etc. Open in summer.

Dragon Palace, Andínoros 3, Pangráti, behind several museums (☎72 42 795; *D5*). Cantonese dishes such as Peking duck. Open in summer.

CZECH

Bohemia, Dhímou Tséliou, Ambelókipi (☎64 26 341; *A5*). Czech beers (of course); open in summer.

Svejk, Roúmbesi 8a, Néos Kósmos, 15-min walk from Koukáki (☎90 18 389; off map, below *G3*). Very rich stew-like entrées, also duck and carp according to season. Closed Mon & Tues.

Fruitopia (formerly *Hlorofíli*), Soultáni 12, corner Solomoú, Exárhia, *C3*. Rare vegetarian/macrobiotic restaurant that has recently reopened. Supper only; closed August.

Rozalia, Valtetsíou 58, Exárhia, *C3*. The best *mezédhes*-plus-grills-type taverna immediately around the platía, and as such usually busy. Supper only; garden in summer.

Strefis Taverna tis Xanthis, Irínis Athinéas 5, in Neápoli behind Lófos Stréfi, *B4*. House specialities include rabbit stew and schnitzel. A pleasant old mansion with a roof garden that offers fine view across northern Athens. Closed Sun.

Neapoli

This district is a long walk or short bus ride up Hariláou Trikoúpi from Exárhia, with a concentration of calmer clubs, bars and cinemas that make it a favourite dining-out target for savvy locals. The food here is good, teetering to either side of the 2000dr divider. Mavromiháli is one street over from Harilaóu Trikoúpi.

O Fondas, Adrianítou 6, just off Mavromiháli. Probably the most expensive of the four listed here, but recently returned to high-quality fare.

I Lefka, Mavromiháli 121. Standard taverna fare, with barrelled retsina. Summer seating in a huge garden enclosed by barrels.

Ta Bakiria, Mavromiháli 117. Similar to the above but a bit cheaper with a more imaginative menu. Atmospheric interior for wintertime and a summer garden. Closed Sun.

O Pinaleo, Mavromiháli 152. Rich *mezédhes* and meaty entrées served up by a young couple from Híos and washed down with unresinated bulk wine. Open Oct–May only.

FRENCH

Prunier, Ipsilándou 63, Kolonáki (☎72 27 379; *D5*). Central and unpretentious bistro.
Calvados, Alkmános 5, Ilísia (☎72 26 291; off map, just past *D5*). Normandy cuisine.

GERMAN

Ritterburg, Formíonos 11, Pangráti (☎72 38 421; off map, past *E/F5*). Schnitzels.
Delicious, Zalakósta 6, Kolonáki (☎36 38 455; *D4*). Tiny bistro with Hamburg seafood and the usual sausages.

ITALIAN

Al Convento, Anapíron Polémou 4–6, Kolonáki. (☎72 39 163; *D5*). Claims to be the oldest Italian eatery in Athens. Speciality pasta and scallopine. Open in summer.
Taormina, Plastíra 116, Néa Smírni (☎94 26 143; off map, at end of #10 trolley). House specials rigatoni and pizza. Open in summer.

JAPANESE

Kyoto, Gariváldi 5, Veïkoú (☎92 32 047; *F2*). A quite reasonable, long-established place; unusual specials as well as the expected *tempura* and *sushi*. Open in summer.
Michiko, Kidathinéon 27, Pláka (☎32 20 980; *E3*). Touristy and with rather ordinary cooking – but very central. Open in summer.

KOREAN

Seoul, Evritanías 8, off Panórmou in Ambelókipi (☎69 24 669; off map beyond *A/B5*). Speciality Korean barbecue. Garden seating in summer.
Orient, Lékka 26, Síndagma (☎32 21 192; *E3*). Also Chinese and Japanese dishes. Open in summer.

SPANISH

Ispaniki Gonia, Theayénous 22, Pangráti (☎72 31 393; off map, past *E5*). Housed in an old mansion near the *Caravel Hotel*. Occasional live music. Open in summer.

Kolonáki and Likavitós

Kolonáki has a ritzy, upmarket reputation that puts off a lot of travellers. Nonetheless, among the boutiques are some surprising finds.

UNDER 2000DR

I Rouga, Kapsáli 7 (in a cul-de-sac), just off Kolonáki square, *D4*. Small taverna open evenings only; menu changes daily. Closed summer and on Sun.

O Vrahos, Likavitoú 8, *D4*. A tiny, sympathetic lunchtime *estiatório*. Not many frills but a bit of character. Open weekdays only.

To Kioupi, Platía Kolonáki, near corner of Skoufá. Subterranean lunchtime taverna.

MORE UPMARKET

Taverna Dhimokrítos, Dhimokrítou 23/corner Tsakálof, *D4*. A bit snooty, but a beautiful building and well prepared food from a huge menu. Open lunchtime and evenings, but closed in late summer and on Sunday.

Rodhia, Aristípou 44, near the base of the téléférique, *D5*. Elegant entrées; open year round; but closed Sun.

To Grafio, Platía Dhexamení, *D4*. Cool, modern *ouzeri* with a wide selection of snacks and dishes; nice location, too.

Pangráti and Méts

These two neighbourhoods feature many of the city's best eating places. All the selections below are a short (if generally uphill) walk across busy Ardhitoú and past the Olympic stadium, or accessible via a #4 trolley ride to Platía Plastíra. **Goúra** is an extension of Méts, just south of the First Cemetery.

UNDER 2000DR

O Megaritis, Ferekídhou 2, corner Arátou, Pangráti, *F5*. Casserole food, barrel wine, indoor/pavement seating. Open all year.

Vellis, Platía Varnáva/corner Stilpónos (between Pangráti and Méts), *F5*. Limited choice, but very characterful little place on the square. One of the last of a dying breed of tradesmen's wine-with-food shops. Evenings only; indoor and outdoor seating.

To Kalivi, Empedhokléous 26/corner Prokloú, above Platía Varnáva, Pangráti, *F5*. Excellent, traditional *mezédhes*-type fare. Closed in summer.

O Ilias, corner Stasínou/Telesílis (near Leofóros Konstantínou), *E5*. A very good and very popular taverna. Tables outside in summer.

MORE UPMARKET

O Virinis, Arhimídhous 11 (off Platía Plastíra), *F5*. Good quality, regular-priced taverna, with its own house wine and a wide variety of *mezédhes*. Garden in summer.

Karavitis, Arktínou 35, off Leofóros Konstantínou, *F5*. Old-style taverna with bulk wine, *mezédhes*, clay-cooked entrées. Indoor and outdoor seating.

O Mandis, Evyeníou Voulgáreos 38, near *Joseph's House* hostel, *F4*. Great for traditional dishes like *spetzofaï* (pepper/sausage stew from Mount Pílion), rabbit stew, snails and also vegetable plates; impeccable service and, by Greek standards, very wacky decor.

Manesis, Márkou Moussoúrou 3, *F4*. Good value, especially if you piece together a meal from their *mezédhes*, which include such novelties as *loukániko flambé*. Walled garden in summer. Evenings only; closed Sun.

Ta Pergoulia, Márkou Moussoúrou 16, *F4*. Delicious, unusual *mezédhes* – order seven or eight and you'll have a fair-sized bill but a big meal. Closed in summer.

To Paragoni, Platía Plíta 3, Goúra, *G5*. A good, slightly upmarket *psistaria*; outdoor seating facing the park in summer.

To Spiti Mas, Dhafnopáti, just off Platía Plíta, *G5*. Features an expensive but imaginative menu and garden dining in summer.

Veikoú/Koukáki

This is one of the most pleasant parts of the city in which to spend the middle of a day or round off an evening, having wandered down from the south slope of the Acropolis or Filopáppou hill. It's very much middle-class, residential Athens – uneventful and a bit early-to-bed. The districts straddle the #1, #5 and #9 trolley lines.

UNDER 2000DR

To Triandaoktó (O Periklis), Veïkoú 38, Veïkoú, *G3*. This walled-in arcade next to a barber-shop becomes, from 8 to11.30pm, one of the cheapest tavernas in the city. Large portions of simple, well-prepared food, and red wine from the barrel. Closed May–Oct.

O Yeros tou Morea, Arváli 4, Koukáki, *G2*. Best for lunch when the oven food and *mezédhes* are fresh. Full of Koukáki bachelors, of all ages, who can eat here more cheaply than at home. Bulk wine from the barrels that form the main decor.

I Gardhenia, Zínni 29, Koukáki, *G3*. Honest, inexpensive casserole food and barrel wine in a cool, cavernous setting. Lunchtime only in summer.

I Gonia, Zán. Moreás 17, corner Andhroútsou, Koukáki, *G2*. One of the cheapest *psistariés* around. Small and popular, so come early for a table. Open lunchtime and evenings.

Ouzeri Evvia, G. Olimbíou 8, Koukáki, off map below *G2*. Hearty food as well as drink served on the new pedestrian way; very reasonable and informal.

To Ikositeróöro, Singroú 42/44, Veïkoú, *F3*. The name means "(Open) round-the-clock", and that's it's main virtue. Fair portions of anti-hangover food such as lamb tongues and *patsás*. At its liveliest after midnight in summer.

MORE UPMARKET

Irodhio, Angelikári 1 (up Rátzieri steps, just off Propiléon at the Acropolis end), Veïkoú, *G3*. Beautiful premises, reasonable *mezédhes*, slightly pricier casseroles.

Ouzedhiko To Meltemi, Zínni 26, Koukáki. A modest-priced *ouzerí* that shields its customers from street traffic with banks of greenery. Stress on seafood. Closed Sun.

To Sokáki, Aryiríou 6 (an alley – *sokáki* in Greek – off Veïkoú, near Zínni), *G2*. Slightly more upmarket *psistariá*; speciality grilled chicken and *mezédhes*. Quiet, outdoor seating.

Áno Petrálona

This old refugee neighbourhood, on the west flank of Filopáppou Hill, is the least touristed district of central Athens. Just why is a mystery: the range of tavernas is excellent, the #9 trolley bus appears regularly, and it's a natural choice for eating after an evening at the Dora Stratou folk-dance theatre. There's a trolley stop on the Platía Áno Petrálona, from where the main artery of Dhimifóndos is a short stroll northwest.

UNDER 2000DR

To Koutouki tou Andhrea, Dhimifóndos 81. Tradesmen's wine-and-food joint.

Ikonomou (no sign displayed), corner Tróon/Kidhandidhón. Basic home cooking served to packed pavement tables in summer.

To Monastiri, Dhimifóndos 46. Very popular, moderately priced neighbourhood place; occasional guitar music on an informal basis after 11.30pm.

MORE UPMARKET

I Avli tou Pikiliou, Dhimifóndos 116. Standard taverna with a garden; closed Mon.

T'Askimopapo, Iónon 61. For many years, this was known as the PASOK (socialists) house taverna. It's still quite popular – and does unusual dishes. Closed Sun.

Breakfasts

A thimbleful of coffee is sufficient for most Athenian **breakfasts**, but if you need a bit more to set you up for the day, it's little problem finding a bakery, yoghurt shop or fruit stall. **Veïkoú** and **Koukáki** are particularly good for this, with the *Tsatsos* **bakery** at Veïkoú 45, another at no. 75 and still another on pedestrianised Olimbíou, just off Platía Koukáki, offering excellent wholegrain bread and milk products. If they don't have the yoghurt or pudding themselves, you'll find it no more than a few doors away.

Alternatively, the city caters well enough for western tastes in and around the Pláka. For a **bacon/egg/juice breakfast**, the cheapest and friendliest place is at Níkis 26 (*E3*); nearby, a second choice is at Kidhathinéon 30, two doors up from Adhrianoú (*F3*), and a third at Kidathinéon 10, near the corner of Moní Asteríou (*E3*).

Around **Omónia**, the *Bretannia* (at the corner of Athinás, *D2*) is a wonderful old café-téria, open twenty hours a day and serving up superb *rizógalo* (rice pudding with cinnamon) and yoghurt. Some of the best *loukoumádhes* – hot puffballs of dough served in syrup – are to be found at the stall near the corner of Panepistimíou and Ippokrátous. Or try one of the places listed under "Tea houses and coffee shops" below.

Snacks

Later in the day, a host of **snack** stalls and outlets get going. If your budget is low you can fill up on them exclusively, forgetting sit-down restaurants altogether. If it's not, you'll still probably indulge. The standard **snacks** are *souvláki me píta* (kebab in pitta bread), *tirópites* (cheese pies) and *spanakópites* (spinach pies), along with *bougátzes* (cream pies) and a host of other speciality pastries.

The best downtown **souvláki stands** cluster at the beginning of Pandhróssou (*E2*), just behind Platía Monastirakíou; other good ones include the unpredictably open *Kostas'*, at Adhrianoú 116 (*E3*), and two facing each other on pedestrianised Dhrákou between Veïkoú and Dhimitrakopoúlou (*G3*).

For the various **pastry snacks**, try two adjacent shops on Kolokotróni, near the corner of Lékka, or – well worth the little bit extra – *Noufara* on Kolonáki square.

Tea houses and coffee shops

With a couple of honourable exceptions, **tea houses** and western-style **coffee shops** are a recent phenomenon in Athens. Quiet, rather consciously sophisticated places, they're essentially a reaction against the traditional and basic *kafenía*. Most are concentrated around the Pláka and in Kolonáki and the more upmarket suburbs.

Floca, Panepistimíou (in the arcade), *D3*. The oldest-established Athenian café-patisseries – and still the best. Their *chocalatina* (cream chocolate cake) is without rival.

Zonar's, Venizélou 9, *D3*. *Floca's* equally traditional rival – still much as it was described, as a haunt of Harriet and Guy Pringle, and Yakimov, in Olivia Manning's *Fortunes of War*.

Koperti, Sína 46, *D3*. A newer entry on the scene, this is a popular, youthful *salon de thé* in a handsome old shop close to the French Institute. Also serves salads, cheese and hot entrées.

De Profundis, Angelikís Hatzimihális 1, Pláka, *E3*. A trendy-looking tea house but surprisingly reasonably priced; herb teas, quiches, small entrées, pastries. Open 5pm–3am; weekends noon –3am. Closed Aug.

Strofes, Hamiltón 7, Platía Viktorías, *B2*. Claims to serve sixty varieties of tea.

To Tristrato, corner Dedhálou/Angélou Yerónda, Pláka, *F3*. Coffee, fruit juices, and salads, eggs, puddings, cakes; comfortable but expensive. Open 10am–midnight.

Oasis (no sign), at the east gate of the National Gardens, just south of the corner of Iródhou Attikoú and V. Sofías. Inexpensive ice cream, hot and cold drinks in a shaded locale.

Ouzerí and bars

Ouzerí – also called *ouzédhika* or *mezedhopolía* – are essentially bars selling *oúzo*, beer and wine (occasionally just *oúzo*), along with *mezédhes* (hors d'oeuvres) to reduce the impact. A special treat is a *pikilía* (usually about 1000dr), a selection of all the *mezédhes* available; this will probably include fried shrimp, pieces of squid, cheese, olives, tongue, cheese pies, sausage, and other delicacies.

The listings in this section also include more western-style – and more expensive – **bars**, which serve cocktails and suchlike. All the places included here put their drinks on at least equal footing with their snacks; certain *ouzédhika* that put more emphasis on the food end of things are listed under "Restaurants" in the previous section.

Apotsos, Panepistimíou 10 (at the end of the arcade), *D3*. Lunchtime-only bar with a wide range of *mezédhes*. A landmark through most of this century, frequented by journalists, politicians, writers and the rest. Highly recommended.

To Athinaikon, Themistokléous 2, corner Panepistimíou, *D3*. An old *ouzerí* in a new location but retaining its style – marble tables, old posters, etc. Variety of good-sized *mezédhes*, such as shrimp croquettes and mussels in cheese sauce. Closed Sun.

Café-Bar Dhodhoni, Sólonos 64 (parallel to Panepistimíou, threee blocks northeast), *D3*. A packed student hangout opposite the law school. Delicious snacks.

Salamandra, Mantzanárou 3, Kolonáki, *D4*. *Mezédhes* bar in a restored neoclassical house. Open evenings as well as lunchtimes; closed Sun.

Dhexameni, Platía Dhexamenís, Kolonáki, *D4*. Unnamed café-*ouzerí* that serves drinks and snacks in summer under the trees. Shaded and moderately expensive.

Ouzeri Finopoulos, corner Athinás/Evripídhou, in the bazaar, *D2*. The drinker's bar. Stand at the dented, water-swilled counter and take your *oúzo* by the tumbler; no food.

Ileana Tounda Centre of Contemporary Art, Armatólon keh Kléfton 48, Néapoli/Ambelókipi border, *B5*. Combination bar/art gallery; fairly expensive.

Balthazar, Vournázou 14/Tsóha 27, Ambelókipi, off map past *B5*. An "in" brasserie (the bar part's more fun) installed amid the palm-tree gardens and on the ground floor of a palatial old mansion. A long list of cocktails, plus snacks and entrées.

Music and nightlife

Traditional **Greek music** – *rembétika* and *dhimotiká* – can, at its best, provide the city's most compelling night-time entertainment. To partake, however, you really need to visit during the winter months; from around May 15 through to October most clubs and *boîtes* close their doors, while the musicians head off to tour the countryside and islands. Most of what remains open is a tourist travesty of over-amplified and over-priced *bouzouki* noise – at its nadir, not surprisingly, in the Pláka.

As for other forms of live music, there are small, indigenous **jazz** and **rock** scenes, perennially strapped for funds and venues but worth checking out. **Classical** music performances tend to form the core of the summer Athens Festival, but with the recent completion of the city's concert hall out on Vassilísis Sofías there's now a long-running winter season as well. **Discos** and **music bars** are very much in the European mould. The clubs in the city, like the Greek music *boîtes*, tend to close during the summer, unless they have roof terraces. Athenian youth, meanwhile, moves out to a series of huge hangar-like disco-palaces in the coastal suburbs.

For **information** and knowledgeable advice on all kinds of Athens music – traditional, rock and jazz – look in at the **record shops** *Philodisc* Emmanuel Benáki 9, Exárhia; *Melody House*, Mitropóleos 88, Monastiráki; or *Pop 11*, Pindhárou 38/corner Tsakálof, Kolonáki. All of these generally display posters for the more interesting events and have tickets on sale for rock, jazz or festival concerts.

Traditional music

An introduction to Greek **traditional and folk music** is included in *Contexts*. In Athens, the various styles can coexist or be heard on alternate evenings at a number of music clubs or *boîtes*. Most gigs start pretty late – there's little point in arriving much before 10.30pm – and stay open until 3 or 4am. After midnight (and a few drinks) people tend to loosen up and start dancing; at around 1am there's generally an interval, when patrons may move to other clubs down the street or across town. Prices tend to be pretty stiff, with expensive drinks (and sometimes food), plus an admission fee or minimum charge.

Rembétika

For anyone with an interest in folk sounds, **rembétika**, the old drugs-and-outcast music brought over by Asia Minor Greeks, is worth catching live. The form was revived in the early 1980s and, though the fad has waned, there are still good sounds to be heard. If possible, phone to make a reservation and check whether veterans are playing.

EXÁRHIA/PLÁKA/BAZAAR

Taksimi, Isávron 29, off Hariláou Trikoúpi, Exárhia, *C3* (☎36 39 919). Crowded salon on third floor of a neoclassical building; no food, no cover, but reckon on 3000dr for drinks. It's very popular – Babis Goles (*tzoura*/song), one of the last few musicians to live something of a rembetic lifestyle, often plays here. Closed Sun and throughout July and Aug.

Frangosyriani, Arahóvis 57, *C3* (☎36 00 693). The house band features a very good female vocalist and performs mainly 1950s material, with a few earlier standards thrown in. No food but a 1500–2000dr minimum charge, depending on the day of the week. Closed Thurs.

Alexandhriani, Lamáhou 3, off Fillelínon, Pláka, *E3* (☎32 45 358). A long-established club whose 1950s-style band is led by Michalis Yennitsaris on *bouzouki*. No food and no minimum, but reckon on around 3000dr per person. Closed Tues.

Rembétika Stoa Athanaton, Sofokléos 19 (in the old meat market), *D2* (☎32 14 362). A new club fronted by veterans Hondronakos and Koulis Skarpelis (*bouzouki*/song). Good taverna food; 2000dr minimum. Open 3–6pm and midnight–6am. Closed Sun.

Akalipti, Sourí/Filellínon, near Síndagma, *D2* (☎32 33 560). Another place to hear some veterans –Anthouia Alifrangi (song) and Theodoros Polykandriotis (*bouzouki*/song). Minimum charge of 2000dr. Closed Mon.

FURTHER AFIELD

Marabou, Panórmou 113, near Leofóros Alexándhras in Ambelókipi (look for a sign with a toucan), off map. One of the first *rembétika* revival clubs, and still one of the most popular – mobbed at weekends. For four nights of the week the music is taped, other times they feature *laterna* (hurdy-gurdy) by an old man aged 74 who was jailed recently for a knife fight over a woman. Expensive food and drink; no reservations. Open year-round.

To Palio Mas Spiti, Odhemissíou 9, Kessarianí (☎72 14 934), off map. Arguably the best and most genuine of all the surviving clubs – a real neighbourhood place with decent food, reasonable drinks, no minimum charge and no amplification. The part-owner, Girogos Tzortzis, plays *baglama*, alongside a *bouzouki*-ist, guitarist and singer; excellent house band album on sale. Closed Sun.

Kosmiko Kendro Dias, Áyiou Meletióu/Leofóros Iónias 25 (☎83 26 800), off map. Large and pretty expensive venue, whose justification is the chance to see Sotiria Bellou, one of the last living legends of *rembétika*; she usually plays at weekends. It's not cheap – with meals and a 4000dr minimum – but recommended nonetheless. Closed Mon and Tues.

Kendro Daskalakis, Leofóros Marathónos (☎66 77 255). Out of town taverna run by vetaran *bouzouki* star Michalis Daskalakis. Open Wed–Sat.

Dhimotiká (folk) music

There's a real mix of styles at these clubs – everything from Zorba-like Cretan *santoúri* music to wailing clarinet from the mountains of Epirus, from ballroom dancing to tunes from Asia Minor. Venues are scattered throughout the city, and are rather pricier than their *rembétika* equivalents; reservations are advisable.

Ravanastron, Dhimitsánas 60, Ambelókipi (☎64 49 534). A newish club, featuring Greek and Turkish traditional music; Ross Daly (see *Contexts*) sometimes plays here. Closed Thurs, & May–Oct. Limited food menu; entrance fee/2000dr minimum most days.

Elatos, Trítis Septemvríou 16 at Platía Lavríou (☎52 34 262). Assorted *dhimotiká*. Closed Wed.

Kriti, Ayíou Thoma 8, Ambelókipi (☎77 58 258). Cretan music. Closed Mon.

To Armenaki, Patriárhou Ioakím 1/corner Piréos, a long walk or short taxi ride from the Venizélou/Távros metro station (☎34 74 716). Island music, with the classic singer Irini Konitopoulou-Legaki often putting in an appearance. Closed Mon and Tues.

Jazz and Latin

Jazz has a rather small following in Greece, and the main club, *Half-Note,* has moved four times in nearly as many years. The main events take place as part of the **Bic Jazz and Blues Festival** at the end of June; information and tickets are available from the Athens Festival box office (see overpage) and select record stores.

Semi-permanent venues include:

Half-Note, Fthiótidhos 68, Ambelókipi, off map beyond *A/B5* (☎64 49 236). Live jazz most nights but closed Tues and for much of the summer.

Latin, Kallidhromíou 69, Exárhia, *C3* (☎36 45 978). A relatively new (and ground-breaking) venue that mixes salsa, Andean folk and occasionally traditional Greek sounds, according to the night of the week.

The French Quarter, Mavromiháli 78, Exárhia, *C4*. Recorded jazz and blues only. Closed in summer.

Take Five, Patriárhou Ioakím 37, Kolonáki, *D5* (☎72 40 736). Supper club with live bands; reservations suggested. Closed Mon and Thurs.

Rock: live venues and music bars

The tiny indigenous Greek rock scene is beset by difficulties. Instruments are the most expensive in Europe, audiences the smallest, and the whole activity is still looked upon with some official disfavour. Clubs pop up and disappear like mushrooms, though there are a number of semi-permanent music bars, especially in Exárhia (*C3*). Many of these host the occasional gig and generally have a dance floor of sorts.

Kittaro, Ipírou 48, between the train stations and Archaeological Museum, *C2*. Open Thurs–Sun only, with live bands most nights.

Rodhon, Márni 24, Platía Váthis, *C2* (☎52 37 418 or 52 47 427). The city's most important venue for foreign and Greek rock, soul and reggae groups. Good atmosphere in a converted cinema. Closed in summer.

Trito Mati, Zozimádhou 10, Exárhia, *C3*. Good small bar with an eclectic choice of music; drinks cheaper than at other bars in the same area. Closed in summer.

Allothi, Themistokléous 66, Exárhia, *C3*. Up-to-date programme of mainly indie/garage/ punk sounds. Reasonable prices.

Green Door Cafe, Kallidhromíou 52, Exárhia, *C3*. One of the longest-established local bars, with classic 1970s and 80s rock sounds.

Decadence, corner Poulherías/Voulgaroktónou, around the corner from *Strefis Taverna tis Xanthis*, *B4*. Features indie/alternative sounds; fairly expensive drinks.

Loft, corner Ermoú and Asomáton, near Thissío metro, *E1/2*. A reasonably priced club playing House and funk to a trendy crowd.

Stadhio, corner Márkou Moussoúrou/Ardhittoú, Méts, *F4*. A high-tech, fashionable bar – extremely pricey, attracting rich, well-dressed young Greeks. However, there's good music, enjoyably exorbitant cocktails and a terrace open to the stars and to views of the Acropolis.

Wild Rose, Panepistimíou 10, *D3*. House soundtrack for fashion-model types and wealthier students from the northern suburbs.

Faze, Doriléon 10–12, Ambelókipi, *off* map past *C5*. Expensive club playing Acid to an upmarket crowd. Closed Mon and Tues.

Discos

The music bars detailed above are probably the most enjoyable of downtown Athens's disco options. The "real" discos, however, take place way out of town – past the airport in the seaside suburbs of Glifádha (16km from Athens) and Voúla (20km). Athens youth moves out here in force at weekends. If you join them, keep in mind that the taxi ride will be only the first major expense; admission prices, however, usually include a first drink.

Aerodhromio, Pergámou 25, opposite the airport, off map. Hippest of a crop of discos around Voúla – the suburb after Glifádha. The dance floor is open-air, so you can watch the planes passing overhead. Open till 4am.

B-52, Vouliagménis 328, Áyios Dhimítrios, off map. A rival of sorts to the above; open Fri and Sat nights only.

Bitchoulas, Vassíleos Yioryioú 66, off map. One of the smaller discos, playing mainly new wave/rock. Just past the airport on the road to Glifádha.

Barbarella, Singrou 253, Néa Smírna, off map but accessible (getting there, at least) by the #10 trolley. Open year round.

Gay discos and clubs

The gay scene is fairly discreet but Athens has a handful of clubs with an established reputation. For further ideas, check the (brief and not entirely reliable) gay section in the listings magazine *Athinorama*.

Alexandher's, Anagnostopoúlou 44, *D4*. Relaxed, slightly middle-of-the-road gay bar in the Kolonáki district.

Grafitti, Xánthou 9, near Omónia. Predominantly gay disco-bar; the music is somewhat abrasive. Open Thurs–Sun.

Granazi, Lembési 20, near Singroú, *F3/4*. Gay bar close by the transvestite cruising area.

Snob, Anapíron Polémou 10, Kolonáki, behind the Yennadhion Library, *C5*. Cocktail bar with food, catering for lesbians and gay men. Closed Tues.

Festival events

The summer **Athens Festival** has, over the years, come to encompass cultural events in just about every sphere: **ancient Greek theatre** most famously (performed – in modern Greek – at the Herodes Atticus theatre on the south slope of the Acropolis), but also established and contemporary dance, classical music, jazz, traditional Greek music, and even a smattering of rock shows. As well as the **Herodes Atticus theatre**, which is memorable in itself on a warm summer's evening, the festival spreads to the open-air theatre on **Likavitós Hill**, the **Veákio amphitheatre** in Pireás and (with special but expensive bus excursions) to the great ancient **theatre at Epidaurus** (for further details on which, see p.152).

Events are scheduled from early June until mid-September. Programmes of performances are best picked up as soon as you arrive in the city, and for theatre, especially, you'll want to move fast to get tickets. The **festival box office** is in the arcade at Stadhíou 4 (*D4*; ☎32 21 459/32 23 111; Mon–Fri 8.30am–1.30pm and 6–8.30pm); the various theatre box offices are open on the day of performance. Schedules of the main drama and music events are available in advance from EOT offices abroad (though they don't handle tickets). For student discounts, you must buy tickets in advance.

Theatre, dance, classical music and cinema

Unless your Greek is fluent, the contemporary **Greek theatre** scene is likely to be inaccessible. As with Greek music, it is essentially a winter pursuit; in summer, the only theatre tends to be satirical and (to outsiders) totally incomprehensible revues. **Dance**, however, is more accessible and includes a fine traditional Greek show, while **cinema** is un-dubbed – and out of doors in summer.

In addition, in winter months, you might catch **ballet** (and **world music** concerts) at the convenient but acoustically awful *Pallas Theatre*, at Voukourestíou 1, or **opera and classical events** in the recently completed *Hall of the Friends of Music*, out on Leofóros Vassilísis Sofías, next to the US embassy. Also worth looking out for are events at the various **foreign cultural institutes**. Among these are the *Hellenic American Union,* Massalías 22 (*D3*), *British Council,* Platía Kolonáki 17 (*D4*), *French Institute,* Sína 29/Massalías 18 (*D3*), and *Goethe Institute*, Omírou 14–16, (*D3*).

Dora Stratou dance shows

On the **dance** front, one worthwhile "permanent" performance is that performed by the **Dora Stratou Ethnic Dance Company** in their own theatre on Filopáppou hill (*G1*). Gathered on a single stage are traditional music, choreography and costumes you'd be hard put to encounter in many years' travelling around Greece. Performances are held nightly at 10.15pm (with an extra show at 8.15pm on Wed and Sun) from June to September. To reach the theatre, walk up the busy Areopayitou street, along the south flank of the Acropolis, until you see the signs. Tickets (900–1300dr) can almost always be picked up at the door; take your own refreshments.

Cinema

Athens is – surprisingly perhaps – a great place to catch up on movies. There are literally dozens of indoor cinemas in the city, many of them moody relics of the 1920s and 30s, whilst in summer **outdoor** screens spring up all over the place – in parks, abandoned lots, anywhere there's space. Unless they have air conditioning or a roll-back roof, the indoor venues tend to be closed between mid-May and October; all-year cinemas include the *Philip, Amalia* and *Alfaville* (see below).

Admission, whether at indoor or outdoor venues, is reasonable: count on 600dr for outdoor screenings, 900–1000dr for first-run fare at a midtown theatre. Films are always shown in the original langauge with Greek **subtitles** (a good way to increase your vocabulary). For **listings**, the listings magazine *Athinorama*, is the most reliable source of weekly programmes if you can decipher Greek script. Films are divided according to category and geographical location of the cinema. The English-language cinema listings in the *Athens News* are notoriously unreliable.

Among **indoor cinemas**, a cluster showing regular English-language films can be found in three main areas: Patissíon/Kipséli; downtown, on the three main thoroughfares connecting Omónia and Síndagma; and Ambelókipi. **Oldies** and **art films** tend to be shown at the *Asti* on Koraï downtown (*D3*); the *Alfaville*, Mavromiháli 168, (*B4*); the *Aavora*, Ippokrátous 180 (*B4*); the *Alkionis,*Ioulianoú 42, Platía Viktorías (*B2*); and the *Studio*, Stavropoúlou 33, Platía Amerikís, Kipséli (off map). Catch **horror/cult films** at the *Pti-Paleh* (corner Vasilíou Yioryíou Víta/Rizári (*E5*); the *Plaza*, Kifissiás 118, Ambelókipi (off map); the *Philip*, Platía Amerikís/Thássou 11 (off map); the *Amalia*, Dhrossopoúlou 197 (off map); the *Nirvana*, Leofóros Alexándhras 192 (*B5*); and the *Rialto*, Kipsélis 54, Kipséli (off map).

The summer **outdoor screens** are less imaginative in their selections – second-run offerings abound – though to attend simply for the film is to miss much of the point. You may in any case never hear the soundtrack above the din of Greeks cracking *passatémpo* (pumpkin seeds), drinking and conversing. The most central and reliable outdoor venues are *Sine Pari*, Kidathinéon 22, Pláka (*F3*); *Zefiros*, Tróön 36, Áno Petrálona (*G1*); and the nearly adjacent *Vox* and *Riviera* in Exárhia, at Themistokléous 82 and Valtetsíou 46 respectively (*C3*).

Markets and shops

You can buy just about anything in Athens and even on a purely visual level the city's **markets** and **bazaar** areas are worth an hour or two's wandering. Among the markets, don't miss the Athinás food halls, nor, if you're into bargain-sifting through junk, the Sunday morning **flea markets** in Monastiráki, Thissíon and Pireás.

The Markets

The **Athens flea market** spreads over a half-dozen or so blocks around Monastiráki square each Sunday from around 6am until 2.30pm. In parts it is an extension of the tourist trade – the shops in this area are promoted as a "flea market" every day of the week – but there is authentic Greek (and nowadays Soviet refugee-Greek) junk, too, notably along (and off) Iféstou and Pandhróssou streets (*E2/3*). The real McCoy, most noticeable at the Thissío metro station end of Adriánou and the *platía* off Kinéttou near the church of Áyios Fílippos, is just a bag of odds and ends strewn on the ground or on a low table: dive in.

For the more seriously inclined, **Pireás flea market** – at similar times on Sunday mornings – has fewer tourists and more goods. There's business antique trading among the stalls, as well as the more simple commerce of ordinary people offloading ordinary (sometimes extraordinarily ordinary) everyday items. The market is concentrated in a couple of streets just behind the Aktí Possidhónios seafront (see the map on p.120).

In addition, many Athenian **neighbourhoods** have a *laikí agorá* – **street market** – on a set day of the week. Usually running from 7am to 2pm, these are inexpensive and enjoyable, offering household items and dry goods for sale as well as fruit and vegetables. The most centrally located ones are: **Monday**, Hánsen in Patissíon (*A20*); **Tuesday**, Lésvou in Kipséli (off map) and Láskou in Pangráti (off map); **Friday**,

Xenokrátous in Kolonáki (*D5*), Tsámi Karatássou in Veïkoú (*B4*), and Arhimídhous in Méts (*F5*); and **Saturday**, Plakendías in Ambelókipi (one of the largest; off map) and Kallidhromíou in Exárhia (*C3*).

Finally, if you're after live Greek **plants or herbs**, there's a Sunday-morning gathering of stalls on Vikéla street in Patissíon (off map) and plants and flowers on sale daily at the Platía Ayía Iríni near Ermoú (*E2*).

Specialist Shops

Selections below include a range of the most enjoyable shops for souvenir hunting – ranging through craft items, records and tapes, and delicacies – plus a few functional shops for those in search of books and outdoor gear.

Crafts and antiques

Greek handicrafts are not particularly cheap but the workmanship is usually very high. In addition to the shops listed below, consider those at the **National Archaeological Museum**, **Benáki Museum** and **Cycladic Art Museum**, which sell excellent, original designs as well as reproductions; and the cluster of antique shops at the base of **Adhrianoú**, near the corner of Kinnéttou, which are good for Ottoman and rural Greek items like backgammon boards, hubble-bubbles, kilims, etc.

National Welfare Organisation, Ipatías 6, corner Apóllonos, Pláka, *E3*. Rugs, embroideries, copperware – traditional craft products made in remote country districts.

EOMMEKH, Mitropóleos 9, Pláka, *E3*. Officially a showroom and wholesaler of the *Hellenic Organisation of Small and Medium Sized Industries and Handicrafts*, but as such a good first stop to gain an overview of the crafts scene – and they won't say no to a sale.

Kokkinos, Mitropóleos 3, Pláka, *E3*. A central outlet for *flokátes*, those hairy-pile wool rugs that are still the best thing to warm up a cold stone floor.

Toh Anoyi, Sotíros 1, Pláka, *E3*. Eclectic stock of craft items.

Argaliou Brailas, Filellínon 7, *E3*. Woollen and cotton designs – both material by the metre and finished goods.

Stavros Melissinos, Pandhróssou 89, off Monastiráki, *E3*. The "poet-sandalmaker" of Athens – see p.87. The sandals perhaps translate better than the poems but nevertheless an inspiring (and not especially inflated) place to be cobbled.

Les Amis de Livres, Valaorítou 9, in the arcade, *D4*. Prints and engravings.

Athens Design Centre, Valaorítou 4, *D4*. A highly original modern potter has her base here. Prices aren't exorbitant considering this is one of the world's best.

Lalaounis, Panepistimíou 6, *D3*. Home base outlet of the world-renowned family of goldsmiths, whose designs are superbly imaginative.

Mati, Voukourestíou 20, *D4*. A small shop that specialises in blue beads to ward off the Evil Eye (*toh mati*), plus blue church lamps, candlesticks and other oddments.

Skyros, corner Makriyánni/Hadzihrístou, Veïkoú, *F3*. Traditional, if not very portable, Greek village furniture (particularly from Skíros), and more practical cushions, lamps, etc.

Records and tapes

If you hear music you like, or want to explore Greek sounds of bygone days (or the present), refer to the discography in *Contexts* and then try the outlets below. When shopping, beware of records warped by poor stacking in the racks. The big advantage of shopping here is that the vinyl industry is still alive and well, not having been totally swamped by CDs; thus you may find pressings discontinued elsewhere.

Xilouris, Panepistimiou 39, in the arcade, *D3*. Run by the widow of the late, great Cretan singer Nikos Xilouris, this is currently the best place for Greek island folk and (of course) Cretan music.

Jazz Rock, Akadhimías 45, *D3*. Specialises in just that, and also a good source of information and tickets for upcoming concerts.

Neodisk, Panepistimíou 25, in the arcade, *D3*. A good shop for classical and more arcane types of world music.

Musiki Gonia, corner Panepistimíou/Ippokrátous, *D3*. The Athenian equivalent of *Tower Records*, with a good range of traditional Greek music, plus rock and jazz.

Mantzourani, Iféstou 41, *E2*. Small corner shop run by two friendly brothers that's excellent for *rembétika*, new Greek art music and *dhimotiká*.

Pop 11, Pindhárou 38/corner Tsakálof, Kolonáki, *D4*. Formerly the best shop in the city, this has deteriorated alarmingly of late, with depleted stocks in all categories.

Books

Compendium, Níkis 28 (upstairs), off Síndagma, *E3*. Friendliest and best value of the English-language bookstores, featuring Penguins, Picadors, *Rough Guides* and other paperbacks, plus a small secondhand section.

Eleftheroudhakis, Níkis 4, *E3*. Probably the best source of books about Greece – in English and Greek – and an extensive general English-language stock, too.

Reymondos, Voukourestíou 18, *E4*. Good for foreign periodicals in particular.

I Folia tou Vivliou, Panepistimíou 25, *D4*, in the arcade and upstairs. The city's biggest selection of English-language fiction; also stocks back issues of the *Korfes* hiking magazine.

Estia-Kollarou, Sólonos 60, *D3*. Big Greek-language bookshop, strong on modern history, politics, folk traditions, fiction, etc.

Vassiotis, Iféstou 24, Monastiráki, *E2*. Huge basement secondhand bookshop with an arrangement that looks like a bomb has just hit.

Sweets and cakes

Greeks devote special shops or stalls to *ksíri kárpi* (dried fruits and nuts) as well as to more decadent sweets.

Floca, Leofóros Kifisías 118, Ambelókipi (off map), corner Panepistimíou/Voukourestíou (in the arcade), *D3*, and just south of junction Veïkoú/Dhimitrakopoúlou, Veïkoú, *F3*. Two branches of the oldest-established Athenian café-pâtisserie.

Aristokratiko, Kolonáki square, *D4* Mountains of chocolates and *loukoúmia* (Turkish delight), sold by weight.

La Chocolatière, Skoufá/corner Dhimokrítou, Kolonáki, *D4*. Exquisite chocolates and cakes. Come for a present if you're invited to a Greek's nameday, or simply to indulge.

Fruit and nuts shop, corner Likavitoú/Alex. Soútsou, Kolonáki, *D4*. A nameless shop – but renowned for its roasted pistachios, almonds, walnuts and *oúzo*.

Health and speciality food

Herbs and herb teas are sold dry and fresh at most street markets and at the Athinás bazaar. Otherwise, the following central outlets are useful.

To Stakhi, Mikás Asías 61–63, Ambelókipi (off map). A new store with wide-ranging stock.

Katerina Pasali, Evripídhou 20, Central Bazaar, *D2*. Good for supplements, vitamins, etc.

Aralus, Sofokléous 17, Central Bazaar, *D2*. Fruits, nuts, wholegrain bread, pasta, etc, lightly wrapped in a manner suitable for trekking.

AB Vassilopoulos Leofóros Kifissías, Psihikó (off map). A gigantic supermarket stocking esoteric ingredients for just about every cuisine or diet – at a price.

Camping, hiking, biking and diving supplies

Army & Navy, Kinettoú 4, on Ayíou Filíppou square, *E2*. Large central store good for ponchos, stoves, mess kits, etc.

Alpamayo, Panepistimíou 44, *D3*. Well-balanced, small hiking' store which also stocks some *Korfes* back issues (see also "Books", above).

Pindhos, Leofóros Alexándhras 4, across from the *Attica KTEL* bus stop on Mavromatéon, *B3*. State-of-the-art hiking/climbing gear: Lowe packs, ice axes, skis, foam pads, etc. There is also a branch at Asklipíou 26 in Neápoli, *C4*.

Adventure, Voukourestíou 11, *D3*. Rather high-tech mountaineering gear.

Kataskinotis, Ayías Triádhos 18, Néa Filadhélfia (off map; take a #18 trolley or the metro). Big barn of a place claiming to be Athens's biggest outdoor activity store.

Iféstou street, off Monastiráki square, *E2*. Numerous stalls along Iféstou sell used, military surplus and off-brand canteens, boots, jungle gear, sleeping bags, duffels, etc.

No-Name Bike Shop, Trítis Septemvríou 40/corner Stournára, C2; **Alberto's**, Patissíon 37 (in the arcade, *B2*); plus many others on same street heading towards Omónia. This is in effect the "bike bazaar", for repairs, parts and sales. For mountain bikes, try **Gatsoulis** at Thessaloníkis 8 in Néa Filadhélfia (off map; #18 trolley bus).

Aegean Dive Shop, Pandhóras 31, Glifádha – on the coast to the southeast. As it says.

Listings

Airlines Almost all the following – Singroú and Eólou addresses apart – are within 100m or so of Síndagma: *Olympic,* ticket office at Óthonos 6, on Síndagma, *E4*; ☎92 92 555, international; ☎92 92 444, domestic; main office at Singroú 96, *G3*; ☎92 92 251; *Alitalia*, Níkis 10, *E3*; ☎32 29 414; *Balkan*, Níkis 23, *E3*; ☎32 26 684; *British Airways*, Óthonos 10, *E4*; ☎32 50 601; *ČSA*, Panepistimíou 15, *D3*; ☎32 32 303; *Dan-Air*, Singroú 206b, *G3*; *Delta*, Óthonos 4, *E4*; ☎32 35 242; *Egyptair*, Óthonos 10, *E3*; ☎32 38 907; *El Al*, Óthonos 8, *E4*; ☎32 30 116; *Kenya Airways*, Stadhíou 5, *D3*; ☎32 47 000; *KLM*, Karayióryi Servías 2, *E3*; ☎32 51 311; *Malev*, Panepistimíou 15, *D3*; ☎32 41 116; *Qantas*, Eólou 104, *D2*; ☎32 39 063; *Sabena*, Óthonos 8, *E4*; ☎32 36 821; *SAS*, Sína 6, *D3*; ☎36 34 444; *Singapore Airlines*, Xenofóndos 8, *E4*; ☎32 39 111; *South African Airways*, Vassilísis Sofías 11, *D/E4*; ☎36 16 305; *Turkish Airlines*, Filellínon 19, *E4*; ☎32 22 569; *TWA*, Xenofóndos 8, *E4*; ☎32 26 451.

Airport enquiries ☎98 11 201 for *Olympic* flight enquiries; ☎96 99 466 for all other carriers.

American Express Poste restante and money changing at the main branch at Ermoú 2 (1st floor), on the corner of Síndagma (*E3*). Mail desk open in summer Mon–Fri 8.30am–7.30pm, Sat 8.30am–1.30pm; shorter weekday hours in winter. Banking facilities open Mon–Thurs 8.30am–2pm, Fri 8.30am–1.30pm, Sat 8.30am–12.30pm.

Banks The *National Bank of Greece* in Síndagma (*E3*) stays open for **exchange** Mon–Fri 8 am–8pm, Sat & Sun. 8am–2pm, as does the nearby, less crowded *Yeniki Trapeza/General Bank* on the corner of Ermoú and Síndagma. **Foreign banks**, keeping normal hours of Mon–Thurs 8am–2pm, Fri 8am–1.30pm, include *Barclays*, Voukourestíou 15, off Panepistimíou, *D4* (☎36 44 311); *Citibank*, Óthonos 8, *E4* (☎32 27 471); *Midland Bank*, Sekéri 1a, Kolonáki, *D5* (☎36 47 410); and *National Westminster*, Stadhíou 24, *D3* (☎32 50 924). *Royal Bank of Scotland* have a branch in Pireás at Aktí Miaoúli 61 (☎45 27 483).

Buses For information on buses out of Athens (and the respective terminals), see "Travel Details" at the end of this chapter.

Camera repair Most central at *Pikopoulos*, Lékka 26 (off Ermoú, *E3*), 3rd floor. All makes; remove easily lost accessories and get an estimate.

Car rental A number of companies are to be found along Leofóros Singroú (*F3*), including *InterRent/EuropCar* (at no. 4), *Thrifty* (no. 24), *Just* (no. 43) and *Autorent* (no. 118); the latter three give student discounts. *Ansa* at no. 33 gets good reports from users.

Car repairs, tyres, and assistance Good for VW van repair is *Stamatis Papageorgiou*, Leof. Singroú 216 (off map). Other (reputably) reliable garages include: *Mavtis*, Leof. Singroú 8, *F3* (Citroens); *Leonidas Fragos*, Mínos 21, Kinosárgous, off Leof. Vougliaménis 104 on the way to the airport, off map (Fiats and Simcas). Mechanics and spares shops for virtually any make are scattered around the Kinosárgous and Néos Kósmos districts, mostly along and between Kallíróis and Vouliagménis. If they don't have the part, or the know-how, they'll refer you to someone who does, further out towards the airport. Tyre shops are grouped between Trítis Septemvríou 60–80 (north of Omónia, *B2*). **ELPA** – the Greek automobile association – gives free **help and information** to foreign motorists at Leof. Mesoyíon 2 (northeast of Likavitós, off map) and at the Athens Tower in Ambelókipi. For **Emergency Assistance** ☎104 (free, though you'll pay for any parts).

Dentists Free treatment at the Evangelismos Hospital, Ipsilándou 45, Kolonáki, *D5* and at the Pireás Dentistry School (*Odhondoiatrikó Skolío*), corner Thivón/Livadhías. For private treatment, check the ads in the *Athens News* or ask your embassy for addresses.

Embassies/Consulates include: *Australia*, Dhimitríou Soútsou 37, 15, *B5* (☎64 47 303); *Britain*, Ploutárhou 1, Kolonáki, *D5* (☎72 36 211); *Canada*, Ioánnou Yennadhíou 4, *D5* (☎72 39 511); *Denmark*, Vassilísis Sofías 11, *D5* (☎36 08 315); *Ireland*, Vass. Konstantínou 7, *E5* (☎72 32 771); *Netherlands*, Vassiléos Konstantínou 5–7, *E5* (☎72 39 701); *Norway*, Vassiléos Konstantínou 7, *E5* (☎72 46 173); *Sweden*, Vassiléos Konstantínou 7, *E5* (☎72 90 421); *USA*, Vassilísis Sofías 91, off map (☎72 12 951). The *New Zealand* embassy has closed and citizens should apply to the British embassy for assistance.

Useful **consulate visa sections** include: *Bulgaria*, Stratigoú Kallári 33a, Paleó Psihikó, off map (Mon–Fri 10am–noon); *Egypt*, Zalakósta 1, *D4* (Mon–Fri 9am–noon); *Hungary*, Kalvoú 16, Paleó Psihikó, off map (Mon–Fri 9am–noon); *India*, Kleánthous 3, *E5* (Mon–Fri 9am–noon); *Kenya*, visa granted by British embassy; *Pakistan*, Loukianoú 6, *D5* (Mon–Thurs 9–11am); *Romania*, Emmanuel Benáki 7, Paleó Psihikó, off map (Mon–Fri 10am–noon); *Sri Lanka*, visa granted by British embassy; *Sudan*, Ayías Sofías 5, Néo Psihikó, off map (Mon–Thurs 10am–noon); *Thailand*, Taïyettou 23, Paleó Psihikó, off map (Mon–Fri 9am–2pm); *Yemen*, Patissíon 9, *C2* (Mon–Fri 8am–4pm); *"Yugoslavia"/Serbia*, Évrou 25, off map (Mon–Fri 9–11.30am).

Note: Unless you are resident in Greece, it may take four weeks or more to obtain an Indian visa; if you need one, it's easier to fly to Nepal or Sri Lanka and obtain it there.

Emergencies Dial the tourist police (☎171; 24hr) for medical or other assistance. In case of a **medical emergency**, if you can travel safely don't wait for an ambulance. Get a taxi straight to the hospital address that the Tourist Police give you. If your Greek is up to it, ☎166 summons an ambulance, ☎105 gets you a rota of night-duty doctors, and ☎106 ascertains the best hospital for you to head for.

Environment *Greenpeace* recently opened an Athens office at Kallidhromíou 44, Exárhia (☎36 40 774). Stop by if you want information, or are staying long-term in Greece and would like to participate in volunteer work and campaigns.

Ferry departure ☎143 gets you an information hotline (in Greek).

Football The Athens team *Panathinaikós*, owned by the shipping magnate Yiorgos Vardinoyannis, is Greece's wealthiest and as a rule most successful club. Catch them at the 25,000-capacity stadium on Leof. Alexándhras (*B5*). Their traditional rival, *Olympiakós* of Pireás (owned until recently by Koskotas, the man at the centre of the Bank of Crete scandal) plays at the Karaïskáki stadium (by the Néo Fáliro metro stop; see the Pireás map on p.120). Also worth looking out for are *AEK*, which has had some recent European success. Football being an obsession in Greece (there are daily sports papers), matches are not hard to discover: just ask at a kiosk or bar.

Gay groups The *Autonomous Group of Gay Women* meet weekly at *The Women's House* (see "Women's movement", below). *AMFI*, the (predominantly male) *Greek Gay Liberation Movement*, has an office at Zalóngou 6 (Mon–Fri 6–11pm).

Greek language courses Try the *Hellenic American Union*, Massalías 22, *D4*; the *Ionic Centre*, Lissíou 4, Pláka, *D4*; the *Athens Centre*, Arhimídhous 48, Pangráti, *F5*; the *Hellenic Language School*, Zalóngou 4, *D4*; or the *XEN* (YWCA), Amerikís 11, *D3*.

Hiking The *EOS* (Hellenic Alpine Club) headquarters is in gorgeous new premises at Milióni 5, Kolonáki *D4*, though they have just a few glossy handouts, mostly in Greek, available. *Trekking Hellas*, Filellínon 7, *E3*, arrange hiking tours throughout Greece.

Hospital clinics For minor injuries the *Hellenic Red Cross*, Trítis Septemvríou/ Kapodhistríou, (*C2*) is fairly good; *The Woman's House* (see below) has addresses of English-speaking gynaecologists. For **inoculations**, try the *Vaccination Centre*, Leofóros Alexándhras 196/corner Vassilísis Sofías, Ambelókipi (off map; open Mon–Fri 8am–noon), where most jabs are free; phone ☎64 27 846 for details.

Laundry Numerous dry/wet cleaners will do your laundry for you, or there are coin-ops at Angélou Yerónda 10, off Platía Fillimoussís Eterías (aka "Platía Plákas", *F3*), at Dhidhótou 46, Exárhia (*C3*) and at Veïkoú 107 (below Platía Koukakíou, off map beyond *G2*).

Lost property The transport police have a lost property office (*Grafío Haménon Andikiménon*) at Ayíou Konstantínou 33, *D2* (☎52 30 111).

Luggage storage Best arranged with your hotel; many places will keep the bulk of your luggage for free or a nominal amount while you head off to the islands. *Pacific Ltd*, Níkis 24 (*E3*) stores luggage for 1800dr per item per month, 600dr per week.

Mount Athos permits See p.335 for details if you're planning a trip to Athos. In Athens, the Ministry of Foreign Affairs, Zalakósta 2, off the beginning of Vassilísis Sofías, *E4* is the first stop in securing a permit; office hours are Mon, Wed & Fri 11am–2pm (Rm 73, 3rd floor).

Opticians Quick repairs at *Paraskevopoulos* in the arcade between Voukourestíou and Kriezótou, by the parcel post office (*D3*). For **contact lenses** try *Bakhtiaroglou-Kondaridhes*, in the arcade, and *Gesoura*, on the street front at Panepistimíou 39.

Parcel post To send home personal effects, use the post office in the arcade between Voukourestíou and Kriezótou (Mon–Fri 7.30am–2.30pm). Paper and string are supplied – *you* bring box and tape. "Surface/air lift" will get parcels home to North America or Europe in two weeks. For souvenirs, a branch at Níkis 37 (*E3*) expedites shipments and minimises duty/declaration problems.

Pharmacies (*farmakía*) The *Marinopoulos* branches (in Patissíon and Panepistimíou streets, *C2/D3*) are particularly good and also sell homeopathic remedies, as does (supposedly) any establishment with a green cross outside. ☎107 for after-hours pharmacies.

Phones You can phone locally from a *perίptero* (kiosk), where you pay afterwards. Blue-topped booths may be quieter but require exact change. International calls can be made from orange-topped phone-kiosks or at the central OTE offices at Stadhíou 15 (*D3*) and Patissíon/ Ikosioktó Oktovríou 85 (*B2*), the latter open 24 hours a day.

Police Dialling ☎100 gets the flying squad; for thefts, etc, contact the **Tourist Police** at Leofóros Singroú 7 (behind the Temple of Olympian Zeus; ☎171).

Post offices (*Tahidhromío*) For ordinary letters and parcels up to 2 Kg, the branch on Síndagma (corner Mitropóleos, *E3*) is open Mon–Fri 7.30am–8pm, Sat 8am–3pm, Sun 9am–1.30pm.

Poste restante Main post office for Athens is at Eólou 100, just off Omónia, *D2* (Mon–Fri 7.30am–8pm, Sat 7.30am–2pm).

Swimming pools There are no public pools at all, though the *Hilton* permits non-guests to use their pool for a 1500dr fee.

Travel agencies Most budget and youth/student agencies are to be found just off Síndagma, in and around Filellínon and Níkis streets. The cheapest ferry tickets to Italy are usually sold through *USIT*, Filellínon 1 (☎32 41 884), or *Transalpino* (Níkis 28), still trading despite the demise of its namesake. Among other agencies, *Highway Express*, Níkis 42, *Periscope*, Filellínon 22, *Himalaya*, Filellínon 7 and *Arcturus* , Apóllonos 20 are worth scanning for air travel deals. For the hardy, the widest range of north-bound coaches is still available at *Magic Bus* , Filellínon 20. All these addresses are *E3/F3*.

Women's movement Most accessible of the women's groups is the *Multinational Liberation Group of Athens* (☎86 70 523); like most other women's organisations, they meet at *The Women's House*, Románou Melódhou 4, Likavitós, *C3* (☎28 14 823).

Work/residence permits/visa extensions at the Aliens' Bureau (*Ipiresía Allodhapón*), Halkokondhíli 9, Platía Káningos, *C3*; open Mon–Fri 8am–1pm but go early or you won't get seen. Also, come armed with small notes for revenue stamps, wads of passport photos, pink personalised bank receipts, and plenty of patience.

AROUND ATHENS: ATTICA

Attica (*Attikí*), the region encompassing the capital, is not much explored by tourists. Only the great romantic ruin of the **Temple of Apollo at Sounion** is on the excursion circuit. The rest, if seen at all, tends to be for the functional reason of escaping to the islands – from the ports of **Pireás**, **Rafína** (whose ferry journeys can be quicker and cheaper to many of the Cyclades), or **Lávrio** (which serves Kéa and Kíthnos).

The neglect is not surprising. The mountains of **Imittós**, **Pendéli** and **Párnitha**, which surround Athens on three sides, are progressively less successful in confining the urban sprawl, and the routes out of the city to the south and west are unenticing to say the least. But if you're planning on a reasonable stay in the capital, a day trip or two, or a brief circuit by car, can make a rewarding break, with much of Greece in microcosm to be seen within an hour or two's ride: mountainside at **Párnitha**, minor archaeological sites in **Brauron** and **Rhamnous**, and the odd unspoiled beach, too.

Pireás (Piraeus)

PIREÁS has been the port of Athens since Classical times. Today it is a substantial metropolis in its own right, containing much of Greater Athens's industry, as well as the various commercial activities associated with a port: banking, import-export, freight, and so on. For most visitors, though, it is Pireás's inter-island ferries that provide the reason for coming.

Getting to Pireás

The easiest way to get to Pireás from Athens is on the **metro**. There are central stops in Athens at Omónia and Monastiráki squares, plus Thissío for those in Veïkou, and Petrálona for those in Koukáki; the journey takes about 25 minutes from Omónia to the Pireás train station stop (the end of the line). Metro trains run from 6am, early enough to catch the first ferries, to midnight, long after the arrival of all but the most delayed boats. Tickets cost 75dr a journey; 100dr if you come from north of Omónia square.

Alternatives are to go by bus or taxi. **Green bus #041** (about every 20min during the day; hourly from 1am to 5am) will deposit you on Vassiléos Konstandínou, half a dozen blocks from the docks, but it's very slow – allow nearly an hour from Síndagma, the most obvious boarding point. The **express buses** (see p.65) are quicker and a particularly useful link with the airport. **Taxis** cost about 1000dr at day tariff from the centre of Athens or the airport – worth considering, especially if you're taking one of the hydrofoils from the Flísvos or Zéa marinas, which are a fair walk from the metro.

The port and city

The port at Pireás was founded at the beginning of the fifth century BC by **Themistocles**, who realised the potential of its three natural harbours. His work was consolidated by Pericles with the building of the **"Long Walls"** to protect the corridor to Athens, and it remained active under Roman and Macedonian rulers. Subsequently, under Turkish rule, the place was deserted – incredibly, there was just one building there, a monastery, by the end of the War of Independence.

From the 1830s on, though, Pireás grew by leaps and bounds. The original influx into the port was a group of immigrants from Híos, whose island had been devastated by the Turks; later came populations from Ídhra, Crete and the Peloponnese. By World War I, Pireás had outstripped the island of Síros as the nation's first port, its strategic position enhanced by the opening of the Suez and Corinth canals – in 1862 and 1893 respectively. Like Athens, the city's great period of growth began in 1923, with the exchange of populations with Turkey. Over 100,000 Asia Minor Greeks decided to settle in Pireás, doubling the population almost overnight – and giving a boost to an already existing semi-underworld culture, whose enduring legacy was *rembétika*, outcasts' music played in hashish dens along the waterside.

The City

The city these days is not much different from Athens – indeed there is little to distinguish it as you approach, with its scruffy web of suburbs merging into those of the capital. Economically, it is at present on a mild upswing, boosted by a couple of go-ahead mayors and the prominence of its local MP, former actress and Minister of Culture, Melina Mercouri. It is, however, an unashamedly functional place, with its port despatching up to sixty ships a day in season, both to the islands and to a range of international destinations. There are few sights, beyond the numbers and diversity of the sailors in the harbour. The ancient walls are long gone, and the junta years saw misguided demolition of most later buildings of character.

On the plus side, there's a nice enough **park** (three blocks back from the main harbour, intersected by Vassiléos Konstandínou); a scattering of genuine antique/junk shops, full of peasant copper and wood, plus a big **Sunday morning flea market**, near Platía Ipodhamías, at the top end of Goúnari (behind the railway station); and a couple of more than respectable museums.

The Archaeological and Naval museums

The **Archaeological Museum** (Hariláou Trikoúpi 31, Tues–Sun 8.30am–3pm; 400dr) is the best time-filler in Pireás, and enthusiasts will certainly want to make a special trip out here. Its exhibits include, most notably, a *kouros* (idealised statue) dedicated to Apollo, which was dragged out of the sea in 1959. Dating from 520 BC, this is the earliest known life-size bronze, and makes a good trio with two other, fifth-century bronzes of Artemis and Athena found in the same manner at about the same time; it is displayed on the upper floor.

On the ground floor are more submarine finds, this time second-century AD stone reliefs of battles between Greeks and Amazons, apparently made for export to Rome. The sea's effect on them was far more corrosive than in the case of the bronzes, but you can still tell that some scenes are duplicated – showing that the ancients weren't above a bit of mass artistic production.

A few blocks away, the **Naval Museum** (Tues–Sat 8.30am–1pm; 100dr) is more specialist, tracing developments with models and the odd ancient piece.

The Ferries

If you're staying in Athens prior to heading out to the islands, it's worth calling in at the EOT office in Síndagma to pick up a **schedule of departures** from Pireás. These are never to be relied upon implicitly, but they do give a reasonable indication of what boats are leaving when and for where; note that the Argo-Saronic sailings are omitted.

The majority of the boats – for Lésvos, Sámos, Ikaría, the Peloponnesian coast and the most popular Cyclades – leave between 6.30 and 9am. There is then another burst of activity between noon and 3pm towards the Cyclades and Dodecanese, and a final battery of sailings from 4 to 10pm (sometimes later), bound for a wide variety of ports, but especially Crete and the western Cyclades. The frequency of sailings is such that, in high season at least, you need never spend the night in Athens or Pireás.

Buying tickets is not necessary until you arrive at Pireás, unless you want a cabin berth or are taking a car on board (in which case consult agents in Athens or Pireás). In general, the best plan is to get to Pireás early, say at 6.30am, and check with the various **shipping agents** around the metro station and along the quayside Platía

Karaïskáki. Keep in mind that many of these act only for particular lines, so for a full picture of the various boats sailing you will need to ask at three or four outlets. Prices for all domestic boat journeys are standard but the quality of the craft and circuitousness of routes vary greatly. If you are heading for Thíra (Santorini) or Rhodes, for example, try to get a boat that stops at only three or four islands en route; for Crete settle for direct ferries only.

Boats for different destinations leave from a variety of points along the main harbour, usually following the pattern in the box opposite, though it's wise to leave time for wayward ships and look for the signs (indicating name of boat and a clockface with departure time) hung in front of the relevant boats on the waterside railings or on the stern of the boats themselves. The ticket agent should know the whereabouts of the boat on the particular day.

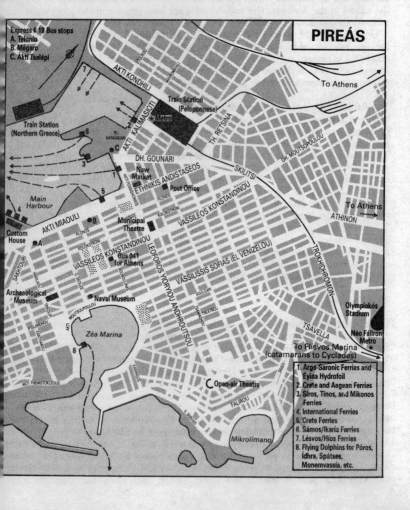

PIREÁS

Express # 19 Bus stops
A. Teloniо
B. Mégaro
C. Ákti Tselépi

1. Argo-Saronic Ferries and Éyina Hydrofoil
2. Crete and Aegean Ferries
3. Síros, Tínos, and Míkonos Ferries
4. International Ferries
5. Crete Ferries
6. Sámos/Ikaría Ferries
7. Lésvos/Híos Ferries
8. Flying Dolphins for Póros, Ídhra, Spátses, Monemvassia, etc.

FERRY DEPARTURE POINTS

Aegean islands (Cyclades/Dodecanese)
These leave from either Aktí Kalimasióti, the quay right in front of the metro station (#2 on the map), or from Aktí Kondhíli (#7, perpendicular to Possidhónios). The big boats going to the major Dodecanese only usually share point (#5) with some of the Cretan ferries.

Crete
Some ferries dock at Aktí Possidhónios (#2) but most use the promontory by Aktí Miaoúli (#5), or even (#7) near the east Aegean departures.

Síros, Tínos, Míkonos
The morning departures, at least, tend to go from (#3), near the Éyina hydrofoils.

Sámos/Ikaría
Boats ending up at these islands use the far end of the dock beyond Platía Karaïskáki (#6).

Híos/Lésvos
The evening services tend to use the far end of Aktí Kondhíli (#7).

Argo-Saronic
Ordinary ferries leave from Aktí Possidhónios (#1), a ten-minute walk from the metro.

International destinations (Limassol, Haifa, Izmir, etc)
These leave farther around the main harbour (#4), towards the Customs House (where you should check passports before boarding).

Hydrofoils
Except for departures direct to Éyina, which leave from Altí Tselepi (#8), hydrofoils for **Argo-Saronic and Peloponnesian** destinations leave from the **Zéa marina** (#9), a twenty-minute uphill walk from the metro.
Tickets are on sale from the *Flying Dolphins* office at the quay from about an hour before departure. To be sure of a particular sailing in season, it is wise to book ahead in Athens. Equally, if your schedule is tight, book your seat back to Pireás when you arrive.

Catamarans
The catamaran, serving the central **Cyclades**, leaves from Flisvos (Troacadero) marina, 8km east of Pireás and best reached by taxi.

Pireás practicalities

Few visitors **stay** in Pireás, and most of the port's **hotels** are geared to a steady clientele of seamen, resting between ships. For this reason, picking a place at random is not always a good idea. A trio of places close by the main harbour, and used to tourists, are the *Hotel Aenos*, Ethnikís Antistaséos 14 (☎41 74 879; ②), the *Hotel Santorini*, Trikoúpi 6 (☎45 521 47; ③), and the *Hotel Acropole*, Goúnari 7 (☎41 73 313; ③), the last of which has a sporadically functioning bar and sunroof. If you have a bit more money to spend, consider the *Hotel Park* (☎45 24 611; ④), a couple of blocks back from the port at Kolokotróni 103, or – at the luxury end of the scale – the very pleasant *Cavo d'Oro* (☎41 13 742; ⑤), overlooking the Mikrolímano yacht harbour.

Sleeping rough in Platía Karaïskáki, as some exhausted travellers attempt to do, is unwise. If thieves or the police don't rouse you, street-cleaners armed with hoses certainly will – at 5am.

Entertainment, restaurants and nightlife

Culturally, there's not a great deal going on at Pireás, though a **summer festival**, run alongside that of Athens, features events in the open-air theatre back from the yacht harbour of Mikrolímano (or Tourkolímano, as it has been called for centuries). In winter there's always **football**: *Olympiakós* are the port's big team, rivals to the capital's *AEK* and *Panathenaïkós*.

Perhaps the most fulfilling pursuit, if you have time to kill, is to check out some of the port's **eating options**. If you're simply looking for food to take on board, or breakfast, you'll find numerous places (as well as several budget restaurants) around the market area, back from the waterside Aktí Miaoúli/Ethnikís Andistáseos, open from 6.30am.

For more substantial meals, there are a string of *ouzerí* and seafood tavernas along Aktí Themistokléous, west of the Zéa marina, most of them pretty good and regularly priced. Alternatively, for a real blowout, try *Vassilenas* at Etolikoú 72 (the street running inland from Aktí Kondhíli). Housed in an old grocery store, its set menu provides *mezédhes* enough to defy all appetites; at 2500dr a head, drinks extra, it's not cheap, but enough Athenians consider it worth the drive out that most evenings you need to book ahead for a table (☎46 12 457). Still more upmarket, but serving excellent seafood, are the line of tavernas around **Mikrolímano** – a nice stroll over the hill.

Finally, a word for the ports best **rembétika venue** (see p.108), the *Café Aman Ontas tis Konstandinas* at Koundouriótou 109 on the corner of Karoli Dhimitríou (☎42 20 459; closed Sun). This is a very friendly taverna, with *rembétika* music each night and a special Smyrna (Asia Minor) show every Tuesday. On Friday and Saturday nights there's a minimum charge of 3500dr per person.

The "Apollo Coast", Cape Sounion and Lávrio

The seventy kilometres of coast south of Athens – the tourist-board-dubbed **"Apollo Coast"** – has some good but highly developed beaches. At weekends, when Athenians flee the city, the sands fill fast, as, by night, do the innumerable bars, restaurants and discos. If this is what you're after, then resorts like **Glifádha** and **Vouliagméni** are functional enough. But for most foreign visitors, the coast's lure is at the end of the road, in the form of the Temple of Poseidon at **Cape Sounion**.

Access to Sounion (Soúnio in the modern spelling) is straightforward. There are buses on the hour and half-hour from the *KTEL* terminal ("B" on the Athens map; *B2*) on Mavromatéon at the southwest corner of Áreos Park; there's also a more central (but in summer, very full) stop ten minutes later at point "D" on Filellínon street, south of Síndagma (corner of Xenofóndos, in front of the *Middle East Airways* office). There are both coastal (*paraliakó*) and inland (*mesoyiakó*) services, the latter slightly longer and more expensive. The coast route normally takes around two hours; last departures back to Athens are posted at the Sounion stop.

For **Glifádha/Voúla** and **Vouliagméni/Várki** – the main resorts – there are additional, more regular, city buses from the Záppion gardens (stop "C" on the Athens map; *F4*). Most frequent are #115, #116 and #117.

The resorts: Glifádha to Sounion

Although some Greeks swim at Pireás itself, few would recommend the sea much before **GLIFÁDHA**, half an hour's drive southeast from the city centre. The major resort along the "Apollo Coast", merged almost indistinguishably with its neighbour **VOÚLA**, this is lined with seafood restaurants, ice-cream bars and discos, as well as a couple of marinas and a golf course. Its popularity, though, is hard to fathom, built as it is in the shadow of the airport. The only possible appeal is in the beaches, the best of which is the Astir, privately owned and with a stiff admission charge; others are gritty. Hotels are all on the expensive side, and in any case permanently occupied in season by package firms; there is a **campsite** at Voúla (☎01/89 52 712).

VOULIAGMÉNI, which in turn has swallowed up **KAVOÚRI**, is a little quieter than Glifádha, and a little ritzier. Set back from a small natural lake, it boasts a waterski school, some extremely chi-chi restaurants, and an EOT pay-beach. Again, budget accommodation is hard to come by, though there is a **campsite** (☎01/89 73 613)– and another EOT pay-beach– just to the south at **VÁRKIZA**.(☎01/89 73 613).

South from Várkiza, there are further beaches en route to Sounion, though unless you've a car to pick your spot they're not really worth the effort. The resorts of **LAGONÍSSI** and **ANÁVISSOS** are in the Glifádha mould, and only slightly less crowded, despite the extra distance from Athens.

Cape Sounion

Site open Mon-Sat 9am until sunset, Sun from 10am; admission 600dr.

Cape Sounion – Akrí Soúnio – is one of the most imposing spots in Greece, for centuries a landmark for boats sailing between Pireás and the islands, and an equally dramatic vantage point in itself to look out over the Aegean. On its tip stands the fifth-century BC **Temple of Poseidon**, built in the time of Pericles as part of a major sanctuary to the sea god.

The Temple of Poseidon

The temple's fame is due above all to **Byron**, who visited in 1810, carved his name on the nearest pillar (an unfortunate precedent), and commemorated the event as the finale of his hymn to Greek independence, the "Isles of Greece" segment of *Don Juan*:

> *Place me on Sunium's marbled steep,*
> *Where nothing, save the waves and I,*
> *May hear our mutual murmurs sweep;*
> *There, swan like, let me sing and die:*
> *A land of slaves shall ne'er be mine –*
> *Dash down yon cup of Samian wine!*

In summer, at least, there is faint hope of solitude, unless you slip into the site before the tour groups arrive. But the temple is as evocative a ruin as Greece can offer. Doric in style, it was probably built by the architect of the Thiseion in the Athens agora. That it is so admired and visited, in contrast to that Athens temple, owes to its site, but also perhaps to its picturesque state of ruin – preserving, as if by design, sixteen of its thirty-four columns. The view from the temple takes in the islands of Kéa, Kíthnos and Sérifos to the southeast, Éyina and the Peloponnese to the west.

The rest of the site is of more academic interest. There are remains of a fortification wall around the sanctuary; a **Propylaion** (entrance hall) and **Stoa**; and, to the north, the foundations of a small **Temple of Athena**.

Beaches – and staying at Sounion

Below the promontory are several **coves** – the most sheltered a five-minute walk east from the car park and site entrance. The main Soúnio beach is more crowded, but has a group of tavernas at the far end – pretty reasonably priced, considering the location.

If you want to stay, there are a couple of **campsites** just around the coast: *Camping Bacchus* (the nearest; ☎0292/39 262) and *Sounion Beach Camping* (5km; ☎0292/39 358). Alternatively, for the more affluent, there's the 1960s-style *Hotel Aegeon* (☎0292/ 39 262; ⑤), right on the Soúnio beach.

Lávrio

Ten kilometres north of Soúnio, around the cape, is the port of **LÁVRIO**. This has daily ferry connections with Kéa and a couple of boats weekly to Kíthnos. It can be reached by **bus** from the Mavromatéon terminal in Athens, or from Soúnio.

The port's ancient predecessor, Laurion, was famous for its silver mines – a mainstay of the Classical Athenian economy – which were worked almost exclusively by slaves. The port today remains an industrial and mining town, though nowadays for less precious minerals – cadmium and manganese – and also hosts the country's principal transit camp for political refugees: mostly Turks and Kurds at present, with a scattering of eastern Europeans, awaiting resettlement in North America, Australia or Europe. The island offshore, **Makrónissos**, now uninhabited, has an even more sinister past: it was here that hundreds of communists were imprisoned in "re-education" labour camps during and after the civil war.

As you might imagine, this is not really a place to linger between buses and ferries. However, if you have time to kill, the site of **ancient Thoriko** is of some interest. It lies down a zigzag track from the village of PLÁKA, 5km north of Lávrio. A defensive outpost of the mining area in Classical times, its most prominent ruins are of a theatre, crudely engineered into an irregular slope in the hill.

East of Athens: the Mesóyia and Brauron

The area east of Athens is one of the least visited parts of Attica. The mountain of **Imittós** (Hymettus) forms an initial barrier, with Kessarianí monastery (see p.99) on its cityside flank. Beyond extends the plateau of the **Mesóyia** (Midland), a gentle landscape whose villages have a quiet renown for their retsina and for their churches, many of which date to Byzantine times. On towards the coast, there is the remote and beautiful site of **ancient Brauron**, and the developing resort of **Pórto Ráfti**.

The Mesóyia

The best-known attraction of the Mesóyia is at the village of **PEANÍA**, on the east slope of Imittós: the **Koutoúki cave** (daily 10am–5.30pm), endowed with spectacularly illuminated stalactites and stalagmites and multicoloured curtains of rock. It is fairly easily reached by taking the Athens–Markópoulo bus, stopping at Peanía, and then walking up. Close by the village – just to the east on the Spáta road – is the chapel of **Áyios Athanásios**, built like so many churches in the region with old Roman blocks and fragments.

MARKÓPOULO, the main Mesóyia village, shelters a further clutch of chapels. Within the village, in a walled garden, stand the twin chapels of **Áyia Paraskeví** and **Ayía Thékla**; ring for admission and a nun will open them up to show you the seventeenth-century frescoes. Over to the west, on the road to **KOROPÍ**, is one of the oldest churches in Attica, tenth-century **Metamórfosi**. The keys to this can be obtained from the church of the Análipsi in Koropí.

Heading east from Markópoulo, the road runs past the unusual double-naved **Ayía Triádha** (2..5km out) and on to the coast at **PÓRTO RÁFTI**, whose bay, protected by islets, forms an almost perfect natural harbour. It's in the throes of development, with an EOT pay-beach and a fair number of tavernas, but remains a good place to stay if you can find a room. On the islet of Rafti, facing the harbour, is a huge, curious Roman statue of a woman tailor, probably intended as a beacon.

From here, if you've your own vehicle, you can make your way along the coast road to the village of VRAVRÓNA and the site of **Ancient Brauron**.

Brauron

Site open daily 8.30am–3pm; museum only Tues, Weds, Sat & Sun same hours; 400dr

BRAURON is one of the most enjoyable minor Greek sites. It lies just outside the modern village of VRAVRÓNA (40km from Athens), in a marshy valley at the base of a low, chapel-topped hill. The marsh and surrounding fields are alive with birdsong only, partly drowned out by traffic noise from the nearby busy road.

The remains are of a **Sanctuary of Artemis**, centred on a vast *stoa*. This was the chief site of the Artemis cult, founded, legendarily, by Iphigeneia (whose "tomb" has also been identified here). It was she who, with Orestes, stole the image of Artemis from Tauris (as commemorated in Euripides's *Iphigeneia at Tauris*) and introduced worship of the goddess to Greece. The main event of the cult was a quadrennial festival, now enshrined in mystery, in which young children dressed as bears to enact a ritual connected with the goddess and childbirth.

The **"Stoa of the Bears"**, where these initiates would have stayed, has been substantially reconstructed, along with a stone **bridge**; both are fifth-century BC and provide a graceful focus to the semi-waterlogged site. Somewhat scantier are the ruins of the temple itself, whose stepped foundations can be made out; immediately adjacent, the sacred spring still wells up, today squirming with tadpoles. Nearby, steps lead up to the chapel, which contains some damaged frescoes. At the site **museum**, a short walk from the ruins, various finds from the sanctuary are displayed.

Getting to Vravróna from Athens will involve a walk if you're dependent on public transport. Bus #304 from the Thissío metro (*E1*) goes to a terminus called "Artémi", from where you must continue along the main road for two kilometres until you see the *stoa* marked by a clump of trees in the middle of the marsh on your left; the museum building is actually more conspicuous, just before it. Bus #305 from the same station is more frequent, but it stops at the beach-village of LOÚTSA, 6km northwest.

At the site, there's just a single **taverna**, *I Artemis*, located midway between the "Artémi" stop and the ruins, from where you've a fine view of the bay.

Rafína, Marathon and Rhamnous

The port of **RAFÍNA** has **ferries** and **hydrofoils** to half a dozen of the Cyclades, as well as to nearby Évvia. It is connected regularly by bus with Athens: a forty-minute trip (from Mavromatéon) through the "gap" in Mount Pendéli.

Boats aside, the appeal of the place is mainly gastronomic. Though much of the town has been spoilt by tacky seaside development, the little fishing harbour with its line of **roof-terrace seafood restaurants** remains one of the most attractive spots on the Attic coast. A lunchtime outing is an easy operation, given the frequency of the bus service. Evenings, when it's more fun, you need to arrange your own transport back, or make for the beachside **campsite** at nearby KÓKKINO LIMANÁKI. The town's half-dozen **hotels** are usually full; best value, if you phone ahead, are the *Rafina* (☎0294/23 460; ②), *Corali* (☎0294/22 477; ③) and *Kymata* (☎0294/23 406; ③), all of which are located in the central Platía Nikifórou Plastíra.

Marathon

The village of **MARATHÓNAS**, 42km from Athens, is on the same bus route as Rafína. Four kilometres before you arrive, the **Tímvos Marathóna** stands to the side of the road: the ancient burial mound raised over 192 Athenians who died in the city's famous victory over the Persians in 490 BC. Although ten metres high, it feels a strangely uninspiring monument.

A kilometre to the west of the burial mound is a small **archaeological museum** (open, as is the mound precinct, June–Aug only Tues–Sun 8.30am–3pm; 400dr), with a sparse collection of artefacts mainly from the local Cave of Pan, a deity felt to have aided the victory. Closer to the town is another burial mound, the **Tímvos Platéon**, built for the Athenians' only allies in the battle.

Marathon village and lake

Marathóna village itself is a dull place, with just a couple of cafés and restaurants for the passing trade. Nearby, though, to the west, and quite an impressive site is **Límni Marathóna** – Marathon Lake – with its huge marble dam. This provided Athens's entire water supply until the 1950s and it is still used as a storage facility for water from the giant Mórnos project in central Greece. A major scandal erupted recently when the reservoir was found to be heavily polluted by leaking sewage.

Skhiniás

The coast around ancient Marathon takes in some good stretches of sand, walkable from the tomb if you want to cool off. The best and most popular beach is to the north at **SKHINIÁS**, a long, pine-backed strand full of windsurfers at the weekends. There is a **campsite**, *Camping Marathon*, midway on the road from Marathónas.

Rhamnous

Further to the north, the ruins of **RHAMNOUS** (Tues–Sun 8.30am–3pm; 400dr) occupy a beautiful and totally isolated site above the sea. Amongst the scattered and overgrown remains is a Doric **Temple of Nemesis**, goddess of retribution. Pausanias records that the Persians who landed nearby before their defeat incurred her wrath by carrying off a marble block – upon which they intended to commemorate their conquest of Athens. There are also the remains of a smaller temple dedicated to Themis, goddess of justice. Rhamnous can only be reached if you have your own transport.

Mount Párnitha and Phyle

Scarcely an hour's bus ride north from the city centre, **Mount Párnitha** is an unexpectedly vast and virgin tract of forest, rock and ravine. If you've no time for expeditions further afield, it will give you a taste of what Greek mountains are all about, including a good selection of mountain flowers. If you're here in March or April, it is certainly worth a visit in its own right. Snow lies surprisingly late on the north side, and in its wake carpets of crocus, alpine squills and mountain windflower spring from the mossy ground, while lower down you'll find aubretia, tulips, dwarf iris, and a whole range of orchids.

There are numerous **waymarked paths** on the mountain (look for red discs and multicoloured paint splodges on the trees). The principal and most representative ones are the approach **to the Báfi refuge up the Houni ravine**, and the walk **to the Skípiza** spring. These, along with a couple of lesser excursions, to the **ancient fort at Phyle** and another legendary **Cave of Pan**, are detailed below.

The hike to the Báfi Refuge

To get to the start of this walk, take bus #726 from the corner of Aharnón and Stournára (top side of Platía Váthi; *C2* on the main Athens map) to Menídhi and change (free transfer) to the #724 on to the suburb of Thrakomedhónes, whose topmost houses are beginning to steal up the flanks of the mountain beside the mouth of the Hoúni ravine. Get off at the highest stop and keep on, bearing left, up Odhós Thrákis to where the road ends at the foot of a cliff beside two new blocks of flats. Keep straight ahead along the foot of the cliff and in a few metres you come on the start of the path. It turns down left into a dry streambed, before crossing and continuing on the opposite bank.

It's about two hours to the refuge, curving slowly leftward up the craggy, well-defined ravine, at first through thick scrub, then through more open forest of Greek fir. You cross the stream two or three times. At a junction reached after about 45 minutes, signposted "Katára–Mesanó Neró–Móla", keep straight ahead. At the next fork, some ten minutes later, keep right. After a further five minutes, at the top of a sparsely vegetated slope, you get your first glimpse of the pink-roofed refuge high on a rocky spur in front of you. Another twenty minutes brings you to the confluence of two small streams, where a sign on a tree points left to Ayía Triádha (see below), and a second path branches right to Móla and Koromiliá. Take the third, middle, path, up a scrubby spur. At the top a broad path goes off left to meet the ring road leading to Ayía Triádha.

From here, turn right, down into the head of a gully, where the path doubles back and climbs up to the **refuge**. Normally the refuge warden provides board and lodging, particularly on weekends, but it would be wise to check opening times and accommodation policy with the Athens EOS (see p.62) in advance as the schedule changes periodically. Water is usually available at the back of the building, except in winter.

To the Skípiza spring

For the walk to the Skípiza spring you need bus #714, again from Menídhi (#726 from Aharnón/Stournári). Get off at the chapel of Ayía Triádha in the heart of the mountains. There are two connections a day: at 6.30am, returning at 8am; and at 2pm, returning at 4pm. If you get stuck, you can continue to the *Hotel Mount Parnes* and take the *téléférique* down if it's operating – otherwise there's a rough trail down a gully near the *Xenia Hotel*, spilling out near the Metóhi picnic grounds.

The **Skípiza spring** is an hour and a half to two hours' walk away. From the bus stop by the chapel, walk west past the *Hotel-Chalet Kiklamina*, continuing straight onto the ring road. After the first ascent and downhill, you come after fifteen minutes to the Paliohóri spring on the right of the road in the middle of a left-hand bend, opposite a piece of flat ground marked with pointed-hat pipes. The path begins by the spring, following the course of a small stream up through the fir woods. It's well-defined, beautiful, and clearly marked by discs on the trees.

From Skípiza you can continue right around the summit to **Móla** (about 90min) and from there, in another hour, back to the Báfi refuge. Alternatively, by setting your back to the Skípiza spring and taking the path that charges up the ridge almost directly behind, you can get to **Báfi** in around forty minutes. Turn left when you hit the tarmac road after about half an hour; follow it ten minutes more down to the ring road and turn left again. In a few paces you are in the refuge car park. To get back to Ayía Triádha by the road it's about 6km (an hour's walk).

Phyle

Over to the west of the main Párnitha trails, another route up the mountain will take you to the nearly complete fourth-century BC Athenian fort of **Phyle**, about an hour and three quarters on foot beyond the village of FILÍ (known locally as HASIÁ). Buses to Filí leave near the Aharnón/Stournára stop on Odhós Soúrmeli (*C2*).

On the way up to the fort you pass the unattractively restored fourteenth-century **monastery of Klistón** in the mouth of the Goúra ravine that splits through the middle of the Párnitha range. The walking, unfortunately, is all on asphalt, but the fort, built to defend the road from Athens to Thebes, is impressive.

The Cave of Pan

Another highly evocative spot for lovers of Classical ghosts is the **Cave of Pan**, which Menander used as the setting for one of his plays. It's not easy to find, but whatever anyone tells you, the easiest access is from the ford where the forest track from Ayía Triádha to Roumáni crosses the Goúra stream. Follow down the true right bank of the stream for five minutes, then, where the gully opens out a bit, cross over and steeply up the left bank. The way is marked by cairns of stones, but they are covered in lichen and don't show up very clearly. About ten minutes later, just downstream from the confluence of two streams and about twenty metres above the water, you come to the cave, a large overhang shaded by a plane tree.

Eleusis and west to the Peloponnese

The main **highway to Kórinthos** (Corinth) is about as unattractive a road as any in Greece. For the first thirty or so kilometres you have little sense of leaving Athens, whose western suburbs merge into the industrial wastelands of first Elefsína and then Mégara. Offshore, almost closing off the bay, is **Salamína** (ancient Salamis), not a dream island in anyone's book but a nicer escape than it looks, and accessible by ferries from the mainland here at KOUMÍNON (and at Peramá, near Pireás).

A train or bus direct to Kórinthos or beyond, though, is perhaps the wisest option. Only the site of **ancient Eleusis** is in any way a temptation to stop, and even this is really for the academic. **Drivers** should note that the Athens–Kórinthos road is one of the most dangerous in the country, switching from four-lane highway to a rutted two-laner without warning, and full of trucks careering along; it is best driven in daytime.

Eleusis

The **Sanctuary of Demeter** at **ELEUSIS** was one of the most important in the Greek world. Here, for two millennia, at the beginning of the Sacred Way to Athens, were performed ritual ceremonies – the mysteries – that had an effect on their ancient initiates the equal of any modern cult. According to Pindar, who undertook the rites in Classical times, and like all others was bound by pain of death not to reveal their content, anyone who had "seen the holy things (at Eleusis) and goes in death beneath the earth is happy, for he knows life's end and he knows the new divine beginning".

The basis of the cult was established in Mycenaean times, perhaps as early as 1500 BC, around the figure of Demeter (Ceres to the Romans), the goddess of corn, and the myth of her daughter Persephone's annual descent into, and resurrection from, the underworld. It was in some ways an ancient prefigurement of the Easter ritual: the earth's crops', and its gods', simultaneous rebirth in the miracle of fertility. By the fifth century BC the cult had developed into a sophisticated annual festival, attracting up to 30,000 from throughout the Greek world. They gathered in Athens, outside the Propylaia on the Acropolis, and, after various rituals, including mass bathing and purification in Phaleron Bay, followed the Sacred Way to the sanctuary here at Eleusis.

The site

The **ruins** (Tues–Sun 8.30am–3pm; 400dr) are obscure in the extreme, dating from several different ages of rebuilding and largely reduced to foundations; any mystic imaginings are further hampered by the spectacularly unromantic setting. The best plan is to head straight for the **museum**, which features models of the site at various stages of its history. This will at least point you in the direction of the **Telesterion**, the windowless Hall of Initiation, where the priests of Demeter would exhibit the "Holy Things" and speak "the Unutterable Words".

To reach the site from Athens, take **bus** #880, #853 or #862 (signposted Elefsína, Skaramangás or Asprópirgos) from Platía Eleftherías ("E" on the main Athens map; *D2*). Ask to be dropped at the *Heroon* (Sanctuary), to the left of the main road, a short way into Elefsína. The trip can easily be combined with a visit to the monastery at Dhafní (see p.99), on the same road and bus routes.

On from Elefsína

Northwest from Elefsína, the **old road to Thebes and Delphi** heads into the hills. This route is covered in the *Central Greece* chapter; it's highly worthwhile, with its detours to **ancient Aegosthena** and the tiny resort of **Pórto Yermenó**. At MÉGARA another, more minor road heads north to reach the sea at the village of ALEPOHÓRI, where it deteriorates to a track to loop around to Pórto Yermenó.

Heading directly west, **on towards the Peloponnese**, there are shingle beaches – more or less clear of pollution – along the old, parallel coastal road at KINÉTA and ÁYII THEÓDHORI. This highway has a small place in pre-Homeric myth, as the route where Theseus slew the bandit, Sciron, and threw him off the cliffs – as he himself had disposed of generations of travellers – to be eaten by a giant sea turtle. The scenery is almost apt for such imaginings, with the Yeránia mountains to the north and those of the Peloponnese across the water.

You leave Attica at ISTHMÍA, a village beside the **Corinth Canal** (see p.135), where most of the buses break the journey for a drink at the café by the bridge. To the north of the canal, LOUTRÁKI and PERAHÓRA are technically part of Attica but, as they are more easily reached from Kórinthos, are covered in *The Peloponnese* chapter following.

travel details

Buses

Attica Buses for most destinations in **Attica** (ie within this chapter) leave from the **Mavromatéon terminal** (250m north of the National Archaeological Museum, at the junction with Leof. Alexándhras, "B" on the Athens map, *B2*). Exceptions are specified in the text.

Destinations include: Sounion (every hour on the half-hour; 1hr); Rafína (every 45min; 1hr); Marathon Tomb (hourly; 1hr).

Peloponnese and western/northern Greece Most buses leave from the terminal at **Kifisoú 100**, easiest reached on the **#051 bus** from the corner of Vilára and Menándhrou (near Omónia; "E" on the map, *D2*).

Destinations include: Áyios Konstandínos (hourly; 2hr 30min); Árgos (hourly; 2hr 45min); Árta (8 daily; 6hr); Corfu (3 daily; 11hr); Igoumenítsa (3 daily; 8hr); Ioánnina (8 daily; 7hr); Kórinthos (hourly; 1hr); Lefkádha (4 daily; 6hr); Mycenae/Náfplio (hourly; 2hr/3hr); Pátra (hourly; 3hr); Olympia (3 daily; 6hr); Pílos (2 daily; 6hr); Thessaloníki (7 daily; 7hr); Spárti (7 daily; 4hr 30min); Trípoli (12 daily; 4hr); Zákinthos (4 daily; 7hr).

Central Greece Buses for most other destinations in central Greece leave from the **Liossíon 260** terminal, easiest reached by **taxi** now that the express buses seem to have given up going there. Alternatively, take either: **bus #024** at the Amalías entrance of the National Gardens (by Síndagma, *E4*), almost to the end of its route (about 25min.; the stop is 200m south of the terminal); or the **metro** from Omónia/Monastiráki to the Áyios Nikólaos station (800m east of the terminal; coming out, go under the rail line, turn left and look out for the coaches).

Destinations include: Delphi (5 daily; 3hr); Halkídha (half-hourly; 1hr); Karpeníssi (2 daily; 6hr); Lamía (hourly; 3hr); Lárissa (6 daily; 5hr); Óssios Loukás (2 daily; 4hr); Thíva/Thebes (hourly; 1hr); Tríkala (7 daily; 5hr); Vólos (9 daily; 5hr).

Trains

Trains for **Kórinthos and the Peloponnese** leave from the **Stathmós Peloponíssou**, those for **northern Greece** from **Stathmós Laríssis**. The stations adjoin each other, just west of Deliyánni (*B/C1*), on the #1 trolley bus route. To reach the Peloponnese station, use the metal overpass next to the Laríssis station.

Tickets and information for trains are available from the OSE office at Sína 6 (*D3*).

Hitching

To Kórinthos/Peloponnese/Patras Bus to Dhafní; National Road 8 starts at the junction of Leof. Athinón and Ierá Odhós.

To Lámia and the north Bus to the Lióssion 260 terminal (as above), then walk north to the start of National Road 1.

Old road to Delphí Bus to Elefsína.

Island Ferries and Hydrofoils

Pireás Ferries and hydrofoils to the Argo-Saronic, Monemvassía, Crete, the Cyclades, Dodecanese and North and East Aegean islands. See p.118 for details on how to get to Pireás.

Lávrio Ferries daily to Kéa; a few weekly to Kíthnos. Bus from Mavromatéon ("B", *B2*).

Rafína Ferries daily to Mármari, Káristos and Stíra on Évia; most days to Ándhros, Tínos, Síros, Míkonos, Páros and Náxos, plus less regularly to Amorgós; two or three weekly to a selection among Astipálea, Kálimnos, Kos, Níssiros, Tílos and Rhodes; and two weekly to Híos, Lésvos and Límnos. Hydrofoils to Évvia (Halkídha, Stíra, Mármari and Karístos), Ándhros, Tínos, Míkonos, Páros, Náxos and beyond.

Most ferries from Rafína to the Cyclades leave in the **late afternoon or evening** – a boon if you've missed the morning Pireás boats.

Bus from Mavromatéon ("B", *D2*).

Information For details of **ferries from Rafína or Lávrio** call their respective port police offices (Rafína: ☎0294/232 888; Lávrio: ☎0292/25 249). For **hydrofoils** call *Ilios Lines* in Pireás (☎01/41 37 725) or Rafína (☎0294/22 888).

International Ferries

From Pireás Destinations include: Alexandria, Egypt (via Iráklion, Crete; 2 weekly); Izmir (once weekly in low season); Kuşadasi (once weekly May–Oct); Ancona (2 weekly); Limassol, Cyprus and Haifa (at least weekly, via Rhodes or Crete); Venice (3–4 monthly).

Domestic Flights

Olympic Airways operate flights from the **west airport** to the following destinations:

Áktion (Préveza), Alexandhroúpoli, Haniá (Crete), Híos, Iráklion (Crete), Ioánnina, Kalamáta, Kárpathos, Kastoriá, Kavála, Kefalloniá, Kérkira (Corfu), Kíthira, Kós, Kozáni, Léros, Límnos, Mílos, Míkonos, Mitilíni (Lésvos), Páros, Ródhos (Rhodes), Sámos, Sitía (Crete), Skíathos, Síros, Sitía, Skíros, Thessaloníki, Thíra (Santoríni) and Zákinthos.

All services are heavily reduced out of season.

CHAPTER TWO

THE PELOPONNESE

The appeal of the **Peloponnese** (*Pelopónnisos* in Greek) is hard to overstate. This southern peninsula, technically an island since the cutting of the Corinth Canal, seems to have the best of almost everything Greek. Its ancient sites include the Homeric palaces of Agamemnon at **Mycenae** and of Nestor at **Pílos**; the best preserved of all Greek theatres at **Epidaurus**; and the lush sanctuary of **Olympia**, host for a millennium to the Olympic Games. The medieval remains are scarcely less rich, with the fabulous Venetian, Frankish and Turkish castles of **Náfplio**, **Methóni** and **Kórinthos**; the strange tower-houses and frescoed churches of the **Máni**; and the extraordinarily preserved Byzantine shells of **Mystra** and **Monemvassía**.

Beyond this incredible profusion of cultural monuments, the Peloponnese is also a superb place to relax and wander. Its **beaches**, especially along the west coast, are among the finest and least developed in the country, and the **landscape** itself is superb – dominated by range after range of forested mountains, and cut by some of the lushest valleys and gorges to be imagined. Not for nothing did its heartland province of Arcadia lend its name to the idea of a classical rural idyll.

A surprise for many first-time visitors is how the big-name sights – though they live up to expectations – turn out not to be the most enduring highlights. The Peloponnese is at its most enjoyable and intriguing when you venture a little off the beaten track: to the old hill towns of Arcadia like **Karítena** and **Dhimitsána**; the bizarre semi-desert of the **Máni** or the castles and beaches of **Messínia** in the south; or the trip along the startling **rack-and-pinion railway** leading inland from **Dhiakoftó** on the north coast.

Itineraries and getting around

The province will amply repay any amount of time that you devote to it. The Argolid, the area richest in ancient history, is just a couple of hours from Athens, and if pushed you could complete a circuit of the main sights here – Corinth, Mycenae and Epidaurus – in a couple of days, making your base by the sea in Náfplio. Given a week, you could add the two sites of Mystra and Olympia, in a leisurely tour. To get to grips with all this, however, plus the wonderful southern peninsulas of the Máni and Messínia, and the hill towns of Arcadia, you'll need at least a couple of weeks.

If you were planning on a combination of **Peloponnese-plus-islands**, you might well be better off limiting yourself to the mainland on a short trip; alternatively, make use of the hydrofoils which link the Argolid, and Pireás, with the **Argo-Saronic** islands. Or explore the island of **Kíthira** – covered in this chapter as it's reached from southern Peloponnesian ports. Or head to **Zákinthos** from the western port of Killíni. Or leave the Peloponnese from Greece's second port city of **Pátra**, gateway to the **Ionian** islands and to southern Italy.

If travelling about the peninsula by **public transport**, you'll be dependent mostly on the **buses**, which are fast and regular on the main routes, and get to most other places at least once a day. The Peloponnese **train line**, now a century old, is in a poor state, especially on its highly scenic southern loop, with trains risking mishaps on defective sleepers if they exceed the leisurely timetable. Renting a **car** is worthwhile if you can afford it, even for just a few days – exploring the south from Kalamáta or Spárti, or Arcadia from Náfplio or Trípoli. **Hitching** can fill in the gaps, though rides from locals tend to be short.

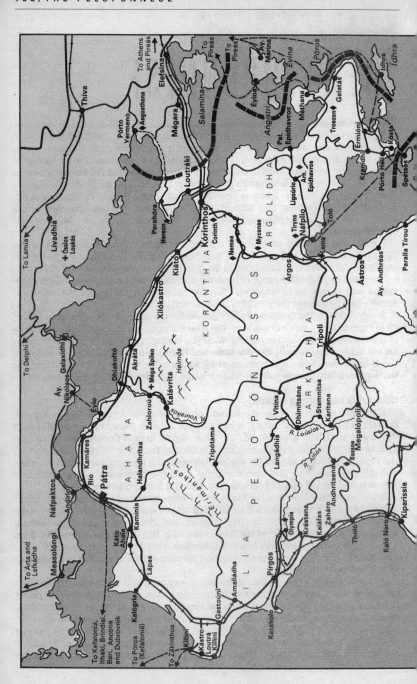

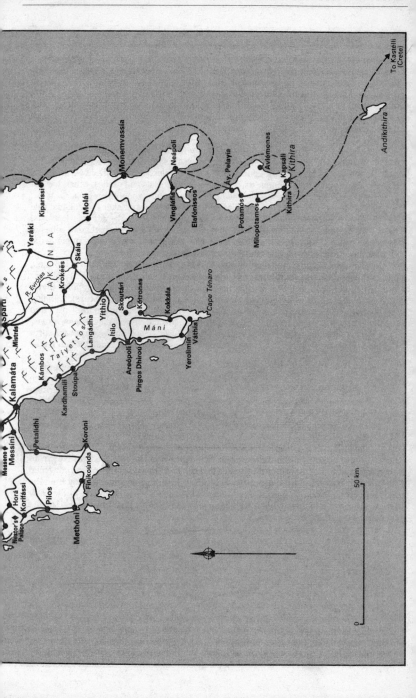

THE PELOPONISSOS-MOREA: SOME HISTORY

The **ancient history** of the Peloponnese is very much that of the Greek mainstream. During the **Mycenaean period** (around 2000–1100 BC), the peninsula hosted the semi-legendary kingdoms of Agamemnon at Mycenae, Nestor at Pylos, and Menelaus at Sparta. In the **Dorian and Classical eras**, the region's principal city-state was Sparta, which, with its allies, brought down Athens in the ruinous Peloponnesian wars. Under **Roman** rule, Corinth was the capital of the southern Greek province. For more on all these periods, see the "Historical Framework" (in the final *Contexts* section of this book) and the individual entries in this chapter.

From the decline of the Romans, through to the Turkish conquest, the Peloponnese – or the **Morea**, as it became known, from the peninsula's map-outline resemblance to the leaf of a mulberry tree (*moréa*) – pursued a more complex and individual course. It is a history of occupations and conquests, with attendant outposts and castles, which has left an extraordinary legacy of castles and medieval remains throughout the region.

The Peloponnese retained a nominally Roman civilisation well after the colonial rule had dissipated, with Corinth at the fore, until, in the sixth century, the city was destroyed by two major earthquakes. Around this time, too, came attacks from barbarian tribes of Avars and Slavs, who were to pose sporadic problems for the new rulers – the **Byzantines**, the eastern emperors of the now-divided Roman empire.

The Byzantines established their courts, castles and towns from the ninth century on, often setting up relations of the emperor – based at Byzantium (Constantinople) – at their head. Their control, however, was only partial, as large swathes of the Morea fell under the control of the Franks and Venetians. The **Venetians** settled along the coast, founding trading ports at Monemvassía, Pílos and Koróni, which endured, for the most part, into the fifteenth century. The **Franks**, led by the Champlitte and Villehardouin clans, arrived in 1204, bloodied and eager from the sacking of Constantinople in the piratical Fourth Crusade. They swiftly conquered large tracts of the peninsula, and divided it into feudal baronies under a Prince of the Morea.

Towards the middle of the thirteenth century, there was a remarkable **Byzantine revival**, which spread from the court at Mystra to exert power over the peninsula once again. A last flicker of "Greek" rule, it was eventually extinguished by the **Turkish conquest**, between 1458 and 1460, and was to lie dormant, save for sporadic rebellions in the Máni, until the nineteenth-century **War of Greek Independence**.

In this, the Peloponnese played a major part. The banner of rebellion was raised near **Kalávrita**, in Arcadia, by Yermanos, Archbishop of Pátra, and the Greek forces' two most successful leaders – **Mavromihalis** and **Kolokotronis** – were natives of, and carried out most of their actions in, the Peloponnese. The battle that decided the war, **Navarino Bay**, was fought off the west coast at Pílos; and the first Greek parliament was convened here, too, at **Náfplio**. After independence, however, power passed swiftly away from the Peloponnese to Athens, where it was to stay. The peninsula's contribution to the early Greek state was a disaffected one, highlighted by the assassination of Capodistrias, the first Greek president, by Maniots.

Throughout the **nineteenth and early twentieth centuries**, the region developed important ports at Pátra, Kórinthos and Kalamáta, but its interior reverted to backwater status. It was little disturbed until **World War II**, during which the area saw some of the worst German atrocities; there was much brave resistance in the mountains, but also some of the most shameful collaboration. The **civil war** left many of the towns polarised and physically in ruins. In its wake there was substantial **emigration** from both towns and countryside, to the US in particular, as well as to Athens and other Greek cities.

Today, the Peloponnese has a reputation for being one of the most traditional – and politically conservative – regions of Greece. The people are held in rather poor regard by other Greeks, though to outsiders they seem unfailingly hospitable. The most significant recent events, sadly, have been **earthquakes**, at Kórinthos in 1981, and at Kalamáta in 1986, the effects of both of which remain visible.

CORINTH AND THE ARGOLID

The usual approach from Athens to the Peloponnese is along the highway through Elefsína and across the Corinth Canal to modern-day **Kórinthos** (Corinth); buses and trains run this way at least every hour, the former halting at the canal (see below). Alternatively – and attractively – you could approach the pensinula by ferry or *Flying Dolphin* hydrofoil, via the islands of the **Argo-Saronic** (see Chapter Six); routes run from Pireás through those islands, with brief hops over to the Argolid ports of Ermióni, Pórto Héli and Náfplio.

The region that you enter, beyond Kórinthos, is known as the **Argolid** (*Argolídha* in modern Greek), after the city of Argos, which held sway in Classical times. In this compact little peninsula – delineated by the main road south from Kórinthos – is the greatest concentration of ancient sites in Greece. Within an hour or so's journey of each other are Agamemnon's fortress at **Mycenae**, the great theatre of **Epidaurus**, and lesser sites at **Tiryns**, **Árgos** and **Lerna**. Inevitably the region, along with the great Roman site at **Ancient Corinth**, draws the crowds, and in peak season you may want to see the sites early or late in the day to realise their magic.

When ruin-hopping palls, there are the small-town pleasures of elegant **Náfplio**, and a handful of nice enough **coastal resorts**. The best beach resorts in these parts, however, are to be found along the coast road south from Árgos – at the Astrós, Tirós and Leonídhi beaches. Technically outside the Argolid, these are easiest reached by bus from Árgos or by *Flying Dolphin* hydrofoil from Náfplio (summer only), Portohéli or the island of Spétses. The southern continuation of these hydrofoil routes takes you on down the coast to the Byzantine remains of Monemvassía.

The Corinth Canal

The idea for a **Corinth Canal**, providing a short cut and safe passage between the Aegean and Ionian seas, dates back at least to Roman times, when the Emperor Nero performed initial excavations with a silver shovel and Jewish slave labour. It was only in the 1890s, however, that the technology became available to cut across the six-kilometre isthmus. Once completed, the canal, along with Suez, its near contemporary, helped establish Pireás as a major Mediterranean port and shipping centre, although its own projected toll revenues were never realised. Today, with supertankers, it is something of an anachronism but a memorable sight nonetheless.

The view from the bridge

Approaching on the main Athens road, you cross the canal near its eastern end. At the **bridge** there's a **café**, where buses from Athens usually stop if they're going beyond Kórinthos. Peering over from the bridge, the canal appears a tiny strip of water until some huge freighter assumes toy-like dimensions as it passes hundreds of metres below. If you were to take one of the few remaining ferries from Pireás to the Ionian, you would actually sail through the canal – a trip almost worthwhile for its own sake.

At the western end of the canal, by the old Kórinthos–Loutráki ferry dock, there are remains of the **diolkos** – platforms onto which boats would be hauled and dragged across the isthmus on logs – used from Roman times to the twelfth century. If you've time to spare, a footpath runs along one bank of the canal for its entire length.

Around the canal

Just to the south of the Corinth Canal is **Ancient Isthmia**, the Greco-Roman port of Corinth. To the northwest are the spa of **Loutraki** and the Classical sanctuary of **Perahora** – the latter with a pleasant beach. Details of these sites, technically in Attica but easiest reached from modern Kórinthos, are to be found on p.140–141.

Kórinthos – modern Corinth

Like its ancient predecessor, the modern city of **KÓRINTHOS** has been levelled on several occasions by earthquakes. The last episode was in 1981 – a serious quake that left thousands in tented homes for most of the following year. Repaired and reconstructed, with buildings of prudent but characterless concrete, the modern city has little of intrinsic interest: it is largely an industrial-agriculture centre, its economy bolstered by the drying and shipping of currant-grapes, for centuries one of Greece's few successful exports (the word currant itself derives from Corinth).

Nevertheless, you could do worse than base yourself here for a night or two, for the setting, with the sea on two sides and the mountains across the gulf, is magnificent, and there are some pleasant quarters along the shore, plus a nice provincial main square. In addition, of course, there are the remains of Ancient and Medieval Corinth – **Arhéa Kórinthos** – 7km to the southwest, as well as access to Perahóra and a couple of other minor sites (see below).

The only particular sight in the modern city itself is a recently opened **Folklore Museum** (daily 8am–1pm; free), located in a tasteful modern building near the harbour. This contains the expected array of peasant costumes, old engravings and dioramas of traditional crafts.

Orientation and transport

Orientation is straightforward. The centre of Kórinthos is its **park**, bordered on the longer sides by Ermoú and Ethnikís Andístassis streets. You'll find the *National* and *Commercial* banks along the latter, and the main **post office** on Adimantoú street, on the north side of the park.

The **bus station for Athens** and most local destinations (including Arhéa Kórinthos, Isthmía, Loutráki and Neméa) is on the Ermoú side of the park, at the corner with Koliátsou. **Longer-distance buses** (to Spárti, Kalamáta, Trípoli, Mycenae, Árgos and Náfplio) use a terminal on the other side of the park, at the corner of Ethnikís Andístassis and Arátou. The **train station** is a couple of blocks towards the waterside.

There's a **tourist police** post on Ermoú, just down from the bus station, and a **taxi rank** (costs to Ancient Corinth are not exorbitant) on the Ethnikís Andístassis side of the park. If you want to rent your own transport, check out *Liberopoulos* (☎0741/72 937) for **mopeds and bikes**, or *Grig Lagos* (☎0741/22 617) for **cars**, at Ethnikís Andístassis 27 and 42, respectively.

Accommodation and meals

At most times of year, **hotels** are reasonably easy to find, with three or four on the main road into town from the train station and a couple of less expensive ones on the waterside. Pick of the options are:

Hotel Belle-Vue, on the waterfront (☎0741/22 088). A popular cheapie that's well worth booking ahead; ask for a room with waterfront balcony. ②

Hotel Acti, on the waterfront (☎0741/23 337). The *Belle-Vue's* somewhat less attractive neighbour. ②

Hotel Byron, Dhimokratías 8, opposite the train station (☎0741/22 631). A functional fall-back – handy for late arrivals or early starts. ②

Hotel Ephira, Vassiléos Konstandínou 52 (☎0741/22 434). Nicely sited, a block back from the park, this is a good mid-budget choice. ③

Alternatively, there are a couple of **campsites** along the gulf to the west: *Corinth Beach*, 3km out at Dhiavakíta (☎0741/27 967) and *Blue Dolphin*, a bit further away at Léheo (☎0741/25 767). Neither has an especially enticing setting, with views of modern Kórinthos's industry, though *Corinth Beach*, at least, is well-equipped; both have tavernas and (not very inspiring) beaches nearby.

Eating out in Kórinthos is quite promising. There are a few tavernas – try the *Anaxagoras* – and rather more fast-food places along the waterfront, all modestly priced. One of the best in the centre of town is *O Moustakias* at Ethnikís Anexartisías 60; it stays open until very late.

Ancient Corinth

Buses to Ancient Corinth, **ARHÉA KÓRINTHOS**, leave modern Kórinthos every hour from 8am to 9pm and return on the half-hour. The ruins of the **ancient city**, which displaced Athens as capital of the Greek province in Roman times, occupy a rambling sequence of sites, the main enclosure of which is given a sense of scale by the majestic ruin of a Temple of Apollo. Most compelling, though, are the remains of the medieval city, which occupy the stunning acropolis site of **Acrocorinth**, towering 565m above.

Staying in Ancient Corinth

To explore both ancient and medieval Corinth you need a full day, or better still, to stay here overnight. A modern **village** spreads around the edge of the main ancient site and there are a scattering of **rooms** to rent in its backstreets – follow the signs or ask at the cafés. If you can afford it, there is also the *Xenia* hotel (☎0741/31 208; ④), built for the archaeologists in a little grove near the remains of an Asclepion.

A rather wonderful alternative, for those with transport or energy for the walk, would be to stay up at the solitary café at **Acrocorinth**, the *Acrocorinthos* (☎0741/31 099 or 31 285; ②); phone ahead, as it only has four rooms.

The Ancient City

The ruins of ancient Corinth spread over a vast area, and include sections of ancient walls – the Roman city had a fifteen-kilometre circuit – outlying stadiums, gymnasiums and necropolises. However, only the central area, around the Roman forum and the Classical Temple of Apollo, is preserved in an excavated state; the rest, odd patches of semi-enclosed and often overgrown ruin, you come across unexpectedly while walking about the village and up to Acrocorinth.

The whole is impressive, if also somewhat obscure, but it only begins to suggest the majesty of this once supremely wealthy city. Ancient Corinth was a key centre of the Greek and Roman world, whose possession not only meant the control of trade between northern Greece and the Peloponnese, but, with the city's twin ports on either

THE SITES: A WARNING ON OPENING HOURS

Summer opening hours for the **sites and museums** in The Peloponnese are included
with some trepidation. They are notorious for changing: without notice, from one season
to another, or from one week to the next due to staff shortages. You may well find sites
listed as closing at 3pm staying open until 7pm in summer – or, equally, vice versa.

To be sure of admission, it's best to visit between 9am and noon, and to be wary of
Monday – when most museums and sites commonly close for the whole day.

side of the isthmus, a link between the Ionian and Aegean seas – the west and eastern
Mediterranean. Not surprisingly, the city's ancient (and medieval) history was
chequered with invasions and power struggles, and in Classical times by Corinth's
rivalry with Athens – against whom it sided with Sparta in the Peloponnesian War.

Despite this, Corinth suffered only one break in its historical continuity, in 146 BC,
when the Romans, having defeated the Greek city states of the Achaean League, razed
the city to the ground. For a century the site lay in ruins before being refounded, on a
majestic scale, by Julius Caesar in 44 BC. This was initially as a colony for veterans,
though it later was made the provincial capital. Once again Corinth grew rich on trade
– with Rome to the west, Syria and Egypt to the east – and its population revived to
300,000 (still down from the extraordinary peak of 750,000 in Classical times).

The new wealth of Roman Corinth was increasingly matched by pleasures, as the
city became a byword for luxury with its access to exotic goods. Sex, too, was part of
the image. Corinthian women were renowned for their beauty and much sought after
as *hetairai* (courtesans); in Corinth itself a temple to Aphrodite/Venus, on the acropolis, was served by over a thousand sacred prostitutes. **Saint Paul** stayed in Corinth for
eighteen months in 54 AD, though his attempts to reform the citizens' ways were met
only by rioting, tribulations recorded in his two *Epistles to the Corinthians*. The city
endured until rocked by two major earthquakes, in 522 and 551, which brought down
the Roman buildings, and again depopulated the site until a brief Byzantine revival in
the eleventh century.

The main excavations

Main excavations open Mon–Fri 8.30am–7pm (5pm off season), Sat & Sun 8am–3pm; 1000dr.

Inevitably, given the waves of earthquakes and destruction, it is remains of the Roman
city that dominate the **main excavated site**, just behind the road where the buses pull
in. The area is entered from the south side, which leads you straight into the **Roman
agora**, an enormous marketplace flanked by the foundations of a huge *stoa*, once multi-
levelled, with 33 shops on the ground floor.

Adjoining the *stoa*, roughly in the middle, is a *bema*, a marble platform used for
public announcements. To the east (right) are remains of a Christian **basilica** and the
starting lines of a Greek **racetrack**, covered in the Roman period by administrative
buildings. Across the agora to the north is another trace of the Greek city, a s**acred
spring**, covered over by a grill but with its bronze lions' head spouts from the fifth
century BC still in situ.

More substantial is the elaborate Roman **Fountain of Peirene**, which stands just
above the starting line of the racetrack. This occupies the site of one of two natural
springs in Corinth – the other is up on the acropolis – and its cool water was channelled into a magnificent fountain and pool in the courtyard. The fountain house was,
like many of Athens's Roman public buildings, the gift of the wealthy Athenian and
friend of the Emperor Hadrian, Herodes Atticus. The waters still flow through the
underground cisterns and supply the modern village. Above the fountain, approached

down a flight of steps, is an excavated stretch of what was the main approach to the city, the **Lechaion Way**. Fifteen metres wide, drained, and paved in marble, this remained in use for centuries; it leads today to the site's exit.

The real focus of the ancient site, though, is a rare survival from the Classical Greek era: the fifth-century BC **Temple of Apollo**, whose seven austere Doric columns stand slightly above the level of the forum, flanked by foundations of another marketplace and baths. Over to their west is the site **museum**, housing a large collection of domestic pieces, some good Roman mosaics and (outside) a frieze depicting the labours of Heracles (Hercules), several of which were performed nearby – at Nemea, Stymphalia and Lerna. The city's other claim to mythic fame, incidentally, is as the home of the infant Oedipus and his step-parents, prior to his travels of discovery to Thebes.

Other excavations

A number of miscellaneous smaller excavations surround the main site. To the west, just across the road from the enclosing wire, there are outlines of two **theatres**: a Roman **odeion** (once again endowed by Herodes Atticus) and a larger Greek amphitheatre, adapted by the Romans for gladiatorial sea battles. To the north, by the (signposted) *Xenia Hotel*, are inaccessible but visible remains of an **Asclepion** (dedicated to the healing god), including a fountain.

Acrocorinth

Rising almost sheer above the lower town, **Acrocorinth** is an amazing mass of rock, and still largely encircled by two kilometres of wall. The ancient acropolis of Corinth, it became during the Middle Ages one of Greece's most powerful fortresses, besieged by successive waves of invaders, who considered it the key to the Morea.

It's a long, four-kilometre climb – or a taxi ride from ancient Corinth, reasonable if shared – to the summit, but unreservedly recommended. Amid the sixty-acre site (unrestricted access) you wander through a jumble of chapels, mosques, houses and battlements, erected in turn by Greeks, Romans, Byzantines, Frankish Crusaders, Venetians and Turks. And looking down over the Saronic and Corinthian gulfs, you really sense the strategic importance of the fortress's position.

The Turkish remains are unusually substantial. Elsewhere in Greece evidence of the Ottoman occupation has been physically removed or defaced. Here, halfway up the hill, you can see a midway point in the process: the still functioning **Fountain of Hatzi Mustafa**, Christianised by the addition of great carved crosses. The outer of the citadel's **triple gates**, too, is largely Turkish; the middle is a combination of Venetian and Frankish; the inner, Byzantine, incorporating fourth-century BC towers.

Within the citadel, the first summit (to the right) is enclosed by a **Frankish keep** – as striking as they come – which last saw action in 1828 during the War of Independence. Keeping along the track to the left, you pass some interesting (if perilous) cisterns, remains of a Turkish bath house and crumbling Byzantine chapels.

In the southeast corner of the citadel, hidden away in the lower ground, is the **upper Peirene spring**. This is fairly easy to find: look out for a narrow, overgrown entrance, from which a flight of iron stairs leads down some three metres to a metal screen. Here, broad stone steps descend to a pool of water (which has never been known to disappear), out of which rises a fourth-century BC arch, seemingly guarding the pool and darkness beyond. To the north of the fountain, on the second and higher summit, is the site of the **Temple of Aphrodite** mentioned above; after its days as a brothel, it saw use as a church, mosque and belvedere.

There are no modern buildings up at Acrocorinth, save for the **café-restaurant**, which does meals and drinks and has a few rooms to rent (see p.137).

Perahóra and other sites around Corinth

Besides the **Corinth Canal**, which you can't help but pass en route between Kórinthos and Athens, a number of minor sites are accessible by bus (at least most of the way) from Kórinthos, both on the Attic and Peloponnese peninsulas. On the Attic side, just south of the canal, is the site of **Isthmia**, the Greek and Roman port of Corinth. To the north – more distant but more rewarding – is the **Sanctuary of Hera** at **Perahóra**.

Back in the Peloponnese proper, **Neméa** – as in the lion of Hercules's labour – is a brief detour southwest of Kórinthos, off the road to Árgos or Mycenae. **Sikyon** is a bit more remote, 25km up the coast towards Pátra, but again accessible by bus.

Ancient Isthmia

The site of ancient **ISTHMIA** (Mon & Wed–Sat 8.45am–3pm, Sun 9.30am–2.30pm; 400dr), Greek and Roman Corinth's eastern harbour on the Saronic Gulf, lies just to the south of the canal. It is located a little before the modern village of ISTHMÍA if you are coming along the road from Kórinthos (from where buses run from the Koliatsoú/Ermoú terminal).

There is nothing very notable to see at the site, though the ancient settlement was an important one, due to its **Sanctuary of Poseidon** – of which just the foundations remain – and Panhellenic Isthmian games. The latter ranked with those of Delphi, Nemea and Olympia, though they have left scant evidence in the form of a **stadium** and **theatre**, plus a few curiosities, including starting blocks used for foot races, in the small adjacent **museum** (same hours and entry ticket as site).

Loutráki and Ancient Perahóra

Six kilometres north of the canal is the spa resort of **LOUTRÁKI**. The epicentre of the 1981 Corinth earthquake, it may once have had its charms but today the concrete line of buildings casts a leaden air over the town. The resort is nonetheless immensely popular, with, astonishingly, the largest concentration of hotels in the Peloponnese. The visitors are virtually all Greek, coming here for the "cure" at the hot springs, and to sample Loutráki mineral water – the country's leading bottled brand – in situ.

There are reasonably priced pensions, some good restaurants, and a long pebbly beach, but with more than a weekend to escape from the capital, it all seems a bit too functional. You may, however, want to use the town as a staging post for getting to the site of **Ancient Perahora** on Cape Melangávi, 20km around the gulf. There is just one morning bus out from Loutráki but you can hire a moped from one of the many outlets along and off the main street. Loutráki itself is connected four times daily in summer by special train with Athens, and by half-hourly bus with Kórinthos (20min).

Cape Melangávi and Ancient Perahora

The **road to Cape Melangávi** is enjoyable in itself, looping above the sea in the shadow of the Y891ránia mountains, whose pine forests are slowly recovering from fire devastation in 1986. En route the road offers a loop through the modern village of PERAHÓRA (11km) before heading out to the cape along the shore of **Lake Vouliagméni**, a beautiful lagoon with sheltered swimming, a couple of tavernas with rooms, and a campsite.

Ancient **PEROHORA** – also known as the Heraion Melangavi – stands right on the tip of the peninsula, commanding a marvellous, sweeping view of the coastline and mountains along both sides of the gulf. The site's position is its chief attraction, though there are identifiable ruins of two sanctuaries, the **Hera Akraia** and **Hera Limenia**, as well as the submerged **stoa** of the ancient port. The latter provides great snorkelling opportunities, but beware the potentially dangerous currents beyond the cove.

The excavation of Perahora is described by Dilys Powell in *An Affair of the Heart*. The site also features in myth, for it was at Perahora that Medea, having been spurned by her husband Jason at Corinth, killed their two children.

East from the cape

If you have a car, there's a grand and rather wild route **east from the cape**, around the Alkionid Gulf to PÓRTO YERMENÓ (see Chapter Three). There are beaches along the way, though little settlement or development, and the final stretch of road beyond KÁTO ALEPOHÓRI is scarcely better than a jeep track.

Ancient Nemea and the Stymphalean Lake

Ancient **NEMEA**, the location for Hercules's slaying of its namesake lion (his first Labour), lies 10km off the road from Kórinthos to Árgos, outside the village of IRÁKLIO. By public transport, take the bus to modern NEMÉA and ask to be dropped en route at *Arhéa Neméa*; moving on from the site, you can walk back down to the Árgos road and try your luck at hitching (or possibly wave down a bus) on to Mycenae.

Like Olympia and Isthmia, Nemea held athletic games – supposedly inaugurated by Hercules – for the Greek world and it was a sanctuary rather than a town. The principal remains at the **site** (Tues–Sat 8.45am–3pm, Sun 9.30am–2.30pm) are of a **Temple of Nemean Zeus**, currently four slender Doric columns surrounded by other fallen and broken drums, but slowly being reassembled by a team of University of California archaeologists. Nearby are a **palaestra** with **baths** and a Christian basilica, built with blocks from the temple. Outside the site, half a kilometre east, is a **stadium** whose starting line has been unearthed. There is also a newly endowed **museum** (same hours), with excellent contextual models and displays relating to the biennial games.

The Stymphalean Lake

If you have transport, it's possible to cut across the hills into Arcadia, via another Herculean locale – the **Stymphalian Lake**. In myth, this was the nesting-ground of man-eating birds, who preyed upon travellers, suffocating them with their wings, and also poisoned local crops with their excrement. Hercules roused them from the water with a rattle, then shot them down – one of the more straightforward of his labours.

The lake is known in modern Greek as **Límni Stimfalías**, though it is really more marsh: an enormous depression with seasonal waters, ringed by woods and the dark peaks of Mount Killíni. There are no buildings for miles around, save for the ruins of the thirteenth-century Frankish Cistercian **Abbey of Zaráka** (east of the road), one of the few Gothic buildings in Greece – and a rather appropriate backdrop to the myths.

If you don't have your own transport, the most promising approach to the lake is from KIÁTO on the Gulf of Kórinthos; the road, much better than that from Neméa, has the occasional bus. The nearest places to stay are the *Hotel Stymfalia* (☎0742/22 072; ②) at **STIMFÁLIA** village, just before the abbey, or the *Xenia* (☎0747/31 283; ④) at **KASTANIÁ**, a mountain village famed for its butterflies, 20km to the west.

Ancient Sikyon (Sikyóna)

Six kilometres inland from KIÁTO (see above), ancient **SIKYON** (SIKYÓNA) is a fairly accessible if little-known site, which deserves more than the few dozen visitors it attracts each year. Six buses a day run from Kiáto (on the bus and train routes from Kórinthos) to the village of VASILIKÓ, on the edge of a broad escarpment running parallel to the sea, from where it's a kilometre's walk to the site.

In ancient history, Sikyon's principal claim to fame came early in the sixth century BC, when the tyrant Kleisthenes kept a court of sufficient wealth and influence to purportedly entertain suitors for his daughter's hand for a full year. After his death the place was rarely heard from politically except as a consistent ally of the Spartans, but a mild renaissance ensued at the end of the fourth century when Demetrios Poliorketes moved Sikyon to its present location from the plain below. The town became renowned for sculptors, painters and artesans, and flourished well into Roman times; it was the birthplace of Alexander the Great's chief sculptor, Lysippus, and, supposedly, of the art of sculptural relief.

The site

The road from Vasilikó cuts through the site, which is fenced off into a number of enclosures. To the right is the **Roman baths museum** (closed at last visit), which shelters mosaics of griffons from the second to third century AD. To the left are the majority of the public buildings, with a theatre and stadium on the hillside above.

As you enter the **main site** (unrestricted access), opposite the Roman baths, the foundations of a **Temple of Artemis** – over which a church was later constructed – are visible to your left. Beyond it are traces of a **bouleuterion** (council chamber) dating from the first half of the third century BC. The most important remains in this section are of the **Gymnasium of Kleinias** in the far right-hand corner, at the base of the hill; this is on two levels, the lower dating from around 300 BC, the other from Roman times.

Although only the first few rows of seats have been excavated, the outline of the **Theatre** – larger than that of Epidaurus – is impressive and obvious. Pine trees have taken root in the upper half, from where you've a marvellous view encompassing the rest of the site, the village of Vasilikó, the lemon and olive groves around Kiáto, plus gulf and mountains in the distance.

Mycenae (Mikínes)

Tucked into a fold of the hills just east of the road from Kórinthos to Árgos, Agamemnon's citadel at **MYCENAE** fits the legend better than any other place in Greece. It was uncovered in 1874 by the German archaeologist Heinrich Schliemann (who also excavated the site of Troy), impelled by his single-minded belief that there was a factual basis to Homer's epics. Schliemann's finds of brilliantly crafted gold and sophisticated tomb-architecture bore out the accuracy of Homer's epithets of "well-built Mycenae, rich in gold".

Mycenaean history and legend

The Mycenae–Árgos region is one of the longest-occupied in Greece, with evidence of Neolithic settlements from around 3000 BC. But it is from a period of three centuries at the end of the second millennium BC – from around 1550 to 1200 BC – that the citadel of Mycenae and its associated drama belong. This period is known as Mycenaean, a term which covers not just the Mycenae region but a whole civilisation that flourished in southern Greece at the time.

According to **legend**, as related in Homer's *Iliad* and *Odyssey* and Aeschylus's *Oresteia*, the city of Mycenae was founded by Perseus, the slayer of the gorgon, Medusa, before it fell into the fated hands of the **House of Atreus**. Atreus brought down the gods' wrath on his descendants with the murder of his nephews and nieces, whom he fed to his brother (and their father) Thyestes – an act of vengeance for Thyestes having seduced Atreus's wife. Thyestes subsequently became the father of Aegisthus (by his own daughter, Pelopia), who then murdered Atreus and restored his father to the throne.

The next generation saw the curse fall upon Atreus's son Agamemnon. On his return to Mycenae after commanding the Greek forces in the Trojan War – a role in which he had earlier consented in the (abortive) sacrifice of his own daughter, Iphigeneia – he was killed in his bath by his wife Clytemnestra and her lover, the very same Aegisthus who had killed his father. The tragic cycle was completed by Agamemnon's son, Orestes, who took revenge by murdering his mother, Clytemnestra, and was haunted by the Furies before Athena finally lifted the curse on the house.

The **archaeological remains** of Mycenae fit remarkably easily with the tale, at least if it is taken as a poetic rendering of dynastic struggles, or, as most scholars now believe, a merging of stories from various periods. The buildings unearthed by Schliemann show signs of occupation from around 1950 BC, as well as two periods of intense disruption, around 1200 BC and again in 1100 BC – at which stage the town, though still prosperous, was abandoned.

No coherent explanation has been put forth for these events, since the traditional "Dorian invasions" theory has fallen from favour, but it seems that war among the rival kingdoms was a major factor in the Mycenaean decline. These struggles appear to have escalated as the civilisation developed in the thirteenth century BC, and excavations at Troy have revealed the sacking of that city – quite possibly by forces led by a king from Mycenae – in 1240 BC. The citadel of Mycenae seems to have been replanned, and heavily fortified, during this period.

The Citadel

Open Mon–Fri 8am–7pm, Sat & Sun 8.30am–2.45pm; 1000dr admission, students 500dr.

The **Citadel of Mycenae** is entered through the famous **Lion Gate**, whose huge sloping gateposts bolster walls termed "Cyclopean" by later Greeks in bewildered explanation of their construction. Above them a graceful carved relief stands out in confident assertion of its powerful and advanced domain: Mycenae at its height led a confederation of Argolid towns (Tiryns, Argos, Asine, Hermione), dominated the Peloponnese, and exerted influence throughout the Aegean. The motif of a pillar supported by two muscular lions was probably the royal symbol of the Mycenaean royal house, for a seal found on the site bears a similar device.

Inside the walls to the right is **Grave Circle A**, the royal cemetery excavated by Schliemann, which he believed to contain the bodies of Agamemnon and his followers, murdered on their triumphant return from Troy. Opening one of the graves, he found a tightly fitting and magnificent gold mask which had preserved the actual flesh of a Mycenaean noble; "I have gazed upon the face of Agamemnon," he exclaimed in an excited cable to the king of Greece. For a time it seemed that Homer's tale had received documentary evidence. In fact, the burials date from at least two centuries before the Trojan war, though given Homer's possible accumulation of different and earlier sagas, there is no reason why they should not have been connected with a Mycenaean king Agamemnon. They were certainly royal graves, for the finds (now in the National Archaeological Museum in Athens) are among the richest archaeology has yet unearthed.

Schliemann took the extensive **South House**, beyond the grave circle, to be the Palace of Agamemnon. However a much grander building, which must have been the **Royal Palace**, was later discovered on the summit of the acropolis. This is an impressively elaborate and evocative building complex; although the ruins are only at ground level, the different rooms are not hard to make out. Rebuilt in the thirteenth century BC, probably at the same time as the Lion Gate, it is centred – as are all Mycenaean palaces – around a **Great Court**. On the south side a staircase would have led via an anteroom to the big rectangular **Throne Room**; on the east, a double porch gave access to the **Megaron**, the grand reception hall with its traditional circular hearth.

The small rooms to the north are believed to have been **royal apartments**, and in one of them the remains of a red stuccoed bath have led to its fanciful identification as the very spot of Agamemnon's murder.

Equally evocative are the **ramparts** – with the sounds of bells drifting down from goats scratching about the mountainside – and, above all, the **secret cistern** at their east end. This was created, presumably in troubled times, in the twelfth century BC; whether it was to withstand siege from outsiders, rival Mycenaeans, or perhaps an increasingly alienated peasantry, is not known. Steps lead down to a deep underground spring, and it's still possible to descend the whole way; you will need a torch – and take care, as there's a seventy-metre drop to the water level (depth unknown) at the final turn of the twisting passageways. Nearby is the **House of Columns**, a large and stately building with the base of a stairway leading to an upper storey.

Outside the walls of the citadel lay the main part of the town; only the ruling elite of Mycenaean society could live within the citadel itself. Extensive remains of **merchants' houses** have been uncovered near to the road, beside a second grave circle. In them were found Linear B tablets recording the spices used to scent oils along with large amounts of pottery, the quantity suggesting that the early Mycenaeans may have engaged in a considerable trade in perfume. The discovery of the tablets has also caused a reassessment of the sophistication of Mycenaean civilisation for they show that, here at least, writing was not limited to government scribes working in the royal palaces as had previously been thought, and that around the citadel may have been a commercial city of some size and wealth.

Alongside the merchants' houses are the remains of another grave circle ("B"), dating to around 1650 BC and possibly representing an earlier, rival dynasty to the kings buried in "A", and two **tholos** (circular chamber-type) tombs, speculatively identified by Schliemann as the **Tombs of Clytemnestra and Aegisthus**. The former, closer to the Lion Gate, dates from around 1300 BC and so may key with the Trojan timescale; the latter is some two centuries earlier.

The Treasury of Atreus

Open Mon–Fri 8am–7pm, Sat & Sun 8.30am–2.45pm; 1000dr admission, students 500dr.

Across the road from the Citadel site is another – and infinitely more startling – *tholos*, known as the **Treasury of Atreus** or "Tomb of Agamemnon". This was certainly a royal burial vault at a late stage in Mycenae's history, contemporary with the "Clytemnestra Tomb", so the attribution to Agamemnon or his father is as good as any – if the king was indeed the historic leader of the Trojan expedition.

In any case, it is an impressive monument to Mycenaean building skills, a beehive-like structure built without any use of mortar. It is entered (on the same ticket as for the main site) through a majestic fifteen-metre corridor. Above the chamber doorway is a great lintel formed by two immense slabs of stone – one of which, a staggering nine metres long, is estimated to weigh 118 tons.

The modern village: transport and accommodation

The modern village of **MIKÍNES** is 2km from the Kórinthos–Árgos road and the train station; the walk in (Athens–Árgos/Náfplio buses usually drop passengers at the turning rather than in the village) is along a beautiful straight road lined with eucalyptus trees, through which glimpses of the citadel appear, flanked by the twin mountains of Zára and Ilías. The site is a further two-kilometre, uphill walk from the village.

Unless you have your own transport, you'll probably want to stay at Mikínes – which is heavily touristed by day but quiet once the site has closed and the tour buses depart. There is quite an array of hotels – most of them named from characters in the House of Atreus saga – as well as a number of signs for rooms.

Options, all along the village's single street, include:

Youth Hostel – above the *Restaurant Iphigeneia* (☎0751/66 285). Easy-going hostel with rather cramped dorm-rooms on the roof. IYHF card required. ①

Rooms Dassis (☎0751/66 385). A pleasant, well organised set-up, operated, along with a useful travel agency, by Greek-Americans. ②

Hotel Belle Hélène (☎0751/66 225). The village's most characterful hotel, converted from the house used by Schliemann during his excavations. Its family owners have had Homeric names over the past three generations – Agamemnon, Menelaus, Achilles, and so on – and appear resplendent in a series of yellowing photos. The hotel also displays signatures from its visitors' book, a motley group including Virginia Woolf, Henry Moore, Debussy and others. Very friendly and a definite first choice. ③

Hotel Klitemnestra, up the hill near the site (☎0751/66 225). Pleasant, modern hotel, outside the village and well positioned for getting to the site at opening time. ③

Mycenae's two **campsites** are both centrally located, in fields just back from the village street. There's not a great deal to choose between them, though *Camping Mycenae* (☎0751/66 247) is smaller and a little closer to the site than *Camping Atticus*, (☎0751/66 221).

The village has plenty of **restaurants**, though all of them are very much geared to the lunchtime bus-tour trade; don't raise your expectations too high.

The Argive Heraion

Four kilometres from Mycenae, on the minor road, east of Árgos, to Náfplio, is the little-visited **Argive Heraion** (daily 8am–3pm; free), an important sanctuary in Mycenaean and Classical times and the site where Agamemnon is said to have been chosen as leader of the Greek expedition to Troy. There are various Mycenaean tombs nearby, but the principal remains of the Heraion are from the fifth century BC – a complex of temples, baths and a *palaestra* (a wrestling/athletics gym) built over three interconnecting terraces.

The Heraion makes an enjoyable afternoon's walk from Mikínes – a little over an hour away if you follow the track southeast from the village, paralleling the road to Monastiráki/Ayía Triádha/Náfplio – or a pleasant diversion for anyone driving between Mycenae and Náfplio. The site is located just above the village of HÓNIKAS, which has the occasional bus to Árgos; AYÍA TRIÁDHA, 4km on, has more frequent connections to Náfplio. The sitekeeper will be delighted to see visitors.

Árgos

ÁRGOS, 12km south of the Mikínes junction, is said to be the oldest inhabited town in Europe. Passing through this workaday farming centre, you wouldn't guess it. However, the city has some pleasant squares and neoclassical buildings, and a brief stop is worthwhile for the excellent museum, Roman ruins and (if you can coincide) the **Wednesday market**, which draws peasants from all the hill villages around.

The **Archaeological Museum** (Tues–Sun 8.30am–3pm) is just off the main market square and makes an interesting visit after Mycenae, with a good collection of Mycenaean tomb objects and armour along with extensive pottery finds. The region's Roman occupation is well represented, too, in sculpture and mosaics.

When you're ready to leave, ask to be pointed in the direction of the town's ancient remains – a few minutes' walk down the Trípoli road, struggling to hold their own next to a tyre yard. The **site** (Mon–Sat 8.30am–3pm, Sun 9am–2.30pm: but not entirely fenced in), once located, turns out to be surprisingly extensive. The **theatre**, built by Classical Greeks and adapted by the Romans, looks oddly narrow from the road, but climb up there and it feels immense. It's estimated to have held twenty thousand spectators – six thousand more than Epidarus and matched on the Greek mainland only by those at Megalopolis and Dodona. Alongside are the remains of an **odeion** and **Roman baths**. If parts of the modern town could be cleared back, other substantial remains would presumably be revealed.

Above the site looms the ancient **acropolis**, capped by the largely Frankish **medieval castle of Lárissa**, built on ancient foundations and later added to by the Venetians and Turks. Massively cisterned and guttered, the sprawling ruins offer the views you'd expect – but they're a long, steep haul up, either on indistinct trails beyond the theatre, or a very roundabout road.

Practicalities: buses and rooms

You may well need to change **buses** in Árgos: its connections are considerably better than those of Náfplio. There are two *KTEL* stands, a block apart from each other and the central square; the one to the south, on Vassiléos Yioryíou Víta, is for buses back towards Athens and various points in the Argolid; the other, at Plíthonos 24, beyond the museum, is for Trípoli, Spárti and down the coast towards Leonídhi.

For a good meal between buses, try the good, very cheap, anonymous **restaurant** twenty metres east of the main square on Nikitára street. Staying overnight shouldn't prove necessary, unless you find Náfplio full – a possibility in high season. Good, modest **hotels** include the *Apollo Inn* (☎0751/28 012; ②) at Papafléssa 13, east of the main square, and the *Theoxenia* (☎0751/27 370; ③) at Tsókri 31, near the ancient site.

Tiryns (Tírinthos)

In Mycenaean times **TIRYNS** stood by the sea, commanding the coastal approaches to Árgos and Mycenae. Today the Aegean has receded, leaving the fortress stranded on a low hillock in the plains – alongside the Argolid's principal modern prison. It's not the most enchanting of settings, which in part explains why this accessible, substantial site is so little visited. After the crowds at Mycenae, however, the opportunity to wander about Homer's "wall-girt Tiryns" in near-solitude is worth taking.

The site lies just to the left of the Náfplio–Árgos road. Buses will drop and pick up passengers, on request, at the café opposite.

The Citadel

Mon–Fri 8am–7pm (5pm winter), Sat & Sun 8.30am–3pm; admission 300dr, students 150dr.

As at Mycenae, Homer's epithets are a remarkable match. Tiryns's dominant aspect is its walls, formed of huge Cyclopean stones. The Roman guidebook writer Pausanias, happening on the site in the second century AD, found them "more amazing than the Pyramids" – a claim that seems a little exaggerated, even considering that the walls then stood twice their present height. But as an example of military architecture, over 3000 years old, the fortress is undeniably impressive.

The sophistication of the site and its unequivocally military purpose (or at least, later adaptation) is clear as soon as you climb up the **entrance ramp** to the citadel. This was wide enough to allow access to chariots, but designed to make any invading force immediately vulnerable. Their right-hand, unshielded side would be exposed along the whole way, and at the top, the ramp forced a sharp turn – again surveyed by defenders from within. The **gateways**, too, were (and remain) considerable barriers to final access to the courtyard; the outer one is similar in design to Mycenae's Lion Gate, though unfortunately its lintel is missing, so there is no heraldic motif to confirm any dynastic link between the two sites.

In the thickness of the courtyard's outer wall is one of the long **stone-vaulted corridors** which are the citadel's most dramatic feature. A passage from the courtyard leads to a large forecourt and from there a staircase continues to a 21-metre-long gallery, off which are numerous storage chambers. Sheep have for years taken refuge from storms in these galleries and the stone walls have been left polished from their movements.

Of the **palace** itself only the limestone foundations survive, but it is somehow more substantial than Mycenae and you can gain a clearer idea of its structure. The walls above would have been of sun-dried brick, covered in stucco and decorated with frescoes. Fragments of these were found on the site: one depicting a boar hunt, the other a life-sized frieze of courtly women (they are now in Náfplio's museum). Entering from the forecourt you emerge on to a spacious **colonnaded court**, with a round sacrificial altar in the middle. A typically Mycenaean double porch leads directly ahead to the **Megaron** (great hall), where the throne, its base surviving, is set before a massive round clay hearth. **Royal apartments**, as at Mycenae, lead off on either side; the women's quarters are thought to have been to the right, while to the left is the bathroom, its floor – a huge, single flat stone – intact.

A tower further off to the left gives access to a **secret staircase**, as at Mycenae, which winds down to an inconspicuous **postern gate**. The site beyond the Megaron is separated by an enormous inner wall and has been fenced off for archaeological exploration after two underground cisterns were discovered at the far end.

Náfplio (Nauplia, Navplion)

NÁFPLIO is a rarity amongst Greek towns. It is lively, beautifully sited and has a rather grand, fading elegance, inherited from the days when it was the fledgling capital of modern Greece. The seat of government was here from 1829 to 1834 and it was in Náfplio that the first prime minister, Capodistrias, was assassinated by vengeful Maniot clansmen; here too that the Bavarian Prince Otho, put forward by the European powers to be the first King of Greece, had his initial royal residence. Today the town is in some danger of becoming too popular for its own good – with hotel rooms and meals at Athens rates and above – but it remains by far the most attractive base for exploring the Argolid and resting up for a while by the sea.

Orientation and accommodation
Wedged between the sea and a fortress-topped headland, Náfplio is an easy town to find your way around. Arriving by **bus** – the train station is now purely ornamental – you are set down at one of two adjacent terminals just south of the interlocking squares, **Platía Tríon Navárhon** and **Platía Kapodhistría**, on Ódhos Singroú. The third main square, further into the old town, is **Platía Síndagma**.

Accommodation is generally overpriced for what you get, though out of season most of the hotel prices drop significantly. In addition to the hotels listed below, there are a fair number of private rooms advertised – and sometimes touted to new arrivals; most of these cluster on the slope south above the main squares. A few other hotels and rooms, generally the last to fill, are located out on the road to Tiryns.

Youth Hostel, Nón Vizandíou/corner of Argonaftón – in the new town (☎0752/24 720). Recently refurbished, the hostel is no longer the last gasp choice it once was. It's run by a friendly couple and offers as-much-as-you-can-eat dinners. Curfew 11pm. ①

Pension Marianna, up by the Íts Kalé; **Rooms Dhimitris Bekas**, above and right of the Catholic church of Metamórfosi. Two recommended budget places. ②

Hotel Emborikon, Plapoúta 31, by the bus station (☎0752/27-339). A bit basic. ②

Hotel Acropole, Vassilísis Ólgas 7 (☎0752/27 796). Just back from the waterfront. The rooms are a bit pokey but clean enough. ③

Hotel Epidavros, Ipsilándou (☎0752/27 541). Central location and spacious rooms. ③

Hotel King Othon, Farmakopoúlou 3 (☎0752/27 585). Highly attractive small hotel, in an old neoclassical mansion just west of Platía Síndagma. ③

Hotel Victoria, Spiliádhou 3 (☎0752/27 585). A second choice near the *Othon*. ④

Hotel Leto, Zigomála 28 – at the base of the Íts Kalé fortress (☎0752/28 093). Another good, old town hotel, with fine view over the town from its balconied rooms, and a nice breakfast terrace; comanaged with the *Othon*. ④

Hotel Park, Dervenakion 1 – off Platía Kapodhístrias (☎0752/28 093). Large, well-run 1960s hotel which may well have space when the smaller old town places are full. ④

The Náfplio municipal campsite closed a couple of years back, though it's still shown on many maps; the nearest **campsites** are 8km east at Toló and Kastráki (see section following).

The Town

There's ample pleasure in just wandering about Náfplio: looking around the harbour-front, walking over to the rocky town beach, and, when energy is sufficient, exploring the great twin fortresses – Palamídhi and Íts Kalé – on the headland.

Palamídhi

The **Palamídhi**, Náfplio's principal fort, was one of the key military points of the War of Independence. The Greek commander Kolokotronis – of whom there's a majestically bewhiskered statue down in the Platía Kapodhistría – laid siege to the castle for over a year before finally gaining control. After independence, ironically, he was imprisoned in the fortress by the new Greek government. Wary of their attempts to curtail his powers, he had kidnapped four of the parliament's members.

To visit the fortress (Mon–Fri 8.30am–4.30pm, Sat & Sun 8.30am–3pm, slightly later closing in summer; 400dr), the most direct approach is by a stairway from the end of Polizídhou street, beside a Venetian bastion, though there is also a circuitous road up from the town. On foot, it's a pretty killing climb – 899 stone-hewn steps – and, when you reach the summit, a bewilderingly vast complex. Within the outer walls are three self-contained castles, all of them built by the Venetians between 1711 and 1714, hence that city's symbol, the Lion of Saint Mark, appears above the various gateways. The middle fort, San Niccolo, was the one used to imprison Kolokotronis; it was later a notorious prison during the civil war.

The fortress takes its name, incidentally, from Náfplio's most famous and most brilliant legendary son – Palamedes, the inventor of dice, lighthouses and measuring scales. He was killed by the Greeks at Troy, on charges of treachery trumped up by Odysseus, who regarded himself as the cleverest of the Greeks.

Íts Kalé and Boúrtzi

The **Íts Kalé** ("Three Castles" in Turkish), to the west of the Palamídhi, occupies the ancient acropolis, whose walls were adapted by the three successive medieval restorers of the name. The fortifications are today far less complete than those of the Palamídhi, and the most intact section, the lower Torrione castle, has been adapted to house a *Xenia Hotel*. There's little of interest, but the hotel has meant a road has been carved out over the headland, and this brings you down to a small **beach**, overcrowded in season but a nevertheless enjoyable spot to cool off in the shadow of the forts. In the early evening it usually has just a few swimmers, though the refreshment stands operate only at peak hours and in season.

Another beach – a slightly longer, rocky stretch – can be reached by following the road clockwise **around the headland** for a few hundred metres. If you were to keep walking along the path, you'd emerge back at Náfplio's port in about half an hour.

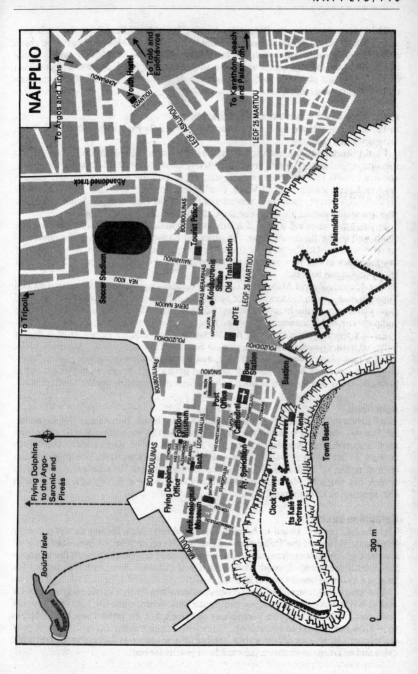

NÁFPLIO

To Argos and Tiryns

To Tolό and Epídhávros

Youth Hostel

ADRIANOU

MIAOULIOU

VIZANTIOU

LEOF. ASKLIPIOU

To Karathóna beach and Palamídhi

LEOF. 25 MARTIOU

Abandoned track

Soccer Stadium

To Trípoli

Tourist Police

BOUBOULINAS

NAVARINOU

NEA KIOU

DERVE NAKION

SIDHIRAS MERARHIAS

Kolokotrónis Statue

Old Train Station

LEOF. 25 MARTIOU

PLATIA KAPODISTRIAS

OTE

POLIZOIDHOU

POLIZOIDHOU

Flying Dolphins to the Argo-Saronic and Pireás

BOUBOULINAS

SINGROU

PL. TRION NAVARHON

Post Office

Bus Station

Bastion

BOUBOULINAS

Folklore Museum

LEOF. AMALIAS

PAPOULIA

Cathedral

PAPANIKOLAOU

Flying Dolphins Office

Bank

OTHONOS

VAS OLGAS

STAIKOPOULOU

VAS KONSTANTINOU

FARMAKOPOULOU

Xenia

KAPODISTRIAS

Archaeological Museum

PLOUTO

PL. SYNTAGMA

Ay. Spirídhon

Clock Tower

Its Kalé Fortress

Town Beach

MIAOULI

Boúrtzi Islet

Palamídhi Fortress

0   300 m

The town's third fort, the **Boúrtzi**, occupies the islet offshore from the harbour – accessible by *kaíkia* (400dr return) in summer. Built in the fifteenth century, the castle has seen various modern uses. In the last century it was the home of the town's public executioner; during this one it was, for a while, a luxury hotel. Actress and politician Melina Mercouri claims in her autobiography (*I Was Born Greek*) to have consummated her first marriage there.

Around the town – mosques and museums

In the town itself, there are a few minor sights – mainly from the Turkish past – and two excellent museums.

Platía Síndagma, the main square of the old town, is the focus of most interest. On the square and in the streets around it survive three converted **Ottoman mosques**: one is a cinema (currently out of use); another, just off the southwest corner, was the modern Greek state's original **Voulí** (Parliament building). A third, fronting nearby Staikopoúlou street, has been reconsecrated as the cathedral of **Áyios Yióryios**, having actually started life as a Venetian Catholic church.

In the same area are a pair of handsome **Turkish fountains** – one abutting the south wall of the theatre-mosque, the other on Kapodhistría, opposite the church of Áyios Spíridhon. On the steps of the latter Ioannis Capodistrias was assassinated by two members of the Mavromihalis clan from the Mani in 1831; you can still see a scar left by one of the bullets.

The **Archaeological Museum** (Tues–Sun 8.30am–3pm; 400dr) occupies a dignified Venetian mansion on the west side of Síndagma. It has some good collections, as you'd expect in a town at the heart of the Argolid sites, including a unique and more or less complete suit of Mycenaean armour and reconstructed frescoes from Tiryns.

Equally worthwhile is the **Folk Art Museum** (9am–2.30pm; closed Tues & during Feb; 300dr) on Ipsilándhou street, just off Sofróni. This won an EC "Museum of the Year" award when it was opened in 1981, and it features some gorgeous embroideries, costumes and traditional household tools and goods – all presented in the context of their use and production. An adjoining shop sells unusually high-quality handicrafts.

Ayía Moní

More handicrafts are on sale at the convent of **Ayía Moní**, 2km east of Náfplio on the Epídhavros road, just south of the village of ÁRIA. The monastic church, one of the most accomplished Byzantine buildings in the Peloponnese, dates back to the twelfth century. From the outer wall bubbles a nineteenth-century fountain, identified with the ancient spring of Kanthanos, in whose waters the goddess Hera bathed each year to restore her virginity. Modern Greeks similarly esteem the water, though perhaps with less specific miracles in mind.

Karathóna beach

The closest "proper" beach to Náfplio is at KARATHÓNA, a fishing hamlet just over the headland beyond the Palamídhi fortress, which can be reached by a short spur off the drive going up to the ramparts. A more direct road around the base of the intervening cliffs was recently opened, along which you can walk there in forty minutes (or there's a morning bus service in season).

The sandy beach stretches for a couple of kilometres, with a single taverna at its far end. It was to have been developed during the junta years, when the old road here was built, along with the concrete foundations of a hotel, but the project was suspended in the 1970s and has yet to be revived. At present Karathóna attracts quite a few Greek day-trippers in season, along with a handful of foreigners in camper-vans; there are cafés and a taverna in summer, plus windsurf boards for rent.

Náfplio practicalities

Náfplio offers the best restaurants and shops in the eastern Peloponnese, plus a range of useful facilities – including car rental and, in summer, hydrofoils down the coast to Monemvassía and to the Argo-Saronic islands.

Restaurants, cafés and nightlife

A good place to start restaurant menu-gazing is the waterside **Bouboulínas** street, where the locals take their early evening *volta*. Wander down **Staïkopoúlou** street, too, off which are many of the most enjoyable tavernas.

For **breakfast**, it's hard to beat the *zaharoplastío* right beside the bus station, which does excellent *loukoumádhes* (puffballs of dough sprinkled with cinnamon) to set you up for the day. Assorted bakeries and juice bars are to be found on, and just off, Platía Síndagma.

Restaurants and tavernas worth checking out include:

Hundalas, Bouboulínas 63. Best value of the waterfront tavernas.

Palia Taverna, Staikopoúlou 6. Nice old-fashioned taverna, just off Platía Síndagma.

O Arapakos, Vassilísis Ólgas 18. Excellent cooking and a varied menu.

Champagne Restaurant, Papanikólaou 32 – parallel to Staïkopoúlou on the Íts Kalé side. Authentic French meals served on a tiny sloping terrace in summer. Expensive but worthwhile.

Nightlife is low-key, with a few late-night bars and the occasional seasonal disco on and around Bouboulínas and Singróu streets. *Sirena*, on the corner of Bouboulínas and Sofróni, has Greek dancing (in summer from 9.30pm).

For a rather more low-key drink, **cafés** on Síndagma square stay open late, too.

Listings

Banks are concentrated around Platía Síndagma and along Amalías street.

Bookshops *Odyssey*, on Platía Síndagma (open summer only), has a good stock of English-language books.

Car rental Pick from: *Safeway*, Eyíou 2 (☎0752/22 155; including convertibles); *Champ*, off Síndagma Platía (☎0752/24 930); or *Ikaros* (☎0752/23 594).

Hydrofoils Náfplio is a stop for *Flying Dolphin* hydrofoils in July and August only. Services connect the town with Spétses and the other Argo-Saronic islands, plus Pireás and Monemvassía; some involve a change at Pórpto Héli. The ticket office is at Bouboulínas 2.

Phones The OTE is on 25 Martíou street. An easier place to make international phone calls, however, is the souvenir shop on Komnínou – opposite the *Hotel King Othon*.

Post office The main branch is on the northwest corner of Platía Kapodhistría.

Moped/motorbike/bicycle rental From *Nikopoulos*, Bouboulínas 49; *Moto Sakis*, Sidhirás Merarhías 15; or *Bourtzi Tours*, next door to the bus station.

Taxis There's a rank on Singroú, opposite the bus station.

Beaches around Náfplio: Tólo (Tolon), Kastráki and beyond

Southeast from Náfplio are the fast-growing resorts of **Tólo** and **Kastráki** – popular and established enough to feature in many British holiday brochures.

Tólo

TÓLO, 12km from Náfplio (hourly buses in season; last back at 8.30pm), is beginning to get too developed for its own good, with a line of thirty or more hotels and campsites swamping its narrow sands. Out of season it can still be quite a pleasant resort, but in summer it is about as un-Greek an experience as you'll find in the Peloponnese. Redeeming features are views of the islets of Platía and Romví on the horizon, and in summer a good range of watersports (windsurfing, waterskiing, paragliding) on offer.

Hotels in Tólo tend to be block-booked through the summer but it's usually possible to find **rooms** by asking around or following the signs. The three **campsites** – *Camping Star, Tolo* and *Lido II* – all charge similar rates and at least one of them should have space at any time of year. In July and August, there are **hydrofoils** to the Argo-Saronic islands of Ídhra (Hydra) and Spétses.

Kastráki and Ancient Assine

A pleasant alternative to Tólo, especially if you're looking for a campsite, is the longer beach at **KASTRÁKI**, 3km to the east; coming from Náfplio by bus, ask to be let off where the road reaches the sea – it forks right to Tólo and left (500m) to Kastráki. Here too development is underway, but it's a fair bit behind that of Tólo, limited to a scattering of small-scale hotels and campsites. *Camping Assini* (☎0752/59 387) is right by the beach with windsurfing equipment for hire.

If you get tired of the water, wander along the beach to the scrub-covered rock by the Náfplio road junction. This is, or was, ancient ASSINE, an important Mycenaean and Classical city destroyed by the jealous and more powerful Argos in retribution for their having sided with the Spartans against them. There's little to see, other than a 200-metre length of ancient wall, but it's an oddly atmospheric spot.

East to Íria

Further around the coast, to the **east of Kastráki**, the road runs on to **DHRÉPANO**, a sizeable village with a **campsite**, *Plaka Beach*, beyond which the **Vivári lagoon** has a couple of good fish tavernas on its shore. If you continue this way for another 10km, you reach a turning and poor track down to the beach and campsite at **ÍRIA**.

For the coast south of here, towards Portohéli, Ermióni, Galatás and Méthana – each local ports for the Argo-Saronic islands – see Chapter Six.

Epidaurus (Epídhavros)

EPIDAURUS is a major Greek site, visited for its stunning **ancient theatre**, built by Polykleitos in the fourth century BC. With its extraordinary acoustics, this has become a very popular annual venue for the Athens Festival productions of **Classical drama** – principally Sophocles, Euripides and Aeschylus – which are staged on Friday and Saturday nights from June through until the last weekend in August. Great spectacles in this setting, they are worth arranging your plans around whether or not you understand the modern Greek in which they're performed.

The theatre, however, is just a component of what was one of the most important sanctuaries in the ancient world, dedicated to the healing god, Asclepius, and a site of pilgrimage for half a millennium, from the sixth century BC into Roman times.

The Ancient Theatre and Asclepion

Site open daily 8.30am–3pm (maybe later if budgets are relaxed); 1000dr. For festival performances you are admitted to the theatre after 7pm, but not to the rest of the site.

The dedication of the sanctuary at Epidaurus to **Asclepius**, the legendary son of Apollo, probably owes its origin to an early healer from northern Greece who settled in the area. There were Asclepian sanctuaries throughout Greece – Athens has ruins of one on the south slope of its Acropolis – and they were sited, rationally enough, alongside natural springs. Epidaurus, along with the island of Kos, was the most famous of them all, and probably the richest.

The sanctuary was much endowed by wealthy visitors and hosted a quadrennial festival – including drama in the ancient theatre – which followed the Isthmian games. Its renown was at a height in the fourth and third centuries BC; Rome, when ravaged by an epidemic in 293 BC, sent for the serpent that was kept in the sanctuary.

This aspect of the site, however, along with most of the associated Asclepian ruins, is incidental for most visitors. For Epidaurus' **Ancient Theatre** is a sight – not a ruin or anecdote – par excellence. With its backdrop of rolling hills, this 14,000-seat arena merges perfectly into the landscape, so well in fact that it was rediscovered and unearthed only last century. Constructed with mathematical precision, it has an extraordinary appearance of balance and, as guides on the stage are forever demonstrating, near-perfect natural acoustics. These are such that you can hear coins – even matches – dropped in the circular *orchestra* from the highest of the 54 tiers of seats.

Aside from repairing these tiers – constructed in white limestone (red for the dignitaries at the front) – restoration has been comparatively minor, retaining the beaten earth stage, for instance, as in ancient times.

The museum

Close by the theatre is a small **museum** (no additional charge), which it's best to visit – if it has reopened after recent maintenance – before exploring the sanctuary. The finds displayed here show a progression of medical skills and cures used at the Asclepion; there are tablets recording miraculous and outrageous cures (like the man cured from paralysis after being ordered to heave the biggest boulder he could find into the sea) and also quite advanced surgical instruments.

Additionally, the museum has some excellent models of the sanctuary, helpful for visualising since most of the ruins are just foundations. In 86 BC, by which time Epidaurus's reputation was probably in decline, the Roman consul Sulla, leader of the forces invading the Peloponnese, looted the sanctuary and destroyed its buildings.

The Sanctuary

The Asclepian Sanctuary, as large a site as Olympia or Delphi, holds considerable fascination, for the ruins here are all of buildings with identifiable functions: hospitals for the sick, dwellings for the priest-physicians, and hotels and amusements for the fashionable visitors to the spa. Their setting, a wooded valley thick with the scent of thyme and pine, is self-evidently that of a health farm.

The **site** has lately been labelled and is still being worked on. It begins just past the museum, where there are remains of Greek **baths** and a huge **gymnasium** with scores of rooms leading off a great colonnaded court; in its centre the Romans built an **odeion**. To the left is the outline of the **stadium**, used for the ancient games. To the right, a small **Sanctuary of Egyptian Gods** reveals a strong presumed influence on the medicine used at the site.

Just beyond the stadium are the foundations of the **Temple of Asclepius** and beside it a rectangular building known as the **Abaton**. Patients would sleep here to await visitation from the healing god, who probably appeared in a more physical manifestation than expected; harmless snakes are believed to have been kept in the building and released at night to give a curative lick.

The strong significance of the serpent at Epidaurus – Asclepius was thought to assume its form – is elaborated in the next building you come to: the circular **Tholos**, one of the best-preserved buildings on the site and designed, like the theatre, by Polykleitos. Its inner foundation walls form a labyrinth which it is believed was used as a snakepit – and according to one theory a primitive form of shock therapy for mental patients. The afflicted would crawl in darkness through the outer circuit of the maze, guided by a crack of light towards the middle, where they would find themselves surrounded by writhing snakes. Presumably, on occasions, it worked.

Epidaurus practicalities

Most people take in Epidaurus as a day trip, though there's a **hotel** at the site, the *Xenia* (☎0753/22 003; ④), and several more modestly priced places – including the *Hotel Koronis* (☎0753/22 267; ②) and *Hotel Asklipios* (☎0753/22 251; ②) – in nearby LIGOÚRIO village, 5km north of the site. Alternatively, it's possible to **camp** in the grass car park on days of performances, though you must wait until an hour after the play's end before setting up a tent. There's alternative beach accommodation at Paléa Epídhavros, 15km northeast (see below).

For meals, the nearest **restaurant** to the site is the *Oasis* on the Ligoúrio road. Much better is *Taverna Leonidhas*, in the village proper, a friendly spot with a garden out the back.

Tickets and transport

Tickets for the plays are available at the site on the day of performance, or in advance in Athens (at the festival box office) or Náfplio (from *Olympic Airways* at Bouboulínas 2). In Athens you can buy all-inclusive tickets for performances and return bus travel. There are also special evening buses from the site to Náfplio after the show. English translations of the plays are available at the site and at the *Odyssey* bookshop in Náfplio.

Normally there are four buses **daily** from Náfplio to the site; they are marked *Asklipion* or *Epidhavros* and shouldn't be confused with those to the modern villages of NÉA or PALÉA EPÍDHAVROS (see below).

Paleá Epídhavros

The closest beach resort to Epidaurus is **PALEÁ EPÍDHAVROS**, which has mushroomed since the recent improvement of the direct coast road in from Kórinthos. Behind the black sands there are at least a dozen **hotels**, as many purpose-built **rooms**, and three **campsites**, all very popular with festival patrons in season. If you want to book ahead, a couple of hotels to try are the *Christina* (☎0753/41 451; ④) and *Epidavria* (☎0753/41 451; ④).

The Saronic ports: Méthana to Porto Héli

The roads across and around the southern tip of the Argolid are slow but scenic rides, but the handful of resorts here are not very characterful and generally overdeveloped. If you've a car then you can pick your beaches and take a leisurely route back to Náfplio, perhaps exploring the site of **Ancient Troezen** and the **Limonódhassos** lemon groves. Otherwise, you'll probably travel this way only if heading for one of the **Argo-Saronic islands**: **Méthana** has local connections to Éyina (Aegina); **Galatás** to Póros; **Ermióni** to Ídhra (Hydra) and Spétses; **Kósta** and **Pórto Héli** to Spétses.

Méthana and its volcano

It's a sixty-kilometre drive from Epidaurus to **MÉTHANA**, the last section along a cliff-hugging corniche road. The town, set on its own peninsula, is a pleasant little spa, whose devotees are attracted by warm sulphur springs. It has half a dozen hotels: the cheapest is the *Aethra* (☎0298/92 420; ②), the most pleasant the seafront *Avra* (☎0298/92 382; ④).

To the west of Méthana town, a road loops around the peninsula to the village of KAIMÉNI HÓRA (Burnt Village), built into cliffs of volcanic rock, from where you can climb – in about half an hour – the pensinsula's **volcano**; follow the mule track signposted "Pros Ifestos".

Ancient Troezen

Close by the village of TRIZÍNA, just south and inland of the turning to the Méthana peninsula, are the ruins of ancient **TROEZEN**, the legendary domain of Theseus and location of his domestic dramas. The cause of these problems was Aphrodite, who, having been rejected by Theseus's virgin son Hippolytus, made Phaedra – Theseus's then wife – fall in love with the boy (her stepson). She too was rejected and responded by accusing Hippolytus of attempted rape. After he fled, and was killed when his horses took fright at a sea monster, Phaedra confessed her guilt and committed suicide. The tragedy is told by Euripides and was reworked by Racine.

Such **remains** as exist of the ancient town are spread over a wide site. Most conspicuous are three ruined Byzantine chapels, constructed of ancient blocks, and a structure known as the **Tower of Theseus**, whose lower half is third-century BC and top medieval. This stands at the lower end of a gorge, the course of an ancient **aqueduct**, which you can follow in half an hour's walk to the **Yéfira tou Dhiavólou** (Devil's Bridge), a natural rock formation spanning a chasm. A rare black butterfly is said to be endemic to the ravine. It's at all events a fine walk.

Galatás and Limonódhassos

GALATÁS lies only 200m across the water from the island of Póros, with which it is connected by skiffs, sailing more or less continuously in the summer months. The town has a cluster of hotels – best value is the *Saronis* (☎0298/22 356; ②) – and **rooms** for rent, plus a handy **bike rental** place, *Fotis Bikes*. The village is connected by a daily bus with Epidaurus and Náfplio.

Equipped with a cycle, the best plan is to follow the coast road south to the beaches of **Pláka** (2km) and **Alíki** (4km). Just back from the latter, a path, signposted *Restaurant Cardassi*, leads into the **Limonódhassos** – a vast, irrigated lemon grove. Though one travel brochure says there are 300,000 lemon trees here, the consensus tallies about 30,000, not that it matters much as you pick your way along the various paths that meander through them, all heading upwards to an inspiringly positioned **taverna**, where a charming old man serves fresh lemonade as you sit on the terrace. Henry Miller recounts a visit here in *Colossus of Maroussi*, hyperbolising that "in the spring young and old go mad from the fragrance of sap and blossom".

Ancient Troezen (see above) is another good cycling target, 9km northwest.

Ermióni, Kósta and Pórto Héli

Continuing anticlockwise around the coast from Galatás, you follow a narrow, modern road, cut from the mountainside to open up additional resorts close to Athens. **PLÉPI** (or Hydra Beach) is a villa-urbanisation, visited by boats from beachless Ídhra opposite. **ERMIÓNI** is better: a real village, enclosed by a rocky bay and saved from development perhaps by lack of a sandy beach. It has two expensive and three modest **hotels**; the latter are the *Nadia* (☎0754/31 102; ③), the *Olympion* (☎0754/31 214; ③) and the *Akti* (☎0754/31 241; ③).

Further round, **KÓSTA** and **PÓRTO HÉLI**, on either side of a bay, are purpose-built resort that have swallowed up their original hamlets and are slowly merging into each other. Each features a rather soulless mix of charter hotels and facilities for yachters exploring the Argo-Saronic islands.

The circuitous **route back to Náfplio** from Pórto Héli runs inland, via attractive KRANÍDHI, scrambling its way up through the mountains. It is covered four times daily by a bus, which usually dovetails with the ferries from Spétses.

The East Coast: Náfplio to Leonídhi

The **coastline south from Náfplio to Leonídhi** is mountainous terrain, increasingly so as you move south towards Monemvassía where the few villages seem carved out from their dramatic backdrop. Considering its proximity to Náfplio – and Athens – the whole stretch is remarkably unexploited, remaining more popular with Greek holidaymakers than with foreign tourists, and enjoyably low-key.

Getting to the beaches – **Parália Ástros**, **Áyios Andréas**, **Parália Tiroú** and **Pláka** – is perhaps best done by car, though there are also **buses** twice daily from Árgos to Leonídhi, while **Pláka** (the port/beach of Leonídhi) is a stop on the *Flying Dolphin* **hydrofoils** from Spétses/Pórto Héli to Monemvassía. However you travel, change money in advance, as there are few banks between Náfplio and Leonídhi.

Right at the beginning of the route, around the coast from Náfplio, the minor site of **Ancient Lerna** makes an interesting halt. If you are travelling by train from Árgos to Trípoli, you could stop off at the station of Míli, only a kilometre distant; alternatively, the site makes a nice ride around the coast if you rent a bike in Náfplio.

Ancient Lerna

The site of ancient **LERNA** (daily 8am–sunset) lies 10km south of Árgos and 15km southwest of Náfplio. The nearest village is MÍLI, at the foot of Mount Pontinus, where buses between Trípoli and Kórinthos break their journey at a group of souvlaki stands, open virtually twenty-four hours. Just beyond the straggle of the village a narrow, signposted lane leads to the site precinct, which is surrounded by an orange grove and close to the sea – a fine picnic spot.

The warden, unused to visitors, may volunteer to show you around this important Bronze-Age settlement, which excavations carried out in the 1950s revealed as one of the most anceint of Greek settlements, inhabited from as early as 4000 BC. This prehistoric settlement is represented by ruins of an early **Neolithic house**, and a well-preserved **fortification wall** from the end of the third millennium BC.

Another large house at the north end of the site is thought to be an early palace. Over it, in about 2200 BC, was built a much larger and more important structure – known as the **House of the Tiles**. This dwelling, possibly another palace, takes its name from the numerous terracotta roof tiles found inside, the earliest known use of this building material. The roof had fallen into the foundations when either lightning or enemy raiders set the building ablaze in approximately 2100 BC. Eighty feet long and thirty feet wide, the house is the most impressive pre-Helladic structure to have been unearthed on the Greek mainland. A symmetrical ground plan of small rooms surrounding larger interior ones is today protected by a canopy, with still-visible stairs mounting to a vanished second storey. The substantial walls, made of sun-dried brick on stone foundations, were originally covered with plaster. Even after its destruction, this palace may have retained some ritual significance, since two Mycenaean **shaft graves** were sunk into the ruins in around 1600 BC, and the site was not completely abandoned until the end of the Mycenaean period.

As implied by the chronology, the founders and early inhabitants of Lerna were not Greeks. Certain similarities in sculpture and architecture with contemporary Anatolia suggest an Asiatic origin but this has yet to be proved conclusively. Excavated finds, however, demonstrate that the Lerneans traded across the Aegean and well up into the Balkan peninsula, cultivated all the staple crops still found in the Argolid, and raised livestock, as much for wool and hides as for food. Elegant terracotta sauce tureens and "teaspoons" hint at a sophisticated cuisine. These treasures may be seen at the Árgos archaeological museum.

According to myth, Hercules performed the second of his labours at Lerna, the slaying of the nine-headed Hydra. As if in corroboration of the legend, the nearby swamps are still swarming with eels.

Ástros and Tirós

The initial section of coast from Náfplio to Ástros and Áyios Andhréas is low-lying: less spectacular than the sections further south, but pleasant enough. The first village of any size is **PARALÍA ÁSTROS**, whose houses are tiered against a headland shared by an ancient acropolis (minor ruins) and medieval fort. Back from the beach, which extends for 6km of sand and gravel south of the fishing harbour, there are half a dozen tavernas, a similar number of room places and a couple of **hotels** – the *Chrissi Akti* (☎0755/51 294; ③) and *Astros* (☎0755/51 294; ③) – and **campsites**.

Just to the south, a trio of surprisingly neat and compact villages – the inland settlements of **ÁSTROS**, **KORAKAVÓUNI** and **ÁYIOS ANDHRÉAS** – perch on the foothills of **Mount Párnon** as it drops to meet the lush, olive-green plain. A little beyond Áyios Andhréas (10km from Ástros), the road curls down to the coast and the first in a series of fine-pebbled swimming coves, crammed between the massive spurs of Párnon. There are seasonal **rooms** at several of the coves, plus a couple of **campsites**. In summer, you could get by here with the occasional makeshift taverna – though outside the season you'd need your own supplies.

PARALÍA TIROÚ is a fair-sized town and quite a popular resort, with a dozen or so hotels, most of them full in summer with middle-aged and older Greeks. For some reason, the younger Greeks tend to go further south on this coast, to Pláka. The resort does feel slightly sedate, with comfortable, mid-range hotels and cafés spread back from its long pebble beach. At **TIRÓS**, now smaller than its old port, set back 3km into the hills, there are numerous **rooms** to rent.

Leonídhi, Pláka and south towards Monemvassía

Gigantic red cliffs which wouldn't look out of place in the American Southwest confine **LEONÍDHI**, the terminus of the Árgos bus route. Set inland, with good agricultural land stretching down to the sea, this is a prosperous and traditional market town, which sees little need to pander to tourists. Most in any case end up down by the sea at Leonídhi's diminutive port, Pláka. If you prefer to stay here, you might find space in the town's one modest **hotel**, the *Alexaki* (②), or the three or four advertised **rooms for rent** (☎0757/22 505 or 22 872; ②). There are some enjoyable, small town tavernas.

Pláka and Poúlithres

PLÁKA, 4km away, is a tiny place, consisting of a harbour, a couple of hotels and restaurants, and a wonderful café. It also has a fine pebble beach, which in recent years has become pretty popular, with Greek and European tourists, plus a sporadic influx of yachties. In summer, it would be wise to phone ahead to reserve a room in the first choice *Hotel Dionysos* (☎0757/22 379; ③), a characterful place with balconied rooms looking out to sea. Alternatives are the pricey apartments of the *Kamaria* (☎0757/22 757; ④) and the rather down-at-heel *Neon* (☎0757/22 383; ②). Both of the seafront tavernas have good food, as does the *Kafenio Mihalis* – painted brilliant blue and a treat of folk art. There are excellent meals to be had on the beach, too, at the taverna twenty minutes' walk to the north along the bay, across the (in summer, dried-up) river bed.

The hamlet of **POÚLITHRES**, 3km south of Pláka around the bay, marks the end of the coast road – which deteriorates to a track as it heads inland. There is a terrace taverna close by the narrow strip of beach, a **hotel**, the *Kentauros* (☎0757/51 214; ③), and a large rooms place by the waterfront.

South: Kiparíssi and Yérakas

South of Leonídhi the coastline is wilder and sparsely inhabited, with just a couple of coastal settlements cut into the cliffs. To reach the two little settlements – Kiparíssi and Yérakas – you are best off on the *Flying Dolphin* **hydrofoil**, which stops at both en route to Monemvassía. By road, it's a very roundabout route (though in better shape than it looks on the map) from MOLÁI, on the Spárti–Monemvassía road.

Both settlements follow the Leonídhi/Pláka model, on a smaller scale, with a main village inland and a little port hamlet, respectively PARALÍA KIPARÍSSI, for KIPARÍSSI, and LIMÉNI YÉRAKAS, for YÉRAKAS. Neither sees many visitors.

Inland from Leonídhi

The route **inland from Leonídhi** is worth taking for its own sake, climbing over a spur of **Mount Párnon**, past the **monastery of Elónis** and the high mountain village of **Kosmás** – quite a temperature shock in the height of summer. It is a decent road for cars, with the few ropier sections recently under repair, and brings you out at the minor Byzantine site of **Yeráki** (aka Pírgos Yerakíou; see p.170); from there, you have a choice of roads – to Spárti, Yíthio (Githion) and Monemvassía.

Without a car, you'll either have to hitch (not impossible) or plan your stay very carefully; **buses** cover the route just twice weekly, currently leaving Leonídhi for Spárti on Tuesday afternoon and Saturday morning (at 6am).

Moní Elónis

The **Moní Elónis** is visible from Leonídhi – a white slash in the mountainside – though as you twist around Mount Párnon, and up a ravine, it drops away from view. The turn-off to the monastery in fact comes 13km from Leonídhi – an approach road that runs downhill, ending at an impregnable gateway. If all looks closed, pull the wire, which passes along the cliff to a large bell. Once admitted, you can wander down to a small chapel crammed with icons and lanterns and to a spring, whose icy-cold water has supposedly curative powers. Most of the monastery – founded in medieval times on the appearance of a miraculous and inaccessible icon – was rebuilt following the War of Independence. It is maintained today by nuns, who sell a classic little history of the monastery's legends and vicissitudes.

Kosmás

Continuing south, past the Elónis turning, you reach **KOSMÁS**, a handsome village set about a grand *platía*, with an inn and a trio of tavernas. Straddling the most important pass of Párnon, at nearly 1200m, it can be a chilly place in spring or winter, but beautiful too, with its streams, cherry and walnut trees, and forests of fir all around.

Beyond the village the road deteriorates into a brief unpaved section, through an uninhabited valley, then lurches slowly down to the village and Byzantine ruins of YERÁKI.

Trípoli: the crossroads

Trípoli is a major crossroads of the Peloponnese, from where most travellers either head **north** through Arcadia towards Olympia, or **south** to Spárti and Mystra or Kalamáta (see below). To the **east**, a very slow road, looping around Mount Ktenías, connects Trípoli with Árgos and Náfplio, via Lerna. To the **west**, you can reach the coast on a reasonably fast road to Kiparissía, via the evocative, scattered ruins of Ancient Megalopolis.

The Peloponnese **railway** also passes through Trípoli, continuing its meandering course from Kórinthos and Árgos to Kiparissía and Kalamáta. Those with passes might be tempted to use the train to Trípoli and then take a bus to Spárti, but it's not a good idea, as Árgos–Sparti buses often pass through Trípoli full; better to take a direct bus, or approach Spárti more enjoyably via the hydrofoil to Monemvassía.

Trípoli

The Arcadian capital doesn't match expectations of the name. **TRÍPOLI** is a large, modern town, and home to one of the country's largest army barracks. It doesn't exactly bombard you with its charm and has no sights to speak of, either. Medieval *Tripolitsa* was destroyed by retreating Turkish forces during the War of Independence, the Greek forces, led by Kolokotronis, having earlier massacred the town's population. The city's ancient predecessors, the rival towns of Mantinea to the north and Tegea to the south, are the only local points of interest (see below).

Getting in and out of the town can be fairly complicated. The major **bus terminal**, serving all destinations in Arkadhía and the northern Peloponnese, is on Platía Kolokotróni, one of the main, central squares. Services to Pátra, Messinía, Kalamáta, the outer Máni, Pílos and Spárti leave from the café directly opposite the train station, at the east edge of town.

If you need to spend a night here, the cheapest **hotel** is the *Kynouria*, Vassilísis Ólgas 79 (☎071/222 463; ②), which is tolerable but not very central. Better, more central and slightly more expensive choices are the *Alex*, Vassiléos Yioryíou 26 (☎071/223 465; ③), or the *Menalon* on Platía Áreos (☎071/222 450; ③).

Mantinea

Ancient **MANTINEA** was, throughout its history, a bitter rival of nearby Tegea, invariably joining in alliance with Athens when Tegea stood with Sparta, and with Sparta when Tegea joined Thebes. Its site stands 6km north of Trípoli, between the road to Dhimitsána/Pátra and the new Kórinthos–Trípoli highway. It is unenclosed, the principal remains being a circuit of fourth-century BC **walls** – still more or less intact, though much reduced in height – and a few tiers of its theatre.

Alongside the site, however, is one of the most bizarre sights in Greece – a modern **church** constructed in an eccentric pastiche of Byzantine and Egyptian styles. It was put together in the 1970s by a Greek-American architect and is dedicated to "The Virgin, the Muses and Beethoven".

Ancient Tegea

Ancient **TEGEA**, 8km south of Trípoli, was the main city of the central Peloponnese in Classical and Roman times, and, refounded in the tenth century, was an important town again under the Byzantines. Its diffuse and partially excavated site lies just outside the village of ALÉA, on the Spárti road.

Local buses from Trípoli stop in the village beside a small **museum** (Tues–Sat 8.30am–2.45pm, Sun 9am–2pm; 400dr), well stocked with sculptures from the site. Take the road to the left as you leave, which leads in 100m to the main remains, the **Temple of Athena Alea**, in whose sanctuary two kings of Sparta once took refuge.

Keeping on the road past the site, it's a twenty-minute walk to the village of PALEÁ EPISKOPÍ, whose church – a huge modern pilgrim shrine – incorporates part of ancient Tegea's theatre and a number of Byzantine mosaics. Ruins of the agora lie to the west. This village also has a couple of tavernas.

THE SOUTH: LAKONÍA AND MESSINÍA

Draw a line on a map from Kalamáta over the Taíyettos mountains, through Spárti and across to Leonídhi. Broadly, everything below this line is **Lakonía**, the ancient territories of the Spartans. It's a dramatic country of harsh mountains and, except for the lush strip of the Evrótas valley, of poor, rocky soil – terrain that has kept it isolated throughout history. **Mount Taíyettos** itself is a formidable barrier, looming ahead of you for miles if you approach from Trípoli, and providing an exciting exit or entrance in the form of the Langádha Pass between Spárti and Kalamáta.

Landscapes apart, the highlights here are the extraordinarily preserved Byzantine towns of **Mystra** and **Monemvassía** – both essential visits for any tour of the Peloponnese – and the remote and arid **Máni** peninsula, with its bizarre history of feuds and unique tower houses and barrel-churches. Monemvassía is a regular stop for *Flying Dolphin* hydrofoils (plus a weekly boat) from Pireás and the Argo-Saronic islands and would make a superb entry point to the peninsula. In summer, the Maniot port of **Yíthio** (Gythion) and tiny **Neápoli**, south of Monemvassía, are additional stops on the hydrofoil and provide the easiest links to **Kíthira**, technically an Ionian island but covered – due to its Peloponnesian access – in this section.

Moving west across the region, you enter **Messinía**, with its mellower countryside and gorgeous, little-developed coast. There are good beaches at Messinía's own duo of medieval sites – the twin fortresses of **Koróni** and **Methóni** – but if you are looking for sands to yourself in the Peloponnese, and you're unbothered by a lack of facilities, you could do no better than explore the **shore north of Pílos**. En route are the remains of **Nestor's Palace**, foundations only, but the most important ancient site in the south and, like Mycenae, keying remarkably well with the Homeric legend.

Spárti (Sparta)

Thucydides predicted that if the city of Sparta were deserted, "distant ages would be very unwilling to believe its power at all equal to its fame". The city had no great temples or public buildings and throughout its period of greatness remained unfortified – Lycurgus, architect of the Spartan constitution, declared that "it is men not walls that make a city". Modern **SPÁRTI**, consequently, has few ancient ruins to speak of – and is today a rather gritty, market and agricultural town. The reason for coming here is basically to see **Mystra** – the Byzantine town, 5km east, which for a while controlled great swathes of the medieval world; an account follows below.

Practicalities

If it is Mystra that brings you to Spárti, and you arrive early in the day, you may well decide to move straight on. Spárti has an appeal in its ordinariness – in its café squares,

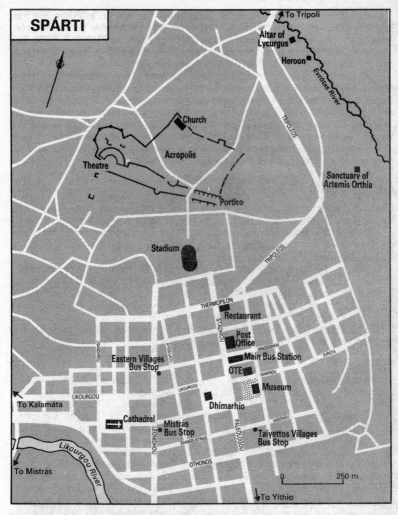

orange trees and evening *volta* – but it isn't the most rewarding of Greek towns. On the plus side, it usually has enough **hotels** to go around, at lower rates than those at Mystra. Choices include:

Hotel Sparti, Ayissiláou 46 (☎0731/21 343). Charges per-person rates. ②
Hotel Kypros, Leonidhíou 72 (☎0731/26 590). ②
Hotel Panhellinion, Konstandínou Paleológou (☎0731/28 031). ②
Hotel Apollo, Thermopílon 14 (☎0731/22 491). ④
Hotel Menelaion, Paleológou 91 (☎0731/22 161). ④
Hotel Lakonia, Paleológou 61 (☎0731/28 951). ④
Hotel Maniatis, corner Paleológou and Likoúrgou (☎0731/22 665). ⑤

There are two **campsites** out on the Mystra road. The nearest, just over 2km from Spárti, is *Camping Mystra* (☎0731/22 724) which has a swimming pool and is open year-round. Two kilometres further on – and thus closer to Mystra – is the new *Camping Castle View*, a very clean, well-managed site with a shop, snack bar, restaurant and slightly lower rates. Take the Mystra bus for either.

Getting out of Spárti is straightforward. The **main bus terminal** (for Trípoli, Athens, Monemvassía, Kalamáta and the Máni) is on Vrassídhou, just off Stadhíou. **Buses for Mystra** leave (hourly on weekdays; less frequently at lunchtime and at weekends) from the corner of the main street Likoúrgou and Ayissiláou; schedules are posted on the window of the café there. Getting to Áyios Ioánnis, trailhead for hikes up **Mount Taïyettos**, you'll need to take a bus from Meneláou, east of Stadhíou.

For **meals**, try the **restaurant** *Kali Kardia* at Ayissiláou 39, or a *psistariá* up at the north end of Stadhíou, just as it begins to bend into Tripoléos.

Ancient Sparta

Descending from the mountains that ring Spárti on all side, you get a sense of how strategic was the location of the ancient city-state of **SPARTA**. The ancient "capital" occupied more or less the site of today's town, though it was in fact less a city than a grouping of villages, commanding the Laconian plain and fertile Evrótas valley from a series of low hills to the east of the river.

The Greek city was at the height of its powers from the eighth to the fourth century BC, the period when Spartan society followed the laws of **Lycurgus**, defeated Athens in the Peloponnesian War, established colonies around the Greek world, and eventually lost hegemony through defeat to Thebes. A second period of prosperity came under the Romans – for whom this was an outpost in the south of Greece, with the Máni never properly subdued – though from the third century AD Sparta declined as nearby Mystra became the focus of Byzantine interest.

The sites

Traces of ancient Spartan glory are in short supply but there are some ruins to be seen to the north of the city: follow the track behind the football stadium towards the old **Acropolis**, tallest of the Spartan hills. An immense **Theatre** here, built into the side of the hill, can be quite clearly traced, even though today most of its masonry has gone – hurriedly adapted for fortification when the Spartans' power declined and, later still, used in the building of the Byzantine city of Mystra. Above the theatre, to the left, are the foundations of a **Temple to Athena**. At the top of the acropolis sits the more substantial Byzantine church and **Monastery of Óssios Nikónas**.

About 500 metres along the Trípoli road, a path descends to the remains of the **Sanctuary of Artemis Orthia**, where Spartan boys underwent endurance tests by flogging. The Roman geographer-travel writer Pausanias records that young men often expired under the lash and adds that the altar had to be splashed with blood before the goddess was satisfied. Perhaps it was this aspect that led the Romans to revive the custom; the main ruins here are of the grandstand they built for the spectacle.

Neither of these sites is enclosed, though this could change as excavation has been resumed and proper walkways laid out.

The Archaeological Museum

All movable artefacts and mosaics have been transferred to the town's small **Archaeological Museum** (Tues–Sat 8.30am–3pm, Sun 9.30am–2.30pm). Among its more interesting exhibits are a number of votive offerings found on the sanctuary site – knives set in stone that were presented as prizes to the Spartan youths and solemnly rededicated to the goddess.

Mystra (Mistrás)

A glorious, airy place, hugging a steep flank of Taíyettos, **Mystra** is arguably the most exciting and dramatic site that the Peloponnese can offer. Winding up the hillside is an astonishingly complete Byzantine city that once sheltered a population of some 42,000; you wander along winding alleys, through monumental gates, past medieval houses and palaces and above all into a sequence of churches, several of which yield superb and radiant frescoes. The effect is of wandering into a massive museum of architecture, painting and sculpture – and into a different age.

Some history

Mystra was basically a Frankish foundation. In 1249, Guillaume II de Villehardouin, fourth Frankish Prince of the Morea, built a castle here – one of a trio of fortresses (the others were at Monemvassía and in the Máni) designed to garrison his domain. The Franks, however, were driven out of Mystra by the Byzantines in 1271, and this isolated triangle of land in the southeastern Peloponnese – encompassing the old Spartan territories – became the **Despotate of Mystra**. This was the last province of the Greek Byzantine empire and for years, with Constantinople in terminal decay, was its virtual capital.

During the next two centuries, there emerged at Mystra a defiant rebirth of Byzantine power. The Despotate's rulers – usually the son or brother of the eastern emperor, often the heir-apparent – recaptured and controlled much of the Peloponnese, which became the largest of the ever-shrinking Byzantine provinces. They and their province were to endure for two centuries before eventual subjugation by the Turks. The end came in 1460 – seven years after the fall of Constantinople – when the despot Demetrius, feuding with his brothers, handed the city over to the Sultan Mehmet II.

Mystra's political significance, though, was in any case overshadowed by its **artistic achievements**. Throughout the fourteenth and the first decades of the fifteenth centuries it was the principal cultural and intellectual centre of the Byzantine world, sponsoring, in highly uncertain times, a renaissance in the arts and attracting the finest of Byzantine scholars and theologians – among them a number of members of the imperial families, the Cantacuzenes and Paleologues. Most notable of the court scholars was the humanist philosopher **Gemisthus Plethon**, who revived and reinterpreted Plato's ideas, using them to support his own brand of revolutionary teachings, which included the assertion that land should be redistributed amongst labourers and that reason should be placed on a par with religion. Although this had limited impact in Mystra itself – whose monks excommunicated him – his followers, who moved to teach in Italy after Mystra's fall, exercised wide influence in Renaissance Florence and Rome.

More tangibly, Mystra also saw a last flourish of **Byzantine architecture**, with the building of a magnificent Despots' palace and a perfect sequence of churches, multi-domed and brilliantly frescoed. It is these, remarkably preserved and sensitively restored, that provide the focus of this extraordinary site. In the painting, it is not hard to see something of the creativity and spirit of Plethon's court circle, as the stock Byzantine figures turn to more naturalistic forms and settings.

The town's **post-Byzantine history** follows a familiar Peloponnesian pattern. It remained in Turkish hands from the mid-fifteenth to late seventeenth centuries, then was taken briefly by the Venetians – under whom the town rose again to prosperity with a population of over 40,000. Decline set in with a second stage of Turkish control, from 1715 on, and destruction with the War of Independence, the site being evacuated after fires in 1770 and 1825. Restoration began in the first decades of this century, was interrupted by the civil war (it was, for a while, a battle site) and renewed in earnest in the 1950s when the last inhabitants were relocated.

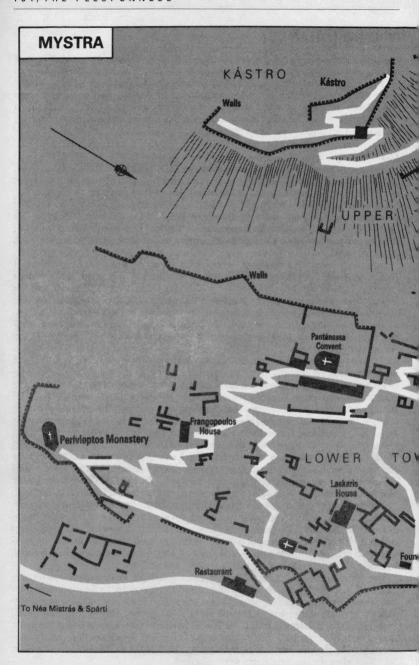

MYSTRA

KÁSTRO

Kástro

Walls

UPPER

Walls

Pantánassa Convent

Frangopoulos House

Perívleptos Monastery

LOWER TOW

Laskaris House

Foun

Restaurant

To Néa Mistrás & Spárti

Parking

Walls

Upper Entrance

Ay. Sofía

Náfplio Gate

Palatáki

kólaos

Despots' Palace

emvassía
Gate

Mosque

0   100 m

Refectory

Afendikó

Vrontohión
Monastery

Ay. Theódhori

Mitrópolis

Walls

Lower
Entrance

Xenia

The Byzantine city

Mon–Fri 8.30am–6pm, closes 3pm in winter, Sat & Sun 9.30am–2.30pm; entrance 1000dr.

The site of the Byzantine city comprises three main parts: the **Katohóra** (lower town), with the city's most important churches; the **Anohóra** (upper town), grouped around the vast shell of a royal palace; and the **Kástro** (castle). There are two entrances to the site: at the base of the lower town and by the Kástro.

A road loops up from the modern village of Néos Mistrás (see below) past both entrances. Buses from Spárti always stop at the lower entrance, and usually go up to the top, too. It's a good idea to stock up on refreshments before setting out; ther's a pricey summer snack bar at the lower gate, but nothing at the upper one or in the site itself.

The Upper Town and Kástro

Following a course from the upper entrance, the first identifiable building you come to is the church of **Ayía Sofía**, which served as the chapel for the Despots' Palace – the enormous structure beyond. The chapel's finest feature is its floor, made from polychrome marbles. Its frescoes, notably a *Pandokrator* (Christ in Majesty) and *Nativity of the Virgin*, have survived reasonably well, protected until recent years by coatings of whitewash applied by the Turks, who adapted the building as a mosque. Recognisable parts of the refectory and cells of its attached monastery also remain.

The **Kástro**, reached by a path direct from the upper gate, maintains the Frankish design of its original thirteenth-century construction, though it was repaired and modified by all successive occupants. There is a walkway around most of the keep, whose views allow an intricate panorama of the town below. The castle itself was the court of Guillaume II de Villehardouin but was used primarily as a citadel in later years.

Heading down from Ayía Sofía, there is a choice of routes. The right fork winds past ruins of a Byzantine mansion, the **Palatáki** or "Small Palace", and **Áyios Nikólaos**, originally a Turkish building. The left fork is more interesting, passing the massively fortified **Náfplio Gate**, which was the principal entrance to the upper town, and the vast, multistoreyed, gothic-looking complex of the **Despots' Palace**.

Parts of the palace (currently closed for restoration) probably date to the Franks. Most prominent among its numerous rooms is a great vaulted audience hall, built at right angles to the line of the building, with ostentatious windows regally dominating the skyline; this was once heated by eight great chimneys and sported a painted facade. Behind it are the ruins of various official public buildings, while to the right of the lower wing, flanking one side of a square used by the Turks as a marketplace, are the remains of a **mosque**.

The Lower Town

At the **Monemvassía Gate**, which links the upper and lower towns, there is a further choice of routes: right to the Pantánassa and Perívleptos monasteries; left to the Vrontohión monastery and cathedral. If time is running out it is easier to head right first, then double back down to the Vrontohión.

When excavations were resumed in 1952, the last thirty or so families, then still living in houses in the lower town, were moved out to Néos Mistrás. Only the nuns of the **Pantánassa** ("Queen of All") **convent** have remained. Its church is perhaps the finest surviving in Mystra, perfectly proportioned in its blend of Byzantine and Gothic. The **frescoes** date from various centuries, with some superb fifteenth-century work including *Scenes from the Life of Christ* in the gallery (entered by an external staircase). David Talbot Rice, in his classic study *Byzantine Art*, wrote of these frescoes that "Only El Greco in the west, and later Gauguin, would have used their colours in just this way". Other of the frescoes in the church were painted between 1687 and 1715, when Mystra was held by the Venetians.

Further down on this side of the lower town is a balconied Byzantine mansion, the **House of Frangopoulos**, once the home of the Despotate's chief minister – who was incidentally the founder of the Pantánassa.

Beyond it is the diminutive **Perívleptos monastery**, whose single-domed church, partially carved out of the rock, contains Mystra's most complete cycle of frescoes, almost all of which date from the fourteenth century. They are in some ways finer than those of the Pantánassa, blending an easy humanism with the spirituality of Byzantine icon traditions. In addition, they give an excellent idea of the structured iconography of a Byzantine church. The position of each figure depended upon its sanctity and so here upon the dome, the image of heaven, is portrayed the *Pandokrator* (the all-powerful Christ in glory after the Ascension); on the apse is the Virgin, and on the higher expanses of wall are depicted scenes from the *Life of Christ in this World*. Prophets and saints could only appear on the lower walls, decreasing in importance according to their distance from the sanctuary.

Along the path leading from Perívleptos to the lower gate are a couple of minor, much-restored churches, and, just above them, the **Laskaris House**, a mansion thought once to have belonged to relatives of the emperors. Like the Frangopoulos House, it is balconied; its ground floor probably served as a stables. Close by, beside the path, is an old Turkish fountain.

The **Mitrópolis**, or cathedral, immediately beyond the gateway, is the oldest of Mystra's churches, built in 1309 under the first Paleologue ruler. A marble slab set in its floor is carved with the double-headed eagle of Byzantium, commemorating the spot where Constantine XI Paleologus, the last Eastern emperor, was crowned in 1448; he was to perish, with his empire, in the Turkish sacking of Constantinople in 1453. Of the church's frescoes, the earliest, in the north aisle, depict the *Torture and Burial of Áyios Dhimítrios*, the saint to whom the church is dedicated. The comparative stiffness of their figures contrasts with the later works opposite. These, illustrating the *Miracles of Christ* and the *Life of the Virgin*, are more intimate and lighter of touch; they date from the last great years before Mystra's fall. A **museum**, adjacent to the cathedral, contains various fragments of sculpture and pottery and a few icons from the various Mystra churches.

Finally, a short way uphill, is the **Vrontohión monastery**. This was the centre of cultural and intellectual life in the fifteenth-century town – the cells of the monastery can still be discerned – and it was also the burial place of the despots. There are two churches attached. **Afendikó**, the further of the two, has been beautifully restored, revealing late frescoes, similar to those of Perívleptos, with startlingly bold juxtapositions of colour.

Néos Mistrás: some practicalities

Buses run regularly through the day from Spárti to the lower Mystra site entrance, stopping (if requested) at the campsites en route (see Spárti), as well as at the modern village of **NÉOS MISTRÁS**. This is quite attractive in its own right: a small roadside community whose half-dozen tavernas, crowded with tour buses by day, revert to a low-key life at night.

In general, staying in Néos Mistrás is worth the bit extra over Spárti, for the setting and early access to the site, though you will need to book ahead, or arrive early in the day, to find a place. Accommodation is limited to a single **hotel**, the *Vyzantion* (☎0731/93 309; ④), which is pleasant but oversubscribed for most of the year, and a small number of private rooms – those run by Dhimitris Bakaviolos (☎0731/93 432; ②) are especially recommended.

The Bakaviolos family also has a decent taverna, while the **restaurant** opposite the hotel, *To Kastro*, is excellent if a bit on the expensive side.

West from Spárti: Mount Taíyettos and the Langádha pass

Moving **on from Spárti** there is a tough choice of routes: west over Mount Taíyettos, either on foot or by road through the dramatic **Langádha Pass to Kalamáta**; south, skirting the mountain's foothills, to **Yíthio and the Máni**; or east to the Byzantine towns of **Yeráki and Monemvassía.**

For anyone wanting to get to grips with the Greek mountains, there is **Mount Taíyettos** itself. This is one of the most dramatic and hazardous ranges, with vast grey boulders and scree along much of its length, but it has one reasonably straightforward path to the highest peak, Profítis Ilías.

Hiking Mount Taíyettos (Taygettus)

Gazing up at the crags above the castle at Mystra, Mount Taíyettos looks daunting and inviting in pretty equal measure. If all you want is a different perspective on the mountain, then the simplest course is to take a bus from Spárti to **ÁYIOS IOÁNNIS**, a little way to the south of Mystra and closer to the peaks. From there a spectacular *kalderími* (cobbled way) leads up from the gravel-crushing mill behind the village to **ANAVRITÍ**, which boasts superb vistas, a single friendly **hotel** (☎0731/21 788 or 91 288; ②) and one very basic taverna aside from the one in the hotel.

An alternative, more popular approach involves following the marked E4 overland route, partly on track, partly on trail, up from Néos Mistrás via the **monastery of Faneroméni**. Neither the E4 nor the *kalderími* take more than two hours uphill, and they can be combined as follows for a wonderful day's outing: bus to Áyios Ioánnis, taxi to rock-crushing mill (2.5km), hike up to Anavrití, have a look around and a meal, then descend via Faneroméni to Néos Mistrás.

Hking beyond Anavrití: the Profítis Ilías area

Most **hikes beyond Anavrití** need experience and proper equipment, including the relevant *Korfes* or *YIS* maps, and should definitely not be undertaken alone – a sprained ankle (or flash floods) could be fatal up here. If you are confident, however, there are various routes to the Profítis Ilías summit and beyond:

● The only straightforward route is to **follow the E4** long-distance footpath, here a forest road, for five hours south to the **alpine refuge at Ayía Varvára** (see below).

● The classic approach to the **Profítis Ilías summit** used to entail a dusty, eleven-kilometre road-walk up from the village of PALEOPANAYÍA, a short bus ride south of Spárti off the Yíthio road, to the spring and ex-trailhead at BÓLIANA, where there's a single ramshackle hut owned by the Dousmanis family that serves drinks and perhaps meals in summer. Since 1988, however, bulldozers have pushed further up the mountain, wiping out most of the former onward trail. After Paleopanayía you now have to proceed past Bóliana towards Anavrití on the E4 track for about half an hour, then bear left near a picnic ground and spring (the last reliable water on the mountain). Another half-hour above this, following E4 blazes, and what's left of the old trail appears on the right, signposted *EOS Spárti Katafíyio*. This short-cuts the new road except for the very last fifty metres to the Ayía Varvára refuge.

● A more challenging option, requiring mountaineering skills, is to adopt the red-dotted trail veering off the E4 early on up to a point just below the 1700-metre saddle described by Patrick Leigh Fermor in *Mani*, where you must choose between dropping to the far side of the range or (very high and very narrow) ridge-walking to the Profítis Ilías summit (2404m).

Crossing the pass would land you at the head of the **Ríndomo gorge**, where you can camp at the chapel-monastery of Panayía Kavsodhematúsa before descending the next day to either GATÍSES or PIGÁDHIA, near the Messinian coast. Keeping to the watershed it is seven tough hours to the peak even in optimum conditions and with a light load, involving exposed rock pinnacles to worm around, sheer drops, and rotten surfaces. This is not a hike to be lightly undertaken.

AYÍA VARVÁRA TO THE SUMMIT

The **Ayía Varvára refuge** (unstaffed, open sporadically – more likely at weekends) sits on a beautiful grassy knoll shaded by tremendous storm-blasted black pines. The conical peak of Profítis Ilías rises directly above; if you can get your climb to coincide with a full moon you won't regret it. There is plenty of room for camping, and the hut has a porch to provide shelter in bad weather.

The **path to the summit** starts at the rear left corner of the refuge and swings right on a long reach. Level and stony at first, it leaves the treeline and loops up a steep bank to a sloping meadow, where it is ineffectually marked by twisted, rusting signs with their lettering long obliterated. Keep heading right across the slope towards a distinct secondary peak until, once around a steep bend, the path begins to turn back left in the direction of the summit. It slants steadily upward following a natural ledge until, at a very clear nick in the ridge above you, it turns right and crosses to the far side, from where you look down on the Gulf of Messinía. Turn left and you climb steeply up to the summit in around 25 minutes.

There is a squat stone chapel and outbuildings on the **summit**, used during the celebrations of the Feast of the Prophet Elijah (Profítis Ilías) on July 18–20. The views, as you would expect, are breathtaking, encompassing the sea to east and west.

The terrain **beyond the peak** is beyond the ambitions of casual hikers. The easiest and safest way off the mountain **towards the Messinian coast** is to follow the E4 from Ayía Varvára to the gushing springs at Pendávli, and then over a low saddle to the summer hamlet of ÁYIOS DHIMÍTRIOS. This takes just a couple of hours and you can camp in the beautiful surroundings. In the morning you're well poised, at the head of the **Víros gorge**, to handle the all-day descent to Kardhamíli through the other great Taiyettan canyon. At one point you negotiate stretches of the **Kakí Skála**, one of the oldest paths in Greece, built to link ancient Sparta and Messene.

Spárti to Kalamáta: the Langádha pass

The **Langádha pass**, the sixty-kilometre route across the Taíyettos from **Spárti to Kalamáta**, was the former alternative to the Kakí Skála and is still the only paved road across the mountain. Remote and barren, with no habitation at all for the central 25-kilometre section, it unveils in a constant drama of peaks, magnificent at all times but startling at sunrise. This was, incidentally, the route that Telemachus took in *The Odyssey* on his way from Nestor's palace at Pylos to that of Menelaus at Sparta. It took him a day's journey by chariot – good going by any standards, since today's buses take three hours.

Heading from Spárti, the last settlement is TRÍPI, 14km out, where there are two small **hotels**, the *Keadas* (☎0731/98 222; ③) and *Trypi* (☎0731/26 387; ③). Just beyond the village, the road climbs steeply into the mountains and enters the **gorge of Langádha**, a wild sequence of hairpins through the pines. To the north of the gorge, so it is said, the Spartans used to leave their sick or puny babies to die from exposure.

Beyond the gorge, close to the summit of the pass, there is a summer-only **hotel**, the *Pension Taiyetos* (③), and a *Tourist Pavilion* serving meals. The first actual village on the Kalamáta side is ARTEMISÍA, where you often have to change buses. Then you enter another gorge before the final zigzagging descent to Kalamáta.

East from Spárti: Yeráki

A kilometre or two north of Spárti, a roadside sign suggests a detour to "visit the Byzantine antiquities" at **YERÁKI**. Such signs in Greece too often make mountains of archaeological molehills, but in this case the advice is sound. With its Frankish castle and fifteen chapels spread over a spur of Mount Párnon, Yeráki stands a creditable – if rather distant – third to the sites of Mystra and Monemvassía.

Medieval Yeráki

Yeráki was one of the original twelve Frankish baronies set up in the wake of the Fourth Crusade, and remained through the fourteenth century an important Byzantine town, straddling the road between Mystra and its port at Monemvássia. The site is spectacular, with sweeping vistas over the olive-covered Evrótas plain and across to Taíyettos. It stands four kilometres outside the current village of Yeráki (see below), on the first outcrop of the Párnon mountains.

Although the site itself is unenclosed, all the main churches are kept locked, and to visit them you should first make enquiries at the café on the village square for the caretaker; he can usually be found here, unless he's already up at the site. You'll be given a tour by him, clambering around the rocks to the best-preserved chapels.

The most substantial remains of the medieval town are of its fortress, the **Kástro**, built in 1256 by the local Frankish baron, Jean de Nivelet, who had inherited Yeráki, with six other lordships, from his father. Its heavily fortified design is based on that of the Villehardouin fortress at Mystra, for this was one of the most vulnerable Frankish castles of the Morea, intended to control the wild and only partially conquered territories of Taíyettos and the Máni. In the event, Jean retained his castle for less than a decade, surrendering to the Byzantines in 1262 and buying an estate near Kórinthos on the proceeds. Within the fortress are huge **cisterns** for withstanding siege, and the largest of Yeráki's churches: the thirteenth-century **Mitrópolis**, also known as **Áyios Yióryios**, which features blackened Byzantine frescoes, a Frankish iconostasis and the Villehardouin arms.

The churches on the slope below also mix Frankish and Byzantine features, and many incorporate ancient blocks from Yeráki's ancient predecessor, Geronthrai. The caretaker is usually prepared to unlock two or three, including **Áyios Dhimítrios**, **Zoódohos Píyi**, and **Áyia Paraskeví** (at the base of the hill), each of which has restored frescoes.

The village

The "modern" village of **YERÁKI** has no regular accommodation, though rooms may be negotiable through the café or taverna in the square. **Buses** run several times daily to Spárti, but not along the splendid route over Mount Párnon to Leonídhi (see p.158).

Near the top of the settlement is a very ancient **acropolis**, preserving stretches of Mycenaean walls, that's now used as a playground.

Monemvassía

After Mystra you half-expect Byzantine sites to be disappointing – or at least low-key like Yeráki. **MONEMVASSÍA** is emphatically neither. Set impregnably on a great island-like irruption of rock, the medieval seaport and commercial centre of the Byzantine Peloponnese is equally as exciting as its spiritual counterpart inland: a place of grand, haunted atmosphere, whose houses and churches are all the more evocative for being populated – albeit on a largely weekend and touristic basis.

The town's name – an elision of *Moni Emvasis* or "single entrance" – is a reference to its approach from the mainland, across a kilometre-long causeway built this century to replace a sequence of wooden bridges. Such a defensible and strategic position gave it control, through the Middle Ages, of the sea-lines from Italy and the West to Constantinople and the Levant. Fortified on all approaches, it was invariably the last outpost of the Peloponnese to fall to invaders, and was only ever taken through siege.

Some history

Founded by the **Byzantines** in the sixth century, Monemvassía became at once an important port. It remained in Byzantine possession for almost seven hundred years, passing only very briefly to the Franks – who took it in 1249 after a three-years' siege but had to ransom it back for the captured Guillaume de Villehardouin. Subsequently, it served as the chief commercial port of the Despotate of the Morea and was to all effects the Greek Byzantine capital. Mystra, despite the presence of the court, was never much more than a large village; Monemvassía at its peak had a population of almost 60,000.

Like Mystra, Monemvassía had something of a golden age in the thirteenth century: a period when it was populated by a number of noble Byzantine families, and reaped considerable wealth from estates inland, from the export of wine (the famed *Malmsey*, mentioned by Shakespeare) and from roving corsairs who preyed on Latin shipping heading for the East. When the rest of the Morea fell to the Turks in 1460, Monemvassía was able to seal itself off, placing itself first under the control of the Papacy, later under the **Venetians**. Only in 1540 did the **Turks** gain control, the Venetians having abandoned their garrison after the defeat of their navy at Préveza.

Turkish occupation precipitated a steady decline, both in prestige and population, though the Venetians revived the town for a second period in the eighteenth century, when for twenty-odd years they took the Peloponnese from the Turks. Monemvassía then again came to the forefront of events during the **War of Independence**. It was the first of the major Turkish fortresses to fall, after a terrible siege and wholesale massacre of the Turkish inhabitants, in April 1821.

After the war, there was no longer the need for such strongholds, and, at the end of the nineteenth century, shipping routes changed, too, with the opening of the Corinth Canal. The population plummeted and the town drifted into a village existence, its buildings for the most part allowed to fall into ruin. By the time of World War II – during which 4000 New Zealand troops were evacuated from the rock – only eighty families remained. Today there are just ten in permanent residence.

The rock: medieval Monemvassía

From the mainland waterfront town of **Yéfira** – where the causeway to **Monemvassía** (or **Kástro**, as locals call it) begins – nothing can be seen of the medieval town, which is built purely on the seaward face of the rock. Little more is revealed as you walk across the causeway, past a spectral-looking garage with a rattling Mobil sign. Then suddenly the road is barred by huge castellated walls. Once through the fortified entrance gate, wide enough only for a single person or donkey, everything finally appears: piled upon one another amid narrow stone streets and alleyways are houses with tiled roofs and walled gardens, distinctively Byzantine churches, and high above, the improbably long castle walls protecting the town on the summit.

The Lower Town

Standing at the **gateway** to the rock there is the same sense of luxury and excitement as at Mystra: the prospect of being able to walk each street, explore every possible turn of this extraordinary place. The **Lower Town** here once numbered forty churches and over eight hundred homes, an incredible mass of building, which explains the intricate network of alleys. A single main street – up and slightly to the left from the gateway – shelters most of the restored houses, as well as a scattering of cafés, tavernas and shops. One of the tavernas is owned by the Ritsos family, relatives of the late Yannis Ritsos, one of Greece's leading poets and a lifelong communist, who was born on the rock; a plaque on a house near the main gate commemorates his birthplace.

At the end of this street is the lower town's main **platía**, a beautiful public space, with a well in its centre, a *kafenío* along one side, and, on the other, the great, vaulted **Mitrópolis** – the cathedral built by the Byzantine Emperor Andronicus II Comnenus when he made Monemvassía a see in 1293. The largest medieval church in southern Greece, it is dedicated to Christ in Chains (*Hristós Elkómenos*). Across the square is the domed church of **Áyios Pávlos**, which was transformed by the Turks into a mosque and now houses a small museum of local finds (open unpredictably). Unusually for Ottoman Greece, the Christian cathedral was allowed to function during the occupation – and must have done so beside this mosque.

Down towards the sea is a third notable church, the **Hrissafítissa**, whose bell hangs from a bent-over old cypress tree in the courtyard. It was restored and adapted by the Venetians in their second – eighteenth-century – occupation. Continuing on here by the sea, past the *Malvasia*, you can get to a small **platform for swimming**.

The Upper Town

The climb to the **Upper Town** is highly worthwhile – not least for the solitude, since most of the day-trippers stay down below. It's also a vast site – much bigger than it looks from below – so to explore at leisure, bring some food and drink (from Yéfira: Monemvássia has no shop). There are sheer drops from the rockface, and unguarded cisterns, so descend before dusk and if you have young children, keep them close.

The fortifications, like those of the lower town, are substantially intact; indeed the **entrance gate** retains its iron slats. Within, the site is a ruin, unrestored and deserted – the last resident moved down in 1911 – though many structures are still recognisable. The only building that is fully intact, however, is the beautiful thirteenth-century **Ayía Sofía**, by the gateway. It was founded as a monastery by Andronikos II, along a plan similar to that of Dhafní, though the outbuildings have long since crumbled to foundations. In the chapel itself, candles still flicker perilously in the wind.

Beyond the church extend acres of ruins: in medieval times the population here was much greater than that of the lower town. Among the remains are the stumpy bases of Byzantine houses and public buildings, and, perhaps most striking, a vast **cistern** to ensure a water supply in time of siege. Monemvassía must have been more or less self-sufficient in this respect. Its weakness was its food supply, which had to be entirely imported from the mainland. In the last siege, by Mavromihalis's Maniot army in the War of Independence, the Turks were reduced to eating rats – and, so the propagandists claimed, Greek children.

Monemvassía and Yéfira practicalities

Monemvassía can be approached by road or sea. There are twice-weekly **ferries** from Pireás, and Kastélli on Crete, and more frequent **hydrofoils** in season, linking the town to the north with Leonídhi, Spétses and Pireás, and to the south with Yíthio, Neápoli and the island of Kíthira. Direct **buses** connect with Spárti three times daily and twice (in season only) with Yíthio; occasionally a change at Mólai is necessary. Out of season it's best to alight at SKÁLA, 17km from Yíthio, and take a bus or taxi or hitch from there.

The boat or hydrofoil will drop you at a mooring midway down the causeway; buses arrive in the town of **YÉFIRA** on the mainland. This is little more than a straggle of rooms, restaurants and hotels for the rock's tourist trade, with a pebble beach.

Rooms and restaurants on the rock

Rooms on the rock are expensive – in season and out – and from June to September, you'll need to book ahead.

The choice is between two very attractive and upmarket **hotels**, each of which has beautifully restored and traditionally furnished rooms. The *Malvasia* (☎0732/61 323; ⑤) occupies two adjoining mansions, between the main street and the sea. The *Byzantio* (☎0732/61 351; ⑤) is similarly characterful, and marginally cheaper. Both are signposted from Monemvassía's main street.

Several other **furnished apartments** on the rock are available for long-term rental. If you ask around at the shops and taverna on the main street, it's just possible that you might get one of these on a more temporary basis, out of season.

Eating out in the old village is enjoyable, though as much for location as food. Establishments run the gamut from *To Kanoni* – a very pricey fish and seafood restaurant – to pizzas at *To Kastro*, down towards the sea.

Practicalities in Yéfira

There's more accommodation in Yéfira, along with various other useful tourist services: a **bank** and **post office**, an **OTE** and a **travel agent**, *Malavasia Travel* (☎0732/61 497), which sells ferry tickets and rents out **bicycles and mopeds**.

Best value of the **hotels** are the *Akroyiali* (☎0732/61 202; ②) and *Aktaion* (☎0732/61 234, ③), both facing the causeway. If these are full, there are plenty of others to choose from, plus dozens of rooms for rent, advertised along the waterfront. The nearest **campsite**, *Camping Paradise* (☎0732/61 123), is around 3.5km to the south, along the coast road. For a **beach** day trip, it's best to head 3–4km north of town.

South to Neápoli and Elafónissos

The isolated southeasternmost "finger" of the Peloponnese to the south of Monemvassía is a bit disappointing, with little of interest in either its villages or landscape. However, the tiny port of Neápoli offers access to the islet of Elafónissos, just offshore, and to the larger Ionian islands of Kíthira and Andíkithira, midway to Crete.

Neápoli

NEÁPOLI is a mix of old buildings and modern Greek concrete behind a grey sand beach – hardly compelling, aside from its ferry and hydrofoil connections. For such an out of the way (and not especially attractive) place, it is surprisingly developed, catering mainly to Greek holidaymakers. Its two good-value **pensions**, the *Aivali* (☎0732/41 287; ③) and *Arsenakos* (☎0732/41 991; ③), are best booked well ahead in summer.

Neápoli **beach** extends north to the village of VINGLÁFIA, where you can negotiate for a fishing boat across the 400-metre channel to the islet of Elafónissos. Alternatively, you can get a small ferry to Elafónissos from Neápoli.

Elafónissos island

Like Neápoli, **Elafónissos** is relatively busy in summer, and again mainly frequented by Greek visitors. Its lone village is largely modern and functional, but has plenty of rooms and some good fish tavernas. The two **pensions**, the *Asteri tis Elafonissou* (☎0732/49 271; ③) and *Elafonissos* (☎0732/49 268; ③), are worth booking.

Although scenically barren, the island has one of the best beaches in this part of Greece at KÁTO NÍSSO, a large double bay of fine white sand; it's 5km southeast of the village, from where a caique leaves every morning in summer. There's one basic sandwich-and-drinks stall, and usually a small community of people camping here. Another beach to the southwest of the village is quieter but less spectacular.

Kíthira island

Isolated at the foot of the Peloponnese, the island of **Kíthira** traditionally belongs to the Ionian islands, and shares their history of Venetian, and later, British rule; under the former it was known as Cerigo. For the most part, the similarities end there. The island architecture, whitewashed and flat-roofed, looks more like that of the Cyclades, albeit with a strong Venetian influence. The landscape is different, too: wild scrub- and gorse-covered hills or moorland sliced by deep valleys and ravines.

Depopulation has left the land underfarmed and the abandoned fields overgrown, for, since the war, most of the islanders have left for Athens or Australia, creating for Kíthira the reputation of being the emigrant island to beat all others. Many of the villages are deserted, their *platías* empty and the schools and *kafenía* closed. Kíthira was never a rich island, but, along with Monemvassía, it once had a military and economic significance – which it likewise lost with Greek independence and the opening of the Corinth Canal. These days, tourism has brought a little prosperity but most summer visitors are Greeks and especially Greek-Australians, whose families come from here. For the few foreigners who reach Kíthira, it remains something of a refuge, with its fine and remarkably undeveloped beaches the principal attraction.

Arriving – and getting around

If you arrive by **boat or hydrofoil** from Pireás or Neápoli in the Peloponnese, you'll probably disembark at AYÍA PELAYÍA in the north of the island. If you're coming from Yíthio or Kastélli on Crete, you'll more likely arrive at KAPSÁLI, below Kíthira's capital, HÓRA, in the south. It's usually possible to find a **taxi** at either harbour, but don't hope for public transport – in summer, the island **bus** runs just once a day between Ayía Pelayía, Potamós, Hóra and Kapsáli, and out of season reverts to its role as the school bus – although you can generally flag it down if you don't mind joining the kids.

Hitching is possible if you have plenty of patience but there isn't a lot of traffic, even on the main road from Hóra to Potamós. Indeed, most places on Kíthira, beaches in particular, are difficult to reach without your own transport, so you're well advised to rent a **moped**, ideal for the island's 30-by-15-kilometre size.

The **airport** is deep in the interior, 8km east of Potamós; taxis meet arrivals.

Ayía Pelayía and northern Kíthira

Most people coming to Kíthira arrive in **AYÍA PELAYÍA**, the island's main port. First appearances aren't too promising, with a line of modern buildings along the waterside and an uninspiring pebble beach. However, it does have a reasonable choice of tavernas, bars and **rooms**, plus the more luxurious *Pension Kytheria* (☎0733/33 321; ④).

There is also a series of excellent **beaches** to the south. Heading out of town, an unpaved road follows the coast for 3km, passing increasingly deserted stretches of pebbles and gritty sand until it arrives at the seaward end of the **Káko Langádhi gorge**. If you're curious, it's possible to explore the entrance to the gorge, though you'd need climbing equipment to reach Paleohóra (see below) at the other end.

Potamós and around

From Ayía Pelayía, the main road winds up the mountainside towards **POTAMÓS**, Kíthira's largest village. It has a few **rooms**, together with **tavernas**, **banks**, a **post office**, *Olympic Airways* office and petrol station. Most of the shops on the island are here, too, as is the **Sunday market**, Kíthira's liveliest regular event. Out of season, it's one of the few places on Kíthira where anything stays open. All in all, it's a pleasant village and with a rented vehicle it could make a good base for exploring the island.

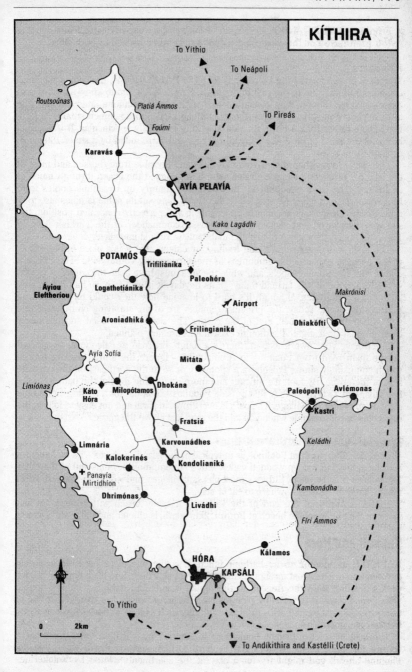

KÍTHIRA

To Yíthio

To Neápoli

To Pireás

Routsoúnas

Platiá Ámmos

Foúrni

Karavás

AYÍA PELAYÍA

Kako Lagádhi

POTAMÓS

Trifiliánika

Paleohóra

Áyiou Eleftheríou

Logathetiánika

Makrónisi

Airport

Aroniadhiká

Frilingianiká

Dhiakófti

Ayía Sofía

Mitáta

Limiónas

Dhokána

Káto Hóra

Milopótamos

Paleópoli

Avlémonas

Kastri

Fratsiá

Keládhi

Limnária

Karvounádhes

Kalokerinés

Kondolianiká

Kambonádha

Panayía Mirtidhíon

Dhrimónas

Livádhi

Fíri Ámmos

Kálamos

HÓRA

KAPSÁLI

To Yíthio

0   2km

To Andíkithira and Kastélli (Crete)

From LOGOTHETIÁNIKA, just south of Potamós, an unpaved road leads down to **Áyiou Eleftheríou** on the west coast, a good sandy beach backed by high cliffs.

Paleohóra

The main reason for visiting Potamós is to get to **PALEOHÓRA**, the ruined medieval capital of Kíthira, 3km to the east of the town. Few people seem to know about or visit these remains, though they constitute one of the best Byzantine sites around. The most obvious comparison is with Mystra: although Paleohóra is much smaller, a forti-fied village rather than a town, its natural setting is equally spectacular. It is set on a hilltop at the head of the Káko Langádhi gorge, and surrounded by a sheer 100-metre drop on three sides.

The site is lower than the surrounding hills and invisible from the sea and most of the island – protection against pirates, who have plagued the island through much of its history. The town was built in the fourteenth century by Byzantine nobles from Monemvassía, and when Mystra fell to the Turks, many of its noble families also took refuge here. Despite its seemingly impregnable and perfectly concealed position, the site was discovered and sacked by Barbarossa, commander of the Turkish fleet, in 1537, and the island's seven thousand inhabitants were sold into slavery.

The town was never rebuilt, and tradition maintains that it is a place of ill fortune, which perhaps explains the emptiness of the surrounding countryside. The hills are dotted with Byzantine chapels, and while the area must have been the centre of medie-val Kíthira, none of it is farmed today. In its heyday, it is said to have had 800 inhabi-tants and 72 churches, although it's hard to imagine how they could have fitted into such a small area. Today, the principal remains are of the surviving churches, some still with traces of frescoes, and of the castle. The site is unenclosed and has never been seriously investigated, although excavations are now planned.

If you have your own transport, there's a rough dirt road to Paleohóra, signposted off the main road from Potamós to Aroniadhiká – ignore the tourist map of Kíthira which confusingly shows Paleohóra a kilometre or so to the northeast on the opposite side of the gorge. By foot, it's quicker and more interesting to take the path from the tiny village of TRIFILIÁNIKA, just outside Potamós – look out for a rusting sign to the right as you enter the village. The path is overgrown in parts and not easy to follow; the ruins only become visible when you join the road just above the gorge.

Karavás

KARAVÁS, 6km north of Potamós, is untypical of the island's villages – its architecture and the setting, in a deep wooded valley with a stream, more reminiscent of the other Ionian islands. It is one of Kíthira's most pleasant villages, and would be a superb base, though there is (as yet) nowhere to eat or stay.

Platiá Ámmos, at the end of the valley, is a sandy beach with a seasonal fish **taverna**. The little pebble beach at **Foúmi**, 2km south, is quieter and more attractive.

Kapsáli and Hóra

KAPSÁLI, in addition to its harbour function, is the one place on Kíthira largely devoted to tourism. Most foreign visitors to Kíthira stay here, and it's a popular call for yachts heading from the Aegean to the Ionian islands and Italy. Set behind double pebble-sand bays, it is certainly picturesque. The larger of its two bays has a line of tavernas and a couple of bars – Kíthira's nightlife, such as it is. The taverna nearest the harbour has good food at reasonable prices.

The best places are usually booked up in summer by a British holiday company; **rooms** for more casual visitors can be hard to find, and expensive when you do. Phoning ahead, you might try for a stay at the apartments owned by Kalokerines

Katikies (☎0733/31 265; ④), Emmanuel Komnenos (☎0733/31 201; ③), or Byron Duponte (☎0733/31 245; ③). Alternatively, there's a **campsite** in the pine trees behind the village. Near the harbour, *Mihalis* (☎0733/31 008) and *Panayiotis* (☎0733/31 004) rent **motorbikes and mopeds**, and the latter also has windsurfboards and canoes.

Hóra

HÓRA (or KÍTHIRA town), a steep 2km haul above Kapsáli, has an equally dramatic site, its Cycladic-style houses tiered about the walls of a Venetian castle. Within the **castle**, most of the buildings are ruined, but there are spectacular views of Kapsáli and, out to sea, to the islet of Avgó (Egg), legendary birthplace of Aphrodite. Below the castle are the remains of older Byzantine walls, and twenty-one Byzantine churches in various states of dereliction. A small museum houses modest remnants of the island's numerous occupiers, in particular Minoan finds from excavations at Paleópoli.

Compared to Kapsáli, Hóra stays quiet. A few **tavernas** open in summer, of which *Zorba* is by far the best, but the climb from Kapsáli discourages the crowds. Out of season, only one café/fast-food place stays open, near the square. **Rooms** are slightly easier to find than in Kapsáli. Two good possibilities are the *Pension Keti* (☎0733/31 318, ③), and *Ta Kithera* at MANITOHÓRI, 2km inland (☎0733/31 563; ③). Other facilities include a couple of **banks**, an **OTE**, **post office**, petrol station, **car rental** firm and a second branch of *Panayiotis* with more **mopeds** for rent.

The Southeast Coast

The beach at Kapsáli is decent but gets very crowded in July and August. For quieter, undeveloped beaches, it's better to head out to the east coast, towards Avlémonas. Be warned, however, that the roads are unpaved and hazardous on moped.

Fíri Ámmos and Kambonádha

Fíri Ámmos, the nearest good sand beach to Kapsáli, is popular but not overcrowded, even in summer. To get there, you can follow a paved road as far as the sleepy village of KÁLAMOS (take the northerly side road between Kapsáli and Hóra); Fíri Ámmos is signposted down a dirt track on the far side of the village.

Fíri Ámmos can also be reached from the inland village of LIVÁDHI, on the Hóra–Arodhiánika road – as can **Kambonádha**, the next beach north.

Paleópoli and Avlémonas

PALEÓPOLI, a hamlet of a few scattered houses, is accessible by a paved road from ARONIÁDHIKA. The area is the site of the ancient city of **Skandia**, and excavations on the headland of **Kastrí** have revealed remains of an important Minoan colony. There's little visible evidence, apart from shards of pottery in the low crumbling cliffs, but happily, tourist development in the area has been barred because of its archaeological significance. In consequence, there's just one solitary **taverna**, the *Skandia* (open June–Sept) on the excellent two-kilometre, sand-and-pebble **beach** that stretches to either side of the headland.

The surrounding countryside, a broad, cultivated valley surrounded by wild hills, is equally attractive. **Paleokástro**, the mountain to the west, is the site of ancient Kithira and a sanctuary of Aphrodite, but again, there's little to be seen today. Heading across the valley and turning right, an unpaved road leads up to a tiny, whitewashed church above the cliffs. From there, a track leads down to **Keládhi**, a beautiful pebble beach with caves and rocks out to sea.

AVLÉMONAS, 2km east of Paleópoli, is a tiny fishing port with two tavernas, a few rooms and a rather unimpressive Venetian fortress. The coast is rocky, the scenery bleak and exposed, and the village has something of an end-of-the-world feel.

Dhiakófti

DHIAKÓFTI, over the mountain to the north of Avlémonas, is equally bleak and remote, but surprisingly has developed into something of a resort for Greek families. The main attraction is a tiny white sand beach with a few fishermen's cottages at the back and views across to the islet of **Makrónisi** – picturesque, but crowded in summer. The village itself has plenty of **rooms**, a few **tavernas**, and prominent "No Camping" signs.

Inland from Hóra

LIVÁDHI, 4km north of Hóra, has **rooms** and tavernas and, nearby (2km out), an oddly English-looking arched bridge – a legacy of the nineteenth-century era when the British had a protectorate of all the Ionian islands. From the village, a fork heads west to KALOKERINÉS, and continues 3km further to the island's principal monastery, **Panayía Mirtidhíon**, set among cypress trees above the wild and windswept west coast. Beyond the monastery, a track leads down to a small anchorage at LIMNÁRIA. There are few beaches along this rocky, forbidding shore.

Milopótamos, Káto Hóra and the Áyia Sofía cave

North of Livádhi, the main road crosses a bleak plateau whose few settlements are near-deserted. At DHOKÁNA it's worth making a detour off the main road for **MILOPÓTAMOS**, a lovely traditional village and a virtual oasis, set in a wooded stream valley; it has one, fairly expensive, **hotel**.

Nearby the village is a waterfall. It's hidden from above by lush vegetation – follow the sign for "Neraidha" past an abandoned restaurant. The valley below the falls is overgrown but contains ruins of the watermill that gave the village its name.

Káto Hóra, 500m down the road, was Milopótamos' predecessor. Now derelict, it remains half-enclosed within the walls of a Venetian fortress. The fortress is small and has a rather domestic appearance – unlike the castle at Hóra, it was built as a place of refuge for the villagers in case of attack, rather than as a base for a Venetian garrison. All the houses within the walls, and many outside, are abandoned. Beyond here, an unpaved and precipitous road continues 5km through spectacular scenery to **Limiónas**, a rocky bay with a small beach of fine white sand.

The reason most visitors come to Milopótamos is to see the cave of **Áyia Sofía**, the largest and most impressive of a number of caverns on the island. It's a half-hour walk, signposted from the village. The cave is only open regularly in the summer (3–8pm), but you could probably find a guide in Milopótamos at other times of the year if you ask at the village taverna. The cave is worth the effort to see, spreading across a series of chambers with stalactites and stalagmites, to a depth of 250m. The whitewashed entrance to the system has been used as a church and has a painted iconostasis.

Andikíthira island

The tiny island of **ANDIKÍTHIRA** has twice-weekly connections in summer only on the Kíthira–Kastélli run. Rocky and poor, it only received electricity in 1984. Attractions include a good birdlife and flora, but don't visit if you want too much company. There are only fifty or so inhabitants, including a resident doctor and teacher (there are three children at the village school, as comparted to 37 twenty-five years ago).

The inhabitants are divided between two settlements, POTAMÓS, the harbour, and SOHÓRIA, the village. Both offer a few rather primitive rooms (no toilet/running water) in summer, though they may need a bit of persuasion to open up out of season. Those in Sohória are by the island shop, which is also basic in the extreme: no wine, produce or eggs, and bread privately baked once a week (on Mondays!).

Yíthio (Gythion)

YÍTHIO, Sparta's ancient port, is the gateway to the dramatic Máni peninsula, and one of the south's most attractive seaside towns in its own right. Its somewhat low-key harbour, with intermittent ferries to Pireás, Kíthira and Crete, gives on to a graceful nineteenth-century waterside of tiled-roof houses. There's a beach within walking distance and rooms are easy to find. In addition, the town has as exotic a site as any in Greece. Out to sea, tethered by a long narrow mole, is the **islet of Marathónissi**, ancient Kranae, where Paris of Troy, having abducted Helen from Menelaus's palace at Sparta, dropped anchor, and where the lovers spent their first night.

The Town

Marathónissi/Kranae is the town's main sight, a nice place to while away an hour or so in the early evening, with swimming off the rocks towards the lighthouse (beware sea urchins). Amid the island's trees and scrub stands a recently restored tower-fortress built in the 1780s by the Turkish-appointed Bey of the Mani to guard the harbour against his lawless countrymen. The building promotes itself as a "Museum of the Mani", though its exhibits are yet to materialise.

For an aerial view of the islet and town, climb up through Yíthio's stepped streets on to the hill behind – the town's ancient acropolis. The settlement around it, known as **Laryssion**, was quite substantial in Roman times, enjoying a wealth from the export of murex, the purple-pigmented mollusc used to dye imperial togas.

Much of the ancient site now lies submerged but there are some impressive remains of a **Roman theatre** to be seen at the northeast end of the town. Follow the road marked *Tahidhromio* (post office) for about 300m. This ends at an army barracks, where a sign in the road says "STOP" and the theatre stands before you – a modest 80m in diameter but with most of its stone seats intact. It shows perfectly how ages blend into one another in Greece: built into the side is a Byzantine church (now ruined) and that, in turn, has been adapted into the outer wall of the barracks.

Practicalities: rooms, meals and transport

Buses drop you close to the centre of town, with the main waterfront street, **Vassiléos Pávlou**, right ahead of you. Orientation couldn't be simpler.

Finding **accommodation** shouldn't be hard, with a fair selection of hotels and private rooms – most along the waterfront, signposted up the steps behind, or facing the Marathónissi islet – to choose from. Hotels include:

Pension Koutsouris, south along the waterfront (☎0733/22 321). Excellent value, friendly and comfortable. ③

Hotel Aktaeon, Vassiléos Pávlou 1 (☎0733/22 294). Old, cavernous and characterful. ③

Hotel Kranae, Vassiléos Pávlou 15 (☎0733/22 249). Comfortable mid-budget hotel. ③

Hotel Laryssion, Grigoráki 7 (☎0733/22 021). Good value C-class hotel, a few blocks back from the front. ③

Hotel Pantheon, Vassiléos Pávlou 33 (☎0733/22 284). Pretty plush. ④

Hotel Githion, Vassiléos Pávlou (☎0733/22 284). Yíthio's finest hotel – rated A class on account of some luxurious suites. Most rooms are not so expensive. ⑤

If you want to **camp**, there are three sites along MAVROVOÚNI beach, which begins 3km south of the town off the Areópoli road. The nearest of these is the *Meltemi* (☎0733/22 833); a couple of kilometres further on are the *Gythion Beach* (open April–Oct only; ☎0733/23 441) and *Mani Beach* (open April–Sept only; ☎0733/23-450).

There is also a C-class **hotel** at Mavrovoúni, the *Milton* (☎0733/22091; ③), along with lots of **rooms** places. Many of the buses serving Yíthio from Spárti routinely continue to Mavrovoúni and these campsites – ask on board.

For **meals**, the waterside is the obvious location – though pick carefully from among the tavernas since most have inflated prices for fish and seafood. A much more genuine local taverna, *Petakos*, is to be found tucked against the sports stadium at the northwest end of town; it's good when they feel like making an effort. *Kostas*, by the bus station and facing the public beach, is also a no-nonsense place.

Other outlets you may want to make use of are the *Ladopoulou* **bookshop** (worth scouring for books on the Máni), and *Motor Mani* (by the causeway, on the Areópoli road; ☎0733/22 853), or *Supercycle* (on the main square; ☎0733/24 407), which rent out **mopeds** by the day and, by negotiation, for longer periods. At least three days is worth considering for an exploration of the Máni and, if you're heading that way, **banks** should also be visited; there are three near the bus station.

Lastly, if you are headed for Kíthira, Pireás, Monemvassía or Crete, you can check **ferry and hydrofoil departures** at the *Rozakis Shipping and Travel Agency* on the waterfront. The agency will also change travellers' cheques and money.

Beaches near Yíthio

For swimming, there are a number of coves within reach of Yíthio, on both sides of which rise an intermittent sequence of cliffs. The **beach** at Mavrovoúni, by the camp-sites detailed above, is one of the best; a smaller one, north of the town, has a nominal admission charge. Alternatively, if you've transport, there are the superb beaches in Váthi Bay, further along, off the Areópoli road (see section following).

The Máni

The southernmost peninsula of Greece, **the Máni** stretches from Yíthio in the east and Kardhamíli in the west down to Cape Ténaro, mythical entrance to the underworld; its spine, negotiated by road at just a few points, is the vast grey mass of Mount Taíyettos and its southern extension, Sangiás. It is a wild landscape, an arid Mediterranean counterpart to Cornwall, say, or the Scottish highlands, and with an idiosyncratic culture and history to match. Nowhere in Greece does a region seem so close to its medieval past – which continued largely unchanged until the end of the last century.

Some Maniot history

The mountains offer the key to Maniot history. Formidable natural barriers, they provided a refuge from, and bastion of resistance to, each and every occupying force of the last two millennia. The Dorians never reached this far south in the wake of the Mycenaeans, Roman occupation was perfunctory and Christianity only took root in the interior in the ninth century (some 500 years after the establishment of Byzantium). Throughout the years of Venetian and Turkish control of the Peloponnese there were constant rebellions, climaxing in the Maniots' uprising on March 17, 1821, a week before Archbishop Yermanos raised the Greek flag at Kalávrita to launch the War of Independence.

Alongside this national assertiveness went an equally intense and violent internal society – at its most extreme in the Maniots' bizarrely elaborate tradition of **blood feuds**. These were the result of an intricate feudal society that seems to have developed across the peninsula in the fourteenth century. After the arrival of refugee Byzantine families, an aristocracy known as **Nyklians** arose and the various clans gradually developed strongholds in the tightly clustered villages. The poor, rocky soil was totally inadequate for the population – even given the Maniots' traditional trade in piracy – and for the next five centuries the clans clashed frequently and bloodily for land, power and prestige.

These feuds became ever more complex and gave rise to the building of strongholds: marble-roofed **tower houses** which, in the elaborate rule-system of the peninsula, could be raised only by those of Nyklian descent. From these local forts the clans – often based in the same village – conducted their vendettas according to strict rules and aims. The object was to annihilate the enemy's tower house completely, as well as the male population of their clan. The favourite method of attack was to smash the prestigious tower roofs; the forts consequently rose to four and five storeys.

Feuds would customarily be signalled by the ringing of church bells and from this moment the adversaries would confine themselves to their towers, firing with all available weaponry at each other. The battles could last for years, even decades, with women (who were safe from attack) shuttling in food, ammunition and supplies. With the really prolonged feuds, temporary truces were declared at harvest times, then with business completed the battle would recommence. Ordinary villagers – the non-Nyklian peasantry – would, meanwhile, evacuate for the duration of the conflict. The feuds could end in two ways: destruction of a family in battle, or by total surrender of a whole clan in a gesture of *psihikó* ("a thing of the soul"). In the latter instance the clan would file out to kiss the hands of enemy parents who had lost "guns" (the Maniot term for male children) in the feud; the victors would then dictate strict terms by which they could remain in the village.

The Maniot feuds were probably prolonged, and certainly exploited, by **the Turks**. The first Maniot uprising against them had taken place in 1571 – a year after the Ottoman occupation – and there were to be renewed attempts, involving plots with Venetians, French and Russians, through the succeeding centuries. But the Turks, wisely, opted to control the Máni by granting a level of local autonomy, investing power in one or other clan whose leader they designated "Bey" of the region. The position provided a focus for the obsession with arms and war and worked well until the nine-teenth-century appointment of **Petrobey Mavromihalis**. With a power base at Liméni he managed to unite the clans in revolution, and his Maniot army, which at one stage had to fight a rearguard action for a foothold in the Peloponnese, was to prove vital in the success of the War of Independence.

Perhaps unsurprisingly, the end of the war and the formation of an **independent Greece** was not quite the end of Maniot rebellion. Mavromihalis swiftly fell out with the first president of the nation, Capodistrias, and, with other members of the clan, was imprisoned by him at Náfplio – an act which led to the president's assassination at the hands of Petrobey's brothers. The monarchy, which was then foisted on the emerging nation by the European powers, initially fared little better. In 1833 King Otho decided to break the anarchic outpost of his kingdom by destroying the Maniot tower houses. His first force of troops was ambushed, stripped naked and ransomed back to the state; a second detachment of 6000 soldiers was also repulsed. In the end a more pragmatic solution was found, with one of the king's German officers visiting the Máni to enlist soldiers in a special Maniot militia. The idea was adopted with enthusiasm, and was the start of an enduring tradition of Maniot service in the modern Greek military. The last full-scale feud, however, took place as late as 1870, in the village of Kítta, and required a full detachment of the regular army to put down.

In this century, sadly, all has been decline, with persistent **depopulation** of the villages. In places like Váthia and Kítta, which once held populations in the hundreds, the numbers are now down to single figures, predominantly the old. Socially and politically the region is notorious as the most conservative in Greece. The Maniots reput-edly enjoyed an influence during the colonels' junta, when the region first received roads, mains electricity and running water; they voted almost unanimously for the monarchy in the 1974 plebiscite; and this is one of the very few parts of Greece where you may still see visible support for the far-right National Party.

Visiting the Máni

The Máni divides into two: Éxo (Outer) and Mésa (Inner, or Deep).

● **Deep Máni** is the classic territory: its jagged coast relieved only by the occasional cove, its land a mass of rocks. It has one major sight, the remarkable caves at **Pírgos Dhiroú**, which are now very much on the tourist circuit. Beyond this point, though, tourists thin out fast. The attractions are in small part the coastal villages, like **Yerolimín** on the west coast, or **Kótronas** on the east; more in the walking, and in exploring the **tower houses** and **churches**.

Of the former, a fair number survive – their groupings most dramatic at **Kítta**, **Váthia** and **Flomohóri**. The churches are harder to find, often hidden away from actual villages, but worth the effort. Many were built during the tenth and twelfth centuries, when the Maniots enthusiastically embraced Christianity; almost all retain primitive-looking frescoes.

● In **Éxo Máni** – the coast up from Areópoli to Kalamáta – the emphasis shifts much more to beaches. Stoúpa and Kardhamíli are both beautiful resorts, developing now but far from spoilt. And the road itself is an experience, threading precipitously up into the foothills of Taíyettos before looping down to the sea.

GETTING AROUND – AND MONEY

Getting around can be time-consuming unless you have your own transport – and you may want to consider renting a **moped or car** from Yíthio, Spárti or Kalamáta (see their entries for addresses). Without a vehicle, you will need to walk or hitch to supplement the buses. In Deep Máni, there are just the following two services:

Areópoli–Yerolimín–Váthia Daily in summer; three times a week out of season.

Areópoli–Kotrónas–Láyia Daily service around the eastern side of the peninsula.

An alternative is to make use of the handful of **taxis**, generally negotiable at Areópoli, Yerolimín and Kótronas, as well as at Yíthio.

Keep in mind also that the Deep Máni has no regular **bank**. Though you can change travellers' cheques at the **post offices** in Yerolimín or Areópoli, it's wise to collect as much as you think you'll need for a visit in advance, at either Yíthio or Kalamáta.

BOOKS

For travelling in the region, two **books** are unreservedly recommended. These are Patrick Leigh Fermor's *Mani* (Penguin), a marvellous study of Maniot history, interwoven with travels in the 1950s, and Peter Greenhalgh and Edward Eliopoulos's *Deep Into Mani* (Faber), an anecdotal and practical guide compiled from a journey in 1980. This latter is invaluable if you want to locate Maniot churches – only a selection of which are detailed in our text. Both books are sporadically available in Yíthio.

Into the Máni: Yíthio to Areópoli

The road from Yíthio into the Máni begins amid a fertile and gentle landscape, running slightly inland of the coast – and the Yíthio/Mavrovoúni beaches – through tracts of orange and olive groves. About 12km beyond Yíthio, the Máni seems suddenly to assert itself as the road enters a gorge below the Turkish **Castle of Passavá**. The castle is one of a pair – with Kelefá to the west – guarding the Máni, or perhaps more accurately guarding against the Máni. It's quite a scramble up, with no regular path, but the site is ample reward, with views out across two bays and for some miles along the defile from Areópoli.

Passavá has hosted a fortress since Mycenaean times; the present version is an eighteenth-century Turkish rebuilding of a Frankish fort (contemporary with Mystra) that the Venetians had destroyed on their flight from the Peloponnese in 1684. It was

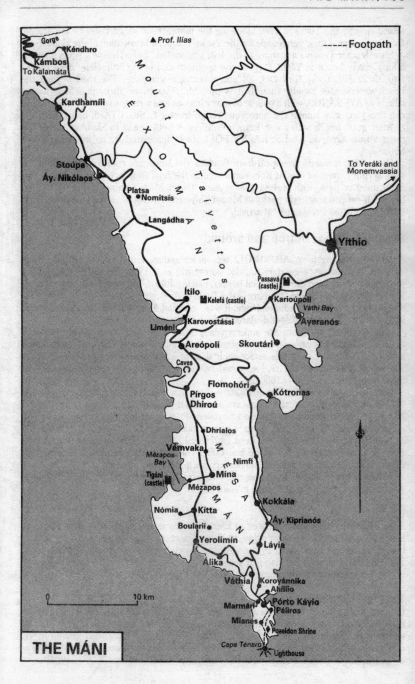

▲ Prof. Ilías   ----- Footpath

Gorge
Kéndhro
Kámbos
To Kalamáta

Kardhamíli

Stoúpa
Áy. Nikólaos

Platsa
Nomitsís

Langádha

Mount Taïyettos

To Yeráki and
Monemvassía

Yíthio

Passavá
(castle)

Ítilo   Kelefá (castle)

Karioúpoli
Vathí Bay

Liméni   Karovostássi

Ayeranós

Areópoli   Skoutári

Caves

Flomohóri

Pírgos
Dhiroú   Kótronas

Dhrialos

Vérnvaka

Mézapos
Bay   Nimfí

Tigáni
(castle)   Mína

Mézapos

Nómia   Kítta

Kokkála

Boularií

Áy. Kiprianós

Yerolimín

Láyia

Álika

Váthia   Koroyánnika
Ahílio

Marmári   Pórto Káyio
Péliros

Mianés

Poseidon Shrine

Cape Ténaro   Lighthouse

0   10 km

THE MÁNI

abandoned by the Turks in 1780 following the massacre of its garrison by the Maniot Grigorakis clan – their vengeance for the Turks' arrest and execution of the clan chief.

Shortly after Passavá a turning to the left, signposted "Belle Hélène", leads down to a long sandy beach at **Váthi Bay**. At the southern end is the little *Hotel Belle Hélène* (☎0733/22 867; open April–Oct; ⑤) and a seasonal campsite. The road beyond the beach deteriorates rapidly though it is possible to continue through woods to the village of AYERANÓS, with a couple of tower houses and a campsite, and thence, if you can find your way among the numerous rough tracks, to SKOUTÁRI, below which is another good beach with some Roman remains. A better road to Skoutári leaves the main Yíthio–Areópoli road at KARIOÚPOLI, itself dominated by an imposing tower house-fort.

Continuing **towards Areópoli** from Passavá, the landscape remains fertile until the wild, scrubby mass of Mount Kouskoúni signals the final approach to Deep Máni. You enter another pass, with **Kelefá Castle** (see "Outer Máni" above) to the north, and beyond it several southerly peaks of Mount Taïyettos. Areópoli, as you curl down from the hills, radiates a real sense of arrival.

Areópoli, Pírgos Dhiroú and around

An austere-looking town, **AREÓPOLI** sets an immediate mood for the region. It was until the last century secondary to Ítilo, 6km north, as the gateway to Deep Máni, but the modern road (and the provincial border, placing Ítilo in Messinía) has made it to all intents the region's centre. Its name – the Town of Ares, god of war – was bestowed for its efforts in the War of Independence: it was here that Mavromihalis (commemorated in a statue in the main square) declared the uprising.

The town's other sights are archetypically Maniot in their apparent confusion of ages. The **Taxiárhis** cathedral, for example, has primitive reliefs above its doors which look twelfth-century until you notice their date of 1798. Similarly, although its tower houses, as throughout the region, could readily be described as medieval, most of them were built in the early 1800s.

One of the towers, the *Pírgos Kapetanakou*, has been restored by the EOT as a "Traditional Guesthouse"; the rooms are beautiful if you can afford the rates (☎0733/51 233; ⑥). Cheaper **rooms** (③–④) are advertised at a number of ordinary houses, mostly grouped around the cathedral; there are some nice ones in the main square (☎0733/51 340; ③), along with the *Pension Kouris* (☎0733/51 307; ③). There is also a **bank** (open Tues & Thurs only), a **post office** and **OTE**. The café-restaurant *Nikola's Corner*, on the main square, does good *meze* dishes: try the general assortment.

Buses leave Areópoli from the main square; if you are heading north, towards Kalamáta, you may need to change in Ítilo.

Liméni

Areópoli stands back a kilometre or so from the sea – an enjoyable walk. The best local beach is at **LIMÉNI**, the town's tiny, traditional port, 3km to the north, whose scattering of houses are dominated by the restored tower house of Petrobey Mavromihalis. There's a taverna, with fine fish and seafood, on the waterside. Further around the bay is another restaurant, with **rooms** (☎0733/51 458; ③).

The Pírgos Dhiroú caves

Driving south from Areópoli, it's 8km to the village of **PÍRGOS DHIROÚ**, where the road forks off to the underground caves – the Máni's major tourist attraction. The village itself has an isolated 70-foot-high tower house, but is otherwise geared to the cave trade, with numerous tavernas and cafés, and dozens of **rooms** for rent. The closest to the caves – and the sea – are at the *Panorama* restaurant (☎0733/52 280; ③).

The **Pírgos Dhiroú caves** (June–Sept 8am–6pm; Oct–May 8am–3pm; 1400dr) are 4km further on from the main village, set beside the sea and a small beach. They are very much a packaged attraction, with long queues for admission in season. However, unless caves leave you cold, they are worth a visit, especially on weekday afternoons when the queues are slight. Visits consist of a half-hour punt around the underground waterways of the **Glifádha caves**, well-lit and crammed with stalactites, whose reflections are a remarkable sight in the two-to-twenty-metre-deep water. You are then allowed a brief tour on foot of the **Alepótripa caves** – huge chambers (one of them 100m by 60m) in which excavation has unearthed evidence of prehistoric occupation.

You should buy a ticket as soon as you arrive at the caves: this gives you a priority number for the tours. On a midseason weekend the wait can be up to four hours, so it's best to arrive as early as possible in the day with gear to make the most of the adjacent beach. If time is short, taxis from Areópoli will take you to the caves, then wait and take you back; prices, especially split four ways, are reasonable. There is a rather unexciting cafeteria by the caves and beach; a picnic would be more fun.

South to Yerolimín

The narrow plain between Pírgos Dhiroú and Yerolimín – 17km along the main road – is one of the more fertile stretches of Deep Máni, and supported, until this century, an extraordinary number of villages. It retains a major concentration of **churches**, many of them Byzantine, dating from the eleventh to the fourteenth centuries. These are especially hard to find, though well-detailed in Peter Greenhalgh's *Deep Into Mani*. The main feature to look for is a barrel roof. Almost all are kept unlocked.

Among Greenhalgh's favourites **on the seaward side** are the church at HAROÚDHA (3km south of Pírgos), Trissákia church by a reservoir near TSÓPOKAS (5km south of Pírgos Dhiroú) and Ayía Varvára at ÉRIMOS (8km south of Pírgos). Equally rewarding is a walk along the **old road** east of, and parallel to, the main road. This begins near the village of DHRÍALOS and rejoins the main road beyond the tower houses at MÍNA. Midway is VÁMVAKA and its eleventh-century church of Áyii Theódhori, with superb carved marbles and decorative brickwork.

Mézapos and the Castle of the Maina

An easier excursion from the main road is to the village of **MÉZAPOS**, whose deep-water harbour made it one of the chief settlements of Máni until the road was built in this century. There are a few rooms and new concrete apartments here, as well as some fine walks – the best of which is to the **Castle** at TIGÁNI (Frying Pan) rock, 4km around the cliffs, past the Byzantine church of Episkopí (which has a well-preserved cycle of frescoes). This fortress, by general consensus, seems to have been the **Castle of the Maina**, constructed like those of Mystra and Monemvassía by the Frankish baron, Guillaume de Villehardouin, and ceded with them by the Byzantines in 1261.

Tigáni is as arid a site as any in Greece – a dry Monemvassía in effect – whose fortress seems scarcely man-made, blending as it does into the terrain. It's a jagged walk out to the castle across rocks fashioned into pans for salt-gathering; within the walls are ruins of a Byzantine church and numerous cisterns.

If you ask at one of the cafés in Mézapos it's sometimes possible to negotiate a boat trip out to Tigáni, or even around the cape to Yerolimín. The nearby village of **STAVRÍ** offers traditional **tower house accommodation** in the *Pírgos Tsitsíri* (☎0733/54 297; ④), lower-priced than the other tower-hotels in Areópoli and Váthia (see below).

Kítta and Nómia

Continuing along the main road, **KÍTTA**, once the largest and most powerful village in the region, boasts the crumbling remains of over twenty tower houses. It was here in

1870 that the last feudal war took place, eventually being suppressed by a full battalion of 400 regular soldiers. Over to the west, visible from the village, are another eruption of tower houses at Kítta's traditional rival, NÓMIA.

Yerolimín and south to Cape Ténaro

After the journey from Areópoli, YEROLIMÍN (YEROLIMÉNAS, GEROLIMENA) has an end-of-the-world air, and it makes a good base for exploring the southern extremities of the Máni. Despite appearances, the village was only developed in the 1870s – around a jetty and warehouses built by a local (a non-Nyklian migrant) who had made good on the island of Síros. There are a few shops, a post office, a couple of cafés and two hotels, run by cousins. Of these the *Akroyali* (☎0733/54 204; ③) is the more comfortable; the *Akrotenaritis* (☎0733/54 205; ②) has slightly cheaper but rather more basic rooms. The best place to eat is the *psistariá* between them.

At the dock occasional boat trips are offered– when the local owners feel like it– around Cape Ténaro (see below). For swimming, the best nearby **beach** is 2km south at an inlet known as Yiáli, overlooked by the ruins of a tower house and windmill.

Boularïí

Two kilometres to the north of Yerolimín, **BOULARÏÍ** is one of the most interesting and accessible villages in Deep Máni. It is clearly divided into "upper" and "lower" quarters, both of which retain well-preserved tower houses and, in varying states of decay, some twenty churches. The two most impressive are tenth-century **Áyios Pantelímon** (roofless and unlocked, with several frescoes) and eleventh-century **Áyios Stratigós** (locked – keys are with the priest at Eliá village), with a spectacular series of frescoes from the twelfth to the eighteenth centuries. Almost any other church you find in the village has its own modest frescoes, too.

Álika and Váthia

South from Yerolimín a good road (and the bus) continues to **ÁLIKA**, where it divides, one fork leading east through the mountains to Láyia (see below), the other on to Váthia and across the Marmári isthmus to Páliros. Between Álika and Váthia there are good coves for swimming. One of the best, reached by following a riverbed (dry in summer) about midway to Váthia, is a place known as KIPÁRISSOS. On the headland above are scattered Roman remains, including (amid the walled fields) the excavated remains of a sixth-century basilica.

VÁTHIA, a group of tower houses set uncompromisingly on a scorching mass of rocks, is one of the most dramatic villages in Deep Máni. It features in the travels of Colonel Leake – one of the best sources on Greece in the early nineteenth century – who was warned to avoid going through it as a feud had been running between two families for the previous forty years. Today it has a ghost-town feel with under a dozen people left, despite the efforts of the EOT, who have restored a couple of the tower houses as restaurant/cafés and guest lodges (☎0733/54 244; ⑤–⑥). Other than these, there's just a café selling drinks.

On to Pórto Káyio

From Váthia the road south to the cape starts out uphill – edging around the mountain in what appears to be quite the wrong direction. It slowly descends, however, bringing you out at the beach and hamlet of **PÓRTO KÁYIO** (7km from Váthia). There are two tavernas here, but no rooms – a deliberate policy on the part of the proprietors who cherish their solitude. Above the village, a track winds west around the headland, capped by ruins of a Turkish castle contemporary with Kelefá, to sandy beaches at the double bay of MARMÁRI.

To the Gates of Hell

Moving on to the Máni's last, barren peninsula, the road continues for a couple of kilometres up to a hilltop church and a parking area. A track from here extends a few hundred metres more to the nearly deserted hamlet of PÁLIROS. Heading for the cape, follow instead the right-hand, southerly track towards MIANÉS, another hamlet with a single-figure population. Beyond here the road descends towards the sea, ending by a knoll crowned with the squat **chapel of Asómati**, constructed largely of materials from an ancient Temple of Poseidon.

To the left (east) as you face the chapel is the little pebbly bay of ASÓMATI, often with a fishing boat at anchor, on whose shores is the small **cave** said to be the mythical entrance to the underworld*. To the right (west) of the Asómati hill, the main path, marked by red dots, continues along the shore of another cove and through the metre-high foundations of a Roman town that grew up around the Poseidon shrine; there is even a good mosaic in one structure. From here the old trail, which existed before the road was bulldozed, reappears as a walled path, allowing 180° views of the sea on its 25-minute course to the lighthouse on **Cape Ténaro**. The keepers here used to welcome visits but, sadly, the lights were automated in 1986.

Láyia, Kótronas and the east coast

The east coast of Deep Máni is most easily approached from Areópoli, whence there's a daily bus through Kótronas, the largest settlement, to Láyia. However, if you have transport, or you're prepared to walk and hitch, there's satisfaction in doing a full loop of the peninsula, crossing over to Láyia from Yerolimín or Pórto Káyio. For much of its course, the landscape is almost remorselessly barren, little more than scrub and prickly pears, for this is the Deep Máni's **"Sunward coast"**, far harsher than the "Shadow coast" of the west side. There are few beaches, with most of the – very scattered – villages hung on the cliffs.

Láyia

From the fork at Álika (3km south of Yerolimín) it is about an hour and a half's walk by road to **LÁYIA**. Coming from Pórto Káyio it takes around three hours, though the route, at times on narrow tracks, is more dramatic, passing the virtually deserted hilltop village of KOROGONIÁNIKA. Láyia itself is a multi-towered village that perfectly exemplifies the feudal setup of the old Máni. Four Nyklian families lived here, and their four independently sited settlements, each with its own church, survive. One of the taller towers, so the locals claim, was built overnight by the four hundred men of one clan, hoping to gain an advantage at sunrise. During the eighteenth century the village was the residence of Deep Máni's doctor – a strategic base from which to attend the war-wounded across the peninsula. Today there is a single taverna, with a limited menu and a few rather overpriced **rooms** for rent.

Áyios Kiprianós and Kokkála

The first village beyond Láyia, over on the east coast, is **ÁYIOS KIPRIANÓS**. Inexplicably towerless, it too has a few rooms, though the proprietor may prove elusive in the off-season.

KOKKÁLA, 5km on, is larger, enclosed by a rare patch of greenery, and boasts a harbour, several café-restaurants, a **pension** (the *Kokkala*, aka *Zaccharias*; ③) and various **rooms** for rent. It has a very pretty cove, a longer beach to the north, and walking

---

*Patrick Leigh Fermor, in *Mani*, writes of another "Gates of Hades" cave, which he swam into on the western shore of Mátapan, just below Marmári. Other claimants to the title, elsewhere in Greece, include the Necromanetion of Ephira, near Párga in Epirus.

possibilities. Three kilometres to the northwest, up on the mountainside, is a spot known as Kiónia (columns), with the foundations of two Roman temples; from there a path reputedly leads over the mountain to Mína.

Kótronas and Flomohóri
KÓTRONAS – easily reached from Areópoli – is frequented by a fair number of tourists (mainly Germans) each summer, and has a trio of pensions; the most pleasant, on the seafront, is the *Kalikardia* (☎0733/55 246; ②). The place is still a fishing village, and its pebble beach (there are sandy strips further around the bay) and causeway-islet make it a good last stop in the region.

The land hereabouts is reasonably fertile, and **FLOMOHÓRI**, half an hour's walk in the hills behind, has maintained a reasonable population as well as a last imposing group of tower houses.

Outer Máni: Areópoli to Kalamáta

The forty kilometres of road between Areópoli and Kalamáta is as dramatic and beautiful as any in Greece, a virtual corniche route between **Mount Taíyettos** and the **Gulf of Messinía**. The first few settlements en route are classic Maniot villages, their towers packed against the hillside; as you move north, with the road dropping to near sea level, there are three or four small resorts – increasingly popular but as yet relatively unspoilt. For walkers, there is a reasonably well-preserved *kalderími* (cobbled track) paralleling (or short-cutting) much of the asphalt route, and a superb gorge hike just north of Kardhamíli.

Ítilo, Karavostássi, the Castle of Kelefá and Nomitsís
ÍTILO (or Vitylo), 11km from Areópoli, is the transport hub for the region. If you are heading towards Kalamáta, either from Yíthio or Areópoli, you'll need to change here. It looks tremendous from a distance, though close up it is a little depressing – its population in decline, and many of the tower houses collapsing into decay. KARAVOSTÁSSI, its seaport, is a better base, if you can afford the *Hotel Itilo* (☎0733/ 51 300; ⑤), or find a private **room**. Ítilo, too, has few rooms for rent on its outskirts.

In better days, Ítilo was the capital of the Mani, and from the sixteenth to the eighteenth century it was the region's most notorious base for piracy and slave trading. The Maniots traded amorally and efficiently in slaves, selling Turks to Venetians, Venetians to Turks, and, at times of feud, the women of each others' clans. Irritated by their piracy and hoping to control the important pass to the north, the Turks built the **Castle of Kelefá**. This is just a kilometre's walk from Ítilo across a gorge and its walls and bastions, built for a garrison of five hundred, are substantially intact.

Also worth exploring from Ítilo is the monastery of **Dhekoúlou**, down towards the coast; its setting is beautiful and there are some fine medieval frescoes in the church.

Langádha, Nomitsís and Thalamés
Continuing north, if you want to walk for a stretch of the route, you can pick up the *kalderími* out of Ítilo – follow the main road initially and look out for the path below. As it continues north the track occasionally crosses the modern road but it is distinct at least as far as RÍGLIA, and probably (we've not tried) beyond to Kardhamíli. The most interesting of the villages along this mountainous leg of the way are **LANGÁDHA**, for its setting, bristling with towers, and **NOMITSÍS**, with a trio of frescoed Byzantine churches strung out along its main street. A couple more are to be found off the road just to the north – in the Metamórphossi are delightful sculpted animal capitals.

Just beyond Nomitsís, you pass the hamlet of **THALAMÉS**, where a local enthusiast has set up a **Museum of Máni Folklore and History** (May–Sept daily 8am–8pm).

The tag "museum" is perhaps a bit inflated for what is really a collection of junkshop items, but it's a nice stop nonetheless and sells superb local honey.

Áyios Nikólaos and Stoúpa

The beaches of Outer Máni begin at **ÁYIOS NIKÓLAOS**, whose quiet little harbour, flanked by old stone houses, seems fated for higher things. At present it's a delightful place, with four tavernas and a scattering of **rooms** and apartments. A good choice, for both rooms and food, is the restaurant *O Lofos*.

STOÚPA, the next resort, just to the north, is much more developed, though justifiably so, for it has possibly the best sands along this coast – two glorious beaches (Stoúpa and Kalogría) separated by a headland, each sloping into the sea and superb for children. Submarine freshwater springs gush into the bay, keeping it unusually clean – if also a bit cold– while banana trees lend an exotic air.

Out of peak season, Stoúpa is certainly recommended. In July and August, you may find the crowds a bit overwhelming, and space at a premium. Accommodation includes numerous **rooms** and apartments (③ but bargainable out of season) for rent, several **hotels**, cheapest of which are the *Lefktron* (☎0721/54 322; ④) and *Stoupa* (☎0721/54 308; ④), and a **campsite**, *Camping Kalogria* (☎0721/94 319), five minutes' walk from Kalogría beach and equipped with a children's playground. There are plenty of tavernas but no bank – though the local supermarket will change money and travellers' cheques.

Kardhamíli

KARDHAMÍLI, 10km north of Stoúpa, is in a similar vein, with a great long pebble beach fronted by acres of olive trees, and a tower-house medieval quarter up on the hill behind. It too is quite a major resort, by Peloponnese standards at least, with ranks of self-catering apartments and pensions, block-booked by the package trade in season, but once again the **beach** – a long pebble strip north of the the village – is superb.

Back from the road, it's a nice walk over to "Old Kardhamíli", on the hillside, where a group of abandoned tower houses are gathered about the slender-spired eighteenth-century church of **Áyios Spíridhon**. Further back is the old acropolis, and a pair of ancient tombs; the Maniot chieftains Kolokotronis and Mavromihalis played human chess here with their troops during the War of Independence.

Among Kardhamíli's **tavernas**, try *Kiki's* or *Lela's* on the beach; the latter also has good sea-view **rooms** (☎0721/73 541; ③; which should be booked well ahead in summer). Other bookable **hotels** include the *Patriarxea* (☎0721/73 366; ④), by the main road but attractive, and the *Kardamyli Beach* (☎0721/73 180; ②) on the beach. There's also a beachside **campsite**, *Camping Meliskina* (☎0721/73 461). Up on the main road and *platía*, you'll find a few low-key bars, a superb ice cream place, a **post office** for changing money (there's no bank), and a **moped rental** outlet.

Inland from Kardhamíli: the Viros gorge

North of Kardhamíli the road leaves the coast, which rises to cliffs around a cape, before dropping back to the sea in the bay around Kalamáta. But before moving on, a day or two spent exploring Kardhamíli's immediate environs **on foot** is time well spent. The giant **Víros gorge** plunges down from the very summit of Taíyettos to meet the sea just north of the village, and a number of tracks penetrate it from various directions.

The path from the acropolis continues to the church and village of AYÍA SOFÍA, and then proceeds on a mixture of tracks and lanes either across a plateau to EXOHÓRI or down into the gorge, where two monasteries nestle at the base of sheer walls. An hour or so inland along the canyon, more cobbled ways lead up to either TSÉRIA on the north bank (taverna but no accommodation) or back towards the hamlet of EXOHÓRI on the south flank. Linking any or all of these points is an easy day's hiking at most; forays further upstream require full hiking gear and detailed local maps.

Kalamáta and beyond

KALAMÁTA is by far the largest city of the southern Peloponnese, spreading for some four kilometres back from the sea, and into the hills. It's quite a metropolitan shock after the small-town life of the rest of the region.

The city has a long-established export trade in olives and figs from the Messinian plain, and, until recently it had a prospering industrial base. In 1986, however, Kalamáta was near the epicentre of a severe **earthquake** that killed twenty people, left 12,000 families homeless and wreaked forty billion drachmas of damage. But for the fact that the quake struck in the early evening, when many people were outside, the death toll would have been much higher. As it was, large numbers of buildings were levelled throughout the town. The intensity of the damage was in part due to the city's position over several subterranean streams, but mostly, it seems, the legacy of poor 1960s construction. The result has been an economic depression across the whole area – and a startling fifty percent drop in the city's former 60,000 population.

The City

The physical effects of the earthquake are still evident in temporary housing around the suburbs of the city, and few visitors are going to want to linger in the city. However, if you are travelling for a while, it is a good place to get things done, and there are other simple pleasures such as eating at untouristed tavernas and watching a decent movie at what must be Messinía's last surviving cinema.

With a little time to fill, the most pleasing area of the city is around the **Kástro** (Mon–Sat 8am–7pm), built by the Franks and destroyed and adapted in turn by the Turks and Venetians; unlike most modern buildings, it survived the quake with little damage. An **amphitheatre** at its base hosts summer concerts. The area is about twenty minutes' walk from the city centre, which is delineated by the interlocking squares of Platía Yioryoú and Platía Konstnadínos Dhiadhóknou.

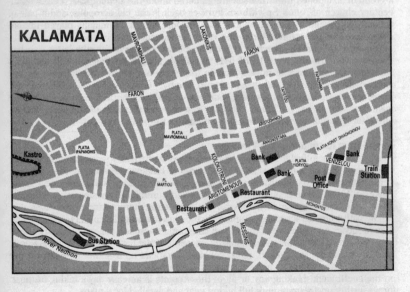

Kalamáta's **beach** – always crowded along the central section – is a ten-minute bus ride (#1) south of the centre, along **Aristoménous** street, the main thoroughfare. The sands are functional but the harbour itself has a welcome touch of life and activity.

Arriving and hotels

Arriving, orient yourself by the main square, **Platía Yioryíou**, which has most of the banks and the post office in the streets around. The **train station** is 300m to the south, with a **tourist police** post; the **bus station** is about 600m north along by the river – follow Nedhóndos street and look out for a large plastic roof.

There are very few central mid-range **hotels** left – cheapest is the *Galaxias*, Kolokotróni 14 (☎0721/86 002; ④). In general you'll do better down by the waterfront, where there are two budget places on Santaróza: *Hotel Nevada* at no. 9 (☎0721/82 429; ③) and *Pension Avra* at no. 10 (☎0721/82 759; ③), and another, the *Plaza* (☎0721/82 590, ③); nearby at Navarínou 17.

The nearest **campsites** are to be found along the stretch of beach to the east of the city. The first, about 2km from the central waterfront, is *Camping Patista* (☎0721/29 525; April–Oct only), which also runs an inexpensive hotel. However, unless stuck, you'd do better heading east towards Petalídhi (see below).

Eating out

The best **restaurants** in the summer months are down by the **harbour**, which is currently being refurbished as a yacht marina. Moving from west to east, you have quite a selection: *Krini* at Evangelistrías 40, a neighbourhood fish-and-wine taverna open most of the year; *Katofli* on Salamínos near the marina, with outdoor summer seating and a huge menu; *Zesti Gonia*, at the corner of Santarósa and Kanári, specialising in innovative vegetable dishes and open most of the year; *Meltemi*, corner of Navarínou and Fáron, a very basic but tasty *psistariá*; and *Akroyiali*, at the seafront end of Navarínou, a pricier ocean-view option with good fish.

Only in winter does the **downtown** area come into its culinary stride. At this time, pick from: *Koutivas*, 100m north of the bus station, with spicy food and bulk wine; *Kannas*, Lakonikís 18, an atmospheric place with occasional live music, which featured in Sheila Kanelli's novel, *Earth and Water*; or *Kioupi*, Alexíki 52 (off the Areópoli road), idiosyncratically decorated and with clay-pot cooking (as the name implies).

If you're not after a full meal, Kalamáta has plenty of *mezedhopolía*, the better among them serving the traditional local **snack** – roast pork and potatoes. Down at the harbour, the *ouzeri* west of the post office does a nice fish *meze*; there's another good one at the intersection of Fáron and Navarínou; and yet another unpretentious one down the street, near a souvlaki stand and video-games arcade, which does an excellent *pikilía* (grand selection of mezes).

Transport and car and moped rental

If you're looking to get transport straight through, arrive early to make connections. The most regular **buses** run north to Megalópoli/Trípoli and south to Koróni; the magnificent route over the Taíyettos to Spárti is covered twice a day, and the one to Kardhamíli and Ítilo (connection to Areópoli) four times daily. Kalamáta is also the railhead for **trains** chugging along the slow but enjoyable route to Kiparissía (and ultimately to Pátra, with a possible detour to Olympia) or inland to Trípoli and Árgos.

Three rival agencies offer **car rental**: *Maniatis*, Iatropoúlou 1 (opposite the post office; ☎0721/27 694), *Theodorakopoulos*, Kessári 2 (☎0721/20 352), and *Stavrianos*, Nedhóndos 89 (☎0721/23 041). By the waterfront, there are two **moped rental** outlets: *Bastakos*, Fáron 190 (☎0721/26 638), and *Moto World*, Virónos (☎0721/81 383).

For the hurried, there are daily **flights** to Athens; tickets are sold at the *Olympic* office across from the train station.

Ancient Messene

The ruins of ancient **MESSENE** (ITHOMI), a fortified capital thrown together by the Messenians as protection against the Spartans, lie 22km northwest of Kalamáta. The city achieved some fame in the ancient world as a showcase of military architecture and the highlights of the widely dispersed site are the outcrops of its giant walls, towers and gates.

The site is a tricky place to get to, unless you're driving. Buses run only twice a day from Kalamáta (one departure is at 6am) and you'll either have to return to the city or try your luck hitching on. With a car it's a fairly easy detour en route to either Kiparissía, Pílos or Petalídhi/Koróni. The site shares the slopes of Mount Ithómi with the pretty village of MAVROMÁTI, and, as you climb higher towards the summit, offers spectacular views of the region of Messinía and the southern Peloponnese.

The site

Messene's fortifications were designed as the southernmost link in a defensive chain of walled cities – others included Megalopolis and Argos – masterminded by the Theban leader Epaminondas to keep the Spartans at bay. Having managed to halt them at the battle of Leuctra in 371 BC, he set about building a nine-kilometre circuit of walls and restoring the Messenians to their native acropolis. The Messenians, who had resisted Spartan oppression from the eighth century BC onwards, wasted no time in re-establishing their capital; the city, so chronicles say, was built in 85 days.

The most interesting of the remains is the **Arcadia gate** at the north end of the site, through which the modern road still runs. It consisted of an outer and inner portal separated by a circular courtyard made up of massive chunks of stone precisely cut to fit together without mortar. The outer gate, the foundations of which are fairly evident, was flanked by two square towers from where volleys of javelins and arrows would rain down on attackers. The inner gate, a similarly impregnable barrier, comprised a huge monolithic doorpost, half of which still stands.

Further south, and signposted "Ithomi: Archaeological site" on the road running northwest from Mavromáti, is a newly excavated **Sanctuary of Asclepius** (Mon–Sat 8.45am–3pm, Sun 9.30am–2.30pm). This site, which was first mistakenly marked out as the *agora*, consisted of a temple surrounded by a porticoed courtyard. The bases of some of the colonnades have been unearthed along with traces of benches. Next to it you can make out the site of a theatre or meeting place.

Other remains are to be seen up Mount Ithómi, an hour's hike along a steep path forking from the road at the Laconia gate. Along the way you pass remains of an Ionic **Temple of Artemis**. At the top, on the site of a Temple of Zeus, is the small, ruinous **Monastery of Vourkanó**, founded in the eighth century but dating in its present form from 800 years later; spread below are the lush and fertile valleys of Messinía.

Towards Koróni: Petalídhi

Beaches stretch for virtually the entire distance southwest from Kalamáta to Koróni, along what is steadily developing as a major resort coast. At present, however, it is more popular with Greeks than foreigners, and the resorts, tucked away in the pines, consist primarily of campsites, interspersed with the odd rooms for rent sign.

The best of the beaches are around **PETALÍDHI**, 40km south of Kalamáta. The **campsites** here – particularly the *Eros Beach* (☎0722/31 209) and *Zervas Beach* (☎0722/31 009) – are geared primarily to car-campers with mini-enclosures as well as a few straw cabins for rent. They cost little less than the price of a room but are well-organised and well-planned. Slightly cheaper are the C-class *Petalidhi Beach* (☎0722/31 154) and *Sun Beach* (☎0722/31 200) sites. All are open from April to October.

Koróni and Methóni

The twin fortresses at **Koróni** and **Methóni** were the Venetians' oldest, and longest-held, possessions in the Peloponnese: strategic outposts on the route to Crete and known through the Middle Ages as "the eyes of the Serene Republic". Today they shelter two of the most attractive small resorts in the south.

If you have transport, the duo form an obvious route either from Kalamáta to Pílos or vice versa. Relying on **buses**, the 47km road across the peninsula can be a problem–Koróni has its connections with Kalamáta (30km) while Methóni's are with Pílos (12km)– though there's the occasional bus in summer between the two, as well as moped rental in Methóni.

Koróni

KORÓNI has one of the most picturesque sites in Greece, stacked against a fortified bluff and commanding grand views across the Messenian gulf to the Taíyettos peaks. The town is beautiful in itself, too, with tiled and pastel-washed houses arrayed in a maze of stair-and-ramp streets that can have changed little since the medieval Venetian occupation. It is not, alas, undiscovered. The Germans arrived in the early 1980s and in recent years have been buying up houses in the town and surrounding countryside. However, the process is decidedly low-key and outside high season Koróni still feels quite unspoilt.

The citadel and beach

Koróni's **Citadel** is one of the least militaristic-looking in Greece, crowning rather than dwarfing the town. Much of it is given over to private houses and garden plots, but the greater part is occupied by the flower-strewn nunnery of **Timíou Prodhrómou**, whose chapels, outbuildings and gardens occupy nearly every bastion.

From the southwest gate of the fortress, stairs descend to the park-like grounds of **Panayía Elestrías**, a church erected at the end of the last century to house a miraculous icon – unearthed with the assistance of the vision of one Maria Stathaki (buried close by). The whole arrangement, with fountains, shrubbery and benches for watching the sunset, is more like the Adriatic than the Aegean.

Continuing downhill, you reach the amazing **Zánga beach**, a two-kilometre stretch of sand and preternaturally clear water that sets the seal on Koroni's superiority as a place to relax, drink wine, and amble about a countryside lush with vineyards, olives and banana trees. There is a line of tavernas on the beach and by night a solitary disco, though all of these close down by mid-September.

Rooms and meals

To be sure of a room in summer, it's worth trying to phone ahead. In the town there are just three **hotels**, the *Flisvos* (☎0725/22 238; ③), *Diana* (☎0725/22 312; ②) and *Auberge de la Plage* (☎0725/22 401; ⑤), the latter almost always booked by groups. Looking for **private rooms** on arrival, try the places to the right of the fishing port as you face the water, and don't leave it too late in the day. There's also a **campsite**, *Camping Koroni*, on the road into town.

There is a reasonable selection of restaurants, including the excellent *To Maistrali* on the waterfront, and some authentic **tavernas** – barrel-wine and oven-food places – along the main shopping street, and the *Panorama* (follow its signs) up by the castle. Many people make wine or raki in their basement and the heady local tipple figures prominently in the nightlife. Otherwise, there is a surprisingly fancy *zaharoplastío* for such a small place, plus two **banks** and a **post office** for money matters.

Finikoúnda

FINIKOÚNDA, 20km west of Koroni, is a small fishing village with a superb cove-beach. Over recent years it has gained a reputation as a largely backpackers' – and especially windsurfers' – resort, with half the summer intake at a pair of campsites on either side of the village, the others housed in a variety of **rooms**. It can be a fun, laid-back place, if you fit this clientele.

To book **rooms** in advance, try the **hotels** *Finikounda* (☎0723/71 208; ③) and *Finisia* (☎0723/71 358; ③), or the restaurant *Moudakis* (☎0273/71 224; ②). The local **campsites** are *Camping Anemomylos* (☎0273/71 360), a kilometre west of the village, and *Camping Animos* (☎0273/71 262), two kilometres to the east.

Methóni

In contrast to the almost domesticated castle at Koróni, the fortress at **METHÓNI** is as imposing as they come – massively bastioned, washed on three sides by the sea, and cut off altogether from the land by a great moat on its fourth. It was maintained by the Venetians in part for its military function, in part as a staging post for pilgrims en route, via Crete and Cyprus, to the Holy Land, and from the thirteenth to the nineteenth centuries it sheltered a substantial town.

Within the **fortress** (Mon–Sat 8.30am–3pm, Sun 9am–3pm; free), entered across a broad moat along a stone bridge, are the remains of a Venetian cathedral – the Venetians' Lion of Saint Mark emblem ubiquitous – along with a Turkish bath, dozens of houses and some awesome underground passages, the last unfortunately cordoned off. Walking around the walls, a sea gate midway along leads out across a causeway to a fortified islet, the **Boúrtzi**.

The modern **village** of Methóni, on the "mainland" below and facing the fortress, is geared more conspicuously to tourism than Koróni and can get very crowded in season. Accommodation, however, is reasonably priced, and rarely too difficult to find if you arrive in good time, or book a day or two ahead. Among budget-priced **hotels**, the most pleasant is the *Iliodyssio* (☎0723/31 225; ③), near the fortress moat. The *Rex* (☎0273/31 239; ③) and *Galini* (☎0273/31 467; ③), on the beach, and the *Dionysos* (☎0273/31 317; ③) in town, are the best fallback choices. In addition, there are a handful of rather more expensive pension/apartments, plus the usual collection of **rooms**, often touted to new arrivals at the bus stop. At the east end of the beach there's also a **campsite**, *Camping Methoni* (☎0273/31 228; April–Oct only), with decent facilities.

The village has a **bank**, **OTE** and **post office**, all easily located in the three-street-wide grid. Here, too, is one of the best **restaurants** you'll come upon anywhere in the Peloponnese, the *Klimataria*, which serves a mouthwatering selection of dishes – including good veggie choices – in a courtyard garden.

Pílos

PÍLOS (PYLOS) is a little like a small-scale, less sophisticated Náfplio – quite a stylish town for rural Messinía, and the more so after Kalamáta. It is fronted by a pair of medieval castles and occupies a superb position on one of the finest natural harbours in Greece, the landlocked Navarino Bay (see box). A better base for exploring this part of the Peloponnese, equipped with a car or moped (both for rent here), is hard to imagine – particularly given its romantic associations with the Battle of Navarino, and, more anciently, with Homer's "sandy Pylos", the domain of "wise King Nestor" whose palace (see below) has been identified 16km to the north. Relying on public transport, however, you'll find the long afternoon gaps in services make day trips difficult.

THE BATTLES OF NAVARINO BAY

Arriving at Pílos your gaze is inevitably drawn to the bay, virtually landlocked by the offshore island of Sfaktiría. Its name, Ormós Navarínou – **Navarino Bay** – commemorates the battle that effectively sealed Greek independence from the Turks on the night of October 20, 1827. The battle itself seems to have been accidental. The "Great Powers" of Britain, France and Russia, having established diplomatic relations with the Greek insurgent leaders, were attempting to force an armistice on the Turks. To this end they sent a fleet of 27 warships to Navarino, where Ibrahim Pasha had gathered his forces – 16,000 men in 89 ships. The declared intention was to coerce Ibrahim into leaving Messinía, which he had been raiding.

In the confusion of the night an Egyptian frigate, part of the Turks' supporting force, fired its cannons and full-scale battle broke out. Without having intended to take up arms for the Greeks, the "allies" found themselves responding to attack and, extraordinarily, sank and destroyed 53 of the Turkish fleet without a single loss. There was considerable international embarrassment when news filtered through to the "victors" but the action had nevertheless ended effective Turkish control of Greek waters and within a year Greek independence was secured and recognised.

Navarino Bay also features in one of the most famous battles of Classical times, described in great detail by Thucydides. In 425 BC, during the Peloponnesian War, an Athenian force encamped in Paleokastro, the old castle of Pílos, laid siege to a group of Spartans on the island of **Sphacteria**, just across the straits. In a complete break with tradition, which decreed fighting to the death, the Spartans surrendered. "Nothing that happened in the war surprised the Hellenes as much as this," commented Thucydides.

The Town

The main pleasures of Pílos are exploring the hillside alleys, waterside streets and fortress. Getting your bearings is easy – it's not a large town – and buses drop you close by the central square, Platía Tríon Navárhon, and the port.

Shaded by a vast plane tree, and scented by limes, **Platía Tríon Navárhon** is a beautiful public square – completely encircled by cafés and very much the heart of the town. At its centre is a **war memorial** commemorating admirals Codrington, de Rigny and von Heyden, who commanded the British, French and Russian forces in the Battle of Navarino (see box above). Nearby, just off the main waterside square on Filellínon street, a little **museum** (Tues–Sun 8.30am–3pm; 200dr) also boasts remains from the battle, along with archaeological finds from the region.

Further memories of the Navarino battles can be evoked by a visit to the **island of Sfaktíria** (Sphacteria), across the bay, where there are various tombs of Philhellenes, a chapel, and a memorial to the Russian sailors. In summer, some of the fishing boats offer trips. If you're interested, enquire at the cafés by the port.

The principal sight in town, however, is the **Néo Kástro** (daily 8.30am–3pm), close by the port on the south side of the bay (off the Methóni road). The "new castle" (the old castle, Paleó Kástro, is away at the north end of the bay – see below), it was built by the Turks in 1572, and allows a 1500-metre walk right around the arcaded battlements.

For much of the last two centuries, it served as a prison and its inner courtyard was divided into a warren of narrow yards separated by high walls (now demolished). Most Greek prisons – internally, at least – are fairly open and this peculiar feature was explained by the fact that it was the nearest garrison to the Máni. So frequently was it filled with Maniots imprisoned for vendettas, and so great was the crop of internal murders, that these pens had to be built to keep the imprisoned clansmen apart. The pens and walls have recently been pulled down as part of an ongoing programme to restore and convert the castle into a museum for underwater archaeology.

Paleó Kástro and the beach

Pílos's northern castle, and ancient acropolis, **Paleó Kástro**, stands on a hill almost touching the island of Sfaktíria, at the end of the bay. It's a seven-kilometre trip from the town, for which you'll need transport (see rental details below). To get there, follow the road out towards Korifássi to the hamlet of ROMÁNOS, then turn off along a track signposted (in Greek) NAVARINO, and over a bridge across a lagoon. If you find your way here, you will end up at one of the best beaches in the Peloponnese – a lovely sweep of sand curling around the **Bay of Voïdhokília**.

Overlooking the bay, the **Paleó Kástro**, known in medieval times as Port Jonch, has substantial walls, and identifiable courtyards and cisterns within; the fortifications are a mix of Frankish and Venetian, set upon ancient foundations.

A path from the castle descends to the **Spíli Nestóros** – Nestor's Cave – which is fancifully identified (due to its stalactite forms) as the grotto in which, in *The Odyssey*, Nestor and Nelesu kept their cows, and in which Hermes hid Apollo's cattle. It is not impossible that the cave sparked Homer's imagination, for this location is reckoned by archaeologists to have been the Mycenaean-era harbour of King Nestor (see below).

The Bay of Voïdhokília encompasses a couple of additional **beaches** and hamlets. GIALÓVA, 4km out of Pílos and the first resort around the bay, has tamarisk-trees shading the sands, a hotel, the *Villa Zoe* (π0723/22 025; ③), a variety of rooms and apartments for rent, and a **campsite**, *Camping Navarino Beach* (π0723/22 761). Just north of here, the beach of MAISTRÓS is a popular windsurfing strip.

Practicalities

Pílos has somewhat limited **accommodation** and in the summer months you should definitely try to phone ahead. In addition to its hotels and pensions, quite a number of **private rooms** are advertised, and there is more on offer – plus camping – around the bay at YIALÓVA (see above) and to the south at Methóni (see previous section).

Pílos **hotels and pensions** include:

Hotel Navarinon, above the south side of the harbour (π0723/22 291). Basic but nice enough – and a fine location. ②

Hotel Trion Navarhon, Platía Tríon Navarhón 24 (π0723/22 206). ③

Hotel Arvanitis (π0723/22 641). ④

Hotel Karalis, Kalamátas 26 (π0723/22 960). An attractive if pricey hotel that may well offer big discounts on its rates outside the summer months. ⑤

For drinks, the Platía Tríon Navárhon cafés are the obvious choice. Among **tavernas**, try *Grigori's*, signposted from the square. Nightlife is pretty much nonexistent, with just a single **music-bar/disco**, *MusicContacts*, by the beach, and a summer **outdoor cinema**.

The *National Bank* is to be found on the waterfront, and the **post office** just back from there on Niléos street. **Mopeds, motorbikes and cars**, ideal for taking in both Methóni and Nestor's Palace, are available at *Venus Rent* (π0723/22 312) on the road north out of town. **Cars** are also rented out at the *Hotel Miramare* (π0723/22 226) and mopeds through the *Verouhis* agency (π0723/22 988).

Nestor's Palace

Both the palace site and museum at Hóra are open Tues–Sun 8.30am–3pm; 200dr admission to each. An excellent site guide by Carl Blegen is on sale.

Nestor's Palace was discovered in 1939 but left virtually undisturbed until after World War II; thus its excavation – unlike Mycenae, or most of the other major Greek sites – was conducted in accordance with modern archaeological techniques. In consequence its remains are the best preserved of all the Mycenaean royal palaces, though they shelter rather prosaically beneath a giant plastic roof.

The palace is located some 16km from modern Pílos, a half-hour drive. Using public transport, take any of the buses from Pílos towards Kiparissía; these follow the main road inland past Korifássi to the site and its museum at HÓRA (3km to the east).

The Palace

Flanked by deep, fertile valleys, **Nestor's Palace** looks out towards Navarino Bay – a location perfectly in keeping with the wise, measured and peaceful king described in Homer's *Odyssey*. The scene of the epic that's set here, is the visit of Telemachus, the son of Odysseus, who journeys from Ithaca to seek news of his father from the king. Arriving at the beach, accompanied by the disguised goddess Pallas Athena, he comes upon Nestor with his sons and court making a sacrifice to Poseidon. The visitors are welcomed and feasted, "sitting on downy fleeces on the sand", and although the king has no news of Odysseus he promises Telemachus a chariot so he can enquire from Menelaus at Sparta. First, however, the guests are taken back to the palace, where Telemachus is given a bath by Nestor's "youngest grown daughter, beautiful Polycaste", emerging, anointed with oil, "with the body of an immortal".

By some harmonious quirk of fate a bathtub was in fact unearthed on the **site**, and the palace ruins as a whole are potent ground for Homeric imaginings. The walls stand to a metre in height, enabling you to make out a very full plan. They were originally half-timbered (like Tudor houses), with upper sections of sun-baked brick held together by vertical and horizontal beams, and brilliant frescoes within. Even in their diminished state they suggest a building of considerable prestige – as indeed might be expected, for Nestor sent the second largest contingent– "ninety black ships"– to Troy. The remains of the massive complex are in three principal groups: the **main palace** in the middle; on the left an earlier and **smaller palace**; and on the right either **guard-houses** or **workshops**.

The basic design will be familiar if you've been to Mycenae or Tiryns: an internal court, guarded by a sentry box, gives access to the main sections of the principal palace. This contained some forty-five rooms and halls. The **Megaron** (throne room), with its characteristic open hearth, lies directly ahead of the entrance, through a double porch. It was here that the finest of the frescoes, depicting a griffin (perhaps the royal emblem) standing guard over the throne, was discovered; this is now in the museum at Hóra. Around are arranged domestic quarters and **storerooms**, which yielded literally thousands of pots and cups during excavations; the rooms may have served as a distribution centre for the produce of the palace workshops. Further back, the famous **bathroom**, its terracotta tub in situ, adjoins a smaller complex of rooms, centred on another, smaller Megaron, identified as the **queen's quarters**.

Archaeologically the most important find at the site was a group of several hundred tablets inscribed in **Linear B**. These were discovered on the very first day of digging in the two small rooms to the left of the entrance courtyard. They were the first such inscriptions to be discovered on the Greek mainland and proved conclusively a link between the Mycenaean and Minoan civilisations – for, like those found by Sir Arthur Evans at Knossos on Crete, the language was unmistakably Greek. The tablets were baked hard in the fire which destroyed the palace around 1200 BC, perhaps as little as one generation after the fall of Troy.

The Museum at Hóra

The museum at **HÓRA** adds significantly to a visit to the site. If you've no transport, it might be better to take a bus here first, and then walk the 25 minutes to the site after viewing the exhibits. In spring or autumn this is a pleasure; in hot weather, or if pressed for time, you can hitch fairly easily or get a taxi.

Pride of place in the display goes to the **palace frescoes**, one of which, bearing out Homer's descriptions, shows a warrior in a boar's-tusk helmet. Lesser finds include much pottery, some beautiful gold cups, and other objects gathered both from the site and from various Mycenaean tombs in the region.

Pílos to Pírgos: Kiparissía and the beaches

The **beaches north from Pílos to Pírgos** are on a different scale to those elsewhere in the Peloponnese, or indeed anywhere else in Greece – fine sands, long enough (and undeveloped enough) to satisfy the most jaded Australian or Californian. That they aren't better known is something of a mystery, though one accounted for in part by the poor communications. For those without transport this entails slow and patient progress along the main "coast" road, which for much of the way runs two or three kilometres inland, and a walk from road junction to beach.

Pílos to Kiparissía

The beaches immediately **north of Pílos** – stretching from GIALÓVA through **Voïdhokília Bay** (see p.196) – are as enjoyable as any on this coast, with a series of ramshackle summer tavernas, a lagoon and sand dunes. Heading north from here, near the turning inland to KORIFÁSSI and Nestor's Palace, you can take a very rough and beautiful track, flanked by orange and olive orchards. This keeps close to the sea for most of the way to Kiparissía, allowing access to isolated beaches and villages.

If you are looking for the rudiments of accommodation and a little more than a village café then Marathópoli and Filiatrá hold most promise. **MARATHÓPOLI** has a long beach – rockier than most along this coast and facing the little islet of Próti. It has a couple of regular **pensions**, some **rooms** for rent, a **campsite**, *Camping Proti*, and two or three summer tavernas by the sea. At **FILIATRÁ**, where the track rejoins the asphalt road – and which is linked by bus with Pílos and Kiparissía – there are two **hotels**, the *Trifylia* (☎0761/32 289; ③) and, down by the beach, the *Limenari* (☎0761/ 32 289; ⑤ – but cheaper out of season).

Fournier's Castle

By one of those quirky patterns of emigration, just as Kíthira is home to Greek-Australians, the villages along the Kiparissía coast have a concentration of returned Greek-Americans, virtually all of them having done a stint of work in New York or New Jersey. Disgraced ex-Vice President Spiro Agnew (1968–1973) was perhaps the most infamous local boy. However, the Greek-American who has left most mark on his home domain is one Haris Fournaki, aka **Harry Fournier**, a doctor from Chicago who came back in the 1960s and started building his fantasies.

In Filiatrá, Fournier constructed a garden-furniture version of the **Eiffel Tower** – illuminated at night by fairy lights – and a mini-replica of the globe from the 1964 New York Expo. His most ambitious project, however, was his **Kastro Ton Paramithia** (Castle of the Fairytales), down by the sea. This is a truly loopy project, with white concrete battlements and outcrops of towers, plus thirty to forty-foot-high statues of the Trojan Horse, Poseidon's steed (flanked by vases of flowers) and the goddess Athena. Within the castle (daily 9am–2pm & 5–8pm; knock hard), you are escorted to galleries of artworks and poetry devoted to Greek War of Independence heroes.

The castle is located right on the sea, near Filiatrá beach, and can reached from Filiatrá by following the road for 4km north, through the hamlet of AGRÍLI. At the nearby **Filiatrá beach**, there is a rocky pool, a couple of restaurants and the *Hotel Limenari* (see above).

Kiparissía

KIPARISSÍA is a small, congenial market town, positioned hard against the Eyaléo mountains. On the range's first outcrop – the hill above town – is a Byzantine-Frankish **castle**, around which is spreads the **old town**, many of whose ochre-hued mansions stand abandoned, having suffered heavy damage in the civil war. A couple of tavernas still function here – lovely old places and very welcoming.

Down below, the modern town goes about its business, with a small harbour and real shops – nothing yet of the tourist boutiques. It's a pleasant place to rest up, and certainly preferable to a night in Kalamáta if you're en route by train or bus to Olympia (Kiparissía is the junction of the Kalamáta and Pírgos lines). Within walking distance of the town, too, are long, near-deserted sands and rocky cliff paths.

The centre of the modern town, a couple of blocks inland from the train station, is is **Platía Kalantzákou**, where you'll find a bank, OTE and post office. Here and in the streets adjacent are a handful of no-nonsense restaurants and pizzerias – though for atmosphere it's better to eat up at the old town, or down at the beach. **Accommodation** consists of a half-dozen hotels, divided between the modern town and the beach. Cheapest of the town hotels is the down-to-earth *Pandohío Trifolia* (②) on Ikosipénde Martíou – one of the few places left in Greece that still uses the name *pandohío* (inn). Other town hotels are the *Vassilikon*, Alexopoúlou 7 (☎0761/22 655; ④); the *Ionion*, Kalantzákou 1 (☎0761/22 511; ④); and the *Artemis*, Doúfa Parália 6 (☎0761/22145; ④). By the beach, the best value is the *Apollon* (☎0761/24 411; ⑤); there is also a **campsite**, *Camping Hani* (☎0761/23 330; open all year).

North towards Pírgos: Kaïáfas

North from Kiparissía the road and rail lines continue a kilometre or so back from the coast, with the occasional **campsite** advertising its particular stretch of beach. There's one by the beach at KÁLO NERÓ, for example, 6km along, and others at YIANNITSOHÓRI and THOLÓ, 12km and 16km beyond; NÉO HÓRI, just past Tholó, has a few rooms to rent, too, as does Yiannitsohóri.

All of these hamlets have superb stretches of sandy beach, edged with olive groves, in the light of which their lack of development seems almost miraculous. One of the nicest of all the beaches is at KAKOVÁTOS, just before the village of Zaháro, which combines breakers with incredibly shallow, slowly shelving waters. There is a beach café here and a few summer rooms – nothing more. At **Zaháro**, the largest village between Kiparissía and Pírgos, and a train stop, there are a few shops and three modest hotels – the *Rex* (☎0625/31 221; ③) and *Nestor* (☎0625/31 206; ③), by the train station, and the *Diethnes* (☎0625/31 208; ③) in the village proper.

Another enormous strand, backed by sand dunes and pine groves, is to be found just before the roads loop inland at **LOUTRÁ KAÏÁFAS**. At the beach there's just a single, rather uninspired taverna and the train station. A couple of kilometres inland, however, the very different atmosphere of a spa takes over. Strung out alongside a lagoon are a dozen or so hotels and pensions, frequented mainly by Greeks seeking hydrotherapy cures. Each morning a small shuttle-boat takes the patients from their hotels to the hot springs across the lagoon.

Getting to Olympia: train connections

If you're **heading to Olympia by train** from this coast, you can save the detour to PÍRGOS (not an exhilarating town) by getting a connection at ALFIÓS, a tiny station at the junction of the Olympia line and as bucolic a halt as any on the network. Opposite the station is a private dwelling that doubles as a *kafenío*, run by a friendly woman who is delighted to have visitors.

ARCADIA AND THE NORTH

Arcadia (*Arkadhía* in modern Greek) lives up to its name. This heartland province of the Peloponnese contains some of the most beautiful landscapes in Greece: rich rolling hills crowned by a string of medieval towns, and the occasional Classical antiquity. The best area of all is around **Andhrítsena** and **Karítena**, where walkers are rewarded with the luxuriant (and rarely visited) **Lousíos gorge**, and archaeology-buffs by the remote, though currently scaffolded, **Temple of Bassae**. En route, if approaching from Trípoli, you may also be tempted by the ancient theatre at **Megalópoli**. The one site everyone heads for is, of course, **Olympia**, whose remains, if at times obscure, are again enhanced by the scenery.

Beaches are not a highlight in this northwest corner, nor along the **north coast** between Pátra and Kórinthos – technically the province of **Ahaía**. However, if you are travelling this way, or are arriving in or leaving Greece at the (modern) port of Pátra, a detour along the **rack-and-pinion Kalávrita railway** should on no account be missed. This takes off through a gorge into the mountains at Dhiakoftó.

If heading for Delphi, or central or western Greece, car-drivers and pedestrians alike can save backtracking to Athens by using the **ferry links** across the Gulf of Kórinthos at either Río-Andírio (the most routine) or Éyio-Áyios Nikólaos.

Megalópoli (Megalopolis)

Modern **MEGALÓPOLI** is an important road and bus junction, and your first thoughts on arrival are likely to be directed towards getting out. Like Trípoli, it's a dusty, characterless place, with a garrison army presence, and little in the way of hotels or food – altogether an empty joke on its adoption of its ancient name, "Great City". However, the impulse should be resisted, at least for an hour or two, for outside the city – 2km to the northwest along the Andhrítsena road – is one of the Peloponnese's most extensive and least touristed ancient sites.

Ancient Megalopolis

Site open daily 9am–6pm; unrestricted access to the theatre.

Ancient Megalopolis was one of the most ambitious building projects of the Classical age, a city intended by the Theban leader Epaminondas, who oversaw construction from 371 to 368 BC, to be the finest of a chain of Arcadian settlements containing the Spartans. However, although no expense was spared on its construction, nor on its extent – nine kilometres of walls alone – the city never took root. It suffered from sporadic Spartan aggression and the citizens, transplanted from forty local villages, preferred, and returned to, their old homes. Within two centuries it had been broken up, abandoned and ruined.

As you approach the site, along a tree-lined track off the Andhrítsena road (signposted "Ancient Theatre"), it seems a past very much in keeping. The countryside is beautiful enough, a fertile valley whose vast power station seems to give it added grandeur, but beyond the riverbed is just a low hill – and no sign of any ruins. Suddenly, though, you round the corner of the hill and its function is revealed: carved into its side is the largest **theatre** built in ancient Greece. Only the first few rows are excavated, but the earthen mounds and ridges of the rest are clearly visible as stepped tiers to the summit where, from the back rows, trees look on like immense spectators.

The theatre was built to seat 20,000 citizens and the **Thersileion** (Assembly Hall) at its base could hold 16,000. Today you're likely to be alone at the site, save perhaps for the custodian (who has plans of the ruins). Out beyond the enclosed part of the site you can wander over a vast area, and with a little imagination make out the foundations of walls and towers, temples, gymnasiums and markets. "The Great City", wrote Kazantzakis in *Journey to the Morea*, "has become a great wasteland" – but it's the richest of wastelands, gently and resolutely reclaimed by nature.

Megalópoli practicalities

Megalópoli has good **bus connections** with Trípoli (and on to Árgos and Athens) and Kalamáta. Arrive at a reasonable hour and you should be able to make either of these connections. Moving north or west **into Arcadia** is slightly more problematic, with just two buses daily to Karítena/Andhrítsena (currently at noon and 7pm). However, hitching is a viable proposition along this route, as local drivers are aware of the paucity of transport, and it's also possible to negotiate a **taxi** to Karítena. The branch rail line to Megalópoli has been closed down but *OSE* operates special shuttle buses to Lefktró for **train connections** west to Kiparissía or east to Trípoli/Árgos.

Should you need to stay in Megalópoli, there are four or five **hotels**, most of them catering to local business travellers rather than tourists. Cheapest are the rather decrepit *Pan*, Papanastassíou 7 (☎0791/22 270; ③), and more enticing *Paris*, next to the bus station at Ayíou Nikólaou 5 (☎0791/22 410; ③). Other facilities – banks, post office, OTE, etc – are to be found around the central square, Platía Gortiniás.

Karítena, Gortys, Stemnítsa and Dhimitsána

North of Megalópoli the best of Arcadia lies before you: minor roads that curl through a series of lush valleys and below the province's most exquisite medieval hill towns. The obvious first stop and most enjoyable base for exploring the region is **Karítena**. From here you can visit the dramatic and remote site of **ancient Gortys** and explore the **Lousíos Gorge**, above which, outrageously sited on 300-metre-high cliffs, is the eleventh-century **monastery of Ayíou Ioánni Prodhrómou**.

Moving **on from Karítena**, there is a choice of roads. The "main" route loops west through **Andhrítsena** (see following section) to Kréstena, from where irregular buses run to Olympia. To the northwest an alternative route (covered overleaf) winds around the edge of the Ménalo mountains to the delightful towns of **Stemnítsa** (Ipsoúnda) and **Dhimitsána**, meeting the main Tripoli–Olympia/Pírgos road at Karkaloú. If you have time on your hands, perhaps the most attractive option is to explore the region north as far as Dhimitsána, then backtrack to Kariténa to proceed on to Olympia via Andhrítsena.

Karítena

Set high above the Megalópoli–Andhrítsena road, **KARÍTENA** may look familiar; with its medieval bridge over the River Alfíos (Alpheus), it graces the 5000-drachma note. Like many of the Arcadian hill towns hereabouts, its history is a mix of Frankish, Byzantine and Turkish contributions, the Venetians having passed over much of the northern interior. It was founded by the Byzantines in the seventh century and had attained a population of some 20,000 when the Franks took it in 1209. Under their century-long rule, Karítena was the capital of a large barony under Geoffroy de Bruyères, the paragon of chivalry in the medieval ballad "The Chronicle of the Morea" and virtually the only well-liked Frankish overlord.

The village these days has a population of just a couple of hundred, though there were at least ten times that figure until the beginning of this century. Approaching, you can stop on the modern bridge over the Alfíos and peer down at the **medieval bridge**, which is immediately adjacent. It is missing the central section but is an intriguing structure nonetheless, with a small Byzantine chapel built into one of the central pillars.

From the main road, there's a winding three-kilometre road up to the village, in the upper part of which is a small central **platía**, with a couple of cafés. Off this square are signposted the Byzantine churches of **Zoödhóhos Piyí**, with a Romanesque belfry, and **Áyios Nikólaos**, to the west, down towards the river; the latter has crumbling frescoes (enquire at the *kafenío* in the square for the keys). Also off the square is the **Frourio**, the castle built by the Franks and with added Turkish towers.

The town has one, unclassified, **hotel**, the *Karítena* (☎0791/31 203; ②), uphill and to the right from the upper *platía*, with hot water in the afternoon, great beds (lots of blankets – nights here are cold), and evening meals on request. There are also two **rooms places**: one signposted opposite the post office, run by Stamata Kondopoulo (☎0791/31 262; ②); the other, a very comfortable apartment a kilometre beyond the upper *platía*, run by Hristos and Athalassia Papodopoulos (☎0791/31 203; ②), who also offer fine evening meals and wine.

Gortys, Prodhrómou and the Lousíos Gorge

The site of **Ancient Gortys** can be approached either from Karítena (9km to the southwest) or from Stemnítsa (7.5km to the northeast). Walkers may want to make a circuit starting or ending in Stemnítsa, possibly camping overnight at Gortys, or staying at the nearby monastery of Prodhrómou.

The most direct road **from Karítena** runs up and through the town to ASTÍLOHOS (11km), a village 2km southwest of Gortys. If you don't have a car, it is easier to follow the road north towards Dhimitsána for 6km to the hamlet of ELLINIKÓ; you may be able to hitch this section of the journey. From the edge of the village a dirt track signposted "Gortys" descends west; after a rough six kilometres it ends at the bank of the Lousíos and you cross to the ruins on the other side via an old bridge.

Ancient Gortys

Ancient Gortys is one of the most stirring of all Greek sites, set beside the rushing river which in ancient times was the Gortynios. The relics are widely sown amongst the vegetation on the west (true right) bank of the stream, but the main attraction, below contemporary ground level and not at all obvious until well to the west of the little chapel of Áyios Andhréas (by the bridge), is the huge excavation containing the remains of a **Temple to Asclepius**, god of healing, and an adjoining **bath**, both dating from the fourth century BC.

The most curious feature of the site is a circular portico enclosing round-backed seats which most certainly would have been part of the therapeutic centre. It's an extraordinary place, especially if you camp with the roar of the Lousíos to lull you to sleep. The only drawback is the climate: temperatures up here plummet at night, no matter what the season, and heavy mists, wet as a soaking rain, envelop the mountains from midnight to mid-morning.

The Lousíos Gorge and Monastery of Prodhrómou

The farmland surrounding Ancient Gortys belongs to the monks of the nearby **Monastery of Prodhrómou**, who have carved a donkey path along the **gorge of the Lousíos** between Áyios Andhréas and the monastery. It's about forty minutes' walk upstream, with at first a gradual and later a steady ascent up a well-graded, switchbacked trail. A set of park benches by a formal gate heralds arrival at the cloister, and the whole area is well stamped about by the monks' mules. If you look up through the trees above the path, the monastery, stuck on to the cliff like a swallow's nest, is plainly visible a couple of hundred metres above.

The interior of the monastery does not disappoint this promise; the local villagers accurately describe it as *politisméno* (cultured) as opposed to *ágrio* (wild). Once inside it is surprisingly small; there were never more than about fifteen tenants, and currently there are twelve monks, four of them very young and committed. Visitors are received in the *arhondaríki* (guest lounge and adjoining quarters), and then shown the tiny frescoed *katholikón* (chapel), and possibly invited to evening services there. The strictest rules of dress apply but the monks welcome visitors who wish to stay the night. The only problem, especially on weekends, is that there are only a dozen or so beds, and people from Trípoli and even Athens make pilgrimages and retreats here, arriving by the carload along a circuitous dirt track from Stemnítsa. Be prepared for this possibility, and arrive in time to get back to level ground to camp.

Beyond Prodhrómou – and towards Stemnítsa

Beyond Prodhrómou the path continues clearly to the outlying monasteries of **Paleá** and **Néa Filosófou**. The older dates from the tenth century but, virtually ruined, is easy to miss since it blends into the cliff on which it's built. The newer (seventeenth-century) one is locked and abandoned, but has fine frescoes inside; ask the monks at Prodhrómou if the rusted lock has been repaired, or content yourself with a peek in through the door grille. North from here the trail becomes almost impassable, though there is a jeep track from near Néa Filosófou upstream to Dhimitsána.

As noted, there is a **jeep road between Prodhrómou and Stemnítsa**, off which forks a branch to Ellinikó (and, with another turning, Gortys), but if you are walking it is pleasant, and quicker, to follow the old **kalderími** (cobbled trail) from Pròdhrómou monastery to Stemnítsa – a climb, but not a killing one, of about ninety minutes through scrub oak with fine views over the valley. Usually one of the monks or lay workers will be free to point out the start of the path; once clear of the roadhead confusion by the modern little chapel at the edge of the canyon, there's little possiblity of getting lost. Descending from Stemnítsa, head out of town on the asphalt road to Dhimitsána and (just after the town-limits sign) bear down and left on to the obvious beginning of the upper end of the path.

Stemnítsa

Fifteen kilometres north of Karítena, **STEMNÍTSA** (or IPSOÚNDA, in its official, but little-used, Hellenised form) was for centuries one of the premier metal-smithing centres of the Balkans. Although much depopulated, it remains a fascinating town, with a small folklore museum, a revived artisan school (and workshop near the bus stop), and a handful of quietly magnificent medieval churches.

The town is divided by ravines into three distinct quarters: the Kástro (the ancient acropolis hill), Ayía Paraskeví (east of the stream) and Áyios Ioánnis (west of it). The **Folklore Museum** (Mon & Wed–Fri 5–7pm, Sat & Sun 11am–1pm & 5–7pm) is in the latter, just off the main road, and repays the trip out in itself. The ground floor is devoted to mock-ups of the workshops of indigenous crafts such as candle-making, bell-casting, shoe-making and jewellery. The next floor up features re-creations of the salon of a well-to-do family and a humbler cottage. The top storey is taken up by the rather random collections of the Savopoulos family: plates by the Asia Minor refugee ceramics master Avramides, textiles and costumes from all over Greece, weapons, copperware, and eighteenth- and nineteenth-century icons. Across the way you can visit an **artisan school**, staffed by the remaining local silver-, gold- and coppersmiths .

Next door to the school is the seventeenth-century basilica of **Tríon Ierarhón**, most accessible of the town's Byzantine churches; its caretaker lives in the low white house west of the main door. To visit the others, all of which are frescoed and locked, requires more determined enquiries to unearth a key. The *katholikón* of the monastery of **Zoödhóhos Piyí**, again seventeenth-century, has perhaps the finest setting, on the hillside above Ayía Paraskeví, but the tiny windows do not permit much of an interior view. The little adjoining monastery hosted the first *yerousía*, or convention, of guerilla captains in the War of Independence, giving rise to the local claim that Stemnítsa was Greece's first capital. Near the summit of the Kástro hill are the two adjacent chapels, tenth- and twelfth-century in turn, of **Profítis Ilías** and **Panayía Vaferón**, the former with a convenient window for fresco-viewing, the latter with an unusual colonnade. The last of the town's five churches, **Áyios Pandelímon**, is located at the western edge of the town, to the left of the asphalt road to Dhimitsána.

Accommodation is limited to the *Hotel Trikolonion* (☎0795/81 297; ③), wich has regular rooms and some luxurious suites in a fine traditional building. For drinks or meals, the place to go is a wonderful no-name **taverna**, at the end of a garden lane (and through a kids' playground) behind the clock tower on the main *platía*; it has fine barrel wine and amazing murals of Classical and revolutionary heroes. **Buses** are restricted to one daily connection with Trípoli; there is no service to Dhimitsána (9km northeast), though hitching would not be difficult.

Dhimitsána

Like Stemnítsa, **DHIMITSÁNA** has an immediately seductive appearance, its cobbled streets and tottering houses straddling a twin hillside overlooking the Lousíos river. Views from the village are stunning. It stands at the head of the gorge, and looking downriver you can just see the stack of the Megalópoli power plant and the bluff that supports Karítena. To the east are the lower folds of Ménalo, most visible if you climb up to the local **Kástro**, whose stretch of "Cyclopean" walls attests to its ancient use.

In the town, a half-dozen churches with tall, squarish belfries recall the extended Frankish, and especially Norman, tenure in this part of the Morea during the thirteenth century. Yet none should dispute the deep-dyed Greekness of Dhimitsána. It was the birthplace of Archbishop Yermanos, who first raised the flag of rebellion at Kalávrita in 1821, and of the hapless Patriarch Grigoris V, hanged in Constantinople upon the Sultan's receiving news of the insurrection mounted by his co-religionist. During the hostilities the ubiquitous Kolokotronis maintained a lair and a powder mill in this then well-nigh inaccessible town. Even before the War of Independence the Kolokotronis clan used the nunnery of **Emyalón** (9am–2pm), 3km towards Stemnítsa, as a hideout.

Accommodation options are a small five-bed inn on a *platía* in the east part of town, whose proprietress is reluctant to let to lone or short-term travellers, and, 1.5km out on the road to Stemnítsa, the very pleasant *Hotel Dimitsana* (☎0795/31 518; ③ – though negotiable out of season). The *Taverna Kallithea*, just across the road from the hotel, is Dhimitsána's best; other than that there's a lone souvláki stall in town, and the eminently avoidable *Vlahos*, a stygian basement dive.

Heading for Olympia

Using public transport towards **Olympia**, keep in mind that through buses are scarce, and you may well need to hitch (or take a taxi) over the first stage, from Dhimitsána to KARAKOLOÚ or VITÍNA, on the main Trípoli–Pírgos road. Once on the road, the most enjoyable halt is **LANGÁDHIA** (18km toward Olympia), whose tiers of houses and bubbling sluices both tumble downhill to the river far below the road. Often you can stop on a late morning bus, eat lunch, and pick up the next through service with little lost time. If you decide to stay the night, there's a couple of modest **hotels**, the *Kentrikon* (☎0795/43 221; ②) and *Langadia* (☎0795/43 202; ③).

You may well find that you have fewer changes and stops backtracking south to join the **Karítena–Andhrítsena route** (see below) and going on to Olympia from there.

Andhrítsena and the Temple of Bassae

Moving west from **Karítena towards Andhrítsena**, the Alfíos river falls away to the north and the hills become mountains – Líkeo and Mínthi, to the south and west respectively. The route, only slightly less remote than the twists of road around Dhimitsána, is a superb one for its own sake, with the added attractions of **Andhrítsena**, a traditional mountain town, and, up in the flanks of Mount Líkeo, the **Temple of Apollo at Bassae**.

Andhrítsena

ANDHRÍTSENA, 28km west of Karítena, is a beautiful stop and the traditional base from which to visit the Temple of Bassae up in the mountains to the south. Though very much a roadside settlement today, it too was a major hill town through the years of Turkish occupation and the first century of independent Greece. It is remarkably untouched, with wooden houses spilling down to a stream, whose clear, ice-cold head-waters are channelled into a fountain – set within a tree – in the central square.

Accommodation is available at the *Hotel Pan* (☎0626/22 213; ②), at the far west end of town by the Shell station, with clean, comfortable rooms, and the fancier, some-what overpriced *Hotel Theoxenia* (☎0626/22 219; ④), on the Karítena side of town. For **meals**, try any of the restaurants on the main square, and especially the one up the steps beside the old (and closed) *Hotel Vassae*.

The Temple of Apollo at Bassae

Fourteen kilometres into the mountains from Andhrítsena, the **Temple of Apollo** at **BASSAE** (VASSÉS, in the modern idiom) has the most remote and arguably the most spectacular site in Greece. In addition, it is, after the Thiseion in Athens, the best-preserved Classical monument in the country, and for many years was considered to have been designed by Iktinos, architect of the Parthenon – though this theory has recently fallen from favour.

There, for the moment at least, the superlatives must cease. For romantic though it was in the past, the temple is swathed for the forseeable future in a gigantic grey marquee supported on metal girders and set in concrete with wire stays; its entablature and frieze lie dissected in neat rows on the ground to one side. No doubt the restoration is badly needed for its preservation – and the marquee is quite a sight in itself – but it has to be said that visitors are likely to be a bit disappointed. If you are not put off – and drivers can cross the mountains to reach the coast at Tholó – the road up to the temple begins to climb from behind the main church in Andhrítsena. The simplest aproach is to share a taxi, which should charge around 1000dr for the round-trip, wait-ing an hour at the site. On foot it's a pretty agonising ascent, with little likelihood of a lift. The site has a daytime guardian but is unenclosed. It's a lonely place, and must have felt even more so in ancient times.

The temple was erected in dedication to **Apollo Epikourios** ("the Succourer") by the Phigalians. It's known that they built it in gratitude for being spared from plague but beyond this it is something of a puzzle. It is oddly aligned on a north–south axis and, being way up in the mountains, is only visible when you are comparatively near. There are oddities too in the architecture: the columns on its north side are strangely thicker than in the rest of the building, and incorporated into its *cella* was a single Corinthian column, the first known in Greece (though now vanished save for its base). Unusually again, the cult statue, probably a four-metre-high bronze, would have stood in front of this pillar.

On from Bassae or Andhrítsena

Leaving the Bassae/Andhrítsena area, you've a number of choices. **From Andhrítsena** there are two daily buses back up towards Karítena/Megalópoli and two down to Pírgos. If you are headed for Olympia, take the Pírgos bus and get off in KRÉSTENA, from where you can hitch or take a taxi along the 12km side road up to the site. You'll certainly save time and maybe some money.

For the adventurous, an unsurfaced track winds through the mountains **from Bassae down to the coast** at THOLÓ (see p.199). It's a dusty, very bumpy ride but for the unhurried there's the opportunity to stop at PERIVÓLIA (10km). This mountain hamlet has a two-kilometre dirt road connecting it with the similarly diminutive FIGALÍA, close by the ruinous but enormous Classical walls of **ancient Phigalia**.

Olympia (Olimbía)

The historic associations and resonance of **OLYMPIA**, which for over a millennium hosted the most important **Panhellenic games**, are rivalled only by Delphi or Mycenae. Its site, too, belongs in this company. For although the actual ruins of the sanctuary are jumbled and confusing, the setting is as perfect as could be imagined: a luxuriant valley of wild olive and plane trees, spread beside twin rivers of Alfíos (Alpheus) and Kládhios, and overlooked by the pine-covered hill of Krónos. Despite the crowds, it demands and deserves a lengthy visit.

THE OLYMPIC GAMES: SOME HISTORY

The origins of the games at Olympia are rooted in **legends** – the most dominant relating to the god **Pelops**, revered in the region before his eclipse by Zeus, and to **Hercules**, one of the earliest victors. Historically, the contests probably began around the eleventh century BC, growing over the next two centuries from a local festival to the quadrennial celebration attended by states from throughout the Greek world.

The impetus for this change seems to have come from the Oracle of Delphi, which, with the local ruler of Elis, **Iphitos**, and the Spartan ruler **Lycurgus**, helped to codify the Olympic rules in the ninth century BC. Among their most important introductions was a **sacred truce**, the *Ekeheiria*, announced by heralds prior to the celebrations and enforced for their duration. It was virtually unbroken throughout the games' history – Sparta, ironically, was fined at one point – and as host of the games, Elis, a comparatively weak state, was able to keep itself away from political disputes, growing rich meanwhile on the associated trade and kudos.

From the beginning, the main **Olympic events** were athletic. The earliest was a race over the course of the stadium – roughly 200 metres. Later came the introduction of two-lap (400m) and 24-lap (5000m) races, along with the most revered of the Olympiad events, the Pentathlon. This encompassed running, jumping, discus and javelin events, the competitors gradually reduced to a final pair for a wrestling-and-boxing combat. It was, like much of these early Olympiads, a fairly brutal contest. Even more so was the Pancratium, introduced, alongside chariot racing, in 680 BC. In this – one of the most prestigious events – contestants fought each other, naked and unarmed, using any means except biting or gouging each others' eyes; the olive wreath had on one occasion to be awarded posthumously, the victor having died at the moment of his opponent's submission. The chariot races, similarly, were extreme tests of strength and control, only one team in twenty completing the seven-kilometre course without mishap.

The great **gathering of people and nations** at the festival extended the games' importance and purpose well beyond the winning of olive wreaths; assembled under the temporary truce, nobles and ambassadors negotiated treaties, while merchants chased

The site and museum

Olympia is one of the largest and most beautiful sites in Greece – a blessing, since it is also one of the most crowded and confusing. The crowds, in fact, are easily absorbed by temples and stadium alike. But the archaeologists, with their zeal for unearthing every last, loose stone, have left ruins that seem to cry out for reconstruction, even on a modest scale. The great temple columns lie half-buried amid the trees and undergrowth: picturesque and shaded, perfect ground for picnics, but offering little real impression of their ancient grandeur or function. Their fame, however, prevails over circumstance and walking through the arch from the sanctuary to the stadium it is hard not to feel in awe of the Olympian history.

The site was from its beginnings a **sanctuary**, with a permanent population limited to the temple priests. At first the games took place within the sacred precinct, the walled, rectangular **Altis**, but as events became more sophisticated a new stadium was built to adjoin it. Additional public buildings, too, spread out from the *Altis*, and as the religious functions of Olympia declined, memorials and palaces were built for Alexander the Great and later for Nero. The whole sanctuary was throughout its history a treasure-trove of public and religious statuary. Victors were allowed to erect a statue in the *Altis* (in their likeness if they won three events) and numerous city states installed treasuries. Pausanias, writing in the fourth century AD, after the Romans had already looted the sanctuary several times, fills almost a whole book of his *Guide to Greece* with descriptions. An idea of this wealth is suggested today not only by the site but by a spectacular collection of sculpture in the **museum**.

contacts and foreign markets. Sculptors and poets, too, would seek commissions for their work. Herodotus read aloud the first books of his history at an Olympian festival to an audience that included Thucydides – who was to date events in his own work after the winners of the Pancratium.

In the early Olympiads, the **rules of competition** were strict. Only free-born – and male – Greeks could take part, and the rewards of victory were entirely honorary: a palm, given to the victor immediately after the contest, and an olive branch, presented in a ceremony closing the games. As the games developed, however, the rules were loosened to allow athletes from all parts of the Greek and Roman world – from as far afield as Sicily and Asia Minor – and nationalism and professionalism gradually crept in. By the fourth century BC, when the games were at their peak, the athletes were virtually all professionals, heavily sponsored by their home states and, if they won at Olympia, commanding huge appearance money at games elsewhere. Bribery, too, became an all too common feature, despite the solemn religious oaths sworn in front of the sanctuary priests prior to the contests.

Under the **Romans**, predictably, the process was accelerated. The palms and olive branches were replaced by rich monetary prizes, and a sequence of new events was introduced. The nadir was reached in 69 AD when the Emperor Nero delayed the games for two years so that he could compete in (and win) special singing and lyre-playing events – in addition to the chariot race in which he was tactfully declared victor despite falling twice and failing to finish.

Despite all this abuse the Olympian tradition was popular enough to be maintained for another three centuries, and the games' eventual **closure** happened as a result of religious dogma rather than lack of support. In 393 AD the Emperor Theodosius, newly converted to Christianity, suspended the games as part of a general crackdown on public pagan festivities. This suspension proved final, for Theodosius's successor ordered the destruction of the temples, a process completed by barbarian invasion, earthquakes and, lastly, by the river Alfíos changing its course to cover the sanctuary site. There it remained, covered by seven metres of silt and sand, until the first excavation by German archaeologists in the 1870s.

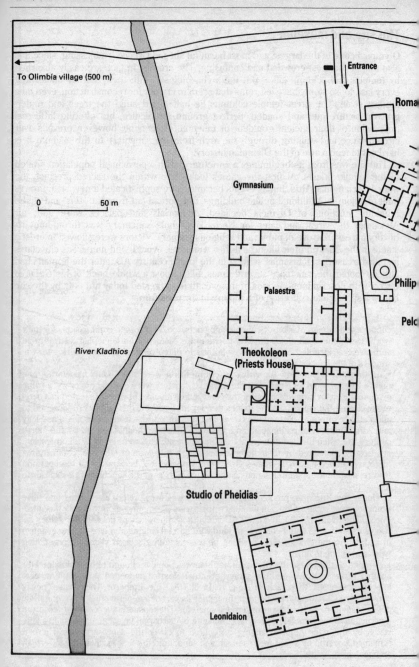

To Olimbía village (500 m)

Entrance

Roma

Gymnasium

0   50 m

Palaestra

Philip

Pelo

River Kladhios

Theokoleon
(Priests House)

Studio of Pheidias

Leonidaion

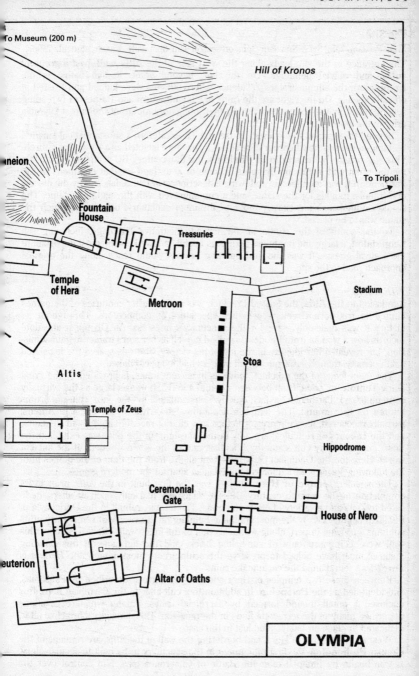

To Museum (200 m)

Hill of Kronos

neion

To Trípoli

Fountain
House

Treasuries

Temple
of Hera

Stadium

Metroon

Stoa

Altis

Temple of Zeus

Hippodrome

Ceremonial
Gate

House of Nero

euterion

Altar of Oaths

OLYMPIA

The Site

Mon–Fri 8am–7pm, Sat & Sun 9am–3pm; off-season 9am–3pm daily. 1500dr, students 750dr.

The entrance to the site leads along the west side of the **Altis wall**, past a group of public and official buildings. On the left, beyond some Roman baths, is the **Prytaneion**, the administrators' residence where athletes were lodged and feasted at official expense. On the right are the ruins of a **Gymnasium** and **Palaestra** (wrestling school), used by the competitors during their obligatory month of training at Olympia prior to the games.

Beyond these stood the Priests' House, the **Theokoleion**, a substantial colonnaded building in the southeast corner of which is a structure adapted as a Byzantine church. This was originally the **studio of Pheidias**, the fifth-century BC sculptor responsible for the great cult statue in Olympia's Temple of Zeus (and for that of Athena in the Parthenon). It was identified by following a description in Pausanias, and by the discovery of tools, moulds for the statue, and a cup engraved with the sculptor's name. The studio's dimensions are exactly those of the inner sanctuary, or *cella*, in which the statue was to be placed.

To the south of the studio lie further administrative buildings, including the **Leonidaion**, a large and doubtless luxurious hostel endowed for the most important of the festival guests. It was the first building visitors would reach along the original approach road to the site.

THE ALTIS

Admission to the **Altis**, the Sacred Precinct, was in the earlier centuries of the games limited to free-born Greeks – whether spectators or competitors. Throughout its history it was male-only, save for the sanctuary's priestess. An Olympian anecdote records how a woman from Rhodes disguised herself as her son's trainer to gain admission, but revealed her identity in the joy of his victory. She was spared the legislated death penalty, though subsequently all trainers had to appear naked.

The main focus of the precinct, today as in ancient times, is provided by the great Doric **Temple of Zeus**. Built between 470 and 456 BC, it was as large as the (virtually contemporary) Parthenon, a fact quietly substantiated by the vast column drums littered on the ground. The temple's decoration, too, rivalled the finest in Athens; partially recovered, its sculptures of Pelops in a chariot race, of Lapiths and Centaurs, and the Labours of Hercules, are now in the museum. In the *cella* was exhibited the (lost) gold-and-ivory cult statue by Pheidias, one of the seven wonders of the ancient world. Here too the Olympian flame was kept alight, from the time of the games until the following spring – a tradition continued at an altar for the modern games.

The smaller **Temple of Hera**, behind, was the first built in the *Altis*; prior to its completion in the seventh century BC, the sanctuary had only open-air altars, dedicated to Zeus and a variety of other cult gods. The temple, rebuilt in the Doric style in the sixth century BC, is the most complete building on the site, with some thirty of its columns surviving in part, along with a section of the inner wall. The levels above this wall were composed only of sun-baked brick, and the lightness of this building material must have helped to preserve the sculptures – most notably the *Hermes of Praxiteles* – found amid the earthquake ruins.

Between these two temples of Hera and Zeus is a grove described by Pausanias, and identified as the **Pelopeion**. In addition to a cult altar to the Olympian hero, this enclosed a small mound formed by sacrificial ashes, among which excavations unearthed many of the terracotta finds in the museum. The sanctuary's principal altar, dedicated to Zeus, probably stood just to the east.

West of the Temple of Hera, and bordering the wall of the *Altis*, are remains of the circular **Philippeion**, the first monument in the sanctuary to be built to secular glory. It was begun by Philip II after the Battle of Chaeronea gave him control over the

Greek mainland, and may have been completed by Alexander the Great. To the east of the Hera temple is a small, second-century AD **fountain house**, the gift of the ubiquitous Herodes Atticus. Beyond, lining a terrace below at the base of the Hill of Kronos, are the **state treasuries**. All except two of these were constructed by cities outside of Greece proper, as they functioned principally as storage chambers for sacrificial items and sporting equipment used in the games. They are built in the form of temples, as at Delphi; the oldest and grandest, at the east end, belonged to Gela in Sicily. In front of the treasuries are the foundations of a fourth-century BC Doric temple, the **Metroön**, dedicated to the mother of the gods.

The ancient ceremonial entrance to the *Altis* was on the south side, below a long **stoa** taking up almost the entire east side of the precinct. At the corner was a house built by Nero for his stay during the games. The emperor also had the entrance remodelled as a triumphal arch, fit for his anticipated victories.

Through the arch, just outside the precinct, stood the **Bouleuterion** or Council House, where before a great statue of Zeus the competitors took their oaths to observe the Olympian rules. As they approached the stadium, the gravity of this would be impressed upon them; lining the way were bronze statues paid for with the fines exacted for foul play, bearing the name of the disgraced athlete, his father and city.

THE STADIUM
In the final outcome, it's neither foundations nor columns that make sense of Olympia, but the 200-metre track of the **Stadium** itself, entered through a football-tunnel-like arch. The starting and finishing lines are still there, with the judges' thrones in the middle and seating ridges banked to either side.

Originally unstructured, the stadium developed with the games' popularity, forming a model for others throughout the Greek and Roman world. The tiers here eventually accommodated up to 20,000 spectators, with a smaller number on the southern slope overlooking the **Hippodrome** where the chariot races were held. Even so, the seats were reserved for the wealthier strata of society. The ordinary populace – along with slaves and all women spectators – watched the events from the Hill of Krónos, then treeless and a natural grandstand to the north.

The stadium was unearthed only in the last war, by German archaeologists, who dug here from 1941 to 1944, allegedly on the direct orders of Hitler. It's a sobering thought to see this ancient site in the context of the 1936 Berlin Olympics.

The Archaeological Museum
Open Mon noon–5pm, Tues–Fri 8am–7pm, Sat & Sun 9am–3pm; 1000dr, students 500dr.

Olympia's site museum lies a couple of hundred metres north of the sanctuary. It contains some of the finest Classical and Roman sculptures in the country, all superbly displayed, and amply justifies the rather high admission fee.

The most famous of the individual sculptures are the **Head of Hera** and the **Hermes of Praxiteles**, both dating from the fourth century BC and discovered in the Temple of Hera. The Hermes is one of the best-preserved of all Classical sculptures, and remarkable in the easy informality of its pose; it retains traces of its original paint. On a grander scale is the **Nike of Paionios**, which was originally ten metres high. Though no longer complete (and currently sequestered for restoration), it hints at how the sanctuary must once have appeared, crowded with statuary.

The best of the smaller objects are housed in Room 4. They include several fine bronze items, among them a **Persian Helmet**, captured by the Athenians at the Battle of Marathon, and (displayed alongside) the **Helmet of Miltiades**, the victorious Athenian general; both were found with votive objects dedicated in the stadium. There is also a superb terracotta group of **Zeus abducting Ganymede** and a group of finds from the workshop of **Pheidias**, including the cup with his name inscribed.

In the main hall of the museum is the centrepiece of the Olympia finds – statuary and scupture reassembled from the **Temple of Zeus**. This includes three groups, all of which were once painted. From the *cella* is a frieze of the **Twelve Labours of Hercules**, delicately moulded and for the most part identifiably preserved. The other groups are from the east and west pediments.

The east, reflecting Olympian pursuits, depicts Zeus presiding over a **Chariot race between Pelops and Oinamaos**. The story has several versions. King Oinamaos, warned that he would be killed by his son-in-law, challenged each of his daughter Hippomadeia's suitors to a chariot race. After allowing them a start he would catch up and kill them from behind. The king (depicted on the left of the frieze) was eventually defeated by Pelops (on the right with Hippomadeia), after – depending on the version – assistance from Zeus (depicted at the centre), magic steeds from Poseidon, or, most un-Olympian, bribing Oinamaos's charioteer to tamper with the wheels.

The west pediment, less controversially mythological, illustrates the **Battle of Lapiths and Centaurs** at the wedding of the Lapith king Peirithous. This time Apollo presides over the scene while Theseus helps the Lapiths defeat the drunken centaurs, depicted – with fairly brutal realism – attacking the women and boy guests.

In the last rooms of the museum are a collection of **objects relating to the games** – including *halteres*, or jumping weights, discuses, weightlifter's stones, and so on. Here, too, are displayed a number of funerary inscriptions, including that of a boxer, Camelos of Alexandria, who died in the stadium after praying to Zeus for victory or death.

Olimbía village: practicalities

Modern **OLIMBÍA** is essentially one long main avenue, **Leofóros Kondhíli**, with a few side streets: a village that has grown up simply to serve the excavations and tourist trade. Nevertheless, it's quite a pleasant place to stay – and certainly preferable to Pírgos (see following) – with the prospect of good countryside walks along the Alfíos river and around the hill of Krónos.

Accommodation

Accommodation is fairly easy to come by, with a swift turnaround of clientele and a range of hotels and private rooms whose prices are kept modest by competition. The cheaper ones tend to have more space for individual travellers, as many of the mid-range and more luxury hotels have block bookings from group tours. As elsewhere, rates can drop substantially out of season.

Among the **hotels and pensions** are:

Pension Possidon (☎0624/22 567); **Pension Achilles** (☎0624/22 931). A pair of decent budget pensions on Ódhos Stefanopoúlou – up behind the *National Bank*; there are also some rooms places on this street. ②

Hotel Heraeum, Kondhíli 39 (☎0624/22 539). Often the cheapest hotel rates in town. ②

Hotel Praxiteles, Spiliopoúlou 7 (☎0624/22 592). ②

Hotel Pelops, Varía 2 (☎0624/22 543). ③

Hotel Hermes, Kondhíli 63 (☎0624/22 577). ③

Hotel Phedias, Spilopoúlou 2 (☎0624/22 667). ③

Hotel Artemis, Tsouréka 2 (☎0624/22 255). ③

If you're travelling alone, the **youth hostel** (on the main street, Kondhíli 18; ☎0624/22 580) is the cheapest option, and the 11.30pm curfew is unlikely to prove frustrating; the hostel is open all day except between 10am and 1pm. Between two people, **rooms** in private houses will end up being better value: you may well be offered one on arrival – otherwise most are signposted on the road parallel to and above Kondhíli.

There are three **campsites**, closest of which is *Camping Diana* (☎0624/22 314), 1km back from the main street, with a pool and good facilities. The others are *Camping Alphios* (☎0624/22 950), 2km up in the hills, and *Camping Olympia* (☎0624/22 745), 2km out on the Pírgos road.

Food and other practicalities

Most of the **tavernas** offer standard tourist meals at mildly inflated prices, though the *Anesis*, at the top of Odhós Avyerínou, is a tasty, authentic *psistariá* specialising in *kondosoúvli*. For picnics, bread from the bakery on the road to Kréstena is excellent.

Among other facilities, Olimbía has two **banks** and an **OTE** on the main street, a **post office** (just uphill) with Saturday and Sunday morning hours. **English-language books** are to be found at the back of the *Galerie d'Orphée* crafts shop and in the *Altis* shop, down towards the sanctuary site. There is a **tourist office**, on the right of the main road, going towards the site, and another in summer at the site itself.

The village itself has little in the way of diversion, save a somewhat dutiful **Museum of the Olympic Games** (Mon–Sat 8am–3.30pm, Sun 9am–4.30pm; 500dr), with commemorative postage stamps and the odd memento from the modern games, including the box which conveyed the heart of Pierre de Coubertin, reviver of the games, from Paris to Olympia – where it was buried.

Transport

Most people arrive at Olympia **via Pírgos**, which is on the main Peloponnese rail line and has frequent bus connections with Pátra and a couple daily with Kalamáta/Kiparissía. **Buses** leave 16 times per weekday (10 on weekends) between Pírgos and Olympia, though with a break between 12.30 and 3.30pm and a last service at 9pm. The last of five daily **trains** from Pírgos to Olympia leaves at 7.10pm.

The only other direct buses to Olympia are **from Trípoli**, via LANGÁDHIA. These run three times daily in either direction. If you are approaching **from Andhrítsena**, either take the bus to Pírgos and change, or stop at KRÉSTENA and hitch or take a taxi the final 12km on from there.

The Coast from Pírgos to Pátra

Despite the proximity of Olympia and Pátra, the **northwest corner** of the Peloponnese is not much explored by foreign visitors. Admittedly, it's not the most glamorous of coasts, but for a day or two's beach stop, either **Kalógria** or the old port of **Katákolo** are functional and pleasant. **Ferry connections** may add further purpose: from Killíni there are regular crossings to Zákinthos, and in summer to Kefalloniá, while Katákolo has (summer-only) *kaíkia* to Zákinthos.

Pírgos

PÍRGOS has a grim recent history. When the Germans withdrew at the end of World War II it remained under the control of Greek Nazi collaborators, who, after negotiating surrender with the resistance, opened fire on their entry to the town. Full-scale battle erupted and for five days the town burned. Today, it's a drab, 1950s-looking place, which few casual visitors have a good word to say about. If you can avoid an enforced overnight stay, do so. The hotels are overpriced, the food uninspiring, diversions nonexistent. The main escape routes are to Pátra, Kiparissía or Olympia (by train or bus); or, closer at hand, to Katákolo by local bus #4. The bus and train stations are around 100m apart, and not hard to find your way between.

Among the **hotels**, the *Olympos* at Karkavítsa 2, on the corner of Vassiléos Pávlou (☎0621/23 650; ③), is cheap and relatively pleasant.

Katákolo

Thirteen kilometres west of Pírgos, **KATÁKOLO** is somewhat more enticing: a decayed, ramshackle old port with good beaches close by. Until the last few decades, and improved road connections with Pátra, it controlled the trade for Ilía province. Today only a few tramp steamers rust at anchor, though the navy calls occasionally and, oddly, the port remains a stop for Italian cruise ships, including the *Orient Express*. What the cruise passengers make of the caved-in warehouses and the little two-street town, before they board their air-conditioned coaches to Olympia, is hard to say, but arriving from Pírgos it feels an easy place to settle into.

There are three **hotels**, best value of which is the *Delfíni* (☎0621/41 214; ③), and several **rooms** establishments at the top of steps leading from the road, with cabins fronted by peach and apricot trees. Try to avoid staying on the main drag, which proves to be incredibly noisy at night, belying the town's torpid daytime appearance. For **meals**, there are a handful of excellent tavernas on the quay.

Beaches

Katákolo's beach, the **Spiátza**, stretches away for miles to the north, a popular spot with Greeks, many of whom own shuttered little cottages set just back from the sea. It is sandy, though hard-packed: more of a spot for football or jogging, with the sea too shallow for real swimming for a long way out.

However, a thirty-minute walk north, past the overgrown Byzantine-Frankish **Castle of Beauvoir**, will take you to much better swimming at **Áyios Andhréas** beach – two hundred metres of sloping, outcrop-studded sand, with views over a few attendant islets and out to Zákinthos. There are summer tavernas here and a few rooms to let. An even better beach is to be found at **SKAFÍDHIA**, 3km north of Katákolo and accessible by road via KORAKOHÓRI. It is a quiet, attractive strand despite the presence of a *Club Med* holiday complex to its north.

To the south of Katákolo there's a pleasant twenty-minute walk out to the **lighthouse**, set on a plateau among arbutus and pine.

Loutrá, Killíni and Hlemoútsi

North from Pírgos, road and rail meander through a series of uneventful market towns. For the coast there are two forks: at GASTOÚNI for the spa of **Loutrá Killínis** (occasional buses from Pírgos and Pátra); and at KAVÁSSILAS where a side road (buses from Pátra) heads down to **Killíni** proper. Take care not to confuse the two.

Loutrá Killínis

At the north end of **LOUTRÁ KILLÍNIS'** long beach you'll find a crop of upmarket (A- and C-class, ③ and ⑤) hotels catering for the resort's spa-trade. But walk south and the development soon gives way to sand dunes, seasonal home to a crowd of unofficial campers, mostly German, French and Italian. Joining them should pose no problems, though there is also a legitimate EOT **campsite**, *Camping Killini* (☎0623/96 270), back on the road towards VARTHOLOMIÓ and GASTOÚNI.

Killíni

Cheerless little **KILLÍNI** (which can be reached by taxi from Loutrá Killínis) has little more to offer than its **ferry connections**. It is the principal port for **Zákinthos** (3–7 departures daily) and in season has boats (4 departures daily) to Póros or Argostóli on

Kefaloniá. Be warned, however, that the two daily bus arrivals/departures are perversely designed to just miss each other, forcing a two to three-hour stopover at the harbour.

If you're stuck the night in Killíni, the choice is between sleeping on the beach, rooms on the main street, or the *Hotel Glaretzas* (☎0623/92 937; ③).

Hlemoútsi Castle

Using Loutrá Killínis or Killíni as a base, it's worth taking time to hitch or walk to the village of **KÁSTRO**, 6km from either town at the centre of the sandy cape. Looming above the village is the Frankish **Castle of Hlemoútsi** (also known as Chlemoutsi or Khlemoutsi), a vast hexagonal structure built by Guillaume de Villehardouin, the founder of Mystra, in 1220. Its function was principally to control the province of Achaia, though it served also as a strategic fortress on the Adriatic. Haze permitting, there are sweeping views across the straits to Zákinthos, and even to Kefalloniá and Itháki, from the well-preserved and restored ramparts.

Kalógria

Midway between Killíni and Pátra, **KALÓGRIA** is an eight-kilometre strand of beach, bordered by a swathe of pine forests. A fair proportion of Pátra descends here at the weekend as it's the nearest good beach to the city, but it's also a respected place (both the sands and, for its birdlife, the forest) and permanent development remains low-key. It is not actually a village – the nearest bona fide town is METÓHI – but instead a cluster of tavernas and stores. At the far north end of the beach there's a large hotel and *Barracuda Club* complex. A novelty for wildlife aficionados are the estuaries nearby in which you may find yourself swimming alongside harmless metre-long watersnakes.

Pátra (Patras)

PÁTRA is the largest town in the Peloponnese and, after Pireás, the major port of Greece: you can go from here to Italy and Turkey (services are suspended to the coast of what-was-Yugoslavia), as well as to certain Ionian islands. The city is also the key for the Greek mainland transport network, with connections throughout the Peloponnese and, via the ferry at Río, across the straits to Delphi or western Greece.

Unless you arrive late in the day from Italy, you shouldn't need to spend more than a few hours in the city. A conurbation of close to 500,000 souls, it's not the ideal holiday retreat: there are no beaches, no particular sights, and traffic noise well into the night and earlier than you'd want to get up. Nor is there much effort to make the place attractive to visitors, save for a financially troubled **summer festival** which sponsors events from July to early September. These include classical plays and the occasional rock concert in the Roman **Odeion**, and art and photographic exhibitions that bring a bit of life to the warehouses by the harbour. **Carnival**, in February/March, is, however, one of the biggest in the country, with a grand parade through the city centre.

At other times, if you've an afternoon to fill the best places to make for are the **castle**, the café-table-studded **Platiía Psilá Alónia** nearby, or the out-of-town Achaïa Clauss winery. The castle is mainly Venetian – not exciting but away from the city bustle, surrounded by a park and only a ten-minute walk up from the water. The local **Archaeological Museum** is deeply uncompelling.

Swimming near Pátra isn't really advisable either, with the sea polluted for some kilometres to the west. Locals go to the **beaches** around Río (7km northeast; bus #6 from Kandakári) or to Kalógria (32km southwest – see above; bus from *KTEL* station).

The Achaïa Clauss factory

To get to the **Achaïa Clauss** factory, 9km southeast of town, take the #7 bus from Kandakári (see map). Tours (daily in season 9am–1pm & 4–7pm; free) show you around its wine- and *ouzo*-making process, and feature some treasured, century-old barrels of *Mavrodhafni* – a dark dessert wine named after the woman Clauss wanted to marry. You're given a glass of this to sample (and a postcard, which they post) on reaching the factory's rather Teutonic bar, an echo of its founder's nationality. Along the walls are signed letters from celebrity recipients of *Mavrodhafni* (first prize for arrogance to the British judge who sent a signed photo).

A shop sells all the factory's products if you want a bottle for yourself.

Practicalities

The **ferry agents**, **train station** and main **KTEL bus terminal** could hardly be easier to find, grouped on the harbour road, **Óthonos Amalías**. At the corner of this street and Karólou, just east of the bus station, is the brand new and useful **Europa Centre** (☎061/434 801), which has tourist information, a café-restaurant and a ticket agency.

The **EOT** office, by the customs house at the harbour, also dispenses information. For **money exchange**, if you arrive late or need to buy last-minute drachmas for embarkation tax, the *National Bank of Greece*, just back from the waterside, keeps special daily evening hours (5.30–8pm). There is also an **OTE** (telephone office) and extended-hours **post office** near the customs station.

Accommodation

If you need to stay, one concentration of low-budget **hotels** is to be found on Ayíou Andhréou street, one block back from Óthonos Amalías; another major hotel street, Áyios Nikólaos, runs back from the sea, near the train station and Platía Tríon Simáhon, the principal waterside square. Don't expect too much in the way of standards or value for money; most of the places cater for a very passing trade and don't make great efforts.

Choices include:

Youth Hostel, Iröön Politehníou 68 (☎061/427 278). The best budget option, housed in a nineteenth-century mansion, a kilometre-plus walk south from the ferry terminal. It's clean and cheap, with roof space as well as dormitory rooms, and has no curfew. ①

Hotel Delphi, Ayíou Andhréou 63 (☎061/273 050). ②

Hotel Theoxenia, Ayíou Andhréou 97 (☎061/222 962). ②

Hotel Megali Brettania, Ayíou Andhréou 95 (☎061/27 3421). A huge, ancient building with lots of rooms. ③

Hotel Parthenon, Ermoú 25 (☎061/277 288). A slightly decrepit building, one block in from Platía Tríon Simáhon. ②

ROOM PRICE SCALES

All establishments listed in this book have been price-graded according to the scale outlined below. The **rates quoted** represent the **cheapest available room in high season**; all are prices for a double room, except for category ①, which are per person rates. Out of season rates can drop by up to fifty percent, especially if you negotiate rates for a stay of three or more nights.

① 1000–1500dr (£3–4.50/US$5.50–8)	④ 5500–7500dr (£17–23/US$30–41.50)
② 2000–3000dr (£6–9.50/US$11–16.50)	⑤ 7500–9000dr (£23–28/US$41.50–50)
③ 3000–5500dr (£9.50–17/US$16.50–30)	⑥ 9000dr (£28/US$50) and upwards

For further explanation of our hotel category system, see p.32.

Hotel Esperia, Zaími 10 (☎061/276 476). Between the main *KTEL* and city bus terminals. ③

Hotel Ilion, Ayíou Nikólaou 10 (☎061/273 161). ②

Hotel Hellas, Ayíou Nikólaou 14 (☎061/273 352). Pleasant, recently refurbished rooms in a nineteenth-century mansion. ③

Hotel Méditerranée, Ayíou Nikólaou 18 (☎061/279 602). ④

Hotel Galaxy, Ayíou Nikólaou 9 (☎061/278 815). Good upmarket option. ⑤

The nearest **campsite** is *Kavouri Camping* (☎061/422 145), 2km east of the city centre, near the public swimming pool; take bus #1 from the waterfront.

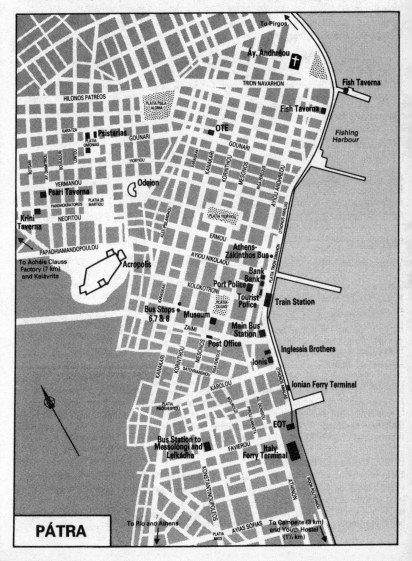

FERRY ROUTES AND COMPANIES

Innumerable ticket agents along the waterfront each sell different permutations of **ferry crossings to Italy** on one or more of the lines detailed below. It is worth spending an hour or so researching these, especially if you're taking a car, since costs, journey times and routes all differ from one company to another. En route to Italy, it is possible to make stopovers on Kefalloniá, Páxi and, most commonly, Igoumenítsa and Corfu (Kérkira). Domestic tickets to these **Greek island stops** (plus Itháki) are also available from Pátra.

A few **general points**:

Fares All companies offer a variety of fares for cabin, aeroplane-type seats, and deck passage, less reductions according to age, student or rail-card status.

Embarkation tax of (currently) 1500dr per person and 1500dr per vehicle is levied on all international departures.

Stopovers are free if you specify them when booking, though you will have to pay re-embarkation taxes.

Checking in at the company's respective port agent is essential if you have booked tickets in advance, or bought them through a travel company other than the official agent. This should be done at least three hours before departure. For companies with no exclusive agent in Pátra, go to the departures hall and look for a booth.

Companies and agents

Fragline Brindisi (18hr 30min) direct; 3 weekly. *Inglessis Bros.*, Óthonos Amalías 12; ☎061/277 676.

Hellenic Mediterranean Lines Brindisi (16hr 30min) via Kefalloniá; daily. Also Brindisi (18.5hr) via Igoumenítsa and Corfu. *Hellenic Mediterranean Lines Co. Ltd*, Sarandapórou 1/corner Athinón; ☎061/429 520.

Restaurants

Pátra's **restaurants** seem to constitute a fairly wretched bunch – fast-food places around Óthonos Amalías and Ayíou Andhréou – until you look away from the city centre. The streets by the castle are the best place to start. Here, *Krini* at Pandokrátoros 57 is an endearingly basic lunchtime place, with wine barrels down one side; around the corner, *Psari* at Ayíou Dhimitríou 75 (open evenings) has a similar feel. For fish, the best places are a couple of tavernas down by the fishing harbour, home to a somewhat half-hearted fleet, while for spit-roast specialities, several *psistariés* are grouped around Platía Omonías and Platía Pirosvestíou.

If you're stuck the night and feel the urge to escape to a quieter stretch of sea, hop on any #5 blue bus labelled "Tsoukaleíka" and alight at either Monodhéndhri or Vrahneíka, 4km south of the city. There are five tavernas or *psistariés* in a row at Monodhéndhri, plus a few more at Vrahneíka – none are uttlerly superlative, but they have reasonable prices and wonderful outdoor tables looking onto the sunset.

Lastly, if you feel an equally strong need to escape Greek food, Pátra has a rare **Chinese restaurant**, the *Peking*, at Iröon Politéhniou at the corner of Terpsithéas (open daily 12.30–3.30pm & 7pm–1am); it's modestly priced and none too bad.

Buses, trains and hitching

Buses go almost everywhere from Pátra: back to Athens, to most points of the Peloponnese, and into central and western Greece (Lefkádha, Ioánnina, etc) via the ferry at Río-Andírio.

● The main **KTEL** station, midway along the waterside, has buses to Athens, Killíni, Pírgos and other towns in the Peloponnese, as well as to Ioánnina.

Adriatica Brindisi (19hr), via Igoumenítsa and Corfu; daily. Also direct to Brindisi (17hr); 3–7 days weekly. No exclusive agent in Pátra.

Ventouris Bari (19hr 30min), via Igoumenítsa and Corfu; daily. Also direct to Bari (18hr 30min). *Express Shipping Agencies Co.*, Óthonos Amalías 85; ☎061/222 958.

Karageorgis Ancona (33–35hr), direct; 4 weekly. *Petropoulos*, Óthonos Amalías 32; ☎061/274 554.

Marlines Ancona (34hr), via Igoumenítsa; 2 weekly. Coming back from Italy a *Marlines* boat leaves Pátra every Sunday noon for Iráklion (Crete), Rhodes and Limassol (Cyprus) – enquire about possibility of domestic stopovers. *Marlines*, Óthonos Amalías 56; ☎061/ 226 666.

Strintzis Ancona (31hr) via Igoumenítsa and Corfu; Mon, Wed, Thurs, Sat. *Tsimaras*, Óthonos Amalías 14; ☎061/277 783.

ANEK Ancona (34hr) via Igoumenítsa and Corfu; Mon, Tues, Thurs, Fri. Continues to Trieste (58hr total) on Thurs.

Minoan Lines Ancona (34hr), via Igoumenítsa and Corfu; 5 weekly. No exclusive agent in Pátra.

European Seaways Brindisi (18hr 30min) via Igoumenítsa and Corfu; daily. *Tsimaras* (see under *Strintzis*).

Poseidon Lines Bari (19hr 30min), via Igoumenítsa and Corfu; daily. No exclusive agent in Pátra.

Mediterranean Line Brindisi (16hr) direct; daily. May stop in Igoumenítsa at peak season, adding 2.5 hours to journey time. *Yannatos*, Óthonos Amalías 47; ☎061/278 022.

Note: Most companies designate a **high season** of early July to mid-September. Frequency of **departures** detailed are for the high season period.

● For Lefkádha (change at Agrínio) and Messolóngi you need the **KTEL Étolo-Akarnanía** on Faviérou, near the domed church above the Ionian island domestic ferry terminal.

● You can pick up the Athens–Zákinthos bus on Óthonos Amalías, just north of the railway station – an alternative to the regular Killíni port departure.

● Heading to **Delphi**, take local bus #6 (from Kandakári, five blocks back from the water-side) to the **Río-Andírio ferry**, cross over and take a local bus to Náfpaktos and then a regular bus on from there.

Moving on by **train** from Pátra, keep in mind the detour along the narrow-gauge line to Kalávrita (see the following section).

Hitching out of the city, for Athens take the Río bus (#6) and walk up to the toll point by the National Road; for central and western Greece, take the ferry across to Andírio and try your luck there; for Pírgos, walk out for 100m or so past the massive modern church of Ayíou Andhréou.

Listings

American Express are handled by *Albatros Trave*l, Óthonos Amalías 48 (☎061/220 993).

Books and newspapers The *Romios Librairie*, on Kapsáli street, behind the main *KTEL* bus station, has a selection of English-language books. English-language papers are available from kiosks on the waterfront.

Car rental *Just*, Óthonos Amalías 37 (☎061/275 495) is good value.

Consulates There are several European consulates in Pátra. These include **Britain** at Vótsi 2, off Othónos Amalías (☎061/276 403).

Poste restante Contact the main post office on the corner of Mesonós and Zaïmi.

The north coast and the Kalávrita railway

From Pátra you can reach Kórinthos in two hours by bus along the **National Highway**, or half an hour longer on the **train** line; Athens itself is only another hour and a half beyond (two-and-a-half by rail). To go this way without taking the time to detour along the **Kalávrita railway from Dhiakoftó**, however, would be to miss one of the best treats the Peloponnese has to offer – and certainly the finest train journey in Greece. Even if you have a car, this railway should still be part of your plans.

Along the coast road: ferries and beaches

The resorts and villages lining the Gulf of Kórinthos are nothing very special, though none too developed either. At most of them you find little more than a campsite and a couple of seasonal tavernas. At **Río** and **Éyio**, you can cross the gulf by ferry. Beyond Dhiakoftó, if you're unhurried, it's worth taking the old **coast road** along the Gulf of Kórinthos; this runs below the new highway, often right by the sea.

Río and Éyio

RÍO, connected by local bus #6 to Pátra, signals the beginning of swimmable water, though most travellers stop here only to make use of the **ferry across the gulf to Andírio**. This runs every fifteen minutes through the day and early evening (hourly or half-hourly thereafter), shuttling cars (800dr) and passengers (80dr) across to the central mainland. It is a long-established crossing, testimony to which are a pair of diminutive Turkish forts on either side of the gulf.

As detailed in the Pátra section, there are onward connections at Andírio for Delphi (via Náfpaktos) and to Messolóngi and Lefkádha to the west. If you are crossing into the Peloponnese from Andírio, you might be tempted to stop by the sea here, rather than at Pátra. There are a couple of **hotels**, the *Georgios* (☎061/992 627; ③) and *Rion Beach* (☎061/992 4212; ③), and three **campsites** on the nearby beach.

Moving east, there are good beaches, and further campsites, around **ÉYIO**. The best sands are at the village of RHODHODHÁFNI, 2km northwest of Éyio; the *Corali Beach* (☎0691/71 558) campsite here is right on the beach. At Éyio itself a **ferry** (cars and passengers) traverses the gulf three times daily (7.30am, 1.30pm & 5pm; passengers 350dr, cars 1700dr) to ÁYIOS NIKÓLAOS, well-poised for Delphi.

Dhiakoftó and beyond

It is at **DHIAKOFTÓ** that the rack-and-pinion railway heads south into the Vouraíkos gorge for Kalávrita (see below). If you arrive late in the day, it's worth spending the night here so as to do the journey in daylight, and the town can in any case be an attractive alternative to staying overnight in Pátra. There are four **hotels**: the *Lemonies* (☎0691/41 229; ②), *Helmos* (☎0691/41 236; ②), *Panorama* (☎0691/41 614; ②) and more upmarket *Chris-Paul* (☎0691/41 715; ④), plus, on the beach, ten minutes' walk across the railway tracks, a bamboo-hut complex called *Camp Engali* (①). For meals, cross the tracks to reach a small harbour with a couple of tavernas.

Beyond Dhiakoftó there are minor resorts at Akráta and Xilókastro. **AKRÁTA**, a small town with a beach hamlet a kilometre distant, is a little crowded with four **campsites** set along a rather drab, exposed stretch of beach. **DHERVÉNI**, another 8km east, is more attractive, though you'll need to camp as there's no official accommodation. **XILÓKASTRO**, a popular weekend escape from Kórinthos, has both good beaches and accommodation, and a pleasant setting below Mount Zíria. Cheapest of its ten **hotels** are the *Hermes*, Ioánou 81 (☎0743/22 250; ③), and *Kyani Akti*, Tsaldhári 68 (☎0743/22 225; ③).

The Kalávrita rack-and-pinion railway

Even if you have no interest in trains, the **rack-and-pinion railway from Dhiakoftó to Kalávrita** is a must. It's a crazy feat of engineering, rising at gradients of up to one in seven as it cuts through the course of the **Vouraïkós gorge**. En route is a toy-train fantasy of tunnels, bridges and precipitous overhangs; midway is the riverside hamlet of **Zahloroú**, a wonderful place to stay the night, with the historic monastery of **Méga Spílio** set in the cliffside above.

The railway was built by an Italian company between 1885 and 1895 to bring minerals from the mountains to the sea. Its steam locomotives were replaced some years ago – one remains by the line at Dhiakoftó – but the line itself retains all the charm of its period. The tunnels, for example, have delicately carved windows, and the narrow bridges zigzagging across the Vouraïkós seem engineered for sheer virtuosity.

It takes about an hour to get from Dhiakoftó to Zahloroú (confusingly listed on timetables as Méga Spílio), and about another half-hour from there to Kalávrita. The best part of the trip is **the stretch to Zahloroú**, along which the gorge narrows to a few feet at points, only to open out into brilliant, open shafts of light beside the Vouraïkós, clear and fast-running even in midsummer. To make the most of it, you could walk back in around three hours – timing your hike to avoid trains in the tunnels. In peak season the ride is very popular, so you'll probably need to buy tickets some hours before your preferred departure (including the return journey).

Zahloroú and Méga Spílio

ZAHLOROÚ is as perfect a railway stop as could be imagined: a tiny hamlet echoing with the sound of the Vouraïkós river, which splits it into two neighbourhoods. It's a lovely, peaceful place with a gorgeous old wooden hotel, the very friendly and very reasonably priced *Romantzo* (☎0692/22 758; ③). The adjacent *Restaurant Messinia* also lets out some rooms in the summer.

The **Monastery of Méga Spílio** (Great Cave) is a 45-minute walk from the village, up a rough donkey track along the cliff, which joins along the final stretch an access drive often chock-a-block with tour coaches. This is reputedly the oldest monastery in Greece but it has burnt down and been rebuilt so many times that you'd hardly guess it. The last major fire took place in the 1930s after a keg of gunpowder left behind from the War of Independence exploded. Visits are allowed to both women and men, though dress conduct is strict: skirts for women and long sleeves and trousers for men. Men are allowed to stay overnight, though the monks like visitors to arrive before 8pm, serving up a rough repast before closing the gates.

The view of the gorge from the monastery is for many the principal attraction. However, the cloister was once among the richest in the Greek world, owning properties throughout the Peloponnese, in Macedonia, Constantinople and Asia Minor. In consequence, its treasury, arranged as a small museum, is outstanding, including among its icons a curiously moving charred black image of the Virgin, one of three paintings in Greece said to be by the hand of St Luke. It was the reason for the monastery's foundation, having been discovered, after a vision, by saints Theodhoros and Simeon, and the shepherdess Euphrosyne, in the large cave behind the church.

Kalávrita and around

From Méga Spílio a huge new road has been hacked down to **KALÁVRITA**. The train line is more in harmony with the surroundings, though coming from Zahloroú the drama of the route is diminished as the gorge opens out. Kalávrita itself is beautifully positioned, with Mount Helmós as a backdrop, though it wears a sad edge. During the last war the Germans carried out one of their most brutal reprisal massacres, killing the entire male population – 1436 men and boys – and leaving the town in flames. Rebuilt, it is both depressing and poignant. The first and last sight is a mural, opposite the station, that reads: "Kalavrita, founder member of the Union of Martyred Towns, appeals to all to fight for world peace". The clocktower on the church stands for ever at 2.34 – the hour of the massacre. Out in the countryside behind the town is a shrine to those massacred, its way gratified with the single word "Peace" (*Ischía*).

The Nazis also burnt the **monastery of Ayía Lávra**, 6km out of Kalávrita and – as the site where Yermanos, Archbishop of Pátra, raised the flag to signal the War of Independence – one of the great Greek national shrines. It too has been rebuilt, along with a small historical museum.

Staying at Kalávrita has a sense of pilgrimage about it for Greeks, though probably not for the casual visitor. If you miss the last train back to Zahloroú (currently at 5.25pm) there are a few **hotels**, among them the *Megas Alexandhros* (☎0692/22 221; ③) and the *Paradissos* (☎0692/22 303; ③). **Buses** also run from Kalávrita to Pátra four times daily, or more interestingly once daily to the recently opened "**Cave of the Lakes**" a half hour's drive southeast.

The "**Cave of the Lakes**" is on the same bus line as the villages of Káto Loussí, Kastriá and Planitéro, and is 2km north of Kastriá. Mineral-saturated water trickling through a two-kilometre cavern system has precipitated natural dams trapping a series of small underground lakes. Only the first 300 metres or so are as yet open to the public but the chambers are still well worth the trip.

Mount Helmós

At 2341m, **Mount Helmós** is the highest peak of the most imposing range of the northern Peloponnese, and only sixty metres short of the summit of Taíyettos to the south. Its highest peaks rear up a dozen or so kilometres to the southeast of Kalávrita. However, the walk from Kalávrita is not an interesting approach, the trail having vanished under an asphalt road and the new ski centre approached by it. To get the most from hiking on the mountain you need to climb up from the village of SÓLOS, on the west side – a five-hour-plus walk which takes you to the **Mavronéri waterfall**, source of the legendary river Styx that the souls of the dead had to cross in order to enter Hades.

The hike from Sólos

To reach the path opening at Sólos, start at AKRÁTA on the Pátra–Kórinthos road. From here it's a slow but beautiful haul up a winding dirt road. Buses run only three times a week, but hitching isn't too difficult in high summer.

SÓLOS is a tiny place, a cluster of stone cottages on a steep hillside just below the fir trees, inhabited only in summer. Facing it across the valley is the larger but more scattered village of PERISTÉRA, past which runs the easiest of the routes to Mavronéri.

Follow the **track through Sólos**, past the inn (all of ten beds), and the *magazí* (café-shop), where you can get a simple meal. Past the last houses the track curves around the head of a gully. On the right, going down its wooded flank, is a good path which leads to a bridge over the river in the bottom. Just beyond (15min; this and all subsequent times are from Sólos), you reach another track. There is a chapel on the left, and, on the wall of a house on the right, a sign saying "Pros Gounariánika"that points up a path to the left. Follow it past a church on a prominent knoll and on to the jeep track again, where, at 75 minutes out, you turn left to the half-ruined hamlet of GOUNARIÁNIKA. From there continue steadily upward along the west (right) flank of the valley through abandoned fields until you come to a stream-gully running down off the ridge above you on your right. On the far side of the stream the fir forest begins. It's an ideal **camping place** (2hr 30min; 1hr 30min going back down).

Once into **the woods** the path is very clear. After about an hour (3hr 30min) you descend to a boulder-strewn **stream bed** with a rocky ravine to the right leading up to the foot of a huge bare crag, the east side of the Neraïdhórahi peak visible from Kalávrita. Cross the stream and continue leftward up the opposite bank. In June there are the most incredible wild flowers, including at least half a dozen different orchids, all the way up from here.

After fifteen-minutes' climb above the bank you come out on top of a grassy knoll (3hr 30min), then dip back into the trees again. At the four-hour mark, you turn a corner into the mouth of the **Styx ravine**. Another five minutes' walk brings you to a deep gully where enormous banks of snow lie late into the spring. A few paces across a dividing rib of rock there is a second gully, where the path has been eroded and you have to cross some slippery scree.

Here you come to a wooded spur running down from the crag on the right. The trail winds up to a shoulder (4hr 20min), descends into another gully, and then winds up to a second shoulder of level rocky ground by some large black pines (4hr 30min), known as *To Dhiásselo tou Kinigoú* (the Hunter's Saddle). From there you can look into the Styx ravine. Continue down the path towards the right until it dwindles at the foot of a vast crag (4hr 45min). You can now see the **Mavronéri waterfall**, a 200-metre-long, wavering plume of water pouring off the red cliffs up ahead.

To get to it, angle across the scree bank without losing altitude – for the track is obliterated soon after the saddle – until you reach the base of the falls (5hr). There's a small cave under the fall, where a rare columbine grows. It is possible to continue up the valley, past some turf next to a seasonal pond where people camp, but the summit area proper is a bit of a let-down after the majesty of the Styx valley. Fairly clear and easy trails lead down from the south side of the watershed to the villages of Káto Loussí or Planitéro; the appropriate *Korfes* or *YIS* maps have more details on these routes .

travel details

Buses

Buses detailed have similar frequency in each direction, so entries are given just once; for reference check under both starting-point and destination.

Connections with Athens Kórinthos (hourly; 1hr); Mikínes (Mycenae)/Árgos/Tíryns/Náfplio (hourly to 9.30pm; 2hr/2hr 15min/2hr 45min/3hr); Spárti (7 daily; 6 hr); Olympia (3 daily; 6 hr);

From Kórinthos Mycenae/Árgos/Tíryns/Náfplio (hourly; 30min/1hr/1hr 15min/1hr 30min); Loutráki (half-hourly; 20min); Neméa (5 daily; 45 min); Trípoli (9 daily; 1hr 30min); Spárti (8 daily; 4hr); Kalamáta (7 daily; 4 hr).

From Árgos Náfplio (half hourly; 30min); Mikínes (Mycenae; 6 daily; 30min); Neméa (3 daily; 1hr); Ástros/Leonídhi (3 daily; 1 hr/3 hr); Trípoli (9 daily; 1hr 20min); Spárti (8 daily; 3hr); Andhrítsena (daily at 10am; 3 hr); Olympia (3 daily on weekdays; 4hr 30min).

From Náfplio Epidaurus (5 daily; 45min); Tólo (half-hourly; 25min); Trípoli (6 daily; 50min).

From Trípoli Megalópoli (8 daily; 40min); Spárti (2 daily; 1hr 20min); Olympia (3 daily, in stages; 5 hr); Pátra (via Lámbia; 2 daily; 4hr); Pírgos (3 daily; 3 hr); Andhrítsena (2 daily; 1hr 30min); Dhimitsána (2 daily; 1hr 30min); Kalamáta (6 daily; 2 hr); Pílos (3 daily; 3hr); Kiparissía (2 daily; 2hr); Megalópoli (8 daily; 35min).

From Spárti Místras (12 daily, 6 on Sunday; 15 min); Monemvassía (2 or 3 daily; 3 hr); Kalamáta (2 daily; 2hr 30min); Yíthio (6 daily; 1hr); Neápoli (3 daily; 4hr).

From Yíthio Areópoli (4 daily; 50min); Láyia (1 daily; 1hr); Monemvassía (2 daily; 2hr 30min).

From Areópoli Yerolimín (daily in season only; 1 hr); Kalamáta (4 daily changing at Ítilo; 2hr 30min) Láyia (1 daily; 1hr).

From Kalamáta Koróni (7 daily; 1hr 30min); Ítilo/ Areópoli (4 daily; 1hr 30min); Pátra (2 daily; 4hr); Pílos (8 daily; 1 hr 20 min); Megalópoli/Trípoli (10 daily; 1 hr/1hr 45min).

From Pílos Methóni (5 daily; 15min); Kalamáta (9 daily; 1hr 20min); Kiparissía (6 daily, but none between 3 and 7pm; 2hr).

From Megalópoli Andhrítsena/Pírgos (2 daily; 3hr/4hr); Trípoli (8 daily; 40min).

From Pírgos Olympia (hourly, but none between 12.30 & 3.30pm; 45min); Andhrítsena (2 daily; 2hr); Pátra (10 daily; 2hr); Kiparissía/Kalamáta 2 daily; 1hr/2hr).

From Pátra Kalávrita (4 daily; 2hr 30min); Zákinthos (3 daily; 2hr 30min including ferry from Killíni); Ioánnina (2 daily; 5hr); Kalamáta (2 daily; 4hr); Vólos (daily; 6hr).

Trains

There are two main Peloponnesian lines:

Athens–Kórinthos–Dhiakoftó–Pátra–Pírgos– Kiparissía–Kalamáta 3 trains daily make the full run in each direction. Another 5 daily run between Athens and Pátra, 2 continuing to Pírgos, the other as far as Kiparissía. Another 2 trains daily cover the route between Pátra and Kiparissía.

Approximate journey times are:

Athens–Kórinthos (2hr)
Kórinthos–Dhiakoftó (1–1· hr)
Dhiakoftó–Pátra (1hr)
Pátra–Pírgos (2 hr 15min)
Pírgos–Kiparissía (1hr–1hr 20min)
Kiparissía–Kalamáta (1hr 40min).

Athens–Kórinthos–Mikínes (Mycenae)– Árgos–Trípoli–Kalamáta 5 trains daily cover the full route, in each direction.

Approximate journey times are:

Athens–Kórinthos (2hr)
Kórinthos–Mikínes (50min)
Mikínes–Árgos (10min)
Árgos–Trípoli (1hr 30min)
Trípoli–Kalamáta (2hr 40min).

In addition, there are the following branch lines:

Pírgos–Olympia 5 daily (40min).

Pírgos–Katákolo Daily at 1.54pm (25min).

Kavássila–Killíni Suspended at time of writing.

Dhiakoftó–Zahloroú–Kalávrita 4 daily; Diakoftó–Zakhloroú (50min); Zahlaroú–Kalávrita (20min).

Lefktró–Megalópoli Service replaced by *OSE* coaches, connecting with services to Lefktró (between Árgos and Kalamáta).

Ferries

Pireás–Monemvassía–Neápoli–Kíthira– Yíthio–Kíthira–Andíkithira–Kastelli (Crete)

Every Monday and Friday at 9am the *Ionion* leaves Pireás, stopping at Monemvassía (8hr), Neápoli (10hr) and Ayía Pelayía (Kíthira; 12hr), then looping back to the mainland at Yíthio (14hr) before finally heading south for Kapsáli (Kíthira), Andíkithira and Kastélli (Crete; 6hr from Yíthio). The Monday boat normally stops at Kiparíssi and Yérakas en route to Monemvassía, as well as at Elafónissos. The boat **returns from Kastélli** on Tuesdays and Saturdays, calling at Neápoli and/ or Monemvassía on its way back to Pireás. Departure times (and ports of call) can, however, fluctuate. For current, reliable information, it's worth contacting the helpful *Rozakis* agency in Yíthio (☎0733/22 229).

From Killíni Zákinthos (3–7 daily; 2hr); Kefalloniá (1-3 daily; 1· hr).

From Pátra Igoumenítsa and Corfu (2 or 3 daily; 7–9hr/9–11hr); Kefalloniá and Itháki (most days; 4–5hr); Paxí (2 or 3 weekly; 6hr); Iráklion (Crete) and Rhodes (weekly on stop-over basis only; 18hr/ 28hr); also to Brindisi, Ancona, Bari, Trieste (Italy), Limassol (Cyprus); unreliably to Split, Croatia; and Kuşadasi (Turkey) as politics, war and shipowner whim permit. See under "Pátra'"for details.

Across the Gulf of Kórinthos Andírio-Río (every 15 min, much less often between 11pm and dawn; 20min); Éyio-Áyios Nikólaos (3 to 5 times daily; 35min).

From Galatás to Póros (every 15min from dawn till past midnight; 5min).

Hydrofoils

'Flying Dolphin' hydrofoils run between the following ports:

Leonídhi/Kiparíssi/Monemvassía to Spétses, Póros and Pireás.

Neápoli/Kíthira to Pireás.

Méthana to Éyina and Póros.

Ermióni to Ídhra (Hydra) and Spétses.

Náfplio (midsummer only) to Monemvassía, Toló, Spétses, Póros and Pireás.

For details and frequencies of services, which vary drastically with season, contact local agents or the Ceres Hydrofoils' main office in Pireás (Themistokléous 8; ☎01/45 27 107).

Summer-only Excursion Boats

From Katákolo Zákinthos (3 times a week; 2hr 30min). **From Portohéli** Water-taxis to Spétses according to demand (20min).

Flights

To/from Athens Kalamáta (2 daily; 50min); Kíthira (daily; 50min).

CHAPTER THREE

THESSALY AND CENTRAL GREECE

U nlike the Peloponnese, Central Greece is a region of scattered highlights – above all the site of the ancient oracle at **Delphi**, and, further, to the north, the unworldly rock-monasteries of the **Metéora**. The area as a whole, dominated by the vast agricultural plain of Thessaly, is less exciting, with rather drab market and industrial towns. For scenic drama – and most of the historic sights – you have to head for the corners.

The southern part of this region, before you enter Thessaly proper, is known as the **Stereá Elládhos** – literally "Greek Continent", a name that reflects its nineteenth-century past as the only Greek mainland territory, along with Attica and the quasi-island of the Peloponnese. It corresponds to the ancient divisions of Boetia and Phocis, the domains respectively of Thebes and Delphi. Most visitors head straight through these territories to Delphi but, if you have time, there are rewarding if minor detours in the monastery of **Óssios Loukás** – with the finest Byzantine frescoes in the country – and **Gla**, the largest and most obscure of the Mycenaean sites. For hikers there is also the opportunity of climbing **Mount Parnassós**, the Muses' mountain.

The central plains of **Thessaly** (*Thessalía*), beyond, formed the bed of an ancient inland sea – rich agricultural land that was ceded reluctantly to the modern nation by the Turks in 1878. The province's attractions lie on the periphery, chained in by the mountain ranges of Ólimbos (Olympus), Píndhos (Pindus), Óssa and Pílion (Pelion). Picking a route is a hard choice. To the east, extending from the major city and port of Vólos, is the slender peninsula of **Mount Pílion**, whose luxuriant woods and beaches are easily combined with island-hopping to the Sporades. To the west, **Kalambáka** gives access to the Metéora (not to be missed) and across the dramatic **Katara Pass** over the Píndhos to Epirus. North, the horizon is increasingly filled with the silhouette of **Mount Olympus** (covered in Chapter Five), the home of the gods.

Looming across a narrow gulf from the Stereá Elládhos, and joined by a bridge at Halkídha, is the **island of Évvia** (Euboea). Though this feels like an extension of the mainland (from where there are three ferry crossings), it is nonetheless a bona fide island and we have detailed its attractions along with the Sporades in Chapter Eleven.

STEREÁ ELLÁDHOS: THE ROADS TO DELPHI AND BEYOND

The inevitable focus of a visit to the Stereá Elládhos is **Delphi**, 150km northwest of Athens. Buses cover the route from the capital several times a day, or can be picked up at Livádhia, the nearest rail terminus. However, if you're in no hurry, there are rewards in slowing your progress: taking the "old road" to Thíva (Thebes), or detouring **from Livádhia** to the Byzantine monastery of Óssios Loukás, or to Mycenaean **Glá**.

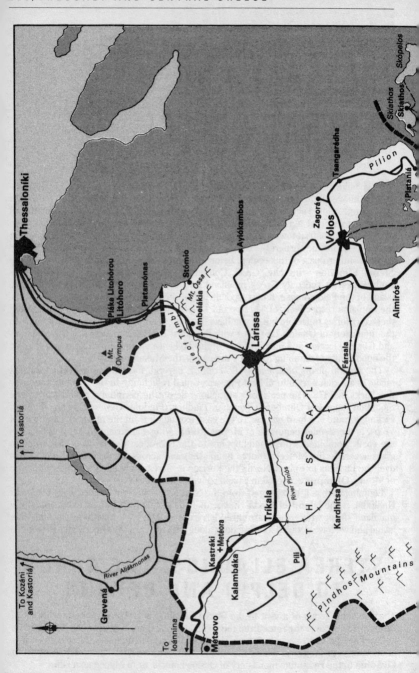

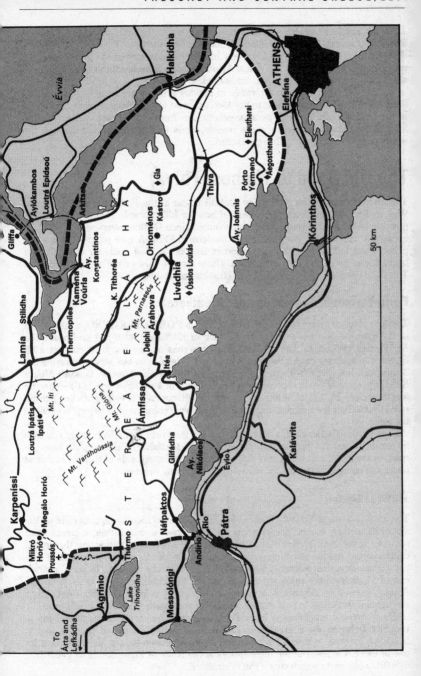

To the northeast of the Athens–Delphi road, traffic thunders along the **National Road #1** towards Lárissa and Thessaloníki, skirting the coast for much of the way, with the long island of Évvia only a few hundred metres across the gulf. Along this route there are ferries over to Évvia at **Arkítsa**, **Áyios Konstandínos** (where you can also pick up ferries or hydrofoils to the Sporades) and **Glífa**.

Moving **on from Delphi**, the range of options grows more complex. Two routes head north into Thessaly – west to the Metéora, east to the Pílion; another, southwest to the Gulf of Corinth, offers an approach to – or from – **the Peloponnese**, via the ferry at Andírio–Río; a fourth, more remote, leads to **Karpeníssi** and through the southern foothills of the Píndhos mountains.

The Old Road to Thebes (Thíva)

The **ancient road from Athens to Delphi** began at the Parthenon as the **Sacred Way to Eleusis**, and from there climbed into the hills towards Thebes (Thíva). It is possible to follow this route, almost unchanged since Oedipus supposedly trod it, by taking the minor road into the hills at modern ELEFSÍNA (see p.129). Leaving the polluted and industrial port, things improve fast, as the road winds up and out into a landscape of pines and grey stony hills. There are two buses daily along this road to Thíva and connections from there on to Livádhia and Delphi.

Pórto Yermenó, Aegosthena and Eleutherai

The first place to tempt you off the Sacred Way is **PÓRTO YERMENÓ**, a little resort at the extreme northeast corner of the Gulf of Kórinthos, with just one **hotel**, the *Egosthenion* (☎0263/41 226; ③), and a few tavernas on the beach. It can get a bit crowded in summer but for those with transport – there is no bus service covering the 23km from the Elefsína–Thíva road – makes a fine detour. Nearby, beneath Mount Kithairon, sprawls the best-preserved circuit of ancient walls anywhere in Greece – the fourth-century BC Classical fort of **Aigosthena**. Historically it is insignificant but the ruins themselves are tremendous, some of the towers rising as high as forty feet above the walls.

Back on the Thebes road, a kilometre on from the Pórto Yermenó turning, you pass by another Classical fortress, fourth-century BC **Eleutherai**. This is visible from the road, to the right, and it is again well preserved. The north side of the fort is almost intact and eight of its circuit of towers survive to varying degrees.

Thíva (Thebes)

The modern town of **THÍVA** (Thebes) lies 20km on from Eleutherai, built right on the site of its mighty, ancient predecessor. For this very reason, however, it boasts scant remains of the past: archaeologists have had little success in excavating the crucial central areas, and the most interesting visit is to the excellent town **museum** (Tues–Sat 8.30am–3pm, Sun 9.30am–2.30pm; 400dr). This is to be found at the far (downhill) end of Pindharoú, the main street; look out for the Frankish tower in its forecourt. Among many fine exhibits is a unique collection of painted *larnakes* (Mycenaean sarcophagi) depicting, in bold expressionistic strokes, women lamenting their dead.

There are no direct **buses** from Thíva to Delphi but services run frequently to Livádhia (whence there are better connections) and a couple of times a day to Halkídha, gateway to Évvia. You're unlikely to have reason to stay, unless waiting for one of these. Cheapest of the three **hotels** is the *Niobe* at Epaminónda 63 (☎0262/27 949; ③), a pleasant enough stop if you're stranded.

Livádhia and around

LIVÁDHIA is a pleasant and prosperous town on the banks of the Herkína, a river of ancient fame which emerges from a dark gorge at the base of a fortress. It is an attractive and curious place to stop, with a unique duo of ancient and medieval sights.

The ancient curiosity is the site of the **Oracle of Trophonios**, a ten-minute walk from the main square, beside an old Turkish bridge. Here the waters of the Herkína rise from a series of springs, now channelled beside a (signposted) *Xenia* restaurant. Above the springs, cut into the rock, are niches for votive offerings – in one of which, a large chamber with a bench, the Turkish governor would sit for a quiet smoke. In antiquity they marked the Springs of Memory and Forgetfulness, where all who sought to consult the Oracle of Trophonios had first to bathe. The oracle, a circular structure which gave entrance to caves deep in the gorge, has been tentatively identified at the top of the hill, near the remains of an unfinished Temple of Zeus. It was visited by the Roman guidebook writer Pausanias, who wrote that it left him "possessed with terror and hardly knowing himself or anything around him".

The **Froúrio**, or castle, again a short walk from the centre (along Odhós Froúrio), provides the medieval interest. In itself it is impressive: a well-bastioned square structure, built in the fourteenth century and a key early conquest in the War of Independence. But it's the history that's most interesting. The castle was the stronghold of a small group of Catalan mercenaries, the Grand Company, who took control of central Greece in 1311 and, appointing a Sicilian prince as their ruler, held it for sixty years. They were a tiny, brutal band who had arrived in Greece from Spain in the wake of the Fourth Crusade. They wrested control from the Franks, who were then established in Athens and Thebes, in a cunning deviation from traditional rules of engagement. As the Frankish nobility approached Livádhia, the vastly outnumbered Catalans diverted the river to flood the surrounding fields. The Frankish cavalry advanced into the unexpected marsh and were cut down to a man.

Practicalities

The town is today a minor, provincial capital with a trade in milling cotton from the area. It is completely off the tourist route and so an enjoyable pause before, or after, Delphi, though in season buses on towards Delphi often arrive and leave full. Arriving by **bus**, you'll be dropped near the central square, **Platía Dhiákou**; the **train station** is 3km out but arrivals may be met by a shuttle bus (or more likely taxis) into town.

Staying, you should have no problem finding a room. There are a couple of modest **hotels**: the very pleasant *Helikon* (☎0261/23 911; ④) on Platía Yioryíou Alpha, and the slightly run-down *Erkyna* (☎0261/28 227) at Láppa 6, overlooking the river. Round the corner from the latter, excellent **meals** are to be had at the *Taverna Tambahna*.

Orhómenos

Just 10km east of Livádhia (10min by hourly local bus) is the site of Ancient **ORHOMENOS**, inhabited from Neolithic to Classical times and, as the capital of the Minyans, a native Thessalian dynasty, one of the wealthiest Mycenaean cities.

Near the middle of the rather drab modern village is the **Treasury of Minyas** (Tues–Sat 9am–3pm, Sun 10am–2pm), a stone *tholos* similar to the tomb of Atreus at Mycenae. Its roof has collapsed but it is otherwise complete and its inner chamber, hewn from the rock, has an intricately carved marble ceiling. Beside it are the remains of a fourth-century BC theatre, and behind, on the rocky hilltop, a tiny fortified acropolis from the same period.

Across the road is the ninth-century Byzantine **Church of the Dormition**, built entirely of blocks from the theatre and column drums from a Classical temple – as is the minute Byzantine church in the main village square.

The Citadel of Gla

Continuing east, in a highly worthwhile diversion, it's a further twenty minutes by bus (5 daily, but they stop early) to the village of KÁSTRO, right next to the National Road to Lárissa. If you walk through the village, cross the highway and then walk for about a hundred metres south along it (towards Athens) you come to an unsignposted road behind a Shell garage and tyre store. This leads in around two hundred metres to the Mycenaean Citadel of Gla.

An enormous and extraordinary site, **GLA** (unrestricted entrance) stands within a three-kilometre circuit of Cyclopean walls – a far larger citadel than either Tiryns or Mycenae. Almost nothing, however, is known about the site, save that it was once an island in Lake Copais (which was drained in the last century) and that it may have been an outpost of the Minyans. The **walls** and **city gates** still stand to five metres in places, and are almost three kilometres in length, despite being damaged when the city fell. Inside, on the higher ground, what is thought to have been a huge Mycenaean **palace** has been revealed; it appears to include a *megaron* (throne room) and various storerooms, though archaeologists are puzzled by differences from the standard Mycenean palace form. Further down, and currently being excavated, is a vast walled area believed to have been the **marketplace**.

Almost anywhere you walk in this rarely visited site, however, you come across evocative traces of its former buildings. One **word of warning** about the site: there are said to be snakes among the ruins, so tread with care.

Chaironeia

Directly north of Livádhia, on the main road to Lamía, is the site of one of the most famous battles of ancient Greece. This is **Chaironeia**, where in 338 BC Philip of Macedon won a resounding victory over an alliance of Athenians, Thebans and Peloponnesians put together by Demosthenes. The defeat was in essence the death of the old city-states, from whom control passed forever into foreign hands: first Macedonian, later Roman.

Set beside the road, at modern HERÓNIA, is a remarkable six-metre-high **stone lion**, originally part of the funerary monument to the Thebans (or, some say, to the Macedonians) killed in the battle. Adjacent is a small museum of local finds, and there are remains of **acropolis** fortifications, with a theatre at its base, above the village. Herónia was a minor ancient town and home of the writer Plutarch.

The site of the battle lies 3km to the east, towards the village of AKONDÍO, where a Macedonian burial mound is still to be seen near the river.

The Oedipus crossroads and Óssios Loukás

West from Livádhia, the scenery becomes ever more dramatic as Mount Parnassós and its attendant peaks loom high above the road. At 24km, about halfway to Delphi, you reach the so-called **"Schist Crossroads"**, junction of the ancient roads from Thebes, Delphi, Daulis and Ambrossos. (The crossroads is today signposted to Dávlia, the modern successor of Daulis; the old road in fact lay below the new one, in the gorge.)

It is this spot that Pausanias identified as the site of **Oedipus's murder of his father**, King Laertes of Thebes, and his two attendants. According to the myth, Oedipus was returning on foot from Delphi while Laertes was speeding in the opposite direction on a chariot. Neither would give way, and in the altercation that followed Oedipus killed the trio, ignorant of who they were. It was, as Pausanias put it mildly, "the beginning of his troubles". Continuing to Thebes, Oedipus solved the riddle of the Sphinx, which had been ravaging the area, and was given the hand of widowed Queen Jocasta, his mother.

Getting to Óssios Loukás: Dhístomo

If you have transport, you can turn left at the crossroads and follow a minor road to Dhístomo, and thence to the **Monastery of Óssios Loukás**. Travelling by bus, you need to take a more roundabout route: first from Livádhia to Dhístomo, then another bus on from there towards Kiriakí – getting dropped at the fork to Óssios Loukás (leaving just a 2.5km walk).

Alternatively, it's possible to charter a taxi in **DHÍSTOMO**, which also has a couple of hotels, the *America* (✆0267/22 079; ③) and *Koutriaris* (✆0267/22 268; ③) if you get stuck overnight. It is a drab place, though, with a tragic wartime history: the Germans shot the entire adult population in 1944, in reprisal for a guerilla attack.

Óssios Loukás Monastery

Open daily summer 8am–2pm & 4–7pm; winter 8am–5pm; 400dr.

The **Monastery of Óssios Loukás** was a precursor of that last defiant flourish of Byzantine art that produced the great churches at Mystra in the Peloponnese. It is modest in scale, but from an architectural or decorative point of view, ranks as one of the great buildings of medieval Greece. The setting, too, is exquisite – as beautiful as it is remote. Hidden by trees along the approach from Dhístomo, the monastery's shady terrace suddenly appears, and opens out on to a spacious sweep of the Elikónas peaks and countryside.

The main structure comprises two domed churches, the larger **Katholikón** of Óssios Loukás and the attendant chapel of the **Theotókos**. They are joined by a common foundation wall but otherwise share few architectural features. Ten monks still live in the monastic buildings around the courtyard, but the monastery is essentially maintained as a museum, with a café-restaurant in the grounds. Skirts or long trousers (no shorts) must be worn.

The Katholikón

The **Katholikón**, built in the early eleventh century, is dedicated to a local beatified hermit, Saint Luke of Stiri (not the Evangelist). Its design formed the basis of Byzantine octagonal-style churches, and was later copied at Dhafní and at Mystra. Externally it is modest, with rough brick and stone walls surmounted by a well-proportioned dome. The inside, however, is startling. A conventional cross-in-square plan, its atmosphere switches from austere to exultant as the eye moves along walls lined in red and green marble to the gold-backed mosaics on the high ceiling. Light filtering through marble-encrusted windows reflects across the curved surfaces of the mosaics in the narthex and the nave and bounces on to the marble walls, bringing out the subtlety of their shades.

The original **mosaics** were damaged by an earthquake in 1659, and in the dome and elsewhere have been replaced by unmemorable frescoes. But other surviving examples testify to their effect. The mosaic of *The Washing of the Apostles' Feet* in the narthex is one of the finest; its theme is an especially human one and the expressions of the Apostles, seen varying between diffidence and surprise, do it justice. This dynamic and richly humanised approach is again illustrated by the *Baptism*, high up on one of the curved squinches that support the dome. Here the naked Jesus reaches for the cross amid a swirling mass of water, an illusion of depth created by the angle and curvature of the wall. The church's original **frescoes** are confined to the vaulted chambers at the corners of the cross plan and, though less imposing than the mosaics, are far more sympathetic in colour and shade to their subjects, particularly that of *Christ Walking towards the Baptism*.

The Theotókos and Crypt

The church of the **Theotókos** (literally "God-Bearing", ie the Virgin Mary) is a century older than the *katholikón*. From the outside it overshadows the main church with its elaborate brick decoration culminating in a highly Eastern-influenced, marble-panelled drum. The interior, though, seems gloomy and cramped by comparison, highlighted only by a couple of fine Corinthian capitals and an original floor mosaic.

Finally, do not miss the vivid frescoes in the **crypt** of the *katholikón*, entered on the lower right-hand side of the building. If you have a torch, bring it, since the same darkness that has preserved the colours also hides them.

Aráhova

Arriving at **ARÁHOVA**, the last town east of Delphi, you are properly in Parnassós country. The peaks stand tiered above, sullied somewhat by the wide asphalt road cut to a ski-resort – the winter weekend haunt of BMW-driving Athenians. If you want to ski, it's possible to hire equipment on a daily basis at the resort and even to get an all-in day package from Athens (see p.47). The resort's main problem is high winds, which often lead to the closure of its ski lifts.

Skiing aside, the town is a delight, despite being split in two by the Livádhia–Delphi road. Its houses are predominantly traditional in style, twisting up narrow lanes into the hills and poised to the south on the edge of the olive-choked Pleistos gorge. It is renowned for its strong wines, honey, *flokáti* (sheep-hide) rugs, and woollen weavings; all are much in evidence in the roadside shops, though some of the goods are nowadays imported from Albania and northern Greece. Also of note is the local **Festival of Áyios Yióryios** (23 April, or the Tuesday after Easter if this date falls within Lent), which is centred on the church at the top of the hill. It's one of the best events to catch genuine folk-dancing – and almost 48 hours of continuous partying.

Practicalities

If you're not making for any other mountain areas, Aráhova is well worth an afternoon's pause before continuing to Delphi (just 11km further on), and if you've got your own transport you might consider staying here as a base for visiting the site. At the cheaper end of the scale, there are two pleasant and modest **hotels**, the *Apollon* (☎0267/31 427; ③) and *Parnassos* (☎0267/31 307; ③), plus a very few rooms in private houses. There are also two excellent **tavernas** – *Karathanasi* and *To Elato*.

For details of **hiking on Parnassós** from Aráhova, see p.239.

Delphi (Dhelfí)

With its site raised on the slopes of a high mountain terrace and dwarfed to either side by the great and ominous crags of Parnassós, it's easy to see why the ancients believed **DELPHI** to be the centre of the earth. But more than the natural setting or even the occasional earthquake and avalanche were needed to confirm a divine presence. This, according to Plutarch, was achieved through the discovery of a rock chasm that exuded strange vapours and reduced all comers to frenzied, incoherent and undoubtedly prophetic mutterings.

The Oracle: some history

The first **oracle** established on this spot was dedicated to **Gea** ("Mother Earth") and to **Poseidon** ("the Earth Shaker"). The serpent **Python**, son of Gea, was installed in a nearby cave and communication made through the Pythian priestess. Python was subsequently slain by **Apollo**, whose cult had been imported from Crete (legend has it that he arrived in the form of a dolphin – hence the name *Delphoi*). The Pythian Games were instigated on an eight-year cycle to commemorate the feat, and perhaps also to placate the ancient deities.

The place was known to the **Mycenaeans**, whose votive offerings (tiny striped statues of goddesses and worshipping women) have been discovered near the site of Apollo's temple. Following the arrival of the **Dorians** in Greece at the beginning of the twelfth century BC, the sanctuary became the centre of the loose-knit association of Greek city-states known as the **Amphyctionic League**. The territory still belonged, however, to the city of Krissa, which as the oracle gained in popularity began to extort heavy dues from the pilgrims arriving at the port of Kirrha. In the sixth century BC the league was called on to intervene, and the first of a series of **Sacred Wars** broke out. The league wrested Delphi from the Krissaeans and made it an autonomous state. From then on Delphi experienced a rapid ascent to fame and respect, becoming within a few decades one of the major sanctuaries of Greece, with its oracle tried and tested and generally thought to be the arbiter of truth.

For over a thousand years thereafter, a steady stream of **pilgrims** worked their way up the dangerous mountain paths to seek divine direction in matters of war, worship, love or business. On arriving they would sacrifice a sheep or a goat and, depending on the omens, wait to submit votive questions inscribed on leaden tablets. The Pythian priestess – a simple and devout village woman, of fifty or more years – would chant her prophecies from a tripod positioned over the oracular chasm. More importantly, an attendant priest would then "interpret" her utterings and relay them to the enquirer in hexameter verse.

Many of the **oracular answers** were equivocal: Croesus, for example, was told that if he embarked on war against neighbouring Cyrus he would destroy a mighty empire – he did and destroyed his own. But it's hard to imagine that the oracle would have retained its popularity and influence for so long without offering predominantly sound advice. Indeed, Strabo wrote that "of all oracles in the world it had the reputation of being the most truthful". One explanation is that the Delphic priests were simply better informed than any other corporate body around at the time. As the centre of the Amphyctionic League, which became a kind of "United Nations" of the Greek city states and, as Peter Levi describes it, "a keystone of their disjointed unity", it amassed a wealth of political, economic and social information. And from the seventh century BC on, Delphi had its own network of informants throughout the Greek world.

The **influence** of the oracle spread abroad with the age of Classical colonisation and as its patronage grew so did its spectrum of informants. It reached a peak in the sixth century BC, attracting powerful benefactors such as Amasis, King of Egypt, and (as mentioned above) the unfortunate King Croesus of Lydia; many of the Greek city-states also dedicated treasuries at this time. The Temple of Apollo was elaborately rebuilt in 548 BC, and the **Pythian Games** were reorganised (along the lines of Olympia) to become one of the four great Panhellenic festivals.

Privileged position and enormous wealth, however, made Delphi an obvious prey to Greek rivalries. The first Sacred Wars left it autonomous but in the fifth century BC the oracle began to be too closely identified with individual states. Worse, it maintained a defeatist, almost treacherous attitude towards the Persian invasions – only partially mitigated when a Persian force, sent by Xerxes to raid Delphi, was crushed at the entrance to the Sanctuary by a well-timed earthquake.

It never quite regained the same level of trust (and consequently of power) after these instances of bias and corruption. However, real **decline** did not set in until the fourth century BC with the resumption of the Sacred Wars and the emergence of Macedonian control. Following prolonged squabbling amongst the Greek city-states the Sanctuary was seized by the Phocians in 356 BC, leading to Philip of Macedon's intervention to restore control to the Amphyctionic League. Seven years later, when the league again invited Philip to settle a dispute, this time provoked by the Amphissans, he responded with the invasion of southern Greece. The independence of the city-states was brought to an end at the Battle of Chaironeia (see p.230); Delphi's political intriguing was effectively over.

Under **Macedonian** and later **Roman** control, the oracle's role became increasingly domestic and insignificant, dispensing advice on marriages, loans, voyages and the like. The Romans thought little of its utterances and of its treasure; Sulla plundered the sanctuary in 86 BC and Nero, outraged by the oracle pronouncing judgement on the murder of his mother, carted away some 500 bronze statues. Finally, with the demise of paganism under Constantine and Theodosius in the fourth century AD, the oracle became defunct.

Excavations

In modern times, the sanctuary site was rediscovered towards the end of the seventeenth century and explored, haphazardly, from the 1840s onwards. Real **excavation** of the site came only in 1892 when the French School of Archaeology leased the land – then occupied by a hamlet – in exchange for a French government agreement to buy the Greek currant crop. There was little to be seen other than the outline of a stadium and theatre but the villagers were persuaded (with the help of an army detachment) to move to the site of the modern village 1km west, and digging commenced. Over the next decade most of the excavations and reconstruction visible today were completed.

The most interesting development in Delphi's recent history came through the efforts of the poet Angelos Sikelianos and his wife Eva Palmer to set up a "University of the World" in the 1920s. The project eventually failed, though it inspired an annual **Delphic Festival**, held now in June of each year with performances of Classical drama in the ancient theatre.

The Sites

Split by the road from Aráhova, the ancient site divides essentially into three parts: the **Sacred Precinct**, the **Marmaria** and the **Castalian spring**. In addition there is a worthwhile (though poorly presented) **museum**. All in all it's a large and complex ruin, best taken in two stages, with the sanctuary ideally at the beginning or end of the day, or at lunchtime, to escape the crowds.

Visiting the sites, make sure you have sturdy footwear as there's a lot of clambering up rough stone steps and paths. And if you're planning to make a full day's visit, take food and drink – consumed, most enjoyably, in the amphitheatre with its seats and panorama of the sanctuary.

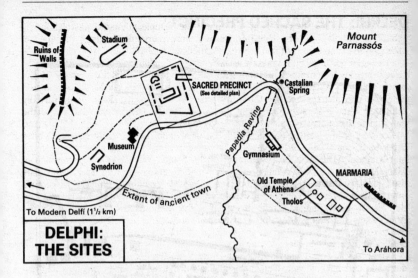

DELPHI: THE SITES

The Sacred Precinct

Open Mon–Fri 7.30am–6.30pm, Sat & Sun 8.30am–3pm; 500dr

The **Sacred Precinct**, or Temenos (Sanctuary) of Apollo, is entered, as in ancient times, by way of a small **Agora**, enclosed by ruins of Roman porticoes and shops for the sale of votive offerings. The paved **Sacred Way** begins after a few stairs and zigzags uphill between the foundations of memorials and treasuries to the Temple of Apollo. Along each edge is a litter of statue bases where gold, bronze and painted marble figures once stood; Pliny counted more than three thousand on his visit, and that was after Nero's infamous raid.

The choice and position of these **memorials** was dictated by more than religious zeal; many were used as a deliberate show of strength or often as a direct insult against a rival Greek state. For instance, the **Offering of the Arcadians** on the right of the entrance (a line of bases that supported nine bronzes) was erected to commemorate their invasion of Laconia in 369 BC, and pointedly placed in front of the Lacedaemonians' own monument. Beside this, and following the same logic, the Spartans celebrated their victory over Athens by erecting their **Monument of the Admirals** – a large recessed structure, which once held 37 bronze statues of gods and generals – directly opposite the Athenian's **Offering of Marathon**.

Further up the path, past the Doric remains of the **Sikyonian Treasury** on the left, stretch the expansive foundations of the **Siphnian Treasury**, a grandiose Ionic temple erected in 525 BC. Siphnos had rich gold mines and intended the building to be an unrivalled show of opulence. Fragments of the caryatids that supported its west entrance, and the fine Parian marble frieze that covered all four sides, are now in the museum. Above this is the **Treasury of the Athenians**, built, like the city's "Offering", after Marathon (490 BC). It was reconstructed in 1904–06 by matching the inscriptions that completely cover its blocks. These include honorific decrees in favour of Athens, lists of Athenian ambassadors to the Pythian Festival, and a hymn to Apollo with its musical notation in Greek letters above the text.

Next to it are the foundations of the **Bouleuterion**, or council house, a reminder that Delphi needed administrators, and a little higher up is a circular area known as the **Threshing Floor**, where a morality play enacting the killing of the serpent was

DELPHI: THE SACRED PRECINCT

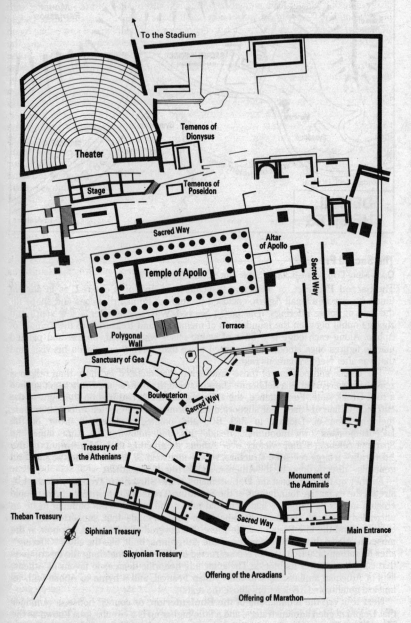

To the Stadium

Theater

Temenos of Dionysus

Stage

Temenos of Poseidon

Sacred Way

Altar of Apollo

Sacred Way

Temple of Apollo

Terrace

Polygonal Wall

Sanctuary of Gea

Bouleuterion

Sacred Way

Treasury of the Athenians

Monument of the Admirals

Theban Treasury

Siphnian Treasury

Sacred Way

Main Entrance

Sikyonian Treasury

Offering of the Arcadians

Offering of Marathon

presented every seventh year. Above is the remarkable **Polygonal Wall** whose irregular interlocking blocks have withstood, intact, all earthquakes. It too is covered with inscriptions but these almost universally refer to the emancipation of slaves; Delphi was one of the few places where such freedom could be made official and public by an inscribed register. An incongruous outcrop of rock between the wall and the Treasuries marks the original **Sanctuary of Gea**. It was here, or more precisely on the recently built-up rock, that the Sibyl, an early itinerant priestess, was reputed to have uttered her prophecies.

Finally, the Sacred Way leads to the Temple Terrace and you are confronted with a large altar, erected by the island of Híos. Of the main body of the **Temple of Apollo** only the foundations stood when it was uncovered by the French; they have, however, re-erected six Doric columns which give a vertical line to the ruins and provide some idea of its former dominance over the whole of the sanctuary. In the innermost part of the temple was the *adyton*, a dark cell at the mouth of the oracular chasm where the Pythian priestess would officiate. No sign of cave or chasm has been found, nor vapours that might have induced a trance, but it is likely that such a chasm did exist and was simply opened and closed by successive earthquakes. On the architrave of the temple – probably on the interior – were inscribed the maxims "Know Thyself" and "Nothing in Excess".

The theatre and stadium used for the main events of the Pythian Festival are on terraces above the Temple. The **Theatre**, built in the fourth century BC with a capacity of five thousand, was closely connected with Dionysos, god of ecstasy, the arts and wine, who reigned in Delphi over the winter months when the oracle was silent. A path leads up through cool pine groves to the **Stadium**, a steep walk which discourages many of the tour groups. Its site was artificially levelled in the fifth century BC, though it was banked with stone seats (capacity 7000) only in Roman times – the gift (like so many other public buildings in Greece) of Herodes Atticus. It easily dwarfs the crowds but if you want further solitude climb up above to the pine trees that have engulfed the remains of fourth-century BC walls.

The Museum

Same hours as main site, except Mon noon–6.30pm; 1000dr, students 500dr.

Delphi's museum contains a rare and exquisite collection of archaic sculpture, matched only by finds on the Acropolis. It features pottery, figures and friezes from the various treasuries, which, grouped together, give a good picture of the sanctuary's riches.

The most famous exhibit, placed at the far end of the central corridor, is **The Charioteer**, one of the few surviving bronzes of the fifth century BC. It was unearthed in 1896 along with other scant remains of the "Offering of Polyzalos", which probably toppled during the earthquake of 373 BC. The charioteer's eyes, made of onyx and set slightly askew, lend it a startling realism, while the demure expression sets the scene as a lap of honour. It is thought that the odd proportions of the body were designed by the sculptor (possibly Pythagoras of Samos) with perspective in mind; they would become "corrected" when the figure was viewed, as intended, from below.

Other major pieces include two huge **Kouroi** (archaic male figures) from the sixth century BC in the second room at the top of the stairs. To the right of this room, in the "Hall of the Siphnian Treasury", are large chunks of the beautiful and meticulously carved **Syphnian frieze**; they depict Zeus and other gods looking on as the Homeric heroes fight over the body of Patroclus, and the gods battling with the giants. In the same room is an elegant Ionic sculpture of the winged **Sphynx of the Naxians** (c. 560 BC). Back along the main corridor is the **Athenian Treasury**, represented by fragments of the metopes, which depict the labours of Hercules, the adventures of Theseus and a battle with Amazons. Further on and to the right, the **Hall of the Monument of Daochos** is dominated by a group of three colossal dancing women, carved from

Pentelic marble around an acanthus column. It is likely that the figures, celebrating Dionysus, formed the stand for a tripod.

The Castalian spring

Site partially fenced in; free admission.

Following the road east of the sanctuary, towards Aráhova, you reach a sharp bend. To the left, marked by niches for votive offerings and by the remains of an archaic fountain house, the celebrated **Castalian spring** still flows from a cleft in the Phaedriades cliffs.

Visitors to Delphi (only men were allowed in the early centuries) were obliged to purify themselves in its waters, usually by washing their hair, though murderers had to take the full plunge. Byron, impressed by the legend that it succoured poetic inspiration, jumped in. This is no longer possible, since the spring is fenced off, and, sadder still, the entire, adjacent base of the Phaedriades cliffs which tower overhead are now swathed in scaffolding to prevent their collapse – the result of traffic vibrations.

The Marmaria

Same hours as main site; free admission.

Across and below the road from the spring is the **Marmaria**, or Sanctuary of Athena, whom the Delphians worshipped as Athena Pronoia ("Guardian of the Temple"). The name *Marmaria* means "marble quarry" and derives from the medieval practice of filching the ancient blocks for private use.

The most conspicuous building in the precinct (and the first visible from the road) is the **Tholos**, a fourth-century BC rotunda. Three of its dome-columns and their entablature have been set up but while these amply demonstrate the original beauty of the building (which is *the* postcard image of Delphi), its purpose remains a mystery.

At the entrance to the sanctuary stood the **Old Temple of Athena**, destroyed by the Persians and rebuilt in the Doric order in the fourth century BC, a hundred metres away; foundations of both can be traced. Outside the precinct on the northwest side (above the *Marmaria*) is a **Gymnasium**, again built in the fourth century BC, but later enlarged by the Romans who added a running track on the now collapsed terrace; prominent among the ruins is a circular (cold) plunge bath used after training.

Dhelfí: the village

The modern village of Dhelfí is entirely geared to tourism. An insubstantial place, its attraction lies in its mountain site, proximity to the ruins, and access to Mount Parnassós (see the following section). Like most Greek site villages, however, it has a quick turnaround of visitors, so finding a place to stay should present few problems.

Accommodation

There are upwards of thirty hotels and pensions and various rooms to let. Touts often meet the buses, offering both hotel and private rooms, though their claims ("I'm the only place open/with vacancies/with hot water") should be greeted with scepticism.

Most of the **hotels and pensions** are reasonable; good value options include:

Pension Maniatis, Issáia 2 (☎0265/82 134). ②
Pension Odysseus, Fillelínon 1 (☎0265/82 235). ②
Hotel Pan, Vassiléos Pávlou 53 (☎0265/82 294). ③
Hotel Athena, Vassiléos Pávlou 55 (☎0265/82 239). ③

The village also has an excellent **youth hostel** (☎0265/82 268; Closed Dec–Feb; ①) at Appollónou 29, the upper road, and two "local" **campsites**: the closest is *Camping Apollon* (☎0265/82 762), 1.5km west on the road out towards Ámfissa; *Camping Delphi* (☎0265/28 944) is almost 4km down the road towards Itéa.

Food and other practicalities

Meals are best at *Taverna Vakhos*, next to the youth hostel, which is incredibly cheap, tasty and has views down to Itéa from its terrace. Among others, try the *Psistaria Arahova*, opposite the *Hotel Pan* at the west end of town, with excellent *kokorétsi* and wine, or *Stammatis*, 200m further out. Other amenities include **banks**, a **post office**, a **tourist office** and an **OTE** along the main street.

There is now a single **bus terminal**, located at the Itéa (west) end of town. Westbound buses go to Ámfissa (whence you can pick up connections north), Itéa and (usually with a change) Náfpaktos, while eastbound services go only to Livádhia or Athens. The main difficulty, since all coaches originate elsewhere, is that seats allocated for the Dhelfí ticket booth are limited and they sell out some hours in advance. If you're going to be stuck standing all the way to Athens, it's better to get off at Livádhia and continue by train – there are three afternoon departures.

Mount Parnassós

For a quick sniff of the Greek alpine scene, **Parnassós** is probably the most convenient peak in the land, though it is no longer a wilderness, disfigured by the ski-station above Aráhova and its accompanying paraphernalia of lifts, snack bars and access roads. The best routes for walkers are those up from Delphi to the **Corycian Cave** (practicable from April to November), or to the **Liákoura summit ascent** (practicable from May to September only).

If you're driving, there are metalled **roads** up the mountain from Aráhova and Graviá and a jeep track from Amfíklia. These could easily be combined with a walk.

Delphi to the Corycian Cave

To reach the **trailhead** for this walk – and the initial path up the mountain – take the right-hand (approaching from Athens), uphill road through Dhelfí village. At the top of the slope turn right on to a road that doubles back to the **museum-house** (Tues–Fri 8am–8pm, Mon, Sat & Sun 9am–3pm) where the poet **Angelos Sikelianos** – he of the briefly revived ancient festival – once lived. There is a bust of him outside.

Continue climbing from here, on a gravel surface, and you reach the highest point of the fence enclosing the sanctuary ruins. Where it ends at a locked gate, adopt a trail on your left, well-marked by black-on-yellow metal diamonds since it's part of the E4 European long-distance trail. Initially steep, the way soon flattens out on a grassy knoll overlooking the stadium, and continues along a ridge next to a line of burnt cypresses.

Soon after, you join up with an ancient, cobbled trail coming from inside the fenced precinct, the **"Kakí Skála"**, which zigzags up the slope above you in broad reaches. The view from here is fantastic, stretching back over the Gulf of Kórinthos to the mountains of the Peloponnese. The cobbles come to an end by a large concrete inspection cover in the Delphi water supply, an hour above the village, at the top of the Phaedriades cliffs. Nearby stand a pair of rock pinnacles, from one of which those guilty of sacrilege in ancient times were thrown to their deaths – a custom perhaps giving rise to the name *Kakí Skála* or "Evil Stairway".

E4 markers remain visible in the valley which opens out ahead of you. You can get simultaneous views south, and northeast towards the Parnassan summits, by detouring a little to the right to a wooden hut and a barn, then to a slight rise perhaps 150m further. The principal route becomes a gravel route bearing northeast; beyond, you take the right fork near a spring and watering troughs, with some shepherds' huts scattered under the trees. The track passes a picnic grounds and a chapel within the next fifteen minutes, and acquires intermittent tarmac surface before skirting a sheepfold and another hut on the left. Some two hours above Dhelfí, you emerge from the fir woods with a view ahead of the rounded mass of the Yerondóvrahos peak (2367m) of the Parnassós massif.

Another fifteen minutes brings you to a spring, followed by another chapel and lean-to on the left, with a patch of grass that would do for camping. Just beyond is a muddy tarn backed by a low ridge. To the left rises a much steeper ridge, on whose flank lies the ancient **Corycian cave**. Scramble up the slope, meeting a dirt road about three-quarters of the way up; turn left and follow it to the end, about 10m below the conspicuous cave mouth.

This was sacred to Pan and the nymphs in ancient times, the presiding deities of Delphi during the winter months when Apollo was said to desert the oracle. Orgiastic rites were celebrated in November at the cave by women acting as the "nymphs", who made the long hike up from Delphi on the Kakí Skála by torchlight. The cavern itself is chilly and forbidding, but if you look carefully with a torch you can find ancient inscriptions near the entrance; without artificial light you can't see more than 100m inside. By the entrance you'll notice a rock with a man-made, circular indentation – possibly an ancient altar to hold libations.

Descending to Dhelfí takes rather less than the roughly three-hour ascent. The marked E4 route, on the other hand, continues almost due north over a mixture of trails and tracks to the village of **EPTÁLOFOS**, on the Aráhova–Graviá asphalt road, where simple **rooms** and meals are available.

The Liákoura summit

Liákoura is Parnassós's highest and finest peak (2457m) and can be aproached either from the Delphi side or from around the mountain to the north. The latter is the best walk, starting **from Áno Tithoréa**, but it involves taking a bus or train and then local taxi to the trailhead – plus camping out on the mountain. If you want a more casual look at Parnassós, it's probably better to walk up **from the Delphi side**. This is very enjoyable as far as the *EOS* (Hellenic Alpine Club) refuge – about six hours' walk – and you could either turn back here or a couple of hours' lower down on the Livádhi plateau (hitching here is possible) if you don't fancy a night on the mountain and the final, rather dull, four hours' slog up to Liákoura.

For the energetic, it's possible to **traverse the whole massif** in around fifteen hours' walking, starting from Delphi and descending at Áno Tithoréa, or vice versa.

Áno Tithoréa to Liákoura via the Velítsa Ravine

This last surviving wilderness route up Parnassós to Liákoura involves first a train or bus to **KÁTO TITHORÉA**, which is on the Livádhia–Amfíklia road and the Athens–Thessaloníki railway. You then need to get to the higher, twin village of **ÁNO TITHORÉA**, a four-kilometre haul easiest accomplished by taxi (usually available; bargain for the price beforehand). It's best to arrive early in the day and plan on camping out on the mountain as lodging can be difficult to find.

From the *platía* in Áno Tithoréa, head southwest out of town until you reach some park benches overlooking the giant Velítsa ravine. Adjacent is a "waterfall", in reality a leak in an aqueduct, which crosses the path beginning here a few minutes above the benches. A hundred metres further, bear left away from what seems to be the main track and descend towards the bed of the canyon. Once you're on the far side you can see the aqueduct again, now uncovered. Follow it until you reach the isolated chapel of Áyios Ioánnis (1hr from Áno Tithoréa).

Once past the chapel, bulldozer scrapings cease and a fine alpine path heads off through the firs before you. The way is obvious for the next ninety minutes, with tremendous views of the crags filing up to the Liákoura summit, on your right across the valley. You emerge on a narrow neck of land, with a brief glimpse over the Ayía Marína valley and namesake monastery to the east (left). The path, faint for an interval, heads slightly downhill and to the right to meet the floor of the Velítsa at the Tsáres spring (3hr 30min). This is the last reliable water, so best fill up.

On the far bank of the river, head up a steep, scree-laden slope through the last of the trees to some sheep pens (4hr), then climb up to another pastoral hut (4hr 30min) at the base of the defile leading down from the main summit ridge. Beyond this point the going is gentler for much of the final ascent to the northwest (top right-hand) corner of this valley. A brief scramble up a rock fall to a gap in the ridge and you are at the base of Liákoura (5hr 30min). Orange paint-splashes – primarily oriented for those descending – stake out most of the approach from the Tsáres spring.

The **final ascent** is an easy twenty-minute scramble more or less up to the ridge line (for a total of about 6hr; allow 4hr 30min to return). On a clear morning, especially after rain, you're supposed to be able to see Mount Olympus in the north, the Aegean to the east, the Ionian to the west and way down into the Peloponnese to the south. The best viewing is said to be in midsummer; all too often you can see only cloud.

Down to the gulf: Delphi to Náfpaktos

The train-less, almost beach-less **north shore of the Gulf of Kórinthos** is even less frequented than the south coast, and the arid landscape, with harsh mountains inland, can be initially off-putting. But there are attractive and low-key resorts in **Galaxídhi** and **Náfpaktos**, both reasonably well connected by bus, and offering connections on south to the Peloponnese, via the ferries at Áyios Nikólaos–Éyio or Andírio–Río.

All buses heading southwest of Delphi towards the Gulf of Kórinthos stop first at ITÉA, a gritty little town (literally, owing to the bauxite-ore dust everywhere) where you may have to change buses for the next leg of the journey. For the continuation of the route west from Andírio to Messolóngi and Agrínio, see p.298.

Galaxídhi

GALAXÍDHI, 17km southwest of Itéa, is a quiet, mirage-like port, with a superb water-front of nineteenth-century shipowners' houses. These have lately become the haunt of Athenian second-homers, plus a smattering of French and Italians. Despite the restorations and a bit of an overt yachtie ethos down at the southern "new" harbour, the town still remains just the right side of tweeness, with an animated market high street and a variety of watering-holes.

There is no real beach – something that's no doubt acted as a healthy brake on development – but strolling around the pine-covered headland you'll find some pebbly **coves**, with chapel-crowned islets offshore. Another good walk is to the thirteenth-century **Moní Metamórfosis**, an archetypal rural monstery looking out over the bay towards Parnassós. It's an hour on foot to the west, through terraced fields and olive and almond groves; take the track under the flyover at the western edge of the village and look out for a footpath to the right after about twenty minutes. In town, there's also a small **archaeological museum** (Wed–Sat 9am–1.30pm, Sun 9.30am–1.30pm), above the new harbour, if you're insistent on more things cultural.

Accommodation is on the pricey side and hard to find in summer. The dead-central *Hotel Possidon* (☎0265/41 271; ③) is the cheapest option but a bit sleazy; better are the *Rooms Galaxidhi* (☎0265/41 198; ③), over the supermarket next to the post office, or more rooms (☎0265/41 349; ③) at the head of the new harbour. Further inland, the hotels *Koukounas* (☎0265/41 179; ④) and *Galaxidhi* face each other across a small square, but they're both modern cement piles, and if you're going to be splurging it's better to go for one of the restored traditional premises. Best situated of these is the *Hirolakas*, on the old, northern harbour of the same name, which has an *ouzeri* downstairs as well as doubles in the ③ range. Top of the range is represented by the *Pension Galaxa* (☎0265/41 620; ⑤), on the promontory above Hirólakas bay, and, a little inland, the delightful Italian-run *Pension Ganimede* (☎0265/41 328; ⑤ but cheaper out of season), with a beautiful garden and home-made jams at breakfast.

Eating out, far and away the best of the tavernas is *O Dervenis* (open May–Sept), near the *Ganimede*, with fair prices and impeccable food. For budget eating, tucked in among the new harbour's quayside boutiques and bistros is the fish-fryer *O Tasos*, the traditional greasy spoon *O Alekos*, and a good *ouzeri* – at the back of the *platía* across the way. For dessert, *To Konaki* on the market street has lethal sweets.

The Áyios Nikólaos–Éyio ferry

West of Galaxídhi is some of the sparsest scenery of the Greek shoreline; there are few villages and none which seems to warrant a stop, despite scrappy beaches. At **ÁYIOS NIKÓLAOS**, however, there's a year-round **ferry across the gulf** to ÉYIO – an alternative approach to the Peloponnese to the crossing at Andírio–Río, 60km further west. The boats leave Áyios Nikólaos three times daily in winter, at 8.30am, 3pm and 6pm, with two additional departures in summer at noon and 6pm; the journey takes 35 minutes, costing 350dr for passengers, 1700dr per car. If you miss the last departure there are **hotels** and a **campsite**.

Náfpaktos

The one place that stands out to the west of Galaxídhi is **NÁFPAKTOS**, a lively resort sprawling along the seafront below a rambling Venetian castle. Two hours by bus from Delphi, and an hour by bus and ferry from Pátra, it's a convenient journey break – though, surprisingly, most of its visitors are Greek.

The **Kástro** provides a picturesque backdrop to the town, and enjoyable rambling to the top of its fortifications. At their base they run down to the sea, enclosing the old harbour and the **beach** – entered through one of the original gates. On the outskirts of town to the west there's a longer stretch of beach with a few tavernas. The castle was long a formidable part of the Venetian defences, and offshore was fought the **Battle of Lepanto** in 1571. Under the command of John of Austria, an allied Christian armada devastated an Ottoman fleet – the first European naval victory over the Turks since the death of the dreaded pirate-admiral Barbarossa; Cervantes, author of *Don Quixote*, lost his left arm to a cannonball in the conflict.

As at Galaxídhi, **accommodation** can be in short supply in summer, though you should end up with a bed at one or other of the dozen hotels or assorted rooms places. Best value of the hotels are the *Aegli*, Ilárhou Tzavéla 75 (☎0634/27 271; ③), and the *Amaryllis*, Platía Liménos (☎0634/27 237; ③). There's a good **campsite**, *Camping Platanitis*, 4.5km west of the town towards Andírio; to get there, catch a blue city bus from the main square (the last one leaves at 10pm).

Moving on, there are **buses** northwest to Agrínio (where you can pick up services to Ioánnina or Lefkádha), and east to Itéa and Ámfissa (for connections north into Thessaly). The local city buses detailed for the campsite run to the ferry at Andírio, or you can sometimes get a seat on a long-distance coach heading to Pátra.

The Andírio–Río Ferry

The ferry at **ANDÍRIO** runs across the Gulf of Kórinthos to Río (see p.220) every fifteen minutes from 6.45am to 10.45pm and every half-hour at night; the trip takes just fifteen minutes; fares are 100dr per passenger, 700dr per car. Once across, you can generally pick up a city bus immediately for Pátra but through bus services between the Delphi area and Pátra have improved in recent years, so if you can get one, do so. If you're driving, count on a wait of half-hour or so in summer. There's a cheapish restaurant across from the little fortress gate on the strait.

North to Lamía

Lamía is a half-day's journey north from Delphi, with a connection at Ámfissa: a slow but pleasant route skirting Mounts Parnassós, Gióna and (to the northwest) Íti. At the historic pass of **Thermopylae** the road joins the **coastal highway** from Athens.

Inland via Ámfissa

The inland road north from Delphi climbs slowly through a sea of olive groves to ÁMFISSA, a small town in the foothills of Mount Gióna. Like Livádhia, this strategic military location was a base for the Catalan Grand Company, who have left their mark on the **castle**. If you have time to fill between buses, its ruins – including remnants of an ancient acropolis – are a short and obvious walk, if only to enjoy the shade of the pine trees and examine a few stretches of Classical polygonal masonry. In town, the **market** quarter is good for a stroll. Ámfissa was once one of the major bell-making centres in the Balkans, and copper-alloy sheep bells are still produced and sold here. The local olives – green and salty – are also acclaimed.

Serious **walkers** may want to use Ámfissa as a jumping-off point for the mountains west and north towards Karpeníssi: **Gióna**, **Vardhoússia**, and **Oxía**. There are routes through from Ámfissa (and from Lidhoríki, west of Ámfissa) **to Karpeníssi**. Most travellers, however, roll north on the dramatic **Lamía road**, dividing Mounts Parnassós and Gióna, or along the **rail line** from Livadhiá to Lamía.

The railway is one of the most dramatic stretches of line in Europe and has a history to match. It runs through the foothills of Mount Íti and over the precipitous **defile of the Gorgopótamos** river, where in 1942 the Greek resistance – all factions united for the first and last time, under the command of the British intelligence officer C.M. Woodhouse – blew up a railway viaduct, cutting one of the Germans' vital supply lines to their army in North Africa.

The coastal highway

The **Athens–Lamía** coastal highway is fast, efficient and generally dull. For the first 90km or so it runs a little inland, though skirting various pockets of inland lake, like Límni Ilíki, north of Thíva. The most interesting stop, along with Thíva, is the Mycenaean citadel of **Glá**, by the village of KÁSTRO (see p.215).

There are various **links with the island of Évvia**: first at HALKÍDHA, where there's a causeway; then by ferry at **ARKÍTSA** to LOUTRÁ EDHIPSOÚ (about every hour in season, every other hour out; last at 9pm; 50min; passengers 350dr, cars 1700dr). Arkítsa itself is a rather upmarket resort, popular mainly with Greeks. A short way to the north of here is the more general port of Áyios Konstandínos, which has ferry connections with the Sporades.

Áyios Konstandínos and Kámena Voúrla

ÁYIOS KONSTANDÍNOS is the closest port to Athens if you're heading for the islands of the Sporades. There are daily car **ferries**, usually just before midday, to Skíathos and Skópelos, with an additional evening departure in season which sometimes continues to Alónissos; for information call the port police (☎0235/31 920). In summer there are also *Flying Dolphin* **hydrofoils** (passengers only) to Skíathos, Skópelos and Alónissos; these are about twice as fast and twice as expensive (☎0235/ 318 74 for information).

There should be no reason to stay in Áyios Konstandínos, but if you're stranded it has eight or so **hotels** – try the *Pension O Tassos* (☎0235/31 610; ②) or *Hotel Poulia* (☎0235/31 663; ③) – and a **campsite**, *Camping Blue Bay* (☎0235/314 25).

A better beach, if you find yourself waiting some time, is at **KÁMENA VOÚRLA**, 9km north; this is, however, very much a resort, used mainly by Greeks attracted by the spas here and at neighbouring Loutrá Thermopilíon (see below).

Thermopylae and its spa

Just before joining the inland road, the highway enters the **Pass of Thermopylae**, where Leonidas and three hundred Spartans made a last stand against Xerxes' 30,000-strong Persian army in 480 BC. The pass was in ancient times much more defined, a narrow defile with Mount Kalídhromo on its south and the sea – which has silted and retreated nearly 4km – to the north.

The tale of Spartan bravery is described at length by Herodotus. Leonidas, King of Sparta, stood guard over the pass with a mixed force of 7000 Greeks, confident that it was the only approach an army could take to enter Greece from Thessaly. At night, however, Xerxes sent an advance part of his forces along a mountain trail and broke through the pass to attack the Greeks from the rear. Leonidas ordered a retreat of the main army, but remained in the pass himself, with his Spartan guard, to delay the Persians' progress. He and all but two of the guard fought to their deaths.

LOUTRÁ THERMOPILÍON, midway through the pass, is named for the hot springs present since antiquity. It retains the grave mound of the fallen Spartans, opposite a modern memorial to Leonidas. The spa and restaurant facilities are intimidatingly built up but there are a few cascades and drainage sluices where you can bathe undisturbed in the open air.

Lamía

LAMÍA is a busy provincial capital and an important transport junction for travellers. It sees few overnight visitors since there are no particular sights – the Catalan castle is still in military use – but if you are in no hurry, it's as good a place as anywhere to get an idea of small-town Greek life.

The town is arranged around three main squares: Platía Párhou, Platía Eleftherías and Platía Laoú. **Platía Párhou** stakes out the shopping area, with **banks** also grouped around. The **buses**, including a local service from the train station (6km out), all arrive nearby, though their terminals are scattered: Ámfissa and Karpeníssi services use a terminal on Márkou Bótsari; those for Lárissa, Tríkala and the north, one on Thermopilón; those for Vólos, one at the corner of Levadhítou and Rozáki-Ángeli.

Most of the **hotels** are also grouped here, with a pair of budget places on Ódhos Rozáki-Ángeli: *Thermopylae* (☎0231/28-840; ③) at no. 36 and *Athina* (☎0231/20 700; ③) at no. 41. A couple of others, nicely sited, are on Platía Laoú (see below): the *Emborikon* (☎0231/22 654; ③) and *Neon Astron* (☎0231/26 245; ③).

Platía Eleftherías is the town's social hub, full of outdoor cafés and restaurants, and the scene of the evening *volta*. The cathedral and town hall occupy two sides of the square, the latter pockmarked by bullets dating from riots during the colonels' junta. Every Sunday the flag above is lowered in solemn ceremony, to the wayward accompaniment of the local band. Steps below the cathedral lead down to an *ouzerí*, good for a *mezé* and a drink. Just to the south of Eleftherías is **Platía Laoú**, shaded by plane trees which in autumn are crowded with migratory birds. Here you'll find the town's main taxi rank and an all-night kiosk. In the paved streets off to the right are a number of very cheap pasta-and-chicken **restaurants**. Even cheaper, and open until 6am, is the restaurant at the base of the steps on the south side of the square, by the fish and meat market; this is used chiefly by prostitutes and their pimps. If you prefer a bit more attention to cuisine, good tavernas elsewhere in town include *Yiorgos* in Markopoúlou, *Foudha* near the Tríkala bus station, and *Psilidhas* on the road out towards Vólos.

For a look at **bread-making** by the oldest of old-fashioned methods, leave Platía Laoú by the road behind the *zaharoplastío* and follow it for 200 metres into the old part of town. The bakery is on the left, recognisable by the quarter-glazed windows and stable door. Another noteworthy bakery, supplying perhaps the best *tirópites* in Greece, is to be found between *platías* Laoú and Eleftherías; look for its blue shutters.

Other diversions in Lamía include live **bouzouki music**, untainted by the sophisticated tastes of Athenians, nor pandering to tourists, on the Stilídha road, opposite the high school; a **theatre** on Ipsilándou, used for art exhibitions and in winter as an art-film cinema; and a scattering of winter-only **"pubs"**, among them *59* on Markopoúlou and *Decadence* on Víronos, both with loud music and not a lot of atmosphere.

On **Saturdays**, the streets below Párhou turn into a **market**, very lively and with everything from goats to plastic combs on sale. And finally, every **Sunday** there is a **puppet show** in the small theatre 200m up the road past the OTE; it's designed for children, telling classic Greek stories that are understandable even with a very hazy knowledge of the language.

North from Lamía

Heading north from Lamía there's a choice of three routes: to Tríkala and Kalambáka, to Lárissa, or around the coast to Vólos. None is especially memorable. FÁRSALA and KARDHÍTSA, on the routes to Lárissa and Tríkala respectively, are small, very ordinary country towns. The **Vólos road**, however, along the coast, has a little more to delay your progress.

Lamía to Vólos

First temptation on the coast road to Vólos is **AYÍA MARÍNA**, 12km north of Lamía, where there are some fine seafood tavernas along the beach – a popular weekend trip for Lamian families.

A couple of kilometres further, **STILÍDHA** was once one of the major ports of the Aegean – it was at the opera house here that Maria Callas's grandfather outsung a visiting Italian star and started a dynasty. The town is today chiefly concerned with olive-oil bottling and cement: not an inspiring prospect, though there is a good beach with a **hotel** (*Stilis Beach*) and **campsite** (*Camping Paras*; April–Oct only; ☎0238/52 802). Look out for nesting herons on the road back to Lamía.

The best beach along this route is at **GLÍFA**, 30km further north, though it is 9km off the highway and hard to get to without your own transport. It has the mainland's northernmost **ferry crossing to Évvia**: seven times daily to ÁYIOKAMBOS (last at 6pm; 30min journey; passengers 250dr, cars 1400dr). Rooms are on offer in private houses and at half a dozen **hotels**, cheapest of which is the *Oasis* (☎0238/61 201; ③). **AKHÍLIO**, 7km north, is less attractive, though it has a **campsite**.

Finally, rounding the Pagasitic Gulf towards Vólos, car-drivers might want to stop at **NÉA ANHIÁLOS**, where five early Christian basilicas have been uncovered. Their mosaics and the small site museum are interesting, though perhaps not enough to make it worth risking a three-hour wait between buses.

West to Karpeníssi – and beyond

The road **west from Lamía** climbs sinuously out of the Sperhiós river valley, allowing glimpses along the way of Mounts Íti, Gióna and Vardhoússia, just 10km to the south. If you're looking to do some **hiking**, there are spectacular routes on Mount Íti (the Classical Oita), easiest approached from the village of Ipáti. The **Karpeníssi valley**, too, lends itself to walking trips amid a countryside of dark fir forest and snow-fringed mountains, which the EOT promote (with some justice) as "the Greek Switzerland". Neither area sees more than a few dozen summer tourists.

Ipáti and paths on Mount Íti

Mount Íti is an unusually accessible mountain. There are buses almost hourly from Lamía to Ipáti, its main trailhead; if you arrive by train, these can be picked up en route at Lamía "local" station, LIANOKLÁDHI, 6km from the town. Be sure not to be get off the bus at the sulphurous spa of LOUTRÁ IPÁTIS, 5km south of Ipá proper.

IPÁTI is a small village, gathered below a castle. It has two **hotels**, catering mainly for Greek families, and both good value – the *Panorama* (☎0231/59 222; ②) and *Panhellinion* (☎0231/59 640; ②). There are also a couple of reasonable tavernas.

Trail-finding on **Mount Íti** can be an ambitious undertaking and requires detailed maps and/or a hiking guidebook. A limited trek, however, should be feasible if you've reasonable orientation skills. From the village, a path loosely marked by red splashes of paint leads in around four hours to an *EOS* refuge known as **Trápeza** (usually locked, but with a spring and camping space nearby). This is a steep but rewarding walk, giving a good idea of Íti's sheer rock ramparts and high lush meadows.

Karpeníssi

The main road west from Ipáti, after scaling a spur of Mount Timvristós, and passing the turnoff to a tiny **ski centre** (uncrowded and with equipment to rent), drops down to the town of **KARPENÍSSI**. Its site is spectacular, huddled at the base of the peak and head of the Karpenissiótis valley, which extends south all the way to the wall-like Mount Panetolikó, though the town itself is entirely nondescript, having been destroyed in World War II by the Germans and again during the civil war. On the latter occasion, in January 1949, it was captured and held for a week by Communist guerillas. During the fighting here an American pilot was shot down, having, as C. M. Woodhouse observes in *Modern Greece*, "probably the unenviable distinction of being the first American serviceman to be killed in action by Communist arms".

Except in midsummer or skiing season, accommodation is easily found. Within a block of the central square a dozen or so **hotels** compete for your attention. The cheapest are the *Panhellinion* at Tsitsára 9 (☎0237/22 330; ②) and *Velouchi* at Zinopoúlou 64 (☎0237/22 264; ②), but there's a broad selection in all categories, the *Helvetia* at Zinopoúlou 33 (☎0237/22 465; ③) being the next notch up. As the provincial capital of Evritanía, the town has most facilities you might need. A couple of passable **tavernas** and a *souvláki* bar are to be found on Etólou, just around the corner from the *Hotel Panhellinion*.

Around Karpeníssi

A pleasant four-kilometre walk from Karpeníssi is the traditional mountain village of **KORISKHÁDHES**, whose stone houses display the ornate wooden balconies typical of the region. It has a single *kafenío* where you can order *mezédhes* and gaze over the trees at Mount Helidhóna. To reach the village, follow the road south out of town (towards Proussós) and look for the turning to the right after about 1km.

If your appetite is whetted for more of this countryside, a twice-daily bus trundles 13km downriver, again along the Proussós road, to **MEGÁLO HORIÓ** and **MIKRÓ HORIÓ** ("Big Village" and "Little Village"). Both have **inns** and the possibility of day hikes up the respective peaks presiding over them.

Beyond these villages, the valley narrows to a gorge, the road loses its asphalt, and only one daily bus braves the hair-raising drive to the monastery and village of **PROUSSÓS** (33km out of Karpeníssi). The **monastery** is large and much rebuilt after a succession of fires (always a hazard with candles), and presently tenanted by just five monks. Visitors are welcomed and shown curiosities in the ninth-century *katholikón* – such as paper made from the skin of goat-kid embryo and an icon of the Panayía with its eyes gouged out. (According to the monks, the Communist *andártes* of the 1940s were responsible for this, though the Turks were wont to perform the same sacrilege, and credulous villagers attributed magical powers to the dust thus obtained.)

In summer the monastery will host men for a one-night stay; otherwise there are a couple of tavernas in the **village** (1km further on) and probably a bed or two – necessary since the bus won't reappear until the following day.

West from Karpeníssi

The roads west from Karpeníssi climb high into the mountains of **Panetolikó**, the southernmost extension of the Píndhos. In winter they're generally impassable, but through the summer they're serviceable, if bone-shaking.

The most remote and dramatic route, with no bus service, is on **south from Proussós** (see above): 33km of dirt track which eventually brings you out at **THÉRMO**, on the shores of Lake Trihonídha. There you are within striking distance (and a daily bus ride) of AGRÍNIO, with its connections to Patrá and Ioánnina.

The direct **Karpeníssi-Agrínio** road is in a better state, though it still takes the one morning bus a good five hours to cover. It breaks for a lunch stop at the tidy village of **FRANGÍSTA**, sandwiched between various river crossings. If you wish to explore the **Ágrafa** wilderness to the north, leave the bus at the nearby turnoff for KERASOHÓRI. Beyond the turning, the bus lumbers past the giant **Kremastón dam** on the Tavropós, Trikeriótis and Ahelóös rivers, skirts Panetolikó, then winds down through tobacco-planted hills to Agrínio. The beauty of the first half of the journey cannot be overemphasised.

THESSALY

The highlights of travelling through **Thessaly** are easily summarised. Over to the east, curling down from the industrial port-city of Vólos, is the **Pílion** (Pelion) mountain peninsula. The villages on its lush, orchard-covered slopes are among the most beautiful in the country: an established resort area for Greeks, though still surprisingly undiscovered by tourists. To the west – a sight not to be missed in any mainland exploration – are the extraordinary "monasteries in the air" of the **Metéora**.

The **central plains** are to be passed through, rather than visited. **Lárissa**, the region's capital, is nothing much in itself, though it provides efficient connections by bus, and rather slower ones by train, to Vólos and to Kalambáka (via Tríkala).

Heading north or west from Lárissa, you will find yourself in one mountain range or another. The dramatic route across the Píndhos, from Kalambáka to Ioánnina, is covered in the following chapter. North from Kalambáka there are reasonable roads, though few buses, into western Macedonia, with the lakeside town of Kastoriá an obvious focus. Most travellers, however, head north from Lárissa towards Thessaloníki, a very beautiful route in the shadow of Mount Olympus (see Chapter Five).

Vólos

Arriving at the port city of **VÓLOS**, you have little hint of the Pílion's promise. This is Greece's fastest-growing industrial centre and a major depot for TIR drivers, who cross with the once-weekly ferry to Tartous in Syria. Except for isolated nooks and crannies, it is not a pretty sight – or smell, when the homegrown *néfos* (pollution cloud) hovers. Physically, it's mainly modern concrete sprawl, rebuilt after a devastating 1955 earthquake, and now edging to its natural limits against the Pílion foothills behind.

That said, you may well find yourself spending a night, or at least a few hours, here, for in addition to serving as a gateway to the Pílion, Vólos is the main **port for the northern Sporades** – Skiáthos, Skópelos and Alónissos. The most attractive place to linger is the eastern waterfront esplanade, between the landscaped **Platía Yioryíou** and the archaeological museum – a highly recommended time filler.

Imaginatively laid out and clearly labelled in English, the **Archaeological Museum** (Tues–Sun 8.30am–3pm) features a unique collection of painted grave *stelai* depicting, in now-faded colours, the everyday scenarios of fifth-century BC life. It also has one of the best European collections of Neolithic pottery, tools and figurines, from the local sites of Sesklo and Dimini (both of which sites – respectively 15km and 3km from Volos – can be visited, though they are of essentially specialist interest).

Ferries, hydrofoils and other transport

Like Áyios Konstandínos, Vólos has both regular ferries and in summer (for nearly double the price) the quicker *Flying Dolphin* hydrofoils to the Sporades.

The **ferries** leave two to four times daily for Skiáthos and Skópelos, with at least one continuing to Alónissos; the last departure is generally 7pm (Sun 1pm); for information phone the port police on ☎0421/38 888 or ☎0421/31 059.

Hydrofoils (☎0421/39 786) run two or three times daily to Skiáthos, Skópelos and Alónissos, continuing two or three times a week to Skíros. In midsummer there are also hydrofils to the islands from **Platanías** at the foot of the Pílion (see p.255).

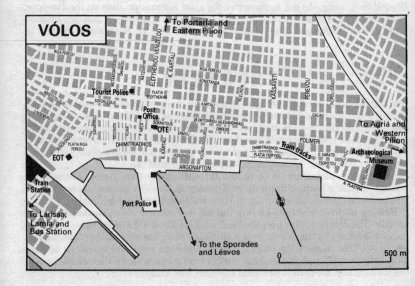

Both ferries and hydrofoils depart from the central **port**, and most other services are found within a couple of blocks. An exception is the **bus station**, off our map on Grigoríou Lambráki and well southwest of the main square, **Platía Ríga Feréou**. Arrayed around the latter are the **train station** and **EOT**, worth a stop to check bus schedules, if you are heading for the Pílion.

If you want to **rent a car** to explore the Pílion, a good agency is *Theofanidhis Hellas* (☎0421/32 360) at Iassónos 137 – parallel to the waterfront, one block inland.

Accommodation
Hotels are fairly plentiful, with a concentration of acceptable ones in the grid of streets behind the port. Options include:

Hotel Iason, Pavlóu Méla 1 (☎0421/26 075). Located near the dock, this is about as rough as you'd want to be – avoid cheaper choices. ②

Hotel Avra, Solonós 6 (☎0421/25 970). One block over from the above and a bit more savoury. ③

Pension Roussas, Tzaánou 1 (☎0421/21 732). Nice location out by the archaeological museum. ②

Hotel Aigli, Argonáfton 24 (☎0421/25 691). Art Deco hotel on the quayside – good for a splash. ④

Restaurants and nightlife
Restaurants are grouped around the ferry jetty – where *Ouzeri Dhelfini* at Argonáfton 37 and *Vangelis*, K. Kartáli 4, can be recommended – and along the refurbished esplanade leading up to the museum. Here you're spoilt for choice, at least in the evening. Two good but somewhat pricey options for lunch are *Remvi*, past the museum at Nikifórou Plastíra 22 and featuring seaside tables, and *Ta Palia Kalamakia*, which specialises in fish; the *Akti Tselepi*, on the corner of F. Ioánnou, is a little cheaper. Inland, there's nothing of note except for *O Haliambalias* on Orféos 8, a casserole taverna that's shut in summer.

As for **nightlife**, there's the *Kafe Santan* on Orféos, though the owners move to Skiáthos during the warmer months, and a good summer cinema, *Exoraístiki*, at one corner of Platía Yioryíou. The local disco, *Archetypo*, is located 5km west of the city, on the beach at Paralía Agriás.

Mount Pílion (Pelion)

There is something decidedly un-Greek about the **Mount Pílion peninsula**, with its lush orchards of apple, pear and nut trees, and dense forests of beech and oak. Scarcely a rock is visible along the slopes, and the sound of water comes gurgling up from crevices beside every track; summer temperatures here are a good 15° cooler than the rest of Thessaly.

Pílion **villages** are idiosyncratic, spread out along the slopes – due to easy availability of water – and with their various quarters linked by winding cobbled paths. They formed a semi-autonomous district during the Turkish occupation, and during the eighteenth century became something of a nursery for Greek culture, which encompassed not only an Orthodox education (imparted through semi-underground schooling) but a revival of **folk art** and **traditional architecture**. There is also, by Greek standards, a strong regional **cuisine**, with specialities such as *spédzofai* (sausage and pepper casserole), *kounéli kokkinistó* (rabbit stew) and *gída vrastí* (goat *pot-au-feu*).

Many of the villages have changed little in appearance over the centuries, and offer rich rewards with their mansions, churches and sprawling *platías* – invariably shaded by a vast plane tree, sheltering the local café. The **churches** are highly distinctive,

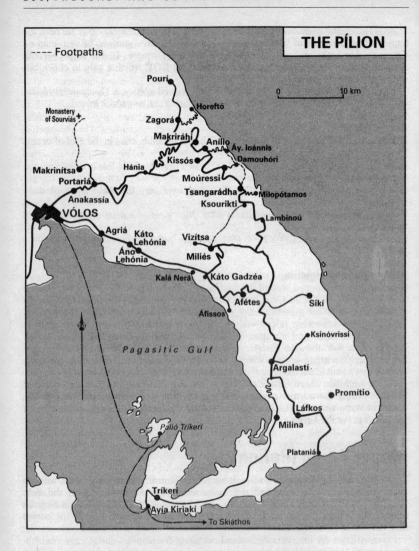

THE PÍLION

---- Footpaths

0   10 km

Pourí

Monastery
of Sourviás

Horeftó

Zagorá

Makriráhi

Anílio

Áy. Ioánnis

Kissós

Damouhóri

Hánia

Makrinítsa

Moúressi

Portariá

Tsangarádha

Milópótamos

Anakassía

Ksourikti

VÓLOS

Lambinoú

Agriá

Káto
Lehónia

Vizítsa

Áno
Lehónia

Miliés

Kalá Nerá

Káto Gadzéa

Afétes

Sikí

Áfissos

Ksinóvrissi

Pagasitic Gulf

Argalastí

Promítio

Láfkos

Palió Trikeri

Milína

Plataniá

Tríkeri

Ayía Kiriakí

→ To Skiáthos

built in a low, wide style, often with a detached belltower and always ornamented with
carved wood. Two communities – **Makrinítsa** and **Vizítsa** – have been designated by
the EOT as protected showpieces of the region, but almost every hamlet boasts a
mansion, church or at least a view.

    Add to the above the presence of a half-dozen or so excellent **beaches**, and you have
a recipe for an instant holiday idyll – or disaster, if your timing is wrong. Lying roughly
midway between Athens and Thessaloniki, the Pílion is all too convenient for Greek
vacationers, and you'd be pushing your luck more than usual to show up in August
without a reservation; prices also are comparatively high for the mainland.

Getting around Pílion

The peninsula breaks into three regions, with the best concentration of traditional villages **north** of Vólos and along the **east coast**. The **west** coast is less scenically interesting, with much more beach development. The **south**, low-lying and sparsely populated, has just one major resort, Plataniás, and a few small inland hamlets.

Travelling between the villages can be tricky without your own transport. **Buses** to the east cover two main routes – Vólos–Haniá–Zagorá (3–5 daily) and Vólos–Tsangarádha–Áyios Ioánnis via Mílies (2 daily) – with just one daily service linking Zagorá and Tsangarádha to allow a complete loop of the peninsula. The far south is equally sparsely served, with just two or three departures a day to Plataniás and Tríkeri, though the respective northern and western highlights of Makrinítsa and Vizítza both have excellent connections.

Alternatives are to **rent a car** in Vólos (especially if you're pushed for time); some very uncertain hitching; or **walking**. The latter means slow progress, since roads snake around ravine contours, seeming never to get closer to villages just across the way, though a limited number of old cobbled **paths** (*kalderími*) provide short cuts.

Leaving the Pílion, you needn't necessarily return to Vólos but can take advantage of a daily summer **hydrofoil from Plataniás** to islands of the Sporades; this seems to have replaced the former *kaíki* service from Plataniás to Koukounariés on Skiáthos.

Makrinítsa and the north

Before crossing over to the east coast on the main Vólos–Zagorá axis, consider pausing en route: both **Portariá** and **Makrinítsa** villages have intrinsic attractions and make good first or last stops out of Vólos.

Anakassía and Portariá

The first of the Pílion villages, **ANAKASSÍA** is just 4km out of Vólos, and few casual visitors give it more than a passing glance. What they miss is a small but very beautiful museum dedicated to the "naive" painter **Theophilos** (1873–1934). A grand eccentric, originally from Lésvos, Theophilos lived for long periods in both Athens and Vólos, where he wandered around, often dressed in traditional costumes, painting frescoes for anyone prepared to either pay or feed him. In the Pílion you find his work in the most unlikely places, mostly unheralded, including a number of village tavernas and *kafenía*. Here, the **museum** (daily 9am–1pm) occupies the **Arhondikó Kondós**, an eighteenth-century mansion whose first floor he entirely frescoed with scenes from the Greek War of Independence – one of his favourite themes.

PORTARIÁ, 10km on, has a more mountainous feel with a startling soundtrack of running streams. Of late, regrettably, it has become tackily commercialised – the areas closest to the busy road at least. Its chief glory, as so often in the Pílion, is its main square, shaded by a tremendous plane tree. If you decide to stay, you can pick from almost a dozen pensions, traditional inns and **hotels**, cheapest among which are the *Filoxenia* (☎0421/99 160; ②) and *Theoxenia* (☎0421/99 527; ④).

Makrinítsa

From Portariá many buses detour northwest to **MAKRINÍTSA**, 17km from Volos and 600m up the mountain. If your time in the Pílion is severely limited, this is perhaps the best single target. Founded in 1204 by refugees from the first sacking of Constantinople, it boasts six outstanding churches and a monastery, and a group of **traditional mansions** – three of which have been restored as lodges by the EOT.

There's a 200-metre altitude difference between the upper and lower quarters of Makrinítsa, so to get a full sense of the village takes a full day's rambling. Most impressive of the churches are **Áyios Ioánnis**, next to the fountain on the shady main *platía*, and the **monastery of Theotókos**, right under the clock tower. Many of the sanctuaries and frescoes here are only a few centuries old but the marble relief work on some of the apses (the curvature behind the altar) is the best of its type in Greece. A few metres on from the Áyios Ioánnis square there are **Theophilos frescoes** in a café. If you are looking for a major walk in Pílion, the village is also the starting point for a long **trail** over to the deserted monastery of Sourviás.

The EOT lodges are very pleasant but expensive **accommodation**. The best is the *Arhondíko Mousli* (☎0421/99 228; ⑤). A somewhat cheaper private operation – again in a traditional mansion – is the *Pilioritiko Spiti* (☎0421/99 194; ③).

The *Kafe-Bar Pantheon*, by the square, is the best place to eat, specialising in the local *spédzofai*.

Hánia

Travelling on over the mountain, beyond Portariá, the road hairpins up to the **Hánia pass**, and the village of the same name, a stark cluster of modern houses. To the south a road leads in 4km to a small, winter **ski resort** (open Jan–March). Once over the Hánia pass, the view suddenly opens to take in the whole east coast, as you spiral down to a fork: leading left to Zagorá, right towards Tsangarádha.

Zagorá and the east

The Pílion's best (and most popular) beaches and lushest scenery are to be found on the Aegean-facing **east coast**. Transport hub for the region is Zagorá.

Zagorá and Pourí

The largest Pílion village, **ZAGORÁ**, has a life more independent of tourism than its neighbours, and is a lot more interesting than first impressions of its concrete main street suggest. In addition to this section of the village, it has two other architecturally well-preserved communities, based around the squares of **Ayía Paraskeví** – to the west above the road – and **Ayía Kiriakí**. Both host a couple of grill-tavernas, of which the most attractive is *O Takis* (open lunchtimes) in Ayía Kiriakí, with seating in the shadow of a giant basilica. An interesting sight, down on the second bend of the road to Horeftó beach, is the **Riga Fereou** "secret school", now an art gallery/folk museum (daily 9.30am–1.30pm & 5.30–8.30pm).

Accommodation in Zagorá comes a little cheaper than elsewhere. There are several rooms advertised and a spruce little hotel, the *Haravghi* (☎0426/22 550; ③), near Ayía Kiriakí. There's also an **OTE**, a **post office** and bank agent – the only such services between here and Tsangarádha, though the nearby coastal resorts are well geared up to change your money.

The road from Zagorá to **POURÍ**, one of the northernmost communities on Pílion, is a spectacular approach and the village itself is regally situated and appealing; it has no accommodation. It used to be a good trailhead for walks, with a path leading into the hills over towards Makrinítsa, via the deserted monastery of Sourviás. Unfortunately this path is now hopelessly jumbled and overgrown.

Horeftó

The nearest sand to Zagorá is eight twisting kilometres down the mountain at **HOREFTÓ** (3 buses daily; hitching – and a few short cuts walking – is possible). There are several beaches here: an enormous one in front of the former fishing village, and another smaller bay (used by nude bathers) around the headland at the north end, where the road stops. If you're still not satisfied, a coastal path continues twenty minutes more to the coves of **Análipsi** – the southerly one a little paradise with a spring, popular with freelance campers, the further road-accessible and rockier.

Horeftó supports half a dozen **hotels** and a lot of rooms for rent. The best value and best-located hotels are the *Votsala* (☎0426/22 001; ③) and *Erato* (☎0426/22 445; ③), both at the quiet, southern end of the coast road. The *Cleopatra* (☎0426/22 606; ③), small, central and noisier, or the *Aegeus* (☎0426/22 778; ③), uphill above the road in from Zagorá, would be second choices, though in high season you'll be lucky to find space at any. The village also has a **campsite**, with decent amenities but rather remote at the extreme south end of the main beach.

Among **restaurants**, the oddly named *Ahilleio OK* on the esplanade is filling if unimaginative. *To Meltemi*, on the beach, has more pretensions to haute cuisine. Two or three bar-pubs provide evening distractions.

Áyios Ioánnis and around

Bearing east at the junction below Haniá, the road winds down from Mount Pílion past MAKRIRÁHI and ANÍLIO, both spoilt by concrete development, towards KISSÓS. This is a much more traditional slice of Pílion – and an enjoyable stop. Set just off the main road, it is virtually buried in foliage, with quarters ascending in terraces and, in eighteenth-century Ayía Marína, one of the finest churches on the peninsula. **Rooms and meals** are available at the *Xenonas Kissos* (☎0426/31 214; ②), which could be a good inland base for exploration. Half-overgrown tracks wander tentatively from the village up towards the ski-lift ridge.

Heading for the coast, it's six kilometres of twisting asphalt down to **ÁYIOS IOÁNNIS**, eastern Pílion's major resort. Despite the sixteen hotels and double that number of private rooms, finding a bed is as problematic as anywhere on the mountain in summer; a small **tourist office** can advise on where there are vacancies, or if necessary on times of buses out. Good budget options include the **hotels** *Kohyli* (☎0426/31 229; ③), *Avra* (☎0426/31 224; ③) and *Armonia* (☎0426/31 242; ③), the last with a decent taverna. There is also a **campsite**, ten minutes' walk south of the village. For a splurge meal, try the elegant *Ostria* taverna, which features traditional Pílion dishes.

The **beach** at Áyios Ioánnis is popular and commercialised, with windsurf boards and waterskis for rent, and the like. For a quieter strand, walk either ten minutes north to **Pláka** beach, with rough camping and for the most part a young, Greek clientele, or fifteen minutes south (past the campsite) to sleepy **Papaneró** beach, fronted by a few rooms for rent and two tavernas.

South from Papaneró, a fairly well-marked mix of tracks and paths leads to **DAMOÚHORI**, a hamlet set amid olive trees and fringing a secluded fishing harbour. It has, alas, been discovered with a vengeance in recent years, following construction of a new road down from Moúressi; spotted here last year was a Greek first – a "No rooms to rent" sign – glimpsed hanging on one of the few buildings that *doesn't* provide accommodation. However, there is a large pebble beach, two pleasant tavernas, and the ruins of a Venetian castle.

From Damoúhori, it's possible to **walk to Tsangarádha** in a little over an hour. At the mouth of the ravine leading down to the larger bay, a spectacular *kalderimi* or stairway begins its ascent, allowing glimpses of up to six villages simultaneously, and even the Sporades on a clear day, from points along the way. The path emerges in the Ayía Paraskeví quarter of Tsangarádha.

Tsangarádha and Moúressi

TSANGARÁDHA is the largest northeastern village after Zagorá, though it may not seem so at first since it's divided into four distinct quarters, scattered along several kilometres of road. Each of these is grouped around a namesake church and *platía*, the finest of which is **Ayía Paraskeví**, shaded by reputedly the largest plane tree in Greece – a thousand years old and with an eighteen-metre trunk. Below it is a *kafenío* and a not very inspired taverna, *I Anatoli*, open only in the evening.

Most **accommodation** around the village is on the noisy main highway. Exceptions include the modern, friendly *Villa ton Rodhon* (☎0426/49 340; ③), on the cobbled path to Damoúhari, and the traditional *Villa Edem* (☎0426/49 377; ③), further down the same way. In **Ayíou Stefánou**, the easternmost district, there are panoramic views from the *Hotel San Stefano* (☎0426/49 213; ③), plus a rather average taverna by the church. There are also some rooms for rent in the southern parish of **Taxiárhes** (linked by a *kalderími* with Ayía Paraskeví), and an acceptable taverna, *To Kalivi*,

In general, better cooking is to be had at **MOÚRESSI**, a few kilometres back on the road. At either *I Dhrosia* or *To Tavernaki* here, you can get specialities like *fasólies hándres* (delicately flavoured white pinto beans) and assorted offal-on-a-spit.

Milopótamos and the coast to Lambinoú

From Tsangarádha a hairpin road (with a daily bus) snakes seven kilometres down to **MILOPÓTAMOS**, a pair of pebble coves separated by a naturally tunnelled rock wall. At the larger bay, there are a couple of tavernas; on the smaller, some interesting rock formations to dive off. They attract a multinational summer crowd, who are catered for by a series of rooms for rent on the approach road.

If you want to swim in more solitude, try **Fakístra beach**, a cliff-girt, white-gravel bay, just to the north. A new road is being constructed down here from Tsangarádha but for the present it's reached by 4km of asphalt and 3km of dirt track, putting off the crowds.

Other beaches on the south side of Milopótamos include **Lambinoú** and **Kalamáki**, both well signposted, along with their inland villages. They have a more open feel since the dramatic terrain is beginning to subside.

En route from Tsangarádha to Lambinoú, the village of KSORÍHTI is the eastern trailhead for an enjoyable three-hour **trail to Miliés**. The path has been marked throughout by a distinctive three-serial-dot tracing. Before the road around the hill via Lambinoú and Kalamáki was built in 1938, this was the principal thoroughfare between the railhead at Míliés and the Tsangarádha area.

Miliés, Vizítsa and the western coast

Lying in the "rain shadow" of the mountain, the western Pílion villages and coast have a drier, more Mediterranean climate, with olives and arbutus shrubs. The beaches, at least until you get past Kalá Nerá, are a bit overdeveloped and in any case lack the character of those on the east side. Inland, however, is a different story, with pleasant foothill villages – and for a change, a decent bus service.

Additionally, scheduled for reintroduction in 1993 are summer **steam locomotive** services on the old *trenaki* – miniature (0.6m) railway – line between Vólos and Miliés. The line, in service until 1972, was laid out early this century by an Italian company.

Miliés

Like Tsangarádha, **MILIÉS** (variously spelled Miléës, Mileaí) is a sizeable village that was an important centre of culture during the eighteenth century. It retains a number of imposing mansions and an interesting church, the **Taxiárhis**, whose narthex (usually kept open) is decorated with brilliant frescoes.

Accommodation is a choice between a handful of inexpensive rooms overlooking the church and *platía*, run by Mihalis Pappas (☎0423/86 207; ②), and *O Paleos Stathmos* (☎0423/86 425; ⑤), a luxury inn and restaurant converted from the old 1920s railway station below the town. Other alternatives for food are a couple of café-restaurants on the village square; a simple grill, *Panorama*; and *To Aloni*, a fancy, over-priced restaurant on the Vizítsa road. The most distinctive food in town emanates from a superb **bakery** down on the road by the bus stop, which cranks out every kind of Pílion bread, pie, turnover and cake imaginable.

Vizítsa

VIZÍTSA, 3km further up the mountain, is preserved as a "traditional settlement" by the EOT. It has a more open and less pickled feel than either Makrinítsa or Miliés, though it draws surprisingly large crowds of day-trippers in summer. The best way to enjoy the place is to stay at one of the **EOT guesthouses**, converted, once again, from the finest of the mansions. For reservations, call ☎0423/86 793 (⑤ in season; ④ out). There are also some cheaper **rooms** establishments, such as that of Kalliroi Dhimou (☎0423/86 484; ③). *O Yiorgaras* is by far the best of three tavernas on the *platía*.

A mere two kilometres of rough farm track separates Vizítsa from the village of PINAKÁTES to the west, terminus of another bus line that threads through ÁYIOS YIÓRYIOS and ÁYIOS VLÁSIOS on its way back to Vólos. While these may not be unadulterated architectural showcases, they merit a brief visit.

Agriá, Káto Gatzéa and inland,

As noted, most of the coast between Vólos and Korópi (below Miliés) is unenticing. At **AGRIÁ**, for example, a cement plant casts its shadow over rashes of hotels and neon-garish tavernas. Heading southeast, things improve temporarily around **KÁTO GATZÉA**, with olive groves lining the road, which now runs well inland; of the two **campsites** here, *Hellas* has the edge over the *Marina*.

A better inland route, if you have your own transport, is through the larger settlements of **DHRAKIÁ** and **ÁYIOS LAVRÉNDIS**. Dhrakiá boasts the Triandafillou mansion and an August 23 festival; Áyios Lavréndis is more homogenous but has the useful *Pension Kentavros* (☎0421/96 224; ③).

The south

Once **south of the loop road** around the mountain, the Pílion becomes more arid and less dramatic, its villages lacking the historic interest and character of their northern counterparts. There are, though, some interesting pockets and, save for a French-run **riding stables** near PROMÍRI, a distinct lack of tourism.

The area can be reached a little tortuously by bus but much easier by sea. In summer, **hydrofoils** from Vólos call at least daily at the port of **Ayía Kiriakí**, and from there you can also catch boats to the little island of **Paleó Tríkeri**.

Argalastí and Plataniá

To get a better idea of the low-lying, olive-grove countryside of the western Pílion, press on south from Kalá Nerá to the junction of **ARGALASTÍ**, the "county town". From here you can get several daily buses to **HÓRTO** (7km) and **MILÍNA** (10km), small beach villages with seasonal **campsites** and rooms for rent.

Argalastí or Kalá Nerá are also the pick-up points for Vólos-based buses passing three times daily on their way to **PLATANIÁ**, a small resort near the end of the Pílion peninsula. The beach is excellent though the resort is often a bit crowded with Greek holidaymakers. Among the half-dozen **hotels**, try the *des Roses* (☎0423/65 568; ③), *Kyma* (☎0423/65 569; ③) or *Platania* (☎0423/65 565; ③).

Tríkeri

Stranded at the far end of the Pílion, the semi-peninsula of **Tríkeri** feels very remote. It was used after the 1946–49 civil war as a place of exile for political prisoners (along with the island of Paleó Tríkeri), and until a few years ago there was no real road connecting it with the rest of the Pílion. There's now an unpaved road from Milína and a daily bus from Vólos, but the area can be reached more conveniently by hydrofoil from Vólos or the Sporades (daily from April to October, going up to twice daily between June and September).

The port of **AYÍA KIRIAKÍ** is still strictly a working fishing village, something of a rarity in modern Greece. Apart from a few **rooms to rent**, there are no concessions to tourism, perhaps because there's no good beach. The village is attractive enough, if you're happy to do little apart from watch the fishing boats. In the local boatyard, large caiques, and occasionally yachts, are built in much the same way they must have been for the last hundred years.

From Ayia Kiriakí, it's a 25-minute walk up to the village of **TRÍKERI**, either by an old *kalderími* or a series of steps that starts behind the port police building or by road. This is a pleasant hilltop village with a scattering of mansions and a tree-shaded *platía* with a *kafenía* and an excellent traditional *ouzeri*. There's also a taverna, with some **rooms** above, by the road down to the harbour.

Paleó Tríkeri

Paleó Tríkeri (or Nisí Tríkeri – Tríkeri island) has a village, a hotel, a couple of tavernas and sand – which perhaps makes it the smallest Greek island with everything you really need. Little more than a kilometre end to end, it consists of a few olive-covered hills and an edge of small, rocky beaches; it is friendly and uncrowded, and has its own charm.

The port and village, **AÏ YÁNNI**, is tiny, with a single shop and a good taverna by the harbour. Around the island from here, there are just donkey tracks. Following the track up from the village, for around ten minutes, you reach the nineteenth-century **Evangelistrías monastery** – and the centre of the island. The monastery is locked and deserted, but you can get a key at a nearby farmhouse. Past here, you reach a large bay and the island **hotel**, the *Paleo Trikeri* (☎0423/91 432; ③), with a restaurant overlooking the beach. There's no problem camping under the olive trees nearby.

The island is connected with Ayía Kiriakí only once a week – currently on Sundays – by *Flying Dolphin* **hydrofoil**, though you may be able to find a fishing boat to take you; standard ferries to and from the Sporades also stop here most days. Information on connections to the island can be hard to come by, since they aren't mentioned in the published *Flying Dolphin* and *Nomicos Line* timetables, and coming from the Sporades you may find that everyone denies the existence of a stop. If all else fails, try calling the port police – *To Limenarhío* – in Vólos (☎0421/38 888).

Lárissa

LÁRISSA stands at the heart of the Thessalian plain: a large market centre aproached across a prosperous but dull landscape of wheat and corn fields. It is for the most part modern and unremarkable, but retains a few old streets (Venizélou, most notably) that hint at its recent past as a Turkish provincial capital. From above the town looms a medieval castle, with the military, as at Lamía, still in residence. Down below, the centre is marked by **Platía Stratoú**, a kilometre from the train station, while the most pleasant place to while away a few hours is the **Alcazar** park, beside the Piniós, Thessaly's major river.

As a major **road and rail junction**, the town has efficient connections with most places you'd want to reach: Vólos to the east; Tríkala and Kalambáka to the west; Lamía to the south; the Vale of Témbi (see below), Mount Olympus and Thessaloníki along the national highway to the northeast.

Should you need to stay in Lárissa, there are numerous **hotels**. Cheapest are a trio of places in the square by the train station: the *Diethnes* (☎041/234 210; ②), *Neon* (☎041/236 268; ②) and *Pantheon* (☎041/236 726; ②). More savoury options include the *Acropole* at Venizélou 142 (☎041/227 843; ③) and the *Atlantic* at Panagoúli 1 (☎041/250 201; ③).

North towards Mount Olympus: the Vale of Témbi and the coast

Travelling north from Lárisssa, the National Highway heads towards Thessaloníki, a highly scenic route through the **Vale of Témbi**, between Mounts Olympus and Óssa, before emerging on the coast. The valley and the best of the **beaches**, east of Mount Óssa, follow; for details on Mount Olympus, see the Macedonia chapter.

Ambelákia

If you have time, or a vehicle, a worthwhile first stop in the Témbi region is **AMBELÁKIA**, a small town in the foothills of Mount Óssa. In the eighteenth century this community supported the world's first **industrial cooperative**, producing, dyeing and exporting textiles, and maintaining its own branch offices as far afield as London. With the cooperative came a rare and enlightened prosperity. At a time when most of Greece lay stagnant under Turkish rule, Ambelákia was largely autonomous; it held democratic assemblies, offered free education and medical care, and even subsidised weekly performances of ancient drama. The brave experiment lasted over a century, eventually succumbing to the triple ravages of war, economics and the industrial revolution. In 1811 Ali Pasha raided the town and a decade later any chance of recovery was lost with the collapse of the Viennese bank in which the town's wealth was deposited.

Until World War II, however, over six hundred mansions survived in the town. Today there are just thirty-six, most in poor condition. You can still get some idea of the former prosperity by visiting the restored **Mansion of George Schwartz**. The home of the cooperative's last president, this *arhondíko* (Tues–Sun 9.30am–3.30pm) is built in grand, old-Constantinople style. Schwartz, incidentally, was a Greek, despite the German-sounding name, which was merely the Austrian bank's translation of his real surname, Mavros (Black).

The town is connected by bus with Lárissa (3 daily); or you can walk up a cobbled way in about an hour from the TÉMBI train station. There is a single **inn**, the *Ennea Mousses* (☎0495/31 405; ③), and a couple of tavernas.

Into the Vale of Témbi

Two kilometres beyond the Ambelákia turn-off, you enter the **Vale of Témbi**, a valley, nearly ten kilometres long, over the eons cut by the Piniós between the steep cliffs of the Olympus (Ólimbos) and Óssa ranges. In antiquity it was sacred to Apollo and one of the few possible approaches into Greece – it was the path taken by both Xerxes and Alexander the Great – and it remained an important passage during the Middle Ages. Walkers might consider a hike along the valley, which can also be traversed by canoe on the Piniós; however, both the National Road #1 and the railway forge through Témbi, impinging somewhat on its beauties.

Halfway through the vale (on the right, coming from Lárissa) are the ruins of the **Kástro tis Oreás** (Castle of the Beautiful Maiden), one of four Frankish guardposts here. Marking the northern end of the pass is a second medieval **fortress** at PLATAMÓNAS, this time built by the Crusaders.

Platamónas marks the beginning of **Macedonia** and heralds a rather grim succession of resorts fronting the narrow, pebbly beaches of the Thermaíkos gulf. The coast south of the castles is a better bet (see below). Inland, the mountain spectacle continues, with **Mount Olympus** (Óros Ólimbos) casting ever-longer shadows. The trailhead for climbing it is LITÓHORO, 7km inland (see p.322).

Stómio and the Óssa Coast

A side road, close by the Kástro tis Oreás, takes you the 13km to **STÓMIO**, an attractive seaside town at the mouth of the river Piniós. The dense beech trees of Óssa march down almost to the shore, giving Stómio almost the appearance of a mountain rather than coastal village. It's a fine spot for birdwatchers.

Outside July and August – when Stómio draws big crowds – you shouldn't have any trouble finding **accommodation**. There are various rooms for rent, self-catering apartments and two hotels, the *Argithea* (☎0495/91 323; ③) and *Drossia* (☎0495/91 365; ③). The free municipal **campsite** behind the beach is a bit squalid, offering cold-water sinks and toilets only, though there are showers on the beach. The best **eats** are in the town centre, where the night-pedestrianised high street has two grill-cafés, facing each other, dishing up chicken and lamb kebab – a Thessalian speciality – by weight.

Down the coast towards the Pílion, **KÓKKINO NERÓ** and **KOUTSÓPIA** have smaller beaches and are both rather scruffy resorts for Larissans and Trikalans. **AYIÓKAMBOS**, southeast of the attractive Óssa hill villages of AYIÁ and MELÍVIA, gets a more international crowd. All three beaches are served by bus from Lárissa, and Ayiókambos boasts a beach, a campsite and several pensions.

West from Lárissa: Tríkala and Píli

West from Lárissa, the road trails the river Piniós to **Tríkala**, a quiet provincial town with a scattering of Byzantine monuments nearby. For most travellers, it is simply a staging post en route to Kalambáka and the Metéora; five buses daily connect it with Lárissa and there are connections on. The railway loops around between Vólos, Lárissa, Tríkala and Kalambáka, via the uninteresting market town of KARDHÍTSA.

Tríkala

TRÍKALA is quite a lively metropolis after the agricultural towns of central Thessaly, spread along the banks of the Lethéos, a tributary of the Piniós. It was the main town of the nineteenth-century Turkish province and retains numerous houses from that era, stacked around the clock tower at the north end of town. Downriver from the bus station, a minaret-less Turkish mosque, the **Koursoum Tzami**, survives too, a graceful accompaniment to the town's numerous stone-built churches.

The liveliest part of town, encompassing the **bazaar**, is in the streets around the central Platía Iróön Politehníou on the riverside; off the square is a **post office** and **OTE**. The **bus station** is on the west bank of the river, 300m southeast of the square; the **train station** is found at the southwestern edge of town, at the end of Odhós Asklipíou. Inside and around the **fortress**, a Turkish adaptation of a Byzantine structure, are attractive gardens and the meagre remains of a **sanctuary of Asclepius**. The cult of the healing god (see p.152) is said, by some accounts, to have originated here.

Rooms and meals

Accommodation should pose few problems, with two decent and inexpensive **hotels** within sight of the main square, across the river: the rock-bottom *Panhellinion*, Vassilísis Ólgas 2 (☎0431/27 644; ②), and rather more comfortable *Palladion*, Víronos 4 (☎0431/28 091; ③). Another mid-range alternative is the *Lithaeon*, Óthonos 18 (☎0431/20 690; ③).

Aside from a rash of *ouzeri*-bars in the old bazaar, **restaurants** are scarce. The best lunch to be had is at *O Elatos*, at the junction of Asklipíou and Víronos in the pedestrian zone behind the hotels; there are also some good *zaharoplastía* in the same area.

Píli

It takes some effort of will to delay immediate progress to Kalambáka and the Metéora. Byzantine aficionados, however, may be tempted by a detour to **PÍLI**, 20km southwest of Tríkala, for the thirteenth-century church of **Pórta Panayía**, one of the unsung beauties of Thessaly, in a superb setting at the beginning of a gorge. Nearby, at the cloistered monastery of **Ayíou Visariónos Dousíkou** (men only admitted) there is a superb cycle of frescoes.

Regular **buses** run to the village from Tríkala. Near the Pórta Panayía and beside a fountain there are two **tavernas** – a far nicer lunch stop than Tríkala; in the village there is a single **hotel**, the *Babanara* (☎0431/22 325; ③). Midway to Píli, a road leads south in 2km to the village of GÓMFI, whose houses incorporate numerous ancient blocks from its Classical and Byzantine predecessors.

The Pórta Panayía

The **Pórta Panayía** (summer 8am–noon & 4–8pm; winter 9am–1pm & 3–5pm; 100dr) is a twenty-minute walk from Píli village. Cross the Portaikós river on either the road or foot bridges, then bear left on the far bank until you see its dome in a clump of trees below the rough road. The caretaker lives in a white house below the nearby tavernas.

The church was completed in 1283 by one Ioannis Doukas, a prince of the Despotate of Epirus. Its architecture is somewhat bizarre, in that the current narthex is a fifteenth-century remodelling of the original dome and transept. The original nave on its west side collapsed in an earthquake, and this replacement to the east gives the whole a "backwards" orientation. The highlights of the interior are a pair of **mosaic icons** depicting Joseph and Mary with the Child, both showing extensive westernising influences, and a marble iconostasis, which unusually (for Orthodox iconography) shows Christ on the left of the Virgin. The frescoes have fared less well and many of the figures are peppered with holes. The most interesting image is next to the tiny font, over Ioannis Doukas' tomb, where a lunette shows the Archangel Michael leading a realistically portrayed Doukas by the hand to the enthroned Virgin with Child.

A kilometre upstream, best reached along the Píli bank of the river (there are savage dogs beyond the church), a graceful **medieval bridge** spans the Portaïkós at the point where it exits a narrow mountain gorge. A couple of cafés and snack bars take advantage of the setting, and you can cross the bridge to follow paths some distance along the gorge on the opposite side.

Ayíou Visariónos Dousíkou

The monastery of **Ayíou Visariónos Dousíkou** – known locally as Aï Vissáris – has a stunning setting, fifteen hundred feet up a flank of Mount Kóziakas. It is an isolation that the small community of monks is keen to maintain, excluding women from visits, and admitting men only with suspicion; in theory, visits are allowed from 8am to noon and 3.30 to 7.30pm. To reach the monastery, cross the road bridge over the Portaïkós as for Pórta Panayía, then turn right instead, then left almost instantly onto a signed dirt track, which leads up in 4km.

The monastery was founded in 1530 by Visarionos (Bessarion), a native of Píli, and contains a perfect **cycle of frescoes** by Tzortzis – one of the major painters on Mount Athos – executed between 1550 and 1558 and recently restored to brilliance. These, and the cloister as a whole, miraculously escaped damage in 1940, when two Italian bombs fell in the court but failed to explode.

Originally, the monastery perched on a cliff as steep as any at Metéora, but in the 1960s the abyss was largely filled in with kitchen gardens and a new road and gate opened. This rendered ornamental the pulleys and ladder on the east, which, like much of the place, had survived intact since its foundation.

The Monasteries of the Metéora

The **Monasteries of the Metéora** are one of the great sights of mainland Greece. These extraordinary cloisters, perched on seemingly inaccessible pinnacles of rock, occupy a valley just to the north of **Kalambáka**; the name *metéora* means literally "rocks in the air". Arriving at the town, your eye is drawn in an unremitting vertical ascent to the first weird grey cylinders. Overhead to the right you can make out the closest of the monasteries, Ayíou Stefánou, firmly entrenched on a massive pedestal; beyond stretch a chaotic confusion of spikes, cones and cliffs – beaten into bizarre and otherworldly shapes by the action of the prehistoric sea that covered the plain of Thessaly around thirty million years ago.

The monasteries: some history

The Meteorite monasteries are as enigmatic as they are spectacular. Legend has it that **Saint Athanasios**, who founded Méga Metéoron (the Great Meteoron), the earliest of the buildings, flew up to the rocks on the back of an eagle. More rational attempts at their history suggest that the villagers of Stáyi, the medieval precursor of Kalambáka, may have become adept at climbing, and helped the original monks up. Whatever, the difficulties of access and building are hard to overstate; a German guide published for rock climbers grades almost all the Metéora routes as "advanced", even with modern high-tech climbing gear.

The earliest religious communities here appeared in the late tenth century, when groups of **hermits** made their homes in the caves that score many of the rocks. In 1336 they were joined by two monks from Mount Athos, **Gregorios**, Abbot of Magoula, and his companion, **Athanasios**. Gregorios returned shortly to Athos but he left Athanasios behind, ordering him to establish a monastery. This Athanasios did, whether supernaturally aided or not, and despite imposing a particularly austere and ascetic rule he was quickly joined by many brothers, including, in 1371, **John Palaeologos**, who refused the throne of Serbia to become the monk Ioasaph.

Such a royal presence was an important aid to the **endowment** of the monasteries, which followed swiftly on all the accessible and many of the inaccessible rocks. They reached their zenith during the Ottoman reign of Suleiman the Magnificent (1520–66), by which time twenty-four of the rocks had been surmounted by monasteries and hermitages. The major establishments accumulated great wealth, flourishing on revenues of estates granted them in distant Wallachia and Moldavia, as well as in Thessaly itself. They retained these estates, more or less intact, through to the eighteenth century, at which time monasticism here, as elsewhere in Greece, was in decline.

During the intervening centuries, numerous disputes arose over power and precedence among the monasteries. However, the principal factors in the Metéora's fall from glory were physical and economic. Many of the buildings, especially the smaller hermitages, were just not built to withstand centuries of use and, perhaps neglected or unoccupied, gradually disintegrated. The grander monasteries suffered depopulation, conspicuously so in the nineteenth century as a modern Greek state was established to the south – with Thessaly itself excluded – and monasticism lost its link with Greek nationalism and resistance to Turkish rule.

In the present century the crisis accelerated after the monastic lands and revenues, already much reduced from their heyday, were taken over by the state for the use of Greek refugees front Asia Minor, after the Greco-Turkish war of 1920–23. By the 1950s, there were just five active monasteries, struggling along with little more than a dozen monks between them – an epoch that's superbly chronicled in a chapter of Patrick Leigh Fermor's *Roumeli*. Ironically, before their expropriation for **tourism** over the last three decades, the monasteries had begun to revive a little, attracting a number of young and intellectual brothers. Today, put firmly on the map by appearances in such films as James Bond's *For Your Eyes Only*, the four most accessible monasteries are today essentially museum-piece monuments. Only two, **Ayía Triádha** and **Ayíou Stefánou**, continue to function with any real monastic purpose.

Kalambáka and Kastráki

Visiting the Metéora demands a full day, which means staying at least one night in **Kalambáka** or at the village of **Kastráki**, 2km to the north. Either makes a pleasant enough base, though Kastráki wins hands down on atmosphere and situation, set as it is right in the shadow of the rocks. It also has the local campsites.

Kalambáka

KALAMBÁKA has no particular appeal, save for its position near the rocks. The town was burnt by the Germans in the last war and very few pre-war buildings remain, save for the old cathedral. This, the **Mitrópolis**, stands a couple of streets above its modern successor, at the top end of the town. It was founded in the seventh century on the site of a temple to Apollo and incorporates various classical drums and fragments in its erratically designed walls. Inside are fourteenth-century Byzantine frescoes and, most unusually in a Greek church, a great marble pulpit in the central aisle.

Arriving by **bus or train**, in season, you are likely to be offered a **room** by waiting householders – often the Totis family, who have three separate premises (☎0432/22 251 or 23 588; ③). If not, there are numerous signs on the road into town from the bus station. **Hotels** are pricier, with above-usual rates reflecting the tourist status of the Metéora. Mid-budget options include the *Odyssion*, Odhós Kastrakíou (☎0432/22 320; ③) and the *Olympia*, Trikálon 97 (☎0432/22 792; ③).

Kastráki

KASTRÁKI is twenty minutes' walk out of Kalambáka; there's a short cut if you follow a footpath out of the northwest corner of the town. In season there are occasional buses.

Along the way to the village you pass *Camping Vrahos* (☎0432/22 293), the first of two **campsites** here. The other, *Camping Boufidhis/The Cave*, is a bit more cramped but incomparably set on the far side of the village, with the monasteries of Ayíou Nikoláou and Roussánou rearing above. Both have swimming pools, as do the other two more distant sites out on the Tríkala and Ioánnina roads.

The village also has a fair number of **rooms** for rent, as well as a rather dilapidated hotel, the *Kastraki* (☎0342/22 286; ③), below the rocks. On Kastráki's central *platía*, *To Kalami* is an authentic local taverna with excellent fare.

The Monasteries

North from Kastráki the road loops around between huge outcrops of rock, passing below the chapel-hermitage of **Doupianí**, the first communal church of the early monastic settlements. This takes around twenty minutes to walk. A further ten minutes and you reach a track to the left, which winds around and up a low rock, on which is sited **Áyios Nikólaos Anapavsá**. A small, recently restored monastery, this has some superb sixteenth-century frescoes in its *katholikón* (main chapel) by the Cretan painter Theophanes. Oddly, the *katholikón* faces almost due north rather than east because of the rock's shape. As well as the Theophanes paintings there are later, naive-style images that show Adam naming the animals, including a basilisk – the serpent of classical legend that could kill by a breath or glance.

Next to Áyios Nikólaos, on a needle-thin shaft, sits **Ayía Moní**, inaccessible now, ruined and empty since an earthquake in 1858.

METÉORA PRACTICALITIES

There are six Metéora monasteries, each open to visits at different hours (see below). To see them all in a day, start early to take in Áyios Nikólaos, Varlaám and Méga Metéoron before 1pm, leaving the rest of the day for Roussánou, Ayía Triádha and Ayíou Stefánou.

The road route from **Kastráki to Ayíou Stefánou** is just under 10km. Walking, you can veer off the tarmac occasionally onto a few short-cut paths; at Ayíou Stefánou the "circuit" stops (the road signposted Kalambáka just before Ayía Triádha is a highly indirect 5km), though there is a walkers' path from here back to Kalambáka. In season there are a couple of daily buses from Kalambáka up the road as far as Méga Metéoron/ Varlaám; even taken just part of the way they will give you the necessary head start to make a hiking day manageable. Hitching is also pretty straightforward.

Before setting out it is worth buying **food and drink** to last the day; there are only a couple of drinks/fruit stalls on the circuit, by the Méga Metéoron. And finally, don't forget to carry money with you: each monastery levies an admission charge – currently 200dr, with half off for students except at Ayía Triádha.

Opening hours for the monasteries are as follows:

Áyios Nikólaos Anapavsá Daily summer 9am–5pm ; winter 9am–1pm and 3–5pm.

Varlaám 9am–1pm & 3–6pm; closed Friday.

Méga Metéoron 9am–1pm and 3–6pm; closed Tuesday.

Roussánou Daily 9am–6pm.

Ayía Triádha Daily 9am–6pm.

Ayíou Stefánou 9am–1pm and 3–6pm; closed Monday.

For visits to all the monasteries, **dress code** is strict. For women this means wearing a skirt – not trousers; for men, long trousers. Both sexes must cover their shoulders. Skirts are usually lent to female visitors, but it's best not to count on this.

Roussánou

Bearing off to the right, fifteen minutes or so further on from Áyios Nikólaos, a trio of well-signed and cobbled paths ascend from various points on the road to the tiny and compact convent of **Roussánou** (also known as Ayías Varváras); the final approach is across a dizzying bridge from an adjacent rock. Again recently restored and opened, Roussánou has perhaps the most extraordinary site of all the monasteries, its walls built right on the edge of a sharp and imposing blade. Inside, the narthex of its main chapel, or *katholikón*, has particularly gruesome seventeenth-century frescoes of martyrdom and judgement, the only respite from sundry beheadings, spearings and mutilations being the lions licking Daniel's feet in his imprisonment, near the window.

A short way beyond Roussánou the road divides, the left fork heading towards Varlaám and the Méga Metéoron. Varlaám is also directly accessible on foot by a path leading off from the road-curve just past Áyios Nikólaos.

Varlaám (Balaam)

Varlaám is one of the earliest-established monasteries, standing on the site of a hermitage established by Saint Varlaam – a key figure in Meteorite history – shortly after Athanasios's arrival. The present building was founded by two brothers from Ioánnina in 1517 and is one of the most beautiful in the valley.

The monastery's *katholikón*, dedicated to Ayíon Pándon (All Saints), is small but glorious, supported by painted beams and with walls and pillars totally covered in frescoes. A dominant theme, well suited to the Metéora, are the desert ascetics; more conventionally, there is a highly vivid *Last Judgement*, with a gaping Hell's Mouth, and, dominating the hierarchy of paintings, a great *Pandokrátor* (Christ in Majesty) in the

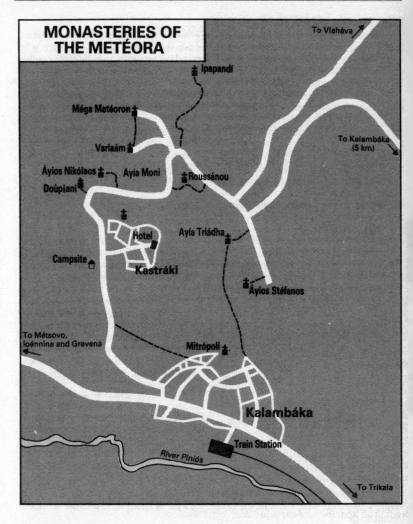

MONASTERIES OF THE METÉORA

To Vlaháva

Ipapandí

Méga Metéoron

To Kalambáka (5 km)

Varlaám

Áyios Nikólaos Ayía Moní Roussánou

Doúpiani

Hotel

Ayía Triádha

Campsite

Kastráki

Áyios Stéfanos

To Métsovo, Ioánnina and Grevená

Mitrópoli

Kalambáka

Train Station

River Piniós

To Trikala

dome; they were painted in 1548 and 1566. In the refectory is a small museum of icons, and elsewhere the monks' original water barrel is displayed.

Varlaám also retains intact its old **Ascent Tower**, with a precipitous reception platform and dubious windlass mechanism. Until the 1920s the only way of reaching most of the Meteorite monasteries was by being hauled up in a net drawn by rope and windlass, or by the equally perilous retractable ladders. Patrick Leigh Fermor, who stayed at Varlaám in the 1950s, reported the anecdote of a former abbot; asked how often the rope was changed, he gave the macabre, if logical, reply: "When it breaks".

Steps were eventually cut to all of the monasteries on the orders of the Bishop of Tríkala, doubtless unnerved by the vulnerability of his authority on visits. Today the ropes are used only for carrying up supplies and building materials.

Méga Metéoron (Great Meteora)

The **Méga Metéoron** (Great Meteora) is the grandest and highest of the monasteries, built on the "Broad Rock" nearly 2000 feet above the ground. It had extensive privileges and held jurisdiction over the area for several centuries; in an eighteenth-century engraving (displayed in the museum) it is depicted literally towering above the others. How Athanasios got onto this rock is a wonder.

The monastery's **katholikón**, dedicated to the Metamórfosi (Transfiguration), is the most magnificent in Metéora, a beautiful cross-in-square church surmounted by a lofty dome. It was rebuilt in the sixteenth century, with the original chapel, constructed by Athanasios and Ioasaph, forming just the *ierón*, the sanctuary behind the *témblon*, or altar screen. The other monastery rooms comprise a vast, arched cluster of buildings. In the refectory is a **museum**, featuring a number of exquisite carved-wood crosses, and the ancient domed and smoke-blackened kitchen can also be visited.

Coming from Varlaám a path short-cuts the road approach to Méga Metéoron.

Ipapandis, Ayías Triádhos and Ayíou Stefánou

If you are visiting the valley in midsummer, you may by this point be impressed by the buildings but depressed by the crowds – which blur much of the wild, spiritual romance of the valley. The remaining monasteries on the "south loop" are less visited, or for a real escape, you can take a path leading north from just past the Varlaám/Great Meteora fork which will bring you out, in around half an hour's walk, at the abandoned fourteenth-century monastery of **Ipapandís**, a cave containing a small church.

Following the main road, it's about thirty minutes' walk from the Varlaám/Great Meteora fork to **Ayía Triádha** (or Ayías Triádhos – Holy Trinity), whose final approach consists of 130 steps carved into a tunnel in the rock. You emerge into a light and airy cloister, recently renovated, though a new winch and water system are still needed. There's a small folk museum of weavings and kitchen/farm implements, but in general less to be seen than elsewhere – many of the frescoes in the *katholikón* are black with soot and damp, a project to clean and restore them having stalled at an early stage. Most tour buses, mercifully, do not stop here, and the life of the place remains essentially monastic – even if there are only three brothers to maintain it.

Ayíou Stefánou, the last and easternmost of the monasteries, is twenty minutes' walk beyond here, appearing suddenly at a bend in the road. Again it is active, occupied this time by nuns, and the buildings are a little disappointing. The *katholikón* is whitewashed and simple, while the rock on which it stands is spanned by a bridge from the road. Its view, of course, is amazing – like every turn and twist of this valley – but if you're pushed for time it's the obvious one to leave out.

Although Ayía Triádha teeters above a deep ravine and the little garden ends in a precipitous drop, there is an obvious, well-signposted **path** at the bottom of the monastery's steps that leads **back to Kalambáka**. This is about three kilometres in length, saving a long trudge back around the circuit; it's a partly cobbled, all-weather surface in decent shape.

On from Kalambáka

West from Kalambáka runs one of the most dramatic roads in Greece, negotiating the **Katára Pass** across the Píndhos mountains to MÉTSOVO and IOÁNNINA. This route, taking you into northern Epirus, is covered at the beginning of the next chapter.

North from Kalambáka a road leads into Macedonia, through GREVENÁ, and then forks: north to KASTORIÁ, or east to SIÁTISTA, KOZÁNI, VÉRIA and THESSALONÍKI (see *Macedonia and Thrace*). The **Grevená road**, despite its uncertain appearance on most maps, is quite reasonable; its only drawback is that there's just one daily bus (mid-morning) to dull Grevená itself, and not a lot of other transport.

travel details

Buses

Buses detailed have similar frequency in each direction, so entries are given just once; for reference check under both starting-point and destination.

Connections with Athens Thíva/Livádhia (hourly; 1hr 30min/2hr 10min); Delphi (4–6 daily; 3hr 30min); Lamía (hourly; 3hr 15min); Karpeníssi (2 daily; 6hr); Vólos (9 daily; 5hr 15min); Lárissa (6 daily; 5hr); Tríkala (7 daily; 5hr 30min).

From Elefsína Thíva [Thebes] (2 daily; 1hr 30min).

From Thíva Livádhia (hourly; 1hr); Halkídha (2 daily; 1hr 20min).

From Livádhia Aráhova/Delphi (6 daily; 40min/1hr); Dhístomo, for Óssios Loukás (10 daily; 45min); Óssios Loukás, direct (daily at 1pm; 1hr).

From Delphi Itéa (5 to 9 daily; 30min); Ámfissa (4 daily; 40min); Náfpaktos (4 daily – not direct; 2hr).

From Itéa Galaxídhi/Náfpaktos (4 daily; 30min/1hr 30min).

From Náfpaktos City bus to Andírio for most connections.

From Andírio Messolóngi/Agrínio (12 daily; 1hr 30min).

From Ámfissa Lamía (3–4 daily; 2hr 30min).

From Lamía Karpeníssi (1 daily; 5hr); Vólos (2 daily; 3hr); Lárissa (4 daily; 3hr 30min); Tríkala, via Kardhítsa (4 daily; 3hr).

From Karpeníssi Agrínio (1 daily; 5hr).

From Vólos Lárissa (hourly; 1hr 30min); Tríkala (4 daily; 2hr 30min); Thessaloníki (4 daily; 3hr 20min); Portaría/Makrinítsa (9 daily; 40min/50min); Zagorá (4 daily; 2hr); Tsangarádha/Áyios Ioánnis (2 daily; 2hr/2hr 30min); Miliés/Vizítsa (6 daily; 1hr/1hr 10min); Plataniás (3 daily; 2hr); Tríkeri (2 daily; 2hr).

From Lárissa Stómio (3 daily; 1hr 25min); Litóhoro junction (almost hourly; 1hr 45min); Tríkala (every half-hour; 1hr 25min); Kalambáka (hourly; 30min).

From Tríkala Kalambáka (hourly; 30min); Kalambáka–Métsovo–Ioánnina (2 daily; 30min/2hr/4hr); Kalambáka–Grevená (1 daily; 30min/2hr).

From Kalambáka Métsovo/Ioánnina (2 daily; 1hr 30min/3hr 30min); Grevená (1 daily; 1hr 30min).

Trains

Athens–Thíva–Livádhia–Lianokládhi (Lamía)–Lárissa
13 trains daily, in each direction.
Approximate journey times:
Athens–Thíva (1hr 20min–1hr 30min)
Thíva–Livádhia (30–40min)
Livádhia–Lianokládhi (1hr 10min–1hr 25min)
Lianokládhi–Lárissa (1hr 30min–2hr).

Lárissa–Kateríni–Thessaloníki 10 daily in each direction.
Approximate journey times:
Lárissa–Kateríni (1hr 10min)
Kateríni–Thessaloníki (1hr 10min).

Vólos–Lárissa–Platamónas–Litóhoro–Kateríni–Thessaloníki 3 daily in each direction.
Approximate journey times:
Vólos–Lárissa (1hr 10min)
Lárissa–Platamónas (45min)
Platamónas–Litóhoro (25min)
Litohoro–Kateríni (15min)
Kateríni–Thessaloníki (1hr 50min).

Lárissa–Vólos 13 daily in each direction (1hr).

Vólos–Fársala–Kardhítsa–Tríkala–Kalambáka 4 daily in each direction.
Approximate journey times:
Vólos–Fársala (1hr 40min)
Fársala–Kardhítsa (1 hr 30min)
Kardhítsa–Tríkala (45min)
Tríkala–Kalambáka (35min).

Ferries

From Áyios Konstandínos Daily to Skíathos and Skópelos (occasionally continuing to Alónissos); weekly (usually Mon) to Áyios Efstrátios, Límnos and Kavála – ☎01/41 78 084 for information.

From Vólos 2–4 daily for Skíathos and Skópelos, at least one continuing to Alónissos – information ☎01/41 78 084 or ☎0421/31 059; weekly (usually Sat evening) to Tartous, Syria.

From Plataniás (Pílion) 1 or 2 daily kaíkia to Koukou-nariés, Skíathos (summer only).

To Évvia Arkítsa—Loutrá Edhípsou (hourly, half as often in winter, last at 11pm/8pm; 50min); Glífa-Ayiókambos (7 daily, 4 in winter; last at 6pm/5pm; 30min).

Across the Gulf of Kórinthos Andírio–Río (every 15min, much less often after midnight; 20min); Áyios Nikólaos–Éyio (3 times daily, 5 in summer; 35min).

Hydrofoils

Flying Dolphins run between the following ports:
From Áyios Konstandínos At least 2 daily in season to Skíathos, Skópelos and Alónissos.

From Vólos 2–4 daily in season to Skíathos, Skópelos and Alónissos, with three weekly continuing to Skíros; last reliable departure to Skíathos usually 7pm, to Skópelos/Alónissos 1pm.

For details of services, which vary drastically with season, contact local agents or the Flying Dolphins' main office in Pireás (Themistokléous 8; ☎01/45 37 107).

CHAPTER FOUR

EPIRUS AND THE WEST

Epirus (*Ípiros* in modern Greek) has the strongest regional identity in mainland Greece. It owes this character to its mountains: the rugged peaks and passes, forested ravines and turbulent rivers of the **Píndhos** (Pindus) **range**. They have protected and isolated Epirus from outside influence and interference, securing it a large measure of autonomy even under Turkish rule.

Because of this isolation, the region's role in Greek affairs was peripheral in ancient times: there are just two archaeological sites of importance, both of them oracles chosen for their end-of-the-world isolation. At **Dodona**, the sanctuary includes a spectacular Classical theatre, at **Ephyra**, the weird remains of a Necromanteion, or "Oracle of the Dead", touted by the ancients as the gateway of Hades.

In more recent times, **Lord Byron** has been the region's greatest publicist. Byron visited in 1809 when the tyrannical ruler Ali Pasha was at the height of his power, and the poet's tales of passionate intrigue, fierce-eyed brigandage and colourful braggadocio came just at the right moment to send a frisson of horror down romantic western spines. The poet later, of course, distinguished himself in the southern extension of the region – the tongue-twistingly named province of **Étolo-Akarnanía** – by taking command of the Greek War of Independence forces, and dying, at **Messolóngi**.

Despite eventual Greek victory in the War of Independence, however, the Turks remained in Epirus, to be ousted finally only in 1913. A disputed frontier territory through the nineteenth century, the region never recovered its former prosperity. When the Italians invaded in 1940, followed by the Germans in 1941, its mountain fastnesses became first the stronghold of the Resistance, then a battleground for rival political factions, and finally, after 1946, the chief bastion of the Communist Democratic Army in the **civil war**. The events of this period – see the box overleaf – are among the saddest of modern Greek history, and continue to reverberate today.

However, the **mountains** are still the place to head for in Epirus. The people are the friendliest and most hospitable you could find and many aspects of their traditional way of life are still in force. Latinate-speaking Vlach and Doric-speaking Sarakatsan shepherds (see "Greek Minorities" in *Contexts*) still bring their flocks to the high mountain pastures in summer. Bears leave footprints on riverbanks or raid beehives, risking an (illegal) bullet in the head, while wolves keep a hungry eye out for stray ewes.

The best single area to visit is around **Mounts Gamíla** and **Smólikas**, with the **Aóös** and **Víkos gorges** to walk and the splendid **villages of the Zagóri**. Buses serve all these villages regularly, if not daily, though walking is the best way to get the full flavour of the place. A number of **hiking routes** are detailed in the text; others, expanded and with fuller maps, are to be found in the specialist guides (see "Books" in *Contexts*). Most of the routes are arduous and lonesome, rather than dangerous. But all the same, this is high mountain country, with rather unpredictable microclimates, and it's inadvisable set off on the longer, more ambitious itineraries unless you are already familiar with basic trekking routines.

Among less strenuous travelling highlights are some of the road routes – above all that negotiating the **Katára pass** across the Píndhos from Kalambáka to Ioánnina. En route is **Métsovo**, perhaps the easiest location for a taste of mountain life, though sadly increasingly commercialised of late. **Ioánnina**, Ali Pasha's capital, is a town of some character, with its island and lake, and the main transport hub for trips into the Zagóri.

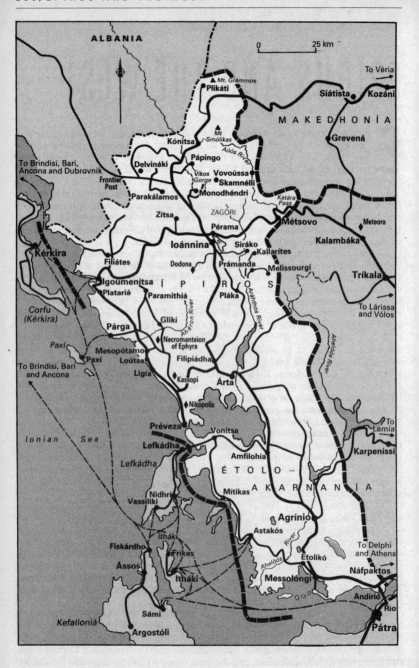

Other than **Árta**, prettily set and with some fine Byzantine churches, there are few other urban attractions.

The coast, both in Epirus and Étolo-Akarnanía, is in general disappointing. **Igoumenítsa** is a useful ferry terminal for Corfu and Italy, but will win few admirers for itself. **Párga**, the major Epirot resort, has been developed beyond its capacity, though **Préveza** has retained some character against the odds and is now a major gateway for charter-package patrons. Between these two towns are a string of functional beaches and a scenic highlight just inland – the **gorge of the Aherónda River**.

South of Préveza, you enter a low, marshy landscape of lakes and land-locked gulfs – of interest mainly to the birdwatcher and fish-dinner enthusiast. For better beach escapes in this part of the world you need islands, fortunately close at hand in the Ionian group – **Lefkádha** (see Chapter Twelve) is actually connected to the mainland by a movable bridge.

WORLD WAR II AND THE CIVIL WAR IN EPIRUS

It was in **November 1940** that the **Italians** invaded Epirus, pushing down from Albania as far as Kalpáki, just south of Kónitsa. United as a nation for the first time in decades, the Greeks repulsed the attack and humiliated Mussolini. However, the euphoria was short-lived as the following April the Germans attacked and rapidly overran Greece.

When parcelling out key portions of the country to their allies for administration, the Germans initially assigned Epirus to the Italians, who trod lightly in the province where they had lately been so soundly beaten, but after Mussolini's capitulation they assumed direct responsibility for Epirus – and conditions markedly worsened. Together with the mountains of central Greece to the south, the Epirote Píndhos was the main staging point for various **guerilla bands**, foremost among them the Communist-dominated **ELAS**. Resistance harassment and ambush of the occupying forces incurred harsh reprisals – including the burning in early 1944 of virtually every Vlach village along the Aöös River.

The wartime flight to the cities from the mountains dates more or less from these atrocities, and the vicissitudes of the subsequent **civil war** (1946–49) dashed any lingering hope of a reasonable existence in the mountains. Victims of reprisals by either the Communists or the Royalist/Nationalist central government, villagers fled to safety in the cities, and many never returned. Wherever you go in the back country you'll hear people talk of these times. Some blame the Communists, others the Nationalists, while those of all persuasions blame the British: "They set us at each other's throats", they say, and with much justice.

Since 1975, many men (and a few women) who fought as communists in ELAS, either as volunteers or conscripts, have returned to their villages – some of them after twenty or thirty years of exile in the USSR and eastern bloc countries. Among them are Greeks who were carried off as children to Albania, and worked in labour camps before being distributed to various east European states. The political Right claim that this *pedhomázema* – the roundup of children – was a cynical and merciless ploy to train up an army of dedicated revolutionaries for the future. The left retort that it was a prudent evacuation of noncombatants from a war zone. Which merely illustrates the futility of arguments over who committed more atrocities.

One thing, however, is certain. The Right won, with the backing of the British and, more especially, the Americans, and they used that victory to maintain a thoroughly undemocratic and vengeful regime for the best part of the following quarter-century. Many Epirot villagers, regardless of political conviction, believe that the poverty and backwardness in which their communities have remained was a deliberate punishment for being part of Communist-held territory during the civil war. They were constantly harassed by the police, who controlled the issue of all sorts of licences and permits needed to find work, travel, put your children in better schools, run a business and so forth. Only in the 1980s did things really change, and the past begin to be treated as another, and separate, age.

THE PÍNDHOS MOUNTAINS

Even if you have no plans to go hiking, the **Píndhos range** deserves a few days' detour. The remoteness and traditional architecture, the air, the peaks – all constitute a very different Greece to the popular tourist image and, despite increasing popularity as a trekking destination, very little spoilt.

The best of the main **routes** is **Kalambáka–Métsovo–Ioánnina**. If you are coming from central Greece, this is a perfect introduction to Epirus; arriving by ferry at Igoumenítsa, it's quite the most attractive route into the mainland. **Walkers** will want to make directly for **Ioánnina**, to the north of which the excitements begin. They range from relatively easy day-walks, such as the increasingly trodden **Víkos gorge**, to the most peak-oriented ramblings you can devise.

Métsovo and the Katára pass

West of Kalambáka, the 1694-metre **Katára pass** cuts across the central range of the Píndhos to link Thessaly and Epirus. This route, the only motor road that is kept open year-round, is one of the most spectacular in the country and worth taking for the sake of the journey alone. It is also, in fact, the shortest east–west crossing in Greece, though distances here are deceptive: the road switchbacks and zigzags through folds in the enormous peaks, rising to over 2300m around Métsovo, and from November to April the snowline must be crossed.

Just two **buses** daily cover the entire route, running between Tríkala and Ioánnina. If you're **driving**, allow half a day for the journey from Kalambáka to Ioánnina (114km), and in winter check on conditions before setting out. Anyone planning on **hitching** from Kalambáka should take a lift only if it's going through to Ioánnina or Métsovo, for there's little but mountain forest in between.

Métsovo

MÉTSOVO spreads just west of the Katára pass, an alpine town built on two sides of a ravine and guarded by a forbidding range of peaks to the south and east. This startling site is matched, albeit in a slightly showcase way, by a traditional architecture and way of life. Immediately below the highway begins a series of eighteenth- and nineteenth-century stone houses, with their wooden balconies and quarried roof slates. The dwellings spill down the slope to and past the main *platía*, where a dwindling number of old men still loiter, especially after Sunday mass, magnificent in full traditional dress, from flat black caps to pompommed shoes; the women, enveloped in rich blue weave and a kerchief over a pair of braids, have a more subdued appearance.

If you arrive outside of the main summer season, stay overnight and take the time to walk in the valley below, the place can seem magical. During the summer, however, your experience may not be so positive. Métsovo has become a favourite target for coach tours, and its beauty veers perilously close to the artificially quaint. Souvenir shops selling "traditional" handcrafts (the weavings often imported from Albania these days) have proliferated, while the stone roofs of the mansions are increasingly replaced by ugly pan-tiles, since the slates were too much bother to maintain and roofs collapsed when their weight was added to by winter snow.

Nonetheless, it would be a shame to pass through Métsovo too speedily, for its history and status as the Vlach "capital" (see "Greek Minorities" in *Contexts*) are unique. Positioned on the only commercially and militarily viable route across the Píndhos, it won a measure of independence, both political and economic, in the earliest days of the Turkish conquest. These privileges were greatly extended in 1659 by a grateful Turkish vizier who, restored to the sultan's favour, wanted to say a proper "thank you" to the Metsovite shepherd who had protected him during his disgrace.

As the town grew in prosperity, the Vlachs – who occupy a score of villages in the surrounding Píndhos as well as Métsovo – traded their sheep products further and further afield. Local merchants established themselves in Constantinople, Vienna, Venice, and elsewhere, expanding into other lines of business: Vlachs played a major role in Balkan mule-back haulage and the hotel trade – specifically the *caravanserais* where the mule convoys halted.

Métsovo's continued prosperity, and the preservation of some of its traditions, are largely due to the munificence of Baron Tositsas, banker scion of a Metsovite family living in Switzerland. He left his colossal fortune to an endowment that has financed sawmills, dairy farms and a small weaving industry, along with the local museum and its small ski resort north of the main road.

Around the town

The Métsovo museum occupies the eighteenth-century **Arhondikó Tosítsa** (8.30am–1pm & 4–6pm closed Thurs; group tours every half-hour; 200dr). This has been restored to its full glory, and with its panelled rooms, rugs and fine collection of Epirot crafts and costumes, gives a real sense of the town's wealth and grandeur in that era.

The **Ídhrima Tosítsa** (Tosítsa Foundation) building down in the square serves as an outlet for contemporary handicrafts of like quality, stocking some of the more tasteful and finely woven cloth, rugs and blankets to be found in Greece, no relation to most of the schlock in the souvenir stalls. They are expensive, but not outrageously so, considering the quality of the hand-weaving.

The other major Métsovo attraction is the relatively remote monastery of **Áyios Nikólaos**, signposted from the main square but in fact twenty minutes' walk below town, just off the half-cemented-over *kalderími* headed for Anílio, the suburb across the ravine. The monastery's main chapel, or *katholikón*, was built in the fourteenth century to a bizarre plan. It is topped by a simple barrel vault and what might once have been the narthex became over time a *yinaikonítis* or women's gallery, something seen nowhere else in Greece except Kastoriá. The brilliant **frescoes**, mostly scenes from Christ's life and assorted martyrdoms, exhibit a highly unusual style dating from the eighteenth century, and were recently cleaned and illuminated courtesy of the Tosítsa Foundation. A warden couple live on the premises and receive visitors until 7pm. You'll be shown the monks' former cells, with insulating walls of mud and straw, and the abbot's more sumptuous quarters; a donation or purchase of postcards is expected.

The **Anílio** ("sunless") quarter is a further half-hour down, then up, and you'll have to make the gruelling trek back the same way. Like Métsovo, its population is Vlach-speaking, and its life more genuinely traditional, but with no pretensions to tourist appeal, its architecture is executed in dull cement. You can, however, get an excellent, reasonably priced lunch at the *platía* before starting back.

Practicalities

Métsovo has a wide range of accommodation – twelve hotels plus quite a few rooms and apartments for rent – and outside of the ski season, or the town's festival (July 26), you should have little trouble in getting a bed. **Budget hotels** include:

Hotel Athinae, just off the main square (☎0656/41 217). Inexpensive and friendly. ②

Hotel Acropolis, at the top end of town, just below the junction of the access road and the main highway (☎0656/41 672). ③

Hotel Kassaros, near the Athinai (☎0656/41 346). Comfortable, compact and quiet. ③

Hotel Egnatia, on the main street (☎0656/41 263). Okay but less characterful – and something of a tour mill. ③

For **meals**, try two simple grills: *Krifi Folia*, on the main *platía*, or *O Kostas*, directly under the post office and entered via a side alley; both function only in the evening. At lunchtime, the *Athinai* does good, reasonably priced casserole food, accompanied by decent house wine, while *To Spitiko*, between the *Egnatia* and the Tosítsa mansion, serves Métsovo specialities at a fair price. Wine buffs may want to try the fabled *Katoí*, available in some of these restaurants – a very expensive five-year-old limited bottling from tiny vineyards down on the Árakhthos River.

Moving on – and the eastern ZagÓri

For a taste of wilder, remoter scenery, and a truer, grittier picture of contemporary mountain life, you might consider breaking the journey from Métsovo to Ioánnina. At the BALDHOUMA junction, 32km west of Métsovo, a road heads north along the valley of the Várdhas River and through the predominantly Vlach villages of the **eastern Zagóri** (see p.252). It's a winding, precipitous dirt road most of the way, but plied by a bus (daily except Wed) from Ioánnina; coming from Métsovo, you can usually pick it up at Baldhoúma at around 2pm (see p.286 for more details).

When **leaving Métsovo by bus**, make sure that your departure loops down to the terminal in the centre; most do, but a few, particularly the Tríkala–Ioánnina through services, merely pass by on the upper road.

Ioánnina

Coming from Métsovo, you approach **IOÁNNINA** through more spectacular folds of the Píndhos, emerging high above the great lake of **Pamvótis**. The town stands upon its edge, a rocky promontory jutting out into the water, its fortifications punctuated by towers and minarets as if to declare its history. For it was from this base that Ali Pasha, "the Lion of Ioannina", carved from the Turks a fiefdom that encompassed much of western Greece – an act of contemptuous rebellion that portended wider defiance in the Greeks' own War of Independence.

Ali Pasha's capital

The major figure in Ioánninan and Epirot history, **Ali Pasha** was a highly ambivalent "heroic rebel". His only consistent policy was that of ambition and self-interest, and as frequent as his attacks on the Turkish Porte were his acts of appalling and vindictive savagery against his Greek subjects.

He was born in 1741 in Albania and rose to power under Turkish patronage, being made Pasha of Tríkala in reward for his efforts in the Sultan's war against Austria. His ambitions, however, were of a grander order and that same year, 1788, he seized Ioánnina, an important town since the thirteenth century, with a population of 30,000 – probably the largest in Greece at the time. Paying sporadic and usually token tribute to the Sultan, he operated from this power-base for the next thirty-three years, allying in turn, and as the moment suited him, with the British, French and Turks.

In 1809, when his dependence upon the Turkish Porte was nominal, Ali was visited by the young **Lord Byron**, whom he overwhelmed with hospitality and attention. (The tyrant's sexual tastes were famously omnivorous, and it is recorded that he was particularly taken with the poet's "small ears", a purported mark of good breeding.) Byron, impressed for his part with the rebel's daring and stature, and the lively revival of Greek culture in Ioánnina (which, he wrote, was "superior in wealth, refinement and learning" to any town in Greece), commemorated the meeting in *Childe Harold*. The portrait that he draws, however, is an ambiguous one, well aware that there are "deeds that lurk beneath" the Pasha's splendid court and deceptively mild countenance that "stain him with disgrace".

In a letter to his mother Byron was more explicit, concluding that "His highness is a remorseless tyrant, guilty of the most horrible cruelties, very brave, so good a general that they call him the Mahometan Buonaparte . . . but as barbarous as he is successful, roasting rebels, etc, etc". Of the rebels, the most illustrious was Katsandonis the Klepht, whom Ali captured wracked by smallpox in a cave in the Ágrafa mountains. He imprisoned the unfortunate wretch in a soaking lakeside dungeon, and finally executed him by breaking his bones in public with a sledgehammer.

Arrival and accommodation

The axis of downtown Ioánnina is the confusing, oddly angled jumble of streeets between the central **Platía Pirroú** and the **Froúrio**, Ali Pasha's old citadel. Near the latter is the old bazaar area – still in part an artesans' marketplace. Around Platía Pirroú are most essential services – the **OTE**, **post office** and **banks**.

Arriving by **bus**, you'll find yourself at one of two terminals. The main station is at **Zozimádhou 4**, north of Platía Pirroú; this serves most points north and west, including Métsovo/Kalambáka, Igoumenítsa, Kónitsa and the villages of the Zagóri. A smaller terminal at **Vizaníou 28** connects Árta, Préveza, Dodona and all villages in the south or east parts of Epirus. It is advisable, especially at weekends, to buy tickets for both coast and mountains the day before. You can check out times and departure points – and get information on accommodation – at the friendly **EOT** office or at the **tourist police**.

Ioánnina **airport** is on the road out to the Pérama cave; it's connected to town by bus #8.

Accommodation

If you arrive early enough in the day, or book ahead, it is worth heading straight out to the **island on Lake Pamvótis** (see below), whose two adjoining inns offer the cheapest, most attractive accommodation available. They are:

Pension Varvara (☎0651/24 396). ②

Pandohío (☎0651/73 494). An unnamed place run by the Della family. ②

In the town, the options include:

Hotel Metropolis, Kristálli 2 on corner Avéroff (☎0651/26 207). Pretty basic. ②

Hotel Tourist, Kolétti 18 (☎0651/26 443). Around the corner – similar but quieter. ③

Hotel Paradissos, Ikosimía Fevrouaríou 15 (☎0651/25 365). Good budget choice near Platía Tzavéla and the southern bus station. ③

Hotel King Pyrros, Goúnari 1–3, just off Platía Akadhimías (☎0651/27 652). Okay mid-range option if you can get a room facing the side street Goúnari; otherwise it's noisy. ④

Hotel Egnatia, Aravandínou 20 on corner Dánglí – towards the lake (☎0651/25 667). Decent hotel favoured by trekking groups. ④

Camping unusually for a city, is here an attractive alternative:

Camping Limnopoula. Pleasant, mosquito-free site, 2km out of town on the Pérama road (city bus #2 or a 15–20min walk from Platía Mavíli). Amenities are okay but it fills early in the day in summer and is a bit cramped at the best of times.

The Town

It is the stories of Ali Pasha's cruelties rather than the glories of his success that seem to hang about the surviving vestiges of his capital. Disappointingly, most of the city is modern and undistinguished – a testimony not so much to Ali, athough he did burn much of it to the ground when under siege in 1820, as to developers in the 1950s. However, the fortifications of Ali Pasha's citadel, the **Froúrio**, survive more or less intact; there are crumbling **mosques**, their minarets capped by storks' nests, to evoke the old Turkish atmosphere; an excellent **archaeological museum**; and Lake Pamvótis, with its village and monasteries, is a delight.

The Froúrio

The **Froúrio** is an obvious point to direct your explorations. In its heyday the walls dropped abruptly to the lake, and were moated on their (southwest) landward side. The moat has been filled, and a quay-esplanade now extends below the lakeside ramparts, but there is still the feel of a citadel.

Once within, signs direct you to the **Popular Art Museum** (daily 8am–3pm; 300dr), a splendidly ramshackle collection of Epirot costumes and jewellery. It displays also photographs and relics from the liberation of Ioánnina from the Turks in 1913, a sobering reminder of the closeness of foreign rule in Greece. The museum is housed in the well-preserved **Aslan Pasha Jami**, allowing a rare glimpse in Greece of the interior of a mosque; it retains the decoration on its dome and the recesses in the vestibule for the shoes of worshippers. Here, in 1801, tradition places Ali's rape and murder of Kyra Phrosyne, the mistress of his eldest son. Her "provocation" had been to refuse the 62-year-old tyrant's sexual advances; together with seventeen of her companions, she was bound, weighted, and thrown alive into the lake.

To the east of the Aslan Pasha Jami is the **inner citadel** of the fortress. This was used for some years by the Greek military and most of its buildings – including Ali's palace where Byron was entertained – have unfortunately been adapted or restored past recognition. A circular tower remains, however, along with the old **Fetiye Jami** (Victory Mosque), currently in the throes of restoration. Close by this mosque is purported to be Ali Pasha's tomb.

The bazaar and archaeological museum

Apart from the Froúrio, the town's most enjoyable quarter is that of the old **bazaar**, a roughly semicircular area focused on the citadel's gate. This has a cluster of Turkish-era buildings, as well as a scattering of copper-, tin- and silver-smiths – the last were for centuries a mainstay of the town's economy.

Just off the central Platía Dhimokratías, set beside a small park and the town's modern cathedral, is the **Archaeological Museum** (Tues–Sat 8.30am–3pm; 400dr), one of the best you'll find in the provinces. It's certainly a must if you're planning a visit to the theatre and oracle of Dodona, for on display here – along with some exceptional crafted bronze seals – is a fascinating collection of lead tablets inscribed with questions to the Oracle.

Nissí and Lake Pamvótis

The island of **Nissí**, on the unfortunately much-polluted **Lake Pamvótis**, is connected by half-hourly motor-launches (half-hourly in summer, hourly otherwise, 6.30am–11pm; 90dr) from the quay northwest of the Froúrio on Platía Mavíli. The beautiful island village, founded in the sixteenth century by refugees from the Máni in the Peloponnese, is flanked by a group of five monasteries, providing a perfect focus for an afternoon's visit. Stay on through the evening and you can eat at a string of restaurants on the waterfront, watching superb sunsets over the encircling reedbeds.

The **Monastery of Pandelímonos**, just to the east of the village, is perhaps the most dramatic of Ioánnina's Ali Pasha sites. In January 1822 he was assassinated here, his hiding place having been revealed to the Turks, who had finally lost patience with the wayward ruler. Trapped in his rooms on the upper storey, he was shot from the floor below. The fateful bullet holes in the floorboards form the centrepiece of a small museum to the tyrant, along with a few prints and knick-knacks like Ali's splendid hubble-bubble.

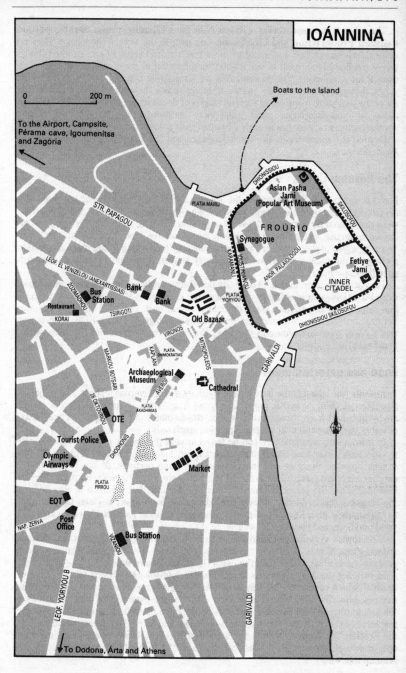

IOÁNNINA

0   200 m

To the Airport, Campsite,
Pérama cave, Igoumenítsa
and Zagória

Boats to the Island

STR. PAPAGOU

PLATIA MÁVILI

DHIONISSIOU

Aslan Pasha
Jami
(Popular Art Museum)

SKILOSOFOU

FROÚRIO

LEOF. EL VENIZELOU (ANEXARTISSIAS)

Synagogue

KARAMANLI

IOUSTINIANOU

ANDR. PALAIOLOGOU

Fetiye
Jami

ZOZMADHOU

Bank

Bus
Station

Bank

INNER
CITADEL

Restaurant

KORAI

TSIRIGOTI

Old Bazaar

PLATIA
YIORYIOU

VIRONOS

DHIONISSIOU SKILOSOFOU

MAROU BOTSARI

KARLANI

PLATIA
DHIMOKRATIAS

MITROPOLEOS

GARIVALDI

Archaeological
Museum

AVEROF

Cathedral

28 OCTOVRIOU

PLATIA
AKADHIMIAS

OTE

DHODHONIS

Tourist Police

Olympic
Airways

PLATIA
PIRROU

Market

EOT

NAP. ZERVA

Post
Office

VIZANIOU

Bus Station

LEOF. YIORYIOU B

To Dodona, Árta and Athens

The other four monasteries – Ayíou Nikoláou Filanthropinón, Stratigopoúlou, Ioánnou Prodhrómou and Eleoússas – are over to the west of the village. They are quite clearly signposted and stand within a few hundred yards of one another along a lovely treelined lane; each is maintained by a handful of nuns, who allow brief visits (knock for admission). The monasteries are attractively situated, with pleasant courtyards, though visits essentially consist of being shown the main chapel, or *katholikón*. All of these feature frescoes, in various stages of decay or preservation. The finest are those of Filanthropinón, portraying some extraordinarily bloody and graphic seventeenth-century scenes of early Christian martyrdoms.

Beyond the monasteries the track loops around the island to bring you out near Pandelímonos.

The Pérama Caves

Five kilometres north of Ioánnina, the village of PÉRAMA boasts what are reputed to be Greece's largest **caves** (daily summer 8am–8pm; winter 8am–4pm; 500dr). They were discovered during the last war by a guerilla in hiding from the Germans and are indeed immense, extending and echoing for kilometres beneath a low hill. Half-hour tours are given of the complex – a little perfunctory (consisting in the main of a student reeling off the names of various suggestively shaped formations), but not enough to spoil the experience.

To reach the caves, take a #8 blue city bus (buy your ticket in advance from a kiosk) from Platía Dhimokratías to Pérama village; the caves are a short walk inland from the bus stop. If you are driving, you can make a circuit of it. The road splits shortly after Pérama: one fork leading north to the mountain village of DHRÍSKOS, with superb views down over Ioánnina and the lake; the other running around the lake, with a beachside café midway.

Food and entertainment

For **meals**, the island is the best location with its trio of tavernas featuring lake specialities like eel (*héli*), crayfish (*karavídhes*) and frogs' legs. If you'd rather not sample anything fished from those murky waters, the farmed trout (*péstrofa*) is cheaper and possibly safer. In winter the tavernas provide lunch only.

In town, more standard fare can be found around the bazaar near the Froúrio gate; try the basic, oven-food *Pantheon* restaurant, or, for grills, the excellent *To Mandio*, exactly opposite the gate and inexpensive with good portions. At lunchtimes there's another excellent *psistariá* on Zozimádhou, below the *Hotel Egnatia*. By night, the liveliest places are the pizzerias around Platía Mavíli. Note that Ioánnina is also home to the *bougatza* (custard-tart), fresh at **breakfast** time from *Select* at Platía Dhimokratías 3. Alternatively, there's an English-style breakfast salon at Avéroff 39, which also does good puddings and yoghurts as well.

The town's very limited **nightlife** is to be found in a group of pubs and cinemas around Platía Mavíli. Thanks to the university students, there is usually quite a decent programme of films, rather than the usual Greek small-town dross.

In summer, the biggest events are part of the *Politístiko Kalokéri* (Cultural Summer) **festival**, which runs from mid-July to mid-August, made up of music and theatre performances, plus the odd cultural exhibition. Most of the events take place in a hillside theatre, known as the **Fróntzos**, just outside the town (there is also a pleasant summer restaurant here, with fine views down to the town and lake). Tickets are available from the Folklore Museum at Mihaíl Angélou 42 or the EOT office. Some years there are one or two performances of Classical drama at the ancient theatre of Dodona (see account following).

Dodona

There is a certain romantic egocentricity in being a tourist which demands that a site should not only be beautiful beyond one's expectations but should also be a personal and private discovery. If you've ever felt like this, go to **DODONA**, 22km southwest of Ioánnina. Here, in a wildly mountainous and once isolated region lie the ruins of the **Oracle of Zeus** – the oldest in Greece – dominated by a vast and elegant theatre that was meticulously restored at the end of the last century.

The Oracle

The **oracle** is a very ancient site indeed. "Wintry Dodona" is mentioned in Homer and the worship of Zeus and of the sacred oak tree here seems to have been connected with the first Hellenic tribes who arrived in Epirus around 1900 BC.

The origins of the site are shadowy: Herodotus gives an enigmatic story about the arrival of a dove from Egyptian Thebes which settled in an oak tree and ordered a place of divination to be made. The word *peleiae* in fact meant both dove and old woman, so it's possible that the legend he heard refers to an original priestess – perhaps captured from the East and having some knowledge or practice of divination. The **oak tree**, stamped on the ancient coins of the area, was central to the cult. Herodotus recorded that the oracle spoke through the rustling of its leaves in sounds amplified by copper vessels suspended from its branches. These would then be interpreted by frenzied priestesses and strange priests who slept on the ground and never washed their feet.

Many oracular inscriptions were found scattered around the site when it was excavated in 1952. Now displayed in Ioánnina's archaeological museum, they give you a good idea of the personal realm of the oracle's influence in the years after it had been eclipsed by Delphi. More interestingly, they also offer a glimpse of the fears and inadequacies that motivated the pilgrims of the age to journey here, asking such everyday domestic questions as: "Am I her children's father?" and, memorably, "Has Pleistos stolen the wool from my mattress?".

The Theatre and Site

Mon–Fri 8am–5pm, may shut 7pm in summer, Sat & Sun 8.30am–3pm; admission 500dr.

Entering the site through the outline of a third-century BC **Stadium**, you are immediately confronted by the massive western retaining wall of the **Theatre**. Built during the time of Pyrrhus (297–272 BC), this was one of the largest on the Greek mainland, rivalled only by those at Argos and Megalopolis. Later, the Romans made adaptations necessary for their blood sports, adding a protective wall over the lower seating and also a drainage channel, cut in a horseshoe shape around the orchestra. What you see today is a meticulous, late nineteenth-century reconstruction, since until then the amphitheatre had been an almost incomprehensible jumble of stones.

The theatre is used occasionally for weekend ancient drama performances during Ioánnina's summer cultural festival (see facing page), which must be terrific, for this is one of the most glorious settings in Greece. The seats face out across a green, silent valley to the slopes of Mount Tómaros, as though one peak is challenging the other. At the top of the *cavea*, or auditorium, a grand entrance gate leads into the **Acropolis**, an overgrown and largely unexcavated area. The foundations of its walls, mostly Hellenistic, are a remarkable four to five metres wide.

Beside the theatre, and tiered uncharacteristically against the same slope, are the foundations of a **Bouleuterion** (council house), beyond which lie the complex ruins of the **Sanctuary of Zeus**, site of the ancient oracle. There was actually no temple at all in the sanctuary until the end of the fifth century BC. Worship centred upon the Sacred Oak, in which the god was thought to dwell, standing alone within a circle of votive tripods and cauldrons. Building began modestly with a small, stone temple precinct, though by the time of Pyrrhus this enclosure was made of Ionic colonnades. In 219 BC the Sacred House was sacked by the Aetolians and a larger temple was rebuilt with a monumental *propylaion*. This survived until the fourth century, when the oak tree was hacked down by Christian reformists.

It is remains of the later precinct that can be seen today. They are distinguishable by an oak planted at the centre by a helpfully reverent archaeologist. Ruins of an early Christian **basilica**, constructed on a Sanctuary of Herakles, are also prominent nearby.

Access

Few people make the detour to Dodona so the site, and DODHÓNI – the little village to the west of it – are completely unspoilt. **Transport**, however, is accordingly sparse, with only two buses a day from Ioánnina, at 6am (8am on Sunday) and 2pm. Hitching back from the site should be feasible in summer (sometimes necessary, if the after-noon bus back fails to materialise), or a round trip by taxi from Ioánnina with an hour at the site can be negotiated for a reasonable amount.

Alternatively, you could always stay the night here. There are some lovely spots to camp, a friendly if basic taverna in the village, and a tiny **pension** at the site, the *Xenia Andromachi* (☎0651/91 196; ③). MELÍGI, the next village beyond, and the road's end, has a good restaurant on its *platía*.

The Zagóri, Víkos Gorge and Mount Gamíla

Few parts of Greece are more surprising, or more beguiling, than **Zagóri**. A wild, infer-tile region, it lies to the north of Ioánnina, bounded by the roads to Kónitsa and Métsovo on the west and south and the Aóös river valley to the east. The beauty of its landscapes is unquestionable: barren limestone wastes, rugged mountains deeply furrowed by foaming rivers and partly subterranean streams, miles of forest. But there is not a cultivatable inch anywhere, and scarcely a job for any of its few remaining inhabitants. The last place, in fact, that one would expect to find some of the most imposing architecture in Greece.

Yet the **Zagorohória**, as the forty-six villages of Zagóri are called, are full of grand stone mansions (*arhondiká*), enclosed by semi-fortified walls and with deep-eaved porches opening on to immaculately cobbled streets. Inside, if you are lucky enough to get a glimpse, the living quarters are upstairs, arranged on the Turkish model. Instead of furniture, low platforms line the rooms on either side of an often elaborately hooded fireplace; strewn with rugs and cushions, they serve as couches for sitting during the day and sleeping at night. The wall facing the fire is usually lined with panelled and sometimes painted storage cupboards called *misándhres*. In the grander houses the intricately fretted wooden ceilings are often painted too.

Though they look older, these mansions are mostly late eighteenth- or nineteenth-century. They were built with money earned abroad. For while they enjoyed privileges similar to the Metsovites, the men of Zagóri were forced by poverty to seek their fortunes away from home, returning only periodically to sire children and build them a home that implied the miseries of *ksenitiá* (living in foreign parts) were worth endur-ing. Though many of the mansions have long fallen into disrepair, the government now ensures that repairs are carried out in the proper materials. Monodhéndhri and Pápingo are the best preserved of the western Zagóri villages, all of which escaped the wartime devastation suffered by their eastern cousins.

As for the countryside, much the best way of savouring its joys is on foot, **trekking** the dozens of still extant paths that, gliding through forest and sheepfold or slipping over passes and hogbacks, connect the outlying villages. The most popular trip – now very much part of the holiday trekking company circuit – is up the awesome **Víkos gorge**. It's not to be missed, though for more of a feel of the back country, you may want to continue north, over towards Mount Gámila, or even loop up to the Víkos via Vovoússa and the remoter Vlach villages of the eastern Zagóri.

If you would rather have things organised and made easy for you, *Robinson Travel* at Ógdhoïs Merarhías 10, Ioánnina (☎0651/29 402), run **group treks** for one of the British hiking companies and welcome walk-in custom. If you phone ahead, or are prepared to wait a few days, they will do their best to fit you in.

The Víkos Gorge and western Zagóri

The walls of the **Víkos gorge** are nearly 1000 metres high in places, cutting right through the limestone tablelands of Mount Gamíla, and separating the villages of western and central Zagóri. It is quite the equal of the famous Samarian gorge in Crete and a hike through or around it, depending on your abilities and time, is likely to be the highlight of a visit to the Zagóri. Since 1975 a national park has encompassed both Víkos and the equally gorgeous Aóös river canyon to the north and, to date at least, various plans for ski centres, téléfériques and dams have been fought off.

Touristic development, however, has proceeded apace since the early 1980s, when British and French trekking companies first began coming here, and today almost every hamlet within spitting distance of the canyon – and indeed any sizeable village elsewhere in the Zagóri – has **rooms** for rent and **tavernas**. Be warned, though, that the area's popularity is such that you won't get a room to save your life in July or August – and bringing a tent can be a useful fallback at any time of year.

HIKING PRACTICALITIES

The **walk along the gorge** is not difficult to follow, since the entire gorge route is waymarked, in parts a bit faintly, by white-on-red stencilled metal diamonds with the legend "O3". This refers to a newly staked-out long-distance path, which begins in Monodhéndhri and as of writing can be followed across Mount Gamíla all the way to Mount Smólikas. Walking the gorge, it takes about five hours at a reasonable pace to clear the narrowest part of the canyon and arrive at the source of the Voïdhomátis river. Another hour will get you as far as the hamlet of VÍKOS, above the north end of the gorge to your left; in two hours from the river sources you can reach one of the PÁPINGO villages, on the opposite flank of the valley.

Despite the gorge's popularity, and recent improvements in trail surface, mapping and marking, it is worth emphasising that the traverse is not a Sunday stroll and that there is still plenty of scope for **getting lost** or worse. In April or May snowmelt usually makes the Monodhéndhri end impassable due to high run-off, and in a rainstorm the sides of the gorge can become an oozing mass of mud, tree-trunks and scree. At the best of times it's not really a hike to be attempted with low-cut trainers and PVC water bottles, as so many do; a stout stick for warding off snakes and belligerent livestock, and purchase on slopes, wouldn't go amiss either.

The Ioánnina EOT hand out photocopies of the *Korfes* magazine's **topo map** of the Víkos gorge area, but this is old (1984–85) and full of dangerous errors. If you are going beyond the gorge, the schematic maps which the EOS rep in Megálo Pápingo keeps on hand are more authoritative and should at least be glanced at.

Monodhéndhri

The usual starting point for the walk is the handsome village of **MONODHÉNDRI**, perched right on the rim of the gorge, near its south end. On weekdays there are two daily buses here from Ioánnina, at 6.30am and 3.45pm. If you take the later one, you can stay the night at the luxury *Ksenonas Vikos* (☎0653/61 232 or 01/68 16 417; ⑨) or at four or five more modest inns, such as the *Monodendri* (☎0653/61 233; ③). For **meals** you have a choice of a *psistaria* by the bus stop in the upper quarter or a taverna in the lower *platía*. Additional accommodation is available at nearby VÍTSA – only fifteen minutes' walk below by a footpath – in a renovated *arhondikó*.

The lane leading off from the far end of the *platía*, signposted "Pros Vikon", leads to the eagle's-nest monastery of **Áyia Paraskeví**, teetering on the very brink of the gorge. If you continue on around the adjacent cliff face – a good head for heights is needed here – the path eventually comes to a dead-end near a well-hidden cave where the villagers used to barricade themselves in times of danger.

Through the gorge

Much the clearest **path into the gorge** starts beside the church in Monodhéndri's lower main square, where a sign reading "Víkos Arísti Pápingo" shows a schematic pedestrian figure and the misleading estimate of "10km" (it's more like 13km by the time you reach Pápingo).

The path is paved for most of the way down to the riverbed, whose stony course you can quite easily parallel for the first hour or so of the walk. There are occasional splashes of red paint directing the way, but in reality all you need to do is keep straight, occasionally crossing from one to the other side of the riverbed or climbing for a while through the wooded banks.

About two and a half hours out of Monodhéndri you draw even with the mouth of the **Mégas Lákkos ravine**, the only major breach in the eastern wall of the gorge; its water is drinkable, and the only reliable source en route. Another forty minutes' level tramping brings you past the small white shrine of **Ayía Triádha** with a recessed well opposite; a further hour yet (around 4hr 30min from Monodhéndri) sees the gorge begin to open out and the sheer walls recede.

On to Víkos or the Pápingos

As the gorge widens you are faced with a choice. Continuing straight, on the best-defined path, takes you close to a beautifully set eighteenth-century chapel of the Panayía, past which the route becomes a well-paved *kalderími* (mule path), climbing up and left to the hamlet of **VÍKOS** (also known as VITSIKÓ). This route has been kept in good repair by the locals and there is a single small inn in the hamlet, run by Kostas Karpouzis (☎0653/41 176; ③).

Most walkers, however, prefer to follow the marked **"O3 route"** to the two **Pápingo villages**, crossing the gorge bed at the **Voïdhomátis springs**. This trail was regraded and rerouted in 1985 and is fairly straightforward to follow. It's about two hours' walk to Mikró Pápingo, slightly less to Megálo, with the divide in the trail nearly ninety minutes above the riverbed crossing. Midway, after an initial steep climb, there's a fine view down into the north end of the gorge in the vicinity of some weathered, tooth-like pinnacles, before the trail traverses a stable rock slide.

MEGÁLO PÁPINGO is, as its name suggests, the larger of the two villages: a sprawl of fifty or so houses along a tributary of the Voïdhomátis river. Despite a blanket preservation order, an enormous cement hotel is creeping towards completion and Megálo has been discovered with a vengeance by wealthy Greeks of late, making it a poor choice of base in high season. It has a seventeen-bed **inn** with a café-grill, run by the Hristodhoulos family (☎0653/41 138 or 41 115; ③), who are also the local EOS representatives. As such they can advise on space in the Astráka hut and walks towards Gamíla (see below). The son, Nikos, speaks English. A second, smaller inn, offering good home-style meals, is run by Kalliopi Ranga (☎0653/41 081; ③). There is also a former EOT-run (and now privately operated) scheme of luxury inns in converted *arhondiká* (☎0653/41 615; ⑥). The most active taverna is across from the Hristodhoulos inn – a surprisingly trendy place with *calzone*, pizza and wine.

MIKRÓ PÁPINGO, around half the size of its neighbour, crouches below an outcrop of grey limestone rocks known as the *Pírgi* (Towers). The village has three **inns** – most conspicuous of which is *O Dhias* (✆0653/41 257; ④), whose proprietor Kostas Tsoumanis is sympathetic to trekkers – and two tavernas. There is also a small British expat colony who've bought and renovated houses.

Pápingo–Ioánnina transport

There is a paved road betwen Ioánnina and the Pápingo villages, via Arísti, on the Ioánnina–Kónitsa road. **Bus links** are rather haphazard: departures **from Ioánnina** are on Monday, Thursday and Friday at 5am and 3pm, turning around for the **return trip** immediately upon arrival; on Sunday the outbound service is 9.30am, back to town in the late afternoon.

If you strike unlucky, the best course is to walk to the village of KÁTO KLIDHONIÁ, on the Kónitsa–Ioánnina highway, which has regular buses. It's around two and a half hours' walk, via the nearly abandoned hamlet of Áno Klidhoniá, on a better than average, marked path.

Hikes across Mount Gamíla

For walkers keen on further, fairly arduous hiking, there are a number of routes on from the Pápingo villages, up and across the **Gamíla** range. These are linked by the newly marked "03" trail.

Astráka: the refuge and around

All onward hikes east into Gamíla begin with the steep but straightforward ascent to the **refuge on Astráka col**, clearly visible from Megálo Pápingo. To reach this you need to start from Mikró Pápingo. Coming from Megálo Pápingo, a marked short cut of the asphalt road, going via an old historic bridge, cuts journey time to half an hour.

From the top of **Mikró Pápingo** the "03" trail resumes – a well-signed, bona fide path. You pass a chapel (Áyios Pantelímon), then head through forest to a spring (Antálki; about 40min from Mikró Pápingo). From here the forest thins as you climb towards a second spring (Tráfos; 1hr 40min from Mikró). Twenty minutes beyond Tráfos, a signposted trail branches right towards the **Astráka summit** – a three-hour round-trip from this point.

If you ignore this path, and keep straight with the "03" markers, you will reach the **EOS refuge**, perched on the saddle joining Astráka with Mount Lápatos, in around 35 minutes (3hr 15min from Megálo Pápingo). The hut is permanently staffed from mid-May to mid-October but space is at a premium and bunks are relatively expensive (1200dr), as are meals. If you want to squeeze in amongst the Greek and foreign trekking/climbing groups, phone the Hristodhoulos store in Megálo Pápingo; they're in radio contact with the hut, who can confirm space.

Northeast of the refuge, on the far side of the boggy Lákka Tsoumáni valley below, the gleaming **lake of Dhrakólimni** is tucked on the very edge of the Gamíla range. This is about an hour from the refuge, along a well-grooved-in and marked path. **Gamíla summit** proper, 2497m, is a good two and a half hours' climb to the east-southeast of the refuge.

The marked **"03" route**, however, veers off south from the final summit approach to negotiate a prominent col between the Karterós and Gamíla peaks, with a nasty scree slide on the far side. This route eventually joins an easier, unmarked trail coming over from Skamnélli (see below) near the usually empty *stáni* (sheepfold) of Kátsanos, before the final descent to **Vrissohóri** (again, see below). Despite the waymarking, this section of the "03" is a strenuous nine-hour hike; it's best attempted only if you're an experienced trekker and equipped with the appropriate maps.

PACKHORSE BRIDGES

A perennial pleasure as you stumble down boulder-strewn ravine beds that are bone-dry an hour after a thunderstorm is coming upon one of the many fine high-arched "pack-horse" bridges that abound in the Zagóri. One-, two- or three-arched, these bridges, and the old cobbled tracks, were the only link with the outside world for these remote communities until motor roads were opened up in the 1950s. They were erected mainly in the nineteenth century by gangs of itinerant craftsmen and financed by local worthies.

Like the semi-nomadic Vlach and Sarakatsan shepherds of Epirus, these wandering construction gangs or *bouloúkia* left home between the feasts of Áyios Yióryios (St George's Day) in April and Áyios Dhimítrios in October. As in other mountainous regions of Europe – the Alps, for example – they came from remote and poor communities, Pirsóyianni and Voúrbiani in particular in the Kónitsa area, and Ágnanda, Prámanda and Houliarádhes southeast of Ioánnina. Closely guarding the secrets of their trade with their own invented private language, they travelled the length and breadth of Greece and the Balkans, right up to World War II.

While you're in the Zagóri region, a good side trip, easiest done from either Vítsa or Tsepélovo, would be to go out to **Kípi** to take a look at the half-dozen fantastic bridges in the vicinity of the village. These span the upper reaches of the Víkos gorge and its tributaries, and constitute the most representative and accessible examples of this vanished craft.

South to Tsepélovo

A more obvious, less demanding **onward trek from Astráka col** is the five-hour route across the Gamíla uplands, via the Mirioúli sheepfold and the head of the Mégas Lákkos gorge, to the village of **TSEPÉLOVO**. There is only one tiny spring en route and for the most part the scenery consists of forbidding limestone-dell-scape but the destination is one of the finest of Zagorohória. In the village, English-speaking Alekos Gouris runs a store and keeps a taverna and **rooms** (☎0653/81 214; ③) on the *platía*; there's also a good value pension, the *Fanis* (☎0653/81 271; ③), run by his cousin. Two buses daily (Mon–Fri) connect the village with Ioánnina; they leave Ioánnina at dawn and at 3.15pm, returning from Tsepélovo an hour or so later.

This side of Mount Gamíla is treeless and rather dull, though there are good day excursions. The adjacent village of SKAMNÉLLI (which has another **pension**, the *Pindos*; ③) is an easy walk, with a medieval monastery en route, and there's another monastery above the canyon immediately to the south. Following this valley downhill brings you to the celebrated cluster of **old bridges** around KÍPI, plus the amazing coiled-spring *kalderími* linking KEPÉSOVO and VRADHÉTO.

Routes to Vrissohóri and the Aóös valley

Beyond **Skamnélli** forest appears, extending north to the **Aóös valley**. The now-dirt road ends at Vrissohóri in the west, and at Láista in the east; two or three days a week the bus continues beyond Skamnélli to both. **LÁISTA** has an incongruously large **hotel**, the *Robolo* (☎0653/81 286; ③), and a fine, though damaged, church.

Rather than following the relatively dull road from Skamnélli to Vrissohóri, you can walk in seven hours over a pass **between the peaks of Karterós and Tsoúka Roússa** – a rather easier walk than the "O3" route col previously described and covered by many of the organised trekking groups. An added bonus of this choice is the unrivalled display of mountain wildflowers in the **Goúra valley**, directly below Tsoúka Roússa. After the approach, **VRISSOHÓRI** is a little anticlimactic, being almost swallowed by the dense woods at the base of Tsoúka Roússa peak. Tiny and ramshackle – this was one of the settlements burnt by the Germans in the war – the village has no proper inn, proper taverna or even a shop. You can camp at the edge of town by one of two springs, to either side of the "O3" coming down from Karterós.

The "O3" trail used to continue **across the Aóös** from **Vrissohóri to Paleosélli** but the path was bulldozed in 1989, extending the road in from Skamnélli. If you are purist about cross-country hiking, you will have to follow a slightly longer, pretty, but as yet unmarked trail via Áyios Minás chapel down to the Aóös, ford it (at low water only), and bushwhack a bit on the other side up to Paleosélli. You would need to allow about three and a half hours. The attraction of trail or road is access to the villages of Palioséli and Pádhes on the southern slopes of Mount Smólikas (see overleaf). From either, you could return to Ioánnina by bus, via Kónitsa.

North of the Aóös: Kónitsa and Mt Smólikas

The region **north of the Aóös river** is far less visited than the Zagóri. Its landscape is just as scenic but its villages are very poor relatives – virtually all those within sight of the river were burnt in the war, accounting for their present jerry-built appearance. The villagers claim that before 1943 their houses exceeded in splendour those of the Zagóri, since they had ample timber to span huge widths and for carved interiors.

The region can be approached on foot **from Mount Gamíla** (as detailed above) or by road from **Kónitsa**, the largest settlement in these parts, just off the road from Ioánnina to Kastoriá.

Kónitsa

KÓNITSA is a sleepy little town, its most memorable features a famous bridge and a view. The **bridge**, over the Aóös, is a giant, built around 1870 but looking far older. The view comes from the town's amphitheatrical setting on the slopes of Mount Trapezítsa; below spreads a broad flood plain where the Aóös and Voïdhomátis rivers mingle with the Sarandáporos before flowing through Albania to the sea.

The town was besieged by the Communist Democratic Army over the New Year in 1948, in a last and unsuccessful bid to establish a provisional capital. Much was destroyed in the fighting, though parts of the old bazaar and a tiny Turkish neighbourhood near the river survive.

If you want to stay, there is a basic but clean **inn** or *ksenónas* in the bazaar, the *Pindhos* (☎0655/22 604; ②), and rooms for rent at the *Psistaria To Dhendro* on the road out to the old bridge. There are also four **hotels**, cheapest of which are the *Tymfi* (☎0655/22 035; ③) and *Egnatia* (☎0655/22 881; ②) on the central *platía*, the latter unsigned at no. 17. More upmarket choices are the *Aoos* (☎0655/22 079; ④) and *Bourazani* (☎0655/22 079; ④). For freelance **camping**, see the Aóös Gorge, below.

Grouped around the central square are a **bank**, a good taverna, *O Makedhonas*, and the **bus terminal** (seven buses daily to Ioánnina and connections to most villages in the sections following).

The Stomíou monastery and Aóös gorge

Kónitsa can serve as a base for a fine afternoon's walking. Beginning at the old **bridge over the Aóös**, either of two interweaving tracks on the south bank lead within around an hour and a half to the eighteenth-century **Monastery of Stomíou**, perched on a bluff overlooking the narrowest part of the **Aóös gorge**. The *katholikón* here is of minimal interest, and the premises have been rather brutally restored, but the setting is sublime, and many visitors camp in the surroundings, with two springs to drink from, after bathing below in the river or under a tributary waterfall.

Beyond Stomíou the slopes are shaggy with vegetation constituting one of the last pristine habitats for lynx, roe deer and birds of prey. A minimally **waymarked path** climbs from the monastery gate up to the **Astráka area** (see preceding sections)

within five hours, rather less than that coming down. This is a very useful trekkers'
link, provided you have a good map: less arduous than the Astráka–Vrissohóri route
and allowing all sorts of loops through both Gamíla and the northern Píndhos.

Around Mount Smólikas

At 2637 metres, **Mount Smólikas**, to the east of Kónitsa, is the second highest peak in
Greece. It dominates a beautiful and very extensive range, covering a hundred square
kilometres of mountain territory, all of it above 1700m, and including a lovely mountain
lake, **Dhrakólimni**. The region is one of the last heartlands of traditional shepherd life,
which is best witnessed in summer at the Vlach village of **Samarína**.

The trailheads: Dhístrato, Paleosélli and Pádhes

From Kónitsa one afternoon bus a day, plus three weekly dawn services, roll through
the mountains to **DHÍSTRATO**, stopping en route at **PALEOSÉLLI** and **PÁDHES**.
Each of these villages has inn-tavernas, the best of which is that run by Sotiris Rouvalis
(π0655/71 216) in Paleosélli. Evening meals can be arranged at these places and there
are also two simple shops in Paleosélli.

Hiking options are varied, once you have reached these villages. **From Paleosélli**
there is a fine trail up to lake Dhrakólimni, from where you can make an ascent of Mount
Smólikas. **From Pádhes** there is actually a road to Dhrakólimni, for those exploring
the mountains with a vehicle or mountain bike; this has bulldozed what used to be a very
nice trail.

From Dhístrato there is also a road north to Samarína and a newly marked long-
distance trail/track, the **"E6"**, along the Aóös to **Vovoússa** (see below); this keeps to
the east (true left) bank of the Aóös and takes a full day to accomplish.

Samarína can be approached on foot, most enjoyably from Dhrakólimni.

Paleosélli to Dhrakólimni, Mount Smólikas and Áyia Paraskeví

The trail from **Paleosélli up to Dhrakólimni** has been waymarked as part of the
"O3" and a **refuge** established midway. Keys for this shelter are available from Sotiris
Rouvalis at the Paleosélli inn; it is located around two hours' walk from Paleosélli at a
spring and sheepfold known as Náneh, an idyllic little spot 1600m up with an external
water supply and toilet; it's also a good place for camping.

Beyond the refuge, the trail becomes less distinct but waymarks lead you up onto a
ridge aiming for the summit of Mount Smólikas – with Dhrakólimni disappearing at the
treeline. At a little over four walking hours from Paleosélli you should emerge into the
little depression containing **the lake**. You can camp here, but level space is at a
premium and you'll need a tent against the cold and damp.

Moving along the ridge above the lake, you can reach the **summit of Smólikas** in
about an hour and a quarter, tackling a rather nasty scree slope of nearly 45°. It is not
unusual to see chamoix near the top.

The easiest way down from Smólikas is a scenic and well-trodden two-and-a-half-hour
path to the hamlet of **Áyia Paraskeví** (also known as Kerásovo). This leads off at a
sheepfold in the vale between the lake and the peak. There are a couple of tavernas in
the village, a grossly overpriced inn (camping near the village tolerated) and a dawn bus
to Kónitsa.

Dhrakólimni to Samarína

If you have a good head for heights, and you're not carrying too heavy a pack, it's possible to walk from Dhrakólimni **along the ridge of Smólikas** much of the way to
Samarína.

It's a lot safer and easier, however, to head **back down to the lake** and follow the course of the stream below it to the southeast. After about an hour's descent you meet the old marked path from Pádhes to Samarína, which is in part paralleled and in part bulldozed over by a jeep track. Bear left (northeast), following sporadic yellow blazes on the rocks, and in another half-hour you pass a couple of sheepfolds on the left, where the new track (at last visit) ends. Here, bear to the right (northeast), towards a gap in the ridgeline, looking for markers on the last dwindling trees or rocks. Once through the "gap" – where you join up with the high ridge route – you've crossed the actual Smólikas watershed, and descend into the rather lunar, northwest-facing cirque which eventually drains down to Áyia Paraskeví.

Next you traverse the base of one of Smólikas's secondary peaks as a prelude to creeping up a scree-laden rock "stair". From the top of this climb – the last en route – the markers change from yellow to red, and a line of small cairns descends diagonally across a broad, flat-topped ridge. Follow these cairns until the path wriggles down through a rocky gully, levelling out on another neck of land. To the left of this is a dry gully (to be avoided) and way off to the right (south) can be glimpsed the other of Smólikas's lakes, as large or bigger than Dhrakólimni but difficult of access. Try not to stray in either direction in poor visibility – there are steep drops to either side.

Beyond, there is a single stunted landmark pine before you encounter the leading edge of the black pine forest, at the foot of Bogdháni peak, which is capped by an altimeter. The trail threads between this knoll and Mount Gorgoloú, at the foot of which lies Samarína. Twenty minutes or so beyond this pass, the Bogdháni spring oozes from serpentine strata. Then you begin to descend once more in earnest through thick forest, with the Soupotíra spring gurgling into a log-trough set in a beautiful mountain clearing. Lower down, the woods end abruptly and you'll emerge on a bare slope directly above Samarína.

Samarína and beyond

Although **SAMARÍNA** looks a bit of a mess – it was burnt during both World War II and the civil war – it's a thriving and friendly place and very proud of its Vlach traditions. It's only inhabited in the summer (at 1450m, it's the highest village in Greece), when it fills up with Vlachs from the plains of Thessaly – and their sheep, some 50,000 of them. The high point of the year is the Feast of the Assumption on August 15, when there is much music and merry-making and the place is swamped by nostalgic Vlachs from Athens and all over the country.

The interior of the main church, the **Panayía**, is superb, with frescoes and painted ceilings and an intricately carved *témblon*, where the angels, soldiers and biblical figures are dressed in mustachios and *fustanélles* (the Greek kilt). Though it looks a lot older, like many other churches in the region, it dates from around 1800. Its special hallmark is an adult black pine growing out of the roof of the apse, and no one can remember a time without it.

The improbably large stone building that confronts you at the top of the village is a **hotel** and there is another basic **inn** by the *platía*, but both of these may well be full during the summer– in which case the only other lodging, with more chance of a vacancy, is the *Hotel Kiparissi*, out on the east edge of town. No one will mind, though, if you camp a bit out of town, and there are numerous *psistariés* (and even an OTE office) on the square.

Leaving Samarína, you have two choices. There is a bus to Grevená from June to September, but not every day, though a lift is not too hard to get if you ask around. Otherwise, just follow the **E6 trail to Dhístrato** via the monastery of Áyia Paraskeví and Goúrna ridge. As indicated under "Dhístrato" above, it's possible to continue along the east bank of the river to Vovoússa, in the Eastern Zagóri (see below).

Vovoússa and the eastern Zagóri

As detailed in the previous section, walkers can make a loop back from Samarína/
Dhístrato via Vovoússa and the **eastern Zagóri**. Alternatively, you could treat this as
an entry into the Píndhos, following the road up towards Vovoússa from HÁNI
BALDHOÚMA on the Ioánnina–Métsovo road. This heads north along the valley of the
Várdhas river and thence to the Aóös, near Vovoússa, past a series of predominantly
Vlach villages. It's a winding, precipitous dirt road for most of the way but plied by a
regular **bus** from Ioánnina. Services are daily from Ioánnina at 2pm except Wednesday
and Saturday, returning to Ioánnina the next morning at 6am; Sunday out from
Ioánnina at 8.15am, returning at 2pm.

Háni Baldhoúma to Vovoússa

From Háni Baldhoúma, the road snakes uphill through a lush landscape of broad-
leafed trees and scrub towards Greveníti, where a black pine forest, extending virtually
to Albania, takes over.

The villages of **GREVENÍTI**, **FLAMBOURÁRI**, **ELATOHÓRI** and beautiful
MAKRINÓ (an hour's glorious walk across the ravine, with a fine monastery) are all
populated by Vlachs. The first three have basic **inns** (*ksenónes*) or rooms and places to
eat. All are badly depopulated, never having recovered from wartime destruction by the
Germans pursuing Resistance fighters. But what is left of them is very attractive:
stone-roofed churches, vine-shaded terraces, courtyards full of flowers and logs
stacked for the winter.

Vovoússa and beyond

VOVOÚSSA lies right on the Aóös river, its milky green waters spanned by a high-
arched eighteenth-century bridge. On either side, wooded ridges rise steeply to the
skyline. There is a large riverside **hotel** in the village, a couple of *psistariés*, and a
single (poorly stocked) shop, all of which are open more or less year-round. If you
prefer to camp, walk for about fifteen minutes downstream to where a stretch of riverbank meadow makes an idyllic site (turn left off the road on to the old path just past
the Vovoússa roadsign), so long as the thought of bears in the vicinity doesn't alarm
you. Fresh prints are often seen in the riverside mud here, but the locals swear they
are timid creatures and avoid contact with humans.

Though the road continues **beyond Vovoússa** to PERIVÓLI and on to Grevená, the
Ioánnina-based bus goes no further. You'd have to walk or hitch to Perivóli (uninhabited from November to May; big summer hotel) to pick up the Grevená province buses.
If you're committed to staying in Epirus, it's better to hike to Dhístrato, where there's
an inn and early morning bus back to Kónitsa (see preceding section).

Mount Grámmos

It was on **Mount Grámmos** that the Democratic Communist Army made its last stand
in the civil war. Their eventual retreat into Albania followed a bitter campaign which
saw tens of thousands of deaths and the world's first use of napalm (supplied by the
United States). The upper slopes of the mountain remain totally bare, and walking in
the range you still see rusting cartridges and trenches from the fighting.

If you want to visit the range, and peer down into the wilds of Albania, the simplest
approach is from Kónitsa. At 2pm each day there's a bus to **Plikáti**, the most useful
base for a day's hike. Coming from the Gámila/Smólikas area, you're best off walking
out to **Áyia Paraskeví**, which has a daily bus to Kónitsa; if you time it right you could
get off at the junction with the main road and flag down the Plikáti bus.

Plikáti and a hike up Grámmos

There's a singularly end-of-the-world feel to **PLIKÁTI** – as indeed there should be, for this is the closest Greek village to the Albanian frontier, and trailhead for Greece's least frequented mountain, Grámmos. It's a traditional-looking place, with stone houses, a tiny permanent population, a couple of **inns** and a combination taverna/general store.

Mount Grámmos is, at 2520m, the fourth loftiest Greek peak. In making the **ascent** – a practicable day trip from Plikáti – the easiest strategy is to angle north-northeast up the gentler slopes leading to Perífano (2442m), second highest point in the range, rather than tackling head-on the badly eroded and steep incline immediately below the main peak. The trail in the indicated direction is clear for the first two hours out of the village, crossing the river and switchbacking up through bushes and then beech trees before it peters out at a sheepfold. Just above this are the last water sources on this side of the ridge – various trickles feeding a pond. Bearing west along a plain trail, you can thread along the crest for roughly an hour to the **summit**, its cairn covered in a babel of multilingual initials and graffiti. Below, to the west, a cultivated Albanian valley stretches to the barns of ERSEKE, 5km distant.

In the opposite direction from Plikáti, you can follow the watershed to the lower **Aréna massif**, which is garnished with a trio of small lakes and clumps of beech trees. The summer-only village visible from the summit ridge is GRÁMMOS, to which a clear trail leads – but from where there's no bus (and little transport) on towards Kastoriá, the nearest town.

INTO ALBANIA

A side road from KALPÁKI, roughly midway between Ioánnina and Kónitsa, leads to KAKÁVI, currently the only authorised land crossing between Greece and Albania. Since the end of the Communist regime in 1991, travel to Albania by most nationals (Americans included) is permitted. However, in practice, most of those using this entry point are Greeks visiting friends or relatives in northern Epirus (as they call the ethnically Greek part of southern Albania). Independent travel – while not impossible – is difficult and, with famine currently stalking the country, a pretty questionable exercise. If you're intent on it, you'd probably be best off in a group, at least for the first few days, then you can decide whether to stay on. In Ioánnina, *Besa Travel*, at Mavroyiánni 37 (☎0651/73 220), organise all-in tours, with transport and accommodation. They also arrange visas, which are still technically required at the border.

For day trips to the Albanian coast, see also Corfu in *The Ionian Islands* chapter.

Villages of the south Píndhos

Most hikers arriving at Ioánnina have their sights firmly set to the north – on the Víkos gorge and the Zagóri villages. If you're feeling adventurous, however, and are not too particular about where you sleep or what you eat, the villages of the **south Píndhos** provide an interesting alternative. On weekdays buses leave from Ioánnina's southern (Odhós Vizaníou) station at 5am and 3.30pm for Ágnanda, Prámanda and other remote villages on the beetling flanks of **Mounts Tzoumérka** and **Kakardhítsa**: two overlapping ridges of bare mountains linked by a high plateau, plainly visible from Ioánnina. There are few special sights, but you'll get a solid, undiluted experience of Epirot life.

Many of the villages can also be approached **from Árta**. Buses run a couple of times daily in either direction along the secondary road between Árta and Ioánnina, stopping at PLÁKA, with an eighteenth-century bridge over the Arakhthós amid stunning scenery. Here you can flag down another two daily Árta-based buses continuing along the side road east into the mountains as far as MELISSOURGÍ.

Prámanda, Melissourgí and hikes

Twelve kilometres into the mountains from Pláka, **ÁGNANDA** is the first village of any size on the bus route. However, it was heavily damaged in the last war so it's not particularly attractive, nor does it have reliable accommodation.

Better to continue on to **PRÁMANDA**, where there's a rather primitive *ksenónas* (inn), a more comfortable pension, the *Tzoumerka* (☎0659/61 336; ③), plus a couple of *psistariés*. The village itself, while no more distinguished architecturally than Ágnanda, enjoys a wonderful setting strewn across several ridges; it is dominated by Mount Kakardhítsa behind and commands fine views of the Kallaritikós valley. Nearby there is a huge cave, inhabited in Neolithic times; any villager will give you directions (ask for *To Spíli*). Some days the bus continues to **MATSOÚKI**, the last village on the provincial route, beautifully set near the head of a partly forested valley and offering easy access to Mount Kakardhítsa as well as a few beds.

MELISSOURGÍ, 6km to the southeast, is much more rewarding, having escaped destruction during the war. Its buildings and large church are a grand if sombre unity in traditional grey schist. There is a taverna and two **inns** – one large, one tiny, though neither not to be counted on in midsummer, when all accommodation is likely to be booked by holidaying relatives from the cities.

If you plan on hiking, Melissourgí is a good jump-off point for rambles on the **Kostelláta plateau** to the south. This upland separates the 2429-metre Kakardhítsa, which looms sheer above the village, from the more pyramidal Tzoumérka (2399m). You can cross these high pastures, heading south, in a day and a half. The initial stretch of path south from Melissourgí is waymarked, and there are intermittent *stánes*, or summer sheepfolds, if you need water or directions. You can descend to the villages of THEODHORIANÁ or DHROSSOPIYÍ, at the edge of the Ahelóös river basin; both have daily early-morning buses buses to Árta, as well as modest **inns** and tavernas.

Kípina and Kallarítes

On days when it doesn't serve Matsoúki, the bus runs instead as far as the hamlet of **KÍPINA**. A famous namesake **monastery**, founded in 1381 but uninhabited today, hangs like a martin's nest from the cliff face a half hour's walk beyond the hamlet.

Beyond this point, you can follow the road for around half an hour to join the remnant of a wonderful *kalderími* (stepped path) climbing up to the village of **KALLARÍTES**, perched superbly above the upper reaches of the Kallaritikós river. One of the southernmost Vlach settlements in the Píndhos, this depleted village was a veritable El Dorado until the close of the last century. Fame and fortune were based on its specialisation in gold- and silver-smithing, and even today the craftsmen of Ioánnina are mostly of Kallaritiote descent – as in fact is Bulgari, one of the world's most celebrated contemporary jewellers.

Though the village is all but deserted except during summer holidays, the grand houses of the departed rich are kept in excellent repair by their descendants. The cobbled *platía*, with its old-fashioned shops and statue commemorating local emigré Kallaritiots, who helped finance the Greek revolution, has probably remained unchanged for a century.

There is a fairly basic **inn** (☎0659/61 251) and two grills on the square.

The Hroússias Gorge and Siráko

Just beyond Kallarítes, the awesome **Hroússias river chasm** separates the town from its neighbour Siráko, visible high up on the west bank but a good hour's walk away. The trail is steep and spectacular, including a near-vertical "ladder" hewn out of the rockface. Down on the bridge over the river you can peer upstream at a pair of abandoned watermills; the canyon walls are steep and the sun shines down here for only a few hours a day even in summer.

SIRÁKO is even more strikingly set than Kallarítes with its fortress-like locale; its well-preserved mansions, archways and churches are more reminiscent of those in the Zagóri. Not to be upstaged by Kallarítes, the village has also erected a number of monuments to various national figures (including the poet Krystallis) who hailed from here. There is a **taverna** whose proprietor (☎0651/53 290) rents out a handful of **rooms** in summer, and a couple of *kafenía*.

There is an alternative route back to Ioánnina from Siráko, **via Mihalítsi**, though it is covered by just three buses a week. These follow a slightly bizarre schedule, leaving Ioánnina on Tuesday at 5.45am and 1.30pm (returning from Sírako at 8am and 3.45pm), and on Friday at 4pm (returning at 6.15pm).

THE COAST AND THE SOUTH

The **Epirot coast** is nothing special, with **Igoumenítsa** a purely functional ferry port and **Párga**, the most attractive resort, overdeveloped and best left for out-of-season travel. Head a little inland, however, and things look up. Close by Párga, the **Necromanteion of Ephyra** is an intriguing ancient detour – the legendary gate of Hades; the **gorge of the Aherónda** offers fine hiking; and the imposing Roman ruins of **Nikópolis** break the journey to Préveza. Best of all, perhaps, is **Árta**, an interesting little provincial town, approached either around the Amvrakikós gulf, or, most impressively, along the plane-shaded Loúros river gorge from Ioánnina.

Moving south into **Étolo-Akarnanía**, the landscape becomes increasingly desolate with little to delay your progress to the island of Lefkádha (see the *Ionian Islands* chapter) or to Andírio, for the ferry to the Peloponnese. For committed isolates, though, there's **Kálamos** islet, south of Vónitsa; and for diehard romantics, **Messolóngi**, though unglamorous, retains its name, its situation and Byron's buried heart.

Igoumenítsa and around

IGOUMENÍTSA is Greece's third passenger port, after Pireás and Pátra, with almost hourly ferries to Corfu and several daily to Italy, and in summer hydrofoils to Corfu, Páxi and Brindisi. In the past, there were regular connections north along the coast of what-was-Yugoslavia – services are suspended at time of writing.

These ferry functions and a lively waterfront apart, the town is pretty unappealing – it was levelled during the last war and rebuilt in a sprawling, functional style. If you can arrange it, try to arrive and get a ferry out the same day. Heading for Italy, you may find this tricky, as most departures are early morning, forcing an overnight stay in or near the port; to get a berth, or take a vehicle on the few afternoon or evening sailings (see details overleaf), it's best to make reservations in advance.

Accommodation

The town is not large and most of the **hotels** – which are plentiful if uninspiring – are to be found either along, or just back from, the waterfront. Choices include:

Hotel Rhodos, Kíprou 19 (☎0665/22 248). Cheap rooms in town; near the main square. ②

Hotel Stavrodhromi, Soulíou 14 (☎0665/22 343). Another budget fallback. ③

Hotel Egnatia, Elefthérias 1 (☎0665/23 648). And another. ③

Hotel Xenia, Vassiléos Pavloú 2 (☎0665/22 282). Good value for its class – very comfortable and nicely sited near the entrance to the town. ④

The closest campsites are at the beaches of KALÁMI or PLATARIÁ, respectively 10km and 12km south (local buses); both have tavernas.

IGOUMENITSA FERRY COMPANIES

If you arrive late and stay overnight in Igoumenítsa, you can at least shop around for tickets; travel offices tend to stay open until around 9pm. Most **ferries** leave for Italy between 7 and 10am, with usually at least one afternoon or evening departure in season. In 1992 **hydrofoils** to Corfu, Páxi and Brindisi were introduced; these are operated by *Ilio Lines* and run in summer only.

A few **general points**:

Fares All companies offer a variety of fares for cabin, "aircraft" seats and deck passage, as well as reductions according to age, student or rail card status. Cars are carried on all ferries.

Embarkation tax of (currently) 1500dr per person and per car is levied on all international departures.

Stopovers Unlike sailings from Pátra, ferries from Igoumenítsa to Italy are not allowed to sell tickets with stopover on Corfu. You can, however, take the regular Corfu ferry over and then pick up most ferry routes on from there.

Checking in If you have bought tickets in advance, or from a travel agent other than the official agent listed below, you must check in (to the respective official agent, or to their booth at the port) at least two hours before departure.

Currency exchange Arriving in Igoumenítsa from Italy or Yugoslavia, a word of warning. If you miss the banks (which all close at 2pm) you're dependent on travel agents for changing money and rates are not good. It's best to buy a few drachmas on board.

International ferry companies and agents

R-Line Otranto (9hr), via Corfu; Tues–Sat only, 10am. *Epirus Travel,* Ethnikís Andistásis 62; ☎0665/24 252.

Fragline Brindisi (10–11hr), via Corfu; Mon, Wed, Fri at 9.30pm; Sat 10pm; Sun

Around Igoumenítsa

If you find yourself stuck for the day in Igoumenítsa, the best escapes are probably to the **beach**. The closest strands are alongside the campsites at KALÁMI and PLATARIÁ (10km and 12km south) and at SÍVOTA, 11km south of Platariá.

SÍVOTA is by far the most attractive – a sleepy resort in the initial stages of development, surrounded by olive groves, and draped over some evocative coastal topography. It's the sort of place Greeks favour for *their* holidays and, accordingly, summer apartments predominate. Best value among the half dozen hotels are the *Acropolis* (☎0665/93 263; ③) and *Hellas* (☎0665/93 227; ③). Down at Sívota's small harbour, there's year-round **car-ferry to Paxí**; contact *Sivota Travel* (☎0665/93 222) for schedules.

Inland: Filiates and Paramithía

Inland, few destinations reward the effort expended to get to them, despite earnest promotion in the EOT brochures. The "traditional village" of **FILIÁTES**, 19km to the northwest, is a drab place, with a paltry number of old Epirot houses and nothing much else – not even a taverna – to redeem it.

The old hill town of **PARAMITHÍA**, 38km to the southeast (2 buses daily), is another disappointment. A castle and Byzantine church are scarcely in evidence, and despite touting as a centre for copper-working, just two mediocre metal shops remain in a tiny bazaar much encroached on by 1960s architecture – nothing comparable to what you'd more easily and conveniently see in Ioánnina. For an inland excursion, your time would be much better spent at the remarkable Necromanteion of Ephyra or the Gorge of the Aherónda (see sections overpage).

11.30pm; Wed, Fri, Sat 6.30am. *Revis Brothers*, Ethnikís Andístassis 34; ☎0665/22 104.

Hellenic Mediterranean Lines Brindisi (10hr); daily at 7 and 8am via Corfu; Ortona via Corfu (20hr) Tues, Thurs and Sat at 8pm. *Hellenic Mediterranean Lines*, Ethnikís Andistásis 30; ☎0665/22 180.

Adriatica Brindisi (10hr), via Corfu; daily at 7am. No exclusive agent.

European Seaways Brindisi (9hr) via Corfu; daily at 6am. *Katsios Shipping*, 44A Ethnikís Andistásis (☎0665/22 409).

ANEK Ancona direct (21hr 30min), Tues, Wed, Sat at 10.30am; Trieste direct (24hr) Sat 9.30am. *Revis Brothers*, Ethnikís Andistásis 34; ☎0665/22 104.

Ventouris Bari (10hr–12hr 30min), via Corfu; daily at 6.30am spring/autumn, 8.30pm summer. *Milano Travel*, Ayíion Apostólon 11B; ☎0665/24 237.

Marlines Ancona (24hr), direct; Thurs 6pm, Tues 8am, Fri 10am. *Marlines*, Ethnikís Andistásis 42; ☎0665/23 301.

Strintzis Ancona (23hr), via Corfu; Mon, Wed (9pm), Fri, Sun (7.15am). *G. Pitoulis*, Ethnikís Andistásis 14; ☎0665/24 252.

Minoan Ancona (23hr 30min), via Corfu; daily except Wed, Sun (11am). No exclusive agent.

All frequencies of ferry crossings detailed are for the high season (early July to mid-September); out of season, all services are reduced.

Domestic ferries

Corfu (2hr); hourly ferries in season from 5.30am to 10pm; tickets from the quay or any agent. Daily hydrofoils in summer.

Paxí, Kefaloniá, Itháki. Sporadic ferry services are operated in July and August only, most years. Paxí is also connected by **hydrofoil** - on a line that continues to Lefkádha, Itháki, Kefalloniá and Zákinthos.

Párga

PÁRGA – if it weren't so popular – would be a wonderful place. Its crescent of tiered houses, set below a Norman-Venetian **castle**, and its superb **beach**, with a trail of rocky islets offshore, constitute as enticing a resort as any in western Greece. However, the last few years have seen all of this swamped by concrete apartment blocks – and the accompanying crowds. The Corfu model, presumably, was just too close. These days, in season at least, it's hard to recommend more than a brief stopover (if you can find a room) before taking the local **ferry to Paxí**. And in July and August even the ferry may need to be reserved a day ahead.

The Town

Párga's fate is sadder still given its highly evocative and idiosyncratic history. From the fourteenth to eighteenth centuries Párga was a lone Venetian toehold in Epirus, complementing the Serene Republic's offshore possessions in the Ionian islands. The Lion of Saint Mark – symbol of Venice – is still present on the bluff-top **Kastro** (open all day). Later, the Napoleonic French took the town for a brief period, leaving additional fortifications on the largest **islet**, a 200-metre swim from the harbour beach.

At the start of the nineteenth century, the town enjoyed a stint of independence, self-sufficient through the export of olives, still a mainstay of the region's agriculture. After that, the British acquired Párga and subsequently sold it to Ali Pasha. The townspeople, knowing his reputation, decamped to the Ionian islands, the area being resettled by Muslims who remained until the exchange of populations in 1924, when they were replaced by Orthodox Greeks from the area around Constantinople.

Beaches and practicalities

Párga's **beaches** line three consecutive bays, split by the headland of the fortress hill. Immediately beyond the castle (and on foot easiest reached by the long stairway from the castle gate) is **Váltos beach**, over a kilometre in length as it sprawls around to the hamlet of the same name. **Lihnós**, 3km in the opposite (southeast) direction, is a similarly huge beach. Both have **campsites**; another, *Parga Camping* (☎0684/31 130), is sited 600m inland to the north among olive groves.

Rooms are plentiful if a little pricey: someone will probably approach you on arrival at the bus station or ferry quay. **Hotels** are generally block-booked in season, but try the *Tourist* (☎0684/31 515; ②), at the base of the fort, or the *Galini* (☎0684/31 581; ③), inland and north of town.

For **meals**, the taverna *To Kantouni*, at the rear of the market on Platía Ayíou Dhimitríou, serves good cheap meals, as does its nearest neighbour across the square. Up by the castle are a couple more decent places to eat. On the waterside, *To Souli* is probably the best of the bunch.

Buses link Párga with Igoumenítsa and Préveza four times daily, more in season; if you've missed a direct departure try hitching the 12km up to the Mórfi junction on the Igoumenítsa–Préveza road. *Parga Tours* and *West Travel*, both just inland from the dock, rent **mopeds** – worth considering for the trip to the Necromanteion of Ephyra detailed below. *Ephira Travel* (☎0684/31 439), near the bus station, does **car rental**. Most tour agents sell tickets for the daily (in season) passenger **ferry to Paxí**.

West Travel also runs **boat tours up the Aherónda river** to the Necromanteion of Ephyra (see below), allowing good views of the delta birdlife en route.

The Necromanteion of Ephyra

The **Necromanteion of Ephyra** (or Sanctuary of Persephone and Hades) is the strangest of all Greek sites. It is sited on a low, rocky hill, above what in ancient times was the mouth of the Aherónda – the mythical Styx, river of the underworld – and from Mycenaean to Roman times it maintained an elaborate Oracle of the Dead.

The oracle never achieved the stature of Delphi or Dodona but its fame was sufficient for Homer, writing (it is assumed) in the ninth century BC, to use it as the setting for Odysseus's visit to Hades. This he does explicitly, with Circe advising Odysseus:

> You will come to a wild coast and to Persephone's grove, where the hill poplars grow and the willows that so quickly lose their seeds. Beach your boat there by Ocean's swirling stream and march on into Hades' Kingdom of Decay. There the River of Flaming Fire and the River of Lamentation, which is a branch of the Waters of the Styx, unite around a pinnacle of rock to pour their thundering streams into Acheron. This is the spot, my lord, that I bid you seek out . . . then the souls of the dead and departed will come up in their multitudes.

The Sanctuary

Open daily 8am–3pm.

The trees of Homer's account still mark the sanctuary's site, though the lake, which once enclosed the island-oracle, has receded to the vague line of the Aherónda skirting the plain: from the sanctuary you can pick out its course from the vegetation. As for the sanctuary itself, its **ruins**, flanked by an early Christian basilica, offer a fascinating exposé of the confidence tricks pulled by its priestly initiates.

According to contemporary accounts, pilgrims arriving on the oracle-island were accommodated for a night in windowless rooms. Impressed by the atmosphere, and by their mission to consult with the souls of the dead, they would then be relieved of their votive offerings, while awaiting their consultation with the dead.

When their turn came, they would be sent groping along labyrinthine corridors into the heart of the sanctuary, where, further disoriented by hallucinogenic vapours, they would be lowered into the antechamber of Hades itself to witness whatever spiritual visitation the priests might have devised.

The remains of the sanctuary allow each of these function room to be identified; there is a plan at the entrance. At the centre is a long room with high walls, flanked by chambers used for votive offerings. And from here metal steps lead to the underground chamber where the necromantic audiences took place. Originally this descent was by means of a precarious windlass mechanism – which was found on the site.

Access – and Kanaláki

The Necromanteion stands just above the village of MESOPÓTAMO, 22km southeast of Párga; it is also signposted from the village of KASTRÍ, 5km east, on the Igoumenítsa–Préveza bus route.

The easiest access is by tour (or rented moped) from Párga. At **KANALÁKI**, 2km southeast of Kastrí, mopeds can also be rented in summer, and there are two basic hotels: the *Ephyra* (☎0684/22 128; ②) and *Aheron* (☎0684/22 241; ②). The village could make a useful base for leisurely exploration of both the Necromanteion and the Soúli area (see below).

The Aherónda gorge and Souliot country

Although it seems hard today to think of the placid **Aherónda**, near the Necromanteion of Ephyra, as the pathway to hell, only a few kilometres to the east the river saws a course through a **mountain gorge**, its water cutting deep into rock strata and swirling in unnavigable eddies. While not in quite the same league as the Víkos, it is certainly a respectable wilderness, and if you're looking for an adventure inland from Párga you won't find better. The trail takes you into the traditional heartland of the **Souliots** – for more on which see the Monastery of Zalongo, below.

The hike up the gorge starts at **GLIKÍ**, near Kanaláki but on another side road between Préveza and Paramithía (one daily bus from the former). The river here, still relatively calm, is flanked on one bank by a reasonable **café-grill** ideal for a lunch before or after the trek, and on the other by a sign reading "Skála Tzavélainas", pointing up a dirt road. Following this, bear left after about one kilometre, towards a chapel, and within ten minutes you'll reach a laboriously wrought tunnel, where the wider track ends and the *skála* – a well-constructed path – begins. Below, the canyon walls have suddenly squeezed together, and upstream a carpet of greenery covers a wilderness, rolling up to the plainly visible castle of **Kiáfa**.

The main trail, waymarked by a Swiss trekking company, **descends to the Aherónda** – spanned on a relatively recent bridge – then immediately takes a much older bridge over a tributary, the outflow of the Tsangariótiko river, known locally as the **Piyés Soulíou** (Souliot Springs). Beyond here the marked route climbs up through the oaks out of the Aherónda valley. (If you want to explore the main drainage, there are faint trails on the north bank, and detailed maps of the area indicate that you would emerge from the narrows below the upstream village of TRÍKASTRON within around two and a half hours).

The main trail, after paralleling the Tsangariótiko, turns up yet another side ravine to reach the tiny, poor hamlet of **SAMONÍDHA** – around two hours from Glikí – where there's a well behind the community office; the nearest *kafenío*/taverna is in the village of SOÚLI, 3km to the north.

From Samonídha a recently bulldozed track leads up within another half-hour to **Kiáfa castle**, one of several the local Souliots erected in their many and protracted wars with the Turks.

South to Préveza

Approaches to Préveza from the Necromanteion and Aherónda area feature a few more minor sites and resorts before edging out on to the landlocked **Amvrakikós (Ambracian) Gulf**, where in 31 BC Octavian defeated Antony and Cleopatra at the Battle of Actium. The most substantial ruin, a bit south of the junction of the coastal, inland and gulf roads, is suitably enough Octavian's "Victory City" of **Nikopolis**.

The coast route: Ammoudhiá and Liyiá

The village of **AMMOUDHIÁ**, 4km due west of the Necromanteion site, is a surprisingly unspoilt little resort, considering it faces Párga across the bay and has an excellent beach. Like other resorts down the coast towards Préveza, it attracts mainly Germans and Italians equipped with campervans.

On the Préveza coast road, the first village of note is LOÚTSA, a still-functioning fishing port. South again for five kilometres and you reach **LIYIÁ**, unmarked on many maps and much the best place to break a journey. There are **rooms for rent**, an impromptu campsite, several tavernas and an enormous, boulder-studded beach – all overlooked by a crumbling castle in the distance.

Two daily **buses** cover this coastal route between Ammoudhiá and Préveza. Note, however, that long-distance buses to and from Párga or Igoumenítsa don't pass this way – heading instead inland at Messopótamo before rejoining the coast road near Nikopolis.

The inland route: Zalóngo and ancient Kassopi

After some 28km on the inland route (National Road #19) from Messopótamo, you pass a turning east to the village of **KAMARÍNA**, which is overlooked by the monastery and monument of Zalóngo and the ruins of ancient Kassopi. These are a steep four-kilometre-climb from the village, though a daily bus from Préveza goes direct to the site each morning at 6am.

The **Monastery of Zalóngo** is a staple of Greek schoolbook history, its fame immortalised by the defiant mass suicide of a group of Souliot women in 1806. The Souliots, an independent-spirited tribe of Orthodox Christians, maintained their village strongholds above the Aherónda gorge and into this range to its south; great mountain warriors, they provided the bodyguard for Lord Byron in the War of Independence. For the last decades of the eighteenth century, and the first of the nineteenth, they had conducted a perennial rebellion against Ali Pasha and the Turks. In the famous 1806 episode, Turkish troops cornered a large band of Souliots in the Zalóngo monastery. As this refuge was overrun, about sixty Souliot women and children fled to the top of the cliff above and, to the amazement of the approaching Muslim troops, the mothers danced one by one, with their children in their arms, over the edge of the precipice.

This act is commemorated by a modern **cement-and-stone sculpture** – one of whose figures is currently headless after a lightning strike. Along with the monastery nearby, it draws regular groups of Greek schoolchildren.

Slightly to the northwest of the monastery, on a similar bluff, are the remains of **Ancient Kassopi** (daily 8am–3pm), a minor Thesprotian city-state. The ruins, dating mainly from the fourth century BC, are at present under excavation, though an excellent site plan helps to locate highlights – most of which are visible from the publicly accessible areas. You can view the walls and column bases of the central *agora*, *stoas*, a tiny theatre and a *katagoyeion* or guest hostelry. Principally, though, Kassopi is memorable for its site – nearly two thousand feet above sea level, with the coast and Ionian islands laid out below you.

Nikopolis

NIKOPOLIS – "Victory City" – was founded by Octavian on the site where his army had camped prior to the Battle of Actium. An arrogant and ill-considered gesture, it made little geographical sense: the settlement was on unfirm ground, water had to be transported by aqueduct from the distant springs of the Loúros mountains, and a population had to be forcibly imported from towns as far afield as Náfpaktos. However, such delusionary posturing was perhaps understandable. At **Actium**, Octavian had first blockaded and then largely annihilated the combined fleets of Antony and Cleopatra, gathered there for the invasion of Italy. The rewards were sweet, subsequently transforming Octavian from a military commander into the Emperor Augustus.

Nikopolis's own history was undistinguished, with much of its original population drifting back to their homes. As the Roman Empire declined, the city suffered sacking by Vandals and Goths. Later, in the sixth century AD, it was restored by Justininan and flourished for a while as a Byzantine city, but within four centuries it had sunk again into the earth, devastated by the combined effect of earthquakes and Bulgar raids.

The Site and Museum

Open Tues–Sun 9am–3pm; 200dr, students 100dr.

Nikopolis's far-flung and overgrown ruins stand either side of the main road from Igoumenítsa/Árta to Préveza – 7km north of the latter. Travelling by bus, you could just ask to be set down here – though it's a long walk back to town; if you can afford it, it would be better to engage a taxi in Préveza for a couple of hours.

The **site** looks impressive from the road. A great theatre stands to the east and as you approach the site museum, past remnants of the baths, there is a formidable stretch of fortified walls. Walking around, however, the promise of this enormous site is unfulfilled; few other remains reward close inspection.

The **museum** (sporadically open) houses a rather miscellaneous array of Roman sculpture. Its caretaker's main function used to be the wardership of the Roman and Byzantine mosaics unearthed amidst the foundations of the sixth-century **basilica of Doumetios** nearby, but these have recently been recovered by a protective layer of sand and polythene. If available, the caretaker will escort you to the Roman **Odeion**, for which he has the keys. This dates from the original construction of the city and has been well restored for use in a summer music festival (see Préveza).

Backtracking past the scant foundations of another sixth-century church, the **basilica of Bishop Alkyon**, it's a three-kilometre walk to the main **theatre**, whose arches stand amidst dangerously crumbling masonry. To the left of this you can just make out the sunken outline of the **stadium**, below the modern village of Smirtoúna. Octavian's own tent was pitched upon the hill above the village, and a massive podium remains from the **commemorative monument** that he erected. On a terrace alongside, recent excavations have revealed the remains of "beaks" (ramming protruberances) of some of the captured warships, which he dedicated to the gods.

Préveza

Modern **PRÉVEZA**, at the tip of the gulf, is a relatively insignificant successor to Nikopolis, but not without its charm. With the advent of charter traffic to nearby Áktio airport in recent years, the town has had a facelift of sorts, and more character remains in the old market than, say, at Párga. In the summer months, the town also has useful *Ilio Lines* **hydrofoils** to Páxi, Lefkádha, Itháki and Kefalloniá.

Charter flights arriving at the **airport** generally have transport laid on to Lefkádha or Párga; otherwise there are taxis. The bus station in Préveza is on Leofóros Irínis, a kilometre north of the ferry dock. **Ferries** across the gulf ply across to Áktio jetty, where you can pick up infrequent buses to Vónitsa and Lefkádha.

None of the half-dozen **hotels** is especially inviting. The cheapest are the *Glaros* on Ammoúdhia street (☎0682/27 123; ②); the *Urania* (☎0682/27 123; ③), near the bus terminal at Irínis 17; and the *Savvas* (☎0682/27 432; ③), on Áyios Thómas. A reasonable mid-range option is the *Dioni* at Kaloú 4 (☎0682/27 432; ④).

The nearest **campsites** are out towards KALAMÍTSI, on the promontory south of the ferry dock: *Camping Indian Village* and *Camping Kalamitsi* here are around 4km from town. In the opposite direction, any bus running through KANÁLI (not to be confused with Kanaláki) will pass the summer-only sites of *Monolithi* and *Kanali*, on either side of the road at Monolíthi beach (11km from Préveza).

Meals, nightlife and culture

There must now be a dozen **tavernas** scattered around the centre of Préveza, many within sight of the clock tower. Some good choices include *Psatha*, Dhardhanellíou 2, up from the main shopping thoroughfare and the clock; *To Panepistimio*, a tiny kitchen at Hrístou Kódou 26, west of the clock; the *Ouzeri Kaiksis* at Parthenagoyíou 9; and *Amvrosios*, specialising in grilled sardines and barrel wine, virtually under the clock. *G. Peponis* offers reasonable waterfront eating on Venizélou, the quay. If you can afford it, *To Dhelfinaki*, behind the *Credit Bank*, specialises in fish. At **night**, the alleys in the bazaar, especially around the fish market building, come alive with an assortment of bars, pubs and cafés.

As for culture, July and August see a range of musical events as part of the **Nikopolia festival**, held at Nikopolis. There is also a **shadow puppet** (*karaghiosis*) theatre – the only one left in the country – on Platía Androútsou, by the port.

Sharing a building on the quay are a **post office** and **tourist office**. The OTE is in a pedestrian grid, near the *Hotel Minos*.

Árta

ÁRTA is one of the more pleasant Greek towns: a quiet place, very much the provincial (Étolo-Akarnanía) capital, with an old centre that retains much of its Turkish bazaar aspect, and some celebrated medieval monuments. It also has a fine situation, in a loop of the broad Árakhthos River, flanked, as you enter town from the west, by a packhorse **bridge** that is the subject of song and poetry throughout the mainland.

Legend maintains that the bridge builder, continually thwarted by the current washing his foundations away, took the advice of a bird and sealed up his wife in the central pier; the bridge finally held but the woman's voice haunted the place thereafter. Nowadays, crudely stitched together with cables, it is not very romantic.

Arriving, accommodation and meals

Arriving by **bus**, you'll be dropped at a terminus on the riverbank, on the northern ouskirts of town, unless you come from Ioánnina (these services leave from a stop closer to the centre). From the main station it's a ten-minute walk along **Odhós Skoufá** to the central **Platía Ethnikís Andistásis**. Skoufá and its parallel streets, Pírrou and Konstandínou, wind through the oldest part of town.

There are just five **hotels**, normally enough for the trickle of tourists and business visitors. Most are close by the Platía Ethnikís Andistásis.

Hotel Rex, Skoufá 9 (☎0655/27 563). Cheap and basic. ②

Hotel Anesis, Mitropolítou Xenopoúlou 7 (☎0655/25 991). A pleasant, old-fashioned small-town hotel. ③

Hotel Chronos, Platía Kílkis (☎0655/28 311). Midway along Pirroú. ③
Hotel Amvrakia, Priovoloú 13 (☎0655/28 311). A bit plusher. ④
Hotel Xenia, Froúrio (☎0655/28 311). Brilliantly sited in the castle. ④

The town's **restaurants** are excellent value, catering for locals rather than tourists. Best of the cheapies is *Averoff*, at the corner of Skoufá and Grimbóvou, with a no-name place at Skoufá 5 a runner-up. Near the intersection of Skoufá and Platía Monopolíou are a number of *souvláki* takeaways and *meze* bars; best in each respective category are *Nikos* and the deceptively down-at-heel café opposite it. For more formal meals, try the *Hotel Amvrakia* at Priovoloú 13 or the *Estiatorio Skarabaios*, next door at no 11.

The town and its monasteries

Árta was known anciently as Ambracia and had a brief period of fame as the capital of Pyrrhus, King of Epirus; it was the base for the king's hard-won ("Another such victory and I am lost") campaigns in Italy – the original Pyrrhic victories. Very sparse remains from this period – the foundations of a **Temple of Apollo** and an **Odeion** – lie on either side of Odhós Pírrou. At the end of the street is the **Froúrio** – the ancient acropolis and the citadel in every subsequent era. Its keep is now occupied by a *Xenia* hotel, an open-air theatre and fragrant citrus trees; the walls are almost entirely Byzantine, and you can pace their circuit.

More substantial monuments date from Árta's second burst of glory, following the 1204 Fall of Constantinople, when it became, like Mystra, an autonomous Byzantine state. This, the **Despotate of Epirus**, which stretched from Corfu to Thessaloníki, was governed by the Angelos dynasty, the imperial family expelled from Constantinople, and it survived until 1449, when the garrison surrendered to the Turks.

Churches in the town

Most striking and certainly the most bizarre of the Byzantine monuments is the **Panayía Paragorítissa** (sometimes rendered Paragorítria; Tues–Sat 8.30am–3pm; 400dr), a grandiose, five-domed cube that rears above Platía Skoufá, at the west end of that street. The interior is almost gothic in appearance, the main dome being supported by an extraordinary cantilever system that looks unwieldy and unsafe. Up top this insecurity is accentuated by a looming *Pandokrator* (Christ in Majesty) mosaic in excellent condition, overshadowing the sixteenth-century frescoes. The church, flanked by two side chapels, was built in 1283–96 by Despot Nikiforos I as part of a monastic complex.

Two smaller Byzantine churches from the same period also survive in the town. Both have a more conventional structure but are enlivened by highly elaborate brick and tile decorations on the outside walls. They're usually locked but this is no tragedy since the exteriors are the main interest. **Ayia Theódhora**, containing the fine marble tomb of the wife of the Epirot ruler Michael II, stands in its own courtyard halfway down Pírrou. A little further north, opposite the produce market, is thirteenth-century **Áyios Vassílios**, a gem ornamented with glazed polychrome tiles and bas reliefs.

Monasteries nearby

Amid the orange groves surrounding Árta a number of monasteries were built during the Despotate, many of them by members of the imperial Angelos dynasty.

Within easy walking distance (2km along Odhós Komméno) stands **Káto Panayía**, erected by Michael II between 1231 and 1271 and a near-twin of the **Pórta Panayía** near Tríkala – understandable when you realise that the builders were father and son. The *katholikón* in a shaded courtyard, (May 1–Sept 15 7am–1pm & 4.30–7.30pm; winter 8am–1pm & 3–6pm) patrolled by peacocks, has extravagant exterior decoration, and frescoes inside showing Christ in three guises.

Rather further out to the northeast, but accessible by a twenty-minute city bus ride from Platía Kilkís (downtown end of Skoufá), is the monastery church of **Vlahérna** in the village of GRAMMENÍTSA. This is based on a rustic twelfth-century design, to which the Despot Michael II added a trio of domes in the next century; one of the several tombs inside is thought to be his. For admission, ask for the custodian at the village *kafenío*.

The Amvrakikós gulf and south to Messolóngi

Árta is a bright spot on the **Amvrakikós gulf**. Further around, and in fact all the way south to the open sea, there is little to prompt a stop. Locals from Árta head at weekends for seafood meals at the fishing villages of MENÍDHI (21km) or KORONÍSIA (25km), the latter also a low-key windsurfing resort. The best extended escape is to **Lefkádha** (see the *Ionian Islands* chapter), which can be reached either via Amfilohía–Vónitsa, or on one of the few direct buses daily from Ioánnina running through Filipiádha and Préveza. If you're approaching from Árta you might try flagging down a Ioánnina–Lefkádha bus at the Filipiádha junction.

Heading **south for Messolóngi** and the gulf of Kórinthos, there is not much more of interest, at least on the direct gulf and inland route. On the coast, however, **Mítikas** has boats across to the tiny islands of **Kálamos** and **Kástos**, while from neighbouring Astakós there's a summer ferry to Itháki (Ithaca).

Around the gulf and the inland route

AMFILOHÍA is promisingly situated at the head of the gulf, but in reality is a very dull small town. The chance for a swim would seem on the map a redeeming feature, but the water here is at its most stagnant. Heading inland to Messolóngi from here, you pass a few swampy patches of lake pumped for irrigating the local tobacco. AGRÍNIO serves as a transport link for this area, with buses to Árta/Ioánnina, Karpeníssi, and south to Andírio, where there are local buses to Náfpaktos, as well as the ferry across the Gulf of Kórinthos to the Peloponnese.

If you needed to stay the night, VÓNITSA, 38km west of Amfilóhia, would be a convenient choice. Again it's not an exciting place, and frustratingly distant from real sea. But there's a quiet waterside, squares lined with plane trees, and a substantial **castle** above. There are four **hotels**, including the modestly priced *Leto* (☎0643/22 246; ③) on Platía Anaktorioú. Infrequent local buses cover the 14km to ÁKTIO, the south ferry terminal across the gulf from Préveza, passing Áktio airport.

The coast

The **coast south from Vónitsa** is bleakly impressive, with a mostly dirt road surface mirrored by the arid wilderness inland. There is just one passably attractive resort, **MÍTIKAS**, whose rows of rickety houses strung along a pebbly shore look out on to the island of Kálamos. As yet development is minimal, confined to a few hotels and tavernas and pitched at Greeks; it's an okay place to break a journey or wait for a boat across to either **Kálamos** or (less reliable and summer-only) **Lefkádha**.

South from here, the coast road runs through ASTAKÓS, a village whose name means "lobster". Patrick Leigh Fermor, in *Roumeli*, fantasises about arriving at this gastronomic-sounding place; it turned out to be a crashing non-event, and it hasn't changed much since. There are three **hotels**: the *Byron* (☎0643/41 516; ③), *Akti* (☎0643/41 135; ③) and *Stratos* (☎0643/41 096; ⑤). You may want to make use of these if you are taking the ferry across to **Itháki**.

Hardly more enticing is **ETOLIKÓ**, perched on a causeway across the Messolóngi gulf. The lagoon is sumpy, the buildings neglected, poverty palpable; its main virtues are two **hotels** that are cheaper than any options in Messolóngi: the *Alexandra* (☎0632/22 243; ③) and *Liberty Inn* (☎0632/22 206; ②). From here Messolóngi itself is just 10km south, past the salt factories that are today the area's mainstay.

Kálamos and Kástos islands

Kálamos is essentially a bare mountain, that rises abruptly from the sea. In summer there are usually a few yachts moored in the small fishing harbour below the main port and village, **Hóra**, but otherwise the island sees few visitors. The only regular connection is a daily **kaíki from Mítikas** on the mainland; currently this leaves Mítikas at noon and returns from the island at 7am the next day. The few rooms in Hóra are usually booked through the summer, so come prepared to camp.

HÓRA, on the south coast, is spread out among gardens and olive groves, and survived the 1953 earthquake – which devastated so much of the Ionian – largely intact. There's a basic *kafenío*/taverna and a "supermarket" by the harbour, and two more cafés higher up, next to a post office where you can change money. The village **beach**, to the southwest, has a couple of tavernas behind a long stretch of shingle; in summer a few people camp beyond the windmills at the end. There's a much better, but less accessible pebble beach fifteen minutes to the east of the harbour.

KÁSTRO, the old fortified main village, is a ninety-minute walk from Hóra. Its walls are surrounded by roofless and abandoned houses and its courtyard is overgrown, used by villagers to keep their hens and sheep. Down towards its harbour, more of the houses are still inhabited, though there's no shop or café.

There are more good beaches between Hóra and EPISKOPÍ, on the north coast facing Mítikas. The island's strip of road runs this way but the beaches can be reached more easily by boat than by scrambling down the forested slopes from the road.

To the southeast of Hóra, a mule track leads to the village of PÓRTO LEÓNE, deserted since the 1953 earthquake. It's a two-hour walk across scrub-covered mountainside, with views across to the neighbouring island of Kástos.

Kástos and Átokos

Kástos has one village with a harbour and taverna. Only a few families still live here permanently and there's no regular *kaíki*. If you want to get across, you could ask around in Mítikas or Kálamos to see if anybody is planning a trip, but you'll probably have to hire a caique to take you. Normally the only visitors are from the occasional yachts calling in at the harbour.

The islet of **Átokos**, to the southwest, has a few ruined houses, but is now completely uninhabited, as are the other islets scattered off the coast to the south.

Messolóngi

MESSOLÓNGI (MISSOLONGI), for most visitors, is irrevocably bound with the name of **Lord Byron**, who died in the town, to dramatic world effect, while commander of the Greek forces during the War of Independence (see box below). The town has an obvious interest in this literary past, though be aware that, as in Byron's time, it's a pretty miserable and desperately unromantic place – wet through autumn and spring, and comprised of drab modern buildings. If you come here on a pilgrimage, it's best to plan on moving ahead within the day.

O LÓRDOS VÍRONOS: BYRON IN MESSOLÓNGI

Byron arrived at Messolóngi, a squalid and inhospitable town surrounded by marshland, in January 1824. The town, with its small port allowing access to the Ionian islands, was the western centre of resistance against the Turks. The poet, who had contributed much of his personal fortune to the war effort, as well as his own fame, was enthusiastically greeted with a twenty-one-gun salute.

On landing, he was made commander-in-chief of the 5000 soldiers gathered at the garrison: a role that was as much political as military. The Greek forces, led by Klephtic brigand-generals, were divided among themselves and each faction separately and persistently petitioned him for money. He had already wasted months on the island of Kefalloniá, trying to assess their claims and quarrels before finalising his own military plan – to march full force on Náfpaktos and from there take control of the Gulf of Corinth – but in Messolóngi he was again forced to delay.

Occasionally Byron despaired: "Here we sit in this realm of mud and discord", he wrote in his journal. But while other Philhellenes were returning home, disillusioned by the squabbles and larceny of the Greeks, or appalled by the conditions in this damp, stagnant town, he stayed, campaigning eloquently and profitably for the cause. Outside his house, he drilled soldiers; in the lagoon he rowed, and shot, and caught a fever. It was, bathetically, the most important contribution he could have made to the struggle. On April 19, 1824, Byron died, pronouncing a few days earlier, in a moment of resignation, "My wealth, my abilities, I devoted to the cause of Greece – well, here is my life to her!"

The news of the poet's death reverberated across northern Europe, swelled to heroic proportions by his admirers. Arguably it changed the course of the war in Greece. When Messolóngi fell again to the Turks, in 1826, there was outcry in the European press, and the French and English forces were finally galvanised into action, sending a joint naval force for protection. It was this force that accidentally engaged the Turks at Navarino Bay (see Pílos), casting a fatal blow to the Turkish navy.

Byron, ever since Independence, has been a Greek national hero. Almost every town in the country has a street – Víronos – named for him; there was once a brand of cigarettes (perhaps the ultimate Greek tribute); and, perhaps more important, the respect he inspired was for many years generalised to his fellow countrymen – before being dissipated in this century by British interference in the civil war and bungling in Cyprus.

The Town

You enter the town by the **"Gate of the Exodus"**, whose name recalls a later event in the War of Independence, when, during the Turks' year-long siege in 1826, 9000 men, women and children attempted to break out. In one wild dash they managed to get free of the town, leaving a group of defenders to destroy it in their wake. But they were betrayed and in the supposed safety of nearby Mount Zígos were ambushed and massacred by a large Albanian mercenary force.

Just inside this gate, on the right, is the **Heroón**, or **Garden of Heroes**, where a tumulus covers the bodies of the town's unnamed defenders. Beside the tomb of the Greek Souliot commander, Markou Botsaris, is a **statue of Byron**, erected in 1881, under which are buried the poet's lungs. The rest of Byron's remains were taken back to his family home, Newstead Abbey, despite his dying request: "here let my bones moulder; lay me in the first corner without pomp or nonsense." Perhaps he knew this would be disregarded. There is certainly a touch of pomp in the carving of Byron's coat of arms with a royal crown above; there had been speculation that Byron would be offered the crown of an Independent Greece.

Elsewhere in the town, traces of Byron are sparse. The **house** in which he lived and died was destroyed during World War II and its site is marked by a clumsy memorial garden. It's on Odhós Levídhou, reached from the central square by walking down to the end of Trikoúpi and turning left.

Back in the central square, Platía Vótsari, the **Dhimarhío** (town hall) houses a small "Museum of the Revolution", with some emotive paintings of the independence struggle – including a reproduction of Delacroix's *Gate of the Sortie* – and a rather desperate collection of Byronia, padded out with postcards from Newstead Abbey and the branch of an elm from his old school, Harrow.

Perhaps more interesting and enjoyable than any of this is a walk down through the **lagoon**. A causeway extends for around five kilometres to the sea, past the forts of Vassiládhi and Kleissoúra, which were vital defences against the Turkish navy.

Practicalities

Lodgings in Messolóngi are a bit cheerless and Etolikó (see p.299), 10km to the west, would be a more enjoyable base for the night. If you need or want to stay in the town, the cheapest of the three **hotels** is the *Avra*, Hariláou Trikoúpi 5 (☎0631/22 284; ③). The others, more comfortable but overpriced, are the *Liberty*, Iróön Politehníou 41 (☎0631/28 050; ③), and the *Theoxenia* (☎0631/28 098; ③).

travel details

Buses

Buses detailed have similar frequency in each direction, so entries are given just once; for reference check under both starting-point and destination.

Tríkala–Kalambáka–Métsovo–Ioánnina (2 daily; 1hr 30min/3hr).

From Ioánnina Athens (10 daily; 7hr 30min); Metsovo (4 daily; 1hr 30min); Dodona (2 daily, 6am/2pm Mon–Sat.; 40min); Igoumenítsa (10 daily; 2hr 30min); Árta (10 daily; 2hr 30min); Préveza (10 daily; 2hr 30min); Kónitsa (7 daily; 1hr 30min); Thessaloníki (5 daily; 8hr); Paramithiá/Párga (1 daily; 2hr/3hr); Kastoriá, via Kónitsa (2 daily, change at Neápoli; 6hr).

From Igoumenítsa Párga (5 daily; 1hr 30min); Préveza (2 daily; 3hr).

From Árta Párga (4 daily; 1hr 30min); Préveza (5 daily; 1hr).

From Préveza Párga (5 daily; 1hr 30min); Glikí (1 daily; 1hr).

From Áktio Lefkádha (5 daily; 45 min)

From Vónitsa Áktio (3 daily; 30 min); Lefkádha (5 daily; 2hr 30min).

From Agrínio Messolóngi–Andírio (12 daily; 1hr /1hr 30min); Karpeníssi (1 daily; 5hr); Corfu (bus/ferry, 2 daily in season; 4hr); Lefkádha (5 daily; 2hr)

Ferries

From Igoumenítsa Corfu (hourly, last at 10pm; 2hr). Also to Ancona, Bari and Brindisi (Italy); Dubrovnik, Hvar, Korçula, Rab, Rijeka, Split and Zadar (Croatia). See "Igoumenítsa and around" for details.

From Sívota Paxí (2 weekly, year-round; 2hr; takes cars).

From Párga Paxí (2 daily June–Sept; 2hr).

Préveza-Áktio Every 20min (9am–9pm); every half hour (6am–9am and 9pm–midnight); every hour (midnight–6am); 10min.

From Astakós Daily (mid-morning) to Itháki, almost year-round.

Hydrofoils (summer only)

From Igoumenítsa to Corfu, Páxi, Lefkádha, Itháki and Kefalloniá. Also to Brindisi, Italy,

From Préveza to Páxi, Lefkádha, Itháki and Kefalloniá.

Flights

Ioánnina–Athens 2 daily
Ioánnina–Thessaloníki 3–5 weekly
Préveza–Athens 5–7 weekly
Also international charters between Préveza (Áktion) and Britain.

CHAPTER FIVE

THE NORTH: MACEDONIA AND THRACE

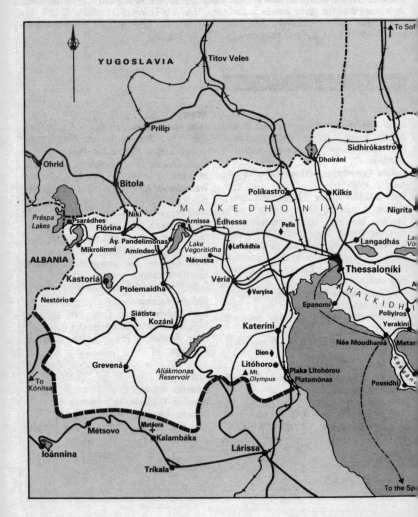

The two northern provinces – **Macedonia** and **Thrace** – have been part of the
Greek state for little more than two generations. Macedonia (*Makedhonía*) was
surrendered by the Turks after the Balkan wars in 1913; Thrace (*Thráki*) only
in 1923. As such, the region stands slightly apart from the rest of the nation –
an impression reinforced for visitors by scenery and climate that are essentially
Balkan. Macedonia is characterised by lake-speckled vistas to the west, and – to the
east, towards Thrace – by heavily cultivated flood plains and the deltas of rivers finishing courses begun in what-was-Yugoslavia or Bulgaria. The climate can be harsh, with
steamy summers and bitterly cold winters, especially up in the Rhodópi mountains that
form a natural frontier with Bulgaria.

These factors, along with a relative dearth of beaches, may explain why the north is
so little known to outsiders, even to those who have travelled throughout the rest of

A NOTE ON MACEDONIA

The name "Macedonia" is a geographical term of long standing, applied to an area that has always been populated by a variety of races and cultures.

The original **Kingdom of Macedonia**, which gained pre-eminence under Alexander the Great and Philip II, was a Greek affair – governed by Greek kings and inhabited by a predominantly Greek population. Its early borders spread south to Mount Olympus, west to present-day Kastoriá, east to Kavála, and north into parts of modern Yugoslavia. It lasted, however, for little more than two centuries. In subsequent years the region fell under the successive control of **Romans, Slavs, Byzantines, Saracens** and **Bulgars**, before eventual subjugation, with southern Greece, under Ottoman **Turkish** rule.

In the late nineteenth century, when the disintegration of the Ottoman Empire began to throw into question future national territories, the name Macedonia denoted simply the region. Its population included Greeks, Slavs and Bulgarians – who referred to themselves and their language as, respectively, *Makedhones, Makedonski* and *Macedoneni* – as well as large numbers of Jews, Serbs, Vlachs, Albanians and Turks. The first **nationalist struggles** for the territory began in the 1870s, when small armies of Greek *andartes*, Serbian *chetniks* and Bulgarian *comitadjis* took root in the mountain areas, coming together against the Ottomans in the first Balkan War.

Following Turkish defeat, things swiftly became more complex. The Bulgarians laid sole claim to Macedonia in the second Balkan War, but were defeated, and a 1912 Greco-Serbian agreement divided the bulk of Macedonian territory between the two states along linguistic/ethnic lines. During World War I, however, the Bulgarians occupied much of Macedonia, along with Thrace, until their capitulation in 1917. After Versailles, a small part of Slavic-speaking Macedonia remained in Bulgaria, and there were exchanges of Greek-speakers living in Bulgaria, and Bulgarians in Greece. This was followed, in 1924, by the arrival and settlement of hundreds of thousands of Greek refugees from Asia Minor, who – settling throughout Greek Macedonia – effectively swamped any remaining Slavophone population.

During World War II the **Bulgarians** again occupied all of eastern Macedonia and Thrace (beyond the River Strímon), as allies of Nazi Germany. Their defeat by the Allies led to withdrawal and seems to have vanquished ambitions. Recent Bulgarian leaders,

the mainland and islands. The only areas to draw more than a scattering of summer visitors are **Halkidhikí**, the three-pronged peninsula trailing below Thessaloníki that provides the city's beach-playground, and **Mount Olympus**, a mecca for walkers in the south of the region. For the rest, few travellers look beyond the dull farmland trunk routes to Yugoslavia and Turkey.

With a more prolonged acquaintance, the north may well grow on you. Part of its appeal lies in its vigorous day-to-day life, independent of tourism, at its most evident in the relaxed Macedonian capital of **Thessaloníki** (Salonica) and its chief port **Kavála**. Another lies, as in Epirus, in the mountain areas of the west, around **Flórina** and the lakeside city of **Kastoriá**.

Monuments are on the whole modest, though the recent discovery of Philip II of Macedon's tomb at **Veryína**, if it is opened to visitors, will change that assessment. Meanwhile, there are lesser Macedonian and Roman sites at **Pella** and at **Philippi**, Saint Paul's first stop in Greece.

If you are male, over 21, and interested enough in monasticism – or Byzantine art and architecture – to pursue the applications procedure, **Mount Áthos** may prove to be a highlight of a Greek stay. This "Monks' Republic" occupies the mountainous, easternmost prong of Halkidhikí, maintaining control over twenty monasteries and numerous dependencies and hermitages. **Women** (and female animals) have been excluded from the peninsula since a decree of 1060, although it is possible for both sexes to view the monasteries from the sea by taking a boat tour.

both Communist and post-Communist, have renounced all territorial claims and "minority rights" for "Greek-Bulgarians". The position of **Yugoslavia**, though, which under Tito established the Socialist Republic of Macedonia in its share of the historical territory, has been more ambiguous. During the decades of its unity there were Yugoslav propaganda attempts to suggest Slav affinities with the ancient Macedonian kingdom, and, by extension, with the present Greek population. When the Yugoslav federation fell apart violently in mid-1991, the issue resurfaced at the top of the Greeks' political agenda. Reaction to a September 1991 referendum, in which the population of Yugoslav Macdonia voted overwhelmingly for independence, was vehement. No effort was spared by Greece, as her ministers made the rounds of many EC capitals, imploring their allies not to recognise any independent entity on the northern frontiers that failed to renounce territorial claims on its neighbours, or even assumed the name of "Macedonia" – a place-name for which Greece virtually exercises a copyright.

This Greek obsession with the **name** is not as irrational as it may at first seem; in the post-war years Tito had cobbled together a Macedonian identity through the designation of one Vardarian dialect as "standard Macedonian", and the establishment of an autonomous Macedonian Orthodox church. The Greeks fear that this could be used as a springboard to irredentist moves to reclaim "Greater Macedonia", which before 1912 extended all the way south to Thessaloníki. Early in 1992 the situation was aggravated when diplomatic recognition of "Macedonia" was contemplated, or actually extended, by Bulgaria, Turkey and Italy, a move that led to recriminations and diplomatic outbursts across the Balkans and the Adriatic, and spurred massive demonstrations in Thessaloníki by enraged citizens proclaiming the Greekness of their city. For the Greeks, it was their worst nightmare coming true: encirclement by their Balkan neighbours and potential reversal of the hard-won territorial gains of 1912–23. At present it is prohibited to refer in print to Yugoslav "Macedonia" within Greece except in inverted commas, and the press refers to the "rump Skopje republic" in terms scarcely less disparaging than those reserved for the "Turkish pseudo-state of Northern Cyprus". At the same time Greece steadfastly refuses to admit the existence of any Slavophone minority within her present borders, for fear that doing so would provide more impetus for nationalist intrigue across existing borders.

THESSALONÍKI AND WESTERN MACEDONIA

Thessaloníki is the fulcrum, and focus, to Macedonian travel. If you are heading for the west of the province – to **Kastoriá**, **Édhessa** or **Flórina** – you will usually do best to go by bus or train from the capital. The train ride between Édhessa and Flórina, edging around Lake Vegoritídha, is one of the most scenic in the country, and Kastoriá, for those who like their towns remote and speckled with Byzantine monuments, is also highly worthwhile. Beyond Flórina, the secluded **Préspa lakes**, straddling the frontiers of three countries, constitute one of the finest wildlife refuges in the Balkans. The biggest attraction in this part of Macedonia, however, has to be **Mount Olympus** (Óros Ólimbos). The fabled home of the gods soars high above the town of Litóhoro, easily approached from the highway or rail line between Lárissa and Thessaloníki.

Thessaloníki (Salonica)

The second city of Greece and administrative centre for the north, **THESSALONÍKI** – or Salonica, as the city was known in western Europe until this century – has a very different feel to Athens: more Balkan-European and modern, less Middle Eastern.

Situated at the head of the Thermaikós gulf, it also seems more open; you're never far from the sea, and the air actually circulates, though this is a bit of mixed blessing since the bay, anywhere near town, is pretty much a sump.

The "modern" quality of the city is due largely to a disastrous 1917 fire, which levelled most of the old labyrinth of Turkish lanes; the city was rebuilt over the next eight years on a French grid plan, with long central avenues running parallel to the seafront. The result is a more liveable, though arguably less interesting city than Athens, with a more cosmopolitan, wealthy aspect, stimulated by its major university and international trade fair. Thessaloníki will have soon outgrown its self-deprecating nicknames of *I Protévoussa ton Prosfigón* ("The Refugee Capital", after the ring of 1920s Anatolian settlements, all prefixed by "Nea", around it) and *Ftohómana* (Poor-Mother).

Before 1923, the city's population was as mixed as any in the Balkans. Besides Turks, who had been occupiers for close to five centuries, there were Slavs, Albanians and the largest European **Jewish** community of the age: 100,000, or over half of the inhabitants, before the first waves of emigration to Palestine began after World War I. Numbers remained at around 70,000 up until World War II, when all but a tiny fraction were deported to the concentration camps, in one of the worst atrocities committed in the Balkans. It was this operation in which Austrian president Kurt Waldheim was involved – or, rather, which he claims not to have noticed.

You can get glimpses of "Old Salonica" today in the walled **Kástra** quarter, on the hillside beyond the modern grid of streets. Even amidst the post-1917 flatlands below, there are pockets of Turkish, and Greek Art Deco, buildings – mostly uncared for, and doubtless earmarked for redevelopment. For most visitors, however, it is Thessaloníki's excellent **archaeological museum**, with its spectacular exhibits from the tombs of Philip of Macedon and others of his dynasty, that stands out. Additionally, if you have developed a taste for Byzantine monuments, a unique array of **churches** dating from Roman times to the fifteenth century constitutes a showcase of the changing styles of Orthodox religious architecture.

The downside, for visitors as well as residents, is a complex of **problems** all too reminiscent of Athens. Industries and residences alike discharge their waste, untreated, into the gulf, and traffic on the main avenues, despite a comprehensive one-way system, is often at a standstill. The former *Néa Dhimokratía* mayor, Sotiris Kouvelas, elected on the promise of a clean-up, had ambitious plans for a metro line and a widening of the waterfront boulevard – never acted on. Indeed his only claim to fame was to defy the central government by being the first official to oversee the introduction of satellite television, officially forbidden in Greece until the late 1980s but now a veritable craze.

> The Thessaloníki phone code is ☎031

Arrival, orientation and information

Arriving in Thessaloníki is fairly straightforward. The **train station** on the west side of town is just a short walk from the central grid of streets and the harbour. The previously scattered provincial KTELs are being gradually gathered into one giant **bus terminal** out at the end of Ikosioktó Oktovríou, in the Sfayiá district (☎513 734), accessible on local bus #31. Coming from the **airport**, there is no longer an *Olympic Airways* bus service, but the gap has been filled in theory by city bus #78, which shuttles back and forth twenty times daily between 6.30am and midnight; the fare is currently 75dr, and the most convenient town stops are the train station and Platía Aristotélous. All **ferries and hydrofoils** call at the passenger port, within walking distance, just south of the centre.

Once within the grid, get your **bearings** by the several main avenues: Ayíou Dhimitríou, Egnatías, Tsimiskí and Mitropóleos. All run parallel to the quay, but confusingly change their names repeatedly as they head east into the city's modern annexe. The divide between the older and newer parts of town is marked by the exhibition grounds and the start of the seaside park strip, dominated by the **Lefkós Pírgos** or White Tower, the city's symbol.

There are two types of **local buses**: the orange "caterpillar" models in which conductors sell you your tickets (50dr) at the rear entrance, and the blue ones with automatic ticket machines requiring 50dr coins. Useful lines include #10 and #11, which both ply the length of Egnatías. From Platía Eleftherías (just behind the ferry port; see map), buses initially run east along Mitropóleos; line #5 takes you to the archaeological and folklore museums, and #22/23 heads north through Kástra to the highest quarter, known as **Eptapirgíou**, the most pleasant part of town. During summer, you can also catch **launches** next to the White Tower for the beaches at Peréa and Ayía Triádha, and also to the restaurant-laden suburb of Néa Kríni.

If you bring your own **car**, it's best to use the free parking area near the fairgrounds, or the fee parking area that occupies all of Platía Eleftherías. Staff will sell you strip tickets for ninety minutes each, which you cancel yourself; buy as many as you need in advance for display in the windscreen. Tokens for the rare kerbside meters are more expensive. Both the parking area and meters are attended 8am to 8pm Monday to Friday, 8am to 3pm on Saturday.

Information

The main **EOT** office, with friendly and helpful staff, is at Platía Aristotélous 8 (Mon–Fri 8am–8pm, Sat 8.30am–2pm). There are also booths in the train station and at the airport. When these are closed, use the **tourist police** post at Dhodhekaníssoun 4, near the harbour.

THESSALONÍKI'S FESTIVALS

The city's festival season begins in September with the **International Trade Fair**, the major event of the year. This is followed almost immediately by a **Festival of Greek Song**, and finally, for the last week of October, by the **Dhimitría** celebrations for the city's patron saint. The Film Festival was moved in 1992 from September to November, merely prolonging the hoteliers' high season. The period of the Trade Fair, particularly, is not a good time to visit. Hotels are full, with across-the-board price increases of up to 80 percent.

Accommodation

Outside of the festival season, reasonably priced hotel rooms are fairly easy to find – if not always very attractively situated. One area to avoid if you can afford to is the Vardári district, haunt of most of the city's prostitutes, transvestites, druggies, etc, centred on the namesake *platía* and creeping west towards the train station, south towards the sea and east along the start of Egnatías.

Modest to comfortable hotels tend to cluster in two areas: around the beginning of Egnatías, although many of the establishments here are plagued by street noise, or in the more agreeable zone between Eleftherías and Aristotélous squares. There are also a couple of good bets near Platía Dhikastiríon.

Lower Egnatías

Argo Egnatías 11 (☎519 770). Basic but acceptable. ②

Atlantis Egnatías 14 (☎540 131). Another, similarly basic hotel, with the better rooms facing a side street. ②.

ROOM PRICE SCALES

All establishments listed in this book have been price-graded according to the scale outlined below. The **rates quoted** represent the **cheapest available room in high season**; all are prices for a double room, except for category ①, which are per person rates. Out of season rates can drop by up to fifty percent, especially if you negotiate rates for a stay of three or more nights.

① 1000–1500dr (£3–4.50/US$5.50–8)   ④ 5500–7500dr (£17–23/US$30–41.50)

② 2000–3000dr (£6–9.50/US$11–16.50)   ⑤ 7500–9000dr (£23–28/US$41.50–50)

③ 3000–5500dr (£9.50–17/US$16.50–30)   ⑥ 9000dr (£28/US$50) and upwards

For further explanation of our hotel category system, see p.32.

Avgoustos, Elénis Svorónou 4 (☎522 550). A block north of Egnatías, so quieter. ③
Alexandhria, Egnatías 18 (☎536 185). ③
Ilios, Egnatías 27 (☎512 620). ③
Atlas, Egnatías 40 (☎537 046). ③

Eleftherías/Aristotélous

Bristol, Ilía Oplopíou 2 (☎ 530 351). Creaky but clean, right near Eleftherías and the port. ②
Continental, Komnínon 5 (☎277 553). A decent hotel, which can sometimes be bargained down a good fifty percent from the official rates. Rooms with and without bath. ③–④
Luxembourgo, Komnínon 6 (☎278 449). Similar pricing policy and facilities to above. ④
Tourist, Mitropóleos 21 (☎270 501). Around the corner from the preceding, two blocks back from the water. Management unfriendly but the rooms are okay. ③
Pallas, Tsimiskí 12 (☎270 855). Fairly fancy but good-value with discounts for longer stays. ④–⑤

Near Dhikastiríon

Lido, Egnatías 60 (☎223 805). Nice location near the central bazaar, within site of the church of Panayía Halkéon. ③
Orestías Kastorías, Agnóstou Stratiótou 14, corner Olímbou (☎276 517). Quiet and excellent value. ③

Hostels

Youth Hostel, Svólou 44 (☎225 946). The official IYHF hostel, noisy, ill-equipped, and charges extra for evening-only showers. It closes from 11am to 6pm and has an 11pm curfew; IYHF card required for the privilege.
XAN (YWCA) at Ayías Sofías 11 (☎276 144). A much better hostel alternative for women – well-run and well-maintained, opposite the cathedral. (Note that the *XEN* or YMCA – marked on the tourist board maps – is a sports hall and has no accommodation).

Camping

The closest **campsites** are at the rather uninspiring beach resorts of Peréa and Ayía Triádha, 20km and 22km away respectively. Take bus #72 from Platía Dhikastiríon, or, in summer, a boat from the quayside by the White Tower park.

Central Thessaloníki

Although scholarly opinion now holds that the main Via Egnatia skirted the ancient city walls, there is no doubt that the modern **Odhós Egnatías** follows the course of an important Roman street or processional way. At some point in your visit you are likely to ride or walk down it, catching glimpses of various monuments that line it.

Near the corner of Platía Dhikastiríon, stands the disused fifteenth-century **Çifte Hamam** or Turkish **bath**, its doorway surmounted by elaborate stalactite ornamentation. The eleventh-century **Panayía Halkéon** just southwest is a classic though rather unimaginative example of the cross-in-square form. Though currently under restoration, you should be able to make out the founder's dedicatory inscription over one door. As the name indicates, it served during the Ottoman occupation as the copperworkers' guild mosque, and in continuation of that tradition three copperware shops, among the last remaining in Thessaloníki, still operate just across the street.

Across the way from Panayía Halkéon, take time to explore the **bazaar** area, bounded roughly by Egnatías on the northwest, Dhragoúmi on the southwest, Aristotélous on the northeast, and Tsimiskí to the southeast. At the very heart of this quad sprawls the **Modiáno**, or the central meat, fish and produce market; jewellery and watches hold forth around the corner of Venizélou and Ermoú, humbler household items are found along the latter street. It is said that until the last war, Ladino (Judaeo-Spanish) was the principal language of commerce here. Down towards the sea at Singroú 35, the old **main synagogue** is no longer used regularly but can be visited by arrangement with the caretaker at the Jewish Community Centre, in the shopping arcade at Tsimiskí 24.

Remains of Salonica's formative years in the early eastern empire are thin on the ground; those that survive are concentrated, appropriately enough, just to either side of Egnatías. Ruins of the **Roman agora** were unearthed in the 1970s in the vast Platía Dhikastiríon, behind Panayía Halkéon; they have yielded little in the way of structures, though they're still being excavated. Rather more prominent is an **odeion** in the north corner of the square.

Tucked just out of sight north of the boulevard, the church of **Panayía Ahiropíitos** is the oldest in the city, featuring arcades, monolithic columns and often highly elaborate capitals – a popular development under Theodosius. Only the mosaics beneath the arches survive, depicting birds, fruits and flowers in a rich Alexandrian style. Further along on the same side of Egnatías, the **Rotunda**, later converted rather strangely to the church of **Áyios Yióryios**, is the most striking single Roman monument – designed, but never used, as an imperial mausoleum (possibly for Galerius) and consecrated for Christian use in the late fourth century by adding a sanctuary, a narthex and rich mosaics. Later it became one of the city's major mosques, from which the minaret remains. Sadly the church's interior has been closed since the 1978 earthquake, and the outside hedged by scaffolding. If it is open – as happens sometimes for special exhibitions – the superb mosaics of peacocks, elaborate temples and martyred saints are definitely worth time.

The Rotunda originally formed part of a larger complex linking the **Arch of Galerius** with a palace and hippodrome. Now also swathed in scaffolding to prevent its collapse from pollution damage, the arch is the surviving span of a dome-surmounted arcade leading to a group of Roman palaces. Built to commemorate the emperor's victories over the Persians in 297 AD, its piers contain reliefs of the battle scenes interspersed with symbolic poses of Galerius himself. The scant remains of **Galerius' palace** can be viewed, below the modern street level, along pedestrianised Dhimitríou Goúnari and its extension, Platía Navarínou.

Between Egnatías and Navarínou, and not to be confused with the city's undistinguished modern cathedral, the eighth-century church of **Ayía Sofia** was consciously modelled on its more illustrious namesake in Constantinople. Its dome, ten metres in diameter, bears a splendid mosaic of the *Ascension*: Christ, borne up to the heavens by two angels, sits resplendent on a rainbow throne; below a wry inscription reads "Ye Men of Galilee, Why stand ye Gazing up into Heaven?" Currently the dome is in the

To Kavála

LANGADHA

Walls

Óssios David

ÁYIAS SOFÍAS

SAKHTOURI

DHIMITRÍOU POLIORKÍTOU

SAKHTOURI

THEOFILOU

Ayía
Ekaterini

OLÍMBIADHOS

Profítis Ílias

K

OLÍMBIADHOS

KASSANDHROU

Ministry of
N. Greece

Áyios Dhi

PLATÍA
DHIKITIRIOU

AY

IFESTONOS

ÁYIOU

DHIMITRÍOU

OLÍMBOU

OLÍMBOU

Dhódheka
Apóstoli

LANGADHA

DHIKITIRIOU

OLÍMBOU

IÓNOS DHRAGOÚMI

EL. VENIZÉLOU

FILÍPPOU

PLATÍA
DHIKASTIRÍON

FI

ANTIGONIDHON

Panayía
Halkéon

Turkish
Bath

E. SVORÓNOU

Train Station

PLATÍA
VARDHARI

EGNATÍAS

BAZAAR

MONASTIRÍOU

SOLÓMOU

ERMO

To Véria
and Édhessa

28 OKTOVRÍOU

ERMOU

DHODHEKANÍSSOU

LEÓNDOS SOFOÚ

VASSÍLIOU IRAKLÍOU

KOMNINON

VENIZÉLOU

ARISTOTÉLOUS

OTE

ANAYENÍSSEOS

POLITEHNÍOU

TSIMISKÍ

Bank

Post
Office

T
XA

28 OKTOVRÍOU

SALAMÍNOS

UK
Consulate

EL.

MITRÓPOLIS

OSE

KOUNDOURIÓTI

PLATÍA
ELEFTHERÍAS

PLATÍA
ARISTOTÉLOUS

EOT

Olympic
Airways

Port

Car Park

NÍKIS

NÍKIS

To the Bus Station,
Lárissa and Athens

To the Sporades, Crete,
Lésvos and Hios

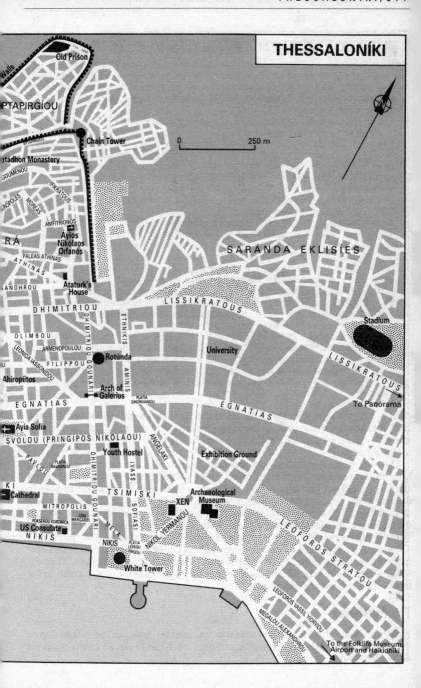

THESSALONÍKI

Walls

Old Prison

PTAPIRGÍOU

Chain Tower

atádhon Monastery

0   250 m

IGÍOU

UMENOU

IFIKRATOUS

ROPOLES   MOREAS

AMFITRIONOS

Áyios
Nikolaos
Orfanós

RÁ

PALEAS ATHINAS

ATHINAS

SANDHROU   Ataturk's
House

SARÁNDA EKLISÍES

DHIMITRIOU

LISSIKRATOUS

ETHNIKIS

OLIMBOU

Stadium

LEONIDA IASSONIDOU   ARMENOPOULOU

FILIPPOU   GOUNARI

Rotúnda

University

LISSIKRATOUS

U

Ahiropíitos

AMINIS

Arch of
Galerius

PLATÍA
SINDRIVANIOU

DHIMITRIOU GOUNARI

EGNATÍAS   EGNATÍAS   To Panórama

Áyia Sofía

SVOLOU (PRINGIPOS NIKOLAOU)

ANGELAKI

PAVLOU

Youth Hostel   Exhibition Ground

PLATÍA
NAVARÍNOU

DHIMITRIOU GOUNARI

IVASS

KI   Cathedral

TSIMISKI

Archaeological
Museum

MITROPOLIS

SOFIAS

XEN

PKSENOU KOROMILA   LORI
MARGARITI

MELA

LEOFOROS

US Consulate   NIKIS

NIKIS

PLATÍA
LEFKOU
PIRGOU

NIKOL YERMANOU

STRATOU

White Tower

LEOFOROS VASSIL VIORYOU

MEGALOU ALEXANDROU

To the Folklife Museum
Airport and Halkidhiki

ROMAN AND BYZANTINE SALONICA AND ITS CHURCHES

Macedonia became a **Roman** province in 146 BC, and Salonica, with its strategic position for both land and sea access, was the natural and immediate choice of capital. Its fortunes and significance were boosted by the building of the *Via Egnatia*, the great road linking Rome (via Brindisi) with Byzantium and the East, along whose course Philippi and Kavála were also to develop.

Christianity had slow beginnings in the city. **Saint Paul** visited twice, being driven out on the first occasion after provoking the Jewish community. On the second, in 56, he stayed long enough to found a church, later writing the two Epistles to the Thessalonians, his congregation. It was another three centuries, however, before the new religion took full root. **Galerius**, who acceded as eastern emperor upon Byzantium's break with Rome, provided the city with virtually all its surviving late Roman monuments – and its patron saint, Dhimitrios, whom he martyred. The first resident Christian emperor was **Theodosius** (375–395), who after his conversion issued here the Edict of Salonica, officially ending paganism.

Under Justinian's rule (527–565) Salonica became the second city of **Byzantium** after Constantinople, which it remained – under constant pressure from Goths and Slavs – until its sacking by Saracens in 904. The storming and sacking continued under the Normans of Sicily (1185) and with the Fourth Crusade (1204), when the city became for a time capital of the Latin Kingdom of Salonica. It was, however, restored to the Byzantine Empire of Nicea in 1246, reaching a cultural "Golden Age" amid the theological conflict and political rebellion of the next two centuries, until Turkish conquest and occupation in 1430.

The most prevalent of Roman public buildings had been the **basilica**: a large wooden-roofed hall, with aisles split by rows of columns. It was ideally suited for conversion to Christian congregational worship, a process achieved simply by placing a canopied altar at what became the apse, and dividing it from the main body of the church (the nave) by a screen (a forerunner to the temblon). The baptistry, a small distinct building, was then added to one side. The upper reaches of wall were adorned with mosaics illustrating Christ's transfiguration and man's redemption, while at eye level stood a blank lining of marble. (Frescoes, a far more economical medium, did not become fashionable until

process of restoration; the rest of the interior decoration was plastered-over after the 1917 fire. Another fine mosaic of the *Virgin Enthroned*, in the apse, may be easier to study; it apparently replaced a Cross, of which traces are visible, dating from the Iconoclast period.

The most prominent central post-Byzantine monument is a short walk southeast of here on the seafront: the **White Tower**, which formed the southeast corner of the city's Byzantine and Turkish defences before most of the walls were demolished late in the nineteenth century. Prior to this, it was the "Bloody Tower", a place of imprisonment and (in 1826) execcution of the Janissaries, until the Ottomans whitewashed both the building and its image. Today it looks a little stagey in its isolation, but is a graceful symbol nonetheless, which for years appeared as the background logo on the evening TV news. It was restored in 1985 for Salonica's 2300th birthday celebrations and now houses a small museum of early Christian art (summer Mon 12.30–7pm, Tues–Fri 8.30am–7pm, Sat & Sun 8.30am–3pm; shorter hours in winter). You can climb to the top for the views and a pleasant café.

The Museums

From the White Tower you are within a few minutes' walk of the archaeological museum. For the folklore/ethnological museum, catch the #5 bus as it runs northeast along Mitropóleos.

much later – during the thirteenth and fourteenth centuries – when their scope for expression and movement was realised.)

By the sixth century architects had succumbed to eastern influence and set about improving their basilicas with the addition of a **dome**. For inspiration they turned to the highly effective Ayía Sofía in Constantinople – the most striking of all Justinian's churches. Aesthetic effect, however, was not the only accomplishment, for the structure lent itself perfectly to the prevailing representational art. The **mosaics and frescoes** adorning its surfaces became physically interrelated or counterposed, creating a powerful spiritual aid. The eye would be uplifted at once to meet the gaze of the *Pandokrátor* (Christ in Majesty) illuminated by the windows of the drum. Between these windows the prophets and apostles would be depicted, and as the lower levels were scanned the liturgy would unfold amid a hierarchy of saints.

The most successful shape to emerge during later experiments with the dome was the **"Greek Cross-in-Square"** – four equal arms that efficiently absorb the weight of the dome, passing it from high barrel vaults to lower vaulted chambers fitted inside its angles. Architecturally it was a perfect solution; a square ground plan was produced inside the church with an aesthetically pleasing cruciform shape evident in the superstructure. Best of all, it was entirely self-supporting.

By the mid-tenth century it had become the conventional form. Architects, no longer interested in new designs, exploited the old, which proved remarkably flexible; subsidiary drums were introduced above corners of the square, proportions were stretched ever taller, and the outer walls became refashioned with elaborate brick and stone patterning.

Almost all the main Byzantine churches can be found in central Thessaloníki, so a "Grand Tour" of them is not difficult – but then it isn't very grand either. Under the Turks most of the buildings were converted for use as mosques, a process that obscured many of their original features and destroyed (by whitewashing) the majority of their frescoes and mosaics. Further damage came with the 1917 fire and more recently with the earthquake of 1978. Restoration seems a glacially slow process, guaranteeing that many of the sanctuaries are locked, or shrouded in scaffolding, or both, at any given moment. But these disappointments acknowledged, the churches of Thessaloníki remain an impressive and illuminating group.

The Archaeological Museum

Mon 12.30–7pm/10.30am–5pm in winter, Tues–Fri 8am–7pm/5pm in winter, Sat & Sun 8.30am–3pm all year; 1000dr.

Whatever else you do in Thessaloníki, find time for the superb **Veryína exhibition** at the archaeological museum. Displayed – and clearly labelled in both English and Greek – are almost all of the finds from the Royal Tombs of Philip II of Macedon (father of Alexander the Great) and others at the ancient Macedonían capital of Aegae (at modern Veryína, see below). They include startling amounts of gold – masks, crowns, wreaths, pins and figurines – all of extraordinary craftsmanship and often astounding richness.

Through these and other local finds, the history of the Macedonian dynasty and empire is traced: a surprisingly political act, for the discoveries at Veryína have been used by Greece to emphasise the fundamental "Greekness" of the modern provinces of Makhedonía and Thráki. Although to an outsider these territories might seem an accepted and inviolable part of Greece, their recent occupation by Turks and Bulgarians is still very much part of Greek political memory. The ancient sites, too, are a significant part of the debate; during the Bulgarian occupation of Macedonia during World War II, for example, there was a deliberate policy of vandalism towards "Greek Macedonian" remains. Archaeology in northern Greece has always been a nationalist as well as an academic issue – the museum itself is a brilliantly executed "educational" endeavour.

"Folklife" (Ethnological) Museum of Macedonia

Vassilísis Ólgas 68. 9.30am–2pm; closed Thurs; 200dr.

This is the best museum of its kind in Greece, with well-written commentaries (in English and Greek) accompanying displays on housing, costumes, day-to-day work and crafts. The exhibits, on weaving and spinning especially, are beautiful. And there is a sharp, highly un-folkloric emphasis on context: on the role of women in the community, the clash between tradition and progress, and the yearly cycle of agricultural and religious festivals. Even the traditional costumes are presented in a manner that goes beyond the mere picturesque.

The collection is housed in an elegant turn-of-the-century mansion, just a fifteen-minute walk (or short bus ride) from the archaeological museum.

Kástra and Eptapirgíou

Above Odhós Ayíou Dhimitríou, hillside **Kástra** is the main surviving quarter of Ottoman Thessaloníki. Although they are gradually becoming swamped by new apartment blocks, the streets here remain ramshackle and atmospheric, a labyrinth of timber-framed houses and winding steps. In the past few years the stigma of the district's "Turkishness" has been overcome as the older houses are bought up and restored, and it is justifiably one of the city's favourite after-dark destinations.

At the very foot of the slope is a massive yet simple church, **Áyios Dhimítrios** (daily 8am–7pm/5pm), conceived in the fifth century though heavily restored since; indeed it was almost entirely rebuilt after the 1917 fire, which destroyed all of it but the apse. It is dedicated to the city's patron saint and stands on the site of his martyrdom. Even if you know that it is the largest church in Greece, its immense interior comes as a surprise. Tall facades supported on red, green and white columns run alongside the nave. However, amid so much space and white plaster, the few small surviving mosaics make an easy focal point; five are grouped to either side of the temblon and of these three date back to the church's second building in the late seventh century. The mosaic of *Áyios Dhimítrios with the Church's Founders* was described by Osbert Lancaster as "the greatest remaining masterpiece of pictorial art of the pre-Iconoclastic era in Greece"; it contrasts well with its contemporary neighbour, a warm and humane mosaic of the saint with two young children. The **crypt** (Tues–Sun 9am–2.45pm), unearthed after the great fire, contains the *martyrion* of the saint – probably an adaption of the Roman baths in which he was imprisoned – and a beautiful column-capital carved with birds.

Around Áyios Dhimítrios are several more churches, utterly different in feel. West along Ayíou Dhimitríou, is the somewhat remote church of **Dhódheka Apóstoli**, built with three more centuries of experience and the bold Renaissance influence of Mystra (see *The Peloponnese* chapter). Its five domes rise in perfect symmetry above walls of fine brickwork, though its interior no longer does it justice. To the west, **Ayía Ekateríni**, contemporary with Dhódheka Apóstoli, has fine brickwork, exploiting all the natural colours of the stones. Fourteenth-century **Áyios Nikólaos Orfanós** (Tues–Sun 9am–2.30pm) is a diminutive basilica to the north of Áyios Dhimítrios, preserving its original imaginative and well-preserved frescoes. **Profítis Ilías**, between Ayía Ekateríni and Áyios Dhimítrios, is in the same vein as Dhódheka Apóstoli, though less imposing, with negligible surviving interior decoration.

Sections of the fourteenth-century **Byzantine ramparts**, constructed with brick and rubble on top of old Roman foundations, crop up all around the northern part of town. The best-preserved portion begins at a large circular keep, known as the "Chain Tower" (after its encircling ornamental moulding), in the northeast angle. It then rambles north around the district of **Eptapirgíou**, enclosing the old acropolis at the top end. For centuries it served as the city's prison, described in a number of plaintive old songs as

"Yediküle" (Turkish for "Eptapirgíou" or "Seven Towers") until abandoned as too inhumane in 1988. On its south side, the wall is followed by Odhós Eptapirgíou and edged by a small strip of park – a good place to sit and scan the town. Nearby, various *psistariés* and *kafenía* come alive in the late afternoon and evening; see "Eating and Drinking".

Although, strictly speaking, the following two monuments lie within Kástra, they are easier to find walking downhill from the Eptapirgíou area. **Óssios Davíd** (daily 8am–noon & 5–7pm), a tiny fifth-century church on Odhós Timothéou, does not really fit into any architectural progression, since the Turks, overzealous in their conversion, hacked most of it apart. However, it has arguably the finest mosaic in the city, depicting a clean-shaven Christ Emmanuel appearing in a vision, to the amazement of the prophets Ezekiel and Habakkuk. Nearby, the **monastery of Vlatádhon** is noteworthy for its peaceful, tree-shaded courtyard, a perfect place to complete a tour; if you can gain entrance to the much-restored *katholikón*, there are fourteenth-century frescoes inside.   If you approach or leave Kástra on its east side, it's worth casting an eye at the Turkish Consulate at the bottom of Apostólou Pávlou. In the pink building beside it **Kemal Ataturk**, first president and creator of the modern state of Turkey, was born. The consulate maintains the house as a small museum, with its original fixtures. To visit you must apply for admission at the main building, with your passport (Mon–Fri 9am–1pm & 4–6pm). Security is tight, and for good reason – Ataturk has been held largely responsible for the traumatic exchange of Greek and Turkish populations in 1923. In 1981 a Turkish celebration of the centenary of his birth had to be called off after a Greek stunt pilot threatened a kamikaze-dive at the house.

Eating and drinking

In recent years there has been an explosion of interesting places to eat and drink in Thessaloníki, paralleling the increasing prosperity of the city; and there's little excuse for wallowing in the fast-food outlets that at first glance seem to dominate the centre. Most of the listings below, categorised both by district and price per person, are within walking distance of Platía Aristotélous, and for those that aren't we've given the appropriate bus or boat connections. Thessalonians take their summer holidays a bit earlier than Athenians, so a notation of "closed in midsummer" tends to mean mid-July to mid-August.

Downtown: between the sea and Odhós Ayíou Dhimitríou

UNDER 1500DR

Thanasis's, in arcade at west end of the Modiáno, near corner Ermoú/E. Venizélou. Grills and *meze*; lunch only.

O Loutros, Komninón 23, corner Vassilíou Iraklíou. Housed in an old Turkish bath near the flower market, this taverna has good fried fish and excellent retsina, compensating somewhat for the abruptness of the staff. Lunch only; closed in summer.

Tsarouhas, Olímbou 78, near Platía Dhikastiríon. Reputedly the best, and certainly the most famous, of the city's *patsatzídhika* – kitchens devoted to that tripe-and-trotter soup. Closed midsummer.

Modiano, Vassilíou Iraklíou 39, corner Aristotélous. Another *patsatzídhiko* near the central meat market, with the advantage of very late opening hours.

Psistaria Megas-Kotsiamanis, Olímbou 83. An excellent and inexpensive grill under the hotel *Orestias Kastorias*; their speciality *soudzoukakia* bear little relation to the usual Greek version, being more like Turkish *inegól kófte*. Outside seating; open in summer.

Ta Koumbarakia, Egnatías 140. Tucked behind the little chapel of the Transfiguration, the outdoor tables of this *ouzeri* are always packed with those dining on Macedonian-style grills, seafood and salads (including *túrsi*, pickled vegetables). Closed Sun and midsummer.

Anapiros, Svólou 20 (formerly Pringípos Nikoláou). Rougher, indoor *ouzeri*, so shut in summer.

To Stenaki, rear of alley opposite cinema *Esperos* at Svólou 22. Another *ouzeri*, rival to its neighbour. Closed Sun but outdoor seating in the cul-de-sac means it's open summer.

O Bekris, D. Goúnari 74, the pedestrian walkway. Speciality sausage and *kopanistí* (spicy cheese mash). Closed Thurs.

Ta Adelfia, Platía Navarínou 9. Lunch and supper rendezvouz for the city's yuppies.

OVER 1500DR

Olymbos Naoussa, Níkis 5. White tablecloths, 1920s atmosphere and service, sea views and excellent, deceptively unadorned food make this a perennial favourite with locals. Lunch only but open in summer.

Rotonda, Patriárhou Ioakím 26, at the Rotunda. Specialising in stuffed cabbage and pastry-coated roast.

Palio Skholio, Iktínou 16, a pedestrian way. Speciality stews and mushroom-based dishes.

Rongotis, corner Kalapotháki and Venizélou. Famous for its *tsoudzoukákia*; businessmen's lunch environment. Closed midsummer.

To Sokaki, Kalapotháki 4, across street from preceding. More of a straight-ahead taverna, with occasional live music in the garden. Shut Sun and midsummer.

Aproöpto, L. Margaríti 11, and **Kapilio**, Proksénou Koromíla 26. Two of the better, hearty-eating *ouzeris* in an area known more for bars and clubs. Both shut Sun.

Limaniotis, Navárhou Vótsi 1/3, next to the Red Cross post and customs hall at edge of the harbour. You pay for the ambience, and the good live *rembétika*, rather than the rather predictable seafood – which is all they serve. Closed Sun; count on nearly 2000dr per person.

Bextsinar, Katoúni 11 (no sign out). A recent *ouzeri*-taverna housed in one of the bazaar's older remaining buildings. Closed midsummer.

Kástra and Eptapirgíou

Most of the following cling to either side of the walls encircling Eptapirgíou district; bus #22 or #23 from Platía Eleftherías spares you the walk.

UNDER 1500DR

Kastroperpatimatia, Steryíou Polidhórou 15, just inside the main gate of the Kástra. Smallish portions of good Greek/Turkish Cypriot food, served alongside the park strip inside the walls.

Metanastis, Steryíou Polidhórou 23. Nearby alternative to the above and more of an *ouzeri*. Closed Mon.

Hiotis and **Paris**, both at Graviás 2, corner Ayíou Pávlou, just inside the second (eastern) castle gate, near the Chain Tower. Goat, kebabs and *kokorétsi* served on the pavement under the ramparts.

Vangos, above Platía Pávlou Melá in the hillside area of Saránda Eklisíes. Tiny hole-in-the-wall, popular with students and slummers, tucked away in an alley; ask in the square for directions.

OVER 1500DR

Tsolias, Eptapirgíou 70, Kástra. On the outer (city view) side of the fortifications, so pricier. Speciality quail.

The eastern suburbs

The establishments below cater primarily to the well-heeled residents of the "better" part of town, so food is consequently more elegant – and routinely more than 1500dr per person.

Krikelas, Ethnikís Andistásis 32, out in Byzándio district, on the way to the airport. A bit of a touristy splurge, but the chef here is one of the best in Greece, drawing on almost half a century of experience. Wide-ranging menu.

Ta Pringiponissia, Krítis 60, near Ikosipénde Martíou, 600m beyond the folklore museum. Delicious Constantinople-Greek food served in a pleasant two-level modern building; you select from proferred trays of hot and cold *mezé*. Closed Sun.

Dheka Vimata stin Ammo, Fléming 16, again near the folklore museum. One of the better indoor *bouzoúki* tavernas. Closed on Mon and all summer.

Ble Parathira, behind the Iraklí soccer field, up by the university. A *rembétika* taverna, open all year except on Tues.

Roma Pizza, Nikifórou Plastíra 21, Hariláou. There are several outlets of this popular chain in the city, but none particularly central and this franchise, for unknown reasons, is the best. Hariláou is a suburb about 3km northeast of the White Tower; best to go by taxi.

Batis, Platía Eleftherías 22, Néa Kríni. Sea view with your grilled octopus; other fish dishes as well. Bus #5 goes there, and in summer special launches from the harbour.

Arhipelagos, Kanári 1, Néa Kríni. A somewhat fancier seafood place.

La Pignatta, Kerasoúndos 2, Kalamariá. Expensive but decent Italian dishes; shut Sun. Kalamariá is the next district beyond Néa Kríni; same bus and launch service.

Breakfast and dessert

Cafe Rafaelo, corner Mitropóleos and Komnínon. With coffees, juices and croissants, this is the fanciest of several *bougátsa* and other filled-pastry establishments along Komnínon, as you walk seaward from the Modiáno.

Corner, Ethnikís Amínis 6, near the White Tower. Not just great desserts, but pizza, sandwiches, draught beer and a full bar, with indoor and outside seating. Very fair priced for what it is: a multidisciplinary, California-bistro-meets-London-pub hybrid.

Andonis Armenakis Boutimata, Egnatías 144; Venizélou 10. A cookies-by-weight stall that is one of the best in Greece, with imaginative varieties that put Mrs Field's and her ilk to shame.

To Kaïmaki, corner Palíou Patrón Yermanoú and Tsimiskí. Good ice cream and nothing but.

Nightlife and entertainment

In winter, after-dark activities tend to focus in the warren of streets behind the quayside boulevard Níkis, and at certain theatres and concert halls near the White Tower. Proksénou Koromilá and Lóri Margaríti, two narrow alleys, essentially continuations of each other, just a block back from the water, are home to a huge number of bars and clubs. During the warmer months, action shifts to various glitzy establishments lining the coast road out to Kalamariá, and to the nightly *vólta* (promenade) that takes place between the Arch of Galerius and the seafront along pedestrianised Dhimitríou Goúnari, which bulges out to include Platía Navarínou.

Bars and clubs

Zythos, Katoúni 5, near the ferry terminal. A pub-like wine bar and *ouzerí*, though you can get plenty of quality beer, as the Greek name ("beer") suggests.

Tottis, Platía Aristotélous 3. A classic "place to be seen", actually as much *ouzerí* as bar.

Mandragoras, Mitropóleos 98. A large and elegant upstairs wine-and-*mezé* bar, run by a man who twice won the state lottery. Closed in summer.

Yuri's, Pávlou Melá 2. Snacks and drinks served to a younger crowd than at *Mandragoras*.

Jack Daniels, corner Proksénou Koromilá and Mitropolítou Iosíf. Typical of the pub-bars in this area.

Banal Entasis, Proksénou Koromilá 29. Bar-café with a partly gay clientele.

Chic, Lóri Margaríti 5. Women-only piano bar; shut in summer.

Pirgos OTE, International Fair Grounds. Not the trendiest place in town, but reasonably priced drinks and snacks up in the tower salon that does a complete turn every half-hour and stays open until 2am.

Events

Winter **dance**, **concert** and **theatre** events tend to take place in the *Kratikó Théatro* (State Theatre) and the *Vassilikó Théatro* (Royal Theatre), within sight of each other behind the White Tower. In summer things move to either the *Théatro Kípou* (Garden Theatre), near the archaeological museum, or well up the hill into the *Théatro Dhássous* (Forest Theatre), in the pines beyond the upper town. At any season the State Theatre will have playbills up to help you decide whether there's a language barrier to be overcome.

Indoor cinemas tend to cluster between the White Tower and the Galerius arch; those known to concentrate on first-run material, rather than porno or kung fu flicks, include *Alexandhros*, Ethnikís Amínis 1; *Anatolia*, D Goúnari 55; *Aristotelion*, Ethnikís Amínis 2; *Ellespondos*, Angeláki 25; *Esperos*, Svólou 22; *Ilisia*, Pávlou Melá 8; *Makedhonikon*, between Ethnikís Amínis and Filikís Eterías; and *Navarinon*, on the namesake plaza. **Summer cinemas** have just about vanished from downtown Thessaloníki, owing to spiralling property values; virtually the only one left is the *Alex*, at Olímbou 106. There is no comprehensive listings magazine on a par with Athens' *Athinorama*, so you'll have to stroll by to see what's playing unless you can read the daily Greek papers.

Listings

Airlines *Lufthansa*, Níkis 31; *JAT*, Mitropolítou Iosíf 8; *Olympic*, Níkis 7. Most other airlines are represented by general sales agents (see below). The airport itself is at Mikrá, 16km out and served by bus #78; ☎411 977 for flight information.

Books *Molho*, Tsimiskí 10, has an excellent stock of English-language books, magazines and newspapers. *Promithevs*, at Ermoú 75, is a good second choice.

Camping gear *Petridhis*, Vassilíou Iraklíou 43.

Car rental *Ansa*, Laskaráta 19; *Budget*, Angeláki 15; *Europcar/InterRent*, G Papandhréou 5; several booths at the airport as well.

Consulates Important for getting letters of introduction for Mount Áthos. *UK/Commonwealth*: honorary consul is at Venizélou 8, 8th floor, by appointment only (☎278 006). *Netherlands*, Komnínon 26 (☎227 477). *USA*, Níkis 59 (☎266 121).

Cultural institutes *British Council*, Ethnikís Amínis 9; free library and reading room, plus various events in the winter months. *USIS Library*, Mitropóleos 34.

Exchange Outside usual banking hours, try the *Ethniki Trapeza* at Tsimiskí 11, which has evening and Saturday morning opening. There's also the post office (see below), or, as a last resort, the booth in the train station.

Ferry tickets For the large *Nomikos* and *NEL* ferries to the northeast Aegean, the Sporades, Cyclades and Crete, buy tickets at Koundourióti 8 on the corner of Vótsi, by the harbour. Hydrofoils to the Sporades are handled by *Egnatia Tours*, Kamvouníon 9 (near the Arch of Galerius). For routes and frequencies, see "Travel Details" at the end of each chapter.

Football Thessaloníki's main team is PAOK, whose stadium is in the east of the city – off our map, though visible in square A5 of the EOT "Thessaloniki/Halkidiki" handout.

Hospitals For minor traumas, the *Érithros Starvrós* (Red Cross) post down at the harbour; otherwise, the *Ippokration* at Konstandinopóleos 49, in the eastern part of town.

Laundries There are three coin-ops spaced fairly close together downtown: *Bianca*, Antoniádhou 3, near Galerius arch; *Zerowatt*, Episkópou 2, around the corner; and *Canadian*, Platía Navarínou.

Ministry of Macedonia and Thrace This is on Platía Dhikitiríou; for processing Mount Áthos permits, make your way to Room 218. Mon–Fri 11am–2pm.

OTE Central OTE branch is at the corner of Ermoú and Karólou Diel. Open daily 24hr.

Post office Main branch (for poste restante and after-hours exchange) is at Tsimiskí 45 (Mon–Fri 7.30am–8pm).

Records Two good stores are *Stereodisc*, Aristotélous 4, and *Studio 52*, Goúnari 46, basement.

Shopping Chic boutiques line Tsimiskí and its perpendicular side streets. For shoes, a city fetish, try *Sevastakis* at no. 23 or *Papadhakis* at no. 38. You won't undercut North American or British prices but you may find something unique. Humbler styles can be found in the central bazaar and along Svólou or Egnatías.

Train tickets All services depart from the giant station down on Monastiríou, the southwestern continuation of Egnatías, well served by buses. If you want to buy tickets or make reservations in advance, the *OSE* office at Aristotélous 18 (Tues–Fri 8am–8pm, Mon & Sat 8am–3pm) is more central and helpful than the station ticket-windows.

Travel agents *Magic Bus* at Tsimiskí 32 (☎283 280) run buses to Istanbul (quicker and more comfortable than the train), and – less recommended – to London via central Europe. Flights out of Thessaloníki are not cheap, but for what they're worth air ticketers cluster around Platía Eleftherías, especially on Kalapotháki, Komnínon and Mitropóleos. More specifically, *Goldair*, Kalapotháki 20, *American World Express*, Iónnos Dhragoúmi 4, and an unnamed premises at Tsimiskí 17, all handle the major airlines.

Out from the centre: woods and beaches

The big weekend escape from Thessaloníki is to the three-pronged Halkidhikí peninsula. To get to its better beaches, however, requires more than a day trip. If you just want a respite from the city, or a walk in the hills, think instead in terms of Thessaloníki's own local villages and suburbs.

Panórama and Hortiátis

On the hillside overlooking the city, 12km east, **PANÓRAMA**, the closest escape from the city, is exactly what its name suggests: a high, hillside viewpoint looking down over Thessaloníki and the gulf. To accompany the views, there are a number of cafés, tavernas and **zakoroplastía**. The best-known of these is *Elenidhi-To Ariston*, which serves up the premier local speciality, *trígona* (custard-filled triangular confections), wonderful *dondurma* (Turkish-style ice-cream) and *salépi* (a beverage made from the ground-up root of *Orchis mascula*). The village can be reached by #59 bus from Platía Dhikastiríon, or (not too expensive) by taxi.

Still more of a retreat is **HORTIÁTIS**, 11km further on, set in an area known as *Hília Dhéndhra* (Thousand Trees). This is accessible on the #61 city bus from Egnatía. Again, it offers sweeping views over the city, some popular places to eat, and good walking among the pines.

Beaches

To swim near Thessaloníki you need to get well clear of the gulf, where the pollution is all too visible – and odorous. This means heading southwest towards Kateríni and the beaches below Mount Olympus (along the fast National Road), or north towards Halkidhikí.

If all you want is a meal by the sea, then you can take local bus #72 or #69 clockwise **around the gulf**. Bus #69 runs to PERÉA (with a campsite, and a good inexpensive grill, *O Fotis*), AYÍA TRIÁDHA (another campsite, and rooms) and NÉA MIHANIÓNA: small resorts, with good seafront tavernas but a rather unpleasant beach. Bus #72 takes you a little further around the bay to ÓRMOS EPANOMÍS, with a better strand and a third, expensive EOT campsite. The first point where the sea is anything like clear, however, is NÉA KALLIKRÁTIA, an hour by bus from the new bus station.

ANASTENARIA: THE FIRE WALKERS OF LANGADHÁS

On May 21, the feast day of Saints Constantine and Helen, villagers at **LANGADHÁS**, 20km north of Thessaloniki, used to (and may still) perform a ritual barefoot dance across a bed of burning coals. The festival rites are of unknown and strongly disputed origin. It has been suggested that they are remnants of a Dionysiac cult, though devotees assert a purely Christian tradition. This seems to relate to a fire, around 1250, in the Thracian village of Kósti: holy icons were heard groaning from the flames and were rescued by villagers, who emerged miraculously unburnt from the blazing church. The icons, passed down by their families, are believed to ensure protection. Equally important is piety and purity of heart: it is said that no one with any harboured grudges or uncon-fessed sins can pass through the coals unscathed. The Greek church authorities, mean-while, refuse to sanction any service on the day of the ritual; it has even been accused of planting glass among the coals to try and discredit this "devil's gift".

Whatever the origin, the rite was until recently still performed each year – lately as something of a tourist attraction, with an admission charge and repeat performances over the next two days. It was nevertheless strange and impressive, beginning around 7pm with the lighting of a cone of hardwood logs. A couple of hours later their embers were raked into a circle and, just before complete darkness, a traditional Macedonian *daoúli* drummer and two *lyra* players preceded about sixteen women and men into the arena. These *anastenarídhes* (literally "groaners"), in partial trance, then shuffled across the coals for about a quarter of an hour.

Recently the cult members were subjected to various scientific tests. The only estab-lished clues were that the dancers' brain waves indicate some altered state – when brain activity returns to normal they instinctively left the embers – and that their rhythmical steps maintain minimum skin contact with the fires. There was no suggestion of fraud, however. In 1981 an Englishman jumped into the arena, was badly burnt, and had to be rescued by the police from irate devotees and dancers. In 1991, however, the rites failed to take place, owing to continued pressure from the church and the *anastenarídhes'* own ire at being viewed merely as freak-show attractions. The ceremony's future seems uncertain, with the likelihood of it taking place, if at all, in private at an undisclosed location.

If the *anastenariá* are taking place in public this year, and you decide to go, arrive early at Langadhás – by 5.30pm at the latest – in order to get a good seat. Be prepared, too, for the circus-like commercialism, though this in itself can be quite fun.

Other *anastenarídhes* used to "perform" at **MELÍKI**, near Véria, and at the villages of **AYÍA ELÉNI** and **ÁYIOS PÉTROS** near Sérres. Crowds, though, were reputed to be just as large and fire-walkers fewer. If you're in Greece, anywhere, and moderately inter-ested, you can catch the show (if it happens) on the **ERT TV news** at 9pm. Their camera-men are at Langadhás, too.

Pella

PELLA was the capital of Macedonia throughout its greatest period and the first real capital of Greece, after Philip II forcibly unified the country around 338 BC. It was founded some sixty years earlier by King Archelaus, who transferred the royal Macedonian court here from Aigai (see Veryína), and from its beginnings was a major centre of culture. The royal palace was decorated by Zeuxis and said to be the greatest artistic showplace since the time of Classical Athens. Euripides wrote and produced his last plays at the court, and here too Aristotle was to tutor the young Alexander the Great – born, like his father Philip II, in the city.

The site today, split by the road to Édhessa, is an easy and rewarding day trip from Thessaloníki. Its main treasures are a series of pebble mosaics, some in the museum, a couple in situ. For an understanding of the context, it is best to visit after looking around the archaeological museum at Thessaloníki.

The Site

Tues–Sat 8.30am–3pm, Sun 9.30am–2.30pm; 400dr.

When Archelaus founded Pella, it lay at the head of a broad lake, connected to the Thermaíkos gulf by a navigable river. By the second century BC the river had begun to silt up and the city fell into decline. It was destroyed by the Romans in 146 BC and never rebuilt. Today its **ruins** stand in the middle of a broad expanse of plain, 40km from Thessaloníki and the sea.

The city was located by chance finds in 1957; preliminary excavations have revealed a vast site covering over one and a half square miles. As yet, only a few blocks of the city have been fully excavated but they have proved exciting. To the right of the road is a grand official building, probably a government office; it is divided into three large open courts, each enclosed by a *peristyle*, or portico (the columns of the central one have been re-erected), and bordered by wide streets with a sophisticated drainage system.

The three main rooms of the first court have patterned geometric floors, in the centre of which were found superb, intricate **pebble mosaics** depicting scenes of a lion hunt, a griffin attacking a deer, and Dionysus riding a panther. These are now in the **museum** across the road (same hours as the site; separate 400dr admission). But in the third court three mosaics have been left in situ; one, a stag hunt, is complete, and astounding in its dynamism and use of perspective. Others represent the rape of Helen and a fight between a Greek and an Amazon.

It is the inherently graceful and fluid quality of these compositions that sets them apart from later Roman and Byzantine mosaics and that more than justifies a visit. The uncut pebbles, carefully chosen for their soft shades, blend so naturally that the shapes and movements of the subjects seem gradated rather than fixed, especially in the action of the hunting scenes and the sloping movement of the leopard with Dionysus. Strips of lead or clay are used to outline special features; the eyes, all now missing, were probably semiprecious stones.

The **acropolis** at Pella is a low hill to the west of the modern village. Excavation is in progress on a sizeable building, probably a palace, but at present it's illuminating mainly for the idea it gives you of the size and scope of the site.

Access

Pella is easiest reached from Thessaloníki. Just take any of the Édhessa **buses**, which run more or less half-hourly through the day and stop by the Pella museum. If you arrive late and want to stay, the nearest **hotel** (C-class) is in the town of YIANNITSÁ, 12km west on the road to Edhessa.

Continuing to **Aegae/Veryína** by public transport, you'll need to get a bus, or walk, back down the Thessaloníki road to the junction at Halkidhóna. From here you can pick up the Thessaloníki–Véria buses.

Dion

Ancient **DION**, in the foothills of Mount Olympus, was the Macedonians' sacred city. At this site – a harbour before the sea receded – the kingdom maintained its principal sanctuaries: to Zeus (from which the name *Dion*, or *Dios*, is derived) above all, but also to Demeter, Artemis, Asclepius, and, later, to foreign gods such as the Egyptians Isis and Serapis. Philip II and Alexander both came to sacrifice to Zeus here before their expeditions. Inscriptions found at the sanctuaries referring to boundary disputes, treaties and other affairs of state suggest that the political and social importance of the city's festivals exceeded a purely Macedonian domain.

Most exciting for visitors, however, are the finds of mosaics, temples and baths that have been excavated over the last five years – work that remains in progress. These are not quite on a par with the Veryína tombs, but still rank among the major discoveries of Macedonian history and culture. If you are heading for Mount Olympus, they are certainly worth a half-day detour. At the village of DHÍON (MALATHRIÁ), just north of Litóhoro beach, take a side road inland, to the east, past the remains of a theatre. The main **site** lies ahead (Mon 12.30–7pm, Tues–Fri 8am–7pm, Sat & Sun 8.30am–3pm; 400dr). The integrity of the site and its finds is due to the nature of the city's demise. At some point in the fifth century a series of earthquakes prompted an evacuation of the city, which was then swallowed up by mud from the mountain. The main visible excavations are of the vast **public baths** complex, and, outside the city **walls**, the **sanctuaries** of Demeter and Aphrodite-Isis. In the latter a small temple has been unearthed, along with its cult statue – which remains in situ. The finest mosaics so far discovered (and which may be on view) are in a former banquet room; they depict the god Dionysus on a chariot. Christian **basilicas** attest to the town's later years as a Roman bishopric in the fourth and fifth centuries AD.

Back in the village, a small **museum** (same hours; admission with site ticket) houses most of the finds. The sculpture, perfectly preserved by the mud, is impressive, and accompanied by various tombstones and altars. Upstairs, along with extensive displays of pottery and coinage, is a collection of everyday items, including surgical and dental tools perhaps connected with the sanctuary of Asclepius, the healing god.

Note that the village cannot be approached directly from Mount Olympus, since an army firing range bars the way.

Mount Olympus (Óros Ólimbos)

The highest, most magical and most dramatic of all Greek mountains, **Mount Olympus** – *Ólimbos* in Greek – rears nigh on 3000 metres straight from the shores of the Thermaíkos gulf. Dense forests cover its slopes and its wild flowers are without parallel even by Greek standards. To make the most of it, you need to allow two to three days' hiking.

Equipped with decent boots and warm clothing, no special expertise is necessary to get to the top in summer (mid-June to October), though it's a long hard pull requiring a good deal of stamina; winter climbs, of course, are another matter. At any time of year Olympus is a mountain to be treated with respect: its weather is notoriously fickle and it does claim lives.

Litóhoro and Olympus practicalities

The best base for a walk up the mountain is the village of **LITÓHORO** on the eastern side. Unexciting in itself, in good weather it affords intoxicating eve-of-climb views into the heart of the range. To reach Litóhoro is fairly easy. There's a train station 9km distant, from where there are frequent taxis and the occasional connecting bus; or you can get the same bus direct from Thessaloníki or Kateríni. The cheapest lodgings are at the **youth hostel** (☎0352/81 311) or D-class *Hotel Park* (☎0352/81 252; ③), respectively above and below the square. A more comfortable **hotel**, well-heated in winter and only marginally more expensive, is the *Myrto* near the main square (☎0352/81 398; ③). For **eating**, in the square there's just a rash of horrible fast-food places; *To Pazari*, at the end of the uphill shopping street Ikosioktó Oktovríou, is a much better bet for a real **taverna**. In any event, avoid the *Olympus* on the main road in, which serves some of the worst and most overpriced food in Macedonia.

Accommodation on Olympus itself is better organised than on any other mountain in Greece. There are two staffed **refuges**: the EOS-run *Spílios Agapitós* at 2100 metres (open May 15–October 15; ☎0352/81 800, reservations recommended in summer), and the SEO-managed *Yiósos Apostolídhis* hut at 2700 metres (open only July–September, though its glassed-in porch is always available for climbers in need). There is no longer a set phone number for this refuge, since the wardership is in a state of flux. Both currently charge 1100dr for a bunk, with lights out and outer door locked at 10pm. Meals at either shelter are expensive at about 1500dr, and mandatory since no cooking is allowed inside; bring more money than you think you'll need, as bad weather can ground you a day or two longer than planned.

For sustenance while walking, you'll need to have bought food in Litóhoro, though water can wait until you're at the vicinity of either of two trailheads (see below). The free leaflet handed out at the EOS kiosk in Litóhoro is quite useless; buy a proper **map**, co-produced by *Korfes* magazine and EOS Aharnés, from the youth hostel.

The mountain

To reach alpine Olympus, you've a choice of road or foot routes. With your own vehicle, you can for the moment **drive** deep into the mountain along a fairly decent road, the first 6km of which is now paved. There is a control/education post at Km2, where your nationality is recorded and you're given some literature advising you of the park rules, but so far there's no admission charge, though this will certainly change in the future. Conservationists are agitating for a total ban on private vehicles within the park, and all and all it is much better to **walk** in from Litóhoro, as far as the ruined monastery of Ayíou Dhionisíou, and beyond to the two trailheads following.

As for the final **ascent routes**, there are two main paths: one beginning at PRIÓNIA, just under 18km up the mountain at the road's end, where a primitive taverna operates by the spring in summer; the other at a spot called DHIAKLÁDHOSI or GORTSIÁ (14km up), marked by a signboard displaying a map of the range. The Priónia path is more frequented and more convenient, the Dhiakládhosi trail longer but more beautiful. A 1.8-km driveway, appearing on the main road about halfway between the two trailheads, leads down to Ayíou Dhionisíou.

The Mavrólongos canyon and Ayíou Dhionisíou monastery

Some years ago the Greek overland-trail committee rehabilitated old paths in the superlatively beautiful Mavrólongos (Enipévs) river canyon to make a fine section of the **E4 overland trail**, thus sparing hikers the drudgery of walking up the road or the expense of a taxi. Black-on-yellow diamond markers begin near the youth hostel, and lead you along a roller-coaster course by the river for three and a half hours to Ayíou Dhionisíou. It's a delightful route, but you'll need basic hiking skills as there are some ladder-assisted scrambles and water crossings.

The **monastery** itself was burned by the Germans in 1943 for allegedly harbouring guerillas, and the surviving monks, rather than rebuilding, relocated to new premises near Litóhoro. On summer weekends the half-ruined structure is a bit of a zoo, with the still-intact cells long since looted of their beds and blankets; a caretaker monk seems rather jaded by those hoping to crash for free, and in season at least the only advantage of an overnight here are the running water taps. Many people prefer to camp along the riverbanks below the perimeter wall (tolerated despite falling within national park territory).

From Ayíou Dhionisíou it's about an hour more along the riverside E4 to Priónia, or slightly less up the driveway and then east to the Dhiakládhosi trailhead.

The ascent from Priónia

The E4 carries on just uphill from the taverna by an EOS signpost giving the time to the refuge as two hours thirty minutes (allow 3hr). You cross a stream (last water before the *Spílios Agapitós* refuge, purification advisable) and start to climb steeply up through woods of beech and black pine. The path, the continuation of the E4, is well-trodden and marked, so there is no danger of getting lost. As you gain height there are superb views across the Mavrólongos ravine to your left and to the peaks towering above you.

The *Spílios Agapitós* **refuge** perches on the edge of an abrupt spur, surrounded by huge storm-beaten trees. Zolotas, the warden, speaks English, but you need to let him know in good time if you want a meal and a bed. It's best to stay overnight here, as you should make an early start for the three-hour ascent to Mítikas, the highest peak at 2917 metres. The peaks frequently cloud up towards midday and you lose the view, to say nothing of the danger of catching one of Zeus's thunderbolts, for this was the mythical seat of the gods. Besides, nights at the refuge are fantastic: a log fire blazes; you watch the sun set on the peaks, and dawn come up over the Aegean; there are billions of stars.

The summit area

The E4 path continues behind the refuge (the last water source on the mountain), climbing to the left up a steep spur among the last of the trees. In an hour you reach a signposted **fork** above the treeline. Straight on takes you across the range to KOKKINOPILÓS village with the E4 waymarks, or with a slight deviation right to Mítikas, via the ridge known as Kakí Skála (1hr 30min). An immediate right turn leads to the Yiósos Apostolídhis hut in one hour, with the option after forty minutes of taking the very steep Loúki couloir left up to Mítikas; if you do this, be wary of rockfalls.

For the safer **Kakí Skála route**, continue up the right flank of the stony featureless valley in front of you, with the Áyios Andónios peak up to your left. An hour's dull climb brings you to the summit ridge between the peaks of Skolió on the left and Skála on the right. You know you're there when one more step would tip you over a 500-metre sheer drop into the Kazánia chasm; take great care. The Kakí Skála (Evil Stairway) begins in a narrow cleft on the right just short of the ridge; paint splashes mark the way. The route keeps just below the ridge, so you are protected from the drop into Kázania. Even so, those who don't like heights will feel pretty uncomfortable.

You start with a slightly descending rightward traverse to a narrow nick in the ridge revealing the drop to Kazánia – easily negotiated. Continue traversing right, skirting the base of the Skála peak, then climb leftwards up a steepish gully made a little awkward by loose rock on sloping footholds. Bear right at the top over steep but reassuringly solid rock, and across a narrow neck. Step left around an awkward corner and there in front of you, scarcely 100 metres away, is **Mítikas summit**, an airy, boulder-strewn platform with a trigonometric point, tin Greek flag and visitors' book.

In reasonable conditions it's about forty minutes to the summit from the start of Kákí Skála; three hours from the refuge; five and a half hours from Priónia.

A stone's throw to the north of Mítikas is the **Stefáni peak**, also known as the Throne of Zeus, a bristling hog's back of rock with a couple of nastily exposed moves to scale the last few feet.

Descending from Mítikas, you can either go back the way you came, with the option of turning left at the signpost (see above) for the Apostolídhis hut (2hr 30min from Mítikas by this route), or you can step out, apparently into space, in the direction of Stefáni and turn immediately down to the right into the mouth of the Loúki couloir. It takes about forty minutes of downward scrambling to reach the main path where you turn left for the hut, skirting the impressive northeast face of Stefáni (1hr), or go right, back to the familiar signpost and down the E4 to Spílios Agapitós (2hr altogether).

The ascent from Dhiakládhosi (Gortsiá)

Starting from the small parking area beyond the information placard, it's critically important to take the narrow path going up and left, not the forest track heading down and right. An hour along, you reach the meadow of **Bárba**, and two hours out you'll arrive at a messy junction with a new water tank and various placards – take left forks en route when given the choice. The signs point hard left to the spring at **Strángo**; right for the direct path to Petróstrounga; and straight on the old, more scenic way to **Petróstrounga**, passed some two and a half hours along.

Beyond this summer pastoral colony, there's a signed right, then the trail wanders up to the base of **Skoúrta** knoll (4hr 15min), above the treeline. After crossing the Lemós (Neck) ridge dividing the Papá Réma and Mavrólongos ravines, with spectacular views into both, five and a quarter hours should see you up on the Oropédhio Musón (Plateau of the Muses), five and a half hours to the Apostolídhis refuge, visible the last fifteen minutes. But you should count on seven hours, including rests, for this route; going down takes about four and a half hours, a highly recommended descent if you've come up from Priónia.

It takes about an hour, losing altitude, to traverse the onward path linking Apostolídhis and the E4, skimming the base of the peaks – about the same as coming the other way as described above.

The southern ridge route

To experience complete solitude on Olympus, continue past Áyios Andónios, the peak just south of Skála and the E4 trail, and begin to ridge-walk the line of peaks that bounds the Mavrólongos to the south. Much of this trek past Metamórfosi, Kalóyeros, and Págos summits is cross-country, but with the recommended map, route-finding is easy on a clear day. It's six and a half walking hours from the Apostolídhis hut to the dilapidated but serviceable, unstaffed shelter at **Livadháki**, with unreliable cistern water only – you'll need to carry at least a couple litres in with you. From Livadháki a good trail descends via the ridges of Pelekoudhiá and Tsouknídha, coming out three and a quarter hours on at the meadow of **Déli**, where you're just above a forest road which leads 7km down to Litóhoro.

Alternatively, a faint but followable trail at Déli dips down into a ravine and up onto **Gólna** knoll, intersecting another, sporadically marked path up from Litóhoro that leads over into the Mavrólongos watershed to join up with the E4. Just above the junction woodcutters have hopelessly messed up the path, but persevere, and you'll suddenly drop down on to the E4 about halfway along its course, some ninety minutes out of Déli. This last section makes a beautiful, if challenging walk. For full details, consult one of the specialist hiking guides (see "Books" in *Contexts*).

Véria and Veryína

The broad agricultural plain extending west from Thessaloníki eventually collides with an abrupt, wooded escarpment, at the panoramic edge of which several towns have grown up. The largest of these, **VÉRIA**, has no particular sites or monuments, but it is one of the more interesting northern Greek communities. Certain central streets preserve much of their old Ottoman atmosphere, including a largely untouched nineteenth-century bazaar, as well as a unique collection of churches, which see few tourists from one year to the next.

The **train station** is hopelessly inconvenient, 3km east of the centre; most arrivals will hike up Odhós Venizélou from the **bus terminal** to Odhós Elías, the short but fashionable street leading in turn to the Belvedere, the escarpment view-park, where there's a municipal **tourist information** post – although with no maps; study the placard nearby. Odhós Anixéos snakes north along the cliff edge to intersect Venizélou, passing en route the **archaeological museum** (Tues–Sun 8.30am–5pm; 400dr). It has a few of the lesser finds from Veryína (see below) but contains mostly Roman oddments from the area. The **ethnographic collection**, which used to be on Odhós Xánthi, has been temporarily disbanded while it looks for a new home.

For the most part, however, Véria is more of a place to wander about, stumbling across some of the fifty or so seventeenth- and eighteenth-century **churches**. These were once disguised as barns or warehouses, but today, often surrounded by cleared spaces, are not hard to find. There is, for example, one on Méga Alexándhrou, within sight of the Belvedere, and two more just beyond – though they are generally locked. One that's not is that of **Hristós** (Tues–Sun 8.30am–3pm), with recently restored four-teenth-century frescoes, near the junction of Elías and Mitropóleos.

Mitropóleos bisects the town, running southwest towards the actual centre, past the new cathedral. The old one, opposite a gnarled plane tree from which the Turks hung the town's archbishop in 1436, is just off Odhós Vassiléos Konstandínou, which links Venizélou and the main square at the far end of Mitropóleos. Near the tree, the old **bazaar** straddles Vassiléos Konstandínou, and a small number of crumbling old houses overlook the river, five minutes' walk west from either the central square or the bazaar.

Practicalities

OTE, the **post office** and most **banks** are on or around Mitropóleos, near the new cathedral. **Hotels** are scattered throughout town: there are two rather rough places, the *Veroi* on the central square (☎0331/22 866; ③), and the *Aristidhis* (☎0331/26 355; ②) on Platía Platamón, a swelling in Vassiléos Konstandínou. There's also a good-value but noisy budget hotel, the *Vasilissa Veryina* at Venizélou 31 (☎0331/22 301; ③), and the pricier and unwelcoming *Politimi* at Megálou Alexándhrou 35 (☎0331/64 902; ③).

Eating out, most authentic option is *To Hriso Pagoni*, a little *ouzerí* with tables in the courtyard of Ayía Anna church, at Tsoúpeli 1, just southwest of Venizélou. Alternatively, try *Pitsaria Porto Fino*, at the corner of Merkouríou Karakostí and Anixéos. Nocturnal **bar** life is mostly confined to the Belvedere park strip, culminating in the expensive but pleasant tourist pavilion by the tourist information post; this district, which takes its name from nearby Odhós Elías, is Véria's wealthiest. Finally, you can get home-made yoghurt and ice-cream nearby from *O Stergios* at Elías 11.

Veryína: ancient Aigai

Excavations at **VERYÍNA**, twenty minutes' drive southwest of Véria, have revolution-ised Macedonian archaeology since the 1970s. A series of chamber tombs, unearthed here by Professor Manolis Andronikos (1919–1992), are now unequivocally accepted as those of Philip II and other members of the Macedonian royal family. This means that the site itself must be that of **Aigai**, the original Macedonian royal capital before the shift to Pella, and later its necropolis. Finds from the site and tomb, the richest Greek trove since the discovery of Mycenae, are exhibited at Thessaloníki's archaeological museum.

The main tombs, however, are still in the process of excavation and documentation, and utterly inaccessible, resembling a construction site while a protective roof is erected (don't hold your breath as to the completion date). The few sites that can be seen here are frankly minor and apt to disappoint – not, on balance, worth much of a detour. As yet the village is not quite geared up for the growing number of hopeful tourists, but there are a few tavernas and rooms to let, and freelance camping is certainly possible in the pleasant surroundings.

The sites

Ancient Aigai is documented as the sanctuary and royal burial place of the Macedonian kings. It was here that Philip II was assassinated and buried – and tradition maintained that the dynasty would be destroyed if any king were buried elsewhere, as indeed happened after the death of Alexander the Great in Asia. Until Andronikos's finds in November 1977 – the culmination of years working on the site – Aigai had long been assumed to be lost beneath modern Édhessa, a theory now completely discarded.

What Andronikos discovered, under a tumulus just outside the modern village of Veryína, were two large and indisputably Macedonian **chamber tombs**. The first had been looted in antiquity but retained a mural of the rape of Persephone by Pluto, the only complete example of an ancient Greek painting that has yet been found. The second, a grander vaulted tomb with a Doric facade adorned by a superb painted frieze of a lion hunt, was – incredibly – intact, having been deliberately disguised with rubble from later tomb pillagings. Among the treasures to emerge were a marble sarcophagus containing a gold casket of bones bearing the exploding-star symbol of the royal line on its lid, and, still more significantly, five small ivory heads, among them representations of both Philip II and Alexander. It was this clue, as well as the fact that the skull bore marks of a disfiguring facial wound Philip was known to have sustained, that led to the identification of the tomb as his.

Buses to modern Veryína stop at a crossroads low down in the village, from where the "Royal Tombs" and other local sites are clearly signposted. Though there's nothing for the tourist at the closed-off main complex except a café and water fountain, the so-called "**Macedonian Tomb**", actually three adjacent tombs and not to be confused with Philip's, can be visited after a fashion. They are about 500 metres uphill and south of the village and, like the Royal Tombs, lie well below the modern ground level, protected by a vast tin roof. When he's around, the guard will let you into the dig, though not into the tombs themselves. Excavated by the French in 1861, the most prominent one has the form of a temple, with an Ionic facade of half-columns breached by two marble doors. Inside you can just make out an imposing marble throne with sphinxes carved on the sides, armrests and footstool. The neighbouring pair of tombs, still under excavation, are said to be similar in design.

A few hundred metres further on, at the end of the same road, the ruins of the **Palace of Palatitsa** (Tues–Sun 8.30am–3pm; 400dr) occupy a low hill. This complex was probably built during the third century BC as a summer residence for the last great Macedonian king, Antingonus Gonatus. It is now little more than foundations, but amidst the confusing litter of column drums and capitals you can make out a triple *propylaion* (entrance gate) opening onto a central courtyard. This is framed by broad porticoes and colonnades which, on the south side, preserve a well-executed if rather unexciting mosaic. Despite its lack of substance it is an attractive site, dominated by a grand old oak tree looking out across the plains, scattered with Iron-Age (tenth- to seventh-century BC) tumuli and who knows what else. The only substantial items dug up to date are the first two tiers of the **theatre** just below, described by Philip's bodyguard as the site of the king's murder.

Édhessa, Lefkádhia and Náoussa

With your own vehicle, the other two escarpment towns can be easily and enjoyably toured in a day or less, with an unspoilt archaeological site – Lefkádhia – in between. Travelling by public transport, however, especially by train, stopping off is time-consuming and probably more trouble than it's worth, in which case Édhessa, astride the main route between Thessaloníki and the far west of Macedonia, is the place you're most likely to halt.

Édhessa

ÉDHESSA, like Véria, is a pleasant stopover, its modest fame attributed to the waters that flow through the town. Coming down from the mountains to the north, they flow swiftly through the middle of town and then, just to the east, cascade down a dramatic ravine, luxuriant with vegetation, to the plain below. From the train station, walk straight for 400m until you see the walled-in river, paralleled by Tsimiskí street. Turn left and you will come to the **waterfalls**, the focus of a park with a *Xenia* hotel (☎0381/ 22 995; ④ but less out of season) and a couple of cafés. For the **Byzantine bridge** turn right from here and follow the river for about 600 metres. Paths also lead down the ravine, providing access to caves below.

The town itself is a little ordinary, but the various riverside parks and wide pedestrian pavements are a rare pleasure in a country where the car is tyrant, and the train and bus stations are both well placed for breaking a journey. If you're looking for budget **accommodation**, the *Hotel Olympia,* 18 Oktovríou 69 (☎0381/23 544; ②), near the train station, is passably clean, friendly and quiet. The *Olympion*, 18 Oktovriou 69 (☎0381/23 544), and *Pella*, Egnatias 30 (☎0381/23 541, ③), by the bus station, are both more comfortable but noisier. Simple but good and inexpensive **food** is served at the taverna *I Varhoula*, again near the train station, at Ikosipénde Martíou 10, at *Tsarouhakis*, Dhekaoktó Oktovríou 32, and at *To Roloi*, near the clock tower and OTE.

Lefkádhia

South of Édhessa, Lefkádhia has not been positively identified with any Macedonian city, but it is thought possibly to have been Mieza, where Aristotle taught. The modern village of **LEFKÁDHIA** lies just west of the main road, but you should turn off east at a sign reading "Two Royal Tombs". There are, in fact, four Macedonian tombs – today quite subterranean like the Veryína group – though only one has a guard, who keeps the keys to the other three.

The staffed one, the so-called **Great Tomb** or **Tomb of Judgement** (Tues–Sun 8.30am–3pm), east of the road just past the train tracks, is the largest Macedonian temple-tomb yet discovered. Despite extensive cement protection, it has been so badly damaged by creeping damp from the very high local water table that there's progressively less to see; plans are afoot to dismantle, consolidate and reassemble the whole thing stone by stone. It dates from the third century BC, and was probably built for a general, depicted on the left, in one of the barely surviving frescoes, being led by Hermes (the Conductor of Souls). Other faded frescoes on the right represent the Judges of Hades – hence the tomb's alias. A once-elaborate double-storeyed facade, half Doric and half Ionic, has almost completely crumbled away; on the entablature frieze you can barely make out a battle between Persians and Macedonians.

The **Anthimíon Tomb**, 150m further along the country road, is more impressive, with its four Ionic facade columns, two marble interior sarcophagi with inscribed lids, and well-preserved frescoes. The typanum bears portraits of a couple, presumably the tomb occupants, though the man's face has been rubbed out. Ornamental designs and three giant *akrokerámata* complete the pediment decoration. Between the double set of portals, the ceiling frescoes are sensually vegetal – or perhaps stylised representations of octopi. Frogs, in fact, live through the summer in the bilge of the pump protecting the site.

The other two local tombs are of essentially specialist interest. The one called **Kinch**, after its Danish discoverer, is on the east side of the road, on the way back towards the village. That of **Lyson-Kallikles** is signed west of the highway, at the end of a 1km dirt track through orchards; to visit you have lower yourself through a usually locked grating in the ceiling, the original entrance having been long since buried.

Náoussa

Four kilometres south of the tombs is a turning west to **NÁOUSSA**, a small country town whose vintners, the **Boutari** company, produce some of Greece's best wines. Along with Véria, the town is also at the heart of the country's main peach-growing region – excuse enough for at least a stop in July – and hosts one of Macedonia's most elaborate pre-Lenten carnivals. That said, Náoussa is generally the sleepiest and least distinguished of the three escarpment towns – a pleasant enough place to live but not necessarily to holiday at. In winter, however, Náoussa is very busy with Greeks enjoying the two superb ski centres overhead on Mount Vermíon.

If you do drop in, the big attraction is the parkland of **Áyios Nikólaos**, 4km beyond town (6km west of the main highway), an oasis of giant plane trees nourished by the streams that boil from the earth here. The riverbanks are lined with several more or less identically priced tavernas featuring farm-raised trout (the *Nisaki* is the most pleasantly set). Just upstream, the *Hotel Vermion* (☎0332/23 013; ③–④) is a small B-class establishment. The torrents eventually cut through the town below, lending it some definition and a green vegetation belt, but it's a distinct miniature of Édhessa. South of the large belfried church, which you pass as you wind up from the main road, there's a small park strip, lined with the bulk of Náoussa's restaurants and bars. If you need to stay here, there are two more hotels, the E-class *Kentrikon* at Konstantinídhi 9 (☎0332/22 409; ③), and the B-class *Hellas* at Megálou Alexándhrou 16; (☎0332/22 006; ③). Leaving, you'll almost certainly be doing so by **bus** or under your own power, since the **train station** is a good 7km distant.

West from Édhessa: Flórina and the lakes

West of Édhessa lies **Límni Vegoritídha**, the first of a series of lakes that punctuate the landscape towards Kastoriá and up to and across the "Yugoslav border". The rail line between Édhessa and Flórina traces the lake's west shore: a fine journey which could be broken at either of the two village train stops, Árnissa and Áyios Pandelímonas.

ÁRNISSA has perhaps the better setting, opposite an islet and amidst apple orchards. The village itself is a little drab, though it does have the convenience of an E-class **hotel**, *Megali Hellas* (☎0381/31 232; ③). To its north rises **Mount Kaimaktsalán**, scene of one of the bloodiest and more important battles of World War I, which raged intermittently from 1916 to 1918 until a Yugoslav force managed to break through the German-Bulgarian lines. The 2524-metre summit marks the Greek–"Yugoslav" frontier and bears a small memorial chapel to the fallen. If you can get a lift to the end of the road at Kalívia, it's a beautiful walk beyond.

The more attractive of the villages, however, is **ÁYIOS PANDELÍMONAS**, with its red-roofed houses crowned by a windmill, and a small beach if you're prepared to swim in the slightly algae-ridden waters. There is a taverna, which may be able to arrange **accommodation**. Otherwise camping should present no problem. The place sees few tourists.

Flórina

FLÓRINA is the last town before the Yugoslav Macedonian border 13km to the north. As such, it is quite a lively market centre, both for Greeks from this region and for "Yugoslavs" in search of goods unobtainable over the frontier. You can get just about anything here, including Yugoslav *dinars* – though they are (currently) sold at better rates across the border.

There is little of intrinsic interest. Other than crossing into "Yugoslav Macedonia", the main reason for a visit is to see the Préspa lakes 40km west, or get onward transport to Kastoriá. If you stay, best of the cheap **hotels** is the unclassified *Hotel Patera*, behind the fruit market; otherwise try the D-class *Hellinis*, Pávlou Méla 61 (☎0385/22 672; ③). For Macedonian food at its best, follow the locals to *Taverna Orea Elladha* on the main square.

Transport to "Yugoslav Macedonia" or Kastoriá

If it's still running, the one, slow daily train from **Flórina to Bitola** (3.30pm), in "Yugoslav Macedonia", sounds like a bad deal compared to the four daily buses (morning and mid-day) to the frontier post at NÍKI. However, it's still 18km to Bitola from the frontier post and you have to hitch the first 6km to MEDZITLIJA, where bus services resume. One consolation at NÍKI is that there's a bank at which you can exchange drachmas for dinars. Rates, however, as at Flórina, are worse than they are across the border, so don't change more than you need for the day.

There's isn't one daily bus direct **to Kastoriá**, along the recently paved road that climbs west out of Flórina through dense beech forests to the 1600-metre Pisodhéri saddle, site of a ski lift. Two kilometres beyond, you can stay if need be at the *Modestios Ksenonas* (☎0385/61 345; ④) in the stone-house hamlet of PISODHÉRI. Since its resurfacing, the road is kept snow-ploughed in winter; it follows the headwaters of the Aliákmonas River, the longest in Greece, most of the way to Kastoriá.

The Préspa lakes

Rising out of the Aliákmonas valley on the recently paved side road towards Préspa, you have little hint of what's ahead until suddenly you top a pass, and a shimmering expanse of water riven by islets and ridges appears. It is not, at first glance, postcard-pretty, but the basin has an eerie, back-of-beyond quality that grows on you with further acquaintance – and a turbulent recent history that belies its current role as one of the Balkans' most important wildlife sanctuaries.

During the Byzantine era, Préspa became a prominent place of exile for troublesome noblemen, thus accounting for the surprising number of ecclesiastical monuments in this backwater. In the tenth century it briefly hosted the court of the Bulgarian Tsar Samuel before his defeat by Byzantine Emperor Basil II. Under the Ottomans the area again lapsed into obscurity, only to regain the dubious benefits of strategic importance in just about every European war of this century, culminating in vicious local battles during the 1947–49 Greek civil war. (In 1988 a forest fire on the eastern ridge treated observers to a dangerous fireworks display, as dozens of unexploded artillery shells were touched off by the heat.) After the last war Préspa lay desolate and largely depopulated, as the locals fled overseas to eastern Europe, North America and Australia, in response to a punitive government policy of forced assimilation against Macedonian-speakers – as all the lake-dwellers are. It is only in the last decade or so that the villages, still relatively primitive and neglected, have begun to refill during the summer, when beans and hay are grown as close to the two lakes as the national park authorities allow.

Mikrí Préspa, the southerly lake, is mostly shallow and reedy, with a narrow fjord curling west to just penetrate Albania. The borders of Greece, Albania and Yugoslavia (however long that concept continues to exist) meet in the middle of deeper **Megáli Préspa**, dividing its waters unequally, making the area doomed to play some role in whatever Balkan uproars lie in the future. During the past few years a steady stream of Albanian refugees used the basin as an exit corridor. Current policy, agreed on by both governments concerned, is for those fleeing to be returned, and almost every day some are caught, taken to an army guard post for a meal, and then sent back the way they came. Considering that for years you needed an official permit to visit Préspa, and the uncertain future, the Greek military presence is surprisingly unobtrusive and sovereignty lightly exercised; it's almost as if they couldn't be bothered investing manpower and money on an indigenously Slavic area of suspect political sympathies.

The core of the **national park**, established in 1971, barely encompasses Mikrí Préspa and its shores, but the peripheral zone extends well into the surrounding mountains, affording protection of sorts to a variety of land mammals. You'll almost certainly see foxes crossing the road, though the wolves and bears up on the ridges are considerably shyer, although it is the **bird life** for which the Préspa basin, particularly the smaller lake, is most famous. There are few birds of prey, but you should see a fair number of egrets, cormorants, crested grebes, and pelicans, which nest in the spring, with the chicks out and about by summer. They feed partly on the large numbers of snakes, which include vipers, whip snakes, and harmless water snakes which you may encounter while swimming. **Observation** towers, for example at the site Opáyia, are marked on orientation placards, but they are virtually all rotten and unclimbable; don't despair, however, since any dawn spent at the edge of the reedbeds with a pair of binoculars will be immensely rewarding (you are not allowed to boat or wade into the reeds).

Finally, while you may arrive from Flórina by bus, the service is unreliably infrequent, and you really can't hope to tour the area without some **means of transport** – either a mountain bike or a car. Similarly, in view of the area's until-recent under-development, don't expect much in the way of **facilities**: food is adequate and inexpensive, but exceedingly simple; the same can be said of most places to sleep.

The way in: Mikrolímni
MIKROLÍMNI, 5km up a side track off the main road into the valley, would be a first conceivable stop. There's just one rooms place/taverna, on the shore square, looking towards sunsets over reedbeds and the snake-infested Vitrinítsi islet, though swimming isn't good here. At the far end of the hamlet is a sporadically used biological observation station, literally the last house in Greece, and beyond that the lake narrows between sheer hillsides on its way to Albania. A prominent trail, much used by fleeing Albanians, leads there, paralleling the long inlet, but it would be unwise to walk its full length.

The main road reaches a T-intersection, 16km from the main Flórina–Kastoriá highway, on the spit which separates the larger and smaller lakes. It's probable that at one time there was just one lake here, but now there's a five-metre elevation difference. Bearing right leads within 4km to ÁYIOS YERMANÓS; the left option splits again at the west end of the spit, bearing south toward the islet of ÁYIOS AHILLÍOS or north-west toward the hamlet of PSARÁDHES.

Áyios Yermanós
ÁYIOS YERMANÓS proves to be a surprisingly large village of tile-roofed houses, very much the district "town", overlooking a patch of Megáli Préspa in the distance. It's worth making the trip up just to see two tiny late Byzantine churches, whose frescoes date from the time when the place belonged to the bishopric of Ohrid and thus display a marked Macedonian influence. The lower church, **Áyios Athanásios**, has been recently renovated but if it's open you can glimpse a dog-faced *St Christopher* among a line of saints opposite the door.

The main thing to see, however, is the tiny, eleventh-century parish church of **Áyios Yermanós** up on the square, hidden behind a new monster awkwardly tacked onto it in 1882. The Byzantine structure has its own unlocked door, and the frescoes, skilfully retouched in 1743, can be lit (switch hidden in narthex). There are more hagiographies and martyrdoms than space allows to list here, but if you read Greek there's a complete catalogue of them by the door. Among the best are the dome's *Pandokrátor*; a *Nativity* and *Baptism* right of the dome; a *Crucifixion* and *Resurrection* to the left; plus the saints *Peter and Paul, Kosmas and Damian, Triphon and Pandelimon* by the door. Less conventional scenes include the *Entry into Jerusalem* and *Simon Helping Christ with the Cross*, opposite the door, and the *Apocalypse*, with the *Succouring of Mary the Beautified by Zozimas*, in the narthex. (Mary was an Alexandrine courtesan who, repenting of her ways, retired to the desert for forty years. She was found, a withered crone on the point of death, by Zozimas, abbot of a desert monastery, and is traditionally shown being spoon-fed like an infant.)

In addition to a **post office** – the only one in the Préspa basin – the village has two places to **stay**: *I Pelikani* (☎0385/51 442; ②), across from Áyios Athanásios and with a bit of lake view from its terrace, or (better) three renovated old houses at the very top of the village, run by a local women's cooperative. Reservations (☎0385/51 320; ③) are strongly advised, especially in August when a folk-dance seminar takes place here. In the evenings an unlikely looking taverna across from the main church dishes up good **meals**.

Across the spit and beyond

At the far end of the causeway dividing the two lakes, 4km from the T-junction, there's a cluster of what passes for touristic development hereabouts: a patch of beach from where you can swim in Megáli Préspa, a free but basic camping area, and a cluster of tavernas. Tents and vans sprout by the "sailing club", actually a sporadically operating taverna of sorts, but *I Koula*, up by the army guard-post, offers the best value. Just below it you can see where Mikrí Préspa drains into the bigger lake, next to a rather silly "private" beach.

If you don't intend to camp, it's best to bear right just above the army post, reaching after 6km the picturesque village of **PSARÁDHES**, whose alleys – and a plaza *kafenío* just inland where the elders gabble away in mixed Macedonian and Greek – make for an hour's stroll. Across the rather stagnant inlet here, tracks and paths lead to a more usable, white-pebble beach, near which are two cave-churches with rock paintings. In the village there are **rooms** to rent, and three of the four **tavernas** are run by people surnamed Papadopoulos; *I Paradhosi* seems the best of the bunch. You won't see the fish fried here anywhere else in Greece; similarly, the cows ambling the lanes of Psarádhes are a locally adapted dwarf variety.

The leftward option at the spit's end takes you, after 2km or so, to the jetty for the islet of **Áyios Ahillíos**, with a hamlet of the same name. With luck you would coincide with a resident's boat across, but even then you could easily be stranded on the other side. Once on the island, you can see the ruins of a monastery, a medieval church and the ruins of a Byzantine basilica, the latter with an egret mosaic in the floor. The hill above the jetty is also an excellent vantage point for spotting live birds in the reedbeds below.

Kastoriá

Set on a peninsula extending deep into a chill-blue lake, **KASTORIÁ** is one of the most interesting and attractive towns of mainland Greece, despite its proliferation of tower blocks. It is a wealthy place and has been so for centuries as the centre of the Greek (and Balkan) fur trade; Kastoriá is not a trapping centre, and never really was, but instead boasts a considerable industry of furriers who make up coats, gloves and other items from fur scraps imported from Canada and Scandinavia. For visitors, the main appeal lies in the town's traces of former prosperity. From the seventeenth to nineteenth centuries, when the town was perhaps at its peak, survive half a dozen splendid *arhondiká* – mansions of the old fur families. Dotted about as well are some fifty Byzantine and medieval churches.

Arriving at the **bus station**, you'll find yourself at the edge of the peninsula. Finding a **hotel** can be a struggle, as the town's business means places are full pretty much year-round. They are also expensive, so if you plan on staying try to phone ahead. There is just one cheapie, the *Palladion* at Mitropóleos 40 (☎0467/22 493; ②), centrally positioned, though don't count on getting a room. Two slightly pricier options are by the bus station on Grámmou: *Anessis* at no. 10 (☎0467/29 410; ③) and *Acropolis* at no. 16 (☎0467/22 537; ②). Another, *Keletron*, is on the street's extension, Éndheka

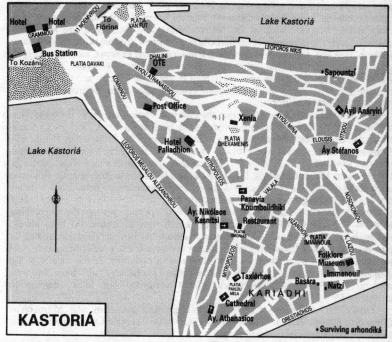

Noemvríou, at no. 52 (☎0467/22 676; ③). The last place to fill is generally the *Xenia du Lac* on Platía Dhexamenís (☎0467/22 565), which, although graded A-class, has out-of-season ③ rates. The best area for **restaurants** is around Platía Omonías. The *Stakhi* bakery, below the square, is good for *bougátzes* (custard tarts), *tirópites* and pizzas. If you need to return to Athens in a hurry, Kastoriá has an **airport**; details of flights can be had from *Olympic Airways* at Megálou Alexandhroú 15 (☎0467/24 455).

The best part of town, for a sense of what Kastoriá must once have been, is the lake-side quarter and former Christian ghetto of **Kariádhi**, around Platía Immanouíl. In nearby Ódhos Kapitán Lázou (at no. 10) the seventeenth-century Aïvazís family mansion has been turned into a **Folklore Museum** (daily 9am–12.30pm & 2–6pm). The house was inhabited until 1972 and its furnishings and ceilings are in excellent repair. It's well worth the visit. The caretaker, on request, will show you some of the other surviving *arhondiká*. The most notable – the nearby **Basára** and **Natzí**, and the **Sapountzí** to the north – are marked on the map.

Kastoriá's **churches** are harder to visit. Although hours of admission are posted on some of the doors, they are irregularly kept. To be sure of entry, it's best to enquire of the two *fílakes* (caretakers) at one of the *kafenía* in Platía Omonías. One has keys for Taxiárhes, Áyios Nikólaos and Koumbelidhikí; the other for Áyii Anáryiri and Áyios Stéfanos. **Áyii Anáryiri** dates from the eleventh century, with three layers of frescoes spanning the following two hundred years. Only one of the frescoes, *Áyios Yióryios and Áyios Dhimítrios*, has been cleared of grime. **Áyios Stéfanos** is of the tenth century and has been little changed over the years. Its frescoes are negligible but it does have an unusual women's gallery, or *yinaikonítis*. Twelfth-century **Áyios Nikólaos Kasnítsi** is currently under restoration, inside and out; when this is complete, its excellent frescoes should have been returned to their former glory. **Taxiárhes**, the oldest (ninth-century) church, hides various treasures beneath layers of soot and damp; some of its more visible frescoes, such as that of the *Virgin and Archangels*, are fourteenth-century. Lastly, the **Panayía Koumbelidhikí**, so named because of its unusual dome (*kübe* in Turkish), has the best-preserved and illuminated frescoes, including a highly unusual portrayal of God the Father in a ceiling mural of the *Holy Trinity*. The building was done in stages, with the apse completed in the tenth century and the narthex in the fifteenth. The dome was meticulously restored after being destroyed by Italian bombing in World War II.

Kastoriá also suffered heavily during the civil war. Platía Ván Flít, by the lakeside at the neck of the promontory, commemorates the US general – Van Fleet – who supervised the Greek Nationalist Army's operations against the Communist Democratic Army in the final campaigns of 1948–49. The town was nearly captured by the communists in 1948, and Vítsi, the conical peak dominating the north shore of the lake, was, together with Mount Grámmos, the scene of their last stand in August 1949. However, most of the destruction of Kastoriá's architectural heritage is not due so much to munitions as to 1950s neglect and 1960s developers.

If tracking down buildings seems too frustrating a pursuit, perhaps the nicest thing to do in Kastoriá is to follow the footpath which runs all around the **lake shore**. Although the lake itself is heavily polluted, the path has been deliberately created by one of Greece's few environmentalists. It has almost a country-park atmosphere, and wildlife abounds – frogs, tortoises and water snakes especially. At the far end of the peninsula, about an hour's walk, is the **Mavrótissa monastery**, with more fine frescoes in its eleventh-century church, and a **campsite** (for those immune to mosquitoes).

Finally, for aficionados, there's a new **Byzantine museum** near Mitropóleos (Tues–Sun 8.30am–2.30pm; find warden for admission), containing an ever-expanding collection of restored Byzantine icons.

Around Kastoriá

If you have transport, you might make a trip 14km west to **OMORFOKLISSIÁ**, an eerie village of mud houses inherited from Turkish peasants. It has a Byzantine church with a high cupola, attached belfry and, inside, a huge, primitive wooden **statue-icon of St George** thought to date from the eleventh century.

Siátista

If for some reason you can't make it to Ambelákia or Kastoriá, then **SIÁTISTA**, draped along a single ridge in a forbiddingly bare landscape 70km south of Kastoriá, is a worthy substitute. Located just above the point where the road splits for Kozáni or Kastoriá, it was, like the latter, an important fur centre, and boasts a handful of eighteenth-century mansions or *arhondiká*, which can be visited.

The eighteenth-century house of **Hatzimihaíl Kanatsoúli** at Mitropóleos 1, near the police station, is still lived in but you can ring to be shown around. The first two floors are occupied; upstairs, a corner room has naive murals of mythological scenes (including Kronos' castration of Ouranos). The dilapidated **Nerantzópoulos mansion** (Mon–Sat 8.30am–3pm, Sun 9.30am–2.30pm) is on the upper square, by the *Ethniki Trapeza*; the warden here has the keys for several other houses, of which the largest and most elaborate is the **Manoúsi mansion**, dating from 1763, in a vale below the Kanatsoúli along with various other surviving *arhondiká*. Ceiling medallions often sport a carved cluster of fruit or a melon with a slice missing, where you'd expect a chandelier attachment point; there are more three-dimensional floral and fruit carvings up at the tops of the walls, which are adorned with stylised murals of pastoral and fictitious urban scenes. The church of **Áyía Paraskeví**, on the lowest *platía*, has soot-blackened seventeenth-century frescoes inside; until the scheduled cleaning occurs, you're better off glancing at the exterior ones.

Almost everything you need – **banks**, **OTE**, **post office** – is along the single main street, including the C-class *Arhondiko* **hotel** (☎0465/21 298; ③), a new building despite the name. Options for **eating** out are limited; the *Psistaria Ouzeri O Platanos*, just below Áyía Paraskeví, has acceptable food but a rather boozy male environment – the hotel is more genteel. The easiest bus connections are with Kozáni.

HALKIDHIKÍ AND EASTERN MACEDONIA

Halkidhikí, easily reached by bus from Thessaloníki, is the clear highlight of Macedonia's eastern half. Its first two peninsulas, **Kassándhra** and **Sithonía**, shelter the north's main concentration of beaches; the third, **Áthos**, the country's finest, though most secretive, monasteries.

Moving east, there are a few more good beaches en route to **Kavála**, but little of interest inland, with a scattering of small market towns serving a population that – as in neighbouring Thrace – produces the main Greek tobacco crop.

Kassándhra, Sithonía and secular Áthos

The squid-shaped peninsula of **Halkidhikí** begins at a perforated edge of lakes east of Thessaloníki and extends into three prongs of land – Kassándhra, Sithonía, and Áthos – trailing like tentacles into the Aegean sea.

Mount Áthos, the easternmost peninsula, is in all ways separate, a "Holy Mountain", whose monastic population, semi-autonomous within the Greek state, excludes all women – even as visitors. For men who wish to experience Athonite life, a visit involves suitably Byzantine procedures which are detailed, with the monastic sights, in the section that follows. The most that women can do is to glimpse the buildings from offshore. It is possible to take *kaíki* rides from the two small resorts on the periphery of the peninsula – Ierissós and Ouranoúpoli, the "secular" part of Áthos covered in this section.

Kassándhra and **Sithonía**, by contrast, host some of the fastest-growing holiday resorts in Greece. Up until the last five years these were popular mainly with Greeks, but they're now in the process of a staggering development, with most European package-tour companies maintaining a presence. On Kassándhra, especially, almost any reasonable beach is accompanied by a crop of villas or a hotel development, while huge billboards advertise campsite complexes miles in advance. A still larger billboard at the entrance to the Kassándhra peninsula reminds you that camping outside the authorised grounds is strictly prohibited, although you may have no other choice if you're so bold as to show up in high season without a reservation. One consolation is that most beaches here are equipped with free freshwater showers.

Both Kassándhra and Sithonía are connected to Thessaloníki by a network of fast new roads which extend around their coastlines; buses run frequently to all the larger resorts. In spite of this, neither peninsula is that easy to travel around if you are dependent on public **transport**. You really have to pick a place and stay there, perhaps hiring a moped for local excursions.

Kassándhra

Kassándhra, the nearest prong to Thessaloníki, is also by far the most developed. Unless you're very pushed for time and want a couple of days' escape from Thessaloníki, it's best to keep on to Sithonía, or, better still, the top end of Áthos. Apart from resorts, there is very little to Kassándhra. Its population took part in the independence uprising of 1821, but was defeated and massacred; as a result, there were only a few small fishing hamlets here until after 1923, when the peninsula was resettled by refugees from around the Sea of Marmara.

On the peninsula's west coast, the first resort you come to, **NÉA MOUDHANIÁ**, has hydrofoils in summer to Skiáthos, Skópelos and Alónissos. The second, **NÉA POTÍDHEA**, at the neck of the peninsula, is a tiny place, overlooked by a medieval watchtower. It is generally jammed to the gills in season, however, as are both **SANÍ** and **POSSÍDHI** with their international campsites. **KALLITHÉA**, just beyond Possídhi, is a slightly better option if you want a straightforward resort. There are a large number of **rooms** to let – not just package hotels – and you can rent bikes and mopeds on the main street, or windsurfers on the beach. Don't expect much character, though.

On the east coast, **HANIÓTIS** has a good long beach and a few ordinary-sized hotels and tavernas; *Camping Kera Maria*, just outside the resort, is low-key. But at both **PALIOÚRI** and **KRIOPIYÍ** it's back to the huge "holiday-campings".

Sithonía

Things improve considerably as you move east across the Halkidhikí and away from the frontline of tourism; the landscape also becomes increasingly green and hilly, culminating in the isolated and spectacular scenery of the Holy Mountain, looming across the gulf lapping Sithonía's east coast. As for the peninsula itself, **Sithonía** is more rugged but better vegetated than Kassándhra, though once again there are few true villages, and those that do exist date from the 1920s resettlement era. Pine forests cover many of the slopes, giving way to olive groves on the coast. Small sandy inlets with relatively discreet pockets of campsites and tavernas make a welcome change from sprawling mega-resorts.

Suitably enough, **METAMÓRFOSI** ("Transfiguration"), at the western base of Sithonía, signals the transformation. Its beach is only adequate but there's good swimming to be had, and the village, while relentlessly modern, has an easy-going air. In addition to one D-class hotel, *Golden Beach* (☎0375/22 063; ③ out of season), and furnished apartments such as *Olympic Bibis* (☎0375/22 558; ④), there's a **campsite**, *Camping Sithon*, a couple of kilometres beyond. A fair number of tavernas cluster in and around the village square.

Moving on to Sithonía proper, it's best to follow the loop road clockwise around the east coast, so that Áthos is always before you. **Bus services** are sparse, however: there are up to five buses daily around the west coast to Sárti, and up to three a day to Vourvouroú, but there's no KTEL connection between these two endpoints. A complete circuit is only really possible with your own transport.

ÓRMOS PANAYÍA, first of the east coast resorts, is nowadays well developed; ranks of villas dwarf the tiny harbour, and the nearest decent beaches are 4km north at **ÁYIOS NIKÓLAOS**, which is marginally more attractive. The only conceivable reason to stop at Órmos would be to catch the excursion boats that sail around Áthos from here, but these are expensive and often pre-reserved for tourists bused in from the big Halkidhikí resorts.

VOURVOUROÚ, 8km downcoast, is not a typical resort, since it's essentially a thirty-year-old vacation-villa project for Thessaloníki professors, built on land expropriated from Vatopédhi monastery on Áthos. There is relatively little short-term **accom-**

modation – the hotels *Dhiaporos* (☎0375/91 313; ⑤) and faded *Vourvourou* (☎0375/91 261, ③) are about the size of it. The strange feel is accentuated by those plot owners who haven't bothered to build villas (so far very scattered) and merely tent down, making it hard to tell which are the real campsites. The setting, with islets astride the mouth of the bay, is very fine, but the beach, while sandy, is extremely narrow, and Vourvouroú is really more of a yachters' haven. **Tavernas** are relatively inexpensive because they're banking on a return clientele (which includes lots of Germans); the *Itamos*, inland from the road, is the best; the *Gorgona*, while the nicest positioned, is rather surly; *Dionisos* is intermediate in position and quality, but has a simple though adequate **campsite**.

Some of Sithonía's best **beaches** line the thirty kilometres of road between Vourvouroú and Sárti: five signposted sandy coves, each with a **campsite** and little else (though the *Armenistis* has a scuba-diving operation). The names of the bays reflect the fact that most of the land here belonged to various Athonite monasteries until confiscated by the civil government to resettle Anatolian refugees.

Concrete-grid **SÁRTI** itself is set well back from its broad, two-kilometre-long beach, with only the scale of the bay protecting it from being utterly overrun in summer by Germans. There are hundreds of **rooms** (though often not enough to go around), and the cheaper of the **tavernas** lining the landscaped, gravel shore esplanade include *Neraida* and *O Stavros*, the latter by the **OTE**. Inland you'll find a short-hours **bank** and a rather tacky square with forgettable tavernas and sleazy sex bars – although it does boast a **moped rental** place. To the south lie a series of small coves, the first of which – **ÁYIOS IOÁNNIS** – supports a campsite so expensive that many people tent down freelance in neighbouring bays.

If you want reasonably priced facilities, **PARALÍA SIKIÁS**, 8km further along, has a beach the equal of Sárti's but is so far undeveloped except for a **campsite** and a few **tavernas**. **KALAMÍTSI**, as many kilometres again to the south, consists of a beautiful double bay sheltered by islets, but one of the two **campsites** monopolises one cove, and the handful of **rooms** and **tavernas** just behind the other sandy beach combines with the habitual crowds to cramp matters. You can easily swim out to the islets for less company, or (taking things to extremes) arrange an excursion with the scuba-diving centre *Nireas* (☎0374/41 436; in winter contact ☎031/812 698).

Sithonía's forest cover has been diminishing since Sárti, and as you round the tip of the peninsula it vanishes completely, with bare hills spilling into the sea to create a handful of deep bays. **PÓRTO KOUFÓ**, just northwest of the cape, is the most dramatic of these, almost completely cut off from the open sea by high cliffs. There's a decent beach near where the road drops down from the east, with two **campsites** – one expensive, one reasonable – just overhead. The north end of the inlet, a kilometre from the beach area, is a yacht harbour with a string of somewhat expensive seafood **tavernas**; *O Pefkos* is a cheaper, though not very inspired alternative.

TORÓNI, 2km north, is the antithesis of this, an exposed, two-kilometre-long crescent of sand, still at the developmental stage where each of the half-dozen **tavernas** doubles as a "**rooms**". It's probably your best Sithonian bet as a base if you just want to flop on a beach for a few days; for more stimulation there is a minimal **archaeological site** on the southern cape, and an open-air **cinema**. Just to the north are more coves especially popular with car-campers, accessible on a dirt coastal track as far as **Aretes**, where most vehicles and people give up. **TRISTINÍKA**, with **rooms** as well as **camping** at the edge of a cow-patrolled swamp (mosquitoes abound), is a more common choice.

Beyond Tristiníka, you edge back into high-tech resort territory, epitomised by Greece's largest planned holiday complex, **PÓRTO CARRÁS**. Established by the Carras wine and shipping dynasty, it takes Spanish Marbella as its model, featuring its own conference hall, shopping centre and vineyards. On the beach outside the complex – 20,000dr per room, incidentally – you can indulge in every imaginable watersport. The nearest "town" to all this is NÉOS MARMARÁS, a concrete eyesore draped over hills above a once-attractive fishing port and small beach; the only thing to recommend it are OTE, banking and postal facilities.

If you're curious as to what Sithonía looked like before all this happened, a dirt road leads 5km from Néos Marmarás to PARTHENÓNAS, the lone "traditional" village on Sithonía, crouched at the base of 808-metre Mount Ítamos. The place was abandoned in the 1960s in favour of the shore, and never even provided with mains electricity; its dilapidated but appealing houses are now slowly being sold off to wealthy Greeks and Germans. A single bistro-disco operates by night at road's end, powered by its own generator.

East to secular Áthos

From Órmos Panayía a partly paved road winds around the coast to Ierissós at the head of the Áthos peninsula. No buses cover this stretch, however, and if you're dependent on public transport you'll have to backtrack as far as YERAKINÍ and then inland to Halkidhikí's capital, POLÍYIROS, a drab market town with an unexciting archaeological museum. Here, or from ÁYIOS PRÓDHROMOS, 20km north, you can pick up buses heading for Áthos via ARNÉA, which has some fine old quarters and a reputation for somewhat touristy weavings; it could be worth a brief stopover, though there's no longer any hotel here.

If all this sounds like too much bother, hitching from Órmos to Ierissós is not out of the question; the thirty-odd kilometres of road as far as GOMÁTI are now mostly paved, with the 10km remaining to the southeast soon to follow suit. The only place you'd think to stop is PIRGADHÍKIA, a hill-set former fishing village now taken over by German holidaymakers.

IERISSÓS, with a good, long beach and a vast, promontory-flanked gulf, is probably the best "secular Athos" resort, although the town itself, set well back from the shore and with room to expand, is a sterile concrete grid dating from after a devastating 1932 earthquake. The only hint of pre-touristic life is the vast caique-building dry dock to the south. There are numerous rooms, two inexpensive hotels – the basic *Akanthos* (☎0377/22 359; ③) and slightly classier *Marcos* (☎0377/22 518; ③) – and two primitive campsites (one at the north edge of town, the other on the way to Néa Ródha). The beach is surprisingly uncluttered, with just a handful of shore tavernas and bars (*Tou Kolatsi* and the one in the northerly campsite are the most old-fashioned). Rounding off the list of amenities, there's a post office, two banks and a summer cinema by the campsite. Ierissós is also the main port for the northeast shore of Áthos; summer sailings take place daily at 8.30am, with only three or four weekly in winter as weather – which can turn very stormy on this side – allows.

The road beyond Ierissós passes through the resort of NÉA RÓDHA, with a small beach and no more claim to architectural distinction than its neighbour, but worth knowing about as an alternative point for picking up the morning boat. Just beyond here your route veers inland to follow a boggy depression that's the remaining stretch of Xerxes's canal, cut by the Persian invader in 48 BC to spare his fleet the shipwreck at the tip of Áthos that had befallen the previous expedition eleven years before. You emerge on the southwest facing coast at Tripití, not a settlement but merely the ferry jetty for the small island of AMOULIANÍ (regular crossings in summer, especially at weekends). On the island's further, southwest side is a beautiful beach, Alikés, with a namesake campsite and small taverna; the island's town itself, after decades of eking out an existence as a refugee fishing community from the Sea of Marmara, is having to adjust to the relatively sudden arrival of well-heeled Greek and foreign visitors – you can even arrange scuba expeditions here.

By contrast to Ierissós, **OURANÓPOLI**, 15km beyond and the last community before the restricted monastic domains, represents a lot of busy-ness crammed into a small space. Its centre is downright tatty, showing the effects of too much Greek-weekender and German-package tourism, and the sandy **beaches**, though stretching intermittently for several kilometres to the north, can be cramped. The pebbly coves in the opposite direction, up to the Athonite frontier, are less used. If you're compelled to stay the night while waiting for passage to Áthos, the best temporary escape would be a cruise, or **self-hire motor boat**, to the mini-archipelago of **Dhrénia** just opposite, with almost tropical sands and tavernas on the larger islets.

The only other conceivable diversion in Ouranópoli is the Byzantine **Phosphori tower** by the bus stop; here for nearly thirty years lived Sydney Loch, author of *Athos: the Holy Mountain*, published posthumously in 1957 but still an excellent guide to the monasteries. Sydney Loch and his wife Joyce, who died in the tower in 1982, were a Scots-Australian missionary couple who devoted most of their lives to the refugees of Halkidhikí. The cottage industry of carpet-weaving, which they taught the local villagers, is unfortunately increasingly less in evidence.

Three **ferries** – the *Ayios Nikolaos*, the *Poseidon* and the *Axion Esti* – take turns calling along the southwest shore of Áthos, and they're probably the main reason you're here. Much of the year there's just one daily departure, at around 9.45am, though in summer there may be two: one earlier, one around 11.30am. If you need to **stay**, there are a fair number of **rooms**, like the *Athos* and *Niki* on the main thoroughfare, and a few cheaper hotels such as the *Galini* (☎0377/71 217; ③), the *Ouranopolis* (☎0377/71-205; ③) or the seafront *Akrogiali* (☎0377/71.201; ③), all fairly used to one-night stands. A **campsite**, better appointed than those in Ierissós, is 2km north of the village, amidst a crop of luxury hotel complexes that have sprung up where there's more space to spread out. Ouranópoli has a Portakabin **post office** and an **OTE** but no bank. The four or five waterfront **tavernas** all tout identical rip-off menus, though you're unlikely to care much about value for money before (or especially after) several lean days on Áthos. If budgeting is an issue, there are a few marginally less expensive places in the inland alleys.

Mount Áthos: the monks' republic

The population of the **Mount Áthos** peninsula has been exclusively male – farm animals included – since an edict, the *Ávaton*, banning females permanent or transient, was issued by the Byzantine emperor Constantine Monomachos in 1060. Known in Greek as the **Áyion Oros** ("Holy Mount"), it is an administratively autonomous part of the country – a "monks' republic" – on whose slopes are gathered twenty monasteries, plus a number of smaller dependencies and hermitages.

Most of the **monasteries** were founded in the tenth and eleventh centuries. Today, all survive in a state of comparative decline but they remain unsurpassed in their general and architectural interest, and for the art treasures they contain. If you are male, over 18 years old, and have a genuine interest in monasticism or Greek Orthodoxy, or simply in Byzantine and medieval architecture, a visit is strongly recommended. It takes a couple of hours to arrange, either in Thessaloníki or Athens (see below), but the rewards more than justify your efforts. In addition to the religious and architectural aspects of Áthos, it should be added that the peninsula, despite some horrific fires and heavy logging in recent years, is still one of the most beautiful parts of Greece. With only the occasional service vehicle, two buses and sporadic coastal boats, a visit of necessity involves walking between settlements – preferably on paths through dense woods, up the main peak, or above what is perhaps the Mediterranean's last undeveloped coastline. For many visitors, this – as much as the experience of monasticism – is the highlight of time spent on the Holy Mountain.

The Theocratic Republic: some history

By a legislative decree of 1926, Áthos has the status of **"Theocratic Republic"**. It is governed from the small town and capital of Kariés by the *Ayía Epistasía* ("Holy Superintendency"), a council of twenty representatives elected for one-year terms by each of the monasteries. At the same time Áthos remains a part of Greece. All foreign monks must adopt Greek citizenship, and the Greek civil government is represented by an appointed governor and a small police force.

Each monastery has a distinct place in the **Athonite hierarchy**: Meyístis Lávras holds the prestigious first place, Kastamonítou ranks twentieth. All other settlements are attached to one or other of the twenty "ruling" monasteries; the dependencies range from a *skíti* (either a group of houses, or a cloister-like structure scarcely distinguishable from a monastery) through a *kellí* (a sort of farmhouse) to an *isikhastírio* (a solitary hermitage, often a cave). As many laymen as monks live on Áthos, mostly employed as agricultural or manual labourers by the monasteries.

The **development of monasticism** on Áthos is a matter of some controversy, and foundation legends abound. The most popular asserts that the Virgin Mary was blown ashore here on her way to Cyprus, and while overcome by the great beauty of the mountain, a mysterious voice consecrated the place in her name. Another tradition relates that Constantine the Great founded the first monastery in the fourth century, but this is certainly far too early. The earliest historical reference to Athonite monks is to their attendance at a council of the Empress Theodoa in 843; probably there were some monks here by the end of the seventh century. Áthos was particularly appropriate for early Christian monasticism, its deserted and isolated slopes providing a natural refuge from the outside world – especially from the Arab conquests in the east, and the iconoclastic phase of the Byzantine Empire (eighth to ninth centuries). Moreover its awesome beauty, which had so impressed the Virgin, facilitated communion with God.

The most famous of the **early monks** were Peter the Athonite and Saint Euthimios of Salonica, both of whom lived in cave-hermitages on the slopes during the mid-ninth century. In 885 an edict of Emperor Basil I recognised Áthos as the sole preserve of monks, and gradually hermits came together to form communities known as *cenobia* (literally "common living"). The year 963 is the traditional date for the foundation of the first monastery, Meyístis Lávras, by Athanasios the Athonite; the Emperor Nikephoros Phocas provided considerable financial assistance. Over the next two centuries, with the protection of other Byzantine emperors, foundations were frequent, the monasteries reaching forty in number (reputedly with a thousand monks in each), alongside many smaller communities.

Troubles for Áthos, after this early growth, began at the end of the eleventh century. The monasteries suffered sporadically from pirate raids and from the settlement of 300 Vlach shepherd families on the mountain. After a reputedly scandalous time between the monks and the shepherdesses, the Vlachs were ejected and a new imperial *chryssobul* (edict) was issued, confirming that no female, human or animal, be allowed to set foot on Áthos. This edict, called the *ávaton*, remains in force today.

During the twelfth century, the monasteries gained an international – or at least, a **pan-Orthodox** – aspect, as Romanian, Russian and Serbian monks flocked to the mountain in retreat from the turbulence of the age. Áthos itself was subjected to Frankish raids during the Latin occupation of Constantinople (1204–61), and even after this faced great pressure from the Unionists of Latin Salonica to unite with western Catholics; in the courtyard of Zográfou there is still a monument to the monks who were martyred at this time while attempting to preserve the independence of Orthodox Christianity. In the early fourteenth century the monasteries suffered two disastrous years of pillage by Catalan mercenaries but they recovered, primarily through Serbian benefactors, to enjoy a period of great prosperity in the fifteenth and sixteenth centuries.

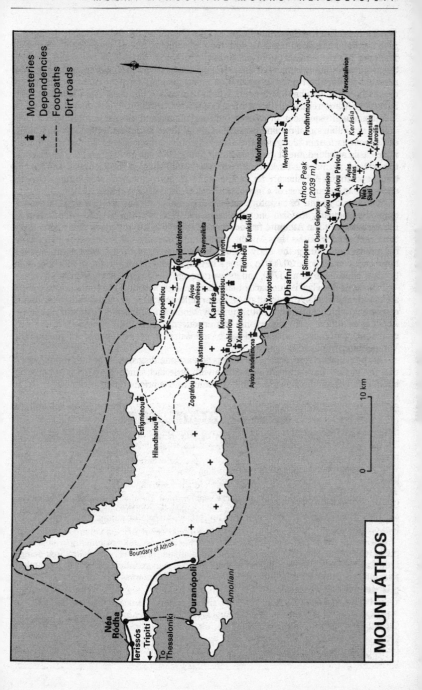

After the fall of the Byzantine Empire to the Ottomans, the fathers wisely declined to resist, maintaining good relations with the early sultans, one of whom paid a state visit. The later Middle Ages brought **economic problems**, with heavy taxes and confiscations, and as a defence many of the monasteries dissolved their common holdings and reverted to an idiorrhythmic system, a self-regulating form of monasticism where monks live and worship in a loosely bound community but work and eat individually. However, Athos remained the spiritual centre of Orthodoxy, and during the seventeenth and eighteenth centuries even built and maintained its own schools.

The mountain's real decline came after the **War of Independence**, in which many of the monks fought alongside the Greek klephts. In Macedonia the insurrectionists were easily subdued, the region remaining under Ottoman control, and the monks paid the price. A permanent Turkish garrison was established on the mountain and monastery populations fell sharply as, in the wake of independence for southern Greece, monasticism became less of a focus for Greek Orthodox Christianity.

At the end of the last century and the beginning of this one **foreign Orthodox** monks, particularly Russian ones (before the 1917 revolution), tried to step in and fill the vacuum. But the Athonite fathers have always resisted any move that might dilute the Greek quality of the Holy Mount, even – until recently – at the expense of its material prosperity. During the early 1960s, numbers were at their lowest ever, barely a thousand, compared to 20,000 in Áthos's heyday. Today, however, the monastic population has climbed to about 1700, and its average age has dropped significantly.

This modest revival is due partly to the increasingly appeal of the contemplative life in a blatantly materialistic age, but more importantly to a wave of rather militant sectarian sentiment, which has swept both the Holy Mountain and world Orthodoxy at large. Active recruitment and evangelising has produced a large crop of novices from every continent, particularly visible in such monasteries as Simópetra, Filothéou and Vatopedhíou.

On the negative side, critics, including at least one disgruntled former monk, assert that the zealots have transformed Áthos with little tact, compelling many supposedly lax idiorryhythmic houses to become cenobitic as the price of their revitalisation. In an

---

ATHONITE TERMS

Arhondáris Guestmaster of a monastery or *skíti*, responsible for all visitors; similarly, *arhondaríki*, the guest quarters themselves.

Arsanás Harbour annexe of each monastery or *skíti*, where the *kaíkia* anchor; they can be a considerable distance from the institution in question.

Dhíkeos The "righteous one" – head of an idiorrhythmic foundation.

Cenobitic/Idiorrythmic This is (increasingly, was) the major distinction between religious foundations on the Mountain. At cenobitic establishments the monks eat all meals together, hold all property in common and have rigidly scheduled days. Those that are idiorrhythmic are more individualistic: the monks eat in their own quarters and study or worship when and as they wish. Over the past decade most of the remaining idiorrhythmic monasteries have reverted to cenobitic status, with Pandokrátoros being the last hold-out. Currently monks wishing to follow a more independent path must take up residence in an idiorrhythmic *skíti* (most of them are) or a *kellí*.

Dhókimos A novice monk.

Fiáli The covered font for holy water in some monastery courtyards; often very ornate.

Igoúmenos Abbot, the head of a cenobitic house.

Katholikón Main church of a monastery.

Kiriakón Central chapel of a *skíti*, where the residents worship together once weekly.

Trapezaría Refectory, or dining room.

echo of the conflicts earlier this century, there has also allegedly been interference with the efforts of the non-Greek foundations to recruit brothers and receive pilgrims from the home country, and in general a confusion of the aims of Orthodoxy and Hellenism. If these tensions appear unseemly in a commonwealth devoted to spiritual perfection, it's worth remembering that doctrinal strife has always been part of Athonite history; that most of the monks still are Greek, and that donning the habit doesn't quell their inborn love of politicking. Also, in a perverse way, the ongoing controversies demonstrate a renewed vitality, inasmuch as Mount Athos, and who controls it, are seen once again as having some global importance.

Permits and entry

Until a few decades ago foreigners could visit Áthos quite easily, but in the early 1970s the number of tourists grew so great that the monasteries could no longer cope. Since then a permit system has been instituted, and only Greeks – and to a lesser extent foreign Orthodox – are exempt from it.

The first step in **acquiring a permit** to visit and stay on Áthos is to obtain a **letter of recommendation** from your embassy or consulate in Athens or Thessaloníki; see those respective city's "Listings" for addresses. The letter should be purely a formality; the US consulate issues it free, UK ones make a £15 charge – though as a courtesy, before charging you, they suggest you contact the relevant Greek ministries first to see if space is available when you want to go. It is best to have yourself described in the text as a university-level scholar or graduate in art, religion or architecture – or as a "man of letters", which description covers just about any published (or hopeful) writer.

Take the consular letter either to the **Ministry of Foreign Affairs in Athens** (Zalakósta 2, Room 73, 3rd floor; Mon, Wed & Fri 11am–2pm) or to the **Ministry of Macedonia and Thrace in Thessaloníki** (Platía Dhikitiríou, Room 218; Mon–Fri 11am–2pm). In exchange for the letter you will be issued a permit valid for four days' residence on Áthos, which must be used "within a reasonable amount of time" and which will have a date specified for the beginning the visit. This may not be the date of your choice in high summer, when it's all but mandatory to apply for permission at least two months in advance. Each of the ministries described above is alotted ten slots for foreigners of all nationalities on each day of the year, for a total of twenty new arrivals on Áthos per day. Therefore if your day, or week, of choice is full up in one city, there is some chance that there may be space in the other, though this can't be relied on.

To get to Áthos, take a Halkidhikí KTEL bus (either from the new joint station or the old terminal at Karakássi 68) to OURANÓPOLI or IERISSÓS (see "East to Secular Áthos", preceding). From Ouranópoli at least one **boat** daily sails as far as **Dháfni**, the main port on the southwestern coast of Áthos, where there's a connecting service onward to the *skíti* of Ayías Ánnas. If you're setting out on the day your permit starts, you'll have to take the earliest (6am) KTEL departure to connect with the boat. At Ierissós, the boat usually leaves earlier in the morning than the first bus will pass through, entailing an overnight here – and a chance to see if bad weather will force a cancellation. Service along the northeast shore always goes as far as the monastery of **Ivíron**, usually up to Meyístis Lávras, and turns around more or less immediately. Ouranópoli–Dháfni takes about ninety minutes; Ierissós–Ivíron more than two hours.

At the first port of call – the *arsanás* (harbour annexe) of Zográfou on the southwest side, the *arsanás* of Hilandharíou on the northeast – all passengers will be ushered off the boat to the police post, where your ministry permit and a fee of 2000dr will be exchanged for a document called the **dhiamonitírion**, which entitles you to stay at any of the main monasteries. You are now free to leave the boat or continue with it to any destination you wish – they stop at the dock for every monastery on their respective coasts. You no longer have to go to Kariés unless you specifically want to, and the new streamlined procedure has in effect granted visitors an extra half-day that was formerly wasted traipsing up to Kariés on the bus from Dháfni or Ivíron for necessary paper-work before setting out for the monasteries.

Many visitors wish to arrange for an **extension** of the basic four-day period. There is little point in asking for one, either at your first landfall or later in Kariés, for the simple reason that it will be routinely denied. In actual fact, however, nobody is terribly both-ered if you stay five days or even a week, except in high summer when monastic accommodation can get quite crowded. It is rare that guestmasters ask to see your *dhiamonitírion*, much less scrutinise it carefully, and the four-day limit was originally enforced to discourage gawkers and others with frivolous motives for visiting. If you are regarded as a sincere pilgrim, and move on to a different monastery each day as the regulations require you to, there are no problems with a do-it-yourself extension. Conversely, if you strike the monks as behaving presumptuously or inappropriately, no amount of time remaining on your permit will persuade them to grant you hospitality. As signs on walls repeatedly remind you, "Hospitality is not obligatory".

The way of life

With *dhiamonitírion* in hand, you will be admitted to stay and eat in the main monaster-ies – and certain *skítes* – free of charge. If you offer money if will be refused, though Orthodox pilgrims are encourgaged to buy candles, incense, icon reproductions and the like at those *skítes* which specialise in their production. **Accommodation** is usually in dormitories, and fairly spartan, but you're always given sheets and blankets; you don't need to lug a sleeping bag around. Áthos grows much of its own **food**, and the monastic diet is based on tomatoes, beans, cheese and pasta, with occasional treats like *helva* and fruit included. After Sunday morning service, wine often accompanies fish in the heartiest meal of the week. Normally only two meals a day are served, the first at mid-morning, the latter about an hour and a half to two hours before sunset. You will need to be partly self-sufficient in provisions – especially dried fruits, nuts, sweets – both for the times when you fail to coincide with meals and for the long walks between monasteries. (If you arrive after the evening meal you will generally be served leftovers set aside for latecomers.) There are a few shops in Kariés, but for better selection and to save valuable time you should stock up before coming to Áthos.

If you're planning to **walk between monasteries**, you should get hold of one of two **maps**: the first simply entitled "Athos", produced in Austria at a scale of 1:50,000 by Reinhold Zwerger and Klaus Schöpfleuthner (Wohlmutstr 8, A 1020 Wien) but usually available for 1500dr in Ouranópoli; the other, a simple sketch map of all the roads and trails on the Mount, by Theodhoros Tsiropoulos of Thessaloníki (☎031/430 196). The *Korfes* magazine map is now obsolete and contains potentially dangerous errors, but it's still more useful than any of the touristic productions sold in Ouranópoli. Even equipped with these, you'll still need to be pointed to the start of trails at each monas-tery, and confirm walking times and path conditions. New roads are constantly being built, and trails accordingly abandoned, and in the jungly local climate they become completely overgrown within two years if not used.

If need be, you can supplement walking with the regular **kaíki services** that ply between the main establishments on each coast. The return time out of Ayías Ánnas to Dháfni is about 8am in summer, with onward connections towards the "border" just after noon. On the other side, the single craft leaves Meyístis Lávras at about 2pm, bound for Ierissós. On alternate days in summer there is also a useful *kaíki* linking Meyístis Lávras and Ayías Ánnas, stopping at the *skíti* of Kavsokalivíon on its way around the south tip of the peninsula.

However you move around, you must reach your destination **before dark**, since all monasteries and many *skítes* lock their front gates at sunset – leaving you out with the wild boars and (it is claimed) a handful of wolves. Upon arrival you should ask for the *arhondáris* (**guestmaster**), who will proffer the traditional welcome of a *tsípouro* (distilled spirits) and *loukoúmi* (Turkish delight) before showing you to your bed. These days guestmasters tend to speak at least some English, a reflection of the increasing numbers of Cypriot, Australian or educated Greek novices on Áthos.

You will find the monastic **daily schedule** somewhat disorienting, and adapted according to the seasonal time of sunrise and sunset. On the northeast side of the peninsula 12 o'clock is reckoned from the hour of sunrise, and on the opposite side clocktowers may show both hands up at sunset. Yet Vatopedhíou keeps "worldly" time, as do most monks' wristwatches. However the Julian calendar, thirteen days behind the outside world, is universally observed, and will be the date appearing on your *dhia-monitírion*. More and more monasteries are getting electric power but this has affected the round of life very little; both you and the monks will go to bed early, shortly after sunset. Sometimes in the small hours your hosts will awake for solitary meditation and study, followed by *órthros* or matins. Around sunrise there is another quiet period, just before the *akolouthía* or main liturgy. Next comes the morning meal, anywhere from 9.30 to 11.30am depending on the time of year. The afternoon is devoted to manual labour until the *esperinós* or vespers, actually almost three hours before sunset in summer (much less in winter). This is followed immediately by the evening meal and the short *apódhipno* or complines service.

A few words about **attitudes and behaviour** towards your hosts (and vice versa), as many misunderstandings arise from mutual perceptions of disrespect, real or imagined. For your part, you should be fully clad at all times, even when going from dormitory to bathroom; this in effect means no shorts, no hats inside monasteries, and sleeves that come down to the middle of the biceps. If you swim, do so where nobody can see you, and don't do it naked. Smoking in most foundations is forbidden, though a few allow you to indulge out on the balconies; it would be criminal to do so on the trail, given the chronic fire danger; you might just want to give it up as a penance for the duration of your stay. Singing, whistling and raised voices are taboo; so is standing with your hands behind your back or crossing your legs when seated, both considered overbearing stances. If you want to photograph monks you should always ask permission, though photography is forbidden altogether in several cloisters. It's best not to go poking your nose into corners of the monasteries where you're not specifically invited, even if they seem open to the public.

Monasteries, and their tenants, tend to vary a good deal in their handling of visitors, and their reputations, deserved or otherwise, tend to precede them as a favourite subject of trail gossip among foreigners. You will find that as a non-Orthodox you may be politely ignored, or worse, with signs at some institutions specifically forbidding you from attending services or sharing meals with the monks. Other monasteries are by contrast very engaging, putting themselves at the disposal of visitors of whatever creed. It is not uncommon to be treated to extreme bigotry and disarming gentility at the same place within the space of ten minutes, making it very difficult to draw conclusions about Áthos in general and monasteries in particular. If you are not even a Christian as well as non-Orthodox, and seem to understand enough Greek to get the message, you'll probably be told at some point during your visit that you'll burn in Hell unless you convert to the True Faith forthwith. While this may seem offensive, considering your probable motivation for being here, it pays to remember that the monks are expecting religous pilgrims, not tourists, and that their role is to be committed, not tolerant. On average, expect those monks with some level of education or smattering of foreign languages to be benignly interested in you, and a very soft-sell in the form of a reading library of pamphlets and books left at your disposal. Incidentally, idiorrhythmic *skítes* (see below) and *kelliá* are not bound by the monastic rule of hospitality, and you really need to know someone at one of these to be asked to stay the night.

The monasteries

Obviously you can't hope to visit all twenty monasteries during a short stay, though if you're able to extend the basic four-day period somewhat you can fairly easily do a once-over of the peninsula's most prominent foundations. Now that you are no longer required to present yourself in Kariés at the outset, you've added flexibility in planning itineraries. The dirt road linking the southwestern port of Dháfni with the northeastern coastal monastery of Ivíron by way of Kariés, the capital, not only cuts the peninsula roughly in two but also separates the monasteries into equal southeastern and north-western groups; the division is not so arbitrary as it seems, since the remaining path system seems to reflect it and the feel of the two halves is very different.

The southeastern group

IVÍRON

The vast **IVÍRON** monastery is not a bad introduction to Áthos, and is well poised for walks or rides in various directions. Although founded late in the tenth century by Iberian (Georgian) monks, the last Georgian died in the 1950s and today it is a ceno-bitic house of 35 Greek monks, some of whom moved here from nearby Stavronikíta. The focus of pilgrimage is the miraculous **icon** of the *Portaítissa*, the Virgin Guarding the Gate, housed in a special chapel to the left of the entrance. It is believed that if this protecting image ever leaves Áthos, then great misfortune will befall the monks. The **katholikón** is among the largest on the mountain, with an elaborate mosaic floor dating from 1030. The frescoes are recent and of limited interest, but not so various pagan touches such as the Persian-influenced gold crown around the chandelier, and two Hellenistic columns from a temple of Poseidon with rams-head capitals which once stood here. There's also a silver-leaf lemon tree crafted in Moscow; because of the Georgian connection, Russians were lavish donors to this monastery. There is also an immensely rich library and treasury, but you are unlikely to be able to see these.

KARIÉS AND AROUND: SOME MINOR MONASTERIES

A look around **KARIÉS** is rewarding: the main church of the Protáton, dating from 965, contains exceptional fourteenth-century **frescoes** of the Macedonian school. Kariés also has a few **restaurants** where you may be able to get heartier fare than is typical in the monasteries, and a simple **inn** – though there seems little reason to patronise it. At the northern edge of "town" sprawls the enormous cloister-like *skíti* of **Ayíou Andhréou**, a Russian dependency of the great Vatopedhíou monastery, erected in a hurry last century but today virtually deserted.

A signposted trail leads up within an hour to **KOUTLOUMOUSÍOU**, at the very edge of Kariés and now fully restored after a recent fire (a frequent occurrence on Áthos). Much the most interesting thing about it is its name, which appears to be that of a Selçuk chieftain converted to Christianity.

From Ivíron a path stumbles uphill, tangling with roads, to reach **FILOTHÉOU**, which was at the forefront of the monastic revival in the early 1980s and hence one of the more vital monasteries. It is not, however, one of the more impressive foundations from an architectural or artistic point of view – though the lawn surfacing the entire courtyard is an interesting touch – and it's one of those houses where the non-Orthodox are forbidden from attending church or eating with the monks.

The same is true of **KARAKÁLOU**, 45 minutes' walk (mostly on paths) below Filothéou, also accessible via a short trail up from its *arsanás*. The lofty keep is typical of the fortress-monasteries built close enough to the shore to be victimised by pirates. Karakálou is currently recovering from a 1988 fire, with limited space in the guest wing.

Between here and Meyístis Lávras the trail system has been destroyed, replaced by a bus-less road that makes for dreary tramping, so it's advisable to continue southeast on the boat, or by arranging a lift with a service vehicle.

MEYÍSTIS LÁVRAS AND THE ATHONITE WILDERNESS

MEYÍSTIS LÁVRAS (the Great Lavra) is the oldest and foremost of the ruling monasteries, and physically the most imposing establishment on Áthos, with no fewer than fifteen chapels within its walls. Although there are a fair amount of additions from the last century, and, more recently, electric current, it has (uniquely among the twenty) never suffered from fire. The treasury and library are both predictably rich, the latter containing over 2000 precious manuscripts, though the ordinary traveller is unlikely to view them; as is usual, several monks (out of the 25 here) have complementary keys which must be operated together to gain entrance. What you will see at mealtime are the superior **frescoes** in the **trapezaría**, executed by Theophanes the Cretan in 1535. Hagiographies and grisly martyrdoms line the apse, while there's a *Tree of Jesse* in the south transept, the *Death of Athanasios* (the founder) opposite, and an *Apocalypse* to the left of the main entry. In the western apse is a *Last Supper*, not surprisingly a popular theme in refectories. Just outside the door stands a huge **fiáli**, largest on the mountain, with pagan columns supporting the canopy. The **katholikón**, near the rear of the large but cluttered courtyard, contains more frescoes by Theophanes.

Beyond Meyístis Lávras lies some of the most beautiful, and deserted country on the peninsula, traced by a beautiful path unlikely to ever be bulldozed. One of Meyístis Lávras's many dependencies, **Skíti Prodhrómou**, is just over an hour's walk to the south, but its formerly Romanian inmates seem to have departed. Nonetheless it is a fairly hospitable house, little visited, and only ten minutes away by marked path there's the **hermitage-cave of Saint Athanasios**, watched over by five skulls.

Most first-time visitors will, however, proceed without delay on what ends up being a five-hour traverse across the tip of Áthos. You might consider dropping down off the main trail to see the *skíti* of **Ayías Triádhas (Kavsokalivíon)**, its *kiriákon* surrounded by many cottages, but the commonest strategy involves heading straight for **Skíti Ayías Ánnas**, whose buildings tumble downslope to a perennial-summer patch of coast capable of ripening lemons. This is the usual "base camp" for the climb of **Áthos peak** itself (2030m) – best left for the next morning, and the months from May to September.

With a (pre-)dawn start, you gain the necessary mercy of a little shade and can expect to be up top just over four walking hours from Ayías Ánnas, with the combination refuge-church of **Panayía** passed a bit over an hour before reaching the summit. Some hikers plan an overnight at this shelter, to watch the sunrise from the peak, but then you must be self-suffcient in **food** – as you may well be at the *skíti*, which being idiorrhythmic does not set a particularly sumptuous table, even allowing for monastic austerities. There's no spring **water** en route – you drink from cisterns at Panayía or at **Metamórfosi**, the tiny chapel atop the peak.

Returning from the peak before noon, you'll still have time to reach one of the monasteries north of Ayías Ánnas; the path continues to be delightful, and affords a sudden, breathtaking view of **AYÍOU PÁVLOU** as you round a bend. Except for the ugly scar of the new access road off to the left, little can have changed in the perspective since Edward Lear painted it in the 1850s. The monastery, just over an hour from Ayías Ánnas, is irregularly shaped owing to the constraints of the inland site at the base of Áthos peak, and is currently home to 36 monks, many of them from the island of Kefalloniá.

THE "HANGING" MONASTERIES

From Ayíou Pávlou it's another hour to **DHIONISSÍOU**, a fortified structure perched spectacularly on a coastal cliff, which has overcome a former grim reputation and is now both one of the better houses to stay at, and among the most richly endowed monasteries, with neat and airy *arhondaríki* that come as a relief after so many claustrophobic facilities. Sadly, it is difficult to make out the sixteenth-century **frescoes** by the Cretan Tzortzis in the hopelessly dim *katholikón*, likewise an icon attributed to the Evangelist Luke; however, those of Theophanes on the inside and out of the **trapezaría** are another story. The interior features *The Entry of the Saints into Paradise* and *The Ladder to Heaven*; the exterior wall bears a version of the *Apocalypse*, complete with what looks suspiciously like a nuclear mushroom cloud. Unusually, you may be offered a tour of the **library** with its illuminated gospels on silk-fortified paper, wooden carved miniature of the Passion week, and ivory crucifixes. You've little chance, however, of seeing Dhionisíou's great treasure, the three-metre-long **chrysobull** of the Trapezuntine emperor Alexios III Comnene. Extensive modernisation has been carried out here, with mixed results: clean electric power is supplied by a water turbine up-canyon, but the old half-timbered facade has been replaced with a rather brutal concrete-stucco one.

The onward path to **OSÍOU GRIGORÍOU** is a bit neglected but still usable, depositing you at the front door within an hour and a quarter. Of all the monasteries and *skítes* it has the most intimate relation with the sea, though every building dates from after a devastating 1761 fire. Some of the guest rooms overlook the water, and the monks are exceptionally hospitable.

The southwest coastal trail system ends just over an hour later at **SÍMONOS PÉTRA** (abbreviated **Simópetra**) or "The Rock of Simon", after the foundation legend asserting that the hermit Simon was directed to build a monastery here by a mysterious light hovering over the sheer pinnacle here. Though entirely rebuilt in the wake of a fire a century ago, Simópetra is perhaps the most visually striking monastery on Áthos. With its multiple storeys, ringed by wooden balconies overhanging sheer 300-metre drops, it resembles nothing so much as a Tibetan lamasery. As at Dhionisíou, of which it seems an exaggerated rendition, the courtyard is quite narrow. Thanks to the fire there are no material treasures worth mentioning, though the monastery rivals Filothéou in vigour, with sixty monks from a dozen countries around the world. Unfortunately, because of the spectacle it presents, and its role as an easy first stop in the days when everyone started out from Kariés, Simópetra is always crowded with foreigners and might be better admired from a distance, at least in season.

Between the local maze of roads and extensive damage from a 1989 bush fire, further walking is inadvisable. Best arrange a lift further up the peninsula, or catch the morning boat in the same direction.

The northwestern group

DHÁFNI PORT AND THE RUSSIAN MONASTERY

Though you may not ever pass through Kariés, at some point you're likely to make the acquaintance of **DHÁFNI**, if only to change boats, since the service on this coast is not continuous. There's a **post office** for mailing your postcards, some rather tacky souvenir shops, and a **customs** post – much more vigilant when you leave than upon entry; all passengers' baggage is inspected to check traffic in smuggled-out treasures. A number of eagle-brooch-capped Athonite police skulk about as well. There's a **taverna** where you can get a beer and bean soup, but no shops adequate for restocking on food and drink.

The *kaíki* usually has an hour's layover here before heading back towards Ayías Ánnas, during which time the captain can often be persuaded (for a reasonable fee) to to take groups as far as the Russian monastery of **AYÍOU PANDELÍMONA** (ROUSSIKÓ), a dull forty-minute walk from the port, allowing a look at the premises before the scheduled departure to Ouranópoli appears. Most of the 38 monks are Russian, an ethnic predominance strongly reflected in onion-shaped **domes** and the softer faces of the frescoes. The majority of the buildings were erected in a hurry just after the mid-1800s, as part of Tsarist Russia's campaign for eminence on the Mountain, and have a utilitarian, barracks-like quality. The sole unique features are the corrosion-green lead roofs and the enormous **bell** over the refectory, the second largest in the world, which always prompts speculation as to how it got there. Otherwise, the small population fairly rattles around the echoing halls, the effect of desolation increased by ranks of outer dormitories gutted by a fire in 1968. If you're an architecture buff, Roussikó can probably be omitted without a twinge of conscience; students of turn-of-the-century kitsch will be delighted, however, with mass-produced saints' calendars, gaudy reliquaries, and a torrent of gold (or at least gilt) fixtures in the seldom-used *katholikón*. If you are permitted to attend service in the top-storey chapel north of the belfry, do so for the sake of the Slavonic chanting, though it must be said that the residents don't exactly put themselves out for non-Slavs. With the collapse of the Soviet Union, Ayíou Panetelímona can now look forward to a material and spiritual renaissance of sorts, and already, in 1991, large groups of Russian pilgrims filled the place in the weeks following the festival of the patron saint.

Actually closer to Dháfni is the square compound of **XEROPOTÁMOU**, with most of its construction and church frescoes dating from the eighteenth century, except for two wings that were fire-damaged in 1952.

GREEK COASTAL MONASTERIES

From the vicinity of Dháfni or Roussikó, most pilgrims continue along the coast, reaching **XENOFÓNDOS** along a mix of trail and tractor track an hour after quitting the Russian monastery. Approached from this direction, Xenofóndos's busy sawmill gives it a vaguely industrial air, accentuated by ongoing, extensive renovations. The enormous, sloping, irregularly shaped court, expanded upward last century, is unique in possessing two *katholiká*. The small, older one – with exterior frescoes of the Cretan school – was outgrown and replaced during the 1830s by the huge upper one, currently shut for repairs. Among its many icons are two fine **mosaic** ones of saints Yióryios and Dhimítrios. The guest quarters occupy a modern wing overlooking the sea at the extreme south end of the perimeter.

A half-hour's walk separates Xenofóndos from **DOHIARÍOU**, one of the more picturesque monasteries on this coast but not conspicuously friendly, and currently in the throes of renovation; this hasn't yet extended to the primitive but clean *arhondaríki*, which see few foreigners. An exceptionally lofty, large **katholikón** nearly fills the court, though its Cretan-school frescoes, possibly by Tzortzis, were clumsily retouched in 1855. Much better are the late seventeenth-century ones in the long, narrow **refectory**, with its sea views some of the nicest on Áthos. Even Orthodox pilgrims have trouble getting to see the wonder-working icon of *Gorgoipikóöu* (She Who is Quick to Hear), housed in a chapel between church and *trapezaría*.

THE FAR NORTHERN MONASTERIES

The direct trail inland and up to Konstamonítou has been reclaimed by the forest, so to get there you have to go in a roundabout fashion 45 minutes along the coast to its *arsanás*, and then as much time again sharply up on tracks and cobbled way. **KONSTAMONÍTOU**, hidden up in a thickly wooded valley, seems as humble, bare and poor as you'd expect from the last-ranking monastery; the *katholikón* nearly fills the quadrangular court where the grass is literally growing up through the cracks. Non-Orthodox and believers are segregated, not that many foreigners make it this far; as a consolation a carillon "concert" of some musicality announces vespers.

From here you can continue on foot ninety minutes to **ZOGRÁFOU**, the furthest inland of the monasteries, today populated by a handful of Bulgarian monks. More than at most large, understaffed houses, you gain an appreciation of the enormous workload that falls on so few shoulders; a walk down the empty, rambling corridors past the seventeenth- and eighteenth-century cells, now unmaintained, is a sobering experience. "Zográfou" means "of the Painter", in reference to a tenth-century legend: the Slavs who founded the monastery couldn't decide on a patron saint, so they put a wooden panel by the altar, and after lengthy prayer a painting of Áyios Yióryios – henceforth the institution's protector – appeared.

Near Zográfou the trail splits, presenting you with a three-fold choice. In two and a half hours along the leftmost option, you arrive at the large, irregularly shaped monastery of **HILANDHARÍOU**, which was in the past patronised by the thirteenth-century Serbian kings and has to this day remained a Serbian house (and lately hotbed of Serbian nationalism). The **katholikón** dates in its present form from the fourteenth century, but its frescoes, similar in style to those in the *Protáton* at Kariés, have been retouched. As you'd expect for a beacon of medieval Serbian culture, the library and treasury are well-endowed.

The central, down-valley route out of Zográfou leads in three hours to **ESFIGMÉNOU**, built directly on the water and reputedly the strictest foundation on the mountain – a banner hung out of the top-storey window reading "Orthodoxy or Death" would seem to confirm this and does not encourage a casual visit. In any case the path veers down the coast for three hours to **VATOPEDHÍOU**, a similar distance away if setting out directly from Zográfou. Exceeding Meyístis Lávras in size, it also vies with it in importance and wealth, and makes a good beginning or farewell to Áthos. The cobbled, slanting court with its freestanding belfry (which can be climbed) seems more like a town plaza, ringed by stairways and stacks of cells for more than 300. The **katholikón**, one of the oldest on the mountain, has the usual array of frescoes painted over for better or worse, but more uniquely two **mosaics** of the *Annunciation* and the *Deisis* flanking the door of the inner narthex. The population of forty monks, mostly young and two-thirds Cypriot (as is the abbot), includes a handful of French novices and a brotherhood of nine Australians who have had to change residence four times (a common drama for non-Greek monks on the peninsula) and hope that this is their last home.

With the proper maps it is just possible to short-cut the dusty track above Vatopedhíou en route to **PANDOKRÁTOROS**, two and a half hours away, the last half of the journey on scenic coastal paths. Other than the setting on a hill overlooking its own picturesque fishing harbour, and the courtyard with its eight Valencia orange trees, there is little of note. But most of the 35 monks are welcoming and unless the community succumbs soon to pressure from its peers, this will be your only chance to experience a large, idiorrhythmic community. The guest wing overlooks the sea and there is a (cold) **shower** – a boon after days of trekking. In a valley above looms the *skíti* of **Profítis Ilías**, a relic of the Russian expansion drive and today home to just nine monks from several different countries.

Continuing on the coastal trail, it's under an hour door-to-door to tiny **STAVRONIKÍTA**, the best example of the Athonite coastal fortress-monastery and distinctly vertical in orientation. Long one of the poorest houses, it has recently been completely redone, and, surrounded by aqueduct-fed kitchen gardens, is pin-neat. Several Australians, including the abbot, number among the fifteen monks, but they're ill-equipped to cope with the relatively large numbers of guests and it no longer rates as one of the more outgoing monasteries. The modernised guest quarters, despite the showers, are similarly meagre, and fill early in the day in summer. There's little chance of a seaside room, though by virtue of its rock-top position Stavronikíta has some of the best views of Áthos peak on the peninsula. The narrow **katholikón** occupies virtually all of the gloomy courtyard, and the **refectory**, normally opposite, had to be shifted upstairs to the south wing, where it's a spartan room with a single window on the water, and fresco fragments by Theophanes of the *Death of Áyios Nikólaos* (the patron) and the *Last Supper*. From here an hour's walk separates you from Ivíron.

The Coast to Kavála

Heading towards Kavála from Sithonía or Áthos is surprisingly tricky, since buses from either peninsula run only back to Thessaloníki. However, the gap between the Thessaloníki–Halkidhikí and Thessaloníki–Kavála services is only 16km wide at one point, with a couple of places you wouldn't mind getting stuck at along the way, so if you're without wheels it's well worth trying to hitch the distance.

To begin, you should descend the Ouranópoli–Thessaloníki bus at the coastal mining town of SRATÓNI, from where a recently paved road glides over the ridge north 15km to the beach resort of Olimbiádha and regular buses to the Thessaloníki–Kavála highway. OLIMBIÁDHA itself is still very low-key, with **rooms**, two official **campsites** north of the village, and three **tavernas** on the southern bay, cheapest and most characterful being the *Kapetan Manolis/Platanos* by the concrete jetty. All along this shore the local speciality is **mussels** (*mídhia*), farmed in floating nursery beds and typically served in a spicy cheese sauce. The small town beaches are okay, but there are far better ones 2–3km back toward Stratóni, behind the promontory with a few cursory walls of **ancient Stayira**, birthplace of Aristotle.

STAVRÓS, 10km north of Olimbiádha – the interval again dotted with semi-accessible coves – is a lively place with a beautiful seafront of plane trees, popular with Greeks, Slavs and Germans. The cheapest of five inexpensive **hotels** is the E-class *Avra Strymonikou* (☎0397/61 278; ②), though you'd be more likely to end up in **rooms** or the official **campsite** behind the town beach.

From here you're just 4km from the main E-90 highway, where the first coastal place of any size – ASPRÓVALTA – will come as a nasty shock after the relative calmness of Halkidhikí. An ugly concrete mess straddling the busy road and fringed by rough rock beaches, it's essentially a summer suburb of Thessaloníki, an impression reinforced by the frequent urban bus service from Platía Dhikastiríon.

Once across the River Strimónas, long-distance buses tend to veer inland to hug the base of Mount Pangéo, but under your own power it's worth following the coast to Kavála. LOUTRÁ ELEFTHERÓN, just 2km inland, is an old-fashioned spa set in a riverside oasis, though the thermal springs themselves are a bit difficult to bathe in, and the old Turkish domed bath has been closed down, leaving only the rather clinical indoor plunge-pools (open in the morning and evening).

Approaching Néa Péramos, a narrow frontage road seaward from the main highway threads past very impromptu **campsites** among vineyards and fine, duney **beaches**, the best in eastern Macedonia. NÉA PÉRAMOS itself, 14km before Kavála, sports an unheralded **castle** at one corner of its sandy, sheltered bay, and isn't a bad place to wait for one of the four daily, well-spaced seasonal ferries to the island of Thássos. *Camping Anatolia* can be recommended if you have to spend the night; the only other **campsites** between here and Kavála are the *Estella*, 5km east, or the expensive, unfriendly EOT site, *Batis*, 10km along and already hedged by Kavála's sprawl.

Kavála

KAVÁLA, backing on to the lower slopes of Mount Simbólon, is the second largest city of Macedonia and the principal port for northern Greece. Coming in through the suburbs, there seems little to commend a stay. But the centre, at least, is pleasant and characterful, grouped about the old nineteenth-century harbour area and its old tobacco warehouses. A citadel towers above from a rocky promontory to the east, and an elegant Turkish aqueduct leaps over modern neighbourhoods into the old quarter on the bluff.

KAVÁLA

0   200 m

The town was known anciently as Neapolis and as such served as a terminus of the Via Egnatía and the first European port of call for merchants and travellers from the Middle East. It was here that Saint Paul landed on his way to Philippi (see below), on his initial mission to Europe. In later years, the port and citadel took on considerable military significance, being occupied in turn by Byzantines, Normans, Franks, Venetians, Turks and (during each of the world wars) Bulgarians.

Old Kavála

Although the remnants of Kavála's Turkish past are understandably neglected, the **Panayía** quarter above the port preserves a scattering of eighteenth- and nineteenth-century buildings, and considerable atmosphere. It is by far the most attractive part of town to explore, wandering amid the twisting wedge of lanes and up towards the citadel.

The most conspicuous and interesting of its buildings is the **Imaret**, overlooking the harbour on Ódhos Poulidhoú. An elongated, multi-domed structure covered in Islamic inscriptions, it was originally an almshouse housing three hundred *softas*, or theological students. After many decades of neglect, it has recently been refurbished, appropriately enough, as a restaurant. The building was endowed by **Mehmet Ali**, the Pasha of Egypt and founder of the dynasty which ended with King Farouk. Born in Kavála in 1769, his birthplace, at the corner of Pavlídhou and Méhmet Alí, is maintained as a monument. It provides an opportunity, rare in Greece, to look over a prestigious Turkish house. To visit its wood-panelled reception rooms, ground-floor stables and first-floor harem, ring for the caretaker.

Another caretaker may escort you through the Byzantine **citadel** (daily 10am–7pm) as you explore the Byzantine ramparts and dungeon; in season it hosts a few festival performances, mainly dance, in its main court. From here, down towards the middle of town, north of Panayía's narrow maze of streets, the **aqueduct**, built on a Roman model in the reign of Suleiman the Magnificent (1520–66), spans the traffic in Platía Nikotsára.

Finally, the other side of the harbour from the old town, there are two museums of moderate interest. The **Archaeological Museum** (Tues–Sun 8.30am–3pm; 400dr), at the west end of the waterfront, just off Erithroú Stavroú, contains a fine dolphin mosaic, a reconstructed Macedonian funeral chamber and many terracotta figurines decorated still in their original paint. Close by, next to an old tobacco warehouse on Odhós Filíppou, is the **Folk Art and Modern Art Museum** (daily 9–11am & 6–9pm). Along with various collections of traditional costumes and household utensils, this has some interesting rooms devoted to the locally born sculptor Polignotos Vigis.

Practicalities

Most points of utility or interest are central. The main **bus station** is on the corner of Mitropolítou and Filikís Eterías, near the main anchorage; buses for Alexandhroúpoli stop some blocks away on Erithroú Stavroú, near the *Okeanis Hotel*. In the main square, Platía Eleftherías, you'll find an **EOT** office, which can provide details (and sell tickets) for the summer drama festivals at Philippi and on Thássos. They can also be of help with schedules for ferries from Kavála (see below), and those from Alexandhroúpoli to Samothráki.

Hotels are in short supply and in season it's wise to phone ahead and book a room. All three of the D-class places are in the grid of streets around Eleftherías: *Attikon*, Megálou Alexándhrou 8 (☎051/222 257; ②), *Parthenon*, Spétson 14 (☎051/223 205; ②), and *Rex*, Kriézi 4 (☎051/223 393; ②). Moving up to C-class, try either the *Acropolis* (☎051/223 543; ③) or *Panorama* (☎051/224 205; ③), respectively at Eleftheríou Venizélou 53c and 32c, west of the square. The only private rooms advertised in the centre are those of *Yiorgos Alvanos* at Anthemíou 35 (☎051/228 412; ②), in the heart of the old Panayía quarter – worth trying for if you arrive early in the day. An alternative place to stay, frequented by many Greeek tourists, is the beach-suburb of Kalamítsa, to the west of town. The closest **campsite** is *Irini*, on the shore 2km east of the port; city bus #2 goes there.

For **meals**, ignore the tourist traps along the waterfront and walk instead a ways up into the Panayía district, where rows of tavernas with outdoor seating on Theodhórou Poulídhou tempt you with good and reasonably priced seafood; this is where the locals eat.

Ferries sail from Kavála to **Thássos** almost hourly in season; most run to the port of Órmos Prínou, though a few continue to the capital, called Thássos or Liménas (an hour-long journey in total). Out of season, when services drop to just two boats daily, or if you're driving a car, you will be better off taking the bus to Keramotí 46km southwest (hourly service) and the car ferry on from there to Thássos/Liménas. If you're heading for Thássos, Keramotí provides an alternative, though unexciting, base. It's a small, rather drab village, with a functional beach, a campsite and three hotels: D-class *Evropi* (☎0591/51 277; ③) and the very cheap E-class *Eleftheria* (☎0591/51 230; ②) and its annexe *Exasteron* (☎0591/51 230; ②).

Other ferry services are less predictable. In season, there are generally two weekly departures to **Samothráki** (Mon & Wed), and five to **Límnos** (Mon, Wed, Thurs, Sat & Sun). Two or three of these continue to various islands, among them Áyios Efstrátios, Lésvos, Híos and Rafína/Pireás, with one weekly line all the way down to Rhodes via major east Aegean islands. Details are available from *Nikos Miliadhes*, Karaóli Dhimitríou 36.

Philippi

As you might expect, **PHILIPPI** was named after Philip II of Macedon, who wrested the town from the Thracians in 356 BC. However, it owed its importance and prosperity to the Roman building of the Via Egnatia. With Kavála/Neápolis as its port, it was essentially the easternmost town of Roman-occupied Europe.

Here also, as at Actium, the fate of the Roman Empire was decided on Greek soil, at the **Battle of Philippi** in 42 BC. Following their assassination of Julius Caesar, Brutus and Cassius had fled east of the Adriatic, and, against their better judgement, were forced into confrontation on the Philippi plains with the pursuing armies of Antony and Octavian. The "honourable conspirators", who could have successfully exhausted the enemy by avoiding action, were decimated by Octavian in two successive battles, and, as defeat became imminent, first Cassius, then Brutus killed himself – the latter running on his comrade's sword with the Shakespearian sentiment "Caesar now be still, I killed thee not with half so good a will".

Saint Paul visited Philippi in 49 AD and so began his mission in Europe. Despite being cast into prison he retained a special affection for the Philippians, his first converts, and the congregation that he established was one of the earliest to flourish in Greece. It furnished the principal remains of the site: several impressive, although ruined, basilican churches.

The Site

Tues–Sun 8.30am–3pm; 400dr.

Philippi is easily reached from Kavála, just 14km distant; buses (which continue to Dhráma) leave at least every half-hour, and drop you by the road that now splits the site.

The most conspicuous of the churches is the **Direkler**, on the left of the modern road. This was an unsuccessful attempt by its sixth-century architect to improve the basilica design by adding a dome. In this instance the entire east wall collapsed under the weight, leaving only the narthex convertible for worship. The central arch of its west wall and a few pillars of reused antique drums stand amid remains of the Roman **forum**. A line of second-century porticoes spreads outwards in front of the church, and on their east side are the foundations of a colonnaded octagonal church which was approached from the Via Egnatia by a great gate. Behind the Direkler, and perversely the most interesting and best preserved building of the site, is a huge monumental **public latrine** with nearly fifty of its original marble seats still intact.

Across the road near the further of the two entrances, stone steps climb up to a terrace passing on the right a Roman crypt, reputed to have been the **prison of Saint Paul** and appropriately frescoed. The terrace flattens out on to a huge paved atrium that extends to the foundations of another awesomely large basilica. Continuing in the same direction around the base of a hill you emerge above a **theatre** cut into its side. Though dating from the original town it was heavily remodelled as an amphitheatre by the Romans – the bas-reliefs of Nemesis, Mars and Victory (on the left of the stage) all belong to this period. It is used for the annual ancient drama festival, held every weekend from mid-July to early August. The **museum** (Tues–Sun 8.30am–5pm; separate 400dr admission), above the road at the far end of the site, is rather dreary.

The best general impression of the site – which is very extensive despite a lack of obviously notable buildings – and of the battlefield behind it can be gained from the **acropolis**, a steep climb along a path from the museum. Its own remains are predominantly medieval.

THRACE (THRÁKI)

Separated from Macedonia to the west by the Néstos river and from (Turkish) Eastern Thrace by the Evros river delta, **Western Thrace** is the Greek state's most recent addition. Under effective Greek control from 1920, the Treaty of Lausanne (1923) confirmed Greek sovereignty over the area, and also sanctioned the exchange of 390,000 Muslims, principally from Macedonia, for more than a million ethnic Greeks from Eastern Thrace and Asia Minor. But the Muslims of Western Thrace, acknowledged as a community of long-standing, were exempt from the exchanges and continue to live in the region.

Thrace was originally inhabited by a people with their own, non-Hellenic, language and religion. From the seventh century BC on it was colonised by Greeks, and after Alexander the area took on a strategic significance as the land route between Greece and Byzantium. It was later controlled by the Roman and Byzantine empires, and after 1361 the Ottoman Turks.

Nowadays, out of a total population of 360,000, there are around 110,000 Muslims, made up of 60,000 **Turkish-speakers**, 30,000 **Pomaks** and 20,000 **Gypsies**. These figures are disputed by Turkish Muslims who put their numbers alone at something between 100,000 and 120,000. The Greek government lumps all three groups together as "a Muslim minority" principally of Turkish descent, and provides Turkish-language education for all the Muslim minorities (despite the fact that the Pomaks speak a language very similar to Bulgarian). Greek authorities also point to the 336 mosques, the Turkish-language newspapers and a Turkish language radio station in Komotiní as evidence of their goodwill. However, since 1968 only graduates from a special Academy in Salonica have been allowed to teach in the Turkish-language schools here, thus isolating Thracian Turks from mainstream Turkish culture, and on various occasions, the Greek authorities have interfered with Muslim religious appointments. In 1985, when the Mufti of Komotiní died, he was replaced by a government appointee. When he resigned, another Mufti was appointed by the authorities. In August 1991, the Greeks appointed a new Muslim leader in Xanthi, again without consulting the Muslim community.

There is no doubt in the minds of local Turks and Pomaks that in secular matters, too, they are the victims of **discrimination**. Muslim villages, they say, receive less help from the state than Greek villages: some are without electricity; many lack proper roads. Muslim schools are underfunded; Muslims are unable to join the police force; and it is extremely difficult for them to buy property or get bank loans – although most ethnic Turks do also acknowledge that they are better off than their counterparts in Turkey.

There have been occasional explosions of inter-communal violence. In January 1990, protests erupted in Komotiní when Sadiq Ahmet, a Muslim leader and briefly a Deputy in the Greek Parliament, was jailed for "inciting violence and dissension". Twenty-one Muslims were injured in the riots that followed; eighteen Greeks were later charged with looting Muslim properties. Matters have only worsened since the re-incorporation, in neighbouring Bulgaria, of the Turkish minority into the commercial and political life of that country, with the Greeks becoming increasingly aware of the potential for unrest. In July 1991 the Greek government put forward a plan to demilitarise the whole of Thrace, including Bulgarian and Turkish sectors. The plan received a positive reply from the Bulgarian government, but ominously Turkey reserved its position, and Greece remains fearful of Turkish agitation in Western Thrace that might lead to a Cyprus-type military operation where Turkish forces "come to the assistance" of an oppressed minority.

As an outsider you will probably not notice the intercommunal tensions, but you will not to able to avoid the large numbers of military installations in the province; some

Muslim areas near the Bulgarian border north of Komotiní and Xánthi are subject to police and army restrictions. However, there are mixed villages where Muslims and Greeks appear to coexist quite amicably, and Thracians, both Muslim and Orthodox, have a deserved reputation for hospitality.

There is little tangible to see, and most travellers take a bus straight through to **Alexandhroúpoli**, for the ferry to Samothráki, or head straight on to **Istanbul**. But Thrace's many rulers left some mark on the area, and there are a few well-preserved monuments, most significant the remains of the coastal cities of Avdira, south of Xánthi, and Maroneia, southeast of Komotiní – Greek colonies in the seventh century BC that were abandoned in Byzantine times when the inhabitants moved inland to escape pirate raids. Otherwise, it's the landscape itself that is of most appeal, the train line forging a circuitous but scenic route below the foothills of the Rodhópi mountains that's at its best in the **Néstos valley** between Paranésti and Xánthi. Indeed if you make time to explore the backstreets of the towns, or venture up the myriad tracks to tiny, isolated villages in the Rhodópi mountains, you'll find an atmosphere quite unlike any other part of Greece.

Xánthi and around

Coming from Kavála, shortly after the turning to KERAMOTÍ you cross the Néstos river, which with the **Rhodópi mountains** forms the border of Thrace. The Greek/Turkish, Christian/Muslim make-up is almost immediately apparent in the villages: the Turkish ones, long established, with their tiled, whitewashed houses; the Greek settlements, often adjacent, built in drab modern style for the refugees of the 1920s.

XÁNTHI (KSÁNTHI), the first town of any size, is perhaps the most interesting point to break a journey. Here the two ethnic groups lived side by side until the riots – and still do, but less easily. There is a busy market area, good Turko-Greek food, and, up the hill to the north of the main café-lined square, a very attractive old quarter. The town also has a recently established university, which lends a lively air to the place, particularly in the area between the bazaar and the campus, where bars, cinemas and bistros are busy in term time. Try if you can to visit on Saturday, the day of Xánthi's **market** – a huge affair, attended equally by Greeks, Pomaks and Turks, held in a large open space behind the new shopping centre on the eastern side of the town.

The narrow, cobbled streets of the Old Town are home to a number of very fine mansions, some restored, some derelict, with painted exteriors, bow windows and wrought-iron balconies; most date from the mid-nineteenth century when Xánthi's tobacco merchants made their fortunes. One of them has been turned into a **Folk Museum** (opening hours erratic). Originally the home of two tobacco magnate brothers, it has been lovingly restored with painted wooden panels and decorated plaster and floral designs on the walls and ceilings, as well as displays of Thracian clothes and jewellery, a postcard collection and cakes of tobacco. Further up, the roads become increasingly narrow and steep, and the Turkish presence is more noticeable: most of the women have their heads covered; the stricter ones wear full-length macs. Churches and mosques hide behind whitewashed houses with red tiled roofs. Orange-brown tobacco leaves are strung along drying frames. At the very top of the town is the **Panagia Convent** (open to the public; bare female legs forbidden) and a derelict monastery, from where there are fine views north into the forested Rhodópi mountains, and south over the town and the green misty plain.

There are a couple of cheap **hotels**, the *Lux* at Stavroú 18 (☎0541/23 004; ②), clean, cheap and friendly, and the *Paris* at Dhimokrítou 12 (☎0541/20 531, ③). For not a lot more, try the *Sissy*, Lefkípou 14 (☎0541/22 996; ③).

North of Xánthi

Much of the countryside north of Xánthi, towards the Bulgarian border, is a restricted zone, and dotted with yellow signs denoting the fact. Greeks will tell you areas like this are controlled because of the sensitivity of the border with Bulgaria: ethnic Turks and Pomaks claim the army uses the border as an excuse to keep tabs on them. It is possible to enter the restricted areas, but you need passes from the police and army in the regional capitals.

If you do venture up into the mountains here, the reward is some magnificent scenery, the road twisting up through forests and tobacco terraces into the highest and wildest part of the Rhodópi range. There are a number of Muslim villages: **SMINTHI**, a large and dispersed Pomak settlement with a mosque and tall minaret, and, further on and much more isolated, **MIKI**, with long single-story stone houses and a large mosque. The road north of here, towards Ehínos, leads into a restricted area, and you will probably need a pass to get through. If you do have one, **EHÍNOS** is a fine-looking town that is the main market for the surrounding Pomak community – Bogomil-Christian Slavs forcibly converted to Islam in the sixteenth century. They still speak a degenerate dialect of Bulgarian with generous mixtures of Greek and Turkish. Otherwise, the most northerly place you can get to without a pass is **OREA**, to the west of Ehínos, another Pomak village, set on a steep hillside with cloud-covered peaks behind and terraces falling away to the riverbed – a dramatic setting in the extreme. It has a mosque and Turkish-language school, but it is grindingly poor: the ground floors of the houses are used for corralling animals or storing farm produce, and it has no bar or taverna, at least not for visitors. If you pass through, don't expect much of a welcome.

South of Xánthi: along the coast

Travelling south from Xánthi is less problematic. The coastal plain, bright with cotton, tobacco and cereals, stretches to the sea. Heading towards Ávdira, you might stop briefly in **GENISSEA**, an unspectacular farming village with a mixed Greek-Turkish population, and, behind its nondescript centre, one of the oldest mosques in Thrace, more than four hundred years old. It's a low whitewashed building, with a tiled roof, and is in daily use, although a wooden portico running round its four sides is dangerously rotten and its minaret has been truncated. Over the road, behind a petrol station, is a second mosque, door locked and windows boarded, though its minaret still stands.

Ávdira and along the coast

A few kilometres further on, regular buses go to the village of **ÁVDIRA**, and, in summer, to the beach resort of the same name, 7km beyond, passing through the ancient site of **Avdira**. The walls of the ancient acropolis are visible on a low headland above the sea, and there are traces of Roman baths, a theatre and an ancient acropolis. However, the best finds been taken off to museums to Kavála and Komotiní, and the remains are unspectacular, and the setting not particularly attractive. If you have time only for one site, you're better off going to Maroneia (see below).

For the most part, the coast between Ávdira and Maroneia is flat and dull. At the southern end of Lake Vistonis is **PORTO LAGO**, a semi-derelict harbour redeemed by the low white monastery of **Áyios Nikólaos** built on a reef in the lagoon. The surrounding marshland is an important site for birdlife, and is more accessible than the Évros delta. Nearby, the small resort of **FANÁRI** has a long beach with two fairly expensive hotels and an EOT campsite, and a number of fish restaurants; it's popular with Komotiniots in the evenings and at weekends. Its beach gets busy in the high summer, but there are less crowded spots east along the coast.

Maroneia and further east

Further along the coast, **ANCIENT MARONEIA** has little more to see than Ávdira, but the site is altogether more attractive. Most of it is still unexcavated, and the visible remains are scattered among the olive trees and undergrowth at the foot of Mount Ísmaros. The founder of the city is reckoned to be Maron, the son of the god of wine, Dionysus (Ísmaros is known locally as the Mountain of Dionysus) and the city became one of the most powerful in all of ancient Thrace. There are traces of a theatre, a sanctuary of Dionysus, and various buildings including a house with a well-preserved mosaic floor. The land walls of the city are preserved to a height of two metres, together with a Roman tower above the harbour. Over time, the sea has done its own excavation, eroding the crumbling cliffs, revealing shards of pottery and ancient walls. There can be fewer more magical places to watch the sun set over the Thracian Sea.

The harbour of **ÁYIOS HARÁLAMBOS**, at the edge of the site, has a couple of cafés and tavernas, plus a few **rooms**. A number of Roman and Byzantine buildings, including baths and a church, have been excavated between the modern houses. There are reasonable beaches in both directions, and in summer the area is popular with Greeks from Komotiní. The pleasant, modern village of **MARÓNIA**, 4km inland, has some fine old Thracian mansions with jutting balconies and some rooms (☎533/41 158). It's connected with Komotiní by six daily buses.

Towards Alexandhroúpoli, there are good beaches at **MESIMVRÍA** and **MÁKRI**, though with few facilities. If you have your own transport, you can continue east to the **Évros delta**, one of Europe's most important wetland areas for birds – and one of Greece's most sensitive military areas, so mind where you point cameras and binoculars.

Komotiní

KOMOTINÍ, 48km east of Xánthi, the road skirting the Rodhópi foothills, is larger and less attractive, with ranks of tower blocks and gridded suburbs to the south and west, and dusty, noisy streets, clogged with traffic. It is more markedly Turkish with its fourteen functioning mosques, and social mixing between the different ethnic groups is less common, although Orthodox and Muslim continue to live in the same neighbourhoods.

During the thirteenth century, the city gained importance and wealth due to its position on the Via Egnatia. When the Ottomans took the city in 1361, they changed its name to Gioumoulzina, which is what it was called during the long centuries of the "tourkokrateia", the period of Turkish rule. In 1912, at the outbreak of the First Balkan War, Komotiní was taken by the Bulgarians; it was liberated by Greek forces in the following year, only to be taken once more by the Bulgarians. It was finally and definitively liberated on the May 14, 1920.

The old **bazaar**, to the north of Plateia Ireni, the central square, is very pleasant, caught between mosques and a fine Turkish clock tower: shady cafés and tiny shops sell everything from carpets to iron buckets, and it's especially busy on Tuesdays when the villagers from the surrounding area come into town to sell their wares. Behind this old quarter, you can see the modern **Cathedral** and the remains of Komotiní's **Byzantine walls.**

Traditionally a city with Greek and Turkish inhabitants, Greek influence began to dominate in the waning years of the Ottoman empire, with rich Greeks funding schools and colleges in the city to develop Greek culture and ideals. Some of these educational foundations still survive: one, the **Hellenic Civic School of Nestor Tanakali**, a neoclassical structure on Ódhos Dhimokritoú, behind the Central Park, is now the official residence of the Dean of the University of Thrace; another, on Ódhos Áyios Yióryos, on the other side of the Park, has become Komotiní's **Folk Museum** (Mon–Sat 11am–1pm), displaying examples of Thracian embroidery, traditional Thracian dress, silverware, copperware and a collection of religious seals. The **Archaeological Museum** (daily 9am–5pm), just off to the right of the main road from Xánthi and well signposted, is also worth a visit, giving a lucid overview of Thracian history, by means of plans and finds from local sites, from its beginnings up to the Byzantine era. On display are a number of statues, busts, bas reliefs, jewellery and artefacts from the archaeological sites around Komotiní.

If you need to stay, choose between the *Astoria* on the main square (☎0531/22 707; ③) or the somewhat pricier *Democritus* at Platía Viziníou 8 (☎0531/22 579; ③); although there are some *pandohía* (workmen's hostels) in the bazaar, the *Hellas* at Dhimokrítou 31 (☎0531/22 055; ②) will probably be as basic as you'd like.

North of Komotiní

If you want to escape the heat and noise, to the north of the city is the forest of **Nymphaia**, well used by the locals for jogging and walking, and home to a number of cafés. Further up the road, you come to the ruins of the Byzantine fortress of **Nymphias**, with a wonderful view over Komotiní down to the sea. It is said that on a clear day, you can see Mount Áthos, more than 100km away over the Thracian Sea.

Alexandhroúpoli and beyond

A modern city, designed by Russian military architects during the Russian-Turkish war of 1878, **ALEXANDHROÚPOLI** – Dedeagatch to the Turks and Bulgars – has little to recommend it: a border town and military garrison, its nearby beaches and summer wine festival seem something of an afterthought. Surprisingly, though, it can get very crowded in season, with overland travellers and Greek holidaymakers competing for limited space in the few hotels and the gritty beach campsites.

The town became Greek in 1920, when it was renamed Alexandhroúpoli after a visit from the Greek King Alexander. There are no obvious sights except for an **ecclesiastical art museum** next to the cathedral of Áyios Nikólaos, and the heavy military presence can be oppressive – especially for single women. The Turkish quarter, literally on the wrong side of the tracks, may whet the appetite for the genuine article across the border. Otherwise it's the seafront that characterises the town best. Dominated by a huge **lighthouse** built in 1880 (and adopted as the town's symbol), the area comes alive at dusk when the Alexandriots begin their evening *volta*. Traffic is diverted and the cafés spill out onto the road and around the lighthouse; makeshift stalls along the pavements sell salted seeds, pirated cassettes and grilled sweetcorn. There is also a little funfair on waste ground between the lighthouse and the harbour.

The best places to stay are the (relatively) inexpensive **hotels** right near the train station: the D-class *Metropolis*, Athanasíou Dhiakoú 11 (☎0551/26 443; ③), and *Majestic*, Platía Troúman 7 (☎0551/26 444; ③), or the E-class *Aktaeon*, Karaóli 74 (☎0551/28 078; ③). **Food** is a bright spot. Excellent meals are to be had at *I Neraidha*, a couple of blocks from the train station and across from the town hall. There's a municipal campsite, *Camping Alexandhroupoli* (bus #5 from the train station or a half-hour walk), which also hosts a **Wine Festival** through July and August. Heading for the island of **Samothráki** (see the "East and North Aegean Islands" chapter), there is at least one daily ferry year-round between 10am and 3pm; Sunday and Tuesday have historically been the days with only one early departure, necessitating an overnight here. Tickets are sold at a cluster of waterfront agencies opposite the ferry dock, which is within sight of the train station.

The Évros Valley and northeastern Thrace

The **Évros Valley**, northeast of Alexandhroúpoli, is a prosperous but dull agricultural area. The towns are in general ugly, modern concrete affairs full of bored soldiers, with little to delay you. If you have time, however, there are a number of possible attractions.

To the southeast, the **Évros Delta** is one of Europe's most important wetlands, and home to more than 250 different species of birds, including sea-eagles. The easiest way to get there (if you have a car) is to drive up to **Loutra Traianopolis**, the site of an ancient Roman spa, and turn right onto the dirt track that runs past the *Hotel Isidora*. It is crisscrossed with tracks along the dykes that are mainly used by farmers taking advantage of the plentiful water supply for growing sweetcorn and cotton. The south is the most inspiring part, well away from the army installations the north, and, the further into the wetlands you go, utterly desolate, with decrepit clusters of fishing huts among the sandbars and inlets. At the mouth of the Delta is a huge saltwater lake called **Límni Dhrakónda**. Obviously what you see depends on the time of year, but even if the bird-life is a bit thin on the ground, the atmosphere of the place is worth experiencing.

Further up the valley, at **FÉRES**, close by the frontier, the exquisite twelfth-century Byzantine church of **Theotokós Kosmosotíra** is also worth a look, originally part of a monastery and founded by a member of the Comnene dynasty. Its interior frescoes are in mediocre condition but the five-domed design is rare in Greece outside of Thessaloníki. If you have to change buses en route to the border post at KÍPI, as sometimes happens, and have some time to wait, it's well worth seeking out. With your own car, there's no excuse for missing it.

DHIDHIMÓTIHO, further north by the border, is the only other stop of any interest. The old part of town is still partially enclosed by the remains of double Byzantine fortifications (hence the name, which means "double wall"), and some old houses and churches survive, but the area has a feeling of decay despite continuing efforts at restoration. Among the buildings is a hard-to-find **synagogue** which the townspeople ransacked during World War II at the instigation of the Nazis – who had spread about the (false) rumour that treasure was secreted in its walls. Outside the old quarter, the most important monument is the fourteenth-century **mosque**, the oldest and second largest in Greece, an unelaborate square stone building with a pyramid-shaped roof. Unfortunately, the interior is closed indefinitely for restoration. Excavations just outside the town have revealed the site of the Roman city of **Plotinoupolis**, but there's really nothing to see.

Further north still, smaller roads take you through isolated villages and beautiful countryside. **METAXÁDHES** is one of the most handsome villages in the area, sited on a steep hill, its large houses built traditionally of stone and wood with red tiled roofs and lush gardens. Fought over by Bulgars and Turks, Metaxádhes used to support a Turkish community but now its population is exclusively Greek, although older residents still speak some Turkish. Beyond Metaxádhes, you descend to the vast, fertile **Arda plain** that dominates the northerneastern tip of Greek Thrace: rich farmland – the main crops are sunflowers, sweetcorn, and (increasingly) sugar beet – that supports a large number of modern villages, many of them populated by settlers from Asia Minor. Hemmed in on three sides by Bulgaria and Turkey, it has been a Greek priority to establish a Greek population in this extremely sensitive corner of Thrace, and, apart from its agricultural importance, the area has great strategic significance. Barracks are liberally scatted through the hinterland and along the eastern border with Turkey; there are numerous surveillance posts, all flying Greek flags, and looking over to the minarets of Turkey across the Évros river valley.

The main town in this northeastern corner is **ORESTIÁDHA**, a busy market town with restaurants, bars and lots of cake shops in its main square. It also has a branch of the *National Bank of Greece*, something worth bearing in mind when returning from Bulgaria or Turkey. You could do worse than spend a night here before/after crossing the border. Hotels include the *Metropolis* (☎0552/22 260; ③), the *Selini* (☎0552/22 636; ③) and the *Vienni* (☎0552/22 578; ④).

On to Turkey or Bulgaria

Crossing into Turkey from Alexandhroúpoli, you are presented with a bewildering choice of routes; currently there's only one daily rail link to Bulgaria.

British passport holders now need a **Turkish visa**, which costs £5 at the border; if you don't have the exact amount in sterling, you'll have to change more. **Bulgarian visas** are required for all nationals and are expensive; prices fluctuate, but count on £20 for a transit pass at the border, somewhat less if you obtain it at a consulate beforehand.

By bus to Turkey

The simplest way to travel from northern Greece to Turkey, if you can get a ticket, is to go by **bus** direct to Istanbul. There are several departures daily, one run by OSE (tickets from the train station), the others by private companies (ask at travel agents). The problem is that most of the buses start in Thessaloníki and by this stage most are full. In addition to buses to Istanbul, there are private buses three or four times a week to Edirne, just across the border; ask for details at travel agents in Xánthi, Komotiní or Alexandhroúpoli.

An alternative is to take a local bus to the border at **KÍPI** (6 daily). You are not allowed to cross the frontier here on foot, but it is generally no problem to get a driver to shuttle you the 500m across to the Turkish post, and perhaps even to give you a lift beyond. The nearest town is IPSALA (5km further on), but if possible get as far as KEŞAN (30km), from where buses to Istanbul are much more frequent.

By train to Turkey

Travelling by **train** to Istanbul should in theory be simpler. However, the only through connection leaves Alexandhroúpoli at 9.18pm, crossing the border at PÍTHIO and taking about eleven hours in total (including a long halt at the frontier) to reach Istanbul. This is nominally an important express, with seat reservations applicable, so try not to leave tickets to the last minute.

You might prefer to go by day, taking a train through Píthio and on to **KASTANIÉS**, opposite Turkish Edirne. The most useful departures are currently at 5.45am and 9.49am; later ones arrive after the border post (daily 9am–1pm) has closed. There's no accommodation in Kastaniés, but unlike Kípi you are allowed to walk across the border (under army escort). Once on the Turkish side, there's bus service to the first Turkish village, 2km beyond the frontier, or you can try hitching the 7km total into Edirne (Adrianoúpoli to the Greeks) – an attractive and historic city with some important Ottoman monuments and frequent buses making the three-hour trip to Istanbul. For more information, there's no better source than *Turkey: The Rough Guide*.

Into Bulgaria

To Bulgaria, from Alexandhroúpoli, there is one just train daily, leaving at 5.45am and reaching Greek Dhikéa just over three hours later, where you then have a nearly two-hour wait before the special twenty-minute connection to SVILENGRAD inside Bulgaria. (Curiously, this turns around to provide a through service to Alexandhroúpoli in the early afternoon.) From Svilengrad (which has just one, five-star, hotel), it is best to plan on moving on the same day towards PLOVDIV.

travel details

Buses

From Thessaloníki to Athens (hourly; 8hr);
Pélla/Édhessa (hourly; 1hr/1hr 15min); Kateríni,
for Mount Olympus (hourly; 1hr 30min); Véria
(hourly; 1hr 15min); Vólos (4 daily; 4hr); Flórina (5
daily; 3hr 30min); Kastoriá (5 daily; 4hr 30min);
Kalambáka/Ioánnina (4–5 daily; 4hr 30min/7hr
30min); Sárti, via Políyiros (4 daily; 4hr 30min);
Vourvouroú, via Políyiros (3 daily; 3hr);
Arnéa–Ierissós/Ouranópoli (5–7 daily; 2hr/3hr
30min); Kavála (hourly; 3hr); Alexandhroúpoli (7
daily; 6hr); Istanbul (daily *OSE* service, others
privately operated; 14hr); Sofia (Thurs & Fri; 7hr
30min).

From Kateríni to Litóhoro (for Mount Olympus)
(4 daily; 45min).

From Véria to Kozáni (8 daily; 1hr); Édhessa, via
Náoussa (6 daily; 1hr 15min).

From Édhessa to Kastoriá (4 daily; 2hr 30min);
Flórina (5–6 daily; 2hr) .

From Kastoriá to Flórina (1 direct, daily; 2hr;
other indirect services via Amíndeo).

From Flórina to Níki, Yugoslav frontier (4 daily;
45min).

From Kozáni to Grevená (8 daily; 1hr); Siátista (4
daily; 30min).

From Kavála to Philippi (every 20min; 20min);
Keramotí (half-hourly; 1hr); Xánthi/Komotiní (half-
hourly; 1hr/2hr); Alexandhroúpoli (5 daily; 3hr).

From Alexandhroúpoli to Dhidhimótiho (8–9
daily; 2hr); Kípi (6 daily; 45min); Istanbul (daily
OSE and other private coaches; 8hr).

Trains

Thessaloníki–Kateríni/Lárissa/Athens

4 express, 6 slower trains daily in each direction
(1hr 30min/2hr 20min/6–8hr).

Thessaloníki–Kateríni/Litóhoro/Platamónas/ Lárissa/Vólos

3 daily in each direction (2hr/2hr
25min/4hr 30min/5 hr).

Thessaloníki–Véria/Édhessa/Amíndeo/ Flórina

5 daily in each direction; connections
between Amíndeo and Kozáni 4 times daily; 2
daily only to Édhessa; 1 train daily leaves Flórina
(3.30pm) for Bitola, Yugoslavia (Thessaloníki–
Véria 1hr 10min; Véria–Édhessa 1hr 15min;
Édhessa–Flórina 1hr 30min).

Thessaloníki–Sérres–Dhráma–Xánthi– Komotiní–Alexandhroúpoli

1 morning express,
4 slower trains daily (Thessaloníki–Dhráma 2hr
45min–3hr 30min; Dhráma–Xánthi/Komotiní 1hr/
15min/2hr 30min; Xánthi–Alexandhropoúli 1hr
30min–2hr).

Thessaloníki–Sofia, via Promahón (2 daily; 8hr
30min).

Thessaloníki–Belgrade–Venice, via
Idhoméni/Gevgéli (3 daily; 12hr/24–28hr). Service
temporarily suspended.

Alexandhroúpoli–Istanbul (Turkey) Semi-
direct (change cars at Píthio) night train (9.18pm),
arriving Istanbul around 8am, after an hour or
longer wait at the border.

Alexandhroúpoli–Dhidhimótiho– Orestiádha–Kastaniés (for Edirne)

7 daily, but
only 2 reach frontier post while open; 2hr/2hr
30min/3hr.

Alexandhroúpoli–Svilengrad (Bulgaria) 1
daily (5.45am); 5hr 20min, including 2hr stopover
at Dhikéa.

N.B. *OSE* also operates **long-distance buses**
from Thessaloníki to Istanbul, Sofia, Belgrade,
Milan, Paris, London, Vienna and towns in
Germany. They're not cheap, though.

Ferries

From Thessaloníki to Límnos, Lésvos and Híos
(2 weekly); to Iraklio via a selection among
Skíathos, Skíros, Tínos, Míkonos, Páros, Íos and
Thíra (2–3 weekly, always Mon & Fri year-round);
to Skíros, Skópelos, Alónissos (3 weekly in
summer).

From Néa Péramos to Thássos (Órmos Prínou)
(4 daily in summer).

From Kavála to Thássos (Órmos Prínou; 7–11
daily, depending on season); to Samothráki (2
weekly in season); to Límnos and Áyios Efstrátios
(3–5 weekly); to Lésvos and Híos (2 weekly); to
Límnos/Lésvos/Híos/Sámos/Ikaría/Léros or
Pátmos/Kálimnos/Kos/Rhodes (1 weekly in
summer). In winter this long-haul service sails out
of Thessaloníki.

From Keramotí to Thássos (Thássos town/
Liménas) (7–12 daily, year-round).

From Alexandhroúpoli to Samothráki (1–2 daily in season, 4 weekly out of season).

Hydrofoils
From Thessaloníki to Skíathos, Skópelos and Alónissos, via Néa Moudhaniá (Halkidhikí) (May-June/Sept 4 weekly, July & Aug daily).
For details of service, contact *Egnatia Tours*, Kamvouníon 9, Thessaloníki (☎031/223 811).

Flights
From Thessaloníki to Athens (5 daily); Ioánnina (3–5 weekly); Iráklion, Crete (2 weekly); Haniá, Crete (1 weekly); Lésvos (4–6 weekly); Límnos (4–6 weekly); Rhodes (2 weekly).
From Alexandhroúpoli to Athens (1–2 daily).
From Kastoriá to Athens (3–4 weekly).
From Kozáni to Athens (3–4 weekly).

PART THREE

THE

ISLANDS

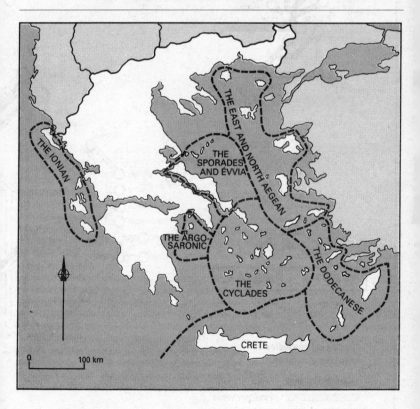

THE IONIAN

THE EAST AND NORTH AEGEAN

THE SPORADES AND ÉVVIA

THE ARGO-SARONIC

THE CYCLADES

THE DODECANESE

CRETE

0   100 km

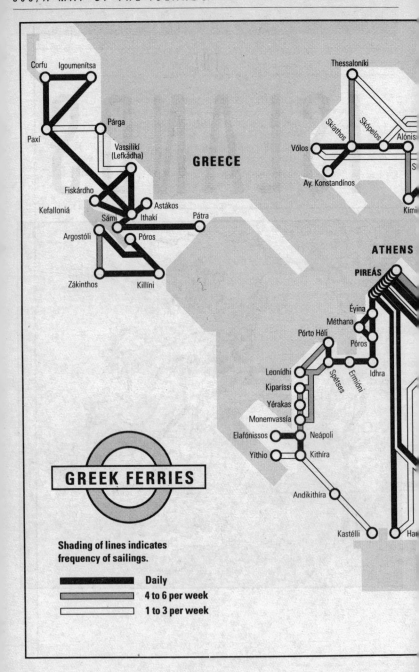

Corfu Igoumenítsa
Thessaloníki
Párga
Paxí
Vassilikí (Lefkádha)
GREECE
Skíathos Skópelos Alónis
Vólos
Fiskárdho
Ay. Konstandínos
Kefalloniá Astákos
Sámi Ithakí Pátra
Argostóli Póros
Zákinthos Killíni
Kími

ATHENS
PIREÁS
Éyina
Méthana
Pórto Héli Póros
Leonídhi Spétses Idhra
Kiparíssi Ermióni
Yérakas
Monemvassía
Elafónissos Neápoli
Yíthio Kithíra
Andikithíra
Kastélli Hai

GREEK FERRIES

Shading of lines indicates frequency of sailings.

— Daily
— 4 to 6 per week
— 1 to 3 per week

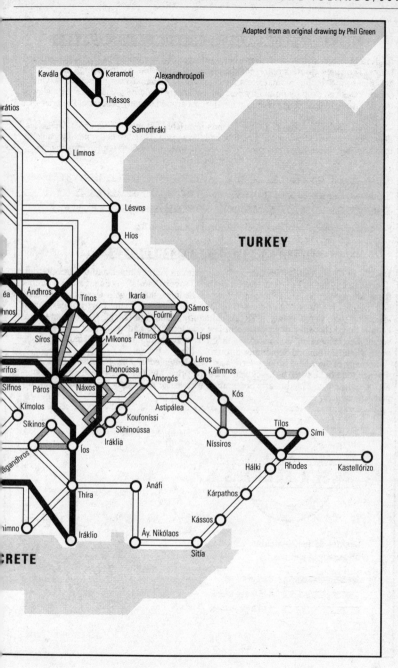

Adapted from an original drawing by Phil Green

Kavála
Keramotí
Alexandhroúpoli
Thássos
rátios
Samothráki
Límnos
Lésvos
Híos
TURKEY
éa
Ándhros
Tínos
Ikaría
Sámos
hnos
Foúrni
Síros
Míkonos
Pátmos
Lipsí
rifos
Dhonoússa
Léros
Kálimnos
Sífnos
Páros
Náxos
Amorgós
Kímolos
Koufoníssi
Astipálea
Kós
Síkinos
Skhinoússa
Tílos
Sími
égandhros
Íos
Iráklia
Níssiros
Hálki
Rhodes
Kastellórizo
Thíra
Anáfi
Kárpathos
nimno
Iráklio
Áy. Nikólaos
Kássos
Sitía
CRETE

ISLAND ACCOMMODATION: ROOM PRICE SCALES

All **hotels** listed in this book have been price-graded according to the scale outlined below. The **rates quoted** represent the **cheapest available room in high season**; all are prices for a double room, except for category ①, which are per person rates. Out of season rates can drop by up to fifty percent, especially if you negotiate rates for a stay of three or more nights. Single rooms generally cost around seventy percent of the price of a double.

Rented **"private rooms"** on the islands invariably fall into the ② or ③ categories, depending on their location and facilities, and the season. They are not generally available from October through to the beginning of March, when only hotels tend to remain open.

① 1000–1500dr (£3–4.50/US$5.50–8)

② 2000–3000dr (£6–9.50/US$11–16.50)

③ 3000–5500dr (£9.50–17/US$16.50–30)

④ 5500–7500dr (£17–23/US$30–41.50)

⑤ 7500–9000dr (£23–28/US$42–50)

⑥ 9000dr (£28/US$50) and upwards

For further explanation of our hotel category system, see p.32.

FERRY ROUTES AND SCHEDULES

Details of ferry routes, together with approximate journey times and frequencies, are to be found at the end of each chapter in the **"Travel Details"** section. Please note that these are for general guidance only. Ferry schedules change with alarming regularity and the only information to be relied upon is that provided by the **port police** in each island harbour. Ferry agents in Pireás and on the islands are helpful, too, of course, but keep in mind that they often represent just one ferry line and won't necessarily inform you of the competition. Be aware, too, that ferry services to the smaller islands tend to be pretty skeletal from mid-September through to May.

In many of the island groups, ferries are supplemented by *Flying Dolphin* **hydrofoils** – which tend to be twice as quick and twice the price. Most of the major hydrofoil routes are operated from May to early September, with lesser ones sometimes running in July and August only.

CHAPTER SIX

THE ARGO-SARONIC

The rocky, volcanic chain of **Argo-Saronic** islands, most of them barely an olive's throw from the Argolid, differ to a surprising extent not just from the mainland but from one another. Less surprising is their massive popularity, with Éyina (Aegina) especially becoming something of an Athenian suburb at weekends.

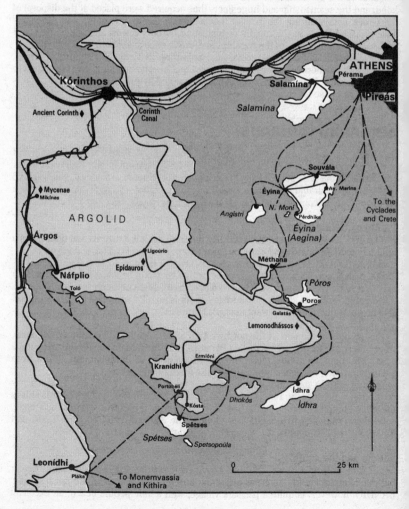

Ídhra (Hydra), Póros, and Spétses are not far behind in summer, though their visitors tends to be predominantly cruise and package tourists. More than any other group, these are islands at their best out of season, when populations fall dramatically and the port towns return to quiet, provincial-backwater life.

Éyina, important in antiquity and more or less continually inhabited since then, is the most fertile of the group, famous for its pistachio nuts, as well as for one of the finest ancient temples in Greece. Its main problem – the crowds – can be escaped by avoiding weekends, or taking the time to explore its satellite isles, **Angístri** and **Moní**.

The three southerly islands, **Spétses**, **Ídhra** and **Póros**, are pine-cloaked and relatively infertile. They were not really settled until medieval times, when refugees from the mainland – principally Albanian Christians – established themselves here. In response to the barrenness of their new home the islanders adopted piracy as a livelihood, and the seamanship and huge fleets thus acquired were placed at the disposal of the Greek nation during the War of Independence. Today foreigners and Athenians have replaced locals in the rapidly depopulating harbour towns, and windsurfers and sailboats are faint echoes of the warships and *kaíkia* once at anchor.

The closest island of the Argo-Saronic, **Salamína**, is virtually a suburb of Pireás, under a mile offshore to its east, and it almost touches the industrial city of Mégara to the west, as well. As you might expect, it is frequented by Athenian weekenders, and is also used as a base for commuting to the capital, but sees very few foreign visitors.

Salamína (Salamis)

Salamína is the quickest possible island hop from Athens. Take a taxi to the shipyard port of Pérama, just west of Pireás, and a ferry (daily 5am–midnight; 80dr) will whisk you across to the little port of Paloukía in a matter of minutes. On arrival, you won't be rewarded by desirable or isolated beaches – the pollution of Pireás and Athens is a little too close for comfort – but you soon escape the capital's *néfos* and and city pace.

Paloukía, Salamína and Selínia

PALOUKÍA is really just a transit point. By the ferry dock is a taverna and opposite is a bus station, with services to Salamína Town (3km), the island capital, and beyond.

SALAMÍNA TOWN (also known as KOULOÚRI) is home to 18,000 of the island's 23,000 population. It's a ramshackle place, with a couple of banks, a fishmarket and an over-optimistic (and long-closed) tourist office. Pretty much uniquely for an island town – and emphasising its absence of tourists – there is no bike or moped rental outlet, and also no hotel (not that you'd want to stay). Fortunately, bus services are excellent, linking most points on the island.

Bus #8 runs to the port at the northwest tip of the island, the **Voudoro peninsula**, where there are ferries across to Néa Peramás, near Mégara on the Athens–Kórinthos road. En route it passes close by the **Monastery of Faneroméni** (6km from Salamína), rather majestically sited above the frustratingly polluted gulf.

Around 6km to the south of Paloukía is a third island port, **SELÍNIA**, which has connections direct to the Pireás ferry dock (8am–2.30pm; 675dr; half-hour trip). This is the main summer resort – not a bad little place, with a pleasant waterfront, a bank, several tavernas and two inexpensive hotels, the *Akroyali* (☎01/46 53 341; ②) and Votsalakia (☎01/46 53 494; ②). It can be reached direct by bus from Paloukía.

Eándio and the south

South from Salamína Town, the road edges the coast towards Eándio (6km; regular buses). There are a few tavernas along the way, but the sea vistas are not inspiring. EÁNDIO, however, is quite a pleasant village, with a little pebble beach, an excellent taverna, the *Isipandisi*, and the island's best **hotel**, the *Gabriel* (☎01/46 62 275; ③). The hotel overlooks the bay, whose waters are again unenticing (probably a health risk) for swimming, but it could be an enjoyable off-season stay.

Two roads continue from Eándio. The one to the southeast runs to the unassuming village resorts of PERÁNI and PARALÍA (both around 4km from Eándio). The more interesting route is southeast to KANÁKIA (8km from Eándio; no buses), over the island's pine-covered mountain, and passing (at around 5km) a monastery – dedicated, like almost all Salamína churches, to Áyios Nikólaos. At the monastery you could turn off the road (left) along a track to the harbour and small-scale resort of PERISTÉRIA (5km). This is a much more attractive settlement than the littered beach and scruffy huts of Kanákia itself.

Éyina (Aegina)

Given its current population of a little over 10,000, it seems incredible to reflect that Éyina (Aegina) was a major power in Classical times – and a rival to Athens. It carried on trade to the limits of the known world, maintained a sophisticated silver coinage system (the first in Greece) and had prominent athletes and craftsmen. However, during the fifth century BC the islanders made the political mistake of siding with their fellow Dorians, the Spartans, which Athens seized on as an excuse to act on a long-standing jealousy; her fleets defeated the islanders' in two separate sea battles and, after the second, the population was expelled and replaced by more tractable colonists.

Subsequent history was less distinguished, with the familiar central Greece pattern of occupation, by Romans, Franks, Venetians, Catalans and Turks, before the War of Independence brought a brief period as seat of government for the fledgeling Greek nation. These days, the island is regarded by Athenians as a beach annexe for their city – it is the closest place to the capital most of them would swim in – though for tourists it has a monument as fine as any in the Aegean in its beautiful fifth-century BC **Temple of Aphaia**. This is located on the east coast, close to the port of **Ayía Marína** and if it is your primary goal, you'd do best take one of the ferries that in season run directly to that port. If you plan to stay, then make sure your boat will dock at **Éyina Town**, the island capital. Ferries also occasionally stop at **Souvála**, between the two ports.

Éyina Town

A solitary column of a Temple of Apollo beckons as your ferry steams around the point into the harbour at **ÉYINA TOWN**. The island capital, it makes an attractive base, with some grand old buildings from the time (1826–28) when it served as the first capital of Greece after the War of Independence. And for somewhere so close to Athens, it isn't especially overrun by foreign tourists, nor are prices unduly inflated.

The **harbour** is workaday rather than picturesque, and all the more appealing for that. Fishermen talk and tend their nets, and *kaíkia* loaded with produce from the mainland bob at anchor. Over to the north are the Apollo Temple column, set on a low hill that was the ancient acropolis and is known – logically enough – as **Kolóna**. Around the temple are some rather overgrown **excavations** (Tues–Sun 8.30am–3pm; 200dr), not very substantial, save for a few stretches of Classical wall, but a pleasant wander for the views out to sea. Just to the north of here is an attractive bay with a small, sandy **beach** – the best spot for swimming in the immediate vicinity of the town.

The town's other sights, such as they are, are the frescoed thirteenth-century church of **Ómorfi Ekklisía**, fifteen minutes' walk east of the port, and a house in the suburb of Livádhi, just to the north, where a plaque recalls the residence of **Nikos Kazantzakis**, when he was writing his most celebrated book, *Zorba the Greek*.

ÉYINA (AEGINA)

Practicalities

Rooms can be hard to come by in Éyina Town, with many of the hotels block-booked by package groups or Athenians in the summer months. You would be well advised to phone ahead, or to take whatever you're offered on arrival, at least for the first night. If looking around on your own, try the streets inland from Platía Ethneyersías, a couple of hundred metres to the left of the jetty as you disembark. Options include:

Sklavenas Hostel, Kapodhístrias 19 (☎0297/223 27). Rooms (②) and roofspace (②).

Hotel Miranda, Ymnastioú 10 (☎0297/22 266). ②

Hotel Plaza, Kazantzáki 4 (☎0297/25 600). ③

Hotel Avra, Kazantzáki 4 (☎0297/22 303). ④

Hotel Toghia, Platía Ethneyersías (☎0297/24 242). ④

The **bus station** is also on Platía Ethneyersías, with an excellent service to most villages, and the largest moped and cycle rental place is just to the north. Cycles are fine for getting around Éyina, and the Temple of Aphaia is a comfortable ride away.

On the waterfront, near the ferry quay, are several decent **tavernas**, and an *ouzerí* where you can have octopus and pistachios (the island's main product) with your drink while you watch the produce and seafood being carried to the **fish market**. Directly behind the market is a particularly good fish taverna, the *Agora*.

There is a **National Bank** on the waterfront and an **OTE** and **post office** inland.

The Temple of Aphaia and Ayía Marína

The Doric **Temple of Aphaia** (Mon–Fri 8.15am–5pm, Sat & Sun 8.30am–3pm; 300dr), Éyina's great monument, lies 17km east of Éyina Town, standing among pines that are tapped to flavour the local retsina. It is one of the most complete and visually complex ancient buildings in Greece, with superimposed arrays of columns and lintels evocative of an Escher drawing. Built early in the fifth century BC – or possibly at the end of the sixth century – it predates the Parthenon by around sixty years. The dedication is unusual: Aphaia was a Cretan nymph who had fled from the lust of King Minos, and seems to have been worshipped almost exclusively on Aegina.

As little as two centuries ago the temple's pediments were intact and virtually perfect, depicting two battles at Troy. However, like the Elgin marbles they were "bought" from the Turks: this time by Ludwig of Bavaria, which explains their current residence in the Munich Glyptothek.

Routes to the temple: Paleohóra

There are buses to the temple from Éyina Town but the best approach is by rented bicycle, which allows you to take the more interesting inland road, past the monastery of **Áyios Nektários** (a local worthy who died only sixty years ago and was canonised in highly irregular fashion) and ruined **PALEOHÓRA**, the island's old capital. This inland town was built in the ninth century as protection against piracy and was only abandoned in 1826, following Greek independence. A dozen or so of its reputed 365 churches and monasteries remain in recognisable state, but nothing of the town itself; when the islanders left, they simply dismantled their houses and moved them to modern Éyina.

The coast road between Éyina Town and the temple runs via the resort of SOUVÁLA: uninteresting but functional for a swim on the way back.

Ayía Marína and Mount Óros

AYÍA MARÍNA, 13km from Éyina town, lies on the south side of the Aphaia temple ridge. It is the island's major resort and in summer its beach is so crowded that it is only really worth coming here for the ferries. Rooms and restaurants are both expensive, though scores of backpackers brave the insect life to camp in the olive groves behind the beach – not a great prospect.

Beyond the town the road continues south to another beach at **PÓRTES**, where the rough road turns inland to cross the island, passing just under Mount Óros and hitting the west coast near **MARATHÓNAS**. This is good hiking country. From Marathónas, you can walk up past PAHÍA RÁHI hamlet on a mixture of jeep tracks and paths to the turning for the final scramble up the Argo-Saronic's highest point, **Mount Óros**.

Mount Óros

Just off the trail, past Pahía Ráhi, are the massive foundations of the shrine of **Ellaníou Dhiós**, Éyina's third temple, with the monastery of Taxiárhes squatting amidst the massive masonry. At the summit of **Mount Óros** (532m, 1700ft), an hour from the road and capped by a chapel, the views stretch over the entire island and much of the Argo-Saronic gulf. You can pick out the hamlets of Vláhides, Anitséou and Sfendóuri, as well as the isolated beach of Kípi.

More **paths** in this largely roadless portion of the island link these points with Pórtes and Pérdhika; there is also a direct path from nearby the ancient temple to Pérdhika. From ALÓNES, a hamlet west of Ayía Marína, you can walk through the settlements of Yiannákidhes and Lazáridhes to the nunnery of **Hrissoleóndissa**.

Pérdhika and Moní islet

The road due south of Éyina Town runs along the west coast of the island to the very attractive beach and fishing village of **PÉRDHIKA** (9km; regular buses). This is the best place to stay on the island, besides the main town, with a pension and a few rooms for rent. Alternatively, if you want to camp, you can get a *kaíki* across to Moní Islet, just a 100-drachma ride across the bay.

On Moní there's an official EOT **campsite**, a seasonal taverna and tremendous skin diving. The campsite is a bit pricey but lively and has plenty of water – a pressing problem back on Éyina where the thirsty pistachios lower the water table several feet annually. On the island, your co-inhabitants include wild peacocks and goats.

Angístri

Angístri, a half-hour by boat from Éyina, is small enough to be overlooked by most island-hoppers, though it's now in a few foreign package-holiday brochures. Beaches, however, remain quieter than on Aegina and out of season the island drops to a quiet village pace, many islanders still making a living from fishing and farming. The yellow headscarves worn by the old women indicate the islanders' Albanian ancestry.

Boats from Éyina and Pireás call at both the main villages, Skála and Mílos. **From Pireás**, the *Manaras Express* runs twice daily in season, once a day out of season: the journey takes two hours. From Éyina (departures from the fish market harbour), there are boats three or four times a day in season, twice a day out of season.

Skála

SKÁLA is essentially a modern resort, with its older settlement, METÓHI, poised on the hillside above. It has Angístri's only sandy beach, which is fronted by a single taverna. There is usually a reasonable choice of rooms for rent and vacancies at the few modest-priced **hotels**, though on July and August weekends the beach fills up with Athenians and accommodation can be hard to find. If you're booking ahead, the *Hotel Andrea* (☎0297/91 346; ②) is recommended, as is its adjacent **taverna**.

A road to the left of the harbour leads to the *Angístri Club*, with a disco-bar on the rocks above the sea. From there, it's ten minutes' walk to a quiet pebble beach backed by crumbling cliffs and pine-covered hills.

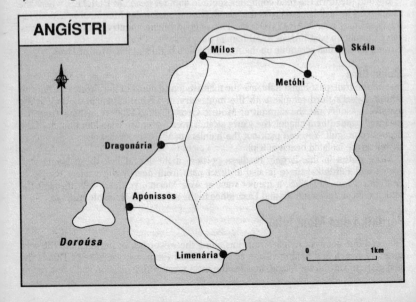

MÍLOS, built in the traditional Argo-Saronic style, lacks a decent beach but is a more attractive village, again with plenty of rented rooms and some **hotels**. The *Mílos Hotel* (☎0297/91 241; ②) is a nice place, worth a try, and *Ta Tria Adhélfia*, in the centre of the village, is the island's best taverna.

Limenária and Apónissos

A regular bus service connects Skála and Mílos with Limenária on the far side of the island – or you could walk from Metóhi along a winding track through the pine forest with views across to Athens, Éyina and the Peloponnese.

LIMENÁRIA is a small farming community, largely unaffected by tourism. There are two tavernas, a few rooms, and a sign pointing misleadingly to the "beach" – in reality just a spot where you can swim off the rocks.

A half-hour walk from here, through olive and pine trees, and past a shallow lake, will bring you to a causeway linking the tiny islet of **APÓNISSOS**. This has a seasonal taverna, nearby which there are usually a few summer campers.

Póros

Separated from the mainland by a 400-metre strait, **Póros** ("the ford") only just counts as an island. But qualify it does, making it fair game for the package tours, while its proximity to Pireás also means a weekend invasion by Athenians. Unspoilt it isn't, and the beaches are few and poor, especially compared to neighbouring Éyina and Spétses. The island town, however, has a bit of character, and the topography is interesting. Póros is in fact two islands, **Sferiá** (which shelters Póros Town) and the more extensive **Kalávria**, separated from each other by a shallow engineered canal. According to one local guide book "the canal reminds you of Venice" – a phrase which must have gained something in the translation.

In addition to its regular ferry and hydrofoil connections with Pireás and the other Argo-Saronics, Póros has frequent boats shuttling across from the mainland port of **Galatás** in the Peloponnese. This allows for some interesting excursions – locally to the lemon groves of **Limonodhássos**, **Ancient Troezen** and the "Devil's Bridge" (see p.155), and further afield to Náfplio, or to performances of ancient drama at the great theatre of Epidaurus (see p.152).

Póros Town

Ferries from the Argo-Saronics or from Galatás drop you at **PÓROS**, the only town, which rises steeply on all sides of the tiny volcanic peninsula of Sferiá. The harbour and town are picturesque from the sea and the cafés and the waterfront have quite an animation about them. There's no special sight, save for a little **archaeological museum** (Mon–Sat 9am–3pm; free) with a display on the mainland site of Troezen.

Just back from the waterfront, two **travel agents**, *Family Tours* (☎0298/23 741) and *Takis Travel* (☎0298/22 048) exchange money, sell island maps and arrange accommodation in **rented rooms**. The quieter and preferable places are in the streets back – and up – from the clocktower, if you want to look around on your own. Prices generally are on the high side. Most of the proper hotels are across the canal on Kalávria. Camping is not encouraged anywhere on the island and there is no official campsite.

Additional facilities around the waterfront include a couple of **moped and bicycle rental** outlets (you can take either across on boats to the mainland), a **bank**, **post office**, and a **bookshop**, *Anita's*, which trades secondhand paperbacks. If you are interested in seeing a play at (or just visiting) Epidaurus, call in at the travel agents to ask about excursions – the simplest and cheapest way of doing it.

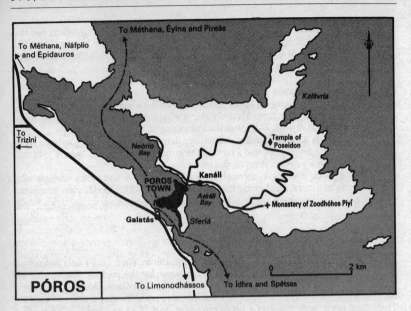

Down on the quayside, good-value **restaurants** include *Grill Oasis* and *Ta Dhilina*, at the far end away from the ferry dock, while up in the town the *Three Brothers* taverna is pricier but recommended.

Kalávria

Most of Póros's **hotels** are to be found on Kalávria, the main body of the island, just across the canal beyond the Naval Cadets' Training School. They stretch for two kilometres or so on either side of the causeway, with some of those to the west ideally situated to catch the dawn chorus – the Navy's marching band. If you'd rather sleep on, head beyond the first bay where the fishing boats tie up.

Alternatively, turn right around **Askéli Bay**, where there are a group of hotels and villas facing good clear water, if not much in the way of beaches. The best island beach is **Kanáli**, near the beginning of the causeway, which usually charges admission – a reflection both of Póros's commercialism and the premium on sand.

The Monastery of Zoödhóhos Piyí and Temple of Poseidon

At the end of the four-kilometre stretch of road around Askéli is the simple eighteenth-century **Monastery of Zoödhóhos Piyí**, whose monks have fled the tourists and been replaced by a caretaker to collect the admission charges. It's a pretty spot, with a couple of summer tavernas under the nearby plane trees.

From here you can either walk up across to the far side of the island through the pines and olives, or bike along the road. Either route will lead you to the few columns and ruins that make up the sixth-century BC **Temple of Poseidon** – though keep your eyes open or you may miss them. Here, supposedly, Demosthenes, fleeing from the Macedonians after taking part in the last-ditch resistance of the Athenians, took poison rather than surrender to the posse sent after him. A road leads on and back down in a circular route to the "grand canal".

Ídhra (Hydra)

The port and town of **Ídhra**, with its tiers of substantial stone mansions and white, tiled houses climbing up from a perfect horseshoe harbour, is a beautiful spectacle. Unfortunately, thousands of others think so too, and from Easter until September it's packed to the gills. The front becomes one long outdoor café, the hotels are full and the discos flourish. Once a fashionable artists' colony, established in the 1960s as people restored the grand old houses, it has experienced a predictable metamorphosis into one of the more popular (and expensive) resorts in Greece. But this acknowledged, a visit is still to be recommended, especially if you can get here some time other than peak season.

Ídhra Town

The waterfront of **ÍDHRA TOWN** is literally lined with mansions, most of them built during the eighteenth century, on the accumulated wealth of a remarkable merchant fleet of 160 ships which traded as far afield as America and, during the Napoleonic Wars, broke the British blockade to sell corn to France. Fortunes were made and the island also enjoyed a special relationship with the Turkish Porte, governing itself, paying no tax, but providing sailors for the Sultan's navy. These conditions naturally attracted Greek immigrants from the less-privileged mainland, and by the 1820s the town's population stood at nearly 20,000, an incredible figure when you reflect that today it is under 3000. During the War of Independence, Hydriot merchants provided many of the ships for the Greek forces and inevitably many of the commanders.

The **mansions** or *arhondiká* of these merchant families, designed by architects from Venice and Genoa, are still the great monuments of the town. If you are interested in looking in at close quarters, ask the tourist police for help in locating, among others, the **Votsís** and **Ikonomoú** houses. The interior of the **Koundouriótis** and **Voulgarís** *arhondiká* can also occasionally be visited. The **Tsombadhoú** villa on the harbour is now a maritime academy, and the **Tombázis** a school of fine arts.

Ídhra is also reputedly hallowed by no less than 365 churches – a total claimed by many a Greek island, but here with some justice. The most important is the cathedral of **Panayía Mitropóleos**, built around a courtyard down by the port, and with a distinctive clocktower.

Practicalities

Staying on Ídhra means finding a room in the port, or, if you're lucky, at Vlíhos (see overpage). There are quite a number of **pensions and hotels** along the waterfront, most of them charging around a third above usual island rates, and your main concern is likely to be finding space rather than quality. In addition, single rooms are pretty much unavailable.

Reasonable-value **hotels** to phone and reserve ahead include: *Hotel Leto* (☎0298/53 385; ③); *Hotel Hydra* (☎0298/52 102; especially recommended; ③); *Hotel Argo* (☎0298/52 452; ③); *Pension Dina* (☎0298/52 248; ③); *Hotel Sofia* (☎0298/52 313; ③); *Pension Angelika* (☎0298/52 360; ③); and the *Pension Douglas* (☎0298/52 599; ②). Most of these are on or just back from the waterfront. If you still have no luck, try asking around the fishermen's quarter of Kamíni, a kilometre to the west.

There is no shortage of **restaurants** around the waterfront. *Ta Tria Adhelfia* is a good, inexpensive, friendly taverna next to the cathedral. The *Ambrosia Café*, back from the front, serves vegetarian meals and excellent breakfasts.

For nightlife, try the **discos** *Heaven*, with impressive views from its hillside site, or the long-established *Kavos*, above the harbour, with a garden for dance breaks.

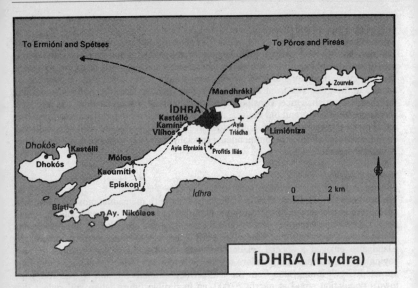

ÍDHRA (Hydra)

Beaches around Ídhra Town

The island's only sandy beach is at **MANDHRÁKI**, 2km east of Ídhra Town along a concrete track; it's the private domain of the *Miramare Hotel*, although the windsurfing centre is open to all.

On the opposite side of the harbour a coastal path leads around to a pebbly but popular stretch, just before **KAMÍNI**, where there's a good year-round taverna, *George and Anna's*. Continuing along the water on the now unsurfaced mule track you'll come to **KASTÉLLO**, another small, rocky beach with the ruins of a tiny fort.

Thirty minutes' walk beyond Kamíni (or a boat ride from the port) will bring you to **VLÍHOS,** a small hamlet with three tavernas, **rooms** and a historic nineteenth-century bridge. **Camping** is tolerated here (though nowhere else closer to town) and the swimming in the lee of an offshore islet is good. Farther out is the islet of **Dhokós**, only seasonally inhabited by goatherds and people tending their olives.

The interior and south coast

There are no motor vehicles of any kind on Ídhra, except for two lorries to pick up the rubbish, and no metalled roads away from the port, for the island is mountainous and its interior accessible only by foot or donkey. The practical result of this is that most visiting tourists don't venture outside the town, so with a little walking you can find yourself in a quite different kind of island. A dampener on this is that the pines that formerly covered the island were devastated by forest fires in 1985 and are only now beginning to recover.

Following the streets of town upwards and inland you reach a path which winds up the mountain (in about an hour's walk) to the **Monastery of Profítis Ilías** (Prophet Elijah) and the **Convent of Ayía Efpraxía**. Both are beautifully situated; the nuns at the convent (the lower of the two) offer hand-woven fabrics for sale. Further on, to the left if you face away from the town, is the **Monastery of Ayía Triádha**, occupied by a few monks (no women admitted). From here a path continues east for two more hours to the cloister of **Zourvás** in the extreme east of the island.

The donkey path continues west of Vlíhos to **Episkopí**, a high plateau planted with olives and vineyards and dotted by perhaps a dozen summer homes (no facilities). An inconspicuous turning roughly half an hour below leads to Mólos Bay, dirty and sea-urchin-infested, and to the more pleasant farming hamlet of **KAOUMÍTI**. From Episkopí itself faint tracks lead to the western extreme of the island, on either side of which the bays of **BÍSTI** and **ÁYIOS NIKÓLAOS** offer solitude and good swimming.

The south coast, too, if you're energetic and armed with a map, is scattered with coves, the best of which, **LIMIÓNIZA** (beyond Ayía Triádha), is also served by **boat excursions** in season from Ídhra town.

Spétses (Spetsai)

Spétses was the island where John Fowles once lived and which he used, thinly disguised as Phraxos, as the setting for *The Magus*. It is today a bit too popular for its own good, with signs for fast food and English breakfasts lining rather too many of the old town lanes. However, as a whole, the island hangs onto its charms pretty well. The island town's architecture is characterful and distinguished – if less dramatic than that of Ídhra – and, despite another bout of forest fire devastation (in 1990), the landscape described by Fowles is still to be seen: the parts "away from its inhabited corner (where it is) truly haunted . . . its pine forests uncanny". Remarkably, too, Spétses's best beach (and arguably the best in the Argo-Saronic), Áyii Anáryiri, has had its development limited, to a scattering of holiday villas.

Spétses Town

SPÉTSES TOWN (also known as Kastélli), is the port and only town. It shares with Ídhra the same history of nineteenth-century mercantile adventure and prosperity, and the same leading role in the War of Independence, which made its foremost citizens the aristocrats of the newly independent Greek state. Pebble-mosaic courtyards and streets sprawl between 200-year-old mansions, whose architecture is quite distinct from the Peloponnesian styles across the straits. Horse-drawn cabs connect the various quarters of town, spread out along the waterfront.

The sights are principally the majestic old houses and gardens. The finest of these is the magnificent Mexis family mansion, now taken over by the local **museum** (Tues–Sun 8.30am–3pm; free) which has a display of relics from the War of Independence, including the bones of the Spetsiote admiral-heroine Lascarina Bouboulina.

Just outside the town, Fowles aficionados will notice **Anáryiros College**, a curious Greek recreation of an English public school where the author was employed and set part of his tale; it is now vacant, save for the occasional conference or kids' holiday programme. Like the massive Edwardian **Hotel Possidonion**, another *Magus* setting, on the waterside, it was endowed by Sotirios Anáryiros, the island's great nineteenth-century benefactor. An enormously rich self-made man he was also responsible for planting the pine forest that now covers the island. His former house, behind the *Hotel Roumani*, is a monument to bad taste, decked out like a pharaoh's tomb.

Perhaps more interesting than chasing *Magus* settings, though, is a walk east from the **Dápia**, the cannon-studded main harbour. At the end of the road you reach the **Baltíza** inlet, where half a dozen boatyards continue to build *kaíkia* in the traditional manner; it was one of these that recreated the *Argo* for Tim Severin's *Jason Voyage* a few years back.

En route, you pass the smaller "old harbour", where the Athenian rich moor their yachts, and the church of **Áyios Nikólaos** with its graceful belfry and some giant pebble mosaics.

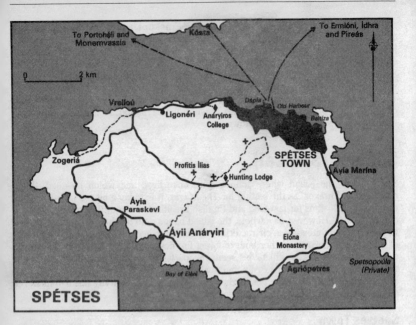

SPÉTSES

Spétses Town practicalities

Nearly all visitors stay in Spétses town and all kinds of **accommodation** are available, from the above-mentioned *Hotel Possidonion* (☎0298/72 208; ⑤ – but surprisingly low rates out of season) to simple **rooms** in people's houses. The best rooms are in a grand old house behind the Sotirios Anaryiros mansion – illustrious quarters and not too expensive. Also well worth trying for is the blue-balconied *Hotel Saronikos* (☎0298/72 646; ③), a lovely old inn just by the *Flying Dolphin* quay at Dápia. Another pleasant hotel is the *Villa Christina* (%0298/72 218; ③), in the backstreets.

If you don't fancy pounding the streets yourself, then go to *Takis's Tourist Office*, fifty paces from the end of the jetty, and see what they can come up with. Takis is mayor and tourist king of the island, and controls more or less all the room and villa accommodation. *Meltemi Travel*, on the waterfront near Takis's, rents out a few studios at the beach of Áyii Anáryiri (see "The Beaches", following).

Food and drink are a bit on the pricey side. Best of the waterfront places are *Ta Tzakia*, 300m to the left of the Dápia, and *Taverna Haralambos,* on Baltíza inlet, by the smaller harbour. The only traditional taverna is *Lazaros*'s (400m inland and uphill from Dápia: ask directions), though it can't cope with large parties. For a splurge, try *Trehandiri*, next to the church of Áyios Nikólaos on the way to the old harbour; it's the best of an expensive group of restaurants there. For vegetarian meals, try *Lirakis*, next to the *Soleil Hotel*, or *Tops*.

By day, Stambolis's *kafenío*, below the *Hotel Saronikos*, remains steadfastly traditional. By night, clubbers divide between the **discos** *Coconuts* and *Figaro* – the latter being the summer base of DJs from the trendy Athenian club *Papagayo*.

The most reliable of the **bike and moped rental outlets** is on the road to the Old Harbour, past the *Rendez-Vous* bar. Bikes are fine for the island, and despite the poor roads you can reach most points or make a circuit without too much exertion.

Finally a word for the two Dápia **crafts shops**, *Pityousa* (behind the *Soleil Hotel*) and *Kaiki* (on the first street in from the front). Both are superior establishments with genuine pieces from the Pireás markets.

Around the island

For **swimming** you need to get clear of the town. Beaches within walking distance are at **Ayía Marína** (twenty minutes east, with a taverna), at various spots beyond the **old harbour**, and several other spots half an hour away in either direction. The tempting islet of **Spetsopoúla**, just offshore from Ayía Marína, is, unfortunately, off-limits. It's the private property of shipping magnate Stavros Niarchos, of dubious repute, who maintains it as a pleasure park for his associates; his yacht (the largest in Greece) can sometimes be seen moored offshore.

For heading further afield, you'll need to hire a **bike or moped**, or use the **kaíkia** rides from the Dápia, which run to beaches around the island in summer. A very expensive alternative are the **waterboat taxis**, though they can take up to ten people. **Walkers** might want to go over the top of the island to Áyii Anáryiri, though this is not so fine a walk since the forest fire, which destroyed most of the pines between Ayía Marína and Áyii Anáryiri. The route out of town starts from behind *Lazaros's Taverna*.

West from Spétses Town

Heading west from the Dápia around the coast, the road is concreted until the houses run out after a kilometre or so; thereafter it is a dirt track which winds through pine trees and around inlets. The forest stretches from the central hills right down to the shore and it makes for a beautiful coastline with little coves and rocky promontories, all shaded by trees.

VRELLOÚ is one of the first places you come to, at the mouth of a wooded valley known locally as "Paradise". It is a fairly apt description except that like so many of the beaches it becomes polluted every year by tourists' rubbish. However, the entire shore is dotted with coves and in a few places there are small tavernas – a good one at **ZOGERIÁ**, for instance, where the scenery and rocks more than makes up for the inadequate little beach.

Working your way anti-clockwise around the coast towards Áyii Anáryiri you reach **ÁYIA PARASKEVÍ** with its small church and beach – one of the most beautiful coves on Spétses and an alternate stop on some of the *kaíki* runs. It has a basic beach café in summer. On the hill above is the house John Fowles used as the setting for *The Magus*, the *Villa Jasemia*. It is owned by one Alkis Botassis, who claims to be the model for the *Magus* character – though Fowles denies "appropriating" anything more than his "outward appearance" and "superb site" of his house. If you're hooked on the book, you can arrange a stay through *Pine Island Holidays* (PO Box 10, Spétses 180.50; ☎0298/724 64) at a somewhat exorbitant rate; the house is distinctly atmospheric.

Áyii Anáryiri

Áyii Anáryiri, on the south side of the island, is the best, if also the most popular, beach: a beautiful, long, sheltered bay of fine sand. It's gorgeous first thing in the morning, though fills up later in the day, with bathers, windsurfers and rather manic speedboat-driving waterski instructors. On the right-hand side of the bay, looking out to sea, there's a sea cave, which you can swim out to and within.

There's a self-service taverna on the beach and, just behind, *Tassos's*, Spétses' finest (and a well-priced) eating establishment. A meal here, prepared with real care and enthusiasm, is not to be missed.

The road and coves continue **east of Áyii Anáryiri**, though often at some distance from each other until you loop back to Ayía Marína.

travel details

Ordinary Ferryboats

From the central harbour at **Pireás** at least 10 boats daily run to Ayía Marína (1hr) and Éyina (1hr 30min); 5 daily to Póros (3hr 30min); 1 or 2 a day to Ídhra (4hr 30min) and Spétses (5hr 30min). About 4 connections daily between Éyina and Póros.

Most of the ferries stop on the mainland at Méthana (between Éyina and Póros) and Ermióni (between Ídhra and Spétses); it is possible to board them here from the Peloponnese. Some continue from Spétses to Portohéli. There are also constant boats between Póros and Galatás (10min) from dawn until late at night, and boat-taxis between Spétses and Portohéli.

NB There are more ferries at weekends and fewer out of season (although the service remains good); they leave Pireás most frequently between 7am and 9am, and 1pm and 6pm. Do not buy a return ticket as it saves no money and limits you to one specific boat. The general information number for the Argo-Saronic ferries is ☎01/45 11 311 or 41 15 801.

Flying Dolphin Hydrofoils

Approximately hourly services from the central harbour at Pireás to **Éyina** only 6am–8pm in season, 7am–7pm out; 40min.

All hydrofoils going beyond Éyina leave from the **Zea Marina**: 4 to 15 times daily to Póros

(1hr), Ídhra (1hr 40min), and Spétses (2–2hr 30min). All these times depend upon the stops en route, and frequencies vary with the season.

Éyina is connected with the other three islands twice a day; Póros, Ídhra, and Spétses with each other 3 to 5 times daily. Some hydrofoils also stop at Méthana and Ermióni and all of those to Spétses continue to Portohéli (15min more). This is a junction of the hydrofoil route – there is usually one a day onwards to Toló and Náfplio (and vice versa; 30 and 45min) in season and another (almost year-round) to Monemvassía (2hr). The Monemvassía hydrofoil continues 2 to 4 times a week to the island of Kíthira.

NB Once again services are heavily reduced out of season, though all the routes between Portohéli and Pireás still run. Hydrofoils are usually twice as fast and twice as expensive as ordinary boats, though to Éyina the price is little different. You can only buy one-way tickets, so if you need to return on a certain day buy your ticket back, *on arrival*, from the local agent. In season, it's not unusual for departures to be fully booked.

Details and tickets available from local agents and in Athens from *Wagons-Lits*, Stadhíou 5, Síntagma (☎01/32 28 650). The Pireás ticket office is at Ákti Themistokléous 8 (☎01/45 27 107). Tickets can also be bought at the departure quays.

CHAPTER SEVEN

THE CYCLADES

N amed for the circle they form around the sacred island of Delos, the **Cyclades** (*Kikládhes*) are the most satisfying Greek archipelago for island-hopping. On no other group do you get quite such a strong feeling of each island as a microcosm, each with its own distinct traditions, customs and path of modern development. Most of these self-contained realms are compact enough to walk around in a few days, giving you a sense of completeness and identity impossible on, say, Crete or most of the Ionian islands.

There is some unity. The majority of the islands – Ándhros, Náxos, Sérifos and Kéa notably excepted – are both arid and rocky, and most share the "Cycladic" style of brilliant-white, cubist architecture. The extent and impact of tourism, however, is dramatically haphazard, so that although some English is spoken on most islands, a slight detour from the beaten track – from Íos to Síkinos, for example – can have you groping for your Greek phrasebook.

But whatever the level of tourist development, there are only two islands where it has come completely to dominate their character: **Íos**, the original hippie-island and still a paradise for hard-drinking backpackers, and **Míkonos**, by far the most popular of the group, with its teeming old town, nude beaches and sophisticated clubs and gay bars. After these two, **Páros**, **Sífnos**, **Náxos,** and **Thíra** (Santoríni) are currently the most popular, their beaches and main towns drastically overcrowded in August. But away from the resort areas even these islands have for the most part escaped the ravages of mass development and seem able to absorb visitors with remarkable ease. To avoid the hordes altogether, the most promising islands are **Síkinos**, **Kithnos**, **Kímolos** or **Anáfi**, or even (going to extremes) the minor islets around Náxos. For a different view of the Cyclades, visit **Tínos** and its imposing church, a major spiritual centre of Greek Orthodoxy, or **Síros** with its elegant townscape, and, like Tínos, large Catholic minority. The one major ancient site is **Delos** (Dhílos), certainly worth making time for: the commercial and religious centre of the Classical Greek world, it's visited most easily on a day trip, by *kaíki* from Míkonos.

When it comes to **moving on**, many of the islands are handily connected with Crete (easier in season), while from Ándhros, Tínos, Náxos or Amorgós you can loop on to the Dodecanese ferry-circuits. Similarly, you can get from Míkonos, Náxos, Síros and Páros to Ikaría and Sámos (in the eastern Aegean). It's worth remembering, however, that the Cyclades often get frustratingly **stormy**, particularly in early spring or late autumn, and they're also the group worst affected by the *meltémi*, which blows sand and tables about with equal ease throughout much of July and August. Delayed and cancelled ferries are not uncommon, so if you're heading back to Athens to catch a flight leave yourself a day or two of leeway.

Kéa (Tziá)

Kéa is the closest of the Cyclades to the mainland and is very popular in summer with Athenians. However, they – and the attendant commercialisation – confine themselves to certain small coastal resorts, leaving most of the interior quiet. During the week, when the city dwellers head back to Athens, the whole of Kéa is an enticing destination, its rocky, forbidding perimeter enlivened inland by oak and almond

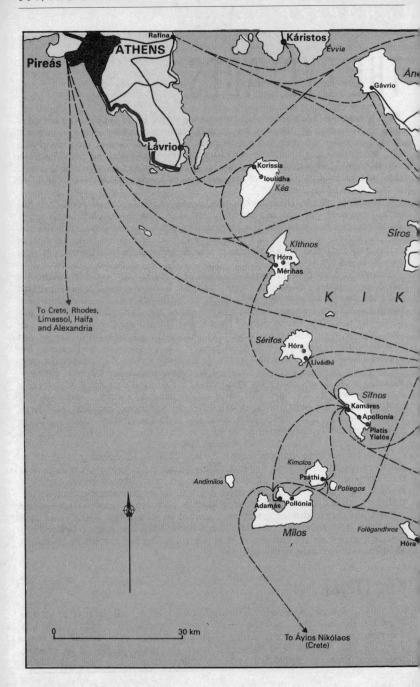

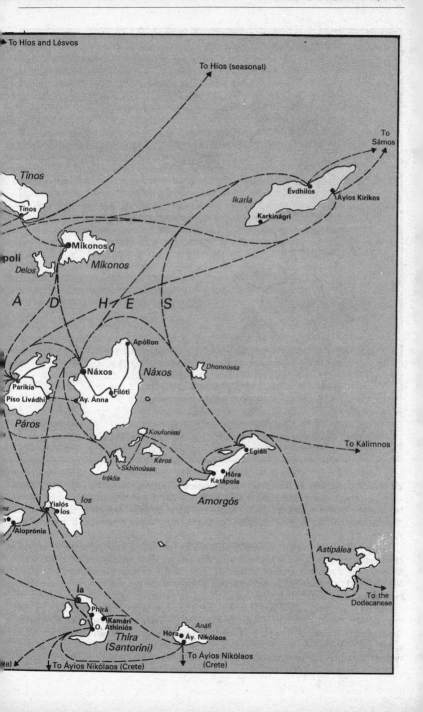

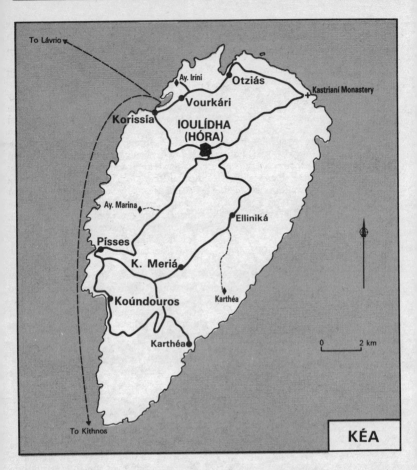

To Lávrio

Ay. Iríni   Otziás

Vourkári   Kastrianí Monastery

Korissía

IOULÍDHA
(HÓRA)

Ay. Marina

Elliniká

Písses

K. Meriá

Karthéa

Koúndouros

Karthéa

0   2 km

To Kithnos

KÉA

groves. As ancient Keos, the island was important, its strategic harbour supporting four cities, a pre-eminence which continued well into the nineteenth century when Síros became the main Greek port. Today tourists account for what sea traffic there is, with regular ferry connections with LÁVRIO on the mainland, only a two-hour bus ride from Athens.

The small northern port of **KORISSÍA** and its handful of hotels, rooms to let and tavernas, has fallen victim to uneven expansion and has little beauty to lose. If you want to stay, the *Pension Korissia* (☎0288/21 484; ③–④) is pricey but recommended. **VOURKÁRI**, a couple of kilometres north, is more attractive, the hangout of the well-heeled yachting set. You might want to stay overnight as there are some good (if expensive) tavernas, and, if you hunt around, a few rooms too. Across the bay, on the promontory, the Minoan site of **Ayía Iríni** has been under excavation since 1960, with the remains of a palace, temple and road unearthed in good condition. Another 3km along, **OTZIÁS** has an unofficial campsite with a small beach, but there's only one taverna here and you're exposed to the prevailing wind. It's better to follow the track beyond Otziás as far as Kéa's only functioning monastery, the eighteenth-century **Panayía Kastrianí** – an hour's walk. It's more remarkable for its fine setting on a high bluff than for any intrinsic interest, but from here you can easily and pleasantly walk on to the island capital, IOULÍDHA, in another two hours.

Fairly regular **buses** link Otziá and Vourkári with the port, and run directly from Korissía to **IOULÍDHA**, the ancient Ioulis and birthplace of the renowned early fifth-century BC poets Simonides and Bacchylides. With its numerous red-tiled roofs it's by no means a typical Cycladic village, but it is beautifully situated in an arc-shaped fold in the hills. The lower reaches stretch across a spur to the **Kástro**, a half-demolished Venetian fortress incorporating stones from an ancient temple of Apollo. Fifteen minutes northeast of town, on the path to Panayía Kastrianí, the road passes the **Lion of Kea**, a sixth-century BC sculpture carved out of the living rock. Six metres long and three high, it's an imposing beast, with crudely powerful haunches and a bizarre facial expression. There are steps right down to it, but the effect is most striking from a distance. Back in town, the **Archaeological Museum** (daily 9am–2pm; closed Tues) displays finds from the four ancient city-states of Kéa, though sadly, as so often, the best items were long ago spirited away to Athens. There's one very good small **hotel**, the *Filoxenia*, above the shoeshop (☎0288/22 057; ③), a fine place to stay if you can get a room. Otherwise there's the *Pension Ioulis* (☎0288/22 177; ③).

Southwest of Ioulídha, reached on a good path from town, the crumbling Hellenistic watchtower of **Ayía Marína** sprouts dramatically from the grounds of a small nine-teenth-century monastery. Beyond, towards the coast, sprawls the lovely agricultural valley of **PÍSSES**, fronted by an excellent and largely undeveloped beach, and home to the only official **campsite** on the island, plus rooms and tavernas too. **KOÚNDOUROS**, the next bay south, is less appealing, a burgeoning bungalow resort catering to Athenian weekenders. The road in from Ioulídha to here has been paved in recent years, and a bus service instituted as far at Písses.

The scant ruins of ancient Poiessa are close to Písses. However, the only remains of any real significance from Kéa's past are at **KARTHÉA**, tucked away on the opposite, southeastern edge of the island at Polis Bay, it's a good three hours' round-trip walk from the hamlets of KATO MERIÁ or ELLINIKÁ.

Kíthnos (Thermiá)

Though perhaps the dullest and most barren of the Cyclades, a short stay on Kíthnos is a good antidote to the exploitation likely to be encountered elsewhere. Few foreigners bother to visit and the island is oddly quiet, even in midsummer, while the inhabitants are overtly friendly – all factors that easily compensate for the dearth of specific diversions. You could use it as a first or last island stop: there are ferry connections once a week with Kéa, and more frequent services (in season) to and from Sérifos, Sífnos and Mílos.

You dock on the west coast at **MÉRIHAS**, a rather functional ferry and fishing port (with a small beach for camping), redeemed by some good tavernas and less likeable – but cheap – blocks of rooms to let. Frankly, though, unless you're arriving late, it's better to let the local **buses** whisk you immediately away to either of the island's two more attractive destinations, HÓRA or DHRIOPÍDHA.

HÓRA is 6km distant, set in the middle of the island; tumbling across an east–west ridge, it's an awkward blend of Kéa-style gabled roofs, Cycladic churches with dunce-cap cupolas, and concrete monsters. Accommadation is limited to rooms above the Koutoulias family shop, near the clock tower; eating is best at *To Kentron* or *Barba Stathis*, near the telephone office. Much of the year electricity is supplied by two wind-mills erected by a German company on the outskirts of the village.

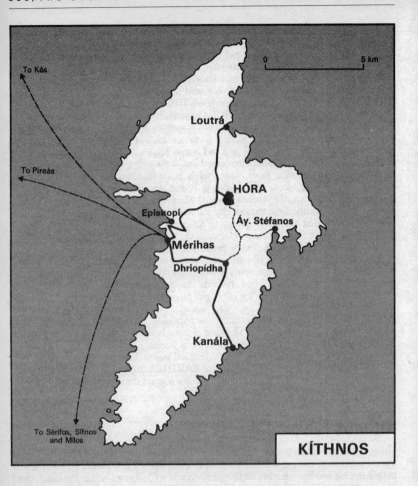

KÍTHNOS

You're handily placed in Hóra to tackle the most interesting thing to do on Kíthnos: the beautiful walk south to **DHRIOPÍDHA**. It takes about an hour, following the obvious old cobbled way that leaves Hóra (though plans are afoot to bulldoze a road over the path). Towards the end the path drops dramatically into Dhriopídha, whose pleasing tiled roofs seem more appropriate to Spain or Tuscany than Greece. It's a surprisingly large place, once the island's capital, and built around a famous cave (the Katafíki) at the head of a valley alive with springs. There are a couple of small tavernas but nowhere to stay. For this you may want to head 6km beyond, to **KANÁLA**, basically some twenty houses and a church on a sea-washed headland, with tavernas and rooms in season.

From Kanála, a succession of small sandy coves extends up the east coast as far as **Áyios Stéfanos**, a chapel-crowned islet tied by causeway to the body of the island. Apart from this stretch, the only other presentable beach on the island is at **EPISKOPÍ**, one bay north of Mérihas.

By way of contrast, the much-vaunted resort of **LOUTRÁ** (3km north of Hóra and named after its thermal baths) is scruffy, its homely nineteenth-century spa closed and decaying beside the sterile modern facility. Once again, there are tavernas on the beach and a few rooms to let.

Sérifos

Sérifos has remained outside the mainstream of history and tourism. Little has happened here since Perseus returned with the Gorgon's head in time to save his mother from being ravished, according to legend. Most would-be visitors are deterred by the apparently barren, little-explored hilly interior, which, combined with the stark, rocky coastline makes the island appear uninhabited from the sea until you turn in to Livádhi. The island is recommended for serious walkers and backpackers, who can camp almost anywhere without hassle.

Modern Serifiotes love seclusion, and, on this island more than any other, you will find homesteads miles from anywhere, with only a goat track to their door. Everyone here seems to keep livestock, and to produce their own wines, and many also cultivate the wild narcissus for the export market. Few islanders speak much English, and they are slow to warm to outsiders.

Livádhi and the main beaches

Most visitors stay in the port, **LIVÁDHI**, set in a wide green bay and handy for the local beaches. It's not the most attractive place on Sérifos – and to stay here exclusively would be to miss some fine walks – but it is certainly the easiest place to find rooms (which elsewhere are very sparse). It is also the one place on the island geared for tourists in any way.

The locals don't bother to meet the boats, apart from the man from the nice but pricey *Hotel Albatros* (☎0281/51 148; ④), who sometimes drives his minibus to the quay to tout for customers. Otherwise you'll have to step lively off the boat to get a decent bed. Try

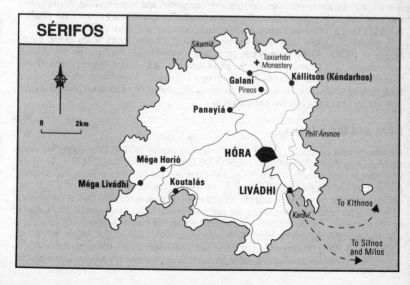

asking in a shop for a likely address or look for hand-painted signs on buildings. As a rule of thumb, the further you've walked, the less you will pay for your room; the rooms on the road to Hóra (turn left at the square) are often a better deal than those on the front. There's a nice block behind the Port Police, run by the Athanasios family, which overlooks a pretty garden (☎0281/51 366). Alternatively, try the friendly *Coral Hotel* just off the waterfront (☎0281/51 484; ③), or the rooms (☎0281/51 318 or 51 134, ③) behind the *Kyklades Hotel*. The cheapest place to stay is the unclassified *Galanos* (☎0281/51 277; ②) above the bakery.

Livádhi is a magnet for island-hopping yachts, whose inmates chug backwards and forwards in dinghies all day (and night). The seafront has a makeshift road running along its length, filled with traffic, restaurants, shops, and all the services you need. The meat market, fruit shop and supermarkets are spread out along the beach, plus there's a new pharmacy and **OTE** station at the foot of the quay. You can **rent a bike or car** at the petrol station, and there are three **boat-ticket agents**, though none is particularly helpful for information.

Eating out in Livádhi, the same rule applies as for accommodation. If you eat near the quay, you'll pay through the nose; walk up the beach, and meals get cheaper. There's a fish restaurant at the *Cavo D'Oro* hotel; *Benny's Taverna* has huge chicken *souvlákia*; the *Kyklades Hotel*'s restaurant is reasonably priced and friendly; the *Maistrali* is cheap and cheerful, *Stamatis* the cheapest in the resort, and the *Sklavanis* at the end of the beach serves good fresh food and has a view of the whole bay.

Nightlife is pretty low-key but better than you'd expect. One place you could try, with an indigestible mix of Greek pop music, heavy metal and disco, is the *Metallein*, although ordinary bars, especially closer to the water, are a better bet. *Vitamin C* and *Froggie's* are always packed, as is *Scorpio's*, a "rock bar" popular with Germans. The *Dolly Pub/Disco* is a half-built shack, while the new *Disco Paradise*, though well appointed, is somewhat inaccessible up a dry, stoney streambed.

Sadly, the **beach** in Livádhi is nothing to write home about. It's long, but dirty and weedy with lots of jellyfish in the water. Walk uphill from the burger bar, or over the southerly headland, to reach the neighbouring, far superior **ÓRMOS LIVADHÁKIA**. This long and golden, tree-fringed beach offers snorkelling and other watersports, a decent taverna, an unobtrusive, carpark-like **campsite**, and some nudism. If you prefer more seclusion, five minutes' stroll across a smaller headland brings you to the smaller **KARÁVI** beach, which is almost totally naturist, cleaner and more sheltered.

A similar 45-minute walk north of the port along a bumpy track leads to the sandy beach at **PSILÍ ÁMMOS**, a white-sand beach considered the best on the island. Accordingly, it's popular, its single good taverna and rooms heavily subscribed. Naturists are pointed towards the next beach beyond, larger and often deserted **ÁYIOS IOÁNNIS**. Both beaches are theoretically visited by *kaíki* from Livádhi, as are two nearby sea-caves, but don't count on it.

Hóra and the interior

An hourly **bus** connects Livádhi with the island capital HÓRA, 2km away, but only manages one daily trip over poor roads to MEGÁLO LIVÁDHI and GALANÍ. You may well want to walk though; it's a pleasant half-hour up a cobbled way to Hóra, visible from the port as you climb. Out of season (ie by the beginning of October) you'll have no choice, since the bus – and nearly everything else – ceases operations during the winter.

HÓRA, precariously sited above the harbour, is one of the most spectacular villages of the Cyclades. The best sights are to be found on the town's borders: tiny churches cling to the cliff edge, and there are breathtaking views across the valleys below. At odd intervals along its alleyways you'll find part of the old castle making up the wall of a house, or a marble statue leaning incongruously in one corner. It's a quiet, atmospheric place, with a couple of tavernas (*Stavros* is the best and has beds, too), the island's **post office** and one place with **rooms** to let (on the track to the cemetery), with more being built. In theory a path leads from the village to Psilí Ámmos, but in fact, once you pass the cemetery, the route degenerates into a maze of walled fields and open countryside.

North of Hóra, the island's high water table frequently breaks the surface to run in delightful rivulets swarming with turtles and frogs; reeds, orchards, and even the occasional palm tree take advantage of the unexpected moisture. This is especially in evidence at **KÁLLITSOS** (Kéndarhos), reached by an hour-plus path from Hóra – this starts in the upper square, following a scrawled signpost. A couple of kilometres beyond Kállitsos the sixteenth-century **monastery of Taxiarhón** has some good frescoes and Byzantine manuscripts stored in the library, but only one monk left in charge; he's often away in Athens. Your best bet is to get a local to phone ahead to find out if it's open.

Looping back towards Hóra, the fine villages of **GALANÍ** and **PANAYIÁ** (named after its tenth-century church) make convenient stops. The church comes alive on its feast day of Ksilopanayía (August 16) when traditionally the first couple to dance around the adjacent olive tree would be the first to marry that year, but unseemly brawls meant that the priest always goes first these days. On foot the circuit will take a full six hours, but there are tavernas and little shops in Kállitsos and Galaní, as well as remote beaches just to the north, such as **SIKAMIÁ**. Note also that the road coming north from Hóra is now paved as far as **PÍRGOS**, between Galaní and Panayiá, so a ride back in a taxi may be more possible than it was.

A little way past Panayiá, you reach a junction in the road. Take a left to return to Hóra, or carry straight on to MEGÁLO HORIÓ – the site of ancient Sérifos, with little else to recommend it. **MEGÁLO LIVÁDHI**, further on, is a remote and quiet beach resort 8km west of Hóra, with a taverna and some rooms. Iron and copper ore were once exported from here, but cheaper African deposits sent the mines into decline and today most of the idle machinery rusts away, though some gravel-crushing still goes on. There's also a rough mulepath from here back to LIVÁDHI, but again, be careful, as it's still very easy to get lost. You can continue across the headland to **KOUTALÁS**, a small mining and fishing port – it's a pretty sweep of bay with a church-tipped rock, a taverna and a tiny beach.

Sífnos

Sífnos is a more immediately appealing island than its northern neighbours: prettier, more cultivated and with some fine architecture. This also means that it's much more popular, and impossibly crowded in August, when hordes of trendy Greeks, French and Italians make rooms nearly impossible to find – be quick to take any offered as you land. In keeping with this somewhat upmarket clientele, freelance camping is discouraged (there are two good organised sites) and nudism is tolerated only in isolated coves.

On the other hand, Sifnos's modest size – no bigger than Kíthnos or Sérifos – makes it eminently explorable, even for the lazy traveller. The bus service is excellent, most of the roads quite decent and there's a network of walled pathways that are fairly easy to follow. Besides pottery (a traditional skill), Sifniote cooking, too, is noted: the island is nationally celebrated for its chefs, and fresh dill flavours everything. Try *stamnás*, a clay-pot speciality with meat, cheese and potatoes, and *revíthia* (garbanzo soup). However, like so many islands, Sífnos is short of both water and fresh produce; it's worth bringing a bag of fruit from Athens.

Ferry connections could be better. The main lines head south, via Mílos and Kímolos, with rare extensions to Thíra and Crete, or north, via Sérifos and Kíthnos to Pireás. The only links with the central Cyclades are provided by the unreliable small

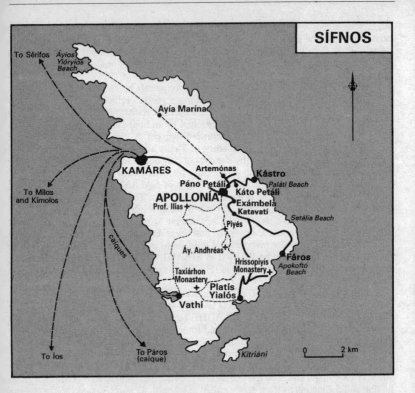

ferry *Margarita*, which sails to Páros most days but is not for the seasick-prone, and the *Páros Express*, which has, in the past, appeared on Tuesday night (at Sérifos too) to deposit you on Síros at a rather uncivilised hour.

Kamáres and the Hóra

KAMÁRES, the port, is tucked away at the base of high bare cliffs in the west which enclose a beach. It's an expensive, somewhat tacky resort, the seafront crammed with bars, travel agencies, gelaterias and fast-food places. You can store luggage at the semi-official **tourist office** while hunting for a room; they also change money and can advise on bed availability throughout the island. Kamáres is an expensive place (in summer accommodation prices double), and outside peak season it is well worth haggling. Try the **rooms** above the *Katzoulakis Tourist Agency* near the quay, as well as the reasonable *Stavros* (☎0284/31 641; ③), just beyond the church. There is also the *Boulis*, above the big waterfront restaurant, not to be confused with a good but expensive namesake across the bay. If desperate, you might try the unofficial **youth hostel** – *Vangelis* – which is further inland. Otherwise, there's a long beach with public showers (small fee), a friendly, well-designed organised **campsite** and more rooms to let right at the end of the sands; these are the last to fill, perhaps because of noise from the adjacent taverna and disco. The sea is, unfortunately, quite polluted and freelance camping is forbidden.

Kamáres is the only place on Sífnos with really lively **nightlife**. Try the *Dolphin Bar* or the *Collage Bar* for your sunset cocktail, **eat** at the *Avra* or the atmospheric *Kapetan*

Andreas and move on to the *Mobilize Dancing Club* or the *Cafe Folie*. On a cultural note, the pottery workshop is worth a look, as is the church of **Áyios Sóstis** which has beautiful frescoes, and the monastery of **Panayía Tóso Neró** ("The Virgin of So Much Water"), built inland to the south by a gushing spring.

An excitingly steep twenty-minute bus ride (hourly service until late at night) takes you up to **APOLLONÍA**, the centre of the *hóra*, an amalgam of three hilltop villages which have merged over the years into one continuous community. Scenic in parts, with white buildings, flowered balconies, belfries, pretty squares, and lovely views, heavy traffic can be a problem, but rooms are plentiful. The island **bank**, **post office OTE** and tourist police are all grouped around the central plaza, but **rooms**, though plentiful, are even more likely to be full than at Kamáres. If you have no luck, ask around at private houses in the outlying districts of Katavatí or Artemónas, respectively 500m north and south of the central *platía,*

On the platía itself, the **Folk Museum** (daily 10am–1pm & 6–9pm; 100dr) is well worth a visit. Most of the exhibits celebrate a certain Kyria Tselemende, who wrote a famous local recipe book (fragments of which are kept here), and there's also an interesting collection of textiles, laces, artwork, costumes and weaponry. A network of stepped marble footways and the main pedestrian street takes off from the square. Odhós Styliánou Prókou has decorated flagstones and is lined with shops, churches and restaurants. The garish, cakebox-cathedral of **Áyios Spíridhon** is here, while the eighteenth-century church of **Panayía Ouranoforía** stands in the highest quarter of town, incorporating fragments of a seventh-century BC temple of Apollo and a relief of Saint George over the door. **Áyios Athanásios**, next to Platía Kleánthi Triandafílou, has frescoes and a wooden *témblon*.

ARTEMÓNAS is worth a morning's look around for the churches and elegant Venetian-era houses alone. **Panayía Gourniá** (key next door) has vivid frescoes; the clustered-dome church of **Kohí** was built over an ancient temple of Artemis; and the seventeenth-century **Áyios Yióryios** contains fine icons. It's also possible to trek half a day beyond across the barren hills to the northwest tip of the island and the exposed **Áyios Yióryios** beach, but this is barely worth the effort except on a calm day.

Hóra in general is becoming commercialised but there are still some good 'genuine' **tavernas**, such as *O Manganas* in Artemónas. The restaurants *Krevatina* and *Sofia* are acceptable, or pay a little extra at the recommended *Cyprus*, with its flower-decked garden and portions of *stamnás* and *stifádho*. **Nightlife**, in contrast to that at Kamáres, is either very genteel or deadly dull depending on your style. The mostly thirtysomething crowd, having dined early by Greek island standards, lingers over its *oúzo* until late. The *Argo* music bar plays lots of Seventies music and is very popular. Finally try also the *Andromeda* club, which bills itself as "more than a bar".

The east coast

Most of Sífnos's coastal settlements are along the less precipitous eastern shore, within a modest distance of Hóra and its surrounding cultivated plateau.

An alternative base with rooms (though there aren't many), **KÁSTRO** is a 3km, traffic-plagued walk (or regular bus ride) below Apollonía on the east coast. Built on a rocky outcrop with an almost sheer drop to the sea on three sides, the ancient capital of the island retains much of its medieval character. Parts of its boundary walls survive, along with a full complement of sinuous, narrow streets graced by balconied, two-storey houses and some fine sixteenth- and seventeenth-century churches with ornamental floors. Venetian coats-of-arms and ancient wall-fragments can still be seen on some of the older dwellings, and there are remains of the ancient acropolis (including a ram's head sarcophagus), as well as a small, free **archaeological museum** (Tues–Sun 9am–3pm) in the higher part of town.

Besides the handful of rooms, there are at least two decent tavernas – *Tzifakis* and *Mengengela* – but no beach right in town; you have to walk to the nearby, pebbly coves of **Serália** and **Paláti**. You can also hike, from the windmills on the approach road, to either the monastery of **Hrisostómou**, or along a track opposite to the cliff face that overlooks the church of the **Eptá Martíres** ("Seven Martyrs"); nudists sun themselves and snorkel on and around the flat rocks below.

At the southern end of the island, around 10km from Apollonía, lies the resort of **PLATÍS YIALÓS**, to which there are (roughly) hourly buses from the capital. Despite claims to be the longest beach in the Cyclades, it can get very crowded at the end near the watersport facilities rental. There are also several tavernas, a pottery workshop, and (expensive) rooms available, but for many the ugly *Xenia* hotel at the southern end of the beach, plus the troublesome winds, rule the place out. The *Pension Angelaki* (✆0284/31 688; ③) near the bus stop is nice, and reasonably priced (for Platís Yialós); alternatively, try the island's oldest official **campsite**, not well signed, near the bus stop. A pleasant walk uphill from Platís Yialós brings you to the convent of **Panayía tou Vounoú**, though it's easy to get lost on the way without the locally sold map. If she's about, the caretaker will let you in.

Less crowded beaches are to be found just to the northeast of Platís Yialós (though unfortunately not directly accessible along the coast). **FÁROS**, with regular bus links to Appollonía, makes an excellent fallback base if you come up empty elsewhere. A small and friendly resort, it has some of the cheapest **accommodation** on the island (✆0284/31 822 & 31 989; both ②) and several early-evening **tavernas**, best of which is *To Kima*. The beaches, though, are not up this standard; the town strand itself is muddy, shadeless and crowded, and the one to the left (northeast) past the headland not much better. Head off in the opposite direction, however, through the older part of the village, and things improve at a longer beach favoured by naturists and snorkellers.

Continuing from there, a fifteen-minute cliffside path leads to **Apokoftó**, with golden sands, a good taverna (*Vasili's*), and, up an access road, the *Pension Flora* (✆0284/31 778; ③) with superb views. Very near Apokoftó, marooned on a rocky sea-washed spit and featuring on every EOT poster of the island, is the disestablished seventeenth-century **Hrissopiyís monastery**, whose cells are let out in summer (✆0284/31 255; ②) – book in advance. According to legend, the cleft in the rock appeared when two village girls fleeing to the spit, menaced by pirates, prayed to the Virgin to defend their virtue.

The interior and Vathí

Apollonía is a good base from which to start your explorations of remoter Sífnos. You can hire **bikes** at *Moto Apollo*, beside the BP station on the road to Fáros, or from *Svikiadhis*, but many are in deplorable condition; besides the best exploration of Sífnos is done on foot.

A short walk out of the village of EXÁMBELA you'll find the active monastery of **Vrísis**, dating from 1612 and home to a good collection of religious artefacts and manuscripts.

Taking the path out from Katavatí (the district south of Apollonía) you'll pass, a few minutes along, the beautiful empty **monastery of Piyés** and (half an hour later) **Áyios Andhréas** – this last offering tremendous views over the islands of Síros, Páros, Íos, Folégandhros and Síkinos. Just below the church is an enormous Bronze-Age archaeological site.

Even better is the walk to **VATHÍ**, around two to three hours from Katavatí and reached by bearing right at a white house ninety minutes past Áyios Andhréas; beyond this junction you pass another small, abandoned Sifniote monastery, **Taxiárhon**, where you can stay in season (✆0284/31 060 or 31 891; ②). However, as at Hrissopiyís, they're usually booked months ahead so pray for a cancellation.

Vathí itself, a fishing and pottery village on the shore of a stunning funnel-shaped bay, is the most attractive base on the island. There are **rooms** to let – though rarely enough, so freelance camping is tolerated – and several summer tavernas. If you've just arrived on the island you could come here directly by well-publicised small boat from Kamáres (three times daily in season – mid-morning, noon & early evening).

From Vathí, an alternative hiking route back to Apollonía winds up towards the ridge of the **Profítis Ilías monastery**, a detour offering even greater views than those from Áyios Andhréas. Or another path (partly duplicating the walk in from Áyios Andhréas) leads directly back to Platís Yialós, from where there are buses until quite late (11pm in season) to Apollonía and on to Kamáres.

Mílos and Kímolos

Mílos has always derived prosperity from its strange geology. Minoan settlers were attracted by obsidian, and other products of its volcanic soil made the island important in the ancient world. Today the quarrying of barite, perlite and porcelain brings in a steady revenue, but it has left deep scars on the landscape. The rocks, however, can also be beautiful – on the left of the bay as the boat enters, two outcrops known as the *Arkoúdhes* ("Bears") face up like sumo wrestlers. Off the north coast, and accessible only by boat, the *Glaroníssia* ("Seagull Isles") are shaped like massed organ pipes, and there are more weird formations on the south coast at Kleftikó. Inland, too, you frequently come across strange, volcanic outcrops, and steaming hot springs.

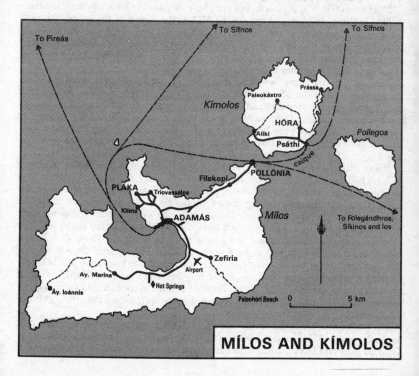

MÍLOS AND KÍMOLOS

ADAMÁS, the cramped little port, was founded by Cretan refugees. Despite sitting on one of the Mediterranean's best natural harbours (created by a volcanic cataclysm similar to, but earlier than, Thira's), it's not a spectacularly inviting place, though just to the right of the quay (facing inland) you can sit in a shady square and watch the island go by. There's no shortage of places to **sleep and eat** in the port, but beds are expensive, and accommodation elsewhere is sparse. Two standard hotel choices, nothing special, are the *Georgantas* (☎0287/41 636; ④), in the square to the left of the quay, and the *Semiramis* (☎0287/41 617; ③), further up and left off the road to Pláka. There are more rooms to let along the harbourfront and in the streets behind, while campers should be all right on the tamarisk-lined sandy beach east of the port (there is no organised site). Back on the quayside, the **tourist office** has information about boat trips, sells maps of the island, and hires out mopeds. Otherwise, Adamás is the hub of the island's bus service; services run hourly to PLÁKA, less regularly to Pollónia, and twice daily to Paleohóri via Zefiría. Incidentally, if you arrive by plane (twice daily from Athens), the **airport** is 5km south of the port, close to Zefiría.

ZEFIRÍA hides among olive groves below the bare hills at the far end of Mílos Bay, and used to be the capital until an eighteenth-century epidemic drove out the population. Much of the old town is still deserted, though some life has returned, especially to the taverna opposite the church. South of here the road deteriorates as it leads past LOUTRÁ PROVÁTA (some good hot springs in a more-or-less natural state), and KÍPOS, with a large Byzantine church. It peters out completely at the remote coarse-sand beach of **PALEOHÓRI**; with only two expensive tavernas and some rooms to let, it's more for day-trippers than for campers.

Most tourists stay in the north, but even here they tend to stick together, and there is little problem dodging the crowds. **PLÁKA** is the capital of the island, the most pleasant of a horseshoe of villages, with various rooms available. A stairway above the town leads up to the old Venetian **Kástro**, its roofs peculiarly sloped to channel precious rainwater into cisterns. This was where the ancient Melians made their last stand against the Athenians before being massacred in 416 BC.

Back in town there are two small museums. An **archaeological** collection (daily except Mon 8.30am–3pm, Sun 9.30am–2.30pm; 200dr) contains Neolithic pottery from the Filakopí site (see opposite) and – more entertainingly – a plaster cast of the world's most famous statue, the *Venus de Milo*, found on the island in 1820 and appropriated by the French (her arms were knocked off in the melée surrounding her abduction). More significantly, the **Folklore Museum** (Tues–Sat 10am–1pm and 6pm–8pm, Sun 10am–1pm; 100dr) displays a whole range of items from Mílotian life.

Below Pláka the road passes the entrance to early Christian **catacombs**, where up to 5000 bodies were buried in tomb-lined corridors. Sadly, the whole ensemble is in imminent danger of collapse and seems permanently closed to visitors. However, the ruins of **ancient Mílos**, extending down from the *kástro* almost to the sea, make the detour worthwhile. There are huge Dorian walls, the usual column fragments lying around and best of all, a well-preserved Roman **amphitheatre** facing out to sea. Two hundred metres from the theatre is a plaque marking where the *Venus de Milo* was found, and promptly delivered to the French consul for "safekeeping" from the Turks; this was the last the Greeks ever saw of the statue until the local copy was belatedly forwarded from the Louvre in Paris. At the very bottom of the vale, **KLÍMA** is one of the best fishing hamlets on the island. There's no beach to speak of, but there is excellent seafood and a good place to both eat and stay, the aptly named *Panorama* (☎0287/ 21 623; ③).

For proper beaches in the north, visit **PLATHIÉNA**, reached by leaving Pláka on a footpath towards ARETÍ and FOURKOVOÚNI; the junction for Plathiéna is signposted. Or head for **POLLÓNIA**, 10km northeast of Adamás, where three or four reasonable fish *tavernas* overlook a working fishing port and a small beach. There are a limited number of **rooms** here, usually oversubscribed since camping on the unprotected shore can be a windy proposition. You might want to head this way since the little island of KÍMOLOS (see below), easily visible, is accessible by a daily (usually early morning) *kaíki* from Pollónia; the boat can be hard to find, so ask at the pier. Just inland at **FILAKOPÍ** the remains of three prehistoric cities lie at the edge of a small cliff. The site was important archaeologically, but it hasn't been maintained and is difficult to interpret.

Kímolos

Of the three islets off the coast of Mílos, Andímilos is home to a rare species of chamois and Políegos has more ordinary goats, but only Kímolos has any human habitation. Like Mílos, it has profitable rocks and used to export chalk (in Greek, *kímolos*) until its supply was exhausted. Today it's a source of fuller's earth, and the fine dust of this stone is a familiar sight on the island. Rugged and barren in the interior, there is some green land on the southeast coast, and this is where the small population is concentrated.

Whether you arrive by ferry, or by *kaíki* from Pollónia, you'll dock at the hamlet of **PSÁTHI**, where there's a good taverna. Around the bay there are a few old windmills and the dazzlingly white **HÓRA** perches on the ridge above them, fifteen minutes' walk up. You'll find most of the island's accommodation here and indeed it seems a surprisingly large town; a maze of tortuous lanes makes it difficult at first to get your bearings. There are only a few cafés and tavernas, a handful of **rooms**, a **post office** – and virtually no tourists, even in August.

Another taverna and a few rooms-to-let can be found at the village of **ALIKÍ** on the southwest coast. This is flanked by a long if rather coarse stretch of sand here, and beyond the headland a smaller, more secluded beach which is better for camping.

More rewarding is the road leading northeast from Hóra to a beach at the village of **KLÍMA,** and beyond that to the radioactive springs at **PRÁSSA**, 7km away. The route takes in impressive views across the straits to Políegos and there are several shady peaceful beaches where you could camp out. Innumerable goat tracks invite exploration of the rest of the island; towards the west coast is **PALEOKÁSTRO**, where the ruins of an imposing Venetian *kástro* ring the church of **Hristós**, the oldest on the island.

Ándhros

Ándhros, the second largest and northernmost of the Cyclades, promises much on a map but is apt to disappoint up close. Thinly populated but prosperous, its fertile, well-watered valleys have attracted scores of Athenian holiday villas whose red-tiled roofs and white walls stand out among the greenery. These have robbed many of the villages of life and atmosphere, turning them into scattered settlements with no nucleus, and created a weekender mentality manifest in noisy Friday and Sunday evening traffic jams at the ferry dock. The island neither needs, nor welcomes, independent travellers, and it can be almost impossible to get a bed in between the block-bookings. On the positive side, the permanent population is distinctly hospitable; traditionally working on ships, they are only too happy to practice their English on you.

Ferries connect the island with Rafína on the mainland, only an hour from Athens on the bus, and you can loop back onto the central Cycladic routes via Míkonos or Síros. The bus service is poor, and even though private traffic on the good road system can be heavy, you'll want to consider hiring a bike as soon as possible to tour the sights – or face doing a lot of walking.

Northern and western Ándhros

All ferries arrive at the main port, GÁVRIO, a nondescript place whose dirty, windswept beach is usually deserted. The sea in the enclosed harbour is so murky that even the wildfowl aren't interested. A converted dovecote houses a sporadically functioning **tourist office**, and the ferry **ticket agent** only opens half an hour before the boats arrive. There's also a part-time **bank**, and a **post office** on the waterfront.

To **stay** here, you'll find the cheapest rooms in a block behind the hatshop, while the *Hotel Aphrodite* (☎0282/71 209; ③) or the *Galaxy* (☎0282/71 228; ③) are clean and reasonable. *Camping Andros*, 2km down the road, advertises an improbable array of facilities for what looks like a simple field, though its café is supposed to be pretty good.

Hotel Aphrodite's **restaurant** serves good food; otherwise try *Three Star Here* (sic), *O Mourikis*, or *O Balmas*, near the port police. For **nightlife**, head for the *Idhroussa Bar*, on Áyios Pétros beach, or see if anybody's turned up at the *Disco Marabout*.

The road north begins behind the *Hotel Gavrion Beach*; after 4km of plain and rolling hills, Vassámia proves to be two sandy coves. On the exposed north coast proper, locals recommend **Zórko** beach (via KALLIVÁRI), if you can find it through a maze of inaccurate signposting. Better, probably, are two beaches named **Féllos**: one reached by veering away from a *Káto Féllo's* sign, and planted with holiday villas, the other hidden beyond the headland and popular with freelance campers. Beyond ÁNO FÉLLOS, the countryside is empty except for a few hamlets inhabited by the descendants of medieval Albanians who settled here and in southern Évvia several hundred years ago.

Most traffic heads 8km south down the coast to BATSÍ, the island's main package resort, with large hotels and discos above its fine natural harbour; *Avra*, ☎0282/41 216; ②) is about the only outfit not on the books of the mostly British package operators. The beautiful, if crowded, beach curves round the port, and the sea is cold, calm and clean (except near the taxi park). For **eating** out, try *O Takis* for reasonable fish. Except for the open-air **cinema**, **nightlife**, as typified by *Disco Blue Sky* or *Chaf*, is slick, expensive and aimed at the couples market. An **OTE** and a **bank** round out the list of facilities.

From Batsí you're within easy walking distance of some beautiful inland villages. At KÁTO KATÁKILOS, one hour inland, three **tavernas** host "Greek nights" organised in Bátsi; a rough track leads to ATÉNI, a hamlet in a lush, remote valley, unvisited by packaged donkey "safaris". A right-hand turning out of Katákilos heads up the mountain to ARNÍ, whose one taverna is often enshrouded in mist. Another rewarding trip is to a well-preserved, 20-metre-high **Classical tower** at AYÍOS PÉTROS, 5km from Gávrio or 9km coming from Batsí.

South of Batsí along the main road are KÁTO and ÁNO APRÓVATO: **Káto** has rooms, a café and a path to a quiet beach. Nearby is the largely unexplored archaeological site of **Paleópolis**.

Hóra and around

A minimal bus service links the west coast with HÓRA or ÁNDHROS town, an hour (35km) from Gávrio. The capital and the most attractive place on the island, this is set on a rocky spur cutting across a huge bay. Much of the town is paved in marble and schist, cut from the still-active local quarries; buildings around the bus station are grand nineteenth-century affairs, and the squares with their ornate wall fountains and gateways are equally elegant. The hill quarters are modern, while the small port acts as a yacht supply station.

The few **hotels** in town are a little expensive and generally filled with Greeks; try the *Aigli* (☎0282/22 303, ③), opposite the big church on the main walkway, or ask around for rooms. There's a seasonal **campsite**, and people also sleep on the sands of Parapórti (the southern) beach below, exposed and none too inviting. For **eating** out,

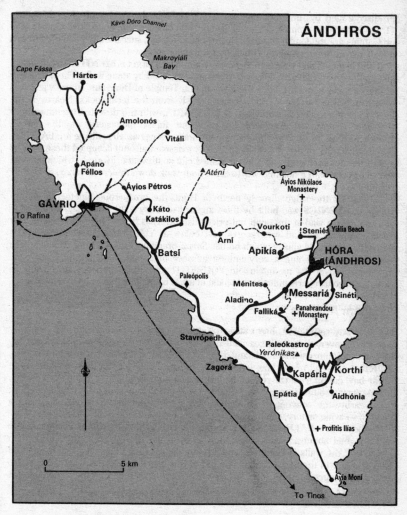

ÁNDHROS

Kávo Dóro Channel

Cape Fássa

Hártes

Makroyiáli Bay

Amolonós

Vitáli

Apáno Féllos

Atení

Áyios Pétros

Áyios Nikólaos Monastery

GÁVRIO

To Rafína

Káto Katákilos

Vourkoti

Steniés Yiália Beach

Arní

Batsí

Apikía

HÓRA (ÁNDHROS)

Paleópolis

Ménites

Messariá

Sinéti

Aladino

Falliká

Panahrandou Monastery

Stavrópedha

Paleókastro
Yerónikas

Zagorá

Kapária

Korthí

Epátia

Aidhónia

Profitis Ilías

0   5 km

Áyia Moní

To Tínos

you've a choice of four tavernas. **Nightlife**, as at a rash of bars plus *Disco Remezzo* and is strongly pitched at a Greek rather than foreign clientele. OTE, the post office and various shops are just off the seafront road.

From the square right at the end of town you pass through an archway and down to windswept **Platía Ríva**, its statue of the unknown sailor scanning the sea. Beyond him lies the thirteenth-century Venetian **Kástro**, precariously joined to the mainland by a narrow-arched bridge, damaged by German munitions in the last world war.

For some inexplicable reason there are three museums in town, two of them endowed by the local Goulandhris family. The **Modern Art Museum** (Wed–Sun 10am–2pm, also 6–8pm in summer; free) has a sculpture garden and a permanent collection including works by Picasso and Braque, as well as temporary exhibits. Don't be discouraged by the stark modern architecture of the **Archaeological Museum** (Tues–Sun 8.30am–3pm; 400dr), well laid out and labelled with instructive models. The prize items are the fourth-century "Hermes of Ándhros", successfully reclaimed from a warehouse in Athens, and the "Matron of Herculaneum".

If hiking inland and west from Ándhros your natural target is **MÉNITES**, a hill village just up the green valley choked with trees and straddled by stone walls. The monastery of the **Panayía** may have been the location of a Temple of Dionysus, where water was turned into wine; water still flows continuously from the local rocks. Nearby is the mostly abandoned medieval village of **MESSARIÁ**, with the deserted twelfth-century Byzantine church of **Taxiárhis** below. The finest monastery on the island, **Panahrándou**, is only an hour's (steep) walk away, via the village of FALLIKÁ. Reputedly tenth-century, it's still defended by massive walls but occupied these days by just three monks. It clings to an iron-stained cliff southwest of Hóra, to which you can return directly with a healthy two- to three-hour walk down the creek valley, guided by red dots.

Hidden by the ridge directly north of Hóra, the prosperous nineteenth-century village of **STENIÉS** was built by the vanguard of today's shipping magnates. Today you can drop a wad at the good but pricey fish tavernas here. There's a small pebbly beach, with a café and watersports, just below at YIÁLIA. Just beyond Steniés is **APIKÍA**, a tidy little village which bottles *Sariza*-brand mineral water for a living; there are a few tavernas and a very limited number of rooms. A delightful track once threaded up over the mountains, to VOURKOTÍ (one basic taverna) and beyond to Arní, but recent reports indicate that most of it has been ploughed under a new road.

Southern Ándhros

On your way south, you might stop at **Zagorá**, a fortified Geometric town, uniquely never built over, that was excavated in the early 1970s. Located on a desolate, flat-topped promontory with cliffs falling away on three sides, it's worth a visit for the view. **KORTHÍ**, the end of the line, is a friendly though nondescript village set on a large sandy bay, cut off from the rest of the island by a high ridge and so relatively unspoilt. It's pleasant enough to merit spending the night at *Pension Rainbow* (☎0282/61 344; ③). Nearby, the convent of Zoödhóhou Piyís, with illuminated manuscripts and a disused weaving factory, can be visited before noon.

To the north is **PALEÓKASTRO**, a tumbledown village with a ruined Venetian castle and a legend about an old woman who betrayed the stronghold to the Turks, then jumped off the walls in remorse, landing on a sparse rock that's now known as "Old Lady's Leap". In the opposite direction out of Korthí are **AIDHÓNIA** and **KAPÁRIA**, dotted with pigeon towers (*peristereónes*) that were introduced by the Venetians. It's these towers, and the *fráktes* or dry-stone walls, which aspire to the status of an art form on the island and are in the end the most compelling monuments on Ándhros.

Tínos

The character of Tínos is determined largely by the grandiose shrine of **Panayía Evangelístria**, erected on the spot where a miraculous icon with healing powers was found in 1822. A Tiniote nun, now canonised as Ayía Pelayía, was directed in a dream to unearth the relic just as the War of Independence was getting underway – a timely coincidence which served to underscore the age-old links between the Orthodox Church and Greek nationalism. Today, there are two major annual pilgrimages, on March 25 and August 15, when (around noon) the icon bearing the Virgin's image is carried in state down to the harbour over the prostrate forms of the lame and the ill.

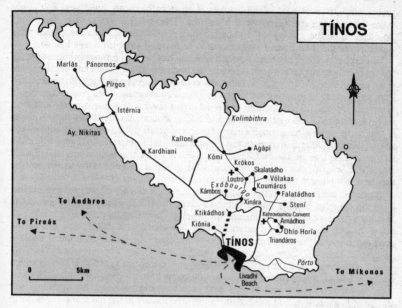

The rest of the island, too, smacks of religion and tradition in varying degrees. The Ottoman tenure here was the most fleeting in the Aegean. **Exóbourgo**, the craggy mount dominating southern Tínos and surrounded by most of the island's sixty-odd villages, is studded with the ruins of a Venetian citadel which defied the Turks until 1715, long after the rest of Greece had fallen. An enduring legacy of the long Latin rule is a persistent Catholic minority (almost half the population), and a sectarian rivalry that is responsible for the numerous graceful belfries scattered throughout the island, Orthodox and Catholic parishes vying to build the tallest. The sky is pierced, too, by distinctive pigeon towers, even more in evidence here than on Ándhros. Aside from all this, the inland village architecture is striking and there's a flourishing folk-art tradition which finds expression in the abundant local marble. If there are weak points to Tínos, they are that the religious atmosphere tends to dampen nightlife, and that beaches are few and far between. However, the islanders have remained open and hospitable to the relatively few foreigners who touch down here; and any mercenary inclinations seem to be satisfied by booming sales in religious paraphernalia to the Greek faithful.

Tínos Town and the southern beaches

Trafficking in devotional articles certainly dominates the busy port town of **TÍNOS**, with the neoclassical **church** (daily 8.30am–8.30pm) towering above at the top of Leofóros Megaloháris. Approached via a massive marble staircase, the famous icon inside is all but buried under a dazzling mass of gold and silver *támmata* (votive offerings); below is the crypt (where the icon was discovered) and a mausoleum for the sailors drowned when the Greek warship *Elli*, at anchor off Tínos during a pilgrimage, was torpedoed by an Italian submarine on August 15, 1940. Museums around the courtyard display more objects donated by worshippers, who inundate the island for the two big yearly festivals.

The shrine aside – and all the attendant stalls, shops, and bustle – the port is none too exciting (a beautiful neoclassical waterfront having been destroyed since the

1960s), with just scattered inland patches of nineteenth-century buildings. You might make time for the **Archaeological Museum** (Tues–Sat 9am–3pm, Sun 10am–2pm, closed Mon) on the way up to the church, which displays finds, including a fascinating sundial, from the local Roman Sanctuary of Poseidon and Amphitrite (see below).

You **arrive** at one of two ferry docks; a new one has been built roughly 600m north of the old one, but thus far it's used primarily in rough weather or when late boats need to make up lost time. When you're leaving, ask your ticket agent which jetty to head for. To have any chance of securing a reasonably priced **room** around the pilgrimage day of March 25 (August 15 is hopeless) you must arrive several days in advance – and even then, be prepared to do a lot of walking and asking around. At other times there's plenty of choice, though nothing is particularly cheap and you'll still be competing with out-of-season pilgrims, Athenian tourists and the sick and the disabled seeking a miracle cure. Of the hotels, the *Thalia* (☎0283/22 811; ③), south of the post office, and *Eleana* (☎0283/22 561; ③), east of the quay about 400m inland at the edge of the bazaar, are the two best low-budget options. The waterfront *Yannis Rooms* (☎0283/22 515; ②) is a conspicuous pension-type option, just in front of the *Thalia*, all the way around the bay from the old jetty. Slightly pricier options include the co-managed *Avra*, a neoclassical D-category relic on the waterfront, and the pension *Favie Souzane* just inland (☎0283/22 693 & 22 242; both ④). The *Vyzantio*, Zanáki Alavánou 26 (☎0283/22 454; ④), on the road out towards Pórto and the villages, is not especially memorable but it and the *Meltemi* at Filipóti 7, near Megaloháris (☎0283/22 881), are the only places open off-season. Otherwise, beat the crowds by staying at *Tínos Camping* (☎0283/22-502) which has tents and a few nice rooms to let; follow the signs from the port, a ten-minute walk.

In recent years many **restaurants and bars** have mushroomed, but anything near the water is expensive, and most of the better tavernas are in the old market area north of Megaloháris – to the left as you face uphill towards the shrine. Good choices include *Nine Muses*, a decent, small *ouzerí*/taverna, *Dionysus*, further along the same lane – in a similar vein but as much bar as restaurant – and, slightly pricier, *O Peristeronas*, again on the same street. Closer to the water and fish-market, *Palea Palada* has the virtue of being open for lunch all year; *O Kipos*, across Megaloháris near the Eleana hotel, is little better despite the atmosphere imparted by its wine barrels. The island, in fact, produces very good retsina, as well as dairy products and sausage from the roving sheep and cattle.

Buses leave from a small parking area in front of a cubbyhole-office on the quay, and are not terribly frequent. A moped is a better strategy for exploring, and *Vidalis*, Zanáki Alavánou 16, is a good rental agency.

Most, though not all, of the island's **beaches** are close to town. **KIÓNIA**, 3km northwest (hourly buses), is functional enough but marred by a luxury holiday complex, though there is a campsite here. More importantly, it's the site of the **Sanctuary of Poseidon and Amphitrite**, discovered in 1902, the excavations yielding principally columns (*kiónia* in Greek), but also a temple, baths, a fountain, and hostels for the ancient pilgrims.

LIVÁDHI, though conveniently close (2km) to the port, is rocky and relatively exposed. **PÓRTO**, 8km east, boasts two good beaches to either side of **Áyios Sostís** headland, with another campsite nearby (and four buses daily), but bring food – development here consists of apartments, villas and rooms, and the nearest tavernas are quite a way back towards town.

Northern Tínos

A good beginning to a foray into the interior is the stone stairway, the continuation of Odhós Ayíou Nikoláou, passing behind and the left of Evangelistría. This climbs for an hour and a half through appealing countryside to **KTIKÁDHOS**, a fine village, now nearly half foreign-owned, with a good sea-view taverna – *I Dhrosia* – that's the focus of coach tours in summer. You can either flag an onward bus up on the main road or stay with the trail until Xinára (see "Around Exóbourgo" below).

Heading northwest from the junction flanked by Ktikádhos, Tripótamos and Ksinára, there's little to stop for – except the fine dovecotes around **KÁMBOS** – until you reach Kardhianí, with a small sandy bay below. **KARDHIANÍ** itself is the most strikingly set and intrinsically beautiful village on the island, with its views across to Síros from amidst a dense oasis. It has recently been discovered by wealthy Athenians and expatriates, and can offer the exotic *To Perivoli* taverna, co-managed by a woman from Martinique. **ISTÉRNIA**, just a little beyond, is not nearly so appealing but it does have a pension at the top of the village and a few cafés, perched above the turning for **Órmos Isterníon**, a comparatively small but overdeveloped beach.

Four daily buses finish up at **PÍRGOS**, a few kilometres further north and smack in the middle of Tínos' marble-quarrying district. A beautiful village, its local artisans are renowned throughout Greece for their skill in producing marble ornamentation; ornate fanlights and bas-relief plaques adorn houses throughout the island but particularly here. With a School of Fine Arts and an attractive shady *platía*, Pírgos is popular in summer, but you should be able to find a **room** easily enough. There are two **tavernas**, *Vinia* by far the more elegant.

The marble products were once exported from **PÁNORMOS** (ÓRMOS) harbour, 4km northeast. There's a tiny beach, more rooms, a taverna and a campsite, though little to keep you there long; its relative overdevelopment is hard to comprehend considering that Kardhianí is both more sheltered and sandier.

Around Exóbourgo

The ring of villages **around Exóbourgo** mountain is the other focus of interest on Tínos. The fortified pinnacle itself, 570m (1800ft) above sea level, with ancient foundations as well as the ruins of three Venetian churches and a fountain, is reached most quickly by steep steps from **XINÁRA** (near the island's major road divide) the seat of the Roman Catholic bishop. Most villages in north central Tínos tend to have mixed populations, but Ksinara and its immediate neighbours are purely Catholic. They also tend to have a more sheltered position on this windy island, with better farmland nearby – the Venetians' way of rewarding converts and their descendants. Yet **TRIPÓTAMOS**, just south of Xinára, is a completely Orthodox village with possibly the finest architecture in the centre of the island – and accordingly bought up and restored by outsiders in the space of a few recent years.

At **LOUTRÓ**, the next community north of Xinára, there's an Ursuline convent and carpet-making school to visit (leave the bus at the turning for SKALÁDHO). From KRÓKOS it's a forty-minute walk to **VÓLAKAS**, one of the highest and most remote villages on the island, a windswept oasis amidst bony rocks. Here, a half-dozen elderly Catholic basketweavers fashion some of the best examples of that craft in Greece. If the workshops are not open, you can have a drink and buy (at fair prices) baskets in the ground-floor café run by a German-Greek couple.

At KÓMI, 5km beyond Krókos, you can take a detour for **KOLIMBÍTHRES**, a magnificent double beach: one wild, huge and windswept, the other sheltered and with a taverna and rooms. There's no camping allowed, even if the mosquitoes from the bog would let you sleep. Any bus marked "Kalloni" will pass through Kómi.

From either Skaládho or Vólakas you can traipse on foot to KOÚMAROS, where another long stairway leads up to Exóbourgo, or skirt the pinnacle towards STENÍ and FALATÁDHOS, white speckles against the fertile plain of Livadhéri. From Stení you can catch the bus back to the harbour (seven daily). On the way down, try and stop off at one of the beautiful settlements just below the important twelfth-century **convent of**

Kehrovouníou, where Ayía Pelayía dreamed of the icon, and the nuns still float through lavender-tinted corridors and under Lilliputian arches. In particular, **DHÍO HORIÁ** has a fine main square where cave-fountains burble; **TRIANDÁROS**, despite being virtually bought up by Germans, has a good, reasonable taverna in *I Levka*.

This is hardly an exhaustive list of Tíniote villages; armed with a map and good walking shoes for tackling the many old trails which still exist, you could spend days within sight of Exóbourgo and never pass through the same hamlets twice. Take warm clothing too, especially if you're on a moped, since the forbidding mountains behind Vólakas and the Livadhéri plain keep things noticeably cool almost year-round.

Míkonos (Mykonos)

Originally visited only as a stop on the way to ancient Delos, Míkonos has become easily the most popular (and the most expensive) of the Cyclades. Boosted by direct air links with Britain and domestic flights from Athens, an incredible 800,000 tourists are reputed to pass through in a good year, producing some spectacular overcrowding in high summer on Míkonos's 75 square kilometres. But if you don't mind the crowds – or you come out of season, a much more attractive proposition – the prosperous capital is still one of the most beautiful of all island towns, its immaculately whitewashed houses concealing hundreds of little churches, shrines and chapels.

The sophisticated nightlife is pretty hectic, amply stimulated by Míkonos' former reputation as *the* gay resort of the Mediterranean – a title lost in recent years to places like Ibiza and Sitges in Spain. Whatever, the locals take this comparatively exotic clientele in their stride, though considerable outrage was provoked a few years ago when Petros the Pelican, the island's official mascot, died after a depraved tourist involved him in an unnatural act. Unspoilt it isn't, but the island does offer excellent, if crowded (and mainly nude) beaches, picturesque windmills, and a rolling brown interior with the sea never very far away. An unheralded Mikonian quirk is the legality of scuba diving, a rarity in Greece, and dive centres have sprung up on virtually every frequented beach.

Míkonos Town

Don't let the crowds put you off exploring **MÍKONOS** town, the archetypal postcard image of the Cyclades. Its sugarcube buildings are stacked around a cluster of seafront fishermen's dwellings with every nook and cranny scrubbed and shown off. Most people head out to the beaches during the day, so early morning or late afternoon are the best times to wander the maze of narrow streets. The labyrinthine design was intended to confuse the pirates who plagued Míkonos in the eighteenth and early nineteenth centuries, and it remains effective – everyone gets lost.

You don't need any maps or hints to scratch around the convoluted streets and alleys of town; getting lost is half the fun. There are, however, a few places worth seeking out if you require more direction to your strolling. Coming from the ferry quay, you'll pass the **Archaeological Museum** (daily except Mon 9am–3pm, Sun 9.30am–2.30pm; 400dr) on your way into town, home to some good Delos pottery – and a superb *souvláki* bar next door. Alternatively, behind the two banks there's the **Library**, with Hellenistic coins and late medieval seals, or, at the base of the Delos jetty, the **Folklore Museum** (Mon–Sat 4–8pm, Sun 5–8pm), housed in an eighteenth-century mansion and cramming in a larger than usual collection of bric-a-brac, including a vast four-poster bed. The museum shares the same promontory as the old Venetian *kástro*, the entrance to which is marked by Míkonos's oldest and best-known church, **Paraportianí**. It's a fascinating hodge-podge, four chapels amalgamated into one with little symmetry. The shore leads around to the area known as "Little Venice" because of its high, arcaded Venetian houses built

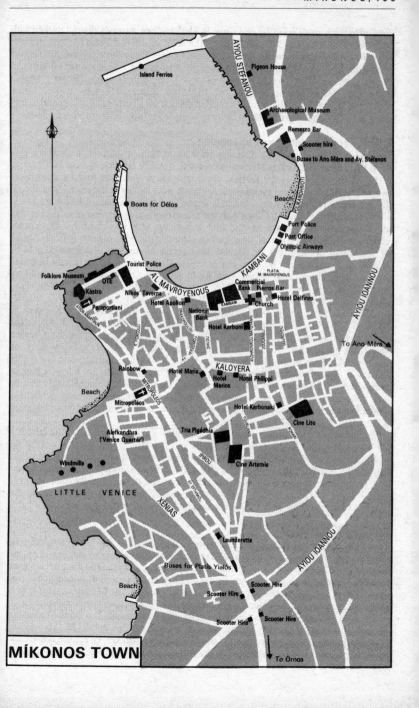

MÍKONOS TOWN

right up to the water's edge. Its real name is **Alefkándhra**, a trendy district packed with art galleries, chic bars and discos. Back off the seafront, behind Platía Alefkándhra, are Míkonos's two **cathedrals**: Roman Catholic and Greek Orthodox. Beyond, the famous **windmills** look over the area, disappointingly shabby but a location for all kinds of photos. Instead of retracing your steps along the water's edge, follow Énoplon Dhinaméon (left off Mitropóleos) to **Tría Pigádhia** fountain. The name means "Three Wells" and legend has it that should a maiden drink from all three she was bound to find a husband, though these days she'd be more likely to end up with a waterborne disease.

Arrival, accommodation and orientation

Arriving is relatively painless. The **airport** is about 3km out of town, a short taxi ride away; there is no longer any shuttle bus service. If you're arriving by boat you'll arrive at the northern jetty, where **ferries** dock, and where you'll be met by a horde of owners hustling hotels and **rooms** which – if you want to stay in the town – you should attempt to procure immediately. Space is limited and rates are high (as they are everywhere on Míkonos); but bus links with the main resorts is good, and most people stay out of town anyway, so you should find something. One establishment that comes recommended is *Villa Giovani*, near the bus station at the edge of town (☎0289/22 485; ④). If you balk at the prices, be warned that a private room here is at least likely to be cheaper than staying in a hotel on any of the nearby beaches. As for **hotels in town**, none are very cheap, with prices doubling in summer. Out of season, you could try *Hotel Delfines* on Mavroyéni (☎0289/22 292; ③–④), *Hotel Karbonis* at Andhroníkou Matoyiánni 53 (☎0289/23 127; ③), *Hotel Apollon* on Mavroyénous (☎0289/22 223; ③–④), *Hotel Maria* at Kaloyéra 18 (☎0289/22 317; ③–④), *Hotel Philippi* at Kaloyéra 32 (☎0289/22 294; ③), *Hotel Karbonaki* at Panahrándou 21 (☎0289/23 127, ③–④), or the *Galini* at Lákka (☎0289/22 626, ③); most are shown on our map. If for some reason you're not approached on arrival, it's worth asking at *O Megas* grocery store on Andhroníkou Matoyiánni – they tend to know who has rooms available. As a last resort, the *Apollo 2001* disco may rent out roof space. Otherwise there are a few organised **campsites** behind various beaches (see below), and, despite the occasional raid, the local police usually allow you to sleep out anywhere except on the beach in Míkonos town itself; the only problem will be persuading a bar or taverna to keep your baggage, as there's no official left-luggage office.

The harbour curves around past the dull, central Polikandhrióti beach; behind it is the **bus station** for Toúrlos, Áyios Stéfanos and Áno Méra. Just beyond, next to the post office, is the *Olympic Airways* office. Continue around the seafront to the southern jetty for the **tourist police** (☎0289/22 482) and *kaíkia* **to Delos**. A second **bus terminus**, for beaches to the south, is right at the other end of the town, beyond the windmills – signposted all over town, and shown on our map. Buses to all the most popular beaches and resorts run very frequently, and until very late in the evening.

Eating and nightlife

Even **light meals** and **snacks** are expensive in Míkonos, but there are several bakeries – the best is *Andhrea's*, just off Platía Mavroyénous – and plenty of supermarkets and takeaways in the backstreets. For example, *Dynasty* on Kaloyéra is a Chinese takeaway, **Rendez-Vouz** serves big pizzas, and **Spilia** on Énoplon Dinaméon does decent burgers, plus there's a *Hard Rock Café*. For **late night** snacks, try *Margarita's* on Flórou Zouganéli, or after 3am head for the port, where *The Yacht Club* is open until sunrise.

The area around Kaloyéra is a promising place for a **full meal**. The *Edem Garden* (top of Kaloyéra) is a popular gay restaurant with an adventurous menu, *El Greco* at Tría Pigádhia is expensive but romantic, and *The Sesame Kitchen* is almost reasonable. Alefkándhra can offer *La Cathedral*, by the two cathedrals on the *platía*, the pricey but well-sited *Pelican*, behind the cathedrals on the water, and *Spiro's* for good fish on the seafront. There's something for most tastes in the Lákka (bus station) area: a variety of salads at *Orpheas*, French cuisine at *Andromeda*, Italian at *Dolce Vita*. Just behind the Town Hall is *Nikos' Taverna* – crowded, reasonable and recommended – and 1km north you can dine by a floodlit pool overlooking the cruise ships at the luxury *Hotel Cavo Tagoo*.

Nightlife in town is every bit as good as it's cracked up to be – and every bit as pricey. There is little for those on a tight budget, so treat yourself for an evening if you can. It's impossible to list every current hot-spot, but you might check one or two of the following. *Remezzo* (near the OTE) is one of the oldest bars, a bit over the hill but a nice place to watch the sunset before the hilarious Greek dancing lessons. Off the main Platía Mavroyénous is *Pierro's* (actually on Matoyánni), once an exclusively gay bar, now mixed and a little tacky. There are more drinking haunts over in the Alefkándhra area. For classical music, try *Kástro's* for an early evening cocktail, moving on later to *Montparnasse*, which is fairly swanky – to the extent of boasting a visitor's book. *Bolero's* and *Piano Bar* have live music, and *Le Cinema* is a newish club worth trying. Save time too for K. Yiorgoúli street, between the sea and Mitropóleos, where the *City Bar* is the campest spot in town, with marble and columns everywhere, a sweeping staircase, and a nightly drag show (there is another one at the *Windmill* next door). Just around the corner, *Scandinavia Bar* is a cheap, jovial and non-stop party bar. Finally, two more discos: *the Famous Mykonos Dance Bar*, with Greek dancing before late-night disco, and the *Rainbow*, young, mixed and sweaty, both at the northern end of Mitropóleos.

Last but not least, the narcissistic beach ethos of Mykonos is well served by an excellent **gym** geared for weight-trainers and body-builders: *The Bodywork Gym*, run by Ankie Feenstra, lets you show with pride those well-oiled cuts.

The beaches

The closest **beaches** to Hóra are those to the north, at TOÚRLOS – 2km away and horrid – and ÁYIOS STÉFANOS (4km, much better), both developed resorts and connected by very regular bus service to Míkonos. There are tavernas and rooms to let (as well as package hotels) at Áyios Stéfanos, away from the beach; try *Elena Gripari*, (☎0289/23 027).

Other nearby destinations include the resorts on the southwest peninsula – fairly undistinguished beaches tucked into pretty bays. The nearest to town, 1km away, is MEGÁLI ÁMMOS, a good beach backed by flat rocks and pricey rooms. Nearby Kórfos bay is disgusting, thanks to the town dump and machine noise. Buses serve ÓRNOS – home to the *Lucky Divers Scuba Club* (☎0289/23 220) – whose beach is okay, though accommodation prices are over-the-top, and ÁYIOS IOÁNNIS, a dramatic bay with a tiny, stony beach and a chapel.

The south coast is the busiest part of the island. *Kaíkia* ply from town to all of its beaches, which are among the straightest on the island, and still regarded to some extent as family strands by the Greeks. You might begin with PLATÍS YIALÓS, 4km south of town, though you won't be alone. One of the longest established resorts on the island, it's not remotely Greek any more, the sand is monopolised by its hotels, and you won't get a room to save your life between June and September. You might find a class vacancy at the *Petinos Dive Club* (☎0289/23 680). PSAROÚ, next door, is very pretty– 150m of white sand backed by foliage and calamus reeds, but covered in sunbathers unless it's dawn, dusk, or out of season. There's another diving club here (☎0289/23 579). The beach is divided up among the various hotels, plus there's waterskiing and windsurfer hire, but absolutely no possibility of finding a room between mid-June and mid-September unless you've reserved well in advance. A dusty footpath beyond Platís

Yialós crosses the deserted fields and caves of the headland, leading to the pale-sand **PARÁNGA** beach, where there's a recently opened official **campsite**, inexpensive and well-appointed. There's some good snorkelling to be done around the east flank of the bay, which is cluttered with volcanic rocks, starfish, and sea urchins. More footpaths continue across the clifftops and drop down to **PARADISE BEACH**, well sheltered by its headland, predominantly nudist, and packed full of beautiful people. The crescent of fine white sand makes it a handsome place to stay; there's an official campsite (April–Oct) with a diving club and two tavernas (*Freddie's* sells English newspapers). The next bay east contains **SUPER PARADISE** beach (officially "Plindhrí"), again, accessible by footpath or by *kaíki*. This has a good, friendly atmosphere, and a couple of tavernas. Its reputation used to be as an exclusive gay/nudist beach, though today it's pretty mixed.

Probably the best beach on Míkonos, though, is **Elía** the last port of call for the *kaíkia*. The longest on the island, though split in two by a rocky area, it's a broad sandy stretch with a verdant backdrop. Almost exclusively nudist, it boasts an excellent restaurant, *Matheos*. If the crowds have followed you this far, one last escape route is to follow the bare rock footpath over the spur at the end of Elía beach (the one with the white house). This cuts upwards for grand views east and west and then winds down to **KALÓ LIVÁDHI** (seasonal bus service), a stunning beach adjoining an agricultural valley scattered with little farmhouses. It hardly seems part of the same island, though even here there's a restaurant (a good one to boot) at the far end of the beach. **LÍA,** further on, is smaller but lovely, with bamboo windbreaks and clear water, plus another taverna.

The rest of the island

If your time is limited, you'll find any of the beaches above good enough for your purposes. There are others, though, further away from Míkonos town, as well as a few other destinations worth making the effort for.

East of Elía, 12km by road from the town, **AYÍA ÁNNA** boasts a shingle beach and taverna, with the cliffs above granting some fine vistas; the place achieved some fame as a location for the film *Shirley Valentine*. **TARSANÁ**, on the other side of the isthmus, has a long, coarse sand beach, with watersports, a taverna and posh bungalows. **KALAFÁTI**, almost adjacent is more of a tourist community, its white-sand beach supporting a few hotels, restaurants and a disco. There's a local bus service from here to **ÁNO MÉRA** (see below), or you can jump on an excursion boat to **Tragoníssi**, the islet just offshore, which boasts spectacular coastal scenery, seals and wild birds. The rest of the east coast is difficult – often impossible – to reach. There are some small beaches, none better than elsewhere and only worth the effort for loners, while the region is dominated by the peak of Profítis Ilías, sadly spoiled by a huge radar dome and military establishment. The **north coast** suffers persistent battering from the *meltémi*, plus tar and litter pollution, and for the most part is bare, brown and exposed. The one notable exception is relatively sheltered **PÁNORMOS BAY**, site of an ancient city of Míkonos. There are two beaches, though both are prone to savage, windy sand-blasting which fails to deter a small colony of (wind)surfers.

From Pánormos, it's an easy walk to the only other settlement of any size on the island – **ÁNO MÉRA** (rooms available), slightly inland and 8km from Míkonos. It works hard at remaining a traditional agricultural village and normal Greek life still thrives here. In the main square there's a proper *kafenío* and fresh vegetables are sold; ouzo and a local cheese are produced; and there's just one hotel. The red-roofed church near the square is the sixteenth-century **monastery of Panayía Tourlianí**, where a collection of Cretan icons and the unusual eighteenth-century marble baptismal font are worth seeing. It's not far, either, to the late twelfth-century **Paleokástro**

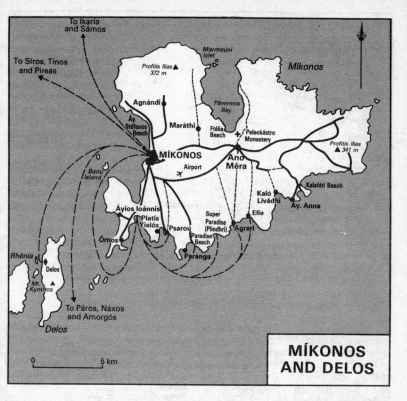

MÍKONOS AND DELOS

monastery (also known as Dárga), just north of the village, in a magnificent green setting on an otherwise barren slope. To the northwest are more of the same dry and wind-buffeted landscapes, though they do provide some enjoyable, rocky walking with good views across to neighbouring islands. Using such tracks as exist, it's a short stroll down to Áyios Stéfanos and buses back to the harbour.

Delos (Dhílos)

The remains of **ancient Delos**, Pindar's "unmoved marvel of the wide world", though skeletal and swarming now with lizards (and tourists), give some idea of the past grandeur of this sacred isle a few sea-miles west of Míkonos. The ancient town lies on the west coast on flat, sometimes marshy ground which rises in the south to **Mount Kínthos**. From the summit – an easy walk up – there's a magnificent view of almost the entire Cyclades; the name of the archipelago means "those (islands) around (Delos)".

The *kaíki* to Delos leaves Míkonos at 9am (2–7 weekly, depending on the season; 900dr round-trip) and returns at 1pm, without loud warning. There is sometimes a larger craft making the trip an hour later, returning an hour later, for a bit more money. Either way, this gives you three hours on the island – barely enough time to take in the main attractions – but sadly the campsite and the tiny *Xenía* lodge have closed, so it's no

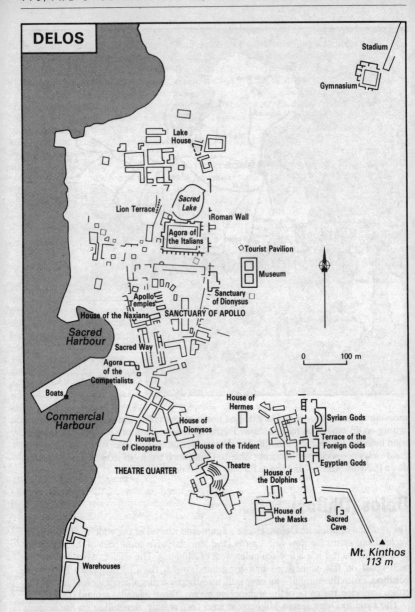

DELOS

Stadium

Gymnasium

Lake House

Sacred Lake

Lion Terrace

Roman Wall

Agora of the Italians

◇Tourist Pavilion

Museum

Apollo Temples

Sanctuary of Dionysus

House of the Naxians

SANCTUARY OF APOLLO

Sacred Harbour

Sacred Way

Agora of the Competialists

Boats

Commercial Harbour

House of Hermes

House of Dionysos

House of Cleopatra

House of the Trident

THEATRE QUARTER

Theatre

Syrian Gods

Terrace of the Foreign Gods

Egyptian Gods

House of the Dolphins

House of the Masks

Sacred Cave

Mt. Kínthos 113 m

Warehouses

0   100 m

longer possible to stay the night. If you want to make a thorough tour of the site, you'll have to come on several morning excursions or take a private afternoon charter tour, both expensive options. In any case take your own food and drink as the tourist pavilion's snack bar is a rip-off.

Some history

Delos's ancient fame was due to the fact that Leto gave birth to the divine twins Artemis and Apollo on the island, although its fine harbour and central position did nothing to hamper development. When the Ionians colonised the island around 1000 BC it was already a cult centre, and by the seventh century BC it had become the commercial and religious centre of the Amphictionic League.

Unfortunately Delos also attracted the attention of Athens, which sought to increase its prestige by controlling the island; the wealth of the Delian Confederacy, founded after the Persian Wars to protect the Aegean cities, was harnessed to Athenian ends, and for a while their officials took over the Sanctuary of Apollo. Athenian attempts to "purify" the island started with a decree that no one could die or give birth on Delos – the sick and the pregnant were taken to the islet of Rheneia – and culminated in the simple expedient of banishing what remained of the native population.

Delos reached its peak in the third and second centuries BC after being declared a free port by its Roman overlords. In the end, though, its undefended wealth brought ruin. First Mithridates (88 BC), then Athenodorus (69 BC), plundered the treasures, and the island never recovered. By the third century AD Athens could not even sell it, and for centuries after every passing seafarer stopped to collect a few prizes.

The site (admission 500dr)

You land with the Sacred Harbour on your left, the Commercial Harbour on your right; straight ahead is the **Agora of the Competialists** – Roman merchants or freed slaves who worshipped the *Lares Competales*, the guardian spirits of crossroads – where there would have been offerings to Hermes in the middle (a round and a square base). The **Sacred Way** leads north from the far left corner; it used to be lined with statues and the grandiose monuments of rival kings. Along it you reach three marble steps which lead into the **Sanctuary of Apollo**. The forest of offerings which covered this entire area – for huge amounts were lavished on the god – has been stripped by plunderers. On your left is the Stoa of the Naxians, while against the north wall of the House of the Naxians to the right there stood in ancient times a huge statue of Apollo. In 417 BC the Athenian general Nicias led a procession of priests across a bridge of boats from Rheneia to dedicate a bronze palm tree; when it was later blown over in a gale it took the statue with it. Three **Temples of Apollo** stand in a row to the right along the Sacred Way: the Delian Temple, that of the Athenians, and the Porinos Naos, the earliest of them (sixth century BC). To the east towards the museum you pass the **Sanctuary of Dionysus**, with its marble phalli on tall pillars.

The best finds from the site are in Athens, but the **museum** (if it's open) still justifies a visit. To the north is the **Sacred Lake** where Leto gave birth clinging to a palm tree. It has lost both its water and its swans, but a modern wall marks where they used to be. Guarding it are the superb **Lions**, their lean bodies masterfully executed by Naxians in the seventh century BC. Of the original nine, three have disappeared and one adorns the Arsenale at Venice; don't try to ride the remaining five, as it is strictly forbidden. On the other side of the lake is the City Wall, built (in 69 BC) too late to protect the treasures. The houses to the north have some mosaics.

Set out in the other direction from the Agora of the Competialists and you enter the residential area, known as the **Theatre Quarter**. Many of the walls and roads remain but there is none of the domestic detail that makes Pompeii, for example, so fascinating. Some colour is added by the mosaics – one in the **House of the Trident**, better ones in the **House of the Masks**, most notably a vigorous portrayal of Dionysus riding on a panther's back. The **Theatre** itself seated 5500 onlookers and, though much ravaged, offers some fine views. Behind the theatre, a path leads past the **Sanctuaries of the Foreign Gods** and up **Mount Kínthos** for more panoramic sightseeing.

Síros (Syros)

Don't be put off by first impressions of Síros. From the ferry it looks grimly industrial, but away from the Neórion shipyard things improve quickly. Very much a working island with no real history of tourism, it's probably the most Greek of the Cyclades; there are few holiday trappings and what there is exists for the locals. You probably won't find, as Herman Melville did when he visited in 1856, shops full of ". . . fez-caps, swords, tobacco, shawls, pistols, and orient finery . . .". But you're still likely to see Síros as a refreshing change from having to compete with the beautiful people. Of course outsiders do come to the island, and the nice beaches are hardly undeveloped. But everywhere there's the underlying assumption that you're on borrowed territory belonging to an inherently private people.

Ermoúpoli

The main town and port of **ERMOÚPOLI** was founded during the War of Independence by refugees from Psará and Híos, becoming Greece's chief port in the nineteenth century. Pireás has left it an age behind, but it's still the largest town in the Cyclades, and the archipelago's capital. Medieval Síros was largely a Catholic island, but there was an influx of Orthodox refugees during the War of Independence, and today the town has two distinct, numerically comparable communities living in their respective quarters, on two hills rising up from the sea.

Ermoúpoli itself, the **lower town**, is worth at least a night's stay, with grandiose buildings a relic of its days as the first port of Greece. Between the harbour and **Áyios Nikólaos**, the fine Orthodox church to the north, you can stroll through its faded splendour. The **Apollon Theatre**, slowly being restored over the last two decades, is a copy of La Scala in Milan and once presented a regular Italian opera season; today local theatre and music groups put it to good use. The long, central **Platía Miaoúli** is named after an admiral of the revolution whose statue stands there; in the evenings the population parades in front of its arcaded *kafenía*, while the children ride the mechanical animals. Up the stairs to the left of the Town Hall is the small **Archaeological Museum** (Tues–Sun 8.30am–3pm; closed Mon) with three rooms of finds from Síros, Páros and Amorgós. To the left of the clock tower more stairs climb up to Vrondádho.

On the taller hill to the left is the intricate medieval quarter of **Áno Síros**, with a clutch of Catholic churches below the cathedral of Saint George. There are fine views of the town below, and, close by, the **Cappuchin monastery of Saint Jean**, founded in 1535 to do duty as a poorhouse. It takes about 45 minutes of tough walking (up Omírou) to reach this quarter, passing the Orthodox and Catholic cemeteries on the way – the former full of grand shipowners' mausoleums, the latter with more modest monuments and French and Italian inscriptions. (You can halve the time needed by turning on to the stair-street named Andhréa Kárga, part way along.)

The other hill, **Vrondádho**, hosts the Orthodox quarter, topped by the wonderful church of the **Anástasi** with its domed roof and great views over Tínos and Míkonos, weather permitting. If it's locked, ask for the key at the priest's house to the left of the church.

Practicalities

The **quayside** is still busy, though nowadays it deals with more touristic than industrial shipping; Síros is a major crossover point on the ferryboat routes. Also down here is the **bus station**, along with the tourist police and several **bike hire** places. Between them shops sell the *loukoúmia* (Turkish delight) and *halvadhópita* (sweetmeat pie) for which the island is famed. **Odhós Híou**, the market street, is especially lively on Saturday when the country people come to town to sell fresh produce.

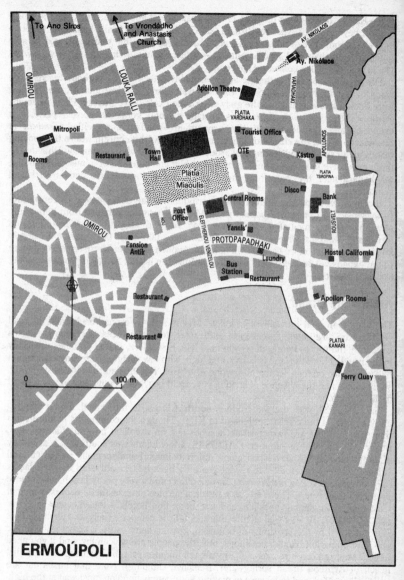

ERMOÚPOLI

Keeping step with a growing level of tourism, **rooms** have improved in quality and number in recent years; many are in garishly decorated (if crumbling) neoclassical mansions. Good choices include *Apollon Rooms* at Odhisséou 8 (☎0281/22 158; ②) and the *Hostel California* around the corner, the *Kástro Rooms*, on Platía Tsiropína (☎0281/ 28 064; ②), or the *Pension Antik* (☎0281/26 849; ③) – follow the little white signposts. A notch up in price and quality, are the well-sited *Hotel Hermes* (☎0281/28 011; ④) on

Platía Kanári, overlooking the port, or for a real slice of good-value opulence the *Xenon Ipatías*, beyond Áyios Nikólaos (☎0281/23 575; ③). Síros is finally beginning to fill up in peak season; at such times the agency *Travel Team* (on the waterfront) may be able to find you unadvertised accommodation – or place you in their very own *Hotel Europe* (☎0281/28 771; ④), a converted convent.

For **meals**, the most authentic and reasonably priced of the harbour tavernas are *Medusa*, at Ándhrou 3, a block in from the water, or *1935*, just inland from the new ferry dock; places actually on the quay tend to be exploitative. Just off Platía Miaoúlis, at Híou 53, the *Estiatorio Syllivani* is virtually the only good, inexpensive place, with oven-food and barrell-wine. Finally, way up in Vrondádho, try either *Tembelis* at Anastáseos 17, on the corner of Kalavrítou, just below the church, where the cooking makes up for the limited seating and grouchy service, or *Folia*, Athanasíou Dhiakoú 2 – more expensive but serving such exotica as rabbit and pigeon. For a musical breakfast, try *Yanni's* near the waterfront; he used to run a guest house and is an island institution.

Incidentally, Síros still honours its contribution to the development of **rembétika** (see "Music" in *Contexts*); *bouzoúki* great Markos Vamvakaris hailed from here and a *platía* has been named after him in Áno Síros. Taverna-clubs such as *Lillis* (up in Áno Síros) and *Rahanos*, with music on weekends, also take their place beside a batch of more conventional disco-clubs down near the Apollon Theatre. There are several more (often expensive) *bouzoúki* bars scattered around the island, mostly on routes heading to beach resorts.

Around the island

The main loop road (to Gallissás, Fínikas, Mégas Yialós, Vári and back), and the road west to Kíni, are good: it's cheapest and easiest to get to these places on the buses which ply the routes hourly in season until late. Elsewhere, expect potholes especially to the **north** where the land is barren and high, with few villages. Here, any exploration has to be done on foot, setting off beyond Áno Síros. But the nature of the meandering, stony tracks and the absence of inviting coves and beaches discourages any real effort in this direction.

Stick, instead, with the well-trodden **south**. Closest to the capital, fifteen minutes away by bus, is the coastal settlement of **KÍNI**. Though the community is more villas than village, there are two separate beaches and an excellent taverna (*Iliovasilema*), rarely overrun even in summer. **GALISSÁS**, a few kilometres south (but reached by different buses), has developed along different lines. Fundamentally an agricultural village, it's been taken over in recent years by backpackers attracted by the island's only **campsites** (*Camping Yianna* plus one other) and a very pretty beach, much more protected than Kíni's. There are, as a result, a surplus of unaesthetic **rooms**, which at least makes bargaining possible, and five bona fide hotels – the cheapest is *Petros* (☎0281/42 067; ③) – as well as mini-markets for the campers. Galissás's identity crisis is exemplified by the proximity of bemused, grazing dairy cattle, a heavy-metal music pub, and upmarket handicrafts shops. Still, the people are welcoming, and if you need to get away, you can hire a moped, or walk ten minutes past the headland to the nudist beach of **Arméos** (fresh springwater, freelance camping). Note that buses out are erratically routed, and to be sure of making your connection you must wait at the high-road stop, not down by the beach.

A pleasant one-hour walk (or ten-minute bus ride) south from Galissás brings you to **FÍNIKAS**, purported to have been settled originally by the Phoenicians (though *fínikas* also means "palm tree" in Greek). It's a more mainstream resort with a narrow and gritty beach, tamarisk-lined but right next to the road. The *Cyclades* (☎0281/42 255; ②)

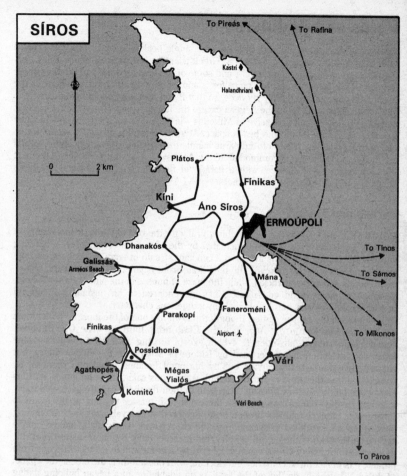

is the cheapest and cosiest of the three reasonable hotels here, and has an acceptble restaurant.

Fínikas is separated by a tiny headland from its neighbour **POSSIDHONÍA** (or Delagrazzia), a nicer spot with some idiosyncratically ornate mansions and a bright blue church right on the edge of the village. It's worth walking ten minutes further south, past the naval yacht club and its patrol boat, to **AGATHOPÉS**, with a sandy beach and a little islet just offshore. **KOMITÓ**, at the end of the unpaved track leading south from Agathopés, is nothing more than a stony beach fronting an olive grove.

The bus and road swing east to **MÉGAS YIALÓS**, a small resort below a hillside festooned with brightly painted houses. The long, narrow beach is lined with shady trees and there are pedal-boats for hire. **VÁRI**, with the adjacent Ahládhi cove, is more – though not much more – of a town, with its own small fishing fleet. Beach-goers are in a fishbowl, as it were, with tavernas and **rooms** looming right overhead, but it is the most sheltered of the island's bays, something to remember when the *meltémi* is up.

Páros and Andíparos

Gently and undramatically furled around the single peak of Profítis Ilías, Páros has a little of everything one expects from a "Greek island" – old villages, monasteries, fishing harbours, a labyrinthine capital – and some of the best nightlife and beaches in the Aegean. It's a favourite starting point for island wanderings: Parikía, the *hóra*, is the major hub of inter-island ferry services, so that if you wait long enough you can get to just about anywhere else in the Aegean except the Ionian group. However, the island is almost as touristed and expensive as Míkonos – in peak season, it's touch-and-go when it comes to finding rooms and beach space. At such times, the attractive inland settlements or the satellite island of Andíparos handle the overflow. If you can coincide, and are lucky enough to get accommodation, the August 15 festival here is one of the best such observances in Greece, with a parade of flare-lit fishing boats and fireworks delighting as many Greeks as foreigners.

Parikía and around

PARIKÍA, the *hóra*, sets the tone architecturally for the rest of Páros, with its ranks of typically Cycladic white houses punctuated by the occasional Venetian-style building and church domes. But all is awash in a constant stream of ferry passengers, and the town is relentlessly commercial. The busy waterfront is jam-packed with bars, restaurants, hotels and ticket agencies, while the maze of houses in the older quarter behind, designed to baffle wind and pirates, has surrendered to an onslaught of chi-chi boutiques and has thus barely retained any indigenous character.

Just outside the central clutter, though, the town has one of the most architecturally interesting churches in the Aegean – the **Ekatondapiliani**, or "The One-Hundred-Gated Virgin" (daily 7am–noon & 4–8pm except on Aug 15 festival). What's visible today was designed and supervised by Isidore of Miletus in the sixth century, but construction was actually carried out by his pupil Ignatius. It was so beautiful on completion that the master, consumed with jealousy, is said to have grappled with his apprentice on the rooftop, flinging them both to their deaths. They are portrayed today kneeling at the column bases across the courtyard: master tugging at his beard in repentance, pupil clutching a broken head. Restored at intervals ever since (including now, when it's swaddled in scaffolding), the church was substantially altered after a severe earthquake in the eighth century, but its essentially Byzantine aspect remains, its shape an imperfect Greek cross. Enclosed by a great wall to protect its icons from pirates, it is in fact three churches interlocking with one another; the oldest, the chapel of Áyios Nikólaos to the left of the apse, is an adaptation of a pagan building dating from the early fourth century BC. Behind Ekatondapiliani, the **Archaeological Museum** (Tues–Sat 8.30am–3pm, Sun 9am–2pm, closed Mon) has a fair collection of antique bits and pieces, its prize exhibits a fifth-century winged Nike and a piece of the *Parian Chronicle*, a social and cultural "history" of Greece up to 264 BC, recorded on marble but now languishing on the floor.

These two sights apart, the real attraction of Parikía is simply to wander the town itself. Arcaded lanes lead past Venetian-influenced villas, traditional island dwellings and the three ornate wall fountains donated by the Mavroyénnis family in the eighteenth century. Of the minor churches, the most interesting is the seventeenth-century one of the **Presentation**, with fine frescoes. The town culminates in a seaward Venetian **Kástro**, whose surviving east wall is constructed of masonry pillaged from ancient temples to Demeter and Apollo. The beautiful, arcaded church of Áyios Konstandínos and Ayía Eléni crowns the highest point, from where the fortified hill drops sharply to the quay in a series of hanging gardens.

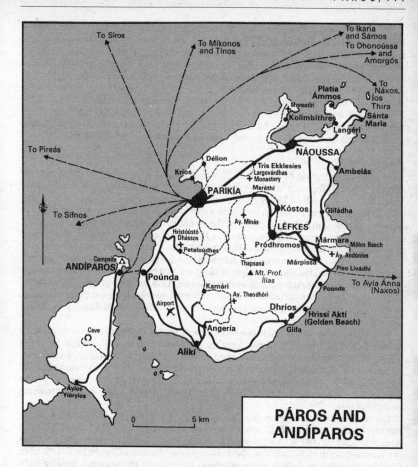

PÁROS AND ANDÍPAROS

If you're staying in town, you'll want to get **out into the surroundings** at some stage, if only to the beach. The most rewarding excursion is the hour's walk up to **Áyii Anáryiri** monastery, perched on the bluff above town and reached along an unsurfaced road which starts just past the museum. It's a great picnic spot, with cypress groves, a gushing fountain and some splendid views.

There are **beaches** immediately north and south of the harbour, though none are particularly attractive when compared to Páros's best. In fact, you might prefer to avoid the northern stretch altogether, though there's a decent if mosquito-plagued **campsite**, *Koula*, about 700m along, and another crowded but mediocre one at KRÍOS, 3km away (regular *kaíki* service). Heading **south** along the asphalt road is better: the first unsurfaced side track you reach leads to a small, sheltered beach; fifteen minutes further on is **PARASPÓROS**, with another, better **campsite** and beach near the remains of an ancient *asklepeion* ("therapy centre"). Continuing for 45 minutes (you'll have taken a bus by now) brings you to arguably the best of the bunch, **AYÍA IRÍNI**. The campsite here, unfortunately, is pretty bad, and badly signposted, but there is good sand and a taverna next to a farm and shady olive grove.

Off in the same direction, but a much longer two-hour haul each way, is **PETALOÚDHES**, the so-called "Valley of the Butterflies", a walled-in oasis where millions of Jersey tiger moths perch on the foliage during the early summer. There's a small admission fee and a snack bar (operating after June 15 only; grounds shut 1–4pm). The trip pays more dividends in conjunction with a visit to the eighteenth-century nunnery of **Hristoú sto Dhássos**, at the crest of a ridge twenty minutes to the north. Only women are allowed in the sanctuary, although men can get as far as the courtyard. The succession of narrow drives and donkey paths linking both places begins just south of Parikía, by the *Ksenon Ery*. Petaloúdhes can be reached from Parikía by bus (in summer), by moped, or on an overpriced excursion by mule.

Practicalities

Ferries **dock** in Parikía by the windmill, which houses a summer tourist information centre. Although there's a bus timetable posted here, the **bus stop** itself is 100m or so to the left – routes extend to Náoussa in the north, Poúnda (for Andíparos) in the west, Alikí in the south, and Dhríos on the island's east coast (with another very useful service between Dhríos and Náoussa). Most of the island is flat enough for bicycle rides, but mopeds are more common and you can hire them at several places in town. The **airport** is around 12km from town, close to Alikí – from where six daily buses run to Parikía.

Polos Tours is one of the more switched-on and friendly **travel agencies**; they effi-ciently issue air tickets when Olympic is shut, act as agents for virtually all boats and offer free luggage storage for customers. *Olympic Airways* itself (no special weekend hours) is at the far end of Odhós Probóne, while the **tourist police** occupy a building at the back of the seafront square. *Scopas Travel* (☎0284/22 300) has a baby-sitting agency.

As for **places to stay**, Parikía is a pleasant and central base, but absolutely mobbed in summer. You'll be met off the ferry by locals offering rooms, even at the most unlikely hours, and late at night it's a good idea to capitulate straightaway. If you arrive on an August day without a reservation, consult the tourist office in the windmill itself which can advise on any (rare) vacancies. Most of the hotels tend to be reserved whole-sale by tour operators, and you'll have to be quick to grab space in the remaining cheaper places.

Less expensive and therefore popular options include *Hotel Dina* near Platía Veléntza (☎0284/21 325; ③), the *Hotel Kondes*, very close to the windmill by the *ITS Travel Agency* (☎0284/21 246; ②), or *Constantine Passos*, which is further up the course of the dry riverbed, on the left-hand side. *Oasis Rooms*, near the post office (☎0284/21 227; ②), is fairly cheap too, and there are more rooms to let along the sea front, turning right (south) from the quayside. In the town centre, try *Maria Aliprandi* (☎0284/21 464, ②) or *Mimikos* (☎0284/21 437, ②). Avoid persistent offers of rooms or hotels to the north; they're invariably a long walk away from town, and mosquitos can be a problem.

Many Parikía **tavernas** are run by outsiders operating under municipal concession, so year-to-year variation in proprietors and quality is marked. However, the following seem to be long-established and/or good-value outfits. Rock-bottom is the *Koutouki Thanasis*, which serves oven food for locals and bold tourists and is tucked in a back street behind the (expensive) *Hibiscus*. The *Possidon*, at the north end of the water-front, and the *Efkalyptos* are both popular with the locals. In the pricier range, the *Stavedo Café*, next to the *Saloon D'Or* bar (see below) is fine for international cuisine, and *To Tamarisko* is an attractive garden taverna. In the exotic department, *Mey Tey* serves average Chinese food at moderate markup; for Italian try *La Barca Rossa* on the seafront or *Bella Italia* across a waterfront square from the (not recommended) *Corfo Leon*. Further out of town, *Nisiotissa* has a highly entertaining chef-proprietor and is rarely crowded; *Delfini*, on the first paved drive along the road to Pounda, is long-established and famous for its Sunday barbecue with live music.

Parikía has a wealth of **pubs**, **bars** and low-key **discos**, not as pretentious as those on Míkonos or as raucous as on Íos, but certainly everything in between. The most popular cocktail bars extend along the seafront, all tucked into a series of open squares and offering competing but staggered (no pun intended) "Happy Hours", so that you can drink cheaply much of the evening until the mandatory 3am closure. *Kafenio O Flisvos*, about three-fourths of the way south along the front, is the last remaining traditional *oúzo/meze* outfit amongst the rash of pizzerias, snackbars, juice and ice-cream joints. A rowdy clientele favours *Ballos, Apollo's* and the conspicuous *Saloon D'Or*, while the *Pirate Bar* features jazz and blues. *Statue Bar, Evinos* and *Pebbles* are more genteel, the latter pricey but with good sunset views and the occasional live gig. The "ethnic" pubs (for want of a better designation) are a bit rough for some; most outrageous is the *Dubliner Complex*, actually four bars, a snack section, disco and common seating area. Other popular **dance** floors include *Disco 7* and *Hesperides*.

Finally, a thriving cultural centre, *Arhilohos* (near Ekatondapilianí) caters mostly to the needs of locals, with occasional **film** screenings. There are also two open-air cinemas, *Rex* and *Páros*, screening foreign films in season.

The north and centre of the island

The second port of Páros, **NÁOUSSA** was until recently an unspoiled, sparkling labyrinth of winding, narrow alleys and simple Cycladic houses. Alas, a rash of new concrete hotels and attendant trappings have all but swamped its character, though down at the small fishing harbour, oblivious of the tourists, fishermen still tenderise octopi by thrashing them against the walls. The local festivals – an annual Fish and Wine Festival on July 2, and an August 23 shindig celebrating an old naval victory over the Turks – are also still celebrated with enthusiasm. Most people are here for the beaches and the relaxed nightlife; there's really only one sight, a **museum** with interesting icons in the church of Áyios Nikólaos Mostrátos.

Despite the development, the town is a good place to head for as soon as you reach Páros; it's noted for its nearby beaches, while **rooms** are marginally cheaper than in Parikía – track them down with the help of Katerini Simitzi's tourist office on the main square. Hotels are much more expensive, though out of season you should haggle for reduced prices at the *Madaki* (☎0284/51 475; ③) the *Drossia* (☎0284/51 213; ③), and the *Stella* (☎0284/51 317; ③). There's an official **campsite**, too, out of town towards Kolimbíthres (see below).

Most of the harbour tavernas are pretty good for a change, specialising in fresh fish and seafood. *Diamante* is reasonably priced, *Mouragio* and *Psariana* are average, and *Limanakis* is cheap-ish and traditional despite looking just like a pub. (Avoid the self-service cafés, which are rip-offs.) The locals drink at *Stratia*, and tourists dance at *Paradise, The Cave, Chez Linardo,* and *Banana Moon* – tacky, but fun. Left-luggage offices, a **bank** by the harbour, a **post office** and an **OTE** round out the roster of amenities.

Some good-to-excellent **beaches** are within walking distance of Náoussa (there's no town beach), and a summer *kaíki* service also connects them. To the west, an hour's tramping brings you to **KOLIMBÍTHRES** ("Basins"), where there are three tavernas and the wind- and sea-sculpted rock formations which give the place its Greek name. A few minutes beyond, **MONASTÍRI** beach – below the abandoned Pródhromos monastery – is similarly attractive, and partly nudist. Go northeast and the sands are better still, the barren headland spangled with good surfing beaches: **LANGÉRI** is backed by dunes; the best surfing is at **SANTA MARÍA**, a trendy beach connected with Náoussa by road; and finally there's **PLATIÁ ÁMMOS** on the northeasternmost tip of the island.

More energetically, you might take the 45-minute walk southeast to **AMBELÁS** hamlet as the start of a longer trek down the **east coast**. Ambelás itself has rooms and hotels, a small taverna and a good beach, and from here a rough track leads south, passing several undeveloped stretches on the way. After about an hour you reach **MÓLOS** beach, impressive and not particularly crowded, and – twenty minutes later – **MÁRMARA**. There are rooms to let here and it's an attractive place to stay, though the marble that the village is built from and named after has largely been whitewashed over.

If Mármara doesn't appeal to you, then serene **MÁRPISSA**, just to the south, may – a maze of winding alleys and aging archways overhung by floral balconies and clinging to the hillside. There are rooms here too, and you can employ a spare hour making the climb up the conical Kéfalos hill, on whose fortified summit the last Venetian lords of Páros were overpowered by the Ottomans in 1537. Today the monastery of **Áyios Andónios** occupies the site and the grounds are locked, so to enjoy the views over eastern Páros and the straits of Naxos fully get the key from the priest in Márpissa before setting out. On the shore nearby, **PÍSO LIVÁDHI** was once a quiet fishing village, but it's been ruined by the concrete mushrooms built to serve package tourism. The main reason to visit is to catch a (seasonal) *kaíki* to Ayía Ánna on Naxos; if you need to spend the previous night here, try *Pension Márpissa* (☎0284/41 288; ③), *Hotel Leto* (☎0284/41 283 or 41 479; ③), or the *Magia* (☎0284/41 390; ③) which may let you sleep on the roof as well; there's also a campsite.

The road runs **west** from Píso Livádhi **back to the capital**, and while there are regular buses back along it you'd do better, if you have time, to return on foot. A medieval flagstoned path once linked both sides of the island, and parts of it survive in the east between Mármara and the villages around Léfkes. **PRÓDHROMOS**, encountered first, is an old fortified farming settlement with more defensive walls girding its nearby monastery. **LÉFKES** itself, an hour up the track, is perhaps the most beautiful and unspoilt village on Páros. The town flourished from the seventeenth century on, its population swollen by refugees fleeing from coastal piracy; indeed it was the island's *hóra* during most of the Ottoman period. Léfkes's marbled alleyways and amphitheatrical setting are unparallelled and, despite the presence of an oversized hotel, a very few rooms, a disco and a taverna on the outskirts, the area around the main square remains unspoilt and the central *kafenío* and bakery observe their siestas religiously.

Half an hour further on, through olive groves, is **KÓSTOS**, a simple village and a good place for lunch in the one taverna. Any traces of path disappear at **MARÁTHI**, on the site of the ancient marble quarries which once supplied much of Europe; with a torch you can poke around the abandoned workings. The last slabs (considered second only to Carrara marble) were mined here by the French in the nineteenth century for Napoleon's tomb. From Maráthi, it's easy enough to pick up the bus on to Parikía, but if you want to continue hiking, strike south for the monastery of **Áyios Minás**, twenty minutes away. Various Classical and Byzantine masonry fragments are worked into the walls of this sixteenth-century foundation, and the friendly couple who act as custodians can put you on the right path up to the convent of **Thapsaná**. From here, other paths lead either back to Parikía (two hours altogether from Áyios Minás), or on up to the island's summit for the last word in views over the Cyclades.

The south of the island

There's little to stop for **south of Parikía** until **POÚNDA**, 6km away, and then only to catch the ferry to Andíparos (see below). What used to be a sleepy hamlet is now a concrete jungle, a far cry from the days when you left the Poúnda church door open to summon the boat over from the smaller island. Neighbouring **ALIKÍ** appears to be permanently under construction – though there's an excellent beachside restaurant here (by the large tamarisk tree) – and the **airport** is close by, making for lots of unwelcome noise. The end of the southern bus route is at ANGERÍA (rooms); about

3km inland is the **convent of Áyii Theodhóri**, whose nuns specialise in weaving locally commissioned articles and are further distinguished as *paleomeroloyítes*, or old-calendarites, meaning that they follow the medieval Orthodox (Julian) calendar, two weeks behind everyone else.

Working your way around the **south coast**, there are two routes east to Dhríos. Either retrace your steps to Angería and follow the (slightly inland) coastal jeep track, which skirts a succession of isolated coves and little beaches; or keep on, across the foothills, from Áyii Theodhóri – a shorter walk. Aside from an abundant water supply (including a duck pond) and surrounding orchards, **DHRÍOS** village is mostly modern and characterless, lacking even a well-defined *platía*. Follow the lane signed "Dhríos Beach", however, and things improve a bit.

Between here and Píso Livádhi to the north are several sandy coves – HRISSÍ AKTÍ (Golden Beach), TZIRDHÁKIA, MEZÁDHA, POÚNDA and LOGARÁS – all prone to pummelling by the *meltémi*, yet all favoured to varying degrees by campers, and wind-surfers making a virtue out of necessity. Hrissí Aktí in particular is strewn with litter left by the numerous day-trippers and users of the semi-official **campsite** and free showers. Note that the only substantial facilities – shops, rooms, and meals – are in Dhríos, though there are tavernas at Golden Beach and Logarás.

Andíparos

In recent years the islet of Andíparos has become something of an open secret among those who consider Páros to be irredeemably sullied. In 1981 the island only had one bar, and as late as 1984 cars were unheard of; now there are at least a dozen places to drink, and in July and August there's a steady stream of vehicles around and through the single village. This is not to say that Andíparos is horrendously commercialised; it isn't – yet. Early in the year it's still a good place to rent a small cottage or a flat, but in high season it can be full of the same young, multi-ethnic clientele that you were trying to leave behind on Páros.

Most of the population of 500 live in the surprisingly large northern **village**, with a long, flagstoned pedestrian street forming its backbone and ending at a double square. One has a giant eucalyptus and several cafés; the other, reached through archways, is a small, exquisite replica of the *Kástro* on Síkinos, with the dwellings on the periphery surviving to their original heights and a central cistern instead of a church. Elsewhere there is the usual complement of domed Cycladic domes and arches – all in all a pleasant surprise for those expecting the generally unremarkable architecture of minor islets.

To get here, you have a choice of summer-only **kaíkia** from Parikía (4–5 daily; 1hr) or the year-round, **barge-ferry** (same frequency; 15min) from Poúnda, which takes vehicles and is also designed to dovetail with the comings and goings of the Páros buses. There are two inexpensive **hotels**, the *Mandalena* (☎0284/61 206; ③) and the *Anargyros* (☎0284/61 204; ③), plenty of **rooms**, plus a very popular **campsite** ten minutes' track-walk northwest, next to its own nudist beach. Of the dozen or so **tavernas**, the *Anargyros*, right on the dock below the namesake hotel, and *Klimataria*, 100m inland, stay open at lunchtime, and *Mario's*, just before the square, features local wine; there's an excellent sweet shop in the eucalyptus-filled *platía* itself. A short-schedule **bank**, a tiny **OTE** booth with morning and evening hours, a **post office**, a **cinema** and several travel agents round out the list of amenities, so that you need never go to Parikía for errands if you don't wish to.

Andíparos's **beaches** begin right outside town: PSARALIDHÁKI, where clothing is optional, is just to the east, and better than "SUNSET" beach on the opposite side of the island, though the latter often hosts evening soccer matches. GLÍFA lies about half-way down the eastern coast, with LIVADHÁKI, its counterpart, to the west. For real seclusion, however, head for ÁYIOS YIÓRYIOS on the southwest side, where fine, small sandy coves remain uncluttered despite incipient villa development. A bus and a mobile food wagon make the journey out here twice daily in high summer.

The great **cave**, before Áyios Yióryios and inland, is the chief attraction for day-trippers. In these eerie chambers the eccentric Marquis de Nointel celebrated Christmas Mass in 1673 while 500 bemused but well-paid Parians looked on; at the exact moment of midnight explosives were detonated at the entrance to emphasise the enormity of the event. Although electric light and cement steps have diminished much of its mystery and grandeur, it remains impressive. Two buses a day run from the port to the cave. Should you miss them it's a stoney ninety-minute hike from the village, or you can jump on one of the morning boats which will transfer you down the coast to within a short, if tiring, walk of it. In the off-season you'll have to fetch the key for the cave from the village.

Náxos

Náxos is the largest and most fertile of the Cyclades, and with its green and mountainous interior seems immediately distinct from many of its neighbours. The difference is accentuated by the unique architecture of many of the interior villages: the Venetian occupation (from the thirteenth to the sixteenth century) left towers and fortified mansions scattered throughout the island, while late medieval Cretan refugees bestowed a singular character upon Náxos's eastern settlements.

Today Náxos could easily support itself without tourism by its production of potatoes, olives, grapes and lemons, but since 1988 has thrown its lot in with mass tourism, so that the island is now almost as busy and commercialised as Páros in season. An airport – the usual criterion in such matters – finally opened in 1991; the runway, however, cannot accommodate large jets, and was built atop a former salt-marsh, so expect it to spend a certain amount of time flooded or buckled.

Few visitors venture away from the harbour and beach area, though more people trickle inland each year, refusing to be scared off by exaggerated tales of the gruffness of the villagers. And the island certainly has plenty to see if you know where to look: intriguing central valleys, a windy but spectacular north coast, and marvellously sandy beaches in the southwest – these last some of the best in Greece.

Náxos Town

A long causeway protecting the harbour on the north connects **NÁXOS** town (or Hóra) with the islet of Palátia, where legend has Theseus abandoning Ariadne on his way home from Crete. The huge stone portal of a **Temple of Apollo** still stands there, built on the orders of the tyrant Lygdamis in the sixth century BC but never completed. Most of the town's life goes on down by the crowded port esplanade or in the commercial streets just behind it; move into the back alleys and there's an almost medieval atmosphere. Claustrophobic, silent alleys behind the harbour lead up past crumbling balconies and through low arches to the fortified **Kástro**, from where Marco Sanudo and his successors ruled over the Cyclades for the Venetians. Only two of the original seven towers – those of the Sanudo and Glezos families – remain, although the north gate (approached up Apóllonos) survives as a splendid example of a medieval fort entrance. The Venetians' Catholic descendants, numbers dwindling, still live in the old mansions which encircle the site, many with ancient coats-of-arms above crumbling doorways. Other brooding relics survive in the same area: a seventeenth-century Ursuline convent, the Roman Catholic Cathedral (restored in questionable taste in the 1950s, though still displaying a thirteenth-century coat-of-arms inside), and one of

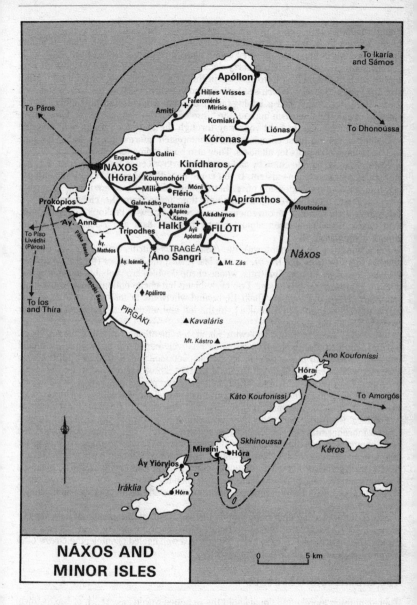

NÁXOS AND
MINOR ISLES

0   5 km

Ottoman Greece's first schools, the French School, opened in 1627 for Catholic and
Orthodox students alike (including, briefly, Nikos Kazantzakis). This now houses an
excellent **Archeological Museum** (daily except Mon 8.30am–3pm; 400dr), whose
wide historical range of finds – mostly pottery – indicates that Náxos was continually
occupied throughout antiquity, from Neolithic to Roman times.

Practicalities

Large ferries dock along the northerly harbour causeway. All small boats including the *kaíkia* to Ayía Ánna and the very useful small ferry, *Skopelitis*, use the jetty in the fishing harbour, *not* the main car ferry dock. The **bus station** is at its landward end: services (up to five daily) run to Apóllon in the far north, via Áno Sangrí, Halkí, Filóti and Apíranthos (for all of which see below), and virtually hourly to the beaches at Ayía Ánna. Here, too, you'll find a left-luggage place and a good bike hire office. In the absence of an official tourism bureau, the **"info"** agency at the base of the ferry jetty – assuming you manage to fight your way through the touts for various pensions and campsites – has the most complete and disinterested information, probably because they're authorised agents for all boats. They also book rooms (expensive).

Rooms can be hard to come by and somewhat overpriced in the old quarter of Hóra, and single rooms are non-existent. If you come up with nothing after an hour of hunting, the new southern extension offers better value, although you are a long walk from most facilities, and there's significant night-time noise from the clubs and discos. Alternatively, there's little inconvenience involved in staying at Prokópios or Ayía Ánna, with buses in each direction almost hourly between 8am and 7.30pm (and *kaíkia* almost as regularly).

For a **hotel**, try (in the old town), the *Panorama* on Afitrítis (☎0285/22 330; ③), the nearby *Anixis* (☎0285/22 112; ③), or, as a last resort, the *Dionyssos* (☎0285/22 331; ①-②) near the *kástro* just off Amfitrítis, whose cheap doubles are probably more bearable than its impromptu youth hostel. Two fairly bland but cheap options close to the quay are the *Hotel Proto*, Protopapadháki 13, behind where the buses park (☎0285/22 394; ③) or the *Hotel Oceanis*, Damiráli 11, to the left and one street back from the water (☎0285/22 436; ③).

The quayside confronts you with about ten identically priced breakfast bars. Further along to the south are a string of relatively expensive but simple oven-food tavernas – *I Kali Kardhia* is typical, acceptable oven food with *híma* wine; if this seems only mediocre, bear in mind that the "Old Market Street" inland, including the vastly overrated *Lucullus*, is far worse. Much better for the money are *Papagalos*, a mostly vegetarian place in the new southern district, almost all the way to Áyios Yióryios bay; *Karnayio*, behind the National Bank, for fish; and *Popi's*, on the front, for roast chicken.

For local fresh fruit and vegetables, something of a rarity in the Cyclades, there's often a morning **market** outside the *Agricultural Bank*. While Athens, Crete and the most popular Cyclades are usually considered the main **sandal-making** centres as far as tourists are concerned, Náxos has some very good craftsmen, particularly Markos Skylakis, near the former market square – now home to breakfast-bars. The island is also renowned for its wines and liqueurs; a shop on the quay sells the *Prombonas* white and vintage red, plus *kítron*, a lemon firewater in three strengths (there's also a banana-flavoured variant).

Much of the evening **action** goes on at the south end of the waterfront, and slightly inland in the new quarter. Nightlife tends more towards tippling than music clubs, though the misnamed *Day Club* belts out jazz to a well-heeled clientele; the *Ocean Club* is more lively, subsisting on pop chart fodder.

The southwestern beaches

There's nothing merely functional about the **beaches** within easy reach of Náxos town; they're considered to be the island's best. For some unusual swimming just to the north of the port, beyond the causeway, **GROTTA** is easiest to reach. Besides the eponymous caves, the remains of submerged Cycladic buildings are visible, including some stones said to be the entrance to a tunnel leading to the unfinished Temple of Apollo.

The finest targets, though, are all **south** of town, the entire southwestern coastline boasting a series of excellent **beaches** accessible by regular bus and *kaíki*. **ÁYIOS YIÓRYIOS**, a lengthy sandy bay fringed by the southern extension of the hotel "colony", is within walking distance. There are several tavernas here and a windsurfing school, plus the first of three **campsites** whose touts you will have no doubt become acquainted with at the ferry jetty.

Skipping the bus, a pleasant hour's walk south through the salt marshes brings you to **PROKÓPIOS** beach (cheapish hotels and rooms and basic tavernas), whose peaceful days are again surely numbered. Or follow the tracks a little further to **AYÍA ÁNNA** (habitually referred to as "Ayi'Ánna"), a small fishing and potato-shipping port where there are plenty of **rooms** to let and a few modest tavernas (plus summer *kaíkia* to Píso Livádhi on Páros). The sea-view *Hotel Ayia Anna* (no phone; ③) and the adjacent *Kapri* taverna both come highly recommended – the latter not inexpensive, but excellent. Away from the built-up area the beach here is nudist, and, again, though there's an official campsite, people set up tents along behind the sand.

Beyond the headland stretch the five lovely kilometres of **PLÁKA** beach, a vegetation-fringed expanse of white sand which comfortably holds the summer crowds of nudists and campers. There are only a couple of buildings right in the middle of Pláka beach, so bring your own provisions. For real isolation, stalk off to the other side of Mikrí Vígla headland (there's a narrow footpath across the cliff edge) to **KASTRÁKI** beach – almost as good, and with a single taverna. Be warned, however, that the sea at the southern end of this beach (at Alikó promontory) catches the sewage swept down from Náxos town. From Kastráki, it's an hour's walk up to the castle of **Apalírou** which held out for two months against the besieging Marco Sanudo. The fortifications are relatively intact and the views are magnificent. Even more remote is **PIRGÁKI** beach, last stop on the coastal bus route and 21km from Náxos town. There's a new hotel complex here but it remains a pretty place.

A word of warning for campers: although this entire coast is relatively sheltered from the *meltémi*, the plains behind are boggy and you should bring some sort of mosquito repellent along, as well as plenty of fresh water.

The rest of the **southern coast** – indeed, virtually the whole of the southeast of the island – is almost completely deserted, and studded by mountains. You'd have to be a very dedicated and well-equipped camper/trekker to get much out of the region.

Central Náxos and the Tragéa

Although buses for Apóllon (in the north) link up the central Naxian villages, the core of the island – between Náxos town and Apíranthos – is best explored by moped or on foot. Much of the region is well off the beaten track, and can be a rewarding excursion if you've had your fill of beaches.

Out of Hóra, you quickly arrive at the neighbouring villages of **GLINÁDHO** and **GALANÁDHO**, forking respectively right and left. Both are scruffy market centres, Glinádho built on a rocky outcrop above the Livádhi plain, Galánadho displaying the first of Náxos's fortified mansions and an unusual "double church". This is a combined Orthodox chapel and Catholic sanctuary separated by a double arch, reflecting both the tolerance of the Venetians during their rule and of the locals to established Catholics afterwards. Continue beyond Glinádho to **TRÍPODHES** (the ancient *Biblos*), 9km from Náxos town. Noted by Homer for its wines, it's an old-fashioned agricultural village with nothing much to do except enjoy a coffee at the shaded *kafenío*. If you're looking for a longer walk, there's a rough road (past the parish church) which leads down the colourful Pláka valley – past an old watchtower and the Byzantine church of Áyios Mathéos (mosaic pavement) – and ends at the glorious Pláka beach (see above).

To the east, the twin villages of **SANGRÍ** are next, on a vast plateau at the head of a long valley. You can also reach them by continuing to follow the left-hand fork, past Galanádho, a route which allows a look at the domed eighth-century church of **Áyios Mámas** (on the left), once the Byzantine cathedral of the island but neglected during the Venetian occupation and now a sorry sight. Either way, **KÁTO SANGRÍ** boasts the remains of a Venetian castle, while **ÁNO SANGRÍ** is a comely little place, all cobbled streets and fragrant courtyards. A half hour's stroll away, on a path leading south out of the village, is a small Byzantine chapel, **Áyios Ioánnis Yíroulas**; the site originally held a Classical temple of Demeter, then a Christian basilica, and there are marble chunks and column fragments all around – plus a breathtaking view down to the sea.

From Sangrí the road twists northeast into the **Tragéa** region, a densely fertile area occupying a vast highland valley. It's a good jumping-off point for all sorts of exploratory rambling, and **HALKÍ** is a fine introduction to what is to come. Set high up, 16km from the port, it's a noble and silent town with some lovely churches. Tourists wanting to stay here are a rarity, although you can get a room in someone's house by asking at the store. The olive and citrus plantations surrounding Halkí are criss-crossed by paths and tracks, the groves dotted with numerous Byzantine chapels (invariably locked) and the ruins of fortified *pírgi* or Venetian mansions. The **Panayía Protóthronis** church with its eleventh- to thirteenth-century frescoes, and the romantic **Grazia (Frangopoulos) pírgos**, both in Halkí itself, are open for inspection, but only in the morning. Between Halkí and Akadhímos, but closer to the latter, sits the peculiar twelfth-century "piggyback" church of **Áyii Apóstoli**, with a tiny chapel (where the ennobled donors worshipped in private) perched above the narthex; there are brilliant thirteenth-century frescoes as well.

A delightful circular path starts from Halkí. There's a footpath north to KALÓXILOS and, beyond, both a track and a road to **MONÍ**. Just before the village, you pass the sixth-century monastery of **Panayía Dhrossianí**, a group of stark grey stone buildings with some excellent frescoes; the monks allow visitors at any time, though there are coach tours too from Náxos town. Moní itself enjoys an outstanding view of the Tragéa and the surrounding mountains, and has three **tavernas** (and **rooms**) from which you can enjoy both. A dirt road leads on to KINÍDHAROS with its old marble quarry, above the village, and a few kilometres beyond a signpost points you down a rough track to the left, to **FLÉRIO** (also commonly called Melanés). This is the most interesting of Náxos's ancient marble quarries, and is home to two famous **koúri** – idealised statues of classical (sixth century BC) youth that were left recumbent and unfinished because of flaws in the material. Even so, they're finely detailed figures, over five metres in length. One *koúros* lies in a private, irrigated orchard, the other up a hillside some distance above; local children will help you to find it.

From Flério you could retrace your steps to the road and head back to the *hóra* via MÍLI and KOURONOHÓRI (with its ruined Venetian castle), both pretty hamlets and connected by footpaths. More adventurously, ask to be directed south to the footpath which leads over the hill to the Potamía villages. The first of these, **ÁNO POTAMÍA**, has a fine taverna and a rocky track back towards the Tragéa. Once past the valley the landscape becomes craggy and barren, the forbidding Venetian fortress of **Apáno Kástro** perched upon a peak just south of the path. This is believed to have been Sanudo's summer home, but the fortified site goes back further if the Mycenean tombs found nearby are any indication. From the fort, paths lead back to Halkí in around an hour. Alternatively you can continue further southwest down the Potamía valley toward Hóra, passing first the ruined **Cocco pírgos** – said to be haunted by one Constantine Cocco, the victim of a seventeenth-century clan feud – on the way to **MÉSO POTAMÍA**, joined by some isolated dwellings with its twin village **KÁTO POTAMÍA**, nestling almost invisibly among the greenery flanking the creek.

At the far end of the gorgeous Tragéa valley, **FILÓTI**, the largest village in the region, lies on the slopes of Mount Zas (or Zeus) – which at 1000m is the highest point in the Cyclades. Essentially agricultural, the village's only concession to tourism is a garish fast-food restaurant; otherwise nights out are spent in the very Greek and friendly tavernas and *kafenía*, sampling the region's locally bottled orange- and lemonade. Water shortages caused a mass exodus in the 1960s, though Filóti seems to have at least partly recovered. There are, perhaps as a consequence, plenty of old houses to let and you could do worse than use Filóti as a long-term base; rooms or hotels on the other hand are virtually non-existent. From the village, it's a round-trip walk of 2 hours 30 minutes to the summit of Zás, a climb which provides an astounding panoramic view of virtually the whole of Náxos and its Cycladic neighbours. From the main Filóti–Apóllon road, take the side road towards Dhánakos until reaching a small chapel on the right, just beside the start of the waymarked final approach trail.

APÍRANTHOS, a hilly, winding 10km beyond, shows the most Cretan influence of all the interior villages. The houses, built of mostly unwhitewashed local stone, present a mottled grey and tan aspect, and the inhabitants are reserved and dignified, though helpful when approached (and reputed to be the best musicians on the island). Among the subdued houses there are two small **museums** and two Venetian fortified mansions, while the square contains a miniature church with a three-tiered belltower. Ask to be pointed to the start of the spectacular path up over the ridge behind; this ends either in Moní or Kalóxilos, depending on whether you fork right or left respectively at the top.

Apíranthos has a beach annexe of sorts at **MOUTSOÚNA**, 12km east. Emery mined near Apíranthos used to be transported here, by means of an aerial funicular, and then shipped out of the port. The industry collapsed recently and the sandy cove beyond the dock now features a growing colony of vacation villas. The coast south of here is completely isolated, the road petering out into a rutted track – ideal for self-sufficient campers, but again take sufficient water.

Northern Náxos

Even if you've got your own vehicle, it really isn't worth trying to push it any further than Apíranthos; leave the concentration to the bus driver while you enjoy the really startling landscape of the route to APÓLLON.

Jagged ranges and hairpin bends confront you before reaching KÓRONOS, the half-way point, where a road off to the right threads through a wooded valley to **LIÓNAS**, a tiny and very Greek port with a pebbly beach. It's not the greatest of diversions and you'd do best to continue, past SKÁDHO, to the high, remote, emery-miners' village of **KOMIAKÍ** – the original home of the *kitron* liqueur. This is a pleasing, vine-covered settlement, the starting-point for perhaps the most extraordinary walk on Náxos. Head up the mountainside and cross the ridge (there is a path) as far as an improbably long marble *kalderími* or staircase, which loses 300m of altitude descending into the valley. It's overwhelmingly tempting to climb down this Jack-and-the-Beanstalk fixture (though bear in mind that you'll need to come back up at some point): the views are marvellous, the experience exhilarating, and the hamlet at the bottom, **MIRÍSIS**, enchanting. People from Komiakí migrate downwards in spring and summer to tend and harvest their crops; there are no amenities and all the food is locally produced in this veritable oasis.

Back on the main road, a series of slightly less hairy bends lead down a long valley to **APÓLLON** (Apóllonas), an embryonic resort, though rather tatty so far, with the beach by turns clean and calm, or marred by washed-up tar. There are, however, **rooms** to let above the shops and tavernas, several **hotels**, and one major attraction – a **koúros**. On the approach to the village, an unsurfaced road leads to this largest of Náxos's abandoned stone figures. Lying in situ at a former marble quarry, it's just over ten metres long, but, compared to those at Flério, disappointingly lacking in detail. Here since 600 BC, it's a singular reminder of the Naxians' traditional skill; the famous Delian lions (see "Delos" preceding) are also made of Apollonian marble. Not surprisingly, busloads of tours descend upon the village during the day, but by nightfall Apóllon is a peaceful place, with a minimal but traditional nightlife. The local festival, yearly on August 29, is one of Náxos's best, though the place is all but shut a month later.

Apóllon is as far as the bus goes, but with sturdy wheels it's possible to loop back to Náxos town on the northern coastal route: windswept, bleak, and far removed from the verdant centre of the island. Make sure that you're equipped for this trip, since there are few settlements along the way. Long-term plans to pave the road and introduce a direct bus service between Hóra and Apóllon have yet to be implemented.

Ten kilometres past Naxos's northern cape sprouts the beautiful **Ayía** *pírgos*, another foundation (in 1717) of the Cocco family. There's a tiny hamlet nearby, and, 7km further along, a track leads off to **ÁVRAM** beach, an idyllic spot with a family-run taverna and **rooms** to let. Just beyond HÍLLIES VRÍSSES, the only real village in this region, is the abandoned **monastery of Faneroménis**, built in 1606. Nearby, there's another deserted beach, **AMITÍ**, and then the track leads inland, up the Engarés valley, to ENGARÉS and **GALÍNI**, only 6km from Hóra. The road at last becomes paved here, and on the final stretch back to the port passes a unique eighteenth-century Turkish fountain-house and the fortified monastery of **Ayíou Ioánni Hrisostómou**, where a couple of aged nuns are still in residence. A footpath from the monastery, or the road below, leads straight back to town.

Four minor Cyclades: Koufoníssi, Skhinoússa, Iráklia and Dhonoússa

In the patch of the Aegean beween Náxos and Amorgós there is a chain of six small islands neglected by tourists, by guidebooks and by the majority of Greeks, few of whom have ever heard of them. **Kéros** – ancient *Karos* – is an important archaeological site but has no permanent population, and **Káto Koufoníssi** is inhabited only by goatherds. However, the other four islands – **Áno Koufoníssi**, **Skhinoússa**, **Iráklia** and **Dhonoússa** – are all inhabited, served by ferry, and can be visited. They have few facilities other than recently installed electricity and (erratic) phones – scarce water, few provisions in the shop(s), limited choice of food at the restaurant(s), usually no post office and no organised method of changing money – though this, of course, is most of the reason why you're going. Some knowledge of Greek, at least to phrasebook-level, is necessary, and you should be prepared to be regarded as a distinct curiosity. However, if you're looking for peace and solitude – what the Greeks call *isikhía*– you should be able to find it.

A few times weekly in summer a Pireás-based **ferry** – usually the *Express Olympia* or *Apollon Express* – calls at each of the islands, linking them with Náxos and Amorgós and (usually) Páros, Síros, Sérifos and Sífnos. A *kaíki*, the *Skopelitis*, is a reliable daily fixture, leaving Náxos in mid-afternoon for relatively civilised arrival times at all the islets.

Áno Koufoníssi and Kéros

Áno Koufoníssi (or just Koufoníssi) is the least primitive of the group, making a good living from its fishing fleet; unlike the rest, it's therefore beginning to attract substantial numbers of Greek holiday-makers and some seasonal travellers. As it's also the smallest of these islands – you can walk around in a morning if you're energetic– *isikhía*, at least in July and August, may not be possible. The (single) village has recently acquired a **post office** and mains electricity. There is a hotel and a number of **rooms** to let, notably at the main taverna, the *Afroessa*, and in a new building, *Soroccos*. On the southeast coast, behind the long sandy stretch of **Fínikas** beach, there's another (seasonal) taverna. Camping hereabouts presents no problems except that you may have to walk some way for fresh water and supplies.

From the beach, it's sometimes possible to take a *kaíki* to Kéros where you can potter around the remains of a Neolithic village. In the north of the island there's a second settlement, in this case an abandoned medieval village.

Skhinoússa

Skhinoússa, a short hop to the west, is probably the quietest of all Cycladic islands, with a winter population of 85 which barely increases throughout the summer. **MIRSÍNI**, its tiny port hamlet, has a simple restaurant and two *dhomátia* places, but the main settlement is at **HÓRA**, concealed on arrival but less than a mile's walk away up the hill. Here, there are two sparsely stocked shops and two similarly endowed tavernas, plus several rooms establishments. Otherwise it's down to camping at the coarse grey beach (others in the group are fine and yellow) of **Tsigoúri**, ten minutes below Hóra on the southwest coast. There are about a dozen other smaller strands on Skhinoússa, accessible by a lacework of trails. Sitting or swimming at any of them, you can gaze out and reflect on the populated and often raucously touristed islands – Páros, Náxos, Amorgós and Íos – visible all around: a strange sensation.

Iráklia and Dhonoússa

Iráklia, at the southwestern end of the chain, and Dhonoússa, slightly isolated to the north, fall somewhere between the previous two – not as equipped for visitors as Koufoníssi nor as primitive as Skhinoússa. They are also a little larger and more mountainous, decent terrain for a good day's walking.

On Iráklia the old *hóra* of **PANAYÍA**, an hour's walk up through the hills, is now superceded by its very attractive harbour, **ÁYIOS YIÓRYIOS**, set in a fertile valley at the head of a deep inlet. The Iráklia beach, **Livádhi**, lies just off the road between the port and Hóra and is pretty much ideal for camping, though only one of the tavernas here has rooms.

An increasing number of people are visiting Dhonoússa each year and the island's capacity to accommodate them has been under severe pressure. With a permanent population of less than a hundred, resources are extremely limited, so don't expect too much in the way of choice at the three tavernas and one shop. Fresh produce is scarce, though there is an excellent (summer only) bakery. The harbour village is the main settlement, and there are rooms available here. Be warned that there are no other facilities of any kind elsewhere on the island.

If you want to camp or swim nude, you'll have to head out of town, about half an hour to the east, to **Kéndros** beach. There's a second good beach, **Livádhi**, a further hour away in the same direction, reached via the hamlets of **HARAVYÍ** and **MIRSÍNI**. The latter has the only springs, orchards and vegetable patches on the island. A final excursion leads northeast to the hamlet of **KALOTARÍTISSA**, three hours from the port along a path giving impressive views of the coastline. A circuit linking all of the points listed could just be done in a long summer's day, though you'd have little time for swims or picnics; better, perhaps, to break the journey with an overnight camp somewhere.

Amorgós

Like Kárpathos in the Dodecanese, Amorgós is virtually two islands. Roads through its splendidly rugged terrain are so poor that by far the easiest way of getting between KATÁPOLA in the southwest and EGIÁLI in the northeast is by ferry, *kaíki* or hydrofoil. Hydrofoils in particular dovetail well with the appearances of the main-line ferries, and have greatly lessened the island's isolation; gone are the days when you were sure to get marooned here, though the brief hop over to the Dodecanese is still not especially easy. Currently all large and most small boats call at both ports, and accept short-hop passengers between one and the other.

The island can get extremely crowded in mid-summer, with a lot of Germans and, lately, Italians and French, who come to pay their respects to the film location of Luc Besson's *The Big Blue*. Few, however, actually venture out to the wreck of the *Olympia* at the island's west end which figured so prominently in the movie. In general it's a low-key, escapist clientele, happy to have found a relatively large, interesting and uncommercialised island with excellent walking.

This may change, however, since provincial authorities have big plans in mind: paving the lengthwise road which seems to get washed out every winter; instituting a proper bus service between the two parts of the island; banning ferries from Egiáli altogether and turning its port into a yacht marina. Already a few kilometres of road have been widened and strewn with gravel in preparation for asphalting. The yacht harbour, at least, would be a disaster, polluting one of the cleanest bays in the Aegean. It seems an incongruous fate for an island which, like Folégandhros, has been used as a neglected place of political exile for thousands of years.

The southwest

KATÁPOLA, set at the head of a deep bay, is actually three separate hamlets: Katápola proper on the south flank, Rahídhi on the ridge at the head of the gulf, and Ksilokeratídhi along the north shore. The beach here won't win many awards except in the opinion of the two dozen ducks who waddle contently across the foreshore, but by virtue of its convenience the place has become a resort of sorts.

There are plenty of small **hotels** and **pensions**, scattered fairly evenly throughout the three districts, and, except in high summer, proprietors tend to meet those boats arriving around sunset (though not necessarily the other contingent that shows up in the small hours). Among the better places is *Dhimitri's* in Rahídhi, an enormous inland compound of interconnecting buildings in an orchard where bathed rooms with use of kitchen go for ②–③ depending on the season and the number of people. The more obvious *Pension Amorgos* (☎0285/71 013; ③) and fancy *Hotel Minoa* on the water (0285/71 480; ④) will be considerably noisier. In Katápola proper, *Mourayio* is the most popular **taverna** with foreigners, though the locals hang out at *O Kamari* mid-quay, which seems to have more sweets than food. A handful of café/pubs make up what **nightlife** there is. *Prekas* is the single, all-in-one boat **boat ticket agency**; plus there's a new **OTE** open until 11pm. You can also rent **mopeds**, though the local bus service is more than adequate and walking trails delightful. Amorgós's one official **campsite** is well signed between Rahídhi and Ksilokeratídhi, and in the latter district are three **tavernas**. The middle one – *Vitzentzos* – is by far the best; avoid *O Gavalas* with its overpriced slop and undrinkable retsina.

Steps, and then a jeep track, lead out of Katápola to the remains of **ancient Minoa**, which are apt to disappoint up close: some Cyclopean wall four or five courses high, the foundations of an Apollo temple, a crumbled Roman structure and bushels of unsorted pottery shards, most recently excavated in 1981 and 1986. It's only the site, in visual contact with Hóra and ancient Arkessíni, that's the least bit memorable. Beyond

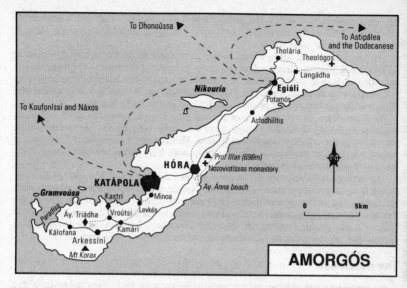

Minoa the track soon dwindles to a trail, continuing within a few hours to ARKESSÍNI (see below) via several hamlets – a wonderful **excursion** with the possibility of catching the bus back.

The **bus** shuttles almost hourly until 11pm between Katápola and Hóra, the island capital; several times daily the service continues to Ayía Ánna via Hozoviótissa monastery, and twice a day there's a run out to the "Káto Meriá", made up of the hamlets of Kamári, Arkessíni and Kolofána. **HÓRA**, also accessible by an hour-long path beginning from behind the Rahídhi campsite, is dominated by a rock plug wrapped with a chapel or two and thirteenth-century Venetian fortifications. Below are countless other bulbous churches, including Greece's smallest, Áyios Fanoúrios, holding just three worshippers – and a line of decapitated windmills beyond. It's a bleak, introverted place, but certainly not without character. Of the half-dozen or so **places to stay**, *Pension Hora* (☎0285/71 110; ④), whose minibus sometimes meets ferries, is the fanciest place, just right of the village entrance, and *Rooms Nomikos* (②), in the rear by the phone antenna, is the most basic. Prices are much the same as in Katápola. In addition to the pair of traditional **tavernas**, *Kastanis* and *Klimataria*, there are several noisy bistro-cafe-pubs, with *To Steki* in the upper plaza perennially popular in the late afternoon. On the same square are the island's main **post office** and a **bank**, though this may not be able to change money.

From the top of Hóra, next to the helipad, a wide cobbled *kalderími* drops efficiently down to two major attractions, effectively short-cutting the road and taking little longer than the bus to reach them. Bearing left at an inconspicuous fork ten minutes' along takes you towards the spectacular monastery of **Hozoviótissa**, which appears suddenly as you round a bend, its vast wall gleaming white at the base of a towering orange cliff. Only three monks occupy the fifty rooms now, but they are quite welcoming considering the number of tour groups and individuals who file through (daily 8am–2pm, also sometimes 5–8pm in summer; donation); you can see the eleventh-century icon around which the monastery was founded, along with a stack of other treasures. The foundation legend is typical for such institutions in outlandish places: during the Iconoclastic period a precious icon of the Virgin was committed to the sea by beleaguered monks at Hózova, somewhere in the Middle East, and it washed up safely at the base of the palisade here. The view from the *katholikón's* terrace, though, overshadows all for most visitors.

The right-hand trail leads down, within forty minutes, to the pebble **beaches** at AYÍA ÁNNA. Skip the first batch of tiny coves in favour of the path to the westernmost bay, where naturists cavort, almost in scandalous sight of the monastery far above. As yet there are no tavernas here, nor a spring (the only one nearby is fenced and locked off above the bus turnaround point), so bring food and water for the day.

For alternatives to Ayía Ánna, take the morning bus out toward modern Arkessíni, alighting at KAMÁRI hamlet (where there's a single taverna) for the twenty-minute path down to the adjacent beaches of **Notiná**, **Moúros** and **Poulopódhi**. Like most of Amorgós's south-facing beaches, they're clean, with calm water, and here, too, a freshwater spring dribbles most of the year.

Archaeology buffs will want to head north from Kamári to VROÚTSI, start of the overgrown hour-long route to **ancient Arkessíni**, a collection of tombs, six-metre-high walls and houses out on the cape of Kastrí. The main path which began at Minoa also passes through Vroútsi, ending next to the well-preserved Hellenistic fort (known locally as the "Pírgos"), just outside modern ARKESSÍNI. The village boasts a single **taverna** with **rooms**, and, more importantly, an afternoon bus back to Hóra and Katápola.

The northeast

Given the sparseness of transport connections between the two halves of Amorgós, and the beauty of the path connecting them, the four-and-a-half-hour **walk** linking Hóra and Egiáli is one of the island's most popular activities, whether out of choice or necessity. Most days in season there's a steady trickle of hikers going in either direction, though it's a good idea to check on the availability of a ferry, hydrofoil or the private **jeep-van** back to your starting-point. The latter is really a shuttle for one of the fancier Egiáli hotels, with preference given to guests, and space must be reserved in advance for its early-morning runs from Egiáli to Hóra (call ☎0285/73 244 or visit a storefront in Egiáli). In theory, they return mid-afternoon.

The photocopy-**map** sold on the island – go for the updated, more expensive edition – is accurate and satisfactory enough for route-finding. On the Hóra side you can start by continuing on the faint trail just beyond Hozoviótissa, but the islanders themselves, in the days before the road existed, preferred the more scenic and wind-sheltered valley route below through TERLÁKI and RIKHTÍ. The two alternatives, and the modern jeep road, more or less meet an hour out of Hóra. Along most of the way you're treated to amazing views of **Nikouriá islet**, nearly joined to the main island and in former times a leper colony. The only habitations on the way are the summer hamlet of ASFODILÍDHI, with well water but little else for the traveller, and POTAMÓS, a double village you encounter on the stroll down towards Egiáli bay.

EGIÁLI (ÓRMOS), smaller than Katápola, is a delightful beach-side place in a 1970s time-warp, epitomised by the fact that you can hire donkeys but not mopeds. Among the better **accommodation** available in the wake of a building boom is the *Hotel Aigaion*, on the east side of town, (rooms with baths at ②–③ rates). You can find even cheaper ones with a sea view by asking at the *Restaurant Korali* or heading down to the far end of the bay past the disco, to two choice "rooms" establishments, one farm selling herbs. Right on the beach is an excellent mid-range option, the *Pensionl Lakki* (☎0285/73 244; ④). Failing that, there's a semi-permanent colony of freelance **campers** on the sand. For **eating out**, the *Korali* has decent fish and the best sunset view, but ultimately loses out to *To Limani* (aka "Katerina's") on the single inland lane, packed until midnight for the sake of its excellent food and barrel-wine, and superb taste in taped music. A few seasonal music bars, such as *Selini*, also attempt to compete with Katerina's.

Unless the scheme to turn the ferry port into a yacht marina pans out, the main Egiáli **beach** is more than serviceable, getting less weedy and reefy as you stroll further north. If it's still not to your taste, a trail here leads over various headlands to an array of clothing-optional bays: the first sandy, the second mixed sand and gravel, the last shingle. There are no facilities anywhere so bring along what you need.

Órmos has its own **bus service** up to each of the two villages visible above and east, with half-a-dozen departures daily up and down, but it would be a shame to miss out on the beautiful **loop walk** linking them with the port. **THOLÁRIA**, reached by the path starting at the far end of the main beach, is named after certain vaulted Roman tombs whose exact location nobody seems to know of or care; a handful of **taverna-cafés**, including a handsome wood-floored establishment near the church, are more contemporary concerns, as is a single rather fancy place with **rooms** (reserve through the *Pension Lakki*). Curling around the head of the vast *kámbos* below is **LANGÁDHA**, the next place you'll arrive at and home to a sizeable colony of expatriates – something reflected in the German-Greek cooking at *Nikos'* **taverna** at the lower end of the village. It also has some **rooms**, as does *Yiannis'* taverna. Langádha – sometimes confusingly referred to as EGIÁLI – supports the only **OTE** booth and **post office** on this end of the island.

Beyond Langádha, another rocky path leads around the base of the island's highest peak, the 821-metre-high **Kríkelon**, passing on the way the fascinating church of **Theológos**, with lower walls and ground plan dating to the fifth century. Somewhat easier to reach, by a slight detour off the main Tholária–Langádha trail, are the church and festival grounds of **Panayía Epanohóri** – not so architecturally distinguished but a fine spot nonetheless.

Íos

No other island is quite like Íos, nor attracts the same vast crowds of young people. The beach is almost as packed with sleeping bags at night as it is with naked bodies by day, and nightlife in the village is loud and long. However, crowded as it is, the island hasn't been commercialised in quite the same way as, say, Míkonos – mainly because few of the visitors have much money. You're either going to decide that Íos (short for "Ireland Over Seas", as some would have it) is the island paradise you have always been looking for and stay for weeks, as many people do, or hate it and take the next boat out – an equally common reaction.

Most visitors stay along the arc delineated by the port – at Yialós, where you'll arrive (there's no airport), in Hóra above it, or at the beach at Milopótamos. It's a small area, and you soon get to know your way around. Three **buses** constantly shuttle between the three places, with a daily service running roughly from 8am to midnight; you should never have to wait more than fifteen minutes, but at least once try the short walk up (or down) the stepped path between Yialós and the Hóra.

Despite its past popularity, **sleeping on the beach** on Íos is worth avoiding these days. Violent crime and police raids are becoming more frequent as the island strains under the sheer impact of youth tourism, and recently the police have been known to turn very nasty – even to the extent of refusing to believe you if you really *have* lost your passport. They prefer you to sleep in the official campsites, which given the problem of theft, is probably good advice. A further problem is the **water shortage**, which has dire effects, above all, on local toilets. Things can get particularly grim in Yialós, and even in the beachside tavernas only the desperate and foolish dare venture out the back. In the village, where there's much more choice, you may find a toilet which flushes, although officially water is too scarce to be used for so frivolous a purpose.

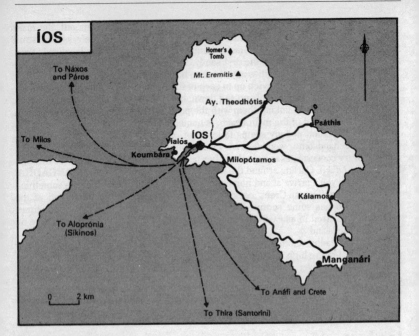

Yialós and Hóra

You might be tempted to grab a **room** in **YIALÓS** as you arrive, though it's the most expensive and least attractive place on the island in which to stay. Owners meet arrivals off the ferries, hustling the town's accommodation; it's up to you whether you take them up on it. Beware that the official campsite here, to the right of the harbour on a scruffy beach, is the worst of the island's three – and mosquito-ridden. From the quayside, **buses** turn around just to the left, while the Yialós **beach** is another five minutes' walk in the same direction. Backed by hotels and rooms-places, it's not peaceful by any means – loud music seems to be accepted on the beach and obligatory in the tavernas, and there are frequent uproarious gatherings – great fun if you like that sort of thing. Yialós has all the other predictable conveniences: a tourist office, a reasonable supermarket (to the right of the bus stop), and a few fairly authentic tavernas. There's also a smaller, less crowded beach at **KOUMBÁRA**, a twenty-minute stroll over the headland, and it's largely nudist. There's also a taverna, and a rocky islet to explore.

Most of the cheaper **rooms** are in **HÓRA**, a twenty-minute walk up behind the port. There's plenty of dormitory space around as well as the usual rooms and hotels – though you've got a better chance of getting something reasonable by haggling if you intend to stay for several days. The old white village is becoming overwhelmed by the crowds of tourists, but with any number of arcaded streets and whitewashed chapels, it still has a certain charm. A bevy of expensive fashion and jewellery boutiques have begun to appear recently, reflecting an increased affluence and consumerism among the once avidly anti-materialist clientele.

What the *hóra* is still really about, though, is **nightlife**. Every evening the streets throb to music from ranks of competing discos and clubs – mostly free, or with a nominal entrance cover charge, though drinks tend to be expensive. In no particular order of importance, some of the best (and longest-established) places to try are: the *Ios Club*, on a peak above the main road, for sunset cocktails and classical music; *Disco Scorpion*, on the road to Milopótamos; the *Sweet Irish Dream* below, where the Pogues and U2 are served at boiling point; *Tomato Bar*, giving a rare island opportunity to shoot pool; the *Why Not?* pub for curries and chili; *Jazz Bar*, sometimes with live music; *Disco 69* for dancing in the street; and the *Village Pub*, with occasional visiting British bands and cheap beer. One to avoid is the *Red Lion* (near the *Sweet Irish Dream*), seemingly a venue for international vomiting contests. There are plenty of places to eat, too: cheapest and best are *I Folia*, near the top of the village, and *Ikoyeniaki Taverna I Stani*, at the heart of town.

Around the island

The most popular stop on the island's bus routes is **MILOPÓTAMOS** (universally abbreviated Milopótas), the site of a magnificent beach and a mini-resort to boot. By day, young people cover every inch of the bus-stop end of the sand, though for a bit more space head the other way, where there are dunes behind the beach. There are two official **campsites**, one at either end of the strip; the first one you come to, *Camping Stars*, is better than *Camping Soulis*. There are **rooms** around (try *Draco Pension* to the right – facing the sea – of the bus stop), and one good self-service **café**, the *Far Out* (so named for the standard reaction to the view on the ride in). You can also walk to Milopótamos from Íos; it takes about 25 minutes, and there are some rooms on the road down.

From Yialós, daily boats depart at around 10am (returning in the late afternoon) to **MANGANÁRI** on the south coast, where there's a beach and a swanky hotel; you can also get there by moped on the newish road. Predominantly nudist, this is the beach to come to for serious tans, although there's more to see, and a better atmosphere, at **ÁYIOS THEODHÓTIS**, up on the east coast. A new **bus** service runs in high season at 10am from Yialós (or ten minutes later from the stop behind the windmills in Hóra), but purists can walk there on a decaying walled track across the heart of the island. This begins just to the north of the windmills; carry water as the hike will take two to three hours. Once there, Áyios Theodhótis boasts a ruined Venetian castle which encompasses the ruins of a marble-finished town and a Byzantine church. If the beach – a good one and mainly nudist – is too crowded (unlikely), try the one at **PSÁTHIS**, an hour's stroll to the southeast. Frequented by wealthy Athenians, this small resort has a couple of pricey tavernas, making it strictly a target for a day-trip rather than a place to stay. The other island beach is at **KÁLAMOS**, another three-hour walk and best reached on a rough road from Hóra. It's very remote indeed, although at PERIVÓLIA – one hour into the walk – there are welcome shady trees and fresh water.

The only cultural diversion on the island is an expensive one. The story goes that, while on a voyage from Samos to Athens, Homer's ship was forced to put in at Íos, the poet subsequently dying on the island. To visit **Homer's "tomb"** you need to hire either a donkey or a *kaíki* – and, ideally, a guide too as it's difficult to find; ask at the tourist office in Yialós. You can walk, but it's a good three hour's slog to the northeastern tip of the island, passing the Psarápirgos tower on Mount Eremítis, until you reach the site of the ancient town of Plakatos. The town itself has long since slipped down the side of the cliff, but the rocky ruins of the entrance to a tomb remain, as well as some graves – one of which is claimed to be Homer's, but which probably dates only to the Byzantine era.

Síkinos

Síkinos has so small a population that the mule-ride or walk up from the port to the village has only recently been replaced by a bus, and until the new jetty was completed it was the last major Greek island where ferry passengers were still taken ashore in launches. With no dramatic characteristics, nor any nightlife to speak of, few foreigners make the short trip over here from neighbouring Íos and Folégandhros or from well-connected Páros, Náxos, or Thíra.

Yet if you spend the required hour walking up from the little harbour of **ALOPRÓNIA**, with its tavernas, handful of rooms (try *Flora*, ☎0286/51 214; ③), and sandy beach, the scenery turns out to be more beautiful than the desolate first impression suggests. The double village of **KÁSTRO-HÓRA**, upon a ridge overlooking the sea, is a charming place, quite untouched by tourism though with just enough rooms to go around – try *Pension Nikos* above one of the *kafenía*. A partly ruined monastery, **Zoödhóhou Piyís** ("Spring of Life", a frequent name on the Cyclades), crowns the rock above, and there are two or three basic tavernas. The architectural highlight of the place, though, is the defensive central quadrangle of **Kástro**, a series of ornate eighteenth-century houses arrayed around a chapel-square, their backs to the exterior of the village.

To the west, an hour's walk (or hired-mule ride) takes you through a landscape lush with olives to **Episkopí**, where elements of an ancient temple-tomb have been ingeniously incorporated into a church dating originally from the seventh century. An hour and a half in the opposite direction lies **Paleokástro**, the patchy remains of an ancient fortress. If you turn down and right (south) from this path you'll come to a pair of beaches, **ÁYIOS YIÓRYIOS** and **ÁYIOS NIKÓLAOS**, which face Íos; the former cove has a well. With somewhat less effort, the pebble beach at **ÁYIOS PANDELÍMONAS** lies just 40 minutes' trail-walk southwest of Aloprónia. All of these beaches are served on occasion by excursion *kaíki* in season.

In addition to the regular ferries there are infrequent local *kaíkia* to and from Íos and Folégandhros. There is no bank, but there is a **post office** up in Kástro-Hóra, near the **OTE**, and you can sometimes change cash at the store in Aloprónia.

Folégandhros

The cliffs of Folégandhros rise sheer in places over 300m from the sea, until the early 1980s a deterrent to tourists as they always were to pirates. It is traditionally an island of political exile, and was used as such in recent decades, but life in the high barren interior has been eased since the junta years by the arrival of electricity and the construction of a road from the harbour to Hóra. A growing number of visitors – mostly German – have begun to tax the island's limited tourist facilities, but rampant commercialisation is still a few years away. **Rooms** are in short supply, however, and since many **ferries** arrive late at night you should be prepared to camp, at least for the first night or two.

KARAVOSTÁSSI, the port, is a popular base, its tavernas and much-sought-after hotel, the *Aeolos* (☎0286/41 205; ③) and rooms a short walk from the pebbly beach. The *Vardia Bay Studios* (②) has excellent rooms overlooking the harbour, with a fine taverna, *The Good Heart*, next door. A little further around, in the next bay, is the hamlet of **LIVÁDHI** and the island's official campsite (sporadically supplied with water); the beach here is fine and shaded, the two seasonal tavernas mediocre.

However, the island's real character and appeal is to be found in the spectacular **HÓRA**, perched on a cliff-top plateau some 45 minutes' walk (or a quick bus ride) from the dock; an hourly bus service runs from morning until late at night. Villagers and foreigners – scores of them in high season – mingle at the tavernas under the trees,

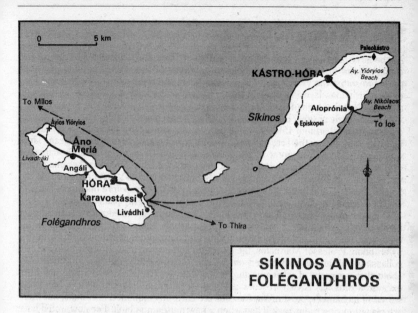

SÍKINOS AND FOLÉGANDHROS

passing the time. Toward the cliff's edge, and entered through an arcade, the defensive core of the medieval **kástro** is marked by ranks of of two-storey houses, whose repetitive, almost identical stairways and slightly recessed doors, are very appealing.

Just above the town, from the square where the bus stops, a zig-zag path with views down to both coastlines leads to the beautiful church of **Análipsi**. Below it is **Hrissospiliá**, a cave with stalactites, but you'll need a boat and close instructions to find it.

In the Kástro, the *Danassis* (☎0286/41 230; ③) is one of the longest established and cheaper **hotels**; it's also the most dramatic place to stay on the island, with some rooms looking directly out on to the alarming drop to the sea. Otherwise, reasonable lodgings include the *Fani-Vevis* (☎0286/41 237; ③) and the *Odysseas* (☎0286/41 239; ③), and a handful of rooms on the outskirts of the village. If you're really stuck for accommodation, *Pavlos's Rooms*, between Hóra and Karavostássi, is often the last outfit to run out of vacancies. A combination **OTE/post office** (no bank) completes the list of amenities.

Northwest of Hóra a road threads its way through **ÁNO MERIÁ**, the other village of the island, deteriorating after several kilometres into what is merely a wide dirt track. There's a taverna about halfway along, an excellent **folk museum** (daily 4–7pm), and, just possibly, rooms. Several times a day the bus trundles out here to drop people off at the footpaths down to the various sheltered beaches on the south and west of the island. Most notable of these is **ANGÁLI** (aka Vathí), an hour's walk west of Hóra. Here you'll find two or three tavernas and some rooms; camping is tolerated but nudism isn't. For that, paths lead twenty minutes east or west to **FIRÁ** or **ÁYIOS NIKÓLAOS** beaches respectively. Alternatively there is a seasonal *kaíki* service once or twice daily between Karavostássi and the Angáli area. **LIVADHÁKI** and **ÁYIOS YIÓRYIOS** beaches, accessible on foot from the last two Áno Meriá bus stops, are more remote and unspoiled. Away from the beaches the countryside is pristine, still largely devoted to the cultivation of barley, which supported many of the Cyclades before the advent of tourism.

Thíra (Santoríni)

As the ferry manoeuvres into the great caldera of Thíra, the land seems to rise up and clamp around it. Gaunt, sheer cliffs loom hundreds of feet above, nothing grows or grazes to soften the view, and the only colours are the reddish-brown, black and gray pumice striations layering the cliff face. The landscape tells of a history so dramatic and turbulent that legend hangs as fact upon it.

From as early as 3000 BC the island developed as a sophisticated outpost of Minoan civilisation, until around 1550 BC when catastrophe struck: the volcano-island erupted, its heart sank below the sea, and earthquakes reverberated across the Aegean. Thíra was destroyed and the great Minoan civilisations on Crete were severely damaged (though probably not destroyed), too. At this point the island's history became linked with legends of Atlantis, the "Happy Isles Submerged by Sea". Plato insisted that the legend was true, and Solon dated the cataclysm to 9000 years before his time – if you're willing to accept a mistake and knock off the final zero, a highly plausible date.

Evidence of the Minoan colony was found near the village of **Akrotíri**, buried under banks of volcanic ash at the southwest tip of the island. Tunnels through the ash uncovered structures, two and three storeys high, first damaged by earthquake then buried by eruption; Professor Marinatos, the excavator and now an island hero, was killed by a collapsing wall and is also buried on the site (Tues–Sat 8.30am–3pm; 1000dr). Only about three percent of what was the largest Minoan city outside of Crete has been excavated thus far. Lavish frescoes adorned the walls, and Cretan pottery was found stored in a chamber; most of the frescoes are currently exhibited in Athens, but there are plans to bring them back if and when a new museum is built. For now, you'll have to content yourself with the (very good) archaeological museum in Firá (see below); Akrotíri itself can be reached by bus from FIRÁ or PERISSA.

These apocalyptic events, though, scarcely concern modern tourists, who are here mostly to stretch out on the island's dark-sand beaches and absorb the peculiar, infernal atmosphere (as recently as a century ago Thíra was still reckoned to be infested with vampires). Though not nearly so predatory as the undead, current visitors have in fact succeeded in pretty much killing off any genuine island life, the island has become a rather expensive and stagey playground .

Coming and going

The arriving ferries, large and small, dock at the somewhat grim port of ÓRMOS ATHINIÓS; SKÁLA FIRÁS and ÍA in the north are reserved for local ferries, excursion *kaíkia* and cruise ships. **Buses**, astonishingly crammed, connect Athiniós with the island capital Firá, and, less frequently, with the main beaches at Kamári and Périssa – disembark quickly and take whatever's going, it's a long walk otherwise. You're also likely to be accosted at Athiniós by people offering rooms all over the island; it can be a good idea to listen to them, given the scramble for beds in Firá especially.

If you alight at Skála Firás, you have the traditional route above you – 580 mule-shit splattered steps to Firá itself. It's not that difficult to walk but the intrepid can also go up by mule or (weather permitting and summer only) by cable car, which runs every fifteen minutes between 7am and 8.30pm. Incidentally, when it comes to **leaving** – especially for summer/evening ferry departures – get to Athiniós a couple of hours in advance, since crowds reminiscent of war-time evacuations gather on the dockside. Note, too, that although the bus service stops around midnight, a shared taxi isn't outrageously expensive. You'll want, in any case, to take one of these to the **airport** near Monólithos, since the shuttle buses connecting with the *Olympic Airways* office in Firá's main square have been suspended.

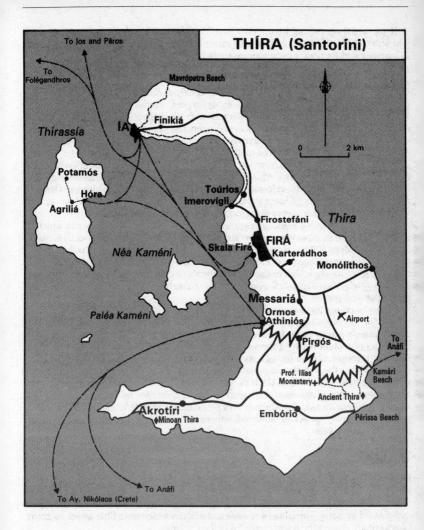

Firá

Half-rebuilt after a devastating earthquake in 1956, **FIRÁ** (Thíra, Hóra) still lurches dementedly at the cliff's edge. A stunningly attractive setting, it appears on postcards and tourist brochures and, naturally, it – and you – pay the price for its position. Besieged by hordes of day-trippers from the cruise boats, it's become incredibly tacky of late, the most grossly commercial spot on what can in summer, at least, seem a grossly commercial island. Gone are the simple restaurants and bakeries of a decade ago, replaced by a mass of supernumerary jewellery and fur boutiques, fast-food places and tourist agencies.

If you insist on staying here, you'll have to move quickly on arrival, particularly if you want one of the better **rooms** with views over the caldera; beds are at a premium in summer and by noon nearly everything is full. Take any reasonable offer, including places just outside the town. Otherwise there are three **youth hostels** in the northern part of town, very cheap, often full to the gills, but not too bad if you have your own bedding and sleep on the roof. Of these, the unofficial *Kamares* hostel is cleaner than the official *YHA* one. In the same neighbourhood, single women can stay at the Dominican convent. Out of season it's easier (and cheaper) to track down rooms; officially, the police only allow hotels to stay open, but you should eventually find someone prepared to put you up. Otherwise, there is the brand-new and well-equipped *Santorini Camping*, a few hundred metres inland from the central square.

For **eating**, try *The Roosters*, along 25 Martiou, which is cheap and unpretentious; *Barbara's*, close by the *Loucas Hotel*, is quite the opposite but worth it. As for **nightlife**, *Bizarre* video bar is youth-orientated, with good music and cheap drinks; *Dionysus Disco* boasts free entry; *Franco's* classical music bar is pricey but great for sunset-watching; while *Enigma*, a soul disco, occupies a converted house and garden.

Firá's cliff-top position is its main attraction but otherwise it's not a place in which to linger. Make time, however, for the **Archaeological Museum** (Tues–Sun 8.30am–3pm, closed Mon; 400dr), near the cable car to the north of town. An excellent collection, it includes a curious set of erotic Dionysiac figures. A separate wing to house finds from the Akrotíri site is due to open soon; there's also an interesting private **Museum Megaro** (daily 10am–1pm & 5–8pm) near the *Kamares* hostel, displaying old engravings, maps and photos.

Buses to points further afield leave Firá from the large square straight ahead from the top of the steps. Timetables are posted in the kiosk at the far end; buses run approximately hourly to Ía, Périssa, Akrotíri, half-hourly to Kamári. There are enough buses to get around between the town and beaches, but if you want to see the whole island in a couple of days hiring a **moped** is useful – try any of the firms on the main road to Ía from the bus station square. One place you can easily **walk** to – in around twenty minutes – is **KARTERÁDHOS**, just south of Firá. It's a small village and a good alternative source of rooms if the capital is full; if there are no rooms, try the *Hotel Albatros* (☎0286/23 431; ③), which is very pleasant. **MESSARIÁ**, another 2km further, is also a possibility for accommodation, although the hotels in this pleasant village are on the expensive side.

The north

Once outside Firá, the rest of Santoríni comes as a nice surprise. The volcanic soil is highly fertile, and every available inch seems terraced and cultivated. Wheat, tomatoes (most made into paste), pistachios and grapes are the main crops, all still harvested and planted by hand. The island's *visándo* and *nikhtéri* wines are a little sweet for many tastes but are among the finest produced in the Cyclades.

ÍA, in the northwest of the island, was once a major fishing port of the Aegean, but it has declined in the wake of economic depression, wars, earthquakes and depleted fish. Partly destroyed in the 1956 earthquake, it presents a curious mix of pristine white reconstruction and tumbledown ruins clinging to the cliff face – by any standards one of the most dramatic towns of the Cyclades. Ía is also much the calmest place on the island, and with the recent introduction of a **post office**, part-time **bank** and bike-hire office there's no longer any reason to feel stuck in Firá. However, **rooms** aren't too easy to come by. The local EOT authorities restored, then privatised, some of the old houses as guest-lodges, all on the exorbitant (⑥) side; far cheaper choices include the troglodytic *Pension Lauda* (☎0286/71 204; ④), the *Hotel Anemones* (☎0286/71 220; ③), and the *Hotel Fregata* (☎0286/71 221; ④) – all fairly reasonable for Santoríni. Recommended

restaurants include *Petros* (for fish) and the popular *Neptune*. If it hasn't already been closed by the police, avoid the rip-off *Café Lotza*, despite its attractive setting on the edge of the abyss. In terms of nightlife, *Strofi* serves as a rock-music bar.

Below the town, 200-odd steps switchback hundreds of metres down to two small harbours: **AMMOÚDHI**, for the fishermen, and **ARMÉNI**, where the ferries dock. Off the cement platform at Ammoúdhi you can swim past floating pumice and snorkel among shoals of giant fish, but beware the currents around the church-islet of Áyios Nikólaos. At Arméni, a single taverna specialises in grilled octopus lunches.

It's 12km from Firá to Ía, easy enough by bus but infinitely more satisfying if you walk the stretch from **IMEROVÍGLI**, 3km out of Firá, using a spectacular footpath along the lip of the caldera. Imerovígli has a taverna and one moderate hotel, the *Katerina* (☎0286/22 708; ③) among the luxury apartments, and if you make the hike on to Ía you'll pass TOÚRLOS, an old Venetian citadel on Cape Skáros, on the way. **FINIKIÁ**, 1km east of Ía, has an excellent unofficial **youth hostel** on the north side of the road, and, among restaurants, the recommended *Markozanes* and the expensive but varied *Finikias*.

The east and south

Beaches on Santoríni, mostly in the east and south, are bizarre – long black stretches of volcanic sand which get blisteringly hot in the afternoon sun. The problem, as always, is that they're no secret and in the summer the crowds can be a bit overpowering. Closest to Firá, **MONÓLITHOS** has a couple of tavernas but is nothing special (though you should be all right camping here, near the airport). Further south, **KAMÁRI** has surrendered lock, stock and barrel to the package-tour operators and there's not a piece of sand that isn't fronted by concrete villas. Nonetheless it's quieter and cleaner than most alternatives, with some beachfront **rooms** available, two inexpensive, co-managed **hotels**, the *Prekamaria* and *Villa Elli* (☎0286/31 266; ③), and a relatively uncrowded **campsite**.

Things are scruffier at **PÉRISSA**, around the cape. Despite (or perhaps because of) being more attractively situated and stocked with lots of cheap rooms, it's noisy and overrun by inconsiderate backpackers, many of whom can't be bothered to cart away their litter after camping rough on the beach, much to the ire of local hoteliers. The official **campsite** is very crowded and not the greatest; it's better, if you're low on funds, to stay in the popular, well-run youth hostel *Anna* (no phone; ①), at the inland entrance to town, open May to October. They also have a few double rooms to let. The beach itself extends almost 7km to the west, sheltered by the occasional tamarisk tree, but it tends to be dirty and wind-buffeted.

Kamári and Périssa are separated by the Mésa Vounó headland, on which stood **ancient Thíra** (Tues–Sun 9am–3pm), the post-eruption settlement dating from the ninth century BC. Expensive taxis and cheaper buses go up from Kamári, but the best route is on foot from Périssa (half an hour) following a clear **path** up past the hillside chapel. Though impressively large, most of the ruins (third–first century BC) are difficult to place, but there are temples and houses with mosaics. The view from the theatre is awesome – beyond the stage there's a sheer drop to the sea. When the city was discovered in the 1890s the uniformed band from Firá trooped all the way up to give a concert. You can continue one hour on the path, soon a cobbled way, down to Kamári, slicing across the switchbacks of the road up. Part way down you pass a huge cave which contains a tiny shrine and a **freshwater spring** – the only one on Thíra and a lifesaver on a hot day.

Inland along the same mountain spine is the monastery of **Profítis Ilías**, now sharing its refuge with Greek radio and TV pylons and antennae of a NATO station, which it will, hopefully, outlive. This used to be open for visits, with a fine little museum of monastic life, but at the end of the 1980s the monks decamped, after a decade of tourgroups, leaving just one of their number to look after the church. He doesn't welcome visitors, save for the annual Profítis Ilías festival, when the whole island troops up here to celebrate. The views are still there to reward you, though, and from near the entrance to the monastery an old footpath heads across the ridge in about an hour to ancient Thíra. On foot, the easiest approach is from the village of PÍRGOS, half an hour's walk below.

PÍRGOS itself is one of the oldest settlements on the island, a jumble of old houses and alleys that also bears the scars of the 1956 earthquake. It climbs to another Venetian fortress crowned by several churches and you can clamber around the battlements for sweeping views over the entire island and its Aegean neighbours. By way of contrast **MESSARIÁ**, a thirty-minute stroll north, has a skyline consisting solely of massive church domes that lord it over the houses huddled in a ravine.

Thirassía and Kaméni

From either Firá or Ía boat excursions run to the burnt volcanic islets of **PALEÁ KAMÉNI** and **NÉA KAMÉNI**, and to the relatively unspoiled islet of **THIRASSÍA**. Néa Kaméni, with its mud-clouded hot springs and shoe-slicing hike to a volcanically active crater, gets mixed reviews, but everybody seems to enjoy Thirassía – part of Santoríni until shorn off by an eruption in the third century BC. There are three small villages on the islet – including the port with its steep stairs up – some tavernas and rooms, and you could live very simply here while waiting for the once-weekly proper ferry. Access is otherwise by excursion boat from Skála Firás or the locals' daily shuttle from Ammoúdhi.

Anáfi

An hour's boat ride to the east of Thíra, Anáfi is the end of the line for most of the ferries which call there, and an excellent retreat from mid-season crowds. Once or twice a week there'll be a boat going on to Crete or some of the Dodecanese so it can prove a useful halting post, too.

It is a small, rather harsh island, with a population of just under 300, almost all of whom live on the south coast, in the port of **ÁYIOS NIKÓLAOS**, with its handful of tavernas serving fresh fish and little crabs, and **HÓRA**, adorning a conical hill a stiff climb above. The cliffs are too steep for a proper road and the mule track up can accommodate nothing more than a motorbike, but in any case there are no cars on the island since there is nowhere else for them to go. Exposed and very windy indeed when the *meltémi* is blowing, Hóra has a few **rooms** to let but only one taverna, one music bar (*I Trelli Garidha* or "The Crazy Shrimp") and surprisingly few *kafenía*; for food and life you're better off in Áyios Nikólaos. It is one of those villages where the men sit inside rather than out to drink their coffee and play backgammon, and at first the place seems a somewhat forbidding ghost town. This impression is slowly dispelled, particularly if you know some Greek, as the people of Anáfi are really very hospitable. There may not be a wide choice of food in the tavernas but the few tiny shops have fresh fruit at the right time of year, there's a good bakery, and also a **post office**.

There is a beach with another taverna at **KLISÍDHI**, a short walk along the cliffs to the east of the harbour, and further along (in the southeast corner of the island) is the empty monastery of **Panayía Kalamiótissa**, built on the site of an ancient temple of Apollo and incorporating part of its masonry. In the mountainous north of the island you come upon a ruined Venetian castle, while numerous tracks lead from Hóra into the interior; most seem to lead nowhere in particular but it's all good walking country. The island is extremely dry, however, and outside the few settlements you'll need to take water with you on any walks.

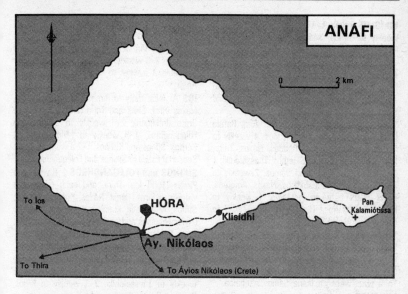

Even if you come to Anáfi in high season you should expect to be marooned here for several days. Although it's nominally the last stop twice a week on various Cyclades ferry routes, the boat may simply skip Anáfi if it's running late – which it generally is. In such a case the only way off the island is by very occasional tourist *kaíki* or, in desperation, a real fishing boat, to Kamári on Thíra.

travel details

Ferries

Most of the Cyclades are served by main-line ferries from **Pireás**, but there are also boats which depart from **Lávrio** (for Kéa, and less often, Síros and Kíthnos) and **Rafína**, which has become increasingly important of late, as the new international airport at nearby Spáta nears completion. At the moment there are regular services from Rafína to Ándhros, Tínos, Míkonos, Síros, Páros, Náxos and Amorgós, with regular extensions of the line into the Dodecanese – a useful link. All three ports are easily reached by bus from Athens.

The frequency of sailings given below is intended to give an idea of services from April to October, when most visitors tour the islands. Expect departures to be at or below the minimum level listed during the winter, with some routes cancelled entirely. Conversely, expect routes to be more comprehensive in spring and autumn, when the government obliges shipping compa-

nies to make extra stops to compensate for numbers of boats still in drydock.

KÉA 1–3 daily to Lávrio (2hr 30min); 1 weekly to Kíthnos.

KÍTHNOS 2–12 weekly to Pireás (4hr); 2–10 weekly to Sérifos, Sífnos, and Mílos; 2–4 weekly to Kímolos, Folégandhros, Síkinos, Íos and Lávrio.

SÉRIFOS AND SÍFNOS 2–12 weekly to Pireás (6hr) and each other; 2–10 to Mílos; 2–4 weekly to Kímolos, Folégandhros, Síkinos, Íos, and Thíra (Santoríni); once weekly to Síros; once weekly to eastern Crete and select Dodecanese; daily (June–Aug) from Sífnos to Páros.

MÍLOS At least daily to Pireás (8hr); 2–8 weekly to Sífnos (2hr), Sérifos and Kíthnos; daily *kaíkia* or ferry to Kímolos; 2–3 weekly to Folégandhros, Síkinos, Íos and Thíra; 1–3 weekly to Crete (Áyios Nikólaos & Sitía); 1–2 weekly to Kássos, Kárpathos, Hálki, Sími and Rhodes (Ródhos).

KÍMOLOS 3 daily *kaíkia* to Mílos (Pollónia); 2–5 weekly to Sífnos, Sérifos, Kíthnos, and Pireás (7hr); 1–2 weekly to Folégandhros, Síkinos, Íos and Thíra.

ÁNDHROS At least 3 daily to Rafína (2hr), Tínos (2hr), and Míkonos; daily to Síros; 1 weekly to Astipálea, Kálimnos, Níssiros, Tílos, Amorgós and the minor islets behind Náxos.

TÍNOS At least 2 daily to Pireás (5hr), Rafína (4hr), Ándhros, Síros and Míkonos; 4 weekly to Páros; 2 weekly to Kos, Rhodes, Náxos, Thíra, Iráklionn (Crete), Skíros, Skíathos, Thessaloníki; 1 or 2 weekly to Ikaría and Sámos; 2 weekly to Astipálea, Kos, Rhodes, Páros, Náxos, Amorgós, minor islets between last two; 1 weekly to Kálimnos, Níssiros, Tílos. Unreliable *kaíkia* to Delos.

SÍROS At least 2 daily to Pireás (4hr), Tínos (1hr), Míkonos (2hr), Náxos, and Páros; 4 weekly to Rafína (3hr 30min), Amorgós and the islets behind Náxos; 3 weekly to Íos, Síkinos, Folégandhros and Thíra; twice weekly to Ikaría, Sámos, Astipálea.

MÍKONOS At least 2 daily to Pireás (5hr), Rafína (3hr 30min), Tínos (1hr), Ándhros (3hr 30min) and Síros (2hr); 2–7 weekly *kaíkia* to Delos; 4 weekly to Amorgós, 2 weekly to Iráklionn (Crete), Thessaloníki, Skíros, Skíathos, Astipálea; 1 weekly to Sérifos, Sífnos, Kálimnos, Níssiros, Tílos.

PÁROS At least 3 daily to Pireás (7hr), Andíparos, Náxos, Íos, Thíra, and Síros; almost daily to Iráklionn (Crete); 3–6 weekly to Ikaría and Sámos; 3 weekly to Amorgós and the islets behind Náxos, and Rafína (5 hr), 3 or 4 weekly to Síkinos and Folégandhros; 3 weekly to Rhodes, Kárpathos, Thessaloníki; 2 weekly to Skíathos, Skíros, Anáfi. Seasonal small ferries to Sífnos and Náxos (Ayía Ánna).

NÁXOS At least 3 daily to Pireás (8hr), Páros (1hr), Síros, Íos and Thíra; 2–3 weekly to Iráklion, Skhinóussa, Koufoníssi, Dhonoússa, and Amorgós; 1–3 weekly to Ikaría and Sámos; 1–2 a week to Crete (Iráklionn), Foúrni, Rafína (6hr 30min). Seasonal *kaíkia* to Páros (Píso Livádhi).

KOUFONÍSSI, SKHINOÚUSSA, IRÁKLIA 1–3 weekly to Pireás or Rafína, Náxos, Páros, Síros, Amorgós, Dhonoússa, and each other; 1 weekly to Astipálea and Kálimnos.

DHONOÚSSA As for the preceding three, plus 2 weekly to Míkonos, Tínos, Síros; 2 extra weekly to Náxos and Páros; 1 weekly to Íos, Thíra and Anáfi.

AMORGÓS 4–6 ferries weekly to Náxos, Páros, and Síros, some of these continuing to Rafína rather than Pireás; 3–4 weekly to Tínos and Míkonos; 2–3 weekly to Dhonoússa; 2 weekly to Astipálea; 1 a week to Kálimnos, Íos, Thíra and Anáfi.

ÍOS At least daily to Pireás (10hr), Páros (5hr), Náxos (3hr), Síros and Thíra (2hr); 3 weekly to Crete (Iráklionn); 2–6 weekly to Síkinos and Folégandhros; 1–3 weekly to Mílos, Kímolos, Sérifos, Sífnos and Kíthnos; 1–2 a week to Anáfi. Seasonal *kaíkia* to Síkinos and Folégandhros.

SÍKINOS and FOLÉGANDHROS 2–6 weekly to Pireás (10hr) Íos, Thíra, and each other; 1–3 weekly to Síros, Páros, Náxos, Kíthnos, Sérifos, Sífnos, Mílos and Kímolos; 1 weekly to Crete (Áyios Nikólaos and/or Sitía), Kássos, Kárpathos, Hálki, Sími and Rhodes; seasonal *kaíkia* to Íos.

THÍRA At least daily to Pireás (10–12hr), Páros, Íos and Náxos; 3–6 weekly to Iráklionn, Crete (5hr); 3–5 weekly to Síkinos and Folégandhros; 3 weekly to Thessaloníki; 2–3 weekly to Milos, Kímolos, Sífnos, Sérifos and Kíthnos; 2 weekly to Skíros, Skíathos, Anáfi; Astipálea, Kálimnos, Kos and Rhodes; 1 weekly to Crete (Áyios Nikólaos and Sitía), Kárpathos, Kássos, Hálki and Rhodes; also weekly to Amorgós and minor islets. Seasonal *kaíkia* to Anáfi and Íos; regular shuttle from Ía to Thirassía.

ANÁFI 2–3 weekly to Thíra (2hr) and Pireás (18hr); 1 weekly to Crete (Iráklionn), Amorgós, Dhonoússa; 2 weekly to Íos, Náxos, Páros, Síros.

Other services

To simplify the lists above, certain strategic **hydrofoil** and **small-boat services** have been omitted. Of these, the *Skopelitis* plies daily in season between Míkonos and Amorgós, spending each night at the latter and threading through all of the minor isles between it and Náxos, as well as Náxos and Páros (Píso Livádhi), in the course of a week. Note that this boat has no café or restaurant on board - so take provisions for what can be quite lengthy journeys. The popular *Íos Express* links Thíra (Skála Firás), Íos, Náxos, Páros and Míkonos daily in season. The *Katamaran*, not a ferry despite its appearance on *EOT* lists but a small-capacity (and expensive) hydrofoil, operates daily out of Flísvos marina in Pireás and connects Síros, Tínos, Míkonos, Páros and Náxos with either the minor isles and Amorgós or a selection from among Íos, Síkinos, Folégandhros,

Thíra and Anáfi (☎0294/22 888 for details). In summer there are *Ilio Line* hydrofoils (*Delfini I, II, III, IV, V*), based in Rafína, which pretty much parallel the large ferry services out of that port. Finally and somewhat unreliable, is the *Nearchos*, a catamaran-type hydrofoil, theoretically linking Páros, Íos and Thíra with either Iráklionn or Réthimnon on Crete.

International ferries
Between May and October, *Minoan Lines* links Páros with Kuşadasi (Turkey) and Ancona (Italy) twice weekly. One domestic stopover – either on Sámos or Kefalloniá – may be allowed.

Flights
There are **airports** on **Míkonos**, **Thíra**, **Páros**, **Náxos**, **Mílos** and **Síros**, listed in decreasing order of flight frequency from Athens. In season, or during storms when ferries are idle, you have

little chance of getting a seat on less than three days' notice. The Mílos–Athens route is probably the best value for money; the other destinations seem deliberately overpriced, in a – usually unsuccessful – attempt to keep passenger volume manageable. Expect off-season (Oct–April) frequencies to drop by at least 80 percent.

Athens–Míkonos (4–8 daily; 50min)
Míkonos–Thíra (4 weekly; 40min)
Míkonos–Iráklionn (3 weekly; 70min)
Míkonos–Rhodes (4 weekly; 70 min)
Athens–Thíra (4–5 daily; 1hr)
Thíra–Iráklionn (3 weekly; 40min)
Thíra–Rhodes (4 weekly; 1hr)
Athens–Páros (4–7 daily; 45min)
Athens–Náxos (3–5 daily; 45min)
Athens–Mílos (4 daily; 45min)
Athens–Síros (3 daily; 35min)

CHAPTER EIGHT

CRETE

rete is a great deal more than just another Greek island. Often, especially in the cities or along the developed north coast, it doesn't feel like an island at all, but rather a substantial land in its own right. Which of course it is: a mountainous, wealthy and at times surprisingly cosmopolitan one. But when you lose yourself among the mountains, or on the less-known coastal reaches of the south, it has everything you could want of a Greek island and more: great beaches, remote hinterlands, and enormously hospitable people.

In history Crete is distinguished above all as the home of Europe's earliest civilisation. It was only at the beginning of this century that the legends of King Minos and of a Cretan society that ruled the Greek world in prehistory were confirmed by excavations at Knossós and Festós. Yet the **Minoans** had a remarkably advanced society, the centre of a maritime trading empire as early as 2000 BC. The artworks produced on Crete at this time are unsurpassed anywhere in the ancient world and it seems clear, wandering through the Minoan palaces and towns, that life on Crete in those days was good. Their apparently peaceful culture survived at least three major natural disasters.

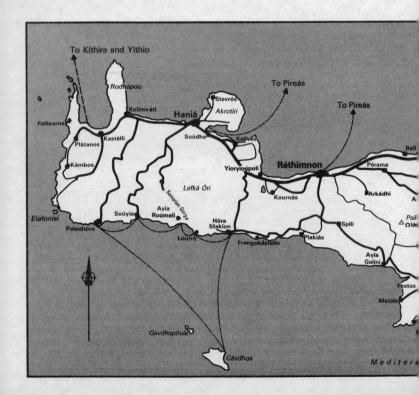

Each time the palaces were destroyed, but they were rebuilt on an even grander scale. Only after the last destruction – probably the result of a massive eruption of Thíra (Santoríni) and subsequent tidal waves and earthquakes – do significant numbers of weapons begin to appear in the ruins. This, together with the appearance of the Greek language, has been interpreted to mean that Mycenaean Greeks had taken control of the island. Nevertheless, for nearly 500 years – by far the longest period of peace the island has seen – Crete was home to a culture well ahead of its time.

The Minoans of Crete came originally from Anatolia; at their height they maintained strong links with Egypt and with the people of Asia Minor, and this position as meeting point – and strategic fulcrum – between east and west has played a major role in Crete's **subsequent history**. Control of the island passed from Greeks to Romans to Saracens, through the Byzantine Empire to Venice, and finally to Turkey for more than two centuries. During World War II the island was occupied by the Germans and attained the dubious distinction of being the first place to be successfully invaded by paratroops. Each one of these diverse rulers has left some mark, and more importantly they have forged for the island a personality toughened by endless struggles for independence.

Today, with a flourishing agricultural economy, Crete is one of the few islands which could probably support itself without **tourists**. Nevertheless, tourism is heavily promoted. The northeast coast in particular is overdeveloped and, though there are parts of the south and west coasts that have not been spoiled, they are getting harder and harder to find. By contrast, the high mountains of the interior are still barely touched, and one of the best things to do on Crete is to rent a vehicle and explore the remoter villages, often only a few kilometres off some heavily beaten track.

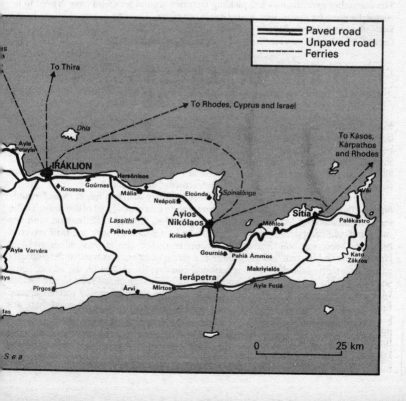

Where to go

Every part of Crete has its loyal devotees and it's hard to pick out highlights, but generally if you want to get away from it all you should head west, towards **Haniá** and the smaller, less well-connected places along the south and west coasts. It is in this part of the island also that the White Mountains rise, while below them yawns the famous **Samarian Gorge**. The far east, around **Sitía**, is also relatively unscathed.

Whatever you do, the first main priority is to leave **Iráklion** (Heraklion) as quickly as possible, having paid the obligatory, and rewarding, visit to nearby **Knossós**. The other great Minoan sites cluster around the middle of the island: **Festós** and **Ayía Triádha** in the south (with Roman **Górtys** to provide contrast), **Mália** on the north coast. Almost wherever you go, though, you'll find a reminder of the island's history – the town of **Gourniá** near the fleshpots of **Áyios Nikólaos**, the palace of **Zákros** in the far east, or the lesser sites scattered around the west. For many people, unexpected highlights include Crete's Venetian forts, dominant at **Réthimnon**, magnificent at **Frangokástello**, and others in various stages of ruin around most of the island; its Byzantine churches, most famously at **Krítsa** but again almost anywhere; and, at Réthimnon and Haniá, the cluttered old quarters full of Venetian and Turkish relics.

Climate

As the southernmost of all Greek islands, Crete has by far the longest summers and you can get a decent tan here right into October and swim at least from May until November. Its agricultural importance, and the several annual harvests, also make it the most promising (if also the most sought-after) location for finding **casual work**. The cucumber greenhouses and pickling factories around Ierápetra have proved to be winter lifelines for many long-term Greek travellers. The one seasonal blight is the *meltémi*, which blows harder here and more continuously than anywhere else in Greece – the best of several reasons for avoiding an **August** visit.

IRÁKLION, KNOSSÓS AND CENTRAL CRETE

Many visitors to Crete arrive in the island's capital, **Iráklion** (Heraklion), but it's not a beautiful city, nor one where you'll want to stay much longer than it takes to get your bearings and visit the **archaeological museum** and nearby **Knossós**. Iráklion itself, though it has its good points – superb fortifications, a fine market, atmospheric old alleys, and some interesting lesser museums – is for the most part an experience in survival: modern, raucous, traffic-laden, overcrowded and expensive.

The area immediately around the city is less touristy than you might expect, mainly because there are few decent beaches of any size on this central part of the coast. To the west, mountains drop straight into the sea virtually all the way to Réthimnon, with just two significant coastal settlements – **Ayía Pelayía**, a sizeable resort, and **Balí**, which is gradually becoming one. Eastwards, the better resorts are at least 40km away, at Hersónissos and beyond, although there is a string of rather unattractive development all the way there. Inland, there's agricultural country, the richest on the island, and a series of wealthy but rather dull villages. Directly behind the capital rises Mount Ioúktas with its characteristic profile of Zeus; to the west the Psilorítis massif spreads around the peak of **Mount Ída** (Psilorítis), the island's highest. On the south coast there are few roads and little development of any kind, except at **Ayía Galíni** in the southwest, a nominal fishing village long since swamped with tourists, and **Mátala**, which has thrown out the hippies that made it famous and is now crowded with package-trippers. **Léndas** has to some extent occupied Mátala's old niche.

Despite the lack of resorts, there seem constantly to be thousands of people trekking back and forth across the centre of the island. This is largely because of the superb archaeological sites in the south: **Festós**, second of the Minoan palaces, with its attendant villa at **Ayía Triádha**, and **Górtys**, capital of Roman Crete.

Iráklion

The best way to approach **IRÁKLION** is by sea; that way you see the city as it should be seen, with Mount Ioúktas rising behind and the Psilorítis range to the west. As you get closer it's the city walls that first stand out, still dominating and fully encircling the oldest part of town, and finally you sail in past the great fort defending the harbour entrance. Unfortunately, big ships no longer dock in the old port but at great modern concrete wharves alongside – which neatly sums up Iráklion itself: many of the old parts have been restored from the bottom up, but they're of no relevance to the dust and noise characterising the city today. These renovations invariably look fake, far too polished and perfect alongside the grime that seems to coat even the newest buildings.

The Town

From the port the town rises overhead, and you can cut up the stepped alleys for a direct approach to Platía Eleftherías (Liberty Square), the tourist office and the archaeological museum. The easiest way to the middle of things, though, is to head west along the coast road, past the main bus station, and then up Odhós 25 Avgoústou. Lined with shipping agencies, travel agents and bike rental places, 25 Avgoústou leads into **Platía Venizélou**. This is crowded with Iráklion's youth, patronising outdoor cafés which are marginally cheaper than those on Eleftherías, and with travellers who've arranged to meet in "Fountain Square". The **fountain** itself, built by Venetian governor Francesco Morosini in the seventeenth century and incorporating four lions which were some 300 years old even then, is not particularly spectacular at first glance (especially as it's usually clogged with mud and cigarette ends) but on closer inspection is really a very beautiful work. From the *platía* you can strike up Dedhálou, a pedestrianised street full of tourist shops and restaurants, or continue on 25 Avgoústou to a major traffic junction. To the right, Kalokerinoú leads west out of the city, the **market** lies straight ahead, and Platía Eleftherías is a short walk to the left up Dhikeosínis.

Platía Eleftherías and the Archaeological Museum
Platía Eleftherías is very much the traditional heart of the city, both in terms of traffic, which swirls around it constantly, and for life in general: lined with expensive cafés and restaurants, and jammed in the evening with strolling hordes. Most of Iráklion's more expensive shops are in the streets leading off the square.

The **Archaeological Museum** (Tues–Sat 8am–7pm, Sun 8am–6pm; though major restoration work may mean some changes) is also just off here, directly opposite the EOT office. Almost every important prehistoric and Minoan find on Crete is included in this fabulous, if bewilderingly large, collection. The museum tends to be crowded – especially when a guided tour stampedes through – but it's worth taking time over. You can't hope to see everything, nor can we attempt to describe it all (several good museum guides are sold here – best is probably the glossy one by J. A. Sakellarakis) but **highlights** include the town mosaics in Room 2 (galleries are arranged basically in chronological order), the famous inscribed disc from Festós in Room 3 (itself the subject of several books), most of Room 4, especially the magnificent bull's head *rhyton* (drinking vessel), the jewellery in Room 6 (and everywhere), and the engraved black vases in Room 7. Save some of your time and energy for upstairs, too, where the Hall of

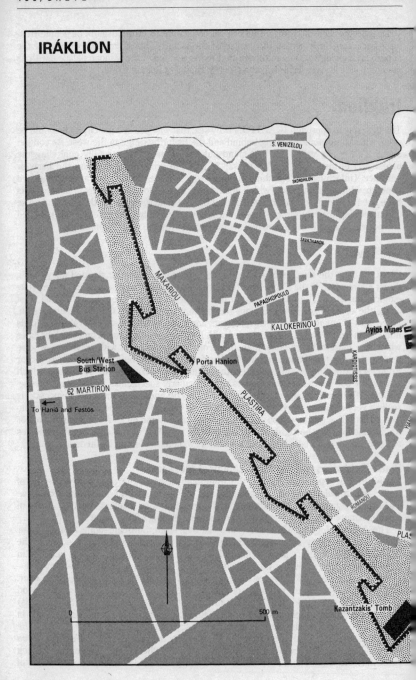

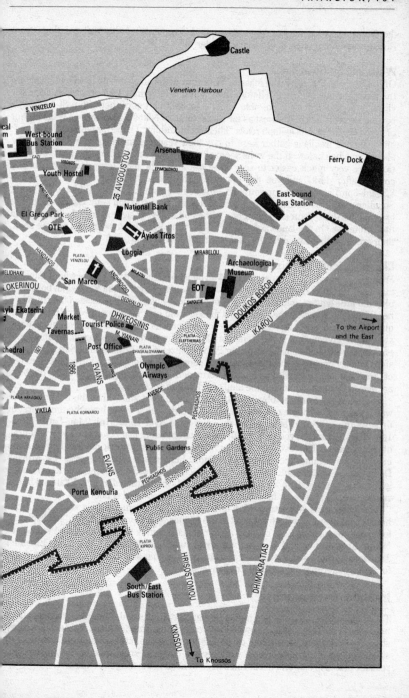

Castle

Venetian Harbour

S. VENIZELOU

cal
m

West-bound
Bus Station

GAZI

Arsenali

EPIMENIDHOU

Ferry Dock

Youth Hostel

VIRONOS

25 AVGOUSTOU

East-bound
Bus Station

National Bank

El Greco Park

OTE

HANDAKOS

MINOTAFOU

Áyios Titos

Loggia

MILATOU

MIRABELOU

Archaeological
Museum

PLATIA
VENIZELOU

ANDHROGEO

EOT

SAPOUTIE

DOUKOS BOFOR

ELIDHAKI

San Marco

DEDHALOU

IKAROU

To the Airport
and the East

OKERINOU

yia Ekaterini

Market

DHIKEOSINIS

PLATIA
ELEFTHERIAS

Tavernas

Tourist Police

M. YIANARI

Post Office

1966

PLATIA
DHASKALOYIANNIS

hedral

EVANS

Olympic
Airways

AVEROF

PEDHIADHOS

PLATIA ARKADIOU

VIKELA

PLATIA KORNAROU

Public Gardens

EVANS

PEDHIADHOS

Porta Kenouria

PLATIA
KIPROU

HRISOSTOMOU

DHIMOKRATIAS

South/East
Bus Station

KNOSOU

To Knossós

the Frescoes, with intricately reconstructed fragments of the wall paintings from Knossós and other sites, is especially wonderful.

Walls and fortifications

Of Iráklion's later history, the massive **Venetian walls**, in places up to 45 feet thick, are the most obvious evidence. Though their fabric is incredibly well preserved, access is virtually nonexistent. It is possible – just – to walk on top of them from St Anthony's bastion over the sea in the west as far as the tomb of Nikos Kazantzakis, Cretan author of *Zorba the Greek*. His epitaph reads "I believe in nothing, I hope for nothing, I am free"; on weekends Iraklians gather here to pay their respects and enjoy a free view of the soccer matches below. If the walls seem altogether too much effort, the **port fortifications** are very much easier to see. Stroll out along the jetty (crowded with courting couples after dark) and you can get inside the sixteenth-century **castle** (Tues–Sun 8.30am–3pm) at the harbour entrance, emblazoned with the Venetian Lion of St Mark. Standing atop this you can begin to understand how Iráklion – or Candia as it was known until the seventeenth century – withstood a 22-year siege before finally falling to the Ottomans. On the landward side of the port the Venetian *arsenali* can also be seen, their arches rather lost amid the concrete road system all around.

Churches, icons and history

From the harbour, 25 Avgoústou will take you up past most of the rest of what's interesting. The church of **Áyios Títos**, on the left as you approach Platía Venizélou, borders a pleasant little square. It looks magnificent principally because, like most of the churches here, it was adapted by the Turks as a mosque and only reconsecrated in 1925; consequently it has been renovated on numerous occasions. On the top side of this square, abutting 25 Avgoústou, is the Venetian **City Hall** with its famous *loggia*, again almost entirely rebuilt. Just above this, facing Platía Venizélou, is the church of **San Marco**, its steps usually crowded with the overflow of people milling around in the square. Neither of these last two buildings has found a permanent role in its refurbished state, but both are generally open to house some kind of exhibition or craft show.

Slightly away from the obvious city-centre circuit but still within the bounds of the walls, there are a couple of lesser museums worth seeing if you have the time. First of these is the collection of **icons** in the church of **Ayía Ekateríni** (Mon–Sat 9.30am–1pm, Tues, Thurs & Fri also 5–7pm), an ancient building just below the ugly cathedral, off Kalokerinoú. This excellent display might inspire you to seek out less-known icons in churches around the island. The finest here are six large scenes by Mihalis Damaskinos, a near-contemporary of El Greco who fused Byzantine and Renaissance influences. Supposedly both Damaskinos and El Greco studied at Ayía Ekateríni in the sixteenth century when it functioned as a sort of monastic art school.

The **Historical Museum** (Mon–Fri 9am–5pm, Sat 9am–2pm) is some way from here, down near the waterfront next to the former westbound bus station. Its display of folk costumes and jumble of local memorabilia includes the reconstructed studies of Nikos Kazantzakis and Cretan statesman (and Greek prime minister) Emanuel Tsouderos); there's enough variety to satisfy just about anyone and comic relief in the form of wonderfully nonsensical English labelling.

Iráklion practicalities

Tourist life focuses on the two main squares, Eleftherías and Venizélou, and the alleys between them. This district, crowded with cafés and restaurants, souvenir and jewellery shops, is also where the entire local population turns out in the evenings to parade or to sit and gossip. Lingering here a while over a coffee is irresistible but expensive. For realistic places to stay and to eat you'll need to head to the fringes of this area.

> The telephone code for Iráklion is ☎081

Accommodation

Finding a **room** can be difficult in season. The best place to look for inexpensive rooms is in the area below Platía Venizélou, along Handhákos and towards the old westbound bus station and the youth hostel. Other concentrations of affordable places are around El Greco park and by the bottom of the market – slightly more expensive and noisy – and off Kalokerinoú, down towards Haniá Gate. There are odd places scattered everywhere, though – take any bed you can find when you arrive and look at leisure the next day if necessary. The dusty part between the main bus station and the harbour is always crowded with the sleeping bags of those who failed to find, or couldn't afford, a room; if you're really hard up, crashing here has the advantage that local farmers come around recruiting casual labour in the mornings – but a pleasant environment it's not.

Youth Hostel, Vironos 5 (☎286 281). In a new location just off 25 Avgoústou: cheap, convenient and likely to have a spare dormitory bed. ①

Yours Hostel, Hándhakos 24 (☎280 858). In the old youth hostel, building, and although it unscrupulously tries to pass itself off as the official youth hostel the place seems well run and is only slightly more expensive. Dorms, single-sex rooms, private rooms and roofspace. ①

Rent Rooms Vergina, Hortátson 32 (☎242 739). Basic but pleasant cheap rooms around a courtyard with an enormous banana tree; English spoken. ②

Rent Rooms Mary, Hándhakos 67 (☎281 135). Decent, cheap rooms place, complete with cold showers and a courtyard to sit and chat. ②

Hotel Rea, Kalimeráki 1 (☎223 638). Between the two above, a friendly, comfortable D-class place: booking essential. ③

Hotel Paladion, Hándhakos 16 (☎282 563). D-class hotel closer to Platía Venizélou with clean but stuffy rooms upstairs, and a pleasant garden at the back with rooms off it. ③

Atlas Guest House, Kandanoleon 6 (☎288 989). Rather run-down old place, in a convenient but noisy alley between Platía Venizélou and El Greco Park. ③

Pension Lion, Andhróyeo 9, alongside San Marco (☎241 194). Across 25 Avgoústou from all the foregoing; pleasant and relatively quiet. ③

Hotel Idaion Andron, Perdhikári 1 (☎283 624). Behind the Venetian Loggia, tiny E-class hotel around a flowery courtyard. Rooms small and very basic, but good value. ③

Hotel Ionia, Evans 5 (☎281 795). At the corner of Evans and Yiánari, also near the market; offers marginally greater comforts and a good restaurant: may by now have been refurbished and upgraded from E-class. ③

ISLAND ACCOMMODATION: ROOM PRICE SCALES

All **hotels** listed in this book have been price-graded according to the scale outlined below. The **rates quoted** represent the **cheapest available room in high season**; all are prices for a double room, except for category ①, which are per person rates. Out of season rates can drop up to fifty percent, especially if you negotiate rates for a stay of three or more nights. Single rooms generally cost around seventy percent of the price of a double.

Rented **"private rooms"** on the islands invariably fall into the ② or ③ categories, depending on their location and facilities, and the season. They are not generally available from October through to the beginning of March, when only hotels tend to remain open.

① 1000–1500dr (£3–4.50/US$5.50–8)
② 2000–3000dr (£6–9.50/US$11–16.50)
③ 3000–5500dr (£9.50–17/US$16.50–30)
④ 5500–7500dr (£17–23/US$30–41.50)
⑤ 7500–9000dr (£23–28/US$41.50–50)
⑥ 9000dr and upwards (£28/US$50 upwards)

For further explanation of our hotel category system, see p.32.

Hotel Christos, Yiamaláki 17 (☎287 390). One of the better choices (E-class) in the side streets off Kalokerinoú. ③

Hotel Dedalos, Dedhálou 15 (☎224 391). Very centrally placed on the pedestrianised alley between Venizélou and Eleftherías. Slightly shabby rooms with balconies, but convenient and reasonably priced; C-class. ④

Camping Iráklion, Amoudhári beach, about 6km west (☎286 380). The only nearby campsite: enormous but not very attractive, with souvenir shop, cafeteria, swimming pool. Strictly run and expensive, it's reached by bus #6, from outside the *Hotel Astoria* in Platía Eleftherías.

Food

Big city as it is, Iráklion disappoints when it comes to eating – and even more when it comes to going out after you've eaten. The cafés and tavernas of the main squares – **Venizélou** and **Eleftherías** – are essential places to sit and watch the world pass, but their food is on the whole expensive and mediocre. One striking exception is *Bóuyatsa Kirkor*, by the fountain in Venizélou, where you can sample authentic, home-made *Bóuyatsa*, a creamy cheese pie served warm and sprinkled with sugar. The cafés and restaurants on **Dedhálou**, the pedestrian alley linking the two squares, are popular with tourists, but again not particularly good value.

For real, sensibly priced **food**, you need to get off this most obvious part of the tourist trail, though not necessarily far. Perhaps the most attractive option is to head for the little alley, Fotíou Theodosáki, which runs through from the **market** to Odhós Evans. It is entirely lined with the tables of rival tavernas, most surprisingly grimy and authentic-looking – check prices, though, as many are not as cheap as they look. Nearby, at the corner of Evans and Yiánari, the taverna under the *Hotel Ionia* is more straightforward, with a wide selection of baked dishes on display.

Other good tavernas are more scattered. Still near the centre, just off Eleftherías at the entrance to **Platía Dhaskaloyiánnis** (where the post office is), are a couple that are cheap and convenient, if not wonderful, and some pleasant cafés – among them *Café Flou*, which has music at night. **Nearer Venizélou**, try exploring some of the backstreets to the east, off Dedhálou and behind the Loggia: the *Cyprus Taverna* and the *Curry House*, for example, are easy to spot and there are others nearby. *Taverna Giovanni*, on an alley parallel to Dedhálou (there's a sign near the *Pizzeria Victoria*), is a friendly place with a varied menu and reasonable prices.

Down **around the harbour** you'll find a number of other, slightly more expensive possibilities. *Ta Psaria*, a fish taverna at the bottom of 25 Avgoústou, has been done up recently and prices have risen accordingly, but it remains a fine place to sit and look out over the castle. Right on the water not far west of here is a short line of others, with glass and plastic screens to keep out the worst of the winds. Also in this area, though without the sea view, *Taverna Rizes* at the bottom of Hándhakos is considerably cheaper – a pleasant, quiet courtyard setting, too.

At the more basic end of the range, **takeaways** abound. There's a group of *souvláki* stalls, for instance, clustering around 25 Avgoústou at the entrance to El Greco Park – the park itself is handy if you need somewhere to sit and eat. For cheese or spinach pies and a variety of other baked items, there are a couple of bakeries at the top of the park, or try the doughnut place on Platía Nikíforos Fókas at the bottom of Odhós 1821.

If you want to buy your own food, the **Market** on Odhós 1866 is the place to go – an attraction in itself, which you should see even if you don't plan to buy.

Bars and nightlife

As for **nightlife**, Iráklion is a bit of a damp squib when compared to many other towns on the island. Much of what does happen takes place in the suburbs or out along the hotel strip to the west. If you're determined, however, there are a couple of city-centre possibilities – and plenty of options if all you want to do is sit and drink.

Bars are mostly to be found in the areas already covered under restaurants. Perhaps the most pleasant place is a quiet square behind Dedhálou (up from the *Taverna Giovanni*), where there are several quietly trendy little bars (including *Flash* and *Avga*) with outdoor tables – popular with students in term time. Around Platía Venizélou are numerous slightly more touristy alternatives: the first-floor "Piano Bar/Ladies Café" *Loggia*, for example, with a pleasant rooftop bar at the top of the same building, and others in basements along Kandanoléon, off El Greco Park. The *Onar* café and tearoom at Hándhakos 36b, north of Venizélou has a small terrace where they serve a wide variety of teas as well as great ices to a gentle jazz background, just the thing when you're winding down around midnight. *Tasos*, on the way down here next to *Yours Hostel*, is a popular hangout for young hostellers, lively at night and with good breakfasts to help you recover in the morning.

Discos proper include *Trapeza*, behind the *Astoria Hotel* down a street opposite the Archaeological Museum, and *Endasie*, on the street behind the Loggia and Áyios Títos – a white marble place with a Cadillac centrepiece and a relatively laid-back atmosphere. For bigger, brighter places less packed with local lads, the resort strip to the west is better – try, for example, *Stathmos* on the road to Gazi, enormous with a breathtaking light show, or *Apollonia*, out near the *Creta Beach* hotel. There are also numerous **cinemas** scattered about; check the posters by the tourist police office. Most enjoyable is the open-air place by *Camping Iráklion*, on the beach to the west.

Information, necessities and car rental

Iráklion's **tourist office** (Mon–Fri 8am–2pm; ☎222 487) is just below Platía Eleftherías, opposite the archaeological museum. The **tourist police** are on Dhikeosínis, halfway between Platía Eleftherías and the market, and the **post office** is just behind here, on Platía Dhaskaloyiánnis. The 24-hour **OTE** office – often with long queues – is next to El Greco Park, in the square immediately north of Venizélou. **Banks** are common – you can find several down 25 Avgoústou, where the **shipping and travel agents** are. You'll also find **motorbike and car rental** down here, but places off the main road offer better prices; try *Motorrad* at Vironos 1 (☎281 670) for bikes, or *Ritz* in the *Hotel Rea* (Kaliméraki 1; ☎223 638) for cars. There are two **launderettes** in the backstreets close to the archaeological museum – follow the signs.

Beaches

Iráklion's **beaches** are some way out, whether east or west of town. In either direction they're easily accessible by public bus, however: #6 west from immediately outside the *Astoria Hotel* in Platía Eleftherías; #7 east from the stop opposite this, under the trees in the centre of the square. **Almirós** (or Amoudhári) to the west has been subjected to a degree of development – the campsite, several medium-size hotels and one giant one (the *Zeus Beach*, in the shadow of the power station at the far end) – and the beach is hard to get to without walking through or past one of these. **Amnissós**, to the east, seems the better choice, with several tavernas and the added amusement of planes swooping in immediately overhead to land. This is where most locals go on their afternoons off – the farthest of the beaches is the best, although new hotels are encroaching here too.

Transport

Iráklion **airport** is right on the coast, 4km east of the city. *Olympic* flights are met by a bus which runs direct to their office in Platía Eleftherías, or the #1 bus (also to Eleftherías) leaves every few minutes from a grassy bit of the car park in front of the terminal; buy your ticket (45dr) at the booth before boarding. There are also plenty of taxis outside, and prices to major destinations are posted; it's about 500dr to the centre of town. If you arrive by **ferry**, you can simply walk into town.

There are four main **bus stations**. Services along the coastal highway to or from **the east** (Mália, Áyios Nikólaos, Sitía etc) use the terminal just off the main road between the ferry dock and the Venetian harbour. Main road services **west**, for Réthimnon and Haniá, run from a brand new terminal right next to this (not from the westbound station marked on most maps, including ours). Buses for the **southwest** – Festós, Mátala or Ayía Galíni – and along the inland roads west (Tílissos, Anóyia) operate out of a terminal just outside Haniá Gate; a very long walk from the centre along Kalokerinoú (or jump on any bus heading down this street). The **southeast**, basically Ierápetra and points en route, is served by the smallest of the stations, just outside the walls in Platía Kíprou at the end of Odhós Evans. **For Knossós**, the #2 local bus sets off every ten minutes from the city bus stop (adjacent to the east bus station), runs up 25 Avgoústou (with a stop by Platía Venizélou) and out of town on Odhós 1821 and Évans.

Knossós

The largest of the Minoan palaces, **KNOSSÓS** reached its cultural peak over 3000 years ago, though a town of some importance persisted here until well into the Roman era. It lies on a low, largely man-made hill some 5km southeast of Iráklion amid hillsides rich in lesser remains spanning twenty-five centuries, starting at the beginning of the second millennium BC.

Barely a hundred years ago the palace existed only in mythology. Knossós was the court of the legendary King Minos, whose wife Pasiphae bore the Minotaur: half-bull, half-man. Here the labyrinth was constructed by Daedalus to contain the monster, and youths were brought from Athens as human sacrifice until Theseus arrived to slay the beast, and with Ariadne's help, escape its lair. The discovery of the palace, and the interplay of these legends with fact, is among the most amazing tales of modern archaeology.

Heinrich Schliemann, the excavator of Troy, suspected that a major Minoan palace lay under the various tumuli here but was denied the necessary permission to dig by the local Ottoman authorities at the end of the last century. It remained for Sir Arthur Evans, whose name is indelibly associated with the site, to do so, from 1900 onwards.

The Site

Mon–Fri 8am–5pm, Sat & Sun 8am–3pm; 500dr.

As soon as you enter the **palace of Knossós** through the West Court, the ancient ceremonial entrance, it is clear how the legends of the labyrinth grew up around it. Even with a detailed plan, it's almost impossible to find your way around the site with any success. My advice is not to try – wander around for long enough and you'll eventually stumble upon everything. If you're worried about missing the highlights you can always tag along with one of the constant guided tours for a while, catching the patter and then backtracking to absorb the detail when that particular crowd has moved on. You won't get the place to yourself – whenever you come – but exploring on your own does give you the opportunity to appreciate individual parts of the palace in the brief lulls between groups.

Knossós was liberally "restored" by Evans, and these restorations have been the source of furious controversy among archaeologists ever since. It has become clear that much of Evans's upper level – the so-called *Piano Nobile* – is pure conjecture. Even so, his guess as to what the palace might have looked like is certainly as good as anyone else's, and it makes the other sites infinitely more meaningful if you have seen Knossós first. Without the restorations, it would be almost impossible to imagine the grandeur of the multistorey palace or to see the ceremonial stairways, strange, top-heavy pillars and gaily painted walls that distinguish the site. For some idea of the size and complexity of

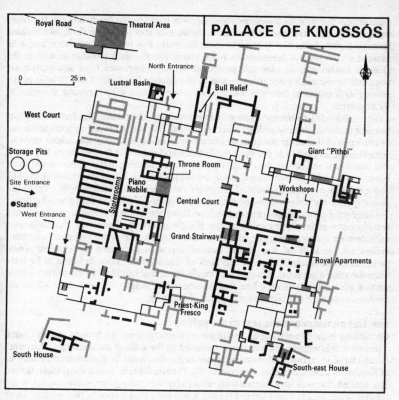

PALACE OF KNOSSÓS

Royal Road — Theatral Area

North Entrance

0   25 m

Lustral Basin

Bull Relief

West Court

Storage Pits

Giant "Pithoi"

Site Entrance

Throne Room

Storerooms

Piano Nobile

Workshops

●Statue

Central Court

West Entrance

Grand Stairway

Royal Apartments

Priest-King Fresco

South House

South-east House

the palace in its original state, take a look at the cutaway drawings (wholly imaginary but probably not too far off) on sale outside.

Royal apartments

The superb **royal apartments** around the central staircase are not guesswork, and they are plainly the finest of the rooms at Knossós. The **stairway** itself is a masterpiece of design: not only a fitting approach to these sumptuously appointed chambers but also an integral part of the whole plan, its large well bringing light into the lower storeys. Light wells such as these, usually with a courtyard at the bottom, are a constant feature of Knossós and a reminder of just how important creature comforts were to the Minoans, and of how skilled they were at providing them.

For evidence of this luxurious lifestyle you need look no further than the **Queen's Suite**, off the grand **Hall of the Colonnades** at the bottom of the staircase. Here the main living room is decorated with the celebrated dolphin fresco (a duplicate; the original is now in the Iráklion archaeological museum) and with running friezes of flowers and abstract spirals. On two sides it opens out on to courtyards that let in light and air; the smaller one would probably have been planted with flowers. In use, the room would have been scattered with cushions and hung with plush curtains, while doors and further curtains between the pillars would have allowed for privacy, and for cool shade in the heat of the day. This, at least, is what they'd have you believe, and it's a very plausible scenario. Remember, though, that all this is speculation and some of it is pure hype – the dolphin fresco, for example, was found in the courtyard, not the room itself, and would have been viewed from inside as a sort of *trompe l'oeil*, like looking through a glass-bottomed boat. Whatever the truth, this is an impressive example of Minoan architecture – the more so when you follow the dark passage around to the Queen's **bathroom**, its clay tub protected behind a low wall (and again probably screened by curtains when in use), and to the famous "flushing" toilet (a hole in the ground with drains to take the waste away – one flushed it by throwing a bucket of water down).

The celebrated **drainage system** was a series of interconnecting terracotta pipes running underneath most of the palace. Guides to the site never fail to point these out as evidence of the advanced state of Minoan civilisation, and they are indeed quite an achievement, in particular the system of baffles and overflows to slow down the runoff and avoid any danger of flooding. Just how much running water there would have been, however, is another matter; the water supply was, and is, at the *bottom* of the hill, and even the combined efforts of rainwater catchment and hauling water up to the palace can hardly have been sufficient to supply the needs of more than a small elite.

Going up the Grand Staircase to the floor above the Queen's domain, you come to a set of rooms generally regarded as the **King's quarters**. These are chambers in a considerably sterner vein; the staircase opens into a grandiose reception chamber known as the **Hall of the Royal Guard**, its walls decorated in repeated shield patterns. Immediately off here is the **Hall of the Double Axes**, believed to be have been the ruler's personal chamber – a double room that would allow for privacy in one portion while audiences were held in the more public section. Its name comes from the double-axe symbol carved into every block of masonry.

The Throne Room and the rest of the palace

Continuing to the top of the grand staircase, you emerge on to the broad **Central Court**. Open now, this would once have been enclosed by the walls of the buildings all around. On the far side, in the northwestern corner of the courtyard, is the entrance to another of Knossós's most atmospheric survivals, the **Throne Room**. Here a worn stone throne sits against the wall of a surprisingly small chamber; along the walls around it are ranged stone benches and behind there's a reconstructed fresco of two griffins. In all probability this was the seat of a priestess rather than a ruler – there's nothing like it in any other Minoan palace – but it may just have been an innovation wrought by the Mycenaeans, since it seems that this room dates only from the final period of Knossós's occupation. The Throne Room is now closed off with a wooden gate, but you can lean over this for a good view, and in the antechamber there's a wooden copy of the throne on which everyone perches to have their picture taken.

The rest you'll see as you wander, contemplating the legends of the place which blur with reality. Try not to miss the giant *pithoi* in the northeast quadrant of the site, an area known as the palace workshops; the storage chambers which you see from behind the Throne Room and the reproduction frescoes in the reconstructed room above it; the Fresco of the Priest-King looking down on the south side of the Central Court; and the relief of a charging bull on its north side. This last would have greeted you if you entered the palace through its north door – here you can see evidence of some kind of gate house and a lustral bath, a sunken area perhaps used for ceremonial bathing and purification. Just outside this gate is the **theatral area** – an open space a little like a stepped amphitheatre which may have been used for ritual performances or dances – and from here the **Royal Road**, claimed as the oldest road in Europe, sets out. Once this probably ran right across the island; nowadays it ends after about a hundred yards in a brick wall beneath the modern road. Circling back around the outside of the palace, you get more idea of its scale by looking up at it; on the south side are a couple of small reconstructed Minoan houses worth exploring.

Food, rooms and onward possibilities

Across a little valley from here, outside the fenced site, is the **Caravanserai** where ancient wayfarers would rest and water their animals. Head out onto the road and you'll find no lack of watering holes for modern travellers either – a string of rather pricey tavernas and tacky souvenir stands. There are several **rooms** places here, too, and if you're really into Minoan culture there's a lot to be said for staying out this way to get an early start. Be warned that it's expensive and unashamedly commercial, though.

If you have transport, the drive **beyond Knossós** can be an attractive and enjoyable one, taking minor roads through much greener country, with vineyards draped across low hills and flourishing agricultural communities. If you want specific things to seek out, head first for **MIRTIÁ**, an attractive village with a small **Kazantzakís Museum** (9am–1pm; Mon, Wed, Sat & Sun also 4–8pm; closed Thurs) in a house where the writer's parents once lived. **ARHÁNES**, at the foot of Mount Ioúktas, is a much larger place that was also quite heavily populated in Minoan times. None of the three sites here is open to the public, but one of them, **Anemospília**, has caused huge controversy since its excavation in the 1980s. Many traditional views of the Minoans, and in particular of Minoan life as a peaceful and idyllic one, have had to be rethought in the light of the discovery of an apparent human sacrifice. From Arhánes you can also drive to the top of Mount Ioúktas to enjoy the panoramic views. At **VATHÍPETRO**, south of the mountain, is a Minoan villa which can be explored.

South: Górtys, Festós and Ayía Triádha

Heading south from Iráklion, the road towards Festós is a pretty good one by the standards of Cretan mountain roads, albeit a dull one too. The country you're heading towards is the richest agricultural land on the island, and right from the start the villages en route are large and business-like. In the largest of them, AYÍA VARVÁRA, there's a great rock outcrop known as the *Omphalos* (Navel) of Crete, supposed to be the very centre of the island. Past here you descend rapidly to the fertile fields of the Messará plain, where the road joins the main route across the south near the village of Áyii Dhéka.

Áyii Dhéka and Górtys

For religious Cretans **ÁYII DHÉKA** is something of a place of pilgrimage; its name, "The Ten Saints", refers to ten early Christians martyred here under the Romans. In a crypt below the modern church you can see the martyrs' tombs, and it's an attractive village to wander around, with several places to eat and even some rooms along the main road.

Within easy walking distance, either through the fields or along the main road, sprawls the site of **GÓRTYS** (Mon–Sat 8am–7pm, Sun 8am–6pm), ruined capital of the Roman province that included not only Crete but also much of North Africa. Cutting across the fields will give you some idea of the scale of this city at its zenith in approximately the third century AD; an enormous variety of other remains, including an impressive theatre, are strewn across your route. Even in Áyii Dhéka itself you'll see Roman pillars and statues lying around in peoples' yards or propping up their walls.

There had been settlement here from the earliest times, but what you find now – and the site has never been systematically excavated – dates almost entirely from the Roman era. At the main entrance to the fenced site, alongside the road, is the ruinous but still impressive basilica of **Áyios Títos**, the saint who converted Crete and was also its first bishop. Beyond this is the *Odeion* which houses the most important discovery on the site, the **Law Code**. These great inscribed blocks of stone were incorporated by the Romans from a much earlier stage of the city's development; they're written in an obscure early Greek/Cretan dialect, and in a style known as *boustrophedon* (ox-ploughed), with the lines reading alternately in opposite directions like the furrows of a ploughed field. About ten metres by three metres in all, this is reputedly the largest Greek inscription ever found. The laws set forth reflect a strictly hierarchical society: five witnesses were needed to convict a free man of a crime, only one for a slave; raping a free man or woman carried a fine of a hundred staters, violating a serf only five.

Míres

Some 20km west of Górtys, **MÍRES** is an important market and focal point of transport for the Messará plain – if you're switching buses to get from the beaches on the south coast to the archaeological sites or the west, this is where you'll do it. There are good facilities including a bank, lots of restaurants and plenty of rooms, though there's no particular reason to stay unless you are waiting for a bus or looking for work (it's one of the better places for agricultural jobs). Heading straight for Festós, there's usually no need to stop.

Festós

Mon–Sat 8am–7pm, Sun 8am–6pm; 300dr.

The **PALACE OF FESTÓS** was excavated by the Italian Federico Halbherr (also responsible for the early work at Górtys), at almost exactly the same time as Evans was working at Knossós. The style of the excavations, however, could hardly have been more different. Here, to the approval of most traditional archaeologists, reconstruction was kept to an absolute minimum – it's all bare foundations, and walls which rise at most a couple of feet above ground level. This means that despite a magnificent setting overlooking the plain of Messará, the palace at Festós is not as immediately arresting as those at Knossós or Mália. Much of the site is fenced off and, except in the huge central court, it's almost impossible to get any sense of the place as it was; the plan is almost as complex as at Knossós, with none of the reconstruction to bolster the imagination.

It's interesting to speculate why the palace was built halfway up a hill rather than on the plain below; certainly not for defence, for this is in no way a good defensive position. Psychological superiority over the peasants or reasons of health are both possible, but it seems quite likely that it was simply the magnificent view – over Psilorítis to the north and the huge plain with the Lasíthi mountains beyond it to the east – that finally swayed the decision. Towards the top of Psilorítis you should be able to make out a small black smudge: the entrance to the Kamáres Cave.

On the ground closer at hand, you can hardly fail to notice the strong similarities between Festós and the other palaces: the same huge rows of storage jars, the great courtyard with its monumental stairway, and the theatral area. Unique to Festós, however, is the third courtyard, in the middle of which are the remains of a furnace used for metalworking. Indeed, this eastern corner of the palace seems to have been home to a number of craftsmen, including potters and carpenters. Oddly enough, Festós was much less ornately decorated than Knossós; there is no evidence, for example, of any of the dramatic Minoan wall paintings.

Ayía Triádha

Mon–Thurs & Sat 8.45am–3pm, Sun 9.30am–2.30pm.

By contrast, some of the finest artworks in the museum at Iráklion came from **AYÍA TRIÁDHA**, less than an hour's walk away, or a short drive. No one is quite sure what this site is, but the most common theory has it as some kind of royal summer villa – smaller than the palaces, but if anything even more lavishly appointed and beautifully

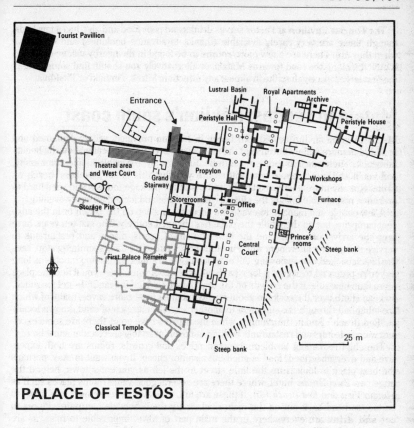

Tourist Pavillion

Lustral Basin   Royal Apartments

Entrance   Archive

Peristyle Hall   Peristyle House

Theatral area
and West Court   Propylon

Grand
Stairway   ← Workshops

Storerooms   Furnace
                        □ □ ← Office

Storage Pits

                        Central   Prince's
                        Court   rooms
                                              Steep bank
First Palace Remains

Classical Temple   0   25 m

                        Steep bank

PALACE OF FESTÓS

situated. In any event it's an attractive place to visit, far less crowded than Festós, with a wealth of interesting little details. Look out in particular for the row of shops in front of what was apparently a marketplace, and for the remains of the paved road that once led down to the Gulf of Messará. The sea itself looks invitingly close, separated from the base of the hill only by Timbáki airfield (mainly used for motor racing these days), but if you try to drive down there it's almost impossible to find your way around the unmarked dust tracks. There's a fourteenth-century church at the site too, worth visiting in its own right for the remains of ancient frescoes.

Practicalities

Take a **tour** from Iráklion or one of the resorts and you'll probably visit Górtys, Festós and Ayía Triádha in a day, with a lunchtime swim at Mátala thrown in. Doing it by public transport you'll be forced into a rather more leisurely pace, but there's still no reason why you shouldn't get to all three sites and reach Mátala within the day; if necessary it is easy enough to hitch the final stretch. **Bus services** to the Festós site are excellent, with some nine a day to and from Iráklion (the last leaves just before the site closes – fewer run on Sunday), five of which continue to or come from Mátala. There are also services direct to Ayía Galíni. If you're arriving in the afternoon, plan to visit Ayía Triádha first, as it closes early.

The **Tourist Pavilion** at Festós serves drinks and poor food and also has a few beds, though these are very rarely available (thanks to advance bookings) and expensive when they are. There are a few more **rooms** to be found in the nearby village of ÁYIOS IOÁNNIS, along the road towards Mátala, or alternatively you should find something in the first larger place you strike in almost any direction: Míres, Timbáki or Pitsídhia.

Mátala to Léndas: Iráklion's south coast

MÁTALA is by far the best-known beach in Iráklion province, widely promoted and included in tours mainly because of the famous caves cut into the cliffs above its beautiful beach. These ancient tombs used to be inhabited by a sizeable hippie community, and you'll still meet people who will assure you that this is *the* travellers' beach on Crete. Not any more it isn't. Today the town is full of package tourists and tries hard to present a respectable image; the cliffs are now cleared and locked up every evening.

A few people still manage to evade the security, or sleep on the beach or in the adjacent campsite, but on the whole the place has changed entirely. The last ten years have seen the arrival of crowds and the development of hotels, discos and restaurants to service them; early afternoon, when the tour buses pull in for their swimming stop, sees the beach packed to overflowing. All of which is not to knock Mátala too much – as long as you're prepared to accept it for what it is– a resort of some size– you'll find the place more than bearable. If the crowds on the town beach – which *is* beautiful – get too much, you can climb over the rocks in about twenty minutes (past more caves, many of which are inhabited through the summer) to another excellent stretch of sand, known locally as "Red Beach". And in the evening, when the trippers have gone, there are some excellent waterside bars and restaurants looking out over invariably spectacular sunsets.

The chief remaining problems concern prices and crowds: rooms are both expensive and oversubscribed, food is good but also not cheap. If you want to **stay**, perhaps the best place to look is up the little street to the left as you enter town, behind the huge new *Zwei Brüder* hotel, where there are several good-value rooms places such as *Matala View* and *Red Beach* (③). If these are full, then everywhere closer in is likely to be too, so head back out on the main road, or try the beachside **campsite**. Places to **eat and drink** are everywhere in the main part of town, impossible to miss, as are most other **facilities** – shops, currency exchange, car and bike rental, travel agents, post office, and an OTE office in a temporary building in the car park behind the beach.

Alternative bases: Pitsídhia and Kalamáki

One way to save some money and also enjoy a bit more peace is to stay at PITSÍDHIA, about 5km inland. This is already a well-used option so it's not quite as cheap as you might expect, but there are plenty of rooms, lively places to eat and an affable, young, international crowd. The beach at KALAMÁKI is a good alternative to Mátala if you're staying here: approximately the same distance to walk, though with far less chance of a bus or a lift. Kalamáki itself is beginning to develop somewhat, with a number of rooms and a couple of tavernas, but so far it's a messy and unattractive little place. The beach stretches for miles, surprisingly wild and windswept, lashed by sometimes dangerously rough surf. At the southern end (easier reached by a path off the Pitsídhia–Mátala road) lies KÓMMOS, once a Minoan port serving Festós and now the site of a major archaeological excavation. As yet there's not a great deal to see, but this is another good beach.

Kalí Liménes and Léndas

Mátala itself was an important port under the Romans, but the chief harbour for Górtys lay on the other side of Cape Líthinon at KALÍ LIMÉNES. Nowadays this is once again a major port – for oil tankers. This has rather spoiled its chances of becoming a major resort, especially when aggravated by the lack of a paved road and proper facilities. Some people like Kalí Liménes: the constant procession of tankers gives you something to look at, there are a number of places offering rooms (best the *Kanavourissia Beach* (③), a kilometre or so east of the village), the coastline is broken up by spectacular cliffs, and as long as there hasn't been a recent oil spill the beaches are reasonably clean and totally empty. But (fortunately) not too many share this enthusiasm.

LÉNDAS, further east along the coast, is far more popular, with a couple of buses daily from Iráklion and a partly justified reputation for being peaceful (sullied by considerable summer crowds). Many people who arrive think they've come to the wrong place: the village at first looks filthy; the beach is small, rocky and dirty, and the rooms are frequently all booked. A number of visitors leave without ever correcting that first impression, for the real attraction of Léndas is not here at all but beyond the point to the west, 3km or so along the coast road. Here there's an enormous, excellent sandy beach, part of it usually taken over by nudists, and a couple of good taverna/bars overlooking it from the roadside. Camping on this beach, or with luck getting one of the few rooms (②–③) at the tavernas, is a considerably more attractive prospect than staying in the village, though after you've discovered the beach even Léndas itself begins to look more welcoming. At least it has most of the facilities you'll need, including a shop which will change money and numerous places to eat. Once you've come to terms with the place, you can also explore some less good but quite deserted beaches eastwards, and the scrappy remains of ancient LEVÍN on a hilltop overlooking them. There was an important *Ascelpion* here around some now-diverted warm springs, but only the odd broken column and fragments of mosaic survive.

If you have your own transport, the roads in these parts are all passable but most are very slow going – there's a line of precipitous hills between the Messará plain and the coast. Along the coast between Léndas and Kalí Liménes there are numerous other little beaches, though nothing spectacular. Public transport is very limited indeed; you'll almost always have to travel via Míres.

East of Iráklion: the package-tour coast

East of Iráklion the startling pace of tourist development in Crete is all too plain to see. The merest hint of a beach is an excuse to build at least one hotel, and these are outnumbered by the concrete shells of resorts-to-be. It's hard to find a room in this monument to the package tour, and expensive if you do. At the city beach of **Amnissós** (#1 bus from Platía Eleftherías) little remains to indicate the once-flourishing port of Knossós aside from a rather dull, fenced-in dig. Nowadays the long stretch of sand is strewn with tourists and litter, but for a day out from Iráklion it's not bad. If you're seriously into antiquities, however, you'll find a more rewarding site in the small villa at HÁNI KOKKÍNI, the first of the full-blown resort developments.

As a general rule, the further you go, the better things get: when the road detours all-too-briefly inland, the real Crete – olive groves and stark mountains – asserts itself. You certainly won't see much of it at **GOÚRNES**, where a US Air Force base has been established for years, its aircraft buzzing the beaches for miles around, or nearby KATO GOÚVES. From the latter, however, you can head inland to the old village of GOÚVES, a refreshing contrast, and the **Skotinó Cave**, one of the largest and most spectacular on the island, less than two hours' walk from the coast.

Not far beyond it is the turning for the direct route up to the Lasíthi plateau, and shortly after that you roll into the first of the big resorts, **HERSÓNISOS** (or, more correctly, Límin Hersonísou; Hersónisos is the village in the hills just behind, also overrun by tourists). If you wanted to stay in a big resort you could do a lot worse than this;

there's plenty of nightlife, enough restaurants to keep prices down, and not bad beaches (the Gulf of Mália generally has some of the island's biggest, sandiest ones, though all highly developed) – but no cheap rooms. While you're here, take a look at the restored Roman fountain overlooking the sea – sole evidence of the ancient town of Chersonesos.

Mália

Without pre-reserved accommodation you'd probably be better off at the still more popular resort of **MÁLIA**, large enough to be a substantial town in its own right. It's very commercial, and the long sandy beach becomes extremely crowded at times, but it's fun if you're prepared to enter into the spirit of things.

For **accommodation** you're best off in the old town, on the landward side of the main road. Simply follow the signs to rooms places here, or backtrack a little towards Iráklion from the T-junction which marks the heart of town to find more places and a new youth hostel (☎081/31 555; ①).

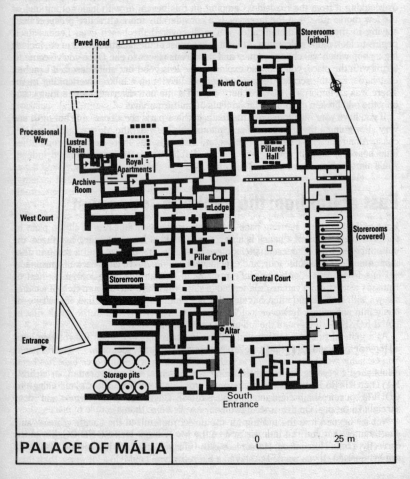

PALACE OF MÁLIA

0   25 m

Virtually every other facility you could need, including dozens of tourist bars and restaurants, can be found, on one of two streets: the main road through town is the more business-like, with banks, shops and travel agents, while the beach road is given over to more frivolous pursuits.

The Palace of Mália

Tues–Sat 8.30am–3pm, Sun 9am–2.30pm; 200dr.

The archaeological site lies forty minutes' walk east of Mália town on the main road. Any bus will stop, or rent a bike for a couple of hours – it's a pleasant, flat ride. Much less imposing than either Knossós or Festós, Mália in some ways surpasses both. For a start, it's a great deal emptier and you can wander among the remains in relative peace. And while no reconstruction has been attempted, the palace was never reoccupied after its second destruction, so the ground plan is virtually intact. It's a great deal easier to comprehend than Knossós and, if you've seen the reconstructions there, it's easy to envisage this seaside palace in its days of glory. There's a real feeling of an ancient civilisation with a taste for the good life, basking on the rich agricultural plain between the Lasíthi mountains and the sea.

From this site came the famous gold pendant of two bees (which can be seen in the Iráklion museum or on any postcard stand), allegedly part of a horde that was plundered and whose other treasures can now be found in the British Museum in London. The beautiful leopard's-head axe, also in the museum at Iráklion, was another of the treasures found here. At the site, look out for the strange indented stone in the central court, which probably held ritual offerings; for the remains of ceremonial stairways; and for the giant *pithoi* which stand like sentinels around the palace. To the south and east, digs are still going on as a large town comes slowly to light.

Moving on

Leaving the archaeological zone, you can follow the dirt track that runs around it to a lovely stretch of near-deserted sand. There's a makeshift taverna here, and usually a couple of camper-vans parked, but considering its position it's an amazingly little-visited patch of beach. You can walk back to Mália from here, along the shore, or out on the main road you should have no difficulty flagging down a bus in either direction.

Head **east**, and it's not long before the road leaves the coast, climbing across the hills towards Áyios Nikólaos. If you want to escape the frenetic pace of all that has gone before, try continuing to SÍSI or MÍLATOS. These little shore villages are bypassed by the main road as it cuts inland, and so far have seen only the beginnings of a tourist industry; each has a few villa/apartments and a couple of tavernas, and there's a campsite at Sísi, the more developed of the two. The beaches aren't great, but they make for a refreshing change of pace.

West of Iráklion: around Psilorítis

Most people heading west from Iráklion speed straight out on the new coastal highway, non-stop to Réthimnon. If you're in a hurry this is not such a bad plan; the road is fast and spectacular, hacked into the sides of mountains which for the most part drop straight to the sea. On the other hand there are no more than a couple of places where you might consider stopping. By contrast the old roads inland are agonisingly slow, but they do pass through a whole string of attractive villages beneath the heights of the Psilorítis range. From here you can set out to explore the mountains and even walk across them to emerge in villages with views of the south coast.

The new road: Ayía Pelayía

Leaving the city, the **new road** runs at first some distance behind a stretch of highly developed coast, where the hotels compete for shore space with a cement works and power station. As soon as you hit the mountains, though, all this is left behind and there's only the clash of rock and sea to contemplate. Look out as you start to climb for the castle of **Paleókastro**, beside a bridge which carries the road over a small cove – it is so weathered as to be almost invisible against the brownish face of the cliff. Some 3km below the road, as it rounds the first point, lies the resort of **AYÍA PELAYÍA**. It looks extremely attractive from above – as indeed it is close up – but it is also very commercial and chi-chi: not somewhere to roll up without a reserved room, though out of season you might find a real bargain at an apartment.

Fódhele

Not far beyond Ayía Pelayía there's a turning inland to the village of **FÓDHELE**, allegedly El Greco's birthplace. A plaque from the University of Toledo acknowledges the claim and, true or not, the community has built a small tourist industry on that basis. There are a number of craft shops and some pleasant tavernas where you can sit outside along the river; there's also "El Greco's house" and a picturesque Byzantine church. None of this amounts to very much but it is a pleasant, relatively unspoiled village if you simply want to sit in peace for a while. A couple of buses a day run here from Iráklion, and there's the odd tour; if you arrive on a direct bus, the walk back down to the main road (about 3km), where you can flag down a passing service, is not too strenuous.

Balí and beyond

BALÍ, on the coast approximately halfway between Iráklion and Réthimnon, also used to be tranquil and undeveloped, and by the standards of this north coast it still is in many ways. The village is built around a couple of small coves some 2km from the main road (a hot walk from the bus), similar to Ayía Pelayía except that the beaches are not quite as good and there are no big hotels. There are, however, lots of rooms – more every month it seems – and a number of what the brochures no doubt describe as "modest hotels". You'll have plenty of company. The last and best beach, known as "Paradise", no longer really deserves the name – it's a beautiful place to splash about, surrounded by mountains rising straight from the sea, but there's rarely a spare inch on the sand.

Continuing along the coast there's one possible further stop before you emerge on the flat stretch leading to Réthimnon, at **PÁNORMOS**. This too is an attractive village with a small sandy beach and a few rooms, but again there are crowds, mostly arriving by boat on day trips from Réthimnon.

Inland routes: Tílissos

Of the **inland routes** the old main road (via Márathos and Dhamásta) is not the most interesting. This too was something of a bypass in its day and there are few places of any size or appeal, though it's a very scenic drive. If you want to dawdle you're better off on the road which cuts up to Tílissos and then goes via Anóyia. **TÍLISSOS** itself has a significant archaeological site (Tues–Sun 8.45am–3pm) where three Minoan houses were excavated; unfortunately its reputation is based more on what was found here (many pieces in the Iráklion museum) and on its significance for archaeologists than on anything which remains to be seen. Still, it's worth a look if you're passing, for a glimpse of Minoan life away from the big palaces, and for the tranquillity of the pine-shaded remains.

Anóyia

ANÓYIA is a much more tempting place to stay, especially if the summer heat is becoming oppressive. Spilling prettily down a hillside close below the highest peaks of the mountains, it looks traditional, but closer inspection shows that most of the buildings are actually concrete; the village was destroyed during the war as one of the German reprisals for the abduction of General Kreipe. The reputation of the place as a handicrafts centre (especially for woven and woollen goods) is at least in part a reflection of the same history – both a conscious attempt to revive the town and the result of grim necessity with so large a proportion of the local men killed. At any rate it worked, for the place is thriving today, thanks at least partly, it seems, to the number of elderly widows keen to subject any visitor to their terrifyingly aggressive sales techniques.

Quite a few people pass through Anóyia during the day but not many of them **stay**; it shouldn't be hard to find a room in the upper half of town. On the other hand there's almost nowhere to **eat**: one taverna on the main road where it loops out of the lower village, and a *souvláki* place near the top of the town, neither of which seem to serve anything other than the barbecued lamb which is a local speciality. Vegetarians are advised to buy their own bread and cheese (local cheese is also excellent).

Psilorítis and its caves

Heading for the mountains, a rough track leads 13km from Anóyia to the Nídha plateau at the base of **Mount Psilorítis**. Here there's a taverna that used to let rooms but seems now to have closed to the public altogether, though it's still used by groups of climbers. A short path leads from the taverna to the celebrated **Idean Cave** (*Idhéon Ándron*), a rival of that on Mount Dhíkti (see p.468) for the title of Zeus's birthplace and certainly associated from the earliest of times with the cult of Zeus. Unfortunately there's a major archaeological dig going on inside, which means the whole cave is fenced off, with a miniature railway running into it to carry all the rubble out. In short you can see nothing.

The taverna also marks the start of **the way to the top** of Crete's highest mountain, a climb that's not for the unwary, but for experienced, properly shod hikers is not at all arduous. The route is well-marked with the usual red dots and it should be a six to seven-hour round-trip to the chapel at the summit – though in spring thick snow may slow you down.

If you're prepared to camp on the plateau (plenty of water but very cold too) or can prevail on the taverna to let you in, you could continue on foot next day down to the southern slopes of the range. It's a beautiful hike – at least while the road they're attempting to blast through is out of sight – and also relatively easy, four hours or so down a fairly clear path to VORÍZIA, where you can pick up buses. If you're still interested in caves there's a more rewarding one above the nearby village of **KAMÁRES**, a climb of some three hours on a good path. Both Vorízia and Kamáres have a few rooms and some tavernas, at least one daily bus down to Míres, and alternate (more difficult) routes to the peak of Psilorítis if you want to approach from this direction.

EASTERN CRETE

Eastern Crete is dominated by **Áyios Nikólaos** and its mass tourism; among most Crete aficionados it has a poor reputation. Yet, though you won't want to stay for long in this highly developed resort, by no means all of the east is like this. Far fewer people venture beyond the isthmus and the road south to **Ierápetra**, and here only **Sitía** and the famous beach at **Vái** ever see anything approaching a crowd. Inland too there's interest, especially on the extraordinary **Lasíthi** plateau – worth a night's stay if only to catch its abidingly rural life.

Neápoli and the Lasíthi plateau

Leaving the palace at Mália, the main road cuts inland towards Neápoli, soon beginning a spectacular climb into the mountains. Set in a high valley, **NEÁPOLI** is a market town little touched by tourism. There is one hotel, some rooms, a modern church and a tiny museum which rarely opens. Beyond the town it's about twenty minutes before the bus suddenly emerges high above the Gulf of Mirabéllo and Áyios Nikólaos, the island's biggest resort. If you're stopping, Neápoli also marks the second point of access to the **Lasíthi Plateau**.

Scores of coach tours drive up here daily to view the "thousands of white-cloth-sailed windmills" which irrigate the high plain, and most groups must be disappointed – there are very few working windmills left, and these operate only for limited periods (mainly in June). This is not to say the trip is not justified – it would be for the drive alone – and there are many other compensations. The plain is a fine example of rural Crete at work, every inch devoted to the cultivation of potatoes, apples, pears, figs, olives and a host of other crops; stay in one of the villages for a night or two and you'll see real life return as the tourists leave. There are plenty of easy rambles around the villages as well, through orchards and past the rusting remains of derelict windmills. You'll find rooms in **TZERMIÁDHO**, the main town, ÁYIOS KONSTANTÍNOS, ÁYIOS YIÓRYIOS (where there's a folk museum and the friendly *Hotel Dias*; ☎0844/31 207; ③), and at Psihró.

PSIHRÓ is much the most visited, as it's the base for visiting Lasíthi's other chief attraction, the **Dhiktean Cave**, birthplace of Zeus (Tues–Sat 8am–6pm, Sun 10am–4pm; watch out for slippery stones inside). In legend, Zeus's father Kronos was warned that he would be overthrown by a son and accordingly ate all his offspring; on this occasion, however, Rhea, having given birth in the cave, fed Kronos a stone and left the child concealed, protected by the Kouretes who beat their shields outside to disguise his cries. The rest, as they say, is history (or at least myth). There's an obvious path running up to the cave from Psihró and, whatever you're told, you don't have to have a guide if you don't want one, though you will need some form of illumination. On the other hand it is hard to resist the guides (they're not expensive if you can get a small group together), and much more interesting to go with one. It takes a Cretan imagination to pick out Rhea and the baby Zeus from the lesser stalactites and stalagmites.

Buses run around the plateau to Psihró direct from Iráklion and from Áyios Nikólaos via Neápoli. Both roads offer spectacular views, coiling through a succession of passes guarded by lines of ruined windmills.

Áyios Nikólaos and around

ÁYIOS NIKÓLAOS ("Ag Nik" to the majority of its British visitors) is set around a supposedly bottomless salt lake, now connected to the sea to form an inner harbour. It is supremely picturesque, and exploits this to the full. The lake and port are surrounded by restaurants and bars, all charging well above normal, and the town itself is permanently crammed with tourists, some distinctly surprised to find themselves in a place with no decent beach at all. If you're after clubs, crowds and expensive souvenirs, this is the place for you (likewise if you want to buy foreign newspapers, phone home, practise your English, or catch a bus to almost anywhere in the east).

Finding a cheap **room** however – finding any room for that matter – is virtually impossible in mid-season. The wonderfully positioned youth hostel at Stratigoú Koráka 3, one of the alleys immediately northeast of the lake, was so bad that it was closed down – though by now it may have reopened under new management. In its absence you face a lot of walking: areas to try are around the bus station, where noise can be a problem; and on the roads parallel to Paleológou as it leads out of town on the other

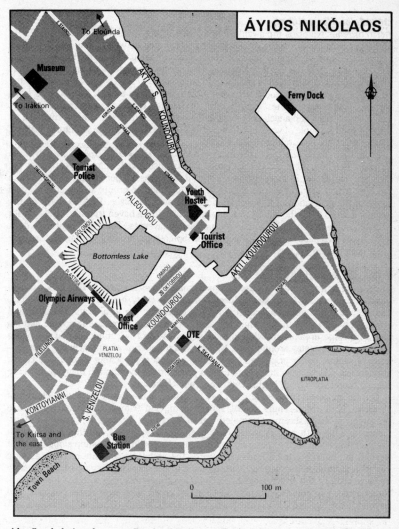

side. Good choices here are *Pension Marilena* at Erithoú Stavroú 14 (☎0841/22 681; ③) or *Pension Katerina* at Stratigoú Koráka 30 (☎0841/22 766; ③). The occasional masochist sleeps on the stony beach right in front of the terminal – but it's not to be advised. Much better, if you're looking to camp, to head southeast for the sandy coves at KALÓ HORIÓ (about 12km) or PAHIÁ ÁMMOS (20km).

The **tourist office** down by the lake (daily 8.30am–10pm) is helpful and has extensive lists of rooms if you're having trouble; they also change money at reasonable rates. Places to eat and drink and other facilities are abundant, with the greatest concentration of shops and travel agents on the hill between the bridge and Platía Venizélou (where there are some cheaper restaurants). The main **ferry agent** is *Massaros Travel* (☎0841/22 267), on Koundoúrou near the post office.

Eloúnda and Spinalónga

North of Áyios Nikólaos the swankier hotels are strung out along the coast road, with upmarket restaurants, discos and cocktail bars scattered between them. **ELOÚNDA**, a resort on a more acceptable scale, is about 8km out along this road. Buses run regularly, but if you feel like renting a moped it's a spectacular ride, with impeccable views over a gulf dotted with islands and moored supertankers. Try *Olous Travel*, next to the post office, if you want a room here. Just before the village a track (signposted) leads across a causeway to the "sunken city" of **Oloús**. There are restored windmills, Venetian salt pans and a well-preserved dolphin mosaic, but of the sunken city itself no trace beyond a couple of walls in about two feet of water. At any rate swimming is good, though there are sea urchins to watch out for.

From Eloúnda, *kaíkia* run to the fortress-rock of **SPINALÓNGA**. As a bastion of the Venetian defence, this tiny islet withstood the Turkish invaders for 45 years after the mainland had fallen; in more recent decades it served as a leper colony. As you watch the boat which brought you disappear to pick up another group, an unnervingly real sense of the desolation of those years descends over the place. **PLÁKA**, back on the mainland, used to be the colony's supply point; now it is a haven from the crowds, with a small pebble beach and a couple of ramshackle tavernas. There are boat trips daily from Áyios Nikólaos to Oloús, Eloúnda and Spinalónga, usually visiting at least one other island along the way.

Kritsá, the Panayía Kirá and Lató

The other excursion everyone from Áyios Nikólaos takes is inland to **KRITSÁ**, a "traditional" village about 10km away. Buses run at least every hour from the bus station, and despite the commercialisation it's still a good trip: the local crafts (weaving and embroidery basically, though they sell almost everything here) are fair value and it's also a welcome break from living in the fast lane at "Ag Nik". In fact, if you're looking for somewhere to stay around here, Kritsá has a number of advantages: chiefly availability of rooms, better prices, and something at least approaching a genuinely Greek atmosphere. There are a number of decent places to eat too, though many of them are regular targets of "Greek Nights Out" from Áyios Nikólaos.

On the approach road, some 2km before Kritsá, is the lovely Byzantine church of **Panayía Kirá** (Mon–Thurs & Sat 9am–3.15pm, Sun 9am–2pm), inside which are preserved perhaps the most complete set of Byzantine frescoes in Crete. The fourteenth- and fifteenth-century works have been much retouched, but they're still worth the visit. Excellent (and expensive) reproductions are sold from a shop alongside. Just beyond the church a track leads off towards the archaeological site of **Lató**, a Doric city with a grand hilltop setting. The city itself is extensive but neglected, presumably because visitors and archaeologists on Crete are concerned only with the Minoan era. Ruins aside, you could come here just for the views: west over Áyios Nikólaos and beyond to the bay and Oloús (which was Lato's port), inland to the Lasíthi mountains.

Gourniá and the road east

Just off the main road about 20km southeast of Áyios Nikólaos, **GOURNIÁ** (daily 8.30am–3pm) slumps in the saddle between two low peaks. The most completely preserved Minoan town, its narrow alleys and stairways intersect a throng of one-roomed houses centred on a main square and the house of the local ruler. Although less impressive than the great palaces, the site is strong on revelations about the lives of the ordinary people ruled from Knossós. Its desolation today – you are likely to be alone save for a dozing guard – only serves to heighten the contrast with what must have been a cramped and raucous community 3500 years ago.

It is tempting to cross the road here and take one of the paths through the wild thyme to the sea for a swim. Don't bother – this seemingly innocent little bay acts as a magnet for every piece of floating detritus dumped off Crete's north coast. There is a slightly better beach, and rooms to rent, in the next valley at **PAHIÁ ÁMMOS**, about twenty minutes' walk, or in the other direction there's the rather bizarre campsite of *Gourniá Moon*, with its own small cove.

This is the narrowest part of the island, and from here a fast new road cuts across the isthmus **to Ierápetra** in the south. In the north, though, the route on **towards Sitía** is one of the most exhilarating in Crete. Carved into cliffs and mountainsides, the road teeters above the coast before plunging inland at Kavoúsi. Of the beaches you see below, only **MÓHLOS** is at all accessible, some 5km below the main road: here there are a few rooms, a hotel or two and a number of tavernas – all expensive. Nearer Sitía the familiar olive groves are interspersed with vineyards, and in late summer the grapes, spread to dry in the fields and on rooftops, make an extraordinary sight in the varying stages of their slow change from green to gold to brown.

Sitía and the far east

The port and main town of the relatively unexploited eastern edge of Crete, **SITÍA** is a pleasant if unremarkable place. It offers a plethora of waterside restaurants, a long sandy beach and a lazy lifestyle little affected even by the thousands of visitors in peak season. There's an almost Latin feel to the town – reflected in (or perhaps caused by) the number of French and Italian tourists – and it's one of those places you may end up staying longer than you intended. For entertainment there's the **beach**, providing good swimming and windsurfing; or in town a mildly entertaining **folklore museum** (Mon–Sat 9.30am–3pm), a Venetian fort and Roman fish tanks to explore, and an interesting **archaeological museum** (Tues–Sun 8.30am–3pm). Look out too for the town's resident mascot, **Níkos the pelican**.

There are plenty of cheap pensions and **rooms**, especially in the streets around the OTE, a **youth hostel** on the main road as it enters town, and rarely any problem about sleeping on the beach (though it is worth going a little way out of town to avoid any danger of being rousted by police). Rooms places to try include *Pension Venus*, Kondhiláki 60 (☎0843/24 307; ②), *Hotel Arhontiko*, Kondhiláki 16 (☎0843/28 172; ③), and *Iris*, Riga Fereou 15, off Sífi (☎0843/22 494; ②); the **tourist office** at the start of the beach road may be able to help if you have difficulty. For **food**, the waterside places are expensive enough to make you careful about what you eat; best value here is *Remegio*, or there are cheaper options in the streets behind, including a couple of excellent ice-cream parlours. **Nightlife** centres on a few bars and discos near the ferry dock and out along the beach. The one major excitement of the year is the August **Sultana Festival** – a celebration of the big local export, with traditional dancing and all the locally produced wine you can consume included in the entrance to the fairground.

To Vái Beach

Vái beach features alongside Knossós or the Lasíthi plateau on almost every Cretan travel agent's list of excursions. For years it has also been a popular hangout for backpackers camping on the sands. This dual role has created something of a monstrosity – with the vast crowds divided into two hostile camps. At the same time it *is* a superb beach, and the trip there is an enjoyable one.

Leaving Sitía along the beach, the Vái road climbs above a rocky, unexceptional coastline before reaching a fork to the **Monastery of Toploú**. The monastery's forbidding exterior reflects a history of resistance to invaders, but doesn't prepare you for the

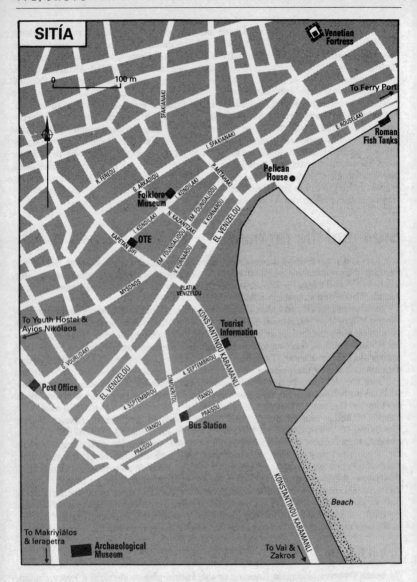

gorgeous flower-decked cloister within. The blue-robed monks keep out of the way as far as possible, but their cells and refectory are left discreetly on view. In the church is one of the masterpieces of Cretan art, the eighteenth-century icon *Lord Thou Art Great*. Outside you can buy enormously expensive reproductions.

VÁI BEACH itself is famous above all for its palm trees, and the sudden appearance of the grove is indeed an exotic shock. Lying on the fine sand in the early morning, the illusion of a Caribbean island is hard to dismiss. During the day, however, the beach fills as buses arrive in quantities hardly justified by a few palm trees. As everywhere, notices warn that "Camping is forbidden by law"; for once the authorities seem to mean it and most campers climb over the headlands to the south or north. If you do sleep out, watch your belongings – this seems to be the one place on Crete with crime on any scale. There's an expensive taverna and a café at the beach, plus toilets and showers. By day you can find a bit more solitude by climbing the rocks or swimming to one of the smaller beaches which surround Vái. **ÍTANOS**, twenty minutes' walk north by an obvious trail, has a couple of tiny beaches and some modest ruins of the Classical era.

PALÉKASTRO, some 9km south, is in many ways a better place to stay. Although its beaches can't begin to compare, you'll find several modest places with rooms, a number of reasonable restaurants (good rooms and food at the *Hotel Hellas*; ☎0843/61 240; ③), and plenty of space to camp out without the crowds – the sea is a couple of kilometres down a dirt track. Palékastro is also the crossroads for the road south to Zákros.

Zákros

ZÁKROS town is a little under 20km from Palékastro, at the end of the paved road. There are several tavernas and a hotel in the village, but the Minoan palace is actually at Káto Zákros, 8km further down a newly paved road to the sea. Most buses run only to the upper village, but in summer a couple every day do run all the way to the site. Part way along you can, if on foot, take a short cut through an impressive gorge (the "Valley of the Dead", named for ancient tombs in its sides) but it's usually not difficult to hitch if your bus does leave you in the village.

The **palace of Zákros** (daily 9am–4pm) was an important find for archaeologists; it had been occupied only once, and abandoned hurriedly and completely. Later it was forgotten almost entirely and as a result was never plundered or even discovered by archaeologists until very recently – the first major excavation began only in 1960. All sorts of everyday objects – tools, raw materials, food, pottery – were thus discovered intact among the ruins, and a great deal was learned from being able to apply modern techniques (and knowledge of the Minoans) to a major dig from the very beginning. None of this is especially evident when you're at the palace, except perhaps in a particularly simple ground plan, so it's as well that it is also a rewarding visit in terms of the setting. Although the site is some way from the sea, parts of it are often marshy and waterlogged: partly the result of eastern Crete's slow subsidence, partly the fault of a spring which once supplied fresh water to a cistern beside the royal apartments and whose outflow is now silted up. Among the remains of narrow streets and small houses higher up, you can keep your feet dry and get an excellent view down over the central court and royal apartments.

The village of **KÁTO ZÁKROS** is little more than a collection of tavernas, some of which rent out rooms (*Poseidon* is perhaps the best; ☎0843/93 388; ③), around a peaceful beach and minuscule fishing anchorage. It's a wonderfully restful place.

Ierápetra and the southeast coast

From Sitía the route south is a cross-country roller-coaster ride until it hits the south coast at **MAKRIYIALÓS**. This little fishing village has one of the best beaches at this end of Crete, with fine sand which shelves so gently you feel you could walk the 200 miles to Africa. Unfortunately in the last few years it has been heavily developed, so while still a very pleasant place to stop for a swim or a bite, it's not somewhere you're likely to find a cheap room.

From here to Ierápetra there's little reason to stop; the few beaches are rocky and the coastal plain submerged under ranks of polythene-covered greenhouses. One exception however is **AYÍA FOTIÁ**, where, hidden from the main road in a wooded valley leading down to a bay, there's quite a travellers' scene going on. Whether you like this depends on just how many other people determined to get away from it all you want to share your solitude with – but at least there are cheap rooms or opportunities to camp out, some café/tavernas with good music, and a fine beach which you reach by walking down the stream bed from the village. Beyond here, beside the road leading in to Ierápetra, are long but exposed stretches of sand, including the appropriately named "Long Beach", along which you'll find a couple of large campsites.

Ierápetra

IERÁPETRA itself is a cheerless modern supply centre for the region's farmers. It also attracts an amazing number of package tourists and not a few backpackers looking for work, especially out of season. The tavernas along the tree-lined front are scenic enough and the beach, its remotest extremities rarely visited, stretches for a couple of miles to the east. But as a town most people find it pretty uninspiring. Although there has been a port here since Roman times, only the Venetian fort guarding the harbour and a crumbling minaret remain as reminders of better days. What little else has been salvaged is in the one-room **museum** (Tues–Sat 9am–3pm, but not always open) near the post office.

If you want to **stay**, head up Kazantzakís from the chaotic bus station and you'll find the *Four Seasons* rooms (☎0842/24 390; ②); or towards the centre on Platía Venizélou there's the *Hotel Creta* (☎0842/22 550; ③). More central, and perhaps better value, is the *Hotel Ligia* (☎0842/28 881; ③) on the square by the post office. You'll find places to eat and drink all along the waterfront, or try the bizarre *Rex*, a restaurant in an old cinema, on Platía Venizélou.

Mírtos, Árvi and beyond

If you're not heading straight back to the north coast by the fast road, there are a number of small resorts along the beach westwards, though little in the way of public transport. **MÍRTOS** is the first that might actually tempt you to stop, and it's certainly the most accessible, just off the main road with numerous buses to Ierápetra daily and a couple direct to Iráklion. Although developed to a degree, it nonetheless remains tranquil and inexpensive, with lots of young travellers (many of them sleeping on the beach, to the irritation of locals). If you want a **room**, try *Angelos* or *Mertini* (☎0842/51 386 for both; ②) – though there are plenty of others. Just off the road from Ierápetra are a couple of excavated **Minoan villas** you might want to explore: Néa Mírtos and Pírgos.

After Mírtos the main road turns inland towards ÁNO VIÁNNOS, then continues across the island towards Iráklion; several places on the coast are reached by a series of rough side tracks. That hasn't prevented one of them, **ÁRVI**, from becoming a larger resort than Mírtos. The beach hardly justifies it but it's an interesting little excursion (with at least one bus a day) if only to see the bananas and pineapples grown down here and to experience the microclimate (noticeably warmer than neighbouring zones, especially in spring or autumn) that encourages them. Two more villages – **KERATÓKAMBOS** and **TSOÚTSOUROS** – look tempting on the map. The first has a rather stony beach and only the most basic of rooms available, but it's popular with Cretan day-trippers and great if you want to escape from the tourist grind for a spell. The second is developed and not really worth the tortuous thirteen-kilometre dirt road in.

If you hope to continue **across the south** of the island, be warned that there are no buses, and that the road toward Míres may still not be complete, despite years of work. It's an enjoyable, rural drive, but progress can be slow; there's very little traffic if you're trying to hitch.

RÉTHIMNON AND AROUND

The relatively low, narrow section of Crete which separates the Psilorítis range from the White Mountains in the west seems at first a nondescript, even dull part of the island. Certainly in scenic terms it has few of the excitements that the west can offer, there are no major archaeological sites as in the east, and many of the villages seem modern and unattractive. On the other hand, **Réthimnon** itself is an attractive and lively city, with some excellent beaches nearby. And on the south coast, in particular around **Plakiás**, are beaches as fine as any Crete can offer – as you drive towards them the scenery and villages improve by the minute.

Réthimnon

In the past ten years or so, **RÉTHIMNON** has seen a greater influx of tourists than perhaps anywhere else on Crete, with the development of a whole series of large hotels extending almost 10km along the beach to the east. For once, though, the middle of town has been spared, so that at its heart Réthimnon remains one of the most beautiful of Crete's major cities (with only Haniá as a serious rival), with an enduringly provincial air. A wide sandy beach and palm-lined promenade border a labyrinthine tangle of Venetian and Turkish houses lining streets where ancient minarets lend an exotic air to the skyline. Dominating everything from the west is the superbly preserved outline of the fortress built by the Venetians after a series of pirate raids had devastated the town.

The Town

With a beach right in the heart of town it's tempting not to stir at all from the sands, but Réthimnon repays at least some gentle exploration. For a start, you could try checking out the further reaches of the **beach** itself. The waters protected by the breakwaters in front of town have their disadvantages – notably crowds and dubious hygiene – but less sheltered sands stretch for miles to the east, crowded at first but progressively less so if you're prepared to walk a bit.

Exploring the streets

Away from the beach, you don't have far to go for the most atmospheric part of town, immediately behind the inner harbour. Almost anywhere here you'll find unexpected old buildings, wall fountains, overhanging wooden balconies, heavy, carved doors and rickety shops, many still with local craftsmen sitting out front, gossiping as they ply their trades. Look out especially for the **Venetian loggia**, now being converted into a library (it used to house the town museum); the **Rimóndi fountain**, another of the more elegant Venetian survivals; and the **Nerandzes mosque**, best preserved of several in Réthimnon, whose minaret you can climb (daily 11am–7pm) for excellent free views over the town and surrounding countryside. Simply by walking past these three you'll have seen many of the liveliest parts of Réthimnon: Ethníkis Andistásis, the street leading straight up from the fountain, is also the town's **market** area.

The old city ends at the Porta Guora at the top of Andistásis, the only surviving remnant of the city walls. Almost opposite are the quiet and shady **Public Gardens**. These are always a soothing place to stroll, but most visitors only bother in the latter half of July, when the **Réthimnon Wine Festival** is staged here. Though touristy it's a thoroughly enjoyable event, with spectacular local dancing as the evening progresses and the barrels empty. As at the more famous festivals on the mainland, the entrance fee includes all the wine you can drink, though you'll need to bring your own cup or else buy one of the souvenir glasses and carafes on sale outside the gardens.

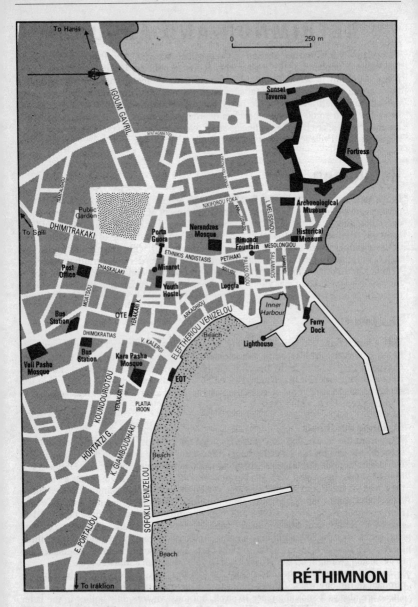

RÉTHIMNON

The museums and fortress

Heading in the other direction from the fountain, you can approach the mighty fortress via two interesting museums. The **Historical and Folk Art Museum** (Mon–Sat 9am–1pm & 7–9pm), on Mesolongíou, is small but tremendously enjoyable – inside, in just two not particularly large rooms, are gathered musical instruments, old photos, basketry, farm implements, an explanation of traditional bread-making techniques, smiths' tools, traditional costumes and jewellery, lace, weaving and embroidery, pottery, knives and old wooden chests. It makes for a fascinating insight into a fast disappearing rural (and urban) lifestyle, which had often survived virtually unchanged from Venetian times to the 1960s, and is well worth a look.

The **Archaeological Museum** (Tues–Sun 8.30am–3pm) occupies a newly converted building almost directly opposite the entrance to the fortress. This was built by the Turks as an extra defence for the entry, and later served as a prison, but it's now entirely modern inside: cool, spacious and airy. Unfortunately the collection is not particularly exciting, and really only worth seeing if you're going to miss the bigger museums elsewhere on the island.

The massive **Venetian Fortress** (Tues–Fri 8am–8pm, Sat, Sun & Mon 9.30am–6pm) is a must, however. Said to be the largest Venetian castle ever built, this was a response, in the last quarter of the sixteenth century, to a series of pirate raids (by Barbarossa among others) that had devastated the town. Inside now is a vast open space dotted with the remains of all sorts of barracks, arsenals, officers' houses, earthworks and deep shafts, and at the centre a large domed building that was once a church and later a mosque. It was designed to be large enough for the entire population to take shelter within the walls, and you can see that it probably was. Although much is ruined, it remains thoroughly atmospheric, and you can look out from the walls over the town and harbour, or in the other direction along the coast to the west. It's also worth walking around the outside of the fortress, preferably at sunset, to get an impression of its fearsome defences, plus great views along the coast and a pleasant resting point around the far side at the *Sunset Taverna*.

The phone code for Réthimnon is ☎0831

Practicalities

Réthimnon has two **bus terminals** – one for long-distance, the other for local services – diagonally opposite each other at the corner of Dhimokratías and Moátsou. From here walk north towards the sea; the waterside **tourist information office** (Mon–Fri 8am–3.30pm; ☎29 148) will be in front of you when you get to the beach. If you arrive by **ferry** you'll be even more conveniently placed, over at the western edge of the harbour.

Accommodation

There's a great number of places to stay in Réthimnon, and only at the height of the season are you likely to have difficulty finding somewhere; though you may get weary looking. The greatest concentration of **rooms** is in the tangled streets west of the inner harbour, between the Rimóndi fountain and the museums; there are also quite a few places on and around Arkadhíou.

Youth Hostel, Tombázi 41 (☎22 848). Cheapest beds in town are in the youth hostel dormitories (or on the roof). It's large, clean, very friendly and popular, and there's food, showers, clothes-washing facilities and even a library of books in an assortment of languages. ①

Pension Vrisinas, Heréti 10 (☎26 092). In a narrow street parallel to Kalérgi, worth checking as you walk from the bus station, but often full. Lovely rooms, though some are noisy. ③

Pension Zania, 3 Pavlou Vlastou (☎28 169). Right on the corner of Arkadhíou by the old youth hostel building, a well-adapted old house, but only a few rooms. ③

Pension Corina, Dambergi 9 (☎26 911). Very friendly place with a couple of good balcony rooms at front, several darker ones behind. ③

Barbara Dokimaki, Plastíra 14 (☎22 319). Strange warren of a rooms place, with one entrance at the above address, just off the seafront behind the *Hotel Ideon*, and another on Dambergi, opposite *Corina*; some excellent rooms. ③

Pension Anna, Katehaki (☎25 586). Comfortable place in a quiet position on the street that runs straight down from the entrance to the fortress to Melissinou. ③

Rooms George, Himáras (☎27-540). Just below the archaeological museum as you head up from town, a new place with a taverna below. ③

Réthimnon Haus, V Kornarou 1 (☎23 923). Very pleasant, upmarket rooms place in an old building just off Arkadhíou. Bar downstairs. ③

Hotel Leo, Vafe 2 (☎29 851). Slightly more expensive than the above, and slightly better, with lots of wood and traditional feel. Price includes breakfast, and there's a good bar. ④

Hotel Ideon, Platía Plastíra 10 (☎28 667). B-class place with brilliant position just north of the ferry dock; little chance of space in season, though. ⑥

Camping Elizabeth (☎28 694). Pleasant, large site on the beach about 4km east of town; all facilities. Take the bus for the hotels (marked *Scaleta/El Greco*) from the long-distance bus station to get there.

Camping Arkadia (☎28 825). Only a few hundred metres from *Elizabeth*, further east along the beach. Bigger and slightly less friendly.

Food, drink and nightlife

Immediately behind the town beach are arrayed the most obvious of Réthimnon's **restaurants**, all with large and colourful illustrated menus out in English, German, French, Swedish or whatever else seems likely to appeal. These are not always bad value – especially if you hanker after an "English breakfast" – but they are all thoroughly touristy. Around the **inner harbour** there's a second, rather more expensive group of tavernas, specialising in fish and in intimate atmosphere – though as often as not this is spoilt by the stench from the harbour itself: *O Zefyros* and *Seven Brothers* are two of the less outrageous of these.

Although they lack the sea views, the cluster of *kafenía* and tavernas **by the Rimóndi fountain** and the newer places spreading into the streets all around generally offer considerably better value. There are a couple of good pizza places here, too, and a number of old-fashioned *kafenía*, a couple of which serve magnificent yoghurt and honey. Places to try here include *Vangela*, a taverna right by the fountain and consequently very well known and patronised, and slightly more expensive than its neighbours; *Agrimi*, a reliable standard on Platía Petiháki; and the *Zanfoti kafeníon* overlooking Rimóndi fountain, relatively pricey, but a great place to people-watch over a coffee; good yoghurt and honey, too. Slightly cheaper places in the surrounding backstreets include *Stelios Soumbasakis*, a simple, friendly taverna at Nikiforou Foka 98, corner of Koronaíou; *Taverna Kargaki Haroulas*, Melissinou by Mesolongíou, for big, cheap breakfasts plus standard taverna fare at reasonable prices; and *Linda & Joe's Snack Bar*, serving cheap grub to hostellers on Tombázi, opposite the youth hostel.

Takeaway food means either **souvláki** – numerous stalls including a couple on Arkadhíou and Paleológou and *O Platanos* at Petiháki 44 – or buying your own ingredients. **Market** stalls are set up daily on Andistásis below the Porta Guora and there are small general stores scattered everywhere, particularly on Paleológou and Arkadhíou; east along the beach road you'll even find a couple of mini supermarkets. The **bakery** *I Gaspari*, on Mesolongíou just behind the Rimóndi fountain, sells the usual cheese pies, cakes and the like, and it also bakes excellent brown, black and rye bread, a godsend for anyone who's been travelling long-term. There's a good *zaharoplasteío* on Petiháki.

Nightlife is concentrated in the same general areas. At the west end of Venizélou, approaching the inner harbour, a small cluster of noisy **music bars** rock the beach – *Rouli's* is one of the liveliest. Several glitzier bar/discos, including *Fortezza* and *Loggia*, gather on an alley between the inner harbour and Arkadhíou: larger **discos** are mostly out to the east, among the big hotels, but there are one or two in town. *Odysseas*, on Venizélou right by the inner harbour, is a touristy Cretan music and dancing place, with live performances every evening from 9.30pm.

Around Réthimnon: Arkádhi

Of all the short trips that can be made out of Réthimnon, the best known is still the most worthwhile. This is to the **monastery of Arkádhi** (daily 6am–8pm), some 25km southeast of the city. Immaculately situated in the foothills of the Psilorítis range, Arkádhi is also something of a national Cretan shrine. During the 1866 rebellion against the Turks the monastery became a rebel strongpoint in which, as the Turks gained the upper hand, hundreds of Cretan guerillas and their families took refuge. Surrounded and, after two days of fighting, on the point of defeat, the defenders ignited a powder magazine just as the Turks entered. Hundreds (some sources claim thousands) were killed, Cretan and Turk alike, and the tragedy did much to promote international sympathy for the cause of Cretan independence. Nowadays you can peer into the roofless vault where the explosion occurred and wander about the rest of the well-restored grounds. The sixteenth-century Rococo church survived, and is one of the finest Venetian structures left on Crete; other buildings house a small museum devoted to the exploits of the defenders of the (Orthodox) faith. The monastery is easy to visit by public bus or on a tour.

Yioryoúpoli, Lake Kournás and the route west

Leaving Réthimnon **to the west**, the main road climbs for a while above a rocky coastline before descending (after some 5km) to the sea where it runs alongside sandy **beach** for perhaps another 7km. An occasional hotel and a campsite (*George*) offer accommodation, but on the whole there's nothing but a line of straggly bushes between the road and the windswept beach. If you have your own vehicle there are plenty of places to stop here for a swim, and rarely anyone else around – but beware of some very strong currents. If you want to stay for any time, virtually the only base is **YIORYOÚPOLI** at the far end, where the beach is cleaner, wider and further from the road. It's not exactly unknown – there are a lot of rooms places and several hotels, well used in mid-season – but neither is it heavily developed. If you're after a base for a few days that's peaceful but not too quiet, you could do a lot worse: most of the better rooms are found by heading for the main square and then looking along the road down towards the beach. Within walking distance inland is **Kournás**, Crete's only lake, set deep in a bowl of hills and almost constantly changing colour. There's a taverna on the shore with a few rooms for rent, or you could try for a bed in the nearby village of MOÚRI.

Beyond Yioryoúpoli the main road heads inland, away from a cluster of coastal villages beyond Vámos. It thus misses the Dhrápano peninsula, with some spectacular views over the sapphire Bay of Soudha, several quiet beaches, and the setting for the film of *Zorba the Greek*. **KÓKKINO HORIÓ**, the movie location, and nearby **PLÁKA** are indeed postcard-picturesque (more so from a distance), but **KEFALÁS**, inland, outdoes both of them. On the exposed north coast there are beaches at **ALMIRÍDHA** and **KALÍVES**, and off the road between them. Both have quite a few apartments but not many rooms available; Almirídha, though, makes an enjoyable lunch stop.

South from Réthimnon

There are a couple of alternative routes south from Réthimnon, but the main one heads straight out from the centre of town, an initially featureless road due south across the middle of the island. About 23km out, a turning cuts off to the right for Plakiás and Mírthios, following the course of the spectacular Kourtaliótiko ravine.

Plakiás and the south coast

PLAKIÁS has undergone a major boom and is no longer the pristine village all too many people arrive here expecting. That said, it's still quite low-key, there's a satisfactory beach and a string of good tavernas around the dock; visitors on the whole are young and travelling light. There are hundreds of **rooms**, but at the height of summer you'll need to arrive early if you hope to find one; the last to fill are generally those on the road leading inland, away from the waterside. If needed, there's a **youth hostel** (☎0832/31 306; ①) on the edge of town, while the beach is long and nobody is likely to mind if you sleep out on the middle section – but Damnóni (below) is far better if that's your plan.

Once you've found a room there's not a lot else to discover here. You'll find every facility – including a temporary post office, bike rental, money exchange, supermarket and even launderette – strung out around the waterfront. Places to **eat** are plentiful too: the attractive tavernas on the waterfront in the centre are a little expensive; you'll eat cheaper further inland, or around the corner at one of the places facing west (*Julia's Place*, here, has good vegetarian food).

Mírthios

For a stay of more than a day or two, **MÍRTHIOS**, in the hills behind Plakiás, also deserves consideration. It's no longer a great deal cheaper, but at least you'll find locals still outnumbering the tourists and something of a travellers' scene based around another popular **youth hostel** (☎0832/31 202; ①), with a friendly taverna, and several rooms places. The Plakiás bus will usually loop back through Mírthios, but check; otherwise it's less than five minutes' walk from the junction. It takes twenty minutes to walk down to the beach at Plakiás, a little longer to Damnóni, and if you're prepared to walk for an hour or more there are some entirely isolated coves to the west – ask directions at the hostel.

Damnóni

Some of the most tempting beaches in central Crete hide just to the east of Plakiás, though unfortunately they're now a very poorly kept secret. These three splashes of yellow sand, divided by rocky promontories, are within easy walking distance, and together go by the name **DAMNÓNI**. At the first, Damnóni proper, there's a taverna with showers and a wonderfully long strip of sand, but there's also a lot of new development including a number of nearby rooms places and a huge new hotel which, if it's open, may well have changed the atmosphere for ever. For the moment, at the far end you'll generally find a few people who've dispensed with their clothes – the little cove which shelters the middle of the three beaches, barely accessible except on foot, is entirely nudist. Beyond this, Ammoúdhi beach has another taverna (with good rooms for rent) and a slightly more family atmosphere. To any of these – all considerably more attractive than Plakiás's own beach – you'd have less far to walk, and probably spend less, staying in the village of LEFKÓYIA, 2km away. The disadvantages are that Lefkóyia is not itself on the coast, and that besides a couple of tavernas and four or five places renting rooms, it has no facilities at all.

Moni Préveli and "Palm Beach"

Next in line comes **PRÉVELI**, some 6km southeast of Lefkóyia. It takes its name from a **monastery** (daily 8am–1pm & 3–7pm) high above the sea which, like every other in Crete, has a proud history of resistance – in this case accentuated by its role in the last war as a shelter for marooned Allied soldiers awaiting evacuation off the south coast. There are fine views and a monument commemorating the rescue operations, but little else to see. The evacuations took place from **"Palm Beach"**, a sandy cove with a small date-palm grove and solitary drink stand where a stream feeds a little oasis right behind the beach. The beach usually attracts a summer camping community and is now also the target of day-trip boats from Plakiás. Sadly, these two groups between them have left this lovely place filthy and it's barely worth the effort: the climb down from the monastery is steep, rocky and surprisingly arduous. If you do come, it's a great deal easier on the boat.

Spíli and Ayía Galíni

Back on the main road south, **SPÍLI** lies about 30km from Réthimnon. A popular coffee break for tours passing this way, Spíli warrants time if you can spare it. Sheltered under a beetling cliff are narrow alleys of ancient houses, all leading up from a square with a famous 24-spouted fountain. If you have your own transport it's a worthwhile place to stay, peacefully rural at night but with several good rooms places (plus the *Green Hotel*; ☎0832/22 056; ③) and a variety of onward options in every direction.

The ultimate destination of most people on this road is **AYÍA GALÍNI**. If heading here was your plan, maybe you should think again – this picturesque "fishing village" is so busy that you can't see it for the tour buses, hotel billboards and English package tourists. It also has a beach much too small for the crowds who congregate here. Having said that, there are some saving graces – mainly some excellent restaurants and bars, plenty of rooms, and a friendly atmosphere that survives and even thrives on all the visitors. Out of season it can be quite enjoyable, and from November to April the mild climate makes it an ideal spot to spend the winter. A lot of long-term travellers do just that, so it's a good place to find work packing tomatoes or polishing cucumbers. If you want somewhere to stay, start looking at the top end of town, around the main road: there are dozens of possibilities, and usually something to be found even at the height of summer.

The coastal plain east of Ayía Galíni, hidden under acres of polythene greenhouses and burgeoning concrete sprawl, must be among the ugliest regions in Crete, and TIMBÁKI the dreariest town. Since this is the way to Festós and back to Iráklion, however, you may have no choice but to grin and bear it.

The Amári Valley

An alternative, slower route from Réthimnon to the south runs via the **Amári Valley**. Very few buses go this way, but if you're driving it's well worth the extra time. There's little specifically to see or do (though hidden away are a number of frescoed Byzantine churches), but it's an impressive drive under the flanks of the mountains and a reminder of how, in places, rural Crete continues to exist regardless of visitors. The countryside here is delightfully green even in summer, with rich groves of olive and assorted fruit trees, and if you **stay** (rooms in THRÓNOS and YERÁKARI) the nights are cool and quiet. It may seem odd that many of the villages along the way are modern; they were systematically destroyed by the Germans in reprisal for the 1944 kidnapping of General Kreipe.

HANIÁ AND THE WEST

The substantial attractions of Crete's westernmost quarter are all the more enhanced by its relative lack of visitors; and despite the now-rapid spread of tourist development, the west is likely to remain one of the emptier parts of the island. This is partly because there are no big sand beaches to accommodate resort hotels, and partly because it's so far from the great archaeological sites. But for mountains and empty (if often pebbly) beaches, it's unrivalled.

Haniá itself is one of the best reasons to come here, perhaps the only Cretan city which could be described as enjoyable in itself. The immediately adjacent coast is relatively developed and not overly exciting; for beaches it's the **south coast** you really need. **Paleohóra** is the only place which could really be described as a resort, and even this is on a thoroughly human scale; others are emptier still. **Ayía Rouméli** and **Loutró** can be reached only on foot or by boat; **Hóra Sfakíon** sees hordes passing through but few who stay; **Frangokástello**, nearby, has a beautiful castle and the first stirrings of development. Behind these lie the **White Mountains** – the *Lefká Óri* – and above all the famed walk through the **Gorge of Samariá**.

Haniá

HANIÁ, as any of its residents will tell you, is the spiritual capital of Crete, even if the nominal title has passed (in 1971) to Iráklion. For many it is also by far the island's most attractive city – especially if you can catch it in spring, when the Lefká Óri's snow-capped peaks seem to hover above the roofs. Although it is for the most part a modern city, you might never know it as a tourist. Surrounding the small outer harbour is a wonderful jumble of half-derelict Venetian streets that survived the wartime bombardments, and it is here that life for the visitor is concentrated. Restoration and gentrification – consequences of the tourist boom – have made inroads of late, but it remains an atmospheric place.

Arrival and accommodation

Large as it is, Haniá is easy to handle once you've reached the centre; you may get lost wandering among the narrow alleys of the old city but that's a relatively small area, and you're never far from the sea or from some other obvious landmark. The **bus station** is on Odhós Kidhonías, within easy walking distance from the action – turn right, then left down the side of Platía 1866 and you'll emerge at a major road junction opposite the top of Hálidhon, the main street of the old quarter leading straight down to the Venetian harbour. **Arriving by ferry** you'll anchor about 10km from Haniá at the port of SOÚDHA: there are frequent buses which will drop you by the market on the fringes of the old town, or you can take a taxi. From the **airport** (about 15km) taxis will almost certainly be your only option, though it's worth a quick check to see if any sort of bus you could gatecrash is meeting your flight – *Olympic* flights are all met, or you may be able to hitch a lift on a package tour bus.

The **tourist office** is now in the new town, just off Platía 1866 at Kriári 40 (suite 14/15, 4th floor; Mon–Fri 7.30am–2.30pm); it may be that the waterfront mosque where the office used to be (and where it's still marked on our map) will be open as a municipal tourist information centre.

> The phone code for Haniá is ☎0821

Accommodation

There must be thousands of **rooms to rent** in Haniá and, unusually, quite a few comfortable **hotels**. Though you may face a long search for a bed at the height of the season, eventually everyone does seem to find something.

HARBOUR AREA

Perhaps the most desirable rooms of all are those **overlooking the harbour**, and, surprisingly, such rooms are sometimes available at quite reasonable rates: be warned that this is often because they're very noisy at night. Most are approached not direct from the harbourside itself but from the alley behind, Zambelíu, or other streets leading off the harbour further around (where you may get more peace). The nicest of the more expensive places are here too, usually set back a little so they're quieter, but often still with the views from upper storeys.

Hotel Piraeus, Zambelíu 10 (☎54 154). One of the oldest in Haniá; basic and somewhat run-down but friendly, English-speaking and excellent value even for a room with a balcony over the harbour. ③

Rooms Antonis, Zambelíu next to *Piraeus*. Very plain rooms, not always too clean, but astonishingly cheap for the location. ②

Rooms George, Zambelíu 30 (☎43 542). Old building with steep stairs and eccentric antique furniture – rooms vary in price according to position and size. ③.

Artemis, Kondiláki 13 (☎21 196). One of many in this touristy street running inland from Zambelíu. ③

Pension Meltemi, Angelou 2 (☎40 192). First of a little row of possibilities in a great situation on the far side of the harbour; perhaps noisier than its neighbours, but ace views and a good café downstairs. ③

Rooms Eleonora, Theotokopóulou 13 (☎50 011). One of several in the backstreets around the top of Angelou: prices are lower at nearby *Eugenia*. ③

Pension Thereza, Angelou 8 (☎40 118). Beautiful old house in a great position with stunning views from roof terrace and some rooms; classy decorations too. More expensive than its neighbours but deservedly so – unlikely to have room in season unless you book. ④

Hotel Amphora, Theotokopóulou 20 (☎43 132). Large, traditional building, beautifully renovated. Worth the expense if you get a view, but probably not for the cheaper rooms with no view. ④

THE OLD TOWN: EAST OF HÁLIDHON

In the eastern half of the old town rooms are far more scattered, and in the height of the season your chances are much better over here. **Kastélli**, immediately east of the harbour, has some lovely places with views from the height. Take one of the alleys leading left off Kaneváro if you want to try these, but don't be too hopeful – they are popular and often booked up.

Pension Kastelli, Kaneváro 39 (☎57 057). Not the prettiest location, but comfortable, modern, reasonably priced, and very quiet at the back. Alex, who runs the place, is exceptionally helpful and also has a few apartments and a beautiful house (for up to 5 people) to rent. ③

Kydonia, Isódhion 15 (☎57 179). Between the Cathedral square and Platía Sindrívani, in the first street parallel to Hálidhon. Rather dark, but good value for so central a position. ③

Pension Lito, Episkópou Dorothéou 15 (☎53 150). Very near the Cathedral; another street with several options. ③

Pension Fidias, Sarpáki 8 (☎52 494). Signposted from the Cathedral. Favourite backpackers' meeting place: rather bizarrely run, but extremely friendly and has the real advantage of offering single rooms or fixing shares. ③

Marina Ventikou, Sarpáki 40 (☎57 601). Small, personally run rooms place in quiet corner of old town. Others nearby. ③

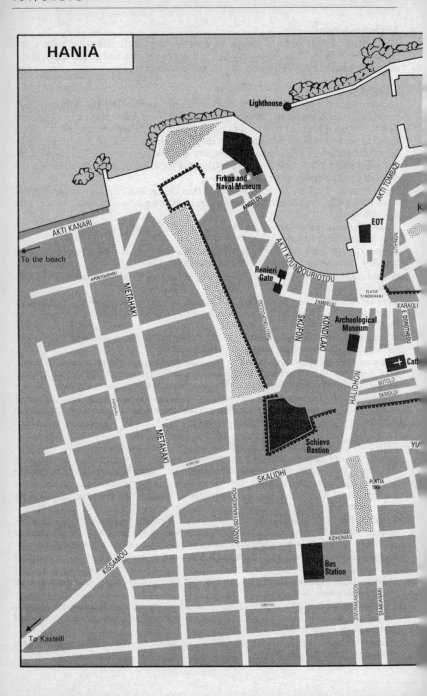

HANIÁ

Lighthouse

Firkas and
Naval Museum

ANGELOU

AKTI KANARI

AKTI TOMBAZI

EOT

To the beach

AKTI KOUNDOURIOTOU

LITHINON

k

APOSTOLIDHOU

Renieri
Gate

ZAMBELIU

PLATIA
SINDRIVANI

KARAOLI

METAHAKI

THEOTOKOPOULOU

SKOFON

KONDILAKI

Archeological
Museum

E DOROTHEOU

Cath

HALIDHON

BOTOLO

SKRIDLOF

PASGHALI

METAHAKI

KIRILOU

Schiavo
Bastion

YIA

SKALIDHI

PLATIA
1866

MANOUSOYANAKODHOU

KIDHONIAS

Bus
Station

KISSAMOU

ZIMVRAKAKIDON

SFAKIANAKI

SMIRIS

To Kastelli

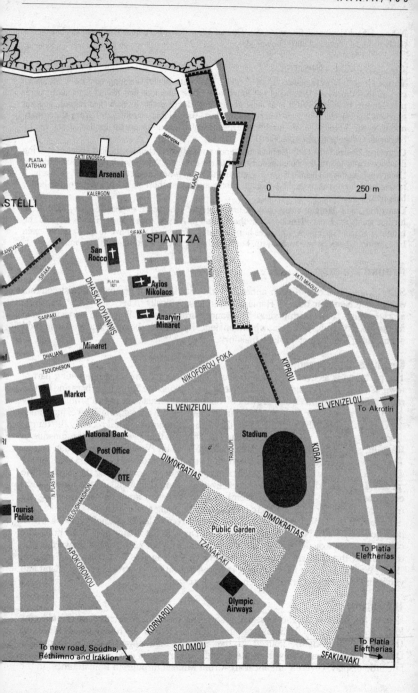

Nikos, Dhaskaloyiánnis 58 (☎54 783). One of a few down here near the inner harbour; relatively modern rooms all with shower. ③

HOSTEL AND CAMPSITES

Youth Hostel, Dhrakoniánou 33 (☎53 565). The youth hostel is a long way from anywhere you might otherwise visit and is not much of a place – four or five rooms with about eight metal bunks in each – but it is at least cheap and friendly, with a good view inland. You get here on the *Ay. Ioannis* bus (every 15min; last, they claim, at midnight) from the square opposite the market – ask for Platía Dhexameni. Organises cheap guided tours to the Samarian Gorge and other places. ①

Camping Hania (☎31 686). Behind the beach some 4km west of Haniá, just about in walking distance if you follow the coast around, but much easier reached by taking the local bus (see "Beaches", below). There's a large sign to warn you where to get off. The site is lovely, if rather basic in terms of facilities; small, shady, and a just short walk from some of the better beaches.

Camping Ayía Marína (☎48 555). A much bigger (and more expensive) site, 4km or so further west on an excellent beach at the far end of Ayía Marína village. This is beyond the range of Haniá city buses, so to get here by public transport you have to go from the main bus station. Check before turning up, because the site is earmarked for redevelopment.

Around the city

Surprisingly for a city of such antiquity – the site has been occupied almost continuously since Neolithic times – Haniá offers little specifically to see or do. It is, however, a place which is fascinating simply to wander around, stumbling upon surviving fragments of city wall, holes in which ancient Kydonia is being excavated and odd segments of Venetian or Turkish masonry.

Kastélli and the harbour

The port area is as ever the place to start, the oldest and the most interesting part of town. It's at its busiest and most attractive at night, when the lights from bars and restaurants reflect in the water and crowds of visitors and locals turn out to promenade. By day, things are quieter. Straight ahead from Platía Sindrivani (aka Harbour Square) lies the curious, domed shape of the **Mosque of the Janissaries**: until recently the tourist office, but currently without a function. The little hill that rises behind the mosque is **Kastélli**, site of the earliest habitation and core of the Venetian and Turkish towns. There's not a great deal left, but it's here that you'll find traces of the oldest walls (there were two rings, one defending Kastélli alone, a later set encompassing the whole of the medieval city) and the sites of various excavations. Beneath the hill, on the **inner (eastern) harbour**, the arches of sixteenth-century Venetian arsenals survive alongside remains of the outer walls; both are currently undergoing restoration.

Following the esplanade around in the other direction leads to a hefty bastion which now houses Crete's **Naval Museum** (Tues, Thurs & Sat 10am–2pm & 4–6pm). The collection is not exactly riveting, but wander in anyway for a look at the seaward fortifications and the platform where the modern Greek flag was first flown on Crete (in 1913). Walk around the back of these restored bulwarks to a street heading inland and you'll find the best preserved stretch of the outer walls.

The old city

Behind the harbour lie the less picturesque but more lively sections of the old city. First, a short way up Hálidhon on the right is Haniá's **Archaeological Museum** (Mon–Fri 8.30am–3pm), housed in the Venetian-built church of San Francesco. Damaged as it is, especially from the outside, this remains a beautiful building and a fine little display, covering the local area from Minoan through to Roman times. In the garden a huge fountain and the base of a minaret survive from the period when the Turks converted the church into a mosque; around them are scattered various other sculptures and architectural remnants.

The **Cathedral**, ordinary and relatively modern, is just a few steps further up Hálidhon on the left. Around it are some of the more animated shopping areas, particularly **Odhós Skrídlof** (Leather Street), with streets leading up to the back of the market beyond. In the direction of the Spiántza quarter are ancient alleys which have yet to feel much effect of the city's modern popularity, still with tumbledown Venetian stonework and overhanging wooden balconies; though gentrification is spreading apace. There are a couple more **minarets** too, one on Dhaliáni, the other in Platía 1821 – a fine traditional square to stop for a coffee.

The new town

Once out of the narrow confines of the maritime district, the broad, traffic-choked streets of the **modern city** have a great deal less to offer. Up Tzanakáki, not far from the market, you'll find the **Public Gardens**, a park with strolling couples, a few caged animals (including a few *kri-kri* or Cretan ibex), and a café under the trees; there's also an open-air auditorium which occasionally hosts live music or local festivities. Beyond here you could continue to the **Historical Museum** (Mon–Fri 9am–1.30pm & 3–5.30pm) but the effort would be wasted unless you're a Greek-speaking expert on the subject; the place is essentially a very dusty archive with a few photographs on the wall. Perhaps more interesting is the fact that the museum lies on the fringes of Haniá's desirable residential districts – continue to the end of Sfakianáki and then down Iróön Politehníou towards the sea for an insight into how Crete's other half lives. There are several (expensive) garden restaurants down here and a number of fashionable café bars where you can sit outside.

Beaches

Haniá's beaches all lie to the west of the city. For the packed **city beach** this means no more than a ten-minute walk following the shoreline from the naval museum, but for good sand you're better off taking the local bus out along the coast road. This leaves from the east side of Platía 1866 and runs along the coast road as far as **Kalamáki** beach. Kalamáki and the previous stop, **Oasis Beach**, are again pretty crowded but they're a considerable improvement over the beach in Haniá itself. In between you'll find emptier stretches if you're prepared to walk: about an hour in all (on sandy beach virtually all the way) from Haniá to Kalamáki, perhaps ten minutes from the road to the beach if you get off the bus at the signs to *Aptera Beach* or *Camping Hania*. Further afield there are even finer beaches at Ayía Marína to the west, or Stavrós (see below) out on the Akrotíri peninsula (reached by *KTEL* buses from the main station).

Food and entertainment

Evenings in Haniá centre around the harbour, and you need not stray an inch from the waterfront walk to find a cocktail before dinner, a meal, a late-night bar and an all-night disco – numerous possibilities for all of these in fact. The most fashionable area these days, particularly with locals, is towards the far end of the inner harbour, around Sarpidóna. If you're on a tight budget, however, you'll need to avoid the waterfront.

Tavernas, restaurants and cafés

You're never far from something to eat in Haniá: in a circle around the **harbour** is one restaurant, taverna or café after another: All have their own character, but there seems little variation in price or what's on offer. Away from the water there are plenty of slightly cheaper possibilities on Kondiláki, Kaneváro and most of the streets off

Hálidhon. For snacks or lighter meals there are also lots of cafés around the harbour – on the whole these serve cocktails and fresh juices at exorbitant prices, though breakfast (especially "English") can be good value. For more traditional places, try around the market and along Dhaskaloyiánnis (*Singanaki* here is a good traditional bakery serving *tiropitta* and the like, with a cake shop next door). Fast food is also increasingly widespread, with numerous *souvláki* places and even a couple of burger joints..

Vasilis, Platía Sindriváni. Perhaps the least changed of the harbourside cafés. Reasonably priced breakfasts.

Karnáyio, Platía Kateháki 8. Set back from the inner harbour near the port police. Not right on the water, but one of the best harbour restaurants nonetheless.

Dino's, inner harbour by bottom of Sarpidóna. One of the best choices for a pricey seafood meal with a harbour view; *Apostolis*, almost next door, is also good.

Neorion, Sarpidóna. Café to sit and be seen in the evening; some tables overlook the harbour. Try an expensive but sublime lemon *granita*.

Hippopotamus Pizzeria, Sarpidóna. Surrounded by trendy bars and patronised by local youth; the pizza and pasta can make a welcome change.

Tamam, Zambelíu just before Renieri Gate. Young, fashionable place with adventurous Greek menu including much vegetarian food. Unfortunately only a few cramped tables outside, and inside it's very hot. Slow service.

Kyttaro, Kondiláki. The first of numerous good places as you head up Kondiláki from Zambelíu. Again, some vegetarian food.

Taverna Ela, top of Kondiláki. Live Greek music to enliven your meal.

Le Saladier, Kaneváro just off Platía Sindriváni. French-run joint offering salads of every kind.

To Dhiporto, Skridhlóf 40. Long-established, very basic taverna amid all the leather shops. Multilingual menu offers such delights as Pigs' Balls – or, more delicately, *Testicules de Porc*.

Pafsilipon, Sífaka 19. Good, standard taverna. Tables on the street and also on the raised pavement opposite.

Boúyatsa, Sífaka 4. Tiny place that serves little except the traditional creamy cheese pie – *boúyatsa* – to eat in or take away.

Pension Lito, Episkópou Dorothéou 15. Café/taverna with live music (usually Greek-style guitar); one of several in this street.

Tasty Souvláki, Hálidhon 80. Seems always to have been here and is always packed despite being cramped and none-too-clean – which is a testimonial to the quality and value of the *souvláki*. Better to take away. There are other *souvláki* places on Karaolí; at the end of the outer harbour, near the naval museum; and around the corner of Plastíra and Yianári, across from the market.

Meltemi, Angelou 2. Slow, relaxed place for breakfast, and where locals (especially expats) sit whiling the day away or playing *tavli*.

Bars and nightlife

There are NATO air force and navy bases out on Akrotíri, which means there are some bars in Haniá that are a lot heavier than you'd expect, full of US and other servicemen. Over the last couple of years some of these places have been closed and others tamed, however, and the troops have been on their best behaviour in the face of local opposition to their presence: tourists and young locals predominate in most places.

The smartest and newest places are on and around Sarpidóna in the far corner of the inner harbour: bars like *Fraise*, on Sarpidóna; and late night disco-bars such as *Berlin Rock Café*, on Radimánthus, just around the corner at the top of Sarpidóna. Heading from here around towards the outer harbour you'll pass others including the *Four Seasons*, a very popular bar by the port police; the *Canale Club*, on the outer harbour, another bar/disco that doesn't open till 11pm; and then reach a couple of the older places including *Remember* and *Scorpio* behind the *Plaza Hotel*. *Fagotto*, Angelou 16, is a pleasant, laid-back jazz bar, often with live performers. Discos proper include *Ariadni*, on the inner harbour (opens 11.30pm, but busy later), and *Agora Club*, a big, bright place on Tsoudherón behind the market, which doesn't really get going until 2am.

A couple of places that offer more traditional entertainment are the *Café Kriti*, Kalergón 22, at the corner of Androgéo, basically an old-fashioned *kafeníon* where there's **Greek music and dancing** virtually every night, and the Fírkas (the bastion by the naval museum), where there's Greek dancing at 9pm every Tuesday – pricey but authentic entertainment. It's also worth checking for events at the open-air auditorium in the public gardens, and for performances in restaurants outside the city, which are the ones the locals will go to. Check for posters, especially in front of the market and in the little square across the road from there.

For **films**, you should also check the hoardings in front of the market. There are open-air screenings at *Attikon*, on El. Venizélou out towards Akrotíri, about 1km from the centre, and occasionally in the public gardens.

Listings

Airlines *Olympic*, Tzanakáki 88 (☎27 701; Mon–Fri 9am–4pm). There's a bus from here connecting with their flights. For airport information phone ☎63 245.

Banks The main branch of the *National Bank of Greece* is directly opposite the market. Convenient smaller banks for exchange are next to the bus station, at the bottom of Kaneváro just off Harbour Square, or at the top of Hálidhon. There are also a couple of exchange places on Hálidhon, open long hours, and a post office van parked through the summer in Cathedral square.

Bike and car rental Possibilities everywhere, especially on Hálidhon though these are rarely the best value. For cars try *Hermes*, Tzanakáki 52, (☎54 418; 20% discount promised to readers), friendly and efficient; for bikes and cars *Duke of Crete*, Sífaka 3, (☎21 651), Skalídhi 16 (☎57 821), and branches in Ayía Marína and Plataniás (15% discount promised for cash).

Boat trips Various boat trips are offered by travel agents around town, mostly round Soúdha Bay or out to beaches on the Rodhópou peninsula. *Domenico's* on Kaneváro offers some of the best of these.

Ferry tickets The agent for *Minoan* is *Nanadakis Travel*, Hálidhon 8 (☎23 939); for *ANEK* on Venizélou, right opposite the market (☎23 636).

Launderette There are three, at Kaneváro 38 (9am–10pm), Episkópou Dorothéou 7 and Áyii Dhéka 18. All do service washes.

Left luggage The bus station has a left luggage office.

Post office The main post office is on Tzanakáki (Mon–Sat 7am–8pm, exchange 8am–2pm). In summer there's a handy Portakabin branch set up in the Cathedral square.

Shopping Shops aimed at tourists are in the old town: jewellery and souvenirs on Hálidhon and all around the harbour. The leather goods on Skridhlóf are excellent value. If you want to buy food or get stuff together for a picnic, the market is the place to head. There are vast quantities of fresh fruit and vegetables as well as meat and fish, bakers, dairy stalls for milk, cheese and yoghurt, and general stores for cooked meats, tins and other standard provisions. When the market is closed there are several small stores down by the harbour square which sell cold drinks and a certain amount of food, but these are expensive (though they do open late). A couple of large supermarkets can be found on the main roads running out of town – particularly *CretaMarket* on the way to Akrotíri.

Taxis The main taxi ranks are in the Cathedral square and, especially, Platía 1866. For radio taxis try ☎29 405 or ☎58 700.

Telephones OTE headquarters is on Tzanakáki just past the post office – open daily 6am–midnight. It's generally packed during the day, but often blissfully empty late at night.

Tourist police Kareskáki 44 (☎24 477). Town and harbour police are on the inner harbour.

Travel agencies For cheap tickets home – *Magic Bus* and student/charter flights – *Bassias Travel*, Skridhlóf 46 (☎44 295), is the place, very helpful for regular tickets too. They also deal in standard excursions. Other travel agents for tours and day trips are everywhere.

Around Haniá: the Akrotíri and Rodhopoú peninsulas

Just **north of Haniá** the **Akrotíri peninsula** loops around to protect the Bay of Soúdha – and a NATO military base and missile-testing area. In an ironic twist, the peninsula's northwestern coastline is fast developing into a luxury suburb – the beach of HORAFÁKIA, long popular with jaded Haniotes, is surrounded by villas and apartments. STAVRÓS, further out, has not yet suffered this fate, and its beach is absolutely superb if you like the calm, shallow water of an almost completely enclosed lagoon. It's not very large so it does get crowded, but rarely overpoweringly so. You can rent rooms here, and there are two tavernas.

Inland are the **monasteries of Ayía Triádha** and **Gouvernétou** (both daily 9am–2pm & 5–7pm). The former is much more accessible and has a beautiful seventeenth-century church inside its pink-and-ochre cloister; it's also one of the few Cretan monasteries in which genuine monastic life continues. Beyond the latter you can clamber down a craggy path to the abandoned ruins of the monastery of Katholikó and the remains of its narrow (swimmable) harbour.

West to Rodhopoú

To the **west of Haniá** extends a coast that was the scene of most of the fighting during the German invasion in 1941. As you leave town, an aggressive diving eagle commemorates the German parachutists, and at **MÁLEME** there's a big German cemetery; the Allied cemetery is in the other direction, on the coast just outside Soúdha. There are also beaches, and considerable tourist development, along much of this shore. At **AYÍA MARÍNA** there's a fine sandy beach, and an island offshore said to be a sea monster petrified by Zeus before it could swallow Crete. Seen from the west, its "mouth" still gapes open. Between **PLATANIÁS** and **KOLIMBÁRI** an almost unbroken strand unfurls, by no means all sandy, but deserted for long stretches between villages. The road here runs through mixed groves of bamboo and oranges; the bamboo windbreaks protect the ripening oranges from the *meltémi*. At Kolimbári, the road to Kastélli cuts across the base of another mountainous peninsula, **Rodhopoú**. Just off the main road here is a monastery, **Goniá** (daily 9am–2pm & 5–7pm), with a view most luxury hotels would envy. Every monk in Crete can tell tales of his proud ancestry of resistance to invaders, but here the Turkish cannon balls are still lodged in the walls to prove it, a relic of which the good fathers are far more proud than of any of the icons.

The Samarian Gorge

From Haniá the **Gorge of Samariá** can be visited as a day trip or as part of a longer excursion to the south. At over 16km it's Europe's longest gorge and is startlingly beautiful. Buses leave Haniá for the top at 6.15, 7.30 and 8.30am, plus 4.30pm, and you'll normally be sold a return ticket (valid from Hóra Sfakíon at any time). It's well worth catching the early bus to avoid the full heat of the day while walking through the gorge, though be warned that you will not be alone – there are often as many as five coachloads setting off before dawn for the nail-biting climb into the White Mountains. There are also direct early-morning buses from Iráklion and Réthimnon, and coach tours from virtually everywhere on the island; despite all the crowds, the walk is hard work, especially in spring when the stream is a roaring torrent.

One way to avoid the early start would be to stay at **OMALÓS**, in the middle of the mountain plain from which the gorge descends (some ordinary rooms places and a

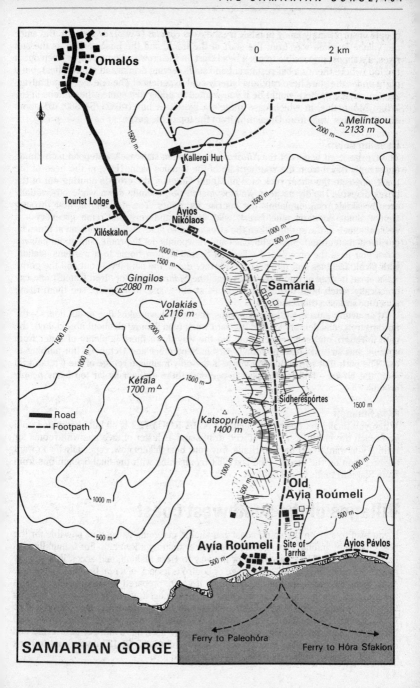

0   2 km

Omalós

1500 m

Kallergi Hut

Tourist Lodge

Xilóskalon

Áyios Nikólaos

1500 m

1000 m

500 m

1000 m

1500 m

Melíntaou
2133 m

2000 m

Gíngilos
2080 m

Samariá

Volakiás
2116 m

2000 m

1000 m

1500 m

Kéfala
1700 m

Sidherespórtes

1500 m

Katsoprínes
1400 m

1000 m

1000 m

Road
Footpath

500 m

Old
Ayia Roúmeli

500 m

1000 m

500 m

Ayía Roúmeli

Site of
Tarrha

Áyios Pávlos

500 m

SAMARIAN GORGE

Ferry to Paleohóra

Ferry to Hóra Sfakíon

couple of surprisingly fancy hotels – try the *Neos Omalos* (☎0821/67 269; ③). But since the village is some way from the start of the track, and the buses arrive as the sun rises, it's almost impossible to get a head start on the crowds. Some people sleep out at the top (where there's a bar-restaurant and stalls serving drinks and sandwiches), but a night under the stars here can be a bitterly cold experience. The one significant advantage to staying up here would be if you wanted to undertake some other climbs in the White Mountains, in which case there's a mountain hut (☎0821/54 560; ①) about ninety minutes'.walk from Omalós or from the top of the gorge.

Heading down

The **Gorge** itself begins at the *Xilóskalo*, or "wooden staircase", a stepped path plunging steeply down from the southern lip of the Omalós plain. Here, at the head of the track, opposite the sheer rock face of Mount Gíngilos, the crowds pouring out of the buses disperse rapidly as keen walkers march purposefully down while others dally over breakfast, contemplating the sunrise for hours. You descend at first through almost alpine scenery: pine forest, wild flowers and very un-Cretan greenery – a verdant shock in the spring, when the stream is also at its liveliest (and can at times be positively dangerous). Small churches and viewpoints dot the route, and about halfway down you pass the abandoned village of **Samariá**, now home to a wardens' station, with picnic facilities and filthy toilets. Further down, the path levels out and the gorge walls close in until at the narrowest point (the *Sidherespórtes* or "Iron Gates") one can practically touch both tortured rock faces at once, and, looking up, see them rising sheer for almost a thousand feet.

At an average pace, with regular stops, the walk down takes five or six hours – the upward trek considerably longer. It's hard work (you'll know all about it next day), the path is rough, and solid shoes vital. On the way down there is plenty of water from springs and streams (except some years in September and October), but nothing to eat. The park that surrounds the gorge is the only mainland refuge of the Cretan wild ibex, the *kri-kri* – but don't expect to see one, there are usually far too many people around.

Ayía Rouméli

When you finally get down, the village of **AYÍA ROUMÉLI** is all but abandoned until you reach the beach, a mirage of iced drinks and a cluster of tavernas with rooms for rent. If you want to get back to Haniá, buy your boat tickets now, especially if you want an afternoon on the beach – the last boat (connecting with the final 6.30pm bus from Hóra Sfakíon) tends to sell out first.

Villages of the southwest coast

If you plan to stay on the south coast you should get going as soon as possible for the best chance of finding a room somewhere nicer than Ayía Rouméli. For tranquillity it's hard to beat **LOUTRÓ**, two-thirds of the way to Hóra Sfakíon, and accessible only by boat or on foot. The chief disadvantage of Loutró is its lack of a real beach; most people swim from the rocks around its small bay. If you're prepared to walk, however, there are deserted beaches along the coast to the east. Indeed, if you're really into walking there's a coastal trail through Loutró which covers the entire distance between Ayía Rouméli and Hóra Sfakíon, or you could take the daunting zigzag path up the cliff behind to the mountain village of ANÓPOLI. Loutró itself has a number of tavernas and rooms (though not always enough of the latter; call ☎0825/91 127 if you want to book one) and space to camp out on the cape by a ruined fort.

HÓRA SFAKÍON is the more usual terminus for walkers traversing the gorge, with a regular boat service along the coast to and from Ayía Rouméli. Consequently it's quite an expensive and not an especially welcoming place; there are plenty of rooms and some excellent tavernas, but for a real beach you should jump straight on the evening bus going toward Plakiás. Plenty of opportunities present themselves en route, one of the most memorable at **FRANGOKÁSTELLO**, a crumbling Venetian attempt to bring law and order to a district which went on to defy both Turks and Germans. Its square, crenellated fort, isolated a few kilometres below a chiselled wall of mountains, looks like it's been spirited out of the High Atlas or Tibet. And speaking of spirits, the place is said to be haunted by ghosts of Greek rebels massacred here in 1829. Every May these *dhrossolítes* (dewy ones) march at dawn across the coastal plain and disappear into the sea near the fort. The rest of the time Frangokástello is peaceful enough, with a superb beach and numbers of tavernas and rooms, but it's on its way to development. Slightly further east – and less influenced by tourism or modern life – are the attractive villages of SKALOTÍ and RODHÁKINO, each with basic lodging and food.

Soúyia

In quite the other direction from Ayía Rouméli, less regular boats also head to **SOÚYIA** and on to Paleohóra. Soúyia, until World War II merely the anchorage for Koustoyérako inland, is low-key with a long, grey pebble beach and mostly modern buildings (except for a church with a sixth-century Byzantine mosaic as the foundation). Since a new road has been completed to Haniá the village has started to expand, but except in the very middle of summer it continues to make a good fallback for finding a room or a place to camp, eating cheaply and enjoying the beach when the rest of the island is seething with tourists.

Kastélli and the western tip

Apart from being Crete's most westerly town, and the end of the main road, **KASTÉLLI** (KÍSSAMOS, or Kastélli Kissámou as it's variously known) has little obvious attraction. It's a busy town with a rocky beach visited mainly by people using the boat that runs twice weekly to the island of Kíthira and the Peloponnese. The very ordinariness of Kastélli, however, can be attractive: life goes on pretty much regardless of outsiders, but there's every facility you might need. The ferry agent's office in Kastélli is right on the main square (*Ksirouksákis*; ☎0822/22 655), and nothing else is far away apart from the dock – a wearying two-kilometre walk (or cheap taxi ride) from town.

Falásarna to Elafonísi

To the west of Kastélli lies some of Crete's loneliest – and for many visitors, finest – coastline. The first place of note on the map is ancient **FALÁSARNA**, city ruins which mean little to the non-specialist except insofar as they overlook some of the best beaches on Crete, wide and sandy with clean water. There's a handful of tavernas and an increasing number of rooms places; otherwise you have to sleep out, as many people do. This can mean that the main beaches are dirty, but they remain beautiful, and there are plenty of others within walking distance. The nearest real town is PLÁTANOS, 5km up the recently paved road, along which there are a couple of daily buses.

Further south, the western coastline is still less discovered, the road is surfaced only as far as Kámbos, and there is little in the way of official accommodation. SFINÁRI has several houses which rent rooms, and a quiet pebble beach a little way below the village.

KÁMBOS is similar, but even less visited, its beach a considerable walk down a hill. Beyond them both is the **monastery of Hrissoskalítissa**, hard to get to (though increasingly visited by tours from Haniá or Paleohóra) but well worth the effort for its isolation and nearby beaches; the bus gets as far as VÁTHI, from where the monastery is another two hours' walk away.

Five kilometres beyond Hrisosskalítissa, the road bumps down to the coast opposite the tiny uninhabited islet of **Elafonísi**. You can easily wade out to the island with its sandy beaches and rock pools, and the shallow lagoon is warm and crystal-clear. It looks magnificent, but daily boat trips from Paleohóra and coach tours from elsewhere on the island ensure that, in the middle of the day at least, it's far from deserted. If you want to stay, and really appreciate the place, there are a couple of seasonal tavernas – bring some supplies unless you want to be wholly dependent on them.

A round trip

If you have transport, a circular drive from Kastélli, taking the coast road in one direction and the inland route through Élos and Topólia, makes for a stunningly scenic circuit. Near the ocean, villages cling desperately to the high mountainsides, apparently halted by some miracle in the midst of calamitous seaward slides. Around them olives ripen on the terraced slopes, the sea glittering far below. Inland, especially at **ÉLOS**, the main crop is the chestnut, whose huge old trees shade the village streets. In **TOPÓLIA** the chapel of Ayía Sofía is sheltered inside a cave which has been known since Neolithic times. Cutting south from Élos, a partly paved road continues through the high mountains towards Paleohóra; on a motorbike, with a sense of adventure and plenty of petrol, it's great: the bus doesn't come this way, villagers still stare at the sight of a tourist, and a host of small, seasonal streams cascade beside or under the track.

Paleohóra

Getting down to Paleohóra by the main road, which is paved the whole way, is a lot easier, and several daily buses from Haniá make the trip. But although this route also has to wind through the western outriders of the White Mountains, it lacks the excitement of the routes to either side. **KÁNDANOS**, at the 58-kilometre mark, has been entirely rebuilt since it was destroyed by the Germans for its fierce resistance to their occupation. The original sign erected when the deed was done is preserved on the war memorial: "Here stood Kándanos, destroyed in retribution for the murder of 25 German soldiers".

When the beach at **PALEOHÓRA** finally appears below it is a welcome sight. The little town is built across the base of a peninsula, its harbour on one side, the sand on the other. Above, on the outcrop, Venetian ramparts stand sentinel. These days Paleohóra has become heavily developed, but it's still thoroughly enjoyable, with a main street filling in the evening with tables as diners spill out of the restaurants, and with a pleasantly chaotic social life. There are scores of places to stay (though not always many vacancies) and there's also a fair-sized campsite; in extremis the beach is one of the best to sleep out on, with showers, trees and acres of sand. Nearby discos and a rock'n'roll bar, or the soundtrack from the open-air cinema, combine to lull you to sleep. When you tire of Paleohóra and the excellent windsurfing in the bay, there are excursions up the hill – to Prodhrómi, for example – or along a five-hour coastal path to Soúyia.

You'll find a helpful **tourist office** (daily 9.30am–1pm & 5.30–9pm) in the town hall on Venizélos, right in the centre of town; they have full accommodation lists and a map (though you'll hardly need this). The OTE, banks and travel agents are all nearby; the post office is on the road behind the sandy beach. **Boats** run from here to Elafonísi, the island of Gávdhos, and along the coast to Soúyia and Ayía Rouméli.

Gávdhos

The island of **Gávdhos**, some fifty kilometres of rough sea south of Paleohóra, is the most southerly landmass in Europe. Gávdhos is small (about 10km by 7km at the most) and barren, but it has one major attraction: the enduring isolation which its inaccessible position has helped preserve. There are now a few package tours (travel agents in Paleohóra can arrange a room if you want one), and there's a semi-permanent community of campers through the summer, but if all you want is a beach to yourself and a taverna to grill your fish, this remains the place for you.

travel details

Air/Sea Connections

Iráklion 2 ferries daily to Pireás (12hr); 1–6 ordinary ferries to Thíra (4hr), also fast boats and hydrofoils (2hr 30min); daily ferries to Thíra, Íos, Náxos and Páros in season; also regular connections with Míkonos and Náxos; at least twice weekly to Tínos, Skíros, Skíathos, Anáfi, Kárpathos and Rhodes. Ferries to Alexandria (Egypt) and Venice (Italy) every 8 days and twice weekly to Limassol (Cyprus) and Haifa (Israel). Many daily flights to Athens; seasonally daily to Rhodes, 3 or 4 weekly to Míkonos, Páros and Thíra; 2 a week to Thessaloníki.

Áyios Nikólaos and Sitía 1–3 ferries a week to Kássos, Kárpathos, Hálki, Rhodes and the Dodecanese; weekly to Anáfi, Thíra, Folégandhros, Mílos, Sífnos and Pireás.

Réthimnon 3 ferries a week to Pireás (12hr); weekly service and seasonal day trips to Thíra.

Haniá 1 or 2 daily ferries to to Pireás (12hr); several flights a day to Athens, weekly to Thessaloníki.

Kastélli (Kíssamos) Ferry once a week to Kíthira, Yíthio (Peloponnese; 8hr), Monemvassía and Pireás; once to Kíthira and Neápoli.

Paleohóra 2 boats a week in season to Gávdhos.

Main Bus Routes on the Island

Kastélli–Haniá (13 daily 6am–8pm; 1hr 30min); Haniá–Réthimnon–Iráklion (27 daily 5.30am–8.30pm; 3hr total); Iráklion–Áyios Nikólaos (24 daily 6.30am–9pm; 1hr 30min); Áyios Nikólaos–Sitía (8 daily 6.30am–7pm; 2hr); Iráklion–Ierápetra (8 daily 7.30am–6.30pm; 2hr 30min); Iráklion–Festós–Ayía Galíni (9 daily 6.30am–5.30pm; 2hr/2hr 30min); Réthimnon–Spíli–Ayía Galíni (6 daily 6.30am–5pm; 45min/1hr 30min); Haniá–Hóra Sfakíon (4 daily 8.30am–3.30pm; 2hr); and Haniá–Paleohóra (5 daily 9am–5pm; 2hr).

Hitching on Crete is poor, rides coming mainly from tourist traffic, so if you can afford it this is one island where **renting bicycles, mopeds or motorbikes** makes a lot of difference. There are rental agencies in all the main towns, and most of them will give quite reasonable discounts if you're going for two or more days.

CHAPTER NINE

DODECANESE

T he most distant of the Greek islands, the **Dodecanese** (*Dhodhekánisos*) lie close to the Turkish coast – some, like Kós and Kastellórizo, almost within hailing distance of the shore. Because of this position, and their remoteness from Athens, the islands have had a turbulent history: they were the scene of ferocious battles between German and British forces in 1943–1944 and were only finally included in the modern Greek state in 1948 after centuries of occupation by Crusaders, Turks and Italians. Even now the threat (real or imagined) of invasion from Turkey is very much in evidence. When you ask about the heavy military presence locals talk in terms of "*when* the Turks come", rarely "*if . . .*".

Whatever the rigours of the occupations, their legacy includes a wonderful blend of architectural styles and of eastern and western cultures. Medieval Rhodes is the most famous, but almost every island has its classical remains, its Crusaders' castle, its traditional villages, and abundant grandiose public buildings. For these last the Italians, who occupied the islands from 1913 to 1943, are mainly responsible. In their determination to beautify the islands and turn them into a showplace for fascism they undertook public works, excavations and reconstruction on a massive scale; and if historical accuracy was sometimes sacrificed in the interests of style, only the expert is likely to complain. A more sinister aspect of the Italian administration was the attempted forcible Latinisation of the populace: spoken Greek and Orthodox observance were banned in public from 1920 to 1943. The most tangible reminder of this policy is the great number of older people who speak Italian – or bastardised variants thereof.

Aside from this frequently encountered bilingualism, the Dodecanese themselves display a marked topographic and economic schizophrenia. The dry limestone outcrops of **Kastellórizo**, **Sími**, **Hálki**, **Kássos** and **Kálimnos** have always been forced to rely on the sea for their livelihoods, and the wealth generated by the maritime culture – especially in the nineteenth century – fostered the growth of attractive port towns. The sprawling, relatively fertile giants, **Rhodes** (Ródhos) and **Kós**, have recently seen their traditional agricultural economies almost totally displaced by a tourist industry attracted by good beaches and nightlife, as well as the Aegean's most exciting ensembles of historical monuments. **Kárpathos** lies somewhere in between, with a (formerly) forested north grafted on to a rocky limestone south; **Tílos**, despite its lack of trees, has ample water, though the green volcano-island of **Níssiros** does not. **Léros** shelters softer contours and more amenable terrain than its map outline would suggest, while **Pátmos** and **Astipálea** at the fringes of the archipelago boast architecture and landscapes more appropriate to the Cyclades.

The largest islands in the group are connected almost daily with each other, and none is hard to reach. Rhodes is the transport hub, with services to Turkey, Israel, Cyprus and (sporadically) Egypt, as well as connections with Crete, the northeastern islands, the Cyclades and mainland.

Kássos

Barren and depopulated, Kássos attracts few visitors despite being a regular port of call for the ferries. What is left of the population is grouped together in five villages in the north, under the shadow of Kárpathos, leaving most of the island unvisited and

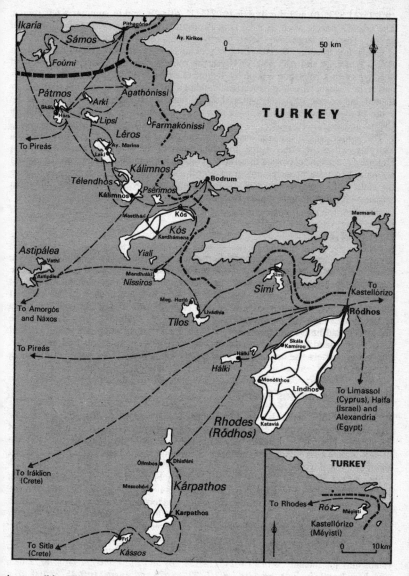

inaccessible. There's little sign here of the wealth brought into other islands by emigrant workers, nor, since the island has little to offer them, by tourists; the crumbling houses which line the village streets and the disused terraces covering the land poignantly recall better days.

It's just ten minutes' walk from **FRÍ**, the capital, to the port at EMBORIÓ; indeed the furthest village, **PÓLI**, is only 3km away. There are two **hotels** in Frí, the *Anagenissis*

(☎0245/41 323; ③) and the *Anessis* (☎0245/41 201; ③), and in summer a few rooms. The island's beach, such as it is, is at **Ámmousa**, the other side of the underused airstrip. There's a large cave (**Selai**) nearby, with impressive stalactites.

Continuing inland, especially if you're seeking isolation, is more rewarding. Between **AYÍA MARÍNA** and **ARVANITOHÓRI**, the route across the island leaves the road heading south. Civilisation is soon left behind in a silence broken only by the goat bells and an occasional wheeling hawk. Smallholdings and olive groves are still sporadically tended, but no one stays long. After about an hour the Mediterranean appears on the south of the island, a desolate mass of water broken only by the odd ship plying to Cyprus and the Middle East.

The higher fork in the way leads to the mountain chapel and monastery of **Áyios Yióryios**, while the other drops gradually down to the coast. It emerges finally at **Helathrós**, a beautiful cove at the end of a cultivated but uninhabited valley. The beach is small and sandy, the swimming great after the walk, and seabirds of every kind circle the cliffs. With plenty of supplies – hard to come by on Kássos which has little fresh produce – it could be a great place to camp.

Kárpathos

Alone of the the the major Dodecanese, Kárpathos was held by the Venetians after the Byzantine collapse and so has no castle of the crusading Knights of Saint John. The island has always been something of a backwater, and despite a magnificent coastline of cliffs and rocky promontories constantly interrupted by little beaches, has succumbed surprisingly little to tourism. Only the two ports, Pigádhia and Dhiafáni, are really prepared for a large influx. Most visitors come here for a glimpse of traditional village life, which had until recently carried on quite unaltered for centuries in the isolated north of the island. Now there's an airport which can take direct international flights; but only a few charters use it as yet, and visitors are concentrated in a couple of resorts in the south.

Pigádhia (Kárpathos Town)

PIGÁDHIA, the capital, is now more often known simply as Kárpathos. It curves around one side of Vróndis Bay, with a harbour where boats dock right in the heart of town, and a long sickle of sandy beach stretches out to the west and north. The town itself is almost entirely modern, and there's really nothing to see, but it does offer just about every facility you might need.

As you get off the ferry you'll almost inevitably be met by people offering **rooms**, and you might as well take up an offer – standards here seem generally good, and the town is small enough that no location is going to be too inconvenient. If you do want to seek out somewhere yourself, walk into town and follow the signs up past the *Hotel Coral* to *Anna's Rooms* (☎0245/22 313; ②) or the *Artemis Pension* (②), both good value and very well positioned. Nearby *Vittoroulis Furnished Apartments* (☎0245/22 639; ③) are available only weekly, but worth it if you are staying that long: other simple rooms establishments include *Sofia's* (☎0245/22 154; ②) and the *Filoxenia* (☎0245/22 623; ②); cheap **hotels** include the *Avra* (☎0245/22 388; ②) and *Anessis* (☎0245/22 100; ②) a little way out past the OTE office. More expensive places are generally further out, towards the beach. If you want to **sleep out**, you'll generally find others doing so out along the beach – particularly under the trees by the ruined fifth-century basilica of **Ayía Fotiní** – though development is gradually spreading along here, with several bars and tavernas and the odd hotel already open.

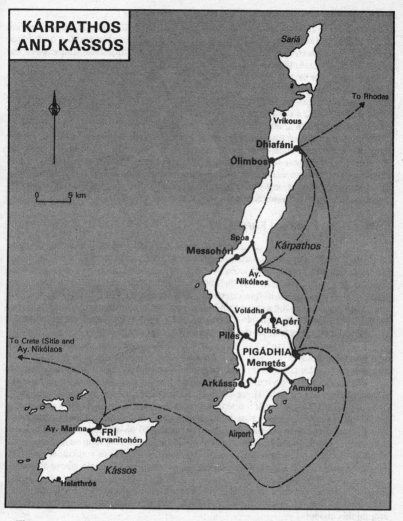

KÁRPATHOS AND KÁSSOS

Sariá

To Rhodes

Vríkous

Dhiafáni

Ólimbos

0   5 km

Spóa

Kárpathos

Messohóri

Áy. Nikólaos

Voládha

Apéri

Piles   Óthos

PIGÁDHIA

To Crete (Sitía and Ay. Nikólaos

Menetés

Arkássa

Ammopí

Ay. Marina   FRÍ

Arvanitohóri

Airport

Kássos

Helathrós

There are **restaurants and bars** all around the harbour front, though they're all rather pricey – *To Kyma* is probably the most reasonably priced place to eat in the main group, and there are some basic grill places further round which are considerably cheaper. In the town, *Kassos* and *El Greco* also serve decent food without the waterfront view for rather less. Some of the best food, though not the most attractive setting, is served at a little place marked simply as *Restaurant Pizza*, up an alley behind *Possi Travel*. *Pan Burger*, on the road up to the post office, is better than you might guess from the name, with excellent *gyros pitta* to take away. For drinking, the livelier places are around the beach end of town: cocktails and music at the *Café Marina*, the discos *Spider* and *Highway* (a little further out), and *Le Mirage* for live Greek or folk music.

Practicalities

There's an **OTE** office (Mon–Sat 7.30am–3.10pm, Sun 9am–2pm) on Platía 5 Oktobríou at the end of Odhós Kárpathos; the *Olympic* office is right by this; and the **post office** is directly behind, in the next street parallel. If you want to get out and explore the island there are four **buses** a day to Pilés, via Apéri, Voládha and Óthos, four to Ammopí, and one or two to Arkássa and Fíniki. **Taxis** aren't too expensive to get to these villages on the paved roads, but can charge a fortune to go anywhere further afield. Cars and bikes are available for rent too – try the places up by the post office like *Holidays* (☎0245/22 813) or *Circle* (☎0245/22 690); be warned that the only fuel on the island is here in town, and the tanks on the small bikes are barely big enough to complete the circuit of the south, let alone head up north. If you are heading for the north it's easier and cheaper to go by boat or on a **tour**: *Olympos Travel* (☎0245/22 993), on the front near the port, offers very good deals on all-in trips (from around 2500dr return trip and one night in the north), though the rival boat (*Chrisovalandou Lines*; pay on board for best deals) is much more attractive. *Olympos* and other agents can also offer trips to Kássos and to isolated east coast beaches.

Southern and central Kárpathos

The flat southern extremity of Kárpathos, towards the airport, is extraordinarily desolate – its natural barenness exacerbated by fires. There are a couple of empty, sandy beaches, but they're not at all attractive and very exposed to any wind that may be blowing. The nicest beach here is the tiny cove by the *Hotel Poseidon*, which has some shelter. You're better off in this direction going no further than **AMMOPÍ**, just 7km from Pigádhia. This is the closest thing on Kárpathos to a developed beach resort: two sandy coves serviced by a couple of tavernas and a few rooms places: the development is scattered and not exactly pretty, but it's far from overwhelming.

The west coast

Heading across the island, there's a steep climb up to **MENITÉS**, a lovely village on the ridge of the hills with handsome old hilltop houses, a tiny folklore museum and a spectacularly sited church. There's a good taverna here, and a memorial with views back to the east. Beyond, you immediately start to descend to **ARKÁSSA** on the west coast, with excellent views across to Kássos as you come down. Arkássa again has a little development, with rooms and restaurants scattered on a rocky coast and beaches both south past the headland and north at Fíniki, neither a very long walk. Signs point along a cement road to Ayía Sofía, just five minutes' walk, where you can see a whitewashed chapel. Around this are various remains of **ancient Arkessia**, above all several mosaic floors with geometric patterns. Some are part buried, including one running diagonally under the floor of a half-buried chapel, emerging from the walls on either side. Various bits of marble, broken statuary and columns are propped up in and around this chapel.

FÍNIKI, just a couple of kilometres away, marks the end of the asphalt road. A tiny fishing harbour, it boasts a small beach, three or four tavernas, and a couple of rooms establishments. If you continue up the west coast the road isn't too bad, and it's being improved – eventually there'll be a tarmac road right round the southern half of the island. There's an attractive beach at LÉFKOS, below the main road, where again there are a couple of tavernas and rooms for rent, and thence you can climb higher to **MESOHÓRI** through one of the few sections of unburnt pine forest. The village falls down towards the sea around narrow, stepped alleys. The road ends at the top of town where there's a snack bar – the only tourist facility here of any sort. Alternatively, you can carry on to Spóa, overlooking the east coast.

The centre and east coast

The lush centre of Kárpathos supports a quartet of villages – **APÉRI**, **VOLÁDHA**, **ÓTHOS** and **PILÉS** – blessed with superb hillside settings and ample running water. In these settlements nearly everyone has "done time" in North America, then returned home with their nest eggs. New Jersey, New York and Canadian car plates tell you exactly where repatriated islanders struck it rich. Staying in Apéri, the largest of them, you can walk to the isolated beaches of **Aháta** and **Kirá Panayía** (where many locals have built villas). Óthos is at almost the highest point of the island, with a huge wind generator up above it. Pilés is perhaps the prettiest of them, with great views to the west.

Beyond Apéri, the road up the **east coast** is extremely rough in places, but a beautiful drive; it passes above beaches all too many of which are tantalisingly inaccessible (though there are boat trips from Pigádhia). **Apella** is the best of these which you can, just about, reach by road. The end of this route is **SPÓA**, high above the shore. Here the road stops by a snack bar at the edge of the village, which you'd have to explore on foot – there's a good traditional *kafenío* a short way down. **Áyios Nikólaos**, 5km below, is an excellent beach with tavernas, and an ancient basilica to explore.

Northern Kárpathos

Northern Kárpathos, though connected since 1979 by road with Spóa, continues to exist almost independently of the richer south. Much the easiest way to get here is by boat – inter-island ferries call at Dhiafáni a couple of times a week or there are smaller tour boats from Pigádhia daily. These take a couple of hours, and are met at Dhiafáni by buses to take you up to Ólimbos, the traditional village that is the main attraction of this part of the island. If your visit is a short one, take the bus.

High in the mountains, **ÓLIMBOS** straddles two small peaks, the ridges above studded by windmills, a couple of them still operational though most are now ruined. Although the road and electricity, together with a growing number of tourists, are dragging the place into the twentieth century, it hasn't fully arrived yet. The women here are immediately striking in their magnificent **traditional dress** and after a while you notice that they also dominate the village: working in the gardens, carrying goods on their shoulders, or tending the mountain sheep. As on several other of the Dodecanese, property inheritance is matrilineal with houses passing down from mother to eldest daughter upon marriage. Nearly all Ólimbos men emigrate or work outside the village, sending money home and returning only on holidays. The long-isolated villagers also speak a unique dialect, said to maintain traces of its Doric and Phrygian origins. Traditional music is still heard regularly and draws crowds of visitors at festival times.

Sadly, the number of day-trippers are increasingly changing the atmosphere here; it's still a very picturesque place, full of photo oportunities, but the traditions are dying fast (or at least they're hard to find in season). On the whole, it's only the older women and those who work in tourist shops who wear traditional dress nowadays; and during the day you'll almost certainly see more visitors than locals. This might be a good reason to stay, either as part of an organised excursion or in one of an increasing number of **rooms** places: the *Ólimbos* and *Posidon* pensions (②) are good. There are also plenty of places to **eat** – *Parthenones*, on the square by the church, is excellent; try their *makarounes*, a local dish of home-made pasta with onions and cheese. Inside the church, which appears modern, are frescoes said to be ancient, though they don't look it.

From the village, the west coast and tiny port and beach at **Frísses** are a dizzy drop below, or there are various walks up into the mountains. It's also possible to walk between Ólimbos and Spóa or Messohóri in the south, a six-to-seven hour trek that unfortunately has been made much less scenic by fires. Perhaps the most attractive option, however, and certainly the easiest, is to walk back down to Dhiafáni – a ravine leads through whatever is left of the forest. A small stream runs beside most of the way, and there is a spring; at your approach snakes slither into hiding and partridges break cover. Even on a day trip there's plenty of time to take a look around, have lunch, and reach the bottom in time for the late afternoon journey back.

Dhiafáni

Although its popularity is growing, rooms in **DHIAFÁNI** are still cheap, and life slow. There's plenty of choice of places at which to stay and eat, shops that will change money and even a small travel agency. There are boat trips to various nearby beaches – as well as to the uninhabited islet of **Sariá** or through the narrow strait to Trístomo anchorage and the ruins of **Vrikoús**, once the island's chief port – or there are several in walking distance. Closest is **Vanánda Beach** to the north; stony but a good place to sleep among the trees. It's a pleasant walk through the pines on a signposted path, but don't believe the ones that say ten minutes: it's nearer half an hour away.

Rhodes (Ródhos)

It's no accident that Rhodes is among the most visited Greek islands. Not only is its east coast lined with sandy beaches, but the kernel of the capital is a beautiful and remarkably preserved medieval city, the legacy of the crusading Knights of Saint John who used the island as their main base from 1309 until 1522. Unfortunately this showpiece is jammed to capacity with up to 50,000 tourists a day, ten months of the year. For some reason Scandinavians predominate, revelling in the cheap drink (extended duty-free status was one of the conditions of Dodecanese incorporation into Greece in 1948); British package tourists are also very much present, as are Italians, particularly in August. Accordingly, *smorgasbord*, fish fingers and pizza all jostle on menus with *moussaka*.

Arrival, orientation and information

All international and inter-island **ferries** dock at the middle of Rhodes's three ports, the commercial harbour; the only exceptions are local **boats** to and from Sími, and the **hydrofoils** to Kós, which use the yacht harbour of Mandhráki. Its entrance was supposedly once straddled by the Colossus, an ancient statue of Apollo; today two columns surmounted by bronze deer are less overpowering replacements.

The **airport** is 17km southwest of town, near the village of Paradhísi; public urban buses make the trip once an hour. Those arriving at an unsociable time of day on a charter may find that the night taxi fare into town is barely any less than the cost of hiring a car for a day at the airport counter.

KTEL **buses** for both the west and east coasts of Rhodes leave from two almost adjacent terminals on Odhós Papágou, within sight of the so-called New Market (a tourist trap). Between the lower eastern station and the **taxi** rank at Platía Rimínis there's a **municipal tourist office**, open daily in season, while some way up Papágou on the corner of Makaríou is the **EOT office** (Mon–Fri 7.30am–3pm), which dispenses bus and ferry schedules plus information sheets on archaeological site times and admissions.

Ródhos Town

RÓDHOS TOWN divides into two unequal parts: the compact old walled city, and the amorphous new town which sprawls around it in three directions. Throughout, the tourist is king. In the **modern district**, especially the part west of Mandhráki yacht harbour, the few buildings which aren't hotels are souvenir shops, car rental or travel agencies and bars – easily a hundred in every category. Around them to the north and

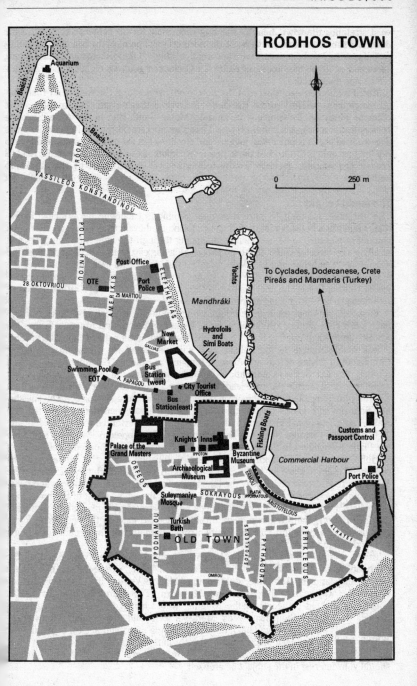

RÓDHOS TOWN

Aquarium

Beach

Beach

VASSILEOS KONSTANDINOU

NÍORÍ

POLITEHNÍOU

0   250 m

28 OKTOVRÍOU

AMERIKIS

Post Office

OTE

25 MARTIOU

Port Police

ELEFTHERÍAS

Yachts

To Cyclades, Dodecanese, Crete
Pireás and Marmaris (Turkey)

Mandhráki

New
Market

GALLIAS

Hydrofoils
and
Sími Boats

Swimming Pool

EOT

A. PAPAGOU

Bus
Station
(west)

City Tourist
Office

Bus
Station (east)

Fishing Boats

Customs and
Passport Control

Knights' Inns

IPPOTON

Byzantine
Museum

Commercial Harbour

Palace of the
Grand Masters

ORFEOS

Archaeological
Museum

ENNIOU

PLATIA
IPPOKRATOUS

Port Police

Suleymaniye
Mosque

SOKRAYOUS

ARISTOTELOUS

Turkish
Bath

IPPODHAMOU

OLD TOWN

SOKRATOUS

PYTHAGORA

PERIKLEOUS

ALHATEF

OMIROU

west stretches the **town beach** (standing room only for latecomers), complete with deckchairs, parasols and showers. At the northernmost point of the island a run-of-the-mill **aquarium** and a museum with apparently rotting stuffed fish and an extraordinary collection of grotesque freaks of nature (a Cyclopean goat, an eight-legged calf, etc) offer some distraction.

About a kilometre southwest of the new town, overlooking the west-coast road, the sparse remains of **Hellenistic Rhodes** – a restored theatre and stadium, plus a few columns of an Apollo temple – perch atop Monte Smith, the hill of Áyios Stéfanos renamed after a British admiral who used it as a watchpoint during the Napoleonic wars. The wooded site is popular with joggers and strollers, but for summer shade and greenery the best spot is the **Rodini park**, nearly two kilometres south of town on the road to Lindos. On summer evenings a wine-tasting festival is held here by the municipal authorities.

The medieval city

The **old town** is infinitely more rewarding. Simply to catalogue the principal monuments and attractions cannot do full justice to the medieval city. There's an enormous amount of pleasure to be had merely in slipping through the nine surviving gates and strolling the streets, under flying archways built for earthquake resistance, past the warm-toned sandstone and lava walls splashed with ochre and blue paint, and over the *hokhláki* (pebble) pavement, the little stones arranged into mosaics in certain courtyards. Getting lost in the alleys is part of the experience, but if you'd rather not, accurate map-placards are posted at strategic junctions.

First thing to meet the eye, and dominating the northeast sector of the city's originally fourteenth-century fortifications, is the **Palace of the Grand Masters** (Tues–Sun 8.30am–3pm; 400dr but free Sun). Destroyed by an ammunition depot explosion in 1856, it was reconstructed by the Italians as a summer home for Mussolini and Victor Emmanuel III ("King of Italy and Albania, Emperor of Ethiopia"), neither of whom used it much. The exterior is as authentic as possible, but inside things are on an altogether grander scale: a marble staircase leads up to rooms paved with Hellenistic mosaics from Kós, and the movable furnishings rival many a northern European palace. On Tuesday and Saturday afternoons (2.45–3pm; 800dr), there's a supplementary tour of the **city walls**, beginning from a gate next to the Palace – the only permitted access, incidentally.

The heavily restored **Street of the Knights** (Odhós Ippotón) leads due east from the Platía Kleovoúlou in front of the Palace; the "Inns" lining it housed the Knights of St John, according to linguistic and ethnic affiliation, until the Ottoman Turks compelled them to leave for Malta after a six-month siege in which the defenders were outnumbered thirty to one. Today the Inns house various government offices and cultural institutions vaguely appropriate to their past, but the whole effect of the renovation is predictably sterile and stagey (and indeed nearby streets *were* used in the filming of *Pascali's Island*). Halfway down, peek through a locked gate on the south side into a garden where a beautiful Turkish fountain runs continuously; the grounds are being restored and may soon be open to the public.

At the bottom of the grade the Knights' Hospital has been refurbished as the **Archaeological Museum** (Tues–Sun 8.30am–3pm; 400dr), where the star exhibit is a Hellenistic statue of Aphrodite, dubbed the "Marine Venus" by Lawrence Durrell. Across the way stands the **Byzantine Museum** (Tues–Sun 8.30am–3pm; 400dr) housed in the old cathedral of the Knights, who adapted the Byzantine shrine of Panayía Kástrou for their own needs. Medieval icons and frescoes lifted from crumbling chapels on Rhodes and Hálki, as well as photos of art still in situ, constitute the exhibits; it's worth a visit since most of the Byzantine churches in the old town and outlying villages are locked continuously. A map-placard locates the rural chapels should your interest in the subject be aroused.

Islamic and Jewish survivals

If you leave the Palace of the Grand Masters going straight south, it's hard to miss the most conspicuous Turkish monument in Rhodes, the candy-striped **Süleymaniye mosque**, rebuilt in the nineteenth century on foundations 300 years older. The old town is in fact well sown with mosques and *mescids* (the Islamic equivalent of a chapel), many of them converted from Byzantine shrines after the 1522 conquest, when the Christians were ejected from the medieval precinct to found the new quarters outside.

A couple of these mosques are still used by the sizeable **Turkish-speaking minority** here, some of them descended from Cretan Muslims deported from that island in 1913 and resettled in the rundown village of Kritiká on the way to the airport. Native Rhodian Muslims are concentrated in the old town, unconcernedly mixing Greek with Turkish in everyday speech; they tend, however, to maintain a low public profile, gravitating towards service trades – pastry chef, *kafenío* owner, haulage and delivery – where they're less likely to come in contact with outsiders. Their most enduring civic contribution is the imposing **hamam** or Turkish bath on Platía Ariónos up in the southwest corner of the medieval city. One of only a few working public baths in Greece, it's deteriorated a bit recently but is still a great place to go on a cool, off-season day (Mon–Sat 7am–7pm; 150dr but 50dr Wed & Sat; soap and towel extra so bring your own).

Heading downhill and east from the Süleymaniye mosque, **Odhós Sokrátous**, once the heart of the Ottoman bazaar, is now the "Via Turista", packed with multiple fur jewellery shops and milling foreigners. Beyond the fountain in Platía Ippokrátous, Odhós Aristotélous leads into the Platía ton Evreón Martirón (Square of the Jewish Martyrs), renamed in memory of the large local community that was almost totally annihilated in late 1943. You can visit the ornate **synagogue** on Odhós Dhosiádhou just to the south; less than a hundred Jews remain on Rhodes, some of whom are recent refugees from Egypt.

Sleeping, eating and drinking

Cheap pensions abound in the old town, contained almost entirely in the quad bounded by Odhós Omírou to the south, Sokrátous to the north, Perikléos to the east and Ippodhámou to the west. Outside peak season lodging is the one thing in Rhodes that's still reasonably priced; ②, sometimes with bath, is the standard budget rate. At crowded times, or late at night, it's prudent to accept the offers of proprietors meeting the ferries and change base next day if necessary – as it often is. On extended acquaintance, most of the pensions turn out to be much of a muchness, with amenities sometimes little changed since the Knights departed. Two establishments that stand out above the ordinary are the *Pension Andreas*, Omírou 28D (☎0241/34 156; ②), French/Greek-run; and the *Hotel S Nikolis*, Ippodhámou 61 (☎0241/34 561; ④), dear but worth it for the warm welcome and excellent breakfasts included in the price. The Danish and Greek owners also manage less expensive self-catering apartments and a cheapish pension; phone bookings are essential for all of them.

Eating well for a reasonable price is a challenge, but not an insurmountable one. As a general rule, the further back from Sokrátous you go, the better value you'll find. From the least expensive to the most, there's the *patsás* (tripe-and-trotter soup) kitchen *O Meraklis* at Aristotélous 32; another, *Patsas Sotiris* and the grill *Apollon* tucked into nameless alleys just beyond Sokrátous; *Yiannis*, Apéllou 41, for Greek oven food; *Le Bistrot*, Omírou 22, run by friendly French and ideal when you're sick of Greek oven food; *Nireas*, Platí Sofokléous 22 (☎0241/21 703), where a family of five dispenses excellent home cooking, though bookings are suggested in the evening; and *Taverna Sea Star*, the *Nireas'* adjacent rival, with good if pricey seafood dished up by a colourful proprietor. If none of the above appeals, get the last evening bus out to *Snack Bar O Yiannis* in the nearby village of Kóskinoú, where *mezé* and wine in a group works out incredibly cheap (though you'll have to take a taxi home). For dessert, the Turkish-run *To Anatolikon* at Sokrátous 9 is unbeatable for ice cream, puddings and sticky cakes; a traditional, wood-fired bakery at Ippodhámou 41 provides interesting bread and biscuits.

As for **nightlife**, you'll have to follow your nose, since venues change seasonally as owners get exhausted and pack up. With few exceptions – notably the gay bar *Valentino*, south of Sokrátous, and the *Cafe Panorama*, on terraces overlooking Platía Ippokrátous – medieval Rhodes is tomb-silent after dark, so most of the action is in the new quarter, particularly on Odhós Dhiákou. Theme nights and various drinks-with cover gimmicks predominate; none, however, can match the bad taste of *Tropical Oasis* at the base of Dhiákou near the tourist office, where deafening music videos, a "Dancing Waters" light show and several exorbitant bars surround a swimming pool to which admission is allegedly free.

Listings

Airlines *British Airways*, Platía Kíprou 1 (☎0241/27 756); *KLM*, Ammohóstou 3 (☎0241/2 010); *Olympic*, Iérou Lóhou 9 (☎0241/24 571). Scheduled flights are exorbitant; there's a very faint chance of picking up an unclaimed return charter seat to northern Europe– ask a the various group tour offices.

Car rental Prices are the island standard, but can be bargained down to about 7000dr a day all-in, out of season. Among the more flexible local outfits are *Holiday*, Iónos Dhragoúmi (☎0241/30 568), and *Just*, Orfanídhou 45 (☎0241/31 895), in the new town, or *Smile* Perikléous 12 (☎0241/30 285), in the old town. Most rental contract insurance specifically excludes damage to the underside of the vehicle, so beware if you're planning to bump over dirt roads in the south of the island.

Exchange Most bank branches are in the new town, keeping weekday evening and Saturday morning hours; at other times use one of the numerous "exchange" booths which have sprung up everywhere. The cashpoint machines of the *Trapeza Pisteos* (Credit Bank) will give cash on a Visa card.

Ferries The best one-stop, full service agency, ticketing virtually every boat and hydrofoil, is *Kouros*, Karpáthou 34 (☎0241/24 377). If that and the tourist office, are shut, schedule information is available at the *limenarheio*, on Mandhráki esplanade near the post office.

Motorbike rental Mopeds will make little impact on Rhodes' huge area, and gain you scant respect from motorists. Sturdier Yamaha 125s, suitable for two persons, go for as little as 3000dr a day. There are plenty of outlets, especially around Odhós Dhiákou.

OTE At the corner of Amerikís and 25 Martíou in the new town, open daily 6am–11pm; also one in the old city near the Archaeological Museum, but only open short "village" hours. Many of the "exchange" booths noted above offer long-distance phone service, but beware of possible surcharges on the basic OTE rates.

Post office Main branch on Mandhráki harbour, mobile office on Órfeos in the old town. Outgoing mail, poste restante and exchange windows at both, open daily 7.30am–8pm.

The east coast

Heading down the coast from the capital you have to go some way before you escape the crowds from local beach hotels, their numbers swelled by visitors using the regular buses from town or on boat tours out of Mandhráki. Nostalgia buffs might look in at the decayed, all-but-abandoned spa of **KALITHÉA**, dating from the Italian period, while most of Rhodes's folk carpets are woven in **AFÁNDOU**; but the ex-fishing village of **FALIRÁKI**, which draws a youngish package clientele, is all too much in the mode of a Spanish *costa* resort. And it must be said that the scenery just inland – arid, scrubby sand-hills at the best of times – was made that much more dreary by a vast 1987 fire that wiped out much of the east's interior vegetation all the way past Líndhos.

The giant promontory of **TSAMBÍKAS**, 26km south of town, is the first place at which most will seriously consider stopping. Actually the very eroded flank of a much larger extinct volcano, the hill has a monastery at the summit offering unrivalled views along some 50km of coastline. A steep, 1500-metre-long cement drive leads to a small car park and a snack bar, from which recently finished concrete steps lead to the summit. The monastery here is unremarkable except for the happier consequences of the September 8 festival: childless women climb up – sometimes on their knees – to be relieved of their barrenness, and any children born afterwards are dedicated to the Virgin with the names Tsambikos or Tsambika, names particular to the Dodecanese.

From the top you can survey **KOLÍMBIA** just to the north, once an unspoiled beach stretching south from a tiny cove ringed with volcanic rocks but now backed by a dozen, scattered, low-rise hotels. Shallow **Tsambíkas bay** on the south side of the headland warms up early in the spring, and the excellent beach, though protected from development, other than a couple of tavernas, teems with people all summer. If it's too much, you can walk further south over another cape to the relatively deserted bay of **Stégna**. This, however, gets a fair bit of traffic from the many tourists staying in **ARHÁNGELOS**, a large village just inland overlooked by a crumbling castle and home to a dwindling leather crafts industry. Though you can disappear into the warren of alleys between the main road and the citadel, the place is now firmly caught up in tourism, with a full complement of banks, tavernas, mini-marts and jewellery stores. A more peaceful overnight base on this stretch of coast would be **HARÁKI**, a pleasant if undistinguished, two-street fishing port with mostly self-catering accommodation (generally ③) overlooked by the stubby ruins of **Feraklós castle**. You can swim off the town beach if you don't mind an audience from the handful of waterfront cafes and tavernas, but most people head north a kilometre beyond the castle – the last stronghold of the Knights to fall to the Turks – to the secluded **Agáthi beach**.

Líndhos

LÍNDHOS, the island's number-two tourist attraction, erupts 12km south of Haráki. Like Ródhos Town itself, its charm is heavily undermined by the commercialism and the crowds, and there are only a few places to stay not booked semi-permanently by British or German tour companies. What with a rash of expensive burger bars and fish-and-chip shops, recommendations for eating out seem equally pointless. Twenty years ago the place was moribund, but since then those village houses not snapped up by the package outfits were bought and refurbished by wealthy British and Italians. High-rise hotels have been prohibited, but the result is not much better – a curiously lifeless, fake resort. At midday dozens of coaches park nose-to-tail on the access road, with even more on the drive down to the beach, strung like beads on an abacus calculating overdevelopment.

Nevertheless, if you arrive before or after the tours, when the pebble streets between the immaculately whitewashed houses are relatively empty, Líndhos can still be a beautiful, atmospheric setting. The **Byzantine church** is covered with eighteenth-century frescoes, and several of the older fifteenth-to-eighteenth-century mansions are open to the public; entrance is free but there's some pressure to buy something, especially the lace for which the village is noted.

On the bluff above the town, the ancient acropolis with its scaffolding-swaddled Doric **Temple of Athena** is found inside the Knights' **castle** (daily 8.30am–5pm; 800dr) – a surprisingly felicitous blend of two cultures. Though the ancient city and original temple, of Líndhos, date from at least 1100 BC, the present structure was begun by the tyrant Kleovoulos in the sixth century BC and completed over the next two centuries.

Líndhos's sandy coves, though numerous, are overrated and overcrowded; if you do base yourself here, better, quieter beaches are to be found at Lárdhos and beyond (see p.511). At the southern flank of the acropolis huddles the small, sheltered **Saint Paul's harbour**, where the apostle is said to have landed to evangelise the island, though he is doubtless turning in his grave at the notion of today's ranks of topless sun-worshipppers.

The west coast

Rhodes's west coast is the windward flank of the island, so it's damper, more fertile and more forested; most beaches, however, are exposed and decidedly on the rocky side. None of this has deterred development and as in the east the first few kilometres of the busy shore road down from the capital have been surrendered entirely to industrial tourism. From the aquarium down to the airport the asphalt is fringed by an uninterrupted line of Miami-beach-style mega-hotels, though such places as TRIÁNDA, KREMASTÍ and PARADHÍSSI are still nominally villages, and appear so in their centres. This was the first part of the island to be favoured by the package operators, and for the old-money, old-style facilities there's a decidedly middle-aged, sedate clientele that often can't be bothered to stir much out of sight of the runways.

Neither the planes buzzing over Paradhíssi or the giant power plant at Soroní are much inducement to pause, and you probably won't want to until reaching the important archaeological site of **KAMIROS**, which with Líndhos and Ialyssos was one of the three Dorian powers that united in the fifth century BC to found the powerful city-state of Rhodes. Soon eclipsed by the new capital, Kamiros was abandoned and only rediscovered in the last century. As a result it is a particularly well-preserved Doric townscape, doubly worth visiting for its beautiful hillside site (daily 8.30am–4pm; 400dr). While none of the individual remains are spectacular, you can make out the foundations of a few small temples, the *stoa* of the *agora*, and a water catchment basin. Because of the gentle slope of the site, there were no fortifications, nor was there an acropolis.

On the beach below Kamiros there are several tavernas, ideal while waiting for one of the two daily buses back to town (if you're willing to walk 4km back to Kalavárda you'll have a better choice of service). There are more tavernas clustered at **SKÁLA KAMÍROU** 15km south, a tiny anchorage which somewhat inexplicably is the hapless target of coach tours come to see Ye Olde Authentic Fishing Village (decals on the windows of the half-dozen restaurants attest to the fact). Less heralded is the daily *kaíki*, that leaves for the island of **Hálki** at 2pm weather permitting, returning the next morning; on some days there's an extra departure at 9am, returning by noon.

A couple of kilometres south of Skála, the "Kastello", signposted as **Kástro Kritínias**, is from afar the most impressive of the Knights' rural strongholds, and the access road is too rough for coaches to pass. Close up it proves to be no more than a shell, with only a chapel and a rubbish-filled cistern more or less intact inside – it's a glorious shell, though, with fine views west to assorted islets and Hálki. You make a "donation" to the little old lady at the car park in exchange for fizzy drinks, oranges or flowers.

RHODES AND HÁLKI

Beyond KRITINÍA itself, a quiet hillside village with a few rooms and tavernas, the main road winds south through the forest to **SIÁNA**, the most attractive mountain settlement on the island, famous for its aromatic pine-sage honey and *soúma*, the local firewater. Bus tours also stop in at the church on the square, with heavily restored eighteenth-century frescoes. The tiered, flat-roofed farmhouses of **MONÓLITHOS**, 4km southwest at the end of the public bus line, are scant justification for the long trip out here, and food at the two **tavernas** is indifferent owing to the tour-group trade, but the view over the bay is striking, and you could use the village as a base by staying in "rooms" or the slightly pricey *Hotel Thomas* (☎0246/61 291; ③). Two possible reasons for an overnight stay are yet another **Knights' castle** 2km west of town, photogenically perched on its own pinnacle and enclosing a couple of chapels, and the fine gravel beach of **Foúrni**, five bumpy, curvy kilometres below the castle, its 800-metre extent unsullied except for a seasonal drinks stand. Beyond the headland, to the left as you face the water, are some caves that were hollowed out by early Christians fleeing persecution.

The interior

Inland Rhodes is hilly, and still mostly wooded despite the recent depredations of arsonists. You'll need a vehicle to see much here, especially as the main enjoyment is in getting away from it all: no one site justifies the tremendous expense of a taxi or the inconvenience of trying to make the best of the schedules of the occasional buses.

In retrospect it will probably be the scenery which stands out, along with the last vestiges of the old agrarian life in the slowly depopulating villages. Young Rhodians that do remain in the interior stay largely to help with the grape harvest in late summer (when there's some chance of work for foreigners too). If you have time to spare, and a bit of Greek at your command, traditional hospitality in the form of a drink at the *kafenío*, or perhaps more, is still very much alive.

Starting from the west coast, turn inland at TRÍANDA for the five-kilometre uphill ride to ancient **Ialyssos** on Filérimos hill. Important as this city was, its visible remains are few; most conspicuous are a subterranean chapel covered with faded frescoes and a Doric fountain. The pine-covered slopes here also shelter the grounds of Filérimos monastery (which you can visit) and a Byzantine-cum-Turkish castle, but the whole ensemble won't take more than an hour of your time.

Beyond Paradhíssi, another side turning leads within 7km to **Petaloúdhes**, the "Valley of the Butterflies" (open daily until sunset; 200dr). It's actually a rest stop for Jersey tiger moths and might more accurately be christened the "Valley of the Tour Buses". Despite the mob, however, it's an appealing place, with trees shading and wooden bridges crossing a little stream.

From the Kolímbia bus stop on the east coast road, it's a three-kilometre walk or drive inland to **Eptá Piyés** (same hours and admission fee as Petaloúdhes), a superb oasis with a tiny reservoir for swimming and an unusual streamside taverna. A trail, or a peculiar, half-submerged tunnel, lead to the pond. Continuing inland, you reach **ELEOÚSSA** after another 9km, in the shade of the dense forest at the east end of Profítis Ilías ridge. Two other undisturbed villages, PLATÁNIA and APÓLLONA, nestle on the south slopes of the mountain overlooking the start of the burned area, but most people keep straight on 3km further to the late Byzantine church of **Áyios Nikólaos Foundoúkli** (St Nicholas of the Hazelnuts). The partly shaded site has a fine view north over cultivated valleys, and locals descend in force for picnics on weekends; the frescoes inside, dating from the thirteenth to the fifteenth centuries, could use a good cleaning but various scenes from the life of Christ are recognisable.

Negotiating an unsignposted but fairly obvious welter of dirt tracks gets you finally to **Profítis Ilías**, where the Italian-vintage chalet-hotel *Elafos/Elafina* (Stag and Doe; ☎0246/22 225; ⑤) hides in deep woods just north of the 798-metre altimeter, Rhodes's third highest point. There's good, low-key strolling around the summit and the namesake monastery, and the lodge's snack bar is generally open in season.

All tracks and roads west across Profítis Ilías more or less converge upon the main road from Kalavárda bound for **ÉMBONAS**, a large and architecturally nondescript village backed up against the north slope of 1215-metre Mount Atáviros, roof of the island. Émbonas, with its two pensions and various tavernas, is more geared to handling tourists than you might expect, since it's the venue for summer "folk dance tours" from Ródhos Town. The village also lies at the heart of the island's most important wine-producing districts, and CAIR – the vintners' cooperative – produce a range of generally excellent varieties: the white *Ilios*, the red *Chevaliers*, and the premium label *Emery*. If you'd like to see what Émbonas would be like without tourists, carry on clockwise around the peak to less celebrated **ÁYIOS ISÍDHOROS**, with as many vines and tavernas, a more open feel, and the **trailhead** for the five-hour return ascent of Atáviros.

There's a mediocre road from here to Siána, and an even worse one that runs the 12km east to Láerma, but the latter is worth enduring if you've any interest at all in Byzantine monuments. In **LÁERMA** proper, the church of Áyios Yióryios, just above the plane-shaded fountain, looks modern but actually contains fourteenth-century frescoes; get the keys from the adjacent *kafenío*. This is just an appetiser for the **monastery of Thári**, lost in pine forests five well-marked kilometres south. The oldest religious foundation on the island, the monastery was re-established as a living community of half a dozen monks in 1990 by a charismatic abbot from Pátmos. The voluble lay sister and cook who also acts as caretaker will usher you into the *kathólikon*, consisting of a long nave and short transept surmounted by barrel vaulting. Despite two recent cleanings, the damp of centuries has smudged the frescoes, dating from 1300 to 1450, but they are still exquisite: mostly various acts of Christ, including such rarely depicted scenes as the storm on the Sea of Galilee, meeting Mary Magdalene, and healing the cripple.

The monastery, dedicated to the Archangel Michael, takes its name from the legend of its foundation. A princess, kidnapped by pirates, was abandoned here by her captors; she saw the Archangel in a dream, and he promised her eventual deliverance. In gratitude, she vowed to build as many monasteries in his honour as the gold ring cast from her hand travelled in cubits. Upon being reunited with her parents the deed was done, but the ring was lost in some bushes, and never found. Thus "Thári" comes from *tharévo*, "I hazard, guess, venture", after the family's futile search for the heirloom. In their pique, apparently only one cloister was founded.

The far south

South of a line connecting Monólithos and Lárdhos, you could easily begin to think you had strayed onto another island – at least until the still-inflated prices brought you back to reality. Gone are the five-star hotels and roads to match, and with them most of the crowds. Gone too are most tourist facilities and public transport. Only one daily bus runs to Kataviá, along the east coast, where deserted beaches are backed by sheltering dunes that offer scope for private camping. Tavernas grace the more popular stretches of sand but there are still relatively few places to stay.

A new auxiliary airport is planned for the area, however, so this state of affairs won't persist indefinitely. Already massive construction is beginning behind the sandier patches south of **LÁRDHOS**, solidly on the tourist circuit despite an inland position between Láerma and the peninsula culminating in Líndhos. The beach 2km south is excellent, with the best of the island's three campsites and the outriders of the small *Lárdhos Bay* complex edging east toward the package resort of PÉFKI.

Asklipío

Nine kilometres further on, a paved side road heads 4km inland to **ASKLIPÍO**, a sleepy village guarded by a crumbling castle and graced by the Byzantine church of **Kímisis Theotókou**, whose frescoes are in far better condition than Thári's owing to the drier local climate. To gain admission, call at the priest's house behind the apse, or if that doesn't work, haul on the belfry rope. The building dates from 1060, with a ground plan nearly identical to that of Thári, except that two subsidiary apses were added during the eighteenth century, partly to conceal a secret school in a subterranean crypt. The frescoes themselves are somewhat later than Thári's, though the priest claims that the final work at Thári and the earliest here were executed by the same hand, a master from Híos.

The format and subject matter of the frescoes is rare in Greece: didactic "cartoon strips" which extend completely around the church in some cases, and extensive Old Testament stories in addition to the more usual lives of Christ and the Virgin. There's a complete sequence from Genesis, from the Creation to the Expulsion from Eden; note the comically menacing octopus among the fishes on the Fifth Day. A seldom-encountered *Revelation of John the Divine* takes up most of the east transept, and pebble mosaic flooring decorates both the interior and the vast courtyard.

To the southern tip

Returning to the coast road, there are ample facilities at **YENNÁDHI**, though tour operators have yet to arrive. The shore is empty again until **PLIMÍRI**, which consists of a single **taverna** on a sheltered, sandy bay; just off the crumbling jetty, a ten-year-old wreck attracts expert scuba divers. Beyond Plimíri the road curves inland to **KATAVIÁ**, nearly 100km from the capital. There are several tavernas at the junction that doubles as the *platía*, and a few rooms to rent; the village, like so many in the south, is three-quarters deserted, the owners of the closed-up houses off working in Australia or North America.

From Kataviá a rough, marked track leads on to **Prássonissi**, Rhodes' southernmost extremity and site of a lighthouse automated only in 1989. From May to October you can stroll across the wide, low sandspit to visit, but winter storms swamp this tenuous link and render Prássonissi a true island. Even in summer the prevailing northwesterly winds drive swimmers to the lee side of the spit, leaving the exposed shore to the world-class windsurfers who come to train here. In season the scrubby junipers rustle with tents and caravans; water comes from two **tavernas** flanking the access road. The outfit next to the old windmill is more characterful, but beware of the fish – tasty, but among the most expensive in Greece.

The southwest coast

West of Kataviá, the island loop road emerges onto the deserted, sandy southwest coast, and soon deteriorates in a long, yet-to-be-improved stretch. If freelance camping and nudism are your thing, this is the place to indulge, though you'll need your own transport, or lots of supplies and a stout pair of shoes. Just before the road shapes up again, there's a turning for the fourteenth-century hilltop monastery of **Skiádhi**, which houses a miraculous icon of the Virgin and Child; in the fifteenth century a heretic stabbed the painting, and blood was said to have flowed from the wound in the Mother of God's cheek. The offending hand was, needless to say, instantly paralysed; the fissure, and suspicious brown stains around it, are still visible. You can stay the night upon arrangement with the caretaker, but as with the beaches below you'll have to bring your own kit and on weekends you'll have plenty of (local) company.

The nearest town is modern and unexciting **APOLAKIÁ**, a few kilometres inland but equipped with a couple of **rooms** and **tavernas** plus a general store, ideal for those beachcombers undaunted by the logistics of staying in southern Rhodes. At the central, badly marked roundabout, there always seem to be a few visiting motorists scratching their heads over maps: northwest leads to Monólithos, due south goes back to Kataviá, and the northeast option is a paved scenic road cutting quickly back to Yennádhi. Just a bit further on is the proudly featured side track to an irrigation dam just north, oddly scenic as these things go and plainly visible from Siána overhead.

Hálki

Hálki is a member of the Dodecanese in its own right, though all but 400 of the population have decamped (mostly to Rhodes or to Tarpon Springs, Florida) in the wake of a devastating sponge blight early in this century. For the moment, though this may soon change, the island is marvellously tranquil compared to Rhodes – the big event of the day is when someone catches a fish.

The first hint of development came in 1983, when UNESCO designated Hálki as the "isle of peace and friendship", and made it the seat of an annual summer international youth conference. (Tílos was approached first but declined the honour.) As part of the deal, 150 crumbling houses in the harbour town of **EMBORIÓ** were to be restored as guest lodges for the delegates and other interested parties, with UNESCO footing the bill. In the event, one hotel was actually finished, after the critical lack of fresh water which had hampered all previous attempts at tourist development, was supposedly remedied by the discovery of ample undersea deposits by a French geological team.

By 1987 the rest of the grandiose plans had still not been seriously acted on. The only tangible sign of "peace and friendship" was an unending stream of UNESCO and Athenian bureaucrats and their dependents occupying every available bed at unpredictable intervals and staging drunken, musical binges under the guise of "ecological conferences". The islanders, fed up with what had obviously turned out to be a scam, sent the freeloaders packing at the end of that year. Since then, in conjunction with sensitive operators such as *Laskarina Holidays*, they are managing the restored houses as a going concern and hope to finish the water projects, thus attracting both package tourists (a few of whom already come) and independent travellers.

For a few years yet you can still enjoy the sleepy atmosphere on this tiny (40 square km) limestone speck. However, in the summer you'll have fierce competition for the handful of rooms in Emborió, and plenty of company at the four tavernas. But if you're staying any length of time, especially off-season, you can rent an entire house ridiculously cheaply. There's a **post office** (open as little as possible), three stores, a bakery, and two beaches nearby, one sandy and minute, with a taverna, the other larger and pebbly.

Three kilometres inland lies the old pirate-safe village of **HORIÓ**, abandoned in the 1950s but still crowned by the Knights' castle. Across the way, the little church of **Stavrós** is a venue for one of the two big island festivals on September 14. There's little else to see or do here, though you can **walk** across the island in an enjoyable couple of hours. The cobble path picks up where the cement "Tarpon Springs Boulevard" mercifully ends; the latter was donated by the expatriate community in Florida to ensure easy Cadillac access to the Stavrós *paniyíri* grounds, though what Hálki really needed (and still needs) is a proper sewage system and salt-free water supply. At the end of the walk you'll come to the monastery of **Ayíou Ioánni Prodhrómou**. The caretaking family there can put you up in a cell (except around August 29, the other big festival date); you'll need to bring supplies. The terrain en route is monotonous, but compensated by views over half the Dodecanese and Turkey.

Kastellórizo (Méyisti)

Kastellórizo's official name, Méyisti (Biggest), seems more an act of defiance than a statement of fact. While the largest of a tiny group of islands, it is in fact the smallest of the Dodecanese, barely more than three nautical miles off the Turkish coast but over seventy from its nearest Greek neighbour (Rhodes). At night you find its lights quite outnumbered by those of the Turkish town of Kaş, across the bay.

Less than a century ago there were 16,000 people here, supported by a fleet of schooners which made fortunes transporting goods from the Greek towns of Kalamaki (now Kalkan) and Andifelos (Kaş) on the Anatolian mainland. But the advent of steam power and the Italian seizure of the Dodecanese in 1913 sent the island into a decline from which it never recovered. Shipowners failed to modernise their fleets, preferring to sell their ships to the British for the Dardanelles campaign, and the new frontier between the island and republican Turkey, combined with the expulsion of all Anatolian Greeks in 1923, deprived any remaining vessels of their former trade. During the 1930s the island enjoyed a brief renaissance when it became a major stopover point for the seaplanes of *Alitalia* and *Air France*, but events at the close of World War II put an end to any hopes of the island's continued viability.

When Italy capitulated to the Allies in the autumn of 1943, a few hundred British commandos occupied Méyisti until displaced by a stronger German force in the spring of 1944. At some stage during the hasty departure of Commonwealth forces, the fuel dump caught fire and an adjacent arsenal exploded, taking with it more than half of the 2000 houses on Kastellórizo. Enquiries have concluded that the retreating Allies did some looting, though it was probably Greek pirates engaging in some pillaging of their own who accidentally or deliberately caused the conflagration. In any event the British are not especially popular here; islanders are further angered by the fact that an Anglo-Greek reparations committee has for almost forty years delayed payment of reparations to the 850 surviving householders.

Even before these events most of the population had left for Rhodes, Athens, Australia and North America, and today there are barely 200 people living permanently on Kastellórizo. These are largely maintained by remittances from the thousands of emigrants and by subsidies from the Greek government, which fears that the island will revert to Turkey should the number diminish any further. The remaining population is concentrated in the northern harbour, **KASTELLÓRIZO** (or MÉYISTI) – the finest, so it is said, between Beirut and Pireás – and its little "suburb" of **Mandhráki**, just over the fire-blasted hill with its ruined castle of the Knights. Locals may not admit it, but the Anatolian influence on the surviving quayside houses, with their tiled roofs, wooden balconies and long, narrow windows, is clearly evident. One street behind the waterfront, though, all is desolation – abandonment having seen to most of the mansions which the 1944 fire missed.

Despite its apparently terminal plight, Kastellórizo may have a future of sorts. During the 1980s the government dredged the harbour to accommodate cruise ships, completed an airport for flights to and from Rhodes, and briefly contemplated making the island an official port of entry, a measure calculated to appeal to the many yachties who call here. The interesting local **History Museum** (Tues–Sun 8am–2.30pm) was moved one building up from the old **mosque**, leaving the mosque itself, briefly slated to be a duty-free shop, locked and abandoned. Each summer, too, the population is swelled by returnees of "Kassie" ancestry, some of whom celebrate traditional weddings in the **Áyios Konstandínos** cathedral with its ancient columns pilfered from Patara in Asia Minor.

There is one overpriced municipal *ksenónas* (☎0241/29 072; ④) and a few other **rooms** for rent (*Paradisos*, ☎0241/29 074, and *Barbara*, ☎0241/29 295; both ②), virtually all deficient in plumbing even by the standards of small, dry islets. Indeed, despite the recent flurry of government activity, Kastellórizo is not prepared for – nor does it get – more than a handful of casual visitors. Water has to be collected in cisterns during the winter, and almost all the food at the two supermarkets and three or four quayside **tavernas** is shipped in at considerable expense from Rhodes, fish being the one relatively cheap exception – best eaten at *To Mikro Parisi*. The **OTE** (often cut off from the outside world) and **post office** share the same building.

If you go **swimming** you'll discover an incredible abundance of multicoloured marine life around these shores, and though there is no beach, the sea is usually clear and flat as glass, perfect for snorkelling off the rocks and steps. Over on the east coast, accessible only by boat, is the grotto of **Parásta**, famed for its stalactites and the strange blue-light effects inside, rivalling those at Capri; it's also inhabited by seals, who can be quite aggressive if you get too close.

Heat (infernal in summer) permitting, you can **walk** south and west of the port on good paths past country chapels to **Paleokástro**, site of the Doric city. From the heights you've tremendous views over the elephant's-foot-shaped harbour and surrounding Greek islets across to Turkey. None of these smaller islands are inhabited today but until recently "The Lady of Rhó", on the islet of that name, resolutely hoisted the Greek flag each day in defiance of the Turks on the mainland; she died a few years ago, at the age of 104.

Kastellórizo has traditionally depended heavily on produce smuggled across from Kaş and for years (during the port captain's siesta, of course) it was fairly easy to arrange a ride over **to Turkey** for the day. Recent reports indicate that this has changed, with the authorities zealously enforcing the rules. This ridiculous bit of Greek nationalism has had the effect of squeezing the island further by requiring the locals to pay the high Rhodes prices plus portage, and they resent it mightily.

The ferry **back to Rhodes** takes six hours, more in bad weather (if it runs at all). Equally infrequent planes to Rhodes are small, expensive STOL craft; in sum Méyisti is not a place to be at the end of a holiday if you're committed to a particular return flight.

Sími

Sími's most pressing problem, lack of water, is in many ways also its greatest asset. If the rain cisterns don't fill in winter, brackish water must be imported at great expense from Rhodes. So however much it might want to, the island can't hope to support more than one or two large hotels. Instead hundreds of people are shipped in daily during the season from Rhodes, relieved of their money and sent back. This arrangement suits both the islanders and the few visitors who stay. If you are among the latter, the former become friendlier once it's clear that you're not a day-tripper. Many foreigners return regularly, or even own houses here – indeed since the mid-1980s the more desirable dwellings, ruined or otherwise, have been sold off in such numbers that the island is well on its way to becoming another Ídhra.

The island's capital – and only proper town – consists of **Yialós**, the port, and **Horió**, on the hillside above, collectively known as **SÍMI**. Incredibly, less than a hundred years ago the town was richer and more populous (30,000) than Ródhos Town. Wealth came, despite the barren land, from expertise in shipbuilding and sponge-diving nurtured since pre-Classical times. Under the Ottomans, Sími, like many of the Dodecanese, enjoyed considerable autonomy in exchange for a yearly tribute in sponges to the sultan; but the 1919–1922 war, the advent of synthetic sponges, and the gradual replacement of the crews by Kalymniotes spelt doom for the local economy. Vestiges of both activities remain, but the souvenir-shop sponges are mostly of North American origin today, and the magnificent nineteenth-century mansions are now largely roofless and deserted, their windows gaping blankly across the fine natural harbour. As on Kastellórizo, a war time ammunition blast – this time set off by the retreating Germans – levelled hundreds of houses up in Horió. Shortly afterwards, the official surrender of the Dodecanese to the Allies was signed here on May 8, 1945: a plaque marks the spot at the present-day *Restaurant Les Katerinettes* (not otherwise recommended), and each year on that date there's a fine festival with music and dance.

Sími town

The 3000 remaining Simiotes are scattered fairly evenly throughout the mixture of Neoclassical and more typical island dwellings, though despite the surplus of properties many have preferred to build anew, rather than restore shells accessible only by donkey or on foot. The port, a protected historical area since the early 1970s, is deceptively lively, especially between noon and 4pm when the excursion boats are in, but one street back from the water it's a sad and desolate tableau that meets the eye. Two massive stair-paths, the *Kalí Stráta* and *Katarráktes*, effectively deter many of the day-trippers and are most dramatically climbed towards sunset; the massive ruins along the *Kalí Stráta* are lonely and sinister after dark, home now only to wild figs and nightjars.

At the top, the hard-to-find island **museum** (Tues–Sun 10am–2pm; free) contains the usual assortment of local archaeological finds, traditional costumes, antiques and kitsch salvaged from better days. At the very pinnacle of things a **castle of the Knights** occupies the site of Sími's ancient acropolis, and you can glimpse a stretch of Cyclopean wall on one side. A dozen churches grace Horió; that of the Ascension, inside the fortifications, is a replacement of the one blown to bits when the Germans torched the munitions cached there. One of the bells in the new belfry is the nose-cone of a thousand-pound bomb, hung as a memorial.

Practicalities

Arrival poses few problems: there are daily excursion boats from Mandhráki in Ródhos Town, but you're under considerable pressure to buy an expensive (about 2500dr) return ticket – not what you want if you're off island-hopping without returning to Rhodes. You can insist on a single, or even better take the islanders' own unpublicised boat, the *Symi I*, which is significantly cheaper: it sails to Rhodes at dawn, returning at 2pm after shopping hours are done. Twice a week there are mainline ferries as well.

Room and hotel proprietors generally meet the boats, on a rota basis worked out among themselves. Best value among these are rooms let by the Australian-Greek Katerina Tsakiris (✆0241/71 813; ③), with a grandstand setting overlooking the harbour. Somewhat more basic are two old budget standbys down by the market area, the *Glafkos* (✆0241/71 358; ②) and the *Egli* (✆0241/71 392; ②) which may only open in high season. If you can afford a bit more, the *Hotel Horio* (✆0241/71 800; ④) is a good new outfit in traditional style up in Horió. If money's no object, the A-class *Aliki* (✆0241/71 665; ⑤), a few paces right from the clocktower, is also a famous monument; the monstrous new municipal inn right by the clock, erected in seeming defiance of the preservaion order, isn't famous and won't be. Failing all of these, you can appeal for help from archrivals *Symi Tours* and *Symian Holidays*, both at the base of the *Kalí Stráta*, though for the restored mansions, windmills and more conventional apartments that they book, a minimum of a week's stay and double occupancy may be required.

When **eating out**, you're best off avoiding entirely the north side of the port, where menus, prices and attitudes have been terminally warped by the day-trade. Matters improve perceptibly as you press further inland or up the hill. At the very rear of what remains of Sími's bazaar, *O Meraklis* has polite service and reasonable prices; *Neraïdha*, well back from the water near the OTE, is delicious and almost cheap. Up in Horió, *Georgios* is a decades-old institution, and still good value despite the crowds; if he's shut (likely at lunch), *Dallaras* next door is okay. Nearly half a dozen pub/cafés satisfy the urge for a **drink** in Yialós, with perhaps half that many up in Horió; there's some conscious catering to the yachties who congregate in the harbour, though *Vapori*, just inland, seems the most consistently popular, with a varied clientele.

The **OTE** and **post office** are open the standard Monday to Friday hours; there's a full service **bank** (the *Ionian*) and designated exchange agents for odd hours. A blue **van**, labelled "The Symi Bus", shuttles between Yialós and Pédhi via Horió at regular intervals; there are also three taxis and the possibility of moped and car **rental**, though this is an island patently ideal for boat and walking excursions. *ANES*, the outlet for *Symi I* tickets, and *Psihas*, the agent for all big inter-island **ferries**, are one alley apart in the marketplace.

Around the island

Sími has no big sandy beaches, but there are plenty of pebbly stretches at the heads of the deep narrow bays which indent the coastline. **PÉDHI**, 45 minutes' walk from Yialós, still has much of the character of a fishing hamlet, with enough water in the plain behind – the island's largest – to support market gardens. The beach is average-to-poor, though, and the giant *Pedhi Beach* hotel has considerably bumped up prices at

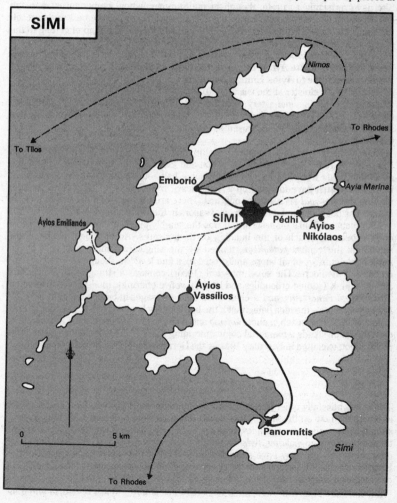

the three local tavernas. Many will opt for another twenty minutes of walking via goat track along the south shore of the almost landlocked bay to **Áyios Nikólaos**, stony but with sheltered swimming and a drinks stall. Alternatively, a marked path on the north side of the inlet leads within an hour to **Ayía Marína**, where you can swim out to a monastery-capped islet.

Around Yialós, you'll find tiny **Nós** beach ten minutes past the boat yards at Haráni, but there's sun here only until lunchtime and it's packed with day-trippers. You can continue along the coastal track here, or cut inland from the Yialós *platía* past the abandoned desalinisation plant, to very average **Emborió** bay, where there's a taverna and a Byzantine mosaic in the courtyard of a church back in the bushes.

Plenty of other, better and more secluded coves are accessible by energetic walkers with sturdy footwear, or those prepared to pay for a boat trip. The tourist map sold on Sími is surprisingly accurate, though in mid-summer, when temperatures approach 100°F, you may prefer to take advantage of the boats. These are the best way to reach the southern bays of **Marathoúnda** and **Nanoú**, and the only method of getting to the spectacular, wall-girt fjord of **Áyios Yióryios Dhissálona**.

On foot, you can cross the island – which has retained patches of its natural juniper forest – in two hours to **Áyios Vassílios**, the most scenic and sheltered of the gulfs, or in a little more time to **Áyios Emilianós**, where you can stay the night (bring supplies) in a wave-lashed cloister at the island's extreme west end. On the way to the latter you might look in at the monastery of **Mihaél Roukouniótis**, Sími's oldest, with lurid eighteenth-century frescoes and a peculiar ground plan: the *kathólikon* is actually two stacked churches, the currently used one built atop an earlier structure abandoned to the damp.

The Archangel is also honoured at the huge monastery of **Taxiárhis Mihaél Panormítis**, Sími's biggest rural attraction and generally the first port of call for the excursion boats from Rhodes. You get a quick half-hour tour with them; if you want more time, you'll have to come on a "jeep safari" from Yialós, or arrange to stay the night in the *ksenónas* set aside for pilgrims. There are numbers of these in summer, as Mihaél has been adopted as the patron of sailors in the Dodecanese.

Like many of Sími's monasteries, it was thoroughly pillaged during the last war, so don't expect too much of the building or its treasures. An appealing pebble court surrounds the central *kathólikon*, tended by the single remaining monk, lit by an improbable number of oil lamps and graced by a fine *témblon*, though the frescoes are recent and mediocre. The small museum (100dr) contains a strange mix of precious antiques, junk (stuffed crocodiles and koalas), votive offerings, models of ships named *Taxiarhis* or *Panormitis*, and a chair piled with messages-in-bottles brought here by Aegean currents – the idea being that if the bottle or toy boat arrived, the sender got his or her wish. A tiny beach, a shop/*kafenío* and a taverna round out the list of amenities; near the latter stands a memorial commemorating three Greeks, including the monastery's abbot, executed in February 1944 by the Germans for aiding British commandos.

Tílos

The small, blissfully quiet island of Tílos is one of the least visited of the Dodecanese, although it's now on the list of (occasional) day trips from Sími and Kós. Why anyone should want to come for just a few hours is unclear: while it's a wonderful place to rest on the beach or go walking, there is nothing very striking at first glance. After a few days, however, you may have stumbled on several of the seven small castles of the Knights of Saint John which stud the crags, or gained access to some of the inconspicuous medieval chapels, some frescoed or pebble-mosaiced, clinging to hillsides. Though rugged and scrubby on the heights, the island has ample water – mostly pumped up

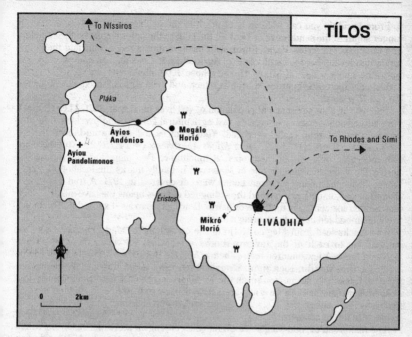

from the agricultural plains – and groves of oak and terebinth near the cultivated areas. The volcano on neighbouring Níssiros has contributed pumice beds and red-lava-sand beaches to the landscape as well. From many points on the island you've fine views across to Sími, Turkey and Níssiros.

A single road runs the seven kilometres from Livádhia, the port village, to Megálo Horió, the capital and only other significant habitation. When boats arrive a red **mini-bus** links the two, and the pension-owners at Eristós lay on their own vehicles, but at other times you walk, charter said minibus, hire a pushbike or hitch – though the last can be slow work since there are only about twenty vehicles on the island.

Of the two settlements, **LIVÁDHIA** is more equipped to deal with tourists and is closer to the best hikes. If there are vacancies **room** and **hotel** owners meet the ferries, with prices starting in the ② range, but in high season it may be worth phoning ahead to some of the following: the E-class *Livadhia* (☎0241/53 266; ②), the C-class *Irini* (fanciest hotel on the island, well inland but excellent; the same management have rather cheaper rooms; ☎0241/53 293; ④), the doubles-only municipal bungalows (☎0241/53-258; ④), and the inexpensive, unsigned *Kastello* (☎0241/53 292; ③). If you come up empty, **camping** is tolerated – even expected – in August, or you can head for Megálo Horió and Eristós.

For **eating out**, visitors distribute themselves between the two best seafront tavernas, the friendly and tasty *Sofia's* or the more predictable but wholesome *Irina*. Inland, near the *platía*, there's the *Soúvlaki Pitta Taverna*, with an unfortunate view of the public toilets but otherwise good and cheap, and a rather expensive but excellent fish place, the *Trata*. The **post office** is the only place to change money; **OTE** consists of a phone box in the larger of two grocery stores; and the jetty *kafenío* sells all **ferry** tickets. There's a bakery, with plenty of produce sold off pickup trucks, and an overall feel of 1970s Greece – though a rash of building sites behind Livádhia's long pebble beach is an ominous sign.

From Livádhia you can walk an hour north to the pebble bay of **Léthra**, or slightly longer south to the sandy cove of **Tholoú**; the path to the latter begins by the cemetery and the chapel of **Áyios Pandelímon** with its Byzantine mosaic court and then curls around under the hard-to-climb castle of **Agriosíkia**. It's less than an hour west by trail up to the ghost village of **Mikró Horió**, whose 1000 inhabitants abandoned it in the 1950s; only the castle-guarded church is intact, and even this is locked except for the August 15 festival.

The rest of Tílos's permanent population of 400 lives in or near **MEGÁLO HORIÓ**, with an enviable perspective over its vast agricultural *kámbos*, and overlooked in turn by the vast Knights' castle overhead. Your choices for **accommodation** are the *Pension Sevasti* (☎0241/53 237; ③) or *Milios Apartments* (☎0241/53 220; ③); there are two **tavernas**, only one of them open at lunchtime. Two more fortresses stare out across the plain: the easterly one of **Massariá** helpfully marks the location of a cave where Pleiocene midget-elephant bones were discovered in 1971. A trail goes there from the road, ending just beyond the spring-fed cypress below the cave-mouth, which was hidden for centuries until a World War II artillery barrage exposed it. The bones are still embedded in the floor; bring a torch.

Two tracks lead from Megálo Horió to the one-kilometre long **Eristós** beach – or rather, one to each of the **taverna-rooms** establishments which divide the trade between them. A few hundred metres before Megálo Horió, bear left onto a signed dirt track for the *Navsika*, then right, straight, then right again through the unmarked maze of tracks and farms. You reach the *Tropikana* via the left fork in the cement just past Megálo Horió. Both tavernas are set well back from the sand, hidden in their orchards, and either way it's a 75-minute walk from Livádhia; beds are cheap (②) because of the remoteness.

The main road beyond Megálo Horió hits the coast again at **Áyios Andónios**, with a single hotel/taverna (the *Australia*) and an exposed, average beach. At low tide you can find more lava-trapped skeletons strung out in a row – human this time, presumably tide-washed victims of a Nissirian eruption in 600 BC, and discovered by the same archaeologists who found the miniature pachyderms.

There's better swimming at isolated **Plaka** beach, 2km west of Áyios Andónios, and the road finally ends 8km west of Megálo Hório at the fortified fifteenth-century monastery of **Ayíou Pandelímonas**, deserted except from July 25 to 27, when it hosts the island's biggest festival. The tower-gate and oasis setting, over 200 forbidding metres above the west coast, are more memorable than the damaged frescoes within; if you want to visit go in a group with the island minibus to guarantee access.

Níssiros

Volcanic Níssiros is noticeably greener than its southern neighbours Tílos, Hálki, and Sími, and unlike them has proved attractive and wealthy enough to retain more of its population, staying lively even in winter. While remittances from abroad (particularly Astoria, New York) are inevitably important, much of the island's income is derived from quarrying; offshore towards Kós the islet of Yialí is a vast lump of gypsum and pumice on which the miners live as they slowly chip it away.

The main island's peculiar geology is potentially a source of even more benefits: DEH, the Greek power company, has sunk one successful **geothermal well**, with plans for four more. Two megawatts of electricity would be available from the one bore alone, four times Níssiros's consumption, with the excess sent by undersea cable to Kós, Kálymnos and Léros. Mindful of DEH's poor behaviour in similar circumstances on Mílos, however, the locals are almost unanimously against the project, fearing noxious fumes, industrial debris and land expropriation as in the Cyclades. Already the

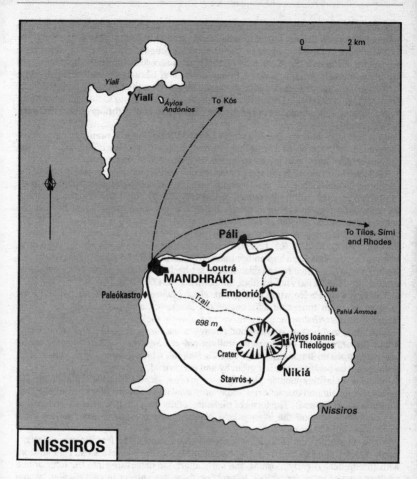

DEH has bulldozed a new road of dubious necessity around the southwest flank of the island, damaging farmland and destroying a beautiful 500-year-old *kalderími* in the process, along with the metal litter of an abandoned well– not an auspicious beginning.

It seems a shame that some kind of *modus vivendi* will probably not be arrived at, since Níssiros has a dire water shortage, and the desalinisation plant stands idle for want of sufficient current to run it. Then again, with water to squander, a heedless mushrooming of tourism could be expected, so perhaps the status quo is the lesser of two evils. The relatively few tourists who stay the night, as opposed to the day-trippers from Kós, find peaceful villages with a minimum of concrete eyesores, and a friendly population.

The north coast

MANDHRÁKI is the port and capital, the wood balconies and windows on its tightly packed white houses splashed in bright colours, with blue swatches of sea visible at the ends of the narrow streets. Except for the drearier fringes near the ferry dock, the bulk of the place looks cheerful, arrayed around the community orchard or *kámbos* and overlooked by two ancient fortresses which also protect it somewhat from the wind.

Into a corner of the first of these, the predictable Knights' castle, is wedged the little monastery of **Panayía Spilianí**, built on this spot in accordance with the instructions of the Virgin herself, given in a vision to one of the first Christian islanders. Its prestige grew after raiding Saracens failed to discover the vast quantities of silver secreted here, in the form of a rich collection of Byzantine icons. On the way up to the monastery, you might stop in at the house restored for the **Historical and Ethnographic Museum** (no set hours).

As a defensive bastion, the 2600-year-old Doric **Paleókastro**, twenty minutes' well-signposted walk out of the Langadháki district, is infinitely more impressive than the Kinghts' castle, and one of the more isolated ancient sites in Greece.

You'll see a handful of **hotels** and **tavernas** on your left as you disembark; best of the mid-range options, helpful and friendly, are the *Hotel/Restaurant Three Brothers* (☎0242/31 344; ③) and the *Romantzo* (☎0242/31 340; ③). In all honesty, though, these are best passed up in favour of establishments in the town proper. Just beyond the public toilets is the simple pension *Maria Intze* (②), across from *Enetikon Travel*, the single **travel agency**. A more popular budget option is the basic but clean *Pension I Dhrosia* (☎0242/31 328; ②), tucked right under the castle on the shore; enquire at Mihalis Orsaris' butcher shop on the main street. If it's full, the same management has slightly more expensive rooms inland. Also set back from the sea, but overlooking the *kámbos*, are Mandhráki's luxury digs, the *Porfiris* (☎0242/31 376; ③).

You've a wide choice when **eating out**. Near *I Dhrosia*, *Kleanthis* is a popular local hangout at lunch time, and adjacent *Mike's* looks, but isn't particularly, tacky. The inland *Taverna Nissiros* is inexpensive and always packed after dark, whereas the *Karava*, next to *Enetikon*, is pricey and empty – a sea view and good menu compensate. About the only places you'd categorically avoid are *Frantzis Special*, a greasy spoon tottering on the brink of extinction, and *To Dhilino*, which despite (or because) of its prime seafront position is rather grouchy and overpriced.

Island **specialities** include pickled caper greens, *pittiá* (chickpea croquettes), and *soumádha*, an almond-extract drink today only available from one store or two tavernas (*Romantzo* and *Karava*). The focus of **nightlife**, oddly enough, is not the shore but various bars and cafés on the lively inland *platía* around the misnamed *Taverna Pizza* (actual speciality roast meat).

Rounding out the list of facilities, there's a short-hours **OTE** near the same *platía*, a **bank agent** and a **post office** at the harbour. Also by the jetty is a small **bus station**, with (theoretically) early morning and early afternoon departures into the interior and another four or so as far as Páli. In practice these are subject to cancellation, so you might consider renting a **moped**: the half-day or overnight rates offered by an inland tourist shop are better than the *Hotel Romantzo's* somewhat expensive full-day rates.

Beaches on Níssiros are in even shorter supply than water – the tour agency here can successfully market excursions to a beach on **Áyios Andónios** islet, just next to the mining apparatus on Yialí. Closer at hand, the black-rock beach of **Hokhláki**, behind the Knights' castle, is impossible if the wind is up, and the town beach at the east edge of the harbour would be a last resort in any weather. Better to head out along the main road, passing the half-abandoned spa of **Loutrá** (hot mineral-water soaks by prior arrangement) and the smallish "**White Beach**", 2km along and dwarfed by an ugly new namesake hotel (☎0242/31 498; generally taken over by tour groups). At the latter the swimming is delightful, but between the biting flies and the ranks of hotel customers you'll soon be wanting to move on.

A kilometre or so further, 45 minutes' walk in all from Mandhráki, the fishing village of **PÁLI** makes a more attractive proposition as a base. Here you'll find the *Hotel*

Hellenís, two **rooms** places (fanciest at the west end of the quay) and arguably the best and cheapest **taverna** on the island, *Afrodíti*, featuring white Cretan wine and home-made desserts. Another dark-sand beach extends east of Páli to an apparently abandoned new spa, but to reach Níssiros's best beaches, continue in that direction for an hour on foot (or twenty minutes by moped), past an initially discouraging seaweed- and cowpat-littered shoreline, to the delightful cove of **Líes**, where the track ends. A ten-minute scramble past a headland to the idyllic expanse of **Pahiá Ámmos**, as broad and sand-red as the name implies, is well worth it.

The interior

It is the **volcano** which gives Níssiros its special character and fosters the growth of the abundant vegetation – and no stay would be complete without a visit. When excursion boats arrive from Kós or Rhodes, the *Polyvotis Tours* coach and usually one of the public buses are pressed into service to take customers up the hill, but if you want to get up there without the crowds it's best to use either the morning and afternoon scheduled buses, a moped or your own feet to get up and back. Tours tend to set off at about 10.30am and 2.30pm, so time yourself accordingly for relative solitude.

Winding up from Páli, you'll first pass the virtually abandoned village of **EMBORIÓ**, where pigs and cows far outnumber people, though the place is slowly being bought up and restored by Athenians and foreigners. New owners are surprised to discover natural **saunas**, heated by volcano steam, in the basements of the crumbling houses; at the outskirts of the village there's a public one in a cave, whose entrance is outlined in white paint. If you're descending to Páli from here, an old cobbled way offers an attractive shortcut.

NIKIÁ, the large village on the east side of the volcano's caldera, is a more lively place, and its spectacular situation offers views out to Tílos as well as across the volcanic crater. Of the three **kafenía** here, the one on the engaging, round *platía* is rarely open, while the one in the middle of town usually has food. There is also **accommodation**, but it's substandard and expensive; not recommended except in an emergency. By the bus turnaround area, signs point to the 45-minute **trail** descending to the crater floor; a few minutes downhill, you can detour briefly to the eyrie-like **monastery of Áyios Ioánnis Theológos**, with a shady tree and yet another perspective on the volcano. The picnic benches and utility buildings come to life at the annual festival, the evening of September 25. To **drive** directly to the volcanic area you have to take the unsignposted road which veers off just past Emborió.

Approaching from any direction a sulphurous stench drifts out to meet you as the fields and scrub gradually give way to lifeless, caked powder. The sunken main **crater** is extraordinary, a Hollywood moonscape of grey, brown and sickly yellow; there is another, less visited double-crater to the west, equally dramatic visually, with a clear trail leading up to it. The perimeters of both are pocked with tiny blow-holes from which jets of steam puff constantly and around which little pincushions of pure sulphur form. The whole floor of the larger crater seems to hiss, and standing in the middle you can hear something akin to a huge cauldron bubbling away below you. In legend this is the groaning of Polyvotis, a titan crushed here by Poseidon under a huge rock torn from Kós. When there are tourists around a small café functions in the centre of the wasteland.

Since the destruction of the old trail between the volcano and Mandhráki, pleasant options for walking back to town are limited. If you want to try, backtrack along the main crater access road for about 1km to find the start of a good, poorly marked path which passes the volcanic gulch of **Káto Lákki** and the monastery of Evangelistrías on its two-hour course back to the port.

Kós

After Rhodes, Kós is easily the most popular island in the Dodecanese, and there are superficial similarities between the two. On Kós as on Rhodes, the harbour is guarded by an imposing castle of the Knights of Saint John, the waterside is lined with grandiose Italian public buildings, and minarets and palm trees punctuate extensive Hellenistic and Roman remains. Once again Scandinavian package tourists predominate, filling the hotels behind the extensive beaches.

Though sandy and fertile, the hinterland of Kós lacks the wild beauty of Rhodes's interior, and it must also be said that the main town, unlike Rhodes, has little charm aside from its antiquities – it looks more like Miami Beach. Rhodes-scale tourist development imposed on an essentially sleepy, small-scale island economy has resulted most obviously in even higher food and transport prices than on Rhodes: where Rhodes is a provincial capital in its own right, Kós is purely and simply a holiday resort – though there's also a strong military presence here. Except for its far west end, this is not an island that attracts many non-package travellers, and in mid-season you'd be lucky to find any sort of room at all.

Kós Town

The town of **KÓS** spreads in all direction from the harbour; apart from the **castle** (Tues–Sun 8.30am–3pm; admission 400dr), its sole compelling attraction lies in the wealth of Hellenistic and Roman remains, many of which were only revealed by an earthquake in 1933, and restored afterwards by the Italians. The largest single section is the ancient **agora**, linked to the castle by a bridge or reached by a signposted walkway from Platía Eleftherías next to the **Archaeological Museum** (same hours as the castle). The **Casa Romana** (same hours), a palatial Roman house at the rear of town, and the sections of the ancient town bracketed by the **odeion** and the **stadium** are more impressive up close. Both have well-preserved fragments of mosaic floors, although the best have been carted off to Rhodes – and what remains tends to be under several inches of protective gravel.

There are, in fact, so many broken pillars, smashed statues and fragments of bas-relief lying around among the ruins than nobody knows quite what to do with them. The best pieces have been taken for safekeeping into the castle, where most of them are piled up, unmarked and unnoticed. A couple of pillars, now replaced by scaffolding, were once even used to prop up the branches of **Hippocrates' plane tree**. This venerable tree has guarded the entrance to the castle for generations, and although not really elderly enough to have seen the great healer, it has a fair claim to being one of the oldest trees in Europe. Just next door is the imposing eighteenth-century **mosque of Hatzi Hassan**, its ground floor, like that of the **Defterdar mosque** on Platía Eleftherías, taken up by rows of shops.

Kós also boasts a rather bogus "old bazaar": a lone pedestrian street, today crammed with tatty tourist boutiques, running from behind the overpriced produce market on Eleftherías as far as Platía Dhiagóras and the isolated minaret overlooking the inland archaeological zone. About the only genuinely old thing here is a capped **Turkish fountain** with an inscription, found where the walkway cobbles cross Odhós Venizélou.

Arrival, orientation and information

Large **ferries** anchor just outside the harbour at a special jetty by one corner of the castle; **excursion boats** to neighbouring islands sail right in and dock all along Aktí Koundouriótou. **Hydrofoils** from as far away as Sámos and Rhodes have their own dock beyond the main archaeological zone, on Aktí Miaoúli. The **airport** is 26km west of Kós Town in the centre of the island; an *Olympic Airways* shuttle bus meets *Olympic*

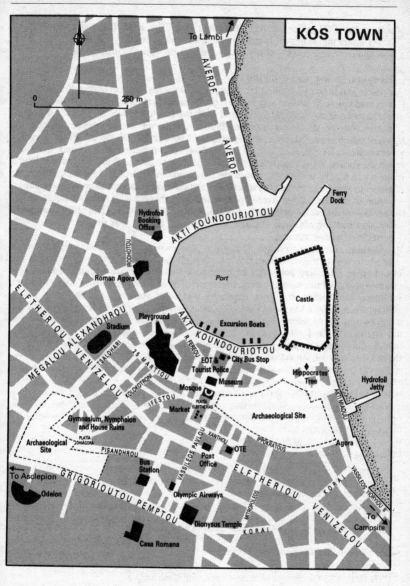

KÓS TOWN

To Lambi

AVEROF

AVEROF

Hydrofoil Booking Office

AKTI KOUNDOURIOTOU

Ferry Dock

IRODHIOTOU

Roman Agora

Port

Castle

ELEFTHERIOU

MEGALOU ALEXANDHROU

VENIZELOU

Playground

Stadium

TSALDHARI

28 MARTIOU

KOLOKOTRONI

R. FEREOU

AKTI KOUNDOURIOTOU

Excursion Boats

EOT & Tourist Police

City Bus Stop

Hippocrates' Tree

Hydrofoil Jetty

IFESTOU

Mosque

Museum

Market

PLATÍA ELEFTHERÍAS

Archaeological Site

AKTI MIAOULI

Gymnasium, Nympheion and House Ruins

PLATÍA DHIAGORA

VASSILEOS PAVLOU

YANTHOU

IPPOKRATOUS

Agora

Archaeological Site

PISANDHROU

Bus Station

Post Office

OTE

ELEFTHERIOU

KORAI

VASSILEOS YIORYIOU B'

To Asclepion

GRIGORIOUTOU PEMPTOU

Olympic Airways

VENIZELOU

Odeion

Dionysus Temple

MITROPOLEOS

KORAI

To Campsite

Casa Romana

0   250 m

flights, but if you arrive on any other flight you'll have to either take a taxi or head towards the giant roundabout outside the airport gate and find a *KTEL* bus – they run from here to Mastihári, Kardhámena and Kéfalos as well as Kós town.

The **KTEL terminal** in town is a series of stops around a triangular park 500m back from the water; the municipality also runs a **local bus** service through the beach suburbs and up to the Asclepion, with a ticket and information office immediately adjacent to the EOT office on Aktí Koundouriótou. The **EOT** (Mon–Fri 8am–3.15pm, longer hours mid-summer) is mainly of use for comprehensive, but not utterly reliable, boat and ferry schedules – which are posted outside when the office is shut.

Sleeping, eating and drinking

If you're just in transit, waiting for a ferry, then it makes sense to **stay** in Kós town. The long-standing rock-bottom option, the E-class *Kalimnos* at Ríga Feréou 9 (☎0242/22 336; ②), has a booming disco on the ground floor; the quietest rooms are on the top floor or at the rear of the lower storeys. Better alternatives in the centre include the *Dodekanissos* around the corner at Ipsilándou 2 (☎0242/28 460; ③), the *Elena*, Megálou Alexándhrou 5 (☎0242/22 740; ③), or the deservedly popular *Pension Alexis*, Irodhótou 9 at the corner of Omírou (☎0242/28 798; ③), across from the Roman *agora*. For longer stays and bigger wallets, the rooms let by Moustafa Tselepi at Venizélou 29, on the corner of Metsóvou (☎0242/28 896; ③) are a good choice, some with cooking facilities.

Across the port, along Avérof, are some other reasonable, if noisy, options: try the *Pension Popi* at no. 37 (☎0242/23 475; ③) or the *Nitsa* at no. 41. The official **campsite** is 2.5km out towards Cape Psalídhi, accessible by the city bus service but open only during the warmer months.

Eating out well and cheaply is likely to pose more problems. You can pretty much write off most of the waterfront tavernas, though the *Romantica*, one of the first as you come from the ferry jetty, and its neighbour the *Limnos*, are within the bounds of reason. None of the myriad eateries seaward of Avérof are particularly cheap or worth singling out. Inland, the least expensive and most authentic establishment is the *Australia Sydney* at Vassiléos Pávlou 29, near *Olympic Airways*, with an amazingly full bar and an ample menu. You might also try the *Troödhon*, next to *Pension Alexis* at Irodhótou 11, and the *Hamam*, housed partly in an old Turkish bath off Platía Dhiagóras – atmospheric, though not too cheap or friendly. If you're craving an English – or even American – **breakfast**, *Pancakes Over 100,000 Served* (sic) serves them and other dishes besides under giant trees on Platía Ayías Paraskevís, behind the produce market: expensive but worth it.

In terms of **nightlife**, you need look no further than the inland pedestrian way joining Platía Eleftherías and the castle; every address is a bar, just choose according to the crowd and the noise level. Otherwise there are two rather moribund **cinemas**, the *Orfevs* and the *Kendriko*.

Listings

Exchange The *Credit Bank* on the waterfront opens on Saturday morning for foreign currency exchange; some other banks open in the evenings. Otherwise you're at the mercy of private agents who will extract a hefty commission.

Ferry tickets Virtually all ferry and excursion boat agents sit within 50m of each other at the intersection of Vassiléos Pávlou and the waterfront. Important exceptions include the head office of *Stefamar*, out on Avérof, for boats to Kálimnos, Psérimos and Níssiros, and the ticket outlet for the expensive hydrofoils to Sámos, Pátmos, Léros and Rhodes, on Platía Iróön Politehníou (the round plaza at the back of the harbour).

Laundry Self-service and attended wash at *Happy Wash*, Mitropóleos 14.

OTE Víronos on the corner of Xánthou, open until 11pm daily.

Post office Venizélou 14; Sat and Sun morning hours in season.

Trips to Turkey Greek morning boats and Turkish afternoon ones shuttle to Bodrum, Turkey, daily from mid-April to mid-October, otherwise according to demand. Prices including tax are currently £13 one way, £17 same day return, and £20 open return – presently the cheapest crossing to Turkey from any island. Sole agent for the Turkish afternoon boat is *DANE*, which also handles the big Dhodekánissos–Pireás liners.

The Asclepion and Platáni

Hippocrates is justly celebrated on Kós; not only does he have a tree named after him, but the star exhibit in the town museum is his statue, and the Asclepion (city bus via Platáni 8.30am–2.30pm, to Platáni only 2.30–11pm; or a 45-minute walk) is a major tourist attraction. Treatments described by Hippocrates and his followers were still used as recently as a hundred years ago, and his ideas on medical methods and ethics remain influential.

The **Asclepion** whose ruins can be seen (Tues–Sun 8.30am–3pm; 600dr) was actually built after the death of Hippocrates, but it's safe to assume that the methods used and taught here were still his. Both a temple to Asclepius (son of Apollo, god of medicine) and a renowned centre of healing, its magnificent setting on terraces levelled from a hillside overlooking the Anatolian mainland reflects early doctors' recognition of the importance of the therapeutic environment: springs still provide the site with a constant supply of clean fresh water. There used to be a rival medical school in the ancient town of Knidos, on the Asia Minor coast southeast of Kós, at a time when there was far more contact across the water than you'll find today.

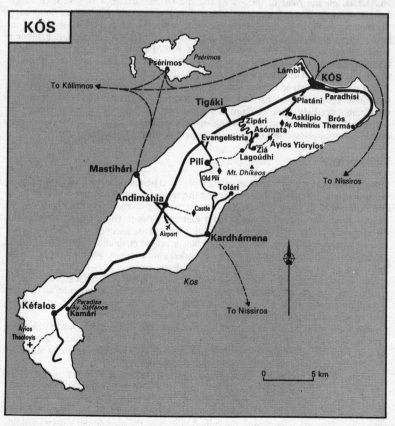

HIPPOCRATES

Hippocrates (c 460–377 BC) is generally regarded as "the father of medicine", and through the Hippocratic oath – which probably has nothing to with him, and is in any case much altered from its original form – still influences doctors today. He was certainly born on Kós, but otherwise details of his life are few and disputed; what seems beyond doubt is that he was a great physician who travelled throughout the Classical Greek world but spent at least part of his career teaching and practising at the Asclepion on the island of his birth. To Hippocrates were traditionally attributed a vast number of medical writings, only a small portion of which he could actually have written; in all probability they were the collection of a medical library kept on Kós. Some probably were Hippocrates' own work – in particular *Airs, Waters and Places*, a treatise on the importance of environment on health, is widely thought to be his. This stress on good air and water, and the holistic approach of ancient Greek medicine, can in the late twentieth century seem positively modern at times.

A mild social segregation still prevails close at hand in the bi-ethnic village of **PLATÁNI**, on the road to the Asclepion; the Greek Orthodox stay in their single *kafenío* while the Muslim majority hold forth at the three establishments dominating the crossroads. All of the latter serve excellent, relatively cheap, Turkish-style food, far better than anything you generally get in Kós Town. There's a working Ottoman fountain nearby, and the older domestic architecture of Platáni is strongly reminiscent of rural styles in provincial Crete – which, as with part of the community on Rhodes, is where many of the Turks here came from early this century.

Just outside Platáni on the road back to the harbour, the Jewish cemetery stands in a dark pine grove, 300m from the Muslim graveyard. Dates on the headstones stop ominously after 1940, after which none were allowed the luxury of a natural death. The old synagogue, locked and crumbling since the deportations to the concentration camps, is back in Kós Town between the ancient *agora* and the waterfront.

Eastern Kós

If you're looking for anything resembling a deserted **beach** near the capital, you'll need to make use of the city bus line connecting the various resorts to either side of town, or else rent a vehicle. Closest is **Lámbi**, 3km northeast towards Cape Skandhári with its military watchpoint, the last vestige of a vast army camp which has deferred to the demands of tourism. On the same coast, 12km west of the harbour, **TIGÁKI** is still just about a village, easily accessible by *KTEL* bus or rented push-bike (a popular option in the flat east end of Kós). As a result it's crowded until evening, when everyone except those lucky enough to have rented a room has disappeared.

The far end of the city bus line beginning at Lámbi is **ÁYIOS FOKÁS**, 8km out, with the unusual and remote **Brós Thermá** 5km further on, easiest reached by moped. Here **hot springs** trickle over black sand into the sea, warming it up for early or late-season swims. There's a small seasonal café but no other facilities.

Inland, the main interest of eastern Kós resides in the villages of **Mount Dhíkeos**, a handful of settlements collectively referred to as Asfendhíou, nestling among the slopes of the island's only forest. They are accessible either via the curvy side-road from Zipári, or a more straightforward turning signed as "Píli".

Modern **PÍLI** is sprawlingly modern and unattractive, and the lack of tourist amenities seems an admission that no-one will stop here. **Old Píli**, signposted inconspicuously as such on a house corner in AMANÍOU, the next hamlet east, gets more attention; a paved road leads up a wooded canyon, stopping by a spring at the base of a crag with a Byzantine castle and the ruined houses of the abandoned village tumbling away from it. The frescoes in the handful of medieval churches are in bad condition, however, and all told the place is more impressive from a distance.

From Amaníou the dirt track leads via the untouristed hamlet of LAGOÚDHI to **EVANGELÍSTRIA**, where there's a taverna and an interesting "suburb", **ASÓMATI**, with fine whitewashed houses. **ZIÁ**, further up the now paved road, is the hapless target of up to six tour buses per night; several rather commercialised tavernas take advantage of the spectacular sunsets, but it's a good idea to clear out immediately afterwards. Beyond Ziá the way deteriorates to dirt once more, continuing to **ÁYIOS YIÓRYIOS**, where only around thirty villagers and a handful of foreigners and Athenians renovating houses live on; there is one tiny store run by an old woman where you can get a drink. **ÁYIOS DHIMÍTRIOS**, 2km beyond, on an exceedingly rough track, was abandoned entirely during the junta years, when the inhabitants went to Zipári or further afield. Indeed, the best reason for coming up this way is to get some idea of what Kós looked like before tourism and ready-mix concrete took root.

Western Kós

Near the centre of the island, a pair of giant roundabouts by the airport funnels traffic northwest towards Mastihári, northeast back towards town, southwest towards Kéfalos, and southeast to Kardhámena.

The beach at **MASTIHÁRI** is smaller than those at Tigáki or Kardhámena, and the small town is increasingly built up, but it is the port for the least expensive *kaíkia* to Kálimnos and the tiny Greek islet of Psérimos (see below), so you may want to come here. In season there are daily morning and mid-afternoon sailings, with an extra late-night departure when charter landings warrant it – though be warned that boats can be fully occupied by package clients.

KARDHÁMENA, on the southeast-facing coast, is the island's second largest tourist playpen, packed in season with Germans, British and the odd Nordic type, and the runaway local development has banished whatever redeeming qualities it may once have had: the clientele is decidedly downmarket. A beach stretches to either side of the town, backed on the east with ill-concealed military bunkers and a road as far as TOLÁRI, where there is a massive hotel complex. Halfway back towards Andimáhia an enormous **castle** (the Knights' again) sprawls atop a ridge. Like Mastihári, Kardhámena is most worth knowing about as a place to catch inter-island *kaíkia*, in this case to Níssiros. There are supposedly two daily sailings in season, at approximately 9am and 5pm, but the municipal **tourism information post** here denies all knowledge of the later service and in practice the afternoon departure takes place any time between 1.30 and 6.30pm.

Outside high season, there are generally a few **rooms** not taken by tour companies available to those showing up on their own, and prices, at ②–③ depending on the facilities and number of people, are not outrageous. The one reasonable **taverna**, *Andreas*, is right on the harbour; inland, a **bakery** (signed with red arrows) does homemade ice cream, yoghurt and sticky cakes, and *Peter's* **rent a bike** across the street is one of the more flexible outfits (*Ilias* is the biggest).

The end of the line for buses is KÉFALOS, which squats on a mesa-like hill looking back down the length of Kós. Most visitors will have alighted long before, either at **KAMÁRI** (plenty of accommodation) or **ÁYIOS STÉFANOS** (ditto), where the exquisite remains of a fifth-century basilica overlook tiny Kastrí islet. The beach begins at Kamári and runs five kilometres east, virtually without interruption, to the cliff-framed and aptly-named **Paradise beach**. Unfortunately the entire area between Kamári and Áyios Stéfanos has been overshadowed by a huge Club Med complex of bungalows surrounding the main luxury hotel.

Kéfalos itself is rather dull but is the staging point for expeditions into the rugged southwest peninsula. To the west, around the monastery of **Áyios Theológos**, you can still find deserted stretches of coastline, but the nearest cove is about 6km distant over rough tracks – and none are as sheltered as the bays on the island's southeast flank.

Psérimos

If it weren't for its proximity to Kós and Kálimnos, which results in day-trippers by the boatload every day of the season, Psérimos could be an idyllic little island. Even in April and October, however, you can be guaranteed at least 100 outsiders a day (which doubles the population), so imagine the scene in high season as the visitors spread themselves along the main sandy beach, which stretches around the bay in front of the twenty or thirty houses that constitute **PSÉRIMOS VILLAGE**. There are a couple of other, less attractive pebbly beaches to hide away on during the day, no more than thirty walking minutes distant – in fact nowhere on Psérimos is much more than half an hour's walk away.

When the day-trippers have gone you can, out of season, have the place to yourself and even in season there won't be too many other overnighters, since there's a limited number of **rooms** available. Of the three small "hotels", the best (for cheapness, cleanliness and friendliness) is the one run by Katerina Fyloura above her taverna on the eastern side of the harbour. She has a total of thirteen beds apportioned over five rooms (③) and the food's good too. Katerina also acts as postmistress if you want to write home, since the island can't support a post office. There's just one small **store**, not very well-stocked, and most of the island's supplies are brought in daily from Kálimnos. **Eating out**, however, won't break the bank and there's plenty of fresh fish in the handful of tavernas.

The island is easily reached from either Kálimnos or Kós: most Kós Town–Kálimnos and Mastihári–Kálimnos excursion *kaíkia* make a stop at Psérimos in each direction.

Astipálea

Both geographically and architecturally, Astipálea would be more at home among the Cyclades – the island can be seen quite clearly from Thíra and Amorgós, and it looks and feels more like them than its neighbours to the east. Despite its butterfly shape, it's not the most beautiful of islands: the barren coastline gives way in parts to fields, citrus groves and decent, mountainous walking country, but the beaches are often stony and litter-strewn.

In antiquity the island's most famous citizen was Kleomedes, a boxer disqualified from an early Olympic Games for killing his opponent. He came home so enraged that he demolished the local school, killing all its pupils. Things have calmed down a bit in the intervening 2500 years and today the capital, **ASTIPÁLEA**, is a quiet fishing port – the catch is locally consumed, as the island is too remote for it to be shipped to the mainland. This is also a reflection of the notoriously poor ferry links; things have improved recently with the introduction of two new lines to the Cyclades, but you still risk being marooned here for an extra day or three. Despite the relative isolation, plenty of people find their way to Astipálea in summer, though relatively few are English-speaking – it seems more popular with French, Italian and Athenian travellers.

Yialós and Hóra

The harbour of **YIALÓS** dates from the Italian era (Astipálea was the first island the Italians occupied in the Dodecanese) and most of the settlement between the quay and the line of nine windmills is even more recent. As you climb up beyond the port,

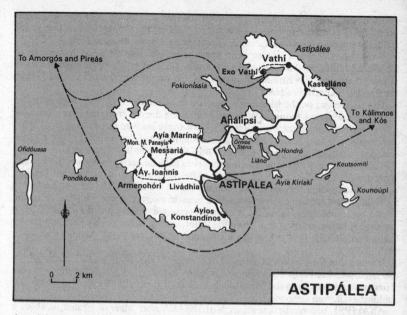

though, the neighbourhoods get progressively older and their steep streets are enlivened by the *poúndia* or colourful wooden balconies of the whitewashed houses. The whole culminates in the fourteenth-century *kástro*, one of the finest in the Aegean. Until well into this century over 3000 souls dwelt within, but depopulation and wartime damage have combined to leave only a desolate shell today; the fine groin vaulting over the entrance and a couple of maintained churches remain an attraction.

There are four inexpensive **hotels** down in the port – the *Astynea* (☎0243/61 209; ③), the *Gallia* (☎0243/61 245; ③), the *Paradisos* (☎0243/61 224; ③) and the *Egeon* (☎0243/61 236; ③) – but if you can get them, **rooms** in the upper town near the windmills that mark the *platía* in Hóra are better. There's a **campsite** halfway to Analípsi, easily reached by bus, and also plenty of unofficial spots around the island. Of the places to **eat**, *To Akroyiali*, *Babis* and *Kali Kardhia* are the local haunts, while the *Astynea*, on the wharf, and *I Monaxia*, behind the generator, are also good. The stepped hill of Maltezána constitutes the business district; here you'll find more places to eat, several discos, shops, the **OTE** and a **travel agency** arranging boat excursions to remote beaches. The **post office** is well up in the Hóra, as are some subdued clubs like *Castle Bar* and *Artemis*. You can change money at the post office or a bank exchange place (there's no bank).

A **bus** runs regularly between Hóra, Skala, Livádhia and Analípsi in Júly and August, less frequently out of season – the posted timetables are far from reliable. There are only two official **taxis**, far too few in season when lots of Athenians visit; several places rent out mopeds. The island **map** sold locally is grossly inaccurate.

Around the island

Half an hour's walk (or a short, frequent bus journey) from the capital is **LIVÁDHIA**, a fertile green valley with a popular, good beach and shaded restaurants by the water-side. You can **camp** here or **rent a room** or bungalow in the beach hamlet – for example from the Kondokatos family (☎0243/61 269; ②) or *Pension Nikolaos*, which has been known to offer a mattress in the local citrus/banana orchards when they're full inside. Among the **tavernas**, *Yiesenia*, *Thomas* and *Kalamia* are all decent.

If the beach here is not to your liking, continue southwest on a footpath to **TZANÁKI**, with nude bathing and fewer people. Continuing to bug-infested, seaweed-strewn Moúra or Áyios Konstandínos coves is less worthwhile, though the shade from the fringing orchards is a plus.

The best outing on the island, however, has to be the two-hour walk from Astipálea to the oasis of **Áyios Ioánnis**. Walk one hour along the dirt track beginning from the fifth or sixth windmill, then bear left at the fork (right leads to the anchorage of **Áyios Andhréas**: one ramshackle taverna, good swimming and snorkelling). After a while, you pass another path going right towards the uninspiring monastery of Panayía Flevariotíssas; carry on through **Arménohori** (a pillaged ancient site) and the farming hamlet of **MESSARIÁ**, before turning left, at the top of a pass, on to a footpath heading for some bony-white rock outcrops. Soon the walled orchards of the farm-monastery of Áyios Ioánnis (not to be confused with a seaside cloister of the same name to the north) come into view. Just below, a ten-metre waterfall plunges into deep pools fine for bathing. A rather arduous trek down the valley ends at a fine pebbly bay, and proper paths lead directly back to Livádhia if you don't fancy a reprise of the jeep tracks you arrived on.

Northeast of the harbour, a series of bays nestle in the "body" of the "butterfly". Of the two coves known as **Marmári**, one is home to the power plant, and the next one, 2.5km out of town, hosts the island's only organised **campsite**. Beyond, at **Stenó**, the middle beach, with clean sand and fresh-water wells, is the best.

ANÁLIPSI, universally known as MALTEZÁNA after Maltese pirates, is about a twelve-kilometre taxi-ride or walk in the other direction. Although the second largest settlement on Astipálea, there's little for outsiders except a narrow, sea-urchin-speckled beach and two small **tavernas** (*Obelix* is excellent), plus quite a few **rooms** – though you can still get away with sleeping under the stars. At the edge of surrounding olive groves are the well-preserved remains of **Roman baths**, with floor mosaics of zodiacal signs and the seasons personified. In high season, Análipsi can be a welcome escape – once you find your way around, there are other beaches accessible around the bay. The road ends at **VATHÍ**, an even sleepier fishing village (one taverna) with a superb harbour, which is where the ferry will dock in winter when Astipálea Town is too exposed to the prevailing southerly winds. At such times, and only then, there is a bus between Vathí and Astipálea. Occasional *kaíkia* shuttle back and forth in season between Vathí and either Áyios Andhréas or Yialós.

Kálimnos

Most of the population of Kálimnos lives in or around the port of Pothiá, a wealthy but not very beautiful town famed for its sponge divers. Sadly almost all the Mediterranean's sponges, with the exception of a few deep-water beds off Italy, have been devastated by disease, and only three or four of the fleet of thirty or more boats can currently be usefully occupied. In response to this economic disaster, the island is attempting to establish a tourist industry – so far little developed. The warehouses behind the harbour, however, still process and sell sponges to tourists all year round. During the Italian occupation houses here were painted blue and white to keep alive the Greek colours and irritate the invaders. The custom is beginning to die out, but is still evident; even some of the churches are painted blue.

Since Kálimnos is the home port of the very useful local ferry of that name (see "Travel Details"), and also where the long-distance ferry lines from the outer Cyclades

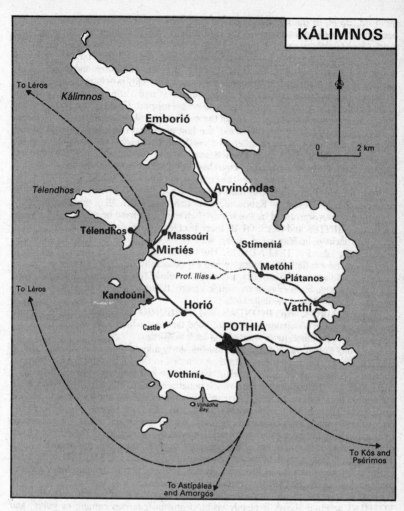

and Astipálea join up with the main Dodecanesian ones, many travellers find themselves here without meaning to, and are initially most concerned with how to move on quickly. The islanders have so far remained welcoming, and indulgent of short stays, perhaps realising that the place won't hold most people's interest for more than a day or two.

Pothiá and around

POTHIÁ, without being particularly picturesque, is colourful and pre-touristically Greek, the overwhelming impression being of the phenomenal amount of noise engendered by the cranked-up sound systems of the dozen waterfront cafés, and the exhibitionist motorbike traffic. **Accommodation** is rarely a problem, since pension keepers usually meet the ferries; otherwise the *Hotel Patmos* (☎0243/22 750; ③), in a relatively quiet sidestreet, or the tersely-named, nearby *Hotel V*, are dependable fall backs. For **eating out**, *Zorba's*, tucked among the row of tourist agencies near the jetty, isn't bad, but for a wider choice the best strategy is to follow the waterfront west past the Italian-built municipal "palace" to a line of **fish tavernas and ouzerís**. The first, nameless joint under the tamarisks is okay, *Barba Petros* at the far end is a bit glitzy, and there's plenty of scope at the establishments in between. The local specialty is octopus croquettes.

Buses run as far as Aryinóndas in the northwest and Vathí in the east, while for more freedom there are plenty of places to rent a **moped**. Chances are you'll want to escape, at least during the day, to one of the smaller coastal settlements.

Heading northwest across the island, the first place you come to is the old capital, **HORIÓ**, sandwiched between an eroded **castle** of the Knights of Saint John and the miniature Byzantine precinct of **Péra Kástro**. The crumbling ruins of the latter are peppered with conspicuously white churches, but it's the castle that especially merits a visit, with its stupendous views over the entire west coast of the island.

From the ridge at Horió the road dips into a cultivated ravine, heading for the consecutive beach resorts of Kandoúni, Mirtiés and Massoúri. All of them are far more developed than is warranted by the scanty shelves of grey sand or pebbles in the vicinity, but at **MIRTIÉS** and **MASSOÚRI** there is at least the possibility of finding a room amid the package-holiday villas, along with views across the strait to the striking, volcanic-plug island of **TÉLENDHOS**. The trip across is arguably the best reason to come to Mirtiés; little boats shuttle to and fro constantly throughout the day. On the islet you'll find a ruined monastery, a castle, a couple of tiny beaches and several tavernas and pensions, all in or near the single village. It's also possible to go from Mirtiés directly to Léros aboard the daily *kaíki*.

Beyond Mirtiés, **ARYINÓNDAS** and **EMBORIÓ** both have empty, decent beaches, the latter alongside a couple of good tavernas which have rooms. If the bus fails you there is sometimes a shuttle boat back to Mirtiés.

East from Pothiá, an initially unpromising, forty-minute ride ends dramatically at **VATHÍ**, whose colour provides a startling contrast to the lifeless greys elsewhere on Kálimnos. A long, fertile valley, verdant with orange and tangerine groves, it seems a continuation of the cobalt-blue fjord which penetrates finger-like into the landscape. In the simple port, known as Rína, there are a handful of *kafenía* and tavernas to choose from, as well as a **hotel** (*Galini*, ☎0243/31 241; ③) and a few **rooms**. For **walkers** the lush valley behind, criss-crossed with rough tractor-tracks and paths, may prove an irresistible lure, but be warned that it will take you the better part of three hours, most of it shadeless once you're out of the orchards, to reach points on the opposite coast. The only facilities en route lie in the hamlets of PLÁTANOS and METÓHI at the head of the valley; once past these, the route divides, with one option going to Massoúri, the other to Aryinóndas via the third hamlet of STIMÉNIA.

Southwest of Pothiá, the attractive little sandy bay of **Vlihádha**, with the village of **VOTHINÍ** perched above, is plainly visible from most ferries coming or going, and considerably less crowded than the northwestern beaches. Local *kaíkia* make well-publicised excursions to the southerly caves of **Kéfalos**, **Skaliá** and **Ayía Varvára**, all nearly as impressive as the photographs they use to tempt you to go there.

Léros

Léros is so indented with deep, sheltered anchorages that during the last world war it harboured (in turn) the entire Italian, German, and British Mediterranean fleets. Unfortunately, these magnificent fjords and bays seem to absorb rather than reflect light, and the island's relative fertility comes across as scruffiness when compared to the crisp lines of its more barren neighbours. These characteristics, coupled with the island's absence until recently from the lists of most major tour operators, mean that barely 10,000 foreigners a year (many of them Italians who grew up on the island), and not many more Greeks, come to stay.

Not that the islanders need, or particularly encourage, tourism; various prisons and sanitariums have long dominated the Lerian economy. Under the junta the island was the site of an infamous detention centre, and today mental hospitals on Léros are still the repository for 2000 of Greece's more intractable psychiatric cases; another asylum is home to hundreds of mentally handicapped children. The island's domestic image problem is compounded by its name, the butt of jokes by mainlanders who pounce on its similarity to the word *léra*, connoting dirt and rascality. Islanders are in fact extremely friendly to those who visit, but their island's role and image seem unlikely to change. In 1989 a major scandal burst forth concerning the administration of the various asylums, with EC maintenance and development funds found to have been embezzled by administrators and staff, and the inmates kept in degrading and inhumane conditions. By 1991 EC inspectors pronounced themselves satisfied that the abuses had stopped, but Léros will be a long time overcoming this additional stigma.

On arrival (invariably at night) the port of **LAKKÍ** is an extraordinary, neon-lit sight, its waterside lined with art deco edifices put up by the Italians. Indeed the whole town, distinctly faded at closer quarters, retains a marvellously seedy elegance in its broad

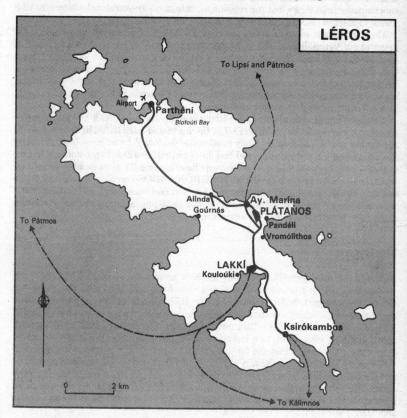

streets laid out around little parks and statues. If you really want to savour it, try the faded grandeur of the *Hotel Léros* (☎0247/22 940; ③), on the front about ten minutes' walk from the jetty. The large rooms here almost all have balconies overlooking the bay. There is nowhere much cheaper in Lakkí, though some places offer more in the way of modern facilities. The beach at **Kouloúki**, where there's a taverna and you can sleep among the trees, is in the opposite (west) direction when you get off the boat, away from town.

Better beaches can be found in the five other huge bays that distinguish the coastline. The one **bus** visits every village a few times a day, and shuttles fairly regularly between Lakkí and the capital at **PLÁTANOS**, about an hour's walk away. **Bicycles** and **scooters** can be hired in Lakkí and in Plátanos, which is a more pleasant and less expensive place to be based for any length of time. Originally built on a low ridge with sea on both sides, and protected by the Byzantine castle above, it has gradually spread in both directions to join up with the fishing villages of **PANDÉLI** and **AYÍA MARÍNA**. Between them the three support a cinema, two discos and a surprisingly lively nightlife in the cafés and bars. It should be easy enough to find a room somewhere here, though not surprisingly amenities are a little better in the two waterside communities. The **castle** (open dawn to dusk), kept in good repair by a series of defenders and once again being restored, is an easy climb above the town. It has superb panoramic views, but for reasons of state security you're not allowed to take photographs; the place is still used as a military observation point.

There's a beach, rooms and two tavernas at **PANDÉLI**, a real fishing village, and a better one at **Vromólithos**, with a taverna further around the bay to the south. North of Ayía Marína the more developed resort of **ALÍNDA** fronts another long beach lined with villas, a popular spot with holidaying Greeks. On the way you pass a cemetery for British soldiers killed in battle in 1943. Across the narrowest part of the island from Alínda and reached by a poorly marked side road, **Gournás** is another popular, sandy beach, but strangely with almost no facilities.

Nowhere in this central part of the island is really too far to walk or cycle if you're reasonably energetic, but **PARTHÉNI** in the north and **XIRÓKAMBOS** to the south are further afield. The former, a tiny hamlet overshadowed by an army base (formerly the junta's political detention centre) and dusty airstrip, has little to recommend it. Five minutes' walk beyond, however, is **Blefoúti Bay**, the island's most isolated (if pebbly) beach, with a lone taverna. On the way to **XIRÓKAMBOS** there's more military development, but the place itself is unaffected; you can find rooms with little difficulty and there are several places to eat and drink, as well as an official (summer only) **campsite** and a good beach. This is also the embarkation point for the Kálimnos-based *kaíkia*.

Pátmos

Arguably the most beautiful, certainly the best known of the smaller islands in the Dodecanese, Pátmos is unique. It was in a cave here that Saint John the Divine (in Greek, *O Theologos*), had his revelation (the Bible's Book of Revelation) and unwittingly shaped the island's destiny. The monastery which commemorates him, founded here in 1088, dominates the island both physically – its fortified bulk towering high above anything else – and, to a considerable extent, politically. While the monks no longer run the island as they did for more than 700 years, their influence has nevertheless stopped Pátmos going the way of Rhodes or Kós. Despite vast numbers of visitors, and the island's firm presence on the cruise and yacht circuits, tourism has not been allowed to take the island over. There are a number of clubs and even one disco around Skála, the port and main town, but everywhere else development of any kind is appealingly subdued.

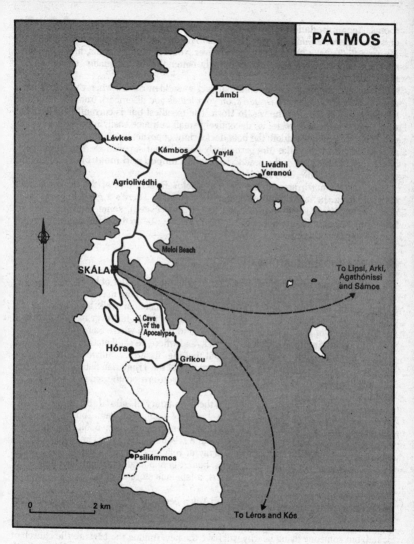

Skála and around

SKÁLA seems initially to contradict this image of Pátmos. The waterside, with its ritzy-looking cafés and clientele, is a little too sophisticated for its own small-town good. In season it's crowded by day with excursionists from Kós and Rhodes; by night with well-dressed cliques of visitors. In winter the shops and restaurants close and most of their owners and staff leave for Rhodes; the town itself taking on a somewhat depressed air, with not so much as a cinema for the kids to roar their motorbikes towards.

If you feel like moving straight out, the most obvious possibility is Méloï Beach (see below); Hóra, a bus or taxi-ride up the mountain, is a more attractive base but has few rooms. **Accommodation** in Skála itself is in demand but there's a reasonable amount of it. The *Hotel Patmion* (☎0247/31 313; ③) is a good, modest-priced choice, as is the *Rex* (☎0247/31 242; ③). More likely, however, you'll end up in rooms, hawked vociferously as ever on the quay; they are mostly better than usual quality, though higher than usual prices, too.

There are plenty of places to **eat**, subject to sudden rushes when the cruise boats arrive – among the best are *Grigori's*, on your left as you disembark from the ferry, and the *Skorpios Creperie*, on the way to Hóra. The trendiest **bar** is currently the barn-like *Café Arion* on the waterside, its deceptively small entrance easily missed. Everything else is near the police station: the boat docks right opposite; **bus and boat timetables** are posted outside; and the (not particularly helpful) tourist police are around the back. South towards the start of the road to Gríkou is a **moped and motorbike** rental outfit; another, more reliable, is by the *Hotel Patmion*.

1500 metres north around the bay lies **Méloï Beach**, one of the best and most convenient on the island, and of course very popular. There's a good but very overpriced **campsite** here (rough camping is not appreciated), some **rooms** – best are those run by Loula Koumendhourou (☎0247/32 281; ③), on the slope south of the bay – and a couple of **tavernas**.

Hóra and the monasteries

For cruise-ship passengers and overnighters alike the first order of business is likely to be heading up to the Monastery of Saint John, sheltered behind massive defences in the hilltop capital of Hóra. There is a bus up, but the half-hour walk by a beautiful old cobbled path puts you in a more appropriate frame of mind. Just over halfway, pause at the **Monastery of the Apocalypse**, built around the cave where Saint John heard the voice of God issuing from a cleft in the rock, and where he sat dictating His words to a disciple. A leaflet left for visitors points out that the "fissure . . . (divides) the rock into three parts, thus serving as a continual reminder of the Trinitarian nature of God", and admonishes pilgrims to "ask yourself whether you are on the side of Christ or of Antichrist".

This is merely a foretaste, however, of the **Monastery of saint John** (erratic hours theoretically Mon 8am–2pm, Tues 8am–1pm & 4–6pm, Wed 8am–2pm & 5.30–7pm, Thurs 8am–1pm & 4–6pm, Fri 8am–2pm, Sat 8am–2pm, Sun 8am–noon & 5–6pm. The cloister of the Apocalypse adheres to the same schedule). Behind its imposing fortifications have been preserved a fantastic array of religious treasures dating back to the earliest days of Christianity: relics, icons, books, ceremonial ornaments and apparel of the most extraordinary richness; in short, a fabulous store of delights. To be sure of admission, "modest" dress is essential.

Outside Saint John's stout walls, **HÓRA** is a beautiful little town whose antiquated alleys shelter over forty churches and monasteries. The churches, many of them containing beautiful icons and examples of the local skill in wood carving, are almost all locked, but someone living nearby will have the key. Among the best are the church of **Dhiassozoússas** and the monastery of **Zoödhóhou Piyís**. You can eat well at *Vangelis* (on the inner square), *Ipiros*, or *Olympia*, all of which are cheaper and probably better than anything in Skála. There are, however, very few places to stay; foreigners here are mostly long-term occupants, and almost a third of the crumbling mansions have been bought up and restored in the past two decades. If you're determined to find somewhere – and there are only a total of twenty beds in one or two signposted buildings – make enquiries in the *platía* early in the day or ring ☎0247/32 114 in advance. Finally, don't miss the **view** from the outer plaza; at dawn or dusk the landmasses to the north, going clockwise, include Ikaría, Thímena, Foúrni, Sámos with the brooding mass of Mount Kérkis, Arkí, and the double-humped Samsun Dag (ancient Mount Mikale) in Turkey.

Around the island

Pátmos, as one locally published guide proclaims, "is immense for those who know how to wander in space and time". The more conventionally propelled may find it easier to get around on foot, or by bus. This is one of the finest islands for **walking**, with a network of paths leading almost everywhere. The overworked **bus** which connects Skála with Hóra, Kámbos and Gríkou is rather less reliable.

After the extraordinary atmosphere and magnificent scenery, it's the **beaches** that are Patmos's principal attraction. From Hóra a good trail heads southeast to the sandiest part of generally overdeveloped **Gríkou Bay** within forty minutes, and a rougher track leads in two hours to the much better beach, with one seasonal taverna, at **Psilí Ámmos** (there's also a summer *kaíki* service from Skála). More good beaches are to be found in the north of the island, most of them accessible on foot by following the old paths which (with the exception of some paved or cross-country stretches) parallel the startling, indented eastern shore.

The first beach beyond Méloï, **Agriolivádhi**, is rocky, algae-ridden and without facilities; the next, **Kámbos**, is not much better. But if you head east from the latter, **Vayiá** and **Livádhi Yeranoú** are considerably more tempting. From Kámbos you can also head north to the bay of **Lámbi**, not so practical for swimming when the wind and surf are up, but renowned for an abundance of multicoloured stones. A hamlet of sorts here has a couple of tavernas and rooms, and this is also the most northerly port of call for the daily excursion *kaíkia* which shuttle constantly around the coast in season.

As is so often the case, you'll find the island at its best out of season. It can get cold in winter, but there is a hard core of foreigners who live here year-round, so things never entirely close down. Many of the long-term residents rent houses in **Léfkes**, a fertile valley just west of Kámbos with a lonely and sometimes wild beach at its end. It was here that a New Age "commune" was based in the late Seventies and early Eighties before its eviction by the authorities, but there has been no shortage of slightly more mainstream tenants to fill the houses they left behind.

Minor Dodecanese Isles: Lipsí, Arkí and Agathónissi

Of the various islets to the north and east of Pátmos, **LIPSÍ** is the largest and most populated, and the one that is beginning to get noticeable summer tourist trade. Deep wells water many small, well-tended farms, but there is only one spring, and pastoral appearances are deceptive – four times the relatively impoverished full-time population of 600 is overseas. Most of the remaining people live around the fine harbour, which is also where most of the food and lodging is located.

You've a choice of **accommodation** between the small hotel *Kalypso* (☎0247/41 242; ③) and several pensions such as the *Flisvos* and *Kolonaki*, the latter the only accommodation actually up in the village. The best **tavernas** are a pair of nameless outfits down on the water: a blue-bannistered *ouzerí* next to the *Kali Kardhia*, and one (probably an annexe of the *Kalypso*) next to the *Asprakis* general store. A Lipsian quirk are the bizarre local **kafenía**: some seem to have a double life as bars and the front rooms of private dwellings; some have garish Italian posters or juke boxes, there are fishermen's joints with nonexistent decor where you'll be served octopus, a wine shop on the jetty where walls of bottles dwarf the patrons, a screaming rock-and-roll ice-cream parlour, and more. There is a **post office** and an **OTE**, and the combination **tourist office** and **Ecclesiastical Museum** is hilariously indiscriminate, featuring such "relics" as oil from the sanctuary on Mount Tabor and water from the Jordan River.

The island's **beaches** are a bit scattered; the most attractive is **Katsadhiá**, a collection of many small, sandy coves south of the port, with a very good, May to September taverna (*Andonis*) just inland. **Kohlakoúras**, on the east coast, is by contrast rather grubby shingle with no facilities. An hour's walk along the road leading west from town brings you to **Platís Yialós**, a small, shallow, sandy bay with no development but sheltered from winds. In high season enterprising individuals run pick-up trucks with bench seats in the loading space to the various coves.

A number of paths provide opportunities for a variety of **walks** through the undulating countryside, dotted with blue-domed churches – you can walk from one end of Lipsí to the other in less than two hours. A **carpet-weaving school** for girls operates sporadically on the quay, and some evenings a *santoúri* (Levantine hammer-dulcimer) player performs. Other than that there's absolutely nothing to do or see, but you won't find many better places to do nothing.

Arkí and Agathónissi

ARKÍ is considerably more primitive (no electricity, no village as such) and about half the size of Lipsí; just thirty inhabitants cling to life here. A desperately poor place, its complete depopulation seems conceivable within the next decade. There's not even a proper beach; the nearest one just offshore is on the islet of **Maráthi**, where a taverna caters to the day-trippers who come a couple of times a week from Pátmos – links with Arkí are unreliable. The taverna also rents some fairly comfortable **rooms**, making Maráthi a better option than Arkí for acting out Robinson Crusoe fantasies.

AGATHÓNISSI is sufficiently remote – much closer to Turkey than Pátmos, in fact – to be out of reach even of these excursions, and its covering of vegetation lives up to its name, which means "Thorn Island". Pebble beaches can be found at the harbour settlement, and at **Katholikó** and **Hokhliá**, reached by walking to opposite ends of the island. There's a bona fide inland village (**MEGÁLO HORIÓ**) with 150-odd people and two stores, but no OTE or post office; there are two pensions and a few rooms in the port, and you won't starve at the three tavernas. But if you do show up, you'll probably be the only foreigner(s) around; best to come with someone you like a lot, as there'll be no escape for a week.

travel details

To simplify the lists below, the Nissos Kalimnos has been left out. For several years this small car ferry has been the most regular lifeline of the smaller islands – it visits them all at least once a week between March and December. Its schedule is currently as follows: Monday and Friday, leaves Kálimnos at 6am for Kós, Níssiros, Tílos, Sími, Rhodes, Kastellórizo and Rhodes; Tuesday and Saturday, departs Rhodes at 10am for Sími, Tílos, Níssiros, Kós and Kálimnos; Wednesday at 6am departs Kálimnos for Léros, Lipsí, Pátmos, Agathónissi, Pithagório (Sámos), Foúrni, Ikaría and back to Kálimnos via the same islands; Thursday at 6.45am from Kálimnos to Kós and back, then to Astipálea and back, then to Kós and back once more at 4pm; Sunday at 6.45am leaves Kálimnos for Léros, Lipsí, Pátmos, Agathónissi, Pithagório and back via the same stops. This ship is poorly publicised on islands other than its home port; for current, disinterested information you're strongly advised to phone the central agency on Kálimnos (☎0243/29 612).

In addition there are now expensive **hydrofoil** services based on Rhodes and Kós; these depart daily in season, weather permitting, between these two islands, with fairly regular (once or twice weekly) services from Rhodes to Sími and from Kós to Pátmos, Léros and Pithagório. Only in very high season do the advertised runs to smaller islands like Tílos and Níssiros actually materialise.

Ferries

KÁRPATHOS (PIGÁDHIA) Twice-weekly connections with Kássos, Rhodes (7hr), Crete (Sitía and Áyios Nikólaos, 6hr), Crete (Iráklion), Mílos and Pireás; once to Hálki, Sími Thíra, Folégandhros, Síkinos and Sífnos.

Note Dhiafáni is served by only one weekly mainline ferry to Crete, select western Cyclades and Rhodes, subject to cancellation in bad weather.

KÁSSOS Twice-weekly with Kárpathos, Rhodes (9hr), Crete (Sitía and Áyios Nikólaos, 6hr), Mílos, and Pireás; once to Hálki, Sími, Thíra, Folégandhros, Síkinos and Sífnos.

RHODES 10 weekly with Pireás (18–20hr); 9 to Kós (4hr) and Kálimnos (5hr); daily to Léros (7hr) and Pátmos (8hr); 3 weekly to Crete (Áyios Nikólaos/Sitía or Iráklion), 2 weekly to Thíra, Páros, Míkonos, Tínos, Ándhros, Rafína; 1 weekly to Tílos, Níssiros, Astipálea, Kálimnos, Hálki, Kárpathos (7hr), Kássos; once weekly to Folégandhros, Mílos, Sífnos, Ikaría, Sámos, Híos, Lésvos, Límnos and Kavála/Thessaloníki. **Excursion boats** twice daily to Sími. **International boat departures** include 2–6 weekly afternoon boats, plus 2–6 weekly morning (8am) boats, to Turkey (Marmaris; 2hr 30min); Single about £15, day return £18, open return £21, plus Greek exit tax. Greek **hydrofoil** in peak season only, 1hr 30min. 2 weekly to Cyprus and Israel, 3 monthly to Egypt.

HÁLKI Once weekly to Crete, select western Cyclades and Rhodes, subject to cancellation in bad weather. Twice daily **kaíki** to Rhodes (Skála Kamírou).

KASTELLÓRIZO (Méyisti) Very tenuous means (ie hitching a yacht) of getting to Kaş on the Turkish mainland opposite. Unreliable service to Rhodes once or twice weekly.

SÍMI 1 weekly (unreliable) to Rhodes, Tílos, Níssiros, Kós, Kálimnos, Astipálea, Amorgós, Páros and Pireás. **Excursion boats** twice daily to Rhodes.

NÍSSIROS AND TÍLOS Same as for Sími, plus 1 weekly between each other, Rhodes, Kós, Míkonos, Tínos, Ándhros and Rafína. **Excursion boats** between Níssiros and Kós as follows: to Kardhámena at 4pm and (unannounced) the islanders' "shopping special" at 7.30am; 4–5 weekly to Kós town (seasonal and expensive).

Excursion boat between Tilos and Kós, 2/3 weekly in season.

KÓS 9 weekly to Rhodes (4hr) and Pireás (at least 12hr); 8 weekly to Kálimnos (1hr), Léros (3hr) and Pátmos (5hr); 2 weekly to Míkonos, Tínos, Ándhros, Rafína; 1 a week to Astipálea, Níssiros, Tílos, Ikaría, Sámos, Híos, Lésvos, Límnos and Kavála/Thessaloníki. **Excursion boats** 3 daily in season from Mastihári to Psérimos and Kálimnos, daily from Kós town to Kálimnos via Psérimos, and Rhodes; 1 or 2 daily from Kardhámena to Níssiros, 4–5 weekly from Kós town to Níssiros; 3 weekly to Pátmos. Exorbitant **hydrofoils** to Léros (2 weekly), Pithagório on Sámos (1 weekly), Pátmos (6 weekly) and Rhodes (daily). **International ferries**: 1–14 boats weekly to Bodrum in Turkey (45min). £13 single, £17 day return, £20 open return, plus Greek port tax.

ASTIPÁLEA Same **ferry** service as Tílos, and Níssiros, plus 2 weekly to Amorgós, Míkonos, Tínos and Síros.

KÁLIMNOS Same **ferry** service as Kós, except only 1 weekly departure for Míkonos, Tínos, Ándhros and Rafína. Expensive afternoon **speedboat** to Kós Town; 2 or 3 daily cheaper **kaikía** to Mastihári, usually via Psérimos. Daily **kaíki** from Mirtiés to Xirókambos on Léros.

LÉROS 7 **ferries** a week to Pireás (12hr), Pátmos (1hr), Kálimnos (2hr), Kós (4hr),and Rhodes (8hr); 1 weekly to Sámos, Ikaría, Híos, Lésvos, Límnos and Kavála/Thessaloníki. Seasonal daily **excursion boats** from Ayía Marína to Lipsí and Pátmos, and from Xirókambos to Mirtiés on Kálimnos.

PÁTMOS Same **ferry** service as Léros, plus daily seasonal **tourist boats** to Sámos, Lipsí, and Maráthi on a daily basis; less often to Arkí.

Flights

KÁRPATHOS 2–7 daily to Rhodes; 3–5 weekly to Kássos; 2/3 weekly to Athens; 1 weekly to Crete (Sitía).

KÁSSOS 2–3 weekly to Kárpathos; 3–7 weekly to Rhodes.

RHODES 4–6 daily to Athens (1hr); 1 daily to Iráklion (40min); 2 daily to Kárpathos (40min); 3–6 weekly to Kássos (40min); 3 weekly to Kastellórizo (45min); 1 daily to Kós (30min;) 1daily to Míkonos (1–2hr); 2 weekly to Lesvos (hr 30min); 3 weekly to Paros (1hr); 4 weekly to Sitía, (45 to 75min); 4 weekly to Thessaloníki (1hr 30min to 3hr); 4 weekly to Thíra (1hr).

KASTELLÓRIZO (MéyÍsti) 2/3 weekly to Rhodes.
KÓS 2 daily to Athens.
LÉROS 3 –7 weekly to Athens.

CHAPTER TEN

THE EAST AND NORTH AEGEAN ISLANDS

The seven substantial islands and four minor islets scattered off the coast of Asia Minor and northeast Greece form a rather arbitrary archipelago. Although there is some similarity in architecture and landscape, virtually the only common denominator is the strong individual character of each island. Despite their proximity to modern Turkey, members of the group bear few signs of an Ottoman heritage, especially when compared to Rhodes and Kós. There's the odd minaret or two, and some of the domestic architecture betrays obvious influences from Constantinople, Thrace and further north in the Balkans, but by and large the enduring Greekness of these islands is testimony to the 4000-year Hellenic presence in Asia Minor, which only ended in 1923.

This heritage is regularly referred to by the Greek government in its propaganda war with the Turks over the sovereignty of these far-flung outposts. The tensions here are, if anything, worse than in the Dodecanese, aggravated by potential undersea oil deposits in the straits between the islands and Turkey. The Turks have also persistently demanded that Límnos, astride the sea lanes to and from the Dardenelles, is demilitarised, but so far Greece has shown no signs of cooperating.

The heavy military presence can be disconcerting, especially for lone woman travellers, and large tracts of land are off-limits as military reserves. But, as in the Dodecanese, local tour operators do a thriving business shuttling passengers for absurdly high tariffs (caused partly by the need for payoffs at both ends) between the easternmost islands and the Turkish coast with its amazing archaeological sites and watering holes, (bear in mind, if you're thinking of making the journey, that, if you have travelled to Greece on a charter flight, your ticket will be invalidated by an overnight stay in Turkey). Many of the islands' main ports and towns are not the quaint picturesque places you may have become used to in other parts of Greece; indeed a number are relatively large and uninteresting university, military and commercal centres. In most cases you should suppress your initial impulse to take the next boat out, and press on into the worthwhile interiors.

Sámos is the most visited of the group, and, if you can leave the crowds behind, is perhaps also the most verdant and beautiful. **Ikaría** to the west is relatively unspoiled, and nearby **Foúrni** is a haven for determined solitaries. **Híos** is culturally interesting, but its natural beauty has been ravaged and the development of tourism has – so far – been deliberately retarded. **Lésvos** is an acquired taste, though once you get a feel for the island you may find it hard to leave – the number of repeat visitors grows yearly. By contrast virtually no foreigners and few Greeks visit **Áyios Evstrátios**, and with good reason. **Límnos** is marginally better, but its appeal is confined mostly to the area around the pretty port town. To the north, Samothráki and Thássos are totally isolated from the others, except via the mainland port Kavála, and it's easiest to visit them en route to or from Istanbul. **Samothráki** has one of the most dramatic seaward

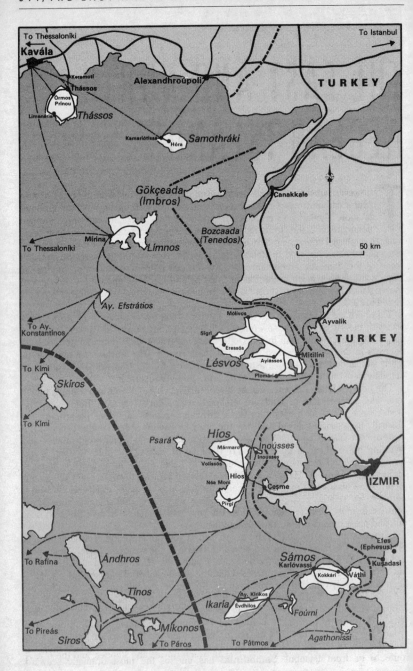

approaches of any Greek island, and one of the more important ancient sites. The appeal of **Thássos** is rather broader, with a varied offering of sandy beaches, forested mountains and minor archaeological sites. Cheaply accessible from the mainland, however, it can be overrun in high season.

Sámos

The lush and seductive island of Sámos was formerly joined to the mainland until sundered from Mount Mycale opposite by Ice Age cataclysms. The strait between the two is now the narrowest distance between the two nations – and heavily militarised.

There's little physical evidence of it today, but Sámos was once the wealthiest island in the Aegean, and, under the patronage of the tyrant Polycrates, home to a thriving intellectual community; Epicurus, Pythagora, Aristarchus and Aesop were among the residents. Decline set in when Classical Athens' star was in the ascendant, though its status was improved somewhat in early Byzantine times when the island constituted its own *theme* (administrative division). Later, towards the end of the fifteenth century, Turkish pirates pillaged and massacred on Sámos, which then remained empty for more than a hundred years until an Ottoman admiral got permission from the sultan to revitalise it with Greek Orthodox settlers, a role which goes far to explain the local identity crisis. Most of the village names are either clan surnames, or adjectives indicating origins elsewhere – constant reminders of refugee status and a rather thin topsoil of culture. There is no genuine Samiote music, dance or dress, and little that's original in the way of cusine and architecture (the latter is a blend of styles from around the Greek mainland and Asia Minor).

The Samiotes compensated somewhat for their deracination by fighting fiercely for independence during the 1820s, but despite their accomplishments in decimating a Turkish fleet in the narrow strait and annihilating a landing army, the Great Powers handed the island back to the Ottomans in 1830, with the consoling proviso that it be semi-autonomous, ruled by an appointed Christian prince. This period, referred to as the *Iyimonía*, was marked by a mild renaissance in fortunes, but union with Greece, the ravages of a bitter World War II occupation and mass emigration effectively reversed that.

Today the Samian economy is increasingly dependent on package tourism, far too much of it in places; the eastern half of the island has pretty much been surrendered to the onslaught of packaged holidaymakers, although the more rugged western part has retained much of its undeveloped grandeur. The rather sedate clientele is overwhelmingly Scandinavian, Dutch and German, couples-orientated, and a far cry from the singles scene of the Cyclades. The absence of an official campsite on such a large island, and phalanxes of self-catering villas, tell you exactly what sort of trade is expected.

Arrival and information

Most ferry lines dock at Vathí, the main town, although a few ferries also dock at Pithagório; the **airport** lies 14km southwest of Vathí, and just 3km from Pithagório. Since the demise of the *Olympic* shuttle coach, you can, if lightly laden, walk to Pithagório to use the reasonable bus service, or take a **taxi** . Taxis are, incidentally, almost impossible to find in Vathí itself, but are your only reasonable options for reaching remote resorts in the southwest of the island.

For travel onwards from Sámos, the most interesting (if also one of the rudest) **agencies** in Vathí is *Pythagoras Tours* (☎0273/27 240), who handle the *Miniotis Line* service to Híos and Foúrni, the *NEL* weekly ferry between Kaválla and Rhodes, and the *G & A*

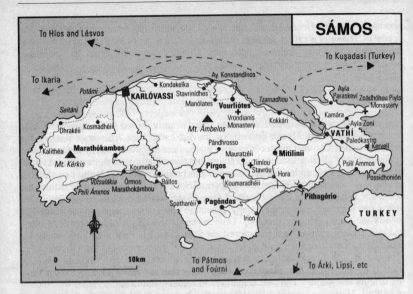

liners to Náxos, Míkonos, Tínos and Síros; they're on the ground floor of the old Catholic church. The *Nissos Kalimnos* line to the Dodecanese is served by an office in Vathí (☎0273/27 337), shared with *Arkadia Lines*; in Pithagório, the municipal **tourism information booth** (☎0273/61 389) sells their tickets as well as dispensing information of a sort. The Vathí **EOT office**, just off the semicircular "Lion" plaza (officially Platía Pithagóras), is fairly useless and open for very limited hours (Mon–Fri 11am–2pm).

Vathí

Lining the steep northeast shore of a deep bay, **VATHÍ** is the main ferry port and provincial capital, founded after 1830 to replace Hóra. It's of minimal interest for the most part, except for an excellent **Archaeological Museum** (Tues–Sun 8.30am–3pm; 500dr), one of the best in Greece, housed in both the old Paskallíon building and a new wing across the way, specially built to house the star exhibit, a majestic, five-metre-tall *kouros*, discovered – like most of the items – out at the Heraion sanctuary. The largest free-standing effigy in the ancient Greek world, despite being dedicated to Apollo, was discovered along with a devotional mirror of Hera, only one of two known in Greece. Other votive offerings of Egyptian design were found simultaneously, proving trade and pilgramage links between Sámos and the Nile delta going back to the eighth century BC. The small-objects collection in the Paskallíon confirms the exotic trend, with visible Mesopotamian and Anatolian influences as well. Most famous are the dozen or so bronze griffin-heads (Sámos was the centre of production in the seventh century); mounted on the edge of bronze *phialai*; they were believed to ward off evil spirits.

The usually malodorous bay is off-limits for swimming. A waterfront curiosity is the old French **Catholic church**, labelled 'ECCLESIA CATOLICA' in Latin, which has been closed except for monthly Masses since 1974 when the last nuns departed the island after having schooled several elite generations since the 1870s. Inland is more rewarding, particularly the museum-like **antique shop** of Mihalis Stavrinos near the lion-square, where if you're feeling flush you can invest in assorted baubles or rescue rare engravings from the silverfish. Still better is **ÁNO VATHÍ**, 150m above sea level, a preserved community of tottering, tile-roofed houses that's the goal of many a day-stroller. Look in at the tiny, central chapel of Áyios Athanásios, with its *témblon* and naive frescoes.

Practicalities

Accommodation proprietors tend not to meet arriving ferries, since so many places are now reserved in advance. Hunting for yourself, the bare-bones options are the waterfront*Parthenon* (π0273/27 234; ②), clean but subject to bar noise from below, or the *Pension Ionia*, a collection of buildings centred around Manóli Kalomíri 5 (π0273/28 782; ②). Try also the *Pension Trova*, Kalomíri 26 (π0273/27 759; ②), or the *Pansion Avli* (π0273/22 939; ②), which offers large rooms in a wonderful old house just above the market. For slightly more comfort, though again prone to noise, the *Artemis*, right off the main lion-square (π0273/27 792; ③), offers rooms with bath. If you can afford it, and can squeeze in between the tour groups, the traditional *Eleana*, 300m north of the ferry jetty at Kefalopoúlou 12 (π0273/28 665; ③), is worth the slight extra cost. If you want to be up the hill a bit, the options are more limited: there's *Pension Pelopidas* at Roíkou 10 (π0273/28 558; ③), also above the dock, but there's only one modest place in Áno Vathí, the *Hotel Aridane G* at Dhimitríou Karídha 2 (π0273/23 320; ③), and it shuts in winter.

When **eating out**, avoid the sleazy places along the central waterfront in favour of less obvious tavernas. *Manolis*, 200m inland from the post office, is a basic grill-fryer with inebriated indoor music sessions in winter and outdoor seating during the warmer months. *Ta Kotopoula*, 250m uphill from here under the giant plane tree at the turnoff for Vlamarí, specialises in roast chicken (as the name implies); it's open from April to October only. Just around the corner, *Fotini Yiannokou*'s grill features cheap main dishes and barrel wine from the village of Idhroússa. If you want a reasonable, convenient lunch before a late afternoon ferry out, *O Stelios*, tucked away a few paces north of the customs building, is acceptable. In the evenings *Psitopolio Alekos*, on the pedestrianised part of the bazaar, is also usually okay. Those willing to spend a bit more might consider *Ta Diodhia*, a kilometre south along the waterfront next to the military garrison, serving pricey but decent seafood at suppertime only. For a more varied, imaginative menu, it's worth driving out 6km west to the hamlet of Kédros, where the *Snack-Bar Ouzerí Yerania* offers such Anatolian-style delicacies as carrot croquettes and *boksadhákia* (bacon-wrapped liver) for reasonable sums. Be warned, though, that quality can suffer in high season, and the place is really at its best in the cooler months (when it's open only Fri and Sat evenings, Sun afternoon).

Vathí **nightlife** revolves around a handful of rather posey bars, with a high management turnover and occasional police closures in response to noise-level complaints. Currently the longest-lived of the summertime pubs is *Number Nine*, on a sea-view terrace at Kefalopoúlou 9 (north of the ferry terminal); this defers to *Cafe Anyway*, almost out of town to the south in Pefkáki district, during the winter months. Another summer favourite is *Cleary's Pub*, Dutch-run by Desireé, just behind the "Lion" plaza.

In terms of transport services, the **KTEL** terminal is a perennially cluttered intersection a block back from the water; service is adequate along the main tourist corridors of Vathí–Kokkári and Vathí–Pithagório, but wretched otherwise. You'll probably want to rent a vechicle at least for a day or two. *Notaras TopCar* is the cheapest place for car rental, although the slightly pricier *Budget*, on the waterfront near the Agricultural Bank, has a larger fleet and better service. For **mopeds and motorbikes**, *Ioannis Azar*, on the water near the Credit Bank, is recommended.

Other amenities of note include several **banks**; an **OTE** office next to the cathedral, open until 11pm much of the year; **Olympic Airways**, roughly halfway between the water and the post office, and two **laundries** – the friendlier (with service wash) is *Alex*, at Yimnasiáarhou Katevéni 17.

Around Vathí

Two kilometres east of Vathí spreads the vast inland plateau of **Vlamarí**, devoted to grapevines and dotted with two hamlets, **AYÍA ZÓNI** and **KAMÁRA**. Both have simple, inexpensive tavernas – *O Kriton* in Kamára is especially recommended. From Kamára you can climb up a cobbled way to the cliff-top monastery of **Zoödhóhou Piyís**, for views across the end of the island to Turkey. At its feet nestles the palm-tree-garnished fishermen's anchorage of **MOURTIÁ**, more picturesque than practical for swimming.

Heading north out of Vathí, the bumpy, narrow road threads through the "Millionaires' Row" of KALÁMI before ending after 6km at the rocky bay of **AYÍ PARASKEVÍ**, where there's another good taverna (*O Fotis*).

Southeast, along the main island loop road, a three-naved chapel marks an important turning, which immediately splits again. Bearing left twice takes you through the hill-top village of **PALEÓKASTRO**, remarkable only for the taverna *Ta Dhilina*, and then beyond within 6km to the quiet, striking bay of **KERVELÍ**, with a small gravel beach, an *ouzerí* and a new hotel. It's not worth proceeding to the road's end at POSSIDHÓNIO, whose tavernas are mediocre and beach nonexistent.

The right-hand option away from Paleókastro leads to the beaches of **MIKÁLI** and **PSILÍ AMMÓS**. The former is in the initial throes of development, with a single taverna and a clutch of villas-to-be behind a kilometre or two of somewhat exposed sand and gravel; the latter (around the headland) is a crowded sandy cove, a featured destination on every tour operator's signboards, with one pre-touristic namesake taverna on the right as you arrive. If you try to swim out to the islet, a tempting target, beware of surprisingly strong currents which crop up in the narrow straits here. There's bus service out here twice daily in season.

Pithagório and around

Most traffic south of Vathí heads for **PITHAGÓRIO**, the island's premier resort, renamed in 1955 to honour its native mathematician. Prior to that it was known as Tigáni (Frying Pan) – in mid-summer you'll learn why. The sixth-century tyrant Polycrates had his capital here, and beyond the cobble-paved core of lanes overshadowed by thick-walled mansions lie acres of archaeological excavations – and dusty modern building sites. The small harbour, fitting more or less into the confines of Polycrates' ancient port, and still using his jetty, is today devoted entirely to pleasure craft and chi-chi bars. Sámos's only surviving attempt at a castle, the nineteenth-century Logothetis *pírgos*, overlooks both the town and the shoreline where this local chieftain commanded decisive victories over the Turks.

Other antiquities include the fairly dull Roman-era **baths** west of town (Tues, Thurs, Fri & Sat 10am–2pm; Wed & Sun 1am–2pm; free), and – much more interesting – the **Evpalínio tunnel**, an aqueduct bored through the mountain just north of Pithagório at the behest of Polycrates. Its midsection has collapsed but you should be able to explore the initial portion of its one-kilometre length with a torch (open sporadic days 10am–1pm). To get there, take the signposted path from the shore road at the west end of town. If you're keen, you can also climb to the five remaining chunks of the Polycratian **perimeter wall**. There's a choice of routes: one leading up from the permanent lagoon west of town, past an **ancient watchtower**, now isolated from any other fortifications, and the other, which is easier, leading from the monastery of **Panayía Spilianí** and the adjacent ancient **amphitheatre**. From the wall fragments atop the hill, you can descend the other side on a jeep track, skirting a military area, to the back opening of the tunnel, which is now being cleaned out and "improved" in anticipation of visits.

If there are any vacancies – and don't count on it in mid-season – **pension** proprietors tend to meet incoming ferries. Otherwise it's a matter of chancing on a spot as you tramp the streets. If you're just waiting for an outbound boat to the Dodecanese, the *Damo* (☎0273/61 303; ④), just above the **OTE** at the base of the ferry jetty, is reasonably quiet if a bit pricey, with sea views. Otherwise there's the *Lakis* apartments (☎0273/61 252; ③), which are good value if you're into self-catering. **Eating out** is frustrating, with value for money a completely alien concept here; you're probably better off going to Hóra or Iréon (see below) for meals. Pithagório also supports two **banks** and a **post office**, both on the main thoroughfare. The flattish country to the west of town is ideal for pedal-bike touring, a popular activity, although if you want to rent a **moped** *Evelin's*, 1500m out of town by the airport junction, is the cheapest and most helpful.

Pithagório's **beach** stretches for several kilometres west of the Logothetis castle, punctuated about halfway along by the end of the airport runway, and the cluster of hotels known as **POTOKÁKI**. Chief of these is the massive but tasteful "Doryssa Bay" complex, which includes a meticulously concocted fake village, guaranteed to confound archaeologists of future eras. No two of the units, joined by named streets, are alike, and there's even a *platía* with an expensive café. If you don't mind the crowds, and the occasional jet overhead, the sand-and-pebble shore is well-groomed and the water clean; if you do, you'll have to head out to the end of the road for some seclusion.

Potokáki is a dead end, with the main island loop road pressing on to the turnoff for the airport and Iréon. Somewhere under today's runway ran the Sacred Way joining the ancient city with the **Heraion**, the massive shrine of the Mother Goddess (Tues–Sun 8.30am–3pm; 500dr), much touted in tourist literature but assuming humbler dimensions – one re-erected column and assorted foundations – as you approach. The modern resort of **IRÉON** nearby is a nondescript grid of dusty streets, though unobjectionable enough except in midsummer. The clientele seems a bit younger, more active and less packaged than in Pithagório, with more independent rooms in evidence; you can also arrange **horse-riding tours** through the surrounding orchards. The most authentic **taverna** is the very last on the end, and there are a series of beach **bars**, the weirdest of which is *To Karavi*, with a mock-up fishing boat as centrepiece.

The island loop road continues to another junction in long, narrow **HÓRA**, the medieval capital and still a lively village packed with military personnel and those working in the nearby tourist industry. It's worth knowing about principally for a handful of **tavernas**, such as *I Sintrofía*, on the road in from Pithagório, a *psistaria* on Platía Ayías Paraskevís, and, most famously, *O Andonis* on the square with the running fountain. None are especially cheap but they are at least better-quality than anything in Pithagório.

Heading straight on from the crossroads takes you through a ravine to **MITILINIÍ**, which initially seems to be an amorphous, working-class sprawl; a brief exploration, however, turns up a fine main square with some atmospheric *kafenía*, a single unmarked taverna opposite them and the island's only remaining indoor **cinema** down a side street. Across from it is the best – if rather overpriced – **copper-antique** store on the island. The **Paleontological Museum** on the top floor of the community offices (Mon–Sat 9am–2pm & 5.30–7pm; 200dr) is essentially a room of barely sorted bones from an Ice Age animal dying-place nearby, and not worth the bother.

The south

Since the circum-island bus only passes through the places below once (sometimes twice) daily, you'll really need your own vechicle to explore them.

Beyond Hóra a turning leads uphill to the monastery of **Timíou Stavroú**, the island's most important monastery, although the annual September 14 festival is more an excuse for a tatty bazaar in the courtyards than any music or feasting. A similarly hidden detour takes off a kilometre further ahead to **MAVRATZÉII**, one of the two

Samian "pottery villages"; this one specialises in *I Koúpa tou Pithagóra*, the "Pythagorean cup", supposedly designed by the sage to leak over the user's lap if he over indulged beyond the "fill" line. More practical wares can be found in **KOUMARADHÉII**, back on the main road. From here you can descend a dirt track past the monastery of **Megális Panayías**, said to contain the finest frescoes on the island but currently closed for restoration, to **MÍLI**, a balmy-winter village submerged in lemon trees, also accessible from the airport. Overhead sprawls **PAGÓNDAS**, a large hillside community with a splendid main square, from where a wild but scenic track curls around the hill to **SPATHARÉII**, rather pokey but set on a natural balcony overlooking the Aegean for the best views this side of the island. From here a road leads back to **PÍRGOS** on the main road, lost in pine forests at the head of a ravine and the centre for Samian honey production. A short distance down the gorge, **KOÚTSI** is a small oasis of plane trees – seventeen of them, according to the sign – shading a gushing spring and a taverna that's an excellent lunch stop if the tour buses haven't beaten you to it.

The rugged and beautiful coast to the south is largely inaccessible, glimpsed by most visitors for the first and last time on the descending airplane in. The lone vehicle approach is via the small village of **KOUMÉÏKA**, with a massive inscribed marble fountain and a couple of *kafenía* in its square. Below extends the long, pebbly bay at **BÁLLOS**, with sand, caves and nudists at the far end. Bállos itself is merely a sleepy collection of summer houses, **rooms** to rent and a few **tavernas**, best of which is the *Cypriot*. Much of the food here is oven-cooked in limited portions; the garrulous couple running it requests advance notice (☎0273/36 394).

There are other tiny coves to the southwest of Bállos, but they are mostly the realm of villas, with no facilities, and not worth the extra trouble to reach. Returning to Kouméïka, the apparently dodgy side road marked "Velanidhiá" is in fact quite passable to any vehicle, and a very useful **short cut** if you're travelling to the beaches around Órmos Marathókambos (see "The West", below).

The north coast

Leaving Vathí on the north coastal section of the island loop road, there's little to stop for until you reach **KOKKÁRI**, the third major Samian tourist centre after Pithagório and the capital. It's also the prime prompter of nostalgia among Sámos regulars; while lower Vathí and Pithagório had little beauty to sacrifice, much has been irrevocably lost here. The town profile, covering two knolls behind twin headlands, is still recognisable, and, amazingly, several families still doggedly untangle their fishnets on the quay, lending some credence to brochure touting of the place as a "fishing village". But in general its identity has been altered beyond recognition. It's now an elegant stage set, expanding slowly inland over vineyards and the abandoned onion fields that gave the place its name. With exposed, uncomfortably rocky beaches close by, buffeted by near-constant winds, it seems an unlikely candidate for further gentrification, although its Germanic promoters seem to have made a virtue of necessity by developing it as a highly successful windsurfing centre.

If you'd like to stay in Kokkári, Yiorgos Mihelios (☎0273/92 456; ③) has a broad range of **rooms** and flats to rent. **Tavernas** are attractively set along the waterfront: *Tó Kima* is the oldest and one of the more reliable ones on the west end of the quay, with a row of newer establishments worth a try at the east extreme. Further inland, on the new bypass road, *To Hrisso Vareli* is more authentic than anything in the town itself. Kokkári now has a short-hours **bank**, an **OTE** portakabin, a **laundry** and the island's only **outdoor cinema**.

The closest half-decent beaches are thirty to forty minutes' walk away to the west, with canoes and windsurfers to rent. **Lemonákia** is a bit too close to the road, with an obtrusive café; the graceful crescent of **Tzamadhoú** (as in Coleridge's Xanadu) figures in virtually every EOT poster of the island. It's a bit more natural, with path-only access, a spring sustaining the large colony of freelance campers, and an expensive but hidden taverna up in the vineyards. The western end of the saucer-shaped-pebble beach is by tacit consensus clothing-optional. There's one more pebbly bay west of **AVLÁKIA** (a mostly Greek resort 6km from Kokkári), called **Tzaboú**, but unless you're passing by and want a quick dip it's not worth a special trip.

Inland between Kokkári and Karlóvassi, an idyllic landscape of pine, cypress and orchards is overawed by dramatic, often cloud-shrouded mountains. Excursions into this quintessentially Romantic countryside are accordingly popular. Despite destructive nibblings by bulldozers, some of the **trail system** linking the various inland villages is still intact, and you can walk for as long or little as you like, returning to the main highway to catch a bus home. Failing that, most of the communities can provide a bed on short notice.

The monastery of **Vrondianís** (Vrondá) is a popular destination, although since the army now uses it as a barracks, the place only really comes alive on the September 8 festival, when *yiórti* – a special cereal-and-meat stew – may be served. **VOURLIÓTES**, a typical hill village of tile-roofed houses sporting beaked chimneys and brightly painted shutters, has a photogenic central square, where the best of several **tavernas** is *Snack Bar I Kiki*, with its two local specialities – *revithokeftédhes* (chickpea patties) and homemade *moskháto* wine, so sweet and heavy that you'll have to dilute it with soda water. (The other Samian delicacy worth trying if you've access to a kitchen are the excellent sausages available from select butchers.) **MANOLÁTES**, further uphill but an hour across a deep river canyon, also has a simple taverna or two, and is the most popular trailhead for the four-hour round-trip up **Mount Ámbelos**, Samos's second highest summit.

From Manolátes you can no longer walk over to STAVRINÍDHES by foot, since the trail was destroyed in 1991, but must plunge straight down, partly on a cobble path, through the shade-drenched gully known as "Aïdhónia" (Nightingales) to **PLATANÁKIA**, with a handful of **tavernas** and **rooms**. *O Paradhisos* is worth eating at here mainly because of their excellent barrel wine, nearly impossible to get on Sámos and always better than the vastly overrated and essentially undrinkable bottled stuff from the co-op.

Platanákia is actually the eastern suburb of **ÁYIOS KONSTANDÍNOS** proper, a case study in arrested touristic development. The surf-pounded esplanade is in a seemingly permanent state of excavation, and there are no usable beaches within walking distance, so the collection of warm-toned stone buildings (increasingly adulterated by concrete blocks) serves as a more peaceful alternative to Kokkári. In addition to modest old standby **hotels** such as the *Ariadne* (✆0273/94 205; ③), the *Four Seasons* and the *Atlantis* (✆0273/94 329; ②) up on the highway, there's a new generation of **rooms** in the numerous concrete blocks, and the **tavernas** of Platanákia – if the two here don't appeal – are not far away.

Once past "Áyios" (as the bus conductors habitually bellow it out), the mountains hem the road in against the sea, and the landscape doesn't relent until near **Kondakéïka**, worth a visit at dusk for its fabulous sunsets, after which you can descend to its diminutive shore annexe **Áyios Nikólaos** for excellent fish suppers.

Karlóvassi

KARLÓVASSI, the second town of Sámos, divides into no less than four, generally unattractive districts: Néo, whose untidy growth was spurred by the influx of post-1923 refugees; Meséo, across the usually dry river bed, draped appealingly on a knoll; and postcard-worthy Paleó, perched above Limáni, the small harbour. Undistinguished as it is, Karlóvassi makes an excellent base from which to explore the west of the island; the name, incidentally, despite a vehement lack of Ottoman legacy elsewhere on Sámos, appears to be a corruption of the Turkish for "snowy plain" – the plain in question being the conspicuous saddle of Mount Kérkis beyond, which is indeed snow-covered in a harsh winter.

Most tourists stay at or near **LIMÁNI**, which has an array of **rooms** and two **hotels**: one luxury, one modest – the *Aktaion* (☎0273/32 356; ②), a neoclassical shoreline relic open only in high season. The port itself, its quay pedestrianised by night, is an appealing place with a boat-building industry at the far end, and all the **ferry ticket agencies** grouped together nearby. **Tavernas** and **bars** are abundant, but steeply priced; only *Andreas*, the first in line, is reasonable and reliably open at lunchtime.

Immediately overhead, the partly hidden hamlet of **PALEÓ** is deceptively large, its hundred or so houses draped on either side of a leafy ravine. The only amenity is the sporadically functioning café *To Mikro Parisi*, which prepares food in summer, and a seasonal taverna on the path down towards **MESÉO**. The latter is a conceivable alternative to Limáni for staying, with one **pension** just behind the playground, and other rooms scattered through the intervening half-kilometre between here and the sea. Lost in the residential streets near the top of Meséo's hill is a simple but satisfying **taverna**, *O Kotronis*, while down on the small square there's an excellent *ouzerí, Para Pende*, the haunt of oldies and Karlóvassi's small university contingent alike. Following the street linking the square to the waterfront, you pass one of the improbably huge turn-of-the-century churches, topped with twin belfries and a blue-and-white dome, which dot the coastal plain here. Just at the intersection with the harbour frontage road you'll find the excellent *Ouzerí To Kima*, the best place in town to watch the sunset over a *pikilía* (the house *mezé* medley).

NÉO has little to recommend it, except for a wilderness of derelict warehouses and mansions down near the river-mouth, reminders of the long-gone local tanning industry which flourished here during the first half of this century. However you'll almost certainly at some point visit one of the two **banks**, the **post office**, **OTE** or the impromptu **KTEL** stop on the main square. Some, though not all, of the departures from Vathí continue down to the harbour; enquire about details. In summer a horse-and-buggy shuttle between Limáni and Néo sometimes functions. While waiting for a bus, one of two traditional **kafenía** might interest you: *O Kleanthis*, on the lower *platia*, or *O Kerketevs*, by the upper *platía*. Any enforced stop in Néo, or Karlóvassi in general, is mitigated somewhat by the fact that the people are a good deal friendlier than in the east of the island.

The west

Visitors put up with Karlóvassi's dullness partly for the sake of western Samos's excellent **beaches**, the closest being **Potámi**, forty minutes on the coast road from LIMÁNI or an hour by a more scenic trail from Paleó. This broad arc of sand and pebbles, flecked at one end with tide-lashed rocks (and a hideous blufftop chapel), gets crowded at summer weekends; near the end of the trail from Paleó stands *To Iliovasilima*, a reasonable and friendly fish **taverna**. There are a few **rooms**, but most of the individuals staying here are **free-camping** up the year-round river that gives the beach its name. A path leads twenty minutes inland, past the eleventh-century church of **Metamorfosís** – the oldest on Sámos – and the tents, to an apparent dead end. From here on you must swim and wade in heart-stoppingly cold water through a fern-tufted rock gallery to a series of **pools and waterfalls**; bring trainers with good tread and maybe rope if you want to explore past the first cascade. You probably won't be alone until the trail's end, since the canyon is well-known to locals and even included in certain tour companies' "Jeep Safaris".

The coast beyond Potámi is the most beautiful and unspoiled on Sámos, supposedly the core of a monk seal refuge which may never in fact have received official sanction. The dirt track at the far end of Potámi bay ends after twenty minutes of walking (or five of driving), from which point you backtrack slightly to find the side trail which runs parallel to the water. Within twenty minutes you'll arrive at **Mikró Seïtáni**, a small pebble cove guarded by sculpted rock walls, and a full hour's walk through ancient olive terraces takes you to **Megálo Seïtáni**, the island's finest beach, at the mouth of an awe-inspiring gorge. You'll have to bring food and water along, though not a swimsuit – there's no dress code here.

Heading south out of Karlóvassi on the loop road, the first place you'd be tempted to stop is **MARATHÓKAMBOS**, a pretty, amphitheatrical village overlooking the epony-mous gulf; there's a **taverna** or two, but no short-term accommodation. **ÓRMOS**, its port, is in the throes of tourist development, though some character shines through in its back alleys and a slow traffic in *kaíkia* shipping bricks to the Dodecanese. The least expensive and most peaceful of a meagre selection of shoreline **tavernas** is *Ormos*, out near the gravel/shingle beach. For better **beaches**, you'll have to continue with the twice-daily bus or under your own power 2km west to **Votsalákia**, Samos' longest, though not perhaps most beautiful beach. Its appeal has been diminished in recent years by wall-to-wall **rooms**, **apartments** and on the whole rather poor **tavernas** behind it, but it's still a vast improvement on the Pithagório environs, and the hulking mass of 1433-metre **Mount Kérkis** behind rarely fails to impress.

If Votsalákia is not to your taste, you can continue a couple of kilometres past the end of the asphalt to **PSILÍ ÁMMOS**, considerably more scenic and not to be confused with its namesake on the other side of the island. The sea shelves gently here – ridiculously so, as you're still knee-high a hundred paces out – and cliffs shelter clusters of naturists from prying eyes. Surprisingly there are only two **tavernas**, one just built, up in the pines. If you want to stay in the immediate area, make for **LIMNNIÓNAS**, a smaller cove 2km west with **rooms** as well as eateries. Swimming there, though, is complicated by a rock shelf slimy with seaweed and the occasional sea urchin, and if you're based in Votsalákia or further afield it's not worth the extra effort to get to.

Gazing up from a supine seaside position, some people are inspired to go and **climb Mount Kérkis** (Kerketévs). The classic route begins just before the end of the asphalt road in Votsalákia, signposted for the convent of **Evangelístria**. After an initial half-hour on tracks through the olive groves, past men tending charcoal pits (a major indus-try hereabouts), the marked path begins in earnest, more or less following power lines up to the convent. One of four friendly nuns will proffer a welcoming *oúzo* and point you up the fairly well blazed continuation up to the peak. The views are tremendous, as you'd expect, though the climb is humdrum once you're out of the trees. Near the top, there's a chapel and, just beyond, in wet years, a welcome spring. Elation at attaining the summit may be tempered somewhat by the knowledge that here on August 3, 1989, one of the worst Greek aviation disasters ever occurred here, when an aircraft flying out of Thessaloníki slammed into the mist-cloaked summit with the loss of all 34 aboard. All told it's a five-to-six-hour outing, there and back, not counting any rests.

Less ambitious walkers might want to circle the base of the mountain, first by vehicle and then by foot. A sturdy dirt bike (*not* a moped), or the twice-weekly noon bus, nego-iates the rough road to **KALLITHÉA** and **DHRAKÉII**, truly back-of-beyond villages with views across to Ikaría. You then proceed from the latter along the majestic two-hour trail down to Megálo Seïtáni, from where it's easy enough to continue to Karlóvassi. People doing this in reverse discover to their cost that the bus (if any; more likely during school term) goes back from Dhrakéii rather early – 2.45pm – compelling them to stay overnight at the expensive **xenónas** in Kallithéa, and dine at the simple *sistariá*. There are no facilities in Dhrakéii except for a *kafenío*, and the only possible spot for a swim is the remote fishing anchorage and boatyard at **Áyios Isídhoros**.

Ikaría

Ikaría, a narrow, windswept landmass between Sámos and Míkonos, is little visited and invariably underestimated or dismissed by travel writers, who usually haven't even gone to see for themselves. Its name is supposed to derive from the unexpected appearance of Icarus, who fell into the sea just offshore after the wax bindings on his wings melted; and (as some locals are quick to point out) the island is clearly wing-shaped.

For years the only substantial tourism was generated by a number of radioactive hot springs on the south coast, some reputed to cure rheumatism and arthritis, some to make women fertile, though others are so potent that they've been closed for some time. The unnerving dockside sign which once read "Welcome to the Island of Radiation" has now been replaced by one proclaiming "Welcome to Icarus' Island", with an extra tag celebrating an aviation jamboree of a few years ago.

Ikaría, along with Lésvos and Sámos, is also one of the Greek Left's strongholds, a tendency accentuated during the long decades of right-wing domination in Greece, when (as in prior ages) the island was used as a place of exile for political dissidents. Apparently the strategy backfired, with the transportees outnumbering, and proseletys-ing, their hosts; at the same time, many Ikarians emigrated to North America, and iron-ically their regular capitalist remittances help keep the island going. It can be a bizarre experience to be treated to a monologue on the evils of US imperialism, delivered by a retiree in perfect Alabaman English.

These are not the only Ikarian quirks, and for many the place is an acquired taste. It is not a strikingly beautiful island except for the forested portions of the northwest; the coastline drops steeply in cliffs and most of the landscape is scrub-coated schist though there is ample ground water. Neither are there many picturesque villages since the rural schist-roofed houses are generally scattered so as to be next to their famous apricot orchards, vineyards and fields, while the community store or taverna is equally hidden. Finally, the people, while not unfriendly – quite the contrary in fact – have resisted most attempts to develop Ikaría for conventional tourism, which splutters along principally between July and September; an airport planned for the northeast tip has got little past the talk stage and won't happen before 1996. Long periods of seem-ingly punitive neglect by Athens has made the locals profoundly self-sufficient and idio-syncratic, and tolerant of the same in others.

Áyios Kírikos

Most though not all ferries call at the south-coast port and capital of **ÁYIOS KÍRIKOS** 2km either side of which are the pair of thermal resorts noted above. Because of the spa trade, beds are at a premium in town; arriving in the evening, as is often the case accept any offers of rooms at the jetty, or – if in a group – proposals of an immediate taxi ride to the north coast, which won't be much more than 5000dr per vehicle to the end of the line. **Buses** set out across the island, in theory, at 9am and noon, but both the bus stop (on the main square) and the vehicle itself are poorly marked, and the service may terminate without explanation well short of the main northern resort of Armenistís.

If you decide to **stay**, there are several hotels – for example the _Isabella_ (☎0275/2 238; ④), or the _Akti_ (☎0275/22 064; ③), on a knoll east of the fishing quay, with view of Foúrni from the garden. Rented rooms fill fast and are not especially cheap: _Adam Pension_ (☎0275/22 418; ③) is about the fanciest of these, and there are three unmarked, spartan ones grouped around the **post office** on Odhós Dhionísou, the inland high street. There are also two **banks**, a limited-hours **OTE**, and assorted ferry **agents**, the most helpful being _Dolihi Tours_ – though all are coy about the daily noon

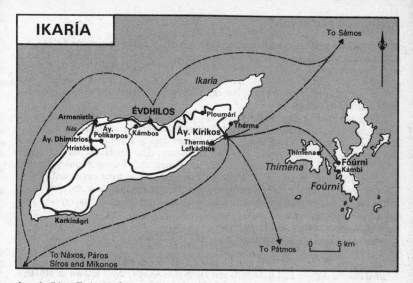

time *kaíki* to Foúrni, whose tickets are sold on board. You can **rent** motorbikes and cars here too, but both are cheaper in Armenistís.

Eating out, you've a better choice than in lodging. On the way from the ferry to the main square you'll pass the barn-like *Ta Adhelfia* and *Seafood Snack Bar*, open only in the evenings; *Snack Bar Psistaria*, inland toward the post office, is a combination *ouzerí* and *loukamádhiko*, while the tiny grill *I Samos*, across from *Dolihi Tours*, is good for *mezé* and the strong local wine. Finally, the giant *I Sinantisi* two doors down is utterly unlike any other *kafenío* in the Greek islands: in a reversal of the norm, young adults play *távli* and cards inside, while outside their elders and assorted foreigners suck on sweets or watch each other – better entertainment by far than anything dished up at the summer cinema.

Évdhilos and around

The twisty road from Áyios Kírikos to Évdhilos is one of the most exhilarating on any Greek island, and the long ridge which extends the length of Ikaría often wears a streamer of cloud, even when the rest of the Aegean sky is clear. KARAVÓSTAMO, with its tiny port, is the first substantial north-coastal place, and has a series of three beaches leading up to **ÉVDHILOS**. Though the island's second town and a ferry stop at least twice weekly in summer, this is considerably less equipped to deal with visitors than Áyios Kírikos. There are two **hotels**, the *Evdoxia* on the slope west of the harbour, and the *Georgios* (☎0275/31 218; ③), plus a few **rooms**. Of the pair of waterfront **restaurants**, *O Kokkos* has the fuller menu but is expensive; try *O Flisvos* next door instead. A **post office** and **OTE**, and a surprisingly good town beach to the east, are also worth knowing about.

KÁMBOS, 2km west, has a small museum with finds from nearby **ancient Oinae**, the sparse ruins of a Byzantine palace used to house disgraced nobles, plus an evening taverna and a large beach; it's also the start and end point of a road loop up through the hamlet-speckled valley inland. MARATHÓ isn't up to much but FRANDÁTO has a summertime taverna; STÉLI and DHÁFNI are good, attractive examples of the little oases which sprout on Ikaría.

Armenistís and beyond

Most travellers won't stop until reaching **ARMENISTÍS**, 57km from Áyios Kírikos, and with good reason: this little resort lies in the heart of Ikaría's finest wooded scenery, with two enormous, sandy beaches – **Livádhi** and **Messakhtí** – five and fifteen minutes' walk east respectively. Numerous campers in the marshes behind each stretch set the tone for the place, but the islanders' tolerance doesn't yet extend to nude bathing, as signs warn you.

Armenistís itself is tiny, and reminiscent of similar youth-orientated spots on the south coast of Crete, though lately gentrification has definitely set in. A disco operates seasonally behind the nearer beach, but nights are mostly about extended sessions in the tavernas and cafés overlooking the anchorage. The *Paskhalia* taverna/rooms (☎0275/41 403; ③) is the cleanest in both categories, with bathed doubles the local standard; the food, including full breakfasts, is good too, and not exorbitant. Should you require more luxury, there's the *Armena Inn* well up the hillside or the new, luxury *Cavos Bay Hotel* (☎0275/41 449; ④) a kilometre or so west. A giant bakery/cake shop caters to sweet teeth for the entire west end of the island, and the *Marabou* travel agency changes money and rents clapped-out mopeds and somewhat sturdier jeeps, although you don't really need either, since the best of Ikaría lies within an hour's walk of the port.

Armenistís is actually the shore annexe of three inland hamlets – ÁYIOS DHIMITRIOS, ÁYIOS POLÍCARPOS and HRISTÓS – collectively known as **RÁHES**. Despite the modern dirt roads in through the pines, they still retain a certain Shangri-La quality, with the older residents speaking a positively Homeric dialect. On an island not short of foibles, Hristós is particularly strange, in which the locals sleep most of the day and send their children to school at night. Near the pokey main square there's a **post office** and a **hotel/restaurant**, but for lunch you'll have to scrounge something at one of the odd *kafenía*, where the slightly spaced-out demeanours of those serving may be attributable to over-indulgence in the excellent home-brewed **wine** which everyone west of Évdhilos makes – strong but hangover-free, and stored in rather disgusting goat-skins which are also used as shoulder bags, sold in some shops.

By tacit consent the hippies, naturists and Greek dope fiends have been allowed to shift 4km west of Armenistís to **Nás**, a tree-clogged river canyon ending in a small but sheltered pebble beach. The little bay is nearly enclosed by weirdly sculpted rock formations, and signs warn you not to swim outside cove limits – sound advice as there have been drownings hereabouts. Other signs are duly ignored, such as the one forbidding access to the impressive foundations of the fifth-century temple of **Artemis Tavropolio** (Patroness of Bulls), overlooking the permanent deep pool at the mouth of the river, or the "no camping" notices defied by a large community of tents upstream. If you continue 45 minutes along this, Ikaría's only year-round watercourse, you'll find secluded rock pools for freshwater dips. Back by the path leading down to the beach from the road are two or three tavernas and as many **rooms** – for instance *Pension Nas* (☎0275/41 255; ②).

Should you be persuaded to rent a vehicle from *Marabou* or join one of their jeep safaris, either will take you through half a dozen villages at the southwest tip of the island. **VRAKÁDES**, with two *kafenía* and a natural-balcony setting, makes a good first or last stop on a tour. A sharp drop below it, the impact of the empty convent of **Evangelistrías** (not to be confused with its namesake above Hristós) lies mostly in its setting amidst gardens overlooking the sea. Nearby **AMÁLO** has two summer tavernas.

The puny mopeds will go down *from* Langádha *to* KÁLAMOS, not the other way around; in any case it's a tough bike that gets all the way to **KARKINÁGRI**, built at the base of cliffs near the southern extremity of Ikaría and a dismal anticlimax to a journey out here. The only thing likely to bring a smile to your lips is the marked intersection of Leofóros Bakunin and Odhós Lenin – surely the only one in Greece – at the edge of town, which boasts two sleepy, seasonal tavernas and a rooms establishment near the jetty. Before the road was opened (the continuation to Manganítis and Áyios Kírikos is stalled at an unblastable rock-face), Karkinágri's only easy link with the outside world was by ferry or *kaíki*, both of which still call at odd intervals in season.

The sole drawback to staying in Armenistís is **getting away**: taxis and buses are elusive and even wealthier travellers may find themselves hitching to Évdhilos or beyond. Lifts, as throughout the island, are generally easy to get, though you should allow a few hours leeway for catching your ferry. Theoretically **buses** descend from Ráhes headed at least as far as Évdhilos – sometimes to Áyios Kírikos – at 7am and 11am, but school kids have priority on the early departure, and the second one is extremely unreliable even by Ikarian standards.

Satellite islands: Foúrni and Thímena

The straits between Sámos or Ikaría are littered with a number of spidery-looking islets. The only ones permanently inhabited are Thímena and Foúrni, the latter home to a huge fishing fleet and one of the more thriving boatyards in the Aegean. As a result of these, and the recent improvement of the jetty to receive car ferries, **FOÚRNI**'s population is stable, unlike so many small Greek islands. The islets were once the lair of Algerian pirates, and indeed many of the islanders have a distinctly North African appearance.

Apart from the remote hamlet of Hrissomiliá in the north, where the island's only road accessible by motor goes, most inhabitants are concentrated in the port and Kámbi hamlet just south. The harbour community is larger than it looks from the sea, with a feel – including the friendliness of the people – reminiscent of 1970s Greece.

There are several **rooms** establishments, the most basic and inexpensive, with cold showers, being those owned by Kostas Ahladhis (✆0275/51 268; ②), immediately to your left as you disembark. Two other waterfront rooms establishments have more amenities, and if these are full you can head inland to the modern blocks of *Evtihia Amoryianou* (✆0275/51 364; ③) or *Maouni* (✆0275/51 367; ③).

Of the three waterfront **tavernas**, the most consistently open and tasty is *O Miltos*, which serves big breakfasts, while *Rementzo* next door is a decent alternative; if you're lucky the local *astakós* or Aegean lobster, actually an oversized saltwater crayfish, may be on the menu. The central "high street", fieldstoned and mulberry-shaded, ends well inland at a little *platía* with a handful of more conventional *kafenía* and a **post office** where you can change money.

Most of the interior appears desolate, except for a lone monastery high above the port; it's best to stay close to the coast. Fifteen minutes of walking south, skirting the cemetery above the harbour and then slipping over the windmill ridge, brings you to **KÁMBI**, a scattered community overlooking a pair of sandy, tamarisk-shaded coves which you'll share with chickens and fishing boats. There are two cafés, the upper one providing filling snacks, the lower one controlling seven **rooms** that are admittedly spartan but have arguably the best views on the island; another family also has some cottages to let. The path continues towards the south end of the island, passing more isolated, sandy bays, which like Kámbi proper are preferred anchorages for wandering yachts.

Heading in the opposite direction via steps, followed by a trail away from the harbour, you'll find more **beaches**: an average one at the fish-processing plant, plus two better ones further on, following the path. Beyond here the coast is beachless and largely inaccessible all the way to the 25 or so houses of HRISSOMILIÁ.

THÍMENA has one tiny hillside settlement, at which the regular *kaíki* calls on its way between Ikaría and Foúrni, but no tourist facilities whatsoever. This **kaíki**, incidentally, leaves Ikaria at about 1pm, stays overnight at Foúrni and returns the next morning. The twice-weekly *kaíki* from Karlóvassi and the larger car ferries which appear at odd intervals are likewise not tourist excursion boats but exist for the benefit of the islanders, so in any case you must plan to stay at least one night.

Híos

"Craggy Hios", as Homer aptly described his (probable) birthplace, has an eventful history and a strong sense of place. It has always been relatively prosperous, in medieval times through the export of mastic and later by virtue of several shipping dynasties. The maritime mandarins and the military authorities have in the past not encouraged tourism, but with the worldwide shipping crisis, resistance is dwindling. Increasing numbers of foreigners are discovering a Híos beyond its large port capital – fascinating villages, an important Byzantine monument and a fair complement of beaches. While not yet heavily over-run with tourists, the local scene has a definitely modernised flavour, courtesy of returned expatriates, and English is widely spoken.

Sadly, the island has suffered more than its fair share of catastrophes in the past two centuries. The Turks perpetrated their most famous, if not their worst, anti-revolutionary atrocity here in 1822, massacring 30,000 Hiotes and enslaving or exiling even more. In 1881, much of Híos was destroyed by a violent earthquake, and throughout the 1980s the natural beauty of the island has been markedly diminished by a series of comprehensive forest fires, which were the culmination of the depredations of generations of shipbuilders. Only in the far north (around Ayiásmata and Amádhes) and the far south (where there's little to burn) have the woods remained unscathed.

In 1988 the first weekly charters from Northern Europe were instituted, an event that signals equally momentous changes for Híos. Unfortunately there are only about 2500 guest beds at present on the entire island, with a concentration in or near the main town. Hotels and rooms are proliferating at a dizzying rate, but barely fast enough – some properties are block-booked by tour operators while still at the foundation stage.

Híos Town

HÍOS TOWN, the harbour city, will come as a shock after other modest island capitals; it's a bustling, concrete-laced commercial centre, with little predating the 1881 earthquake. Any time spent exploring is amply repaid, however, with a large and fascinating bazaar, a museum or two, some good and authentic tavernas, and on the waterfront Greece's largest evening *volta* (promenade).

The marvellously vibrant **bazaar** extends south and east of the main square, officially Plastíra but known universally as **Vournakíou**. The old **mosque** (Tues–Sun 10am–1pm; free) opposite the Vournakíou taxi rank is now used as an archaeological warehouse and workshop, littered with marble fragments and Turkish, Jewish and Armenian gravestones. The actual **Archaeological Museum**, at Porfirá 4 behind the Handris hotel (Tues–Sun 9am–3pm; 400dr), contains a rather limp assortment of Hellenistic relics, coins and finds from Káto Fána. More worthwhile is the **Argenti Museum** (Mon–Fri 8am–2pm & Fri 5–7pm, Sat 8am–noon; free), housed on the top floor of the Koraï Library building at Koraï 2 and endowed by a leading Hiote family. Accordingly there's a rather ponderous gallery of Argenti genealogical portraits, showing if nothing else the local aristocracy's compulsion to ape English dress and artistic conventions in every era. The other wing boasts a hall of costumes and embroidery, kitsch figurines in traditional dress, and carved wooden objects from the time when the island was more forested. Among multiple replicas of Delacroix's *Massacre at Hios* are engravings of eighteenth-century islanders and several views of the Genoese *kástro*,

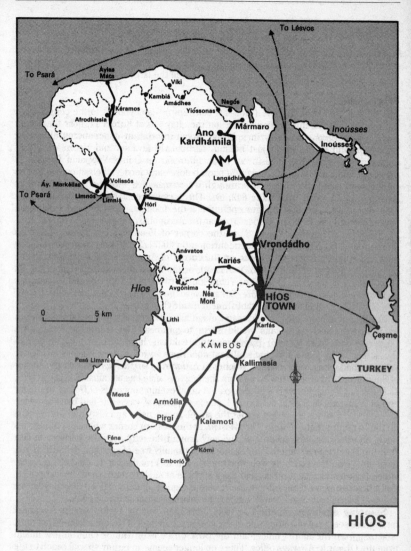

To Lésvos

To Psará

Áyios Máta

Víki

Kambiá

Amádhes

Kéramos

Nagós

Afrodhíssia

Yióssonas

Mármaro

Áno Kardhámila

Inoússes

Inoússes

Áy. Merkélias

Volissós

Langádhia

To Psará

Limnós

Limniá

Hóri

Vrondádho

Anávatos

Kariés

Híos

Avgónima

Néa Moní

HÍOS TOWN

0   5 km

Líthi

Karfás

Çeşme

KÁMBOS

Pasá Limaniá

Kallimasía

TURKEY

Mestá

Armólia

Pirgí

Kalamotí

Fána

Kómi

Emborió

HÍOS

which, until the earthquake, was quite clearly intact; thereafter developers razed the seaward walls, filled in the moat to the south and made a fortune selling off the real estate created around present-day Platía Vournakíou. You can enter the **kástro** at the gate giving on to the square next to the town hall. It's home these days to a small **Byzantine Museum** (Tues–Sun 9am–8pm; free), up some stairs in a medieval structure, housing a satisfying collection of unusual local icons and mosaics. The **old quarter** inside the castle walls, formerly the Turkish and Jewish neighbourhoods, is well worth a wander; among the wood-and-plaster houses are assorted Turkish monuments in various states of decay, including a few dry inscribed fountains and a former dervish convent converted into a church after 1923. The Ottomans relinquished control of Híos, like all of the islands covered in this chapter, only in 1912.

Finally, the **Omírio**, on the south side of Platía Vournakíou, is a cultural centre and events hall well worth looking in at: there are changing exhibitions, and foreign artists often come here after a stop in Athens to perform in the large auditorium.

Practicalities

The helpful official **EOT** office (Mon–Fri 8am–2pm) – as opposed to the conspicuous but private "Tourist Information Office" on the quay – is at Kanári 11, near the *Ionian and Popular Bank*. Relatively inexpensive **accommodation** concentrates along the waterfront and in the alleys just behind, particularly Livánou and Venizélou. Rock-bottom is the exceedingly basic but clean *Filoxenia* on Odhós Voupálou (☎0271/22 813; ②), really only for quick overnight stays before early ferries; the same goes for the conspicuous *Acropolis* on the quay, though it's co-managed with the more salubrious *Apollonio* just behind (☎0271/24 842; ③). The various pensions are better value for extended stays. The best budget options are the friendly, New Zealander-managed *Rooms with a View* (☎0271/20 364; ②), near the Acropolis, or the cramped but accepta-ble *Welcome* at Neofítou Vámva 3, on the corner of Venizélou (no phone; ②). With more money, try *Neoclassico* at Koundouriótou 6 (☎0271/23 297; ③), with painted ceil-ings and a huge garden, the *Anesis*, on the corner of Aplotarías and Vassilikári in the bazaar but quiet at night (☎0271/24 572; ③), or the *Ionia* at Prokymea (Quayside) 98 (☎0271/22 759; ③). The *Tsouklis* at Venizélou 72 (☎0271/24 730; ③), and *Taousannis* at Livánou 42–46 (☎0271/27 433; ③), are also good. The *Rodhon*, at Zaharíou 17 (☎0271/24 335; ③) is the only establishment inside the castle.

Eating out is more pleasurable than the initially obvious rash of fast-food places run by returned Greek-Americans would seem to promise. For tremendous yoghurts (imported daily from Mitilíni), puddings and breakfasts, head for the milkshop behind the *Acropolis/Apollonio* inns; the stall next door does *loukoumádhes*. Further into town, you get good, cheap oven-cooked lunches at *Estiatorio Dhimitrakopoulos* on the corner of Sgoutá and Valtarías, a few steps from the long-distance bus terminal. For carnivores, *O Thiveos* at Venizélou 80 is a decent grill. A good evening option is *O Hotzas*, at the far end of the bazaar at Stefánou Tsourí 74, an excellent *mezé*, casserole and barrelled-wine taverna with a summer garden across the street. Inexpensive and tasty night-only-spots on the harbour are the *Ouzerí Theodhosiou*, at the western corner where the big ferries dock, and the nameless taverna all the way around the jetty near the harbour mouth (not the Handris end) and fishing anchorage, blissfully free of cars and exhaust. If you have your own transport it's well worth a trip out to Vrondádhos to dine at *To Kyma*, which features excellent pizzas and daily specials at slightly more than typical prices. For a before-or-after-dinner drink, the *Iviskos* is a good modern café on the quay with a range of juices, coffee and booze, but just one of many other bars and pubs.

Shipping agencies, whether for the short hop over to Turkey or the long-haul ferries, are scattered on either side of the customs building; **OTE**, open 6am–11pm only, is across from the tourist office, and the **post office** is on Odhós Omírou just inland from the **Olympic Airways** office. There no longer seems to be any special coach to the airport, 4km south, so you should take a blue **urban bus** marked "KALLIMASIA" from the terminal on the north side of the public gardens which take up much of Platía Vournakíou. **Karfás**, also reached by frequent blue bus services, is the closest decent beach to town, 7km away, though be warned that the sand is now dwarfed by massive new developments behind. The standard green **long-distance buses** leave from a terminal on the opposite side of the park, behind the *Omírio*, though services to the centre and northwest of the island are particularly sparse, so it's well worth renting a moped or car, or sharing a taxi (a very common practice). Among **car rental** agencies, the *Europcar* franchise on Evyeníou Handrí (☎0271/29 754) can be recommended.

Southern Híos

The dry valleys of the southern part of the island are home to the mastic bush, *Pistacia lentisca* to be precise, which here alone in Greece produces an aromatic gum of marketable quantity and quality. The plant itself resembles an ugly miniature baobab, but the resin scraped from it was for centuries the base of paints, cosmetics and chewable jelly beans which became a somewhat addictive staple in Ottoman harems. Indeed the interruption of the flow of mastic from Híos to Istanbul by the revolt of 1821 was one of the root causes of the brutal Ottoman reaction the next year. The wealth engendered by the mastic trade supported a half-dozen *mastihohoriá* (mastic villages) from the time the Genoese set up a monopoly in the substance during the fourteenth and fifteenth centuries, but the end of imperial Turkey, and the industrial revolution with its petroleum products, knocked the bottom out of the mastic market. Now it's just a curiosity, to be chewed – try the sweetened *Elma* brand gum – or drunk as a liqueur called *Mastiha*, and the *mastihohoriá* live mainly off their tangerines, apricots and olives. The towns themselves, the only settlements on Híos spared in 1822, are architecturally unique, planned by the Genoese but distinctly Middle-Eastern-looking, and at the first opportunity you should jump on a bus headed in their direction.

Once past the turnoff for VAVÍLI and its Byzantine church of **Panyía Krína**, you'll reach **ARMOLIÁ**, the first, smallest and least imposing of the mastic villages. Its main virtue is a pottery industry – two-thirds kitsch, one-third useful objects – and two café-snack bars: the *Kástro* on the road, and another in the centre, both open daily all year (out of season it can be difficult to get anything to eat in the south of the island).

PÍRGI, 24km from the port, is perhaps the liveliest and certainly the most colourful of the communities, its houses elaborately embossed with *ksistá*, geometric patterns cut into the plaster and then outlined with paint. On the northeast corner of the central square the twelfth-century Byzantine church of **Áyii Apóstoli**, embellished with much later frescoes, is tucked under an arcade; it's open erratic hours – Tuesday to Thursday and Saturday only, 9am–2pm. The giant church of the **Assumption** on the square boasts a *témblon* in an odd folk style dating from 1642, and an equally bizarre carved figure peeking out from the base of the pulpit. Pírgi has a handful of **rooms**, the most expensive of which are bookable through the *Women's Agricultural and Tourist Cooperative* (☎0271/72 496; ③). Try also *Rita's Rooms*, though you may want to write in advance (to 82102 Prigí, Híos). There's also a **bank**, a **post office**, a miniscule **OTE**, and a couple of **tavernas**; try the *Pi & Fi*, just across from the belfry of the Assumption.

OLÍMBI, 7km further on the same bus route, is the least visited of the villages but not devoid of interest; the tower-keep, which at Pírgi stands virtually abandoned away from the modern main square, is here bang in the middle of the square, its ground floor occupied by *kafenía*. By now you will have grasped the basic layout of a mastic village: an originally rectangular warren of stone houses, the outer layer doubling as the town's perimeter fortification and pierced by just a few gates. More recent additions, although in traditional style, will straggle outside the original defences.

MESTÁ, 11km from Pírgi, has a more sombre feel and is considered the finest example of its genre. From the main square, dominated by the church of the **Taxiarhis**, the largest on the island, a bewildering maze of cool, shady lanes, provided with anti-earthquake buttresses and tunnels between the usually unpainted houses, leads off in all directions. But most streets end in blind alleys, except the critical half-dozen leading to as many gates; the northeast one still has an iron grate in place. There's an EOT-run scheme of **rooms** in restored traditional dwellings (☎0271/76 319 or 76 217; ④), though they're on the pricey side; as at Pírgi unaffiliated rooms are somewhat cheaper. The place, unfortunately, has been discovered (by Híos standards) for some years, and, with boutiques, arty bars and the occasional film crew, is verging on the twee. The handful of **tavernas** on the square are now only average value, though it's worth asking for the locally produced raisin **wine**: heavy, semi-sweet and sherry-like.

Beachless **LIMÁNI MESTÓN,** 3km north, has come down considerably in the world since ferry service here ceased some years ago, and you wonder who stays in the handful of rooms; it's only worth a trip for the fish tavernas. The closest **beach** worthy of the name to Mestá is at **Merikoúnda,** 4km west. Closer to Olímbi, **Káto Faná** offers the scanty ruins of an Apollo temple as well as swimming and unhassled free camping, but Pírgi is really the most convenient base to the best coastal resorts in this corner of the island.

The nearest of these is **EMBORIÓ,** an almost land-locked harbour with a few tavernas and (expensive) rooms; there's a British-excavated archaeological zone nearby, the ancient Hiotes not being slow to realise the advantages of the site as a trading-post. Four hundred metres beyond Embório, the first **Mávra Vótsala** (sometimes Mávra Vótsala) cove is rather too manicured and hemmed in by cement, but if you follow the trail over the second headland you'll come to another dramatic pebble beach, twice the size and backed by impressive cliffs. Signs warn you not to pilfer the red-and-black volcanic stones, but it's hard to resist. If you want sand, you'll have to go to **KOMÍ,** accessible by bumpy dirt track from Emborió or via a roundabout paved route through Armólia and Kalamotí. With a handful of rooms and restaurants, it's the most developed of the resorts hereabouts, though with little character and difficult to reach with your own transport. In summer there are some direct buses to Embório, and rather fewer to Kalamotí, which is off the main road, but at any time of the year it's easy to get stranded.

The only other coastal town in the south, as opposed to scrappy, anonymous villa clusters, is **KATARÁKTIS,** remarkable mainly for its pleasant waterfront with balconied houses, genuine fishing port and a few tavernas; there are no appreciable beaches nearby. Just inland and up a considerable hill are the substantial villages of NÉNITES and VOUNÓ, worth a detour with your own vehicle.

Central Híos

The **Kámbos,** a vast plain fertile with citrus groves, extends southwest from Híos town as far as the village of HALKIÓ. Exploring it with a bicycle is apt to be less frustrating than going by car, since the unsignposted roads degenerate into a web of lanes sandwiched between high walls; behind these you catch fleeting glimpses of ornate old villas built out of a tawny, peanut-brittle masonry. Courtyards are paved in pebbles or alternating light-and-dark tiles, and most still contain a *manganós* or water-wheel once used to draw water up from deep wells. The district was originally settled by the Genoese in the fourteenth century and remained a preserve of the local aristocracy until 1822. Many of the the the sumptuous, three-storey dwellings, constructed in a hybrid Italo-Turko-Greek style unique in the country, have languished in ruins since 1881, but the ancestral home of the Argenti has been renovated as a traditional inn, the *Villa Argentikon* (☎0271/31 599; ⑥), where, for a staggering £200 or so per day, you can have your every whim catered for by trained chefs, valets and waiters. A somewhat more reasonable alternative is the *Perivoli* (☎0271/31 513; ④). Other mansions are venues for the annual summer Greek language and culture course offered by the **Ionic Centre** (for information, write to: Lissíou 11, Plaka, Athens).

Beyond Halkió, the road (and a daily bus) continues towards a cluster of villages nearly as distinctive as the *mastihohoriá*, though less casbah-like. ÁYIOS YIÓRYIOS on its ridge has been adulterated by new construction, but **VÉSSA,** beyond, is still a gem, more open than Mestá or Pírgi but still homogeneous. Honey-coloured buildings are arrayed in a vast grid punctuated by numerous belfries; there's a *kafenío* but no other facilities. The bus line turns north to **LITHÍ,** a friendly village of whitewashed buildings perched on a forested ledge overlooking the sea. There are tavernas and cafés near where the bus turns around, but the only places to stay are down at windswept, dreary Lithí harbour 2km below, a weekend target of Hiotes for the sake of its poor beach. For decent swimming you'll have to press north along a rough dirt road that passes first a sand-and-gravel cove at **Kastélla** and then another expanse of the same at the deeply indented **Elínda** bay. All along this coast are peculiar watchtowers erected by the Genoese to look out for pirates; the only significant habitation is **SIDHIROÚNDA**, which enjoys a spectacular hilltop setting overlooking the entire west Hian coast.

Néa Moní

Almost exactly in the physical middle of the island, the monastery of **NÉA MONÍ**, founded by the Byzantine emperor Constantine Monomachos IX in 1049 where a miraculous icon was discovered, is among the most beautiful and important medieval monuments on any of the Greek islands. Its mosaics rank with those of Dháfni and Óssios Loukás as being among the finest expressions of their age, and its setting, high in the mountains west of the port, is no less memorable. There's a direct bus only on Wednesdays; at other times you have to take a blue city bus as far as KARYÉS (7km out) and then walk or hitch an equal distance further. Taxis, however, are not prohibitive at about 4000dr a carload, and a suitable wait while you look around is included in the price.

Once a powerful and independent community of 600 monks, Néa Moní was pillaged during the atrocities of 1822 and most of the inmates put to the sword. The 1881 tremor caused devastating damage (skillfully repaired) and exactly a hundred years later one of the recent forest fires nearly gutted the grounds. Today the monastery, with its giant refectory and vaulted water cisterns, is inhabited by just three elderly nuns and an equal number of lay workers. Just inside the main gate (daily 8am–noon & 4–8pm) is a chapel-charnel house containing the bones of those who met their death here in 1822; axe-clefts in children's skulls attest to the savagery of the attackers. The *kathólikon*, with the cupola resting on an octagonal drum, is of a design seen elsewhere only in Cyprus; the frescoes in the exonarthex are badly damaged – the holes are from Turkish bullets, it is said – but the **mosaics** are another matter. The narthex contains portrayals of the *Saints of Hios* sandwiched between the *Washing of the Feet* and *Judas' Betrayal*; in the dome, which once contained a complete Life of Christ, only the *Baptism*, part of the *Crucifixion*, the *Descent from the Cross*, the *Resurrection*, and the *Evangelists Mark* and *John* survived the earthquake.

With your own transport, you should proceed 5km west to **AVGÓNIMA**, a jumble of houses on a knoll perched above the west coast; some are being restored but the permanent population is six. A returned Greek-American family runs an excellent **taverna/kafenío** here, *O Pirgos*, but there's no place to stay. The road, improved recently, continues another 7km to **ANÁVATOS**, whose empty, dun-coloured dwellings, soaring above pistachio orchards, are almost indistinguishable from the 300-metre bluff on which they're built. During the 1822 insurrection the 400 inhabitants threw themselves over this cliff rather than surrender to the besieging Turks, and it's still a preferred suicide leap. Anávatos is four persons larger than Avgónima, but with an utter lack of facilities and an eerie, traumatised atmosphere; it's no place to be stranded after dark.

Northern Híos

Northern Híos never really recovered from the Turkish massacre, and the desolation left by the fires of 1981 and 1987 will dampen the spirits of inquisitive travellers. The villages are deserted much of the year, which means that bus services are accordingly sparse. About one-third of the former population now lives in Híos Town, venturing out only on the dates of major festivals or to tend their grapes and olives, time which barely adds up to four months of the year. The balance of the northerners, based in Athens or the US, visit their ancestral homes for just a few weeks in the summer, making for a very brief, intense "season".

The blue buses run only as far as **VRONDÁDHOS**, an elongated coastal suburb which is the favoured residence of the island's many seafarers. Homer is reputed to have lived and taught here, and just above the little fishing port and pebble beach you can visit his purported lectern, strangely incorporated into a probable shrine of Cybele and surrounded by terraced park. Many of the buses out here are labelled "Dhaskalópetra" ("Teacher's Rock").

LANGÁDHA is probably the first point on the coast road where you might be tempted to leave the bus. Set at the mouth of a deep valley, this attractive little harbour has half a dozen **rooms** and two or three waterside **tavernas** but no beach anywhere nearby; the tempting cove to the north is an off-limits naval base. There is sometimes an expensive, supplemental *kaíki* service to Inoússes from here; contact Hristos Moudhalos on ☎0272/51 568. The island's only organised **campsite** is inconveniently tucked away at the bay of **Áyios Isídhoros**, past SIKIÁDHA and PANDOUKÓS.

Just above Langádha an important side road leads up to **PITIOÚS**, an oasis in a mountain pass presided over by a single tower-keep, but the main flow of traffic continues to **ÁNO** and **KÁTO KARDHÁMILA**, 37km out of the main town. Positioned at opposite edges of a fertile plain rimmed by mountains, they come as welcome, green relief from Homer's crags. Káto, better known as **MÁRMARO**, is larger, its waterside streets flanked by the hillside districts of Ráhi and Perivoláki, and indeed it's the second largest community on the island, with a **bank, post office** and **OTE** branch. However, neither town is particularly geared up for visitors, nor is there really much to attract them other than some pastel, neoclassical architecture. The fishing harbour, fully exposed to the *meltémi*, is strictly businesslike, and the tiny beach has to be regularly supplemented with sand.

By way of **hotels**, there's just the luxury *Kardamyla* (☎0272/22 378; ④), and the even more expensive *Hiona* (☎0272/22 036; ⑤), which also offers a programme of cultural and natural history tours of the island. Otherwise there's an unmarked **pension** in RÁHI (☎0272/23-183; ②; call beforehand or drop in at the *Markaki* sweet shop) and three other **rooms** establishments. For **eating out**, try the *Kafenio Akroyali* on the waterfront for pizzas and *mezédhes*; Áno Kardhámila has a single *psistariá/ pizzeria* and, while it has no accommodation, makes a good destination for rambles on dirt tracks up through the local orchards.

For good swimming head west past the harbour-mouth windmill for an hour along a coastal cement drive to **Nagós**, a tiny cove at the foot of a gorge choked with greenery; the sea here is chilled by a creek running into it. A lingering water problem in Híos Town was supposed to have been solved by tapping the springs with a giant pipeline which parallels the entire northeast coast road, but the project has been stalled due to lack of funds. You can eat at a single **taverna** and occupy one of two adjacent, unmarked **rooms**, right behind the 300-metre pebble beach. The place-name is a corruption of *naós*, after a large Poseidon temple that once stood at the base of the cliff behind; centuries of orchards, pilfering, and organised excavations after 1912 have ensured that nothing remains visible. **Yióssonas**, a fifteen-minute walk west, is a rockier and less sheltered beach but warmer for swimming, and your only chance of relative solitude in July and August, when Nagós is packed around the clock.

Few outsiders venture beyond Yióssonas, although an early-afternoon bus covers the twenty kilometres between Mármaro and Kambiá. AMÁDHES and VÍKI are attractive villages at the base of the 1297-metre **Pilinéon**, the island's summit, easiest climbed from Amádhes. **KAMBIÁ**, overlooking a chapel-strewn ravine, has very much of an end-of-the-line feel to it; go to one of the *kafenía* by the main church to be pointed along the one-hour path across the canyon to AGRELOPÓ, an abandoned hamlet. From the church here a system of jeep tracks leads in another ninety minutes to the tumbledown pier and seaweed beach at Ayiásmata.

AYIÁSMATA is one of the strangest spots on Híos, consisting of perhaps twenty buildings (four of them churches), including the miraculous grey-and-white **baths** (summer only daily 6–11am), after which the place is named. You can stay either at a stone-built **hotel** or in **rooms** at the west end of the bay, where working-class islanders establish a virtual colony for weeks on end. Amenities are sparse, but the sea view compensates. There are no real tavernas, and the "colony"'s store is rudimentary, since it's assumed you've come prepared with supplies.

The road south out of Ayiásmata passes through strikingly beautiful countryside. Without your own transport, walking is generally obligatory as far as KÉRAMOS and AFRODHÍSSIA, the more attractive of the two. Here something approximating a north-west coastal road leads off to **ÁYIO GÁLA**, where a fourteenth-century Byzantine church with a *témblon* nearly as old is lodged in one of a cluster of deep caves. The most direct tarmac road continues south through HÁLANDHRA and NÉA POTAMIÁ – the latter conceivably the ugliest village on the island – for a total twenty-kilometre traverse to Volissós.

VOLISSÓS was once the most important of the northern villages, and its old stone houses still curl beneath the crumbling hilltop Genose fort. Today it carries a distinctly depressed air, with the bulk of its remaining, mostly elderly residents living in newer buildings around the main square. Here there's a **post office** (but no bank), two shops and an evenings-only **taverna**. Since the bus only comes this way four times a week, you'll have to plan on staying. This should cause no dismay, since the area has simply the best beaches on Híos, unspoiled because the adjacent property owners have thus far refused to sell land to developers.

There is no accommodation in Volissós itself but you can ask here about bungalows in Limniá, 1500m below (☎0272/31 400; ③). **LIMNIÁ** also has two **tavernas** (one seasonal, one permanent) and above the latter are a few **rooms**. It's a lively and authentic little fishing anchorage, with *kaíki* skippers coming and going from Pasará (Mon, Wed & Fri at mid-morning) and sometimes Plomári on Lésvos. You're not far from the fabled beaches either. A kilometre southeast, at HORÍ, begins an almost boundless sand-and-pebble beach where nudism will go unremarked upon, and the more intimate **LÍMNOS** (not to be confused with Limniá) is just a ten-minute jeep-track walk over the headland north of the harbour (or approachable by a longer asphalt road from Volissós). At Límnos there's a single **rooms** establishment (☎0272/31 436; ③) where the dirt track joins the asphalt, and a *psistariá* on the larger of the two excellent sandy coves.

AYÍA MARKÉLLA, 5km further north, stars in many of the local postcards: a long, stunning beach fronting the monastery of the same name – not particularly interesting but there is a summer **taverna** and **rooms** in the grounds. You can skip the "hot" springs out on the headland beyond, however, which turn out to be a tiny cavity of tepid, iron-stained water; after a wet winter there should be enough water in the creek behind the sand to wash the salt off. Indeed most of the beaches hereabouts seem tailor-made for camping – tolerated due to the scarcity of rooms – and except around July 22, the local saint's festival and the big island celebrations, you'll have little company.

Satellite islands: Psará and Inoússes

There's a single settlement, with beaches and the odd rural monastery, on both of Hios's satellite isles, but each is surprisingly different from the main island. **Inoússes**, the closer one, has daily ferries from the main harbour in season; **Psará** is served six days a week, with services on alternate days from Híos town and Limniá.

Psará

The birthplace of revolutionary war hero Admiral Kanaris, **PSARÁ** devoted her merchant fleets – the third largest in 1820s Greece after Ídhra and Spétses – to the cause of independence, and paid dearly for it. Vexed beyond endurance, the Turks landed overwhelming forces in 1824, to stamp out this nest of resistance. Perhaps 3000 of the 30,000 inhabitants escaped in small boats which were rescued by a French fleet, but the majority retreated to a hilltop powder magazine and blew it, and themselves, up rather than surrender. The nationalist poet Solomos immortalised the incident in famous stanzas:

> *On the Black Ridge of Psará,*
> *Glory walks alone.*
> *She meditates on her heroes,*
> *And wears in her hair a wreath*
> *Made from a few dry weeds*
> *Left on the barren ground.*

Today the year-round population barely exceeds 400, and it's a sad, stark place, never having really recovered from the holocaust; the Turks burnt whatever houses and vegetation the blast had missed. The only positive recent development is a decade-long revitalisation project instigated by a French-Greek descendant of Kanaris and a Greek team. The port has been improved, mains electricity and pure water provided, a secondary school opened, and cultural links between France and the island established, though so far this has not been reflected in increased tourism or massive tourist facilities.

Arriving can be something of an ordeal: the regular ferry from Híos Town takes four hours to cover the 35 nautical miles of habitually rough sea. Use Limniá to cross in at least one direction if you can; it takes half the time at half the price.

Since few buildings in the east-facing harbour community predate this century, it's a strange hotchpotch of ecclesiastical and domestic architecture that greets the eye on disembarking. There's a distinct southerly feel, more like the Dodecanese or the Cyclades, and some strange churches, no two alike in style, in and out of town. If you **stay** overnight, your choices are limited to a single studio behind the dockside string of *kafenía* and tavernas; some rooms let by the priest's wife; the overpriced municipal inn for about 1500dr a person, and the EOT *ksenónas* in a restored prison, usually with vacancies at 2500dr each. For **eating**, the best and cheapest place by far is the EOT-run *Spitalia*, housed (as the name indicates) in a restored medieval hospital at the edge of town. Other more obvious tavernas tend to be mediocre and expensive. A **post office**, bakery and shop complete the tally of amenities; there's no bank.

Psará's **beaches** are decent, getting better the further northeast you walk from the port. You quickly pass Káto Yialós, Katsoúni and Lazoréta with its off-putting power station; **Lákka**, fifteen minutes along, seems to be named after its grooved rock formations in which you may have to shelter, as much of this coast is windswept, with a heavy swell offshore. **Límnos**, 25 minutes out along the coastal path, is big and pretty, but there's no reliable taverna here or at any of the other beaches. The only other thing to do on Psará, really, is to walk north across the island to the monastery of the **Assumption**.

Inoússes

INOÚSSES also has a permanent population of a few hundred, down from twice that number since the last war, but a very different history from Psará's. For generations it has provided the Aegean with many of her wealthiest shipping families: in fact the richest Greek shipowner in the world, Kostas Lemos, was born here. This helps explain the large villas and visiting summer yachts in an otherwise low-key Greek island.

Only on Fridays and Sundays is it possible to make a day-trip from Híos; the rest of the week the local **ferry** arrives at 4pm, returning the next morning. An unusually protected harbour is guarded by church-tipped islets; the single town is surprisingly large, draped over hills and ravines. Despite the wealthy reputation, it's of unpretentious appearance, similar to Turkish Ildır just across the water, the houses in a variety of vernacular and modest neoclassical styles. The two **hotels**, *Thalassoporos* (☎0272/51 475; ③) and *Prasonisia* (☎0272/51 313; ③), are also rather plain, since most seasonal visitors have ancestral homes to stay in. You can **eat** at a pair of simple tavernas, one by the water, the other well up the hill, and drink at a handful of *kafenío*/bars on the quay. Inoússes has a **post office**, **OTE** branch, and – not surprisingly – its very own **bank**.

The rest of the island, or at least the southern slope, is peaceful, green and well tended; there are no springs, so water comes from a mix of fresh and brackish wells. The sea is extremely clean, and calm on the lee coast; among the sheltered **beaches**, the choice is between **Farkeró** east of the port, or **Zepága**, **Biláli** or **Kástro**, five, twenty and thirty minutes' walk west respectively. As on Psará, there are no facilities at any of the beaches.

At the end of the road, beyond the *Kástro*, stands the somewhat macabre convent of **Evangelismós**, endowed by the Pateras family of shipping magnates. Inside is the mummified body of the lately-canonised daughter, Irini, whose prayers to die of cancer in place of her terminally ill father Panagos were answered on account of her virtue and piety; he's entombed here too, having outlived Irini by some years. The abbess, presiding over a dozen novices, is Mrs Pateras.

Lésvos (Mitilíni)

Lésvos, the third largest Greek island after Crete and Évia, is not only the birthplace of Sappho, but also of Aesop, Arion and more recently the Greek primitive artist Theophilos, the poet Odysseus Elytis and the novelist Stratis Myrivilis. Despite these artistic associations, it may not at first strike the visitor as particularly beautiful or interesting; much of the landscape is rocky, volcanic terrain, dotted with thermal springs and alternating with vast grain fields, salt pans or even near-desert. But there are also oak and pine forests as well as vast olive groves, some of which are as much as 500 years old. The island tends to grow on you with prolonged acquaintance, especially if you have the time and patience to hitchike or the funds to rent a car.

Lovers of medieval and Turkish architecture certainly won't be disappointed. Genoese castles survive at the main town, Mitilíni, Mólivos and Ándissa: these date from the late fourteenth century, when Lésvos was given as a dowry to a Genoese prince of the Gatelouzi clan following his marriage to the niece of one of the last Byzantine emperors. Along with Crete, Lésvos was the only Greek island where the Turks settled appreciably in rural villages (they usually stuck to the safety of towns), so driving along you encounter the odd Ottoman bridge or crumbling minaret. Again, unusually for the Aegean islands, there was an approximation of a post-Byzantine Greek Orthodox aristocracy here, who built rambling mansions and tower-houses, some of which have survived destruction which claimed the rest in this century. The mild climate and suggestive contours of the landforms seem to have always had a civilising effect on occupiers: Turks and Greeks got along well here right up until 1923, and the World War II Axis occupation was among the most lenient in the Aegean.

Social and economic idiosyncracies persist: anyone who has attended one of the vast, lengthy village *paneyíria*, with music for hours on end and tables in the streets groaning with food and drink, will not be surprised to learn that Lésvos has the highest alcoholism rate in Greece. Breeding livestock, especially horses, is disproportionately important, and traffic jams caused by tethered mounts instead of parked cars are not unheard of. Until recently another local quirk was an overwhelming tendency to vote Communist, in part a reaction to the well-developed medieval feudalism here. But lately there's been a shift to the right, with leftist incumbents being chucked out in favour of *Néa Dhimokratía* candidates.

Historically, the olive plantations, *oúzo* distilleries, animal husbandry and a fishing industry supported the inhabitants, but with these enterprises relatively depressed, mass-market tourism is beginning to make inroads. However, there are few large hotels outside the capital, rooms still outnumber villa-type accommodation, and the first official campsites opened just a few seasons ago. Public buses tend to radiate out from the harbour for the benefit of working locals, not tourists who may want to do an out-and-back day trip. Carrying out such excursions is next to impossible anyway, owing to the size of the island – about 70km by 45km at its widest points – and the frequently appalling roads. Furthermore, the topography is complicated by the two deep gulfs of Kalloní and Yéra, which means that going from A to B usually involves an obligatory change of bus at either the port capital, on the east shore, or Kalloní Town, in the middle of the island. In short, it's best to decide on a base and stay there for at least a few days, exploring its immediate surroundings on foot or by vehicle, rather than constantly trying to move on.

Mitilíni and around

MITILÍNI is the port and capital, and in Greek fashion sometimes doubles as the name of the island, something to watch out for when travelling by ferry or plane. The town sprawls around two broad bays divided by a promontory where the **Genoese fortress** sits – open much of the day but not to be photographed since it's a military area. Further inland, the town skyline is dominated in turn by the Germanic spire of **Áyios Theodhóros** and the mammary dome of **Áyios Therapón**, together expressions of the post-Baroque taste of the nineteenth-century Ottoman Greek bourgeoisie. They stand more or less at opposite ends of the **bazaar**, whose main street, Odhós Ermoú, links the town centre with the north harbour. On its way there Ermoú passes a cluster of antique shops and the roofless **Yeni Jami**, now a venue for art exhibits. Between Ermoú and the castle lies a maze of atmospheric lanes lined with grandiose Belle Époque mansions and elderly vernacular houses, suitable for wandering around.

More formal stimulation is provided by the excellent **Archaeological Museum** (Tues–Sun 8.30am–3pm; 400dr), currently housed partly in the mansion of a large estate just behind the ferry dock (although a large modern installation is under construction) and a perfect time-filler before departing on one of the boats. Among the more interesting of the well labelled and well lit exhibits are a complete set of mosaics from a Hellenistic dwelling, rather droll terracotta figurines, votive offerings from a sanctuary of Demeter and Kore excavated in the *kástro*, and Neolithic finds from present-day Thermi. A specially-built annexe at the rear contains stone-cut inscriptions of various edicts and treaties, and – more interesting than you'd think – *stelae* featuring *nekródhipna* or portrayals of funerary meals. There's also a **Byzantine Art Museum** behind Áyios Therapón (Mon–Sat 9am–1pm; 100dr), and a small **Folk Art Museum** (sporadic hours) on the quay next to the blue city-bus stop.

Practicalities

This may sound like a lot but in fact the town's pleasures are easily exhausted in half a day, and most visitors, repulsed by the general urban bustle, get out as soon as possible. Mitilíni returns the compliment by being in fact a very impractical place to base yourself. You should pause long enough at the **tourism police/information post** behind the customs building (daily 8.30am–5.30pm) to get hold of their excellent town

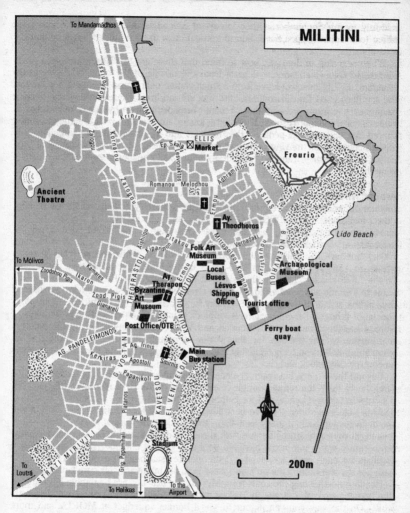

and island maps and brochures. Finding **accommodation** is in any case difficult: the obvious waterfront hotels are exorbitant, and there are few singles to speak of. If you insist on staying here, it's best to hunt for rooms behind Áyios Therapón, or along Ermoú past the Yeni Jami, where quieter, cheaper establishments between the north harbour and fortress advertise themselves. Another mid-range option with some character is the neoclassical *Rex* at Katsakoúli 3 (☎0251/28 523; ④), behind the Archaeological Museum. **Eating out** is an even more insoluble problem: restaurants, with the exception of the oven-food-serving *I Lesvos* in the bazaar, consist of a half-dozen mediocre grills flanking the quay.

If you're stuck here involuntarily, awaiting a dawn-departing ferry, some consolation can be derived from the town's good **entertainment**: indoor/outdoor **cinemas** with good first-run films, and the musical events of the *Lesviakó Kalokéri* in the castle from mid-July to mid-September. Other important amenities include the **OTE** and **post office** (conveniently open Sat & Sun mornings), next to each other a block behind the central park.

When **arriving or leaving**, bear in mind that there are two **bus stations** in town. The *astikó* (blue bus) service departs from the middle of the quay, while *iperastikó* (standard *KTEL*) coaches leave from a small station near Platía Konstandinopóleos at the southern end of the harbour, all the way around from where ferries dock. Service frequency has improved slightly in recent years, with up to five daily departures in summer for the major resorts. There is no longer any bus link with the **airport**, and a shared taxi (among four people – they're dear) into Mitilíni is the only link. The only other alternative for moving on is **car rental**, offered by somewhat dodgy local franchises or *Europcar* – though it's generally better and cheaper to rent at the resort of your choice.

Around Mitilíni

Just south of the town, on the road to the airport, you can visit various *pírgi* (tower-mansions) at HRISSOMALOÚSSA and AKLIDHÍOU, relics of the nineteenth-century gentry, but the most rewarding single targets are a pair of museums at VARIÁ. The **Theophilos Museum** (Tues–Sun 9am–1pm & 4.30–8pm; 100dr) honours the naive painter born in this village, while the adjacent **Teriade Museum** (Tues–Sun 9am–2pm & 5–8pm) is the brainchild of another native son, Stratis Eleftheriades. Leaving the island at an early age for Paris, he Gallicised his name to Teriade and went on to become a renowned art publisher, convincing some of the leading artists of the twentieth century to participate in his ventures. The displays consist of lithographs, engravings, woodblock prints and watercolours by the likes of Mirò, Chagall, Picasso, Léger, Rouault and Villon, either annotated by the painters themselves or illustrations for the works of prominent poets and authors – an astonishing collection for a relatively remote Aegean island. Near the two museums is an enterprising snack bar.

Beyond the airport, but reached easiest by taking a blue city bus as far as LOUTRÁ (and then a taxi), the remote double-cove beach of **Áyios Ermoyénis** is attractive, but it's crowded on weekends, and for bathing near Mitilíni (the fee-entry town "beach" at TSAMÁKIA is mediocre) you're best advised to make for **Loutrá Yéras**, 8km along the main road to Kalloní (daily 8am–8pm; 150dr) – just the thing if you've spent a sleepless night on a malodrous ferry – with three ornate spouts that feed just-above-body-temperature water into a marble-lined pool in a vaulted chamber (there are separate facilities for each sex). A snack-bar/café operates seasonally on the very roof of the bath house, overlooking the gulf, and there is an old inn nearby for cure fanatics.

Heading north along the coast from Mitilíni, the beaches are negligible but the startling views across the straits to Turkey make the trip towards Mandamádhos worthwhile. On the way you can detour to see a Roman aqueduct at **MÓRIA**, and more tower-mansions (all difficult to find) at PÁMFILLA, PIRGÍ, and THERMÍS, but the most compelling attraction is again some **baths**, at **LOUTRÓPOLI THERMÍS**, more sunken indoor pools overarched by great vaults. There's a frequent blue bus service to them, but enquire first before boarding since the spa is periodically closed for repairs.

Southern Lésvos

The southernmost portion of the island is indented by two great inlets, the gulfs of **Kalloní** and **Yéra** – the first curving in a northeasterly direction, the other northwesterly, thus creating a fan-shaped peninsula at the heart of which is the 968-metre Mount Ólimbos. Both shallow gulfs in turn are almost landlocked by virture of very narrow outlets to the open sea.

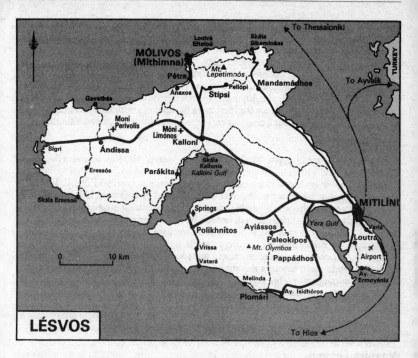

Plomári and Ayiássos

PLOMÁRI is the only sizeable coastal settlement, the second largest on Lésvos, and presents an odd mix of beauty and its famous *oúzo* distilling industry. Despite a lack of sandy beaches nearby, it's besieged in summer by hordes of Scandinavian package tourists, but you can usually find a room or two free near the middle of the old, charmingly dilapidated town. Unfortunately, finding a decent meal is considerably harder, with the taverna at the central plane tree often unbearably busy, and those lining the waterfront just plain bad. You'll get better food at **ÁYIOS ISÍDHOROS**, 3km east, which is where most tourists actually stay; try the westernmost establishment there, *Dhilina*, or, further inland toward Playiá, *I Karidhia*. Áyios Isídhoros itself has rather functional **rooms** and a long, if popular pebble beach with fine swimming. Committed misanthropes can walk ninety minutes west of Plomári past isolated coves in the direction of **Melínda**, the closest sandy beach; back in town the *Okeanis Hotel*, principally home to tour groups, also offers car rental and runs boat trips to the still-better beaches of **Tárti** and **Vaterá** (see below). The local *paniyíri* season kicks off in mid-July with the **Oúzo Festival**, culminating on the 27/28 of the month with celebrations in honour of Áyios Harálambos, featuring such rurally focused activities as horse races and a bull sacrifice.

The bus line into Plomári runs via the pretty villages of PALEOKÍPOS and SKÓPELOS (as well as Áyios Isídhoros), but if you're hitching or have your own vehicle you can take a slight shortcut by using the daytime-only ferry at PÉRAMA, across the neck of the Yéra Gulf. The road north from Plomári to Ayiássos has paving and public transport, only up to MEGALOHÓRI, rough dirt and your own transport thereafter.

AYIÁSSOS, nestling in a wooded valley under the crest of Mount Ólimbos, is the most beautiful hill town on Lésvos – the many traditional houses lining the narrow, cobbled streets are all protected by law. Don't be put off by the huge batteries of kitsch wood and ceramic souvenirs, aimed mostly at Greeks, but continue past the central church to the old bazaar, with its *kafenía* and unusually graphic butcher stalls. Regrettably, redundant video arcades have made inroads, but in certain cafés bands of *santoúri*, clarinet, lap-drum and violin play on weekend afternoons, accompanying inebriated dancers on the cobbles outside. Rather more packaged are the products of *santoúri* player Ioannis Kakourgos, who plays and sells cassettes from his little studio by the church. Not surprisingly the August 15 festival here is one of the liveliest on Lésvos, and there are **rooms** available for the increasing number of visitors; the best **restaurant** is the nameless place on your left as you enter the village from the extreme south end.

Routes to Vaterá

A different bus route from Mitilíni leads to Vaterá via the inland villages of POLIHNÍTOS and VRÍSSA. The former is rather dreary, and its famous hot springs are currently shut, but try the working ones of **Áyios Ioánnis** at nearby LISVÓRI. **VATERÁ** itself is a huge, seven-kilometre-long sand beach, backed by vegetated hills, which could easily accommodate the whole island if need be; the swimming is delightful and warm. The **campsite** here is slightly inland, but the half-dozen or so **tavernas** line the shore road, and, because the clientele is mostly local weekenders, they're cheap and good – for example *Ta Kalamakia*. There are a couple more out towards the cape of Áyios Fókas, where there are traces of an ancient **temple of Dionysus**. So far indoor **accommodation** tends more towards the studio/villa type than rooms, but you should find something suitable. If you intend to stay here you'll really need your own transport, as the closest shops are 4km away at Vríssa; in the other direction a fair-to-poor dirt road leads via STAVRÓS and hidden AMBELIKÓ to either Ayiássos or Plomári within an hour and a half. Leaving the area towards Kalloní, the short cut via the military base at AHLADERÍ is worth using and passable to all but the more underpowered mopeds.

Western Lesvos

The main road west of Loutrá Yéra is surprisingly bare, with little to stop for before Kalloní other than the traces of an Aphrodite temple at MÉSA, or the turning for the AYÍA PARASKEVÍ, where a bull-sacrifice rite is observed at the end of June – though both require your own transport to reach. At other times the village presents an intriguing tableau of nineteenth-century bourgeois architecture.

KALLONÍ itself is an unembellished agricultural and market town more or less in the middle of the island, but it's hard to avoid spending some time here since it's the intersection of most *KTEL* routes. Not all buses depart from the busy main street, so if you're waiting to make a connection, check where your bus is leaving from. If you have a lot of time to spare, you might make the hour walk to **SKÁLA KALLONÍS** with its large if coarse beach and several restaurants. The gulf is noted for its *avthríni*, a sort of cross between sardine and anchovy, and a grilled plateful makes a delicious lunch.

Inland monasteries and villages

West of Kalloní the road winds uphill to the monastery of **Limónos**, founded in 1527 by one Ignatios. It is a huge complex, with just a handful of monks and lay workers to maintain three storeys of cells ringing the giant courtyard, adorned with huge urns sporting potted plants and strutting peacocks. Beside, behind and above are respectively an old-age home, a lunatic asylum, and a hostel for pilgrims; the *katholikón*, with its carved-wood ceiling and archways, is in Asia-Minor style. A former abbot established a **museum** (daily 9am–1pm & 5–7.30pm; 100dr) on two floors of the rear wing; the ground-floor ecclesiastical collection is fine enough, but you should prevail upon the keeper (easier done in large groups) to open the upper, ethnographic hall. The first room is a recreated Lesvian salon, while the next is crammed with an indiscriminate mix of kitsch and priceless objects – Ottoman copper trays to badly stuffed rotting egrets by way of brightly painted trunks – donated since 1980 by surrounding villages. An overflow of farm implements is stashed in a corner storeroom below, next to a chamber where giant *pithária* (urns) for grain and olive oil are embedded in the floor.

Beyond, the road west passes through FÍLIA, where you can turn off for a time-saving short cut to SKOUTÁROS and the north of Lésvos, but be warned that cars with low clearance may not manage the incredibly rutted road. Most traffic continues through to **SKALOHÓRI**, its houses in tiers at the head of a valley facing the sea and the sunset, and **VATOÚSSA**, the most landlocked but also the most beautiful of the western settlements. Eight kilometres beyond a short track leads you to the frescoed seventeenth-century monastery of **Perivolís** (daily 8am–noon & 3–7pm), built as the name suggests in the midst of a riverside orchard. ÁNDISSA nestles under the west's only pine grove and its castle, looking 6km north toward the beach of **Gavathás**, narrow and exposed, although the setting's fine and there are a couple of rooms and tavernas. **Kámbos**, one headland east, is better but equally unsheltered; one promontory further east, and haphazardly signposted, are the remains of **ancient Ándissa**.

Just beyond modern Ándissa there's an important junction. Keeping straight leads you past the still-functioning monastery of **Ipsiloú**, founded in 1101 atop an extinct volcano and still home to five monks. The *katholikón*, tucked in one corner of a large, irregular courtyard, has a fine wood-lattice ceiling and good frescoes, but most of the place (including a museum) is in the throes of restoration for the time being. Ipsiloú's patron saint is John the Theologian, a frequent dedication for monasteries overlooking apocalyptic landscapes like the surrounding parched, boulder-strewn hills.

Near here is one of the main concentrations of specimens from Lésvos' rather over-rated **petrified forest**, indicated by forest service placards which also warn of severe penalties for pilfering souvenirs. For once modern Greek arsonists cannot be blamed for the state of the trees, created by the combined action of volcanic ash and hot springs some 15 million years ago. The other main cluster is south of Sígri (see below), but locals seem amazed that anyone would want to trudge though the barren country-side in search of them; upon arrival you may agree, since the mostly horizontal, three-metre-long chunks aren't exactly one of the world's wonders.

Sígri and Eressós

SÍGRI, near the western tip of Lésvos, has an appropriately end-of-the-line feel, accentuated since foreign travellers have forsaken it in the wake of the general Aegean tourism slump. The bay here is guarded both by a Turkish **castle** and the long island of Nissopí athwart its mouth which protects the place somewhat from prevailing winds. A vaguely Turkish-looking church is in fact a converted **mosque**, and the town itself is an odd mix of old and cement dwellings. The nearest beach, to the south, is narrow and scrappy, though better ones – glimpsed on the way in – lie within walking distance in the opposite direction. If you want to **stay**, there's a mid-range hotel (✆0251/22 340; ③), and a handful of rooms; among an equal number of **tavernas**, *Remezzo* has the best setting and the fanciest menu, but the more central and traditional *Australia* and *Kavolouros* seem quite acceptable.

However, most visitors to western Lésvos park themselves at **SKÁLA ERESSOÚ**, accessible via the southerly turning between Ándissa and Ipsiloú. The beach here runs a close second to the one at Vaterá, and consequently the place is beginning to rival Plomári and Mólivos in tourist numbers. Behind stretches the largest and most attractive agricultural plain on Lésvos, a welcome green contrast to the volcanic ridges above. Coming south from the junction there's no hint of the approaching oasis, something that adds to its idyllic quality as it erupts suddenly just beyond the inland town of ERESSÓS. This is well worth a look too, but only during the cooler hours of the day – in summer half of the population is down at Skála.

Skála has a **post office** and an **OTE** in addition to countless **rooms**, not all of them reserved en bloc. Should everywhere be full, there's a semi-official **campsite** to the west, behind the sand. **Tavernas**, some with elevated wooden dining platforms, crowd the beach; the most central, with complete menus as opposed to breakfast and snacks, include *To Aigaion* and *I Paralia*, on the square with the bust of Theoprastus – a renowned botanist who hailed from **ancient Eressós**. This was not, as you might suppose, on the site of the modern village, but atop the bluff at the east end of the beach; you can still see some crumbled bits of citadel wall from a distance. Another famous reputed native was **Sappho**, and there are often appreciable numbers of gay women here, paying homage.

Returning to the main island crossroads at Kallóní, don't be tempted to complete a loop from Eressós along the western shore of the Gulf of Kallóní until the asphalting program is completed; the indifferent scenery and characterless villages on the way don't justify the punishment cars suffer from the hacked-up road. Pavement currently resumes just south of **PARÁKILA**, which boasts a ruined mosque, an Ottoman bridge and a small, decent beach.

Northern Lésvos

MÓLIVOS (MÍTHIMNA) is arguably the most attractive spot on Lésvos, something that's less of a secret with every passing year. Except in August, however, the town's vine-canopied streets seem to readily absorb all of the package clientele and individual tourists who make their way here. Tiers of sturdy, red-tiled houses, some standing defensively with their rear walls to the sea, mount the slopes between the picturesque harbour and the Genoese **castle**. Closer examination reveals a half dozen weathered **Turkish fountains** along flower-fragrant, cobblestoned alleyways, and you can try to gain admission to the **Krallis** and **Yiannakos mansions**; the **library/art gallery** is usually open. Until proper excavations begin (unlikely), **ancient Mithimna** to the northwest is of essentially specialist interest, though a necropolis has been unearthed next to the bus stop; it's mainly the use of the classical name that has been revived.

Modern dwellings and hotels have been banned from the preserved municipality, and while this inevitably has engendered some tweeness the overall result is worth it – too few Greek towns appreciate what they have and take steps to protect it. There are plenty of **rooms** to let, and a **tourist office** by the bus stop to help you find them if necessary – though if there are any vacancies when you arrive, the various landladies will be quick to find you. The main thoroughfare, straight past the tourist office, heads towards the harbour, where a couple of small **hotels** overlook the water at the end of the road; they are understandably quite pricey and often filled with tour groups. You might instead want to take the street heading upwards from just beyond the tourist office, past houses with shaded courtyards and – if you're lucky – you'll find vacancies to go with them. One of the nicest, cheapest, quietest (but highest up) are those run by Varvara Kelesi (☎0253/71 460; ③). If all else fails there is now an official **campsite** 2km northeast of town.

Also around the tourist office are several **moped and car rental** places – useful if you're planning to spend a few days here – as well as a **bank**, **post office** and an **OTE** station. Choose carefully when **eating out**; the obvious sea view tavernas on the main uphill market street are all expensive, with miniature portions, and you're probably better off forsaking the panorama for Australian-run *Melinda's* on the lower *agora*, where the food's good, different and no more expensive than elsewhere; it's also the only place open between October and May. On the lower port road, the adjacent *Manolis' Garden* and *Vasilis'* tavernas can be recommended; on the harbour itself, only *To Khtapodhi*, strategically placed by the channel entrance, has affordable seafood. For dessert, try the sweet shop across the street and downhill from *Melinda's*.

In terms of **nightlife**, midsummer sees a short festival of musical and theatrical events up in the castle (otherwise Tues–Sun 7am–3pm; free), overshadowing in all senses the rather sporadic pub activity in the alleyways. The single incongruous note is introduced by an abusively noisy disco down by the water, which has thundered for years to empty floors but which can't be closed since the owner has influence with the police.

If or when the pleasures of the town pale, you may care to visit the **Karuna Meditation Retreat Centre** (811 08 Míthimna, Greece) about 3km out of town. This is run by Yiorgos Kassipidhes and his Nepali wife, Yosoda; write in advance for details of their changing April-to-October programmes in the healing arts and yoga, or simply to reserve a place to stay.

Pétra

Since there are both practical and political limits to the expansion of Mólivos, which in any case has a rather mediocre beach, many package companies are now shifting emphasis to **PÉTRA**, 5km due south and marginally less busy. The town is beginning to sprawl untidily behind its good sand beach and seafront square, but the core of old stone houses, many with Levantine-style balconies overhanging the street, remains. Pétra takes its name from the giant rock monolith located some distance inland and enhanced by the eighteenth-century church of the **Panayía Glikofiloússa**. Other local attractions include the sixteenth-century church of **Áyios Nikólaos** and the intricately decorated **Vareltsidena** mansion, which can be visited daily except between 1pm and 4pm.

There are plenty of **rooms** plus a few small hotels, and as at Pirgí on Híos a *Women's Agricultural Tourism Cooperative*, formed by Pétra's women in 1984 to offer something more unusual for visitors. In addition to opening a **restaurant** on the square (which also serves as a **tourist office**, crafts shop and general information centre), they arrange accommodation where it's possible to participate in the proprietors' daily routine and learn a bit about village life. Advance reservations are usually needed (☎0253/41 238; ③).

Aside from the cooperative's eatery, **tavernas** are generally a bit tatty, and you're probably better off at one of a pair of *ouzerís* 100–200 metres south of the square along the shore road. There are also a few tavernas outside Pétra, away from the usual tourist beat, so it's worth continuing along this unpromising-looking road, past the ugly new hillside villas and military sentry post, and picking your way along stretches of coast until you find them. **ÁNAXOS**, 3km away, is the principal developed spot, with half-a-dozen restaurants (including a 24hr pub) behind a kilometre of sand. From anywhere along here you enjoy beautiful sunsets between and beyond three offshore islets.

Around Mount Lepétimnos

East of Mólivos, the villages of **Mount Lepétimnos**, flanked by tufts of poplars, offer a day or two of rewarding exploration. The first stop, though not exactly up the hill, might be **Loutrá Eftaloú**, some rustic (and extremely hot) **thermal baths** 5km along the road to the campsite. These are housed in an attractive, old domed building, which despite a summer admission fee is badly in need of maintenance; rumour has it that when it has deteriorated sufficiently a pretext will be found to build a glitzy new spa in its place. Nearby there are already a growing number of unsightly villas and luxury hotels, as wells as two tavernas. In the opposite direction, behind the baths, is a pebble beach for taking a cooling-off dip (clothing optional).

The main road around the mountain first heads 6km east to **VAFIÓS**, with a well-advertised taverna featuring live music some nights, before curling north around the base of the peaks. This stretch is in the process of being tarmaced, but currently the asphalt, and the bus service back toward Mitilíni, does not resume until just before the exquisite hill village of **SIKAMINIÁ** (SIKAMIÁ), the birthplace of the regional novelist

Stratis Myrivilis. Below the "Plaza of the Workers' First of May", with its two traditional *kafenía* and views north to Turkey, one of the imposing basalt-built houses is marked as his childhood home. A fine *kalderími* short cuts the twisty road down to **SKÁLA SIKAMINIÁS**, easily the most picturesque fishing port on Lésvos. Myrivilis used it as the setting for his best-known book, *The Mermaid Madonna*, and the tiny rock-top chapel at the end of the jetty will be instantly recognisable to anyone who has read the novel. On a practical level, Skála has a few **rooms** and three or four **tavernas**, but only the rather average beach of **Káyia** just east, so it's perhaps better as a planned lunch stop. A fairly rough, roller-coaster track follows the coast back to Mólivos, its condition not deterring a steady stream of vehicles.

Continuing in the opposite direction, you soon come to **KLIÓ**, set attractively on a slope down which six kilometres of dirt road, better than maps suggest, descend to **Tsónia** beach. This proves to be 600 metres of beautiful pink volcanic sand, but with negligible facilities other than a café or two; occasionally boat trips from Mólivos come here.

South of Klió, the route forks at **KÁPI**, from where you can complete a loop of the mountain by bearing west along an indifferent road. **PELÓPI** is the ancestral village of the unsuccessful 1988 US presidential candidate Michael Dukakis, and sports a former mosque now used as a warehouse on the main square. Garden-swathed **IPSILOMÉTOPO**, the next village along, is punctuated by a minaret (but no mosque) and hosts revels on July 17, the feast of Ayía Marína. By the time you reach sprawling **STÍPSI**, you're almost back to the main Kalloní–Mólivos road; consequently there's pavement and a sporadic bus service out again, as well as a large **taverna** at the edge of town where coachloads of tourists descend in season for "Greek Nights". There are also **rooms** to let and it makes a good base for rambles along Lepétimnos' steadily dwindling network of trails; of late donkey trekking has become more popular than walking, and you'll see outfitters advertising throughout the north of the island.

The main highway south from Klió and Kápi leads back to the capital through **MANDAMÁDHOS**. This rather nondescript town is famous for its pottery, including the Ali-Baba style *pithária* (urns) seen around the island, but more so for the "black" icon of the Archangel Michael, whose monastery is the powerful focus of a thriving cult. The image (legendarily made from a mixture of mud and the blood of monks slaughtered in a massacre) is really more idol than icon, both in its lumpy three-dimensionality and in the manner of veneration which seems a hold-over from pagan times. First there is the custom of the coin-wish, whereby you press a coin to the Archangel's forehead – if it sticks, then your wish will be granted. It's further believed that in carrying out his various errands to bring about the desires of the faithful, the Archangel wears through enough footwear to stock a small shoeshop. Accordingly the icon was until recently surrounded not by the usual *támmata* (votive medallions) but by piles of miniature gold and silver shoes left by those he had helped. The ecclesiastical authorities, perhaps embarrassed by these "primitive" practices, apparently removed all of the little shoes in 1986. Just why his devotees should want to encourage this perpetual motion is uncertain, since in Greek folklore the Archangel Michael is also the one who comes for the souls of the dying.

Límnos

Límnos is a prosperous agricultural island that makes few concessions to tourism. Most visitors are Greek, and as a foreign traveller, you're still likely to find yourself an object of curiosity and hospitality; the island's remoteness, inconvenient ferry schedules and lack of obvious attractions mean that this is unlikely to change. Among Greeks, Limnos has a reputation for being dull, perhaps due to its unpopularity as an

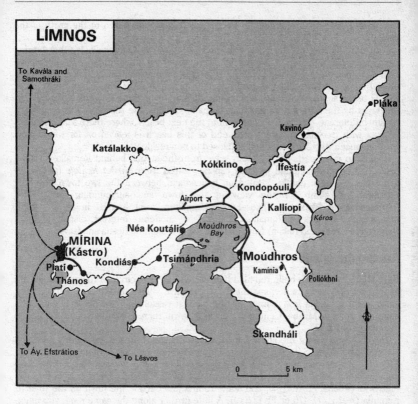

LÍMNOS

To Kavála and Samothráki

Pláka

Kavinó

Katálakko

Kókkino

Ifestía

Kondopóuli

Airport ✈

Kallíopi

Kéros

Néa Koutáli

Moúdhros Bay

MÍRINA
(Kástro)

Kondiás

Tsimándhria

Moúdhros

Platí

Kamínia

Poliókhni

Thános

Skandháli

To Áy. Efstrátios

To Lésvos

0   5 km

army posting. In recent years, the island has been a focus for disputes between the Greek and Turkish governments, and there is a very conspicuous military presence: Turkey has a longstanding demand that Límnos should be demilitarised and Turkish aircraft occasionally overfly the island, serving to worsen already tense Greek-Turkish relations.

Límnos is almost divided in two by the bays of Bournía and Moúdhros, the latter one of the largest natural harbours in the Aegean. The west of the island is rocky and mountainous, while the east is low-lying and speckled with ponds popular with duck hunters where it's not occupied by cattle, combine harvesters and rolling cornfields. However, there are few trees, and in summer the landscape can seem very dry and barren. With many long sandy beaches around the coast, it's easy to find a stretch to yourself, deserted apart from the odd pillbox or military outpost. The coast can be hard to reach however, as most services leave Mírina (the main town and port) in the morning and return in the early afternoon, although there are mopeds and cars to rent.

Mírina

MÍRINA (locally KÁSTRO), on the west coast, has the atmosphere of a provincial market/garrison town rather than a resort. It's pleasant enough, if not picturesque, apart from some old stone houses dating from the Turkish occupation. Mírina is fairly large for an island town, but most things of interest are on the main shopping street that stretches from the harbour to **Romaïkós Yialós**, the beach to the north of the castle.

You may be met off the boat with offers of a **room**. Otherwise, try the *Aktaion* (☎0254/22 258; ③), noisily located by the harbour, or the slightly more expensive *Poseidon Apartments* (☎0254/23 982 or 51 304; ④), behind Romaïkós Yialós. There's no official campsite here, but you could use the beach at AVLÓNAS, 2km north, or at PLATÍ to the south, which also has rooms. Back in town, there's a choice of good fish **tavernas** by the harbour, while along Romaïkós Yialós, the restaurants and bars are mostly indifferent – it's better to walk on to the next beach, where there's a reasonable taverna with tree-shaded tables. The end of this beach is fenced off for the luxury, Swiss-financed *Akti Marina* complex (closed to non-residents).

Buses to most parts of the island leave from the station behind Romaïkós Yialós, while cars, motorbikes and bicycles can be **rented** from *Mirina Rentals* (☎0254/24 476). The Genoese **castle**, located on a headland between the two town beaches, warrants the climb for the view of the town and surrounding coast. The **Archaeological Museum** (Tues–Sun 8.45am-3pm; free) housed in an old stone mansion at the back of Romaïkós Yialós, is of moderate interest, displaying finds (labelled in Greek and Italian) from excavations at Poliókhni, Ifestía and Kavivió .

Around the island

KONDIÁS, with stone-built, red-tiled houses, set in a semi-circle of rocky, wooded hill 11km east of Mírina, is perhaps the most attractive village on Límnos. It has a very basic *psistariá* and a few rooms, but the nearest reasonable beaches are 3km back along the road to Mírina. Continuing towards town, there is another good bay below the village of **PLATÍ**.

Beyond here, along the shores of Moúdros bay, the beaches are muddy and best avoided. **MOÚDROS** itself, the second largest town on Límnos, is of no great interest. The only reason you might want to stay here is as a base to visit the beaches and archaeological sites around the eastern part of the island. There's a **hotel**, the *Filoxenia* (☎0254/71 407; ④), and some rooms just outside the town on the road to Kamínia (☎0254/71 470 or 71 422; ③). A little further along the same road, you unexpectedly come to a military cemetery maintained by the Commonwealth War Graves Commission, its neat lawns and rows of white headstones incongruous in such barren surroundings. In 1915, Moúdros Bay was the principal base for the disastrous Gallipoli campaign. Of the 36,000 Allied dead, around 800 are buried here – mainly battle casualties who died after having been evacuated to the base hospital at Moúdros.

Indications of the most advanced Neolithic civilisation in the Aegean have been found at **Poliókhni**, 3km from the village of KAMÍNIA. Italian excavations in the 1930s uncovered four layers of settlement, the oldest from the fourth millennium BC, predating Troy on the Turkish coast opposite. The remains are rather confusing, and the site essential only for dedicated archaeologists, but the setting, on a low cliff above a long rock and sand beach, is attractive enough. A sporadic bus service connects Moúdros with Kamínia and SKANDHÁLI in the extreme southeast of the island, where there are mediocre beaches.

Ifestía and Kavírio, the other significant ancient sites on Límnos, are most easily reached from the village of KONDOPOÚLI, north of Moúdros. **Ifestía**, in Classical times the most important city on the island, took its name from Hephaistos, god of fire and metal-working. According to legend, Hephaistos landed on Límnos after being hurled from Mount Olympus by Zeus, the fall leaving him lame forever. Much of the site remains unexcavated, but there are scant remains of a theatre and a temple dedicated to the god. **Kavírio**, on the opposite side of Tigáni Bay, is a little more evocative. The remains are of a sanctuary connected with the cult of the Kabiroi on Samothraki, although the site on Límnos is probably older. Only the groundplan of the sanctuary and the bases of a row of Doric columns survive, but the setting – on a headland with views over much of the north coast – is impressive. Both sites are rather remote, and really only feasible to visit if you have your own transport.

The beach at **Kéros**, below KALLIÓPI and KONDOPOÚLI on the east coast, is one of the best on the island. A long stretch of sand with dunes and shallow water, it attracts a number of Greek tourists and Germans with camper vans and windsurfers, but is large enough to remain uncrowded. There are more good beaches near the village of **PLÁKA** at the northeastern tip of the island.

Áyios Efstrátios (Aï Strátis)

Áyios Efstrátios is one of the most isolated islands in the Aegean. Historically, the only outsiders to stay here have been those who were compelled to do so – it was a place of exile for political prisoners under both the Metaxas regime of the 1930s and the various right-wing governments that followed the civil war. It's still unusual for travellers to make it to the island, and, if you do, you're sure to be asked why you came.

You may well ask yourself the same question, for **ÁYIOS EFSTRÁTIOS** village – the only habitation on the island – is perhaps one of the ugliest in Greece. Devastated by an earthquake in 1967, it was grimly rebuilt as rows of concrete prefabs, a concrete church and a deserted shopping centre. The remains of the old village – a few mostly derelict houses surrounded by heaps of rubble – overlook the modern village from a neighbouring hillside. Sadly, most of the destruction was caused by army bulldozers rather than the earthquake: the building contract went to a company with junta connections, and the islanders were prevented from returning to their homes, although many could have been repaired. All in all, the village is a sad monument to the corruption of the junta years. If you're curious, there's an old photograph of the village, taken before the earthquake, in the **kafenío** by the harbour.

Architecture apart, Áyios Efstrátios is still a very traditional fishing and farming community. There are two very basic tavernas and a single pension in one of the few surviving old houses, which is likely to be full in the summer, so call in advance (☎0254/93 202). Nobody will object, however, if you camp on the beach in front of the village.

As you walk away from the village – there are no cars and no real roads – things improve rapidly. The landscape, dry hills and valleys scattered with oak trees, is deserted apart from wild rabbits, sheep, an occasional shepherd, and some good beaches where you can camp in desert island isolation – perhaps the only reason you're likely to visit the island. **Alonítsi**, on the north coast, a ninety-minute walk from the village following a track up the north side of the valley, is a two-kilometre stretch of sand with rolling breakers and views across to Límnos.

South of the village, there's a series of greyish sand beaches, most with wells and drinkable water, although with few real paths in this part of the island, getting to them can be something of a scramble. **Lidharío**, at the end of an attractive wooded valley, is the first worthwhile beach, but again, it's a ninety-minute walk, unless you can persuade a fisherman to take you by boat. Some of the caves around the coast are home to the rare Mediterranean monk seal, but you're unlikely to see one.

Ferries between Límnos and Rafína, Kími and Kavála call at Áyios Efstrátios every two or three days. In summer, there's also a *kaíki* from Límnos twice a week. The harbour is too shallow for the ferries, which anchor outside and transfer passengers and cargo to a boat from the village. This procedure feels hazardous enough at the best of times, and in bad weather you could end up stranded here for longer than you bargained for.

Samothráki (Samothrace)

After Thíra, Samothráki has the most dramatic profile of all the Greek islands. Originally colonised by immigrants from Sámos (hence the name), it rises abruptly from the sea in a dark mass of granite, culminating in 1600-metre Mount Fengári. Seafarers have always been guided by its imposing outline, and in legend its summit provided a vantage point for Poseidon to watch over the siege of Troy. The forbidding coastline provides no natural anchorage, and landing is still very much subject to the vagaries of the wind. Yet despite these difficulties, for over a millennium pilgrims journeyed to the island to visit the **Sanctuary of the Great Gods** and to be initiated into its mysteries. The Sanctuary is still the outstanding attraction of the island, which, home to under 3000 people and too remote for most tourists (although July and August can be busy), combines an earthy simplicity with its natural grandeur.

Kamariótissa and Hóra

Boats dock at the little port of **KAMARIÓTISSA**, where there are **rooms for rent** and a long pebble beach where you could unofficially and uncomfortably camp. The seafront is lined with tavernas and bars, which, with a couple of nearby discos, constitute the island's only real **nightlife**. There's a **bank** and a couple of places renting out **motorbikes and mopeds**, near where the boat docks. Otherwise, Kamariótissa isn't a picturesque or particularly interesting village, and you're unlikely to want to stay long. **Buses** run hourly in season (but only twice weekly in winter) along the north coast to Thermá via Palaeópoli (the site of the Sanctuary) and inland to **HÓRA**, the only other village of any size, an attractive community of whitewashed Thracian-style houses overshadowed by the western flanks of Mount Fengári and the ruins of a Byzantine fort. Hóra, too, has **rooms**, along with another bank, the **post office**, the **OTE** branch and three tavernas. A track leads north to the hamlet of **PALEÓPOLI**, and, in a stony ravine between it and the plunging, northeasternmost ridgeline of Mount Fengári, lie the remains of the **Sanctuary of the Great Gods**.

The Sanctuary of the Great Gods

From the late Bronze Age to the last years of the Roman occupation, the mysteries and sacrifices of the cult of the Great Gods were performed on Samothráki. The island was the spiritual focus of the northern Aegean, and its importance in the ancient world was comparable (although certainly secondary) to that of the Mysteries of Eleusis.

The religion of the Great Gods revolved around a hierarchy of ancient Thracian fertility figures: the Great Mother, a subordinate male deity known as Kadmilos, and the potent and ominous twin demons, the *Kabiroi*. When the Samian colonists arrived (traditionally c 700 BC) they simply syncretised the resident deities with their own – the Great Mother became Demeter, her consort Hermes, and the *Kabiroi* were fused interchangeably with the *Dioskouroi*. Around the nucleus of a sacred precinct the newcomers made the beginnings of what is now the Sanctuary.

The mysteries of the cult were never explicitly recorded, since ancient writers feared incurring the wrath of the *Kabiroi*, but it has been established that two levels of initiation were involved. Incredibly, both ceremonies, in direct opposition to the elitism of Eleusis, were open to allcomers, including women and slaves. The lower level of initiation may, as is speculated at Eleusis, have involved a ritual simulation of the life, death and rebirth cycle; in any case, we know that it ended with joyous feasting and can conjecture, since so many clay torches have been found, that it took place at night by their light. The higher level of initiation carried the unusual requirement of a moral standard (the connection of theology with morality – so strong in the later Judeo-

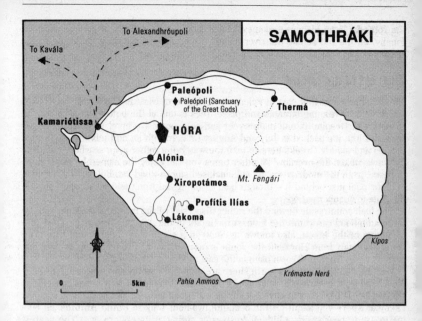

Christian tradition – was rarely made at all by the early Greeks). This second level involved a full confession followed by absolution and baptism in bull's blood.

The Site

The site (Tues–Sun 8.30am–3pm; 200dr) is clearly labelled, simple to grasp and strongly evocative of its proud past. It's a good idea to visit the **museum** (open approximately the same hours as the site) first, where typical sections of the buildings have been reconstructed and arranged with friezes and statues to give you a fuller idea of their original scale. An excellent guide by Karl Lehmann – the American excavator of the site – is on sale.

The first structure you come to is the **Anaktoron**, the hall of initiation for the first level of the mysteries, dating in its present form from Roman times. Its inner sanctum was marked by a warning *stele* (now in the museum) and at the southeast corner you can make out the libation pit. Next to it is the **Arsinoeion**, the largest circular ancient building known in Greece. Within its rotunda are the walls of a double precinct (fourth century BC) where a rock altar, the earliest preserved ruin on the site, has been uncovered. A little further on, on the same side of the path, you come to the **Temenos**, a rectangular area open to the sky where the feasting probably took place, and, edging its rear corner, the conspicuous **Hieron**. Five columns and an architrave of the facade of this large Doric edifice which hosted the higher level of initiation have been erected; dating in part from the fourth century BC, it was heavily restored in Roman times. Its stone steps have been replaced by modern blocks but the Roman benches for spectators remain *in situ*, along with the sacred stones where confession was heard.

To the west of the path you can just discern the outline of the **theatre**, and above it on a ridge is the **Nike fountain**, famous for the exquisitely sculpted marble centrepiece – the *Winged Victory of Samothrace* – which once stood breasting the wind at the prow of a marble ship. It was discovered in 1863 by the French and carried off to the Louvre, with a copy belatedly forwarded to the local museum. Higher up along the ridge, opposite the rotunda, is an elaborate medieval fortification made entirely of antique material. Finally, on the hill across the river stands a monumental **gateway** dedicated to the Great Gods by Ptolemy II; many of its blocks lie scattered across the ravine.

The rest of the island

Nine kilometres further east of Paleópoli on the north coast is **THÉRMA**, (LOUTRÁ) which with its running streams and plane trees is one of the better places to stay on Samothráki. Despite its one main street and sole expensive hotel (also with cheaper rooms to let), it's packed in July and August (mainly with an odd mixture of German hippies and elderly Greeks here to take the waters); a rather grim seashore campsite 2km away takes the overflow. At other times you can enjoy the namesake hot springs in peace, from the modern spa, an old, enclosed stucco-wood bathhouse, or a warmish outdoor pool just behind it – though bear in mind you won't find much open outside the June to October period.

The lush countryside beyond the rather dispersed village is fine for walking, and the more ambitious can climb the highest mountain in the Aegean, **Mount Fengári** (the Mountain of the Moon, also known as *Sáos*) in a six to eight hour round trip. (You could also start from Horá but the route is more difficult.) From the top, a clear day permits views from the Trojan plain in the east to Mount Athos in the west.

Beaches on Samothráki's north shore are uniformly pebbly and exposed; for better ones head for the warmer south flank of the island. A couple of daily buses go as far as **PROFÍTIS ILÍAS**, an attractive hill village with good tavernas but no place to stay, via Lákoma, where you alight for the beautiful two-hour walk to **Pahiá Ámmos**, an 800-metre sandy beach with a hidden freshwater spring at its eastern end. The nearest supplies are at LÁKOMA, but this doesn't deter big summer crowds who also arrive by excursion *kaíki*. These also continue past the Krémasta Nerá coastal waterfalls to **Kípos**, another good sandy beach with fresh water nearby, at the extreme southeast tip of the island.

Thássos

Just twelve kilometres from the mainland, Thássos has long been a popular resort for northern Greeks, and in recent years has been attracting considerable numbers of foreign (mainly German) tourists. Without being spectacular, it's a very beautiful island, its almost circular area covered in gentle slopes of pine, olive and chestnut that rise to a mountainous backbone and plunge to a line of good sandy beaches. It's by no means unspoiled, but visitors tend to be spread over six or seven fair-sized villages as well as the two main towns, so enclaves of bars and discos haven't swamped the ordinary Greek life of nut-, olive- or fruit-harvesting, marble-quarrying and beekeeping. Beehives often line the roadsides, and many types of local honey can be bought all over the island, as can walnut jam, a thick, treacle-like speciality. Among the less pleasant wildlife is the ubiquitous mosquito, so come prepared. Also, most of the inland forests were ravaged by fire in 1985, so do heed the many forest-fire prevention warnings and be extra careful if camping. Despite the many "No Camping" signs, the island is ideal for this, and it's still possible to pitch a tent discreetly in most places.

Thássos Town

THÁSSOS TOWN, or LIMÉNAS/LIMÍN as it's also known, is the island capital and nexus of life, though not the main port. (Kavála-based ferries usually stop down the coast at Órmos Prínou, but a few each day continue on here – a trip worth making for the pine-clad mountain views.) The town, though largely modern, is partly redeemed by its pretty fishing harbour, a popular sand beach just to the east, and the substantial remains of the ancient city which pop up between and above the streets. If you want to stay, there are several cheap **hotels and pensions**: choose from the *Astir* (☎0593/22 160; ③), *Diamando* (☎0593/22 622), *Viky* (☎0593/22 314; ③) and *Angelika* (☎0593/22 387; ③). There are also reasonably plentiful **rooms**, though in summer you should take the first thing offered on arrival. For **Eating**, menus tend to be expensive and bland.

For exploring, the best plan is to rent a moped to circle the island, then use the bus system once you've pinpointed favourite spots. **Car rental** is available but as expensive as anywhere else in Greece; **mopeds or motorbikes** go for standard rates. **Bicycles** are also available, though be aware that there's little flat terrain. **Hitching** is generally good, since distances are usually small. The **bus station** is on the front, near the ferry mooring. The service is good, with about five buses per day doing the full island circuit in season, and several more to and from different villages, with a bias towards the west coast. The "grand tour" costs well under half the price of a hired scooter. There's a

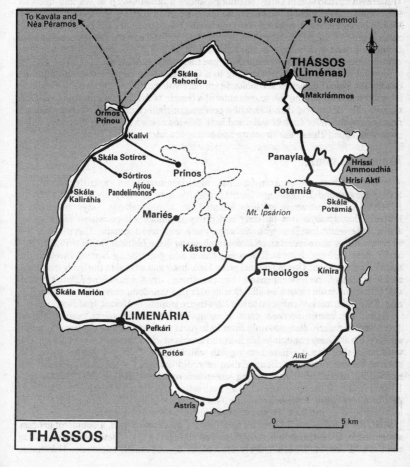

THÁSSOS

privately-run **tourist office** near the old port, with the usual maps, timetables and trips, and also a **tourist police** office (open during high season only) near the bus station.

Ancient **Thássos** abounded in mineral wealth, controlled goldmines on the Thracian mainland and had two safe anchorages, assets which ensured prosperity through Classical, Macedonian and Roman rule. The ruins surrounding the modern town – Limín, incidentally, means "the harbour" – show traces from each phase of this development. The main excavated area is the **agora**, the entrance is beside the town **museum** (Tues–Sat 8.30am–3pm, Sun 9.30am–2.30pm), a little way back from the modern harbour. The site is fenced but not always locked and, taking advantage of this, is best seen towards dusk when a calm, slightly misty air often descends. Prominent are two Roman *stoas* but you can also make out shops, monuments, passageways and sanctuaries from the remodelled Classical city. At the far end of the site (away from the sea) a fifth-century BC passageway leads through to an elaborate sanctuary of Artemis, a good stretch of Roman road and a few seats of the *odeion*.

Above the town, roughly in line with the smaller fishing port, steps spiral up to a **Hellenistic theatre**, fabulously positioned above a broad sweep of sea and used for performances of ancient drama every Saturday between late July and mid-August; tickets can be purchased in advance from the tourist police or from EOT in Kavála. On the same corner of the headland as the theatre, you can still see the old-fashioned *kaíkia* being built, and gaze across to the uninhabited islet of Thassopoúla. It's possible to **rent boats**, self-skippered or not, to take you there and elsewhere.

Beyond the theatre, a path winds on to a **Genoese fort**, constructed out of numerous stones from the ancient acropolis. From here you can follow the circuit of **walls** to a high terrace supporting the foundations of a temple of Apollo and onwards to a small rock-hewn sanctuary of Pan. Below it a precarious, sixth-century BC "secret stairway" descends to the outer rank of walls and back into town. It's a satisfying itinerary, which gives you a good idea of the structure and extent of a fairly typical Classical city.

Around the coast

The first beach clockwise from Liménas, **Makriámmos**, is an expensive, restricted-access playground for package tourists, and it's best to carry on to **PANAYÍA** or **POTAMIÁ**, two attractive villages situated on a mountainous ledge overlooking Potamiá Bay. Panayía is a bustling and pretty mountain village where life revolves around the central square with its large plane tree and fountain. There are a few souvenir shops, and several small **hotels** – cheapest is the *Helvetia* (☎0593/61 231; ③) – and **rooms** for rent, but you'll also see sheep and goats being herded through the middle of the village. This is an ideal place for a drink and a meal in the lively evenings, and food tends to be less expensive than elsewhere – try the *Kostas* or *Ethitrio* restaurants. Potamiá proper has a small folk museum (8.30am–3pm, closed Tues), as well as one of the best, marked paths up to the 1204-metre summit of **Mount Ipsárion**.

There are more tavernas (and a campsite) at the excellent, sandy **Hrissí Ammoudhiá** beach, 4km downhill from Panayía at the north end of the bay. No buses go here but it's easy enough to hitch from Panayía or cheap enough to get a taxi. The walk looks short but it's quite heavy going with luggage. Once you get there you can choose between indoor accommodation or rough camping – the latter popular and untroubled except for early-morning sheep-bell reveilles. **SKÁLA POTAMIÁS** (aka HRISSÍ AKTÍ), at the opposite end, is less attractive with its rocky beach; every building seems to be a souvenir shop, hotel, cafeteria or "rooms to let". Skála's main virtue is the local fishing fleet and the corresponding quality of the seafood restaurants.

KÍNIRA is a tiny hamlet further south with a moderate beach, a couple of grocery stores and hotels – cheapest is the *Athina* (☎0593/31 314; ③) – a few rooms and a lot of beehives. **"Paradise Beach"**, nicely situated, sandy, and mainly nudist, lies 1km south, and there are more beautiful and deserted coves beyond in the same direction if you're willing to explore.

The south-facing coast of Thássos has most of the island's best beaches. **Alikí** faces a double bay which almost pinches off a headland. The mixed sand-and-pebble spit gets too popular for its own good in high season, but the water is crystal-clear and the beach-side taverna offers good food. The hamlet here (one rooms establishment) is at least worth a stopover. Nearby were ancient marble quarries which supplied the Greek city-states and later the Romans, and on the western cove the pillars of a Doric sanctuary are still visible. It is possible to walk away from the crowds and find some excellent spots for snorkelling, sunbathing and picnics, using the slabs of marble that are scattered around the headland, both above and below the waterline; these have occasionally been eroded into convenient bathtub shapes.

At the extreme south tip of Thássos, **ASTRÍS** has two excellent beaches set in a stunning cliffscape, but the best-appointed local resort – and virtually the only one to function outside of summer – is **Potós**, where there are two modest **hotels**, the *Io* (☎0593/51 216; ③) and *Katerina* (☎0593/51 345; ③), a **campsite**, and a fine one-kilometre sandy beach facing the sunset. **Pefkári**, 1km west, is essentially an annexe of Potós but the manicured sand has been overwhelmed by the touristic development behind.

As an alternative to Liménas you can base yourself in the marginally quieter and quainter **LIMENÁRIA**, the island's second town, built to house German mining executives brought in by the Turks at the turn of the century. Their remaining mansions lend some distinctive character, but this apart it's a rather ordinary tourist resort, handy mainly for its **banks**, **post office** and **OTE** station. There are nearly a dozen cheap **hotels**, and numerous **rooms**, so you'll eventually find something affordable and vacant.

Continuing clockwise from Limenária to Thássos, the bus service is more frequent, but there's progressively less to stop off for. The various *skáles* (coastal annexes of villages built inland during piratic ages) such as Skála Marión, Skála Kaliráhis and Skála Sotíros, are bleak, straggly and windy, uninviting even on the rare occasions when the shore is sandy.

ÓRMOS PRÍNOU has little to recommend it, other than the ferry connections to Kavála. Buses are usually timed to coincide with the ferries, but if you want to stay, numerous (not very cheap) rooms, hotels and quayside tavernas beckon. There's a good, official **campsite** near SKÁLA RAHONÍOU, between here and Thássos town (though the beach is mediocre), as well as rooms, hotels, and good fish restaurants.

The interior

Few people get around to exploring inland Thássos, but there are several worthwhile rambles around the hill villages besides the aforementioned walk up Mount Ipsárion from Potamiá. From Potós you can hitch or take a bus up to **THEOLÓGOS**, a linear community of old houses founded by refugees from Constantinople, which was the island's capital under the Turks (the last of whom only departed, as was the case in most islands covered in this chapter, after 1923). It has a small square with a couple of cafés under a tree, and a few rooms are available.

From Theológos you can walk down to Kínira on the east coast on a gravel jeep track, or take your chances with narrower trails leading north through whatever remains of the forest. The most interesting return to Potós involves a westward trek, on a variety of surfaces, to **KÁSTRO**, the most naturally fortified of the anti-pirate redoubts. Thirty houses and a church surround a rocky pinnacle which is a sheer drop on three sides; summer occupation is becoming the rule after total abandonment in the last century. You could perhaps be put up for the night – there's one taverna, one phone, no power – but without transport you will have to walk or hitch 15km down a dirt road to Limenária.

From Kalívi on the west coast a rough road leads 4km up to **MIKRÓ ÁNO PRÍNOS**, start of the signposted, one-hour walk up to Ayíou Pandelímona nunnery. From there you can press on to **SOTÍR**, an untouched old village to the west, or take the much more confusing way (on lumber roads) to **MARIÉS** in the direction of the *Kástro*. You can often hitch down from the inland villages with people who've been tending their beehives, but take food along for the day – there are often no facilities at all.

travel details

To simplify the lists that follow we've excluded a regular sailing of the *NEL* company, which once a week runs a service, usually the Áyios Rafael but sometimes the Alcaeos, linking Thessaloníki or Kavála with Límnos, Lésvos, Híos, Sámos, Ikaría, Pátmos, Kálimnos, Kós and Rhodes. Each one-way trip tends to take place over a 36-hour period between Sunday and Wednesday night – exact days subject to change according to season.

SÁMOS (Vathí) 3–7 weekly to Ikaría, Páros, Pireás (14hr); 2–3 weekly to Híos; 1–2 weekly to Foúrni, Náxos, Míkonos, Tínos, Síros.
SÁMOS (Karlóvassi) As for Vathí, plus 2 weekly *kaíki* departures, usually early Mon and Thurs afternoon, to Foúrni.
SÁMOS (Pithagório) 1–2 weekly to Foúrni, Ikaría, Pátmos; 1–2 weekly to Agathónissi, Lipsí, Pátmos, Léros, Kálimnos, with onward connections to all other Dodecanese (see the "Nissos Kalimnos" summary in *The Dodecanese*). Also expensive excursion *kaíkia* daily in season to Pátmos, and even costlier hydrofoils twice weekly to Kós.
IKARÍA 3–7 weekly to Sámos (both northern ports), Páros and Pireás (at least 2 weekly services via Évdhilos year-round); 1– 2 weekly to Foúrni, Náxos, Míkonos, Tínos, Síros; 1–2 weekly to Foúrni and Pátmos; 4–5 weekly, from Áyios Kírikos, to Foúrni.
FOÚRNI 1–2 weekly ferries, usually Wed or Sun, to Sámos (northern ports), Páros and Pireás; smaller ferries twice weekly (often Tues and Fri) to Sámos (Pithagório), Ikaría, Pátmos; morning *kaíki* to Ikaría, Mon, Wed, Fri, Sun, and on Sat only by demand; twice weekly (usually Mon and Thur) morning *kaíki* to Karlóvassi (Sámos).
HÍOS 4–7 weekly to Pireás (10hr) and Lésvos (4hr); 2 weekly to Rafína, Límnos, Sámos, Psará; 2 weekly to Sámos (5hr), Foúrni and Pátmos; 1 weekly to Thessaloníki, Vólos, Áyios Efstrátios, Kavála. Daily afternoon *kaíki* to Inoússes; 2

weekly to Psará (4hr), 2 weekly on different days from Limniá to Psará (2hr). Also *Flying Dolphin* connections with Lésvos (Mitilíni) (1hr 45min) and Pátmos (2hr 50min).
LÉSVOS 4–7 weekly to Pireás (12hr direct, 14hr via Híos); 4–7 weekly to Híos (4hr); 2–4 weekly to Áyios Efstrátios (4hr 30min); Límnos (7hr) and Thessaloníki (17hr); or Kavála (15hr); 2 weekly to Rafína; 1 weekly to Vólos.
LÍMNOS 5 weekly to Kavála; 2 weekly to Pireás; 1 weekly to Thessaloníki; 4 weekly to Áyios Efstrátios, Mitilíni, Híos, and Rafína; 2 weekly to Pireás and Thessaloníki. Also a summer-only *kaíki* to Áyios Efstrátios twice weekly.
ÁYIOS EFSTRÁTIOS 4 weekly to Límnos, Rafína; 3 weekly to Kavála; 1 weekly to Mitilíni, Híos.
SAMOTHRÁKI 1–2 daily ferries to/from Alexandhroúpoli (2hr) in season, dropping to 5–6 weekly out of season. Also a connection with Límnos once a week throughout the year (originating in Alexandhroúpoli), and with Kavála (and therefore other North Aegean islands) once a week, currently on Fri, returning on Sat.
THÁSSOS 7–15 ferries daily (depending on season) between Kavála and Órmos Prínou (1hr), with a few of these services extending to Liménas. Similar frequencies between Liménas and Keramotí (45min). No direct connections with any other island; you must travel via Kavála.

International Ferries
Váthi (Sámos)–Kuşadaşi (Turkey) At least 1 daily, late April to late October; otherwise a Turkish boat only by demand, usually Fri or Sat. Morning Greek boat (passengers only), afternoon Turkish boats (usually 2 – they take 2 cars apiece). Rates are £20 one-way including taxes on both the Greek and Turkish sides, £26 round-trip all-in; no day return rate. Small cars £30 one-way. Journey time 1hr 30min. Also infrequent (1– 2 weekly) services in season from Pithagório.

Kuşadası (Turkey)–Páros–Kefalloniá–Corfu–Ancona (Italy) 1–2 weekly *Minoan Lines* boats, in the past the *Ariadne*. One stopover allowed between Italy and Turkey with prior notice.

Híos–Cesme (Turkey) 2–12 boats weekly, depending on season. Thurs night and Sat morning services run year-round. Rates are £15 one-way, £20 day return, £30 open return, including Greek taxes. Journey time 45min.

Mitilíni (Lésvos)–Ayvalik (Turkey) 5 weekly in season morning only; winter link unreliable. Note that if initially embarking from the Greek side you are only allowed to use the Greek boat, and cannot board the Turkish afternoon boat, owing to a long-standing feud between the tourist industries of the two communities. A replacement line to Dikili, a few kilometres south of Ayvalik, is supposed to start in 1993. The current rates are about £16 one-way, £24 return. Small cars cost £30 each way. Journey time 1hr 30min.

Flights
Sámos–Athens (3–4 daily; 1hr)
Híos–Athens (3–4 daily; 1hr)
Lésvos–Athens (3–7 daily; 45min)
Lésvos–Thessaloníki (4–6 weekly; 1hr)
Límnos–Athens (2–5 daily; 1hr)
Límnos–Mitilíni (4 weekly; 40min)
Límnos–Thessaloníki (4–6 weekly; 1hr)

CHAPTER ELEVEN

THE SPORADES AND ÉVVIA

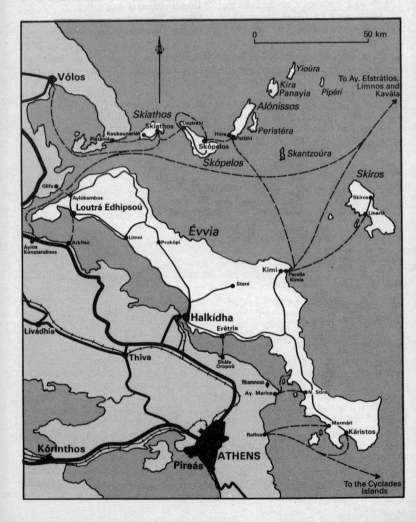

The three northern **Sporades**, Skíathos, Skópelos and Alónissos, are scattered (as their name suggests) head-to-tail with each other, just off the mainland. They're archetypal holiday islands, with a wide selection of good beaches, transparent waters and thick pine forests. They are all very busy in season, though Skíathos is the only one that's sacrificed its entire character to tourism. None has any prominent historical sites, nor much history until the Middle Ages – Skíathos town is nineteenth-century, Skópelos town older in parts – so there's no pressure to do much sightseeing. They're also an easy group to island-hop, well connected by bus and ferry both with Athens – via Áyios Konstantínos or Kími – and with Vólos, though the only ferry connection to Skíros is from Kími, plus, in summer, a "Flying Dolphin" service from Vólos via the other Sporades (3–5 times weekly).

Skíathos has the best beaches, although it is also by far the busiest island in the group. These days **Skópelos** gets crowded too, although it does preserve a certain amount of character. **Alónissos** is the quietest of the three, and has the wildest scenery, but it's only really worth a visit if you stay outside the ugly, post-earthquake main town. **Skíros**, further southeast, retains more of its traditional culture than the other three islands, though development is now well under way: the main town doesn't yet feel like a resort, but is not uncommercialised either. Unlike the other three islands, the only good beaches are those close to the main town.

To the south, the huge island of **Évvia** (or Euboea) runs for 150km alongside the mainland with which it is linked by a bridge (at its capital, Halkídha), and by a series of shuttle-ferries. Perhaps because it lacks any real island feel or identity, it is explored by few foreign tourists. Athenians, in contrast, visit in force, unbothered by such scruples and attracted to half a dozen or so major resorts.

Skíathos

The commercialisation of **Skíathos** is legendary among foreigners and Greeks – it's a close fourth to that of Corfu, Míkonos and Rhodes. But if you've some time to spare, or a gregarious nature, you might still break your journey here in order to sample the best, if most overcrowded beaches in the Sporades. Along the south and southeast coasts, the road serves an almost unbroken line of concrete villas, hotels and restaurants, and although this isn't enough to take away the island's natural beauty, it makes it difficult to find anything unspoilt or particularly Greek about it all. However, as almost the entire population lives in Skíathos town, a little walking soon pays off, though camping outside official sites is strongly discouraged: summer turns the dry pine-needles to tinder – a problem to be aware of on each of the Sporades islands.

Getting around the island

Skíathos offers an unusually wide range of transport choices for those with unlimited budgets. A large number of competing rental outlets in town, most on the front behind the ferry harbour, offer bicycles, mopeds, motorbikes, cars and motorboats for rent: the lowest priced, beach buggy-type cars go for around 7000dr a day, motorboats for 10,000dr a day; fuel and insurance are extra. At a slower pace, several travel agents organise "round the island" mule trips (2500dr a day), or there's horse riding at the *Pinewood Riding Club* on the road to Aselinós beach. Buses and taxis also ply from near the ferry harbour. To Koukounariés, the bus is the cheapest option; the last one returns at 10pm. *Aselinos Tours* run a private bus to Aselinós beach once a day, leaving at 11am from outside their office, close to the official bus stop and returning at 4.30pm (150dr). If shared among a few people, taxis should work out only a little more expensive – though ask the fare first.

You could also get your bearings on a boat trip around the island. These cost 2000–2500dr and leave around 10am. Or try a boat trip to the islet of Tsougria, opposite Skíathos town (where there's a good beach and a taverna): beware that boats leave from the fishing harbour beyond the Boúrtzi, and not the yacht anchorage to the north of the ferry harbour.

If you're interested in seeing more of Skíathos on foot, the locally produced Skíathos guide by Rita and Dietrich Harkort has detailed instructions and maps for walks all over the island. It's a good way to escape the crowds, although you're never going to get away from it all completely.

Skíathos town and around

SKÍATHOS TOWN, where the ferries dock, looks great from a distance, but as you approach, the tourist development becomes all too apparent. Even the little offshore Boúrtzi fortress houses a taverna, and the old quarters (on the slopes away from Odhós Alexándhrou Papadhiamánd) are in danger of being overwhelmed by ranks of hotels, restaurants and "English" pubs. Skíathos has earned its recent reputation as "the straight Míkonos".

Most facilities of interest are on A Papadhiamándi, including the OTE, post office, banks and *Olympic Airways* office. Most of the island's accommodation is in Skíathos town: the few reasonably priced **hotels or pensions** will be full in season, though you can usually find a room, albeit slightly more expensively than on most islands. At other times, supply exceeds demand and you can find very cheap rooms with a little bargaining. There is no official accommodation bureau but there are several tourist agencies. For an honest and helpful approach, try Dimitris Mathinos, a former sea captain with an office at the bottom of A Papadhiamándi, though avoid lodgings in the flatlands to the rightnorthas they tend to be noisy. The best location for accommodation is beyond the *Stamatis* taverna (pricey but worth it), overlooking the fishing harbour – walk high above the water, but parallel to it. There's another concentration of good rooms on Kapodhistríou 14. The island now has four official **campsites** – at Koliós, Koukounariés, Aselinós and Xanémos beach. Koliós is okay, but Koukounariés and Aselinós are probably the best choices. Xanémos beach is 3km northeast of Skíathos town, right next to the airport runway, and, apart from being within walking distance of the town, has little to recommend it.

A good and unusual place to **eat** is the English-run *Lemon Tree Restaurant*, just off A. Papadhiamándi, which does good Indian and vegetarian food. *Taverna Vrahos* has excellent views of the harbour and serves great lobster and fish dishes. The *Banana Bar* is a decent **disco bar**. If that's not your style, the *Kirki Bar* nearby plays good jazz and blues.

As for sights, there aren't any, apart from the excellent **Galerie Varsakis**, near the fishing port on Platía Tríon Ierarhón – one of the best folklore displays in Greece. Many of the older items on display would do the Benaki Museum proud, and Mr Varsakis neither expects, nor wants, to sell the more expensive of these.

Around Skíahos town

The **Monastery of Evangelístria** (daily 8am–noon & 5–7pm), which is an hour on foot out of Skíathos town, is also accessible by rented moped, car or mule. The Greek flag was raised here in 1827, and, among other heroes of the War of Independence, Kolokotronis pledged his oath to fight for freedom here. It is exceptionally beautiful, even beyond the grandeur of isolation you find in all Greek monasteries. To reach it, walk out of the centre of town on the road towards the airport until, at the point where the asphalt veers to the right, a prominently signposted and waymarked track veers left.

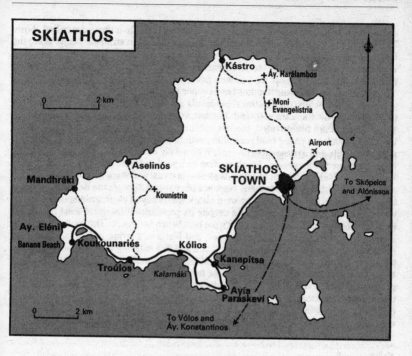

Beyond Evangelístria, a mule track continues to the disused **Monastery of Harálambos**, from where it's possible to walk across the island to the old ruined capital of **Kástro** along another dirt road, taking about two hours. From Skíathos town, it's quicker to take the direct road; the turning is signposted on the road behind town, some distance beyond the turning for Evangelístria. You can take a moped or car to within a thirty-minute walk of Kástro – a spectacular spot, built on a windswept headland. In the past, the entrance was only accessible by a drawbridge (now ruined), which has been replaced by a flight of steps. The village was built in the sixteenth century, when the people of the island moved here for security from pirate raids. It was abandoned 300 years later in 1830, following independence from Turkey, when the population moved back to build the modern town on the site of ancient Skíathos. The ruins are largely overgrown, and only three churches survive intact, the largest still retaining some original frescoes. From outside the gates, a path leads down the rocks to a good pebble **beach**. With a stream running down from the hills and a daytime café (with slightly overpriced food and drinks), it wouldn't make a bad place to camp. However, for an apparently inaccessible spot, it does attract a surprising number of people. All the island excursion boats call here, and even when they've gone, there's little chance of having the ruins or beach to yourself.

The island's beaches

The real business of Skíathos, is **beaches**. There are reputed to be over sixty of them on the island, as there need to be to soak up the numbers of summer visitors: at the height of season, the resident population of 4500 can be eclipsed by up to 50,000 outsiders. The beaches on the northeast coast aren't easily accessible, unless you pay for an excursion *kaiki* or are ready for much more arduous treks than those described above. The bus, though, runs along the entire south coast, and from strategic points along the way you can easily reach a good number of beaches. The prevailing summer *meltemi* wind blows from the north, so the beaches on the south coast are usually better protected. Most of the popular beaches have at least a drinks/snacks stall; those at Vromólimnos, Aselinós and Troúlos have proper tavernas.

The beaches before the Kalamáki peninsula are unexciting, but on the promontory itself, flanked by the campsite and Kanapítsa hamlet, **Rígas, Áyia Paraskeví** and **Vromólimnos** are highly rated, the last offering windsurfing and waterskiing. Beyond here, fom Troúlos, a paved road runs 4km north to **Mégas Aselinós**, a very good beach with a campsite and a reasonable taverna. With a daily bus and excursion boats stopping here, it's crowded in season. An alternative fork leads, via the convent of **Kounístria** (complete with snack bar) to **Mikros Aselinós**, just east and somewhat quieter.

KOUKOUNARIÉS, the last bus stop, is a busy resort, though the beach is excellent if you don't mind the crowds. There's a majestic sandy bay of clear, gradually deepening water, backed by acres of pines, and despite its popularity it merits at least one visit if only to assess the dubious claim that it's the best beach in Greece. The road runs behind a small lake at the back of the pine trees, and features a string of hotels, rooms and restaurants, as well as a good campsite. If you feel like entering into the spirit of things, jetskis, motorboats, windsurfing and waterskiing are all available off the beach. **Banana Beach** (aka **Krássa**), the third cove on the far side of Poúnda headland, is the trendiest of the island's nudist beaches. For the less adventurous, the turning for **Ayía Eléni**, the penultimate bus stop (ie before you reach Koukounariés), leads one kilometre to the pleasant beach (with a drinks stall). Or ask the driver to set you down before here, at the start of the thirty-minute path to **Mandhráki** beach, which has similar facilities.

Skópelos

More rugged and better cultivated than Skíathos, Skópelos is also very much more attractive. Not that its beaches are any better, its pine forests any thicker, nor its accommodation any less crowded in high season. But it does manage to maintain a character, at least in part, that's independent of tourism. It is a well-watered place, harvesting olives, plums, pears and almonds. Glóssa and Skópelos, its two main towns, are also among the prettiest in the Sporades, clambering uphill along paved steps, their houses distinguished by attractive wooden balconies and grey slate roofs.

A number of nationalities have occupied the island at various stages of its history, among them the Venetians, the French, Romans, Persians and, of course, the Turks. Indeed one Turkish admiral, Barbarossa (Redbeard), had the entire population of the island slaughtered in the sixteenth century.

Loutráki, Glóssa and the west

Most boats call at both ends of Skópelos, stopping first at the small port of **LOUTRÁKI** with its thin pebble beach, couple of hotels and few rooms for rent. It's been spoilt a little by developments at either end, but it's still not a bad place to stay if you're after peace and quiet; try the simple *Pension Flisvos*, or the fancier *Hotel Avra*. Unfortunately most of the quayside tavernas are a rip-off, although the café/shop in the square by the harbour is shrouded by beautiful chestnut trees and sells a highly recommended home-made retsina.

High above Loutráki, **GLÓSSA** is perhaps a preferable base, a sizeable and quite beautiful town, totally Greek, with several *kafenía*, a taverna and a very few rooms to let – try Kostas and Nina's place (☎0424/33 686; ②), which has simple and clean rooms,

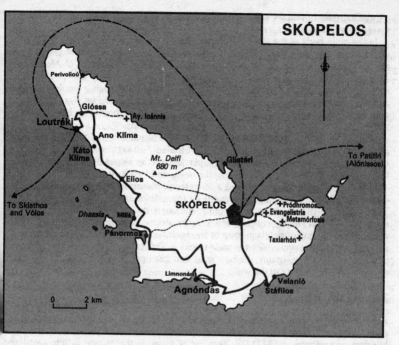

some with a view; they also rent out studios longer-term. Eating, there's one taverna, *To Agnandi*, a lively and authentic place, full most evenings. Incidentally, it's a good idea to accept offers of a taxi ride up to Glóssa from Loutráki; it's a stiff walk up even if you know the path short cuts, and taxi drivers will know which pensions have vacancies.

Ninety minutes' walk from Glóssa, across to the north coast, will bring you to a beach the locals call **Perivolioú**. The walk itself is worthwhile, passing a monastery next to a hollow stone cairn containing masses of human bones and skulls. There's also a huge hollow oak tree here, in the heart of which is a small tank of drinking water. The beach, when you get there, is nothing out of the ordinary, but there's spring water and a cave for shade.

East of Glóssa, a new dirt road leads to the amazing monastery of **Áyios Ioánnis**, accessible at the bottom of a vertiginous flight of steps. This is another beautiful, peaceful walk (again about 90min), with hawks and nightingales for company. The monastery has a truly dramatic setting, perched on the top of a rock high above the sea, though the buildings themselves are modern and rather ugly. There's a water cistern on the rock, and below it a small sandy cove for swimming.

Skópelos town

If you stay on the ferry beyond Loutráki – and this is probably the best plan – you reach **SKÓPELOS TOWN**, sloping down one corner of a huge, almost circular bay. The best way to arrive is by sea, with the town revealed slowly as the boat rounds the final headland. Be prepared, though, for the crowds: although still well behind Skiathos, Skópelos town has seen enormous commercialisation over recent years, with a huge increase in visitors and prices, and the centre is a mass of boutiques and pricey tavernas, with an untidy sprawl of new hotels to the southeast.

In the main body of the town there are dozens of **rooms** for rent; take up one of the offers when you land, since most are otherwise unadvertised. The best places to **eat** are the three tavernas at the jetty end of the quay: *Ta Kymata*, *O Molos* and *I Klimataria*, although, like much else on Skópelos, they're hardly cheap. Nightlife is more subdued than on Skíathos, though there is an ever-increasing number of discos and a dozen or so bars, including a rather expensive jazz bar, *O Platanos*, by the tavernas. Inland, the bookshop/gallery/café *Armoli* is one of the best of its kind in Greece, with numerous Greek titles in foreign-language translations.

Within the town, spread below the oddly whitewashed ruins of a Venetian **kástro**, are an enormous number of churches – 123 reputedly, though some are small enough to be mistaken for houses. Outside town, perched on the slopes opposite the quay, are two convents, **Evangelístria**, in view of the town, and **Pródhromos** (daily 8am–1pm & 4–7pm, 5–8pm at Pródhromos), and a monastery, **Metamórfossi**. The last was abandoned in 1980 but is now being restored by the monks and is open to visitors again. You should of course dress respectfully, although the hospitable nuns at the two convents will lend you leg-covering if necessary. Access is simplest by following an old road behind the line of hotels in town to Evangelístria (an hour's walk). From there it's an extra half hour's scramble over mule tracks to Pródhromos, the remotest and most beautiful of the three. Ignore the new road that goes part way – it's longer and takes away most of the beauty of the walk.

Around the island

Buses cover the island's one asphalt road between Skópelos and Loutráki (via Glóssa) about six times daily between 7am and 6pm, stopping at the paths to all the main beaches and villages. **STÁFILOS**, 4km out of town, is the closest beach, small and rocky (one taverna rents rooms). It is getting increasingly crowded, but the taverna, shaded by a vast pine tree, is a very pleasant spot. Also worth a mention is the *Terpsis* taverna halfway between Skópelos and Stáfilos, which serves an incredible stuffed chicken that must be booked twelve hours in advance.

There's a very prominent "No camping" sign at Stáfilos, but to pitch a tent you can just walk five minutes around the coast to **VELANIÓ**, whose pines and surf always draw a small summer community (often nudist). There is spring water in the area and a campsite near the beach.

Further around the coast, the beachless fishing anchorage of **AGNÓNDAS** (with a combination restaurant/rooms) is the start of a fifteen-minute path (or 2km road) to **LIMNONÁRI**, 100 metres of fine sand set in a rather grim and shadeless rock-girt bay. There are a couple of places to stay and eat, but camping would be a bit cramped.

A more promising base, if you're after isolation and happy to walk to a nearby beach, is **PÁNORMOS**, a pleasant little hamlet with rooms, tavernas and a campsite (where people of all income levels may find themselves at times when Skópelos is chock-full). The beach here is gravelly and steeply shelving, but there are small secluded bays close by and, slightly further on at **MILIÁ**, a tremendous, 1500m sweep of tiny pebbles beneath a bank of pines, facing the islet of Dhasía. There's one taverna and just a couple of houses in this languid setting; nudist swimming is possible at a lovely 500 metre-long beach a little way north. Further north, **ELIOS**, 9km short of Glóssa, is a medium-sized resort in its own right, and not a particularly pleasant one either, although its beach is nice and there's a reasonable taverna, *Theophilos*, with good, if pricey fish. Beyond here, the virtually abandoned village of **PALEO KLIMA** marks the start of a beautiful forty-minute trail to Glóssa, via the earthquake-ruined settlement of AYII ANARYIRI and the oldest village on the island, ATHÉATO.

West of Skópelos town various jeep tracks and old paths wind through olive and plum groves toward **Mount Dhélfi** and the Vathiá forest, or skirt the base of the mountain northeast to Revíthi hill with its fountains and churches, and Karyá, with its "**Sendoúkia**" or ancient tombs. Tracks on the north flank of Dhélfi, beyond Karyá, might ust conceivably lead all the way to the Klíma villages, but the main, old trans-island donkey track ends disappointingly in the vicinity of Élios.

To the northwest of Skópelos town, **GLISTÉRI** is a small pebble beach with no shade but a taverna much frequented by locals on Sundays. A fork off the Glistéri and Mount Dhélfi tracks can be followed across the island to Pánormos within ninety minutes; it's a pleasant walk though the route isn't always obvious. As usual, local maps of the island are mostly very inaccurate, a situation aggravated by the many new tracks bulldozed across the island since the maps were printed – making exploration interesting but sometimes frustrating.

Alónissos and some minor islets

The most remote of the Sporades, **Alónissos** is also, on initial appearance, the least attractive. It has an unfortunate recent history. The vineyards were wiped out by disease in 1950 and the *hóra* was damaged by an earthquake in 1965. Although its houses were mostly repairable, corruption and the social control policies of the new junta were instrumental in the village's forcible abandonment and the transfer of virtually the entire population down to the previously unimportant anchorage of Patitíri, although many emigrated too. The result is a little soulless, but on closer acquaintance the island turns out to be one of the most traditional – and one of the most friendly – in Greece. Take time and explore.

Around the island

PATITÍRI is one of the least attractive island towns. The flat-roofed concrete buildings are relieved only by a row of bars and near-identical restaurants along the seafront. Although Alónissos attracts fewer visitors than Skíathos or Skópelos, most stay in Patitíri, and from mid-July to the end of August it can get very crowded. Travelling independently, there seems little reason to stay longer than you have to. Paliá Alónissos and the beaches to the north of Patitíri are better targets, although accommodation and other facilities are limited. However, if you do stay, rooms are easy to find; you'll probably be approached with offers as you get off the ferry, sometimes by older women wearing traditional blue and white costumes. The local room owners association (☎0424/65 577) has an office on the front, and can find you a room in Patitíri or nearby Vótsi, but you'll end up paying more. Restaurants along the front are reasonably priced, but the food is nothing special. The *ouzerí To Kamáki* is good and not too expensive. There's a campsite among the pine trees, ten minutes' walk (south) along the road to Marpoúnda beach, though in season, with its' open-air disco, it's not the most peaceful place to stay.

MARPOÚNDA features a large hotel and bungalow complex and a rather grim beach. Better to turn left after the campsite towards Megálos Mourtiás, a pebble beach with three tavernas overlooked by Paliá Alónissos, 200m above. Just before Megálos Mourtiás, a path heads down through the pine trees to **VÍTHISMA**, a much better sand and shingle beach that's hardly visible from above. A windsurfing school operates here in the summer.

To the north, Patitíri merges into the adjoining settlements of Roussoúm Yialós and Vótsi. **ROUSSOÚM YIALÓS** holds nothing of interest, while **VÓTSI**, despite the post-earthquake architecture, has an attractive harbour and is a better and quieter place to stay than Patitíri.

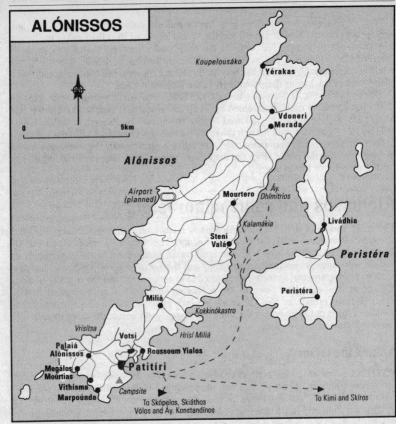

PALIÁ ALÓNISSOS is a fine but steep thirty-minute walk via a donkey track –
signposted on the left just outside Patitíri. Alternatively, there's a bus twice daily,
currently at 11am and 7pm, returning at 1pm and 9pm. Although many houses are still
derelict, much of the village has been restored, mainly by the English and Germans
who bought the properties at knock-down rates. Only a few local families continue to
live here, which gives the village a rather odd and un-Greek atmosphere, but it is picturesque. Most of the owners only come here in July and August, and for the rest of the
year their houses are closed up. Accommodation is in short supply so expect to pay
well over the odds, particularly in season. *Alonissos Travel*, in Patitíri (☎0424 65 511),
can do bookings for a limited number of rooms and apartments. Otherwise, ask
around; nobody seems to put up "room for rent" signs, but there are a few places. The
village has a bar, two shops, and a few tavernas. The *Paraport* taverna is good, though
not especially cheap, and has one of the best views on the island. The nearest beaches
are twenty minutes' walk downhill to the small cove of Vrisítsa to the north or Megálos
Mourtiás to the south.

The best beaches on Alónissos are well to the north of Patitíri, mostly on the eastern
side. There's no bus, and they can be reached most easily by excursion *kaíki* from
Patitíri. You could also rent a moped or motorbike in Patitíri (prices are reasonable),
although beyond Vótsi the roads are unpaved and should be ridden with care. A couple

of the rental places also rent out motorboats and dinghies. On foot, it's easy enough to hitch along the main road, but you'll probably have to walk down to the beaches.

HRISÍ MILIÁ, the first good beach, has pine trees down to the sand and a taverna; there are a couple of new hotels on the hillside above, and it can get crowded in summer. At **KOKKINÓKASTRO**, over the hill to the north, excavations have revealed the site of ancient Ikos and evidence of the oldest known prehistoric habitation in the Aegean. There's nothing much to see, but it's a beautiful spot with a good pebble beach, and, in July and August, a daytime *kantina*.

STENÍ VÁLA, opposite the island of Peristéra, is perhaps the most obvious place to stay. It's almost a proper village, with a shop, a few houses, a bar, rooms and three tavernas, one of which stays open more or less throughout the year. There's a campsite (☎0424/65 258) in an olive grove by the harbour, a long pebble beach and other beaches within reasonable walking distance in either direction. **KALAMÁKIA**, to the north, also has a couple of tavernas. If you want real solitude, **ÁYIOS DHIMITRIOS**, **KOUPELOUSÁKO** and **YÉRAKAS**, much further north, are recommended. However, before committing yourself, take one of the round-the-island trips available, and return the next day with sufficient groceries.

THE MEDITERRANEAN MONK SEAL

The **Mediterranean Monk Seal** has the dubious distinction of being the European mammal most in danger of extinction. Perhaps 800 survive in total worldwide, the majority around the Portuguese Atlantic island of Madeira and the coast of the West African state of Mauritania, and in small numbers in the Ionian and Aegean seas, having disappeared entirely from the Mediterranean. The largest population, an estimated 25–30 seals, lives around the deserted islands north of Alónissos.

Monk seals can travel up to 200km a day in search of food, but they usually return to the same places to rear their pups. They have one pup every two years, and the small population is very vulnerable to disturbance and the possibility of mother seals being separated from and losing their pups. Originally, the pups would have been reared on sandy beaches, but with increasing disturbance by man, they have retreated to isolated sea caves, particularly around the coast of the remote islet of Pipéri.

Unfortunately, the seals compete with fishermen for limited stocks of fish, and, in the overfished Aegean, often destroy nets full of fish. Until recently it was common for seals to be killed by fishermen. This occasionally still happens, but in an attempt to protect the seals, the seas around the northern Sporades have been declared a marine wildlife reserve: fishing is restricted in the area north of Alónissos and prohibited within 5km of Pipéri. On Alónissos, the conservation effort and reserve have won a great deal of local support, mainly through the efforts of the *Hellenic Society for the Protection of the Monk Seal*, based at Stení Vála. The measures have won particular support from local fishermen, as tighter restrictions on larger, industrial-scale fishing boats from other parts of Greece should help preserve fish stocks and benefit them financially.

Despite this, the government has made no serious efforts to enforce the restrictions, and boats from outside the area continue to fish around Pipéri. There are also government plans to reduced the prohibited area around Pipéri to 500m. On a more positive note, the *Society for the Protection of the Monk Seal*, in collaboration with the *Pieterburen Seal Creche* in Holland, has raised three separately abandoned seal pups – all of which have been successfully released in the seas north of Alónissos.

For the moment, your chances of actually seeing a seal are remote, unless you plan to spend a few weeks on a boat in the area. It's recommended that you shouldn't visit Pipéri or approach sea caves on other islands which might be used by seals, or encourage boat owners to do so. Spear fishing, by tourists or professional fishermen, is a particular threat near caves used by seals and is strongly discouraged.

Beyond Alónissos: some minor islets

Northeast of Alónissos half a dozen tiny islets speckle the Aegean. Virtually none of these has any permanent population, nor any ferry service, and the only way you can reach them – at least Peristéra, Kirá Panayía and Yioúra – is by excursion *kaíkia*, and even then only in high season (the excursion boats serve primarily as fishing boats from September to May) and as weather permits. Considerably more powers of persuasion will be required to get the fishermen to take you to the other, more remote islets. It is possible to be left for a night or more on any of the islands, but when acting out your desert-island fantasies, be sure to bring more supplies than you need; if the weather worsens you'll be marooned until such time as small craft can make it out to you.

Peristéra is the closest islet to Alónissos, to which it was once actually joined, but subsidence (a common phenomenon in the area) created the narrow straits beween the two. It is graced with some sandy beaches and there is rarely anyone around, though some Alonissans do come over for short periods to tend the olive groves, and in season there are the regular evening "barbecue boats" from the main island. The water supply is uncertain, but the islanders must originally have provided wells or cisterns near their small farmhouses. As on Alónissos, a few unofficial campers are tolerated, but there is only one spot, known locally as "Barbecue Bay", where campfires are allowed.

Kirá Panayía (also known as Pelagós) is the next islet out and is equally fertile and wooded. It's owned by the Orthodox Church and there are two monasteries here, one inhabited as recently as 1984. Boats call at a beach and anchorage on the south shore, one of many such sandy stretches and coves around the island, which is popular with yachters. There's no permanent population other than the wild goats. The island boasts a stalactite cave reputed to be that of Homer's Polyphemus (the Cyclops).

Nearby **Yioúra** has a similar, larger cave with perhaps better credentials as the one from which Odysseus and his companions escaped. The main feature, though, is a herd of rare wild goats, distinctive enough to have earned the island the status of a reserve. Two middle-aged couples live here as wardens; part of their job is to unlock the cave for visiting parties and provide a hurricane lamp. You'll need more than a single source of illumination to see much, however, and getting down into the cavern is fairly strenuous. Apart from the tourist boats, the wardens' only contact with the outside world is a twice-monthly mail-and-provisions boat, which, like all other craft, cannot land at the primitive jetty in rough seas.

Pipéri, near Yioúra, is a sea-bird and monk seal refuge, and permission from the EOT (in Athens) is required for visits by non-specialists. Tiny, northernmost **Psathoúra** is dominated by its powerful modern lighthouse, although here, as around many of these islands, there's a submerged ancient town, brought low by the endemic subsidence. Roughly halfway between Alónissos and Skíros, green **Skantzoúra**, with a single monastery (still inhabited by one monk) and a few seasonal shepherds, seems a lesser version of Kirá Panayía.

Skíros (Skyros)

Despite its closeness to Athens, Skíros had until recently remained a very traditional and idiosyncratic island. Any impetus for change had been neutralised by the lack of economic opportunity (and even secondary schooling), forcing the younger Skyrians to live in Athens and leaving behind a conservative gerontocracy. A high school has at last been provided, and the island has been "discovered" in the past decade. It's very much of a scene now, the haunt of continental Europeans, chic Athenians and British, many of whom check in to the "New Age" Skyros Centre (see below), catering to those who feel Skíros by itself isn't enough to "rethink the form and direction of their lives".

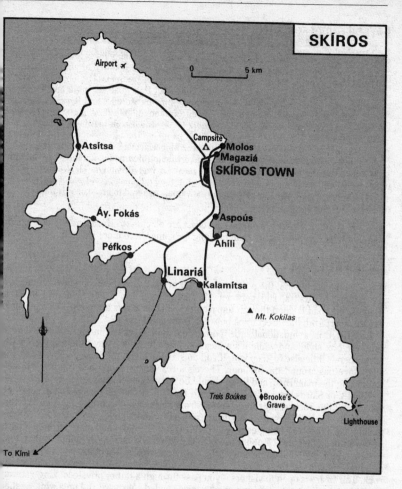

Meanwhile, Skíros still ranks as one of the most interesting places in the Aegean. It has a long tradition of ornate woodcarving – a *Salonáki Skirianí* (handmade set of chairs) is still considered an appropriate partial dowry for any young Greek woman – and a very few old men still wear the vaguely Cretan traditional costume of cap, vest, baggy trousers, leggings and *trohádhia* (Skyrian clogs), but this is dying out. Likewise, old women still wear the favoured yellow scarves and long embroidered skirts.

The theory that Skíros was originally two islands seems doubtful, but certainly the character of the two parts of the island is very different. The north has a greener and more gentle landscape, and away from the port and town it retains much of its original pine forest. The sparsely inhabited south is mountainous, rocky and barren; there are few trees and the landscape is more reminiscent of the Cyclades than the Sporades. Compared to Skíathos, Skópelos and Alónissos, Skíros isn't a great place for out of the way beaches. Most beaches along the west coast attract more than their fair share of sea-borne rubbish, and, although the scenery is sometimes spectacular, the swimming

GOAT DANCES AND WILD PONIES

If you can coincide with them, Skíros also has some particularly lively, even outrageous festivals. The **Apokriatiká** (pre-Lenten) **carnival** here is structured around the famous **"Goat Dance"** performed by masked revellers in the village streets. The foremost character in this is the Yéros, a menacing figure concealed by a goatskin mask and weighed down by garlands of sheep bells. Accompanying him are Korélles and Kyriés (transvestites – only the men participate – and Frangi (maskers in "Western" garb). For further details, read Joy Coulentiano's *The Goat Dance Of Skyros*, available in Athens and occasionally on the island.

The other big annual event takes place near Magaziá beach on August 15, when children race domesticated members of a herd of **wild ponies** native to Skíros and said to be related to the Shetland pony (if so, it must be very distantly). They are thought, perhaps, to be the diminutive horses depicted in the Parthenon frieze, and at any time of the year you might find some of the tame individuals tethered to graze near Hóra.

isn't that good. The beaches on the east coast are all close to Hóra, and the best option is probably to stay here rather than heading for somewhere more isolated.

Linariá and Hóra

A road connects Linariá, the port, to Hóra, 10km away, and then continues round, past the airport, to Atsítsa, and between Ahíli and Kalamítsa. From Kalamítsa to Treis Boukés, the road is good though unpaved. Most other roads are passable on a rented moped, apart from the direct track between Hóra and Atsítsa.

LINARIÁ is a functional little port. Most buildings are in the modern Greek concrete box style, and while it's a pleasant place to while away time waiting for the ferry, there's little else to keep you. If you do stay the night, there are rooms, a bar, and a few tavernas around the harbour. There's a reasonable sandy beach a few minutes walk along the main road, and there should be no problem if you want to camp here.

HÓRA, or Skíros town, with its decidedly Cycladic architecture, sits on the landward side of a high rock rising precipitously from the coast. According to legend, King Lycomedes pushed Theseus to his death from its summit. It has a workaday feel without feeling like a resort or being especially picturesque; the older and more intriguing parts of town are higher up, climbing towards the **kástro**, a mainly Byzantine rather than Venetian building, built on the site of the ancient acropolis. There are few traces of this although remains of the Classical city walls survive belown the seaward side of the rock. The *kástro* is open to visitors – you pass through a rather private-looking gateway into the monastery, then through an attractive shaded courtyard and up a whitewashed tunnel to the upper part of the *kástro*. There's little to see at the top, apart from a few churches in various states of ruin, but there are great views over the town and this part of the island, and the climb up takes you through the quieter and more picturesque part of town, with glimpses into traditionally decorated houses and ancient churches.

Perhaps equally striking, and splendidly incongruous, is the **Memorial to Rupert Brooke** – a bronze nude of "Immortal Poetry"– at the northern end of town (whose nakedness caused a scandal among the townspeople when it was first set up). Brooke, who visited the south of the island very briefly in April 1915, died shortly after of blood poisoning on a French hospital ship anchored offshore and was buried in an olive grove above Treis Boukés Bay. (The site at Treis Boukés can be reached on foot from Kalamítsa, by *kaíki*, or, less romantically, by taxi.) Brooke has become something of a local hero, despite his limited acquaintance with Skíros, and ironically was adopted by Kitchener and later Churchill as the paragon of patriotic youth despite his forthrightly expressed socialist and internationalist views.

Just below the Brooke statue are two museums: the **Archaeological Museum** (Tues–Sat 9am–3.30pm, Sun 9.30am–2.30pm; free), which has a modest collection of pottery and statues from excavations on the island, as well as a reconstruction of a traditional Skíros house interior, and the more interesting, privately run **Faltaitz Museum** (daily 10am–1pm & 5.30pm–8pm; free), in a nineteenth-century house built over one of the bastions of the ancient walls, with a collection of domestic items.

Practicalities

Arriving in Hóra, the bus from Linariá leaves you by the school, just below the main square; the OTE, post office and bank are all nearby. You'll probably be met off the bus with offers of **rooms**. *Skíros Travel* (☎0222/91 123 or 91 600), on the main street above the square, can provide information and advice and can find a room or hotel; in high season, it's a good idea to phone them in advance. The square and the main street running by it are the centre of village life, with a couple of noisy pubs and a wide choice of *kafenía*, tavernas and fast-food places. There are few outstanding places to eat – most are overpriced, or serve rather average food. *O Glaros*, just below the square, is an exception, and many of the local people eat here. It's a very basic taverna with a limited menu, but the owners are friendly and the food is good and reasonably priced. Generally, this is a busier and more modern part of town.

Magaziá and Mólos and some beaches

A path leads down past the archaeological museum towards the small coastal village of **MAGAZIÁ**, coming out by the official **campsite**. From Magaziá, an 800 metre-long sandy beach stretches to the adjacent village of **MÓLOS**; indeed in recent years, a sprawl of new development between the road and the beach has more or less joined the two villages together. Despite this, the beach is good, and if you don't feel like walking down from Hóra to go swimming, it would be a good place to stay. The beachfront tavernas compare favourably to those in town: a small taverna in a converted windmill at the Mólos end of the beach has good food and the best view.

For quieter beaches, take the road past Mólos, or better, try the excellent and undeveloped beach directly below the *kástro*. The path down to it is about 150m beyond the disco *Skiropoula* – it isn't obvious from above. However, following the road beyond here, the beaches are disappointing until you reach **Méalos** beach, known more commonly as **Aspoús**, with a couple of tavernas and rooms to rent, and **Ahíli**, just to the south, which used to have one of the best beaches on the island until it was effectively destroyed by the construction of a new marina. South of Ahíli, the coast is rocky and inaccessible, although you can take a *kaíki* trip down to the bay of **Treis Boukés**, passing some interesting sea caves on the way. **Kalamítsa**, on the west coast across from Ahíli, is okay, but the beach and sea aren't that clean. There's a better and more remote beach halfway along the road to Treis Boukés with absolutely no facilities.

Around the rest of the island

There are a few moped and motorbike rental places in Hóra, in the area around the main square. Hitching is easy, even to remote spots like Treis Boukés, though in summer, the whimsical bus service visits the more popular beaches if that's all you want to do. Otherwise it's best to direct your footsteps (or moped) due west, following Kifissós Creek into the pine-filled heart of this half of Skíros, which contrasts sharply with the barren rockiness of the rest.

The dirt track from **Hóra across to Atsítsa** is well worth the effort (3–4hr walk), but isn't practical with a moped – there's a much less scenic tarmac road past the airport to Atsítsa. The track, beyond Áyios Dhimítrios, is clear enough. **ATSÍTSA** is an attractive bay with pine trees down to the sea (tapped by the Skyrian retsina industry), but the beach is rocky and isn't great for swimming. There's a small sandy beach fifteen minutes' walk to the north at **Kirá Panayiá**, but it's nothing special. Elsewhere in the coniferous north, **Áyios Fokás** and **Péfkos** bays are easiest reached by a turning from the paved road near Linariá, though there is (more difficult) access from Atsítsa. Áyios Fokás is even more primitive that Atsítsa, but Péfkos boasts a taverna (it's only open in season, as are all other tavernas away from Linariá, Hóra and Magaziá and Mólos) and rooms. The bay is beautiful and the beach reasonable but not that clean – the beaches around Hóra are much better for swimming.

Évvia (Euboea)

The second largest Greek island (after Crete), Évvia seems more like an extension of the mainland. At Halkídha the connecting bridge has only a seventy-metre channel to span, the island having reputedly been split from the mainland by a blow from

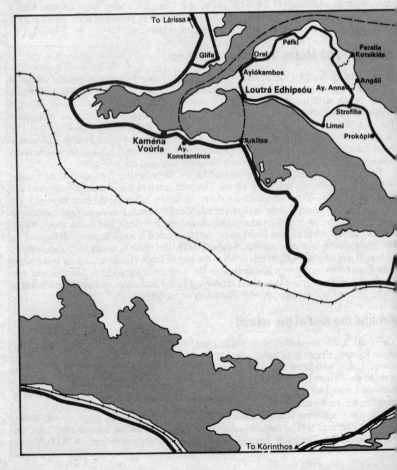

Poseidon's trident. There are ferry crossings at no fewer than six points along its length, and the south of the island is closer to Athens than it is to northern Évvia.

Nevertheless, Évvia *is* an island and in places a very beautiful one. The north, a rolling fertile countryside, is most popular among Greeks, who value its greenery, its beaches and the mineral waters at Loutrá Edhipsoú. The east coast is barren, rocky and largely inaccessible, but the west, right down to Káristos, is much gentler and more cultivated, though increasingly disfigured by industrial operations. All public transport is biased towards this side of the island.

Halkídha

The island capital of **HALKÍDHA** (more formally known as **HALKÍS**), is by far the largest town on Évvia, heavily industrial, with a shipyard, railway sidings, and cement works. For visitors, it seems a dire place apart from the old Turkish quarter of **Kástro** and its waterside. The entrance to the *kástro* is marked by the mosque now housing the **Byzantine Museum**, and beyond are the remains of the old fortress, an arcaded

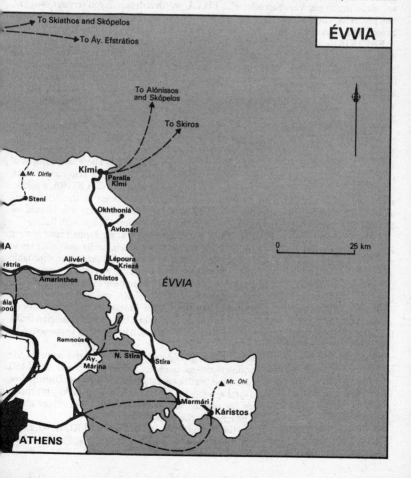

aqueduct and the unique basilican church of Áyia Paraskeví, an odd structure converted by the Crusaders in the fourteenth century into a Gothic cathedral. There's also a market here for ten days every year at the end of July.

The **waterside** overlooks the Evripós, the narrow channel whose strange currents have baffled scientists for centuries. You can stand on the bridge that spans the narrowest point and watch the water swirling by like a river. Every few hours the current changes and the tide reverses. Aristotle is said to have thrown himself into the waters in despair at his inability to understand what was happening, so if you're puzzled you're in good company. A few *ouzerí* south of the bridge serve grilled octopus, the only other reason for stopping. There's a good **bus service** from Halkídha, serving most parts of the island from a station in the middle of town – head straight inland from the bridge.

South from Halkídha

The coast road heading southeast out of Halkídha is a bad introduction to Évvia. There are some intriguing Venetian towers at **FÍLLA**, worth a detour if you've your own car, but just what the package tour companies see in the disappointing scenery around Erétria and Amárinthos, save easy connections to Athens, is hard to imagine.

ERÉTRIA is more notable, with its ancient site, much of which lies under the modern town. A few visible remains are dotted around the centre, most conspicuously an **agora** and a **Temple of Apollo**, but more interesting are the excavations in the northwest corner, behind the small museum. Here the **theatre** has been uncovered and from its orchestra steps descend to an underground vault used for sudden appearances and disappearances. Beyond the theatre are the ruins of a **gymnasium** and **sanctuary**.

Beyond **ALIVÉRI** and its cement factories the route mercifully heads inland for LÉPOURA junction, the crossing point for travellers going between Káristos and Kími. Just to the south, the ancient city of **DHÍSTOS** lies by the shore of a marshy lake (Évvia's largest) 5km south of the modern city town of KRIEZÁ. There are remains of fifth-century BC houses and walls, while on the acropolis perches a Venetian fortress. Continuing south on the main road brings you to the turning for **NÉA STÍRA**, a nondescript seaside resort with a handy ferry connection to Ayía Marína on the Attic peninsula (which gives access to nearby ancient Rhamnous). Much the same can be said for **MARMÁRI**, a few kilometres south, except in this case the ferry link is with Rafína.

Rafína ferries also serve **KÁRISTOS**, at the southern end of the asphalt road system but a vast improvement on the rest of this region. It's a small, pretty port with some good, reasonably priced restaurants. Unfortunately there's a shortage of affordable accommodation, although a nearby sandy beach (to the right as you face the sea) offers the possibility of freelance **camping**. Káristos is also a good base for hikes inland. The most popular destinations are the villages of PÁLEO HÓRA and MÍLI, graced with orchards and fountains, and beyond these the barren **Mount Óhi**. This is Évvia's second highest (1398m) peak, capped by the ancient schist blocks of a Pelasgian building of uncertain function; known as the "Dragon's House", it is popularly supposed to be haunted.

The northerly fork of the road junction at Lépoura meanders across some of the most peaceful and beautiful countryside in Greece. Just off the road at **HÁNI AVLONARÍOU** stands the Romanesque twelfth-century basilica of **Áyios Dhimítrios**, Évvia's finest. A huge Venetian tower crowns the tiered old houses of Avlonári proper, 2km east. In the same vicinity is the turning for **OKHTHONIÁ**, a hill village above some of the finest deserted sand beaches on the island.

Most travellers, though, stay on the bus until the end of the line at **KÍMI**, built on a green ridge overlooking the sea and its port of Paralía Kími, 4km below. Part way down to the harbour you can visit the **Folklore Museum**, and in the upper town there are a couple of cheapish hotels, the *Kími* (③) and the *Krínonn* (③), plus some unadvertised rooms, and good tavernas where you can sample the products of the local vineyards. Despite its name, **PARALÍA KÍMI** has no real beach, although if you're overnighting before a **ferry across to Skíros** there are plenty of rooms at reasonable prices, and one hotel.

To get up into the rugged country west of Kími you must walk along the forest paths or return to Halkídha for the bus service up to **STENÍ**, a large and beautiful village at the foot of Mount Dhírfis, with a few cheap *psistariés* and two expensive hotels. It's a good area for hiking, most notably to the peaks of Dhírfis and Ksirovoúni and the isolated beach hamlets of HILIADHOÚ and AYÍA IRÍNI, though you'll need a specialist hiking guide to do this (see "Books" in *Contexts* for details of the best ones).

North from Halkídha

The main road north from Halkídha crosses flat farmland for a few kilometres, after which it climbs steeply among forested hills. The village of **PROKÓPI** lies beyond the summit in a valley enclosed by the rich and beautiful woods that are one of its claims to fame, the others being a **castle** on a precipitous rock and the church of **St John of Russia**, whose relics are kept there. These were brought here by Orthodox Turks from Cappadocia in the 1923 population exchange, and Prokópi is still occasionally referred to by its old name of Ahmet Aga.

North of here, at **STROFILIÁ**, it's possible to take a left fork to **LÍMNI** on the west coast, a small resort with **rooms**, and shingle beaches curving gently around its bay. There are also a couple of cheap **hotels** and tavernas, and the possibility of outings to the monastery down the coast at Galatáki or inland through some spectacular gorges.

The coast road north towards Loutrá Edhipsoú is dangerous and infrequently used. Most traffic bears north (right) at Strofiliá, and if you've your own car the beaches below **AYÍA ÁNNA** are some of the island's best. Otherwise, the bus can take you to **PÉFKI**, a seaside resort with rooms, tavernas and a long beach. It's mobbed with Greeks in summer but at such times you can always strike out west along the coast between here and **OREÍ**, a fishing village with two inexpensive hotels and a small beach. A little further along the coast from Orei, **AYIÓKAMBOS** has tavernas and rooms for rent, and **GLÍFA** has bus links to Vólos.

South of here, **LOUTRÁ EDHIPSOÚ**, besides being an important ferry and bus terminal, attracts older Greeks (104 hotels full of them) who come to bathe at the spas renowned since antiquity for curing everything from gallstones to depression. You should perhaps stay long enough to buy a few bottles of this wonder-water, but that's about it.

travel details

Alkyon Tours, in cooperation with *Loucas Nomicos* ferry lines, hold a virtual monopoly on conventional ferry services to the northern Sporades, and they exploit it. Fares are almost double those on Cyclades or Dodecanese lines. On the plus side, *Alkyon* maintain an Athens office (Akhadimías 97) for purchase of ferry (and combined bus and ferry) tickets.

Between April and October, "Flying Dolphin" and "Flying Icarus" hydrofoils operate between various mainland ports and the Sporades. These are pricier than the ferries but cut journey times virtually in half.

SKÍATHOS, SKÓPELOS AND ALÓNISSOS
Ferries
From Áyios Konstantínos 9 weekly to Skíathos (3hr); 7 weekly to Skópelos (5hr), 3 continuing to Alónissos (6hr).

From Kími 4 times a week to Alónissos (3hr) and Skópelos (3hr 30min), continuing to Skíathos (5hr 30min) twice a week.

From Vólos 3–4 boats a day to Skíathos (3hr) and Skópelos (4hr); at least one boat every day to Alónissos (5hr). This is the most consistent service out of season, and is always the cheapest.

"Flying Dolphins" (April–Oct only)

From Áyios Konstantínos to Skíathos, Glóssa, Skópelos and Alónissos; 1–2 departures daily in April, May & Oct; 2–3 daily June–Sept.

From Vólos to Skíathos, Glóssa and Skópelos; 2 departures daily in April, May & Oct; 4 daily June–Sept. At least one service daily continues from Skópelos to Alónissos between April & Oct.

From Thessaloníki to Skíathos, Glóssa, Skópelos and Alónissos; 4 departures weekly in May–June & Sept–Oct; daily departures July–Aug.

From Moudhanía (Halkidhikí) to Skíathos, Skópelos and Alónissos; 5–6 departures weekly June to mid-Sept.

From Marmarás (Halkidhikí) to Skíathos, Skópelos and Alónissos; 5–6 departures weekly June–mid-Sept.

From Pefkí (Évvia) to Skíathos, Skópelos and Alónissos; daily June to mid-Sept.

From Tríkeri (Pílion) to Skíathos, Skópelos and Alónissos; daily April, May & Oct, 2 daily June to mid-Sept.

From Platanías and Tríkeri (Pílion) to Skíathos, Skópelos and Alónissos; daily June to mid-Sept.

Flights

Athens–Skíathos 3 flights daily.
Thessaloníki–Skíathos 3 flights weekly.

SKÍROS

Ferries

Skíros is served by conventional ferry, the *FB Lykomides*, from **Kími** ((2hr 20min). Services are at least twice a day June to mid-Sept (usually at 11am & 5pm), once daily (5pm) the rest of the year. There is a directly connecting bus service from the Liossíon 260 terminal in Athens (leaving at 12.30pm).

"Flying Dolphins"

In summer the Vólos-based **hydrofoil** links Skíros with the other Sporades. Services are 3 weekly in June and the first half of Sept, 5 weekly in July & Aug.

Flights

Athens–Skíros 6 weekly June–Sept, 2 weekly the rest of the year.

ÉVVIA

Buses

From Athens (Liossíon 260 terminal) to Halkídha (every half-hour; 1hr 40min); Kími (every 2hr; 3hr 40min); Karístos (daily at 4.30pm).
There is a good bus service from Halkídha to most towns and villages in Évvia.

Trains

From Athens (Laríssis station) to Halkídha (19 daily; 1hr 25min).

Ferries

Rafína–Káristos (1–2 daily; 2hr).
Rafína–Marmári (1–2 daily; 1hr).
Áyia Márina–Néa Stíra (7 daily; 50min).
Skála Oropoú–Erétria (hourly 5am–10pm; 25min).
Arkítsa–Loutrá Edhipsoú (12 daily 6.45am–11pm; 50min).
Glífa–Ayiókambos (every 2hr 6am–7pm; 30min).

*Connecting buses run **from Athens to Rafína** from the Mavromatéon terminal (every half-hour; 1hr 30min). They also run to Skála Oropoú from the same terminal, and to Arkítsa and Glífa from the Liossíon terminal.*

CHAPTER TWELVE

THE IONIAN

The six **Ionian islands**, shepherding their satellites down the west coast of the mainland, are both geographically and culturally a mixture of Greece and Italy. Floating on the haze of the Adriatic, their green, even lush, silhouettes come as a shock to those more used to the stark outlines of the Aegean. The fertility is a direct result of the heavy rains which sweep over the archipelago – and especially Corfu – from October to March, so if you visit in the off-season, come prepared.

The islands were the Homeric realm of Odysseus (centred on Ithaca – modern Itháki – or Lefkádha, according to rival theories) and here alone of all modern Greek territory the Ottomans never held sway (except on Lefkádha). After the fall of Byzantium, possession passed to the **Venetians** and the islands became a keystone in that city state's maritime empire from 1386 until its collapse in 1797. Most of the population must have remained immune to the establishment of Italian as the official language and the arrival of Roman Catholicism, but Venetian influence remains evident in the architecture of the island capitals, despite damage from a series of earthquakes.

On Corfu, the Venetian legacy is mixed with that of the **British**, who imposed a military "protectorate" over the Ionian at the close of the Napoleonic Wars, before ceding the archipelago to Greece in 1864. There is, however, no question of the islanders' essential Greekness: the poet Dionissios Solomos, author of the National Anthem, hailed from the Ionians, as did Nikos Mantzelos, who provided the music, and the first Greek president, Ioannis Kapodistrias.

Today, **tourism** is the dominating influence, especially on **Corfu (Kérkira)**, which was one of the first Greek islands on the package holiday circuit. Its east coast is one of the few stretches in Greece with development to match the Spanish *costas*, and in summer even its distinguished old capital, Kérkira Town, wilts beneath the onslaught. However, the island is large enough to retain some of its charms and is perhaps the most scenically beautiful of the group. Parts of **Zákinthos (Zante)** – which with Corfu has the Ionians' best beaches – seem to be going along the same tourist path, following the introduction of charter flights from northern Europe, but elsewhere the pace and scale of development is a lot less intense. Little **Páxi** is a bit too tricky to reach and lacks the water to support a large-scale hotel, while **Lefkádha** – which is connected to the mainland by a causeway and "boat bridge" – has a so-far quite low-key straggle of resorts. Perhaps the most rewarding duo for island-hopping are **Kefalloniá** and **Itháki**, the former with a series of "real towns" and a life in large part independent of tourism, the latter, Odysseus's rugged capital, protected by an absence of sand.

Corfu (Kérkira)

The seductive beauty of **Corfu (Kérkira** in Greek) has been a source of inspiration for generations. It is thought that Shakespeare took tales of the island as his setting for *The Tempest*; Lawrence Durrell echoed this tribute by naming his book about the island *Prospero's Cell*; and Edward Lear enthused that it made him "grow younger every hour". Henry Miller, totally in his element, became euphoric, lying for hours in the sun "doing nothing, thinking of nothing".

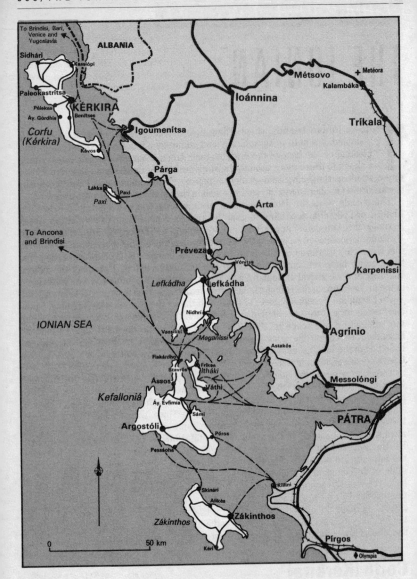

The islands of **Kíthira** and **Andíkithira**, isolated at the foot of the Peloponnese, officially belong to the Ionian group. However, as they have no ferry connections with other Ionian islands, and are most easily reached from Yíthio or Neápoli, they are covered in the Peloponnese chapter.

Likewise, the islet of **Kálamos**, the most distant of Lefkádha's "satellites" is covered in the Thessaly and Central Greece chapter, as it is reached only from the port of Mitíkas.

The island's natural appeal, the shapes and scents of its lemon and orange trees, its figs, cypresses and, above all, its three million olive trees, all remain an experience – if sometimes a beleaguered one, for Corfu has more package hotels and holiday villas than any other Greek island. Yet for all the commercialism – and the wholesale spoiling of its northeast coast – it remains an island where you can still leave the crowds behind, and where almost everyone seems to end up having a good time.

Kérkira town

Corfu's scale of tourism is apparent the moment you arrive in **KÉRKIRA TOWN** (Corfu Town). It is a graceful, elegant town – almost a city – sandwiched between a pair of **forts** and with a gorgeous esplanade, the **Spianádha**, where the Corfiotes play cricket – one of the town's more obvious British legacies. However, the crowds in summer are overpowering, and in season, at least, you'll probably find a night or two here at the beginning or end of your stay is time enough.

Arriving and accommodation

Arriving by boat, you'll find yourself at one or other of the **ferry docks**, on either side of the Néo Froúrio (New Fort); most ferries from Italy use the New Port, to its west, with ferries to and from the mainland (Igoumenítsa, Párga, etc) using the Old Port just to its east. Coming from the **airport**, 2km south of the centre, you can walk (about 40min), get a taxi (500dr – but agree the fare in advance; ☎0661/33 811 for radio taxis), or catch the occasional *Olympic Airways* bus from the terminal, or local #5 or #6 blue bus, which leave from 500m north of the terminal gates.

There are usually **accommodation** touts meeting the boats – and taxi drivers, too, will often know of rooms for rent – but for a more considered choice use the left-luggage office opposite the main harbour and head for the very professional **tourist office**, just east of the Igoumenítsa ferry dock, where you can pick up free maps of the town and island, bus timetables, a list of hotels and campsites and information on **rooms for rent**. The last are the likeliest form of summer accommodation; the tourist office won't make reservations but rentals are handled by several agencies along Odhós Vassiléos Konstandínou – or you can just pick up the lists and approach places direct.

Hotels worth phoning ahead, or trying early in the day and/or off season, include:
Hotel Kypros, Áyion Patéron 13 (☎0661/40 675). ②
Hotel Elpis, Néo Theotóki 4 – in an alley off the street (☎0661/30 289). ③

ISLAND ACCOMMODATION: ROOM PRICE SCALES

All **hotels** listed in this book have been price-graded according to the scale outlined below. The **rates quoted** represent the **cheapest available room in high season**; all are prices for a double room, except for category ①, which are per person rates. Out of season rates can drop by up to fifty percent, especially if you negotiate rates for a stay of three or more nights. Single rooms generally cost around seventy percent of the price of a double.

Rented **"private rooms"** on the islands invariably fall into the ② or ③ categories, depending on their location and facilities, and the season. They are not generally available from October through to the beginning of March, when only hotels tend to remain open.

① 1000–1500dr (£3–4.50/US$5.50–8)   ④ 5500–7500dr (£17–23/US$30–41.50)
② 2000–3000dr (£6–9.50/US$11–16.50)   ⑤ 7500–9000dr (£23–28/US$41.50–50)
③ 3000–5500dr (£9.50–17/US$16.50–30)   ⑥ 9000dr and upwards (£28/US$50 upwards)

For further explanation of our hotel category system, see p.32.

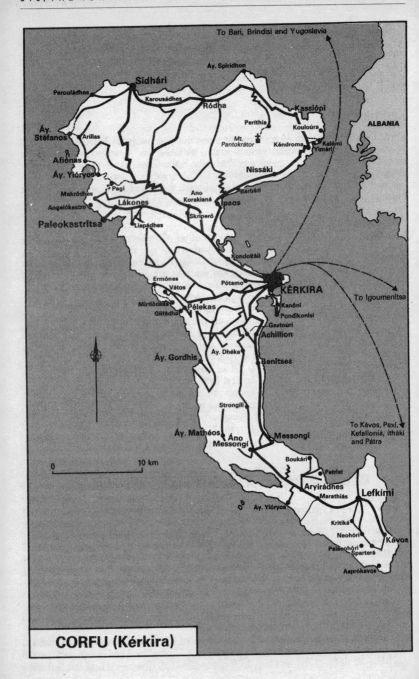

To Bari, Brindisi and Yugoslavia

ALBANIA

Áy. Spiridhon

Perouládhes

Sidhári

Karousádhes

Ródha

Kassiópi

Perithia

Kouloúra

Áy.
Stéfanos

Arillas

Mt.
Pantokrátor

Kéndroma

Kalámi
Yimári

Afiónas

Áy. Yióryos

Nissáki

Pagi

Makrádhes

Áno
Korakianá

Barbáti

Angelókastro

Lákones

Ipsos

Paleokastrítsa

Liapádhes

Skriperó

Kondokáli

Ermónes

Pótamo

KÉRKIRA

To Igoumenítsa

Vátos

Kanóni

Mirtiótissa

Pélekas

Pondikonísi

Glifádha

Gastoúri

Achíllion

Áy. Gordhis

Áy. Dhéka

Benítses

Strongilí

To Kávos, Paxí,
Kefalloniá, Itháki
and Pátra

Áy. Mathéos

Áno
Messongí

Messongí

0   10 km

Boukári

Petríxi

Aryirádhes

Lefkími

Marathiás

Áy. Yióryos

Kritiká

Neohóri

Kávos

Pelaeohóri

Sparterá

Asprókavos

CORFU (Kérkira)

Hotel Criti, Néo Theotóki 23 (☎0661/38 691). ②
Hotel Constantinoupolis, Zavitsánou 11 (☎0661/39 826). ③
Hotel New York, Ipapandís 21, off Zavitsánou (☎0661/39 922). ③
Hotel Europa, Néo Limín – the new harbour (☎0661/39 304). ③
Hotel Hermes, Markóra 14 (☎0661/30 289). ④
Hotel Bretagne, Yioryáki 27 (☎0661/30 274). ④
Pension Phoenix, H. Smirnís 2 (☎0661/42 290). ④
Pension Anthis, Kefalomandoúko (☎0661/25 804). ④

At Kondokáli village, 4.5km north of town, there is a **youth hostel** and **campsite** (☎0661/91 202); the camping is the closest to the town.

The Town

A stroll around the old parts of town offers a fascinating blend of Venetian, French, British and occasional Greek architecture. The most obvious sights are the forts, the **Paleó Froúrio** and **Néo Froúrio**, whose designations (*paleó* – "old", *néo* – "new") reflect the tenth-century origins of the former. In fact, what you see of the older structure was begun by the Byzantines in the mid-twelfth century, a mere century before the Venetians began work on the newer citadel. They have both been modified and damaged by various occupiers and besiegers since, the last contribution being the neoclassical shrine of **St George**, built by the British in the middle of Paleó Froúrio during the 1840s. The Paleó Froúrio is open from 8am to 7pm daily (free) and hosts a sound-and-light show most evenings; the Néo Froúrio is home to the Greek navy and off-limits to the public.

The **Spianádha** (Esplanade) has a leisured and graceful air – it reminded Evelyn Waugh of Brighton – and it's worth paying slightly above normal for a drink to watch people coming and going. Try one of the cafés facing the **Listón**, an arcaded legacy of the brief French occupation, built by the architect of Paris's Rue de Rivoli. If paying luxury tax on your *tsíntsi bírra* (ginger beer – another British influence) puts you off, stroll along the far side of the promenade close to the fort, where in the splendid flower gardens you can join groups of women chatting and lace-making in the evening sun.

Fronting the north end of the Spianádha is the **Palace of St Michael and St George** (Mon & Wed–Sat 8.30am–3pm, Sun 9.30am–2.30pm; 400dr, students 200dr), a solidly British edifice built for the residence of their High Commissioner, one of the last of whom was the future Prime Minister William Gladstone, and later used as a palace by the Greek monarchy. Its former staterooms house a large collection of Asiatic art, together with Byzantine relics from the island. Outside is a row of Doric columns bookended by monumental arches, with reliefs of the Ionian islands and Odysseus's rudderless ship. Through the archway is the loggia of the Corfu Reading Society, which has exhibitions of manuscripts, maps and art (daily 9am–1pm, plus 5–8pm on Thurs & Fri), and close by is a Venetian landing stage and city gate, framing the Vido islet.

Towards the south of the Spianádha is the **Maitland Rotunda**, a graffiti-covered bandstand commemorating the first British High Commissioner, and, just beyond it a statue of **Ioannis Kapodistrias** (1776–1831), first president of modern Greece and an agitator for the union of Greece with the Ionian islands. A little way beyond here, through a gate in the walls is an **Archaeological Museum** (Mon & Wed–Sat 9am–3pm, Sun 10am–3pm; 200dr, students 100dr), a modest but interesting collection whose prize exhibit is a 2500-year-old gorgon's-head pediment. Keep heading south from here and you will come to **Mon Repos**, the town's **public beach**, a sand and shingle strip with a little jetty and a snack bar.

The most atmospheric part of town is the area known as **Campiello** – a maze of Venetian-era alleyways between the Palace of St Michael and St George and the old port. At the edge of the quarter, on the waterfront at Arseníou 41, is the **Solomos**

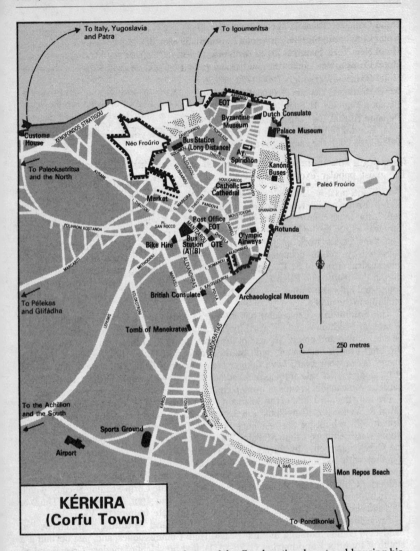

To Italy, Yugoslavia
and Patra

To Igoumenítsa

EOT

Byzantine
Museum

Dutch Consulate

Palace Museum

Customs
House

Néo Froúrio

Bus Station
(Long Distance)

Áy.
Spirídhon

Kanóni
Buses

Paleó Froúrio

To Paleokastrítsa
and the North

Catholic
Cathedral

Market

Post Office

San Rocco

EOT

Bus
Station
(A)(B)

OTE

Olympic
Airways

Rotunda

Bike Hire

To Pélekas
and Glifádha

British Consulate

Archaeological Museum

Tomb of Menekrates

To the Achillion
and the South

0   250 metres

Sports Ground

Airport

Mon Repos Beach

KÉRKIRA
(Corfu Town)

To Pondikonísi

Museum (Mon–Fri 5–8pm), former home of the Greek national poet and housing his archives and memorabilia. Nearby is the sixteenth-century Antivouniótissa church, which houses a little **Byzantine Museum** (Mon & Wed–Sun 9am–3pm) of icons.

To the southwest of the quarter is Corfu's **Cathedral**, packed with icons, including a fine sixteenth-century painting of *St George slaying the Dragon* by the Cretan artist Michael Damaskinos. The building shares religious precedence with the church of **Áyios Spirídhon**, a few blocks to the east on Odhós Vouthrótou, where you will find the silver-encrusted coffin of the island's patron saint, Spirídhon – Spiros in the diminutive – after whom about half the male population is named. Four times a year (Palm Sunday and the following Saturday; August 11; first Sunday in November), to the accompaniment of much celebration and feasting, the relics are paraded through the streets of Kérkira. Each of the days commemorates a miraculous deliverance of the island credited to the saint – twice from plague during the seventeenth century, from a famine of the sixteenth century and (a more blessed release than either of those for any Greek) from the Turks in the eighteenth century.

Another twisted grid of streets, south from the cathedral and backing onto the new fort, was the town's **old Jewish quarter**, home to a community of some five thousand from the sixteenth century until 1940, when they were rounded up by the Germans and sent off to the death camp at Auschwitz. A **synagogue** survives on Velissáriou street, at the southern edge of the ghetto.

Near Corfu Town: Vlahérna, Pondikoníssi and the Achillion Palace

The most popular excursion from Corfu Town is to the islets of Vlahérna and Pondikoníssi, just offshore from the plush suburb of **Kanóni**, four kilometres south of town (local bus from the Spianádha). Both feature heavily on postcards – and indeed almost seem designed for the purpose. The closer is **Vlahérna**, capped by a small monastery and joined to the mainland by a short causeway. Just beyond, a boat trip, swim or pedalo-push will bring you to **Pondikoníssi** (Mouse Island). Tufted with greenery and a small chapel, this is legendarily identified with a ship from Odysseus's fleet, petrified by Poseidon in revenge for the blinding of his son Polyphemus.

Three kilometres further to the south, past the resort sprawl of PERAMÁ, is a rather more bizarre attraction: the **Achillion**, a palace built in a (fortunately) unique blend of Teutonic and neoclassical styles in 1890 by Elizabeth, Empress of Austria. Henry Miller considered it "the worst piece of gimcrackery" that he'd ever laid eyes on and thought it "would make an excellent museum for surrealistic art". Aptly, the palace was the birthplace of the Greco-German Prince Philip (aka the Duke of Edinburgh, consort to the Queen of England). It is today a casino by night, though you can just visit the gardens in the daytime. If you are driving, you might combine a visit with a **meal** at the *Taverna Tripas* – one of the island's most imaginative, and not overpriced for the quality of its fare – at the village of KINOPIÁSTES, 3km inland.

Events, meals, bars and clubs

Corfu Town has no shortage of bars, restaurants and clubs, and during the summer there's a fair amount of **open-air concerts** and **cultural events**. For details of events, check the *Corfu News*, which is published by and available from the tourist office, or tune into *Radio Rama* (96.3 FM; Mon–Sat 3–5pm), with news and chat in Greek and English and spirited DJ-ing. Best of the town's **cinemas** – all of which show undubbed English/American films – is the one on G. Theotokí. The *Corfu News* is also useful for details of services (launderettes, doctors and dentists, etc); branches of most of the major **banks** are dotted throughout the town.

Eating out, you need to pick your way through the tourist joints if you want to find anywhere vaguely Greek in style and price; for picnics, the best place is the produce **market** on Odhós Dhessilá. Good **restaurant** choices include:

Yisdhakis, Solomoú 20, off N. Theotóki. As authentic a restaurant as they come.

Unnamed psistariá, Áyíon Pándon 44, just off Voulgaréos. Budget-priced grills.

Rex, Kapodhístriou. Inexpensive local hangout.

Hrissi Kardhia, Sevastianoú 44, near Kapodhístrias. Pleasant backstreet restaurant.

Averof, Old Port. Traditional Greek dishes – a bit pricey but well-prepared and presented.

Orestes, Stratioú 78, by the New Port. Excellent seafood.

The most popular **clubs** are to the south of town, along towards the beach of Mons Repos. *Bora Bora* and *Apokalypsis* are two of the best, the latter with wildly over-the-top decor of pyramids and Olympic torches, plus an Italian DJ in summer. The *Hippodrome* has a pool and giant video screen but a reputation for *kamákia* (lecherous locals on the hunt for women tourists).

Transport

All the islands **buses** start and finish in Corfu Town. There are two terminals: one on Platía San Rócco for numbered **blue bus** routes to the suburbs and across the island, the other on Platía Néou Frouríou, just below the fort, for **green buses** to more remote destinations. For schedules, consult the tourist office or check the terminal boards. If you are heading for Athens, you can buy combination bus and ferry tickets for the trip (at least daily in season) from the Néo Froúrio bus terminal.

Mopeds, bicycles and cars are available for rent in the town, and at most of the island's main resorts. Most of the agencies here are to be found around the Old and New Ports and along Leofóros Alexándhras. As everywhere in Greece, vehicles get savaged by drivers during the season, so look for agencies with newer ones. Motorbikes are more reliable than mopeds and less likely to have been pushed beyond their capacity but only take them if you're an experienced rider. An incredible number of people have accidents on the gravelly, potholed tracks. Note that almost all of the petrol/gas stations on the island are closed on Sundays.

In season there are also a few excursion **kaíkia** boats to certain beaches on the southern coast of the island – easier and more pleasant access than the buses.

The northeast coast

The coastline **north of Kérkira Town** has been remorselessly developed and the initial stretches are probably best written off. The concentration of hotels, villas and campsites give little sense of being in Greece, the beaches vary between pebbly and rocky and are often sullied with rubbish washed up from the mainland, and the sea looks murky and polluted, too. Things improve considerably, however, as you progress north and especially once you round the coast beyond Kassiópi.

Kérkira Town to Píryi

The first resort past Corfu Town's suburbs is **KONTOKÁLI**, where the islands youth hostel and the town's nearest campsite are located (see Corfu Town accommodation). Their siting is uninspired, to say the least– a sprawling, built-up area, with the stench of a sewage plant blowing in on the wind. Tourists are shuttled through en route to the **Danilia Village** (9am–1pm & 6pm–dawn), five minutes up the main road, a slick operation supposed to look like nineteenth-century Corfu, with daytime shops, workshops and museum, and evening entertainment.

Next stop around the bay is **GOÚVIA**, off the main road but on the routes of most green buses (plus blue bus *Dassia #7*) and with lots of inexpensive rooms for rent. The resort hugs the edge of the huge bay once used by the French fleet to hide from Nelson, though the downflow from Kontokáli means that the sea is absolutely filthy. Still, it's a friendly place and has an attractively low-key nightlife.

Continuing north, it's best to bypass **Cape Komméno**, which looks lovely from the distance, with thick foliage on the promontory, but up close turns out to be just a trio of dirty beaches, fronted by *Dionysos Camping* and a cluster of large hotels. There are further campsites at the next resort, **DÁSSIA**, a touristic sprawl with little to recommend it. For a bit more life, you'd do better at **ÍPSOS**, every inch the package resort, with an esplanade, fish and chips, water-slides, and bars named *Irish Shamrock, Coach House* and *Pig and Whistle*. There are quite a few rooms for rent and two campsites. To swim, wander over to **PÍRYI**, a village which has more or less merged with Ípsos, fronted by a better and sandy beach. From Píryi, too, a road trails up Mount Pandokrátor (see overleaf).

North to Áyios Stéfanos

North of Píryi, a rather different island emerges, as you move from package hotel to villa country. Resorts are small, and seem haphazardly chosen from pebble beaches far below the road. The sea is cleaner, too, and away from the main road, there's still a hint of the Corfu of Gerald Durrell's books, which were set on this coast.

BARBÁTI is the first resort of note – a former fishing hamlet, surrounded by hills and woods, and still identifiable Greek, despite a sizeable package hotel and taxi-boats to and from Ípsos. The few rooms for rent here are mainly located in the new hamlet area, a hundred steep metres above the sea. A kilometre to the north is **Glíffa**, a pebble beach with a taverna.

The next focal point is **NISSÁKI**, a rather sprawly village with a number of coves, the first and last accessible by road, the rest only by track. There's a vast hotel, a *Club Med* complex and a tiny stony beach, plus good watersports. Rooms in summer are like gold dust, but if you can find a bed, it's a good base. If you're prepared to walk, you can pick your way along the coast to find a number of quiet bays. **Kéndhroma**, a kilometre out, has a few rooms for rent. Beyond here, there are more rooms at the villages of **YIMÁRI** – though this has poor swimming and a pebble, kelpy beach – and **KAMINÁKI**, where there's a limestone cave full of bats. Past these outlying developments is a series of small rocky coves.

KALÁMI, set on a curved bay, was the site of Lawrence Durrell's *Prospero's Cell* – which he wrote at the *White House*. A once-pretty hamlet, it's being developed fast, with a rash of villas threatening to stamp out the charm of the grand old houses. There are a number of rooms for rent – including, if you're organised and reasonably affluent, the *White House* (bookable by the week though *CV Travel* in London, ☎071/581 0851). In summer, excursion boats sail from here for Albania (see box below).

There are more little coves around the headland between Kalámi and **KOULOÚRA**, a pretty resort set beside a deep, U-shaped bay enclosed by tall cypresses, palm and eucalyptus trees. It's postcard-pretty and has a small, shingle beach, a lovely taverna, but no rooms for rent. Another good taverna, *Nikos's*, is to be found at the tiny nearby hamlet of Agnistíni, and there are lovely beaches down some of the tracks around; **Kerásia**, down a very grotty track, is a large shady cove with a beach café.

The deep bay of **ÁYIOS STÉFANOS** looks better from the distance. It's a pretty cove with clear water but flanked by a rather too well-heeled resort, marred by some insensitive hotels. Organised excursion ferries ply across the slim channel to Albania (again see box below).

Kassiópi and around the coast to Ródha

KASSIÓPI has a resort history dating back to Tiberius, who had a villa here. It's quite developed but retains pockets of old village life and an ancient plane tree dominating its main square. There are numerous **rooms** for rent and some excellent restaurants – try the *Kassiopi Star* or the harbourside *Three Brothers*. Nightlife includes some decent bars (best are *Illusions* and *The Waves*), a couple of discos, and, fifteen minutes' walk out of town, a *bouzoukia* joint, the *Kan Kan*. People bathe from the promontory below Kassiópi's fortress, around the promontory to the west, but all the beaches are out of town. The closest, around ten minutes' walk, is known as **Imerólia**; beyond it is **Avlídhi**, stony, more secluded and reached from a rough track off the main road. Footpaths and boat excursions give access to other rocky coves and sand.

West of Kassiópi, the coast is initially barren, and one of the quietest stretches in Corfu. **Avláki**, a long stretch of mixed sand and shingle, has a taverna and attracts a few windsurfers, and **Kalamáki**, a pebbled beach, has a few rooms for rent. Just beyond here a road (near the petrol/gas station) turns off up **Mount Pandokrátor**, past the tumbledown and overgrown village of PERITHÍA, with its beehives, nut trees and a taverna, the *Capricorn Grill*; from the village a footpath leads to the summit.

Back on the coast, the first settlement of any size is **ÁYIOS SPIRÍDHON**, where there are a few rooms and a small, sandy beach. If you continue on a little way you'll see a sign to **Almirós** beach, the start of a continuous strand that sweeps around to Ródha. At this end it's very quiet, with just one taverna and the occasional camper van ignoring conspicuous "No Camping" signs. Nearby, a small channel leads through to the Antinióti lagoon, an oasis-like cove with tepid water and wild birds.

Halfway to Sidhári is **AHARÁVI**, a staid tourist community that straggles along a huge, sandy beach. It's purpose-built and a bit soulless, the hotels and beach packed to the brim with young families. There are two decent bars, *Skandros* and *The Barn*, but little in the way of rooms for rent, and camping would not be encouraged. **South from Aharávi** a road heads back to Píryi, skirting the western foothills of Mount Pandokrátor. It runs past EPISKEPSÍS, a farming community strung out along a ridge, with a couple of cafés and a three-storey Venetian manor, and on to SPARTÍLAS, whose square and bar (with superb local wine) is shaded by a vast elm tree. Off the main route a side road leads up to Pandokrátor's 906-metre summit, via STRINÍLAS, which is served by a twice daily bus from Corfu Town.

RÓDHA was once a small village but has been taken over by British tour operators. In addition to a range of watersports on the narrow, shelving beach, it features horse-riding and tennis courts. Hotels are generally block-booked but there's a fair **campsite**, *Roda Camping* (☎0663/93 120). A pleasant road heads inland from here to join the Troúmpeta Pass junction, passing nearby traditional villages like NIMFÉS (with a nice taverna, and a nearby cave-chapel and spring) and VALANIÓN (with an abandoned monastery and lovely pool).

Just down the coast from Ródha, **ASTRAKÉRI** has the first "Rooms for Rent" signs for miles, a trio of **hotels** – best value are the *Sandra* (☎0663/31 120; ③) and *Astrakeri Beach* (☎0663/31 238; ③) – and a campsite. It's a little windswept but has some nice coves nearby as well as a fishing harbour. The west end of the bay merges into the beginning of Sidhári's resort development (see below).

Paleokastrítsa and the northwest

The topography of **PALEOKASTRÍTSA** – a perfect, sand-fringed natural harbour between cliff-headlands – has led it to be identified with Homer's *Scheria*, where Odysseus was washed ashore and escorted by Nausica to the palace of her father Alcinous, King of the Phaeacians. It's a stunning site, though as you would expect, one that's long been engulfed by tourism. The hotels spread ever further around the bay, and have been boosted by the construction of a marina. On the plus side, there are excellent watersports: the bay is superb for snorkelling and there's one of the few Greek opportunities for scuba diving (equipment and lessons from the *Baracuda Club*; ☎0663/ 41 211). **Rooms** are pricey but there are some good **campsites** (best is *Paleokastritsa Camping*, ☎0663/41 204), excellent fish restaurants, mopeds for rent, and an impressive range of boat trips.

If you're staying in town, caique rides provide the easiest access to **beaches to the south** – such as cliff-backed Áyia Triádha, Yérifa and Stiliári; by road, these can be reached via LIAPÁDHES (which has rooms for rent). From here you can walk to the Rópa Plain and bougainvillaea-covered village of YIANÁDHES. Inland, the most popular local excursion is to **Theotokos Monastery** (daily 7am–1pm & 3–8pm), impressively sited on an outcrop of Mount Arákli, but overrun by tourists. More enjoyable is a walk up to the Byzantine fortress of **Angelokástro**, reached by a cobbled path from LAKÓNES or MAKRÁDHES, to the northwest of town (see below).

North of Paleokastrítsa

To the north of Paleokastrítsa are the inland villages of **MAKRÁDHES**, lost in the olives, and **LAKÓNES**, increasingly a suburb of Paleokastrítsa; both offer rooms for rent and access to the superb bay of **Áyios Yióryios**, a long sweep of sand set beneath towering limestone cliffs. There's no village as such at Áyios Yióryios, but a fair bit of package accommodation, a line of tavernas (best are the *Marina* and *Nafsika*), two discos, a relaxed atmosphere and lots of watersports.

Around Áyios Yióryios bay to the north is **AFIÓNAS**, which is more developed, and up the coast from there, **ARILÁS**, a fairly low-key resort backing another wide bay. Nearby **MAGOULÁDHES** is a small, pretty village with an old convent, **Móni Ithamíni**, and a monk's hermitage, **Móni Ipsíi**, which has some valuable icons.

At windswept, dry **ÁYIOS STÉFANOS** (not to be confused with the west coast resort), there are enjoyable breakers – making this an up-and-coming watersports centre. At present the resort boasts a handful of hotels and a fair scattering of **rooms** for rent. Hordes of day-trippers descend most mornings, but leave the village almost empty at night. Stroll north for seclusion, or into the hills for views to Gravía islet and the north of the island.

PEROULÁDHES, around the corner, is quite a surprise. For a start it's a genuine, somewhat run-down village. Then there's the beach, reached by a steep path to the brick-red sand below spectacular, wind-eroded cliffs. There's also a restaurant nearby and views across to some of the islets off Corfu's northwest coast. The absence of buses, plus afternoon shade over the beach keeps the place distinctly low-key.

All of which is in dramatic contrast to **SIDHÁRI**, whose long beach, shallow water and picturesque rock forms have made it a packaged family favourite resort. It's not, in fact, very attractive: there are lots of mosquitoes, murk seeps from the river onto the beach, and crowds fill the two main roads. The best restaurants are *Oasis* (a little way out of town) and *Sophocles*, the best bar *Legends*, and the best dance floor *Remezzos*. As it's a flat part of the island, there are bicycles for rent. You can also escape by excursion boat to the offshore islets of Othóni, Erikoússa and Mathráki (see p.619-620).

Central and southern Corfu

Two natural features divide the centre and south of Corfu. The first is the **Plain of Rópa**, whose bleak landscape harbours an inaccessible coast. Settlements and development stop a little to the south of Paleokastrítsa and only resume around **Ermónes** and **Pélekas** – a quick bus ride across the island from Corfu Town. Down to the south, a second dividing point is the **Korissíon lagoon**, beyond which a single road trails the interior, with sporadic side roads to resorts on either coast. The landscape here is flat, with salt pans forming an undistinguished backdrop for a series of relatively undefiled beaches – and, in the far south, **Kávos**, Corfu's big youth resort.

Ermónes to Lake Koríssion: the west coast
ERMÓNES has one feature that must be unique in Greece: a lift down to the beach, linked to the Corfu Golf Club and a large hotel complex. The beach, below heavily wooded cliffs, has pebbly sand and freshwater streams; anther strand at nearby **Kóndo Yiálo** is small, sheltered, basic and beautiful.

Just inland is **VÁTOS**, an unspoilt village with **rooms** for rent and a **campsite**, *Vatos Camping* (☎0661/94 393); both tavernas, as so often on Corfu, are called *Spiro's*. Down a steep track cut into the cliffs is **Mirtiótissa Beach**, one of the best on the island. It has a nudist section at one end, a monastery at the other, and rooms halfway down the path. You can walk from the beach to Trialos, an abandoned hamlet. It's greatly preferable to the next resort, **GLIFÁDHA**, dominated by a huge hotel and its customers, and seemingly under permanent construction.

PÉLEKAS is likewise busy, as the main crossroads in the west-centre of the island, and its beach is usually packed solid. The village above, however, has remained quite pleasant, with unpretentious tavernas, a hostel, cheapish rooms, and freelance camping near the beach. During the evenings, coached in tourists arrive to watch the sunsets; if you're not the tour-bus sort, take the #11 bus from Platía San Rócco in Corfu Town.

Heading south, the next real resort is **ÁYIOS GÓRDHIS** and it's arguably the nicest on the island. Vines spread down from pine-clad cliffs to a mile-long, sandy coastal strip, with Plitíri point behind, and jagged rocks thrusting skyward below the one big hotel. The resort's disco is part of the bizarre *Pink Palace*, an American-run holiday complex that keeps itself to itself. The rest of the resort is like stepping back ten years, with only the beginnings of commercialism and plenty of rooms for rent.

Mount Áyios Dheka – Corfu's second peak – casts its shadow over this central part of the island, and the roads on its west side are a bit erratic. Edging through a landscape of cypresses, citrus and olive groves, you eventually reach a long swathe of beaches beside a calm sea leading down to the Korissíon lagoon. On its north side is PARAMÓNAS, with rooms for rent and a sand and pebble beach. A little further on is PRASOÚNDA, an amphitheatre-shaped beach with a single taverna. The road south of here becomes a track, leading to a more isolated beach with another taverna, and to the thirteenth-century **Gardiki castle**, an octagonal structure on a low knoll, still partly intact. The Korissíon lagoon itself has sand dunes, freelance camping (and mosquitoes) and snack bars at the north end.

Benítses to Messónghi: the east coast
The **east coast** of the island, from Corfu Town's suburb-resorts of Kanóni and Pérama south to Messónghi is almost as developed as the stretch north of the capital. Kanóni, with its islets, and the crazy Germanic folly of the Achillion have been described under Corfu Town. South from them is **BENÍTSES**, which is *the* Corfu package resort. Only slightly more bearable for having engulfed a genuine village, and a beach littered with beer cans in the evening, and an olive grove with a fish-and-chip shop and a go-kart track. The clientele is mainly British families with teenagers; bars and discos have names like *Pat's Place* and *Posers*. You have been warned.

Things don't improve much until you reach **MESSÓNGHI**, which is fast merging with **MORAITÍKA**, along a sandy stretch of beach, separated from the road by a line of low-rise hotels, restaurants and discos. There are, at least, a lot of **rooms** for rent – some of the best value at the *Hotel Three Stars* (☎0661/92 457; ②) – and a **campsite**, *Sea Horse Camping* (☎0661/65 364). Bars are better than those of Benítses, too.

The road immediately south of Messónghi is due to be surfaced to Boukári, though at present it's a bit rough. If you make it, **BOUKÁRI** rewards with a small hotel and a taverna, and fishermen who still fish. For swimming, walk some way around the coast towards the north, as there are various crude sewage outlets near the village.

Alternatively, head for **PETRITÍ**, a working fishing port – reached by a side road off the Boukári–Aryirádhes road – where you can share a rather modest strand with a few villa dwellers. It is also quite an easy place to find rooms.

Southern Corfu

The roads from west and east coasts join at **ARYIRÁDHES**, a small town that could make a nice inland base if you have transport to visit the local beaches. It has a few rooms for rent advertised, as does **KOUSPÁDHES**, on the Boukári road.

At **ÁYIOS YIÓRYIOS**, on the west coast 3.5km from Aryirádhes, a short walk north will take you to a beautiful undeveloped stretch of surf-pounded sand. The village proper is an expanding straggle of hotels, apartments and restaurants, with a few rooms for rent. Its drawback is daily excursion boat invasions from Paleokastrítsa.

Further south down the central main road is **MARATHIÁS** and its beach (also known as Santa Barbara), which is a long trek down a dirt road. The strand is a continuation of the one at Áyios Yióryios, but made somewhat unenticing by a couple of open sewers. It's better to stay at one of the rooms places a little inland, and walk to the far end of the beach to swim; there are several tavernas. There's even less of note at ugly **LEFKÍMI**, the main town and administrative centre of the south, which has a dirty beach to the east. ALIKES is to the north – still small-time, with a sandy beach, as is MOLOS, which is plain, simple and, well, plain.

At **KÁVOS**, near the southern tip of the island, young British package tourists have invaded and made the place the nightlife capital of Corfu: most of the "rave" crowd that come here don't leave until it's time to go home. The resort is huge, stretching for a couple of miles and encompassing eighty bars and clubs. Good restaurants include *O Naftis*, *Karavas* and *Krinos*; bars, the *Two Georges* and *Ship Inn*; discos *42nd Street*, *The Hacienda*, and – perhaps the island's best – the *Future Pace*. The beach is fair, with lots of watersports on offer.

An hour's walk from Kávos, following the path beside the *Bar Metaxa*, brings you to **Cape Asprokavos** and the ruined **monastery of Arkoudhílas**. This path also offers a view of Arkoudhílas beach, which can be reached on foot via quiet **SPARTÉRA**, a hamlet which rents rooms to the respectable. If you take this road, and loop around to the west coast, you reach the village of **DRAGOTÍNA**, which has a handful of rooms for rent and a couple of tavernas. A half-hour's walk along a track (impossible for mopeds) leads to one of Corfu's best beaches – secluded, isolated and virtually empty, with just a single summer beach-taverna.

Corfu's satellite islands: Eríkousa, Mathráki and Othoní

Northwest of Corfu there are three small and little-known satellite isles – **Eríkousa**, **Mathráki** and **Othoní**. They get few visitors and, if you go, you'll probably have to stay a couple of days between ferries. There'll be little to do besides swim, lie on the beach and relax; choices of accommodation and places to eat are very limited, and there's nowhere to change money. These are islands for those in search of peace and solitude – *ischia*, as the Greeks put it.

Development of the islands has been restricted largely by their scarcity of water rather than anything lacking in the way of scenery and beaches. Without much land or tourism, job prospects on the islands are few and, since the 1950s, most of the island populations have left – usually for New York. Many of those still living here have spent part of their lives in America, and almost everybody speaks a few words of English.

Each of the islands is connected to Corfu town by **car ferry** and to Sidhári by **kaíki** (see "Travel Details" at the end of this chapter).

Eríkousa (Merlera)

Of the three islands, **Eríkousa** attracts most visitors. Caiques from Sidhári bring day-trippers several times a week, while the *Hotel Eríkousa* (☎0663/71 555; ④) and a few cheaper rooms cater for those staying longer. There's a good long sandy beach in front of the island port and village, and even when the excursion boats have arrived, you can walk further on and have the end of the beach to yourself. If this isn't isolated enough for you, there's a longer and totally empty beach beyond the headland to the east.

The small village is pleasant enough, without being particularly picturesque. There's a shop, a couple of *kafenía* and a single taverna on the beach which takes advantage of its monopoly by charging over the odds. Inland, a couple of smaller, more traditional settlements stand amid hills covered by cypress and olive trees.

Mathráki (Samothráki)

Mathráki is smaller than Eríkousa, and apart from returning Greek Americans, who swell the population in summer, very few people come here. This is quite fortunate, for its sandy beach, stretching from the harbour for the length of the eastern side of the island, is a nesting site for the endangered loggerhead turtle (see p.630). It's important not to camp anywhere near the beach – and not to make any noise there at night.

From the harbour, a road climbs the hillside up to the tiny village of **KÁTO MATHRÁKI**, where brightly painted houses are scattered amongst the olive groves. There are very few rooms to rent – don't count on finding one – and a combination shop-*kafenío*-taverna at the top of the hill overlooking the sea; the food is good, but the choice is limited to say the least, and you'd do well to bring some supplies with you. The scenic island road takes you to the slightly larger village of **ÁNO MATHRÁKI** at the other end of the island, with a single, old-fashioned *kafenío* next to the church. From here, a path leads down to the far end of the beach.

Othoní (Fano)

Othoní is the largest, and, at first sight, the least inviting of Corfu's satellite isles. Around the harbour, the landscape is dry and barren, and the village has a definite end-of-the-line feel. There are no great sandy beaches, and most people swim from the shingle in front of the village. Inland, however, there's some fine scenery, and on closer acquaintance you'll find that the village has an enjoyable atmosphere. A small foreign community usually gathers during the summer, and there are always a few yachts moored in the bay. Among a handful of *kafenía* and tavernas, try *O Mikros* for Greek standards, and the Italian-run *La Locanda dei Sogni* for pricier meals – and nice **rooms** (☎0663/71 640; ③). In addition, there are a few cheaper private rooms in the village.

To explore the island, follow the old donkey track up the valley to the left of the harbour, which leads to the main inland village, **HORIÓ**. This route takes you through a landscape of rocky peaks and valleys with hillsides cloaked by cypress trees. Horió, like other inland villages, is heavily depopulated – only about sixty people still live on the island through the winter – but it's very attractive, and the architecture is completely traditional. From the road, a track leads down to the far side of the island and some more rocky and isolated beaches.

Paxí (Paxos) and Andípaxi (Antipaxos)

Paxí is just 12km by 4km in extent and devoted almost completely to olive cultivation. Like Corfu's northern satellite isles, a dire water shortage has prevented construction of all but one luxury hotel, though it is not exactly remote – or unvisited. There are ferries almost every day in season from Corfu and from Sívota and Párga on the mainland, and seats on the latter crossing must be reserved a day ahead in summer. The

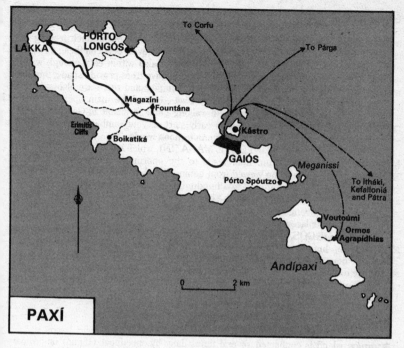

PAXÍ

island's population of just over two thousand is often matched in season by visitors (many of them Italian). However, there are plenty of places to escape to, and by evening most of the calm has returned. For the most part it remains quiet and rural.

Gaíos

Most people stay in or around the main harbour and village of **GAÍOS**, whose three- and four-storey pastel-tinted houses front a channel of water, giving the impression of being built on a river. Opposite is the islet of **Kástro**, endowed with an inevitable ruined Venetian fort; it can be reached by boat and offers the best view of the town – one not much changed since it was sketched by Edward Lear a hundred years ago.

Unless you're exceptionally unlucky, you should be able find a **room** in or around Gaíos. If you're not met on arrival with offers, go through the square away from the waterside and take the road that leads out of the town. When you get to the edge of the built-up area, turn left at the crossroads/bus stop up a steep concrete road and keep an eye out for the signs. Don't be afraid to haggle.

Food is slightly overpriced, but no more than you would expect on a small island with a short tourist season. Some of the best-value meals are to be had at *Spiro's*, also called *Beautiful Paxi. Dodo's* is also recommended. For **drinks**, try *Costa's Kafenion* just off the main square, where you'll pay about one-fifth of the price charged at the trendier bars used by the foreign yachting crowds.

The island's only sandy beach is **Mogoníssi**, half an hour's walk to the south, and flanked by an open-air taverna which boasts "Theo and Pan, probably the best Greek dancers in the world", and a varied menu. A free bus/boat service leaves Gaíos for the beach every evening at 7.30pm, and there's unofficial camping behind the beach.

Around the island

Paxí's single main road splits halfway up the island, with one branch leading from Gaíos to Lákka and the other to Pórto Longós. A **bus** travels between these three main communities about six times a day, though they're also within easy enough walking distance – as is everywhere on the island. Plentiful olive trees provide shade; the island homes are scattered, forming many tiny communities; and there are also said to be over seventy churches. The *Greek Islands Club* – one of the main operators to this island – puts out a useful wildflower and walking guide, available in Gaíos and Lákka, which details hard-to-find paths. Get an early start on your ramblings, as all of Paxí's beaches are exposed to prevailing summer afternoon winds.

Midway point on the road to Lákka is **MAGAZÍNI**, which has a friendly taverna with rooms. A pleasant trail from here leads to the enormous chalk-coloured cliffs of **Erimítis**, which can also be viewed from behind the church in BOIKATIKÁ. **LÁKKA** itself has a population of around two hundred, a few tavernas, rooms for rent and a pebbly cove for swimming, though the bay in general is rather stagnant. It also hosts an **aquarium**, showing locally caught marine exhibits, which are released at the end of the season and replaced the following year.

PÓRTO LONGÓS, facing northeast, is prettier, with better tavernas, but its accommodation is limited to foreign-chartered holiday villas. This housing shortage, however, doesn't concern the multitudes at the island's premier unofficial **campsite**, one cove to the south. That, and two more coves southwest of Pórto Longós, constitute the highest concentration of (pebbly) swimming spots on Paxí, along with a like concentration of Italian and Greek holidaymakers.

Andípaxi

Andípaxi island is connected several times daily by speedboat (15min) or ordinary *kaíki* service from Gaíos. The trip – a very popular day excursion – seems expensive for what it is, but the route takes in the spectacular caves on the rocky southern tip of Paxí on the way, and you might see a few flying fish into the bargain. The boat stops at a couple of superb beaches (sandy and better than any on Paxí) before going on to the main anchorage and village – such as it is – known as ÓRMOS AGRAPÍDHIAS.

There are two tavernas at the first beach (one has a campsite), while the second has a bar with food and a panoramic view. The beaches are connected by a dirt road and there are paths all over the island. There are no rooms to be rented and, if you camp, the tavernas are not likely to stay open just for you in the evening, so bring provisions.

Lefkádha (Lefkas)

Lefkádha is an oddity. Connected to the mainland by a long causeway through salt marshes, it barely feels like an island – and in fact, historically it isn't. It is separated from the mainland by a canal cut by Corinthian colonists in the seventh century BC that has been redredged (after silting up) on various occasions since, and today is connected by a thirty-metre boat-drawbridge built in 1986.

Lefkádha was long an important strategic base, and approaching the causeway you pass a series of fortresses, climaxing in the fourteenth-century castle of **Santa Maura** – the Venetian name for the island. These defences were too close to the mainland to avoid an Ottoman tenure, which began in 1479, but the Venetians wrested back control a couple of centuries later. They were in turn overthrown by Napoleon in 1797 and then the British took over as Ionian protectors in 1810. It wasn't until 1864 that Lefkádha, like the rest of the Ionian archipelago, was reunited with Greece.

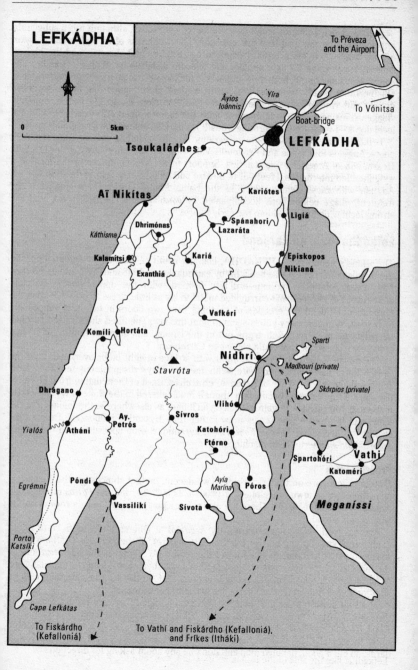

At first glance Léfkadha is not overwhelmingly attractive, although it is a substantial improvement on the mainland just opposite. The whiteness of its rock strata – *Lefkás* means "white" – is often brutally exposed by roadcuts and quarries, and the highest ridge is bare except for ugly military and telecom installations. With the marshes and sumpy inlets all around, both mosquitoes and foul smells can be a midsummer problem. On the other hand, the island is a pretty verdant place, supporting cypresses, olive groves and vineyards, particularly on the western slopes, and life in the mountain villages remains relatively untouched, with the older women still wearing traditional local dress – two skirts (one forming a bustle), a dark headscarf and a rigid bodice.

Lefkádha has been the home of various literati, including two prominent Greek poets, Angelos Sikelianos and Aristotelis Valaoritis, and the short-story writer Lefcadio Hearn, son of American missionaries. Support of the arts continues in the form of a well-attended international **festival** of theatre and folk-dancing lasting the bulk of each August, with most events staged in the Santa Maura castle. On a smaller scale, frequent village celebrations accompanied by *bouzouki* and clarinet ensure that the strong local wine flows well into the early hours.

Lefkádha town and around

The island's main town, **LEFKÁDHA**, lies just south of the shallow lagoon, opposite the mainland fortress. It was badly hit by earthquakes in 1948 and 1953, and its **houses** have been rebuilt in an extraordinary fashion, with the upper storeys typically constructed of plywood and corrugated metal to lay as little stress as possible upon the foundations; indeed the erection of anything over two floors in height is supposedly forbidden, although a few hotels seem to flout this law. The tilted shutters and porches on stilts, the numerous **fish traps** out in the lagoon, and summer flotillas of yachts, complete a portscape that could almost be Caribbean.

The business district, festive at night with strings of light bulbs overhead, lines the town's long, narrow thoroughfare, with narrow alleys disappearing to either side. Scattered about are a score of Italianate **churches**, most of them dating from just after the start of the Venetian occupation, though much altered in the wake of various earthquakes. If you manage to gain entrance you'll find, as elsewhere in the Ionian, that the icons and frescoes show Renaissance rather than Byzantine influences. Take a look also at the self-styled *Mousio Fonografou*, an antique shop specialising in old 78rpm records and wonderful horn-machines.

Practicalities

Hotels in town are on the pricey side. Two decent, budget choices are the *Vyzantion*, near the entry to town at Delpherd 4 (☎0645/22 692; ②), and the *Patras* on the main square (☎0645/22 539; ②). There are also a few signs pointing towards **rooms** on the lagoon shore-road.

Among town centre **restaurants**, try *Regantos* at Dhimárhou Verióti 17 (a minor commercial street going north from the main square), or the *Psistaria O Mitas*, by the southern yacht harbour. At the start of the road to Aï Nikítas is the *Adriatica*, one of the more elegant restaurants on the island; it's not cheap but it features unusual vegetarian dishes, an excellent fish pie and various seafood dishes. For entertainment (in addition to the August festival) there are two summer **cinemas**.

The **bus station** faces the southern yacht anchorage. There are regular services to the main resorts of Nidhrí, Vassilikí and Aï Nikítas, as well as the interior settlement of Kariá. To get anywhere else efficiently you'll need to **rent** a car or a very tough motorbike. Incidentally, Lefkádhan road-signing is atrocious, even by Greek island standards, so get a good, detailed map and don't be shy about asking for directions.

Around Lefkádha town

The closest decent beach to the capital is at **Áyios Ioánnis**, the spit bordering the Yíra lagoon on its west – about 45 minutes away if you choose to walk. It's sandy but also has pebbles that the wind-churned surf can hurl with bruising force. Continuing clockwise around the Yíra from here would bring you to a calmer, north-facing bay and the inexpensive *Estiatorio/Psitopolio Yira*, serving good fare to a mainly local clientele. From there it's easy enough to complete a loop back to town, past the bridge.

West of the harbour, you can follow the Aï Nikítas road up to **Faneroméni monastery**. It's no longer inhabited but has beautiful views and retains its old *símandro* (oxen's yoke and hammer), which was used to call the monks to prayer when first the Turkish, and later German, occupying forces forbade the use of bells.

Inland, a confusion of roads lead from the port to a welter of mostly tiny villages in the north-centre of the island, overlooking a broad agricultural upland whose existence you hardly suspect gazing up from sea level. Possible targets here include the rickety hilltop hamlet of SPANOHÓRI, near the thriving crossroads town of LAZARÁTA with its *platía* tavernas, or the embroidery centre of KARIÁ, with a fine *platía*, expensive lace for sale and a few rooms for rent.

More badly marked roads wiggle between the dozen or so settlements here, and eventually down either flank of the island.

The east coast to Vassilikí

Heading south from Lefkádha town along the eastern shore, there's little initially to compel a halt except for **campsites** at KARIÓTES and EPÍSKOPOS, where there's a rocky beach. Only LIGIÁ, with its fishing port, has retained any village feel, and most of this coast is dotted with small, nondescript resorts patronised mostly by Greeks.

Few foreigners, in fact, stop before **NIDHRÍ**, built on the site of a swamp drained after the war. The swimming off the tiny beach here is very average, worse if the ever-present yachts have been draining their bilges; and the only redeeming feature is the view out towards moonrise over various islets. **Rooms** are generally reserved in advance by tour companies, but the tourist agencies on the front might turn up something for you. There is no shortage of cocktail bars, discos or **restaurants**, though the last present few gastronomic surprises.

The German archaeologist **Wilhelm Dörpfeld** believed Nidhrí, rather than Itháki, to be the site of Odysseus's capital, and did indeed find Bronze Age tombs on the plain nearby. His theory identifying ancient Ithaca with Lefkádha fell into disfavour after his death in 1940, however, although his obsessive attempts to give the island some status over its neighbour are honoured by a statue on Nidhrí's quay. His tomb is tucked away at AYÍA KIRIAKÍ on the opposite side of the bay, near the house in which he once lived, visible just above the chapel and lighthouse on the far side of the water.

VLIHÓS, 3km south of Nidhrí at the head of an all-but-landlocked bay, is essentially an annexe of the bigger resort, though the presence of more old buildings, a quieter setting away from the road, and summer *bouzouki* events count in its favour. The bay is unsuitable for swimming; there is a **campsite** on the far side at DESÍMI.

Beyond Vlihós, the main island road twists through or past the attractive hill villages of KATOHÓRI, FTÉRNOS and PÓROS, all of which have at least one evening taverna apiece. The main resort in this corner of the island is the deep bay of **Ayía Marína** below PÓROS, which has **rooms** and a rather luxurious **campsite**. The pebble beach, however, gets both busy and dirty in July and August.

The next inlet to the west, **SÍVOTA**, has no beach to speak of and is really just a yacht harbour – albeit a fairly scenic one. A brief evening visit is perhaps best, when the five fish tavernas get going. A more functional swimming beach and a semi-official campsite can be found at **KASTRÍ**, at the end of a well-marked side road between MARANDOHÓRI and KONDARÉNA.

The southeastern bus route ends around 40km from Lefkádha town at **VASSILIKÍ**, which enjoys a fine setting with the island's largest agricultural strip just behind the broad bay. However, the beach is drab and the town tacky, dominated by a role as one of Europe's premier windsurfing centres. If you've not come on an instructional package, you can usually find a stray board to rent, but beginners may be forced to confine their efforts to the morning hours since afternoon gusts off the plain behind sweep all except experts from the water.

For anyone not a devotee of the windsurf-cult, Vassilikí is of most interest for its **ferry connections** south to Kefalloniá. The **campsite** behind the beach is well appointed but relatively expensive; alternatively there are various rooms, a **post office** (but no bank), and an **OTE** station with handy evening and Sunday afternoon hours. **Eating out**, you're advised to try **Póndi**, a quieter district a kilometre distant on the far side of the bay, where the *Kamares Restaurant* is a possible alternative.

ÁYIOS PÉTROS, 4km inland and north, has some unusual half-timbered houses and a lively main square, on and around which are several tavernas. *Ta Batsanakia* is a good, characterful grill with palatable local wine.

The west coast

Starting out from Lefkádha Town, the west coast begins with rather more promise. Past the Móni Faneroméni (see above) and beach resort of TSOUKALÁDHES, you arrive at **AÏ NIKÍTAS**, a fine, little developed hamlet, with a single, flagstoned main street flanked by a half-dozen **tavernas**, about as many **rooms**, a campsite (just inland) and a pair of bars. It is a superb base and a ten-minute boat ride around the headland, or an hour's hike through scrub and bushes, will bring you to the glorious **Mílos beach** – a mile-long sweep of sand and shingle.

The next stop south is **Káthisma beach**. This attracts large numbers of freelance campers, though thus far there is just one proper taverna-rooms, plus a trio of snack-caravans with showers and toilets. More substantial facilities are to be found (well up the hill) at **KALAMÍTSI**, host to dozens of **rooms** and a few **tavernas**. This has its own large beach, too, connected by a particularly steep track, which threatens grief to camper-vans. There is no road directly between Káthisma and Kalamítsi beaches; between the two main bays, however, you can walk through several inviting coves frequented by nudists, and past a freshwater spring.

Visible just inland from Kalamítsi are two unspoilt communities reachable by meandering roads: **DHRIMÓNAS**, something of an architectural showcase with its uniform, old stone houses, and **EXÁNTHIA**, as good or better in its amphitheatrical arrangement. Neither has any tourist facilities.

Heading south again on the main route, a right turn at KOMÍLI leads to **ATHÁNI**, another popular beach staging point, with plenty of **rooms** and **tavernas**. The choice of nearby beaches consists of **Yialós**, 4km south and marked after a fashion; **Egrémni**, 6km distant and currently unsignposted; and, most picturesque (but also most crowded), **Pórto Katsíki**, 10km along an increasingly bumpy road, at the base of high cliffs and with a single taverna.

If the west wind is up, none of these coves will be inviting, and you might make the best of things and drive past the monastery of Áyios Nikólaos to the Lefkadhan "Land's End" at **Cape Lefkátas** (Doukato), which drops 75 abrupt metres into the sea. Byron's Childe Harold sailed past this point, and "saw the evening star above, Leucadia's far projecting rock of woe: And hail'd the last resort of fruitless love". The fruitless love is a reference to Sappho, who in accordance with the ancient legend that you could cure yourself of unrequited love by leaping into these waters, leapt – and died. In her honour the locals termed the place *Kávos tis Kirás* (Lady's Cape), and her act was imitated by the lovelorn youths of Lefkádha for centuries afterwards. And not just by the lovelorn, for the act (known as *katapontismós*) was performed annually by scape-goats – always a criminal or a lunatic – selected by priests from the Apollo temple whose sparse ruins lie close by. Feathers and even live birds were attached to the victim to slow his descent and boats waiting below took the chosen one, dead or alive, away to some place where the evil banished with him could do no further harm.

The rite continued into the Roman era, when it degenerated into little more than a fashionable stunt of decadent youth. These days, Greek hang-gliders hold a tourna-ment from the cliffs every July. Weather permitting, there are *kaíki* trips out of Vassilikí for the more sedentary or those without vehicles capable of reaching the cape overland.

Lefkádha's satellites: Meganíssi and other islets

Lefkádha has a string of satellite islets – Spartí, Madourí, Skórpios and Meganíssi – over to the east of the island. **Meganíssi** is the only one with a village population and public access, from the port of Nidhrí.

Meganíssi

Meganíssi, a twenty-minute ferry or excursion-boat crossing from Nidhrí, has been for some time a closely guarded secret among island aficionados, without a postcard or souvenir shop in sight. The British company *Ilios Island Holidays* has now discovered it and rents villas there, though their comparatively small operation should do little damage to the island's charms. A severe water shortage, and little scope for more ambi-tious building, is likely to thwart any of the major operators from following suit. For the present, **rented rooms** are readily available and cheap.

The main ferry stop is **VATHÍ**, a fishing port, whose harbour entrance is flanked by chapels to bless all boats and grant safe passage. That aside, it's a rather scruffy place, moving at its own slow pace. A road leads up from here to the more attractive village of **KATOMÉRI**, where visitors are likely to be greeted with a free *oúzo* at the taverna and an invitation to join in a game of cards. Here also is the island's first **hotel**, the *Meganiss* – small, simple and very pleasant.

The road continues in a westerly loop to **SPARTOHÓRI**, an immaculate village with whitewashed buildings and an abundance of bougainvillaea. The locals live from farm-ing and fishing and are genuinely welcoming. There are a few tavernas, with limited fare, but excellent cooking and decent prices. Through the village and at the end of the island road is PÓRTO SPÍLIO, a stop for some of the Nidhrí excursion boats.

Several tracks lead over the hills of the island and down through the olive-grove terracing to secluded bays. The most popular of these is **Ambelákia**, which attracts visiting yacht flotillas. One tour company over-optimistically set up a Club-Med-type operation here; it has now closed down, though the grass huts are still there. You might also persuade a boat to take you to the caves on the southwest coast which reputedly sheltered submarines during World War II.

Private isles

Of the other Lefkádha satellites, **Skórpios** is the retreat of the (now almost extinct) Onassis family and their staff, with landing still strictly forbidden. It was here that Aristotle married Jackie Kennedy.

Landing is also forbidden on **Madourí**, the property of the poet Nanos Valaoritis and his family. The third islet, **Spartí**, is uninhabited and covered in scrub.

Kefalloniá (Cephallonia, Kefallinía)

Kefalloniá is the largest of the Ionian islands – a place that has "real" towns as well as resorts and which, until the late 1980s, paid scant regard to tourism. Perhaps this was in part a feeling that the island could not easily be marketed. Virtually all of its towns and villages were levelled in the 1953 earthquake, and these masterpieces of Venetian architecture had been the one touch of elegance in a severe, mountainous landscape. A more likely explanation, however, for the island's late emergence on the Greek tourist scene is the Kefallonians' legendary reputation for insular pride and stubbornness. Even Greek visitors are bemused by the fact that buses from Kefalloniá to Athens usually have the island town Lixoúri on the front: apparently the drivers, born in Lixoúri, won't have it any other way.

Having decided on the advantages of an easily exploitable industry, however, Kefalloniá is at present in the midst of a tourism boom. Long favoured by Italians, it has begun attracting British package companies, for whom a new "international" airport terminal has been constructed, while virtually every decent beach has been endowed with a sprinkling of restaurants. There are certainly adequate attractions, with some beaches as good as any in the Ionian, and a fine, if pricey, local wine, the dry white *Rombola*. Moreover, the island seems able to soak up a lot of people without feeling at all crowded, and the magnificent scenery can speak for itself, the escarpments culminating in the 1632-metre bulk of **Mount Énos**, declared a national park to protect the fir trees (*Abies cephalonica*) named after the island.

The size of Kefalloniá, a poor bus service and a distinct shortage of summer rooms makes **moped or car rental** almost a must for exploring the island. Fortunately, most of the towns and larger resorts have a rental outlet. If you are depending on the buses, be warned that there's only a basic grid of services: Sámi, the main port, to Argostóli, the island capital, and Fiskárdho (in the north); and Argostóli to the resorts of Skála and Póros in the southeast. If you use a moped, drive with discretion as the terrain is very rough in places – almost half the roads are unsurfaced – and the gradients can sometimes be a bit challenging for underpowered machines.

Sámi and around

Most boats dock at the large and not very characterful port and town of **SÁMI**, built and later rebuilt near the south end of the Ithaki straits, more or less on the site of ancient Sámi. This was the capital of the island in Homeric times, when Kefalloniá was part of Ithaca's maritime kingdom: today the administrative hierarchy is reversed, Itháki being considered the backwater. With ferries to most points of the Ionian, and several companies introducing direct links to Italy – and one even to Piraeus, Samos and Turkey – the town is clearly preparing itself for a burgeoning future.

For the moment, though, most arriving passengers tend to get out as fast as possible. In addition to moped rentals (mainly on the waterfront), there are three daily buses to Argostóli, plus one bus (change at Dhiviráta) and a ferry to Fiskárdho. If you need or decide to stay, the town has a few **rooms** for rent and four budget hotels: the waterfront *Hotel Kyma* (☎0674/22 064; ③), *Hotel Melissáni* (☎0674/22 464; ③), *Hotel Ionion* (☎0674/22 035; ③) and *Hotel Krinos* (☎0674/32 002; ②).

Karavómilos Beach and the Melissáni and Dhroghoráti caves

More rooms and a **campsite**, *Karavómilos Beach* (☎0674/21 680), are to be found at **Karavómilo Beach**, 2km to the north of Sámi. The beach itself is not very exciting but there is the opportunity of a boat ride to the **Spíli Melissáni**, a blue-tinged sea-cave partly submerged in brackish water. You're taken into an inner lake-grotto, whose waters, amazingly, emerge from an underground fault which leads the whole way under the island to a point near Argostóli. At this point, known as Katavóthres, the sea gushes endlessly into a subterranean channel – and until the 1953 earthquake disrupted it the current was used to drive seamills. That the water, now as then, still ends up in the cave has been shown with fluorescent tracer dye.

Another, more conventional, cavern, the **Spíli Dhrogaráti**, is to be found 4km inland of Sámi, just off the main road to Argostóli (open dawn to dusk). A stalagmite-bedecked chamber, it is occasionally used for concerts thanks to its marvellous acoustics.

Áyia Evfimía

At **ÁYIA EVFIMÍA**, 10km north of Sámi, the road (and bus) turns inland towards Fiskárdho. You could do worse than stop at this pretty port town, which seems to have just about the right mixture of locals and visitors, and boasts the best restaurant on the island, *Stavros Dendrinos's taverna*. To find it, walk round the harbour past the main dock and 500m on to the so-called **Paradise Beach**. The small pebble beach is fine for swimming, and, on a terrace above, the multilingual Stavros serves an unusual range of excellently prepared food – and great house wine. There are **rooms** (③) available above the premises, but they suffer from the heat and noise generated by a busy restaurant. This is a shame, because the view is superb, and rooms back in Áyia Evfimía are not easy to find, especially for short stays.

Note also that in summer there is a useful daily **ferry link** from Áyia Evfimía to Itháki and on to Astakós on the mainland.

Southeast Kefalloniá

Heading directly **southeast from Sámi** by public transport is impossible; to get to **Skála** or **Póros** you need to get one bus to Argostóli and another on from there; five daily run to Skála, three to Póros. With your own vehicle, the backroads route from Sámi to Póros is an attractive option. It's eighty percent dirt track but negotiable with a decent moped; the road is signposted to the left just before the Dhrogaráti cave.

Póros

PÓROS was one of the first resorts on the island to wake up to the idea of tourism, providing the shortest and most popular ferry link with the mainland (to Killíni in the Peloponnese, with three boats a day in season). Several foreign tour operators maintain offices in the village, and a few rooms to rent are available for independent tourists but the place hasn't really changed that much. With its houses encroaching onto the dark green hillsides, the long beach, a small separate bay for boats, and nearby shady coves, it's a more attractive entry point than Sámi.

A dirt road twists 12km around the rocky coastline from **Póros to Skála** at the southern extremity of the island. It's a lovely, isolated route, with scarcely a building en route, save for a small chapel, 3km short of Skála, next to ruins of a **Roman temple**.

Skála

SKÁLA was described in the last edition of this guide as an up-and-coming beach resort. These days it has well and truly arrived, though it has to be said that the tourists have livened things up a bit, with a good range of restaurants, bars and shops. At the north end of town, opposite the *Hotel Skála* on Odisséas street, the remains of a **Roman villa** are on show, featuring finely detailed mosaics.

Rooms aren't easy to find in summer, as British package companies have cleaned up on accommodation in both hotels and village houses. If you're stuck, ask at the small *Koinotiko Grafeio* (Council Office) on the main street, or try at RATZÍKLI, 3km from Skála on the Argostóli road – a little inland from the sea.

LOGGERHEAD TURTLES

The Ionian islands harbour the Mediterranean's main concentration of **loggerhead sea turtles** (*Caretta caretta*). These creatures, which lay their eggs at night on sandy coves, are under direct threat from the tourist industry in Greece. Each year, many turtles are injured by motorboats, their nests are destroyed by bikes ridden on the beaches, and the newly hatched young die entangled in deckchairs and umbrellas left out at night on the sand. The turtles are easily frightened by noise and lights, too, which makes them uneasy cohabitants with freelance campers and discos.

The Greek government has passed laws designed to protect the loggerheads, but, in addition to the thoughtlessness of visitors, local economic interests tend to prefer a beach full of bodies to a sea full of turtles. On Kefalloniá, the island's principal nesting ground is **Potomákia Beach**, 5km to the west of Skála, and here the British wildlife charity, *Care for the Wild*, has set up an annual project, monitoring and protecting the breeding population. They accompany small groups of tourists on visits, so that they can actually see and touch nesting turtles and hatchlings. There is development on the way but hopefully the locals will appreciate the usefulness – and increasingly the uniqueness – of the turtles themselves as a tourist attraction.

If you are interested in taking part as a volunteer on the Kefalloniá Turtle Project, contact Care for the Wild, 1 Ashfolds, Horsham Road, Rusper, West Sussex, RH12 4QX. The project runs from June to September and volunteers are asked to devote a minimum of three weeks .

Skála to Argostóli

Skála is edged by a fine stretch of sand, which continues around the headland and on to the south coast of the island. For the first few kilometres, the road runs a little inland and there is little development. At **Potomákia Beach**, 5km along the coast from Skála and reached by a turning at Ratzíkli, there are breeding grounds of loggerhead turtles (see box above). The sands and dunes are popular with locals at weekends and development looks set, with large clearings of land in preparation for tavernas and hotels. If you visit, or stay, leave the beach to the turtles at night.

The Argostóli road meets the sea midway around Loúrdha Bay at **KÁTO KATELION**, where an absurd number of restaurants compete for the seasonal occupants of purpose-built apartments and a few freelance campers. One possible attraction is that the local **moped rental** agency arranges **scuba dives**.

Continuing west, the road heads inland again, past **MARKÓPOULO**, where the **Assumption of the Virgin festival** (Aug 15) is celebrated in unique style at the local church with small, harmless snakes with cross-like markings on their heads. Each year, at least, so everyone hopes, they converge on the site to be grasped to the bosoms of the faithful; a few, in fact, are kept by the priests for years when they don't naturally arrive. The celebrants are an interesting mix of locals and gypsies – some of whom come over from the mainland for the occasion. It's quite a spectacle.

Further on, rooms are available at VLAHÁTA and MOUSSÁTA, and from the former a track winds its way up to the 5000-foot summit of Mount Énos. On a clear day, you might not quite see forever, but should at least get a glimpse of neighbouring Zákinthos. Note that the main access route is from the Argostóli–Sámi road.

There are more rooms and unofficial summer camping at **LOURDHÁTA**, a little village just inland from its beach – which is flanked by a trio of tavernas. It's an attractive base, and just beyond the beach, across some rocks, a tall overhanging tree directs a trickling freshwater-fall into the sea. Further west, there's another good beach and a taverna at **ÁYIOS THOMÁS**. At **PESSÁDHA** a ferry plies in the summer months to Skinariá on Zákinthos; the minute, uninhabited harbour is some way below the village.

Argostóli, Lixoúri and the west

ARGOSTÓLI, Kefallonia's capital, is a large and thriving town, virtually a city, with a marvellous site on a bay within a bay. It was totally rebuilt after the earthquake but has an enjoyable streetlife that remains defiantly Greek, especially during the evening *volta* around Platía Metaxá – nerve centre of the town.

A couple of museums are worth a little time. The **Historical and Cultural Museum** (Mon–Sat 8.30am–2.30pm; 100dr) is strong on photographic documentation of Argostóli, including the British and French occupations and the 1953 earthquake

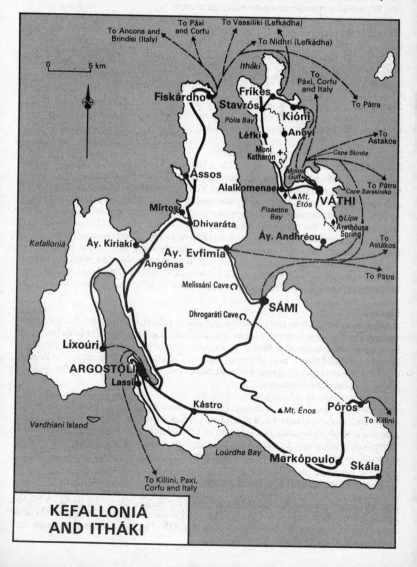

KEFALLONIÁ AND ITHÁKI

and its aftermath. A bit less imaginative is the **Archaeological Museum**, a block down on G. Veryóti (Tues–Sun 8.30am–3pm; 200dr); it consists mainly of pottery, including pieces from a number of Mycenaean tombs discovered in the village to the south.

The **EOT**, on the waterfront Metaxá street, keeps a list of **rooms for rent** and will phone to book for you – assuming there are vacancies. If you'd rather look around yourself, try Spiros Rouhatas at Metaxá 44 (☎0671/23 941 or 24 936; ②), who has rooms above his café opposite the Lixoúri ferry quay, or the restaurant *Adherphi Tzivras* (③), on the side street V. Vandaroú, opposite the petrol pumps by the bus station. All of the **hotels** are pretty expensive, though the *Olga*, Metaxa 82 (☎0671/26 981; ④), is a nice splurge, and good value off season.

More mundane and harder work is the **campsite**, a two-kilometre walk (no bus) to the end of the promontory at Fanári. The site is just after the **Katavóthes**, the point at which the sea drains into the ground to re-emerge at Karavómilos (see Sámi).

For **meals**, the *Adherphi Tzivras* (above) is recommended, with regular dishes and local house wine. For something fancier, try one of the places around Platía Metaxá.

Buses run from Argostóli to most points of the island and *KTEL* tries to make up for (or exploit) the shortcomings of its network by offering tours, and trips to nearby islands and Olympia. As for ferries, there is one daily boat to Killíni and three boats a week to Zákinthos. The walk-on ferry to Lixoúri leaves every hour. Numerous agencies on the waterfront rent out **cars and mopeds**.

South of Argostóli: beaches and Kástro

For a swim, locals and visitors alike take a bus to to LÁSSI, across the headland from Argostóli. Flanking the village, on either side of a hill, are two excellent but crowded beaches: **Platís** (wide) and **Makrís** (long) Yiálos. Both are lined with package hotels and numerous tavernas. For details of the coast to the west, see the previous section.

With a moped, the best inland excursion is to **Kastro** (also known as Áyios Yióryos or San Giorgio), the medieval Venetian capital of the island. The old town here supported a population of 15,000 until its destruction by an earthquake in the seventeenth century: substantial ruins of its castle, churches and houses can be visited on the hill above the modern village. Byron was impressed by the view from the summit in 1823, when he lived for a few months in the village of METAXÁTA, some kilometres below; sadly, as at Messolónghi, the dwelling where he stayed no longer exists.

Lixoúri

A quick ferry hop across the bay will bring you to LIXOÚRI, the only sizeable centre on Kefalloniá's rugged western peninsula. The town itself is a bit downbeat, but would be a quiet and inexpensive base if you could get one of the rooms at the *Estiatoria Maria* on Kósti Palamá, near the main square. The restaurant is basic to the point of scruffy, and won't suit all tastes. For a bit more class try *Antony's* opposite the quay, or one of the places on the square.

Walking south of Lixoúri, you reach the first of a series of sand-and-seaweed beaches after about thirty minutes. Proceed along these (and along tracks where necessary), and eventually you'll reach **Cape Áyios Yióryios**. Around the cape, ninety minutes' walk from Lixoúri, is a splendid and completely undeveloped stretch of sand, facing Vardhiani island. Getting down to it requires a detour along the dirt road. There is no café for miles around, so bring provisions.

The west coast and the road north

From Argostóli, most people board a bus bound for **Fiskárdho** in the north – a highly scenic journey that passes side roads to several excellent beaches. The first of these is **Áyia Kiriakí**, reached by a 2km track from ANGÓN. The next, **Mírtos**, is signposted just past DHIVARATÁ, and reached along a steep track. Seen from the cliff road above, it is one of the most spectacular beaches in Greece – a strip of almost pure white sand – and in summer it attracts a fair number of day-trippers and campers. It's not an ideal place to stay, however, as it has no shade (apart from the cave at one end), and no toilet facilities. A seasonal bar rustles up sandwiches and drinks – overpriced, of course, but the alternative is a 4km slog up to Dhivaratá's two grills and a shop.

The main road, hacked out of the palisades on this road, continues north to **ÁSSOS**, a fishing village built on a narrow isthmus that links it with a castle-crowned headland. There are more shops and cafés than there used to be here, and plenty of daytime visitors, but it is far from spoilt and would make a fine base if you could get one of the few rooms for rent.

Fiskárdho

Kefalloniá's picture-postcard village, **FISKÁRDHO**, is notable mainly for having escaped damage in the earthquake, preserving intact its eighteenth-century Venetian houses. It is pretty but also totally dominated by tourism, with a yacht club, lots of boutiques, and the sort of restaurants that push expensive fish and bottled wine. The richer and dumber you look, the more likely you are to be taken for a ride. If you're going to eat anywhere, try *Nikolas's Taverna*; at least he does it all with good grace and a twinkle in his eye. **Rooms** here in season are like gold dust, with only the odd cancellation from a package company on offer. Particularly nice ones are offered by Anna Barzouka (☎0674/51 572; ③); to find her, ask, as the streets are not named.

Close to the town, there's reasonable swimming off a mixture of rock and pebble beaches, but watch out for oil, which has washed up here and at Ássos recently. Daily **ferries** run to Vassilikí and Nidhrí on Lefkádha, as well as to Itháki and down the coast to Sámi. There are also **kaíkia** to Itháki in season.

Fiskárdho hosts a monk seal conservation project (see p.597 for more on seals).

Itháki (Ithaca)

Rugged **Itháki**, Odysseus's legendary homeland, has had no substantial archaeological discoveries but it fits Homer's description to perfection: "There are no tracks, nor grasslands . . . it is a rocky severe island, unsuited for horses, but not so wretched, despite its small size. It is good for goats."

Despite the romance of its name, and its proximity to Corfu, very little tourist development has arrived to spoil the place. This is doubtless in part accounted for by a dearth of beaches, though the island is good walking country, with a handful of small fishing villages and various pebbly coves to swim from.

Váthi

Ferries from Pátra, Kefalloniá, Astakós, Corfu or Italy land at the main port and capital of **VÁTHI** (ITHÁKI TOWN), sited at the mouth of a bay so deep it seems to close completely around. In size the capital is hardly more than a village, its old tiled houses either undamaged or faithfully rebuilt after the terrible 1953 earthquake. Dozens of yachts and cruise ships stop here for a couple of hours but not many people actually stay – tourist development is for once at a virtual standstill.

Rooms for rent are, however, inconspicuous and in short supply. If nobody meets you off the ferry, try looking around the backstreets south of the ferry quay. Alternatively, head for one of the two hotels, the *Odysseus* (☎0674/32 381; ③) and the *Mentor* (☎0674/32 433; ③), at opposite ends of the long quay. There's a little more choice for meals, with seven or eight **tavernas**, though all seem remarkably similar in price and fare. Among the more reliable are the *Psistaria Athinaiki Gonia* (popular because it's the only grill), *To Trehandiri* (cheap casserole food in the bazaar) and *To Thiaki* and *To Kantouni* (adjacent next to the water, near the ferry dock). For dessert, the island speciality, is *ravaní*, a syrupy sponge cake.

In season the usual small boats shuttle tourists from the harbour to a series of tiny coves northeast of Váthi – a service that's particularly useful, as road links around the island are very poor. The pebble-and-sand **beaches** between Cape Skinós and Sarakinikó Bay are excellent, many people learning of them too late as the ferry they're departing on steams past. Most of those closer to town are little more than concrete diving platforms, though you might reflect that Byron enjoyed daily swims off the Lazzaretto islet in mid-harbour during his visit of 1823.

With some determination, you can walk out to the better beaches when the *kaíki* aren't running, but as long as you have good footwear you may prefer to spend your time hiking out to a handful of nearby sites tentatively identified with Homeric locations, or to head further north on Itháki for swimming or more sedentary pastimes.

Odysseus sites

Two paths to "Odysseus sites" are signposted from Váthi and either of them makes for an easy morning's walk across beautiful country of cypress, olives and vineyards.

The Arethoúsa spring and Perahóra

The **Arethoúsa spring**, ninety minutes' walk south from the port, is down to a trickle in summer but interestingly positioned. Immediately above towers a crag known locally as *Korax* (the raven), exactly as described by Homer in the meeting between Odysseus and his swineherd Eumaeus, on his return to the island to fight the suitors. To reach it, take the wide donkey track south out of Váthi, following signs marked *Krini Arethousas*, and turn down and left on to a narrower path after an hour; the final approach is signalled by occasional red dots on the stones.

If you miss the turning, the main thoroughfare continues on to the **Maráthia plateau** (today called Perapigádhi after its capped well), where Eumaeus had his pigsties, but fails to reach remote **Ayíou Andhréou Bay** (accessible only by sea), where Telemachus disembarked to avoid Penelope's suitors who were lying in ambush for him on Asteris Island (the modern Dhaskalío). Below Arethoúsa, more tiny paths drop down to a pair of good swimming coves in the lee of Lípa islet.

Perapigádhi shouldn't be confused with **PERAHÓRA**, an old pirate-proof inland village some 2km above Váthi. The upper settlement – with one *kafenío*/taverna and a rooms place – makes a good return option from Arethoúsa or a trip in itself; obvious paths lead up to it from the olive-swathed plain or there's a direct track, signposted from Váthi's Odhós Penelópis.

The Grotto of the Nymphs and ancient Alalkomenae

Of equally questionable authenticity but fun to visit in any case is the **Grotto of the Nymphs** (known locally as *Marmarospíli*), a large cavern about a kilometre southwest of Váthi, where local lore suggests Odysseus, on the advice of Athena, hid the treasure he had with him on his return to Ithaca. It was certainly known anciently and seems to have once been used as a place of worship. If its attribution is correct then the **Bay of Dhexiá** (west of Váthi and below the cave) would be where the Phaeacians put in to deposit the sleeping Odysseus and which he failed to recognise as his homeland.

Further to the north, **Mount Etós** looms over the head of the Molos gulf. On its summit are the ruins of **ancient Alalkomenae**, excavated by Schliemann (of Mycenae fame) and mistakenly declared to be the "Castle of Odysseus"; it in fact dates from at least five centuries after Homer. The site is almost impossible to find, and the search for others is complicated by the studiously inaccurate "Odysseus maps" sold on Itháki. A side road skirts the base of the mountain and crosses the narrowest point on the island to get to pebbly **Pisaetós Bay**, nearly 7km in all from Váthi but with some of the best swimming near town.

Northern Itháki

The main road out of Váthi continues across the isthmus to the northern half of Itháki, serving the villages of **Léfki**, **Stavrós**, **Fríkes** and **Kióni**. There are three evenly spaced daily **buses**, though the north of Itháki is excellent moped country. Once a day a *kaíki* also visits the last two of those communities – a cheap and scenic ride used by locals and tourists alike to meet the main-line ferries in Váthi.

Stavrós

STAVRÓS, near the base of arid Mount Korífi (or officially Mount Nisíti – a re-adoption of its old Homeric name), is a fair-sized village with a couple of rather pricey tavernas and some rooms. **Pólis Bay**, fifteen minutes' walk below it, has rocky swimming; people camp here though there are no facilities whatsoever. Supported by a few nearby Mycenaean remains, the bay is the archaeologists' current candidate for the main port of ancient Ithaca.

One kilometre north of Stavrós, more Mycenaean remains have been found amid the ruins of a Venetian fort, on a hill known as **Pelikáta**. This could perhaps have been the site of Odysseus's palace and capital: speculation that is supported by the fact that it enjoys a marvellous simultaneous view over Pólis Bay and Fríkes Bay. For an even better personal vantage point over much of Itháki, make your way up the four-kilometre track to the all-but-abandoned village of EXOYÍ in the northwest corner of the island.

Fríkes, Kióni and Anoyí

FRÍKES is a half-hour walk downhill beyond Stavrós, smaller than the latter but with a handful of tavernas, a hotel (*Nostos*, ☎0674/31 644; ④), a few rooms and a pebbly strip of beach. Seasonal ferries dock here to and from Lefkádha and Fiskárdho on northern Kefalloniá. The port is linked by bus to Váthi.

Around three kilometres east, at the end of the road, is the village of **KIÓNI**, one of the more attractive bases on the island, though its few rooms (including the luxurious *Kioni Apartments*, ☎0674/31 362; ⑤) seem to be booked en masse for the summer by British holiday companies. There's good swimming nearby, free of sea urchins, at the end of the path to Áyios Ilías chapel to the southeast.

With Kióni as your starting point, you can also walk or go by moped due south to the still inhabited **convent of Katharón**, via the inland village of **ANOYÍ**, where the proprietress of the one taverna will lend you the keys to the fourteenth-century village church and its excellent frescoes.

Zákinthos (Zante)

Zákinthos, which once exceeded Corfu itself in architectural distinction, was hit hardest by the 1953 Ionian earthquake, and the island's grand old capital was completely destroyed. Rebuilt, it feels a rather sad, soulless town, and the island's attractions lie more in the thick vineyards, orchards and olive groves of the interior, and some excellent beaches scattered about the coast. In contrast to Itháki, the island is one of the fastest-growing tourist resorts in Greece, following the arrival of an international runway at the airport, and its adoption in the brochures of a dozen or more British and north European package holiday companies.

Pessimists mutter darkly of Zákinthos being turned into another Corfu, and with upwards of 300,000 visitors a year that's understandable. Most tourists, though, are conveniently housed in one place – Laganás, on the south coast. As well as the foreign visitors, July and August also sees an influx of Greek holidaymakers, attracted by the island's proximity to the mainland. If you avoid those months, and steer clear of Laganás and the developing resort villages of Argási and Tsilívi, there is still a peaceful Zákinthos to be found.

The island, incidentally, is self-supporting of its resident population, and you'll even see the occasional tropical plant, such as banana or bamboo, growing. Spring's the time to see the flowers, and autumn if you want to eat the produce. Any time's a good time for the local **wines**, such as the white *Popolaro*, which is among the best in the Ionians. For dessert or a snack, try *mandoláto*, the ubiquitous and delicious honey/egg/almond nougat, or the very strong and pungent *grapéria* cheese. From late August to mid-March, beware the local hunting season – everywhere in the island you'll see what look like little playhouses on stilts; these are the hunters' blinds.

Zákinthos Town

The town, like the island, is known as both **ZÁKINTHOS** and **Zante**. This former "Venice of the East'" (*Zante, Fior di Levante*, "Flower of the Levant", in an Italian jingle), rebuilt on the old plan, has bravely tried to recreate some of its style, though quake-reinforced concrete can only do so much.

The most tangible hints of former glory are to be found in **Platía Solómou**, the grand and spacious main square. At its north (waterside) corner stands the beautiful fifteenth-century sandstone church of **Áyios Nikólaos**, while paintings and icons salvaged from here and other island churches are displayed in the imposing **Neo-Byzantine Museum** (Tues–Sun 8.30am–3pm; 200dr, students 100dr) by the town hall. This collection is exceptional for during the seventeenth and eighteenth centuries Zante became the centre of an Ionian School of painting, given impetus by Cretan refugees unable to practice under Turkish rule.

The square itself is named after the island's great poet **Dionissios Solomos**, who was responsible for introducing demotic Greek (the spoken language of the people) as a literary idiom and who also wrote the words to the Greek national anthem. A small museum (daily 9am–2pm; free) is dedicated to him in the nearby Platía Ayíou Márkou, two blocks up; it is worthwhile for its glimpses of Zante's strong artistic life as well as to see photographs of the town taken both before and after the earthquake.

Elsewhere in town, look in at the large church of **Áyios Dhioníssios** (daily 7am–noon & 4.30–9pm), one of the very few buildings left standing after the earthquake, and with impressive frescoes. And, if you've a few hours to fill, walk up an old cobble path to the town's massive **Venetian fortress** (open 8am–8pm; 100dr), which has views south to Pílos and north to Messolóngi. En route to the fortress lies the suburb village of **Boháli**, occupying a natural balcony overlooking the harbour, and with a number of popular if slightly expensive tavernas. In season these are the venues for *kantádhes*, an Italianate style of trio-singing accompanied by guitars and mandolins.

Practicalities

Since most people stay closer to the beaches, **accommodation** in Zákinthos Town is relatively easy to come by and reasonably priced. It tends to be hotel-based, however, with rooms for rent not much in evidence unless you entrust yourself to the people who meet ferries – and who usually have something to offer out of town as well. At the cheaper end in town, try the **hotels** *Nea Zakynthos* at Filíkou 7 (②) and *Oasis* at Koutózi 58 (☎0695/22 287; ②). For a bit of a splurge, the *Xenia* at Róma 60 (☎0695/22 232; ④) and *Pension Kryoneri* at Krionerioú 86 (☎0695/28 000; ④) are worth trying.

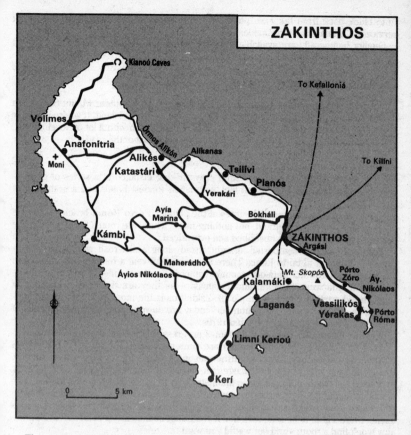

ZÁKINTHOS

The **tourist office** on Platía Solómou, next to the imposing National Bank, will give advice on rooms and hotels but cannot make reservations. The one time you'll stand little chance is around August 24, the feast of Áyios Dioníssios, when even some of the Greek visitors have to resort to sleeping outside the church for lack of a room. The **tourist police** also have information about accommodation (and bus services); they're to be found in the police station on the front, sandwiched between Tzouláti and Merkáti streets, near the church of Áyios Dhioníssios.

Restaurants and tavernas are a bit thin on the ground. The *Taverna Arekia* comes strongly recommended, a fair walk north along the east road past the EOT beach and next to a tiny church on the left-hand side of the road. You can also work up an appetite by walking a good way in the opposite direction to the *Malavetis Restaurant* at Ayíou Dhionissíou 4 (an approach road to the church); it has a limited menu but it's good and cheap. More central is the *Kalliniko*, best value of the places on Platía Solómou. For a snack, try *To Posto* at Róma 59, or *psistariés* such as *Strouza*, Thesillá 22, or another midway up the main arcaded street at Vassilísis Konstandínos 24.

Since the island is mostly flat, Zákinthos is an ideal place to hire a **pedal bike**, available along with **mopeds** and **motorcycles** from *Motorakis* on Leofóros Dhimokratías, opposite the OTE, and other agencies. **Buses** depart from a station on Odhós Filitá (one block back from the *Fina* pump on the main waterside road), with a frequent service to Laganás, and reasonable ones to Tsilívi and Alikés.

Quality handicrafts are available from the *Zakynthos Women's Cooperative*, just off the waterfront.

The south and west

The road heading southeast from Zákinthos harbour passes under Mount Skopós on its way to some of the finest scenery and best beaches on the island. If you're just after a quick swim, avoid the first village, ARGÁSSI, a poor beach with a lot of development, and head for the beach at **Pórto Zóro**, just to the northeast of the road.

Vassilikó and around to Laganás

Further south, **VASSILIKÓ** lies within easy striking distance of a series of good-to-excellent beaches and has a good feel, with a few modest hotels and a scattering of rooms for rent.

Campers congregate under the trees at the popular **Pórto Róma** beach, just to the east – a pleasant enough strand, but nothing more. There are rooms here, too, but the seasonal tavernas are oversubscribed and overpriced.

Yérakas beach is signposted straight ahead along a dirt road where the asphalt turns abruptly left to Pórto Róma. There are **rooms** for rent around here and much of the way down toward Yérakas, though camping is strictly illegal on this and the beaches to the west – Dephní and Kalamáki – as they are the nesting grounds of **loggerhead turtles** (see box on p.630). Zákinthos is the most important Ionian location for the turtles, though local numbers today are down to about 800, roughly half of what they were as recently as the mid-1970s.

West of **Kalamáki**, the beach becomes progressively muddier and more commercialised until new heights (or depths) are demonstrated at the resort of **LAGANÁS** proper. Around the bay, there are further nesting grounds for the **loggerhead turtles**, though the majority now lay their eggs on two small beaches, whereas until recently they used the whole of the fourteen-kilometre bay. In recent years, Greek marine zoologists, attempting to protect and document the turtles, have come into violent dispute with locals, uneasy at restrictions on developing their land for tourism. As for Laganás itself – there's little to be said, save that if you're not booked into a hotel here, you probably won't find a room – and nor would you want to.

Kerí

KERÍ, in the southwest corner of the island, retains some of its pre-earthquake houses and, more curiously, natural **tar pools** commented on by both Pliny and Herodotus and still used for caulking boats. (There is quite a lot of oil under the Ionian sea floor and it's only a matter of time before extraction efforts are undertaken.) You can also visit the lighthouse nearby and various beaches, the best at **Limní Kerioú**, a few kilometres east, where as at Kerí you can stay, eat and drink inexpensively and in generally local company.

Maherádho and Kámbi

If you have transport, an enjoyable route away from Laganás or Kerí is the mountain road, which leads ultimately to Alíkes in the north. Around 15km from either is the village of **MAHERÁDHO**, which shelters the spectacularly ornate church of Ayía Mávra. It is certainly the place to be if you're on the island for her feast day, which usually falls on the first weekend in July.

The road from here to the rural mountain village of **ÁYIOS NIKÓLAOS** is just about passable for a 50cc scooter, but only the sturdiest of dirtbikes – *not* a moped –

can traverse some of the mountain roads west – over to Kámbi. As well as the state of the roads, you also have the local maps to contend with – possibly the most inaccurate on sale in the whole of Greece, which is saying a lot. Roads rated as major on these are often little more than goat tracks, or even nonexistent; some of the newer and better roads are not shown, while others are placed inaccurately.

The effort of such safaris can be worth it, though, as the sunsets to be viewed from the clifftops on the rocky western coast are spectacular. **KÁMBI** is the favoured place for organised "Sunset Trips", when the busloads turn up at a taverna teetering 300m above the sea on the cliff's edge; there's no denying that the performance here is stunning and you might have the place almost to yourself on an "off" night. Even higher than the taverna is an enormous cross, erected to commemorate the deaths of islanders who were thrown off the cliffs during the 1940s, some say by the Nazis, others by nationalist troops in the civil war.

The north

North and west from Zákinthos Town, the roads thread their way through luxuriantly fertile farmland, punctuated with tumulus-like hills. **TSILÍVI**, 4km out, is the closest beach to town worthy of the name, shallow and sandy with warm water, though the evening breeze whips up the surf. There's also a **campsite**, *Camping Dafni*.

Alikón bay

Ormós Alikón, 13km further north, is a huge, gently sloping expanse of sand washed by good breakers. At its eastern end, the village of **ALÍKANAS** has a single shop and one exceedingly slow taverna. Villas are block-booked here by a couple of tour companies, and though the place hasn't yet been spoilt there's an alarming amount of building going on. Nearby, however, are two excellent **restaurants**. *Ta Neraidha*, with a great setting on Alíkanas harbour, always has fresh, well-cooked fish. A friendly family runs *Mantalena*, on the road to Alikés and arguably the best eatery on the island: a variety of delicious traditional dishes from the kitchen, a genuine house wine from the proprietors' own grapes, and water from a well on the premises.

Towards the northwest end of the bay, **ALIKÉS** is an increasingly busy package resort with rooms, restaurants and mopeds for rent. There are half a dozen hotels, but as yet nothing on the scale of Laganás. A drawback, however, is the presence of rats and mosquitoes, aggravated by the stagnant water laughingly described as a river. Plans are afoot to get this flowing again, and hopefully this will sort out the mosquitoes without carting away too much of the fine sand that is the bay's main asset.

A pleasant excursion by moped – or even on foot – from Alikés is to the small cove of **Koróni**, where sulphur springs discharge into the sea. Swimming is quite an experience, if you don't mind the smell, with a few inches of cool, fresh seawater on the surface and warm tracts below. Butterflies abound here in summer.

Another good trip is a ride by **kaíki** to the extreme northern tip of the island, where the **Kianóu (Blue) Caves** are some of the more realistically named of the many contenders in Greece. They're terrific for snorkelling, and when you go for a dip here your skin will appear bright blue.

Inland: Katastári and Ayía Marina

KATASTÁRI, the island's largest community after the capital, lies just inland from Alikés. It's a workaday place, of interest for a chance to witness ordinary island life; stop here and you're likely to be waved over to the *kafenío* to have an *oúzo* plonked in front of you. With a moped, you might be tempted to head 18km northwest to **Anafonítria** monastery. This withstood the earthquake remarkably well and is today tenanted by a few nuns who will show you the frescoed *katholikón*, a medieval tower, and the purported cell of Saint Dionissós, the patron of Zákinthos whose festivals are on August 24 and December 17.

AYÍA MARÍNA, a few kilometres south of Katastári, has a church with an impressive Baroque altar screen, and a belfry that's being rebuilt from the remnants left after the 1953 earthquake. Like most Zákinthos churches, the belltower is detached, in Venetian fashion. Just above Ayía Marína is a taverna rightly boasting one of the best views on the island. From it you can see the whole of the central plain from beyond Alikés in the north to Laganás Bay in the south.

There are more fine views from the hilltop village of **ÁNO YERAKÁRI**, one of three Yerakári-settlements within a few hundred yards of each other, over towards Alikés, and also one of the few interior villages offering **rooms**.

travel details

There are two invaluable boats if you're island-hopping within this group. These are the *Ionis* and *Ionian Glory*, operated by *Seven Islands Line*, which between them sail daily or nearly so from early June to mid-September from Patras to Brindisi and vice versa, stopping at Kefalloniá (Argostóli 3hr), Itháki (4hr 30min), Paxí (8hr 30min) and Corfu (11hr 30min), reaching Brindisi after 18 hr. This route is not included in the island-specific details below.

CORFU (KÉRKIRA) Roughly hourly (5.30am–10pm) **ferries** from Igoumenítsa to Corfu and vice versa (2hr). Additionally, most of the ferryboats plying between Italy and Greece (especially those from Brindisi) call at Corfu; stopover is free if specified in advance.

Several **flights** daily between Corfu and Athens (45min) London and other British airports. Seasonal flights (twice weekly) to/from Kefalloniá and Zákinthos.

PAXÍ Year-round there is a twice-weekly car and passenger **ferry**, the *Kamelia*, from Corfu (3hr), which usually calls at Sívota (also known as Moúrtos) on the mainland en route; information from *Sívota Travel* (☎0665/93 222). From June to September, there are also daily *kaíkia* from Corfu (3hr) and Párga (2hr), and *Ilio Line* **hydrofoils** from Igoumenítsa, Préveza and Lefkádha.

ERÍKOUSA, MATHRÁKI AND OTHONÍ A car **ferry**, the *Alexandros II*, runs from Corfu town to all the islands twice weekly, currently leaving Corfu on Tues and Sat at 6.30am. The route is Corfu–Eríkousa–Mathráki–Othoní–Mathráki–Eríkousa–Corfu. The ferry leaves Corfu Town from opposite the *BP* station on Eleftheriou Venizelou street, midway between the Igoumenítsa and the Italy ferries. Tickets and information from *Star Travel Agency* (☎0661/36 355), Eleftheriou Venizeloú 4, Corfu Town. *Star Travel* also run an excursion boat to Eríkousa and Othoní on Sundays in season.

Kaíkia leave Eríkousa and Othoní for Sidhári early on Mon and Thurs morning, returning to Eríkousa at about 11am, and to Othoní, via Mathráki, at about 1pm. These are primarily supply boats for the local people. To check days and times, ask at Sidhári's jetty, or call Stamatis Zoupanos (☎0663/95 141) at *Budget Travel* in Sidhári, who can also give you information on excursion boats from Sidhári to Eríkousa.

LEFKÁDHA 4 **buses** daily to and from Athens (7hr) and regular services from Áktio (near Préveza). At least daily **boats**, in season, from Nidhrí to Meganíssi, Kefalloniá (Fiskárdho) and Itháki (Fríkes); from Vassilikí to Kefalloniá (Fiskárdho and Sámi). From June to September *Ilio Line* **hydrofoils** link Lefkádha with Préveza, Paxí, Corfu, Itháki and Kefalloniá.

ITHÁKI (ITHACA) and KEFALLONIÁ Daily **ferry** connection between Pátra, Itháki (Váthi – 5hr 30min), and Kefalloniá (Sámi). Year-round daily ferries between Astakós on the mainland and Váthi on Itháki, usually continuing to/from Ayía Evfimía on Kefalloniá. Also 3 ferries daily in season (once daily out) between Póros (southeast tip of Kefalloniá) and Killíni (Peloponnese); 2 daily in season (1 out) between Argostóli on Kefalloniá and Killíni; 2 daily in season between Pessádha (Kefalloniá) and Skinári (Zákinthos); daily in season ferries from Fiskárdho (Kefalloniá) to

Fríkes and Váthi on Itháki and Nidhrí and Vassilikí on Lefkádha.

From June to September *Ilio Line* **hydrofoils** link Itháki and Kefalloniá with Lefkádha, Préveza, Páxi, Pátra and Zákinthos.

Kefalloniá is also on an international *Minoan Lines* route, whose *Ariadne* ferry runs weekly (mid-June to mid-October) from **Ancona** to the island, then on to Pireás, Sámos and Turkey.

Daily **flights** between Argostóli (Kefalloniá) and Athens (45min); useful seasonal link to/from Zákinthos and Corfu; international flights to Argostóli.

ZÁKINTHOS (ZANTE) Up to 7 **ferries** a day in summer (3 out of season; 1hr 30min) between Zákinthos and Killíni (Peloponnese). Difficult, twice-daily connection in summer from Skinári to Pessádha (Kefalloniá), as described above.

From June to September *Ilio Line* **hydrofoils** link Zákinthos with Pátra, Itháki and Kefalloniá, and beyond there with Lefkádha, Préveza, Paxí, and Corfu.

Daily **flights** between Athens and Zákinthos (45min). Twice weekly **flights** to/from Kefalloniá and Corfu; only charter flights between Zákinthos and northern Europe.

PART FOUR

THE
CONTEXTS

THE HISTORICAL FRAMEWORK

This Historical Framework is intended just to lend some perspective to travels in Greece, and is heavily weighted towards the era of the modern, post-Independent nation – especially the twentieth century. More detailed accounts of particular periods (Mycenae, Minoan Crete, Classical Athens, Byzantine Mystra, etc) are to be found in relevant sections of the guide.

NEOLITHIC, MINOAN AND MYCENAEAN AGES

Other than the solitary discovery of a fossilised Neanderthal skull near Thessaloníki, the earliest **evidence of human settlement** in Greece is to be found at Néa Nikomedhía, near Véria. Here, traces of large, rectangular houses dated to around 6000 BC have been excavated.

It seems that people originally came to this and in the eastern Mediterranean in fits and starts, predominantly from Anatolia. These **Proto-Greeks** settled in essentially peaceful farming communities, made pottery and worshipped Earth/Fertility goddesses – clay statuettes of whom are still found on the sites of old settlements. This simple way of life eventually disappeared, as people started to tap the land's resources for profit and to compete and exchange in trade.

MINOANS AND MYCENAEANS

The years between around **2000 and 1100 BC** were a period of fluctuating regional dominance, based at first upon sea power, with vast **royal palaces** serving as centres of administration. Particularly important were those at **Knossos** in Crete, and **Mycenae**, **Tiryns** and **Argos** in the Peloponnese.

Crete monopolised the eastern Mediterranean trade routes for an era subsequently called the **Minoan Age**, with the palace at Knossos surviving two earthquakes and a massive volcanic eruption on the island of Thíra (Santoríni), at some undefinable point between 1500 and 1450 BC. The most obvious examples of Minoan culture can be seen in frescoes, in jewellery, and in pottery, the distinctive red-and-white design on a dark background marking the peak period of Minoan achievement. When Knossos finally succumbed to disaster, natural or otherwise, around 1400 BC, it was the flourishing centre of **Mycenae** that assumed the leading role (and gives its name to the civilisation of this period), until it in turn collapsed around 1200 BC.

This is a period whose history and remains are bound up with its **legends**, recounted most famously by Homer. Knossos was the home of King Minos, while the palaces of Mycenae and Pylos were the respective bases of Agamemnon and Nestor; Menelaus and Odysseus hailed from Sparta and Ithaca. The Homeric and other legends relating to them almost certainly reflect the prevalence of violence, revenge and **war** as increasing facts of life, instigated and aggravated by trade rivalry. The increasing scale of conflict and militarisation is exemplified in the massive fortifications – dubbed Cyclopean by later ages – that were built around many of the palaces.

The Greece of these years, certainly, was by no means a united nation – as the Homeric legend reflects – and its people were divided into what were in effect a series of splinter groups, defined in large part by sea and mountain barriers and by access to **pasture**. Settlements flourished according to their proximity to and prowess on the sea and the fertility of their land; most were self-sufficient, specialising in the production of particular items for **trade**. Olives, for example, were associated with the region of Attica, and minerals with the island of Mílos.

THE DORIAN AND CLASSICAL ERAS

The Mycenaean-era Greek states had also to cope with and assimilate periodic influxes of new peoples and trade. The traditional view of the collapse of the Mycenaean civilisation has it that a northern "barbarian" people, the **Dorians**, "invaded" fom the north, devastating the existing palace culture and opening a "dark age" era. These days, archaeologists see the influx more in terms of shifting trade patterns, though undoubtedly there was major disruption of the palace cultures and their sea powers during the eleventh century.

Two other trends are salient to the period: the almost total supplanting of the mother goddesses by **male deities** (a process begun under the Mycenaeans), and the appearance of an **alphabet** still recognisable by modern Greeks, which replaced the so-called "Linear A" and "Linear B" Minoan/Mycenaean scripts.

CITY STATES: SPARTA AND ATHENS

The ninth century BC ushered in the beginnings of the Greek **city-state** (*polis*). Citizens – rather than just kings or aristocrats – became involved in government and took part in community activities and organised industry and leisure. Colonial ventures increased, as did commercial dealings, and the consequent rise in the import trade was gradually to give rise to a new class of manufacturers.

The city-state was the life of the people who dwelt within it and each state retained both its independence and a distinctive style, with the result that the sporadic attempts to unite in a league against an enemy without were always pragmatic and temporary. The two most powerful states to emerge were Athens and Sparta, and these were to exercise a rivalry over the next five centuries.

Sparta was associated with the Dorians, who had settled in large numbers on the fertile Eurotas (Évrotas) river plain. The society of Sparta and its environs was based on a highly militaristic ethos, accentuated by the need to defend the exposed and fertile land on which it stood. Rather than build intricate fortifications, the people of Sparta relied upon military prowess and a system of laws decreed by the (semi-legendary) **Lycurgus**. Males were subjected to military instruction between the ages of seven

and thirty. Weak babies were known periodically to "disappear". Girls too had to perform athletic feats of sprinting and wrestling, and even dwellings were more like barracks than houses.

Athens, the fulcrum of the state of Attica, was dynamic and exciting by contrast. Home of the administrations of **Solon** and **Pericles**, the dramatic talents of Sophocles and Aristophanes, the oratory of Thucydides and Demosthenes, and the philosophical power of Socrates and Plato, it made up in cultural achievement what it lacked in Spartan virtue. Yet Sparta did not deserve all the military glory. The Athens of the sixth and fifth centuries BC, the so-called **Classical period** in Greek history, is the Athens which played the major part in repelling the armies of the Persian king Darius at Marathon (490 BC) and Salamis (480 BC), campaigns depicted later by Aeschylus in *The Persians*.

It was also Athens which gave rise to a tradition of **democracy** (*demokratia*), literally "control by the people" – although at this stage "the people" did not include either women or slaves. In Athens there were three organs of government. The *Areopagus*, composed of the city elders, had a steadily decreasing authority and ended up dealing solely with murder cases. Then there was the Council of Five Hundred (men), elected annually by ballot to prepare the business of the Assembly and to attend to matters of urgency. The Assembly gave every free man a political voice; it had sole responsibility for law-making and provided an arena for the discussion of important issues. It was a genuinely enfranchised council of citizens.

This was a period of intense creativity, particularly in Athens, whose actions and pretensions were fast becoming imperial in all but name. Each city-state had its **acropolis**, or high town, where religious activity was focused. In Athens, Pericles endowed the acropolis with a complex of buildings, whose climax was the temple of the Parthenon. Meanwhile, the era saw the tragedies of Sophocles performed, and the philosophies of Socrates and Plato expounded.

Religion at this stage was polytheistic, ordering all under the aegis of Zeus. In the countryside the proliferation of names and of sanctuary finds suggests a preference for the slightly more mundane Demeter and Dionysus.

THE PELOPONNESIAN WARS

The power struggles between Athens and Sparta, allied with various networks of city-states, eventually culminated in the **Peloponnesian Wars** of 431–404 BC. After these conflicts, superbly recorded by Thucydides and nominally won by Sparta, the city-state ceased to function so effectively.

This was in part due to drained resources and political apathy, but to a greater degree a consequence of the increasingly commercial and complex pressures on everyday life. Trade, originally spurred by the invention of **coinage** in the sixth century BC, continued to expand; a revitalised Athens, for example, was exporting wine, oil and manufactured goods, getting corn in return from the Black Sea and from Egypt.

The amount of time each man had to devote to the affairs of government decreased and a position in political life became a professional job rather than a natural assumption. Democracy had changed, while in philosophy there was a shift from the idealists and mystics of the sixth and fifth centuries BC to the Cynics, Stoics and Epicureans – followers, respectively, of Diogenes, Zeno and Epicurus.

HELLENISTIC AND ROMAN GREECE

The most important factor in the decline of the city-states was meanwhile developing outside their sphere, in the kingdom of Macedonia.

MACEDONIAN EMPIRE

Based at the Macedonian capital of Pella, **Philip II** (359–336 BC) was forging a strong military and unitary force, extending his territories into Thrace and finally establishing control over Athens and southern Greece. His son, **Alexander the Great**, in an extraordinarily brief but glorious thirteen-year reign, extended these gains into Persia and Egypt and parts of modern India and Afghanistan.

This unwieldy empire splintered almost immediately upon Alexander's death in 323 BC, to be divided into the three Macedonian dynasties of **Hellenistic Greece**: the Antigonids in Macedonia, the Seleucids in Syria and Persia, and the Ptolemies in Egypt. Each were in turn conquered and absorbed by the new Roman empire, the Ptolemies – under their queen Cleopatra – last of all.

ROMAN GREECE

Mainland Greece was subdued by the Romans over some seventy years of campaigns, from 215 to 146. Once in control, however, **Rome** allowed considerable autonomy to the old territories of the city-states. Greek remained the official language of the eastern Mediterranean and its traditions and culture coexisted fairly peacefully with that of the overlords during the next three centuries.

In central Greece both **Athens** and **Corinth** remained important cities but the emphasis was shifting north – particularly to towns, such as **Salonica** (Thessaloníki), along the new *Via Egnatia*, a military and civil road engineered between Rome and Byzantium via the port of Brundisium (modern Brindisi).

THE BYZANTINE EMPIRE AND MEDIEVAL GREECE

The shift of emphasis to the north was given even greater impetus by the decline of the Roman Empire and its apportioning into eastern and western empires. In the year 330 AD the Emperor Constantine moved his capital to the Greek city of Byzantium and here emerged Constantinople (modern Istanbul), the "new Rome" and spiritual and political capital of the **Byzantine Empire**.

While the last western Roman emperor was deposed by barbarian Goths in 476, this oriental portion was to be the dominant Mediterranean power for some 700 years, and only in 1453 did it collapse completely.

CHRISTIANITY

Christianity had been introduced under Constantine and by the end of the fourth century was the official state religion, its liturgies (still in use in the Greek Orthodox church), creed and New Testament all written in Greek. A distinction must be drawn, though, between perceptions of Greek as a language and culture and as a concept. The Byzantine Empire styled itself Roman, or *Romios*, rather than Hellenic, and moved to eradicate all remaining symbols of pagan Greece. The Delphic Oracle was forcibly closed, and the Olympic Games discontinued, at the end of the fourth century.

The seventh century saw **Constantinople** besieged by Persians, and later Arabs, but the Byzantine Empire survived, losing only Egypt, the least "Greek" of its territories. From the ninth to the early eleventh centuries it enjoyed an archetypal "golden age", in culture, confidence and security. Tied up in the Orthodox Byzantine faith was a sense of spiritual superiority, and the emperors saw Constantinople as a "new Jerusalem" for their "chosen people". It was the beginning of a diplomatic and ecclesiastical conflict with the Catholic west that was to have disastrous consequences over the next five centuries. In the meantime the eastern and western patriarchs mutually excommunicated each other.

From the seventh through to the eleventh centuries **Byzantine Greece**, certainly in the south and centre, became something of a provincial backwater. Administration was absurdly top-heavy and imperial taxation led to semi-autonomous provinces ruled by military generals, whose lands were usually acquired from bankrupted peasants. This alienation of the poor provided a force for change, with a floating populace ready to turn towards or cooperate with the empire's enemies if terms were an improvement.

Waves of **Slavic raiders** needed no encouragement to sweep down from the north Balkans throughout this period. At the same time other tribal groups moved down more peaceably from **central Europe** and were absorbed with little difficulty. According to one theory, the nomadic **Vlachs** from Romania eventually settled in the Píndhos Mountains, and later, from the thirteenth century on, immigrants from **Albania** repopulated the islands of Spétses, Ídhra, Ándhros and Évvia, as well as parts of Attica and the Peloponnese.

THE CRUSADES: FRANKISH AND VENETIAN RULE

From the early years of the eleventh century, less welcome and less assimilable western forces began to appear. The **Normans** landed first at Corfu in 1085, and returned again to the mainland, with papal sanction, a decade later on their way to liberate Jerusalem.

These were only a precursor, though, for the forces that were to descend en route for the **Fourth Crusade** of 1204, when Venetians, Franks and Germans turned their armies directly on Byzantium and sacked and occupied Constantinople. These Latin princes and their followers, intent on new lands and kingdoms,

settled in to divide up the best part of the Empire. All that remained of Byzantium were four small peripheral kingdoms or **despotates**: the most powerful in Nicaea in Asia Minor, less significant ones at Trebizond on the Black Sea, and (in present-day Greece) in Epirus and around Mystra in the Peloponnese (known in these times as the Morea).

There followed two extraordinarily involved centuries of manipulation and struggle between Franks, Venetians, Genoese, Catalans and Turks. The Paleologos dynasty at Nicaea recovered the city of Constantinople in 1261 but little of its former territory and power. Instead, the focus of Byzantium shifted to the Peloponnese, where the autonomous **Despotate of Mystra**, ruled by members of the imperial family, eventually succeeded in wresting most of the peninsula from Frankish hands. At the same time this despotate underwent an intense cultural renaissance, strongly evoked in the churches and the shells of cities remaining today at Mystra and Monemvassía.

TURKISH OCCUPATION

Within a generation of driving out the Franks the Byzantine Greeks faced a much stronger threat in the expanding empire of the **Ottoman Turks**. Torn apart by internal struggles between their own ruling dynasties, the **Palaeologi** and **Cantacuzenes**, and unaided by the Catholic west, they were to prove no match. On Tuesday, May 29, 1453, a date still solemnly commemorated by the Orthodox church, Constantinople fell to besieging Muslim Turks.

Mystra was to follow within seven years and Trebizond within nine, by which time virtually all of the old Byzantine Empire lay under Ottoman domination. Only the **Ionian islands** and the **Cyclades**, which remained Venetian and a few scattered and remote enclaves – like the Máni in the Peloponnese, Sfákia in Crete and Soúli in Epirus – were able to resist the Turkish advance.

OTTOMAN RULE

Under what Greeks refer to as the "Dark Ages" of **Ottoman rule**, the lands of present-day Greece passed into rural provincialism, taking refuge in a self-protective mode of village life that has only recently been disrupted. Taxes and discipline, sporadically backed up by the genocide of dissenting communities, were inflicted from the Turkish Porte but estates passed into the hands of local chieftains who often had considerable independence.

Greek identity, meanwhile, was preserved through the offices of the **Orthodox church** which, despite instances of enforced conversion, the Sultans allowed to continue. The **monasteries**, often secretly, organised schools and became the trustees of Byzantine culture, though this had gone into stagnation after the fall of Constantinople and Mystra, whose scholars and artists emigrated west, adding impetus to the Renaissance.

As Ottoman administration became more and more decentralised and inefficient, individual Greeks rose to local positions of considerable influence and a number of communities achieved a degree of autonomy. Ambelákia village in Thessaly, for example, established an industrial cooperative system to export dyed cloth to Europe, paying only direct taxes to the Sultan. And on the Albanian repopulated islands of the Argo-Saronic, a **Greek merchant fleet** came into being in the eighteenth century, permitted to trade throughout the Mediterranean. Greeks, too, were becoming organised overseas in the sizeable expatriate colonies of central Europe, which often had affiliations with the semi-autonomous village clusters of Zagória (in Epirus) and Mount Pilion.

THE STRUGGLE FOR INDEPENDENCE

Opposition to Turkish rule was becoming widespread, exemplified most obviously by the **Klephts** (brigands) of the mountains. It was not until the nineteenth century, however, that a resistance movement could muster sufficient support and firepower to prove a real challenge to the Turks. In 1770 a Russian-backed uprising had been easily and brutally suppressed but fifty years later the position was different.

In Epirus the Turks were over-extended, subduing the expansionist campaigns of local ruler **Ali Pasha**; the French revolution had given impetus to the confidence of "freedom movements"; and the Greek fighters were given financial and ideological underpinnings by the *Filikí Etería*, or "Friendly Society", a secret group recruited among the exiled merchants and intellectuals of central Europe.

This somewhat motley coalition ... and theorists launched their insurrection... monastery of **Ayia Lávra** near Kalávrita in Peloponnese, where on March 25, 1821, the Greek banner was openly raised by the local bishop, Yermanos.

THE WAR OF INDEPENDENCE

To describe in detail the course of the **War of Independence** is to provoke unnecessary confusion, since much of the rebellion consisted of local and fragmentary guerila campaigns. What is important to understand is that Greeks, though fighting for liberation from the Turks, were not fighting as and for a nation. Motives differed enormously: landowners assumed their role was to lead and sought to retain and reinforce their traditional privileges, while the peasantry saw the struggle as a means towards land redistribution.

Outside Greece, prestige and publicity for the insurrection was promoted by the arrival of a thousand or so European **Philhellenes**, almost half of them German, though the most important was the English poet, **Lord Byron**, who died while training Greek forces at Messolóngi in April 1824.

Though it was the Greek guerilla leaders, above all Theodoros **Kolokotronis**, "the old man of the Morea", who brought about the most significant military victories of the war, the death of Byron had an immensely important effect on public opinion in the west. Aid for the Greek struggle had come neither from Orthodox Russia, nor from the western powers of France and Britain, ravaged by the Napoleonic Wars. But by 1827, when Messolóngi fell again to the Turks, these three powers finally agreed to seek autonomy for certain parts of Greece and sent a combined fleet to put pressure on the Sultan's Egyptian army, then ransacking and massacring in the Peloponnese. Events took over, and an accidental naval battle in **Navarino Bay** resulted in the destruction of almost the entire Turkish-Egyptian fleet. The following spring Russia itself declared war on the Turks and the Sultan was forced to accept the existence of an autonomous Greece.

In 1830 Greek independence was confirmed by the western powers and **borders** were drawn. These included just 800,000 of the 6 million Greeks living within the Ottoman empire, and the Greek territories were for the most part the poorest of the Classical and Byzantine lands, comprising Attica, the Peloponnese and the islands of the Argo-Saronic and Cyclades. The rich agricultural belt of Thessaly, Epirus in the west, and Macedonia in the north, remained in Turkish hands. Meanwhile, the Ionian islands were controlled by a British Protectorate and the Dodecanese by the Venetians (and subsequently by the new Italian nation).

THE EMERGING STATE

Modern Greece began as a republic and **Ioannis Kapodistrias**, its first president, concentrated his efforts on building a viable central authority and govenment in the face of diverse protagonists from the independence struggle. Almost inevitably he was assassinated – in 1831, by two chieftains from the ever-disruptive Máni – and perhaps equally inevitably the great western powers stepped in. They created a monarchy, gave limited aid, and set on the throne a Bavarian prince, **Otho**.

The new king proved an autocratic and insensitive ruler, bringing in fellow Germans to fill official posts and ignoring all claims by the landless peasantry for redistribution of the old estates. In 1862 he was eventually forced from the country by a popular revolt, and the Europeans produced a new prince, this time from Denmark, with Britain ceding the Ionian islands to bolster support. **George I**, in fact, proved more capable: he built the first railways and roads, introduced limited land reforms in the Peloponnese, and oversaw the first expansion of the Greek borders.

THE MEGÁLI IDHÉA AND WAR

From the very beginning, the unquestioned motive force of Greek foreign policy was the **Megáli Idhéa** (Great Idea) of liberating Greek populations outside the country and incorporating the old territories of Byzantium into the kingdom. In 1878 **Thessaly**, along with southern Epirus, was ceded to Greece by the Turks.

Less illustriously, the Greeks failed in 1897 to achieve *énosis* (union) with **Crete** by attacking Turkish forces on the mainland, and in the process virtually bankrupted the state. The island was, however, placed under a High Commissioner, appointed by the Great Powers, and in 1913 became a part of Greece.

It was from Crete, also, that the most distinguished Greek statesman emerged. **Eleftherios Venizelos**, having led a civilian campaign for his island's liberation, was in 1910 elected as Greek Prime Minister. Two years later he organised an alliance of Balkan powers to fight the **Balkan Wars** (1912–13), campaigns that saw the Turks virtually driven from Europe. With Greek borders extended to include the northeast Aegean, nothern Thessaly, central Epirus and parts of Macedonia, the *Megáli Idhéa* was approaching reality. At the same time Venizelos proved himself a shrewd manipulator of domestic public opinion by revising the constitution and introducing a series of liberal social reforms.

Division, however, was to appear with the outbreak of **World War I**. Venizelos urged Greek entry on the British side, seeing in the conflict possibilities for the "liberation" of Greeks in Thrace and Asia Minor, but the new king, Konstantinos I, married to a sister of the German Kaiser, imposed a policy of neutrality. Eventually Venizelos set up a revolutionary government in Thessaloníki, and in 1917 Greek troops entered the war to join the French, British and Serbians in the **Macedonian campaign**. On the capitulation of Bulgaria and Ottoman Turkey, the Greeks occupied **Thrace** and Venizelos presented at Versailles demands for the predominantly Greek region of Smyrna on the Asia Minor coast.

It was the beginning of one of the most disastrous episodes in modern Greek history. Venizelos was authorised to move forces into Smyrna in 1919, but by then Allied support had evaporated and in Turkey itself a new nationalist movement was taking power under Mustafa Kemal, or **Atatürk** as he came to be known. In 1920 Venizelos lost the elections and monarchist factions took over, their aspirations unmitigated by the Cretan's skill in foreign diplomacy. Greek forces were ordered to advance upon Ankara in an attempt to bring Atatürk to terms.

This so-called **Anatolian campaign** ignominiously collapsed in summer 1922 when Turkish troops forced the Greeks back to the coast and a hurried evacuation from **Smyrna**. As they left Smyrna, the Turks moved in and systematically massacred whatever remained of the Armenian and Greek populations before burning most of the city to the ground.

THE EXCHANGE OF POPULATIONS

There was now no alternative but for Greece to accept Atatürk's own terms, formalised by the Treaty of Lausanne in 1923, which ordered the **exchange of religious minorities** in each country. Turkey was to accept 390,000 Muslims resident on Greek soil. Greece, mobilised almost continuously for the last decade and with a population of under five million, was faced with the resettlement of over 1,300,000 Christian refugees. The *Megáli Idhéa* had ceased to be a viable blueprint.

Changes, inevitably, were intense and far-reaching. The great agricultural estates of Thessaly were finally redistributed, both to Greek tenants and refugee farmers, and huge shantytowns grew into new quarters around Athens, Pireás and other cities, a spur to the country's then almost nonexistent industry.

Politically, too, reaction was swift. A group of army officers assembled after the retreat from Smyrna, "invited" King Konstantinos to abdicate and executed five of his ministers. Democracy was nominally restored with the proclamation of a republic, but for much of the next decade changes in government were brought about by factions within the armed forces. Meanwhile, among the urban refugee population, unions were being formed and the Greek Communist Party (KKE) was established.

By 1936 the Communist Party had enough democratic support to hold the balance of power in parliament, and would have done so had not the army and the by then restored king decided otherwise. King Yiorgos (George) II had been returned by a plebiscite held – and almost certainly manipulated – the previous year, and so presided over an increasingly factionalised parliament.

THE METAXAS DICTATORSHIP

In April 1936 George II appointed as prime minister **General John Metaxas**, despite the latter's support from only six elected deputies. Immediately a series of KKE-organised strikes broke out and the king, ignoring attempts to form a broad liberal coalition, dissolved parliament without setting a date for new elections. It was a blatantly unconstitutional move and opened the way for five years of ruthless and at times absurd dictatorship.

Metaxas averted a general strike with military force and proceeded to set up a state based on **fascist** models of the age. Left-wing and trade union opponents were imprisoned or forced into exile, a state youth movement and secret police set up, and rigid censorship, extending even to passages of Thucydides, imposed. It was, however, at least a Greek dictatorship, and though Metaxas was sympathetic to Nazi organisation he completely opposed German or Italian domination.

WORLD WAR II AND THE GREEK CIVIL WAR

The Italians tried to provoke the Greeks into **World War II** by surreptitiously torpedoing the Greek cruiser *Elli* in Tínos harbour on August 15, 1940. To this, they met with no response. However, when Mussolini occupied Albania and sent, on October 28, 1940, an ultimatum demanding passage for his troops through Greece, Metaxas responded to the Italian foreign minister with the apocryphal one-word answer *"óhi"* (no). (In fact, his response, in the mutually understood French, was *"C'est la guerre"*). The date marked the entry of Greece into the war, and the gesture is still celebrated as a national holiday.

OCCUPATION AND RESISTANCE

Fighting as a nation in a sudden unity of crisis, the Greeks drove Italian forces from the country and in the operation took control of the long-coveted and predominantly Greek-populated northern Epirus (the south of Albania). However, the Greek army frittered away their strength in the snowy mountains of northern Epirus rather than consolidate their gains or defend the Macedonian frontier, and coordination with the British never materialised.

In April of the following year Nazi mechanised columns swept through Yugoslavia and across the Greek mainland, effectively reversing the only Axis defeat to date, and by the end of May 1941 airborne and seaborne **German invasion** forces had completed the occupation of Crete and the other islands. Metaxas had died before their arrival, while King George and his new self-appointed ministers fled into exile in Cairo; few Greeks, of any political persuasion, were sad to see them go.

The joint **Italian–German–Bulgarian Axis occupation** of Greece was among the bitterest experiences of the European war.

Nearly half a million Greek civilians starved to death as all available food was requisitioned to feed occupying armies, and entire villages throughout the mainland and especially on Crete were burned and slaughtered at the least hint of resistance activity. In the north the Bulgarians desecrated ancient sites and churches in a bid to annex "Slavic" Macedonia.

Primarily in the north, too, the Nazis supervised the deportation to concentration camps of virtually the entire **Greek-Jewish population**. This was at the time a sizeable community. Thessaloníki – where the former UN and Austrian president Kurt Waldheim worked for Nazi intelligence – contained the largest Jewish population of any Balkan city, and there were significant populations in all the Greek mainland towns and on many of the islands.

With a quisling government in Athens – and an unpopular, discredited Royalist group in Cairo – the focus of Greek political and military action over the next four years passed largely to the **EAM**, or National Liberation Front. By 1943 it was in virtual control of most areas of the country, working with the British on tactical operations, with its own army (**ELAS**), navy, and both civil and secret police forces. On the whole it commanded popular support, and it offered an obvious framework for the resumption of postwar government.

However, most of its membership was communist, and the British Prime Minister, **Churchill**, was determined to reinstate the monarchy. Even with two years of the war to run it became obvious that there could be no peaceable post-liberation regime other than an EAM-dominated republic. Accordingly, in August 1943 representatives from each of the main resistance movements – including two non-communist groups – flew from a makeshift airstrip in Thessaly to ask for guarantees from the "government" in Cairo that the king would not return unless a plebiscite had first voted in his favour. Neither the Greek nor British authorities would consider the proposal and the one possibility of averting civil war was lost.

The EAM contingent returned divided, as perhaps the British had intended, and a conflict broke out between those who favoured taking peaceful control of any government imposed after liberation, and the hard-line Stalinist ideologues, who believed such a situation should not be allowed to develop.

In October 1943, with fears of an imminent British landing force and takeover, ELAS launched a full-scale attack upon its Greek rivals; by the following February, when a ceasefire was arranged, they had wiped out all but the EDES, a right-wing grouping suspected of collaboration with the Germans. At the same time other forces were at work, with both the British and Americans infiltrating units into Greece in order to prevent the establishment of communist government when the Germans began withdrawing their forces.

CIVIL WAR

In fact, as the Germans began to leave in October 1944, most of the EAM leadership agreed to join a British-sponsored "official" **interim government**. It quickly proved a tactical error, however, for with ninety percent of the countryside under their control the communists were given only one-third representation, the king showed no sign of renouncing his claims, and, in November, Allied forces ordered ELAS to disarm. On December 3 all pretences of civility or neutrality were dropped; the police fired on a communist demonstration in Athens and fighting broke out between ELAS and **British troops**, in the so-called **Dhekemvrianá** battle of Athens.

A truce of sorts was negotiated at Várkiza the following spring but the agreement was never implemented. The army, police and civil service remained in right-wing hands and while collaborationists were often allowed to retain their positions, left-wing sympathisers, many of whom were not communists, were systematically excluded. The elections of 1946 were won by the right-wing parties, followed by a plebiscite in favour of the king's return. By 1947 guerilla activity had again reached the scale of a full **civil war**.

In the interim, King George had died and been succeeded by his brother Paul (with his consort Frederika), while the **Americans** had taken over the British role, and begun putting into action the cold war **Truman doctrine**. In 1947 they took virtual control of Greece, their first significant postwar experiment in anti-communist intervention. Massive economic and military aid was given to a client Greek government, with a prime minister whose documents had to be countersigned by the American Mission in order to become valid.

In the mountains US "military advisers" supervised **campaigns agains ELAS**, and there were mass arrests, court-martials, and imprisonments – a kind of "White Terror" – lasting until 1951. Over three thousand executions were recorded, including a number of Jehovah's Witnesses, "a sect proved to be under communist domination", according to US Ambassador Grady.

In the autumn of 1949, with the Yugoslav–Greek border closed after Tito's rift with Stalin, the last ELAS guerillas finally admitted defeat, retreating into Albania from their strongholds on Mount Grámmos. Atrocities had been committed on both sides, including, from the left, widescale destruction of monasteries, and the dubious evacuation of children from "combat areas" (as told in Nicholas Gage's virulently anti-communist book *Eleni*). Such errors, as well as the hopelessness of fighting an American-backed army, undoubtedly lost ELAS much support.

RECONSTRUCTION AMERICAN-STYLE: 1950–67

It was a demoralised, shattered Greece that emerged into the Western political orbit of the 1950s. It was also perforce American-dominated, enlisted into the Korean War in 1950 and NATO the following year. In domestic politics, the US Embassy – still giving the orders – foisted a winner-take-all electoral system, which was to ensure victory for the right over the next twelve years. All leftist activity was banned; those individuals who were not herded into political "re-education" camps or dispatched by firing squads, legal or vigilante, went into exile throughout Eastern Europe, to return only after 1974.

The American-backed, highly conservative **"Greek Rally"** party, led by General Papagos, won the first decisive post-civil war elections in 1952. After the general's death, the party's leadership was taken over – and to an extent liberalised – by **Konstantinos Karamanlis**. Under his rule, stability of a kind was established and some economic advances registered, particularly after the revival of Greece's traditional German markets. However, the 1950s was also a decade that saw wholesale **depopulation of the villages** as migrants sought work in Australia, America and western Europe, or the larger Greek cities.

The main crisis in foreign policy throughout this period was **Cyprus**, where a long terrorist campaign was waged by Greeks opposing British rule, and there was sporadic threat of a new Greek–Turkish war. A temporary and unworkable solution was forced on the island by Britain in 1960, granting independence without the possibility of self-determination or union with Greece. Much of the traditional Greek–British goodwill was destroyed by the issue, with Britain seen to be acting with regard only for its two military bases (over which, incidentally, it still retains sovereignty).

By 1961, unemployment, the Cyprus issue and the imposition of US nuclear bases on Greek soil were changing the political climate, and when Karamanlis was again elected there was strong suspicion of a fraud arranged by the king and army. Strikes became frequent in industry and even agriculture, and King Paul and autocratic, fascist-inclined Queen Frederika were openly attacked in parliament and at protest demonstrations. The far right grew uneasy about **"communist resurgence"** and, losing confidence in their own electoral influence, arranged the assassination of left-wing deputy **Grigoris Lambrakis** in Thessaloníki in May 1963. (The assassination, and its subsequent cover-up, is the subject of Vassilis Vassilikos's thriller *Z*, filmed by Costa-Gavras.) It was against this volatile background that Karamanlis resigned, lost the subsequent elections and left the country.

The new government – the first controlled from outside the Greek right since 1935 – was formed by **Yiorgos Papandreou**'s Centre Union Party, and had a decisive majority of nearly fifty seats. It was to last, however, for under two years as conservative forces rallied to thwart its progress. In this the chief protagonists were the army officers and their constitutional Commander-in-Chief, the new king, 23-year-old **Konstantinos (Constantine) II**.

Since power in Greece depended on a pliant military as well as a network of political appointees, Papandreou's most urgent task was to reform the armed forces. His first Minister of Defence proved incapable of the task and, while he was investigating the right-wing plot that was thought to have rigged the 1961 election, "evidence" was produced of a leftist conspiracy connected with Papandreou's son

Andreas (himself a minister in the government). The allegations grew to a crisis and Yiorgos Papandreou decided to assume the defence portfolio himself, a move for which the king refused to give the necessary sanction. He then resigned in order to gain approval at the polls but the king would not order fresh elections, instead persuading members of the Centre Union – chief among them **Konstantinos Mitsotakis**, the current premier – to defect and organise a coalition government. Punctuated by strikes, resignations and mass demonstrations, this lasted for a year and a half until new elections were eventually set for May 28, 1967. They failed to take place.

THE COLONEL'S JUNTA: 1967–1974

It was a foregone conclusion that Papandreou's party would win popular support in the polls against the discredited coalition partners. And it was equally certain that there would be some sort of anti-democratic action to try and prevent them from taking power. Disturbed by the party's leftward shift, King Konstantinos was said to have briefed senior generals for a *coup d'état*, to take place ten days before the elections. However, he was caught by surprise, as was nearly everyone else, by the **coup of April 21, 1967**, staged by a group of "unknown" colonels. It was, in the words of Andreas Papandreou, "the first successful CIA military putsch on the European continent".

The **Colonels' Junta**, having taken control of the means of power, was sworn in by the king and survived the half-hearted counter-coup which he subsequently attempted to organise. It was an overtly fascist regime, absurdly styling itself as the true "Revival of Greek Orthodoxy" against western "corrupting influences", though in reality its ideology was nothing more than warmed-up dogma from the Metaxas era.

All political activity was banned, trade unions were forbidden to recruit or meet, the press was so heavily censored that many papers stopped printing, and thousands of "communists" were arrested, imprisoned, and often tortured. Among them were both Papandreous, the composer Mikis Theodorakis (deemed "unfit to stand trial" after three months in custody) and Amalia Fleming (widow of Alexander). The best-known Greek actress,

Melina Mercouri, was stripped of her citizenship in absentia and thousands of prominent Greeks joined her in exile. Culturally, the colonels put an end to popular music (closing down most of the Pláka *rembétika* clubs) and inflicted ludicrous censorship on literature and the theatre, including (as under Metaxas) a ban on production of the Classical tragedies.

The colonels lasted for seven years, opposed (especially after the first year) by the majority of the Greek people, excluded from the European community, but propped up and given massive aid by US presidents **Lyndon Johnson** and **Richard Nixon**. To them and the CIA the junta's Greece was not an unsuitable client state; human rights considerations were considered unimportant, orders were placed for sophisticated military technology, and foreign investment on terms highly unfavourable to Greece was open to multinational corporations. It was a fairly routine scenario for the exploitation of an underdeveloped nation.

Opposition was from the beginning voiced by exiled Greeks in London, the United States and western Europe, but only in 1973 did demonstrations break out openly in Greece. On November 17 the students of Athens **Polytechnic** began an occupation of their buildings. The ruling clique lost its nerve; armoured vehicles stormed the Polytechnic gates and a still-undetermined number of students were killed. Martial law was tightened and junta chief **Colonel Papadopoulos** was replaced by the even more noxious and reactionary **General Ioannides**, head of the secret police.

RETURN TO CIVILIAN RULE: 1974–81

The end of the ordeal, however, came within a year as the dictatorship embarked on a disastrous political adventure in **Cyprus**. By attempting to topple the Makarios government and impose *énosis* (union) on the island, they provoked a Turkish invasion and occupation of forty percent of the Cypriot territory. The army finally mutinied and **Konstantinos Karamanlis** was invited to return from Paris to again take office. He swiftly negotiated a ceasefire (but no solution) in Cyprus, withdrew temporarily from NATO, and warned that US bases would have to be removed except where they specifically served Greek interest.

In November 1974 Karamanlis and his *Néa Dhimokratía* (New Democracy) party was rewarded by a sizeable majority in **elections**, with a centrist and socialist opposition. The latter was comprised by PASOK, a new party led by Andreas Papandreou.

The election of *Néa Dhimokratía* was in every sense a safe conservative option but to Karamanlis's enduring credit it oversaw an effective and firm return to democratic stability, even legitimising the KKE (Communist Party) for the first time in its history. Karamanlis also held a **referendum on the monarchy** – in which 59 percent of Greeks rejected the return of Constantine – and instituted in its place a French-style presidency, which post he himself occupied from 1980 to 1985 (and has done so again from 1990). Economically there were limited advances although these were more than offset by inflationary defence spending (the result of renewed tension with Turkey), hastily negotiated entrance into the EC, and the decision to let the drachma float after decades of its being artificially fixed at 30 to the US dollar.

Crucially, though, Karamanlis failed to deliver on vital reforms in bureaucracy, social welfare and education; and though the worst figures of the junta were brought to trial the ordinary faces of Greek political life and administration were little changed. By 1981 inflation was hovering around 25 percent, and it was estimated that tax evasion was depriving the state of one-third of its annual budget. In foreign policy the US bases had remained and it was felt that Greece, back in NATO, was still acting as little more than an American satellite. The traditional right was demonstrably inadequate to the task at hand.

PASOK: 1981–89

Change – *allayí* – was the watchword of the election campaign which swept Andreas Papandreou's Panhellenic Socialist Movement, better known by the acronym **PASOK**, to power on October 18, 1981.

The victory meant a chance for Papandreou to form the first socialist government in Greek history and break a near fifty-year monopoly of authoritarian right-wing rule. With so much at stake the campaign had been passionate even by Greek standards, and PASOK's victory was greeted with euphoria both by the generation whose political voice had been silenced by defeat in the civil war and by a large proportion of the young. They were hopes which perhaps ran naively and dangerously high.

The victory, at least, was conclusive. PASOK won 174 of the 300 parliamentary seats and the Communist KKE returned another thirteen deputies, one of whom was the composer Mikis Theodorakis. *Néa Dhimokratía* moved into unaccustomed opposition. There appeared to be no obstacle to the implementation of a radical **socialist programme**: devolution of power to local authorities, the socialisation of industry (though it was never clear how this was to be different from nationalisation), improvement of the social services, a purge of bureaucratic inefficiency and malpractice, the end of bribery and corruption as a way of life, an independent and dignified foreign policy following expulsion of US bases, and withdrawal from NATO and the European Community.

A change of style was promised, too, replacing the country's long traditions of authoritarianism and bureacracy with openness and dialogue. Even more radically, where Greek political parties had long been the personal followings of charismatic leaders, PASOK was to be a party of ideology and principle, dependent on no single individual member. Or so, at least, thought some of the youthful PASOK political enthusiasts.

The new era started with a bang. The wartime resistance was officially recognised; hitherto they hadn't been allowed to take part in any celebrations, wreath-layings or other ceremonies. Peasant women were granted pensions for the first time – 3000 drachmas a month, the same as their outraged husbands – and wages were indexed to the cost of living. In addition, civil marriage was introduced, family law reformed in favour of wives and mothers, and equal rights legislation was put on the statute book.

These popular **reformist moves** seemed to mark a break with the past, and the atmosphere had indeed changed. Greeks no longer lowered their voices to discuss politics in public places or wrapped their opposition newspaper in the respectably conservative *Kathimeriní*. At first there were real fears that the climate would be too much for the military and they would once again intervene to choke a dangerous experiment in democracy, especially when Andreas Papandreou assumed the defence portfolio himself in a move strongly reminiscent of his father's attempt to remove the king's appointee in 1965. But he went out of his way to soothe **military susceptibilities**, increasing their salaries, buying new weaponry, and being super-fastidious in his attendance at military functions.

THE END OF THE HONEYMOON

Nothing if not a populist, **Papandreou** promised a bonanza he must have known, as a skilled and experienced economist, he could not deliver. As a result he pleased nobody on the **economic** front.

He could not fairly be blamed for the inherited lack of investment, low productivity, deficiency in managerial and labour skills and other chronic problems besetting the Greek economy. On the other hand, he certainly aggravated the situation in the early days of his first government by allowing his supporters to indulge in violently anti-capitalist rhetoric, and by the prosecution and humiliation of the Tsatsos family, owners of one of Greece's few modern and profitable businesses – cement, in this case – for the illegal export of capital, something of which every Greek with any savings is guilty. These were cheap victories and were not backed by any programme of public investment, while the only "socialisations" were of hopelessly lame-duck companies.

Faced with this sluggish economy, and burdened with the additional charges of (marginally) improved social benefits and wage indexing, Papandreou's government had also to cope with the effects of **world recession**, which always hit Greece with a delayed effect compared with its more advanced European partners. **Shipping**, the country's main foreign-currency earner, was devastated. Remittances from emigré workers fell off as they joined the lines of the unemployed in their host countries, and tourism receipts diminished under the dual impact of recession and Reagan's warning to Americans to stay away from insecure and terrorist-prone Athens airport.

With huge quantities of imported goods continuing to be sucked into the country in the absence of domestic production, the **foreign debt** topped £10 billion in 1986, with inflation at 25 percent and the balance of payments deficit approaching £1 billion. Greece also began to experience the social strains of **unemployment** for the first time. Not that it didn't existed before, but it had always been concealed as under-employment by the family and the rural structure of the economy – as well as by the absence of statistics.

The result of all this was that Papandreou has had to eat his words. A modest spending spree, joy at the defeat of the right, the popularity of his Greece-for-the-Greeks foreign policy, and some much needed reforms saw him through into a **second term**, with an electoral victory in June 1985 scarcely less triumphant than the first. But the complacent and, frankly, dishonest slogan was "Vote PASOK for Even Better Days". By October they had imposed a two-year wage freeze and import restrictions, abolished the wage-indexing scheme and devalued the drachma by 15 percent. Papandreou's fat was pulled out of the fire by none other than that former bogeyman, the **European Community**, which offered a huge two-part loan on condition that an IMF-style **austerity programme** was maintained.

The political fallout of such a classic right-wing deflation, accompanied by shameless soliciting for foreign investment, was the alienation of the Communists and most of PASOK's own political constituency. Increasingly autocratic – ironic given the early ideals of PASOK as a new kind of party – Papandreou's response to **dissent** was to fire recalcitrant trade union leaders and expel some 300 members of his own party. Assailed by strikes, the government appeared to have lost direction completely. In local elections in October 1986 it lost a lot of ground to *Néa Dhimokratía*, including the mayoralties of the three major cities: Athens, Thessaloníki and Pátra.

Papandreou assured the nation that he had taken the message to heart but all that followed was a minor government reshuffle and a panicky attempt to undo the ill-feeling caused by an incredible freeing of **rent controls** at a time when all wage-earners were feeling the pinch badly. Early in 1987 he went further and sacked all the remaining PASOK veterans in his cabinet, including his son, though it is said, probably correctly, that this was a palliative to public opinion. The new cabinet was so un-Socialist that even the right-wing press called it **"centrist"**.

WOMEN'S RIGHTS IN GREECE

Women's right to vote wasn't universally achieved in Greece until 1956, and less than a decade ago adultery was still a punishable offence, with cases regularly brought to court. The socialist party, PASOK, was elected for terms of government in 1981 and 1985 with a strong theoretical progamme for **women's rights**, and their women's council review committees, set up in the early, heady days, effected a landmark reform with the 1983 **Family Law**. This prohibited dowry and stipulated equal legal status and shared property rights between husband and wife.

Subsequently, however, the PASOK governments did little to follow through on **practical issues**, like improved child care, health and family planning. Contraception is not available as part of the skeletal Greek public health service, leaving many women to fall back on abortions – only recently made legal under certain conditions, but running (as for many years past) to an estimated 70–80,000 a year.

The **Greek Women's Movement** has in recent years conspicuously emerged. By far the largest organisation is the *Union of Greek Women*. Founded in 1976, this espouses an independent feminist line and is responsible for numerous consciousness-raising activities across the country, though it remains too closely linked to the scandal-ridden opposition party, PASOK, for comfort. As a perfect metaphor for this, Margaret Papandreou felt compelled to resign from the Union following her well-publicised divorce from ex-Premier Andreas, leaving it without her effective and vocal leadership. Other, more autonomous groups, have been responsible for setting up advice and support networks, highlighting women's issues within trade unions, and campaigning for changes in media representation.

None of this is easy in a country as polarised as Greece. In many rural areas women rely heavily on traditional extended families for security, and are unlikely to be much affected by legislative reforms or city politics. Yet Greek men of all classes and backgrounds are slowly becoming used to the notion of women in positions of power and responsibility, and taking a substantial share in child-rearing – both postures utterly unthinkable two decades ago, and arguably one of the few positive legacies with which PASOK can at least in part be credited.

Similar about-faces took place in **foreign policy**. The initial anti-US, anti-NATO and anti-EC rhetoric was immensely popular, and understandable for a people shamelessly bullied by bigger powers for the past 150 years. There was some high-profile nose-thumbing, like refusing to join EC partners in condemning Jaruzelski's Polish regime, or the Soviet downing of a Korean airliner, or Syrian involvement in terrorist bomb-planting. There were some forgettable embarrassments, too, like suggesting Gaddafi's Libya provided a suitable model for alternative Socialist development, and the Mitterand-Gaddafi-Papandreou "summit" in Crete, which an infuriated Mitterand felt he had been inveigled into on false pretences.

Much was made of a strategic opening to the Arab world. Yasser Arafat, for example, was the first "head of state" to be received in Athens under the PASOK government. Given Greece's geographical position and historical ties, it was an imaginative and appropriate policy. But if Arab investment was hoped for, it never materialised.

In stark contrast to his early promises and rhetoric, the "realistic" policies that Papandreou pursued were far more conciliatory towards his big Western brothers. This was best exemplified by the fact that **US bases** remained in Greece, largely due to the fear that snubbing NATO would lead to Greece being exposed to Turkish aggression, still the only issue that unites the main parties to any degree. As for the once-reviled **European Community**, Greece had become an established beneficiary and its leader was hardly about to bite the hand that feeds.

SCANDAL

Even as late as mid-1988, despite the many betrayals of Papandreou, despite his failure to clean up the public services and do away with the system of patronage and corruption, and despite a level of popular displeasure that brought a million striking, demonstrating workers into the streets (February 1987), it seemed unlikely that PASOK would be toppled in the following year's **elections**.

This was due mainly to the lack of a credible alternative. Konstantinos Mitsotakis, a bitter personal enemy of Papandreou's since 1965, when his defection had brought down his father's government and set in train the events that culminated in the junta, was an unconvincing and unlikeable character at the helm of *Néa Dhimokratía*. Meanwhile, the liberal centre had disappeared and the main communist party, KKE, appeared trapped in a Stalinist timewarp under the leadership of Harilaos Florakis. Only the *Ellenikí Aristerá* (Greek Left), formerly the European wing of the KKE, seemed to offer any sensible alternative programme, and they had a precariously small following.

So PASOK could have been in a position to win a third term by default, as it were, when a combination of spectacular **own goals**, plus perhaps a general shift to the right, influenced by the cataclysmic events in Eastern Europe, conspired against them.

First came the extraordinary cavortings of the Prime Minister himself. Towards the end of 1988, the seventy-year-old Papandreou was flown to Britain for open-heart surgery. He took the occasion, with fear of death presumably rocking his judgement, to make public a year-long liaison with a 34-year-old *Olympic Airways* hostess, **Dimitra "Mimi" Liani**. The international news pictures of an old man shuffling about after a young blonde, to the public humiliation of Margaret, his American-born wife, and his family, were not popular (Papandreou has since divorced Margaret and married Mimi). His integrity was further questioned when he missed several important public engagements – including a ceremony commemorating the victims of the 1987 Kalamáta earthquake – and was pictured out with Mimi, reliving his youth in nightspots.

The real damage, however, was done by **economic scandals**. It came to light that a PASOK minister had passed off Yugoslav corn as Greek in a sale to the EC. Then, far more seriously, it emerged that a self-made conman, **Yiorgos Koskotas**, director of the **Bank of Crete**, had embezzled £120m (US$190m) of deposits and, worse still, slipped though the authorities' fingers and sought asylum in the US. Certain PASOK ministers and even Papandreou himself were implicated in the scandal. Further damage was done by alegations of illegal **arms dealings** by still more government ministers.

United in disgust at this corruption, the other left parties – KKE and *Ellinikí Aristerá* – formed a coalition, the *Synaspismós*, taking support still further from PASOK.

THREE BITES AT THE CHERRY

In this climate of disaffection, an inconclusive result to the **June 1989 election** was no real surprise. What was less predictable, however, was the formation of a bizarre **"katharsis" coalition** of conservatives and communists, united in the avowed intent of cleansing PASOK's increasingly Augean stables.

That this coalition emerged was basically down to Papandreou. The *Synaspismós* would have formed a government with PASOK but set one condition for doing so – that Papandreou stepped down as Prime Minister – and the old man would have none of it. In the deal finally cobbled together between the left and *Néa Dhimokratía*, Mitsotakis was denied the premiership, too, having to make way for his compromise party colleague, **Tzanetakis**.

During the three months that the coalition lasted, the *katharsis* turned out to be largely a question of burying the knife as deeply as possible into the ailing body of PASOK. Andreas Papandreou and three other ministers were officially accused of involvement in the Koskotas affair – though there was no time to set up their **trial** before the Greek people returned once again to the polls. In any case, the chief witness and protagonist in the affair, Koskotas himself, was still imprisoned in America, awaiting extradition proceedings.

Contrary to the right's hope that publicly accusing Papandreou and his cohorts of criminal behaviour would pave the way for a *Néa Dhimokratía* victory, PASOK actually made a slight recovery in **November 1989 elections**, though the result was still inconclusive. This time the left resolutely refused to do deals with anyone and the result was a consensus caretaker government under the neutral aegis of an academic called Zolotas, who was pushed into the Prime Minister's office, somewhat unwillingly it seemed, from Athens University. His only mandate was to see that the country didn't go off the rails completely while preparations were made for yet more elections.

These took place in **April 1990** with the same captains at the command of their ships and with the *Synaspismós* having completed its about-turn to the extent that in the five single-seat constituencies (the other 295 seats are drawn from multiple-seat constituencies in a complicated system of reinforced proportional representation), they supported independent candidates jointly with PASOK. Greek communists are good at about-turns, though; after all, composer Mikis Theodorakis, musical torchbearer of the left during the dark years of the junta, and formely a KKE MP, was by now standing for *Néa Dhimokratía*.

On the night, *Néa Dhimokratía* scraped home with a majority of one, later doubled with the defection of a centrist, and **Mitsotakis** finally got to achieve his dream of becoming Prime Minister. The only other memorable feature of the election was the first parliamentary representation for a party of the Turkish minority in Thrace, and for the ecologists — a focus for many disaffected PASOK voters.

A RETURN TO THE RIGHT: MITSOTAKIS

Since assuming power, Mitsotakis has followed a course of **austerity measures** to try and revive the chronically ill economy. Little headway has been made, though given the world recession, it is hardly surprising. Greece still has **inflation** up around 20 percent and a growing **unemployment** problem.

The latter has been exacerbated, since 1990, by the arrival of thousands of impoverished **Albanians**. They have formed something of an underclass, especially those who aren't ethnically Greek, and are prey to vilification for all manner of ills. They have also led to the first real immigration measures in a country whose population is more used to being on the other side of such laws.

Other conservative measures introduced by Mitsotakis include laws to combat strikes and **terrorism**. The terrorist issue had been a perennial source of worry for Greeks since the appearance in the mid-1980s of a group called **17 Novembriou** (the date of the Colonels' attack on the Polytechnic in 1973). They have killed a numer of industrialists and attacked buildings of military attaches and airlines in Athens, so far without any police arrests. It hardly seems likely that Mitsotakis's laws, however, were the solution. They stipulated that statements by the group could no longer be published and led to one or two newspaper editors being jailed for a few days for defiance — much to everyone's embarrassment.

The **anti-strike laws** threaten severe penalties but seem equally ineffectual, as breakdowns in public transport, electricity and rubbish collection all too frequently illustrate.

As for the **Koskotas scandal**, the villain of the piece was eventually extradited and gave evidence for the prosecution against Papandreou and various of his ministers. The trial was televised and proved as popular as any soap opera, as indeed it should have been, given the twists of high drama — which included one of the defendants, Koutsoyiorgas, dying in court of a heart attack in front of the cameras. The case against Papandreou gradually petered out and he was officially acquitted in early 1992. The two other surviving ministers, Tsovolas and Petsos, were convicted and given short prison sentences.

The trial, all in all, could not be considered a great success for the government, and in its wake it is Mitsotakis who finds himself embattled amidst social and political unrest, and the usual round of strikes, ignoring calls for new elections.

The news is even worse on the foreign affairs front, as Greece pits itself against the EC in denying recognition to the former-Yugoslav territory of **Macedonia** on the grounds that their northern province has a copyright on the name, for fear of redrawing borders — and, not least, for distracting the electorate with nationalist posturing. There is no progress, either, on the **Cyprus** dispute, although in the summer of 1992 Mitsotakis at least met his Turkish counterpart face to face. Ironically, the one move in international relations is the American decision to close its **Greek bases**, except for Soúdha Bay on Crete: Greece's diminishing role in NATO having done what 17 years of posturing could not achieve.

If Mitsotakis can hold out until the end of his term, in 1994, he may yet get re-elected, for the opposition is scarcely dynamic. The left is again in disarray, following the break-up of the *Synaspismós* and the departure of KKE to revert to its own Communist title. Which again leaves the only realistic alternative as PASOK and its old battlehorse, Papandreou, who stolidly refuses to go out to pasture with his now legal spouse, Mimi.

And yet the eighty-year-old, for all his scandals, may yet have the last laugh on his old enemy Psilós ("tall one"), as Mitsotakis is nicknamed. A by-election that took place in the Athens seat of the disgraced Tsovolas in summer 1992 saw PASOK increase its vote by an astonishing margin of 104,000.

THE GREEK MINORITIES

The Greek minorities – Vlachs, Sarakatsáni, Albanians, Turks, Jews and other
relict communities – are little known,
even within Greece. Indeed to meet
Vlachs or Sarakatsáni who remain true to
their roots you'll have to get to some fairly
remote parts of Epirus. Greco-Turks are
another matter, a sizeable (and recently
problematic) community living, as they
have done for centuries, in Thrace. The
Jews of Greece, as ever, have the saddest
history, having been annihilated by the
Nazi occupiers during the latter stages of
World War II.

THE VLACHS

The **Vlachs'** homeland is in the remote fast-
ness of the **Píndhos Mountains** in northwestern Greece near the Albanian frontier.
Traditionally they were transhumant shepherds, although some have long led a more
settled existence in villages, notably Métsovo.
They are an ancient, close-knit community with
a strong sense of identity, like their rival shepherd clan, the *Sarakatsáni*, whom they despise
as "tent-dwellers" and who, in turn, just as
passionately despise them for living in houses.

Unlike the Sarakatsans, however, their
mother tongue is not Greek, but Vlach, a
Romance language, which even today is full of
words that anyone with a little Latin can easily
recognise: *loop* for wolf, *mulier* for women,
pene for bread. When the Italians invaded
Greece in World War II, Vlach soldiers were
often used as interpreters.

It used to be thought that the Vlachs were
Slavs, descendants of Roman legionaries
stationed in the provinces of Illyria and Dacia,
who over the centuries had wandered down
through the Balkans in search of grazing for
their sheep and finally settled in northern
Greece, where they had been trapped by the
creation of modern frontiers on the disintegration of the Austro-Hungarian and Ottoman
empires. Because of these supposed Slav
connections and the old Greek anxieties about
the Slavophile, separatist tendencies of the
peoples of northern Greece, the Vlachs have

been objects of suspicion to the modern state.
To their chagrin many villages with Slav-
sounding names were officially renamed during
the Metaxas dictatorship of the 1930s, and
Vlach schoolchildren forbidden to use their
mother tongue.

There is, however, a new theory about their
origins, which argues that the Greek Vlachs are
of Greek descent and have always inhabited
these same regions of the Píndhos Mountains;
that during Roman times the Romans found it
convenient to train local people as highway
guards for the high passes on the old Roman
road, the Via Egnatia, which connected Constantinople with the Adriatic. Thus the Vlachs
learned their Latin through their association
with the Romans and preserved it because of
the isolation of their homeland and the exclusive nature of their pastoral way of life.

Sadly, though probably inevitably, the
Vlachs' unique traditions are in danger of extinction. Only fifty or so years back, a prosperous
Vlach family might have 10,000 sheep, and
when they set off on the annual migration from
their lowland winter pastures to the mountains
it was like a small army on the march, with two
or three complete generations together with all
their animals and belongings. Nowadays few
flocks number more than 250 ewes, and the
annual migration takes place in lorries – though
a few veterans still do it on foot. Hundreds of
Vlachs have sold their flocks and moved to the
town or emigrated; many a sheepfold boasts a
former Volkswagen-factory hand. There are
depressingly few young men among the remaining shepherds. The hardships of their life are
too many and the economic returns too small.

JEWS AND TURKS

Jews and Turks in Greece are, for historical
reasons, conveniently considered together.
Since the decline of the Ottoman empire, these
two Greek minorities have often suffered similar fates as isolated groups in a non-
assimilating culture. Yet it seems that enclaves
of each will endure for the forseeable future.

ORIGINS AND SETTLEMENTS

The **Greek Jewish community** is one of the
oldest established in Europe, dating back to the
late Classical period. During the Roman and
Byzantine eras, the Jews were termed

Romaniot and colonies flourished throughout the Balkans. In Greece these included Corfu, Zákinthos, Pátra, Kórinthos, Athens, Halkídha, Véria, Crete and, most importantly, Ioánnina.

The most numerically significant Jewish communities in Greece, however, date back to shortly after the taking of Constantinople by the **Ottomans**. In 1493 Sultan Beyazit II invited Spanish and Portuguese Jews expelled from those countries to settle in the Ottoman empire. The great influx of *Sephardim* (Ladino-speaking Jews) soon swamped the original Romaniot centres, and within two centuries, Ladino, a mix of medieval Spanish and Portuguese with Turkish, Hebrew and Arabic augments, had largely supplanted Greek as the lingua franca of Balkan Jewry. However, *Ladinismo* (the medieval Iberian Jewish culture) never penetrated the Romaniot enclaves of Ioánnina and Halkídha, a few small communities of which remain to this day.

Turkish officials and their families fanned out across the Balkans to consolidate imperial administration, thus sowing the seeds of the numerous **Muslim communities** in present-day Bulgaria, Albania, Yugoslavia and Greece. The Ottoman authorities often appointed Jews as civil servants and tax collectors; one, Joseph Nassi, became governor of the Cyclades.

As a result Jews became identified with the ruling hierarchy in the eyes of the Orthodox Christian population, and at the outset of the 1821 **War of Independence** the Jewish quarters of Pátra, Kórinthos, Athens and virtually all others within the confines of the nascent Greek state, were put to the sword along with Turkish villages. Survivors of the various massacres fled north, to the territories that remained under Ottoman control. Within the new Greek kingdom, a small community of Ashkenazi Jews arrived in Athens, along with the Bavarian king Otho, in the 1830s.

UNDER THE GREEK STATE

The **expansion of the Greek nation** thereafter resulted in the decline of both the Greek-Jewish and Greek-Turkish populations. New annexations or conquests (Thessaly in 1878, Epirus, Macedonia, the northeast Aegean and Crete in 1913) provoked a wave of forced or nervous Judaeo-Turkish migration to the other side of the receding Ottoman frontier. While Jews were never forbidden to stay in newly

occupied territory, rarely were they explicitly welcomed. The Turks – or more correctly, Muslims, since "Turk" was a generic term for any Muslim, including ethnic Greeks who had converted to Islam for economic advantage – were subject to various expulsion orders.

Between 1913 and 1923 the **Muslims of Crete**, mostly converted islanders, were forced to choose between apostasy to Christianity or exile. (The newly Orthodox can today often be distinguished by their ostentatiously Christian surnames, such as Stavroulakis, Hristakis, etc.) Those who opted to stand by their faith were summarily deposited in the closest Turkish-Muslim settlements on Greek islands just over the Ottoman border; Kós Town, the nearby village of Platáni, and Rhodes Town were three of the more convenient ones.

When the Italians formally annexed the **Dodecanese** after World War I, the **Muslims** were allowed to remain and they were thus rendered exempt from any of the provisions of the Treaty of Lausanne (which stipulated the wholescale exchange of "Turk" and "Greek" populations in the wake of the Asia Minor war). It is not certain exactly how or when the Dodecanese Muslims learned Greek, which they today mix unconcernedly in conversation with Turkish. Education in Greek, which has been compulsory since 1948, when the Dodecanese were reunited with Greece, must have played a part. But it's likely that the Muslim refugees from Crete, when they were not actually converted to Greek Orthodoxy, knew enough Greek both to communicate with neighbouring Christians and to teach any purely Turkish villagers the new tongue.

In **Rhodes** there is a long tradition of co-operation between the Muslim and the Jewish communities. In Ottoman days Jews were the only *milet* (subject ethnic group) allowed out after the city gates were closed at dusk, and more recently Muslim and Jewish leaders have consulted on how best to counter government strategies to deprive each of their rights and property. The dilapidated refugee village of Kritiká ("the Cretans") still huddles by the seaside on the way to the airport, and walking through Rhodes' old town it's easy to spot Turkish names on the marquees of various sandalmakers, *kafenía*, and kebab stands. Those Turks who live in the old town itself, however, have in some cases been there since the sixteenth century and will proudly tell you that they have every right to be considered native Rhodians.

In **Kós**, Cretan Muslims settled both in the port town – where they seem to have gravitated to the antique and shoe-making trade – and at Platáni, which still has a mixed Greek Orthodox and "Turkish" population.

During the early 1900s, the same era as the Cretan deportations, the status of mainland Jews and Turks in the path of Greek nationalism was more ambivalent. Even after the respective 1878 and 1913 acquisitions of **Thessaly**, **Epirus** and **Macedonia**, Muslim villages continued to exist in these regions. The Tsamidhes, an Albanian Muslim tribe localised in Epirus and Thesprotía, were left alone until World War II, when they made the grievous error of siding with the invading Axis armies; they were hunted down and expelled forthwith by first the National Army and later guerrilla bands.

Thessaloníki in the late nineteenth century was one of the largest Jewish towns in the world. Jews made up seventy-five percent of the population, and dominated the sailing, shipping and chandlery trades. In addition there were numerous *Dönmeh*, descendants of the false seventeenth century messiah Sabbatai Zvi, who were outwardly Muslims but practiced Judaism in secret. When the city passed to Greek control, the authorities allowed the "pure" Jews to stay but insisted on the departure of the *Dönmeh*, along with other Turkic Muslims. The *Dönmeh* (Turkish for "turncoats", after Zvi's conversion to Islam at swordpoint) insisted that they were "really" Jews, but to no avail. After 1913 the city began rapidly to lose its Hebraic character; the fire of 1917, emigration to Palestine and the arrival of the Nazis effectively brought an era to a close.

The same period, around the time of World War I, also saw the end of Muslim enclaves on the islands of **Thássos**, **Samothráki**, **Límnos**, **Lésvos** and **Híos**, where the Turks themselves, in a dog-in-the-manger mood, destroyed their fine Turkish bath before leaving. On **Sámos** there is a special, tiny Jewish cemetery with the graves of two brothers – apparently Ashkenazi merchants who died between the world wars; otherwise there had not been a significant Jewish community here since Byzantine times, and Muslim Turks were uniquely forbidden to settle here after the seventeenth century.

Western Thrace, the area from the Néstos River to the Évros, was always home to large numbers of Greek Muslims, and it remained their last bastion after the 1919–1922 Asia Minor War. The **Treaty of Lausanne** (1923) confirmed the right of this minority to remain in situ, in return for a continued Greek Orthodox presence in Istanbul (still known to Greeks as Konstantinoúpoli), the Prince's Islands, and Tenedos/Imvros Islands.

Over the years the Turks have repeatedly abrogated the terms of the pact and reduced the Turkish Greek Orthodox population to five percent of pre-1923 levels. The Greeks have acted comparatively leniently, and today Muslims still make up a third of the population of Greek Thrace, being highly visible in the main towns of **Alexandhroúpoli**, **Komotiní** and **Xánthi**. Muslims control much of the tobacco culture hereabouts and the baggy-trousered women can be glimpsed from the trains which pass through their fields.

The loyalty of these Thracian "Turks" to the Greek state was amply demonstrated during the **World War II**, when they resisted the invading Bulgarians and Nazis side by side with their Christian compatriots. In return the two occupying forces harassed and deported to death camps many local Muslims. During the 1946–49 civil war Thracian Muslims suffered again at the hands of ELAS, who found the deep-seated conservatism of these villagers exasperating and laboured under the misconception that all local Muslims were traitors.

Only the **Pomaks**, a non-Turkic Muslim group of aboutly 40,000 centred around Ehinós, north of Xánthi, collaborated to any extent with the Bulgarians, probably on the basis of ethnic affinity. The Pomaks as a group were probably Christian Slavs forcibly converted to Islam in the sixteenth century; they speak a degenerate dialect of Bulgarian with generous mixtures of Greek and Turkish. The authorities still keep them on a tight rein; they require a travel permit to leave their immediate area of residence around Ehínos, and visitors require a permit for their villages, too.

As if the foregoing were not complex enough, there is also a small (several thousand strong) population of **Gagauz**, Christian Turks, around Alexandhroúpoli.

Until recently, the Orthodox and "Turkish" Thracian communities lived in a fairly easy (if distant) relationship with each other, but in early 1990 a series of ugly intercommunal incidents, and official prosecution of Turkish political leaders cast doubt on the carefully cultivated international image of Greece's toleration of its minorities. It has, in fact, always been true that treatment of these Muslims functions as a barometer of relations at a more general level between Greece and Turkey, and as a quid pro quo for perceived maltreatment of the remaining Greek Orthodox in Turkey.

But it is the **Jews** rather than the Muslims who have suffered greater catastrophes during and since **World War II**. Eighty-five percent of a Jewish population of around 80,000 was rounded up by the Nazis in the spring of 1944, never to return. Greek Christians often went to extraordinary lengths to protect their persecuted countrymen, overshadowing the few instances of sordid betrayal. The city council of Zákinthos and the bishops of Athens and Halkídha, for example, put themselves at risk to save many who would otherwise have been killed.

Those Jews who remained in the country either went into hiding or joined the guerrillas in the hills. **Athens Jewry**, indistinguishable from their Orthodox neighbours in appearance and tongue, fared best, but the Ladino-speaking Jews of northern Greece, with their distinctive surnames and customs, were easy targets for the Nazis. It must also be said that certain portions of the Greek business community in **Thessaloníki** benefited greatly from the expulsion of the Jews, and needed little encouragement to help themselves to the contents of the abandoned Jewish shops. Jewish sensibilities were further offended in the post-war era when the German desecration of the huge Jewish cemetery was completed by the construction of the University of Thessaloníki on the site.

The paltry number of survivors returning from the death camps to Greece was insufficient to form the nucleus of a revival, and emigration to Israel was often a preferable alternative to living with ghosts. **Currently** barely 6000 Jews remain in Greece. In Thessaloníki there are around 1100 Sephardim, while small Ladino communities continue in Kavála, Sérres, Dhidhimótiho, Tríkala and Véria. Lárissa has a modest number who are still disproportionately important in the clothing trade. However young Jewish women outnumber their male counterparts, with the result that they tend to marry into the Orthodox faith. In Ioánnina, once a major centre of Jewry, less than 100 Romaniot Jews remain. Only 75 or so of the original community of Rhodes survived the war (that at Kós was completely wiped out), and these are almost outnumbered by recent Egyptian Jewish refugees.

The *Platía ton Evreón Martirón* (Square of the Jewish Martyrs) is a memorial to the 2000 Jews of Kós and Rhodes slaughtered by the Germans; it occupies the site of the (mostly demolished) old Jewish quarter. Three thousand of today's Greek Jews live in Athens, which is also the home of the **National Jewish Museum** (see p.82).

250 YEARS OF ARCHAEOLOGY

Archaeology until the second half of the nineteenth century was a very hit-and-miss affair. The early students of antiquity went to Greece to draw and make plaster casts of the great masterpieces of Classical sculpture. Unfortunately, a number soon found it more convenient or more profitable to remove objects whole-sale, and might be better described as looters than scholars or archaeologists.

EARLY EXCAVATIONS

The British **Society of Dilettanti** was one of the earliest promoters of Greek culture, financing expeditions to draw and publish antiquities. Founded in the 1730s as a club for young aristocrats who had completed the Grand Tour and fancied themselves arbiters of taste, the Society's main qualification for membership (according to most critics) was habitual drunkenness. Its leading spirit was Sir Frances Dashwood, a notorious rake who founded the infamous Hellfire Club. Nevertheless, the Society was the first body organised to sponsor systematic research into Greek antiquities, though it was initially most interested in Italy. Greece, then a backwater of the Ottoman Empire, was not a regular part of the Grand Tour and only the most intrepid adventurers undertook so hazardous a trip.

In the 1740s, two young artists, **James Stuart and Nicholas Revett**, formed a plan to produce a scholarly record of the ancient Greek buildings. With the support of the society they spent three years in Greece, principally Athens, drawing and measuring the surviving antiquities. The first volume of *The Antiquities of Athens* appeared in 1762, becoming an instant success. The publication of their exquisite illustrations gave an enormous fillip to the study of Greek sculpture and architecture, which became the fashionable craze among the educated classes; many European neoclassical town and country houses date from this period.

The Society financed a number of further expeditions to study Greek antiquities, including one to Asia Minor in 1812. The expedition was to be based in Smyrna, but while waiting in Athens for a ship to Turkey, the party employed themselves in excavations at **Eleusis**, where they uncovered the Temple of Demeter. It was the first archaeological excavation made on behalf of the Society, and one of the first in Greece. After extensive explorations in Asia Minor, the participants returned via Attica, where they excavated the Temple of Nemesis at **Rhamnous** and examined the Temple of Apollo at **Sounion**.

Several other antiquarians of the age were less interested in discoveries for their own sake. A French count, **Choiseul-Gouffier**, removed part of the **Parthenon frieze** in 1787 and his example prompted **Lord Elgin** to detach much of the rest in 1801. These were essentially acts of looting – "Bonaparte has not got such things from all his thefts in Italy", boasted Elgin – and their legality was suspect even at the time.

Other discoveries of the period were more ambiguous. In 1811, a party of English and German travellers, including the architect CR Cockerell, uncovered the **Temple of Aphaia** on **Aegina** (Áyina) and shipped away the pediments. They auctioned off the marbles for £6000 to Prince Ludwig of Bavaria and, inspired by this success, returned to Greece for further finds. This time they struck lucky with twenty-three slabs from the **Temple of Apollo Epicurius** at **Bassae**, for which the British Museum laid out a further £15,000. These were huge sums for the time and highly profitable exercises, but they were also pioneering archaeology for the period. Besides, removing the finds was hardly surprising: Greece, after all, was not yet a state and had no public museum; antiquities discovered were sold by their finders – if they recognised their value.

THE NEW NATION

The **Greek War of Independence** (1821–28) and the establishment of a modern Greek nation changed all of this – and provided a major impetus to archaeology. Nationhood brought an increased pride in Greece's Classical heritage, nowhere more so than in **Athens**, which succeeded Náfplio as the nation's capital in 1834 largely on the basis of its ancient monuments and past.

As a result of the selection of Prince Otho of Bavaria as the first king of modern Greece in 1832, the **Germans**, whose education system laid great stress on Classical learning, were in the forefront of archaeological activity.

One of the dominant Teutonic figures during the early years of the new state was **Ludwig Ross**. Arriving in Greece as a student in 1832, he was on hand to show the new king around the antiquities of Athens when Otho was considering making the town his capital. Ross was appointed deputy keeper of antiquities to the court, and in 1834 began supervising the **excavation and restoration of the Acropolis**. The work of dismantling the accretion of Byzantine, Frankish and Turkish fortifications began the following year. The graceful Temple of Athena Nike, which had furnished many of the blocks for the fortifications, was rebuilt, and Ross's architect, Leo von Klenze, began the reconstruction of the Parthenon.

The Greeks themselves had begun to focus on their ancient past when the first stirrings of the independence movement were felt. In 1813 the **Philomuse Society** was formed, which aimed to uncover and collect antiquities, publish books and assist students and foreign philhellenes. In 1829 an orphanage on the island of Éyina, built by Kapodistrias, the first President of Greece, became the first Greek **archaeological museum**.

In 1837 the **Greek Archaeological Society** was founded "for the discovery, recovery and restoration of antiquities in Greece". Its moving spirit was **Kyriakos Pittakis**, a remarkable figure who during the War of Independence had used his knowledge of ancient literature to discover the Clepsydra spring on the Acropolis – solving the problem of lack of water during the Turkish siege. In the first four years of its existence, the Archaeological Society sponsored excavations in Athens at the **Theatre of Dionysus**, the **Tower of the Winds**, the **Propylaia** and the **Erechtheion**. Pittakis also played a major role in the attempt to convince Greeks of the importance of their heritage; antiquities were still being looted or burnt for lime.

THE GREAT GERMANS: CURTIUS AND SCLIEMANN

Although King Otho was deposed in 1862 in favour of a Danish princeling, Germans remained in the forefront of Greek archaeology in the 1870s. Two men dominated the scene, Heinrich Schliemann and Ernst Curtius.

Ernst Curtius was a traditionally Classical scholar. He had come to Athens originally as tutor to King Otho's family and in 1874 returned to Greece to negotiate the **excavations of Olympia**, one of the richest of Greek sanctuaries and site of the most famous of the ancient panhellenic games. The reigning German Kaiser Wilhelm I intended that the excavation would proclaim to the world the cultural and intellectual pre-eminence of his three-year-old empire. Curtius took steps to set up a **German Archaeological Institute** in Athens and negotiated the **Olympia Convention**, under the terms of which the Germans were to pay for everything and have total control of the dig; all finds were to remain in Greece, though the excavators could make copies and casts; and all finds were to be published simultaneously in Greek and German.

This was an enormously important agreement, which almost certainly prevented the treasure of Olympia and Mycenae following that of Troy to a German museum. The Europeans were still in very acquisitive mode. French consuls, for example, had been instructed to purchase any "available" local antiquities in Greece and Asia Minor, and had picked up the Louvre's great treasures, the *Venus de Milo* and *Winged Victory of Samothrace*, in 1820 and 1863 respectively.

At **Olympia**, digging began in 1875 on a site buried beneath many feet of river mud, silt and sand. Only one corner of the Temple of Zeus was initially visible, but within months the excavators had turned up statues from the east pediment. Over forty magnificent sculptures, as well as terracottas, statue bases, and a rich collection of bronzes were uncovered, together with more than 400 inscriptions. The laying bare of this huge complex was a triumph for official German archaeology.

While Curtius was digging at Olympia, a man who represented everything that was anathaema to orthodox Classical scholarship was standing archaeology on its head. **Heinrich Schliemann**'s beginnings were not auspicious for one who aspired to dig for ancient cities. The son of a drunken German pastor, he left school at fourteen and spent the next five years as a grocer's assistant. En route to seeking his fortune in Venezuela, he was left for dead on the Dutch coast after a shipwreck. Later, working as a bookkeeper in Amsterdam, he began to study languages. His phenomenal memory enabled him to master four by the age of 21. Following a six-week study of Russian, Schliemann was sent to Saint Petersburg as a trading agent and had amassed a fortune by the time he was 30. In 1851 he visited California, opened a bank during the Gold Rush and made another fortune.

His financial position secure for life, Schliemann was almost ready to tackle his life's ambition – **the search for Troy** and the vindication of his lifelong belief in the truth of Homer's tales of prehistoric cities and heroes. By this time he spoke no less than seventeen languages, and had excavated on the island of **Ithaca**, writing a book which earned him a doctorate from the University of Rothstock.

Although most of the archaeological establishment, led by Curtius, was unremittingly hostile to the millionaire amateur, Schliemann sunk his first trench at the hill called Hisarlik, in northwest Turkey, in 1870; excavation proper began in 1871. In his haste to find the city of Priam and Hector and to convince the world of his success, Schliemann dug a huge trench straight through the mound, destroying a mass of important evidence, but he was able nevertheless to identify nine cities, one atop the next. In May of 1873 he discovered the so-called **Treasure of Priam**, a stash of gold and precious jewellery and vessels. It convinced many that the German had indeed found Troy, although others contended that Schliemann, desperate for academic recognition, assembled it from other sources. The finds disappeared from Berlin at the end of World War II and survive now only in photographs.

Three years later Schliemann turned his attentions to **Mycenae**, again inspired by Homer, again following a hunch. Alone among contemporary scholars, he sought and found the legendary graves of Mycenean kings *inside* the existing cyclopean wall of the citadel rather than outside, unearthing in the process the magnificent treasures that today form the basis of the prehistoric collection in the National Archaeological Museum in Athens.

He dug again at Troy in 1882, assisted by a young architect, Willhelm Dörpfeld, who was destined to become one of the great archaeologists of the next century (though his claim for Lefkádha as ancient Ithaca never found popular acceptance). In 1884 Schliemann returned to Greece to excavate another famous prehistoric citadel, this time at **Tiryns**.

Almost single-handedly, and in the face of continuing academic hostility, Schliemann, in pursuit of his dream, had revolutionised archaeology and pushed back the knowledge of Greek history and civilisation a thousand years. Although some of his results have been shown to have been deliberately falsified in the sacrifice of truth to beauty, his achievement remains enormous.

The last two decades of the nineteenth century saw the discovery of other important Classical sites. Excavation began at **Epidaurus** in 1881 under the Greek archaeologist **Panayotis Kavvadias**, who made it his life's work. Meanwhile at **Delphi**, the French, after gaining the permission to transfer the inhabitants of the village to a new town and demolishing the now-vacant village, began digging at the sanctuary of Apollo. Their excavations began in 1892, proved fruitful and continued non-stop for the next eleven years; they have gone on sporadically ever since.

EVANS AND KNOSSOS

The beginning of the twentieth century saw the domination of Greek archaeology by an Englishman, **Sir Arthur Evans**. An egotistical maverick like Schliemann, he too was independently wealthy, with a brilliantly successful career behind him when he started his great work and recovered for Greek history another millennium. Evans excavated the **Palace of Minos** at **Knossos** on Crete, discovering one of the oldest and most sophisticated of Mediterranean societies.

The son of a distinguished antiquarian and collector, Evans read history at Oxford, failed to get a fellowship and began to travel. His chief interest was in the Balkans, where he was special corrspondent for the *Manchester Guardian* in the uprising in Bosnia. He took enormous risks in the war-torn country, filing brilliant dispatches and still finding time for exploration and excavation.

In 1884, at the age of 33, Evans was appointed curator of the Ashmolean museum in Oxford. He travelled whenever he could, and it was in 1893, while in Athens, that his attention was drawn to **Crete**. Evans, though very shortsighted, had almost microscopic close vision. In a vendor's stall he came upon some small drilled stones with tiny engravings in a hitherto unknown language; he was told they came from Crete. He had seen Schliemann's finds from Mycenae, and had been fascinated by this prehistoric culture. Crete, the crossroads of the Mediterranean, seemed a good place to look for more.

Evans visited Crete in 1894 and headed for the legendary site of **Knossos**, where a Cretan had already done some impromptu digging, revealing massive walls and a storeroom filled with jars. Evans bought a share of the site and five years later, after the Turks had been forced off the island, returned to purchase the rest of the land. Excavations began in March 1899 and within a few days evidence of a great complex building was revealed, along with artifacts which indicated an astonishing cultural sophistication. The huge team of excavation workers unearthed elegant courtyards and verandahs, colourful wall paintings, pottery and jewellery and sealstones – the wealth of a civilisation which dominated the eastern Mediterranean 3500 years ago.

Evans continued to excavate at Knossos for the next thirty years, during which time he established, on the basis of changes in the pottery styles, the system of dating that remains in use today for classifying Greek prehistory: Early, Middle and Late Minoan (Mycenean on the mainland). He published his account of the excavation in a massive six-volume work, *The Palace of Minos*, which appeared intermittently from 1921 to 36. Like Schliemann, Evans attracted criticism and controversy for his methods – most notably his decision to reconstruct parts of the palace – and many of his interpretations of what he found. Nevertheless, his discoveries and his dedication put him near to the pinnacle of Greek archaeology.

INTO THE 20TH CENTURY: THE FOREIGN INSTITUTES

In 1924 Evans gave to the **British School of Archaeology** the site of Knossos, along with the Villa Ariadne (his residence there) and all other lands within his possession on Crete. At the time the British school was one of several foreign archaeological institutes in Greece; founded in 1886, it had been preceded by the **French school**, the **German Institute** and the **American School**.

Greek archaeology owes much to the work and relative wealth of these foreign schools and others that would follow. They have been responsible for the excavation of many of the most famous sites in Greece: the **Heraion on Sámos** (German), the sacred island of **Delos** (French), sites on **Kós** and in **southern Crete** (Italian), **Corinth** and the **Athenian Agora** (American), to name but a few. Life as a resident foreigner in Greece at the beginning of the century was not for the weak spirited (one unfortunate member of the American school was shot and killed by bandits while on a trip to visit sites in the Peloponnese), but there were compensations in unlimited access to antiquities in a countryside as yet unscarred.

The years **between the two world wars** saw an expansion of excavation and scholarship, most markedly concerning the **prehistoric civilisations**. Having been shown by Schliemann and Evans what to look for, a new generation of archaeologists was uncovering numerous **prehistoric sites** on the mainland and Crete, and its members were spending proportionately more time studying and interpreting their finds. Digs in the 1920s and 1930s had much smaller labour forces (here were just 55 workmen under Wace at Mycenae, as compared to hundreds in the early days of Schliemann's or Evans' excavations) and they were supervised by higher numbers of trained archaeologists. Though perhaps not as spectacular as their predecessors, these scholars would prove just as pioneering as they established the history and clarified the chronology of the newly discovered civilisations.

One of the giants of this generation was **Alan Wace,** who while Director of the British School of Archaeology from 1913–23 conducted excavations at Mycenae and established a chronological sequence from the nine great tholos tombs on the site. This led Wace to propose a new chronology for prehistoric Greece, and put him in direct conflict with Arthur Evans. Evans believed that the mainland citadels had been ruled by Cretan overlords, whereas Wace was convinced of an independent Mycenaean cultural and political development. Evans was by this time a powerful member of the British School Managing Committee, and his published attacks on Wace's claims, combined with the younger archaeologist's less than tactful reactions to

Evans' dominating personality, resulted in the abrupt halt of the British excavations at Mycenae in 1923 and the no less sudden termination of Wace's job. Wace was pressured to leave Greece, and it was not until 1939 that he returned. In the interval his theories gained growing support from the archaeological community, and are today universally accepted.

Classical archaeology was not forgotten in the flush of excitement over the Mycenaeans and Minoans. The period between the wars saw the continuation of excavation at most established sites, and many new discoveries, among them the sanctuary of Asclepius and its elegant Roman buildings on **Kós**, excavated by the Italians from 1935 to 1943, and the Classical Greek city of **Olynthos**, in northern Greece, which was dug by the American school from 1928 to 1934. After the wholesale removal of houses and apartment blocks that had occupied the site, the American school also began excavations in the **Athenian Agora**, the ancient marketplace, in 1931, culminating in the complete restoration of the Stoa of Attalos.

The advent of **World War II** and the invasion of Greece first by the Italians and then the Germans called a halt to most archaeological work, although the Germans set to work again at **Olympia**, supposedly due to the personal interest in the site of Hitler.

A few Allied nation archaeologists also remained in Greece, principal among them **Gorham Stevens** and **Eugene Vanderpool**, of the American School, both of whom did charitable work. Back in America and Britain, meanwhile, archaeologists were in demand for the intelligence arm of the war effort, both for their intimate knowledge of the Greek terrain and their linguistic abilities, which proved invaluable in decoding enemy messages.

POST-WAR EXCAVATIONS

Archaeological work was greatly restricted in the years after World War II, and in the shadow of the Greek civil war. A few monuments and museums were restored and reopened but it was not until 1948 that excavations were resumed with a Greek clearance of the Sanctuary of Artemis at **Brauron** in Attica. In 1952 the American School resumed its activities with a dig at **Lerna** in the Peloponnese. Greek archaeologists began work at the Macedonian site of **Pella**, the **Necromanteion of Ephyra**, and, in a joint venture with the French, at the Minoan site of **Kato Zakros** on Crete.

These and many other excavations – including renewed work on the major sites – were, by comparison with earlier digs, relatively minor operations. This reflected a modified approach to archaeology, which laid less stress on discoveries than on documentation. Instead of digging large tracts of a site, archaeologists concentrated on small sections, establishing chronologies through meticulous **analysis** of data. Which is not to say that there were no **finds**. At Mycenae, in 1951, a second circle of graves was unearthed; at Pireás (Piraeus), a burst sewer in 1959 revealed four superb Classical bronzes; and a dig at the Kerameikos (cemetery) site in Athens in 1966 found 4000 potsherds used as ballots for ostracism. Important work has also been undertaken on **restorations** – in particular the **theatres** of the Athens Acropolis, Dodona and Epidaurus, which are used in summer festivals.

The two great post-war excavations, however, have been as exciting as any in the past. At **Akrotiri** on the island of **Thíra** (Santorini), Spiros Marinatos revealed, in 1967, a Minoan-era site that had been buried by volcanic explosion around 1550 BC. The buildings were two and three storeys high and superbly frescoed.

A decade later came an even more dramatic find at **Vergina**, in northern Greece. Here, Manolis Andronikos found a series of royal tombs dating from the fourth century BC. Unusually, these had escaped plundering by ancient grave robbers and contained an astonishing hoard of exquisite gold treasures. Piecing together clues – the hurriedness of the tomb's construction, an ivory head, gilded leg armour – Andronikos showed this to have been the tomb of Philip II of Macedon, father of Alexander the great. Subsequent forensic examination of the body supported historical accounts of Philip's limp and blindness.

It was an astonishing and highly emotive find, as the artifacts and frescoed walls showed the sophistication and Hellenism of ancient Macedonian culture. With the background of an emerging Macedonian state on Greece's northern border, archaeology had come head to head with politics.

WILDLIFE

Greek wildlife – and in particular flora – may well prove an unexpected source of fascination. In spring, the colour, scent and sheer variety of wild flowers, and the resulting wealth of insect life, are breath-taking. Isolated areas, whether they are true islands or remote mountains such as Olympus, have had many thousands of undisturbed years to develop their own individual species. Overall, there are some 6000 species of flowering plants (three times that of Britain, for example), many of them unique to Greece.

SOME BACKGROUND

Around 8000 years ago, Greece was thickly forested. Aleppo and maritime (Calabrian) pines grew in coastal regions, giving way to Cephallonian and silver fir or black pine up in the hills and low mountains. But early civilisations changed all that, and most of Greece, like most of Europe, is an artificial mosaic of habitats created by forest clearance followed by agriculture, either row crops or stock-grazing. As long ago as the fourth century BC, Plato was lamenting the felling of native forests on the hills around Athens. This wasn't all bad for wildlife, though: the scrubby hillsides created by forest clearing and subsequent grazing are one of the richest habitats of all.

In this century, Greece has on the whole escaped the intensification of agriculture so obvious in Northern Europe. For the most part,

crops are still grown in small fields and without excessive use of pesticides and herbicides, while flocks of goats graze the hillsides in much the same way as they have done for the last few thousand years. On the minus side is damage from rapid development of industry, logging and tourism, all carried out with little sympathy for the environment. The pollution around Athens and Pireás, in particular, is appalling, while new hotels and resorts have often destroyed rich wildlife areas. In the Ionian, for example, the breeding grounds of the loggerhead turtle have been put under threat by tourist development of beaches.

One peculiarly Greek bonus to the naturalist is that wildlife here probably has the longest recorded history of anywhere in the world. Aristotle was a keen naturalist, Theophrastus in the fourth century BC was one of the earliest botanists, and Dioscorides, a physician in the first century AD, wrote a comprehensive book on the herbal uses of plants.

FLOWERS

What you will see of the Greek **flora** depends on where and when you go. Plants cease flowering (or even living, in the case of annuals) when it is too hot and dry for them – the high summer in Greece does the same to plants as does the winter in northern Europe. So, if you want to see flowers in high summer, head for the mountains.

The best time to go is **spring** – which comes to the south coast of Crete in early March, to the northern Píndhos mountains as late as the end of June. In early **summer**, the spring anemones, orchids and rockroses are replaced by plants like brooms and chrysanthemums. The onset of summer ranges from late April in southern Crete to late August or even early September in the high northern mountains.

Once the worst heat is over, there is a burst of activity on the part of **autumn** flowering species such as cyclamens and autumn crocus, flowering from October in the north into December in the south. And the first of the spring bulbs flower in January!

SEASHORE

You might find the spectacular yellow horned poppy growing on shingled banks, and sea stocks and Virginia stocks among the rocks behind the beach. A small pink campion, *Silene colourata*, is often colourfully present.

Sand dunes are rare in Greece, but sometimes there is a flat grazed area behind the beach; these can be fertile ground for orchids. Tamarisk trees often grow down to the shore, and there are frequent groves of Europe's largest grass, the giant calamus reed, which can reach 4m high.

In the autumn, look for the very large white flowers of the sea daffodil, as well as autumn crocuses on the banks behind the shore. The sea squill also flowers in early autumn, with tall spikes of white flowers rising from huge bulbs.

CULTIVATED LAND

Avoid large fields and plantations, but look for small hay meadows. These are often brilliant with annual **"weeds"** in late spring – various chrysanthemum species, wild gladiolus, perhaps wild tulips (especially in Crete and the central Peloponnese), and in general a mass of colour such as you rarely see in northern Europe. (Hot summers force plants into flowering simultaneously.) Fallow farmland is also good for flowers; you can often find deserted terraces full of cyclamens, anemones and orchids.

LOW HILLSIDES

This is a versatile habitat. The trees and shrubs are varied and beautiful, with colourful brooms flowering in early summer, preceded by bushy rockroses – *Cistaceae* – which are a mass of pink or white flowers in spring. Scattered among the shrubs is the occasional tree, such as the Judas tree, which flowers on bare wood in spring, making a blaze of pink against the green hillsides, and stands out for miles.

Lower than the shrubs are the **aromatic herbs** – sage, rosemary, thyme and lavender – with perhaps some spiny species of *Euphorbia*. These occur principally on the *frígana*, limestone slopes scattered with scrubby bushes. (The other hillside type, *maquis*, with its dense prickly scrub, is better for birds.)

Below the herbs is the ground layer; peer around the edges and between the shrubs and you will find a wealth of orchids, anemones, grape hyacinths, irises and perhaps fritillaries if you are lucky. The **orchids** are extraordinary;

some kinds – the *Ophrys* species – imitate insect colouration in order to attract them for pollination, and have delicate and unusual flowers. They're much smaller and altogether more dignified than the big blowsy tropical orchids that you see in florists' shops. The **irises** are beauties, too; of them, a small, blue species called *Iris sisyrinchium* only flowers in the afternoon, and you can actually sit and watch them open around midday.

Once the heat of the summer is over, the **autumn bulbs** come into their own, with species of crocus and their relatives, the colchicums and the sternbergias, more squills and finally the autumn cyclamens flowering through into early December. Heather (genus *Erica*) provides a blaze of pink on acidic slopes around the New Year.

MOUNTAINS

These are good to visit later in the season, with flowers until June in water-scarce Crete, and well into August on Olympus and in the Píndhos. The rocky mountain gorges are the home of many familiar garden rock plants, such as the aubretias, saxifrages and alyssums, as well as dwarf bellflowers and anemones.

The mountains are also the place to see the remaining Greek native coniferous and deciduous forests, and in the woodland glades you will find gentians, cyclamens, violets and perhaps some of the rare and dramatic lilies, such as the crimson *Lilium heldrecheii*. Above 1700m or so the forests begin to thin out, with treeline at about 1900m, and in some of these upland meadows you will find the loveliest crocuses, flowering almost before the snow has melted in spring. As in the lowlands, autumn-flowering species of crocus make a visit worthwhile later in the year.

BIRDS

Greece has a large range of the resident **Mediterranean species**, plus one or two very rare ones such as the Ruppells warbler and the lammergeier vulture, which have most of their European breeding strongholds in Greece.

The great thing about birdwatching here is that, if you pick your time right, you can see both resident and **migratory species**. Greece is on the main flyway for species that have wintered in East Africa, but breed in northern

Europe; they migrate every spring up the Nile valley, and then move across the eastern Mediterranean, often in huge numbers. This happens from mid-March to mid-May, depending on the species and the weather. The return migration in autumn is less spectacular because less concentrated, but still worth watching out for.

On the outskirts of towns and in the fields there are some colourful residents. Small **predatory birds** such as woodchat shrikes, kestrels and red-footed falcons can be seen perched on telegraph wires, and lesser kestrels nest communally and noisily in many small towns and villages. The dramatic pink, black and white hoopoe and the striking yellow and black golden oriole are sparsely represented in woodland and olive groves, and Scops owls (Europe's smallest owl) can often be heard calling around towns at night. They repeat a monotonous single "poo" sound, sometimes in mournful vocal duets.

Look closely at the **swifts and swallows**, and you will notice a few species not found in northern Europe; some of the swallows will be red-rumped, for example, and you may see the large alpine swift, which has a white belly. The Sardinian warbler dominates the rough scrubby hillsides, the male with a glossy black cap and an obvious red eye.

Wetlands and coastal lagoons are excellent bird territories, especially at spring and autumn migration. Both European species of pelican breed in Greece, and there is a wide variety of herons and egrets, as well as smaller waders such as the avocet and the black-winged stilt, which has ridiculously long, pink legs. The coast is often the best place to see migration, too. Most birds migrate up the coast, navigating by the stars; a thick mist or heavy cloud will force them to land, and you can sometimes see spectacular "falls" of migrators.

The most exciting birds, however, are to be seen in **the mountains**. Smaller birds like blue rock thrush, alpine chough and rock nuthatch are pretty common, and there is a good chance of seeing large and dramatic birds of prey. The buzzards and smaller eagles are confusingly similar, but there are also golden eagles. The Greek mountains contain all four European species of **vulture**. The small black and white Egyptian vulture, with a one-metre wingspan, is the commonest, but you might also see the **black** or the **griffon vulture**, which have three-metre wingspans and look like flying tables. The final vulture is the **lammergeier**, also with a three-meter wingspan but narrower wings, once almost extinct in Europe but now recovering slowly.

MAMMALS

Greek mammals include the usual range of rats, mice and voles, and some interesting medium-sized creatures, like the beech marten. There is also a fairly typical range of European species such as fox, badger, red squirrel, hare and so on, though the Greek hedgehog is distinctive in having a white breast.

Again it's the **mountains** that host the really exciting species. In the north, the ranges are home to some of the last remnants of big mammals that used to be widespread in the European forests and mountains. **Wolves**, **brown bears**, **lynx**, **chamois** and **wild boar** are all present, though the chance of the average traveller seeing one are slim to say the least. The Rhodhópi hills, north of Xánthi on the Bulgarian border, and the Elatía (Kara Dere) valleys north of Dhráma, are good places to go to try to see these rare mammals, as are the Píndhos around mounts Gamíla and Smólikas, between Ioánnina and Kónitsa. A rare **ibex**, known locally as the kri-kri, is found around the Samaria gorge in Crete, as well as on some of the islets offshore.

The extremely rare Mediterranean **monk seal** (see p.597) also breeds on some stretches of remote coast; if spotted, it should be treated with deferent distance – it's endangered and easily scared away from its habitat.

REPTILES AND AMPHIBIANS

A hot, rocky country like Greece suits reptiles well and there are over forty indigenous species, half of the European total. Many of these are **wall lizards**. Most of the islands have their own species, all confusingly similar: small lizards with a brownish striped back, often with an orange or yellow belly. Sit and watch a dry, sunny wall almost anywhere in Greece and you're bound to see them.

On a few islands, notably the Dodecanese and the northern Cyclades, you may see the **agama** or **Rhodes dragon**. Growing up to

30cm, though usually smaller, they really do look like miniature, spiny-backed dragons with a series of pale diamonds on a brown or grey background.

In the bushes of the maquis and *frígana* you may see the **Balkan green lizard**, a truly splendid, brightly tinted animal up to half a metre long, most of which is tail; you can often spot it running on its hind legs, as if possessed, from one bush to another.

At night, **geckos** replace the lizards. Geckos are small (less than 10cm long), have big eyes, and round adhesive pads on their toes which enable them to walk upside down on the ceiling. Sometimes they come into houses, in which case welcome them, since they will keep down the mosquitoes and other biting insects. The **chameleon** is found infrequently in eastern Crete and some of the northern Aegean islands such as Sámos. It lives in bushes and low trees, and hunts by day; its colour is greenish but (obviously) variable.

All three European **tortoises** occur in Greece. They have suffered to varying extents from collection for the pet trade but you can still find them easily enough, on sunny hillsides. The best time is mid-morning, when they'll be basking between the shrubs and rocks. They come in all sizes depending on age – from 5cm to 30cm long. A good way to find them is by ear; they make a constant rustle as they lumber around, and if you find one, look for more, since they often seem to stick together.

A closely related reptile is the **terrapin**, which is basically an aquatic tortoise. Again, both European species occur in Greece, and they're worth looking for in any freshwater lakes or ponds, including on the islands. There are also **sea turtles** in the Ionian; you might be lucky and see one while you're swimming or on a boat, since they sometimes bask on the surface of the water. The one you're most likely to see is the **loggerhead turtle** (*Caretta caretta*), which can grow up to a metre long. It is endangered, and protected (see p.630).

The final group of reptiles are the **snakes**. Greece has plenty of them, but (as in most habitats) they're shy and easily frightened. Although most snakes are non-poisonous, Greece does have a number of viper species, which are front-fanged venomous snakes, including the nose-horned viper, as poisonous as they come in Europe.

Snakes actually cause only a handful of deaths a year in Europe but they should nonetheless be treated with with respect. If you get bitten, sit and wait to see if a swelling develops. If it doesn't, then the snake was harmless or didn't inject venom. If it does, move the area bitten as little as possible, and get medical attention. Don't try anything fancy like cutting or sucking the wound, but bind the limb firmly so as to slow down the blood circulation (but not so tightly as to stop the blood flow).

Greek **amphibians** either have tails (newts and salamanders) or they don't (frogs and toads). Newts can be seen in a few alpine tarns; search for salamanders in ponds at breeding time, and under stones and in moist crevices outside the breeding season.

You can't miss the frogs and toads, especially in spring. Greece has the **green toad**, which has an obvious marbled green and grey back, as well as the common toad. **Tree frogs** are small, live in trees, and call very noisily at night. They have a stripe down the flank and vary in colour from bright green to golden brown, depending on where they are sitting – they can change colour like a chameleon.

INSECTS

About a third of all insect species are **beetles**, and these are very obvious in Greece. You might see one of the dung beetles rolling a ball of dung along a path like the mythological Sisyphus, or a rhinoceros-horned beetle digging a hole in a sand dune.

The **grasshopper** and **cricket** family are well represented, and most patches of grass will hold a few. Grasshoppers produce their chirping noise by rubbing a wing against a leg, but crickets do it by rubbing both wings together. **Cicadas**, which most people think of as a type of grasshopper or locust, aren't actually related at all – they're more of a large leafhopper. Their continuous whirring call is one of the characteristic sounds of the Mediterranean noontime, and is produced by the rapid vibration of two cavities called tymbals on either side of the body. If you have time to look closely at bushes and small trees, you might be rewarded with a stick insect or a **praying mantis**, insects that are rarely seen because of their excellent camouflage.

The most obvious Greek insects are the **butterflies**. Any time from spring through most of the summer is good for butterfly-spotting, and there's usually a second flight of adults of many species in the autumn.

Dramatic species include three species of **swallowtail**, easily distinguished by their large size, yellow and black shading, and long spurs at the back of the hind wings. **Cleopatras** are large, brilliant yellow butterflies, related to the brimstone of northern Europe, but larger and more colourful. Look out for **green hairstreaks** – a small green jewel of a butterfly that is particularly attracted to the flowers of the asphodel, a widespread plant of overgrazed pastures and hillsides.

One final species typical of southern Greece and the islands are the **festoons**, unusual butterflies with tropical colours, covered in yellow, red and black zigzags.

FLORA AND FAUNA FIELD GUIDES

MEDITERRANEAN WILDLIFE

Pete Raine *Mediterranean Wildlife* (Penguin, UK). A good overview of Mediterranean wildlife, written by the author of the preceding essay, which it expands upon, along with a site by site guide to the best Greek wildlife habitats.

FLOWERS

Anthony Huxley and William Taylor *Flowers of Greece and the Aegean* (Hogarth Press, UK). Best book for flower identification. It doesn't describe all the Greek flowers – no book does – but it's an excellent general guide with quality photographic illustrations.

Oleg Polunin *Flowers of Greece and the Balkans* (Oxford University Press, UK/US). Good on the mountain biomes.

Paul and Jenne Davies *The Wild Orchids of Britain and Europe* (Chatto & Windus, UK). A splendid book for orchid freaks, with details on where to look for them – including sites in Greece.

BIRDS

Petersen, Mountfort and Hollom *Field Guide to the Birds of Britain and Europe* (Collins, UK/ Stephen Green Press, US); **Heinzel, Fitter and Parslow** *Collins Guide to the Birds of Britain and Europe* (Collins, UK/Stephen Green Press, US). There are no specific reference books on Greek birds. These two European field guides have the best coverage, with the former, ageing but excellent, retaining an edge.

Michael Shepherd *Let's Look at North-East Greece* (Ornitholidays). Useful short guide published by a British holiday company.

MAMMALS

Corbet and Ovenden *Collins Guide to the Mammals of Europe* (Collins, UK/Stephen Green Press, US). As good a guide as they come.

INSECTS

Michael Chinery *Collins Guide to the Insects of Britain and Western Europe* (Collins, UK/Stephen Green Press, US). Although this doesn't include Greece, it gives good general information about the main insects you may see.

Higgins and Riley *A Field Guide to the Butterflies of Britain and Europe* (Collins, UK/Stephen Green Press, US). A field guide that will sort out all the butterflies for you, though it's a bit detailed for the casual naturalist.

REPTILES

Arnold and Burton *Collins Guide to the Reptiles and Amphibians of Britain and Europe* (Collins, UK/ Stephen Green Press, US). A useful guide which, infuriatingly for Greek travellers, excludes the Dodecanese and eastern Aegean islands.

MUSIC

Music, like most Greek cultural traditions, is a mix of East and West. The older songs, invariably in Eastern-flavoured minor keys, have direct precedents in the forms and styles of both the religious chants of the Byzantines and of medieval Turkey and Iran, and almost all native Greek instruments are descendants, or near-duplicates, of ones used thoughout the Islamic world. To this Middle Eastern base both Slavs and Italians have added their share, and as a result the repertoire of traditional and more modern Greek pieces is extraordinarily varied.

REGIONAL FOLK MUSIC

The most promising times to hear regional folk music are at the numerous **summer festivals** – local saints' day ones, as well as larger cultural programmes – when musicians (who are often based in Athens or city clubs in winter) tour the islands and villages.

CRETE, KÁSSOS AND KÁRPATHOS

This arc of southern islands is the most promising area in Greece for hearing live music at any season of the year. The main instrument here is the **lyra**, a three-stringed fiddle directly related to the Turkish kemençe. This is played not on the shoulder but balanced on the thigh, often with tiny bells attached to the bow, which the musician can jiggle for rhythmical accent. The strings are metal, and since the centre one is just a drone the player improvises only on the outer two – a unique, intriguing sound.

Usually the *lyra* is backed up by one or more **laoúta**, similar to the Turkish/Arab *oud* and not unlike the medieval lute. These are rarely used to their full potential but a good player will find the harmonics and overtones of a virtuoso *lyra* piece, at the same time coaxing a pleasing, chime-like tone from his instrument. A *laoúto* solo is an uncommon treat.

In several places in the southern Aegean, notably traditional Kárpathos, a primitive bagpipe, the **askómandra** or **tsamboúna**, joins the *lyra* and *laoúto*. During the colonels' dictatorship the playing of the bagpipe in the Cyclades further north was banned lest anyone think the Greeks too primitive – though hopefully, all concerned have recovered from any sense of cultural inferiority. If you remember Kazantzakis's classic novel (or the movie), Zorba himself played a **santoúri**, or hammer dulcimer, for recreation. Today, accomplished players are few and in *Kritikí* (Cretan music), *nisiotiká* (island songs) and *rembétika* (see below), it's been relegated to a supporting role.

On older recordings you may hear solos on the *voúlgari*, a stringed instrument, essentially a small *saz* (Turkish long-necked, fretted lute), which has all but died out today.

OTHER AEGEAN ISLANDS

On most of the Aegean islands, and particularly the Cyclades, you'll find the *lyra* replaced by a more familiar-looking **violí**, essentially a western violin. The music is lyrical and usually uptempo. Backing is again often provided by *laoúto* or *santoúri*, though these days you're more likely to be confronted with a rock-'n'-roll-type, bass-guitar-and-drum rhythm section. Hilltop shepherds sometimes pass the time fashioning a reed-wailer known as the *karamoúza*, made from two goat horns.

Unlike on Crete, where you can often catch the best music in special clubs or *kéndra*, Aegean island performances tend to be spontaneous and less specialised. Festivals and saints' days in a village square are as usual the most promising times and venues

IONIAN ISLANDS

Alone of all modern Greek territory, the Ionian islands never saw Turkish occupation and have a predominantly western musical tradition. The indigenous song-form is Italian both in name, (**kantádhes**) and instrumentation (guitar, mandolin); it's most often heard these days on **Lefkádha** and **Zákinthos**.

THE PELOPONNESE, CENTRAL GREECE AND EPIRUS

The folk lyrics of the the Peloponnese, central and western Greece generally hark back to the years of Turkish occupation and to the War of Independence. The main type of music is **paleá dhimotiká**, traditional folk ballads with very basic accompaniment on the klaríno (clarinet). Kithára (guitar), laoúto, violí, and toumberléki (lap drum) or défi (tambourine) can also add to the backing.

The music of **Epirus** still exhibits strong connections with that of neighbouring Albania and (ex-)Yugoslav Macedonia, particularly in the polyphonic pieces sung by both men and women. They tend to fall into three basic categories, which are also found further south: **mirolóyia** or laments (the instrumental counterpart is called skáros); drinking songs or **tis távlas**; and various danceable melodies. As throughout the mainland, the clarinet tradition is almost wholly the domain of gypsies.

Most pieces are danceable, and they are divided by rhythm into such categories as kalamatianó, tsámiko, hasaposérviko or syrtó. Those that are not include the slow, stately kleftikó, similar to the rizítiko of Crete, both of which relate, baldly or in metaphor, incidents or attitudes from the years of the Ottomans and the rebellions for freedom.

Since the paleá dhimotiká are strongly associated with national identity, it's not surprising that they were for many years pressed into political service. During election campaigns each party's local storefront-headquarters or soundtrucks blasted out continuous paleá dhimotiká interspersed with political harangues. Since 1989, however, this practice has been (officially) banned.

THRACE AND THE NORTH

Thrace and **Macedonia** were in the hands of the Ottomans until the beginning of this century, with a bewilderingly mixed population, so music here – louder and less lyrical than in the south – has an unremitting Oriental feel.

The Thracian **kavál**, or end-blown flute, is identical to the Turkish article (and to the disappearing floyéra of the south mainland); so, too, is the northern bagpipe, or **gaída**.

In Macedonia you'll find the **zournás**, a screechy, double-reed oboe similar to the Islamic world's shenai. It's much in evidence at local festivals, as is the **daoúli**, or deep-toned drum. The klaríno and toumberléki are not unknown, either, but even in their presence dances are fast and hard-stamping.

REMBÉTIKA

Rembétika began as the music of the Greek urban dispossessed – criminals, refugees, drug-users, defiers of social norms. It has existed in some form in Greece since at least the turn of the century. But it is as difficult to define or get to the origins of as jazz or blues, with which it shares marked similarities in spirit and circumstance.

The themes of the songs – illicit love, drug addiction, police oppression, disease and death – and the tone of the delivery – resignation to the singer's lot, coupled with defiance of authority – will certainly be familiar. But even the word "rembétika" is of uncertain derivation, the most likely one being rembet, an old Turkish word meaning "of the gutter", and searches for the birth of rembétika must be conducted in the Asia Minor of the last years of the Ottoman empire as well as in Greece proper.

Most outsiders equate Greek music with the **bouzoúki**, a long-necked, fretted lute derived from the Turkish saz and baglamá, though early in this century only a small proportion of Greek musicians used it. At the same time, across the Aegean in Smyrna and Constantinople, musical cafés had become popular. Groups usually featured a violinist, a santoúri (hammer dulcimer) player and a female vocalist, who usually jingled castanets and danced on stage. The style was known as café-amanés or just **amanédhes**, after both the setting and the frequent repetition of the exclamation aman aman (alas, alas), used both for its sense and to fill time while the performers searched their imaginations for more explicit lyrics.

Despite a sparse instrumentation, this was an elegant, riveting music, and a style of singing requiring considerable skill, harking back to similar vocalisation in Central Asia. Some of its greatest practitioners included **"Dalgas"** (Wave), so nicknamed for the undulations in his voice; **Rosa Eskenazi**, originally from Istanbul;

her contemporary **Rita Abatzi**, from Smyrna; and **Dhimitris "Salonikiye" Semsis**, a master fiddler from Macedonia.

The 1923 **exchange of populations** was a key event in the history of *rembétika*, resulting in the influx to Greece of over a million Asia Minor Greeks, many of whom settled in shanty-towns around Athens and Pireás. The musicians, like most of the other refugees, were, in comparison to the Greeks of the host country, extremely sophisticated; many were highly educated, could read and compose music, and had even been unionised in the towns of Asia Minor. It was galling for them to live on the periphery of the new society in poverty and degradation; most had lost all they had in the hasty evacuation, and many, from inland Anatolia, could speak only Turkish. In their misery they sought relief in another Ottoman institution, the *tekés* or hashish den.

In the **tekédhes** of Pireás, Athens and Thessaloníki, a few men would sit on the floor around a charcoal brazier, passing around a *nargilés* (hookah) filled with hashish. One of them might begin to improvise a tune on the *baglamá* or the *bouzoúki* and begin to sing. The words, either his own or those of the other *dervíses* ("dervishes" – many *rembetic* terms were a burlesque of those of mystical Islamic tradition), would be heavily laced with slang, in the manner of the Harlem jive of the same era – a way of keeping outsiders at bay. As the *taksími* (long, studied introduction) was completed, one of the smokers might rise and begin to dance a **zeibékiko**, named after a warrior caste of western Anatolia. It would be a slow, intense, introverted performance following an unusual metre (9/8), not for the benefit of others but for himself.

Markos Vamvakaris was one of the greatest performers to emerge from the *tekés* culture. His proficiency on the *bouzoúki* was indisputable, though he protested to his friends that his voice, ruined perhaps from too much hash-smoking, was no good for singing. But he bowed to their encouragement and his gravelly, unmistakeable sound set the standard for male vocals over the next decade.

This "Golden Age" of *rembétika* – as indeed it was, despite the unhappy lives of many performers – was short-lived. The association of the music with this underworld would prove its undoing. The harder-core musicians, with their uncompromising lyrics and lifestyles, were blackballed by the recording industry; hashish was outlawed in the early 1930s, and police harassment of the *tekédhes* was stepped up after the Metaxas dictatorship took power in 1936. Even possession of a *bouzoúki* or a *baglamá* became a criminal offence. Most of the big names served time in jail.

For a while, the persecution failed to dim the enthusiasm of the **mánges** (roughly translatable as "wide boys" or "hep cats"). They were notoriously generous and impulsive, if occasionally violent and unscrupulous, and appeared to enjoy life to the fullest. Beatings or prison terms were taken in their stride; time behind bars could be used, as it always had been around the Aegean, to make *skaptó* (dug-out) instruments. A *baglamá* could easily be fashioned from a gourd cut in half (the sound box), a piece of wood (the neck), catgut (frets), and wire for strings. Jail songs were composed and became popular in the underworld; the excerpt below (very freely translated from the *mangiká* or argot) is typical:

I Lahanádhes (The Pickpockets)

Down in Lemonádhika there was a ruckus
They caught two pickpockets who acted innocent
They took 'em to the slammer in handcuffs
They'll get a beating if they don't cough up the loot.
Don't beat us, coppers, you know very well
This is our job, and don't ask for bribes.
We lift purses and wallets so we can
Have a regular rest in jail.

Kostas Roukounas (1934)

Not too surprisingly, the *rembétes* suffered from the disapproval of the puritanical left as well as the puritanical right; the growing Communist Party of the 1930s considered the music and its habitués hopelessly decadent and counter-revolutionary. There was some overlap, however, in the 1940s, as the singers of *andártika* (resistance songs) learned the lesson of referring in code to issues that were not publicly discussable. Another exception from the later decade was Sotiria Bellou, a *rembétissa* (female rembetic musician) and active Communist.

In general, however, the Metaxas era and World War II signalled the decline of the authentic *rembetic* tradition. Worthwhile material was certainly composed and recorded between 1936 and 1955 – notably the work of

Ioanna Yiorgakopoulou, **Vassilis Tsitsanis** and **Marika Ninou** – but by the 1950s the music was most often characterised by maudlin lyrics and over-orchestration. The addition of an extra string to the *bouzoúki*, and its subsequent electrification, turned a delicate, lightly strung instrument into an overamplified monstrosity. The presentation, in huge, barnlike clubs, became debased and vulgarised. Virtuoso *bouzoúki* players, assisted by kewpie-doll-type female vocalists, became immensely rich. The clubs themselves, also called *bouzoúkia*, were clip-joints where Athenians paid large sums to break plates and to watch dancing whose flashy steps and gyrations were a travesty of the simple dignity and precise, synchronised footwork of the old style.

Ironically, the original *rembétika* material was rescued from oblivion by the colonels. Along with dozens of other highpoints of Greek culture, *rembetik* verses were banned. The younger generation coming of age under the dictatorship took a closer look at the forbidden fruit and derived solace, and deeper meanings, from the nominally apolitical lyrics. When the junta fell in 1974 – and even a little before – there was an outpouring of reissued recordings of the old masters.

Over the next decade live *rembétika* also enjoyed a revival, beginning with a clandestine 1979 club whose *rembetik* credentials were validated when it was raided and closed by the police. Today, however, the fashion has long since peaked, and only a handful of clubs and bands remain from the dozens which made their appearance between 1978 and 1986.

NÉO KÍMA, THEODORAKIS AND CONTEMPRARY MUSIC

Néo Kíma (New Wave) music emerged in small Athenian clubs, or *boîtes*, during the early 1960s. It was in part a rediscovery of the forms of *rembétika*, in part a politicised folk movement with connections to such trends as the Latin American *Nueva Canción*. Like them, its young, improvisatory composers strongly identified with the Communists, whose revolutionary songs from the 1940s they revived and adapted. Like *rembétika* bars, most of the *Néo Kíma* boites were closed down during the 1967–74 military junta.

Although not directly associated with the *Néo Kíma* movement, Mikis Theodorakis and Manos Hadzikakis, the two best-known modern Greek composers – had much in common with its spirit.

Theodorakis's international reputation is perhaps a bit overblown, due to his overplayed soundtrack for *Zorba the Greek*. However, he is an interesting character – a long-time Communist dissident and MP who suddenly shifted right to become a *Néa Dhimokratía* (conservative) Minister Without Portfolio – and he deserves a listening for his astonishing settings of poetry by **Odysseas Elytis**, and his work with the *Horodhia Trikalon* (The Trikala Choir) and vocalist **Maria Farandouri**. Farandouri, like Theodorakis a member of the Greek-Turkish Friendship Society, has also appeared on a few popular albums in the 1980s with Turkish protest musician Zülfü Livaneli.

Hadzidakis has mostly steered clear of political statements; instead he launched, during the 1980s, his own record label, *Sirios*, to provide a forum for various non-mainstream musicians. Like Theodorakis, his own compositional weakness is a tendency towards quasi-symphonic, highly arranged instrumentation.

Somewhat less well known, but perhaps more interesting, are the more vernacular Greek sounds of the third big composer to emerge in the 1960s, the Cretan **Ioannis Markopoulos**. His material mixes authentic folk material and instruments in juxtapositions never heard in their natural environment.

Perhaps the first musician to break out of the *bouzoúki* mould was **Dhionisios Savvopoulos**, who appeared on the scene in the mid-1960s with his maniacal, rasping voice and elliptical, angst-ridden lyrics, his persona rounded out by shoulder-length hair and outsized glasses. Because his material was not overtly political, Savvopoulos was one of the few "protest" artists able to perform under the junta, and was something of a consolation and password to the generation coming of age under it; Thessaloníki born, he paid due homage to the gypsy tradition in Greek music. Recently, however, he did a bit of a Cliff Richard, with a much-publicised return to the Orthodox Church and a new image celebrated in a recent album, *To Kourema* – The Haircut.

A more explicit tip of the hat to the gypsies was made by **Nikos Ksidhakis and Nikos Papazoglou** in their landmark 1978 pressing, *Ekdhikosi tis Yiftias* (The Revenge of

Gypsydom). The spirited, defiant lyrics and highly rhythmic melodies were both homage to and send-up the sort of music beloved by the itinerant truck-drivers who peddle cheap bedding and potted plants in rural Greece. The pair later edged more explicitly into the territory of urban folk and even *rembétika* without completely forsaking gypsydom. More recently, Ksidhakis collaborated with Ross Daly (see below) and vocalist Eleftheria Arvanitaki on *Konda sti Doxa mia Stigmi* – which is simply one of the best Greek discs ever.

Also from northern Greece came *Himerini Kolimvites*, a group of architects led by Aryiris Bakirtzis, whose eponymous first album has acquired enduring cult status in the decade since its 1981 release. *Rembetik*, mainland pop and even island models are set on their ear with rich, drunken harmonies drawn out on both bowed and plucked strings, and utterly surreal lyrics. A Greek Pogues, if you will.

Less easily categorised is the work of **Stamatis Kraounakis and Lina Nikolakopoulou**, whose 1985 *Kykloforo keh Oploforo* was a thoughtful, if slick, exploration of the boundary between rock, jazz-cabaret and *éntehno* (art composition) styles; their more recent collaboration, *Mama Yernao* features veteran Tania Tsanaklidou on vocals in her last professional appearance.

Another Greek approach in the 1970s and early 80s was to combine **folk and Byzantine traditions**. Instrument maker and arranger **Hristodhoulos Halaris** followed up a version of the Cretan epic *Erotokritos* with a film soundtrack, *O Megalexandros* (Alexander the Great), that introduced **Hrisanthos**, a male singer with a distinctive high-register voice. Halaris has gone on to concentrate exclusively on Byzantine chants, reworking the hymns of Constantinople composer Petros Peloponnisios.

Medieval – rather than Byzantine – Constantinopolitan was the emphasis of **Vosforos**, a group coordinated in Istanbul by **Nikiforos Metaxas** to preserve and play Ottoman classical, devotional and popular music. Their specific appeal and pertinence to Grecophiles was demonstrated by the contents

A SELECTIVE DISCOGRAPHY

Excellent recordings of Greek music are available from all eras. All releases below are Greek, unless another country of origin is stated.

TRADITIONAL MAINLAND MUSIC

Songs of . . . (Society for the Dissemination of National Music; SDNM). A series of sixteen albums, each covering the traditional music of one region. All contain information in English.

Greek Folk Music (Peloponnesian Folklore Foundation; 2 vols). A wonderful introduction to *paleá dhimotiká*.

Greek Traditional Music: A Musical Atlas of Greece (EMI Odeon 3C 064 17966, Unesco Musical Atlas series #8). Don't be put off by the subtitle, this is an excellent collection – as are most of the UNESCO projects.

Yiorgos Mangas (GlobeStyle CDORB 021, UK). Clarinet virtuoso, with backup band, playing traditional music in a modern, slightly jazzy style.

Inedit-Grèce–Epire: **Takoutsia, musiciens de Zagori** (Maison des Cultures du Monde, France). Drinking songs, dance tunes and laments recorded live by one of the last working gypsy clans.

Grèce –Chants polyphoniques et musique d'Epire (Ocora 558631, France). One of the best recordings from Epirus. *Klarino*, frame drums and bells for the dances; polyphonic chorus for ballads and laments. French release but widely available.

I Protomastores, 1920–1940 (AEME TC117-8; double LP/cassette). A collection of old songs from Asia Minor, Epirus, central Greece and the Peloponnese. Sheer delight from beginning to end.

TRADITIONAL CRETAN AND ISLAND MUSIC

I Protomastores, 1920–1940 (AEME 11/12). The best Cretan music from between the wars, played on instruments that in cases have all but died out.

Greek Music from the Island of Crete (Lyrichord LLST 7293). A good mixture of ballads and dance tunes, played on *lyra*, *laoúto* and *askómandhra*.

Songs and Dances of the Aegean Islands (Minerva 22042). Hard to find but highly recommended collection of songs and dances from Crete, the Dodecanese and Cyclades islands.

Nikos Skevakis *Fotia me Kaei keh Pono* (Panivar 5283). One of the best all-round Cretan recordings, with everyone playing like they mean it.

and packaging of their first album *Vosforos*, subtitled "Greek Composers of the City" (ie Contantinople) and concentrating on the contribution of Greek and other non-Turkish musicians to the Ottoman courtly tradition. In more recent concerts and recordings the group varied the programme with west Anatolian dance pieces and even Istanbul taverna songs from the turn of the century.

Ross Daly, whose interests and style frequently overlap those of *Vosforos*, is also worth looking out for on disc or live, both in Athens clubs or on tour. English-born but Irish by background, Daly plays a dozen traditional instruments and has absorbed influences not only from Crete, where he was long resident, but from throughout the Near East. Alone or with his group, his vaguely New Age/contemporary interpretations of folk tunes or original compositions are unmistakeable.

More modest in scale and aims is **Dhinameis tou Egeou**, a trio (later increased to five musicians) who, despite some ill-advised noodling with bells, sitar and Egyptian *ney*, are the most accessible folk/island/*Smyrneika* revival group currently going. Their original compositions are often as interesting as the older material – a good omen for the future.

Finally, this round-up would be incomplete without a mention of **Yiorgos (George) Dalaras**, a musical phenomenon in Greece for the last twenty years – and often dubbed the "Greek Springsteen". Born in 1950, the son of a Pireás *rembétika* player, Dalaras has spanned the gamut of Greek music, recording over forty LPs, ranging through Asia Minor and *dhimotiká* songs, the works of Theodorakis, Hadjidakis and Markopoulo, and, most recently, collaborations with the flamenco guitarist Paco de Lucia and American blues star, Al De Meola.

Although something of a national institution, Dalaras remained through the junta years a fierce supporter of popular struggles and has scrupulously avoided the banalities of the *bouzoúki* pop scene. In Greece, his concerts pack 80,000 at a time into football stadiums – rather more than the football teams themselves – and they produce rivers of tears.

Musica Populare del Dodecaneso (Albatros VPA 8295, Italy). A variety of dances, laments and dirges from the Dodecanese, including some wonderful dances from Kos.

Irini Konitopoulou *Athanata Nisiotika* (Perennial Island Songs); also known as *Nisiotikes Epitihies* (Island Successes). The tape(s), often bootlegged, that are beloved of every island bus driver, and no less good for all that.

REMBÉTIKA

I Rembétiki Istoria 1922–1955 (EMI 70364-66, 70378-80; 6 vols). A superb anthology – volumes 1 and 4, are entirely old pieces from Smyrna and Anatolia; the others are more of a mixed bag.

I Megali tou Rembetikou (Margo 8000 series). A series of over 20 discs, arranged by the artist rather than chronologically. Highlights are #1 (Early performers), #2 (Apostolos Hadzikhristos), #5 (the great Sotiria Bellou), #6 (Markos Vamvakaris) and #8 (Kostas Roukounas).

Vangelis Papazoglou, 1897–1943 (Falirea Brothers 1132-3). A double album of classic songs from the 1930s written by Papazoglou and sung by many of the great stars of the era including Stellakis, Rosa Eskenazi, Kostas Roukounas and Rita Abatzi.

Anestis Delias, 1912–1944 (Falirea Brothers 98). A superb collection from the 1930s by one of the best songwriters of the period.

Greek Orientale (Polylyric 9033). Great selection of Asia Minor *rembétika* from the 1920s and 1930s, with interesting sleeve notes and translations of some lyrics.

Amanedhes (Margo 8222). Anthology of a very early *rembetik* form, influenced by Iran and Turkey.

Vasilis Tsitsanis, 1938-1955 (EMI 70193). A good collection of Tsitsanis, with singers like Stella Bellou, Marika Ninou and Stratos.

Mihalis Yennitsaris *Saltadoros* (Trikont US-0168-26, Germany). A live recording by one of the last surviving composers from the early days. He appears on this collection with singer Maria Nalbandi and the group Prosekhos.

Opisthodhromiki Kompania (Retrogade Company) *Live from Xanthi, Ayiniteio, the "Kos" Armory* (Lyra 3347). Contemporary renditions of many Ninou and Hadzikhristos standards.

Rembetiko (CBS 70245). Soundtrack of the film, with music mainly by Stavros Xarhakos, lyrics by the poet Nikos Gatsos. Virtually the only original *rembétika* to be composed in the last thirty years, it carried the film.

SELECTIVE DISCOGRAPHY (contd)

NÉO KÍMA

Mikis Theodorakis and Maria Farandouri (MSM 193). One of the best LPs from their long collaboration; recorded in the mid-1970s.

Mimis Plessas *O Dhromos* (Lyra), and **Linou Kokotou** *To Thalassino Trifili* (Lyra 3576, 1972). Although these may initially sound like tourist *bouzoúki* discs, they were influential in their time and are well written; the latter disc comprises settings of Odysseas Elytis poetry, with Rena Koumioti and Mihalis Violaris singing.

Ioannis Markopoulos *Afieroma* (EMI 2J062 70180) and *Parathiro sti Mesoyio* (MSM 464,). Two of his most worthwhile, from 1975 and 1983.

NEW GREEK MUSIC

Dionysios Savvopoulos *Dheka Hronia Kommatia* (Lyra 3715). Retrospective of the singer's first (and best) ten years.

Nikos Ksidhakis and Friends *I Ekdhikissi tis Yiftias* (Lyra 3308), *Konda sti Doxa mia Stigmii* (Lyra 3460), *Cairo–Nafplio–Khartoum* (Lyra 4504). If you're trying just one, get the huanting *"Konda sti Doxa . . ."*, which is influenced by gypsy forms, *Néo Kíma*, Greek pop and *rembétika* by turn. It features multi-instrumentalist Ross Daly and vocalist Eleftheria Arvanitaki.

Nikos Papazoglou *Haratsi* (Lyra 3369), *Meso Nefon* (Lyra 3340). *Rembétika*-rock crossovers by another Ksidhakis collaborator.

Heimerini Kolymvites (1981). First and best recording by a group of architects from Thessaloníki and Kavála, drawing on *rembétika*, pop and Ionian island traditions.

Stamatis Kraounakis and Lina Nikolakopoulou *Kykloforo keh Oploforo* (Polydor 827589, 1985) and *Mana Yernao* (CBS 461 195/2). Rock, jazz-cabaret and *éntehno* crossovers.

Thanos Mikroutsikos and Haris Alexiou *Agapi eeneh Zali* (Minos MSM 613). More poppy but similar in approach to Kraounakis and Nikolakopoulou, whom they sometimes work with.

Nikos Ksilouris, Tania Tsanaklidhou, Hristodhoulos Halaris *Erotokritos* (EMI 14C 062 70270). Setting of the epic Cretan poem.

Hristodhoulos Halaris *I Melodhi tou Pathous* (EMI 162 1701101). Reworking of hymns by Constantinople composer Petros Peloponnisos.

Vosforos *Vosforos* (EMI 064 170421), *Live at the Irodhio, 1990* (Anima 33001). The first contains their versions of Greek court composers from Ottoman Constantinople; the second more of a mix of Turkish sounds.

Ross Daly *Ross Daly* (Pop 11) is a good introduction to his "crossover" style, with hypnotic rhythms influenced by Turkish and Indian forms. More recent albums include *Anadhisi* (Sirios, 1987), an anthology of Pontic, Turkish, Cretan and original compositions; *Okto Tragoudhia keh ena Semai* (BMG Ariola) and *Hori* (BMG Ariola), Cretan and Turkish pieces; and *O Kiklos sto Stavrodrhomi* (BMG Ariola, 1991), Cretan solo instrumentals.

Dhinameis tou Egeou *Dhinameis tou Egeou* (Lyra 3308), *Ihos Veeta* (EMI 062 1701 371), *Anatoliko Parathiro* (Sirios SMH 89.004, 1989). Folk/island/*Smyrneika* revivalists.

Savinna Yiannatou *Nanourismata* (Lyra 3396). Traditional lullabies with traditional instrumental backing given a modern twist.

Domna Samiou *Seryiani* (Sirios 86-003, 1986). "New" traditional music by a woman folk music collector interpreter and revivalist.

Annabouboula *Burn Down the Coffehouse* (BMG Ariola, 1988). Greeks in New York reworking *rembetik* material as House and rock; a minor underground sensation in Greece.

*For suggestions on **record hunting** in Greece, see the Athens shop listings (p.113). In Britain, the best source is **Trehantiri**, 367 Green Lanes, London N4; (☎0 81/802 6530). In the USA, try **Moundanos** on Eddy St in San Francisco, CA, or **Down Home Music** on San Pablo Avenue in El Cerrito, CA.*

BOOKS

Publishers are detailed below in the form "British Publisher/American Publisher", where two editions exist. Where books are published in one country only, this follows the publisher's name.

O/p signifies an out-of-print – but still highly recommended – book. University Press is abbreviated as UP.

TRAVEL AND GENERAL ACCOUNTS

MODERN CLASSICS ON GREECE

Patrick Leigh Fermor *Roumeli; Mani* (both Penguin/Viking Penguin). Leigh Fermor is an aficionado of the vanishing minorities, relict communities and disappearing customs of rural Greece. These two books, written in the 1950s, are not so much travelogues as scholarship interspersed with strange and hilarious yarns. They are perhaps the best books written on any aspect of modern Greece.

Henry Miller *The Colossus of Maroussi* (Minerva/New Directions). Corfu and the soul of Greece in 1939, with Miller, completely in his element, at his most inspired.

Peter Levi *The Hill of Kronos* (Collins Harvill/ NAL–Dutton, the latter o/p). Beautifully observed landscape, monuments and eventually politics as Levi describes how he is drawn into resistance to the colonels' junta.

Kevin Andrews *The Flight of Ikaros* (Penguin/ Viking Penguin). Intense and compelling account of an educated, sensitive archaeologist loose in the backcountry during the aftermath of the civil war.

Lawrence Durrell *Prospero's Cell* (Faber & Faber/Viking Penguin); *Reflections on a Marine Venus* (Faber & Faber/Viking Penguin); *The Greek Islands* (Penguin/Viking Penguin). Durrell lived before the last world war with his brother Gerald on Corfu, the subject of *Prospero's Cell* (and the setting of **Gerald Durrell**'s sparkling *My Family and Other Animals*, published by Penguin/Viking Penguin). *Marine Venus* recounts Lawrence's wartime experiences and impressions of Rhodes and other Dodecanese Isands. *Greek Islands* is a dated, lyrical and occasionally bilious guide to the archipelagos.

OLDER ACCOUNTS

Edward Lear *Journals of a Landscape Painter in Greece & Albania* (Century/Trafalgar Square). Highly entertaining journals of two journeys through Greece and Albania in autumn 1848 and spring 1849, by the famous landscape painter and author of *The Book of Nonsense*. Further doses of Lear, *The Corfu Years* and *The Cretan Journal*, have recently been published by Denise Harvey, Athens, Greece.

James Theodore Bent *The Cyclades, or Life Among Insular Greeks* (o/p). Originally published in 1881, this remains the best account of island customs and folklore; it's also a highly readable, droll account of a year's Aegean travel, including a particularly violent Cycladic winter.

Nikos Kazantzakis *Journey to the Morea* (o/p). Slightly stilted translation of the Cretan novelist's journey around the Peloponnese and his increasing alienation from 1930s Greece.

Robert Byron *The Station* (Century/Trafalgar Square, the latter o/p). Travels on Mount Áthos in the 1930s, by one of the pioneering scholars of Byzantine art and architecture.

Sidney Loch *Athos, The Holy Mountain* (reprinted by Molho, Thessaloniki, Greece). A resident of Ouranópoli, on the periphery of Mount Áthos, from 1924 to 1954, Loch recounts the legends surrounding the various monasteries, as gleaned from his years of walking through the monastic republic.

Terence Spencer *Fair Greece, Sad Relic: Literary Philhellenism from Shakespeare to Byron* (Denise Harvey, Athens, Greece). Greece from the Fall of Constantinople to the War of Independence, through the eyes of English poets, essayists and travellers.

CLASSICS, HISTORY AND ETHNOGRAPHY

THE CLASSICS

*Many of the classics make good companion reading for a trip around Greece – especially the historians, **Thucydides** and **Herodotus**. It is hard to beat **Homer**'s Odyssey, either, for reading when you're battling with or resigning yourself to the vagaries of island ferries. One slightly less well-known Roman source, which you might consider taking on travels, especially to the Peloponnese, is **Pausanias**'s fourth-century AD Guide to Greece, annotated by Peter Levi in its Penguin edition with notes on modern identifications of sites mentioned.*

The following are all available in Penguin Classic paperback editions:

Homer *The Odyssey, The Iliad.*

Herodotus *The Histories.*

Pausanias *The Guide to Greece* (2 vols).

Plutarch *The Age of Alexander; Plutarch on Sparta; The Rise and Fall of Athens.*

Thucydides *History of the Peloponnesian War.*

Xenophon *The History of My Times.*

ANCIENT HISTORY

A. R. Burn *Pelican History of Greece* (Penguin/ Viking Penguin). Probably the best general introduction to ancient Greece, though for fuller and more interesting analysis you'll do better with one or other of the following.

M. I. Finley *The World of Odysseus* (Penguin/ Viking Penguin). Good on the interrelation of Mycenaean myth and fact.

Oswyn Murray *Early Greece* (Fontana/ Stanford UP). The Greek story from the Mycenaeans and Minoans through to the beginning of the Classical period.

John Kenyon Davies *Democracy and Classical Greece* (Fontana/Stanford UP). Established and accessible account of the period and its political developments.

F W Walbank *The Hellenistic World* (Fontana/ Harvard UP). Greece under the sway of the Macedonian and Roman empires.

Robin Lane Fox *Alexander the Great* (Penguin/Viking Penguin). An absorbing study, which mixes historical scholarship with imaginative psychological detail.

BYZANTINE, MEDIEVAL AND OTTOMAN

John Julius Norwich *Byzantium: the Early Centuries* and *Byzantium: the Apogee* (Penguin/ Viking Penguin). Perhaps the main surprise for first-time travellers to Greece is the fascination of Byzantine monuments, above all at Mystra; these first two volumes of Norwich's history of the empire are terrific narrative accounts.

Steven Runciman *The Fall of Constantinople, 1453* (Cambridge UP, UK/US), *Byzantine Style and Civilisation* (Penguin/Viking Penguin), *Mistra* (Thames & Hudson, UK/US). Again, good narrative history, with more of a slant towards the art, culture and monuments.

Michael Psellus *Fourteen Byzantine Rulers* (Penguin/Viking Penguin). A fascinating contemporary source, detailing the stormy but brilliant period from 976 to 1078.

Nicholas Cheetham *Medieval Greece* (Yale UP, US/UK). General survey of the period and its infinite convolutions in Greece, with Frankish, Catalan, Venetian, Byzantine and Ottoman struggles for power.

Molly Mackenzie *Turkish Athens* (Ithaca, Press/Paul & Co). Readable monograph, drawing on primary sources, that's the best single introductory volume to a neglected topic.

MODERN GREECE

Richard Clogg *A Short History of Modern Greece* (Cambridge UP, UK/US). A remarkably clear account of Greece from the decline of Byzantium to the 1980s; the emphasis is on the events of the last decades.

C M Woodhouse *Modern Greece, A Short History* (Faber, UK/US). Briefer and a bit dryer than Clogg, with a span from the foundation of Constantinople in 324 to the present. Woodhouse was active in the Greek Resistance during World War II; his perspective is rightwing but he is scrupulous with facts. A fifth, updated edition was published in 1992.

Douglas Dakin *The Unification of Greece, 1770–1923* (Ernest Benn/St Martin's Press, o/p). Account of the foundation of the Greek state and the struggle to extend its boundaries.

John S. Koliopoulos *Brigands with a Cause* (Oxford UP, UK/US). History of the brigandage in newly independent Greece and its significance in the struggle for the recovery of territory from Turkey in the nineteenth century.

Michael Llewellyn Smith *Ionian Vision, Greece in Asia Minor, 1919–22* (Allen Lane/St Martin's Press, o/p). Standard work on the Anatolian campaign and the confrontation between Greece and Turkey leading to the exchange of populations.

C.M. Woodhouse *The Struggle for Greece, 1941–49* (Hart-Davis/Beekman, the former o/p). Masterly and by no means uncritical account of this crucial decade, explaining how Greece emerged without a Communist government.

C.M. Woodhouse *The Rise and Fall of the Greek Colonels* (Granada/Watts, the former o/p). The (horror) story of the dictatorship.

ETHNOGRAPHY

T J Winnifrith *The Vlachs: The History of a Balkan People* (Duckworth/St Martin's Press). Rather heavy-going hotchpotch on the existing Vlach communities in Greece and the rest of the Balkans, but the only easily available study.

J.K. Campbell *Honour, Family and Patronage* (Oxford UP, UK/US). A good companion to the above, this is a classic on the Sarakatsáni communities in the mountains of northern Greece, shedding much light on wider aspects of Greek society.

Rae Dalven *The Jews of Ioannina* (Cadmus Press, US; also Lycabettus Press, Greece). History and culture of the thriving pre-Holocaust community, related by a poet and translator of Cavafy, herself an Epirot Jew.

Hugh Poulton *The Balkans: Minorities and States in Conflict* (Minority Rights Group/Paul & Co). Only one chapter is specifically devoted to Greece in this general survey but it is all background of increasingly direct relevance.

Gail Holst *Road to Rembétika: Songs of Love, Sorrow and Hashish* (Denise Harvey, Greece). The predominant Greek urban musical style of this century, evocatively traced by a Cornell University musicologist.

BIOGRAPHY

George Psychoundakis *The Cretan Runner* (John Murray/Transatlantic Arts, the lattter o/p). Narrative of the invasion of Crete and subsequent resistance, by a participant, who was a guide and message-runner for all the British protagonists, including Patrick Leigh Fermor, translator of the book.

Oriana Falacci *A Man* (Pocket Books, US, o/p). Account of the junta years, relating the author's involvement with Alekos Panagoulis, the anarchist who attempted to assassinate Colonel Papadopoulos in 1968. Issued as a novel in response to threats by those who were named.

Vassilis Vassilikos *Z* (Four Walls Eight Windows, US). Another "novel" based very closely on events – the political assassination of Gregoris Lambrakis in Thessaloníki in 1963. It was brilliantly filmed by Costa-Gavras.

Nicholas Gage *Eleni* (Collins Harvill/Ballantine). Controversial account by a Greek-born *New York Times* correspondent who returns to Epirus to avenge the death of his mother, condemned to death by an ELAS tribunal in 1948. Superb descriptions of village life, but very blinkered political "history" – and the basis of a truly forgettable movie. The book inspired a response by a Greek leftist, Vassilis Kavathas, whose family had been decimated by the Right, entitled *I Alli Eleni* (The Other Eleni), not as yet translated into English.

ARCHAEOLOGY AND ART

Gisela Richter *A Handbook of Greek Art* (Phaidon, UK). Exhaustive survey of the visual arts of ancient Greece.

Sinclair Hood *The Arts in Prehistoric Greece* (Yale UP, US/UK); **Reynold Higgins** *Minoan And Mycenaean Art* (Thames & Hudson, UK/US). These are both clear illustrated round-ups.

Colin Renfrew *The Cycladic Spirit* (Thames & Hudson, UK). A fine, illustrated study of the meaning and purpose of Cycladic artefacts.

Peter Warren *The Aegean Civilizations* (Phaidon, UK). Illustrated account of the Minoan and Mycenaean cultures.

Roger Ling *Classical Greece* (Phaidon, UK). Another useful and illustrated introduction.

R.R.R. Smith *Hellenistic Sculpture* (Thames & Hudson, UK/US). Modern reappraisal of the art of Greece under Alexander and his successors.

John Beckwith *Early Christian and Byzantine Art* (Yale UP, US/UK). Illustrated study placing Byzantine art within a wider context.

David Talbot Rice *Art of the Byzantine Era* (Thames & Hudson, UK/US). Talbot was, with Robert Byron, one of the pioneering scholars in the "rediscovery" of Byzantine art; this is an accessible, illustrated study.

MODERN GREEK FICTION

Demetrios Vikelas *Loukas Laras* (Doric Publications, UK, o/p). Classic nineteenth-century novel set mainly on Híos.

Alexandros Papadiamantis *The Murderess* (Writers & Readers, UK/US). Turn-of-the-century novel set on the island of Skíathos. Also available is a collecton of Papadiamantis short stories, *Tales from a Greek Island* (Johns Hopkins UP, US).

Nikos Kazantzakis *Zorba the Greek; Christ Recrucified* (published in the US as *The Greek Passion*); *Report to Greco; Freedom or Death* (*Captain Mihalis* in the US); *The Fratricides* (all Faber & Faber/Simon & Schuster). The most accessible (and Greece-related) of the numerous novels by the Cretan master. Even with inadequate translation their strength, especially that of *Report to Greco*, shines through.

Stratis Haviaras *When the Tree Sings* (Picador/Ballantine, the former o/p) and *The Heroic Age* (Penguin/Viking Penguin, the former o/p). Two-part, faintly disguised autobiography about coming of age in Greece in the 1940s. Written in English "because the experiences depicted in these pages are still too painful to set down in Greek".

Stratis Myrivilis *Life in the Tomb* (Quartet/New England UP). A harrowing and unorthodox war memoir, based on the author's experience on the Macedonian front during 1917–18, well translated by Peter Bien. Completing a kind of trilogy are two later novels, set on the north coast of Lésvos, Myrivilis's homeland: *The Mermaid Madonna* and *The Schoolmistress with the Golden Eyes* (Efstathiadis, Athens, Greece). Translations of these are not so good.

Yiorgos Yatromanolakis *The History of a Vendetta* (Dedalus/Hippocrene). Greek magic realism as the tales of two families unravel from a murder in a small Cretan village.

Petros Haris *The Longest Night: Chronicle of a Dead City* (Nostos Books, Athens, Greece). Short stories set in Athens during the 1940–44 German occupation.

Eugenia Fakinou *The Seventh Garment* (Serpent's Tail, UK). The modern history of Greece – from the War of Independence to the colonels' junta – is told through the life stories (interspersed in counterpoint) of three generations of women. It is a rather more succesful experiment than Fakinou's *Astradeni* (Kedros, Greece*), in which a young girl – whose slightly irritating narrative voice is adopted throughout – leaves the island of Sími, with all its traditional values, for Athens.

Dido Sotiriou *Farewell Anatolia* (Kedros, Greece*). A classic since its initial appearance in Greece three decades ago (it is now in its 52nd printing), this is an epic chronicle of the traumatic end of Greek life in Asia Minor, from the 1912 Balkan War to the catastrophe of 1922. The narrator is a fictionalised version of the author's father.

Maro Douka *Fool's Gold* (Kedros, Greece*). Describes an upper-class young woman's involvement, and subsequent disillusionment, with the clandestine resistance to the junta and her pompous male colleagues.

Alki Zei *Achilles' Fiancée* (Kedros, Greece*). A recent bestseller, exploring identity and values amid a maze of timeshifts, from the German occupation to the civil war, exile in Tashkent and Paris, and a return to Greece.

*These books are part of a new and highly recommended "Modern Greek Writers" series, currently numbering eight titles, issued by the Athenian company, Kedros Publishers. They are distributed in the UK by Forest Books.

POETRY

With two Nobel laureates in recent years – George Seferis and Odysseus Elytis – modern Greece has an extraordinarily intense and dynamic poetic tradition. Translations of all of the following are excellent.

George Seferis *Collected Poems, 1924–955* (Anvil Press/Princeton UP). Virtually the complete works of the Nobel laureate, with Greek and English verses on facing pages.

Odysseus Elytis *The Axion Esti* (Anvil Press/Pittsburgh UP); *Selected Poems* (Anvil Press/Viking Penguin, the latter o/p); *The Sovereign Sun* (Bloodaxe Books/Dufour). English-only text editions.

C. P. Cavafy *Collected Poems* (Chatto and Windus/Princeton UP). The complete works of perhaps the most accessible modern Greek poet, resident for most of his life in Alexandria.

George Pavlopoulos *The Cellar* (Anvil Press, UK). Less well-known poet from Pírgos in the Peloponnese. English translation by Peter Levi.

Yannis Ritsos *Exile and Return, Selected Poems 1967–1974* (Anvil Press/Ecco Press).

Modern Greek Poetry (Efstathiadis, Athens, Greece). Decent anthology of translations, predominantly of Seferis and Elytis.

SPECIFIC GUIDES

ARCHAEOLOGY

Evi Melas (ed) *Temples and Sanctuaries of Ancient Greece: A Companion Guide* (Thames & Hudson, UK o/p; published in the US as *The Greek Experience: A Companion Guide to the Major Architectural Sites and an Introduction to Ancient History and Myth*, Dutton). Excellent collection of essays on the main sites, written by archaeologists who have worked at them.

A.R. and Mary Burn *The Living Past of Greece: A Time Traveller's Tour of Historic and Prehistoric Places* (Penguin/Schocken, the former o/p). Unusual in extent, this covers sites from Minoan through to Byzantine and Frankish, with good clear plans and lively text.

Stuart Rossiter (ed) *The Blue Guide Greece* (A & C Black/W W Norton). Definitive reference guide for the ancient sites.

REGIONAL GUIDES

Peter Greenhalgh and Edward Eliopoulos *Deep Into Mani* (Faber & Faber, US/UK, o/p). A former member of the wartime resistance revisits the Máni forty years after first hiding there, and 25 years after Patrick Leigh Fermor's work, in the company of a British scholar. The result is a superb guide to the region and excellent armchair reading.

Neville Lewis *Delphi and the Sacred Way* (Michael Haag/Hippocrene Press). An account, with ample description of contemporary conditions, and some walking tips, of the route from Athens to Mount Parnassós, followed in ancient times by religious devotees.

John Fisher *The Rough Guide to Crete* (Penguin, UK). An expanded and practical guide to the island by the affable and eccentric contributor of the Crete chapter in this book.

Lycabettus Press Guides (Athens, Greece). This series takes in many of the more popular islands and certain mainland highlights; most pay their way both in interest and usefulness – in particular those on Páros, Pátmos, Náfplio, and the travels of Saint Paul.

GROC's Candid Guides . . . (Ashford, Buchan & Enright, UK). The quirkiest guides in the business, giving exhaustive information on the various groups of Greek islands, along with author and editor G.R. O'Connell's rambling and often bizarre observations. Useful nonetheless.

HIKING

Marc Dubin *Trekking in Greece* (Lonely Planet, UK/US). Fully revised and expanded version of its predecessor *Greece on Foot*, by another of the authors of this guide. It features a comprehensive selection of mainland and island day-hikes and treks, plus extensive preparatory and background information.

Tim Salmon *The Mountains of Greece: A Walker's Guide* (Cicerone/Hunter). The emphasis in this highly practical walkers' handbook (by yet another contributor to this guide) is more specifically on the mountains, with only Sámos covered among the islands. The highlight is a superb walk from Delphi to Albania.

Landscapes of . . . (Sunflower Books/Hunter). A series of walking and car-tour titles devoted to Crete, Rhodes, Sámos, and Corfu. Strong on maps but a little pedestrian and timid in the choice of routes.

FERRIES

Frewin Poffley *Greek Island Hopping* (Thomas Cook, UK). User-friendly guide to the networks of Greek ferries.

BOOKSHOPS

Athens has a number of excellent bookshops, at which many of the recommendations above should be available: see p.114 for addresses. In **London**, the *Hellenic Bookservice*, 91 Fortess Rd, Kentish Town, London NW5 1AG (☎071/267 9499), and *Zeno's Greek Bookshop*, 6 Denmark St, W1 (☎071/836 2522), are knowledgeable and well-stocked specialist dealers in new, secondhand and out-of-print books on all aspects of Greece.

LANGUAGE

So many Greeks have lived or worked abroad in America, Australia and, to a much lesser extent, Britain, that you will find someone who speaks English in the tiniest island village. Add to that the thousands attending language schools or working in the tourist industry – English is the lingua franca of most resorts, with German second – and it is easy to see how so many visitors come back having learnt only half a dozen restaurant words between them.

You can certainly get by this way, but it isn't very satisfying, and the willingness and ability to say even a few words will transform your status from that of dumb *tourístas* to the honourable one of *ksénos*, a word which can mean foreigner, traveller and guest all rolled into one.

LEARNING BASIC GREEK

Greek is not an easy language for English speakers but it is a very beautiful one and even a brief acquaintance will give you some idea of the debt owed to it by western European languages.

On top of the usual difficulties of learning a new language, Greek presents the additional problem of an entirely separate **alphabet**. Despite initial appearances, this is in practice fairly easily mastered – a skill that will help enormously if you are going to get around independently (see the alphabet box following). In addition, certain combinations of letters have unexpected results. This book's transliteration system should help you make intelligible noises but you have to remember that the correct **stress** (marked throughout the book with an acute accent) is crucial. With the right sounds but the wrong stress people will either fail to understand you, or else understand something quite different from what you intended.

Greek **grammar** is more complicated still: nouns are divided into three genders, all with different case endings in the singular and in the plural, and all adjectives and articles have to agree with these in gender, number and case. (All adjectives are arbitrarily cited in the neuter form in the following lists.) Verbs are even worse. To begin with at least, the best thing is simply to say what you know the way you know it, and never mind the niceties. "Eat meat hungry" should get a result, however grammatically incorrect. If you worry about your mistakes, you'll never say anything.

LANGUAGE LEARNING MATERIALS

TEACH-YOURSELF GREEK COURSES

Breakthrough Greece (Pan Macmillan; book and two cassettes). Excellent, basic teach-yourself course – completely outclasses the competition.

Greek Language and People (BBC Publications, UK; book and cassette available). More limited in scope but good for acquiring the essentials, and the confidence to try them.

Anne Farmakides *A Manual of Modern Greek* (Yale/McGill; 3 vols). If you have the discipline and motivation, this is one of the best for learning proper, grammatical Greek; indeed, mastery of just the first volume will get your a long way.

PHRASEBOOKS

Greek Travelmate (Drew, UK). The most functional of the pocket phrasebooks. Phrases are contemporary and laid out in dictionary form.

DICTIONARIES

The Oxford Dictionary of Modern Greek (Oxford University Press, UK/US). A bit bulky but generally considered the best Greek–English, English–Greek dictionary.

Collins Pocket Greek Dictionary (Harper Collins, UK/US). Very nearly as complete as the Oxford and probably better value for the money.

KATHARÉVOUSSA, DHIMOTIKÍ AND DIALECTS

Greek may seem complicated enough in itself, but its impossibilities are multiplied when you consider that for the last century there has been an ongoing dispute between two versions of the language: **katharévoussa** and **dhimotikí**.

When Greece first achieved independence in the nineteenth century, its people were almost universally illiterate, and the language they spoke – **dhimotikí**, "demotic" or "popular" Greek – had undergone enormous change since the days of the Byzantine Empire and Classical times. The vocabulary had assimilated countless borrowings from the languages of the various invaders and conquerors, from the Turks, Venetians, Albanians and Slavs.

The finance and inspiration for the new Greek state, and its early leaders, came largely from the diaspora – Greek families who had been living in the sophisticated cities of central and eastern Europe, or in Russia. With their European notions about the grandeur of Greece's past, and lofty conception of Hellenism, they set about obliterating the memory of subjection to foreigners in every possible field. And what better way to start than by purging the language of its foreign accretions and reviving its Classical purity.

They accordingly set about creating what was in effect a new form of the language, **katharévoussa** (literally "cleansed" Greek). The complexities of Classical grammar and syntax were reinstated, and Classical words, long out of use, were reintroduced. To the country's great detriment, *katharévoussa* became the language of the schools and the prestigious professions, government, business, the law, newspapers and academia. Everyone aspiring to membership in the elite strove to master it, and to speak it – even though there was no absolute and defined idea of how many of the words should be pronounced.

The *katharévoussa/dhimotikí* debate has been a highly contentious issue through most of this century. Writers – from Sikelianos and Seferis to Kazantzakis and Ritsos – have all championed the demotic in their literature. Meanwhile, crackpot right-wing governments forcibly (re-)instated *katharévoussa* at every opportunity. Most recently, the **colonels'** **junta** of 1967–1974 reversed a decision of the previous government to teach in *dhimotikí* in the schools, bringing back *katharévoussa*, even on sweet wrappers, as part of their ragbag of notions about racial purity and heroic ages.

Dhimotikí returned once more after the fall of the colonels and now seems here to stay. It is used in schools, on radio and TV, in newspapers (with the exception of the extreme right-wing *Estia*) and in most official business. The only institutions which refuse to bring themselves up to date are the church and the legal professions – so beware rental contracts.

This is not to suggest that there is any less confusion. The Metaxas dictatorship of the 1930s changed scores of village names from Slavic to Classical forms and these official **place names** still hold sway on most road-signs and maps – even though the local people may use the *dhimotikí* form. Thus you will see "Leonídhion" or "Spétsai" written, while everyone actually says Leonídhi or Spétses.

DIALECTS AND MINORITY LANGUAGES

If the lack of any standard Greek were not enough, Greece still offers a rich field of linguistic diversity, both in its dialects and minority languages. Ancient **dialects** are alive and well in many a remote area, and some of them are quite incomprehensible to outsiders. The dialect of Sfákia in Crete is one such. *Tsakónika* (spoken in the east-central Peloponnese) is another, while the dialect of the Sarakatsáni shepherds is said to be the oldest, a direct descendant of the language of the Dorian settlers.

The language of the Sarakatsáni's traditional rivals, the **Vlachs**, on the other hand, is not Greek at all, but a derivative of early Latin, with strong affinities to Romanian. In the Yugoslav and Bulgarian frontier regions you can still hear Slavic **Macedonian** spoken, while small numbers of Sephardic Jews in the north speak **Ladino**, a medieval form of Spanish. Until a few decades ago there were **Albanian**-speakers in certain villages on Attica's Mount Párnitha, and lately the clock has been turned back as throngs of Albanian refugees circulate in Athens and other parts of the country. In Thrace there is also a substantial **Turkish**-speaking population, as well as some speakers of **Pomak** (a relative of Bulgarian with a large Greco-Turk vocabulary).

GREEK WORDS AND PHRASES

Essentials

Yes	*Néh*	Yesterday	*Khthés*	Big	*Megálo*
Certainly	*Málista*	Now	*Tóra*	Small	*Mikró*
No	*Óhi*	Later	*Argótera*	More	*Perisótero*
Please	*Parakaló*	Open	*Aniktó*	Less	*Ligótero*
Okay, agreed	*Endáksi*	Closed	*Klistó*	A little	*Lígo*
Thank you	*Efharistó (polí)*	Day	*Méra*	A lot	*Polí*
(very much)		Night	*Níkhta*	Cheap	*Ftinó*
I (don't)	*(dhen) Katalavéno*	In the morning	*To proí*	Expensive	*Akrivó*
understand		In the afternoon	*To apóyevma*	Hot	*Zestó*
Excuse me, do	*Parakaló, mípos*	In the evening	*To vrádhi*	Cold	*Krío*
you speak	*miláte angliká?*	Here	*Edhó*	With	*Mazí*
English?		There	*Ekí*	Without	*Horís*
Sorry/excuse	*Signómi*	This one	*Aftó*	Quickly	*Grígora*
me		That one	*Ekíno*	Slowly	*Sigá*
Today	*Símera*	Good	*Kaló*	Mr/Mrs	*Kírios/Kiría*
Tomorrow	*Ávrio*	Bad	*Kakó*	Miss	*Dhespinís*

Other Needs

To eat/drink	*Trógo/Píno*	Stamps	*Gramatósima*	Toilet	*Toualéta*
Bakery	*Foúrnos, psomádhiko*	Petrol station	*Venzinádhiko*	Police	*Astinomía*
Pharmacy	*Farmakío*	Bank	*Trápeza*	Doctor	*Iatrós*
Post office	*Tahidhromío*	Money	*Leftá/Hrímata*	Hospital	*Nosokomío*

Requests and Questions

To ask a question, it's simplest to start with *parakaló*, then name the thing you want in an interrogative tone

Where is the bakery?	*Parakaló, o foúrnos?*	How many?	*Pósi?*
Can you show me the	*Parakaló, o dhrómos*	How much?	*Póso?*
road to . . . ?	*ya . . ?*	When?	*Póte?*
We'd like a room for two	*Parakaló, éna dhomátio*	Why?	*Yatí?*
	ya dhío átoma?	At what time . . . ?	*Ti óra . . . ?*
May I have a kilo of	*Parakaló, éna kiló*	What is/Which is . . . ?	*Ti íneh/pió íneh..?*
oranges?	*portokália?*	How much (does it cost)?	*Póso káni?*
Where?	*Pou?*	What time does it open?	*Tí óra aníyi?*
How?	*Pos?*	What time does it close?	*Tí óra klíni?*

Talking to People

Greek makes the distinction between the informal (*esí*) and formal (*esís*) second person, as French does with *tu* and *vous*. Young people, older people and country people nearly always use *esí* even with total strangers. In any event, no one will be too bothered if you get it wrong. By far the most common greeting, on meeting and parting, is *yá sou/yá sas* – literally "health to you".

Hello	*Hérete*	My name is . . .	*Meh léne . . .*
Good morning	*Kalí méra*	Speak slower, please	*Parakaló, miláte pió sigá*
Good evening	*Kalí spéra*	How do you say it in	*Pos léyete sta Eliniká?*
Good night	*Kalí níkhta*	Greek?	
Goodbye	*Adhío*	I don't know	*Dhen kséro*
How are you?	*Ti kánis/Ti kánete?*	See you tomorrow	*Tha se dho ávrio*
I'm fine	*Kalá ímeh*	See you soon	*Tha se dho se lígo*
And you?	*Keh esís?*	Let's go	*Páme*
What's your name?	*Pos se léne?*	Please help me	*Parakaló, na me voithíste*

Greek's Greek

There are numerous words and phrases which you will hear constantly, even if you rarely have the chance to use them. These are a few of the most common.

Éla	Come (literally) but also Speak to me! You don't say! etc.	*Po-po-po!*	Expression of dismay or concern, like French "O la la!"
Oríste	What can I do for you?	*Pedhí mou*	My boy/girl, sonny, friend, etc.
Bros!	Standard phone response	*Maláka(s)*	Literally "wanker", but often
Ti néa?	What's new?		used (don't try it!) as an infor-
Ti yíneteh?	What's going on (here)?		mal address.
Étsi k'étsi	So-so	*Sigá sigá*	Take your time, slow down
Opá!	Whoops! Watch it!	*Kaló taxídhi*	Bon voyage

Accommodation

Hotel	*Ksenodhohío*	Cold water	*krío neró*
A room . . .	*Éna dhomátio . . .*	Can I see it?	*Boró na to dho?*
for one/two/three people	*ya éna/dhío/tría átoma*	Can we camp here?	*Boróume na váloumeh ti*
for one/two/three nights	*ya mía/dhío/trís vradhies*		*skiní edhó?*
with a double bed	*meh megálo kreváti*	Campsite	*Kamping/Kataskínosi*
with a shower	*meh doús*	Tent	*Skiní*
hot water	*zestó neró*	Youth hostel	*Ksenodhohío neótitos*

On the Move

Aeroplane	*Aeropláno*	Where are you going?	*Pou pas?*
Bus	*Leoforío*	I'm going to . . .	*Páo sto . . .*
Car	*Aftokínito*	I want to get off at . . .	*Thélo na katévo sto . . .*
Motorbike, moped	*Mihanáki, papáki*	The road to . . .	*O dhrómos ya . . .*
Taxi	*Taksí*	Near	*Kondá*
Ship	*Plío/Vapóri/Karávi*	Far	*Makriá*
Bicycle	*Podhílato*	Left	*Aristerá*
Hitching	*Otostóp*	Right	*Dheksiá*
On foot	*Meh ta pódhia*	Straight ahead	*Katefthía*
Trail	*Monopáti*	A ticket to . . .	*Éna isistírio ya . . .*
Bus station	*Praktorío leoforíon*	A return ticket	*Éna isistírio me epistrofí*
Bus stop	*Stási*	Beach	*Paralía*
Harbour	*Limáni*	Cave	*Spiliá*
What time does it leave?	*Ti óra févyi?*	Centre (of town)	*Kéndro*
What time does it arrive?	*Ti óra ftháni?*	Church	*Eklisía*
How many kilometres?	*Pósa hiliómetra?*	Sea	*Thálasa*
How many hours?	*Póses óres?*	Village	*Horió*

Numbers

1	*éna/mía*	12	*dhódheka*	90	*enenínda*
2	*dhío*	13	*dhekatrís*	100	*ekató*
3	*trís/tría*	14	*dhekatéseres*	150	*ekatón penínda*
4	*téseres/tésera*	20	*íkosi*	200	*dhiakósies/ia*
5	*pénde*	21	*íkosi éna*	500	*pendakósies/ia*
6	*éksi*	30	*triánda*	1000	*hílies/ia*
7	*eftá*	40	*saránda*	2000	*dhío hiliádhes*
8	*okhtó*	50	*penínda*	1,000,000	*éna ekatomírio*
9	*enyá*	60	*eksínda*	first	*próto*
10	*dhéka*	70	*evdhomínda*	second	*dhéftero*
11	*éndheka*	80	*ogdhónda*	third	*tríto*

The time and days of the week

Sunday	*Kiriakí*	Saturday	*Sávato*	Five minutes past seven	*Eftá keh pénde*
Monday	*Dheftéra*	What time is it?	*Ti óra íneh?*	Half past eleven	*Éndheka keh misí*
Tuesday	*Tríti*	One/two/three o'clock	*Mía/dhío/trís óra/óres*	Half-hour	*misí óra*
Wednesday	*Tetárti*			Quarter-hour	*éna tétarto*
Thursday	*Pémpti*	Twenty minutes to four	*Tésseres pará íkosi*		
Friday	*Paraskeví*				

THE GREEK ALPHABET: TRANSLITERATION

Set out below is the Greek alphabet, the system of transliteration used in this book, and a brief aid to pronunciation:

Greek	Transliteration	Pronounced
Α, α	a	a as in cat
Β, β	v	v as in vet
Γ, γ	y/g	y as in yes, except before consonants and a, o or long i, when it's a breathy, throaty version of the g in gap.
Δ, δ	dh	th as in then
Ε, ε	e	e as in get
Ζ, ζ	z	z sound
Η, η	i	ee sound as in feet
Θ, θ	th	th as in theme
Ι, ι	i	i as in bit
Κ, κ	k	k sound
Λ, λ	l	l sound
Μ, μ	m	m sound
Ν, ν	n	n sound
Ξ, ξ	ks	ks sound
Ο, ο	o	o as in hot
Π, π	p	p sound
Ρ, ρ	r	rolled r sound
Σ, σ, ς	s	s sound
Τ, τ	t	t sound
Υ, υ	i	long i, indistinguishable from η
Φ, φ	f	f sound
Χ, χ	h	harsh h sound, like the ch in loch
Ψ, ψ	ps	ps as in lips
Ω, ω	o	o as in hot, indistinguishable from o

Combinations and dipthongs

ΑΙ, αι	e	e as in get
ΑΥ, αυ	av/af	av or af depending on following consonant
ΕΙ, οι	i	long i, exactly like η
ΟΙ, οι	i	long i, identical again
ΕΥ, ευ	ev/ef	ev or ef depending on following consonant
ΟΥ, ου	ou	ou as in tourist
ΓΓ, γγ	ng	ng as in angle
ΓΥ, γυ	g/ng	g as in goat at the beginning of a word; ng in the middle
ΜΠ, μπ	b	b as in bar
ΝΤ, ντ	d/nd	d at the beginning of a word; nd in the middle
ΤΣ, τσ	ts	ts as in hits

A GLOSSARY OF TERMS

ANCIENT/HISTORICAL

ACROPOLIS Ancient, fortified hilltop.

AGORA Market and meeting place of an ancient Greek city.

AMPHORA Tall, narrow-necked jar for oil or wine.

APSE Curved recess at the altar end of a church.

ARCHAIC PERIOD Late Iron Age period, from around 750 BC to the start of the Classical period in the fifth century BC.

ATRIUM Open, inner courtyard of a house.

BASILICA Colonnaded, "hall-" or "barn-" type church, most common in northern Greece.

BEMA Rostrum for oratory (and later the chancel) of a church.

BOULOUTERION Senate (BOULE) hall.

BYZANTINE EMPIRE Created by the division of the Roman Empire in 395 AD, this, the eastern half, was ruled from Constantinople (modern Istanbul). In Greece, Byzantine culture peaked twice: in the eleventh century, and again at Mystra in the early fifteenth century.

CELLA Sacred room of a temple, housing the cult image.

CLASSICAL PERIOD Essentially from the end of the Persian Wars in the fifth century BC until the unification of Greece under Phillip II of Macedon (338 BC).

DORIAN Northern civilisation that displaced and succeeded the Mycenaeans and Minoans through most of Greece around 1100 BC.

DORIC Primitive columns, dating from the Dorian period.

ENTABLATURE The horizontal linking structure atop the columns of an ancient temple.

EPARHÍA Greek Orthodox diocese, also the smallest subdivision of a modern province.

FORUM Market and meeting place of a Roman-era city.

FRIEZE Band of sculptures around a temple. Doric friezes consist of various tableau of figures (METOPES) interspersed with grooved panels (TRIGLYPHS); Ionic ones have continuous bands of figures.

FROÚRIO Medieval castle.

GEOMETRIC PERIOD Post-Mycenaean Iron Age era named for the style of its pottery; begins in the early eleventh century BC with the arrival of Dorian peoples. By the eighth century BC, with the development of representational styles, it becomes known as the ARCHAIC period.

HELLENISTIC PERIOD The last and most unified "Greek empire", created in the wake of Alexander the Great's Macedonian empire and finally collapsing with the fall of Corinth to the Romans in 146 BC.

HEROON Shrine or sanctuary, usually of a demigod or mortal.

IONIC Elaborate, decorative development of the older DORIC order; Ionic temple columns are slimmer with deeper "fluted" edges, spiral-shaped capitals, and ornamental bases. CORINTHIAN capitals are a still more decorative development.

IKONOSTÁSI Screen between the nave of a church and the altar, often covered in icons; entrance is reserved for the priest.

JANISSARY Member of the Turkish Imperial Guard, often forcibly recruited in childhood from the local population.

KÁSTRO Any fortified hill (or a castle), but most usually the oldest, highest, walled-in part of an island HÓRA.

KATHOLIKÓN Central chapel of a monastery.

KOUROS Nude statue of an idealised young man, usually portrayed with one foot slightly forward of the other.

MACEDONIAN Empire created by Philip II in the mid-fourth century BC.

MEGARON Principal hall or throne room of a Mycenaean palace.

METOPE see FRIEZE

MINOAN Crete's great Bronze Age Civilisation, which dominated the Aegean from about 2500 to 1400 BC.

MOREA Medieval term for the Peloponnese; the outline of the peninsula was likened to the leaf of a mulberry tree, *moreá* in Greek

MYCENAEAN Mainland civilisation centered on Mycenae and the Argolid from about 1700 to 1100 BC.

NARTHEX Vestibule or church entrance hall.

NEOLITHIC Earliest era of settlement in Greece, characterised by the use of stone tools and weapons together with basic agriculture. Divided arbitrarily into Early (c 6000 BC), Middle (c 5000 BC), and Late (c 3000 BC).

ODEION Small amphitheatre, used for musical performances, minor dramatic productions, or councils.

ORCHESTRA Circular area in a theatre where the chorus would sing and dance.

PALAESTRA Gymnasium for athletics and wrestling practice.

PANDOKRÁTOR Literally "The Almighty", but generally refers to the stern portrayal of Christ in Majesty frescoed or in mosaic in the dome of many Byzantine churches.

PEDIMENT Triangular, sculpted gable below the roof of a temple.

PERISTYLE Gallery of columns around a temple or other building.

PIRGOS Tower or bastion.

PITHOS (plural PITHOI) Large ceramic jar for storing oil, grain etc. Very common in Minoan palaces and used in almost identical form in modern Greek homes.

PROPYLAION Portico or entrance to an ancient building; often used in the plural, *propylaia*.

STELE Upright stone slab or column, usually inscribed; an ancient tombstone.

STOA Colonnaded walkway in Classical-era marketplace.

TEMENOS Sacred precinct, often used to refer to the sanctuary itself.

THEATRAL AREA Open area found in most of the Minoan palaces with seat-like steps around. Probably a type of theatre or ritual area, though this is not conclusively proven.

THOLOS Conical or beehive-shaped building, especially a Mycenaean tomb.

TRIGLYPH see FRIEZE

TYMPANUM The recessed space, flat or carved in relief, inside a pediment.

GENERAL TERMS

ÁYIOS/AYÍA/ÁYII Saint or holy (m/f/pl). Common place name prefix (abbreviated Ag. or Ay.), often spelt AGIOS or AGHIOS.

AGORA Market and meeting place of an ancient city.

ÁNO Upper; as in upper town or village.

ASTIKÓ (intra) city, municipal, local; used of phone calls and bus services.

DHIMARHÍO Town hall.

HÓRA Main town of an island or region; literally it means "the place". An island HÓRA may also known by the same name as the island.

IPERASTIKÓ Inter-city, long-distance – as in phone calls and bus services.

KAFENÍO Coffee house or café; in a small village the centre of communal life and probably serving as the bus stop, too.

KAÍKI (KAÍKIA) A caique, or medium-sized boat, traditionally wooden and used for transporting cargo and passengers; now refers mainly to island excursion boats.

KALDERÍMI Cobbled mule and footpaths.

KÁMBOS Fertile agricultural plateau, usually near a river mouth.

KÁTO Lower; as in lower town or village.

MELTÉMI North wind that blows across the Aegean in summer, starting softly from near the mainland and hitting the Cyclades, the Dodecanese and Crete full on.

MONÍ Monastery or convent.

NÉOS, NÉA, NÉO "New" – a common part of a town or village name.

NOMÓS Modern Greek province – there are more than fifty of them. Village bus services are organised according to their borders.

PALEÓS, PALEÁ, PALEÓ "Old" – again common in town and village names.

PARALÍA Beach or seafront promenade.

PANAYÍA Virgin Mary.

PANIYÍRI Festival or feast – the local celebration of a holy day.

PERÍPTERO Street kiosk.

PLATÍA Square, plaza. KENTRIKÍ PLATÍA central square.

SKALA The port of an inland island settlement, nowadays often larger and more important than its namesake but always younger since built after the disappearance of piracy.

ACRONYMS

ANEK *Anonimí Navtikí Etería Krítis* (Shipping Co of Crete, Ltd), which runs most ferries between Pireás and Crete, plus many to Italy.

EA Greek Left (*Ellenikí Aristerá*), formerly the Greek Euro-communist Party (*KKE-Esoterikoú*).

ELAS Popular Liberation Army, the main resistance group during World War II and the basis of the communist army in the civil war.

EK Fascist party (*Ethnikó Kómma*), consisting mostly of adherents to the imprisoned junta colonel, Papadopoulos.

ELTA The postal service.

EOS Greek Mountaineering Federation.

EOT *Ellinikós Organismós Tourismoú*, the National Tourist Organisation.

KKE Communist Party, unreconstructed.

KTEL National syndicate of bus companies. The term is also used to refer to bus stations.

ND Conservative (*Néa Dhimokratía*) party.

NEL *Navtikí Etería Lésvou* (Lesvian Shipping Co), which runs most of the northeast Aegean ferries.

OSE Railway corporation.

OTE Telephone company.

PASOK Socialist party (Pan-Hellenic Socialist Movement).

SEO Greek Mountaineering Club.

INDEX

PLACE NAME SPELLINGS

Throughout the guide, we've used a largely phonetic transliteration **system**, with *Y* rather than *G* for the Greek gamma, and *DH* rather than *D* for delta, in the spelling of all modern Greek place names; if you're looking for Gytheion/Githion or Geraki, for example, you'll find them under Yíthio and Yeráki. We have, however, retained the accepted "English" spellings for the **ancient sites**, and for more familiar places like Athens (Athiná, in modern Greek).

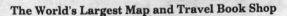

You are
A STUDENT

You travel
THE WORLD

You want
TO SAVE MONEY

Here's how

The International Student Identity Card

Available at Student Travel Offices Worldwide.

Entitles you to discounts and special services worldwide.

BEFORE YOU TRAVEL THE WORLD, TALK TO AN EXPERIENCED STAMP COLLECTOR.

At STA Travel we're all seasoned travellers so we should know a thing or two about where you're headed. We can offer you the best deals on fares with the flexibility to change your mind as you go – without having to pay over the top for the privilege. We operate from 120 offices worldwide. So call in soon.

74 and 86 Old Brompton Road, SW7, 117 Euston Road, NW1. London.
Manchester. Leeds. Oxford. Cambridge. Bristol.
North America **071-937 9971.** Europe **071-937 9921.** Rest of World **071-937 9962**
(incl. Sundays 10am-2pm). **OR 061-834 0668 (Manchester)**

WHEREVER YOU'RE BOUND, WE'RE BOUND TO HAVE BEEN. STA

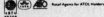

STA TRAVEL